The Encyclopedia of
Motor Sport

Advisory Editor:
Albert R. Bochroch

Foreword by Stirling Moss

The Encyclopedia of
Motor Sport

Edited by G. N. Georgano

A Studio Book The Viking Press New York

This book was designed and produced by
Rainbird Reference Books Ltd.,
Marble Arch House, 44 Edgware Road, London W2,
Published in 1971 by The Viking Press, Inc.
625 Madison Avenue, New York, N.Y. 10022

House Editor: Peter Coxhead
Designer: Michael Mendelsohn

SBN: 670-29405-5
Library of Congress Catalog Card Number: 73–162664

The text was photoset and the monochrome illustrations
were originated by Oliver Burridge Filmsetting Ltd.,
Crawley, Sussex, England
The color plates were originated and the book was
printed and bound by Dai Nippon Printing Co Ltd.,
Tokyo, Japan

Printed in Japan

Foreword

by Stirling Moss OBE

Although I had not met Nick Georgano until after I was asked to write the foreword to *The Encyclopedia of Motor Sport*, I had heard very good reports about a previous book, which Georgano had edited several years ago.

Well, I must say I think that he has done it again! *The Encyclopedia of Motor Sport* appears to me to be the most comprehensive of all reference books on motor sport; more than that, it also seems to be accurate; I suppose I should have expected this when I realized the calibre of the book's writers and photographers.

Many of the 25 contributors who are responsible for the 1,700 photographs and nearly half-a-million words are known to me personally. With experienced motoring journalists such as Denis Jenkinson, Cyril Posthumus and America's Al Bochroch, this volume reflects the best in motor racing reporting and photography.

The book could not have come out at a better time; motor racing, or as our American neighbors call it, automobile racing, is booming all over the world. The need for reliable international information is urgent. Even though there are no lack of reference books, I believe this encyclopedia is the first one that goes back to the beginning of motor sport and puts it altogether in one place. High speed travel now makes it possible to race in Europe one weekend, America, Australia or Africa the next. This can make things a bit confusing, even for those of us who closely follow motor racing. However, I think this book will help us keep better informed.

I did not approach the encyclopedia only as a former racing driver, but also as someone who is now involved with the business side of our sport. As some of you may know, since 1966 I have been working with the Johnson Wax people, the major backers of the fabulous Can-Am series, as their racing director. Reviewing this handsome volume reminds me of how fortunate I am to remain close to the sport, that in so many ways, has become part of me.

Contents

Color plates

Acknowledgments

The Editors would like in particular to thank Michael Sedgwick and Helen Marshall, who not only wrote a considerable portion of the book, but also read the entire manuscript and made many helpful suggestions, and John Bishop, President of the International Motor Sports Association, for his counsel and for reading the American contribution. Other contributors who gave valuable help beyond their own entries include Doug Nye and Cyril Posthumus.

For the generous loan of many rare photographs from their private collections, we are very grateful to Bill Boddy, Hugh Conway, Arnold Farrar, Peter Helck, T. A. S. O. Mathieson, Wilson McComb, Doug Nye and Cyril Posthumus. We would also like to thank Peter Coxhead of Rainbird Reference Books Ltd, London, and Miss Abby Robinson of The Viking Press Inc, New York, for their patience and understanding in seeing the book through the press. Others who have given much valuable help include:

Brian Bolton
Michel Bonnerot
Miss Mary Cattie, curator of the McKean Collection, Free Library of
    Philadelphia
John Conde, American Motors Corporation
Jacques Dorizon
Bill Emery
Yves Giraud-Cabantous
Peter Helck
Linn Hendershot, formerly Public Relations Director, United States Auto Club
Dr Alfred Lewerenz
The Hon Patrick Lindsay
Bill Longley
Countess Maggi
Jack Murrell
Harold Nelson
Jean Plisson
Duncan Rabagliatti
Gianni Restelli
Philipe Rochat
Geoff Rumble
Bob Russo, Director of Press Relations, National Hot Rod Association
Mike Shingler, Manager of Hednesford Hills Raceway

David Warwick
Andrew Whyte, Jaguar Cars Ltd
James Wright

We would also like to thank the following museums, journals and libraries for making available photographs from their collections:

Autocar, London: Peter Garnier, Editor; James Lee
Autosport, London: Simon Taylor, Editor; Ian Phillips
Indianapolis Motor Speedway: Al Bloemker
Montagu Motor Museum, Beaulieu, Hants: Lord Montagu of Beaulieu; Michael Ware, Curator
Motor Sport, London: Laurence Morton; John Dunbar
Veteran Car Club of Great Britain, London: Dennis C. Field, Librarian; Mrs Joan Das, Secretary

The total number of books consulted in preparing this Encyclopedia runs into hundreds, but the editors and contributors have found the following to be of particular help:

The Story of Brooklands   William Boddy
The Golden Age of the American Racing Car   Griffith Borgeson
Power and Glory   William Court
Ferrari   Fitzgerald and Merritt
Racing Voiturettes   Kent Karslake
The Dust and the Glory   Leo Levine
Grand Prix Racing, Facts and Figures   George Monkhouse and Roland King-Farlow
Italian High Performance Cars   Anthony Pritchard and Keith Davey
A Record of Motor Racing, 1894–1908   Gerald Rose

NICK GEORGANO
ALBERT R. BOCHROCH
London, April 1971

Abbreviations

AAA	American Automobile Association	**CASC**	Canadian Automobile Sports Club
ACO	Automobile Club de l'Ouest	**cc**	cubic centimetres
ACGBI	Automobile Club of Great Britain and Ireland	**ci**	cubic inches
		CV	cheval vapeur (French: horsepower)
ADAC	Allgemeine Deutsche Automobil Club	**CSI**	Commission Sportive Internationale
AIACR	Association Inter-nationale des Auto-mobiles Clubs Reconnus	**DIN**	Deutsche Industrie Normen
		dohc	double overhead cam-shaft
ACF	Automobile Club de France	**eoi**	exhaust over inlet (valves)
ACCUS	Automobile Competition Committee for the United States	**ET**	elapsed time
		FEMA	Fédération Européene du Modélisme Automobile
aiv	automatic inlet valve(s)	**FF**	Formula Ford
ALAM	Association of Licensed Automobile Manu-facturers	**FFSA**	Fédération Française du Sport Automobile
AMOC	Aston Martin Owners' Club	**FIA**	Fédération Inter-nationale de l'Auto-mobile
ARCA	Automobile Racing Club of America	**FISA**	Federazione Italiana delle Scuderie Automobile
AVUS	Automobil-Verkehrs- und Übungs-Strasse	**FJ**	Formula Junior
		ft	feet
BARC	British Automobile Racing Club	**ftd**	fastest time of the day
BBC	British Broadcasting Corporation	**4wd**	four wheel drive
		fwd	front wheel drive
bhp	brake horsepower	**GP**	Grand Prix
BMC	British Motor Cor-poration	**GPDA**	Grand Prix Drivers' Association
BRDC	British Racing Drivers' Club	**GT**	Gran Turismo
		hp	horsepower
BRSCC	British Racing and Sports Car Club	**ht**	high tension (magneto ignition)
BRTDA	British Rally and Trials Drivers' Association	**ifs**	independent front sus-pension
CRA	California Racing Association	**IMCA**	International Motor Contest Association
		in	inch(es)

ioe	inlet over exhaust (valves)		**RSAC**	Royal Scottish Automobile Club
irs	independent rear suspension		**SAE**	Society of Automotive Engineers
JCC	Junior Car Club		**sec**	second(s)
kg	kilogram(s)		**Spl**	Special
km	kilometre(s)		**sv**	side valve(s)
KNAC	Koninklijke Nederlandse Automobiel Club		**SCCA**	Sports Car Club of America
kph	kilometres per hour		**swb**	short wheelbase
lt	low tension (magneto ignition)		**TT**	Tourist Trophy
lwb	long wheelbase		**USAC**	United States Automobile Club
MCC	Motor Cycling Club		**VSCC**	Vintage Sports Car Club
min	minute(s)		**yd**	yard(s)
mm	milimetre(s)			
moiv	mechanically operated inlet valve(s)			

Abbreviations used in the section on cars to indicate the country of manufacture:

mpg → **A**	miles per gallon → Austria

mpg miles per gallon
mph miles per hour
MRP Midland Racing Partnership
NACC National Automobile Chamber of Commerce
NART North American Racing Team
NASCAR National Association for Stock Car Auto Racing
NORRA National Off Road Racing Association
ohc overhead camshafts
ohv overhead valve(s)
oiv overhead inlet valve(s)
PS Pferde Stärke (German: horsepower)
psi pounds per square inch
RAC Royal Automobile Club (England)
RN Route Nationale
rpm revolutions per minute

Abbreviations used in the section on cars to indicate the country of manufacture:

A	Austria
AUS	Australia
CDN	Canada
CH	Switzerland
CS	Czechoslovakia
D	Germany, West
DDR	Germany, East
E	Spain
F	France
GB	Great Britain
I	Italy
J	Japan
NL	Holland
NZ	New Zealand
PL	Poland
S	Sweden
SU	Union of Soviet Socialist Republics
US	United States of America
ZA	South Africa

Introduction

On 22 July 1894 twenty-one assorted vehicles rumbled out of Paris on their
way to Rouen, and the world's first motor competition had begun. Soon the
sport divided into reliability trials on the one hand, and out-and-out races on
the other. From the former grew today's rallies, while racing has proliferated
from a handful of town-to-town races in France to today's confusing variety
of Grands Prix and sports car events with an enthusiastic and world-wide
following. For many years it was looked on as a minority sport, a pastime for
rich amateurs with, perhaps, more money than sense. Especially in Great
Britain and the United States of America motor racing had a small following
compared with that for football, baseball, cricket and horse racing, and received correspondingly little attention in the popular press. Since World War
2, however, enthusiasm for motor sport has expanded dramatically; whole
new spheres such as Drag Racing and Stock Car Racing have mushroomed to
become major attractions with their own specialized following, while drivers
such as Stirling Moss, Mario Andretti and Jackie Stewart have become household names in five continents.

This surge of interest has led to a complex variety in the sport, with a be-
wildering series of Formulas, Groups and Classes. Part One of this encyclopedia serves as a guide to the sport as it is today, with separate articles on each
of the Formulas, the major American clubs which organize the Can-Am and
Trans-Am series, and more specialized aspects of the sport such as Autocross
and Rallycross, Trials, Vintage Car Racing and Model Car Racing. The geo-
graphical breakdown is not watertight and we are well aware that, for instance,
Formula One racing according to FIA rules now takes place in the American
continent and will play an increasingly important role there in years to come.

Part Two consists of 161 entries on the major venues and events in the fields
of racing, hill-climbing and rallying. This has been organized on a basis of
places rather than events, so that the German Grand Prix is covered under
AVUS and Nürburgring, the Belgian Grand Prix under Spa, and so on. A few
exceptions to this should be noted: the French Grand Prix has had such a long
history at so many different venues (14 between 1906 and 1970, with a new
one, Ricard-Castelet, in 1971) that it was thought worthy of an entry of its
own. This also applies to the Tourist Trophy, while an event such as the Bol
d'Or has a more coherent history on its own than if it were divided among the,
sometimes insignificant, circuits on which it was held. The coverage is not
claimed to be complete, but includes most places where international, or

otherwise important, events have taken place. The choice of hill-climbs and rallies has had to be more restricted: the former have been limited to two or three per country including, where applicable, the venues for the European Hill-Climb Championship, while for rallies a representative selection of the world's major events has been included. It should be noted that the Lap Record, whether for circuit or hill-climb, indicates the fastest time set up during racing, and does not cover times set up in practice, unless this is specifically mentioned.

In the third part, on drivers, we were faced with the far more daunting task of choosing from the countless numbers of men and women who have ever driven a car in race or rally a satisfactory cross section numbering not more than 360. Had we given only five line entries we could clearly have included far more, but it was thought to be more interesting to give biographies of reasonable length. Our selection covers every era of motor racing from the great pioneers such as René de Knyff and Fernand Gabriel to the current Grand Prix stars. Every winner of the Indianapolis 500 is included, as well as many of the stars of the board track era, and leading names in NASCAR and Trans-Am stock car racing. With rally drivers we have concentrated largely on the men and women prominent in the last ten years, when rallying became the highly competitive and specialized sport that it is today. Apart from drivers, we have included a few outstanding men from the fields of design and sponsorship such as Ettore Bugatti, Ferdinand Porsche, Andy Granatelli and Ken Tyrrell. Tables of principal successes are given for all World Championship Drivers and also for a number of outstanding men from earlier days such as Tazio Nuvolari and Louis Chiron. Drivers are listed alphabetically, but the following points should be noted:

1 Names beginning with Mc such as McLaren are listed at the beginning of the letter M.
2 Names beginning with 'de' or 'von' are listed under the name proper; thus de Portago is found under P, and von Delius under D. An exception is made to this rule for Americanized names such as DePalma and DePaolo which are found under D.

Part Four covers the cars themselves and here again the coverage is, of necessity, incomplete, but every make of any significance will be found. Individual makes are not given for Formula Vee, Karts and USAC Midgets, unless the manufacturer also built other classes of machinery. The realm of the 'special' presents difficulties; clearly record breakers such as the Blue-birds and Thunderbolt must be included, but for racing and hill-climb specials we have insisted that they be either distinctive and original in their conception (Fuzzi) or remarkably successful in competition (Maybach). The rallying activities of a make are covered in the Part Four entries, but road cars which are sporting in conception but have not been used for competitive work, such as the Lamborghini Miura, are not included in the book.

The nationality of each make is indicated by the letter(s) used by the International Conventions of 1926 and 1949 (see list of Abbreviations on page 12). Cars which have dual nationality in that their engines and chassis were made in one country and bodies in another, such as the Franco-Spanish AS, are indicated thus: (F/E). Cars whose nationality changed for political reasons, such as those Austro-Hungarian makes which became Czech after 1918, are indicated thus (A;CS). The makes are listed alphabetically, but the following points should be noted:

1 Names beginning with Mc such as McLaren are listed at the beginning of the letter M.
2 Names beginning with De are listed under D. Thus De Coucy is found under D, not C.
3 Names beginning with Le or La are listed under L. Thus La Perle is found under L, not P.
4 Names having Christian names as part of their make-up are listed under the Christian name. Thus, Georges Irat, not Irat, Georges.
5 Names with modified letters (eg: ü or ø) are treated alphabetically as if they had unmodified letters.

Every effort has been made to keep the book as up to date as possible. New models introduced up to the end of March 1971 are included, and race results and lap records up to the end of April. The Editors would be grateful to receive any corrections or additions which readers may think suitable for future editions. They should be sent to G. N. Georgano, c/o Rainbird Reference Books Ltd, Marble Arch House, 44 Edgware Road, London W2, England.

Contributors

The initials in parentheses are those
used at the end of the entries

Geoffroy de Beauffort (GdeB)
Al Bloemker (AB)
Albert R. Bochroch (ARB)
W. Boddy (WB)
Colin Campbell
H. G. Conway (HGC)
John Davenport (JD)
David Filsell (DF)
Thomas B. Floyd (TBF)
G. N. Georgano (GNG)
C. P. Greenslade (PG)
David R. Hardcastle (DH)
Vladimír Havránek (VH)
David Hodges (DWH)
Peter Hull (PMAH)
Denis Jenkinson (DSJ)
T. A. S. O. Mathieson (TASOM)
F. Wilson McComb (FWMCC)
Hans-Otto Neubauer (HON)
Doug Nye (DCN)
Cyril Posthumus (CP)
José M. Rodriguez-Viña (JRV)
Michael Sedgwick (MCS)
David Thirlby (DAT)
Ron Wakefield (RW)

The Organization of Motor Sport

Western Europe

FIA History

Motoring competition began in 1894 with a reliability run from Paris to Rouen, and the first acknowledged race, where speed was all important, was held in 1895 from Paris to Bordeaux. France was the premier nation in the early days of automobile manufacturing so it was natural that they should be the first to promote motoring competitions. America was not far behind, and in 1899 James Gordon Bennett offered the Automobile Club of France a trophy for an annual event to be organized by them. This series continued until 1905, by which time the French felt their manufacturers were being restricted by the Gordon Bennett rules, which allowed only three cars to represent each country. The French instigated their own race to their own rules in 1906, when they held the first recognized Grand Prix race. They endeavoured to get the agreement of all competing countries when they drew up the rules each year, and thus an international commission was formed with its headquarters in Paris, under the leadership of the Automobile Club of France. With motoring as well as racing spreading rapidly, this body of specialists also took on the control of touring and all its aspects. Until 1914 the Grand Prix of the Automobile Club of France was the only one each year, though the Germans organized their Kaiserpreis and the Italians their Targa Florio.

While Europe was at war between 1914 and 1918 racing continued in the United States and the Americans went their own way as regards racing and regulations. After the war France and Great Britain agreed not to start racing until 1921, Germany and Italy being in no state to take part in any discussions. In 1922 the Association Internationale des Automobile Clubs Reconnus or AIACR formed an International Sporting Commission to specialize in looking after motor racing and all its aspects, leaving other international matters such as roads, touring and frontiers to the parent body. One of the tasks of the commission was to draw up rules for racing, in particular Grand Prix racing, as this was the most important category. Other types of racing were left to the individual countries, and in fact, the Sporting Commission made a point of delegating authority to national clubs where racing of a national character was concerned. In Great Britain the Royal Automobile Club was the accepted controlling body. As long as the general rules of racing were observed national clubs could organize any type of event they liked, but if it was to be of an international status then it had to conform with AIACR rules.

Until the cessation of racing in Europe with the outbreak of the war in 1939 the AIACR drew up international racing rules, changing them every so often, depending on the success or otherwise of the existing rules and the desires of the manufacturers—especially the French manufacturers for the centre of activity was still in Paris. Racing resumed immediately after the war, in France in 1945 and 1946, and other countries soon afterwards. In 1947 the AIACR was reconstituted and renamed the Fédération Internationale de l'Automobile or FIA for short, and the international subcommittee or Commission Sportive Internationale (CSI) controlled the racing rules and drew up the various classes of racing to be held at international level. Great Britain and Italy were very strong in the post-war years, and developed their own national racing on a well-organized scale.

The principal interest of the CSI was Grand Prix racing, regarded as the premier category, and sports car racing and other events were left to the national clubs, but in 1947 it was apparent that the sport was growing rapidly and something more than Grand Prix racing was going to be needed internationally. Racing was therefore divided into groups or formulas. With the serious resumption of racing in 1947 the Grand Prix category was known as Formula 1, and what had been the voiturette category became Formula 2. When 500cc racing flourished in Great Britain and other countries took an interest, it was accepted as an international category and called Formula 3.

As Great Britain, Germany, Italy, the Netherlands, Belgium and other countries became more and more involved in motor racing, the management of the CSI became much more internationally-minded and more democratic, though still based in Paris. Over the years since 1947 the international racing rules have become highly organized and in some aspects very complicated, but motor racing has developed on such an enormous scale throughout the world that simple word-of-mouth, or 'gentleman's' rules can no longer control it all, and the international rules of motor racing fill a considerable book. The basic text is still in French, as a mark of respect to the originators of motor racing, and in all disputes the French text is binding.

Today international racing is divided into nine categories, numbered simply 1 to 9, and called Groups. They embrace every form of recognized racing vehicle and are subdivided into classes according to engine capacity. These classified definitions and specifications come under the heading of 'Appendix J of the International Sporting Code', the present set of rules being drawn up in 1966, and altered or amended as time goes by in the light of events. The nine FIA Groups for 1970 are shown on p. 20.

In the various groups there are capacity subdivisions. From 1 January 1972 Groups 5 and 6 will be amalgamated to form Sports Cars Group 5 with a limit of 3,000cc, without a minimum production. Group 8 has its own Formula rules, recognized by the CSI.

All cars taking part in any of these categories have to be registered with the CSI to see that they conform to

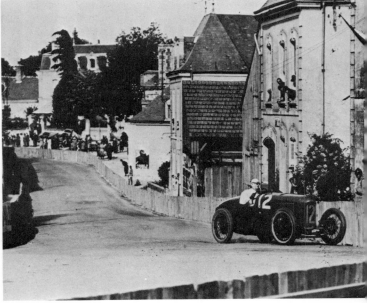

the requirements, and this recognition is known as homologation. Each category and group has a bookful of rules and regulations with which to conform and these are all laid out in the FIA Year Book of Automobile Sport, an annual publication covering all aspects of international motor racing. Among the many jobs that the FIA or its various subcommittees do is to draw up a list of FIA Graded Drivers each year, these being internationally successful drivers in Grand Prix and Sports Car racing. This select list of about 25 drivers is something that every driver racing in international FIA events tries to achieve, by good placings in World Championship races. Certain of the lesser categories of motor racing, such as Formula 2, are barred to these Graded Drivers, but the European Formula 2 champion is subject to certain conditions, automatically graded the following year.

When the organization of racing began on an international scale it involved only a handful of European countries. Today there are 70 member countries in the FIA, which gives some idea of the growth of motoring and motor sport since the turn of the century. In the CSI there are 19 countries represented, some of the larger and more active having two representatives, and for various specialized subjects subcommittees from within the CSI have had to be formed. DSJ

World Championships

When the international body was set up in 1922 to govern racing a number of Grand Prix events in Europe were chosen to count for a manufacturers' championship. This died towards the years of the world slump, in 1929–30, but upon the re-emergence of Grand Prix racing on its new scale in 1934 a driver was nominated each year as the Champion of Europe, chosen by a committee for his performances during the season. The holders were Caracciola, Rosemeyer and Lang.

In the immediate post-war years when international sport was re-organized, a properly conducted Drivers' World Championship and a Manufacturers' Championship were inaugurated, in which points could be scored in a number of different races throughout the season. As races for these championships were held in South America

Left, 1908 Grand Prix: Salzer's Mercedes at Eu. *Photo: Montagu Motor Museum*

Right, 1923 French Grand Prix: Segrave's Sunbeam. *Photo: Montagu Motor Museum*

FIA Groups (1970)

Category A. Recognized Production Cars (numbers in brackets are those of the required minimum production in twelve consecutive months).

Group 1:	Series-Production Touring Cars (5,000)
Group 2:	Special Touring Cars (1,000)
Group 3:	Series-Production Grand Touring Cars (1,000)
Group 4:	Special Grand Touring Cars (500)
Group 5:	Sports Cars (25)

Category B. Experimental Competition Cars

Group 6:	Prototype Sports Cars

Category C. Racing Cars

Group 7:	Two-seater Racing Cars
Group 8:	Formula Racing Cars (Formula 1, 2 etc.)
Group 9:	Formule Libre Racing Cars (Formula 5000 etc.)

as well as in Europe it was felt that the title World Championship was justified. The first series was held in 1950: Farina was the first winner of the award for drivers; Alfa Romeo won the award for manufacturers. DSJ

FIA World Championship of Drivers

Starting in 1950, when Farina was World Champion, the series have been held every year since that date, the number of events counting towards the championship varying over the years. At first, events were only held in Europe and South America, but later other nations joined in and today the Drivers' Championship covers most of the world, including Europe, South Africa, Canada, United States and Mexico, and Japan, South America and Australia are all endeavouring to join in. To begin with the number of events counting towards the Championship was fairly small, in the order of six or seven, but today that number has risen to thirteen, and the Championship season is divided into two parts, of seven and six races; points are scored to the system of 9, 6, 4, 3, 2, 1 for the first six places in each race, and each driver takes his best five scores from the first part and his best six from the second part, if the total should be thirteen. For any other total he scores from one less than the total in each half.

Although a driver does not receive anything more than the title and a trophy from the FIA for becoming World Champion, such a title does enable him to further his career in motor racing in all manner of directions. DSJ

FIA International Cup for Formula 1 Manufacturers

This FIA award began in 1950 along with the Drivers' Championship on a similar points system, but only the highest placed car of any make could score points. It was the usual thing for the winning manufacturer to supply the car to the driver who was World Champion, such as Alfa Romeo in 1950 and 1951, for Farina and Fangio, and Ferrari in 1952 and 1953 for Ascari. There were exceptions to this, however: in 1954, for example, Fangio was champion driving for Maserati and Mercedes-Benz, the latter winning the Manufacturers' Championship; in 1958 when Hawthorn was champion driving for

FIA World Championship of Drivers

Year	Driver	Car
1950	Giuseppe Farina	Alfa Romeo
1951	Juan Manuel Fangio	Alfa Romeo
1952	Alberto Ascari	Ferrari
1953	Alberto Ascari	Ferrari
1954	Juan Manuel Fangio	Mercedes-Benz and Maserati
1955	Juan Manuel Fangio	Mercedes-Benz
1956	Juan Manuel Fangio	Lancia-Ferrari
1957	Juan Manuel Fangio	Maserati
1958	Mike Hawthorn	Ferrari
1959	Jack Brabham	Cooper
1960	Jack Brabham	Cooper
1961	Phil Hill	Ferrari
1962	Graham Hill	BRM
1963	Jim Clark	Lotus-Ford
1964	John Surtees	Ferrari
1965	Jim Clark	Lotus-Ford
1966	Jack Brabham	Brabham-Repco
1967	Denny Hulme	Brabham-Repco
1968	Graham Hill	Lotus-Ford
1969	Jackie Stewart	Matra-Ford
1970	Jochen Rindt	Lotus-Ford

FIA International Cup for Formula 1 Manufacturers

1950	Alfa Romeo
1951	Alfa Romeo
1952	Ferrari
1953	Ferrari
1954	Mercedes-Benz
1955	Mercedes-Benz
1956	Lancia-Ferrari
1957	Maserati
1958	Vanwall
1959	Cooper
1960	Cooper
1961	Ferrari
1962	BRM
1963	Lotus-Ford
1964	Ferrari
1965	Lotus-Ford
1966	Brabham-Repco
1967	Brabham-Repco
1968	Lotus-Ford
1969	Matra-Ford
1970	Lotus-Ford

FIA International Championship for Makes

Sports Car Championship

1953	Ferrari
1954	Ferrari
1955	Mercedes-Benz
1956	Ferrari
1957	Ferrari
1958	Ferrari
1959	Aston Martin
1960	Ferrari
1961	Ferrari.

	Prototype Championship	GT Championship
1962	Ferrari	Ferrari
1963	Ferrari	Ferrari
1964	Porsche	Ferrari
1965	Ferrari	Cobra
1966	Porsche	Porsche
1967	Ferrari	Porsche

World Sports Car Manufacturers' Championship

1968	Ford
1969	Porsche
1970	Porsche

Ferrari, it was the Vanwall team that won the manufacturers' award, because they scored more victories than Ferrari, but with different drivers. In fact, 1958 was the first time a British manufacturer had won the award, and in the following two years it was won by Cooper, though they used Coventry-Climax engines, so in reality the award should have been shared.

With the introduction of the 1,500cc Formula for Grand Prix racing in 1961 there were many competitors using the proprietary Coventry-Climax engine, and the FIA marked time on the Manufacturers' Championship, undecided whether it should go to the chassis builder or the engine builder. A decision was taken that where a competitor used an engine he did not build himself the car name should incorporate the two manufacturers' names, with the car builder first and the engine builder second, and in the event of winning the championship the award would go to the car builder. This decision helped to cause Coventry-Climax to lose interest in building racing engines.

Today a Manufacturers' Cup is still awarded at the end of each season, but the glamour of the individual driver battling for World Championship honours has overshadowed the Manufacturers' Championship in Formula 1. DSJ

FIA International Championship for Makes

In the 1950s the Manufacturers' Championship in Formula 1 was all-important, with Ferrari, Alfa Romeo, Maserati, Mercedes-Benz and others all battling for the honours. More or less as a sideline there was a Trophy for Speed and Endurance competed for in a small number of classic long-distance races for sports cars, such as the Mille Miglia, and Le Mans 24-Hour Race. Although this championship had a certain following, it was not as glamorous or important as the Grand Prix Championship. During the early 1960s the Drivers' Championship assumed increased importance in Formula I, and interest in the Sports Car Championship grew. In 1961 this championship lapsed as such, and was replaced by two championships, one for prototype sports cars and one for Grand Touring cars of which at least 100 had to be built. This figure was reduced to 50 in 1966. In 1968 the FIA combined the two championships into one, the World Sports Car Manufacturers' Championship. Both Group 5 (sports cars, minimum of 25 made), and Group 6 (prototype sports cars) can compete for this. Because the award is for manufacturers such firms as Porsche, Ferrari and Matra give strong support to their teams. The growing importance of the Manufacturers' Championship is shown by the increasing number of qualifying events. In 1970 there were ten: the Daytona 24 Hours, the Sebring 12 Hours, the Brands Hatch 1,000 Kilometres, the Monza 1,000 Kilometres, the Targa Florio, the Spa 1,000 Kilometres, the Nürburgring 1,000 Kilometres, Le Mans 24 Hours, Watkins Glen 6 Hours and the Österreichring 1,000 Kilometres. Winners of the various championships since 1953 are given on the left. DSJ

FIA Rally Championships

Two rally championships are organized annually by the FIA, the International Rally Championship for Makes (IRCM), and the European Rally Championship for Drivers (ERCD), covering a total of thirty events. The IRCM is the most important, and in 1970 comprised seven events, the Monte Carlo, Swedish, San-Remo-Sestriere, East African Safari, Austrian Alpine, Acropolis and RAC Rallies. Scoring is on the same principle as in the Formula 1 World Championship, with 9, 6, 4, 3 and 2 points for the first five places respectively. In 1970 the IRCM saw an exceptionally close fight between Porsche and Alpine, the result being in doubt until the final event, the RAC Rally. Porsche won with 28 points to Alpine's 26, Lancia being in 3rd place with 16 points.

The ERCD is decided on a much more complicated system involving classes and numbers in the class at the start. In 1970 there were 22 events in the Drivers' Championship, ranging from long, tough rallies to relatively simple ones. The winner was J-C. Andruet (Alpine) with 70 points, followed by Gilbert Staepelaare (Ford Escort TC) with 55 points. GNG

FIA European Hill-Climb Championship

Although the pre-World War 2 series of mountain championships was well supported, with those classic uphill battles between the might of Mercedes-Benz and Auto-Union, the sport was in a sad state of decline after the war. Not until 1957 was the Mountain Championship revived, providing for six qualifying rounds on hills of not less than 3·75 miles (6·035km) length, with a minimum gradient of 5%. A sliding scale of points was adopted by which the winner of each round was given a higher score if a large number of competitors contested his class, but this did not prove very satisfactory in practice, and the scheme was dropped in 1958. From the beginning, the championship was for sports cars up to 2 litres, with subdivisions for touring and GT machines, and the complex early scoring system was soon resolved into an F1 World Championship-style 9, 6, 4, 3, 2, 1 point system for the fastest six times overall.

The 1957 series consisted of six mountain 'races', run at Mont Ventoux, Freiburg-Schauinsland, Gaisberg, Lenzerheide, Aosta-Great St Bernard and Mont Parnes. By 1969 the series had more or less settled, using Montseny, Mont Ventoux, Cesana-Sestriere, Trento-Bondone, Schauinsland, Mont Dore and Sierre-Montana-Crans. The original post-war title was won by the Swiss private contender, Willy Peter Daetwyler, in a Maserati, but later the Porsche and Ferrari works backed serious Mountain Championship programmes, and dominated most of the 1960s competitions, Scarfiotti and Mitter putting up brilliant performances for the Italian and German manufacturers respectively. DCN

FIA European Hill-Climb Championship

1957	Willy Daetwyler	Maserati
1958	Wolfgang von Trips	Porsche
1959	Edgar Barth	Porsche
1960	Heini Walter	Porsche
1961	Heini Walter	Porsche
1962	Lodovico Scarfiotti	Ferrari
1963	Edgar Barth	Porsche
1964	Edgar Barth	Porsche
1965	Lodovico Scarfiotti	Ferrari
1966	Gerhard Mitter	Porsche
1967	Gerhard Mitter	Porsche
1968	Gerhard Mitter	Porsche
1969	Peter Schetty	Ferrari
1970	Johannes Ortner	Abarth

FIA European Challenges for Touring Cars

This international competition was initiated in 1964, and was an extremely complicated championship reserved for the drivers rather than their cars. It was for Group 1 and 2 saloons, and was split into three divisions, each with two capacity subdivisions. Points were awarded on both overall results and on placings in each

class, and a series of races and hill-climbs throughout the Continent were included, the hill-climbs scoring only 50% of the race points scale. For 1969 the Challenge catered for Group 5 machines, then with the change in international groupings for 1970 it reverted to Group 2. Abarth and Alfa Romeo have done particularly well in the Challenge. In 1970 the Challenge was won by Toine Hezemans (Alfa Romeo GTA). DCN

Formula I

The rules for the construction and racing of Grand Prix cars in international events are laid down by the FIA and can be changed at intervals, with adequate warning, the basic decisions being made in the light of experience and current conditions. Formula 1 is the title given to the top class of international single-seater racing, and

was called by that name in 1947 when motor racing organization was reconstituted after World War 2. Previously it had been called the Grand Prix Formula, and the idea of having a set of fixed rules originated with the 1,000kg weight limit for heavy racing cars imposed for the 1902 season. The Automobile Club of France drew up the first Grand Prix rules, after consultation with racing car manufacturers, for their first Grand Prix event in 1906. Each year modifications were made, in the light of the experience being gained in those pioneer days, and in 1922 a special subcommittee of the Association Internationale des Automobile Clubs Reconnus, was formed for the express purpose of looking after such things as Grand Prix rules and regulations.

Most of the time the main limitation was engine capacity, such as 2,000cc in 1922-5 and 1,500cc in 1926-7,

Left above, Formula I: Bira's Maserati 4CLT at Silverstone in 1949. *Photo: Motor*

Above, Formula I: I·5-litre cars in the 1961 French GP. Baghetti's Ferrari followed by the Lotuses of Clark and Ireland. *Photo: David Hodges Collection*

Formula I: Graham Hill's Lotus-Ford 49 at Monaco in 1969. *Photo: Ford of Britain*

but occasionally a weight limit was imposed, such as the formula for 1934–7 which imposed a maximum weight limit of 750kg. In 1938 an equivalence formula was drawn up with engine limits of 3,000cc with supercharger, and 4,500cc without supercharger. In 1947, when the title Formula 1 was first used, the limits were a maximum engine capacity of 1,500cc supercharged and 4,500cc without supercharger; this proved to be a reasonably good choice, for equality of the two types was very close. In 1954 the formula was changed to 2,500cc without supercharger and 750cc with supercharger, but this was unbalanced and the 2,500cc unsupercharged engines swept the scene. A modification was made in 1958 when fuel was limited to straight aviation petrol, any form of alcohol fuel being banned, and this formula lasted until 1960.

where C = capacity of piston engine equivalent, (i.e. 3,000cc for Formula 1), and R = ratio of the compression of the turbine engine, obtained by multiplying together a value for each stage of the compressor. For the Wankel-NSU type of rotary-piston engine the equivalent capacity is twice the volume determined by the difference between the maximum and minimum capacity of the working chamber.

All races counting for the Drivers' World Championship are run under the rules of Formula 1 and it is generally accepted that this class of racing is the pinnacle in both design and driving, where road-racing cars are concerned.

All Formula 1 races for the Championship must run for a distance of at least 300km and at the most 400km, unless the FIA grant a special waiver. DSJ

Left above, Formula 2: Mike Hawthorn's 1952 Cooper-Bristol. *Photo: Geoffrey Goddard*

Above, Formula 2: two Brabhams and a Lotus in the 1967 F2 race at Reims. *Photo: Geoffrey Goddard*

Speeds had been rising all the time and authorities everywhere were becoming concerned about safety so a new formula was introduced with an upper engine capacity limit of 1,500cc and superchargers were banned. This formula ran until 1965 and in 1966 the present 3-litre formula started, received with enthusiasm by everyone, for the small limit had not been very popular. Coming into force on 1 January 1966 the formula was intended to run until 31 December 1972, but it will almost certainly be prolonged because of its success. The rules limit engine capacity to 3,000cc without supercharger, or 1,500cc with supercharger, using normal fuel and it has produced some of the fastest Grand Prix cars ever built. The 1954-60 formula virtually ruled out the use of the supercharger, especially when fuel was limited to normal petrol, and the art of supercharging has never been revived all design work being concentrated on 3,000cc engines. This formula will continue for some time, with the modification in 1971 of a limit to the number of cylinders to twelve. The minimum weight of Formula 1 cars is set at 500kg, plus 30kg allowance for mandatory safety features such as fire-extinguishing apparatus, roll-over crash bars and safety fuel tanks.

Within the Formula 1 rules there is an equivalence formula to permit the use of gas-turbine and rotary-piston engines, such as the German Wankel, the same formula applying to other categories of racing. For turbines it is:

$$A = \frac{C \times 0.09625}{(3.10 \times R) - 7.63}$$

Formula 2

Almost from the beginning of racing there has been a class at meetings for cars inferior to those in the main event. The early events had classes for *voitures légères* or light cars, and later when the French were running their Grand Prix for giant racers in the pre-World War 1 days, there was a class for 3-litre engines for the Coupe de l'Auto. During the 1920s and 1930s there were races for *petites cylindrées* or voiturettes, the size depending on the main formula in use at the time. Sometimes it was an 1,100cc capacity limit, sometimes a 1,500cc limit, but always very inferior to the main formula. When the sport was re-organized in 1947, with the new title of Formula 1 being given to Grand Prix racing, the voiturettes, *petites cylindrées* or light cars were put under the title of Formula 2. By common consent, and availability of cars, the formula imposed a limit of 2,000cc without supercharger or 1,100cc with supercharger, and this was well received as many firms and individuals could not afford the expense of Formula 1; which was the basic reason for a secondary formula.

In 1952 when Grand Prix racing was going through a bad period the existing 2,000cc Formula 2 took over the major events and received general support in 1952 and 1953. However, with the successful new Formula 1 in 1954 there was no apparent need for a second formula. But in 1957 this need arose and a new Formula 2 was drawn up for cars with a cylinder capacity limit of 1,500cc without supercharger, and since then Formula 2 has been as well supported as Formula 1. After a period

of 1,000cc limitation, at a time when Formula 1 was limited to 1,500cc, a new Formula 2 came into force on 1 January 1967, to run to 31 December 1971. The engine limits are 1,300cc to 1,600cc, with a maximum limit of six cylinders, and the engine cylinder block must be from a production car manufactured in a quantity of at least 500 in twelve consecutive months. Gearboxes are limited to a maximum of five forward speeds, and a minimum weight is set at 450kg (including 30kg for the mandatory safety measures as in Formula 1). Formula 2 races are held for a Drivers' Championship, from which graded Formula 1 drivers are banned, though they may take part in the actual races, and this is called the European Formula 2 Championship. It is a very good training ground for drivers before they attempt Formula 1: Jackie Ickx, Jean-Pierre Beltoise and Johnny Servoz-Gavin all entered Grand Prix racing with a European Formula 2 Champion title to their credit. The 1970 Champion was Clay Regazzoni (Tecno-FVA). DSJ

Formula 3

The origins of Formula 3 can be traced back to a 'class within a class' from the early days of motor racing. Even in the voiturette class in the 1920s there would usually be a 750cc subdivision within a 1,100cc category, for example, for no matter what class is planned there will always be someone who cannot afford to take part, and is looking for a simpler and cheaper form of racing. In the post-World War 2 2,000cc category there was a subcategory of 1,100cc to begin with, but England produced a national formula for cheap racing, for cars with engines limited to 500cc capacity, mostly using motor-cycle engines. This became so popular that it was accepted internationally by the FIA in 1950, classified as Formula 3 and continued for many years, providing a nursery for such drivers as Peter Collins, Stirling Moss, Ivor Bueb, Stuart Lewis-Evans and many more.

Despairing of competing against the British in Formula 3 the Italians thought up their own national formula, using small 1,100cc FIAT engines, or similar, and this was called Formula Junior. At the time the existing Formula 3 was reaching a condition of stalemate and something else was needed, so the FIA took the basis of the Italian rules and Formula Junior took over from Formula 3. Later the capacity limit was reduced to 1,000cc; the 1964–1970 Formula 3 still used this capacity limit, but with many other restrictions, all aimed at keeping down cost and performance, such as the use of production cylinder blocks and cylinder heads, only one carburettor, (with a 36mm throttling flange between the carburettor and the engine), a production gearbox with not more than four forward speeds and a minimum weight of 420kg (including 20kg for the safety requirements).

This formula came into being on 1 January 1964 and continued until the end of 1970. On 1 January 1971 a new Formula 3 came into operation, limited as before to reciprocating piston engines only, but with an upper limit of 1,600cc and a maximum of four cylinders, the basic engine being a production unit (minimum of 5,000 built in 12 months). Induction is free but all the

Formula 3: an assortment of 500cc machines at Goodwood. From left to right (front row): Cooper, Marwyn, Monaco, FHB, Cooper. *Photo Autosport*

Formula 3: Roy Pike's Lotus-Holbay 59 leads Tim Schenken's Brabham BT28 into North Tower Crescent, Crystal Palace, 1969. *Photo: Doug Nye*

air or mixture must pass through a 20mm diameter throttling flange, and the gearbox may have up to five speeds. A minimum wheelbase of 200cm is specified and a minimum track of 120cm. Weight is a minimum of 440kg, including 30kg for safety equipment as laid down in the general rules for the construction of single-seater racing cars. The 1970 Shell *Motor Sport* Championship was won by Tony Trimmer (Brabham BT28). DSJ

Formula 4

This is a British national formula for small single-seater cars, thought up by people unable to afford to compete in international categories. It imposed a limit of 250cc for racing engines, the idea being to use motor-cycle engines, but was subsequently modified to allow the use of 875cc engines from production cars, such as the Hillman Imp and the BMC Mini. In 1970 engines up to 1,000cc were permitted. Anyone manufacturing a car for this formula must offer it ready to race for not more than £950, less the engine and gearbox. This class of racing is limited and, from 1971 onwards Formula 4 was organized by the 750 Motor Club, providing relatively cheap racing for the amateur driver. In 1970 the formula was dominated by Alec Bottam's Vixen-Imps, in particular those driven by Mike Wilds and Bernard Unsett. DSJ

Formula Ford

Supported by the British Ford Motor Company this class of single-seater racing aims to permit people to race on a very limited budget, yet to enjoy all the activi-ties of the higher forms of racing, such as taking part in international events, competing on Grand Prix circuits, and so on. It stipulates the use of the 1,600cc Ford cross-flow engine, tuned within strictly defined limits, and cars must run on standard road tyres, special racing tyres not being permitted. Backed by the trade and the industry this national formula has received enormous support from amateurs and with promotion by the Ford Motor Company it has spread throughout motor racing countries, taking on an almost circus-like aspect, and is almost accepted as an international formula. Officially it comes under FIA Group 9 (National Formulas) and has been adopted by many countries as a 'beginners' racing class. In 1970 the Les Leston Championship for Formula Ford cars was won by Colin Vandervell (Merlin Mk 17). DSJ

Formula Junior: typical cars of the front-engined phase were the Taraschi and the De Sanctis, seen here with Zannini and De Sanctis respectively at the wheel, on the Vallelunga circuit in 1958. *Photo: Adriano Ceci*

Left, Formula 4: a race of 250cc cars. *Photo: Patrick Benjafield*

Right, Formula Ford: Jeremy Gambs (No 35, Lotus) leads Andy Rouse (No 32, Dulon) and Peter Lamplough (No 54, Palliser) at Castle Combe in July 1970. *Photo: Autosport*

Formula Junior

Failing to come to grips with the British, or even the Germans, in the International 500cc Formula 3 class of racing during the 1950s, the Italians produced their own 'baby-car' racing rules and ran a national class they called Formula Junior. This was in 1958 and at the time the 500cc movement was beginning to wane, because of lack of suitable proprietary engines from the racing motorcycle world, so the Italian formula was put up to the FIA for consideration as an international formula and a possible substitute for the existing Formula 3. The rules called for a 1,100cc production engine, such as the popular FIAT, it banned overhead camshafts, and encouraged construction along conventional racing car lines, as distinct from the 500cc Formula which had developed cars that were like 4-wheeled motorcycles.

In 1959 Formula Junior was recognized as an International Formula and for one year it overlapped with Formula 3. But by 1960 it had become the recognized small car formula and went from strength to strength, eventually taking over the title of Formula 3. DSJ

Formula 5000

A recent addition to single-seater class racing is Formula 5000, which calls for cars using mass-production engines of not more than 5,000cc capacity, which almost automatically implies an American V-8 engine. A list of approved engines is published by the RAC and the formula has been accepted at international level. Up to 1971 the formula was banned to drivers who had scored points in the Formula 1 World Championship series. Popular in Great Britain and America (where it is called Formula A) this class of racing is providing the opportunity for people to race cars that are more closely akin to expensive Formula 1 cars than any other type. It gives drivers an excellent opportunity to become accustomed to the use of as much as 450bhp with all the attributes of a Grand Prix car, such as racing tyres, brakes, suspension and chassis design, although the weight of the production engines reduces the actual performance to below that of a Formula 1 car. Its popularity is spreading, especially to countries like Australia and South Africa where American V-8 engines and tuning equipment are fairly easily obtained. The most successful builders of F 5000 cars have been Lola, McLaren, and Surtees. The Guards F5000 Champion in 1970 was Peter Gethin (McLaren M10B). DSJ

Formula Vee

Sometimes written as Formula V, this class of single-seater racing is sometimes misinterpreted as Formula Five. The Vee stands for Volkswagen, the German firm giving support to this class of racing that calls for single-seater cars to be built from Volkswagen components, similar to the Ford Motor Company's idea in Formula Ford. The rules specify the use of standard components such as engine, gearbox, suspension, steering, wheels and tyres. Because of this the cars have little in common with accepted racing car design, but some drivers, such as Helmut Marko, have progressed from Formula Vee to more important classes of racing.

Naturally enough, this form of racing is very popular in Germany, Austria and Holland, near the home of Volkswagen, but it also has a strong following in America. Two prototype VW-engined racing cars were built by Nardi of Italy in 1959 for Hubert Brundage, a VW-Porsche dealer of Jacksonville, Fla. With encouragement from Col. George Smith, the Sports Car Club of America first sanctioned Formula Vee racing in 1963, and in 1965 made it a separate class. With 3,200 Vees in the United States, this Formula constitutes the largest of all American racing classes.

In 1970 the traditional 1,200cc Vee (1,300cc in Europe) was challenged by the introduction of a new class, the 1,600cc 140mph (225kph) Super Vee, which also allowed freer chassis and suspension design. A ten race Super Vee Championship was announced by the British Automobile Racing Club for 1971, and at the beginning of the year at least four British firms were offering Super Vees

Left, Formula 5000: 1971 Lola T192. *Photo: Geoffrey Goddard*

Right, Formula Vee: the first Super Vee, the Beach Mark 16, built by Eugene Beach's Competition Components of Clearwater, Fla. *Photo: Volkswagen of America Inc*

Formula Vee: clothed and unclothed views of a typical Formula Vee car, showing the standard VW suspension. *Photo: Doug Nye*

(Hawke, Lola, Palliser and Royale). On the Continent the ten race Volkswagenwerk Gold Cup series was scheduled to take place in nine countries. Leading US Formula Vee builders are Autodynamics, Beach, Dickson, Lynz, Zeitler and Zink; among European constructors are Austro-Kaimann (Austria) and McNamara (Germany).

Harry Ingle (Zink) was 1970 US National Vee champion, and Tom Davey (Zeitler) won the SCCA Super Vee title. British Formula Vee champion in 1970 was Mike Hayselden (Monaco Vee); the European Champion was Erich Breinsberg (Austro-Kaimann). DSJ/ARB

Formula Intercontinental

When it was proposed to end the successful 2,500cc Formula 1 in 1960 and substitute a 1,500cc limit there was much opposition, especially from people in Great Britain. They had cars and engines well proven in the old formula and were reluctant to change, even though design work had stagnated. In addition few of them really believed that the 1,500cc limit would take effect, and consequently were unprepared for it. In an attempt to keep the old 2,500cc Formula going and defeat the FIA's proposed new rules Formula Intercontinental was devised, encouraging the use of old Formula 1 engines and allowing an increase in capacity to 3,000cc. The only support for this 'pirate' formula came from private teams or individuals, with no real factory backing and certainly no self-supporting means of producing engines. It was doomed to failure and after a few poorly supported events, with obsolete competing machines, it quietly faded away. Meanwhile all the serious Grand Prix contenders were getting on with the new 1,500cc Formula 1, even though they were not wildly enthusiastic about it. DSJ

Formule France

This French national formula is another fairly recent development in much the same style as Formula Ford. But whereas the British-inspired class quickly received international acceptance and support, Formule France remains very much a national school-room division.

The regulations demand open-wheeled single-seater chassis powered by standard tune 1,300cc Renault-Gordini engines. A nation-wide French Championship is run and this has proved extremely successful and well-supported. The racing is close and exciting, if rather slow, and has brought several promising French drivers to the fore. Manufacturers supporting the class include Serge Aziosmanoff's GRAC concern and Jean-Pierre Beltoise's Elina marque, built at his tuning establishment near Paris. The Formule France Champion in 1970 was François Laccarau (Martini). DCN

Formula 850

This is a class of racing limited to single-seaters built around FIAT components, rather like Formula Vee and Volkswagen, and it is a strictly Italian national affair, providing sport for many young people who cannot afford to take up serious motor racing. It is even run at night on a floodlit circuit at Monza, a specially built short circuit being provided for these little cars. DSJ

Formula 750

The British 750 Motor Club had just started when World War 2 broke out, but its members' determination to start a racing formula for Austin Seven-based specials survived the conflict. The September 1949 edition of the magazine *Motor Sport* carried a 'suggestion for inexpensive racing', outlining a class for Austin Seven-based specials with bodies complying with the current RAC trials and rally car regulations.

Holland Birkett, Jack French and Arthur Mallock were among the formula's prime movers, and the first 750 race took place at the Eight Clubs' Silverstone meeting on 3 June 1950, and was won by an Ulster driven by Charles Bulmer, later to edit *Motor* magazine. The class went from strength to strength in the 1950s, with such notables as Colin Chapman, Eric Broadley, Len Terry, Derrick White, Jem Marsh and Derek Bennett all beginning their successful careers with 750 specials.

Regulations demanded the use of the Austin Seven frame, rear axle, crankcase, block and gearbox; supercharging was prohibited. In 1963 a move began to broaden the division's scope, and the Reliant 600cc ohv engine was admitted for the 1965 season. Chassis restrictions were relaxed in 1967, the only stipulation remaining that they be 52in (1·3208m) long members of 2in × 3in (50·8mm × 76·2mm) tubular section, and in 1968 back axle and suspension restrictions were modified to demand only a bevel-type differential (this virtually ruled out rear-engined designs without a great degree of complexity). The Reliant engine's admission was a great success for it proved to be on a par with a well-developed sv unit. Reliant induction was restricted to a 22mm choke, while ingenious amateur tuners produced Austin engines with 'de-siamesed' 8-port heads, double twin-choke carburettors and two plugs per cylinder. The class is essentially inexpensive and yet sees a degree of ingenuity and encourages much talent seldom evident in more exotic formulas. The F750 Champion in 1970 was Stuart Gerrell (Gerrell-Reliant). DCN

Formula 1172 (1200)

Following the success of Formula 750, the 750 Motor Club devised a big brother class for inexpensive motor racing, using the 1,172cc sv Ford 4-cylinder engine. No restrictions were made on chassis or suspension design, and so the amateur constructor was given much more scope for his ingenuity and expertise. In the 1960s the 1,200cc ohv Ford engine was admitted as the side-valves were becoming rather rare, and under the new title of Formula 1200 the class continued to flourish at an amateur club level. It is notable for the tremendous variety of designs and ideas used, with front- and rear-engined specials both being popular. Cost is limited by the prohibition of Hewland specialist transmissions, for example, although production Renault, VW and Imp gearboxes may be used in rear-engined designs. The F1200 Champion in 1970 was Jonathan Rope (Claydon-Ford). DCN

Formula F100

This class was evolved by Motor Racing Developments —a race management and promotional body connected

with the Brands Hatch, Mallory Park, Oulton Park and Snetterton group of circuits in England—in conjunction with the Firestone tyre company. Their F100 radial tyre had proved extremely successful and well-suited to Formula Ford racing, and the idea was to provide a kind of two-seat Formula Ford, with sports cars powered by Ford Escort 1300cc engines mated to Hewland transaxles. The result was an expensive formula which was not much faster than the Clubmans classes with which it was in direct competition. Royale, Beattie and other similar small constructors produced F100 cars for the formula's start in 1970, and despite initial criticism from Clubmans' Formula supporters, regular fields of cars were being seen by the end of the year. Ray Allen (Royale) was 1970 Champion. DCN

Formula Clubman

Another of the British 'poor man's' club racing formulas, Clubman began with the Radio Caroline Championship of 1964 which catered for sports cars normally constructed from kits and similar vehicles. This fairly lucrative competition attracted a lot of support from Lotus 7 and Mallock U2 owners and Formula Clubman, run in 1,000cc and 1,500cc classes, evolved from this. BMC 1-litre and Ford 1- and 1·5-litre engines are popular and the cars, many of them one-off specials, have proved very fast, occasionally approaching and bettering Formula 3 single-seater records. The 1970 Clubman Champion was Tim Goss (Lotus 7X). DCN

Formula Atlantic

Announced in August 1970 this was in essence an anglicized version of the SCCA Formula B for single-

Formula Clubman: C. Sturdgess (Lotus-Ford) leads R. Reader (Terrier-Ford) in the Lady Caroline Race at Mallory Park in 1965. *Photo: Ronald Hunt*

Below, Formula 750: David Coombs' Reliant Special at Lydden Hill, July 1970 *Photo: Bob Kidby*

Bottom, Formula 1172: Mike Eyre's Pegasus Special. *Photo: John D. Farlie*

seater racing cars with homologated production engines of not more than 1,600cc capacity. The idea was to have an intermediate formula between the existing Formulas 2 and 3, with cars costing about £3,000. A National Championship of about twenty races was planned for 1971, with the possibility of a European Championship in 1972. There is also the chance of a year-round transatlantic series of races. GNG

Saloon Car Racing

Present-day saloon car racing in Great Britain can be traced back to the BRDC's production car races, run at Silverstone during the club's International Trophy meetings. The first International Trophy meeting was in August 1949, and the 1-hour production car race held then was dominated by open sports cars, being won by Leslie Johnson's Jaguar XK from the similar car of Peter Walker and Culpan's Frazer Nash. But in among the open cars were three 2·5-litre Riley saloons and a pair of Jowett Javelins which delighted the crowd and showed up surprisingly well amid their more exotic rivals. They were handicapped by unrealistic international regulations which demanded that they run with the driver's window open and the rear window removed—presumably to aid ventilation—but the seeds were sown.

In May 1950 the Silverstone meeting saw closed cars from Jowett, Healey, Aston Martin, Riley and Lea-Francis running in the production car race, and by 1952 a separate 50-mile (80·47km) production touring car race was run, supporting another 50-miler for production sports models. Stirling Moss won in a Jaguar Mk VII, beginning the make's long-lasting domination of British saloon car racing, and winning from Wharton's Healey and Allard's Allard.

These events proved immensely popular with the crowd, for the antics of these basically standard cars when pushed to the limit made very entertaining racing. The idea had caught on, and saloon car events grew in importance during the 1950s, with various Jaguar models nearly always dominant overall, culminating in the long-lasting run of success for the 3·8-litre Mk I and Mk II saloons.

Left, Saloon Car Racing: B. A. Wood (Ford Anglia) leads J. V. Brownlee (DKW) through the chicane at Goodwood in 1961. *Photo: Michael Ware*

Right, Saloon Car Racing: the Pinter/ Berger Alfa Romeo GTAm passes the Searle/Nichols Ford Escort in the 1970 Spa 24 Hours Race. *Photo: Autosport*

In 1958 the British Racing & Sports Car Club organized their first British Saloon Car Championship, and this has since become the class's premier competition in the United Kingdom. Points were awarded in each of the up to 1,000cc, 1,001-1,300cc, 1,301-2,000cc and over 2,000cc classes, and in this way the overall champion could be a consistent class winner rather than an occasional winner overall, evening up the chances of the smaller car drivers with the Jaguar brigade. Jack Sears won that first year's competition, driving an Austin A105, and in 1959 Jeff Uren's Ford Zephyr took the title. G. S. Shepherd's Austin A40 was a popular winner in 1960, and Sir John Whitmore's works Cooper-Mini won in 1961. John Love scored BMC's third consecutive title in 1962, but great change came in 1963.

That season the John Willment Ford dealership team introduced a 7-litre Ford Galaxie to the fray. Dan Gurney had frightened the Jaguars at Silverstone with a Chevrolet Impala in 1961, and privately-entered American sedans had shown promise in 1962. Now Willment ran a seriously prepared car, and the 1963 May Silverstone meeting saw the rumbling Galaxie blow off the 3·8 Jaguars quite easily. However, they ran into considerable scrutineering problems concerning the full roll-over cage built into the monster saloons, and Jack Sears completed a season with points scored from both Galaxie and Cortina GT successes to take his 2nd title.

In 1964 all the major British meetings were enlivened by the sight of top-line drivers running in most of the minor events, and Jim Clark took the title in his works Lotus-Cortina. The light and easily handled Ford saloons dominated their classes. BMC ran their Coopers in the 1-litre and 1,300cc divisions, and Jack Sears, Sir Gawaine Baillie and Jack Brabham all drove Galaxies. Jaguar were now *passé*, and with Sunbeam's Rapiers and BMC's Riley 1·5s fading from the scene, saloon car racing had developed into a straight fight between Ford and BMC (Austin/Morris), with the crowd-pleasing Minis facing a formidable array of highly-tuned Anglias, Cortinas and Galaxies. The lighter Mustang was introduced in 1965, Roy Pierpoint winning a popular Championship with one, despite some acrimonious disputes with rival teams.

These Championships had been run to Group 2 International regulations, and in 1966 the BRSCC ran a Group 5 Championship, although the European Touring Car Challenge competition remained Group 2. Team Broadspeed moved to Ford after running BMC Mini-Coopers for two seasons (during which they often beat the works cars), and John Fitzpatrick won the title in one of their impeccably-prepared, F3-engined Anglias. Ford Falcons were introduced during the season, supplanting the Mustang, and in 1967 Frank Gardner's Alan Mann-entered Falcon dominated the Championship. The Australian repeated this performance in 1968, running a Cortina-FVA and Escort TC, again in Mann's red and gold colours. BLMC fought back in 1969 with Irishman Alec Poole's 1-litre Equipe Arden Mini snatching the title.

As a straight Ford/British Leyland battle, the Championship had lost some of its appeal, but the many thousands of pounds spent on Group 5 saloon car development made the competition interesting from the engineering viewpoint. Both superchargers and turbochargers were used on some of the cars, and revised valve gear drives and suspension systems (including the substitution of coil springs for leaves, etc.) added a lot of interest. For 1970 the Championship was changed to cater for Group 4 saloon cars, and many of the exotic additions and modifications of Group 5 had to be deleted. Rootes/Chrysler UK achieved a surprise Championship win with Bevan's private Imp driven by Bill McGovern. DCN

Stock Car Racing*

The British, Continental and Scandinavian interpretation of a stock car is very different indeed from that of the Americans and Canadians. In their terminology, 'stock' means standard or unmodified and the phrase was originally coined to describe the racing of production sedans on concrete, oval tracks. Progress has meant an influx of technology and money, and the current NASCAR or Trans-Am sedan is now a very highly developed machine capable of lapping at averages of up to 200mph.

East of the Atlantic the stock car might be described

*For American stock car racing see NASCAR, SCCA and USAC

Left, Stock Car Racing: a Formula I car at Hednesford Hills Raceway, Staffordshire. *Photo: Hednesford Hills Raceway*

Right, Stock Car Racing: a typical scene at Hednesford Hills. *Photo: Hednesford Hills Raceway*

as having gone the other way: instead of becoming more sophisticated, European stock cars started to employ chassis from commercial vehicles and mere approximations of bodywork.

In Britain, stock car racing has suffered through never having been governed by one strong, authoritative body, intent on national promotion. The state has been reached where there are two organizations, each with its regular 'circus' of drivers and cars, issuing two sets of competition licences, both of them now recognized by the RAC. As well as these two—centred on Hednesford Hills Raceway, Brownhills, Staffordshire, and Spedeworth Stadium, Aldershot—there are non-RAC organizations holding events for very cheap cars on shale, concrete or grass tracks. One such is the Sturton and Stow Motor Sports Association of Lincolnshire, which holds Autocross-type meetings and has properly constituted rules, producing safe, popular racing for cars like Jaguar Mk VIIs, Morris Isis and Riley 1·5 saloons. All glass is removed, roll bars are compulsory and the car must have no front passenger door—an effective escape hatch.

Other organizers, however, hold races in which the prime object is to eliminate all opposition by smashing the cars or driving them off the track. These races often leave much to be desired from the safety aspect, if not from local spectator appeal.

By the popular national definition, a Formula 1 stock car is a single-seat saloon with a body 'resembling' a standard production car, a stout separate chassis (usually commercial) and a 6-cylinder Jaguar or American V-8 engine. Quarter-mile oval circuits of cinders have produced few suspension developments but the winning cars may have engines costing many hundreds of pounds. A Formula 2 or Junior stock car is a similar machine, but with a 1,172cc sv Ford engine. In both cases, drivers are graded according to success and identified by different coloured roofs. Novice drivers always start in front on the rolling grid and much of the skill for the fast men is involved in getting through the slower cars.

The latest development from stock cars has been the rapid growth of 'hot rods', highly modified production cars with no bumper protection, but with fast and ex-

pensive engines. This is also now an RAC sport: according to old rules, no RAC competition licence holder could enter any non-RAC sport. Starting money is invariably paid and prize money is much greater than in RAC-backed club racing. The Cooper S is a popular hot rod, and so is the 1650cc Anglia, the Viva and the Zephyr. Lap times of 14secs for the $\frac{1}{4}$ mile are frequently recorded — the cars racing in very close company indeed.

In Scandinavia, stock car racing after World War 2 was often held on circuits ploughed out on frozen lakes, with old cars providing thrills for drivers and spectators at relatively low speeds. Anything with smooth tyres on sheet ice must be exciting. But ice racing, as it came to be known, grew rapidly in sophistication and respectability and now properly recognized and commercially sponsored events produce national champions. It is a major business as well as a sport, particularly in Sweden where British-prepared Ford Escort Twin Cams and Vauxhall Viva GTs compete with regular success against Saabs, Volvos, Opels and Porsches.

Other European countries went in for stock cars, France being notable for old Renaults and the national transport — the Citroën 2CV — jostling each other round short, open-air circuits. But mostly these events were held in conjunction with local fairs and holidays, there being little interest in promoting them for their own sake. Rallying and circuit racing developments soon ousted most stock car interests and few Continental events of the British type now remain. DH

Vintage Car Racing

The Vintage Sports Car Club was founded in England in 1934 with the primary purpose of organizing competitions for cars built before 1931: cars like Bentleys, Vauxhall 30/98s and Alvis 12/50s, which soon became known as 'vintage' cars. At that time pre-1905 cars, or 'veterans' were catered for by the Veteran Car Club, and in 1936 the VSCC introduced their 'Edwardian' class, for cars built between 1905 and 1915. In the mid-1930s a car like the 1908 GP Itala could be bought for £25, so a spur for the preservation of such machines was timely. Today the Edwardian Class comes under the wing of the Veteran Car Club as well as the VSCC, and the VCC date has been extended to include cars made up to and including 1918.

Trials, speed trials and race meetings, often in conjunction with other clubs, were organized by the VSCC before World War 2, and it was the VSCC which discovered Prescott Hill in Gloucestershire and suggested it as a sprint venue to the Bugatti Owners Club, as the VSCC itself was too small to finance such a venture.

VSCC membership was approximately 200 at the outbreak of war in 1939, but this had more than trebled by the end of 1946. Possibly the Club was at its most influential in those early post-war years as it was one of the first to organize speed events, notably the Elstree Speed Trials of Easter 1946, the Gransden Lodge Race Meeting (with the Cambridge University Automobile Club) in 1947, and the Luton Hoo Speed Trials in 1948, the last-named at a period when no petrol was allowed in Britain for pleasure purposes and no other meetings were held. Most of the spectators had to come by bus, and the competitors' cars burned racing fuel instead of the banned pump petrol.

On 23 April 1949, the VSCC held the first club meeting ever at Silverstone, a kilometre sprint with the cars running in pairs, to which the public was not invited.

After the war it had been decided to admit certain

approved sporting and expensive luxury cars of the 1930s to a new class in the VSCC to be known as Post Vintage Thoroughbreds or PVTs. The cars to be included in this category were decided by a referendum among the members. Up until 1951, modern cars had been allowed to take part in VSCC events alongside the Vintage and PVT ones, but after another referendum as a result of a motion put forward at the 1951 Annual General Meeting, it was decided that future VSCC events should be confined to Vintage and PVT cars. At the same time the Historic Racing Car class was instituted, for racing cars which were fifteen or more years old. In 1963 the age was reduced to twelve years, and in 1965 it was decided that the class would include Formula 1 Grand Prix cars up to 1960, provided they were front-engined, and this rule is likely to remain for the foreseeable future.

In 1970 the VSCC had approximately 6,000 members. A typical year's programme consists of four race meetings, two sporting trials, one in Wales and the other in the Lake District or Yorkshire, a speed hill-climb at Prescott and a speed trial at Curborough, plus various driving test meetings and navigational road rallies, of which the Measham Rally, held at night in January and centred on Church Stretton, Shropshire, is the toughest. The Pomeroy Trophy Contest, held at Silverstone in the early spring and purporting to find 'the ideal touring car' on formula (with a bonus for age, smallness of engine capacity and distance between the pedals and back axle) is a series of acceleration, handling and braking tests, plus a one-hour high-speed trial for cars of any age, including moderns in this case, of over 1950cc capacity. To date (1970) the Trophy has been won twice by an Edwardian (1914 TT Sunbeam) and three times by post-war cars (1954 Triumph TR2, 1956 Aston Martin DB

Vintage Car Racing: the start of the VSCC Boulogne Trophy Race at Silverstone, July 1969. Left to right (front row), Neil Corner (Sunbeam Tiger), G. S. St John (Bugatti Type 35B), P. Morley (Bentley 4½-litre). *Photo: Studio 3*

Right above, Vintage Car Racing: a typical pre-war GN Special, the Chawner-GN built in about 1930, driven by P. J. A. Evans at Silverstone in 1969. *Photo: Studio 3*

Right, Vintage Car Racing: a Delage 14/40 sports tourer at a VSCC Hill Climb at Prescott, Gloucestershire. *Photo: Studio 3*

and 1962 Ferrari GTO). Vintage and PVT cars have won the other 12 Trophies.

In VSCC racing, Type 35B 2·3-litre GP Bugattis have been the most successful vintage racing cars, followed by 3-litre Bentleys fitted with 4·5-litre engines, weight of numbers helping these marques. The main races are the Vintage Seaman Trophy at Oulton Park (23 laps or 100 kilometres until 1963, but 10 laps thereafter) and the 10-lap Itala Trophy and Boulogne Trophy races at Silverstone.

In races for Pre-war Historic Racing Cars, 1·5 and 2-litre ERAs have been supreme since 1950, only a 1935 8C-35 3·8-litre Alfa Romeo and a 1934 2·9-litre 8CM Maserati having beaten them in the main race, the Seaman Historic Trophy. These victories were at Silverstone, before the race was moved to Oulton Park in 1956.

The majority of the races at VSCC meetings are 4- or 5-lap handicaps for sports and racing cars, with the handicaps based on known performance—the same system that was used at Brooklands.

Of the post-war cars, the most successful contenders over the years have been GP Aston Martins, 250F Maseratis, Lotus 16s, A-type Connaughts and Cooper-Bristols. Since the inception of the main race for this type of car, the 15-lap Hawthorn Trophy at Silverstone, in 1965, 250F Maseratis have won the race three times, and Lotus 16s twice.

Such is the popularity of the spectacle of Historic Car racing that VSCC members have been invited to put on races with their cars abroad, at Rouen in France, Karlskoga in Sweden and Roskilde in Denmark.

Though speed events for pre-war cars are occasionally held in Australasia, Singapore, USA, France and Italy, they are necessarily on a smaller scale than VSCC

meetings in the UK, where more old racing cars are preserved than in any other country. PMAH

Trials

The history of the British endurance-type trial goes back, along with racing, virtually to the first primitive motorcars and motorcycles. Thus the first organizing body to look at in this context must be the Motor Cycling Club which, inspite of its title, has catered for the trialling interests of 2-wheel and 4-wheel enthusiasts since 1901. Despite changing tastes and economic climates, it is fascinating to note that three of this club's original long-distance events, the Edinburgh, the Land's End and the Exeter, are still thriving and attracting more entries every year. Indeed, one event now enjoys the sponsorship of a national magazine, and another national motoring magazine regularly enters drivers on these occasions.

Now known in club circles as the Classic Trials, these three are open to solo motor cycles, combinations, and cars and vehicles of estate car type to which any modification (apart from a limited slip differential) may have been made. Four-wheel-drive vehicles are not allowed. A typical entry would consist of most types of everyday road car, a selection of older MGs, HRGs, Austins and the like, with a preponderance of supercharged 1,172cc Ford Populars, Hillman Imps, Volkswagens and Morgans.

Front-wheel-drive cars never seem to fare very well, as the competitive sections consist of little-used lanes, usually very steep and rough and sometimes incorporating an obligatory stop and restart half-way up. These sections (which must be traversed without stopping, to avoid penalties) are linked by long, easily-timed road sections.

Other trials which were popular in pre-war days included the Scottish Six Days—a real mud marathon attracting drivers from all over the country. Then, as now, at least one passenger had to be carried to read the fairly easy route card provided, check the timing and bounce to assist traction when the going was very doubtful.

From these early events—which promoted much friendly rivalry, still one of the most heartening features of the sport at club level—activities branched off into Sporting Trials (for specially built, open two-seater cars), Production Car or Standard Car Trials (for road cars unmodified in any way) and Rallies (with the accent on speedy driving and navigation over meandering minor roads.

The two trials branches both concentrated themselves on very closely grouped hills, away from roads altogether, running up grassland, moorland or through woods. This meant that much less travelling had to be done, so costs came down, yet techniques remained the same and everyone was happy.

Hills are divided into sections (usually 12) by marker poles either side of the hill, numbered from 12 at the bottom to 1 at the top. If a driver comes to rest with the hub of one or both front wheels beyond, say, the 3 flags, he would be in section 2 and thus score only 2 penalty points. If he is lucky enough to be able to drive out of the top of the hill without having 'ceased forward motion' up it, then there are no penalties. Most hills are attempted once before lunch and once after in quite a leisurely fashion—but with no practising of course—and the man with least penalties at the end of the day wins. This formula has proved itself successful and is still used

Trials: a 1935 Singer Le Mans negotiating a watersplash in a pre-war trial. *Photo: Montagu Motor Museum*

Opposite, Saloon Car Racing: In front, Ray Calcutt driving the Ian Fraser Team Imp followed by a Mini-Cooper S and a Ford Anglia at Brands Hatch. *Photo: Geoff Goddard*

Trials: S. J. Onslow Bartlett's special of 1952 was distinctly unusual in employing a rear-mounted JAP V-twin engine. *Photo: Autosport*

wheels and actuated by two levers, usually placed just outside the cockpit on the offside, one for each rear wheel. They enable the driver to lock a wheel while the other turns under power, thus helping to twist the car round tight, slow bends on soft surfaces. Watching the experts do this on an impossible gradient where the spectator can hardly stand in an upright position is indeed an education. Another trick of the trade is to let the rear tyres down to a very low pressure to 'spread them out' over as wide an area as possible. To prevent them being torn off in motion they are actually bolted to the wheel rim.

Until recently, cars had to be legally usable on the road (with lights and other Ministry of Transport requirements, etc); most of them now arrive at venues on trailers and are now no longer required to drive on roads from one muddy climb to the next. It is said that only about fifty such cars exist in England, but if this is so, every one of them must be in full use during the trialling season. Many of them are immaculate and most seem to be Cannons (see page 390). However, driver skill, and many years' experience, play a much larger part in trials success than mechanical innovations, which makes it one of the cheapest branches of the sport in which to become involved. The 750 Motor Club organizes championships.

The same can be said for production car trials, run on exactly the same lines, but needless to say, with rather smoother hills — though cars in both branches of trialling have been known to turn over on steep gradients. In production trialling, cars are classed according to their engine and drive layout, with no subdivisions on capacity. Success seems to vary from type to type according to whether the going is firm or soft. Gerry Evans, who was British Trials and Rally Drivers' Association Champion in 1969 in an Austin 1300, obviously found fwd quite satisfactory, yet past champions have used Simcas, Hillman Imps and Volkswagens. DH

Autocross and Rallycross

Autocross — or cars racing in pairs against the clock over grass or loose earth surfaces — must have enjoyed the fastest growth rate of any branch of motor sport. Origins are badly documented, possibly because the first enthusiasts took part in very informal timed hill-climbs on mud, using hand-held stopwatches and no RAC permit. It is clear, however, that they developed in the United Kingdom shortly after World War 2 in the South of England — the element of time being introduced to what would otherwise have been just a normal production car trial up a grassy hill.

It did not take long for the promoters to turn the hill into a circuit and decide that two cars racing together were more exciting than one. Ken Wharton, a brilliant driver, whose name is now linked with a leading annual driving test (or autotest) meeting, was an early winner and cars included specials such as his own, family saloons of the day, MG Midget sports cars, HRGs, Allards and American-inspired Ford Pilot V-8s.

Special preparation and specific RAC rules were still unknown, and the sport grew steadily over the next ten years until the British Trials and Rally Drivers' Association formed the first National Championship. This coincided with the advent of the Mini as a cheap, easily handled car so the success of Autocross was assured. Then Players Cigarettes backed a Midlands Championship in 1966 with maximum press coverage and the sport had suddenly 'arrived'.

today, with only a few small variations at lower-status local events. In the event of two or more drivers tieing, the one who is proportionally better than the best 50% in his class is the winner.

The sporting trial two-seaters (the hills for which may often incorporate a stream, mounds of heather and the remains of drystone walls) are now constructed to very specific RAC regulations. The passenger must be 'normally seated', although bouncing is permitted and the size of chassis and position of engine in it is closely regulated. Austin 7 engines are no longer obligatory.

Mostly, sv Ford engines with 3-speed gearboxes are used and all the cars have the ingenious 'fiddle-brake' system. These are handbrakes operating on the rear

The following year—and right up to 1970—the same company sponsored a National Championship, with qualifying rounds throughout England, Scotland and Northern Ireland. First National Champion was Peter Watkin, a private investigator who drove a Lotus Elan on which, it was said, £500 had been spent on modifications. Much of this would probably have gone into strengthening the car, for in the final it scored a decisive victory on a hilly and extremely muddy track.

Although the Mini must be the most universally popular car for autocross, it is interesting to note that at the time of writing, every National Autocross Champion has driven a front-engine, rwd car. Following the Elan, there was Rod Chapman (who used two Lotus-Cortinas and a Ford Escort during his winning year) and then Mike Day, a Kent fruit farmer, in a TVR Tuscan sports car with American Ford Cobra engine.

On the other hand, the BTRDA title has been taken twice in rear-engined Volkswagens, once by the journalist Laurie Manifold and once by a Bournemouth garage proprietor Jim Taylor. The latter's car featured a Porsche engine and close ratio gearbox, which illustrates how car preparation has changed since drivers merely wound down the windows of the family Hillman Minx to avoid them breaking in the event of a roll-over. Although very fast and spectacular, fwd cars have never enjoyed much national success in autocross, in spite of taking more fastest times of day at lesser meetings than probably any other type of car.

Main class divisions in the sport are by power and drive layouts, with subdivisions according to capacity. Thus fwd cars are divided into 850cc, 850–1,000cc (excluding S-type Minis) and over 1,000cc at most meetings. Front-engine, rear-drive cars are split at the 1,300cc mark (producing technical innovations like 1,300cc twin-cam Lotus-Cortinas and Escorts); sports and GT cars are divided in the same way; there is a class for Specials of all capacities, and one for rear-engined cars of all capacities.

This rear-engined class has been the cause of some controversy, as 875cc Hillman Imps (a popular car in lower-grade autocross) have traditionally had the thin end of the wedge from their 998cc counterparts and 1,600cc Volkswagens. In the Specials group, technical innovation has always been impeded by the handicap of $2\frac{1}{2}\%$ or 5% on times on 4-wheel drive vehicles.

Tony Fisher's Bufi-Mowog, with a Cooper S engine at the front and a supercharged 1100 unit at the rear (each driving the appropriate pair of wheels) came closest to victory overall but when he returned the following year with the wheelbase lengthened by about a foot for better handling, the car hardly ever figured in the results again. People still keep trying, however, and it is a credit to ingenuity that machines like Howard Parkin's 4-wheel-drive, 4-wheel-steering Special still pound the turf. While topless Mini saloons seem the favourite Special variant in Northern Ireland, 1,275cc S engines in tiny, home-made frames are most popular in England, Eric Clegg's Leda 1, which has taken awards in speed hill-climbs and Rallycross as well, being a typical example.

Very few sports cars have made a lasting mark in autocross, Mike Day's TVR being the outstanding exception. The Porsche 911 of Sid Reekes has been a consistent winner in the smoother Sandocross events, held regularly at Ainsdale Beach, Lancashire, by the Liverpool Motor Club, and an extremely well-prepared Mk I Sprite has scored in autocross and rallycross in the

Autocross: a mid-engined autocross special with a big-engined Ford Anglia at a Players National Championship qualifier near Bradford, Yorkshire. Just after the photo was taken, the cars collided, bending the Anglia's front wing. *Photo: David Hardcastle*

Opposite, RAC Trials: A 1965 RAC Trials Championship event. *Photo: Geoff Goddard*

Autocross: Colin Hargreaves' Flymo, powered by a BMC 1·3-litre engine, at Morecombe, Lancashire, in July 1970. *Photo: Peter McFadyen*

hands of Nick Ramus.

Autocross is now very much part of the established British sporting scene, with well over 30 meetings per weekend throughout the country in the summer months. Attendances at the larger, better-promoted ones can exceed 6,000, with trade exhibitions, demonstration drives by top names and performance car shows being incorporated with the largest. Up to 120 entries per meeting are allowed, with the vast majority of top contenders being towed to the meeting in true racing style.

With the increase in popularity, costs have inevitably risen. A guaranteed class winner will probably have a limited slip differential, close ratio box, magnesium alloy wheels, lightened and strengthened bodywork and a fully race-tuned engine. Indeed, the only differences between it and its smooth surface counterpart could be the strengthening, chunky-tread tyres and slightly smaller valve sizes to retain the torque essential for muddy surfaces. But with the generosity of sponsors, like Players, and Guards Cigarettes (and local newspapers in many cases) among them, prize money has risen as well. This is still not on a par with racing, of course, with a class victory being worth perhaps £6.

Although two cars chasing each other round a circuit of, say, 1,000yd, with sharp and gentle left- and right-hand bends, sounds like guaranteed excitement, in many cases such events turn out to be processional, with the better driver or faster car getting in front at the start and staying there. Thus a criticism levelled at autocross is that it can, in fact, be boring for the spectators (though hardly for the drivers—it is a foolish man indeed who does not fit a stout roll-over bar inside his car, along with a full harness seat belt).

This has resulted in venues being specially prepared for four-at-a-time autocross, with the RAC-stipulated increases in track width, bankings for the safety of spectators, and so on. Another more controversial solution was put forward by a sponsor, that of making each two-car run a knock-out: the first past the flag goes on to race the next, the loser dropping out each time. After discussion with drivers, club officials etc, this was modified for 1970 so that the fastest four only in each

sponsorship again comes from major companies. Minis are again predominant and Hugh Wheldon, like Mike Day a Kent fruit farmer, beat all the works-backed cars to take the last Wills Championship in his own battered 1,293cc Cooper S. Drivers now tend to move up to rallycross after a season or two in autocross, while the sport itself is moving up to international level. Demonstrations by British drivers abroad have sparked off championships in many countries, Austria being one of the most enthusiastic. DH

Karting

Karting is the simplest and cheapest form of motor sport available. The tiny vehicles with 5in (127mm) wheels and completely devoid of bodywork may cost as

Left, Autocross: John Taylor's works Ford 1800 Escort at Croft in November 1970. *Photo: Autosport*

class 'knock out', times still being taken in order to determine the ftd winner. Many participants, as well as the motor sporting press, are worried that this may produce much wilder driving with consequently greater hazards to vehicles and drivers.

Rallycross—four cars racing against each other over a variety of surfaces, such as those found on an average rally special stage—is entirely a product of television. The sport was devised when several leading personalities in TV and the press (including Robert Reid and Barry Gill, the latter now employed by Fords) watched a replay of what TV had salvaged from the remains of the 1967 RAC International Rally of Great Britain. This had been cancelled at the very last minute owing to travelling restrictions imposed by a disastrous outbreak of foot and mouth disease. A southern forest special stage was to have been televised, and competitors were invited to run their cars through the stage, purely for the benefit of TV. Many of them did, and the result produced such an enthusiastic response from viewers that something similar was obviously worth repeating.

So Reid, Gill and the others devised an event which would put rally drivers up against each other on a circuit consisting of tarmac, earth, chalk and grass, the first man past the flag to win. Venues became established at Lydden Hill and Croft racing circuits, with Cadwell Park (perhaps the best of all) being used briefly. TV coverage—chiefly by the British Broadcasting Corporation—attracted factory-backed entries from Ford, British Leyland and, initially, Rootes—and a wealth of machines from leading rally, autocross and racing clubmen.

Speeds are generally much higher in rallycross than autocross, the tracks being longer and wider, and

Above, Karting: a scene at the Kart Track, Guernsey, Channel Islands. *Photo: Guernsey Press*

Left, Karting: Irving Jacobs on a Class IV Piranha. *Photo: Autosport*

little as £170, yet have a maximum speed of over 100mph (160kph). The first kart was built in Los Angeles in August 1956. It used a 2·5hp West Bend 750 lawn-mower engine and was the work of Art Ingels, a mechanic at Frank Kurtis' racing car workshops, and gasoline distributor Lou Borelli. Within a year Karts were in production at several factories, and racing began at the Rose Bowl, Pasadena. The Go Kart Club of America was formed in December 1957, and a set of rules drawn up which have remained virtually unchanged since. The karts' wheelbase had to be between 40 and 50in (1·016 and 1·27m), and the track not less than ⅔ of the wheelbase. Engine capacities were in three classes, 84cc, 168cc, and 270cc. These were subsequently changed to 100cc, 200cc and 270cc. The popularity of karting spread rapidly across America, and arrived in Britain in 1959 via the United States Air Force. Within a year Britain had over 120 kart manufacturers, but as so often happens the boom collapsed, and the number stabilized at about 16 to 20. Since 1960 kart meetings have been held at over 100 tracks in the United Kingdom, including several 'big car circuits' such as Silverstone, Brands Hatch and Oulton Park. Karting is currently popular in almost every country in Europe, in the Soviet Union, Australia, New Zealand, and in many other places such as Hawaii, Brunei, Kuwait, the Philippines, Thailand and Hong Kong.

Although chassis dimensions are standardized, capacity limits vary from one country to another. Generally, however, kart engines are single-cylinder air-cooled 2-stroke units of between 100cc and 250cc. Gearboxes are forbidden in the smaller karts (Class I, 100cc in Britain) and compulsory on the larger machines (Class IV, 250cc). Frames vary from the simple ladder type to complicated multi-tubular chassis. The maximum overall length of the kart must not exceed 72in (1·829m), 60in (1·524m) in the United States). Springs and shock absorbers are not forbidden, but unsprung frames have proved to be the most appropriate to karts. However, the chassis can be made to flex up to 3in (76·2mm). Any form of bodywork is forbidden; apart from aesthetic reasons it is difficult to see any advantages in fitting bodies to karts. They would increase the weight and price, and be more likely to trap the driver in the event of an accident. At kart speeds the aerodynamic advantages would be negligible, and offset by the increased weight.

Karting originally took place on tracks with straights of no more than 100yd (now 150yd), but more experienced drivers familiar with the world of motorcycle racing soon demanded bigger circuits. Karting is now organized on many motor racing circuits where speeds compare favourably with those of cars: at Brands Hatch a Class IV Matador Bultaco kart lapped at 72mph (115·87kph), compared with 71·54mph (115·13 kph) for a 875cc Hillman Imp saloon, and 67·84mph (109·17kph) for a JW-4 Formula 4 racing car. The shorter kart races are not more than 5 miles (8km), but long-distance races of 6 hours, 9 hours, and even 24 hours also take place. The winner of a 9-hour Class IV race at Snetterton in 1966 averaged 64·74mph (104·18kph).

Karting can be enjoyed by a wider age range than any other form of motor sport. There is a recognized Junior Class for drivers of between 13 and 16, and the British Outright Champions have varied between 16 and 56 years of age. GNG

Model Car Racing

Racing with model cars began in the United States in the late 1930s, using engines from model aircraft. These were nearly always 10cc air-cooled single-cylinder 2-stroke units by Hornet, McCoy, or Dooling. Some cars were sold as construction kits and reached speeds of 100mph (160kph). Later, smaller units of 1·6, 2·5, 3·2, and 5cc were made.

During World War 2 American servicemen brought the sport to Europe, and it became particularly popular in France, Italy, and Sweden. In February 1952 the Fédération Européenne du Modélisme Automobile (FEMA) was founded under the leadership of Gustavo Clerici (Italy) and Philipe Rochat (Switzerland). Four classes were established, 1·5, 2·5, 5, and 10cc, and these still prevail today. For novices a special category has been set up known as the Monza. For this only one type

of car is used, a magnificent Ferrari model with very simple controls. Engine capacity is 2·5cc, and speeds of 150kph have been attained. Engines are vertical single-cylinder 2-stroke units running at speeds of up to 25,000rpm, and developing power at the rate of 200bhp per litre. For comparison, current Formula 1 engines develop at most 150bhp per litre. Speeds attained by the model cars run up to 160mph (255kph): see table. Ignition on current models is by incandescent plug (Glow Plug) except on some 5 and 10cc engines which use a magneto or even electronic ignition. Compression ratios are in the region of 12:1. All models take the same general form, with fuel tank at the front (capacity of 20 to 120cc according to engine size), followed by the device for cutting off the flow of fuel to the engine (the only method of stopping the cars at the end of a race), then the engine, and behind that final drive by shaft and bevel, without differential. Front-wheel drive was tried one time, but has been abandoned in favour of rear-wheel drive for reasons of weight distribution and wheel adhesion. Bodies are made of duralumin or fibreglass.

Since the foundation of FEMA in 1952 the following countries have become members: Italy, Switzerland, France, Germany, Sweden, Denmark, Great Britain, Belgium, the Netherlands, Poland, Czechoslovakia. They will probably soon be joined by the Soviet Union. From April to October races are held every Sunday, and the European Championship is held at the beginning of August in turn by the most active countries. Some European enthusiasts cross the Atlantic, but Americans only race in the 10cc category.

Races are held on circular courses under the following

Above, Model Car Racing: contributor Geoffroy de Beauffort starting his 5cc car by means of a special fork holding a battery which gives the initial ignition. *Photo: Geoffroy de Beauffort Collection*

Left above, Model Car Racing: Freddy Streun, 1967 European 10cc champion, with his car which achieved nearly 230kph at the Basle track. *Photo: Philipe Rochat*

Model Car Racing: a 2·5cc car, capable of 190kph at an engine speed of 22,000rpm. *Photo: Geoffroy de Beauffort Collection*

conditions: the diameter of the track is 65·32ft (19·91m) which, with eight laps, gives a race of 1,640·42ft (exactly 500m). The cars are attached to a central pylon by a steel thread whose thickness varies according to the car's capacity. Cars run one at a time; the competitor is allowed 3 minutes in which to warm up his engine before the timekeeper gives the starting signal. After eight laps have been completed—at speeds of over 140mph (225kph) a lap is covered in less than one second—the time is taken, and the competitor is allowed a further ten laps in which to bring his car to a standstill. Time-keeping has to be very accurate as the outcome of a championship can rest on 1/100th of a second.

L'automodélisme is a truly amateur sport, receiving no subsidies from industry or advertisers. It offers the chance of finding original solutions to the problems of speed without great expense, and its enthusiasts can reflect with pride that when Surtees lapped Monza at 140·43mph (226kph) a model car on the nearby 'miniature Monza' lapped at 147·26mph (237kph). GdeB

Model Car Racing: Absolute Records on 1 January 1971

Class	Holder	Speed
1·5cc	Oerkenyi (Hungary)	111·856mph (180·90kph)
2·5cc	Mme Mondani (Italy)	133·651mph (215·56kph)
5cc	Peto (Hungary)	136·787mph (220·85kph)
10cc (Europe)	Zetterström (Switzerland)	151·050mph (243·57kph)
(USA)	Torrey jun	158·489mph (255·39kph)
Monza	Zaugg (Germany)	96·331mph (155·03kph)

Voiturette Racing

The term voiturette was first used by Léon Bollée for his 3-wheeler of 1895, but soon came to be applied by manufacturers and journalists to any small car. The first appearance of a voiturette class in racing was in the Paris-Amsterdam-Paris race of 1898, when cars of under 400kg had a separate class. Most of the town-to-town races from 1900 onwards had a voiturette class, supplemented by a class for *voitures légères* (400 to 650kg).

The most widely-supported era of voiturette racing lasted from 1906 to 1910 when the Coupe de l'Auto (or Coupe des Voiturettes as it was sometimes called), Grand Prix des Voiturettes, Sicilian Cup and Catalan Cup attracted nearly forty manufacturers of small cars to enter their products. Most were singularly unsuccessful, but the races saw the first successes of such well-known makes as Delage, Hispano-Suiza, and Sizaire-

Voiturette Racing: Bédélia, Super and Duo cyclecars at the start of the 1913 Cyclecar Grand Prix at Amiens. *Photo: T. A. S. O. Mathieson Collection*

Model Car Racing: Speeds attained. *FEMA*

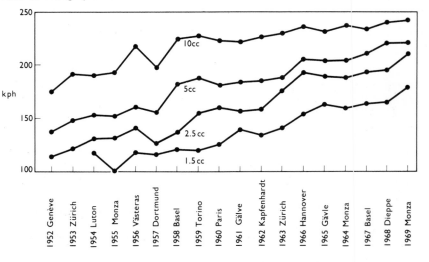

Naudin. The definition of a voiturette depended on the cylinder bore and varied from year to year, but, except in 1909, no restrictions were made on the stroke. This resulted in freak designs such as the 1910 Lion-Peugeot VX-5 with dimensions of 80 × 280mm and a bonnet so high that the driver had to peer round it. From 1911 to 1914 the Coupe de l'Auto was for cars of 3-litres' capacity and was supported by such firms as Vauxhall, Sunbeam, and Peugeot. These were very fine racing cars, hardly voiturettes in the usual sense, and were quite capable of holding their own with Grand Prix cars as Rigal's 3rd place in the 1912 Grand Prix demonstrated. Just before the outbreak of World War 1, a new class of small car appeared, the cyclecar. A number of races were held for these spidery little machines, with a capacity limit of 1,100cc. The most celebrated were the Cyclecar Grands Prix of Amiens and Le Mans, both held in 1913. In the early 1920s voiturette races were held at Le Mans, Boulogne, Brescia and other places, to a 1,400cc limit in 1920 and 1,500cc thereafter.

In 1926 1,500cc became the limit for Grand Prix cars, and no smaller class emerged immediately. The term voiturette had long since passed out of use for touring cars, and ceased to have a precise definition in racing. During the 1930s when Grand Prix cars were built to Formule Libre or the 750kg limit, a number of races were held for cars of 1,100 or 1,500cc, and these were frequently called voiturette races. Examples were the Comminges Voiturette Races, Picardy Voiturette Races, and the Masaryk Voiturette Grand Prix at Brno. The term practically died out after 1939, although a few post-war Formula 2 events were called voiturette races. GNG

Eastern Europe

Peace Cup

Motor sport in Eastern Europe is governed by FIA rules as in the West, although the variety of events is much smaller. The most popular class of racing is Formula 3, and an international trophy called the Peace or Friendship Cup was instituted in 1964. Teams of four members each from the Soviet Union, Bulgaria, Czechoslovakia, Hungary, the German Democratic Republic, Poland and Rumania have taken part in these races. Races are held on various circuits in each of the countries. The 1970 results are as follows:

Below, Czechslovakia: Vladimir Valenta's Formula Junior Mustang, 1962 *Photo: Vladimír Havránek Collection*

Right, German Democratic Republic: Paul Greifzu in his BMW Special. *Photo: Vladimír Havránek Collection*

Peace Cup: 1970

1st	Czechoslovakia	74 points
	Vladimír Hubaček	*Lotus-Ford*
	Vladimír Ondřejik	*Lotus-Ford*
	Jaroslav Mlček	*MGK-Wartburg*
	Zdeněk Smatlánek	*Melkus-Wartburg*
2nd	Poland	68 points
3rd	German Democratic Republic	62 points
4th	U.S.S.R.	30 points

Best individual performances during 1970 were as follows:

1st	Vladimír Ondřejik (CS)	*Lotus-Ford*
2nd	A. V. Andrejev (SU)	*Estonia-Ford*
3rd	Vladimír Hubaček (CS)	*Lotus-Ford*

Regulations for 1971 are uncertain, as Czechoslovakia has introduced her own Formula Skoda, and Hungary inclines towards Formula Vee as the basis for the Peace Cup. VH

Bulgaria

Before World War 2 political and economic conditions in Bulgaria did not encourage the growth of motor sport, but a small club existed in Sofia. After the war activities for motorcycles took priority for a number of years, but recently rallies have begun to be organized. This development has been stimulated by the licence production of Renault and, more recently, Alpine cars in Bulgaria. The leading rally organized by the Bulgarian Automobile and Touring club is the three-day Zlatni Piassatzi Rally. VH

Czechoslovakia

Before World War 2 Czechoslovakia had a number of major races, particularly the Masaryk Grands Prix held on the Brno circuit, which attracted drivers of international fame. This race continued as a Formula 1 event with international participation until 1949, but after that it became a Formule Libre race with largely local drivers. The shortage of suitable factory-built cars led to the appearance of a large number of privately-made cars, some of which were of very interesting design. At first most cars were based on the 2-cylinder Aero Minor (which was seen at Le Mans and elsewhere in 1949), but later Skoda and Fiat 1100 engines were used. One of the neatest and more successful of the Fiat-based cars was the Magda, built and driven by Jaroslav Vlcek of Prague. With the coming of Formula Junior in 1960, a new generation of privately-made racing car appeared, mostly with rear-mounted Wartburg engines. The first of these was the Mustang, built by Vladimir Valenta of Brno. Output was 80bhp and speed 125mph (200kph). A more unusual car was Jiri Gajdos' Delfin, the only air-cooled Formula Junior car in the world. It used one half of a Tatra 603 V-8 engine, reduced to 1,100cc capacity. The clutch came from a Volga, and transmission from a Fiat 600D. Output was 80bhp at 8,500rpm, and maximum speed over 125mph (200kph). When Formula Junior became the new Formula 3 in 1964, a further crop of home-built cars appeared, mostly using Wartburg engines and transmissions. From 1966 to 1969 the Skoda factory ran a team of Formula 3 cars which competed in the Peace Cup.

During 1970 a new formula, Formula Skoda, was announced. This was for single-seater cars based on the Skoda 100/110 and 1000 and 1100MB engines. Only limited modifications were allowed to the engine, and gearbox, steering, suspension components and front disc brakes had to be derived directly from the production car. As in Formula Ford, monocoque construction was not permitted. Minimum weight was 400kg. Stand-

Hungary

Hungary has long been a country more famous for horses than for motorcars, and before World War 2 there were only two race circuits, at Budapest and at Pecs. Only in one year (1936) was an international Grand Prix held on the Budapest circuit. The most celebrated Hungarian driver was Ferenc Szisz (1873–1970) who won the first French Grand Prix of 1906, but among others who completed between the wars were Count Rudolf Kinský, Count Tivadar Zichy, Marcel Hofer, Alan Szénássy and Viktor Szmik who drove a Hungarian-built Weiss Manfred into 2nd place in the 1929 Monte Carlo Rally, Hofer drove an MG in the 1936 Budapest GP.

After World War 2 motorcycling took priority for a few years, but in 1950 a number of home-built cars based on Fiat Balilla, Alfa Romeo and BMW machines began to appear in local races. A few races were held for Formula Junior cars in the early 1960s, but there were too few machines to make this a success, and Formula 3 held out more possibilities. Hungarian amateurs began to build F3 cars powered by Wartburg engines, and from 1964 joined other East European countries in competing for the Peace Cup. Later, Formula Vee attracted even more Hungarian competitors. Leading Hungarian drivers in F3 and FVee today include Tibor Szeles, Ferenc Kiss, Istvan Sulyok, Ferenc Demmel and Michel de Sergo.

Rallies are also popular in Hungary, including the Rally Cordatic. VH

ard wheels with road tyres were obligatory, and equipment had to include seat harnesses, electric circuit-breakers and fire-extinguishing equipment. Formula Skoda was intended to replace Formula 3 in Czechoslovakia in 1971, and also to be extended to Poland and Hungary. VH

Czechoslovakia: Jaroslav Vlček's Fiat-engined Magda, 1954. *Photo: Vladimír Havránek Collection*

German Democratic Republic

The first competition cars to appear in the new republic in East Germany came from Rennkollectiv Johannesthal outside Berlin. Work began in 1950, and in 1952 both Formula 2 and sports cars appeared under the name EMW and later AWE, by which time the works had moved from Johannesthal to Eisenach. One of the leading private racing car builders was Paul Greifzu whose BMW-engined car won the first race held in East Germany, at Leipzig in 1951. Later cars from East Germany included the SEG and the Melkus, both using the 3-cylinder 2-stroke Wartburg unit which has been a boon to constructors in Eastern Europe generally.

There are a number of good circuits in East Germany, of which the best-known are the Sachsenring, Dessau, Schleizer Dreieck and the Halle-Saale-Schleife. In early post-war years Formula 3 was the most popular, followed by Formula 2 and sports car events, Formula Junior from 1962 and the new Formula 3 from 1964. A number of these races attracted international participation, with such cars as Cooper, Lola and Lotus Formula Junior and Formula 3 competing against the local SEG and Melkus machines.

East German rallies include the DDR, Sachsenring, and Wartburg events. VH

Czechoslovakia: Jiří Gajdoš' Formula Junior Delfin, 1964. *Photo: Vladimír Havránek Collection*

Poland

There have been a number of famous racing drivers of Polish origin, such as Count Eliot Zborowski and his son Louis, Count Czaykowski and others, but they were either born or became famous outside their own country. The most celebrated native Polish driver of the pre-World War 2 period was Henryk Liefeldt (1894–1937) who drove Hispano-Suiza and Austro-Daimler cars. The leading events of the period were the Polish Rally, which began in 1921 with a 280-mile (450km) route and by 1939 had been extended to 2,800 miles (4,500km), and the Lwów Grand Prix, held from 1930 to 1933. The first Grand Prix was won by Liefeldt on his Austro-Daimler, but thereafter foreign competitors dominated the event.

After World War 2 the Polish Rally was revived, and continues today as one of the leading East European rallies, but racing took much longer to become re-established. Under the inspiration of Jerzy Jankowski the Rak Formula 3 racing cars appeared in 1963, and international races for F3 cars began at various circuits, of which the most famous is Cracow. VH

Rumania

Motor sport has never been very prominent in Rumania, and before World War 2 only a very limited number of hill-climbs and races were organized. Among these was the Formule Libre Bucharest Grand Prix held in 1937 and 1939 over 82 miles (132km). The leading Rumanian driver before the war was Jean Calcianu who drove Maserati and Duesenberg cars, finishing 2nd in the 1937 Bucharest GP in the latter. Zamfirescu and Cristea won the 1936 Monte Carlo Rally in a Ford V-8, and were well placed in other years.

After World War 2 motorcycling became popular, and since the early 1960s rallies and hill-climbs have been organized. The leading rally is the Danube which attracts international competition. Hill-climbs take place at Ploest and Cluj. Rumanian drivers have competed in the Peace Cup, but there are no Rumanian-built racing cars.

Top, German Democratic Republic: the start of a Formula 3 race at the Sachsenring. *Photo: Vladimír Havránek Collection*

Above, Soviet Union: drivers lined up before the Le Mans-type start of a sports car race at Minsk in 1958. *Photo: Keystone Press Agency Ltd*

Jim Kaser of SCCA and Bob Hanna of CASC, directors of motor sport in the United States and Canada, 1969–70. *Photo: Al Bochroch*

Soviet Union

No private cars were built in the Soviet Union for ten years after the Revolution of October 1917, and there was virtually no motor sport in the country during that period. It is recorded that a motor race was held in Moscow in 1924; this, like the Leningrad-Tiflis-Moscow Trial of 1925, must have attracted only foreign machines. The first Soviet racing car was the GL-1 of 1938, based on the contemporary 3·6-litre GAZ M-1 sedan. It had a maximum speed of nearly 100mph (160kph), but was a test-bed rather than a competition car.

During the 1950s Soviet attention was concentrated on the building of some successful record-breaking cars such as the Zvezdas and the Kharkovs. Russia joined the FIA in 1958, and only after this date were Soviet records officially accepted as International Records. Racing did not get under way until the late 1950s. At first Russian races were Formule Libre events, with a wide variety of sports and racing cars competing against each other, all using components from production cars such as the 1·2-litre Moskvitch, 2·5-litre Volga, and 5·4-litre ZIS. Formula Junior cars appeared in 1959, the first being a Moskvitch-engined machine built by Leningrad taxi-driver Valentin Kozenkov, who later made a number of replicas for other drivers. Other Formula Junior cars were produced by the Estonia workshops in Tallinn. During the period 1958 to 1963 private constructors in Russia also built Formula 3 (500cc) cars, and larger machines of 1,600cc, 3,000cc and unlimited capacity. Since 1964 Russian sportsmen have concentrated on the contemporary Formula 3 (1,000cc), as it is only in these cars that they can compete with other East European countries. Formula 4 and karting are also popular in Russia. Circuits include a road course using part of the Minsk-Leningrad highway, the horseshoe-shaped Kirov Stadium at Leningrad, and tracks at Moscow, Tallinn, Riga, Odessa, and over twenty other cities in the Soviet Union. Motor sport also takes place on horse-racing tracks, and on ice.

Rallies were first formalized in the Soviet Union in 1957, and since then a wide variety of events, both local and national, have taken place. They are normally of 500–1,000km length for local events, and 2,500–3,000km for national, or All-Union events. In recent years Russian teams have taken part in international rallies such as the London–Sydney Marathon, and the World Cup Rally. In both rallying and racing, Russian drivers are classified in four grades. Grade 3 is relatively simple, and can be gained as a result of a successful performance in a local rally or driving-test meeting. Admission to Grades 2 and 1 is on the basis of points scored during a season; the coveted title Master of Sport is only given to the winner of an All-Union Championship event, and even then only in a Championship in which a given number of other Masters are competing.

All Soviet motor sport is organized by the Federation of Automobile and Motor Sport of the USSR, whose president has a seat on the Commission Sportive Internationale of the FIA. This national federation delegates authority to the main clubs in the various Soviet Republics, who in turn govern the smaller local clubs. VH/GNG

USA and Canada

United States Racing Organizations

Motor racing in the United States is complicated by lack of a single, national rule-making, race-sanctioning organization. Until 1955, when the American Automobile Association dropped all racing activity, the AAA was the ACN (Automobile Club Nationale) of the United States. But the AAA's prime interest was the Indianapolis 500 and Land Speed record supervision. It cared little about road racing or stock cars and left the door open for other sanctioning groups to be started. In 1947, Bill France, who lived through stock car racing's gypsy days as a driver and promoter, helped to establish the National Association for Stock Car Auto Racing in a Daytona, Fla., motel room. In February 1944 a small group of New England enthusiasts formed the Sports Car Club of America, now the dominant body in American road racing. And in 1951, the National Hot Rod Association began to steer drag racing from the streets to the strips. USAC, the United States Auto Club, with the Indianapolis 500 as its prize, was founded in 1956 to assume the AAA's racing and record-keeping responsibilities.

There are other sanctioning organizations, some specializing in a single type of competition, but USAC, SCCA, NASCAR and NHRA are America's big four and together constitute ACCUS-FIA.

ACCUS-FIA

Founded in 1957, ACCUS, the Automobile Competition Committee for the United States-FIA, is American representative of the Paris based, Fédération Internationale de l'Automobile, the world body, that through its Commission Sportive Internationale (CSI) establishes race-car specifications and supervises the international racing calendar.

In the United States ACCUS-FIA delegates authority to sanction FIA events to its member clubs, USAC, SCCA, NASCAR and NHRA. John Oliveau, ACCUS executive director has his headquarters in Stamford, Conn. ARB

Can-Am Championship *see SCCA*

CASC

In 1951 three Canadian motor sports clubs combined to form the CASC. Until October 1967, when the CASC became the Automobile Club Nationale, the Royal Automobile Club of Great Britain represented Canada in the Fédération Internationale de l'Automobile. Professional sports car racing at Mosport and St Jovite attracted outstanding European drivers, leading to the Canadian-American Challenge Cup which was first held at St Jovite on 11 September 1966. Since 1967 world championship Formula 1 races have alternated between Mosport, Ontario, and St Jovite, Quebec. Can-Am races are also held at Edmonton, Alberta.

Since 1962 Canadian national racing champions have been: 1962 Francis Bradley, Lotus 19; 1963 Dennis Coad, Lotus 19; 1964 Ludwig Heimrath, Cooper-Ford; 1965 Bob McLaren, Lotus 23; 1966 George Chapman, Lotus 23B; 1967 Ross de St Croix, McLaren; 1968 Horst Kroll, Porsche; 1969 Eppie Wietzes, Lola; 1970 Eppie Wietzes, McLaren 10B.

Blessed with considerable open country and a continental motoring outlook, Canadian motor clubs stage several rallies rivaling the European classics. Organized by the British Empire Motor Club, the Canadian Winter Rally has been held since 1953. The 1970 results show a 3-way tie between Boyce and Woods (Datsun), Kuehne and Potts (SAAB) and Gozzard and Gozzard (Renault). Held from 1961 until 1968 the Shell 4000 attracted internationalists such as Oliver Gendebien, Roger Clark and Rosemary Smith. Usually run from Vancouver to Montreal, the Canadian Rockies and long stretches of prairie 'gumbo', combined with closed sections through forest reserves and national parks provided tests comparable to world championship events. In 1968, after years of trying, Scott Harvey and R. Beckman (Barracuda), won the final event.

Over 100 clubs with more than 8,000 members are represented by CASC; the executive director is Robert Hanna, of Willowdale, Ontario. ARB

Drag Racing *see NHRA and AHRA*

NASCAR

The National Association For Stock Car Auto Racing is largely the work of William Henry Getty France. Born in Horse Pasture, Va., on 26 September 1909, Big Bill France began to drive and promote stock cars in their 'outlaw' years before World War 2. During the winter of 1947 France formed NASCAR at a meeting in a Daytona motel room. The Southerner showed an evangelist's zeal as he fought for guaranteed purses and better racing conditions. He dreamed of a paved track free of Daytona's tides where fans could sit in grandstands. In 1950 a 1·25-mile (2·012km) banked oval—enlarged to 1·38 miles (2·221km) in 1953—opened in Darlington, S.C. and stock car racing was soon adopted as the Southeastern United States very own sport. That

NASCAR: Pre-war Ford coupés in a dirt-track race, c. 1951. *Photo: NASCAR*

a few of stock car racing's early heroes also used their specially set-up sedans to haul moonshine, and that their talent for outrunning government revenue agents apparently sharpened their racing skills, helped to build interest in the budding sport.

In the beginning most stock car racing was on dirt tracks of half a mile or less. By 1970 only three dirt tracks remained on NASCAR's schedule of 50 Grand Nationals. Nine of 33 GN circuits (about half hold two events annually) are considered superspeedways. In addition to Darlington they are: Daytona 2·5 miles (4·023km); Rockingham, N.C. 1·017 miles (1·636km); Atlanta, Ga. 1·552 miles (2·497km); Talladega, Ala. 2·66 miles (4·281km); Charlotte, N.C. 1·5 miles (2·414km); the multi-purpose speedways of Ontario 2·5 miles (4·023km), Michigan International 2 miles (3·219km) and Texas International 2 miles. Almost all NASCAR sites are oval tracks, some with banking as abrupt as 33°. The majority of Grand Nationals range from 150 to 300 miles with superspeedway events usually running a minimum of 400 miles.

During the 1960s NASCAR ventured briefly onto northern road courses, but by 1970 the Riverside 500 was the single Grand National on a road circuit. NASCAR late model stock car races, in many respects the most popular racing in the United States, is largely confined to seven Southeastern states.

Throughout the United States are hundreds of small half-mile or less, often unpaved tracks holding weekly races. Modified stock cars—older sedans with modified engines—demolition derbys, figure-eight races, three-

NASCAR: Hudson Hornet and Chrysler New Yorker at a 1951 NASCAR Grand National. *Photo: American Motors Corporation*

NHRA: Don Prudhomme's Top Fuel Eliminator AA Dragster, 1968. *Photo: NHRA*

Below, NHRA: two Funny Cars at Indianapolis Raceway Park; Mickey Thompson's Mach I Mustang and Candies & Hughes' car. *Photo: NHRA*

Right below, NHRA: Funny Car in action. At right is a 'Christmas Tree'. *Photo: NHRA*

matched in a series of side-by-side, two-car-at-a-time elimination runs. Four of the National Hot Rod Association (NHRA) eight categories are Professional and four are Sports Racing. Professional starts are 'heads-up', even starts, not utilizing the time handicap system required in each of the four Sport categories, where a variety of classes with wide horsepower differences make it desirable to provide slower cars with time advantages.

NHRA 1970 Professional categories are:

Top Fuel and Top Gas Eliminator—the fastest machines in drag racing. Top Gas requires the use of pump gasoline; Top Fuel uses nitromethane or other exotic fuels.

Funny Cars—plastic-bodied replicas of late model production cars powered by modified and supercharged engines using exotic fuels.

Pro Stock, new in 1970—open to modified late model production sedans.

The four Sports categories, all racing under the handicap start system, are:

Modified Eliminator—modified but non-supercharged machines.

Competition Eliminator—both supercharged and non-blown engines with a choice of fuel or gasoline in dragsters, roadsters and coupés built strictly for acceleration.

Super Stocks—late model high-performance production sedans made up of 16 classes, eight for manual transmission and eight using automatic transmission.

The Stock Category—most popular in terms of total entries, this consists of 35 classes including early and late model production vehicles with both stick shift and automatic transmission.

The Top Fuel Eliminator AA Dragster is the special attraction in this sport. Consistently performing in the 225mph (362kph) range, covering the quarter mile in seven seconds or less, a first-class AA/FD cost up to $30,000. Most of the cars have a single engine producing up to 1,500hp, but two engines are permitted. In 1970 the 850ci engine displacement limit was removed.

More than $2,000,000 in prize money is paid at the seven NHRA championship events: Winternationals, Los Angeles Fairground; Springnationals, Dallas Motor Speedway; Nationals, Indianapolis Raceway Park; World Finals, Dallas Motor Speedway; Gatornationals, Gainsville, Fla; Summernationals, York, Pa; Supernationals, Ontario, Calif.

'Big Daddy' Don Garlits, three time national champion, was the first to exceed 180mph (288kph) and the greatest money winner so far in drag racing. Prominent among the big winners are Connie Kalitta; Hawaiian-born Danny Ongias, who drives for designer-builder and former hot rod champion Mickey Thompson; Hank Westmoreland; Tommy Allen; and Ronnie Sox.

Don Prudhome was the first to break the 7 second 'barrier', recording a 6·92 ET in May 1967 at Carlsbad, Calif. And Prudhome's Chrysler-powered AA/Fueler won the 1969 NHRA Nationals in which John Mulligan succumbed to injuries after he had set a record 6·437 ET during an early round. Prudhome was again National Champion in 1970, his third consecutive success.

By 1930 Americans everywhere were tuning and channelling (lowering the body) their family cars. But Southern California's open spaces and favourable climate, coupled with a lack of public transport in the Los Angeles area that made it dependent on the automobile, created a hot rodders' Eden. Before using abandoned World War 2 airfields for improvised drag strips, California hot rodders raced on the dry bed of Muroc Lake, 90 miles north of Los Angeles. Now a US air base, Muroc's 10-mile-wide, 20-mile-long (16km by 32km) surface, washed smooth each year by melting mountain snows, produced many prominent drivers and engine-builders. In 1924 Tommy Milton reached

151mph (243kph) in a 3-litre Miller and in 1927 Frank Lockhart's 1·5-litre supercharged Miller was clocked at 164mph (263·9kph) over the Muroc sands.

The engine-builder Clay Smith and the camshaft expert Ed Winfield; Fran Hernandez and Phil Remington, who were to play vital roles in Ford's high performance programme; Traco's Frank Coon and NHRA founder Wally Parks, then active in the pioneer hot rod Southern California Timing Association, were among many who helped create drag racing. After World War 2, speed record attempts moved to Bonneville and hot rodders to drag strips. The Santa Barbara Acceleration Association opened the first strip at Goleta, Calif., in 1948 and Santa Ana, Calif., followed in 1950.

Until 1951, when Wally Parks established the NHRA, the hot rodder was the harassed maverick of American automobile racing. Enlisting the help of civic groups and law enforcement agencies, the Los Angeles-based NHRA and its president, Wally Parks, led the drive that turned hot rodding into a responsible sport. With 450,000 participants and six million spectators, drag racing is the fastest growing segment of American motor sport. ARB

SCCA

In February 1944 the Sports Car Club of America was founded by seven enthusiasts in Boston, Mass. Cameron Argetsinger organized the first Watkins Glen in October 1948; West Coast enthusiasts found a spectacular natural road course at Pebble Beach, Calif.; Alec Ulmann launched Sebring in December 1950 and the American road racing renaissance was under way.

During its early years the SCCA's big problem was finding a place to race. In 1952 a benefactor appeared in the unlikely person of USAF General Curtis LeMay, who permitted, in fact encouraged, the SCCA to use air force bases. In the next two years, 14 race meets were held under the joint auspices of the Strategic Air Command and the SCCA. In 1961 SCCA reversed its amateur policy, which prohibited drivers accepting cash awards, and in 1963 it organized the United States Road Racing Championship, first of the professional series that now dominate the Club's activities. This change in policy made it possible for the SCCA to sanction four FIA World Championships in 1962: the Daytona Continental, Sebring 12 Hours, Bridgehampton Double 500, and the United States GP at Watkins Glen.

US Road Racing Championships were won by Bob Holbert, Cobra-Ford and Porsche in 1963; Jim Hall, Chaparral-Chevrolet, 1964; George Follmer, Lotus-Porsche, 1965; Chuck Parsons, Genie and McLaren-Chevrolet, 1966; Mark Donohue, Lola-Chevrolet, 1967; and Mark Donohue, McLaren-Chevrolet, 1968. The USRRC was discontinued after the 1968 season when the Canadian American Challenge Cup was

Left, NHRA: Connie Kalitta with his Mustang Funny Car. The plastic bodied rig is powered by a 429ci (7,030cc) 'shotgun' hemi engine equipped with a supercharger and running on special fuel. Photo: NHRA

Right, NHRA: a Plymouth running in the Super Stock category. Note the contrast between front and rear tyres. Photo: NHRA

SCCA: the Caldwell/Posey 1970 Dodge Challenger Trans-Am Championship car. Photo: Autodynamics

expanded from six to 11 races. in 1969, with 10-race schedules in 1970 and 1971.

Trans-American Championship. A series of 12 or 13, 1hr 45min minimum (2hr 30min until 1970) endurance races for manufacturers of under 2-litre (2·5-litre from 1971) and up to 5-litre small sedans.

Trans-Am sedans over 2·5 litres — Ford-Mustang, Chevrolet-Camaro, AMC-Javelin, Plymouth-Barracuda, etc. — are limited to a 116in (2·9464m) wheelbase, 3,200lb (1,451·5kg) — 2,900lb (1,315·4kg) until 1970 — 5 litre (305ci; 4,998cc) single carburettor engines with 22 (US) gallon (83·28-litre) capacity fuel tanks. Production requirements for over 2-litre sedans require a minimum of 2,500 units or 1/250th of the preceding year's total production. Engines must be advertised options with a minimum of 500 examples installed in the model to be recognized. Sturdy steel tubing roll cages not only contribute to drivers safety but add desirable body-frame stiffness. Suspension changes and considerable engine tuning are permitted. Cars under 2·5 litres, such as Alfa Romeo, Ford-Cortina, BMW and, until 1970, Porsche 911, are limited to fuel tanks of 15 (US) gallons (56·78 litres).

Heavily promoted by American automobile manufacturers as an entry to the booming youth market, the small (by US standards) Trans-Am sedan series was a success from its beginning in 1966 when Ford-Mustang and Alfa Romeo won their categories. Led by Jerry Titus, Mustang repeated their success in 1967 with Porsche 911s winning the under 2-litre class. In 1968, Mark Donohue, driving a Camaro prepared by former road racing star Roger Penske, now a Chevrolet dealer, won 10 of 13 Trans-Ams to bring the Chevrolet Division of General Motors the championship. Porsche repeating as under-2-litre champion in 1968. Ford retaliated in 1969 by entering two car teams for Carroll Shelby, with Peter Revson and Horst Kwech, and for Bud Moore Eng., whose drivers were former Indy winner Parnelli

Jones and road-racing champion George Follmer. Penske countered by adding Ronnie Bucknum to back up Donohue. Other serious contenders included a works Javelin team headed by Ron Grable and a privately entered Pontiac Firebird for former Mustang mainstay Jerry Titus.

Although slow to start in 1969, beginning with Bryar, Donohue won six of the next seven Trans-Ams. Camaro and Porsche, with Floridian Peter Gregg accounting for six of Porsche's 11 victories, were again Trans-Am champions. SCCA's success with Trans-Am racing encouraged NASCAR to add a Grand Touring Championship in 1968 (changed to Grand American Challenge in 1970) and in 1970 USAC opened its stock-car division to small sedans.

The Chaparral designer, builder and driver, Jim Hall, entered the 1970 Trans-Am with Camaros for himself and veteran Ed Leslie, as Penske, with drivers Donohue and Peter Revson, moved to Javelin. Chrysler participated in the 1970 Trans-Am with a Dodge Challenger driven by Sam Posey to 3rd place in the series, and with Gurney-prepared Plymouth Barracudas, driven by Swede Savage and, on occasion, by Gurney himself. Ford Mustangs captured the 1970 Trans-Am Championship as Parnelli Jones won five, and George Follmer one, of the 11-race series. Mark Donohue earned 2nd place for Javelin with three victories. Alfa Romeo earned under 2-litre honours, with private entries scoring nine victories.

Trans-Am points are awarded on a 9-6-4-3-2-1 basis for highest finishing position in each division; the championship is based on nine best finishes.

Canadian American Challenge Cup. CASC, Canadian Automobile Sports Clubs, sanctioned professional races at Mosport and St Jovite which combined with the traditional autumn races at Riverside and Laguna Seca were the Can-Am nucleus. When Bridgehampton relinquished its FIA-Manufacturers' Championship date (later taken over by Watkins Glen) and the Las Vegas' Stardust Raceway was added as the sixth circuit, the Can-Am blossomed into being at St Jovite on 11 September 1966.

From its beginning the successful Can-Am Group 7 sports racing car has been an Anglo-American hybrid. Except for Jim Hall's winged Chaparral 2E, first seen at Bridgehampton in September 1966 and winner that year at Monterey and the Tony Dean Porsche 908 that won at Road Atlanta in September 1970, all Can-Am victories during its first five years have gone to Lola (6) and McLaren (31). Powering Lola and McLaren chassis are considerably reworked American stockblock engines. Again, with the exception of Dan Gurney's Lola-Ford victory at Bridgehampton in September 1966, and Dean's Porsche, all Can-Am winners have been Chevrolet-powered. However, late in 1969 Ford's 484ci (8-litre) lightweight block began to produce results when Andretti finished 4th at Monterey and 3rd at Riverside. Excluding Chaparral, American constructors Group 7 efforts—Shelby's King Cobra, Autodynamic's solid axle D7 and 7B, Holman Moody's Honker and the McKee Wedge—all have been uniformly dismal.

After less than all-out Can-Am attacks by Ferrari in 1967-68, 1969 saw Chris Amon campaign with the 4-cam, V-12 612, its 6-litre engine the largest ever built by Ferrari. Also in 1969, McLaren's Can-Am monopoly was threatened by GP star Siffert driving a factory-supported, open version of the 4·5-litre Porsche 917. In 1970 BRMs with Chevrolet power became challengers.

SCCA: a typical field of Can-Am cars at Riverside in November 1969. Jackie Oliver (Autocoast) in the lead, followed by Mario Andretti (No 1 McLaren), Dan Gurney No 48 McLaren), Frank Gardner (No 2 Ford) and Pete Revson (No 31 Lola). *Photo: SCCA*

Below, SCCA: the most successful make in Can-Am racing has been the McLaren. This is an M6B driven by Denny Hulme. *Photo: SCCA*

Bottom, SCCA: one of the less successful Can-Am cars was the Holman & Moody Honker. *Photo: SCCA*

With no limits on engine size, serious Can-Am entrants use fuel-injected, dry-sump, aluminum block Chevrolet engines of 427 to 488ci (7 and 8 litres). California engine specialists Traco (Travis and Coons) and Al Bartz handle much Can-Am engine work, but several teams, including McLaren and Chaparral, do their own.

With more than 600hp, the 1,500lb (680kg) Can-Am car reaches 100mph (160kph) in less than six seconds and exceeds 200mph (320kph) on longer circuits. The cars carry 60 gallons (227 litres) of pump fuel in rubberized safety bladders and it is frequently a near thing to

SCCA: Mike Eyerly, 1969 and 1970 Formula B/C champion, in his 1970 Chevron B17b. *Photo: SCCA*

complete 200-mile Can-Ams without taking on additional gasoline. The SCCA, albeit regretfully, concurred with the FIA ban on wings, 1970 Can-Am cars depending on truncated noses and aerodynamic wedge shapes to keep their enormous tyres, often with more than 16in 'footprints', on the road. Following the 1970 season, during which the Chapparal 2J won several qualifying honours but failed to finish in a single race, the SCCA declared the 'ground effects' machine legal, only to be over-ruled by the CSI in December 1970.

A comparison of the times of Formula1, Formula A and Indianapolis cars on road courses on which they have all competed shows Can-Am racing to be the world's fastest.

Can-Am attendance in 1970 was reported at 370,967; an average starting field was 28 cars. Can-Am purses, highest of any road-racing series, attracts top international talent. In the six-race 1966 series, Can-Am Champion John Surtees and runner-up Mark Donohue earned $48,100 and $28,850. The 1970 purse of $885,900 which includes the Johnson Wax sponsored point fund, is the highest of any road racing series. Denny Hulme, 1970 champion, earned $162,202.

Formula A-Continental. Third of SCCA professional championships is the 10 to 12 Continental series for

Formula A/5000 single-seaters. Introduced for smaller displacement engines as Formula SCCA in 1967, Formula A, like the British Formula 5000, is based on 305ci (5-litre) American production, push-rod V-8 engines. In 1970 minimum engine production requirements were reduced from 5,000 to 1,000 units. Also eligible in Formula A/5000 single-seaters. Introduced for smaller displacement engines as Formula SCCA in 1967, Formula and 2-wheel drive is mandatory. FA minimum weight is 1,250lb (566·99kg) without fuel and driver; safety fuel tanks of a maximum 30 (US) gallons (113·56 litres) are required. Considerable engine tuning is permitted but cylinder heads may not be substituted or the location of camshafts changed.

Leading FA builders are Eagle, McLaren, Surtees, Lola and Lotus. Chevrolet engines were universal until 1970 when George Follmer's Lotus-Ford won at Mt Tremblant and Mid-Ohio.

Tony Adamowicz (Eagle), David Hobbs (Surtees) and Sam Posey (McLaren) finished the 1969 Continental Championship 1-2-3. John Cannon (McLaren), Gus Hutchinson (Brabham and Lola) and David Hobbs (Surtees) finished 1st, 2nd and 3rd respectively in the 1970 Continental Championship.

Other SCCA Formulas include:
Formula B. For engines between 1,100 and 1,600cc; 848lb (384·65kg) minimum. Mike Eyerly, Brabham BT18 and Chevron B17, was 1969 and 1970 champion.
Formula C. Usually raced with FB, up to 1,100cc; 750lb (340·19kg) minimum.
Formula Vee. Two classes, 1,200cc and, beginning 1970, a Super Vee category for 1,600cc, Volkswagen-engined single seaters (see page 26).
Formula Ford. Single-seaters based on the 1,600cc English Ford engine. In the United States, Formula Ford racing is sanctioned by International Motor Sports Association, as well as SCCA.

SCCA Club Racing is held on divisional and national levels. Car classifications, in addition to Formula cars, cover sedan, Production and Sports Racing.
Sedans range from class A—2,500 to 5,000cc; B—1,300 to 2,500cc; C—1,000 to 1,300cc; D—under 1,000cc.

Production Categories are based on performance potential *not* engine size. Examples of 1970 classes are: class A—Cobra 427, Corvette 427 and Porsche 904; class B—Ferrari 275GTB, Jaguar 3·8 and 4·2 and Porsche 911S; class C—Lotus-Elan, MGC and TR-5; class D—Alfa-Romeo Duetto 1750 and Triumph TR-4; down to class H where 948cc MG Midgets and Austin Healey Sprites race with 600cc Hondas and 1,200cc Fiat Spyders. Close to 200 models of production sport cars are classified. To be classified production usually requires a minimum model run of 500. Minor coachwork, engine modifications and a weight tolerance of minus 5% are permitted.

Sports Racing is in four classes, formerly known as SCCA modified category, governed by engine size: A—over 2,000cc; B—1,300 to 2,000cc; C—850 to 1,300cc; D—under 850cc. The sports racing category comes under FIA Group 7 rules; engines may be highly modified, coachwork must provide for two passengers, fenders and windshield.

ARRC. Since 1964 national club racing championships have been determined at American Road Race of Champions. Each of SCCA's seven geographic divisions send a minimum of three drivers in each of 21 classes.

SCCA: D Production club racing; John Morton's Datsun and Bob Hindson's Porsche 914. *Photo: SCCA*

USAC Stock Car: Norm Nelson's 1970
Plymouth. *Photo: USAC*

The ARRC November venue has alternated between
Daytona and Riverside until 1970 when Road Atlanta
became the permanent site.

SCCA Driver's Schools. About 70 highly regarded driver
training schools are conducted annually. The beginner,
after passing physical and blackboard examinations, is
given a minimum of six hours on-track instruction from
senior drivers. They are granted a novice licence, per-
mitting racing in local events under observation,
followed by regional and national competition licences.

National Rally Championship and Solo Events. These
art part of SCCA activities. The National Rally programme consists of about 60 national and divisional
rallies, usually of 450-mile 2-day maximum duration.
In 1969 and 1970 factory supported Ford-Mustangs won
the SCCA manufacturers championship. In 1970 Roger
and Kathy Bohl, in addition to an outstanding record in
US rallies, became the first Americans to win the Mexican
24 Hours. In 1971 the 'Press On Regardless' rally, run
each autumn over the logging trails of Northern
Michigan, was granted an FIA listing. Solo events,
primarily a single car against the clock, include hill-
climbs and gymkhanas calling for manoeuvrability
rather than speed.

SCCA Membership is about 18,500 of whom 5,500 hold a
form of competition licence. Divided into 105 regions,
club policy is determined by a Board of Governors
elected by the general membership. SCCA headquarters
is in Westport, Conn.; Tracy Bird is executive director,
Henry Loudenback director of professional racing. ARB

Trans-Am Championship *see SCCA*

USAC

Founded in 1956 after the American Automobile
Association dropped its motor sports functions, the
United States Auto Club sanctions racing in four
divisions; Stock car, Sprint, Midget and Championship.
Beginning in 1971 separate Championship car divisions
were established for oval track, road course and
dirt track events. Twelve oval track races, including
three 500 mile races at Indianapolis, Ontario and
Pocono, constitute USAC's Championship Trail, its
premier series. It also conducts record and product
certification tests and, until 1970 sanctioned Pikes
Peak, the one major United States hill-climb.

USAC officers are William Smyth, executive director.
Charles Brockman president. Headquarters are in
Indianapolis.

USAC Stock Car. Specifications were similar to
NASCAR, except that, in 1970, USAC opened its stock-
car division to small sport sedans and in 1971, when
NASCAR reduced its new model engine displacement
from 430ci to 366ci, USAC retained the 1970 specifications. Standard and intermediate Detroit sedans must
not be more than three years old, of 3,900lb (1,769kg)
minimum weight with a single-carburettor, 430ci
(7,046cc) engine. The 'small' sedan is limited to a 116in
(2·946m) wheelbase, 3,200lb (1,451·5kg), 305ci (4,998cc)
production sedan, such as Camaro, Mustang and
Javelin in the SCCA's Trans-Am and the NASCAR
Grand American categories. Run on paved ovals, dirt
ovals and a few road courses, the popularity of USAC
Stock Car racing has never approached that of NASCAR.

A. J. Foyt won the title in 1968 in a Ford. Another Indy
veteran, Roger McCluskey, was the 1969 and 1970

champion, driving the Plymouth Road Runner of the
four-time USAC stock-car title-holder, Norm Nelson.

Sprint Cars. Sentimental favourites of American oval
track fans. Before sports car and Grand Prix drivers
began invading the Speedway, it was in the Sprint class
that the majority of Indy drivers learned their trade. A
series of 30 or more races, on tracks ranging from one-
tenth mile indoor ovals to half-mile paved and dirt ovals,
make up an average sprint car season. The majority of the
84in (2·1336m) wheelbase, front-engined roadsters are
powered by 256ci (4,195cc) Chevrolet and Offenhauser
engines. Production stockblock and supercharged 171ci
(2,802cc) engines are permitted but seldom used.
Beginning 1971 USAC Sprint cars were equipped with
roll-cages. Larry Dickson was 1970 Sprint Champion.

Midgets. For the past 35 years midget racing has served
as a training ground for many American oval track stars.
Not to be confused with the more modestly powered
'TQ' three-quarter midget, the championship midget is
a potent race car using 114ci (1,868cc) ohc engines,
usually Offenhauser, Chevrolet, Ford Falcon or Sesco,
the last of these derived from the right bank of a small
Chevrolet V-8. Stock-block engines of 155ci (2,540cc)
are permitted and midget wheelbase requirements are
66in (1·676m) minimum and 76in (1·930m) maximum.
Regulations for 1971 make roll-over cages mandatory
in USAC midget racing.

Midget racing began in 1933 and received American
Automobile Association sanction in 1934. Future
Indianapolis winners such as Sam Hanks, Bill Vukovich
and Johnnie Parsons were among those running several
nights each week, both outdoors and indoors, usually on
small dirt tracks. The AAA began awarding national
championship points in 1948, and in 1956 after the AAA
had dropped motor racing, USAC formed its midget
division. Running between 60 and 70 events annually
on circuits that vary from 0·1-mile (0·1609km) indoor
ovals, to 1-mile (1·609km) paved ovals, the midget is most
at home on 0·25 to 0·5-mile (0·402 to 0·805km) dirt tracks.
Top prize on the midget circuit in 1970 was the $31,000
Astro Grand Prix (in 1969 the 2-day Astro GP offered
a purse of $60,000), a 100-lap feature race, plus the usual
preliminary heats, over a 0·25-mile dirt oval in the
Houston Astrodome. In 1970 A. J. Foyt collected a
record midget purse of $5,750.00 in winning the second
annual Astro GP. Bob Tattersall, who races in Australia
during the American winter, was 1969 midget champion,
Jimmy Caruthers earning the crown in 1970. More than
200 machines and over 100 drivers campaign in USAC
midgets alone.

Championship Cars. Minor engine specification changes
in Indianapolis Championship Cars, effective from 1
January 1970 until 1 January 1972, call for non-supercharged ohc engines of 256ci (4,195cc); supercharged
ohc 161·703ci (2,650cc); stockblock (minimum 5,000
production) engines 320·355ci (5,250cc). On 1 January
1972 the non-supercharged ohc engine goes from 256
(4,195cc) to 274ci (4,490cc) while supercharged ohc
engines remain at 161·7ci (2,649cc). In January 1972,
production stockblock engines increase from 320 to
355ci (5,244 to 5,817cc). At that time supercharged stock-
blocks will be cut from 203ci (3,327cc) to 177·5ci
(2,909cc). Special rocker arm, single non-ohc, non-
supercharged engines will be raised from 305ci (4,998cc)
to 320ci (5,244cc).

The 1960s were a turbulent time for USAC. Led from
1956, until his resignation in 1968, by the Indianapolis

Below, USAC Sprint Cars: Gary
Bettenhausen and Larry Dickson race
wheel-to-wheel. *Photo: USAC*

Bottom, USAC Midget Car: Bob Tattersall,
1969 Midget Champion. *Photo: USAC*

Top, USAC Championship Car; A. J. Foyt's Offenhauser-engined Sheraton-Thompson Special, 1964 Indianapolis winner. Photo: Al Bochroch

Above, USAC Championship Cars: contrast between the traditional front-engined roadster (Federal Engineering Special) and rear-engined car (American Red Ball Special), at the Trenton Speedway in 1967. Photo: Al Bochroch

Opposite top, Autocross: J. Homewood's Imp Californian at Bredhurst Track, near Rainham, Kent in 1968. Photo: Charles Pocklington

Opposite bottom, Can-Am: Jackie Oliver's Autocoast (No 22) and Mario Andretti's MacLaren-Ford M6B (No 1) at Riverside in 1969. Photo: Motor Sport

Below, Off-the-road Racing: Parnelli Jones' Ford Bronco 'Crazy Colt'. Photo: Don Emmoms, Dune Buggies and Hot VWs Magazine

Bottom, Off-the-road Racing: Miller-Havens buggy in the 1970 Mexican 1000. Photo: Dune Buggies and Hot VWs Magazine

industrialist Tom Binford, the USAC Board of Directors repeatedly acted to maintain the status quo. Indianapolis car owners had lived with the traditional front-engined, Offenhauser roadster—and had such substantial investments in them—that the rear-engined, lightweight car revolution, triggered by Jack Brabham driving a 2·7-litre Cooper-Climax to 9th place at the Speedway in 1961, was fiercely resisted. Before the 1960s were over, USAC and Andy Granatelli were to engage in a monumental controversy over turbine power which resulted in restrictions that left turbines uncompetitive. USAC also banned 4-wheel drive, which appeared particularly efficient on the Speedway's shallow, 9°, banked turns. Until a separate division was made for road racing, and dirt tracks began to be phased out, a driver going after USAC's premier championship needed points from ovals, road circuits and dirt tracks. To be competitive he needed a chassis set-up especially for road courses, one for his bread and butter racing on oval tracks and a sturdy front-engined roadster that looked like, but was slightly larger than, a Sprint car.

Until 1971 a typical USAC national Championship— the Championship Trail—consisted of 20 to 25 events, including the month long sojurn at Gasoline Alley which included two weekends of Indy qualifying. In September 1970, the precedent breaking California 500 was added to the Championship Trail and in July 1971 the Pocono 500, with Indy and California, became USAC's multi-million dollar 'Triple Crown'.

USAC championship purses range from a minimum $25,000 or 40% of admissions, to the record $1,000,002.02, paid at Indianapolis in 1970. Contributing to the Indy total is over $300,000 in accessory money and more than $40,000 in lap prizes. The inaugural California 500 carried USAC's second largest purse, $727,500, with winner Jim McElreath earning $146,850. Al Unser, winner of 10 USAC championship races in 1970, including the 500, earned a record $510,000 of which $271,697 represented Speedway earnings. The younger Unser brother also surpassed Mario Andretti's 1969 record breaking annual point total of 5,025 with 5,130. Three time Indianapolis winner A. J. Foyt tops all U.S. driver earnings having collected over three million dollars in his 12 year career.

Off-the-Road Racing

Until the first Mexican 1000 in November 1967, off-the-road racing in the United States was without a rule-making, race-sanctioning organization.

Four-wheel-drive vehicles and motorcycles had been holding trials, hill-climbs and record runs in the western deserts, and dune buggies were becoming popular on both coasts. Most often sold as 'do-it-yourself' kits, competition dune buggies frequently make up more than half the entries in off-road races. Based on shortened, 78 to 84in (1·98 to 2·13m) wheelbase, Volkswagen floor pans with fibreglass panels and moulded plastic seats, usually powered by 1,200cc Volkswagen, Corvair or Porsche engines pushing giant rear tyres, the dune buggy became young America's go anywhere, do anything transport of the 1960s.

In 1962 record runs on the primitive Baja peninsula in Mexico began attracting Southern California motor sportsmen. From Tiajuana at the US border to La Paz on Baja's southern tip was 952·7 miles (1,533·23km). Except for 64 miles (103km) of four-lane highway after Tiajuana (later abandoned and the start moved to Ensenada) the Baja route consists largely of unmarked,

boulder-strewn, pot-holed, car-breaking ruts. It is perhaps the most severe of all motoring tests.

From 1962 until 1967, Honda and Triumph motorcycles earned fastest times with just under 40-hour runs. In April 1967, Bruce Meyers and Ted Mangels used a VW-engined, Meyers/Manx dune buggy to cover a 919·1 mile (1,479·2km) route in 34 hours 45 minutes, a 26·45mph (42·57kph) average speed. Four months later the Rambler sedan of veteran Baja competitors, Spencer Martin and Ralph Poole, finished in 31 hours even. General interest in Baja was high and record attempts were being held so frequently that NORRA, the National off-the-Road Racing Assoc., was formed with Ed Pearlman as president.

The new organization's first act was to give official recognition to the Martin and Poole record. In 1969 Larry Minor and Rodney Hall won the Mexico 1,000, their 4wd Ford Bronco covering 832 miles (1,338·97km) in 20 hours 48 minutes. The Mexico 1,000 has become the Indianapolis of off-road racing. Support crews are flown along the route by American industry. Movie stars and racing celebrities such as Indy veteran Parnelli Jones, who won the 1970 Mexican 500 in a Ford Bronco with Bill Stroppe, and international rally champion Eric Carlsson are among the entrants. Drino Miller and Vic Wilson won the November 1970 Baja, their special 2,200cc VW-engined single-seater buggy covering 832 miles in a record 16hr 7min.

In addition to motorcycles, NORRA classes include: (1) production 2-wheel-drive passenger cars; (2) production 2-wheel-drive utility vehicles; (3) production 2-wheel-drive buggies; (4) modified and non-production 2-wheel-drive vehicles; (5) production 4-wheel-drive vehicles and (6) modified and production 4-wheel-drive vehicles. In classes 1, 2 and 5, 'production' is defined as a minimum of 500 vehicles built in a 12-month period. In class 3 production is a minimum of 10 complete vehicles or 50 complete kits built in 12-month period. Engines in class 3 must be Volkswagen, 4-cylinder Porsche, Corvair or Ford/Saab V-4.

In addition to sanctioning the Mexican 1000, NORRA inaugurated the Baja 500 in June 1969. A third major off-road race, the Mint 400, is staged in the desert near Las Vegas, Nev. In March 1970, it attracted 293 starters, of which fewer than 100 finished.

Snowmobile Racing. America's newest off-the-road racer is the snowmobile. More than one million small, caterpillar-tracked vehicles, using one or two steering skis, have been sold in the United States and Canada. They are powered by 2-stroke engines, primarily in the 300cc to 444cc, 20bhp to 40bhp range and snowmobile races with up to 250 entries and 25,000 spectators are staged in Canada and the United States. In 1970 68 professional racing teams were supported by the snowmobile industry. Of several race-sanctioning organizations, the USSA, the United States Snowmobile Association, of Minneapolis, Minn., is the largest. ARB

Board Track Racing

One of the most important and exciting eras of automobile racing in the United States spanned a period of approximately twenty years, beginning in 1915, when the board track superspeedways were at the peak of their popularity. Twenty tracks of this type, ranging in length from 1 to 2 miles (1·609 to 3·219km), were constructed of 2 × 4in (51 × 102mm) timbers laid on edge. The most common design was a 1·25-mile (2·012km)

oval, with the turns of some tracks banked as steeply as 52° for maximum speed. This, combined with the development of 2-litre and 1·5-litre supercharged dohc Miller and Duesenberg engines in the mid-1920s, made it possible for drivers to win some board track races at average speeds 30 to 35mph (48 to 56kph) faster than on the brick course at the Indianapolis Motor Speedway.

The board tracks, consequently, were responsible for a tremendous increase of interest in auto racing as a spectator sport. The stands were filled to capacity for almost every event during these golden days of high-speed competition. But maintenance costs were high and expensive repairs usually were necessary before any track was more than three years old. By the start of the 1930 season, only the one at Altoona, Pa., was in operation; and it gave way to a new dirt track two years later. One board track in Florida was demolished by a hurricane soon after its inaugural event. Two in California were destroyed by fire. Several—including those at Beverly Hills, Calif., Cincinnati, Ohio, New York and Chicago—were built close to highly populated areas on ground which appreciated in value at such a rapid rate that they were absorbed quickly as part of important real estate developments. Others simply were abandoned when race promoters lacked the cash for alterations and repairs needed to meet the safety requirements of the American Automobile Association's Contest Board.

Only the most skilful of America's top-ranking drivers were able to win consistently on the boards. The most successful were Tom Milton and Jimmy Murphy, who had served his apprenticeship as Milton's riding mechanic. Ralph DePalma's nephew Pete DePaolo, who rode in several races with his uncle before becoming a prominent driver himself, also was outstanding on the 'toothpick saucers' with DePalma, Louis Chevrolet, Ralph Mulford, Earl Cooper, Frank Lockhart, Eddie Hearne, Louis Meyer and Harry Hartz sharing the spotlight. The challengers from Europe, other than Dario Resta, enjoyed little success in this type of competition.

Five years before any of the other nineteen board tracks were nearing completion in other parts of the nation, the first of the 'wooden saucers' was erected in 1910 at Playa del Rey near Los Angeles, Calif. It was a 1-mile (1·609km) circular course banked at a uniform angle of 20° and designed by Jack Prince, whose previous promotional experience had been limited chiefly to bicycle racing. A vast amount of timber, in the form of boards 16ft (4·877m) long, were used in its construction with a supporting framework of 4 × 6in (102 × 152mm) timber. Ray Harroun drove a Marmon to victory in the 100-mile feature event of the inaugural programme on 8 April. His time was 1hr 25min 22·1sec, more than seven minutes better than Louis Strang's 1hr 32min 40·8sec performance in a Buick for a similar distance on the occasion of the Indianapolis Motor Speedway's official opening the previous year. New American records for shorter distances preceding Harroun's victory included: Barney Oldfield, Benz, 1 mile (1·609km), 36·22sec; Ben Kirscher, Darracq, 2 miles (3·219km), 1min 18·29sec; Ralph DePalma, Fiat, 5 miles (8·047km), 3min 15·62sec; George Robertson, Simplex, 10 miles (16·09km), 6min 31·37sec; and DePalma, Fiat, 15 miles (24·14km), 8min 15·62sec. One week later, while completing 148 miles (238·2km) in a 2-hour race, Harroun was clocked at 1hr 16min 21·9sec for 100 miles (160·0kph) on the same course. Most of the subsequent racing activities at Playa del Rey, however, were pre-

Board Track Racing: Ralph Mulford in a Peugeot at Sheepshead Bay, N.Y., 1916. Photo: Indianapolis Motor Speedway

sented in the nature of record runs for short distances, match races and actual contests of not more than 50 miles (80·417km). It burned to the ground in 1912.

It was not until 1915 that interest in board track racing was revived in dramatic manner with Prince also building most of the seven new speedways of this type erected before America's entry into World War 1—and then joining forces with Art Pillsbury for additional expansion beginning in 1920.

The 2-mile Chicago oval, with turns banked at 19° and 29′, was the first of the new 'superspeedways' to begin operation, holding its inaugural event four weeks after Resta had forced DePalma to a new record of 89·84mph (144·58kph) in the fifth running of the Indianapolis 500. The date was 26 June 1915, and a tremendous crowd was on hand to watch those two stars renew their bitter rivalry in another 500-mile battle. Mechanical trouble, however, forced DePalma to withdraw his Mercedes and Resta won in impressive manner at an average speed of 97·58mph (157·04kph) at the wheel of a Peugeot against a strong field which also included Stutz, Sunbeam, Maxwell, Delage and Duesenberg entries.

One week later the top racing talent was split because of a conflict in dates involving the new 1·25-mile (2·012km) board track at Omaha, Nebr., and the 2-mile course at Tacoma, Wash., where the original dirt racing strip had been resurfaced with wooden planking. Eddie Rickenbacker won the Omaha inaugural 300-mile race at an average speed of 91·74mph (147·64kph) with Eddie O'Donnell's Duesenberg trailing by almost 12 minutes; and the unheralded Guy Ruckstell drove a Mercer to victory over such veterans as Earl Cooper, Eddie Pullen, Bob Burman and Barney Oldfield at Tacoma by averaging 84·8mph (136·47kph) for 250 miles (402·3km).

Ralph Mulford in a Duesenberg won the 300-mile opener on the new 1-mile board track at Des Moines, Iowa, early in August and the season reached its climax on 9 October when all the top cars and drivers converged on the magnificent new parabolic 2-mile (3·219km) board speedway at Sheepshead Bay, N.Y., for a 350-mile (563.3km) contest. Resta, as expected, was the early leader. But the over 100mph (160kph) pace was too much for him and his three Peugeot team-mates. All were eliminated by mechanical trouble along with such outstanding entries as Rickenbacker's Maxwell, Oldfield's Delage and half of the 4-car Stutz team, DePalma and Cooper. Only eight of the twenty starters were running at the finish as Gil Anderson averaged 102·56mph (165·10kph) to beat his fellow Stutz driver Tom Rooney by 47sec with Eddie O'Donnell's Duesenberg 15min back in 3rd place. It was the fastest race run up to that time anywhere in the world.

A 2-mile (3·219km) oval at Cincinnati, Ohio, and a 1·125-mile (1·811km) course at Uniontown, Pa., were the new board tracks built in 1916. John Aitken and Louis Chevrolet won the inaugural events, respectively, at distances of 300 miles (482·8km) and 112·5 miles (181km). It was Resta, however, who enjoyed the most successful season with two major victories at Chicago and one at Omaha in addition to his triumph on the bricks at Indianapolis. America's war effort prevented the construction of any board tracks in 1917, when Cooper and L. Chevrolet dominated the curtailed racing programme.

Chicago, Omaha and Des Moines were no longer in operation when racing was resumed in 1919. The 300ci (4,916cc) piston displacement limitation, introduced in

1915, was still in effect; and none of the twelve board speedways still to be built would be ready for use until 1920. Gaston Chevrolet, driving a Frontenac, was the only veteran to score more than one major victory.

The all-new 3-litre cars stimulated interest in the sport with the start of the 1920 campaign, however, and new board tracks at Beverly Hills and Fresno (both in California) replaced Sheepshead Bay and Cincinnati on the championship circuit. The 1·25-mile (2·012km) Beverly Hills speedway, built with money subscribed by members of the wealthy Hollywood film colony, was the finest of its kind anywhere in the world. With turns banked at 37°, it promised greater speed than ever had been attained on a closed course and Murphy made his debut in first-class competition by qualifying at slightly better than 115mph (185kph) and averaging 103·2mph (166·1kph) in a Duesenberg to win the inaugural 250-mile event. Murphy also won the Fresno (mile track) inaugural for Duesenberg, but it was Milton who carried off most of the laurels during the remainder of the season.

Hearne, lured from retirement, and Roscoe Sarles were the principal challengers of Milton and Murphy as three more 1·25-mile board tracks were built in 1921: Kansas City, Mo., and at San Carlos and Cotati in California. Altoona opened its gates for the first time in 1923 and two more tracks were completed during each of the next three years to end the board track building era. With few exceptions, each new track was designed for slightly greater speed than those already in existence. Culver City, Calif., opened in 1924, increased its turn banking to 45° and the tracks at Rockingham, N.H., and Laurel, Md., were banked at 52°. Average speeds,

Board Track Racing: Jimmy Murphy leads Tommy Milton past Frank Elliott's wrecked car at San Carlos, Calif., in 1922. *Photo: Indianapolis Motor Speedway*

Board Track Racing: drivers and officials before the start of the 300-mile inaugural race on the Kansas City board track, 1922. *Photo: Indianapolis Motor Speedway*

consequently, continued to increase despite a reduction in piston displacement to 2-litres in 1923 and to 1·5-litres in 1926. After Murphy's death in a 1924 dirt track accident, DePaolo became Milton's chief rival on the boards. When Milton retired at the close of the 1925 campaign, DePaolo's principal challengers were Hartz, Lockhart, Meyer and Billy Arnold.

Miller and Duesenberg had eliminated all rivals as the board track era neared its close and AAA records reveal Hartz as the fastest of all board track drivers by virtue of his 134·091mph (215·742kph) average at the wheel of a Miller Special in a 300-mile race on the 1·5-mile course at Atlantic City in 1926. Lockhart was timed at 147·7mph (237·7kph) for a single lap on the same track one year later, however, in a race against the clock.

The location, length of track and years of operation for all board speedways one mile or more long follow:

track	length of course	years of operation
Playa del Rey, Calif.	1 mile (1·609km)	1910–12
Chicago, Ill.	2 miles (3·219km)	1915–18
Omaha, Nebr.	1·25 miles (2·012km)	1915–17
Tacoma, Wash.	2 miles (3·219km)	1915–22
Des Moines, Iowa	1 mile (1·609km)	1915–17
Sheepshead Bay, N.Y.	2 miles (3·219km)	1915–19
Cincinnati, Ohio	2 miles (3·219km)	1916–19
Uniontown, Pa.	1·125 miles (1·810km)	1916–22
Beverly Hills, Calif.	1·25 miles (2·012km)	1920–4
Fresno, Calif.	1 mile (1·609km)	1920–5
Kansas City, Mo.	1·25 miles (2·012km)	1921–5
Cotati, Calif.	1·25 miles (2·012km)	1921–2
San Carlos, Calif.	1·25 miles (2·012km)	1921–2
Altoona, Pa.	1·25 miles (2·012km)	1923–31
Charlotte, N.Car.	1·25 miles (2·012km)	1924–6
Culver City, Calif.	1·25 miles (2·012km)	1924–7
Laurel, Md.	1·125 miles (1·810km)	1925–6
Rockingham, N.H.	1·25 miles (2·012km)	1925–9
Miami, Fla.	1·25 miles (2·012km)	1926
Atlantic City, N.J.	1·5 miles (2·414km)	1926–8

Among the shorter board tracks measuring less than one mile in length were those at Woodbridge N.J., Bridgeville, Pa. and Akron, Ohio. AB

Australasia

Tasman Series

The Tasman Series of international motor races began in 1964 to promote world class motor racing in Australia and New Zealand. It was a logical progression from the individual international races several promoters had been running since 1960 in the two countries. However, although drivers race for the Tasman Cup—awarded on a points score basis over the series—prize money is still paid individually by each promoter at each meeting. The series is loosely run in cooperation by six or seven promoters in the two countries—each of whom evaluate their purse each year to decide whether they can afford to participate.

The Tasman Series is open only to monoposto racing cars, and it has drawn the world's top F1 drivers to Australia. Former world champion Jim Clark won the series three times: in 1965, 1967 and in 1968, only two

Above, Tasman Series: Chris Amon (March 701) and Ken Bartlett (Mildren) lead the field in the hairpin at Levin, 1971. *Photo: Euan Sarginson*

Right above, Temporada Series: Andrea de Adamich (Dino Ferrari), winner of the San Juan race, 1968. *Photo: Dr Vicente Alvarez*

Tasman Series Winners

1964	Bruce McLaren	*Cooper*
1965	Jim Clark	*Lotus*
1966	Jackie Stewart	*BRM*
1967	Jim Clark	*Lotus*
1968	Jim Clark	*Lotus*
1969	Chris Amon	*Ferrari V-6*
1970	Graham Lawrence	*Ferrari V-6*
1971	Graham McRae	*McLaren M10B*

Right, Temporada Series: Andrea de Adamich (Dino Ferrari) leads Jochen Rindt at Cordoba, 1968. *Photo: Dr Vicente Alvarez*

months before he was killed at Hockenheim in Germany. Each time Clark was driving a Lotus. Until 1970 victory in the series had eluded resident Australasian drivers who found their own cars were no match for the far more refined 2·5-litre versions from overseas—virtually 'sleeved-down' versions of the current 3-litre F1 cars. The results of the Tasman Series are shown on the left.

Until 1970 the Tasman Series was restricted to a capacity class of 2·5 litres—the Australian National F1. But in 1970 the ruling was altered to include F5000 V-8 cars as well as the 2·5s. At the same time organizers declined to pay overseas drivers starting money in preference to paying bonus amounts for fastest laps and increasing the final purse. Under these regulations top-line overseas drivers did not appear in Australasia in 1970. New Zealander Graham Lawrence won the series driving the ex-Chris Amon championship-winning Ferrari—and took more than $30,000 in prize money. Organizers say they are quite happy with the new class arrangements and they will stand for at least a few years. And they are expected to draw top drivers from overseas. TBF

South America

Temporada Races

International motor racing began in the Argentine in 1947 when a short series of three Formula Libre events were organized with the blessing of Premier Peron. The Peron Cup races at Buenos Aires were 75 miles (120·70km) in length and were both won by Luigi Villoresi's Maserati. The third event was at Rosario, and Villoresi was beaten there by Varzi's Alfa Romeo.

The series was continued in 1948, and the name Temporada was used because of the tremendous heat in which the events were run. Crowd control was a major problem on the open-street circuits, and there were many accidents involving serious and often fatal injury to spectators. The 1948 series included two races at Buenos Aires, one at Mar del Plata and one at Rosario. The 1949 series was overshadowed by Wimille's fatal crash in a Simca while practising for the Peron Cup races.

In 1951 the Peron Cup was moved out of Buenos Aires to Costanera, where Gonzales won both rounds in his Ferrari, Lang, Kling and Fangio taking 2nd and 3rd

places with their pre-World War 2 Mercedes. The new Autodrome was being built in the Argentine capital and this was used for the two 1952 Peron races.

Argentine International motor racing was now concentrated on the BA Autodrome, the Argentine GP being held there from 1953–8 and in 1960; the BA City GP was run there in 1953–5, and 1957–8. This event was moved to Mendoza in 1956 and Cordoba in 1960. Meanwhile the Buenos Aires 1,000km sports car race was an important round in the International calendar, and was run at the Autodrome in 1954–6, 1958 and 1960, and at Costanera in 1957. These races were held early each year, in the height of the Argentine summer, and were extremely hard on both driver and car, shared drives being the rule rather than the exception. It was in the 1958 Argentine GP that Moss scored his first great victory in Walker's tiny Cooper-Climax, beating the Ferraris of Musso and Hawthorn.

But after the 1960 events the series lapsed through lack of finance, being revived in 1964 with a poorly-supported F2 series run at BA Autodrome, Rosario and Cordoba. The Swiss Silvio Moser won all four events. In 1966 a major Formula 3 series was run, under the direction of J. M. Fangio, with races at Buenos Aires, Rosario, Mendoza and Mar del Plata, and Charles Crichton-Stuart won the Championship in a Brabham-Ford. The following year massive support from the state YPF fuel company attracted the cream of Formula 3, and Beltoise's works Matra-Ford won all four events at Buenos Aires, Mar del Plata and Cordoba. But both these Series had been marred by accidents involving spectators, and when

Fangio came to Europe in mid-1968 to attract support for an F2 Temporada it was stated that all events would be held on closed, permanent circuits. The series was run in December to avoid a clash with the Tasman Championship, and Ferrari Dinos won at Buenos Aires, Cordoba (Oscar Cabalen Autodrome), and San Juan (Circuit of Zonda) in the hands of Brambilla and De Adamich. Courage's Brabham won the final round back at the capital and De Adamich took the title.

In January 1970 the Temporada was run for Group 5 and 6 cars, two races being held at the BA Autodrome. The first was a revival of the 1,000km, and the second a two-heat 200 miles. Fangio was again behind the organization, with YPF sponsorship. DCN

Winners of Temporada Races

Year	Race	Winner
1947	Peron Cup, Buenos Aires	Luigi Villoresi *Maserati*
		Luigi Villoresi *Maserati*
	Rosario GP	Achille Varzi *Alfa Romeo*
1948	Peron Cup, Buenos Aires	Luigi Villoresi *Maserati*
		Luigi Villoresi *Maserati*
	Mar del Plata GP	Giuseppe Farina *Maserati*
	Rosario GP	Jean-Pierre Wimille *Simca*
1949	Peron Cup, Buenos Aires	Alberto Ascari *Maserati*
		Oscar Galvez *Alfa Romeo*
	Mar del Plata GP	J. M. Fangio *Maserati*
	Rosario GP	Giuseppe Farina *Ferrari*
1950	Peron Cup, Buenos Aires	Alberto Ascari *Ferrari*
		Luigi Villoresi *Ferrari*
	Mar del Plata GP	Alberto Ascari *Ferrari*
	Rosario GP	Luigi Villoresi *Ferrari*
	Rafaela Circuit	Juan Manuel Fangio *Talbot*
1951	Peron Cup, Costanera	Froilan Gonzales *Ferrari*
		Froilan Gonzales *Ferrari*
1952	Peron Cup, BA Autodrome	Juan Manuel Fangio *Ferrari*
		Juan Manuel Fangio *Ferrari*
1953	Argentine GP, Autodrome	Alberto Ascari *Ferrari*
	BA City GP, Autodrome	Giuseppe Farina *Ferrari*
1954	Argentine GP, Autodrome	J. M. Fangio *Maserati*
	BA City GP, Autodrome	Maurice Trintignant *Ferrari*
	BA 1,000km, Autodrome	Giuseppe Farina/ Umberto Maglioli *Ferrari*
1955	Argentine GP, Autodrome	Juan Manuel Fangio *Mercedes-Benz*
	BA City GP, Autodrome	Juan Manuel Fangio *Mercedes-Benz*
	BA 1,000km, Autodrome	E. Valiente/P. Ibanez *Ferrari*
1956	Argentine GP, Autodrome	Luigi Musso/J. M. Fangio *Lancia-Ferrari*
	BA City GP, Mendoza	Juan Manuel Fangio *Lancia-Ferrari*
	BA 1,000km, Autodrome	S. Moss/C. Menditeguy *Maserati*
1957	Argentine GP, Autodrome	J. M. Fangio *Maserati*
	BA City GP, Autodrome	J. M. Fangio *Maserati*
	BA 1,000km, Costanera	M. Gregory/C. Perdisa/ E. Castelotti/L. Musso *Ferrari*
1958	Argentine GP, Autodrome	Stirling Moss *Cooper*
	BA City GP, Autodrome	J. M. Fangio *Maserati*
	BA 1,000km, Autodrome	P. Collins/P. Hill *Ferrari*
1960	Argentine GP, Autodrome	Bruce McLaren *Cooper*
	BA City GP, Cordoba	M. Trintignant *Cooper*
	BA 1,000km, Autodrome	P. Hill/C. Allison *Ferrari*
1964	Buenos Aires, One	Silvio Moser *Brabham-Ford*
	Rosario GP	Silvio Moser *Brabham-Ford*
	Cordoba	Silvio Moser *Brabham-Ford*
	Buenos Aires, Two	Silvio Moser *Brabham-Ford*
1966	Buenos Aires, One	Chris Irwin *Brabham-Ford*
	Rosario GP	Silvio Moser *Brabham-Ford*
	Mendoza City Autodrome	Charles Crichton-Stuart *Brabham-Ford*
	Mar del Plata GP	Eric Offenstadt *Lola-Ford*
1967	Buenos Aires, One	J.-P. Beltoise *Matra-Ford*
	Mar del Plata GP	J.-P. Beltoise *Matra-Ford*
	Cordoba	J.-P. Beltoise *Matra-Ford*
	Buenos Aires, Two	J.-P. Beltoise *Matra-Ford*
1968	Buenos Aires, One	E. Brambilla *Ferrari Dino*
	Cordoba Autodrome	A. de Adamich *Ferrari Dino*
	San Juan, Zonda	A. de Adamich *Ferrari Dino*
	Buenos Aires, Two	Piers Courage *Brabham-Cosworth*
1970	BA 1,000km, Autodrome	Jean-Pierre Beltoise/ Henri Pescarolo *Matra*
	BA 200 Milla, Autodrome	P. Courage/A. de Adamich *Alfa Romeo*
1971	BA 1,000km, Autodrome	J. Siffert/D. Bell *Porsche 917K*
	Argentine GP	Chris Amon *Matra-Simca MS120*

Land Speed Record

Before November 1964, the Land Speed Record was confined to flying mile and flying kilometre records set by wheel-driven automobiles as defined by the Fédération Internationale de l'Automobile. Jet-powered vehicles did not fall within the official FIA definition of an automobile as they were not driven through the wheels. In November 1964 the Land Speed Record became available to any vehicle depending on the ground for support, controlled by an on-board driver. At the same time the FIA established a new LSR category for conventional internal combustion, axle-driven vehicles, known as the World Record for Automobiles.

From its beginnings, between 18 December 1898 and 29 April 1899, when the Count de Chasseloup-Laubat and Camille Jenatzy drove electrics at Achères near Paris, to raise the flying kilometre record from 39·29mph (63·23kph) to 65·79mph (105·87kph), LSR history reads like a series of duels. Not only duels between drivers but contests between makes, suppliers and nations.

On 21 July 1903 the Frenchman Rigolly on a Gobron-Brillé became first to exceed 100mph (160kph), recording a one-way run of 103·55mph (166·68kph) at Ostend in Belgium. Although his result was not recognized as an official LSR, Fred Marriott drove a Stanley Steamer at 127·66mph (205·50kph) at Daytona Beach on 26 January 1906, becoming the first man to travel faster than two miles a minute. In March 1910, Barney Oldfield reached 131·72mph (211·93kph) in a Benz at Daytona. Later that year the Automobile Club of France (until 1927 the French refused to recognize any LSR unless conducted under ACF jurisdiction) revised LSR rules to require two-way runs over the same course.

From 1924 until 1947, Sir Malcolm Campbell, Sir Henry Segrave, J. G. Parry Thomas, the American Ray Keech, Captain George Eyston and John Cobb pushed the record from 146·16mph (235·30kph) to 394·20mph (634·40kph). Beginning on the sands at Pendine, in Wales, in a supercharged 4-litre Sunbeam, the LSR scene first shifted to Daytona Beach, Fla., where Segrave passed the 200mph (320kph) barrier on 29 March 1927, then to the Bonneville Salt Flats in Utah, where Campbell became the first man to exceed 300mph (480kph) with his 301·13mph (484·65kph) run on 3 September 1935.

Rolls-Royce and Napier aircraft engines powered most of the record-breakers until Americans Craig Breedlove and Art Arfons introduced the jet age. On 5 August 1963, Breedlove achieved 407·45mph

Land Speed Record: Comte de Chasseloup Laubat's electric car of 1899. *Photo: Cyril Posthumus Collection*

Land Speed Record: Camille Jenatzy's 'La Jamais Contente', which reached a speed of 65·79mph (105·87kph) in April 1899. *Photo: Cyril Posthumus Collection*

(655·68kph) at Bonneville in the 3-wheeled, jet-powered 'Spirit of America', to receive the official world record for *motorcycles*. The following July, Donald Campbell set a 403·1mph (648·8kph) record for conventional (wheel-driven) automobiles in his aircraft turbine-powered Proteus Blue Bird at Lake Eyre, Australia. On 15 November 1965, the 4-wheeled 'Spirit of America —Sonic I', averaged 600·601mph (966·602kph) for its two runs over the flying mile. A General Electric J–79 turbojet, capable of 15,000 pounds thrust, propelled Breedlove and his aluminium and fibreglass capsule over the Utah desert 24·148mph (38·863kph) faster than the short-lived LSR set by Art Arfons' 'Green Monster' on 7 November. Three days before Breedlove's run, the LSR for axle-driven, internal combustion engine automobiles, 409·277mph (658·621kph), was made by Bob Summer's 32ft (9·754m) long Goldenrod. Each of Goldenrod's four, 426ci (6,981cc) Chrysler V-8 engines produced 600hp; the front pair driving the front wheels, the rear pair the rear wheels.

Shortly before noon on 23 October 1970, Gary Gabelich, of Long Beach, Calif., a 31-year-old drag racer and former power-boat champion, became the world LSR holder when he guided The Blue Flame to a 622·407mph two-way run over Utah's Bonneville Salt Flats. Sponsored by America's natural gas industry, the half-million dollar, rocket-powered Blue Flame was constructed by Reaction Dynamics to use liquefied natural gas and hydrogen peroxide as propellants. After 5 weeks frustration, on his 26th run, Gabelich bettered Breedlove's record with runs of 617·602mph and 627·287mph to average 622·407, 21mph beyond the old mark. Measuring 38ft 2·6in in length, 8ft 1·5in to the top of the tail fin, and weighing 6,500lb without fuel, The Blue Flame's engine is similar to those used in the U.S. space programme. Both body and chassis are largely aluminium; four 8·00 × 34·75 Goodyear tyres are used on 25in diameter forged aluminium wheels, although the narrow, 8·75in, front track gives the impression of being a single front wheel. The Blue Flame engine is rated at 22,000lb thrust, modified to 16,000lb for the 1970 subsonic run.

Although he never held the absolute Land Speed Record, Mickey Thompson, the versatile Californian hot rodder, designer and builder, established 485 national and international class records over his distinguished 20-year career. Thompson's 'Challenger I', driven by four modified Pontiac V-8 engines, made a record of 406·60mph (654·40kph) one-way run at Bonneville on 9 September 1960, a broken half-shaft preventing a return run. The closed-course record belongs to the Dodge sedan of NASCAR champion Bobby Isaac. Established on 24 November 1970 on the highly banked 2·66-mile (4·281km) Talladega Raceway, Ala., Isaac's speed was 201·104mph. The LSR for electrically-powered automobiles was set by Jerry Kugel at Bonneville in November 1968 when the Ford-Autolite 'Lead Wedge' recorded 138·862mph (223·503kph). The Howmet Turbine Mk II, driven by its designer Ray Heppenstall, set six standing start turbine acceleration records on 21 August 1970 near Talladega, Ala. Two records, formerly held by Russia's Pioneer II and England's Rover, were taken with runs of 105·599mph and 93·505mph. ARB

Land Speed Record

Year	Driver	Car	Speed (mph)
1898	G. de Chasseloup-Laubat	Jeantaud	39·24
1899	C. Jenatzy	Jenatzy	41·42
1899	G. de Chasseloup-Laubat	Jeantaud	43·69
1899	C. Jenatzy	Jenatzy	49·42
1899	G. de Chasseloup-Laubat	Jeantaud	57·60
1899	C. Jenatzy	Jenatzy	65·79
1902	L. Serpollet	Serpollet	75·06
1902	W. Vanderbilt	Mors	76·08
1902	H. Fournier	Mors	76·60
1903	G. Hourgieres	Mors	77·13
1903	A. Duray	Gobron-Brillié	83·47
1903	A. Duray	Gobron-Brillié	84·73
1904	H. Ford	Ford	91·37
1904	W. Vanderbilt	Mercedes	92·30
1904	L. Rigolly	Gobron-Brillié	94·78
1904	P. de Caters	Mercedes	97·25
1904	L. Rigolly	Gobron-Brillié	103·55
1904	P. Baras	Darracq	104·52
1905	A. Macdonald	Napier	104·65
1905	V. Hemery	Darracq	109·65
1909	V. Hemery	Benz	125·95
1910	B. Oldfield	Benz	131·72
1922	K. Lee Guinness	Sunbeam	133·75
1924	R. Thomas	Delage	143·31
1924	E. Eldridge	Fiat	146·01
1924	M. Campbell	Sunbeam	146·16
1925	M. Campbell	Sunbeam	150·87
1926	H. Segrave	Sunbeam	152·33
1926	J. Parry Thomas	Thomas Special	169·30
1927	J. Parry Thomas	Thomas Special	171·02
1927	M. Campbell	Napier-Campbell	174·88
1927	H. Segrave	Sunbeam	203·79
1928	M. Campbell	Napier-Campbell	206·96
1928	R. Keech	White-Triplex	207·55
1929	H. Segrave	Golden Arrow	231·44
1931	M. Campbell	Bluebird	246·09
1932	M. Campbell	Bluebird	253·97
1933	M. Campbell	Bluebird	272·46
1935	M. Campbell	Bluebird	276·82
1935	M. Campbell	Bluebird	301·13
1937	G. Eyston	Thunderbolt	312·00
1938	G. Eyston	Thunderbolt	345·50
1938	J. Cobb	Railton-Mobil	350·20
1938	G. Eyston	Thunderbolt	357·50
1939	J. Cobb	Railton-Mobil	369·70
1947	J. Cobb	Railton-Mobil	394·20
1964	D. Campbell	Bluebird	403·01
1964	T. Green	Wingfoot Express	413·20
1964	A. Arfons	Green Monster	434·20
1964	C. Breedlove	Spirit of America	468·72
1964	C. Breedlove	Spirit of America	526·28
1964	A. Arfons	Green Monster	536·71
1965	C. Breedlove	Spirit of America	555·10
1965	A. Arfons	Green Monster	576·55
1965	C. Breedlove	Spirit of America	600·60
1970	G. Gabelich	The Blue Flame	622·41

Below, Land Speed Record: Craig Breedlove's Spirit of America. *Photo: Al Bochroch Collection*

Bottom, Land Speed Record: Gary Gabelich's rocket-propelled Blue Flame setting up a new Record of 622·4mph 1,001·6kph) in November 1970.

Circuits, Races, Rallies and Hill-Climbs

Acropolis Rally

Like many of the best rallies now held in Europe, the Acropolis Rally started its distinguished history after World War 2. In 1952, the Automobile Touring Club of Greece organized a national rally which started and finished in Athens and comprised several special stages incorporated in difficult road sections. It was won by Pezmazoglou, the local GM agent, in a Chevrolet and proved so successful that the next year it achieved international status. For a few years, little interest was shown by European drivers from other countries. However, the national tourist board saw it as a way of promoting Greece as a holiday place, and other starting places besides Athens were introduced. Mercedes sent cars and the following year they were joined by Lancia and BMC.

The rally is still primarily decided on its special stages but the road sections are not easy: they incorporate some of the roughest mountain roads in Europe. The rally has dropped the multiple starts and now is based in Athens for the start and finish. It lasts about 58 hours non-stop and though this is not as long as the classic Liège–Sofia–Liège, it has replaced that rally as the toughest on-the-road event at present held in Europe. JD

Aintree Circuit

Liverpool's motor racing circuit was opened in May 1954, running outside the Grand National steeplechase course and sharing the permanent grandstand facilities it offered. With a lap distance of 3 miles (4·828km) it was the longest of the British circuits and was covered anti-clockwise in the opening meeting, the more normal clockwise direction being adopted from the second meeting on. Generally flat and featureless, Aintree's corners were mainly tight and slow, but the long Railway Straight on the return leg led into a very tricky left/right kink at Melling Crossing which had to be negotiated correctly in order to line up on the tight right-hander at Tatts immediately afterwards. A shorter club circuit measured just 1·64 miles.

Aintree was the scene of the British GP in 1955, 1957, 1959, 1961 and 1962, and Aintree 200 Formula 1 events were held from 1956 to 1964, although there was no event in 1957 and the 1960 race was for Formula 2 cars. The first 200 in 1954 was for Formula Libre cars, including the V-16 BRMs and Vandervell's 4·5-litre Thinwall Special Ferrari, and this was run in two 17-lap heats and a 34-lap final, totalling 204 miles. The F2 event was over a distance of 150 miles (or 241km) and the 1961–3 events were just on 125 miles (200km) in length. At the 1964 event a Formula 2 class ran concurrently with the F1 machines; Pilette's slow car baulked Clark's new Lotus-Climax 33 at Melling and sent the World Champion off into the straw bales, writing off the new monocoque.

Left and right, Phoenix Park: Caracciola (Mercedes-Benz SSK) winning the 1930 Irish GP. *Photo: Montagu Motor Museum*

Oustanding events were the 1955 British GP in which Moss led home the similar Mercedes W196s of Fangio, Kling and Taruffi; and the 1957 GP in which Brooks and Moss shared the winning Vanwall—the first all-British victory in this race. Jim Clark scored his second Championship victory in 1962, the last time the GP was held at Aintree, which went out of regular use at the end of 1964. Mrs Mirabelle Topham, the landowner, wanted to sell her property, but in the wrangling which followed horseracing continued once a year (the Grand National) and motor racing not at all. However since 1966 a few club meetings have been held, and in May 1970 the lap record was established by Ken Fildes (Crosslé-Cosworth F2) at 101·8mph (163·8kph); 58secs. DCN

Albi Circuit

Circuit racing began at this southern French town in 1934, using the fast tree-lined 'Les Planques' public road course beside the river Tarn. This followed the

Left, Acropolis Rally: René and Claudine Trautmann (Lancia Fulvia) at the start of the 1966 rally. *Photo: John Davenport*

Right, Aintree: Reg Parnell (Ferrari) at the opening meeting in May 1954. *Photo: Associated Press Ltd*

Aintree: Jack Fairman (BRM) leads Carlos Menditeguy (Maserati) and Stirling Moss (Vanwall) at Tatts Corner; British GP, 1957. *Photo: Autosport*

classic, roughly triangular shape of these road circuits, and had a lap length of 8·8km (5·52 miles). Formule Libre races were run there in 1933 and 1934, won by Braillard's Bugatti and 'Buddy' Featherstonehaugh's

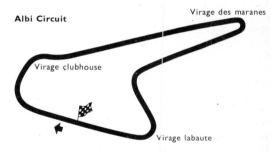

Albi Circuit

Virage des maranes
Virage clubhouse
Virage labaute

Maserati respectively; the speed of the circuit can be judged from the original race winning average of 89·74mph (144·42kph). From 1935-9 the Albi Grand Prix was for 1500cc Voiturettes.

The race was revived in 1946, when Nuvolari's F1 Maserati won at 91.57mph (147·36kph). The Formula 1 Albi race was held annually (apart from 1954) until 1955. Not until 1959 was the race run again—on a narrow airfield circuit in a suburban field. This new course, just 3·636km (2·26 miles) in length, lies alongside the RN88 road between Albi and Toulouse, and was used for Formula Junior races in 1959-63 and for Formula 2 races and supporting F3 and minor class events since then.

Albi was proposed as the scene of the 1970 French GP, an almost universally unpopular move owing to the narrowness of the circuit and its slipstreaming characteristics, with just two very slow corners to break the field up. The meeting was moved to Clermont, reportedly because of lack of funds by the Albi circuit promoters. Lap record: Jochen Rindt (Brabham BT 23C); 111·72 mph (179·81kph); 1min 12·8secs; 1968. DCN

Alpine Rally

The rally known today as the Coupe des Alpes has a history stretching back to the Austrian Alpine Trials of pre-1914 days. During the 1920s these continued on a local basis, and in 1929 were reconstituted as the International Alpine Rally. The route ran across the national

frontiers of the Alps, to include parts of Austria, France Germany, Italy, Switzerland and Yugoslavia. The exact routes varied, but the map of the 1934 rally shows a typical itinerary. The French section, over the Allos, Izoard, Lautaret and Galibier passes to Geneva, became so familiar that it was known to rally drivers as the Milk Run. Before World War 2 there were no outright winners; competitors were awarded a Coupe des Alpes or Coupe des Glaciers (1931–4 only) for penalty-free performances, and in 1950 the special award of a Coupe des Alpes en Or (Golden Alpine Cup) was instituted for competitors who had won three Coupe des Alpes in succession. The number of Cups won gave an idea of the relative severity of the rallies, which varied greatly from year to year. In 1933 only three drivers won Coupes des Glaciers (Walter Delmar, Bugatti Type 43; René Carrière, Alfa Romeo 1750; H. J. Aldington, Frazer Nash), whereas in 1934, nearly 70 cars came through without penalty. Delmar and Aldington had respectively four and three deficit-free runs in a row between 1931 and 1934, and so would both have qualified for a Coupes des Alpes en Or if such an award had been made then.

In 1935 the Alpine Rally was cancelled at the last moment by the French organizers for that year, due to the currency difficulties of the German entrants. H. J. Aldington, managing director of Frazer Nash cars, in an unparalleled offer, stated that he would finance the whole of the German entry, but by this time the French had cancelled the rally.

The 1936 event was held exclusively in Switzerland, and the next Alpine did not take place until 1946 when the route was confined to France and no penalty-free runs were achieved. The 1947 rally also took place in France. Only two Coupes des Alpes were won, by Clermont in a Lancia and Descollas in a Bugatti Type 43 which must have been at least 16 years old. This was undoubtedly the greatest post-war sporting success by a Bugatti car. Two Coupes des Alpes en Or were won in the 1950s, by Ian Appleyard (Jaguar XK 120) for penalty-free runs in 1950, 1951 and 1952, and by Stirling Moss (Sunbeam-Talbot and Alpine) for similar performances in 1952, 1953 and 1954. Following the Le Mans disaster of 1955 that year's Alpine was cancelled but it was revived in 1956, the route going into Yugoslavia for the first time since 1934. It was cancelled in 1957 but held again in 1958 when the Shell

Left, Alpine Rally: Gripper and Aldington's Frazer Nashes in the 1933 event. *Photo: Thirlby Collection*

Right, Alpine Rally: Butler-Henderson's Frazer Nash on the Col du Vars in 1933. *Photo: Thirlby Collection*

Alpine Rally: Ian Appleyard's Jaguar XK 120 descending the southern flank of the Stelvio Pass, 1950. *Photo: Jean Sejnost (Photo Junior)*

Film Unit directed by John Armstrong made a magnificent film of the event. In 1961 only one Alpine Cup was won, by the Morley twins in a works Austin-Healey 3000. They were among the only five winners in 1962, and seemed all set to win a Gold in 1963 when they suffered a broken rear axle. This year was the last time that the rally went into Italy, and from 1964 onwards its route was confined to France. It was now officially called the Coupe des Alpes rather than Rallye des Alpes, and covered many little-known passes in the south-eastern corner of France, in addition to famous ones such as the Galibier, Lautaret. Izoard and Vars. The 1970 event was cancelled as it was thought that tourist traffic would be too heavy during its proposed dates of 1–6 September, and with the present crowded rally calendar no suitable alternative dates could be found.

Outright winners for the General Classification have been named in some, though not all, post-war years, and these are given overleaf. DAT

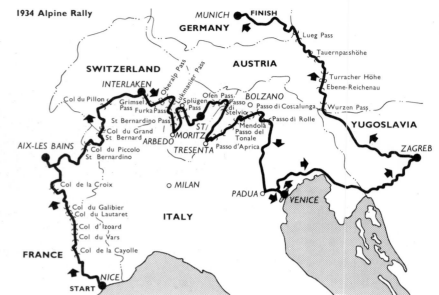

1934 Alpine Rally

Outright Winners, General Classification, of the Alpine Rally

1946	Huguet	Hotchkiss 686
1950	Appleyard	Jaguar XK 120
1951	Appleyard	Jaguar XK 120
1952	Von Falkenhausen	BMW 328
1958	Consten and de Langeneste	Alfa Romeo Giulietta Zagato
1960	de Langeneste and Greder	Alfa Romeo Giulietta
1961	D. Morley and E. Morley	Austin Healey 3000
1962	D. Morley and E. Morley	Austin Healey 3000
1963	Rolland and Angias	Alfa Romeo Giulietta TZ
1964	Rolland and Angias	Alfa Romeo Giulia TZ
1965	Trautmann and Bouchet	Lancia Flavia Zagato
1966	Rolland and Angias	Alfa Romeo GTA
1967	Hopkirk and Crellin	BMC Cooper S
1968	Vinatier and Jacob	Alpine-Renault
1969	Vinatier and Jacob	Alpine-Renault

Alpine Rally: Frazer Nash Le Mans clocking out at the summit of the Galibier Pass, 1951 *Photo: Motor*

Left, Alpine Rally: Citroën DS and Alfa Romeo at a tricky corner on the Vivione Pass, 1966. *Photo: Jean Sejnost (Photo Junior)*

Right, Alpine Trials, Austrian: August Horch driving one of the successful Audi cars, 1914. *Photo: Neubauer Collection*

Alpine Trials, Austrian

The Austrian Alpine Trials were open to fully-equipped four-seater touring cars. The first trial, held in June 1910, was a national event; the distance of 532 miles (856km), mostly on Alpine roads and including the Katschberg and Tauern passes, had to be covered in four days. It attracted little attention and only 16 competitors because it was held in the same month as the Prince Henry Trial. All the competitors completed the event successfully, Laurin & Klement winning the team prize and their class. Other class winners were a Mathis and an NAG. The 1911 trial, with 51 starters, covered about 885 miles (1,424km) and also lasted for four days. Austro-Daimler won the team prize with their 16/25hp Alpine model, while 11 competitors (five Austro-Daimler, two Nesselsdorf, and one each of NAG, Daimler-Knight, Laurin & Klement and Puch) finished without penalty points. For 1912 the event was extended

Alpine Trials, Austrian: James Radley's Rolls-Royce Continental tourer at Riva in the Dolomites, 1913. *Photo: Autocar*

American Grand Prix: Len Zengle in an Acme Six at Savannah in 1908. *Photo: Peter Helck Collection*

to 1,488 miles (2,395km), including 13 difficult passes, and seven days. There were 84 starters, and only 25 of the 72 finishers were unpenalized. These included four Austro-Daimlers, three each of the Fiat, Opel, and Benz, and two Audis. Opel and Fiat won the team prize.

In 1913 the distance was extended still farther, to 1,620 miles (2,607km) and 19 passes. Only nine cars finished with clean sheets: three Audis, and one each of Rolls-Royce, Minerva, Horch, Laurin & Klement, Benz, and Raba. Audi won the team prize. The last major trial was held in 1914, this time lasting for eight days and 1,828 miles (2,942km). It was the most arduous of the series, with a timed climb of the Katschberg and a three-mile speed trial elsewhere. There were 75 starters including several American cars — three Overlands, three Cadillacs, and a Chevrolet. Nineteen cars finished without penalty: five Audis, three each of Austro-Daimler and Fiat, two Minervas and one each of Graf & Stift,

Rolls-Royce, Laurin & Klement, Benz, Praga, and Opel. Audi won the Challenge Trophy. For four years the Austrian Alpine had been the major touring event in Europe; it was revived after the war, but only attracted local participation. HON

American Grand Prize

Up to 1908 the Vanderbilt Cup races had been organized by the American Automobile Association, but as a result of differences of opinion between them and the Automobile Club of America, the latter held another race, a month after the Vanderbilt, called the Grand Prize of the ACA. Unlike the Vanderbilt, the Grand Prize conformed to the prevailing European regulations of a 755cm² (117·02sq in) piston area, and the first event of 1908 attracted top European drivers. It was held over a twisty road course of 402 miles (647km) near Savannah, Ga. The winning car was Wagner's Fiat, from Hemery's Benz and Nazzaro's Fiat. There was no race in 1909, but a new course was laid out in 1910, largely by convict labour who were rewarded by a special enclosure on race day. The 1910 and 1911 Savannah races were Formula Libre events, and saw vast cars such as Bruce-Brown's 14·1-litre Fiat S.74 which won from Hémery's 920ci Benz and DePalma's 12·8-litre Mercedes.

For 1912 the Grand Prize moved to a road circuit at Milwaukee, Wisc., and from then until the end of the series in 1916 it used the same circuit as the Vanderbilt Cup. The 1912 event was marred by the death of Bruce-Brown in practice, and serious injury to DePalma in the race. The Formule Libre was replaced by a 450ci (7,374cc) capacity limit in the 1915 Grand Prize which now conformed with other road and board track race regulations. That year the race was won by Dario Resta's 1913 Peugeot with which he also took the Vanderbilt Cup: the only time the same car and driver won both events. Peugeot were again victorious in the last Grand Prize, held in 1916 at Santa Monica, Calif. This was a 300ci event, and three 1914 Grand Prix Peugeots took part. Aitken broke down on the first lap so he took over Wilcox's car and won in it. Wilcox, however, was declared the winner. Though held on several different courses, all the Grand Prize races were of approximately 400 miles (640km) length. GNG

Ardmore Circuit

The New Zealand Grand Prix venue from 1954 to 1962, Ardmore was a 2-mile (3·219km) artificial road circuit on a disused aerodrome about 20 miles (32km) south of Auckland. New Zealand International Grand Prix (Inc) was formed to promote an annual international meeting, the Grand Prix being the feature, and, apart from two minor meetings in 1958 and 1960, it was not used otherwise. Rather rough by current standards, Ardmore was generally wide and comprised three fast curves and four slower corners, including a hairpin, with three straights of moderate length. Stirling Moss (Lotus-Climax) set the ultimate lap record of 90·5mph (145·65kph) in 1961.

The first two races were run in counter-clockwise direction, but subsequent ones were run in the reverse direction which provided a faster and safer course. For the first three years the Grand Prix was over a distance of 200 miles (321·9km). In 1957 the distance was 240 miles (386·6km) and subsequent races were of 150 miles (241·4km) although, because of torrential rain, the final race in 1962 was cut to 100 miles.

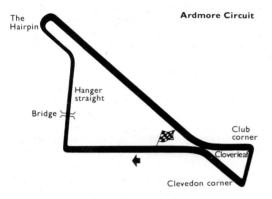

New Zealand's first full-scale international meeting was held at Ardmore on 9 January 1954, entrants including Ken Wharton, Peter Whitehead, Horace Gould and Fred Tuck from Britain, Stan Jones, Lex Davison, Lou Molina, Tom Hawkes and Jack Brabham from Australia. Jones, driving the Maybach Special, won at 72·5mph (116·68kph) from Wharton (BRM V-16), Gaze (HWM) and Gould (Cooper-Bristol). From 1958 onwards the Grand Prix was dominated by Brabham and Moss, the Australian, Cooper-mounted, winning in 1958, 1960 and 1961. Moss won in 1959 and 1962 in Rob Walker cars, a 2,014cc Cooper-Climax and 2,500cc Lotus-Climax respectively. Bruce McLaren drove his first international race at Ardmore in 1958 but retired. Subsequently, driving works Coopers, he finished 3rd in 1959 and 1962 and 2nd in 1960 and 1961. Wharton died from injuries received when his Ferrari Monza crashed in a sports car race in 1957, this being the only fatality in the history of Ardmore, which was reinstated as an operational aerodrome in 1962. PG

Ards Circuit see Tourist Trophy

Australian Grand Prix

The first Australian Grand Prix was held at Phillip Island in Victoria in 1928. Run over 100 miles (160·9km) around a 6·5-mile dirt track, it was won by the British driver, Capt. A. C. Waite, driving a 747cc Austin Seven. Captain Waite was later to become a director of the Austin Motor Company in Britain. The first Grand Prix was watched by more than ten thousand spectators in blinding dust — and it carried prize money of

£30. The Australian GP continued at Phillip Island until 1935, and in that time was won three times by Melbourne driver Bill Thompson, twice in a Type 37A Bugatti and once in a 1,098cc Brooklands Riley.

Capt. Waite was the last non-Australian driver to win the GP until 1956, when Stirling Moss took an easy victory at Albert Park in Victoria driving a 250F Maserati. Moss brought true professionalism to Australia for the first time, leaving a trail of broken cars behind him as local drivers tried to keep up with his 95·9mph (154·34kph) average. In 1964 Australian drivers were far better equipped but they were still no match for the sophisticated machines and experience of the internationals, contesting the GP as part of the annual Tasman Series. Since that year the Australian GP has always been won by an international driver — although twice the winner was Australian Jack Brabham, now living in Europe.

Only one driver has won the Australian GP four times. He was Lex Davidson, killed in practice for the Sandown Park international race in 1965. Davidson won in 1954 driving an HWM Jaguar, in 1957 and 1958 in a Ferrari and in 1961 in a Cooper-Climax. A trophy bearing a silver model of Waite's Austin Seven is now presented annually in memory of Davidson to the winner of the Australian GP. Another three drivers have won the GP three times: Jack Brabham, Doug Whiteford and Bill Thompson.

In 1970 the Australian Grand Prix reverted to being a race seperate from the Tasman Series, throwing it open once more to local competition. TBF

Austrian Alpine Trials see Alpine Trials, Austrian

Austrian GP see Zeltweg

Avus Circuit

The idea of the AVUS (*Automobil-Verkehrs- und Übungs-Strasse*) was mooted in 1907. A company was founded and registered in 1909 and the track planned for the Grünewald, near Berlin. Construction started in

AVUS: the start of a Formula 3 race, held in 1967. *Photo: Doug Nye Collection*

1913 but work was interrupted by World War 1 and it was not finished until 1920. The circuit consisted of two parallel straights with a very narrow turn on the south end and a wider bend of the north giving a total length of 12·43 miles (20km). The opening meeting was held in 1921 and won by Fritz von Opel in an Opel. His average speed was 79·8mph (128·43kph). In 1926 the first German Grand Prix was held on the AVUS; the winner was Caracciola in a 2-litre 8-cylinder supercharged Mercedes. His average speed over 20 laps was 85mph (136·79kph). It became evident that the two long straights and the surfacing — mostly of asphalt — were not ideal. The later German Grands Prix were held on the Nürburgring, but the Avusrennen (AVUS races) took place on the circuit every year. In 1927 the famous super-elevated north bend was built, banked at an angle of 43°. In 1938 only a sports car race was held; the AVUS was integrated in the national autobahn network and no further races were run.

After World War 2 the circuit was divided into two parts by the Berlin zonal borders. When plans were made to resume the Avusrennen the circuit was shortened to 5·151 miles (8·3km) and a new south curve was built. The first post-war race was held in 1951. The formula 2 race was won by Paul Greifzu in his 2-litre BMW-Special at an average speed of 112·6mph (181·2kph). The German Grand Prix was held at the AVUS in 1959. Tony Brooks won in a Ferrari and drove the fastest lap at 149mph (239·8kph). Only minor events were held at the AVUS circuit in the following years. The north bend was used for the last time in 1967 in connection with a rally, and was later dismantled. During the last few years there have been rumours that the AVUS circuit may be rebuilt. Lap record: Bernd Rosemeyer (Auto Union); 171·75mph (276·38kph); 1937. HON

Autodromo de la Ciudad de Mexico *see* Mexico, Autodromo de la Ciudad de

Bahamas Races *see* Nassau Speed Weeks

Barcelona Circuits
Racing has taken place in or near Barcelona on three separate circuits: the Circuito Villafranca del Panades Manjos-Almunia (1921–3); the Circuit del Parque de Montjuich (1933–6 and 1966 to the present day); and the Circuito de Pedralbes (1946–54). The Villafranca circuit was the longest, with a lap distance of 9·19 miles (14·79km), and saw the first three Penya Rhin Grands Prix for 1·5-litre cars. The road circuit in Montjuich Park has a lap of 2·35 miles (3·79km); it was used for the next four Penya Rhin GPs, which were run for Formula Libre or 750kg cars, and for Formula 2 or Formula 1 (non-championship) cars today. From 1946 to 1950 Penya Rhin races were held on the 2·774-mile (4·464km) Pedralbes Circuit which was also used for the 1951 and 1954 Spanish Grands Prix. Lap Record (Montjuich): Jacky Ickx (Ferrari 312B); 99·64mph (160·35kph); 1min 25·1sec; 1970. GNG

Bari Circuit
The seaport of Bari, on the Adriatic coast of Italy, Apulia, has long had an enthusiastic Automobile Club who organized races on a circuit that ran through the streets of the town, over a distance of 8·93 miles (5·55km), the whole town coming to a virtual standstill on race day. Although flat, it was an exacting circuit with all the natural hazards of a city along its route, with fast and

slow corners, hairpins and fast straights. The post-war boom in motor racing allowed the club to hold their first race in 1947, starting with a full-blooded Grand Prix event, won by Achille Varzi (Alfa-Romeo 158) at 65·15mph (105·275kph).

The circuit was used every year until 1957, with one break in 1953, but there were signs of difficulty by 1952 when the Bari race had to be held for sports cars as Grand Prix racing was beginning to become too costly for a small club to organize. A Grand Prix was tried again in 1954, but the final two years saw the Automobile Club of Bari forced to revert to sports car races. Ever ambitious, they organized night races in 1955 with the main straight floodlit and the rest of the circuit illuminated by the normal street-lighting. The growing concern with spectators' safety after the Le Mans catastrophe of 1955 had many side effects on motor racing, one being stricter rules by governments and governing bodies, so that the Bari street circuit could no longer comply with international requirements. After struggling for one more year Bari finally had to abandon international motor racing, being unable to afford the outlay on safety precautions and modifications demanded. Lap record: Onofre Marimon (Maserati); 90·124mph (144·104kph); 1954. DSJ

Bathurst Circuit
One of the most historic, spectacular and difficult circuits of the world is the 3·8-mile (6·116km) Mount Panorama circuit at Bathurst, 130 miles (209km) west of Sydney, Australia. The only public road circuit now left in the country, it is for all but two meetings — seven days of the year — a 35mph-limit (56kph) scenic drive around Mount Panorama, rising 800fr (243·84km) over rolling plains patched with orchards and farms. Bathurst has a special quality about it unmatched by any other Australian circuit. There is the frightening mile-long downhill Conrod Straight, which has claimed three lives, including that of 69-year-old Brooklands veteran Tom Sulman in April 1970. And there is the equally daunting Skyline, which the racing cars approach at about 130mph with the effect of running straight out into nothingness as the road drops away. The record for the 3·8 miles is around 2min 9sec, with top speeds just over 180mph (290kph). The circuit opened in 1938 with a bare-headed Peter Whitehead winning the Australian GP in an ERA on a dusty gravel road, and has operated continuously since, apart from the war years. The Australian Grand Prix has been run there four times. Drivers revere

Bathurst Circuit

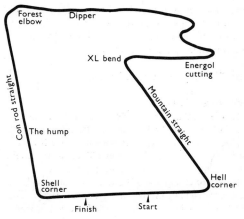

Bathurst as the most demanding yet most exciting of circuits, with sheer drops at the edge of the road in many places, thick trees and high clay walls looming everywhere.

Since 1963 Bathurst has been the home of the classic 500-mile annual race for stock-standard production sedans, racing in five classes according to retail price. There has not been a classic Grand Prix run there since 1958, although organizers' plans include an application for a World Championship round in the future. TBF

Bay Park Raceway

Scene of the first international Formula A/5000 race to be held in New Zealand, in December 1968, Bay Park Raceway is a 1.3316-mile (2.1348km) permanent circuit owned by Bay Park Raceways Ltd. The promoting club for the annual major international meeting each December is the Bay of Plenty Motor Racing Association Inc. The circuit, which provides terraced seating and a full view of the course for 8,000 spectators, is 7 miles from Tauranga, a major North Island resort town on the east coast. It is a predominantly left-turning circuit with well-cambered corners. Maximum number of entries for single-seater events and saloon events are 18 and 24 respectively.

Although the Bay Park International does not qualify as a Tasman Championship event, most Tasman contenders competed in the 1969 race and the promoters of the meeting contributed to the overall prize money pool for Tasman Formula races in New Zealand and Australia in the 1970 series. Lap record: Graham McRae (McLaren M1OA); 89·73mph (144·41kph); 53·4sec; 1969. PG

Belgian GP see Spa-Francorchamps

Belgian Touring Car GP see Spa-Francorchamps

Berne Circuit

Also known as the Bremgarten circuit this was situated on the western outskirts of the Swiss capital, and was often described as beautiful and dangerous. It was a true road circuit, for the most part running through a publicly-owned forest, made up of a succession of very fast bends, with hardly any true straights, more testing for men than for machines. It was first used, for motor-

Bay Park Raceway

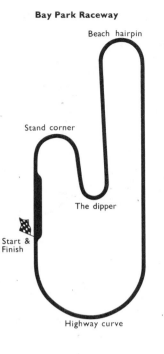

Beach hairpin

Stand corner

The dipper

Start & Finish

Highway curve

Berne: Fangio and Kling (Mercedes-Benz W196) lead away at the start of the 1954 Swiss GP. *Photo: Motor*

Berne: the start of the 1955 Prix de Berne, showing the famous stands which survived the circuit by 15 years. *Photo: ATP Bilderdienst*

Left, Bay Park: Mike Goth (Surtees) leads Ulf Norinder (Lola T190) out of Beasley corner, December 1969. *Photo: Trakshots*

Right, Berne: the problems of Berne are summed up in this photo of the 1949 Swiss GP; narrow roads with varying surfaces, little run-off space and confusing patterns of shade and sunlight. *Photo: Motor*

cycle racing, in 1931; the first car races were run in 1934, and it was the venue of 14 Swiss Grands Prix before the Federal Government banned all racing in Switzerland in 1955.

Roughly diamond-shaped, the 4·52-mile (7·28km) circuit ran almost flat to Bethlehem corner, then dropped to Quarry, climbed to the fairly sharp right-hand Eicholz, and then ran down through the very fast sequence of bends known collectively as Jorden. The Eymatt and Tenni right-handers both had inconsistent radii (the former really being two corners). After Tenni the forest closed in, and through it fast swerves and bends followed in quick succession as the circuit climbed to the Forsthaus right angle. A gentle fast curve past the pits completed the lap. The pits were almost a prototype for modern practice, but unusual for their time, as the pit road was separated from the circuit. The circuit was exacting in itself, and complicated by ever-varying light

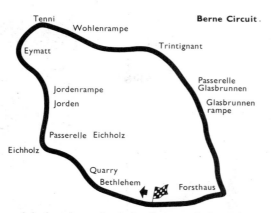

Berne Circuit .

Tenni
Wohlenrampe
Eymatt
Trintignant
Jordenrampe
Passerelle Glasbrunnen
Jorden
Glasbrunnen rampe
Passerelle Eichholz
Eichholz
Quarry
Bethlehem
Forsthaus

and shade and, save for the last few races, by inconsistent road surfaces.

The Bremgarten circuit had more than its share of accidents, H. C. Hamilton being killed there in the inaugural Swiss GP of 1934, and Varzi and Kautz died there in 1948 — the former in practice and the latter in the race. Caracciola's crash in the 1952 Prix de Berne sports car race ended his career.

Apart from the GP, the most important event was the Prix de Berne, for 1·5-litre cars from 1934 to 1939, for F2 cars in 1948 and 1950, and for sports cars in 1952. Lap record: J. M. Fangio (Mercedes-Benz W196); 101·97mph (162·56kph); 2min 39·7sec; 1955. DWH

Bol d'Or

The race for the Bol d'Or (Golden Bowl) was the first 24-hour race in Europe, as it was instituted in 1922, one year before the more famous sports car event at Le Mans. It was open to cars of up to 1,100cc, and there was also a class for 3-wheelers and for motorcycle combinations. Unlike Le Mans, only one driver was allowed for the whole 24 hours, but he could take a passenger to keep him company and help with repairs if he wished. A rest period of four hours was allowed, and the cars had to have covered at least 90km (55·923 miles) at the end of the third hour to qualify. This meant an average of nearly 32kph (20mph), which seems modest enough, but some of the cars had engines as small as 350cc. The first race of 1922 was won by an Amilcar driven by André Morel, followed by the Salmsons of Benoist and Bueno. It was held on a 5km (3·1069 miles) circuit in the

Bol d'Or: Salmson, Amilcar and MG at the start of the 1936 race. Photo: Cyril Posthumus Collection

forest of St Germain near Paris, used every year until 1937, with the exception of 1927 when a circuit at Fontainebleau was employed. During the 1920s the Bol d'Or was very popular with both works and private entrants of the well-known light French sports cars such as Amilcar, Salmson, Sénéchal, and BNC, but some real miniatures did well in their classes: for example the 350cc Villard which won its class in 1926, hotly pursued by two Microns of the same capacity. From the late 1920s onwards the race became the favourite preserve of private entrants who sometimes figured quite high in the results with home-made specials. These were often of unusual design, employing twin engines, fwd, and so on, and it is a tribute to their constructor/drivers that such spidery machines as the 350cc Sphinx-Staub 3-wheeler lasted the 24 hours. Driven by Cheret, the Sphinx-Staub won its class in 1931, the day after Cheret had won a 24-hour motorcycle race.

In 1937 the Bol d'Or moved to the road circuit at Montlhéry near Paris. That year's race was notable for Rigoulot and Giraud-Cabantous' 1st and 2nd places with revamped 10-year-old 'Tank' Chenard-Walckers. The capacity limit went up to 1·5 litres in 1938, when Amédée Gordini won in a Fiat. The last pre-World War 2 race went to Contet in an Ulster Aston Martin.

The first two post-war races (1947 and 1948) were held at St Germain again, as was the 1951 event, but all other Bols d'Or took place at Montlhéry. Simcas and Gordinis dominated the first few post-war races, but from 1950 onwards DBs and various special-bodied 4CV Renaults took the leading places. As in pre-war days the Bol d'Or still gave a chance to the small constructor, and the 1952 race saw a 425cc Rovin minicar finish 12th overall. Another small maker to do well was Germain Lambert, who finished 3rd in the 1,100cc class in 1949, and won it in 1951. In 1954 there was a sharp break with tradition, in that two drivers were allowed for the first time. This race was won by Sigrand and Celérier in a special Peugeot-MD. The last Bol d'Or was in 1955, with capacity limit up to 2 litres. Porsches were 1st and 2nd, with a Maserati in 3rd place. GNG

Boulogne Races

The first racing at Boulogne took place in 1909 when the Coupe de l'Auto was held on a 23·5-mile (37·82km) circuit beginning on the outskirts of the town. The course included a 13km (8·078 miles) straight with several hills giving a switchback effect, and a 9km (5·59 miles) narrow road through the Forêt de Boulogne. The same circuit was used for the 1910 Coupe de l'Auto, but a new 32-mile (51·50km) circuit was chosen for the 1911 and 1913 events. The fastest lap in a Coupe de l'Auto race was made by Jules Goux in a Peugeot in 1913. From 1921 to 1928 Boulogne was the site of the Speed Week during which a series of sprints and races were held for sports and racing cars. There were also driving tests, a hill-climb in the streets of the town, and a Con-cours d'Elégance. The latter and the driving tests were held at nearby Le Touquet in later years. The races were held over a 23-mile circuit substantially the same as the original one of 1909. The best known race was the Georges Boillot Cup for sports cars, won by Hispano-Suiza in 1921 and 1922, Chenard-Walcker in 1923, 1924, 1925 and 1926, Ariès in 1927 and Alfa Romeo in 1928. The distance varied between 232 (373·4km) and 372 miles (598·7km), and for the first three years the Cup was awarded under complex rules for regularity. The main events for racing cars were the Boulogne Light Car

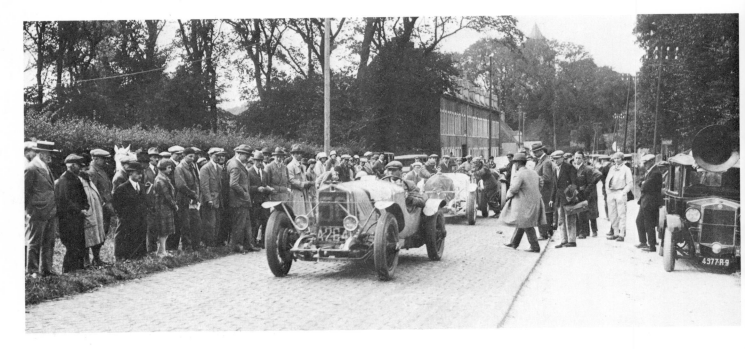

and Voiturette Grand Prix with awards for 1100cc and 1500cc competitors, and the National Trophy held in 1928 was only for 2-litre cars, was the final event. GNG

Brands Hatch Circuit

The Brands Hatch circuit lies in a natural fold in the North Downs, 20 miles (32·19km) south-east of London, and right beside the main A20 Dover road, near Farningham. It was first used, as a motorcycle grass track, between the wars, and was revived in 1949. A short, roughly kidney-shaped track was surfaced and the 500 Club, later to grow into the British Racing & Sports Car Club, ran a number of highly-successful 500cc F3 races on this track, circulating anti-clockwise, in the early 1950s.

Attendances were nearly always good, and in 1954 the circuit's amenities were improved and an extra loop added up the hill to Druids Hairpin. The mouldering asphalt of the original track still remains at the foot of Druids Hill, but the 1·24-mile (1·996km) circuit was the scene of some excellent racing. The BRSCC grew

rapidly to become Britain's most go-ahead and enterprising motor sporting organization, and in 1960 a long awaited extension was built to bring the circuit up to GP length. The new loop disappeared over the hill south of Kidney Bend, dropping into the next valley and climbing on to a ridge before returning to rejoin the 'club' circuit at Clearways. Now with a lap length of 2·65 miles (4·265km) Brands Hatch became the venue for many major international race meetings, while the club circuit was used increasingly for sprints and club races.

In the early 1960s Brands was the scene of the *Motor* 6-hour saloon car races, and the circuit promoters' association with Guards Cigarettes produced a long string of top quality Guards Trophy sports car races. The Formula 1 Race of Champions was instituted at the circuit in 1965, and the British GP was held there in 1964, 1966, 1968 and 1970, alternating with Silverstone. In 1965 a Guards double-500-mile race took place, developed into the Ilford 500 6-hour event the following year. In 1967 BOAC took over sponsorship and the

Boulogne Races: André's Georges Irat at the start of the 1928 Georges Boillot Cup.
Photo: Montagu Motor Museum

Left, Brands Hatch: R. G. Bicknell (Revis) leads a field of Formula 3 cars round Paddock Bend, 1954. *Photo: Central Press Photos Ltd*

Below, Brands Hatch: Jackie Stewart in John Coombs' Jaguar E-type leads a field of sports cars, 1964. *Photo: Mercury Photos*

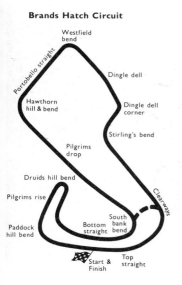

Brands Hatch Circuit

Brands Hatch: the start of the British Grand Prix, 1966. *Photo: Sport and General*

event became a World Championship of Makes qualifying round, developing into a full 1,000km race in 1970.

Brands Hatch is an exceptionally tricky circuit, with its change of gradient and selection of corners with a fairly bumpy surface putting a great strain on the cars. It has also proved fairly dangerous, for there are few spaces to spin on to, and if a car goes off it hits a bank. Brands Hatch went through a bad period for fatal accidents in the mid-1960s; the blind downhill corner at Paddock Bend had a particularly bad record. Subtle changes were made which improved the circuit's record, but it remains one of the most difficult of the British circuits. Exceptional visibility makes it one of Europe's most attractive circuits for the spectator. Lap record (GP circuit): Jack Brabham (Brabham BT33); 111·91mph (180·10kph); 1min 25·8sec; 1970. (Club circuit): Graham McRae (McLaren-Chevrolet M10B); 97·89mph; 45·6sec; 1970. DCN

Bremgarten Circuit *see* Berne Circuit

Bridgehampton Race Circuit

Bridgehampton is yet another American race track that had its beginnings on public roads. In 1949, following a lapse of 29 years, sports-car races were held on a 4-mile (6·44km) combination of Bridgehampton streets and nearby country lanes. Within a few years police were unable to control the crowds and the present 2·855-mile (4·595km) circuit opened in 1957.

Bridgehampton Circuit

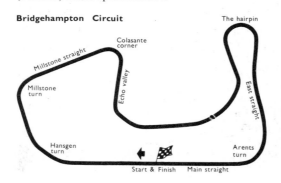

Although spectator amenities or garage facilities are poor, many drivers consider the 'Bridge' America's best road course, including the Swiss Jo Siffert, who on first seeing it thought it the US track most like those in Europe, and said that he could surprise people there. The next day Siffert's Porsche 917 finished 3rd, on the same lap with the all-conquering Hulme and McLaren, the best finish in the entire 1969 Can-Am series for the works Porsche. During the first four years of the Can-Am, Bridgehampton was the single circuit where American drivers held their own, Dan Gurney and Mark Donohue winning in 1966 and 1968.

Rolling over giant sand dunes overlooking Peconic Bay and the old whaling village of Sag Harbor, Bridgehampton may be the only race course where spectators can watch sailing-boat and automobile racing at the same time. Located near the tip of Long Island, 100 miles (160km) east of New York City, the track is 6 miles (9·66km) from the seashore villages of Southampton and Bridgehampton.

The minimum circuit width is 30ft (9·144m), with track elevations ranging from 132 to 265ft (40·234 to 80·772m) above sea-level. In addition to club meets, Bridgehampton was the site of Trans-Am and Can-Am events. Financial problems closed the track in Sept. 1970, the Sept. 13th Can-Am originally scheduled for Bridgehampton going to the new Road Atlanta circuit. It was reopened under new management in 1971.

Lap record: Bruce McLaren (McLaren-Chevrolet); 118·949mph (191·374kph); 1min 26·64sec; 1969. ARB

British GP *see* Aintree, Brands Hatch *and* Silverstone Circuits

Brno Circuit

The first international road races in Czechoslovakia were held on the Brno circuit, otherwise known as the Masaryk, from 1930 onwards. The original circuit measured 29·147km (18·109 miles) per lap, with 47 right-hand corners and 36 left-hand corners. Races were held anti-clockwise. The most interesting, and difficult, part of the circuit was a series of corners at Ostrovačice,

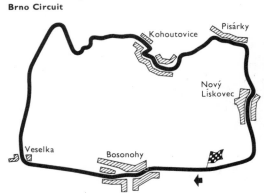

Brno Circuit

Kohoutovice

Pisárky

Nový Lískovec

Veselka

Bosonohy

about 16km (10 miles) from the start. Races on this course were held until 1937, but when competitions began again after World War 2, in 1949, the course had been shortened to 17·801km (11·06 miles), and the Ostrovačice area was eliminated. There were now 28 right-hand and 22 left-hand corners. The most interesting part of the circuit was a series of corners in the Žebětín and Kohoutovice woods. In 1964 it was further shortened to 13·941km (8·663 miles).

From 1930 to 1937 the Masaryk Grand Prix, or Czechoslovak Grand Prix, was a major event. Many well-known drivers competed there, Chiron winning three times in succession (1931, 1932, 1933); from 1934 the great German teams dominated the results, Stuck and Rosemeyer winning for Auto Union in 1934 and 1935, and Caracciola for Mercedes-Benz in 1937. A Voiturette Grand Prix, for cars of up to 1·5 litres capacity, was held from 1930 to 1937. Bugattis were mainly the victors, although Dick Seaman won in an ERA in 1935. After the war, only two Formula 1 races were held, in 1949 when Peter Whitehead won in a Ferrari, and in 1950 when Václav Hovorka drove a Maserati to victory. There was then no racing until 1962 when the Czechoslovak Grand Prix became a Formula Junior event, won by Kurt Ahrens on a Cooper-Ford in 1962 and by Kurt Barry in the same make of car in 1963. From 1964 to the present day it has been a Formula 3 event with such cars as Lotus, Wartburg, Brabham and Tecno sharing the honours. In 1971 it was proposed to shorten the course still further, to make a lap of exactly

7km (4·349 miles). Lap records for the various circuits are as follows: 1930–37 circuit — Rudolf Caracciola (Mercedes-Benz); 142·7kph (88·67mph). 1949–63 circuit — B. Bira (Maserati); 132·41kph (82·27mph). 1964–9 circuit — Freddie Kotullinsky (Lotus); 156·75kph (97·40mph). VH

Brno—Soběšice Hill-Climb

This hill was first used for motor sport in 1924, following the popularity of Prague's Zbraslav-Jíloviště hill-climb. The course was 2·3 miles (3·7km) long, with a maximum gradient of 8% and a height differential of 525ft (160m). At first it proved more popular than the Prague venue, with twice as many competitors in the first year's event. This was won by the Austrian driver Wetzke in an Austro-Daimler at a speed of 49·46mph (79·6kph). Honours in later years were shared among: Čeněk Junek (Bugatti), 57·41mph (92·4kph); Eliška Junek (Bugatti), 56·73mph (91·3kph); and Milos Bondy (Bugatti), 68·97mph (111kph), the last result being the final record for the hill. Foreign drivers such as Caracciola and Von Morgen also competed at Brno, but were never as successful as the local drivers. In 1930 the Masaryk circuit was opened, also in Brno, and the hill-climb was discontinued. VH

Brooklands Motor Course

Brooklands Motor Course, the first proper car race track in the world, was built at his own expense by H. F. Locke King in order to provide the British motor

Far left, Brno: Stuck, Varzi and Rosemeyer (Auto Unions) at the start of the 1934 Masaryk Grand Prix. *Photo: Vladimír Havránek Collection*

Above, Brno: Jurg Dubler (Chevron B17) in the 1970 Formula 3 Grand Prix. *Photo: Zavrel Zdenek*

Brno-Soběšice: an Austro-Daimler in a 1927 hill-climb. *Photo: Vladimír Havránek Collection*

industry, which at the time was hampered by a universal 20mph (32kph) speed limit and police action, with somewhere to test their products unhindered. Work was started on the Brooklands estate at Weybridge, Surrey, close to the main London and South-Western railway line, in the autumn of 1906 and their ambitious project, involving a 2·75-mile (4·426km) banked circuit of concrete, was ready for use by the following summer, a feat of construction which astonished even the Americans. Building the track involved diverting the River Wey in two places, demolishing farms, felling woodland and moving a vast amount of earth.

The track had been designed by Col. Holden of the Royal Engineers and its construction was supervised by a railway engineer, Donaldson. The width of the track was 100ft (30·48m) and the pear-shaped circuit had a short banking (the Home, or Members') struck at a mean radius of 1,000ft (304·8m) and a longer banking (the Byfleet) struck at a radius of 1,550ft (472·4m). The straight beside the main railway line, known as the Railway straight, was half a mile (0·805km) long, coupling the two bankings, and the Byfleet banking ran on to flat ground with a reverse curve which coupled it to the beginning of the Members' banking, this slight right-handed curve in an otherwise fast circuit being necessary to clear the works of the Itala Motor Company, where the Vickers aircraft sheds were built right beside the track in 1915. The bankings were composed of shallow concrete on earth embankments, but the steep Members' banking had to be taken over the River Wey

Left, Brooklands: S. F. Edge in the 24-Hour Record Napier, June 1907. *Photo: Veteran Car Club of Great Britain*

Right, Brooklands: 1910 Straker-Squire, typical of the stripped touring cars which ran at Brooklands before 1914. *Photo: William Boddy Collection*

Left, Brooklands: the special-bodied Prince Henry Vauxhall, KN2, taking the World 300-Mile Record at 92·11mph in 1913. A. J. Hancock at the wheel. *Photo: William Boddy Collection*

Right, Brooklands: paddock scene in the early 1920s. *Photo: Montagu Motor Museum*

on an elaborate Hennebique bridge of ferro-concrete. Apart from the outer circuit, a finishing straight ran from the reverse curve aforementioned to the end of the Members' banking, this straight making the total track distance 3¼ miles (5·23km), of which 2 miles were level. Towards the upper end of the 991yd (906·2m) finishing straight, on its Byfleet banking side, the concrete paddock was situated, and here a substantial clubhouse with observation balcony was built. In the paddock 75 simple shelters were provided for the racing cars.

Brooklands being an innovation and constructed in the horse age it was natural that horse race tactics should have been widely operated there: hence the finishing straight. In the formative years, too, the cars were not numbered but their drivers wore different coloured jockey's silks for identification; and races were started by Hugh Owen, ex-starter to the Jockey Club. Nevertheless, in spite of this seemingly naive approach to motor racing, Brooklands was a most elaborate undertaking, its Clubhouse equipped with restaurants, bars, changing rooms, billiard room and a weighing court. The Brooklands Automobile Racing Club ministered to motor racing at the new track from its offices at Carlton House in London.

The first race meeting took place on 6 July 1907. Six races were contested, the most important of which was the First Montagu Cup Race over 30·5 miles, for which the first prize was £1,400 and a cup valued at an additional £200. The winner was J. E. Hutton in a Mercedes. The cars raced in an anti-clockwise direction, coming

Brooklands Circuit

Railway Straight
Railway turn
Solomon's straight
Aerodrome curve
Sahara straight
Byfleet banking
Howel's corner
Campbell straight
Fork bend
Banking bend

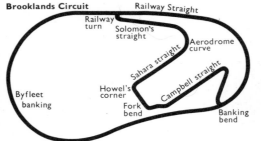

up the finishing straight at the end of the final lap.

Brooklands was not at first a success and was considerably hampered by an action brought by local residents against the noise, and a fatal accident to the mechanic of one of the faster cars. It had, however, received useful publicity before even the first race meeting had been held when S. F. Edge booked the new track for an attack on the World 24-Hour Record, driving a 60hp Napier single-handed round and round the track, the circumference of which was picked out at night by innumerable red lanterns, with flares illuminating the top of the banking. This same S. F. Edge later put up a series of challenges to publicize Napier cars, which drew further attention to events at the new motor course and it was not long before its value as a testing ground to the motor industry was fully appreciated. All-out running on the track imposed a severe strain on engine bearings, valves, pistons, etc. and especially on cooling systems and tyres. Some manufacturers, such as Sunbeam, Vauxhall and Talbot, built special cars with which to combat these conditions, usually fitting them with extremely narrow single-seater bodies for effective streamlining.

The races, with the important ones taking place on public holidays, were usually of short duration, and handicapped on an individual basis, which enabled a wide variety of cars, of different types and speeds, to compete successfully, a system retained to the end of racing at Brooklands. The first Clerk of the Course was E. de Rodakowski, who was succeeded in later years by Col. Lindsay Lloyd and A. Percy Bradley. The legendary handicapper and starter over almost the entire period of the track's history was the one and only 'Ebby' — A. V. Ebblewhite. His Majesty the King became Patron of the BARC.

Apart from racing, a great deal of record-breaking activity went on at the Weybridge track, special electrical timing apparatus being installed, actuated by inflated rubber contact strips laid across the surface of the course. Although the noise dispute put paid to attacks at Brooklands on the 24-Hour Record, a new category known as the 'Double-Twelve' was substituted in which the car made its record bid running for twelve hours and was locked up during the night before resuming its run. A notable record established in the early years of Brooklands was that of Percy Lambert who, driving an sv 25hp Talbot single-seater, was in 1913 the first driver to exceed 100 miles (160km) in one hour; unfortunately in trying to regain this record Lambert was killed when a tyre burst and the Talbot overturned on the Members' banking.

During World War 1, Brooklands was taken over by the RFC and RAF and their heavy lorries played havoc with the track's surface, although the airfield, where flying had been pioneered since the year 1910, proved of great value to them, and to Vickers, Sopwith and Blériot, who manufactured aircraft there. Only one race meeting was held during the war years but after the Armistice extensive repairs were put in hand and Brooklands was reopened in May 1920.

Racing continued much as before, the BARC Bank Holiday meetings being the occasion for short and long handicap races under the former handicapping system, even the longer races being usually of less than 10 miles (16km). Cars were grouped roughly on their speed capabilities and run together in races termed the 75, 90, and 100mph handicaps, with the very fastest competitors taking part in the dramatically named Lightning Short and Long Handicaps. This was the age of the new cyclecars and small cars, which were encouraged by the Brooklands authorities, so that GN, AC, Morgan 3-wheeler, Hillman, Calthorpe, AV, and other such makes raced there. At the opposite extreme it was the era of giant aero-engined cars such as the V-12 350hp Sunbeam single-seater, the now immortal Chitty-Chitty-Bang-Bangs of Count Zborowski, the Wolseley Viper, and the Isotta-Maybach. Small cars used Brooklands to demonstrate the remarkable advances in speed from small engines possible in the 1920s, 100mph being achieved over short distances, then for a full lap, and then for an hour by the AC, and long-distance records of up to 2,000 miles being accomplished by AC and Aston Martin light cars.

In 1921 the ambitious Junior Car Club staged Britain's first important long-distance race, a 200-mile event for cars not exceeding 1,500cc, the winner of which was Segrave in a two-seater Talbot-Darracq at 88·82mph (142·94kph). This long-distance race caused a great deal of interest and was repeated in the same form in 1922, 1923 and 1924, the respective winners being K. Lee Guinness in a Talbot-Darracq at 88·06mph (141·72kph); C. M. Harvey in an Alvis at 93·29mph (150·13kph); and Guinness in a Darracq at 102·27mph (164·61kph). (There had been a 500-mile motorcycle race in 1921 but this was never repeated.) Up to 1924 the Brooklands outer circuit had been universally employed, with different start and finish lines, and the finishing straight ignored for the faster races. In 1924 the noise hazard again arose and to appease local inhabitants special Brooklands silencers had thenceforth to be used on all racing cars and motorcycles competing at the track. In 1925 the JCC decided to bring a road racing atmosphere to Brooklands by introducing artificial sandbank and other corners into its 200-mile light car race, which that year was won by Segrave in a Darracq at 78·89mph (126·96kph). This innovation proved popular and was followed by many other clubs. Long-distance races were also run over the outer circuit, those of 1925 being the Essex MC 100-mile handicap won by Purdy's Alvis at 86·77mph (139·64kph) and the *News of the World*

Far left, Brooklands: one of the aero-engined specials which enlivened racing in the 1920s was the Wolseley-Viper, powered by a V-8 Hispano-Suiza engine of 11,762cc. *Photo: William Boddy Collection*

Above, Brooklands: before the start of the 1929 Double Twelve; fwd Alvis, Lea-Francis and Talbot. *Photo: William Boddy Collection*

Right, Brooklands: 1929 Double Twelve, Alvis, Lea-Francis and Rileys taking the turn from the Finishing Straight into the Railway Straight. The timekeepers' bus is in the foreground. *Photo: William Boddy Collection*

Below right, Brooklands: Members' Banking and Bridge. *Photo: Montagu Motor Museum*

Brooklands: 1925 200 Mile-Race. *Photo: William Boddy Collection*

100-mile handicap, won by J. G. Parry Thomas in his 1·5-litre Thomas Special at 98·23mph (158·09kph).

Parry Thomas, who resided at Brooklands, had become an institution at the Weybridge track, winning a great many races and establishing the lap record with his straight-8 Leyland Thomas cars. At this period Brooklands was the great centre for the British sporting motorist who was allowed to take his touring car and motorcycle on the track when racing was not in progress. BARC members could watch the races from the natural hill encircled by the Members' banking, and enjoyed facilities that enabled them to regard the place as a country estate with the added attraction and excitement of motor racing. A special car badge for those who had lapped at 120mph or over was instituted, the first driver to receive such recognition being K. L. Guinness with the V-12 Sunbeam, followed by Parry Thomas and his Leyland. Later this was changed for a 130mph badge, seventeen drivers qualifying for this including two women drivers, Mrs Stewart with the Derby-Miller and Mrs Petre with the 10·5-litre V-12 Delage. By the 1930s the offices of the BARC had been transferred from London to the Clubhouse in the paddock, but Kenneth Skinner retained the post of Secretary.

In the latter part of the 1920s long-distance races for sports cars were an important feature of the Brooklands curriculum. The JCC ran its Production Car Race in 1926, won by Hazelhurst's Salmson at 62·9mph (101·23kph), and its Sporting Car Race in 1927, the winner of which was Harvey in an Alvis at 63·2mph (101·71kph). In that year the Essex MC organized a 'miniature Le Mans' with its Six-Hour Endurance Race, of which the winner was George Duller in a 3-litre Sunbeam at 64·3mph (103·48kph). Even more significant, the RAC had permitted the British Grand Prix to be run over an artificial road course at Brooklands in 1926 and this race was again held at Brooklands in 1927, the respective winners being Sénéchal and Wagner in a Delage at 71·61mph (115·25kph) and Benoist (Delage) at 85·5mph (137·60kph).

The Essex MC Six-Hour Endurance Race was repeated in 1928, and won by Ramponi in an Alfa Romeo at 69·57mph (111·96kph). The Junior Car Club 200 miles race continued to be held annually, until 1928, the winner in 1926 being Segrave's Talbot at 75·56mph (121·61kph); in 1927 Malcolm Campbell's Bugatti at 76·62mph (123·31kph); and in 1928 Campbell's Straight-8 Delage 78·34mph (126·07kph). In 1929 the BARC itself took over the Six-Hour Endurance Race, the winning

car that year being a Bentley driven by Woolf Barnato and Jack Dunfee which averaged 75·88mph (122·12kph). In the same year, 1929, the JCC put on another ambitious Brooklands race in the form of a Double-Twelve contest for sports cars; the second twelve hours' racing was completed on the Saturday (Sunday racing was not allowed at Brooklands). The first of these Double-Twelves was won by Ramponi's Alfa Romeo at 76·0mph (122·31kph). The race survived a serious accident to two of the Talbot team in 1930, in which two fatalities occurred; the winner that year was the Bentley of Barnato and Clement at 86·88mph (139·82kph). In 1931 the MG Midget driven by the Earl of March and C. S. Staniland won at an average of 65·62mph (105·60kph). After this the JCC, finding the Double-Twelve a rather too expensive race to attract entries, changed it to a single-day, 1,000-mile sports car race, of which the winners were two girls, Mrs Elsie Wisdom and Miss Joan Richmond from Australia who shared a Brooklands-model Riley Nine and averaged 84·41mph (135·85kph).

Another classic long-distance race at Brooklands was the 500 Miles Race of the British Racing Drivers' Club, for racing cars and run over the outer circuit on a class handicap basis. It was instituted in 1929, the first of the series being won by Barclay and Clement at 107·32mph (172·73kph) in a 4½-litre Bentley. The subsequent winners of this annual race were S. C. H. Davis and the Earl of March in a stripped Ulster Austin Seven at 63·42mph (102·06kph); Jack Dunfee and Cyril Paul in a Bentley at 118·39mph (190·54kph); R. T. Horton and J. H. Bartlett in an MG at 96·29mph (154·96kph); E. R. Hall in an MG Magnette at 106·53mph (171·45kph); Freddie Dixon in a Riley at 104·8mph (168·7kph); Cobb and Rose-Richards in the 24-litre Napier-Railton at 121·28mph (195·13kph); and Dixon and Martin in a Riley at 116·86mph (188·10kph). In 1937 the length of this race was reduced from 500 miles to 500km and it was won by Cobb and Bertram at 127·05mph (204·48kph) this being the fastest long-distance race in the world at the time.

Apart from all the foregoing races, the Light Car Club held a Relay Race every year at Brooklands for teams of cars; the JCC in 1933 started its series of International Trophy races, which used an ingenious method of handicapping by channelling the competing cars into corners of varying severity once every lap; and the BRDC staged its British Empire Trophy Races at the Weybridge track.

Some semblances of road racing was obtained by

Left, Brooklands: a Singer Nine on the Test Hill, 1935. *Photo: William Boddy Collection*

Above, Brooklands: the big cars at the start of the 1934 500-Mile Race; Alfa Romeo, Marker-Bentley and Bugatti. *Photo: William Boddy Collection*

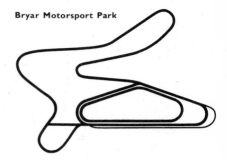
Bryar Motorsport Park

making up artificial turns and using various combinations of circuit by including or omitting certain parts of the track and lapping it either clockwise or anti-clockwise. However, from 1930 another circuit which called for braking and accelerating out of corners was devised, by taking the cars up the finishing straight, right-handed on to the Members' banking, whence they hairpinned right at the fork to regain the finishing straight. Because this circuit encircled the Members' Hill it was known as the Mountain circuit and a Mountain Championship was instituted. Then, in 1937, Sir Malcolm Campbell, who was one of the directors of the company which owned the track, gave his name to a new road circuit. This turned off the railway straight and wound across the grounds to a new straight at the fork which ran parallel with the old finishing straight, and from there wound up to the middle of the Members' banking. This Campbell circuit enabled yet another variation in the possible courses which could be brought into use. It was on this circuit that spectators were involved in another accident resulting in fatalities, but racing at the track was not terminated.

Yet another amenity at Brooklands was a special test hill, wide enough to accommodate one car, which was built in 1909, rising from the finishing straight opposite the paddock to the Members' Hill, at a point close to the bridge which took cars over the Members' banking. Access to the paddock was by means of a tunnel under this banking and there was a footbridge over the Byfleet banking.

In 1930, races for veteran cars, encouraged by the newly formed Veteran Car Club, formed part of the attraction of the Bank Holiday race meetings. In any case, old racing cars were for many years a feature of the Weybridge track because the handicapping system employed made it possible for pre-World War 1 Fiats, Lorraine-Dietrichs, Grand Prix Opels and similar cars to compete successfully with much more modern machines, stripped sports cars, and specials in the ordinary Brooklands races. Attractions of a special kind were frequently introduced at the Bank Holiday meetings, such as demonstrations on the track of land speed record cars like Segrave's 200mph 1,000hp twin-engined Sunbeam and Sir Malcolm Campbell's Bluebirds.

Brooklands proved a very valuable national asset, has been described as 'the eighth wonder of the World', and gave employment and enjoyment to many thousands of people in the years 1907 to 1939. Unfortunately, it was badly cut up for the purposes of aircraft manufacture by Vickers Armstrong Ltd during World War 2, after which it was sold to that company for the sum of £330,000. Those responsible included Sir Malcolm Campbell and C. W. Hayward, but ever since many motor racing enthusiasts have expressed deep regret at the demise of the historic motor course. The creator of Brooklands died in 1926, virtually unrewarded for his great enterprise, but his wife, Dame Ethel Locke King, who took a very active interest in the track, lived until 1956, to the age of 90. Vickers Armstrongs Ltd held a party at Brooklands in 1957 to mark its 50th anniversary and erected a large memorial to the old track, which faces the railway.

The ultimate outer circuit lap record is that established by John Cobb in the Napier-Railton in a time of 1min 9.44sec: 143.44mph (230.76kph). Raymond Mays holds the lap records for both the Mountain and Campbell circuits, respectively at 84.31 (135.69kph) and 77.79mph (125.19kph), with his supercharged ERA cars. The Test

Hill record is held by R. G. J. Nash's Frazer Nash in a time of 7.45sec: 32.444mph (52.206kph); and the fastest speed ever recorded at Brooklands was that by Cobb's Napier-Railton, which in 1935 covered a flying kilometre at 151.97mph (244.51kph). The ladies' lap record, discontinued after 1935, belongs to Mrs Gwenda Stewart, whose 1.9-litre Derby-Miller lapped at 135.95mph (218.78kph) WB

Bryar Motorsport Park
This Loudon, N.H., track is best known as the site of Laconia national motorcycle championships. Located in attractive New Hampshire resort country, 95 miles (152km) north of Boston, the 1.5-mile (2.414km) circuit follows hillside contours. Trans-Am Sedan series events are held here. Lap record: Ed Leslie, (Camaro); 78.38mph (126.14kph); 1min 13.9sec. 1969. ARB

Budapest Circuit
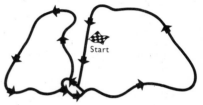
Budapest Circuit

The only important event in pre-war Hungary was the 1936 Budapest Grand Prix, held in a park in the city. The circuit was in a figure-of-eight form, with start and finish in the central portion. The race was over 155.4 miles (250km), or 50 laps of exactly 5km each. The leading international drivers took part, including Caracciola and von Brauchitsch in Mercedes-Benz, Rosemeyer in an Auto Union, and Nuvolari in an Alfa-Romeo. There were also a number of Hungarian drivers with such diverse cars as Bugatti, Steyr, BMW, and Salmson. Caracciola retired, and the race was won by Nuvolari at 69.52mph (119.9kph) from Rosemeyer and Varzi on Auto Unions.

The Budapest Grand Prix was never held again, and post-war events have been run on a modified circuit of 5.3km per lap. They have included races in the European Touring Car Championship, and international and national races for Formula 3 and Formula Vee. Lap record: Dieter Quester (BMW 2002); 2min 27.1sec; 130kph (80.78mph); 1969. VH

Bulawayo Circuit
After many seasons' racing at the Kumalo airfield circuit in Rhodesia, the Bulawayo Motor Racing Association decided to build a permanent course during 1969. With help from the Smith regime and the city authorities the new circuit was completed in time for the Bulawayo 3-Hours race in December 1969. Measuring 2.535 miles (4.080km) to the lap, the course lies in a natural depression and has wide run-off areas on either side for almost its complete length, making it very safe. The new surface was to prove very abrasive, however, and off-road excursions scattered pebbles on the track. The first 3-Hours meeting was successful, Love's Lola-Chevrolet T70 GT winning from De Udy's similar car. Lap record: Helmut Marko (Lola T210); 99.0mph (159.33kph); 1min 32.2sec; 1970. DCN

Canadian GP see Mosport Park; St Jovite

Cape Town Circuits
Under this general heading may be grouped three circuits, starting with the course used for the Grosvenor GP from 1937 to 1939. This was financed by A. O. Edwards from the Grosvenor House concern in London, and was laid out over 4.5 miles (7.242km) of quite fast roadway at Pollsmoor, near Muizenberg. Von Delius' Auto Union won the first Grosvenor GP there in 1937, from Rosemeyer and Howe, averaging 80.37mph

(129·34kph). Howe's ERA won the following year from the Maseratis of Taruffi and Villoresi and Cortese's Maserati won in 1939 from Aitken's ERA.

Post-war South African motor sport was in a bad way, and not until 1956 did the Gunners Circle course open near Cape Town, measuring 3·25 miles (5·231km) to the lap. The Cape Grand Prix there was won on handicap by Phillips' MG despite the presence of Bill Holt's Connaught, but the circuit was not a success.

In 1960 the authorities tried again, with a slow and narrow 2-mile (3·219km) course at Killarney. The Cape GP was run there on 17 December 1960, with Moss and Bonnier in Porsches leading von Trips' Lotus home on a circuit they did not like. The circuit is used today, providing annual rounds in the National Championship and the International Springbok sports car series. It was here in 1967 that Beltoise scored Matra's first Formula 1 victory, driving a ballasted F2 car in an open F1 event. DCN

Carrera Pan Americana
In March 1949 the Association Mexicana de Caminos, the Mexican Highway Asso., and two Mexican Automobile Clubs, announced that a road race would be held to celebrate completion of the Mexican section of the Pan American Highway. Linking Ciudad Juarez, near El Paso, Texas, and El Ocotal, on the Guatemala border, the route's 2,135 miles (3,346km) was to be covered in nine stages over six days. Known variously as the Carrera Pan Americana Mexico de Frontera de Frontera, the Pan American Road Race, the Prueba Internacional de Velocidad, or simply as the Mexican Road Race, the first event started on 5 May 1950, a national holiday. Handicapped by a United States AAA Contest Board regulation calling for minimums of 50 units sold and 500 on order, European entries in 1950 were limited to 6; 21 of the 126 starters were Cadillacs. A 1950 Oldsmobile driven by Hershal McGriff and Ray Elliot was the winner; Deal and Cresap in a Cadillac were 2nd; Pikes Peak regulars Al and Roy Rogers finished 3rd in their 1949 Cadillac, and the Alfa Romeo coupé of Piero Taruffi and Isidore Geroli finished 4th. Bill France and Curtis Turner failed to finish and over a million Mexicans lined the mountain and desert road. The start of the 1951 marathon shifted to Tuxtla Guttierez and covered 1,932 miles (3,109km). Under new sports car entry regulations, Ferrari Vignale coupés took the first two places. Taruffi and Chinetti won with a 88·04mph (141·68kph) race average followed by Ascari and Villoresi, with Bill Sterling's Chrysler 3rd. It was Mercedes' year in 1952, Kling covering 2,093 miles (3,369km) and recording a 102·8mph (165·5kph) winning average, with Lang's 300 SL 2nd and the Chinetti Ferrari 3rd.

Shortened to 1,912 miles (3,077km) and reduced to eight laps over four days, the 1953 race began on 19 November with a record 197 entries. The Lancias of Fangio, Taruffi and Castelotti finished 1-2-3, with Fangio, who did not lead a single stage, setting a 105·8mph (170·3kph) average. Maglioli's Ferrari coupé achieved a 138mph (222·1kph) average for the 223-mile (358·9km) final stage. Lincolns, with 18 of the 46 sedans in their class, won the stock car division. The Ferrari spyders of Maglioli and Phil Hill ran 1-2 in 1954, the Italian veteran averaging a record 107·96mph (173·7kph) in winning the last of the Carreras. Hans Herrmann brought a 1·5-litre Porsche home 3rd overall and first in class, with GP veteran Louis Chiron 4th in an Osca and Ray Crawford's Lincoln 5th. In five years more than 20 drivers and spectators had perished and the race was abandoned.

Contrary to popular belief the Mexican constabulary did a professionally ruthless job of maintaining order, shooting cattle and poultry that wandered near the highway and keeping a firm rein on unruly spectators. Unfortunately it was nearly impossible to patrol 2,000 miles of highway. ARB

Castle Combe Circuit
The prettiest village in England nestles in a valley, and the motor racing circuit which takes its name lies around the perimeter of a wartime grass airfield on top of a hill alongside it. The enthusiastic Bristol Motor Car & Light Car Club were responsible for its inception, and the 1·84-mile (2·9km) circuit was used quite extensively in the early 1950s. It was opened in July 1950, when Shawe-Taylor's ERA won the fastest race of the day at 81·23mph (130·37kph).

But after the Le Mans disaster the RAC laid down minimum safety regulations which Castle Combe's financial position made impossible. Circuit racing ceased after 1955, but the course was still occasionally used for minor speed events. In 1962 it was resurrected by the BRSCC and used regularly for club race meetings, sprints and so on. Lap Record: Peter Gethin and Howden Ganley (McLaren-Chevrolet M10Bs); 117·03mph (188·35kph); 56·6sec; 1970. DCN

Cesana-Sestrière Hill-Climb
This European Hill-Climb Championship venue is controlled by the Turin Automobile Club and is situated on Strada Statale 23 and 24 crossing the Italian border into France. The course starts in the town of Cesana-Torinese and climbs for 10·4km (6·46 miles), rising from a height of 1,350m (4,429ft) to 2,033m (6,669ft) above sea-level. In 1969 Peter Schetty won the climb in his flat-12 2-litre Ferrari 212E, the sixth of his seven consecutive victories in securing the title of Mountain Champion that year. Record: P. Schetty (Ferrari 212E); 79·318mph (127·65kph); 4min 53·3sec; 1969. DCN

Charade Circuit see Clermont-Ferrand Circuit

Chesapeake International Raceway
A major 3-mile (4·828km) road-racing circuit, under construction near Elkton, Md., approximately 50 miles (80km) from Philadelphia, Pa. and Baltimore, Md. Originally scheduled to open in May 1971, but delayed by financing problems, CIR and Sports Car Club of America announced a unique advance agreement providing CIR exclusive 125-mile radius territorial rights to Trans-Am, Formula A Continental and Can-Am events.

The driver Mark Donohue, who is on the CIR Board of Directors, designed the circuit. ARB

Chimay Circuit
The small town of Chimay lies close to the border with France in south-west Belgium. Jules Buisseret owns the main café and the casino in Chimay and with the help of the local Auto-Moto Club Beaumont-Chimay he is the power behind the Grand Prix des Frontières, held traditionally at Whitsun time. Over the years it has been held for Grand Prix cars, sports cars, various forms of Formula 2; today it is a regular Formula 3 fixture. The 6·75-mile (10·870km) circuit is just north of the town and uses the public roads, Belgian law allowing the closure of roads for racing purposes. It is roughly rectangular in shape, run clockwise, and is long and fast, few conces-

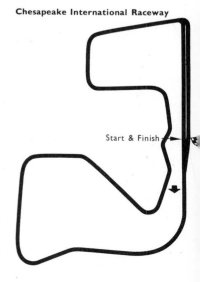

Chesapeake International Raceway

Start & Finish

Chimay: 1968 Formula 3 race. *Photo: Autosport*

sions being made to competitors' whims. It takes the sharp righthand bend by the shops on the northern edge of the town, soon after the start and runs out into the country on a very fast leg with some flat-out curves in it, and turns right in a neighbouring village and then again right. On the return leg it heads straight for a small wayside chapel, passes it on the left by mere feet, runs through two fast left-handers, an S-bend and down to a sharp right corner which brings it on to the main Beaumont to Chimay road, where it ends in a downhill rush past the pits. It is road-racing in its purest form and the hazards are there for drivers to see and appreciate.

The organizers have never aspired to great 'status' events or entries, being content to run their annual meeting on simple lines where all involved enjoy themselves. Being located not too far from the English Channel ports, the race has always attracted numerous British competitors, as well as neighbours from France, and was one of the first events in the post-war revival of motor racing in 1946. It is also an important event in the Belgian national racing calendar. Lap record: John Hunt (Lotus 59); 117·0mph (188·3kph); 3min 19·8sec; 1970. DSJ

Circuit des Ardennes

This was the first important race organized by the Automobile Club de Belgique, and also the first race in which several laps of a closed circuit were covered; thus it was the ancestor of all circuit racing which has followed since. It was also important as a long distance race without the control points which had caused so much argument in events such as the Paris–Berlin. Six laps of 85·30km (53 miles) had to be covered, a total of 511·8km (318 miles). In the first event of 1902 75 racing cars took part, as well as some touring cars; as all were on the circuit at the same time, there was much more passing than there had ever been in the town-to-town races. Dust was a severe problem, but the race was better

value to spectators, who could see their heroes no less than six times instead of merely once. The heavy car class was won by Charles Jarrott's 70hp Panhard at 86·90kph (54mph), from the 60hp Mors of Fernand Gabriel and W. K. Vanderbilt. The light car class went to Rigolly's 18hp Gobron-Brillié, and the voiturette class to Corre's 8hp Corre. In 1903 a Panhard again won, driven by Pierre de Crawhez who had suggested the race in the first place. The 1904 race involved five laps of a longer circuit, giving 590·6km (367 miles). There was a large entry and a very close finish, Heath winning by less than a minute from Teste, both on 90hp Panhards. Le Blon's 90hp Hotchkiss made the fastest lap at 103·00kph (64mph). The 1905 entry was disappointingly small, with only 13 cars in the heavy class; it was won by Hémery's Darracq at 99·14kph (61·6mph). The 1906 event was very fast, seven cars averaging 96kph (60mph). The winner was Duray's 120hp de Dietrich at 105·89kph (65·8mph).

In 1907 two races were held, one for Kaiserpreis cars (8-litre limit) and the other for Grand Prix cars. The first race was a Minerva benefit; these cars finished 1st, 2nd, 3rd and 6th (Moore-Brabazon, Koolhoven, Lee-Guinness, Warwick Wright). The race for Grand Prix cars had a very small entry of six cars, and was interesting only in that it gave Baron de Caters (Mercedes) his first important victory after driving gamely in every kind of car for nearly ten years. The Circuit des Ardennes was not held after 1907. GNG

Circuit des Routes Pavées

Most race organizers look for a reasonably-surfaced route, but the Automobile Club du Nord deliberately chose a circuit composed entirely of granite pavé (cobblestones or Belgian blocks) when they planned the race known as the Circuit des Routes Pavées. It was held in the suburbs of Lille, an industrial town in the north-

east of France, and there were eight miles per lap. When it was first held in 1923, large cars (over 1·5 litres) had to cover 24 laps, and small cars 22. The first race was won by a Georges Irat driven by Rost at an average speed of 49·13mph (79·07kph). This combination of car and driver won again in 1925; were 3rd in 1926; and won on distance in 1927, though beaten on handicap by Doré's La Licorne. There were classes for two and four-seater cars, as well as various capacity classes down to 1,100cc, so several drivers had a chance of carrying off prizes each year. The organizing committee took a perverse pleasure in difficult conditions; in 1925 it was reported that 'to the disappointment of the organizers the weather was kind, so that grease and mud did not cover the worn paving stones.' In addition to well-known makes such as Chenard-Walcker, Darracq, Excelsior, and in later years Alfa-Romeo and Bugatti, the Circuit saw many obscure makes competing, such as Omega Six, Génestin, Delfosse and Louis Chenard. An improbable car in any race was a Delaunay-Belleville which actually won the 4-litre class in 1930.

From 1927 onwards the race was a 6-hour event; Alfa Romeo won in 1928 and 1929 (Ivanowski and Zehender respectively), and the 1930 race went to a Type 37 Bugatti driven by Joly. Second was another rare car, a Ford-engined Montier Special. The last Circuit des Routes Pavées was held in 1931, when Zehender won again on a 1750 Alfa Romeo, from Fourny (Bugatti) and Joly (Bugatti). The winner's speed was now 65·4mph (105·25kph). An Alfa crashed killing one spectator and injuring ten. Because of the accident no further races were held. GNG

Circuit du Nord

Several competitions were held in France during 1901 to demonstrate the suitability of alcohol fuel for motor-cars. In 1902 a race was organized, sponsored by the Minister of Agriculture, to encourage the use of this domestically produced fuel. Known at the time as the Concours du Ministre, it has come to be known generally as the Circuit du Nord. It was held over two days, with a 537-mile route in Northern France, starting and ending in Paris. Ten heavy cars, 26 light cars, and 11 voiturettes took part, and there were also classes for touring cars and commercial vehicles. For the heavy cars it was the

first race held under the new 1,000kg rules; only one of the season's new cars, Réné de Knyff's 70hp Panhard, was entered. The race was won by Maurice Farman's 40hp Panhard, from Jarrott's similar car, and no less than four Serpollet steam cars. The drivers of the latter complained that the alcohol fuel reduced their performance by almost 20% compared with the paraffin normally burnt. The internal combustion cars did not do well as they would have done with petrol, so as a demonstration of alcohol fuel the event was not a success. GNG

Clermont-Ferrand Circuit

In 1908 Chevalier Réné de Knyff led an ACF technical committee in exploring the Puy de Dôme area near Clermont, with a view to establishing a 48km (30-mile) motor-racing circuit having permanent stands, pits and other facilities. The scheme came to nothing, but 50 years later a circuit did appear in the area, albeit a much shorter one.

This is the Charade, alias Louis Rosier circuit, sited around the volcanic remains of the Puy de Gravenoire and Puy de Charade west of Lyons and east of Limoges, in central France. The Automobile Club d'Auvergne co-operated with the local authorities in developing the public roads around these long-extinct volcanic plugs into a beautiful and tricky circuit, extensive resurfacing and the building of some 2km of new link road forming the 8·055km (5·005-mile) course. It includes no less than 51 corners, three of them sharp hairpins, and there is 180m (590ft) between the highest and lowest points; maximum gradient is 1 in 10. The circuit is fairly difficult to learn and its high-speed swoops and plunges can take as much toll of a driver's stomach as of his car.

It was opened on 27 July 1958, when Trintignant won both inaugural events, averaging 117·54kph (73·04mph) in his F2 Cooper-Climax. The course was relatively little used, with 1·5-litre F2, sports and later FJ, F2 and F3 races being run there. In 1965 the French GP was held at Clermont-Ferrand for the first time. Clark won the race for Lotus at 143·580kph (89·22mph). The event returned there in 1969 when Stewart's Matra dominated the meeting, winning at 157·251kph (97·72mph) and 1970 when Jochen Rindt won at 158·390kph (98·419mph). Lap record: Jack Brabham (Brabham BT33/1); 99·5mph (160·431kph); 3min 00·75sec; 1970. DCN

Circuit des Routes Pavées: a Lancia Lambda on the characteristic cobblestones. *Photo: Montagu Motor Museum*

Clermont-Ferrand Circuit

Comminges Circuit

This French circuit on public roads was in use as long ago as 1925, and lasted until the mid-1950s when racing in France underwent a radical overhaul. It was roughly rectangular in shape and ran clockwise, with the start just before a steep climbing right-hand bend; on the outside of this the natural banks were used for the grandstands, which can still be seen today. This curve brought the course to a sharp right-hand corner on the western edge of the town of St Gaudens, south-west of Toulouse towards the Pyrenees. After a short straight along the edge of the town, the road turned right and plunged downhill on to a long fast straight, with flat-out swerves, running parallel with the river Garonne. Another right-hand bend, a short straight and a fast right hander brought it on to Route Nationale 117 heading east towards St Gaudens. It was then a full-throttle long straight back to the start. The original length was 16·156 miles (26km) but in 1933 this was reduced to 6·835 miles (11km) by the construction of a new link road from the Pont de Valentine. In that year Luigi Fagioli won the Comminges Grand Prix in a 2·3-litre Alfa Romeo at 88·23mph (143kph).

The circuit was the scene of the Comminges Grand Prix, sports car races, and motorcycle races, and was twice used for the French Grand Prix (in 1928 and 1949). When road closure and police control became more difficult the circuit was shortened by cutting out the run into the country and back, using the town end only with a lap of 2·487 miles (4·4km), but this only staved off the end for the Comminges circuit. The Automobile Club du Midi, who ran the races, could not afford the expense of bringing the safety measures up to the new standards, and the last race was an F2 in 1952. DSJ

Continental Divide Raceway

A tight, rolling, 2·66-mile (4·281km) road course at Castle Rock, Colo., 30 miles (48km) south of Denver, near Pikes Peak. Here are held Formula A Continental and Indianapolis championship car road races. On 28 June 1970 Mario Andretti won his 31st USAC Championship race and the STP-McNamara's first, with a 84·109mph race average. Lap record: Al Unser (Ford) 91·461mph (147·19kph); 1min 44·7sec; 1970. ARB

Copenhagen Cup and Copenhagen GP see Roskilde Ring

Coppa Acerbo see Pescara Circuit

Coppa Florio

The first race for Vincenzo Florio's Cup was held on a

Left, Clermont-Ferrand: start of the 1970 French GP; Jackie Ickx in the lead. *Photo: David Phipps*

Right, Coppa Florio: André Boillot's Peugeot, 1922. *Photo: T. A. S. O. Mathieson Collection*

Crystal Palace Circuit

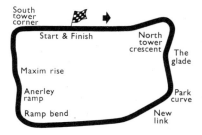

circuit at Brescia, in 1900 six years before his more famous Targa Florio event, which has always been held in Sicily. The Coppa Florio was to be competed for seven times, 'the winner of the greatest number of seven annual races to become the absolute owner of the trophy'. Because of various vicissitudes it was well over seven years before the final victor was found. The race was held at Brescia in 1900, 1904, 1905 and 1907, and at Bologna in 1908, and each time was won by a different make of car (Panhard, Fiat, Itala, Isotta-Fraschini, and Berliet respectively). In 1914 it was run on the Madonie circuit in Sicily, a week after the Targa Florio; the victor was Nazzaro on one of his own cars. In 1922 the Coppa Florio was again held on the Madonie circuit, after the Targa, and in 1924 and 1925 it was run concurrently with the more famous event, but over one more lap, making a race of 335 miles (539km) compared with the Targa's 268 miles (431km).

On aggregate of placings over the years, Peugeot and Itala had equal honours, and the Cup was to go to whichever of these marques was in the lead at the end of the fourth lap in 1925. This turned out to be the Peugeot driven by André Boillot who had won in 1922.

This was not quite the end of the Coppa Florio races, for although they had won the cup outright, the Peugeot company put it up again in 1927, on condition that the race was held in France. A triangular 6·5-mile (10·461km) circuit near St Brieuc in Brittany was chosen, and the race was to go to the competitor who maintained the best regularity. A wide variety of sports and racing cars took part, and the winner was Laly in a 3-litre Ariès sports car. It was proposed to hold the race again in 1928, in Sicily, but these plans did not materialize. GNG

Crystal Palace Circuit

London's only motor-race circuit was built in the shadow of the Crystal Palace itself, on Sydenham Hill, but when it opened in 1937 that glass edifice was a charred ruin.

In original form it was 2 miles (3·219km) in length, the start being on the present bottom straight and a very slow twisty section running past the lake at North Tower Crescent. Fairfield in an ERA won the 1937 Coronation Trophy at 53·77mph (86·53kph) and 'Bira' took the Imperial Trophy at 57·80mph (93·020kph). The Siamese excelled at the circuit before the war, winning six major events there in his ERAs.

Motor racing returned to the Palace in 1953. The RAC ruled that the existing course was too twisty and narrow, and so the New Link section was built, cutting out the tight infield loop past Big Tree Bend. The result was a faster but still tricky circuit, very attractively laid out among the rhododendron bushes of the park, sleeper-

flanked for much of its length and just 1·39 miles (2·237km) in length. Formula 1 races were held at the circuit until 1962, when Formula Junior and later F2 and F3 took over as the major class contested there. As there are dwelling houses close by only a handful of car and motorcycle meetings can be run each year, but they are usually very well attended and see some excitingly close racing.

Despite its compact size and daunting nature, the Palace's lap speed is quite fast. Lap record: Jochen Rindt and Jackie Stewart (Lotus 69 and Brabham BT30); 100·89mph (162·36kph); 49·6sec; 1970. DCN

Coupe de l'Auto and Coupe des Voiturettes
see Voiturette Racing (in the section: Organization of Motor Sport)

Coupe des Alpes see Alpine Rally

Dakar Circuit
This French-sponsored circuit in the Senegalese port of Dakar was one of the fastest in the world and was

Top, Crystal Palace: Alfa Romeo 8C 2900B and Riley, 1938. *Photo: Montagu Motor Museum*

Centre, Crystal Palace: Raymond Mays (ERA), Percy Maclure (Riley) and A. C. Dobson (ERA) in the 1938 Imperial Trophy. *Photo: Montagu Motor Museum*

Left, Crystal Palace: Cliff Allison's Lotus in the 1961 London Trophy. *Photo: Associated Press Ltd*

similar to AVUS in many respects. It was laid out along a stretch of tarmac dual carriageway and comprised two parallel straights 2¾ miles in length joined by triangular loops at either end, the lap distance totalling 6·5 miles (10·46km).

The first major race to be held there was in 1955, when the 228-mile (366·9km) sports car Dakar GP was won by Carini's Ferrari at 118·55mph (190·78kph). Rosier's Ferrari set fastest lap at 122·4mph (197kph), and in 1956 Trintignant won from Schell and Behra (the first two in Ferraris and Behra in a Maserati). In 1963 the Dakar 6 hour race was won by Noblet and Guichet (Ferrari). The circuit has followed a sporadic career with long-distance race meetings being held there, but little of real international importance. DCN

Dallas International Motor Speedway
A combination drag strip and road circuit in Lewisville, Texas, 20 miles (32km) from Dallas. It opened in 1969 with a championship drag meet, and in 1970, the 2·7-mile (4·345km) road course had planned to hold USAC Championship Trail, SCCA Trans-Am and Formula A events.

Dallas International Motor Speedway

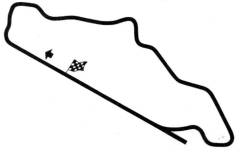

The 26 April 1970 Trans-Am was cancelled following practice when torrential rains resulted in snakes occupying course marshal stations and unsafe track conditions. On 5 July 1970 Gus Hutchison won the 102·5-mile Continental driving a Brabham BT26-Cosworth Ford, the first Formula A-Continental victory for a 3-litre Formula 1 machine in a series dominated by 5-litre stock-block American engines. USAC cancelled its Aug. 1970, 200-mile race for Indy championship cars 'due to unfavorable track conditions.' Lap record: John Cannon (McLaren Formula A); 104·408mph (168·027kph); 1min 26·2sec; 1970. ARB

Daytona International Speedway
The 2·5-mile (4·023km) Daytona, Fla., tri-oval opened in 1959 as the showpiece of American stock car racing. In 1962 Daytona became a major road racing site when the 3·81-mile (6·132km) road circuit, a combination of 1·31 miles (2·108km) of flat infield roadways and 2·5 miles (4·023km) of 31° banked ovals, became the site of the Daytona Continental.

When Dan Gurney won the 3-hour Continental in 1962 by using a combination of his Lotus-Ford starter motor and gravity to crank over the finishing line, he triggered the FIA regulation requiring race cars to finish under their own power. In 1964 the Continental went to 2,000km and in 1966 it became a 24-hour race, the longest in the United States.

Indy veteran Lloyd Ruby and Ken Miles brought the Ford GT-40 its first-ever victory in 1965 and in 1966 the same pair led a 1-2-3 sweep of 7-litre Ford Mark II's,

Miles and Ruby setting a record 107·51mph (173·02kph) race average that stood until 1970. Ferrari's P-4s finished 1-2-3 in 1967 and Porsche's long-tailed 907s did the same in 1968. When John Wyer's Fords and works Porsches failed to last the 1969 24-hours, Mark Donohue and Chuck Parsons nursed Roger Penske's Lola-Chevy coupé home 1st in spite of its spending over two hours in the pits. In 1970 a works 4·5-litre Porsche 917, driven by Pedro Rodriguez and the young Finnish rallyist, Leo Kinnunen, covered a record 2,755·63 miles (4,435·05km), averaging 114·866mph (184·91kph) for the 24 hours.

Stock car races are Daytona's bread and butter. In February over 200,000 fans watch the month long carnival of sports cars, stock car preliminary races and time trials that culminate in the annual Daytona 500. Qualifying record for the 428ci, 7-litre, 4,000lb, late model Detroit sedans is 194·015mph (312·228kph) set by Cale Yarborough, Mercury Cyclone, in February 1970 while earning the pole for the 500. A week later Yarborough established a record for closed-course racing when he captured one of two, 125-mile preliminary races, with a 183·295mph (294·948kph) average.

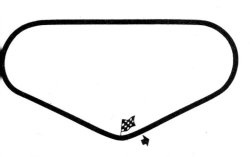

In 1970, the 500 was won by Peter Hamilton with a 149·601mph (240·82kph) race average. Hamilton's Plymouth was entered by two-time Daytona 500 winner Richard Petty, whose father, Lee, won the first Daytona in 1959, his Oldsmobile averaging 135·521mph (218·132kph). The record race average, largely dependent on the number of yellow caution flags displayed, is 160·627mph (258·541kph) set by Richard Petty's Plymouth in 1966.

Left, Daytona Speedway: the infield roads that make up part of the road circuit are covered with parked cars in this photograph. *Photo: Daytona International Speedway*

Right, Daytona Speedway: a Dodge and two Fords on the banking during a NASCAR Grand National event. *Photo: Daytona International Speedway*

In addition to the 24-hours and 500, Daytona is the site of the Firecracker 400 stock car Grand National, motorcycle championships and, until 1970, held the American Road Race of Champions, SCCA's amateur run-off. Lap record (road circuit): Mark Donohue (Ferrari 512M); 133·92mph (215·52kph); 1min 42·42sec; 1971. ARB

Donington Park Circuit

Donington Park lies about 10 miles (16km) from Derby, near the village of Castle Donington, and forms the grounds of the 17th-century Donington Hall. The landowner, Mr J. G. Shields, backed Fred Craner and his Derby & District Motor Club in developing a race circuit through these grounds, first used for motorcycle events in 1933 and measuring 2·19 miles (3·525km) to the lap. The Hall with its 80 bedrooms became a clubhouse. After that first season the circuit was lengthened to 2·55 miles (4·104km). The result was a delightful road circuit, passing a farm at Coppice Corner and going through woods and an impossibly narrow-looking bridge just beyond Starkey's Corner. Considerable alterations were made in 1937, adding an extra loop to

Donington Park Circuit

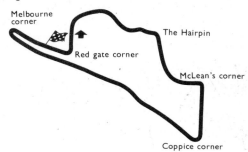

bring lap distance up to 3·125 miles (5·03km) and thinning out much of the surrounding undergrowth to give better spectator viewing.

The Nuffield Trophy, a 1·5-litre handicap event, was run at Donington from 1934–9 and was won every time by ERA, while between 1935 and 1938 the Donington Grand Prix was held, being first won by Shuttleworth's Alfa Romeo at 63·97mph (102·95kph), and attracting the German works team in 1937–8, Rosemeyer winning

the earlier event in his Auto Union at 82·85mph (133·33kph), and Nuvolari the latter at 80·49mph (129·53kph). In 1936 both the BRDC Empire Trophy and JCC 200 Miles came to Donington, and the RAC TT moved there from Ards in 1937.

On the outbreak of war in 1939, the Park was requisitioned by the Army. It was intended to restart racing in 1957 with an even longer 4·5-mile (2·796km) circuit but nothing came of this.

In 1971 the course was bought by Leicester builder and racing car collector Tom Wheatcroft, who plans to re-open it and build a museum there. Lap record: Bernd Rosemeyer (Auto Union) and Manfred von Brauchitsch (Mercedes-Benz W125); 82·26mph (132·38kph); 1937. DCN

Donnybrooke Speedway

A 3-mile (4·8km) circuit opened in August 1968 and located 140 miles (225km) northwest of Minneapolis-St Paul, near Brainerd, in northern Minnesota lake country. It is the site of Trans-Am and Formula A Continental races, and, beginning 1970, one of the Canadian American Challenge Cup series. Lap record: Denis Hulme (McLaren-Chevrolet M8D); 120·67mph (194·19kph); 1min 29·5sec; 1970. ARB

Donnybrooke Speedway

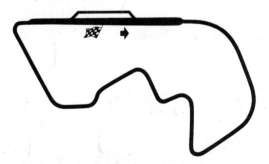

Douglas, Isle of Man Races

From 1933 to 1937 the RAC organized a series of races in and near Douglas in the Isle of Man. They were 'round the houses' events, imitating the Monaco Grand Prix. From 1933 to 1935 they were known as the Mannin Moar and the Mannin Beg (Great Man and Little Man in the Manx language), the former being a Formule Libre race, and the latter for 1·5-litre cars. The 1933 route covered 230 miles (370km) of a difficult circuit of 4·6 miles (7·403km) per lap, with many sharp corners and narrow streets. Tramlines (streetcar tracks) made it especially tricky in the wet. The first Mannin Beg was won by Freddie Dixon's Riley Nine at 54·41mph (87·57kph), with D. K. Mansell's MG Midget in 2nd

Left, Donington Park: Luigi Villoresi (Maserati 8CTF) in the 1938 International Donington GP. *Photo: Motor*

Right, Douglas, Isle of Man: Reg Parnell leads David Murray, both in Maserati 4CLTs in the 1949 British Empire Trophy Race. *Photo: Autosport*

place. All six MG Magnettes retired. The first Mannin Moar was held two days later; there was a good entry of 14 cars, including Alfas and Bugattis. The race was won by Brian Lewis (Alfa Romeo).

In 1934 the course was reduced to 3·7 miles (5·955km) per lap and a total distance of 183 miles (294·5km). This was to avoid the closing of main shopping streets which had caused resentment in 1933. There were now only three acute bends, and a 1·25-mile straight. Brian Lewis again won the Mannin Moar at 75·34mph (121·24kph), while Norman Black won the Mannin Beg in an MG Magnette. The 1935 Mannin Moar went to Brian Lewis for the 3rd time, this time in a Type 59 Bugatti. The Mannin Beg was won by Pat Fairfield's ERA at 67·29mph (108·29kph).

In 1936 there was only one race, known as the International Light Car Race, for cars of up to 1·5 litres. It was held on a new circuit on the outskirts of Douglas, with more corners, and a lap of just under 4 miles. Total race distance was 193 miles. Although called an international race, the only foreign entries were Bira's ERA and Christian Kautz' Maserati. The race was won by Dick Seaman's 10-year-old Delage at 69·76mph (112·27kph), a remarkable feat in that he beat all the works ERAs. This make took all the other places, Bira being 2nd, Cyril Paul 3rd, Fairfield 4th, and Marcel Lehoux 5th. The 1937 International Light Car Race was held on yet another circuit, but about the same length at 195 miles. ERAs finished 1-2-3 (Bira, Mays, Fairfield) in pouring rain.

After World War 2 the Isle of Man circuit was used as the venue of the British Empire Trophy, a Formula 1 event until 1950, and a sports car race from 1951 to 1953 when it was transferred to Oulton Park. It was very much an ERA benefit, this make being 1st and 2nd every year from 1947 to 1950. A number of shorter races were also held as curtain raisers, the Manx Cup for Formula 2 cars, and the Formule Libre Castletown Trophy. GNG

Dunedin Circuit

'Round-the-houses' racing in New Zealand was pioneered by the Otago Sports Car Club which conducted the New Zealand Road Racing Championship on two different circuits laid out in city streets between 1953 and 1960, and subsequently organized Dunedin Festival road races in 1961, 1962 and 1965. The original course, about 1½ miles (2·4km) in length, was extremely tight with mainly right-angled corners, an overbridge on which some cars 'bottomed', and a short section of surfaced road. Ron Roycroft dominated the first three races, winning with the ex-Nuvolari P3 Alfa Romeo in 1953 and 1955 and his Jaguar-engined Bugatti 35B in 1954.

East African Safari: Peugeot 504 driven by Nick Nowicki and Paddy Cliff in the 1970 event. *Photo: UPI*

A new fully-surfaced circuit with two fast straights, a hill section, and a winding back leg, also about 1½ miles in length and closer to the city centre, was used from 1960 to 1962. In 1962 John Mansel, driving a Scuderia Centro Sud Cooper-Maserati suffered fatal injuries following a crash late in the race and this was the last time the circuit was used.

In 1965 the club staged a round-the-houses race on yet another circuit in Dunedin. It was also about 1½ miles in length and had one fast straight and a number of tight turns, as well as a bumpy section which took in a flyover bridge. The winner was Jim Boyd, who covered the 51·2 miles (82·40km) in 41min 59·2sec in the Lycoming Special. This was the last race to be held in Dunedin. PG

Dutch GP see Zandvoort Circuit

Dundrod Circuit see Tourist Trophy

East African Safari

Few rallies outside Europe have achieved the status of the East African Safari. Since its inception in 1953, when it was called the East African Coronation Safari, it has become a symbol of all that is roughest and toughest in modern rallying. Originally the rally was for standard production touring cars which were put into classes according to their price in East Africa. This system had many attractions, not least of which was to encourage car importers to bring in their wares at the lowest prices.

The original rally route passed through all three countries of East Africa — Kenya, Uganda and Tanzania — but more recently, political differences have confined it to the first two. The kind of cars competing have

changed too. In 1960 the classes by price were dropped in favour of the international capacity class system, but the idea of using just standard cars persisted a lot longer and during the 1960s, the cars that were entered had to conform to the Group 1 category of Appendix J. The big break with tradition came in 1969, when the rally allowed cars of Group 2 — improved touring cars — for the first time. This led to its inclusion in the 1970 International Rally Championship, the only non-European event to qualify for this.

In character the Safari is a high-speed event run through uncertain country where rain, floods and animals can all play their part in providing hazards for the cars and drivers. Fatigue is also a big factor in the event as it lasts three and a half days with only a break of six to eight hours in the middle. Some indication of the severity of the event can be obtained from considering that when Nick Nowicki won the rally for the second time in 1968, the weather was so bad that only seven cars got through to the finish and even he, the winner, was penalized for being twelve hours late. East African drivers have always won the event despite competition from Europeans and there is now a substantial prize fund accumulating for the first overseas driver to win the rally. JD

East London Circuit

The Prince George road circuit at this South African holiday port was first used in 1934 as the venue of the South African GP. It was laid out over 15·2 miles (24·46km) of public roads and included what was known as the West Bank section, through the outskirts of a village. The race, run on handicap over 91 miles,

was won by Straight's Maserati at 85·68mph (137·89kph) and was marred by a near-fatal accident to Richard Shuttleworth, in an Alfa Romeo.

The course was used again in 1936, but had been shortened to 11 miles 57 yards (17·752km) in order to bypass the village, the new link road being named Potter's Pass after the civil engineer responsible for the work. The circuit was used in this form in 1936-9.

Motor racing took a long time to recover in post-war South Africa, and in 1960 the local club decided to restart racing on the East London circuit. Initially the plan was to base a modern course on the long straight of the Prince George circuit, but building developments prevented this and eventually a 2·43-mile (3·911km) circuit was adopted, running towards the city from Potter's Pass and using a natural amphitheatre on the coastline plateau to advantage. Local authorities backed the project enthusiastically to the amount of £30,000 and the circuit was opened in July 1959 with a local

Opposite top, Trans-Am: Dan Gurney driving a Plymouth Barracuda in the 1970 Riverside event. Photo: Al Bochroch

Opposite bottom, USAC: Sprint cars on the high banking at Winchester, Indiana, 1960. Photo: Al Bochroch

Below, Elgin Races: cars lined up for the start, 1911 National Trophy. No 2 National, in the foreground, was the eventual winner, driven by Len Zengle. Photo: Courtesy Edward F. Gathman

Bottom, Elgin Races: Earl Cooper's Stutz rounding Graveyard Bend, 1915. Photo Courtesy Edward F. Gathman

Winter Handicap meeting. On 1 January 1960, the sixth South African GP took place, won by Frère's ENB F2 Cooper. The race was a Championship round from 1962 to 1965. A non-Championship GP was held in 1966 but in 1967 the South African GP had outgrown the east coast resort, and was moved to the more populous and richer area of Johannesburg (see Kyalami). DCN

Eifelrennen see Nürburgring

Eireann Cup see Phoenix Park Circuit

Elgin Races

These were held over an 8½-mile circuit just outside Elgin, Ill., for stock cars in various sizes. They were held from 1910 to 1920 (excepting 1916-18), and again in 1933. The most important event was for the Elgin National Trophy, a silver trophy worth about $4,000 and presented by the Elgin Watch Company. It was for cars in the 600ci (9,832cc) class. Smaller classes were for cars of 300 and 230ci (4,916 and 3,769cc). The National Trophy attracted famous cars and drivers such as Ralph Mulford (Lozier), Ralph DePalma (Mercedes), Gil Anderson (Stutz), and Tommy Milton (Duesenberg). However the Elgin races were perhaps more important because they gave an opportunity to lesser-known drivers with stock cars of modest capacity to win the numerous prizes offered. Cars such as Abbott-Detroit, Marion, Overland and Jackson figured among the winners. Model T Fords were banned in 1910 as being too light, but they were allowed from 1911 onwards. The series lapsed after 1920 because of the danger of the course, and also because ordinary motorists objected to public roads being closed for two days. It was revived in 1933 as a race for stock cars of up to 231ci (3,785cc) capacity. The first three places were taken by Fords. GNG

Elkhart Lake see Road America Circuit

Enna Circuit

The super-fast Sicilian circuit at Enna is laid out around the Lago di Pergusa, measures 2·981 miles (4·797km) in length and of its very fast curves only the one after the pits really calls for the brakes. It was first used for a major meeting in 1961, when Boffa's Maserati sports car won at 112·01mph (180·26kph). In 1962 the first Mediterranean GP was held there, Bandini's F1 Ferrari V-6 winning at 129·06mph (207·7kph). A regular race fortnight developed with sports and FJ/F3 events one weekend and the F1 GP the next; Formula 2 cars also raced at the circuit in this period.

Siffert excelled in the course's high-speed curves and won two F1 Mediterranean GPs, in 1964 and the last event in 1965. Surtees won in a Ferrari in 1963 when Taylor had one of his tremendous Lotus accidents. Many a driver has had to be rescued from the swamps lining the circuit, which also teem with snakes.

In recent years the Enna Cup sports car race has been run regularly, and the circuit also has an important annual round in the European Formula 2 Championship Lap record: Jochen Rindt (Brabham-F2); 147·42mph (237·244kph); 1min 12·7sec; 1968. DCN

Finnish GP see Helsinki Circuit

Flowers Rally see Italian Rally

Four-Inch Race see Tourist Trophy

Opposite, Alpine Rally: Jean Vinatier and Jean-François Jacob (Alpine-Renault) on their way to victory in the 1968 event. *Photo: Motor Sport*

Freiburg Hill-Climb

First used in 1925 the Schauinsland course just outside Freiburg-Guntertal in Germany is one of the most sinuous of the European Hill-climb Championship, and is 6·959 miles (11·2km) in length. The start is at a height of 1,378ft (420m) and the road then climbs through the tight Forsthaus Kurve to the S-bends at Diesendobel, zigzagging its way up the mountainside through a very tight hairpin to the finish at 3,937ft (1,200m) above sea-level. Record: Rolf Stommelen (Brabham F2); 78·76mph (126·764kph); 5min 18·07sec; 1970. DCN

French Grand Prix

The Grand Prix de l'Automobile Club de France was born of French nationalism, out of frustration with the Gordon Bennett Cup, to which only one team representing each country was admitted. It was first proposed in 1904, and first run in 1906.

The first Grand Prix was run over an immense triangular circuit east of Le Mans, six 64·12-mile (103·18km) laps having to be completed on each of two consecutive days. Two of the roads making up the triangle were good, undulating and with no sharp bends; the linking stretch was narrow and rough, and in part made up of temporary plank roads. The rules imposed a maximum weight limit of 1,007kg. On 26 June 1906, 32 cars representing three countries and thirteen makes (ten of them French) started individually at 90-second intervals, and the best drivers lapped in under an hour. Dust, tar and the plank roads were hazards, and frequent tyre changes added to drivers' physical problems. At half-distance 17 cars were still running, led by the Renault of Szisz. He held his position, ahead of 10 other finishers, to win in 12hrs 14min at 62·88mph (101·20kph).

In 1907 and 1908 the race was shortened, and run on single days over 10 laps of a 47·84-mile (76·98km) circuit outside Dieppe. Again a triangle, this was made up of better roads (although the surface broke up badly in 1907). Facilities and grandstands were fairly elaborate, and in 1908 team servicing points were arranged in a divided trench—thus 'pits' entered motor racing terminology. The 1907 race was run to a fuel consumption formula (equalling about 9·4mpg), the 1908 event to a weight/bore formula (1,100kg minimum/155mm for 4-cyclinder engines, or 127mm for sixes). In 1907 Nazzaro clearly reversed his 1907 position vis-à-vis Szisz, winning for FIAT at 70·61mph (113·64kph). Then in 1908 a sweeping German triumph dismayed the French: Lautenschlager won for Mercedes at 69·05mph (111·12kph), and Hémery and Hanriot took 2nd and 3rd places for Benz.

In part because of this, the Grand Prix was allowed to lapse until 1912, when the Dieppe circuit was again used, for a two-day, 956-mile (1,538km) race run concurrently with the Coupe de *l'Auto*. The only restriction on GP cars was on width—69in (1·75m), while the Coupe was for 3-litre, 800kg (minimum) cars. Entries ranged from 'old-style' muscle-bound Fiats to sophisticated Peugeots. Altogether, 47 cars started. At the end of the first day Bruce-Brown (Fiat) led Boillot (Peugeot) by 2min 3sec; at the end of the race Boillot won by 13min 11sec from Wagner's Fiat, at 68·45mph (110·16kph).

The 1913 Grand Prix was run over 29 laps (579 miles; 931·8km) of a shorter 19·65-mile (31·62km) and simpler circuit outside Amiens, to a fuel consumption/weight formula (14·12mpg, 800-1,100kg). Twenty cars started, and 11 finished, with Peugeots (Boillot, Goux) well

ahead of a Sunbeam and two Delages.

The sixth Grand Prix has a firm place in racing lore, even in dispassionate history, as one of the great motor races. It was run over 20 laps—467·68 miles (752·73km) of the demanding 23·38-mile (37·63km) Lyons-Givors circuit, for 1,100kg maximum weight cars with engines of up to 4·5 litres. The outward leg of the circuit followed the twists of the River Gier; the return leg was faster, largely straight and undulating, until it reached the famous Piège de la Mort hairpin and dropped to the start line. Most of the 37 cars which started were technically advanced, but, perhaps of greater moment, the event had abundant drama. For the first time cars were started in pairs, at 30-second intervals. For two hours Sailer led in a Mercedes. As he retired the French favourite Boillot took the lead, closely harried by Lautenschlager; on lap 17 the German regained the lead, and Boillot's Peugeot expired. Mercedes enjoyed a 1-2-3 triumph, Lautenschlager winning at 65·66mph (105·67kph), and Goux' 4th place for Peugeot did little to salvage French pride.

The series was revived in 1921, from which point it has to be regarded as the *French* Grand Prix. The circuit chosen was Le Mans, and the formula 3 litres/800kg minimum weight. This race, too, has its secure place in history, as it was won by an American team, Murphy averaging 78·10mph (125·69kph) for the 30 laps (321·68 miles; 517·69km) in his Duesenberg.

From 1922 to 1925 the race was for 2-litre, 650kg cars; at Strasbourg in 1922, and Tours in 1923 when Segrave in a Sunbeam gave Britain her first and last GP win until 1955.

A shortened (14·38-mile; 23·14km) version of the Lyons-Givors circuit was used in 1924, for another outstanding race between Alfa Romeo (P2), Bugatti (T35), Delage, Fiat (805), Miller, Schmid and Sunbeam; all save the Miller works cars were in the tradition of the race, which was not to have such a scintillating entry for decades. Five drivers and three makes led at various times in the race, and at the end of the 503 miles (809km) Campari won for Alfa, at 70·97mph (114·21kph) with V-12 Delages second and third.

An artificial circuit, Montlhéry, was used for the 1925 and 1927 races (1926 was the year of the three-Bugatti Miramas fiasco). Delage won both, although in 1925 only after the dominant Alfa P2s were withdrawn following Ascari's fatal accident. Then the race fell on hard times: sports cars in 1928 and 1930 (Comminges and Pau); fuel consumption formula in 1929 (Le Mans); a 10-hour race in 1931 (Montlhéry). The 1932 race was better (run at Reims for the first time, as a 5-hour event, and won by Nuvolari in a Type B Alfa), as was the 1933 event, when Campari drove a Maserati to victory in a 500km race at Montlhéry.

A return to the works-entries-only tradition came in 1934, when the 750kg Formula Mercedes-Benz and Auto Union teams raced outside Germany for the first time, and at Montlhéry failed. Only the three Ferrari Alfa Romeos completed the 500km, Chiron winning at 85·05mph (136·87kph). Mercedes at least made no mistakes over the same distance in 1935; their opposition broken, Caracciola and von Brauchitsch cruised to win at 77·42mph (124·59kph).

Sports car GPs were run in 1936 and 1937, at Montlhéry, but the last two pre-war races were for Formula cars, and at Reims. Von Brauchitsch won the first for Mercedes at 101·137mph (162·761kph), Müller the second for Auto Union at 105·25mph (169·38kph).

French Grand Prix: Duray's de Dietrich, 1907. Photo: Montagu Motor Museum

French Grand Prix: Lautenschlager's Mercedes passing the Lyon stands, 1914. Photo: David Hodges Collection

French Grand Prix: Murphy's Duesenberg winning at Le Mans, 1921. Photo: David Hodges Collection

French Grand Prix: Hawthorn (Ferrari) challenging Fangio (Maserati) at Reims in 1953. Photo: David Hodges Collection

The French GP was resumed in 1947, and run for a miscellany of pre-war cars, and two post-war white elephants (the CTA-Arsenal and E-type ERA) over 314·2 miles (505·6km) of the odd Lyons–Parilly circuit —virtually the two carriageways of a ring road, 4·49 miles (7·226km) to the lap. Chiron drove a canny, tactical race to win at 78·09mph (125·67kph) in a Talbot. In 1948 came a return to Reims, and complete Alfa Romeo domination, Wimille leading his team-mates Sanesi and Ascari home at 102·96mph (165·70kph). The 1949 race was for sports cars, but the Formula machines ran again at Reims in 1950, and this time Fangio won for Alfa Romeo, at 104·84mph (168·76kph) for the 60 laps: 309·16 miles (497·60km). He took over Fagioli's 159 to win at Reims again in 1951, at 110·97mph (178·51kph) for 77 laps: 374 miles (601·9km) and break Lang's record at last: 118·29mph (190·34kph).

The 1952 3-hour GP for 2-litre cars at Rouen was undistinguished (Ascari winning for Ferrari in that year), but the 1953 event at Reims was a classic hard-fought race, won by Hawthorn in a Ferrari at 113·65mph (182·98kph), by one second from Fangio and Gonzalez (Maseratis).

Mercedes-Benz chose the French race at Reims for their GP return in 1954, Fangio and Kling winning as they pleased in 2·5-litre W196s, at 115·67mph (186·21kph) for the 61 laps: 311·21 miles (500·82km). The 1955 race was cancelled, and at Reims in 1956 there was Schell's startling Vanwall challenge and then another team-controlled finish, this time Ferrari's, with Collins leading Castellotti over the line at 122·21mph (196·62kph).

Rouen was used again in 1957, when Fangio (Maserati 250F) won at 100·02mph (160·93kph). The race at Reims in 1958 fell to Hawthorn. Success for front-engined GP cars was rare by 1959, but Brooks won the French race for Ferrari (Dino 246) at 127·43mph (205·05kph), after 50 laps at Reims in extremely testing conditions—the excessive heat was hardly bearable in itself, and it softened the road surface so that men and machines were scarred by flying stones. Coopers dominated the last year of the 2·5-litre Formula, Brabham winning even on the high-speed Reims circuit: still over 50 laps. covered in 1960 at 131·93mph (212·25kph).

Reims was used only twice for the GP in the five years of the 1·5-litre Formula. In 1961, GP novitiate Baghetti won in an FISA Ferrari, at 119·84mph (192·86kph) for the 52 laps, and by one fifth of a second from Gurney (Porsche). In 1963, Clark won a race packed with minor incidents, at 125·31mph (201·72kph). The 1962 and 1964 GPs were run at Rouen: in the first Gurney gained for Porsche that company's only grande épreuve victory, in the second he gained for Brabham their first grande épreuve victory; speeds were 101·89mph (163·94kph) and 108·77mph (175·01kph) respectively. Another new circuit, Clermont-Ferrand, was used in 1965, when Clark (Lotus 33) was unchallenged on his way to winning the 40-lap, 200-mile (320km) race at 89·22mph (143·58kph).

For the first French GP of the 3-litre Formula, at Reims, Ferraris were clear favourites. However, the race fell to Brabham, who thus became the first driver to win a grande épreuve in a car bearing his own name. His speed for 48 laps was 136·90mph (220·30kph). The desire of people in Sarthe to make Le Mans the venue of the French GP again were satisfied in 1967, when the race was run on a circuit 'around the car parks', and won by Brabham at 98·92mph (159·19kph).

Revolutionary talk was loud in French motor racing

Above, French Grand Prix: Auto Union, Mercedes-Benz and Bugatti in the dead car car park, Montlhéry, 1934. *Photo: Motor*

Right, French Grand Prix: period of transition between front and rear-engined cars; Brabham's Cooper alongside Brooks' Ferrari at Reims in 1959. *Photo: David Hodges Collection*

Below, French Grand Prix: start of the 1966 race, in which Jack Brabham was the first driver to win a Grand Prix in a car bearing his own name. *Photo: David Hodges Collection*

circles in 1968, and one outcome was that the Grand Prix was of the FFSA rather than of the ACF. It was run at Rouen, where in the rain Ickx scored for Ferrari their only win of the season at 100·45mph (161·66kph) over 40 laps. The 1969 race at Clermont-Ferrand was a low-water mark in the 3-litre Formula in that only 13 cars started, but the result was important, at least for France, as Matras were 1st and 2nd, Stewart covering the 38 laps at 97·71mph (157·25kph). The 1970 race, again run on the Charades circuit, attracted a full field (20 cars, plus three which failed to qualify to start), and was clearly led by V-12 cars—a Ferrari and a Matra—until their mechanical troubles let Rindt through, to win in a Lotus 72 at 98·42mph (158·39kph). DWH

French Touring Car Grand Prix

These races were held from 1922 to 1925 either the day before, or the day after, the French Grand Prix for

Below, French Touring Car Grand Prix: the start at Lyon, 1924. No 27 is a La Buire, No 31 a Steyr and No 38 a Peugeot. *Photo: Montagu Motor Museum*

Bottom, French Touring Car Grand Prix: Bugatti and Cottin-Desgouttes at Montlhéry in 1925. *Photo Autocar*

racing cars, and on the same circuit. There were separate classes for two-, four-, and five-seater cars, and although no mechanics were carried, each car had to carry ballast equivalent to the weight of one, three or four passengers. There was a fuel consumption limit which varied from year to year. In 1923 it was 47·1mpg for two-seaters, 28·3mpg for four-seaters, and 18·8mpg for five-seaters. Although nominally for standard touring cars, some very specialized machines appeared, including the first closed cars seen in European racing. The 1924 Peugeots had retractable headlamps and faired-in rear wheels; the 1924 La Buire and 1925 Peugeots both had stream-lined saloon bodies.

The introduction of Le Mans in 1923, a longer race for the same type of car, spelled the end of the Touring Car Grands Prix, which were not held after 1925. Races for touring cars were held at a number of other circuits, including Spa, Monza, and San Sebastian, but all had been dropped by 1930, or as at Spa, became sports car events. There was then virtually no racing for the ordinary family car until after World War 2. GNG

Frontières GP *see Chimay Circuit*

Fuji International Speedway

This speedway is situated about 62 miles (100km) west of Tokyo, and some 40 miles (64km) north-west of Yoko-hama, taking its name from Mount Fuji itself. Circuits available include distances of 3·726 miles (6·0km) and 2·67 miles (4·3km), and the course's first big event was the 200-mile Indianapolis-type race of 1966, won by Stewart's Lola T90.

Fuji is now the scene of the annual Group 7 Japanese Grand Prix, and a 'Can-Jap-Am' G7 event has also been held in recent years, inviting entries from the Can-Am series in America. The Japan Automobile Federation Grand Prix for single-seaters is another major meeting held in the spring, and in 1970 this was won by Stewart's Coombs-entered F2 Brabham-Cosworth BT30, from Graeme Lawrence's Tasman 2·4 Dino V-6. The current lap record stands to Moto Kitano's Nissan R382 G7, which circulated in 1min 44·77sec at 129·05mph (207·7kph) in 1969.

In the Japanese GP that year works Nissans and Toyotas beat works-supported Porsches, Vic Elford sharing the 4th-place Toyota. DCN

Fuji International Speedway

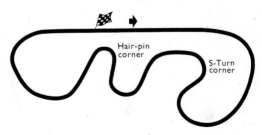

Hair-pin corner

S-Turn corner

Gaisberg Hill-Climb

The Austrian hill-climb at Gaisberg is situated near Salzburg, off the Munich-Vienna Autobahn, and is one of the fastest courses used in the Championship. It is quite short, at 5·376 miles (8·652km) and has a modest average gradient from the start at 1,968ft (608m) to the finish at 4,209ft (1,280m). Record: Rolf Stommelen (Porsche Bergspyder); 88·25mph (142·03kph); 3min 39·2sec; 1967 DCN

Geneva Circuits

The principal Geneva races were the Grands Prix des Nations run in 1946, 1948 and 1950; earlier, events of little account had been run at Geneva, the first of three Swiss Lac Leman towns where racing took place (races were later held at Lausanne and Montreux). The first races were run on the triangular Meyrin circuit just outside Geneva in 1924 for 1·5-litre and 1,100cc voiturettes. The first Geneva GP in 1931 attracted attention chiefly because of Czaykowski's accident (a spectator was killed and the count briefly placed under house arrest in hospital). The 155-mile (250km) race was won by Lehoux (Bugatti), and the supporting 1,100cc event by Benoist (Amilcar).

With the possible exception of the St Cloud race, the 1946 Grand Prix des Nations marked the return of real GP racing after the Second World War. The 1·83-mile (2·94km) Geneva circuit was made up of boulevards and streets, part-tarmac and part-concrete surfaced, with the complication of tram (streetcar) tracks in two stretches. The start was near the Palace of the League of Nations, whence the circuit dropped past the International Labour Monument (a very slow corner), down the Rue de Lausanne, left onto a short stretch of a wide avenue by the Wilson gardens almost to the lakeside. This last stretch was divided, and from a hairpin the return leg ran up the opposite of the avenue to a slow chicane at the junction with the Lausanne road, from there climbing back up to the pits.

Alfa Romeo 158s dominated the 1946 race, Farina winning at 64·10mph (103·16kph). Farina won again in 1948 in a Maserati 4CLT, while the last Geneva GP of 1950 went to Fangio (Alfa Romeo). In 1948 and 1950 there were supporting events for 1,100cc and 2-litre F2 cars and for sports cars. DWH

German GP see Avus Circuit and Nürburgring

Goodwood Circuit

Goodwood's motor race circuit was one of Britain's first airfield courses, laid out around the perimeter track of the old Westhampnett fighter base of the World War 2 years. The ground was part of the Duke of Richmond and Gordon's Goodwood estate in Sussex, and the circuit stood at the foot of the South Downs within sight of Chichester.

The 2·38-mile (3·83km) circuit combined a number of varied and difficult corners with a reasonably long straight, and in some measure belied its airfield ancestry by having a reasonable change in gradient. It was adopted as the home of the British Automobile Racing Club — this organization combining the remnants of the old Brooklands ARC and the Junior Car Club — and was opened on 18 September 1948. Reg Parnell won the Goodwood Trophy in his Maserati at 80·56mph (129·65kph), and Dennis Poore took the Woodcote Cup at 77·74mph (125·11kph) in his Alfa Romeo. An artificial chicane was put into the left-hand curve just before the pits, first being used on 14 April 1952, and this brought the lap length to 2·4 miles (3·862km). Regular international and club meetings were held in the early 1950s, and a 9-hour sports car race was held from 1952–5. Aston-Martin won all three and began their unfortunate tradition of setting fire to their pits.

The RAC Tourist Trophy moved to Goodwood in 1958 and some highly successful races were held there until the TT began its decline and moved to Oulton Park in 1965. Moss won the Goodwood TT in four successive

Below, Goodwood: Mike Hawthorn (Cooper-Bristol) takes the lead in the 1952 Chichester Cup. Photo: Motor

Bottom, Goodwood: C. D. Boulton spins his Connaught at Woodcote Corner, 1954. Photo: Charles Dunn

attempts, and then had his near-fatal and inexplicable accident there in early 1962. Club racing at Goodwood continued and Clark won the last F1 race there on Easter Monday, 1965, averaging 105·026mph (169·089kph). In 1966 the last major meeting at the circuit was the *Sunday*

Goodwood Circuit

Lavant corner — Lavant straight — Woodcote corner — St. Mary's — Paddock bend — Start & Finish — Fordwater — Madgwick corner

Mirror Trophy for F2 cars, won by Brabham in his Brabham-Honda at 99·51mph (162·201kph. The Duke of Richmond announced that he was fearful that rising speeds on his narrow circuit would cause a major accident, and at the end of the year Goodwood passed into limbo as a racing venue. It was still widely used as a test track by many manufacturers and teams, notably Bruce McLaren Motor Racing who developed their successful F1 and Can-Am cars there. Despite Bruce's tragic accident while testing the G7 Can-Am car in June 1970, the McLaren organization continues to use the track. Today, apart from these activities, it lies fallow and the BARC have moved their home to Thruxton. Lap record: Jackie Stewart (BRM) and Jim Clark (Lotus); 107·46mph (172·94kph); 1min 20·4sec; 1965. This is the final record, but the time has been lowered unofficially to below 1min 14sec by McLaren cars on test at the circuit. DCN

Gordon Bennett Cup, The

This was the first international series of motor races, for a trophy awarded by James Gordon Bennett, expatriate proprietor of the *New York Herald,* in July 1899. Specifications of competing cars were governed by prevailing formulas for *grandes voitures,* the 1,000kg limit being imposed for the 1902 race. Other regulations, though viable enough in 1899, were bound to spark off acrimony once motor-racing caught on. For instance, the Cup was to be contested, not between drivers or works teams, but between teams of three cars, each nominated by a recognized national club, while every part of a competing car had to be made in the country which it represented. There were, however, no rules to specify that it had to be designed there: though the use of foreign tyres caused the 50hp Napier to be disqualified in 1901, Mercedes were able to hedge their bets in 1904 and 1905 by running identical cars in German and Austro-Hungarian colours, and Darracq tried to get into the British and German teams as well as the French in 1904. National racing colours were also specified under the original rules, though rigid adherence to these was not found before 1903, when the so-called British Racing Green first appeared. The ACF was accorded the honour of staging the first race in 1900, but thereafter responsibility would devolve upon the winning club.

Nobody took the Gordon Bennett seriously at first. In 1900 five entries (three from France, one from Belgium and one from the United States) contested the Cup over a 353-mile (568km) course between Paris and Lyons (actually the longest of all the six races), but only two finished, Charron's Panhard being the victor at 38·6mph (62·12kph). Even worse was 1901, for the French team were the only starters, and the event was combined with the Paris-Bordeaux, a policy also pursued in 1902 when the Gordon Bennett was a subdivision of the 352-mile (566km) Paris–Vienna marathon. This year the only challenge came from Britain (one Napier and one Wolseley), but though the winner's average speed 31·8mph (51·18kph) was the lowest to date, the honours went to S. F. Edge on the 30hp Napier, and the British Club was faced with the task of organizing the 1903 event. Parliamentary sanction proved difficult to obtain, and in the end a closed circuit at Athy in Ireland had to be used. The field was the best so far — three British Napiers, challenged by three Mercedes from Germany, a Winton and a Peerless from America, and two Panhards and a Mors from France, and the British club found it necessary to stage eliminating trials. By 1904 France had followed suit, their *éliminatoire* at Mazagran

being a big affair with 29 entries from eleven factories. The 1903 winner was Jenatzy's 60hp Mercedes, which averaged 49·2mph (79·18kph), and the newly awarded Montagu Cup for the best team performance went to France. The German Gordon Bennett of 1904 was held over a closed circuit at Homburg in the Taunus, and was patronized by Wilhelm II and his Kaiserin. By this time the Gordon Bennett was big business, France, Germany and Britain being challenged by the Mercedes of Austria-Hungary, the Fiats of Italy, the Pipes of Belgium and a solitary Dufaux from Switzerland, which failed to start. The winner was Théry's Richard-Brasier for France, followed home by a German Mercedes, a French Turcat-Méry, and another Mercedes.

The manufacturers—and this, effectively, meant French manufacturers—were by this time exasperated with the Gordon Bennett rules, and from a vast amount of acrimonious talk there emerged a French plan to replace the race by a Grand Prix with fairer representation, based on manufacturers' teams rather than narrow national quotas. Though differences were resolved in time for the 1905 race to be staged at Clermont-Ferrand, and this was supported by 18 cars from six countries (the United States again challenged this season), it was the last of the series. Théry again repeated his victory at 48·4mph (77·89kph), followed home by the Fiats of Nazzaro and Cagno. The first Grand Prix was staged in 1906 and James Gordon Bennett gave his name to another Cup—this time for the gentler sport of long-distance balloon racing. MCS

GP des Voiturettes see Voiturette Racing in section: Organization of Motor Sport

Grands Prix de France

This title has been spasmodically applied to races which should not be confused with the classic French Grand Prix (Grand Prix de l'Automobile Club de France), although in 1949 a Grand Prix de France was to all intents and purposes the French GP and in 1952 one race of a series of Grands Prix de France was the French GP.

The first three races were run on a 33·55-mile (53·99km)

Le Mans circuit. The 1911 event was an ACF-blessed attempt to revive Grand Prix racing in the face of an agreement among European manufacturers to abstain, and as entries failed to materialize was run to a completely free formula. Thus an odd collection of 14 cars, ranging from a 1·5-litre Bugatti to an 18-litre 1906 GP Lorraine-Dietrich started in this 'Grand Prix des Vieux Tacots' on a torridly hot July day. Hémery won on a 10·5-litre Fiat, while 2nd place went to Friderich on the Bugatti of one seventh the capacity. The 1912 GP de France was a 3-litre event won by Zuccarelli's Lion-Peugeot, and the 1913 a Formule Libre race won by Bablot's Delage.

The title Grand Prix de France was revived in 1934 by the Moto Club de France for a 55-mile race at Montlhéry for cars of the current 750kg formula. Neither this nor the 1935 event attracted many leading drivers or cars, and the title lapsed until 1949 when it was applied to a Formula 1 race at Reims. This was an important event as that year's French GP proper was a sports car race, and the Reims contest attracted such drivers as Villoresi, Bira and Fangio. It was won by Louis Chiron in a Talbot.

In 1952 a series of eight Formula 2 Grands Prix de France were held, at Rouen (the official French GP), La Baule, Comminges, Marseilles, Montlhéry, Pau, Reims, and Les Sables d'Olonne. DWH

Grands Prix des Nations see Geneva Circuit

Gunners Circle see Cape Town Circuits

Hämeenlinna Circuit

This Finnish circuit lies about 62 miles (100km) north of Helsinki in the Hämeenlinna suburb of Ahvenisto, and was opened with an international F3 meeting on 16 July 1967. It was built at a cost of some Finnmarks 2 millions and was sponsored by the town of Hämeenlinna, the Finnish AC and Gulf Oil. The area in which the circuit stands was being developed as a sports centre, and the 1·8-mile (2·9km) course looped around two disused sandpits, one of which was the site of a large and very well-equiped paddock with a log-cabin restaurant, changing rooms and so on. The pine-clad slopes around the course give an excellent view for the spectators, but when F2 cars raced there for the first time—in September 1967—they found the circuit rather tight and narrow. Rindt won from Brabham and Clark, but thereafter meetings were confined to F3 sports and national classes. In May 1970 a 2-litre European Sports Car

Hämeenlinna Circuit

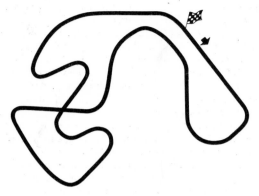

Championship round was held there. Lap record: Jack Brabham (Brabham F2); 78·74mph (127kph); 1min 20·06sec; 1967. DCN

Helsinki Circuit

After a tentative start at Munkkiniemi in 1932, international motor racing in Finland moved to Helsinki's Eläintarha circuit for the 1937 Finnish GP. Hans Ruesch won in an Alfa Romeo from Ebb's Mercedes SSK and Bjørnstadt's ERA, and in 1938 BMWs dominated the sports car event. The following year Westerblom's Alfa won the second Finnish GP, and then World War 2 and the Russo-Finnish conflict stopped all sport.

In the early 1950s motor racing was revived on the 1·23-mile (2·0km) parkland circuit, usually for sports cars. From 1960 the event was run for Formula Junior cars, winners including Lincoln's Cooper-BMC, Bremer's Elva-BMC and Nygren's Cooper-BMC Ian Raby's Merlyn did well in 1963 but the course was proving too tight and bumpy for the modern lightweight cars. It had a half-mile main straight, but the rest of the circuit was very twisty and slow, and the surface was loose in places. It ran around a sports stadium, and the 1952 Olympic Games stadium stood just outside the course, but within the park. Eläintarha has now lain fallow for several years, Finnish motor racing moving to Keimola and Hämeenlinna north of the city. DCN

Hockenheim Circuit

The local authorities in this small south German town built themselves a motor-racing circuit which was opened in 1939, although not used for any important meetings before World War 2. Sited 8·7 miles (14km) south-west of Heidelberg, 21·75 miles (35km) north of Karlsrühe, the circuit was 4·8 miles (7·72km) in length and comprised two long straights joined by a fast curve and a slow hairpin, running through flat woodland.

In 1939 Mercedes used the circuit for testing their 1·5-litre W165 Tripoli voiturettes, and continued to utilize it after the war. In 1947 one of the first post-war German motor race meetings took place there, Stuck's single-seater Cisitalia 1100 winning at 87·9mph (141·46kph). The course was used regularly until 1951, always attracting huge crowds, for the area is densely populated and there are 33 sizeable towns within a 60-mile radius. The 1948 crowd was a record 280,000, but between 1951 and 1955 there were no meetings of any importance. The Rhine Cup sports car races moved there briefly in 1955. Mercedes used the circuit for testing their F1 and sports cars that season, Kling and Moss setting an unofficial lap record of 2min 15sec, 128mph (206·0kph). But in the mid-1950s a plan was projected for a new autobahn to Karlsrühe, which would bisect the circuit. It seems that the local authorities held out until they claimed sufficient compensation to rework their circuit, and in the early 1960s it was closed as work on the autobahn began. By the start of the 1966 season the new course was ready, shortened to 4·2 miles (6·768km) in length with a very twisty section around the pit area, before a huge concrete grandstand. A short circuit within this stadium measured 1·64 miles (2·634km) and was to be used for minor national events.

The result was a very fast slipstreaming course through the trees, with place changing and innumerable incidents taking place on the stadium 'Mickey Mouse' section, and the circuit immediately proved extremely unpopular among drivers. But it had 500km sports car races, F3 Internationals and eventually two Formula 2 races in 1967. In 1968 Jim Clark lost his life on the wooded back curve, and in 1969 and 1970 the F2 round was known as the Jim Clark Memorial race. In 1970 the German GP was held there. Lap record: Jackie Ickx (Ferrari 312B); 131·7mph (211·95kph); 2min 0·05sec; 1970. DCN

Hockenheim: Brian Redman (de Tomaso-Ford) during practice for the 1970 German Grand Prix. *Photo: Motor*

Hockenheim Circuit

Grosser Kurs

Index of Performance and **Index of Thermal Efficiency** *see* Le Mans

Indianapolis Motor Speedway

The Indianapolis Motor Speedway, oldest race track in the world operated continuously since its construction, was built in 1909 on the northwest edge of Indianapolis, Ind. After being used for races of shorter duration at frequent intervals during the first two years of its existence, it was the scene of the first international 500-mile event for a purse of $25,100 on 30 May 1911; and the '500' series has been continued annually, except during the years of World War 1 and World War 2, with increasing success.

The 1970 renewal attracted approximately 300,000 spectators and the entrants of the 33 cars in the starting line-up divided prize money totalling just over one million dollars, the winner receiving $271,697.

Carl G. Fisher, whose success as an Indianapolis businessman was linked closely to the rapid growth of the young automotive industry, realized the need for a race track of major importance in the United States after witnessing the early Vanderbilt Cup Races on Long Island and the 1905 Gordon Bennett Cup Race in France.

When no one else appeared to be interested in building the type of speedway he had proposed, Fisher decided to tackle the project himself with the financial help of James Allison and two other Indianapolis businessmen: Arthur C. Newby of the National Motor Vehicle Company and Frank H. Wheeler of the Wheeler-Schebler Carburetor Company. Together they formed the Indianapolis Motor Speedway Corporation on 8 February 1909, capitalized at $250,000 with Fisher as president, and paid $72,000 for a tract of ground which was exactly 1 mile long and $\frac{1}{2}$ mile wide. On it they started construction of a rectangular 2·5 mile (4·023km) race course made by covering a 2in layer of gravel with 2in of crushed limestone and taroid. The four identical 0·25-mile turns were banked at an angle of 9° 12′, separated by two long straights measuring five-eights of a mile (1·0058km) each and two shorter straights each one-eighth of a mile (0·2012km) long.

Hopefully, they scheduled their first series of auto races for the holiday weekend of 4 July, but encountered unexpected construction problems which delayed the actual opening day until 19 August. Fisher, however, had made arrangements for the national balloon races to be held at the speedway as early as 5 June, while construction work was still in progress; and also had promised use of the facilities to members of the Federation of American Motorcyclists for their national championship events, on 14 August. Both programmes were held as planned while the finishing touches were being applied to the course and the auto racing fraternity converged on the track for practice laps beginning 16 August.

The main events of the inaugural programme were won by Buicks (drivers Bob Burman and Lewis Strang), but the track began to disintegrate on the third day of the competition. Conditions finally became so bad that officials ended the scheduled 300-mile Wheeler-Schebler trophy race at the 235-mile mark. Lee Lynch, driving a 4-cylinder Jackson, was averaging 55·61mph (89·50kph) in first place at the time.

Undaunted, Fisher and his associates admitted their construction mistakes and announced plans immediately to install guard rails and resurface the course with

Winners of the Indianapolis 500

Year	Driver	Car
1911	R. Harroun and C. Patschke	Marmon
1912	J. Dawson and D. Herr	National
1913	J. Goux	Peugeot
1914	R. Thomas	Delage
1915	R. de Palma	Mercedes
1916	D. Resta	Peugeot
1919	H. Wilcox	Peugeot
1920	G. Chevrolet	Monroe-Frontenac
1921	T. Milton	Frontenac
1922	J. Murphy	Duesenberg-Miller
1923	T. Milton and H. Wilcox	Miller
1924	L. Corum and J. Boyer	Duesenberg
1925	P. de Paolo and N. K. Batten	Duesenberg
1926	F. Lockhart	Miller
1927	G. Souders	Duesenberg
1928	L. Meyer	Miller
1929	R. Keech	Miller
1930	W. Arnold	Miller
1931	L. Schneider	Miller
1932	F. Frame	Miller
1933	L. Meyer	Miller
1934	B. Cummings	Miller
1935	K. Petillo	Miller
1936	L. Meyer	Miller
1937	W. Shaw	Gilmore-Offenhauser
1938	F. Roberts	Miller
1939	W. Shaw	Maserati
1940	W. Shaw	Maserati
1941	F. Davis and M. Rose	Noc-Out Hose Clamp Spl
1946	G. Robson	Thorne
1947	M. Rose	Blue Crown Spl
1948	M. Rose	Blue Crown Spl
1949	W. Holland	Blue Crown Spl
1950	J. Parsons	Wynn Friction Proof Spl
1951	L. Wallard	Belanger Spl
1952	T. Ruttman	Agajanian Spl
1953	W. Vukovitch	Fuel Injection Spl
1954	W. Vukovitch	Fuel Injection Spl
1955	B. Sweikert	John Zink Spl
1956	P. Flaherty	John Zink Spl
1957	S. Hanks	Belond Exhaust Spl
1958	J. Bryan	Belond Exhaust Spl
1959	R. Ward	Leader Card Spl
1960	J. Rathmann	K. Paul Spl
1961	A. J. Foyt	Bowes Seal Fast Spl
1962	R. Ward	Leader Card Spl
1963	A. P. Jones	Agajanian Spl
1964	A. J. Foyt	Sheraton-Offenhauser
1965	J. Clark	Lotus-Ford
1966	G. Hill	Lola-Ford
1967	A. J. Foyt	Coyote-Ford
1968	R. Unser	Eagle-Offenhauser
1969	M. Andretti	Hawk-Ford
1970	A. Unser	Colt-Ford

3,200,000 paving bricks at a cost of $155,000. The work was completed in 63 days and the speedway was re-opened for a series of record attempts on the weekend of 17–18 December. That programme also was curtailed —because of severe cold weather, with a thermometer reading of 9°F—but not until after Strang had established an unofficial American 5-mile record of 91·813mph (147·765kph) for a closed course with a clocking of 111·86mph (180·0kph) (also unofficial) for a quarter mile on the straight; and the speedway owners looked forward optimistically to 1910.

They scheduled attractive events for the holiday weekends of 30 May, 4 July and Labor Day, attracting a tremendous crowd estimated at 60,000 for the initial programme. Ray Harroun became the popular home-town hero of the day by winning the 200-mile feature at the wheel of a 6-cylinder Marmon; and feature events of similar length later in the season were won by Joe Dawson on 4 July in another Marmon and John Aitken in a National on 5 September. The second programme attracted only half as many spectators as the first one, however, and another drop in attendance was evident for the Labor Day series.

Convinced that they had been offering the public 'too much racing,' the speedway founders decided to concentrate their 1911 promotional efforts on one big race to be held on 30 May. They gave serious consideration to various distances up to 1,000 miles, as well as a 24-hour event, but finally settled on the 500 figure so that the entire operation could be concluded during daylight hours. Formal announcement of the race—limited to cars with engines of not more than 600ci (9,832cc) and run under the supervision of the Contest Board of the American Automobile Association—was greeted enthusiastically by automobile manufacturers and 46 entries were received. Forty of them met the minimum requirement by averaging 75mph (120kph) or better for a distance of 440yd (402·3m) on the main straightaway during the week prior to the race; and they were assigned starting positions, in rows of five abreast, according to the order in which they had filed their entries.

A crowd estimated at 80,000 overflowed the five grandstands to watch the contest involving the outstanding American racing teams and a number of European cars entered by some of the nation's most prominent sportsmen. Aitken's National, Spencer Wishart's Mercedes, Fred Belcher's Knox, David Bruce-Brown's Fiat and Ralph DePalma's Simplex were the early leaders. By the time the half-way mark had been reached, however, the race had developed into a battle between Harroun's Marmon and Ralph Mulford's Lozier. With the advantage of less tyre wear, Harroun, riding without a mechanic, finally took command only 19 laps before the finish and defeated Mulford by 1min and 43sec. His time was 6hr 42min 8sec for an average speed of 74·59mph (120·04kph). Harroun's earnings, including special accessory awards, totalled $14,000.

Because of the tremendous financial success of the first 500, the purse for 1912 was increased to $50,000 for cars of similar engine size, with riding mechanics mandatory. Two other important changes were announced. One limited entries to not more than two cars of the same make until after mid-April, at which time additional entries would be accepted to fill out the field. The other innovation provided that no more than 33 cars would be permitted to compete, in compliance with an AAA safety ruling, based on one car for every 400ft (121·92m) of race track (13 on a 1-mile track, 20 on a 1·5-mile

Indianapolis Motor Speedway

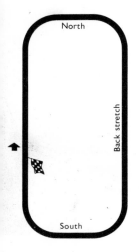

track, 26 on a 2-mile track, and so on). Except for a three-year experimental period, beginning in 1931, this same 33-car limitation always has been followed. Forty cars started the 1931 and 1932 events, and 42 formed the Race Day field in 1933—as a concession to entrants demanding a better chance of earning starting positions —but speedway officials then resumed the 33-car formula because of an increase in the number of accidents. The custom of starting the cars in three-abreast formation has remained unchanged since 1922. Before that the cars had been started five-abreast in 1911 and 1912, and four abreast from 1913 through 1921.

As the deadline for the 1912 race arrived only National, Stutz, Mercedes, Lozier and Case were represented by two-car teams and 15 other manufacturers represented by single entries. Stutz and National then entered a third car each and 24 of the 27 cars answered the starter's flag. DePalma, this time at the wheel of a Mercedes, took the lead on the third lap and increased it steadily for an advantage of more than 12 miles as the race neared its close. Many spectators already had left the grounds when DePalma's car rolled to a stop because of a broken connecting rod with only one and a half laps to go and Dawson roared home in a National for a second straight all-Indianapolis victory while the Mercedes was being pushed to its pit.

Europe began to show increasing interest in the 500 the following year, when the engine size was cut to a maximum of 450ci (7,374cc), and Jules Goux carried the colours of France across the finish line first with a 448ci (7,341cc) ohc Peugeot. The second-place Mercer, driven by Wishart, trailed by approximately 16 miles.

With engine specifications unchanged for 1914, Europe provided 15 of the 45 entries and dominated the contest. Long before the half-way mark was reached, the only question was which of the invaders would win. René Thomas of France provided the answer in the cockpit of a 380ci (6,227cc) Delage and the next three finishers were Arthur Duray in a Peugeot of only 183ci (2,999cc), Albert Guyot in another Delage and Goux in a Peugeot. The first American to finish was Barney Oldfield in a slower but durable 434ci (7,112cc) Stutz.

Fisher made a personal trip to Europe a few weeks after the race in an effort to interest more manufacturers in the next Indianapolis event for cars of not more than 300ci (4,916cc), but his visit was cut short by the advance rumblings of World War 1. The 1915 entry list was closed in April with only 31 cars listed. One of them, however, was a new Mercedes which DePalma had managed to get aboard ship before the outbreak of hostilities. Another was a Peugeot assigned to Dario Resta; and it was a two-car race most of the way with DePalma five miles ahead at the finish and Gil Anderson a distant 3rd in a Stutz.

The racing outlook for 1916 was even more discouraging. Although America was not actively engaged in the conflict, most of the nation's automobile manufacturers were already producing battlefield equipment. There was little possibility of obtaining any new race cars except three Frontenacs and three Crawfords already under construction by Louis Chevrolet and Billy Chandler, respectively. Drastic action was necessary and Fisher wasted no time. He purchased two Peugeots and two Maxwells; persuaded the Premier company to build three cars, similar in design to the Peugeots; obtained the pledge of several individual car owners that they would participate; and reduced the scheduled distance from 500 to 300 miles (804·7 to 482·8km).

DePalma's attempt to file a post-entry was ignored, after he had tried unsuccessfully to obtain 'appearance money' from the speedway. The race also lacked some of its usual lustre in that none of the new cars lived up to expectations. Resta won without being extended at any time and only 10 of the other cars in the starting field of 21 (smallest in Indianapolis history) were running at the finish. With America's entry into the war becoming more imminent each day, the management then sought additional 1916 revenue by planning a special 'Harvest Auto Racing Programme' for 9 September with a 100-mile event as the feature attraction. Although only 10,000 spectators turned out to watch 10 other cars compete against six owned by the speedway, the day resulted in some profit as Johnny Aitken earned $5,900 of the $12,000 posted prize money in a speedway-owned entry. Then the track suspended operations for the duration and made its facilities available to the war effort as a landing field and repair depot for aircraft.

Immediately after the signing of the Armistice in 1918 —and with the assurance of new cars from France and England, as well as from some American manufacturers —Fisher moved quickly to resume the 500 series on the traditional 30 May date the following spring. Most of the new equipment, however, developed various mechanical ailments and Howdy Wilcox was the winner in one of the four-year-old 274ci (4,490cc) speedway-owned Peugeots, which had been reconditioned with Goux's help. Goux also drove the Peugeot sister car for the speedway, coming 3rd behind Eddie Hearne in a Durant, and one of the new Ballots managed 4th place.

The rapid development of American racing equipment during the next decade—as displacement was cut steadily from a maximum of 300ci (4,916cc) to 183ci (2,999cc), to 122ci (1,999cc) and finally to 91·5ci (1,499·4cc)—included high compression engines, 4-wheel hydraulic brakes, low pressure tyres, exotic fuels, superchargers and hydraulic shock absorbers. With the creation of improved racing engines, however, the principal manufacturers withdrew from racing because of their inability to compete successfully against the specials built for individual sportsmen by Louis Chevro-

Indianapolis: the field behind the La Salle pace car on the back straight in 1937. The winner, the Gilmore, is in the centre of the front row. *Photo: Indianapolis Motor Speedway*

Indianapolis: Mauri Rose (Blue Crown) leads the field into the first turn at the start of the 1947 race. *Photo: Indianapolis Motor Speedway*

Indianapolis: Jim Clark (Lotus-Ford) laps Len Sutton (Vollstedt-Ford) in 1965. *Photo: Indianapolis Motor Speedway*

let, the Duesenberg brothers (Fred and August) and Harry Miller.

During the three years of the 183ci formula, Gaston Chevrolet won in 1920 with one of his brother's 4-cylinder Frontenacs (under Monroe sponsorship); Tommy Milton scored the first 500 victory with an 8-cylinder engine (another Frontenac) in 1921; and Jimmy Murphy set a new race record of 94·48mph (152·05kph) in 1922 with a Miller engine in a Duesenberg chassis. Milton used a Miller engine in his HCS Special to win the first race for 122ci entries in 1923, starting a seven-year period without riding mechanics, before Duesenberg won two consecutive races, with Pete DePaolo breaking the 100mph barrier by averaging 101·13mph (162·66kph) in 1925. But the Millers re-asserted their superiority by winning three of the four races during the 91·5ci era from 1926 to 1929, inclusive.

Eddie Rickenbacker—a former race driver and America's ace of aces in World War 1, who had purchased the speedway from its founders during the summer of 1927—then attempted to interest the nation's passenger car manufacturers in racing again by banning super-chargers and raising the maximum engine size to 366ci (5,981cc) for the eight-year period beginning with the 1930 event. Riding mechanics again were made mandatory. Many cars with modified stock block engines were entered, but none was able to finish better than 3rd in any race despite factory support from such companies as Ford and Studebaker. The 8-cylinder Millers, and then the 4-cylinder Offenhausers, invariably won decisively.

Two other changes of short-lived duration also were introduced during the Rickenbacker regime. One, inaugurated in 1933 for a seven-year period, increased the distance of the official time trials to determine starting positions from 10 miles to 25 miles. The entrants expressed increasing opposition to this procedure every year, however, and the 10-mile distance was restored in 1939. The most drastic change involved the establishment of limitations on the quality and quantity of fuel, previously unrestricted on both counts. Each car was limited to 45 gallons (170·34 litres) of fuel in 1934, 42·5 gallons (160·88 litres) in 1935 and 37·5 gallons (141·95 litres) in 1936. During each of these three years, several prominent contenders ran out of fuel while running with the leaders late in the race. Beginning in 1937, entrants again were permitted an unlimited amount of fuel, but they were required to use commercial gasoline for the 1937 event. Then, with the adoption of the new international racing formula in 1938, the last of the fuel restrictions was abandoned. When the fuel restrictions were established in 1934, however, the speedway had also ruled that no car could use more than 6·5 gallons (24·605 litres) of oil during the race. This restriction also was lifted in 1938, but a new rule was imposed—and still is in effect—limiting each car to the amount of oil in the car at the start of each race. No additional oil may be added for any reason, once the race is under way; and an additional safety precaution gives the chief steward of the 500 the right to disqualify any car for spewing fuel or lubricant or coolant in sufficient quantity to create a hazard.

Even the adoption of the international formula in 1938 for supercharged and non-supercharged engines up to 183ci (2,999cc) and 274ci (4,490cc), respectively, in single-seated cars resulted in the interruption of the steady string of Offenhauser triumphs on only three occasions between that date and the development of the

Indianapolis: although no drivers were hurt, this multiple accident at the start of the 1966 race eliminated one third of the 33 participants. *Photo: Indianapolis Motor Speedway*

Indianapolis: Mario Andretti, with his wife Dee Ann in Victory Lane, receives the Borg Warner trophy after winning the 1969 race. *Photo: Indianapolis Motor Speedway*

Ford racing engines which won for the first time in 1965. The exceptions came in 1939 and 1940, when Wilbur Shaw gained the distinction of scoring two consecutive victories for the first time with a supercharged 8-cylinder Maserati; and in 1946 when George Robson led the field home at the wheel of a 6-cylinder supercharged Thorne Engineering Special in the first event following the purchase of the track from Rickenbacker by Anton Hulman, Jr, of Terre Haute, Ind.

During the four-year suspension of all racing activities in the United States, because of World War 2, the speedway facilities had deteriorated to such an extent that Rickenbacker was not interested in attempting to reopen the track because of the tremendous expense involved. At one time in 1945 it appeared almost certain that the big plant, which had been greatly expanded in area, would be absorbed by an ambitious real estate development. Shaw, however, worked untiringly to find an interested sportsman willing to assume the financial risk of re-establishing the 500 as a fixture on the international racing calendar; and it was Hulman who finally accepted the challenging assignment with no thought of personal financial gain. All speedway income in excess of operating expenses would be used to improve the facilities and increase the prize money.

With Shaw in the rôle of speedway president until his death in a 1954 aircraft crash, when Hulman assumed personal charge of the track's destiny, the 500 has grown in importance and prestige at a really astonishing rate. The aged wooden grandstands have been replaced with massive structures of steel and concrete, many of them of the double-deck type, with the number of reserved seats increased to approximately 230,000. The entire racing strip has been resurfaced and the pit area rebuilt for safety reasons. A new control tower has been added for race officials. Thirteen lanes of traffic tunnel under the track and new interior roads lead to free infield parking space for 25,000 vehicles.

Of equal importance is the fact that prize money has been increased steadily from a high figure of slightly under $100,000 before the start of the Hulman regime to the astonishing total of over $1,000,000 for the 1970 event.

The racing fraternity has responded in like manner,

The **Jarama Circuit** diagram is labelled at top right.

building safer and faster cars for each renewal of the 500. Bill Holland became the first 120-plus mph race winner by averaging 121·327mph (195·241kph) with an Offenhauser-powered fwd Blue Crown Spark Plug Special in 1949; Bill Vukovich reached 130·84 (210·56kph) with an 'Offy' Fuel Injection Special in 1954; Rodger Ward averaged 140·293mph (225·745kph) with another Offenhauser engine in 1962; and Jimmy Clark of Scotland lifted the race average to 150·686mph (242·63kph) three years later in a rear-engine Lotus powered by a V-8 Ford racing unit. Mario Andretti, driving another rear-engine entry with a turbocharged V-8 Ford engine, set the present race record of 156·867mph (252·511kph). In 1970, Al Unser's winning speed of 155·749mph (250·653kph) was slightly slower, but his prize money of $271,697.72 was the biggest ever. AB

Irish GP *see* Phoenix Park Circuit

Italian GP *see* Monza Autodrome

Italian Rally (Sestrière; San Remo)

The Italian Rally, which is now that country's contribution to the international rally championship, was formed in 1970 by the amalgamation of the Sestrière and San Remo events. These were two of Italy's best rallies. The Sestrière was the older, being first run in 1950, but lapsing after 1959. However, in 1968 FIAT and the city of Turin were looking round for a rally. The Turin Automobile Club revived the Sestrière and thanks to FIAT were able to endow it with a substantial prize fund.

The San Remo Rally — or as it was then known, the Flowers Rally — was first run in 1961 and very quickly became a popular international event. Erik Carlsson won it in 1964 when it was first included in the European championship and from that point it never looked back. It utilized many of the same roads as the renovated Sestrière, so that combining the two events as one was a logical step. JD

Jarama Circuit

The Jarama artificial circuit, built in the arid and hilly area some 16 miles (25·6km) north of Madrid, was inaugurated in July 1967. Within its 2·1-mile (3·4km) lap, designer Hugenholtz packed eleven named corners — several following in quick succession — two identifiable swerves and only one worthwhile straight, of roughly half a mile. In this respect it is only just acceptable as a Grand Prix venue; on the other hand facilities such as pits are excellent, and spectators are well catered for.

Indianapolis: Dan Gurney, 2nd in 1969, makes a 21sec pit stop for fuel. Photo: Indianapolis Motor Speedway

Winners of the Italian Rally

Sestriere

1950	Emilio	*Lancia Aprilia*
1951	Villoresi	*Lancia Aurelia*
1952	Valenzano	*Lancia Aurelia*
1953	Seibert	*Citroën 15*
1954	Valenzano	*Lancia Aurelia*
1955	Gatta	*Lancia Aurelia*
1956	Schock	*Mercedes 300 SL*
1957	Borghesio	*Dyna Panhard 750*
1958	Cussini	*Fiat Abarth 750*
1959	Castellina	*Fiat Abarth 750*
1968	Pat Moss	*Lancia Fulvia*
1969	Munari	*Lancia Fulvia*

San Remo

1961	De Villa	*Alfa Romeo Giulietta*
1962	Frescobaldi	*Lancia Flavia*
1963	Patria	*Lancia Flavia*
1964	Carlsson	*Saab 850*
1965	Cella	*Lancia Fulvia*
1966	Cella	*Lancia Fulvia*
1967	Piot	*Renault Gordini*
1968	Toivonen	*Porsche 911 T*
1969	Kallström	*Lancia Fulvia*

Italian Rally

1970	Therier	*Alpine-Renault*
1971	O. Andersson	*Alpine-Renault*

The first international race at Jarama was the 1967 Formula 2 Madrid GP, won by Clark in a Lotus at 81·8mph (131·64kph). In November 1967 the Spanish GP was revived, as a non-championship race to test the organization for a race of this status. Again Clark (Lotus) was the winner; some inadequacies (in for example safety barriers) were shown up in incidents. These shortcomings were rectified in time for the next Spanish GP held in May 1968, and won by Graham Hill.

The F2 Madrid GP was repeated in 1968, Beltoise (Matra) winning and setting a lap record which was not broken in the F1 race a month later, this demonstrating the nature of the circuit. In 1969 the Madrid GP was contested by eight second-line F1 and F5000 cars, Holland winning in a Lola; the 1969 F2 race was won by Stewart in a Matra at 84·9mph (136·63kph). Jarama was the venue of the 1970 and 1971 Spanish GPs, which were both Championship events. Lap record: Jack Brabham (Brabham BT33); 92·45mph (145·381kph); 1min 24·3sec 1970. DWH

Johannesburg Circuit *see* Kyalami Circuit

Jyllands Ringen

Denmark sees very little motor racing, and after the demise of Roskilde, where the Copenhagen GP was held regularly in the 1960s, this central Jutland circuit, lying 5 miles (8km) east of Silkeborg and some 24 miles (38km) west of Århus, is an interesting 'autodrome' offering a number of alternative, but all very short, courses. Lap length is only 1·062 miles (1·701km) and few important meetings take place there. Lap record: Kurt Ahrens (Brabham BT21); 75·64mph (121·9kph); 50·2sec; 1967. DCN

Kaiserpreis Race

This race, for a prize offered by the German Emperor, was for medium-powered cars, nominally tourers, whose engines were not to exceed 8 litres capacity. It was held in 1907 only, over a course in the Taunus mountains near Frankfurt, in Germany, which included part of the 1904 Gordon Bennett circuit. As the entry list was so large (92 cars) it was decided to have two Eliminating Trials, half of the entries in one and half in the other. The first 20 cars in each Trial started in the race itself. Many of the makes entered were not normally seen in competitions, and included Gräf und Stift, Eisenach, Argus, Sun, and Martin-Lethimonnier. However, as might be expected, it was the well-known makes that reached the final. The winner was Nazzaro in a Fiat. Second was Hautvast in a Pipe, with Joerns and Michel 3rd and 4th in Opels. HON

arlskoga Circuit

he Karlskoga Motorstadion is in central Sweden, bout 155 miles (250km) west of Stockholm and in the ndustrial centre from which it takes its name. The annon Race, or Karlskoga Kanonloppet, was insti- ated in 1955, at first for sports cars. Gunnar Carlsson a Ferrari won the first race from Musy in a Maserati nd Bonnier in an Alfa Romeo. Carlsson won again in 956 and the following year Lotus swept the board with 1-2-3 finish led by Peter Ashdown. Moss won the orts car Cannon Races from 1958 to 1960, then in 961 the Karlskoga Motorklubb ran the first of three 1 races at the 1·864-mile (3km) stadium circuit. Moss a Lotus won the first event at 72·46mph (116·62kph), nd in 1962 Gregory scored a victory in the UDT Lotus- limax V-8 at 78·25mph (125·93kph). Clark won the last 1 Kanonloppet in 1963 at 69·27mph (111·48kph), and hereafter the races were for Formula 2. The last major 2 meeting at the stadium was in 1967 when Stewart's Matra matched Rindt's Brabham for the first time, and indt left the lap record at 1min 17·2sec, 86·8mph 39·69kph). Wisell's Tecno won the feature F3 event 1968, Piper's Ferrari taking the sports car race. In 969 Redman's Lola-Chevrolet won from Piper's orsche 908 in one of the Nordic Cup rounds. Lap ecord: Chris Craft (McLaren M8C); 88·06mph 41·73kph); 1min 16·2sec; 1970. DCN

Kyalami: Jim Clark is leading the field so far that he seems to be alone in the race. South African Grand Prix, 1968. *Photo: Alton Berns*

Left, Karlskoga: John Surtees (Lola) and Masten Gregory (Lotus-BRM) in the 1962 Formula 1 Kannonloppet. *Photo: Rolle Eneflod*

Right, Kyalami: John Surtees and Jack Brabham in the 1967 South African Grand Prix. *Photo: David Phipps*

Kumalo Circuit

The Rhodesian GP has been held at Bulawayo's motor racing circuit at Kumalo since 1962, when motorcyclist Gary Hocking won in a Lotus. The James McNeillie Circuit is 2·06 miles (3·316km) in length, is based on an airfield and is only used a few times each year. Most difficult corner on the course is the 20mph (32kph) first-gear hairpin, and at one point the straight doubles back on itself and for some distance there is only a 20ft wide strip separating racing cars travelling in opposite directions. Player's Cigarettes normally sponsored the annual Rhodesian GP until the unilateral declaration of independence, but the race continues with the blessing of the Smith regime. DCN

Kyalami Circuit

The Kyalami circuit at Johannesburg replaced the South African city's Grand Central course in the early 1960s, and has since become the scene of the annual Kyalami 9 Hours—longest race in the Springbok series—and more recently of the South African GP.

The circuit has a lap distance of 2·54 miles (4·088km) and its first big meeting was in 1961, when the Rand GP was won by Clark's Lotus-Climax at 90·55mph (145·73kph). In 1962 the Rand 9 Hours moved to Kyalami from Grand Central, and Piper scored his first of five consecutive victories in Ferraris.

Karlskoga Circuit

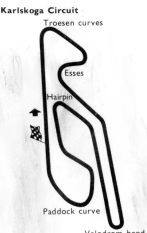

Troesen curves

Esses

Hairpin

Paddock curve

Velodrom bend

Keimola Motor Stadium

he Keimola Moottoristadion was built just 11 miles 18km) north of Helsinki in 1966, and its first big meeting was on 3 September the following year when the Finnish 2 Grand Prix was held there. The organizing club was mall and short of money, and negotiations were handled y veteran Finnish driver and circuit administrator, urt Lincoln, and his son-in-law, Jochen Rindt. They ttracted quite a good field for this non-Championship vent and the race was won by Clark in a Lotus 48.

Today Lincoln handles all the circuit's affairs and it has been the scene of several good national open and nternational F3 and sports car meetings. Lap length is ·05 miles (3·3km); a tricky return section, with a right- and hairpin following a downhill left-hander, is its main feature. Lap record: Jochen Rindt (Porsche 908); 6·74mph (155·70kph); 1min 16·3sec; 1969. DCN

Kyalami Circuit

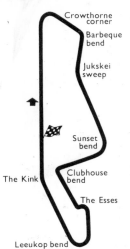

Crowthorne corner

Barbeque bend

Jukskei sweep

Sunset bend

Clubhouse bend

The Kink

The Esses

Leeukop bend

The South African Grand Prix moved to Kyalami from East London in 1967, and Rodriguez in a Cooper- Maserati won this first event there at 97·09mph (156·25kph). Hulme's Brabham setting fastest lap at 1min 29·9sec.

Kyalami is some 5,000ft (approx. 1,520m) above sea-level, lying on the open plateau some 15 miles (24km) north of Johannesburg. Its permanent facilities are very good, and in recent years it has been used increasingly for extensive Formula 1 car testing during Northern Hemisphere winters. The surface was very abrasive but has now improved somewhat, and fine weather can be virtually guaranteed months in advance. Lap record: Dave Charlton (Lotus 49C); 114·5mph (182·7kph); 1min 20·2sec; 1970. DCN

Lady Wigram Trophy see Wigram Circuit

Laguna Seca Raceway

Laguna Seca Raceway opened in 1957, after the closing of the nearby 1·8-mile (2·897km) Pebble Beach (1950-1956)

Killarney Circuits see Cape Town Circuits

Klondike 200 see Speedway Park

Laguna Seca Raceway

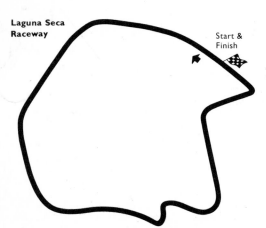

Start & Finish

Opposite top, Acopolis Rally: Pauli Toivonen and Marti Kolari (Porsche 911S) on their way to victory in the 1969 event. *Photo: John Davenport*

Opposite bottom, Indianapolis Motor Speedway: The start of the 5000-Mile Race in 1960. *Photo: Al Bochroch*

which ran over public roads. Laguna Seca lies within the grounds of Fort Ord US Army Base, 5 miles (8km) east of Monterey, Calif. The 1·9-mile (3·058km), 30ft (9·1440m) wide asphalt, track rises from 700ft (213·36m) above sea-level in the pit area to 940ft (286·512m), offering excellent spectator visibility from hillsides within the circuit. Stirling Moss, winner of the 1960 and 1961 Monterey GP, regards Laguna Seca as one of racing's best short circuits. The track is operated by SCRAMP, the Sports Car Racing Association Monterey Peninsula, who lease the land from the U.S. Army and turn all profits over to charity. Laguna Seca is the site of Can-Am, Trans-Am and Formula A events, the three foremost American road racing series.

In 1970 Vic Elford earned the pole with a record 58·8sec qualifying lap but failed to start when the Chaparral 2J broke its engine on race day during practice. Denis Hulme won the 80 lap, 152-mile 1970 Monterey-Castrol Can-Am with a 105·068mph average, finishing 1·2sec in front of Jackie Oliver's Ti-22-Chevy. Lap record: Denis Hulme (McLaren-Chevrolet); 109·980mph (176·93kph); 1min 2·19sec; 1969. ARB

Lakeside Circuit

The 1·5-mile (2·414km) Lakeside circuit lies about 15 miles (24km) north of Brisbane in Queensland. It is an international-standard Australian circuit developed and run by the Queensland Motor Sporting Club. It was built on an old dairy farm, mainly by club members using borrowed equipment, and owes much to the support and enthusiasm of Sidney Sakzewski, a business-man and senior club member.

The track opened in 1961, at a time when Queensland's only existing circuit, a wartime airstrip at Lowood, was declining (the club's previous track at Strathpine, closer to Brisbane, had been reclaimed for housing, and the Southport road circuit, where the 1954 Australian GP had been held, was not available). Lakeside was an immediate success because of unparalleled spectator viewing and a relatively high lap speed despite the short distance.

In 1961 Australia had seen the first of its annual visits by international drivers—visits that led to the instigation of the Tasman Cup—and in 1962 Lakeside took the bold step of retaining the drivers imported by Warwick Farm and the new circuit of Sandown Park, Victoria. Jack Brabham won the circuit's first international race in a 2·5-litre Cooper-Climax at an average speed of 90mph (144·84kph). However, Lakeside's most memor-able race came the next year, when tropical rain poured down for most of the 99 miles (159·33km). It ended in a

heroic victory for John Surtees in a Bowmaker-Yeoman Credit Lola, with Graham Hill 2nd in a 4wd Ferguson P99 prototype he took over for the series. With a very fast sweeping back straight and a main straight with a 140mph (224kph) sweeper near the end, the circuit now produces 100mph (160kph) lap averages, but its place as a Tasman Cup venue has been taken for a time at least by Surfers Paradise.

The circuit underwent major modifications in 1968-9 when a local water supply project raised the level of the adjoining lake. However, Lakeside, still under club control, continues to play an important part in most Australian championship series, generally running six meetings a year. Lap record: Chris Amon (Ferrari Dino); 102·27mph (164·65kph); 52·8sec; 1969. TBF

Le Mans Circuits

Le Mans has been a centre of motor sport since the beginning of the century, and it is also a centre of the French insurance industry: the two might appear to be irreconcilable, but in fact the prosperity of the second has contributed to the prosperity of the Automobile Club de l'Ouest (ACO). This was founded in 1906 as the Automobile Club de la Sarthe, became a wider regional club, and the most powerful single motor club in France.

The first Sarthe circuit was the 64·12-mile (103·18km) triangle used for the first Grand Prix de l'ACF in 1906. The start and finish point was at Pont de Gennes on RN 23, one side of the triangle, the others being RN 157 and the less-important St Calais—le Ferté-Bernard road (St Calais and Vibraye, roughly halfway along this leg, were bypassed by plank roads). The western hairpin was about 4 miles (6·4km) outside Le Mans.

For the 1911–13 Grands Prix de France, and lesser races for cars and motorcycles, a 33·55-mile (54km) circuit south of Le Mans was used. Its northern hairpin was at Pontlieue, and thence it ran down RN 158, along the stretch which was later to become famous as the Mulsanne straight, past Mulsanne itself and on to the outskirts of Ecommoy. The east-west leg ran to le Grand-Lucé, whence the circuit ran back to Pontlieue through Parigné-l'Evêque. The start line was between Pontlieue and the present Tertre Rouge (the 1911 race was run anti-clockwise).

Today's *Circuit Permanent de la Sarthe* was devised by the ACO in 1919, and first used for the Coupe Inter-nationale des voiturettes in 1920, won by Friderich, Bugatti, at 57·6mph (92·70kph). This race was run for the next three years. The French Cyclecar GP was run at the same meetings in 1920-22, as were motorcycle races. Other Sarthe events included a GP de la Consom-mation, the Bugatti GPs (1928–30) and GPs de l'ACF, in 1921, 1929 and 1967. The latter was run on the Bugatti circuit. This 2·7-mile (4·345km) circuit uses a stretch of the main circuit from the pits almost to the S-bends before looping back on itself again, and again, and again; however suitable it might be for lesser classes, it is certainly not a GP circuit.

Above all, the Sarthe circuit has been the venue of the 24-hour race, and since that was first run has been modified several times, although at least the line of the original circuit is followed from Tertre Rouge to the pits. From 1920 to 1928 the lap was 10·72 miles (17·262km), the circuit running almost straight from the start line into the suburbs of Le Mans, where it turned back through the Pontlieue hairpin onto the Tours road, to Tertre Rouge and the Mulsanne straight. In 1929 a link road cut out the hairpin, and cut the lap distance to

Lakeside Circuit

Lucas corner

Neptune corner

Shell corner

BP bend

BMC corner

10·16 miles (16·360km), and for 1932 the circuit took its present 8·36-mile (13·492km) form with the completion of the stretch from the pits through the S-bends to Tertre Rouge. Subsequent alterations have fundamentally changed the nature of the circuit — wide and smooth, it is far removed from the rough original — but no its basic configuration (the first bend was slightly re-aligned in 1956, and the Virage Ford chicane before the pits was introduced in 1968).

From the start the modern circuit swings right between banks to the S-bends, and thence through the Tertre Rouge right angle on to the Mulsanne straight (which is not straight). This ends at the Mulsanne right angle, which is followed by a near-straight to Indianapolis (so named because it was once pavé-surfaced). The Arnage right angle is the slowest corner, and is followed by fast curves past White House and on back to the pits: a stretch which was a fast straight until the Virage Ford was introduced to slow cars passing the pits.

The early rudimentary pits were slowly improved, but with all other facilities were destroyed during World War 2. Permanent constructions were completed for 1949, and after the 1955 accident new three-tier pits were built, on a line which meant that road width in front of them was doubled (little more than a decade later, this was recognized to be inadequate from the safety point of view). As a further move to reduce activity in front of the pits a signalling station was set up at the exit from Mulsanne in 1956. Public facilities are generous, yet because the 24-hour race attracts such vast crowds they always seem inadequate despite steady development.

Le Mans 24-Hour Race

This is undoubtedly the most widely-known motor race in the world, a standing which it is sometimes difficult to justify and which is at least in part due to the fascination it has for British and American enthusiasts. It was conceived by Charles Faroux and Georges Durand in response to Emile Coquille's suggestion that a new race be established, and since then, with occasional variations in timing, has always adhered to their conception of a 24-hour road race through one of the shortest nights of the year. Other fundamental points have long since been abandoned: for example, that it should be a race for practical touring cars.

Early regulations required that 30 cars identical to the entry should have been built, and all cars over 1,100cc had to have four-seater bodies (above 1·5 litres after 1930, a minimum of two comfortable seats in 1937). Ballast equivalent to passengers had to be carried at first, together with tools and spares to be used (early on, only one driver was allowed to work on a car), the efficacy of hoods had to be demonstrated from 1924 to 1927, and refuelling stops were restricted.

There have always been contests within the 24-hour race: indeed, the first race was not intended to be an end in itself, but the first round in the Rudge-Whitworth Triennial Cup. This was superseded by a biennial competition, which lingered on after World War 2, although overshadowed by the Index of Performance. The Index is calculated quite simply:

$$\frac{\text{distance actually covered}}{\text{predetermined distance, according to capacity}}$$

but more complicated and variable formulae have been used to calculate minimum distances required. An outright winner was recognized by the ACO only in 1928.

The first race started at 4pm on 26 May 1923, and was

Opposite, St Jovite Circuit: The start of the 1968 Canadian GP. Chris Amon (Ferrari) leads Jo Siffert (Lotus). *Photo: Motor Sport*

Winners of Le Mans 24-Hour Race

1923	A. Lagache and R. Leonard *Chenard-Walcker*
1924	J. Duff and F. C. Clement *Bentley*
1925	H. de Courcelles and A. Rossignol *Lorraine-Dietrich*
1926	R. Bloch and A. Rossignol *Lorraine-Dietrich*
1927	J. D. Benjafield and S. C. H. Davis *Bentley*
1928	W. Barnato and B. Rubin *Bentley*
1929	W. Barnato and H. R. S. Birkin *Bentley*
1930	W. Barnato and G. Kidston *Bentley*
1931	Earl Howe and H. R. S. Birkin *Alfa Romeo*
1932	R. Sommer and L. Chinetti *Alfa Romeo*
1933	R. Sommer and T. Nuvolari *Alfa Romeo*
1934	L. Chinetti and P. Etancelin *Alfa Romeo*
1935	J. S. Hindmarsh and L. Fontes *Lagonda*
1937	J. P. Wimille and R. Benoist *Bugatti*
1938	E. Chaboud and J. Tremoulet *Delahaye*
1939	J. P. Wimille and P. Veyron *Bugatti*
1949	L. Chinetti and Lord Selsdon *Ferrari*
1950	L. and C. Rosier *Talbot*
1951	P. D. Walker and P. N. Whitehead *Jaguar*
1952	H. Lang and F. Riess *Mercedes-Benz*
1953	A. P. R. Rolt and J. D. Hamilton *Jaguar*
1954	J. F. Gonzalez and M. Trintignant *Ferrari*
1955	J. M. Hawthorn and I. Bueb *Jaguar*
1956	R. Flockhart and N. Sanderson *Jaguar*
1957	R. Flockhart and I. Bueb *Jaguar*
1958	P. Hill and O. Gendebien *Ferrari*
1959	R. Salvadori and C. Shelby *Aston Martin*
1960	P. Frere and O. Gendebien *Ferrari*
1962	P. Hill and O. Gendebien *Ferrari*
1963	L. Scarfiotti and L. Bandini *Ferrari*
1964	J. Guichet and N. Vacarella *Ferrari*
1965	M. Gregory and J. Rindt *Ferrari*
1966	B. McLaren and C. Amon *Ford*
1967	A. J. Foyt and D. Gurney *Ford*
1968	P. Rodriguez and L. Bianchi *Ford*
1969	J. Ickx and J. Oliver *Ford*
1970	R. Attwood and H. Herrmann *Porsche*

largely a French affair, run in conditions of rain and hail which were hardly propitious. Two 3-litre Chenard-Walckers led throughout, the winning Lagache and Leonard car covering 1,372·94 miles (2,209·53km) at a 57·2mph (92·055kph) average. Only three of the 33 starters failed to finish and — of an importance of the event which could hardly have been foreseen — Duff's works-blessed 3-litre Bentley was 5th after assorted misadventure. This car was the only overseas entry in 1924; driven by Duff and Clement, it took the lead early on Sunday morning, and won by just over 10 miles from two Lorraine-Dietrichs, covering 1,290·79 miles (2,077·32km) at 53·78mph (86·55kph). Only 14 of the 41 starters were running at the end.

The race was more international in 1925, when the 49 starters included two Chryslers, two Bentleys, two Sunbeams, Diattos, O.M.s and an Austin Seven. It also saw the first 'Le Mans Start', drivers being required to run to their cars and erect folded hoods before starting their engines.

The legend of the Bentleys at Le Mans really dates from 1927. Initially, the three Bentleys (a '4½' and two 3-litres) led, but then all were involved in the famous multiple accident at White House. The somewhat battered survivor, driven by Davis and Benjafield, pursued the Chassagne and Laly Ariès through the night and on into Sunday. With less than two hours to go, the Ariès retired, and the Bentley went on to win over 1,472·52 miles (2,369·8km) at 61·35mph (98·73kph), ahead of only six other cars. Bentleys won again in 1928, 1929 and 1930.

An Alfa Romeo period started in 1931, when in a 2·3 Howe and Birkin covered 3,000km for the first time (1,875·1 miles, 3,017·2km at 78·13mph, 125·73kph); Alfas won each year until 1935 when a 4½ litre Lagonda driven by Hindmarsh and Fontès was victorious.

The remaining pre-war races (1937–9 — the event was cancelled in 1936) fell to French cars. Wimille and Benoist dominated the 1937 race in a T57S Bugatti. By the grace of a long Delage pit stop in 1939 Wimille and Veyron won in a T57C. In 1938 the first Coupe à l'indice de performance went to a 568cc Simca Cinq (the first small French car to win on index since 1928, and a pointer to the future).

From appearances there might well have been no more than a year's interval as the 1949 entry lined up: large French cars, Talbot, Delage, Delahaye, seemed to be the outright contenders (the only other large car was a Bentley), while save for the admission of prototypes, the regulations were largely carried over (minimum distances were again increased), and there were even 12 starters qualifying for the 1939/49 Biennial Cup. But there were also two 2-litre V-12 Ferraris, and one of these, driven for 22 hours by Chinetti and for two hours by Lord Selsdon, won outright.

The old order had one last victory, in 1950, when Talbots were 1st and 2nd, and in the winning car Rosier pushed the lap record over 100mph: 102·84mph (165·56kph).

Jaguar won in 1951 and 1953, while the 1952 race saw Mercedes-Benz in 1st and 2nd positions. In the latter event Pierre Levegh led the race driving his Talbot single handed until 1¼ hours from the finish when he made a mistake through sheer fatigue. One result of this was the introduction of regulations restricting the time that any one driver might be at the wheel: 18 hours in 1953, 60 consecutive laps since 1960.

In the 1955 race, Levegh's Mercedes-Benz 300SLR

hit an Austin-Healey in his 42nd lap, and was deflected into the crowd opposite the pits. Levegh and over eighty spectators died in motor racing's worst disaster which had far-reaching repercussions on the sport all over Europe.

As a result the regulations were overhauled for 1956: prototypes were restricted to 2·5 litres, fuel consumption restrained by maximum tank sizes and minimum distances between refuelling, and unrealistic bodies ruled out. In the following year the fuel consumption and capacity restrictions were lifted (and the race thereby restored to Championship status).

In 1959 a new competition was introduced, roughly of the same standing as the Index of Performance. This Index of Thermal Efficiency (*Indice au rendement energétique*) took into account average speed, weight and fuel consumption, the actual formula used to determine placings varying from year to year. The basic

formula is: $Ir = \dfrac{Em}{Er}$, where Er is the fuel consumption

and Em has been obtained from a varying formula, e.g:

$$Em = 1\cdot5 + \frac{(P+1)V^3}{4 \times 105} \text{ (in 1962)}, \quad Em = \frac{P \times V^3}{2 \times 10^5} \text{ (in 1966)},$$

V being the average speed, and P the weight of the car.

Le Mans: start of the first 24-Hour Race, 1923. Two Excelsiors and a Lorraine leading. *Photo: Autocar*

Far left, Le Mans: Ravel, Rolland-Pilain and SARA between Arnage and La Maison Neuve, 1926. *Photo: Autocar*

Left, Le Mans: Barnato and Birkin's leading Speed Six Bentley in 1929. *Photo: David Hodges Collection*

In 1959 it went, as did the Index, to a 745cc DB, but thereafter by no means predictably to small cars.

Another innovation in 1959 was a spring test weekend for entrants (then in conjunction with a motorcycle meeting). Most of the leading teams have taken advantage of this, for in theory it means that only fine modifications should be necessary during official practice (normally on Wednesday and Thursday before the race weekend). Rather belated recognition of the dangers inherent in mixing cars with vastly different speeds in the same race came with the imposition of a minimum engine size of 1 litre in 1964. Further to this, minimum lap times have to be achieved in practice.

In the early 1960s there was little outright challenge to Ferrari—fierce but fragile Maseratis, Jaguars and Aston Martins which basically were ageing, and perhaps Porsche. So Ferrari won, in 1960, 1961, 1963 and 1964. This, of course, was not the whole story: the capacity limit was lifted for GT cars in 1960, and this meant that American cars appeared again (Corvettes in that year); the capacity limit for experimental cars (by ACO definition) was lifted in 1962; a gas turbine car (Rover-BRM) ran with the others in 1963 and raced against them in 1965, when it was classified 10th; the Index of Performance went to DB in 1960-1, and to Panhard in 1962, but to the overall winning Ferraris in 1963-4; the Thermal Efficiency award went to Lotus in 1960 and 1962, Sunbeam in 1961, Bonnet in 1963 and Alpine in 1964; in 1964 a 2-litre car (Porsche 904) lapped the Le Mans circuit in under four minutes for the first time.

However, 1964 was a significant year: Ford GT40s, conceived by the American company for this race above all, made their Le Mans debut. It ended in failure, and the Cobra victory in the GT category can have been little compensation. A massive Ford effort failed in 1965, and so did the Ferrari works team; three works-backed (rather than purely private) Ferraris took the leading places.

Ford achieved their objective in 1966, when McLaren/Amon and Hulme/Miles in a Mk 2 tied for first place; covering 3,009·30 miles (4,842·50km) at 125·38mph (201·79kph)—three milestones passed in one race. Fords won again in 1967, 1968 and 1969.

New international regulations, French-influenced and therefore ACO-influenced, ruled out sports cars (Group 4) with engines over 5 litres in 1968, and restricted prototypes (Group 6) to 3 litres. Although at Le Mans there were, therefore, French entries (in the latter category) which on paper were outright winners, for the first time in nearly two decades, Porsche came to the race as favourites, and their principal opposition was the Gulf-

Top, Le Mans: the winning Alfa Romeo (Birkin/Howe) followed by BNC, MG and Bentley, 1931. *Photo: David Hodges Collection*

Above, Le Mans: the start in 1939; Dobson's Lagonda V-12 is just pulling away, with Heldé's Darracq on the left, and another Lagonda behind. *Photo: Motor*

Below, Le Mans: the start in 1949; Aston Martin leading, followed by two Ferraris. *Photo: Motor*

Below right, Le Mans: although almost at the exit of the Esses, Fangio still has the air-brake of his Mercedes-Benz 300SLR raised; 1955. *Photo: Louis Klementaski*

sponsored JWA team of GT40s. Because of mid-summer political preoccupations, the 24-hour race was run at the end of September. The German team's 908s proved mechanically fragile. A semi-works 907 was the best-placed Porsche, 2nd behind the sole GT40 to run the distance—Rodriguez and Bianchi, 2,727·02 miles at 115·29mph (185·54kph).

The 1969 race saw the last 'Le Mans start' as such, for in order that all drivers should start with safety harness done up, in 1970 cars were lined up in echelon in front of the pits, with drivers in their cockpits, so that they simply had to switch on their engines as the flag dropped. The start lacked drama, the race lacked excitement, save that

Porsche at last achieved their outright win (Herrmann and Attwood in a 917, 2,863·15 miles), and won the Indexes of Performance and Thermal Efficiency, and the GT category. Although 16 cars were running at the finish, 9 were eliminated as they failed to complete the minimum distance set, for the ACO distance formula took account only of capacity, not of category:

$$D_1 = 4400 \times \frac{C - 200}{C + 150}$$

In this D_1 is the distance to be covered, and C is engine capacity. Lap record: Vic Elford (Porsche 917); 149·89mph (241·235kph); 3min 21·05sec; 1970. DWH

Levin Circuit

The Levin circuit some 50 miles (80km) north of Wellington, New Zealand's capital city, was conceived by R. W. A. Frost, a notable Formula 3 and motorcycle racing exponent in Britain before he settled in New Zealand. Opened in 1956, the original circuit was one mile (1·609km) in length but was subsequently extended to 1·2 miles (1·931km). It is laid out inside a horse-racing track and spectator amenities include covered grandstands and elevated terraces. The circuit is roughly kidney-shaped, the main start-finish straight being comparatively short. Minimum width is 30ft (9·144m). It was an ideal circuit for the motorcycle-engined Coopers and their variants in the late 1950s, and soon became one of the most popular clubman circuits in the country. Chris Amon, Denis Hulme, Bruce McLaren,

Left, Le Mans: Ford GT40s finish 1, 2, 3 in 1966, the McLaren/Amon car in the lead. *Photo: Motor*

Right, Le Mans: the Le Mans start, introduced in 1925 and discontinued after 1969. This is the 1967 start. *Photo: David Hodges Collection*

Le Mans 24-Hour Race Circuit

John Surtees of Team Lotus. Bonnier (Lotus-Climax) won the feature event from Clark. Since then an international race has been run annually. The inaugural Tasman Championship race was run at the circuit in 1964 and won by Hulme. Except for 1966, Levin has been included in the Tasman series every year since then. Lap record: Jochen Rindt (Lotus-Ford 49T); 93·77mph (150·97kph); 45·3sec; 1969. PG

Liège—Rome—Liège Rally see Marathon de la Route

Liège—Sofia—Liège Rally see Marathon de la Route

Limbourg GP see Zolder Circuit

Lime Rock Park Circuit

A rolling 1·53-mile (2·462km) road course in the Connecticut hamlet of Lime Rock, overlooking the Berkshire Hills, 110 miles (176km) north of New York City. Opened in 1957, Lime Rock became famous in July 1959 when the Indianapolis veteran, Rodger Ward, drove his oval-track, Offenhauser-powered midget to victory over George Constantine's Aston Martin DBR-2. Unlike the great majority of United States circuits, racing at Lime Rock is held on Saturdays, as legal action by local residents bans Sunday events. Lime Rock is the site of Trans-Am and Formula A Continental races. Lap record: David Hobbs (Surtees TS-5A); 108·42mph (174·48kph); 50·8sec; 1970 ARB

Levin Circuit

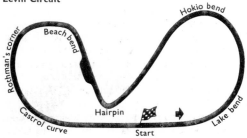

Lime Rock Park Circuit

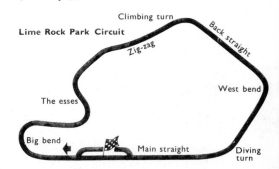

the 1970 Tasman champion Graeme Lawrence and the well-known Formula 5000 driver Graham McRae did much of their early racing at Levin. The first international meeting in 1961 attracted the Yeoman Credit team of Jo Bonnier and Roy Salvadori, as well as Jim Clark and

London to Mexico Rally see World Cup Rally

London to Sydney Marathon

The London to Sydney Marathon, co-sponsored by the London *Daily Express* and the Sydney *Daily Telegraph*, was a pioneer in a type of rally which may turn out to be the event of the future. Just as modern racing and rallying sprang out of the great European town-to-town races like the Paris–Madrid, it seems likely that if the classic rallies cannot survive on the crowded roads of Europe, then long-distance marathon events may take the high-speed driving into the less inhabited parts of the world.

The basic plan of the London-Sydney was simple: to have the competitors drive from London to Sydney through Europe, Asia and Australia. Once it was clear that works teams were interested and that many private entrants would find sponsorship for such an expensive trip, the organizers decided to include some more difficult sections so that a proper classification would be easily obtained.

The rally started from London in late November and went through easy sections to Turkey, where on the first difficult section of some three hours, the works Lotus Cortina of Roger Clark and Ove Andersson took the lead from the works BMC 1800s, Porsches and Citroëns. After another shorter difficult section in Afghanistan, the Ford still held the lead and received all the publicity during the crossing from Bombay to Perth by boat.

Results of the London to Sydney Marathon

1	Andrew Cowan	Hillman Hunter
2	Paddy Hopkirk	BMC 1800
3	Ian Vaughan	Ford Falcon
4	Sobieslaw Zasada	Porsche 911 S
5	Rauno Aaltonen	BMC 1800
6	Brian Hodgson	Ford Falcon

Below, London–Sydney Marathon: Andrew Cowan's winning Hillman Hunter in the Khyber Pass. Photo: Daily Express

Bottom, London–Sydney Marathon: A. Ipatsenko's Moskvitch 408 passing through an Afghan village. Photo: Daily Express

In Australia, the leading Ford ran into engine trouble and Lucien Bianchi and Jean-Claude Ogier took the lead with a Citroën DS 21, but they were hard pressed by Simo Lampinen and Gilbert Staepelaere in a Ford Taunus 20 MRS entered by Ford of Germany. Just before the end of the rally, both these cars were involved in accidents and the works-entered Hillman Hunter of Andrew Cowan, Colin Malkin and Brian Coyle found that after a steady rally they were the winners. The biggest talking point for this event had been the choice of two or three-man crews: whereas the rally leaders for most of the way had been two-man crews, the ultimate winners and the 2nd-place crew, Paddy Hopkirk, Tony Nash and Alec Poole (BMC 1800), both had three men in the car.

A good proportion of the starters reached the finish for most of the going had been relatively easy. However, 10,000 miles in a car is a long way and the 57 cars who finished from almost 100 starters attracted a lot of publicity and paved the way for more comprehensive events in the future. JD

Louis Rosier Circuit see Clermont-Ferrand Circuit

Lourenço Marques Circuit
The Portuguese overseas province of Mozambique has seen international motor racing at the Lourenço Marques circuit, just two miles outside the city. The course is 2·1 miles (3·38km) in length and based on public roads, the main 800m-long straight being formed from a section of the coast road heading north. The circuit's return loop was very slow, running through a number of tight corners, while breaks in the sand dunes along the main straight fostered gusty cross-winds which could cause problems for the faster cars. The first Lourenço Marques 3-Hour race was held in 1966 as part of the Springbok series of sports and GT events, and was won by the Serrurier and Pierpoint Lola-Ford T70.

In July 1967 seven spectators were killed and seven badly injured when Botha's Brabham crashed during a minor meeting, but racing continued with few extra safety measures. Hawkins' Lola-Chevrolet T70 GT won the 3-Hour that year, followed by the Guthrie and Hailwood Mirage in 1968 and De Udy and Gardner's Lola GT in 1969. Organization is in the hands of the Touring Automobile Club of Mozambique. DCN

Lwów Circuit
Although hill-climbs had been held in the country for many years, Poland did not have a road circuit until 1930, when the Lwów Grand Prix was first held. This took place on the streets of the town, a 1·865-mile (3·045km) course involving narrow roads, sharp corners, and slippery basalt blocks which led to many accidents. The race was held for only four years, and each year the number of laps was increased so that whereas the 1930 distance was only 32 miles (51·50km), by 1933 it was 189 miles (304·2km). The first Grand Prix was won by the Polish champion Henryk Liefeldt in an Austro-Daimler at a speed of 50·53mph (81·82kph); the sports car race went to Tadeus Skolimowski on an Alfa-Romeo at 47·125mph (75·84kph). Hans Stuck won in 1931 on an SSK Mercedes-Benz at 48·55mph (78-12kph) from two Bugattis and a 1·5-litre Wikov, the latter being a remarkable performance considering that it was virtually a stock sports car running in the racing car class. The 1931 sports car event was won by Georgeu Nadu on a Bugatti.

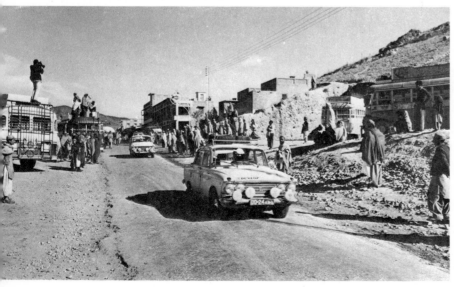

Lwów Circuit

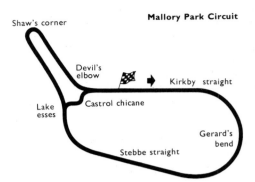

Mallory Park Circuit

In 1932 and 1933 a voiturette race for cars of up to 1·5-litres was held alongside the Grand Prix, winners being L. Hartmann and P. Veyron respectively, both on Bugattis. The last two Grands Prix were won by Caracciola and E. Björnstadt, both on Alfa Romeos.

The organizing club, the Malopolski Klub Automobilowy of Lwów, had constant financial difficulties in arranging the races, which lapsed after 1933. Less important races took place in Poznan and Krakow, but the Lwów GP remains the only internationally famous motor race held in Poland. Since 1945 Lwów (Lvov) has been part of the Soviet Union. VH

Lyons–Charbonnières Rally

The full title of this rally today is the Lyons-Charbonnières/Stuttgart-Solitude Rally for in 1961 the two rallies of the title were amalgamated and run as one. This was mainly because the Germans did not have a rally that was competitive enough to qualify for the European Championship for the simple reason that the German police did not allow them to set a high enough average speed. The most selective aspect of the Solitude Rally, first held in 1953, was the test at the Solitude circuit just outside Stuttgart. By combining with the Lyons-Charbonnières, which had been held first in 1949, it was possible to use French territory where the police were more helpful. Since 1961, the rally has comprised a test at Solitude followed by a series of hill-climbs and selective sections in the French hills terminating at the casino of Charbonnières. JD

Winners of the Lyons–Charbonnières Rally

1961	Oreiller	Alfa Romeo Zagato
1962	Oreiller	Ferrari
1963	Trautmann	Citröen
1964	Trautmann	Lancia Flavia
1965	Vinatier	Renault Gordini
1966	Hanrioud	Alpine Renault
1967	Elford	Porsche 911 S
1968	Andruet	Alpine-Renault
1969	Vinatier	Alpine-Renault
1970	Andruet	Alpine-Renault
1971	Nicolas	Alpine-Renault

Mallory Park: start of a Formule Libre race, 1960. In front row, three Cooper-Climaxes and a Lola-Climax. *Photo: Michael Ware*

Mallory Park Circuit

The pretty Leicestershire village of Kirkby Mallory is about 9¾ miles (15·3km) from Leicester, and shortly after World War 2 a pony-trotting track was laid out in a bowl-like valley which forms the grounds of the local Hall. Trotting did not catch on with the British public, and the Leicester Query Club rented the site for grass-track motorcycle racing on the egg-shaped course. In 1954 the ACU National Grass Track Championship was held there, and about that time Mallory Park was bought by Clive Wormleighton, a builder from nearby Earl Shilton.

The grass track was 1,660yd (1,517·9m) long, and in 1955 the solo motorcycle standing start record was 71·35mph (114·83kph), and side-cars 66·16mph (106·48kph). Wormleighton and Mr J. E. Shaw of the Leicester Club surfaced the course, adding a loop which ran up beside the old stable buildings of the Hall almost into the village, and the resulting 1·35-mile (2·172km) road circuit was opened on 25 April 1956. Really good viewing was provided by the hillside flanking the bottom straight, and lakes, which had been drained when the trotting track was built, were restored for water-sport and for landscaping.

Since then the BRSCC, Nottingham SCC and several other clubs have run many very successful club and international meetings at the Park, and it has also been used extensively for motorcycle races. It has become something of a home for Formule Libre with the Bob Gerard Championship for the class being held there, and in recent years has known some excellent sports and F3 racing. In 1962 the International 2000 Guineas F1 race was won by Surtees in a Bowmaker Lola at 93·38mph (150·28kph), and in 1963 Amon scored a rare win for his Parnell Lola in an FL event there. Rindt astonished the F2 circus with his performance at Whitsun 1964, and this tight but surprisingly quick little course became a 100mph (160kph) circuit in the late 1960s. A club circuit has been evolved by using a short link road between the lake S-bends and the foot of Devil's Elbow. The course is one of the best spectator venues in the country. Lap record: Peter Gethin (McLaren M1OB); 113·55mph (182·74kph); 42·8sec; 1970. DCN

Mannin Beg *and* Mannin Moar *see* Douglas

Marathon de la Route

The rally organized by the Royal Motor Union of Liège under the title of the Marathon of the Roads is recognized by all rally drivers as being *the* classic event. During the 1950s and the early 1960s it was the epitome of all that is tough and arduous in rallying, both for the car and the crew. The last time that it was run as a road event was in 1964, but its tradition lives on in an 84hr regularity race held each year at the Nürburgring.

The Marathon de la Route was first held as the Liège-Rome-Liège in 1931 over a route of 2,800 miles which started in Liège and went through western Germany and Austria to the Brenner Pass, through the Dolomites and then down over the Apennine chain to Rome, returning to Liège via the French Alps. The main features of the rally which made it different from the others were the fact that it was run practically non-stop, and that the overall average speed was about 32mph (51kph). In 1931, 21 cars started and 12 finished and that was probably the highest proportion of finishers that the event ever had. An overall winner was announced, but the classification was primarily for classes and victory in the class depended on sticking closest to the average speeds set over the stretches of road for that class.

After World War 2, the Marathon was first held again in 1950 and it became immediately obvious to the organizers that cars had improved, for the best drivers got through the Dolomites without 'demerits', as the penalties used to be called. They decided to make it a bit harder and by 1952 the total distance had gone up to 3,204 miles and speed tests were included on a number of passes, among them the infamous Stelvio in Italy and the Cols of Vars and Galibier in France. Whereas 58 out of 128 had finished the year before when Johnny Claes had won with a Jaguar, only 24 of the 116 starters were classified in 1952. The organizers' idea was to keep increasing the toughness of their event, and once M. Garot, the Clerk of the Course, stated that the ideal Marathon should just have one finisher. In 1953, the average speeds on some of the passes had gone up to almost 40mph (64kph) and again it was a victory for Johnny Claes, this time in a Lancia Aurelia, who drove the last 1,700 miles single-handed when his co-driver, Traesenster, fell ill.

As the 1950s went on and names such as Gendebien, Strahle and Mairesse headed the prize lists, it became clear that running such a high speed endurance event on the roads of Europe was not easy, and even by 1955, Austria was insisting that the average speed on sections there be kept to 25mph (40kph). Italy insisted that 31mph (50kph) be the highest average in the Apennines, but left the Dolomites free of speed restrictions. After Pat Moss won the rally in 1960, the organizers announced that the rally was now going to be called the Liège-Sofia-Liège. This came as no shock as for the last few years the event had gone into Yugoslavia as far as Zagreb in search of new freedoms, and now it was to use all of Yugoslavia and part of Bulgaria. Four classic events came out of this new formula, but eventually in 1965 even the Yugoslavs cried enough and the Marathon went to its present home at the Nürburgring.

As a road event, the Marathon may be dead but it will always be remembered as the toughest of them all: an event where to finish was an achievement in itself, and where the organizers were so confident that their course was a full test of man and machine that they allowed any modification at all to the car, and never had to resort to coefficients or driving tests to find the winner. JD

Marne GP see Reims Circuit

Masaryk GP see Brno Circuit

Mediterranean GP see Enna Circuit

Melbourne Motordrome
The history of the Motordrome, which stood on the site

Winners of the Marathon de la Route

Year	Winner	Car
1931	Toussaint	Bugatti
1932	Orban	Bugatti
1933	Georges	F.N.
	Von Guillaume	Adler
1934	Evrard	Bugatti
	Peeters	Bugatti
	Lahaye	Renault
	Bahr	Imperia
	Van Naemen	Lancia
	Thirion	Bugatti
	Bernet	Mercedes-Benz
1935	Trasenster	Bugatti
	Lahaye	Renault
1937	Haeberle	Hanomag
1938	Trasenster	Bugatti
1939	Trasenster	Bugatti
	Trevoux	Hotchkiss
1950	Dubois	Peugeot
1951	Claes	Jaguar
1952	Polensky	Porsche
1953	Claes	Lancia
1954	Polensky	Porsche
1955	Gendebien	Mercedes-Benz
1956	Mairesse	Mercedes-Benz
1957	Storez	Porsche
1958	Hebert	Alfa Romeo
1959	Buchet	Porsche Carrera
1960	Moss	Austin-Healey
1961	Bianchi	Citröen
1962	Bohringer	Mercedes-Benz
1963	Bohringer	Mercedes-Benz
1964	Aaltonen	Austin-Healey

Nürburgring 84 Hours

Year	Winner	Car
1965	Greder	Ford Mustang
1966	Vernaeve	MG B
1967	Herrmann	Porsche
1968	Linge	Porsche
1969	Fall	Lancia
1970	Stuck Jr/ Schickenstanz	BMW

now occupied by Melbourne's Olympic Park, dates back to the mid-1920s. When first opened, the Motordrome consisted on a 586yd (536m) concrete bowl some 63ft (20·7m) in width. The original 'Prince' design called for two further additions of 60ft (18·3m) to the edge of the bowl giving it a vertical wall. These additions were never made because it was felt the cars and motorcycles would never stay on the circuit.

The Motordrome was Melbourne's premier racing car venue, where such historic makes as Amilcar, Bugatti and Bullard competed regularly. Motorcycle races were also featuring Douglas, AJS, Norton and Imperial marques—and Louis Geisler a World Champion cyclist, raced on the bowl. However, the death toll rose alarmingly with the higher speeds and the concrete bowl had its last race in 1934.

The Motordrome was, in that year, made into a 586yd speedway oval with a special gravel surface. Motorcycle racing dominated the new oval until 1936 when the first midget speedway racing cars became popular. 'World Derby' races in the late 1930s attracted crowds of over 40,000 to watch international drivers as Paul Swedberg (America) Paul Simmonds and Bill Reynolds (Britain) race against Australian drivers. For most part, the speedway cars were powered by twin motorcycle engines, only moving up to 4-cylinder in-line units at the end of the decade. Paul Swedberg introduced the first Offenhauser to Australia in 1939 at the Motordrome.

World War 2 was responsible for closing the Motordrome in 1940, and it was demolished when work started on the Olympic Park complex for the 1956 Olympic Games. TBF

Mexican GP see below

Mexico, Autodromo de la Ciudad de
The flat, 3·2-mile (5·150km) Grand Prix circuit within the municipal sports park on the eastern edge of Mexico City is distinguished by private garages in the rear of the pits and an almost total lack of crowd control. First run in 1962, the Gran Premio de Mexico has become the final round in the World Championship for Drivers.

Although Mexico City's 7,500ft (2,286m) altitude, coupled with track temperatures often above 100°F (38°C), results in special engine tuning problems, the hospitality of the host automobile club, RODA, makes the Mexican GP popular with participants.

Beginning in 1971, the circuit is to be known as Autodromo Ricardo Rodriguez, after the young Mexico City driver who lost his life during practice for the 1962 GP.

Autodromo dela Ciudad de Mexico

Start

111

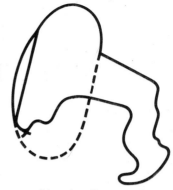

MIS, a part of American Raceways Inc., owners of Texas International Speedway and part owners of Atlanta and Riverside Raceways, was reorganized in 1970. Lap record (3·31 mile road circuit): Denis Hulme (McLaren-Chevrolet); 112·382mph (180·833kph); 1min 36·1sec; 1969. ARB

Mid-Ohio Sports Car Course

Opened in 1962, this tight, rolling 2·4-mile (3·862km) circuit is near Lexington, 50 miles (80km) from Columbus, Ohio. Continental Championship, Trans-Am Sedan and Can-Am races are held here. In September 1970 George Follmer's Lotus 70-Ford won the 42 lap, 100·8 mile (161·06km) Formula A/Continental in 1hr 28·6min for a record 97·52mph average. Lap record: Chris Amon (Ferrari 612); 100mph (166·9kph); 1min 26·4sec; 1969. ARB

Lap record: Jacky Ickx (Brabham-Ford); 108·54mph (174·68kph); 1min 43·05sec; 1969. Ickx won the 1970 Mexican GP with a record average speed of 106·780mph, driving a Ferrari 312B. However his 1970 fastest lap, 108·491mph, just missed setting a new mark. ARB

Top, Mexico: Bandini's 12-cylinder Ferrari, 1964. *Photo: Bernard Cahier*

Above, Mexico: 1967 Mexican GP. *Photo: Doug Nye Collection*

Michigan International Speedway

Located 65 miles (104km) west of Detroit, in Irish Hills near Jackson, Mich., MIS combines a 2-mile (3·219kph) banked oval and a 3·31-mile (5·327km) road course.

The oval opened in October 1968 with the 250-mile United States Auto Club national championship won by Ronnie Bucknum, 161·812mph (260·423kph) being the race average. The fastest qualifier was Mario Andretti at 183·720mph (295·630kph).

Following the 1969 Trans-Am and Can-Am over the MIS road course, in January 1970 ARI announced it was dropping road races to concentrate on stock and Indianapolis championship cars.

Mille Miglia

When the French inaugurated the Le Mans 24-Hours race for sports cars in 1923 they started more than a classic long-distance race, for it fired the imagination of a group of Italians who sought to run an even bigger and better event. These were Aymo Maggi, Franco Mazzotti, Giovanni Canestrini and Renzo Castagneto, the last named being the secretary of the Brescia Automobile Club, in northern Italy. Their plan was to run an event on the normal public roads, from Brescia to Rome and back, in the form of a figure-of-eight with the crossing point at Bologna over a distance of approximately 1,600 kilometres, equal to one thousand old Roman miles, or *miglia*, hence the title of the race, the Mille Miglia. It was an audacious project calling for the assistance of automobile clubs throughout the country, the police, the military and indeed the government. The plan reached fruition with enthusiasm and the first event took place on the 26/27 March 1927, the route running anti-clockwise, covering every type of road imaginable, including mountain passes. The winners were Minoia and Morandi with an OM car, built in Brescia. This was a return to the town-to-town races that flourished at the turn of the century, and the race was run on a time basis with competitors starting at intervals and being clocked at various points around the course, the start and finish being in the centre of Brescia.

Winners of the Mille Miglia

Year	Drivers	Car
1927	Minoia and Morandi	OM
1928	Campari and Ramponi	Alfa Romeo
1929	Campari and Ramponi	Alfa Romeo
1930	Nuvolari and Guidotti	Alfa Romeo
1931	Caracciola and Sebastian	Mercedes-Benz
1932	Borzacchini and Bignami	Alfa Romeo
1933	Nuvolari and Compagnoni	Alfa Romeo
1934	Varzi and Bignami	Alfa Romeo
1935	Pintacuda and della Stufa	Alfa Romeo
1936	Brivio and Ongaro	Alfa Romeo
1937	Pintacuda and Mambelli	Alfa Romeo
1938	Biondetti and Stefani	Alfa Romeo
1940	von Hanstein and Baumer	BMW
1947	Biondetti and Romano	Alfa Romeo
1948	Biondetti and Navoni	Ferrari
1949	Biondetti and Salani	Ferrari
1950	Marzotto and Crosara	Ferrari
1951	Villoresi and Cassani	Ferrari
1952	Bracco and Rolfo	Ferrari
1953	Marzotto and Crosara	Ferrari
1954	Ascari	Lancia
1955	Moss and Jenkinson	Mercedes-Benz
1956	Castelotti	Ferrari
1957	Taruffi	Ferrari

The race was held annually and its following grew strong, but mostly from Italian firms for it was such a specialized event that competing was a formidable task for anyone not living in Italy. In 1931 Mercedes-Benz broke the Italian hold when Caracciola and Sebastian won with an SSK, but after that Italian drivers and Alfa Romeo got a firm grip on the race once more. Each year the route was more or less the same, with minor deviations, running from Brescia to Bologna, over the mountains to Florence, down to Rome, across the Abruzzi Mountains to Ancona on the Adriatic coast, up to Rimini, inland to Bologna once more and then back to Brescia via Padua and Vicenza. In 1938 the southern loop of the route was altered considerably, turning to the Mediterranean coast from Florence and then follow-

Mille Miglia Circuit

Secondary paved roads
Main roads
Mountain passes and poor roads

Above right, Mille Miglia: Mario Tadini (Alfa Romeo) in 1934. *Photo: Motor*

Below left, Mille Miglia: Luigi Arcangeli (Maserati) in the 1929 event. *Photo: Cyril Posthumus Collection*

Mille Miglia: Antonio Brivio (Alfa Romeo 8C 2900A), winner of the 1936 event. *Photo: David Hodges Collection*

ing the coast road down to Rome. That year the Alfa Romeo string of successes was continued with Biondetti and Stefani winning with a 2·9-litre Tipo B, but the race was marred by a serious accident in which a car went off the road and killed a number of spectators. This caused a certain amount of Government opposition to the race so that it was not held in 1939, and then the European war began. Italy continued to organize motor racing and in 1940 the Brescia club held a race on a triangular circuit from Brescia to Cremona, across to Mantua and back to Brescia; though it was called the Brescia GP it was subtitled the 13th Mille Miglia to keep the old classic race alive.

Held on 28 April 1940 it was the last in the series until after the war, when the real Mille Miglia was revived in all its former glory on 21/22 June 1947, this time running clockwise more or less on the 1938 route, with the addition of an extension to Turin and back across Milan to Brescia. It covered 1,118·5 miles (1,800km) and was the longest route used throughout the series and once again Biondetti was the winner with the same type of Alfa Romeo he had used in 1938. He lived on the route, just north of Florence, and made the race his speciality, winning again in 1948 and 1949, in these two years with the new Ferrari cars. In 1949 the race was run anti-clockwise once more, and cut out Bologna, going over the Appenines to La Spezia, down the coast to Rome, across the Abruzzi to Pescara and up the Adriatic coast

Above, Mille Miglia: Umberto Maglioli about to start in 1954 in a Ferrari 375 Plus. The car's number indicates a starting time of 5.45am. *Photo: Cyril Posthumus Collection*

Right, Mille Miglia: Stirling Moss and Denis Jenkinson (Mercedes-Benz 300SLR), winners in 1955. *Photo: David Hodges Collection*

Below, Mille Miglia: Piero Taruffi (Ferrari 315MM), winner of the 1957 event, on the Futa Pass. *Photo: Yves Debraine*

and back by way of Ravenna and Padua. It was in this year that the system of numbering the cars according to their starting time was inaugurated, i.e. 001 started at 1 minute past midnight and the last car 649, started at 06 49 which made it simple for anyone around the route to know the progress of the race.

Enthusiasm ran high for the race, and in 1950 there was an all-time record entry of 743, with many other nationalities joining in, including British Jaguars, though smaller British firms had entered in the numerous categories for many years, back to Austin in 1931. In 1950 the route was run clockwise and it remained that way until the final race in 1957, and in 1952 it settled to the route Brescia, Rimini, Pescara, Rome, Siena, Florence, Bologna, Piacenza, Brescia. In 1952 Mercedes-Benz made a concerted attack once again, Kling and Klenk finishing 2nd with a 300SL, and in 1955 they attacked the Ferrari, Lancia, Alfa Romeo, Maserati stronghold once more, Moss and Jenkinson winning with a 300SLR, their winning average speed of 97·897mph (157·550kph) being an all-time record.

In 1957 disaster struck the race when the Marquis de Portago and Edward Nelson crashed into the spectators, killing themselves and eleven others. By this time traffic congestion in Italy had grown enormously and it had become difficult to close the roads for the race, the resultant confusion causing a lot of opposition. This accident was the last straw, and the Government banned the race. Piero Taruffi (Ferrari) won the last race, and in 1958 a regularity rally was held around Brescia and called the Mille Miglia. In 1959 it expanded a little and included some timed sections, but the Mille Miglia was dead, never to be revived, the last true race in the series being the 1957 event. It was the end of an heroic chapter in the history of motor racing. DSJ

Modena Circuit

Before World War 2 the Automobile Club of Modena held races on a circuit that ran round the park in the centre of the town. These started in 1927 and continued up to 1938, but they were very much of a local nature that did not develop much above national status, although some of the great names in Italian racing made their mark there, among them Fagioli, Nuvolari, Trossi and Cortese. During the war a military airfield was built on the edge of the town, and in 1950 the Automobile Club of Modena re-instated the Modena GP with a Formula 1 race, won by Alberto Ascari (Ferrari) in 2hrs 47min 31·8sec at an average speed of 67·65mph (108·875kph), on a circuit combining the airfield perimeter track and the single central runway, with a lap time of just under 2 minutes. This was continued in 1951 and again Ascari won with a Ferrari.

For the next two years the course was shortened by deleting the loop that went down one side of the runway and back up the other, making the circuit roughly a rectangular shape with one corner radiused off. This increased the race average from 72·267mph (116·302kph) in 1951 to 77·209mph (124·256kph) in 1952, when Luigi Villoresi won in a Ferrari. In 1953 Fangio won for Maserati, and then there was a interval in the history of the Modena GP until 1957. By this time the 1·47-mile (2·366km) perimeter-track circuit, run anti-clockwise and incorporating an artificial S-bend at the end of the pits straight, had become known as the Aeroautodromo di Modena and was used continuously for testing by Ferrari and Maserati, for local club events, and for motorcycle racing.

In 1957 the Grand Prix was started again, Jean Behra winning for Maserati, against strong Ferrari opposition, and the average speed was up to 81·09mph (130·503kph) with the lap record down to 1min 02·2sec. This was a difficult time in Italian racing history, with new and stringent government laws being passed and the Grand Prix of Modena did not take place again until 1960, when it was run as a 1·5-litre Formula 2 race, Bonnier winning for Porsche and beating Ferrari on their home ground, with a lap record shared with von Trips (Ferrari) in 58·1sec. The 7th and last Modena GP was held in 1961, for the new 1·5-litre Grand Prix cars, when Stirling Moss won with a Lotus-Climax.

During its use as a test circuit the Modena Aeroautodromo has seen a great deal of activity and some unfortunate accidents. Eugenio Castellotti lost his life when he crashed at the S-bends in a Lancia-Ferrari in 1957, and Giulio Cabianca was killed when he crashed through a gateway onto the main road. Since the last race the circuit has been used for club events, such as local saloon and sports car races, gymkhanas and driving tests, as well as motorcycle races. With the rapid post-war expansion of the city of Modena the airfield is now in the centre of a built-up area, but it is still the focal point for Modenese racing enthusiasts, and test-lap records are down to about 50 seconds for the flat perimeter-track circuit. DSJ

Monaco Circuit; Monaco Grand Prix

This most durable of all round-the-house circuits was conceived in 1928 by Antony Noghès and first used, for the first Monaco GP, in the following year. It owes its origins to the aspirations of the Automobile Club de Monaco, for only by running a race of front-line status on Principality soil could its claim to be a national, rather than provincial French, club be sustained. So Noghès devised a street circuit, which has survived periods of change in racing which have seen others come, and usually go. It has remained virtually unaltered since 1929: in this, too, it is now unique among championship circuits.

The pits are beneath trees between a harbour-side promenade and an everyday road. From the start-line the 1·95 mile (3·145km) circuit curves gently right into the fairly fast Ste Dévote right-hand corner. This is followed by the 1 in 8·5 climb to the long Massenet corner, swinging left into the Place du Casino. Here the circuit turns right again, and over a brow which is a quite abrupt bump at racing speeds, begins its descent to sea-level past the best-known bars in Monte Carlo. This is followed by a series of slow corners and short linking stretches of varying gradients: upper Mirabeau

Left, Modena: start of the 1957 Modena F2 GP: left to right — Schell (Maserati) Musso (Ferrari) and Behra (Maserati), the eventual winner. *Photo: Hans Tanner*

Right, Monaco: Nuvolari (Alfa Romeo) leading Varzi (Bugatti) through Station hairpin in 1933. *Photo: David Hodges Collection*

Monaco: start of the first Monaco GP, 1929. *Photo: David Hodges Collection*

(a 90° right-hander), Station (a hairpin), lower Mirabeau (similar to its upper counterpart). Now on the level, the circuit passes under the old railway bridge, and again turns right through 90° to a long gentle curve which continues through the famous 130yd (117m) tunnel. Through this drivers continue to accelerate into the fastest part of the circuit, until it straightens and dips to the chicane, where it leaves everyday roads for the *quais*. The first of these ends at the 25ft (7·6m) wide Tabac corner, only a few feet from and below Ste Dévote. A broader stretch of *quai* leads to the Gasholder hairpin; thence drivers accelerate past the pits.

These are rudimentary structures; their counters once faced the harbour, when the start-line was on the *quai* (it reverted to the parallel road after an inevitable first-lap accident at the Gasholder hairpin, in 1962). Since World War 2 the chicane has been as near to the tunnel as possible, and its angle and width have varied. Otherwise the circuit changed only when the tram (streetcar) tracks and cobblestones were lifted in 1932 (although landmarks such as the gasholders and station have disappeared).

Above all other circuits, Monaco demands absolute

concentration, and opportunities even to glance at instruments are few. It is also utterly demanding on machines, particularly transmissions and brakes.

In drama, Monaco races have often matched their setting. The first GP was won by 'Williams' (Bugatti T35B) at 49·83mph (80·2kph), and the 1930 and 1931 events also fell to Bugattis, in 1931 to a T51 driven by Monégasque Louis Chiron. In a works 8C Monza Alfa Romeo Nuvolari then ended the run of Bugatti successes, and in 1933 he fought out an intense duel with Varzi over virtually the whole race distance. Nuvolari led for 66 laps, Varzi for 34; both drivers over-revved on the 100th and last lap—Nuvolari's Monza engine blew up, the Bugatti engine held together and Varzi won.

In 1935 the Mercedes team ran at Monaco for the first time and one of their cars, Fagioli's, lasted to win. The 1936 race was run in the wet, and produced the first Monaco multiple pile-up, at the chicane. The last pre-war race was dominated by W125 Mercedes, and won by Brauchitsch after an internercine duel with Carraciola, who set a lap record of 1 min 46·5sec, 66·79mph (107·48kph), which was to stand for 18 years.

The Monaco GP was not run again until 1948, when Farina beat a mediocre field. The promise in the first-rate entry in 1950 was not fulfilled in the race, as eight cars were eliminated in a first-lap multiple accident at the Tabac corner. Grand Prix cars returned to the circuit five years later, when Mercedes suffered a rare defeat, when 1929 fears were at last realized and a car crashed into the harbour (Ascari's Lancia), and Trintignant won in an obsolescent Ferrari. Moss drove a Maserati 250F impeccably to win his first *grande épreuve* in the 1956 race, but in the following year he, Hawthorn and Collins were eliminated in a single accident at the chicane and Fangio won in a Maserati.

The 1958 Monaco GP was the occasion of the first *grande épreuve* appearance of Team Lotus, and the first European Championship race victory for a rear-engined

Left, Monaco: Graham Hill (BRM) leading the field up Beau Rivage hill, 1963. *Photo: David Hodges Collection*

Above, Monaco: the Tunnel. *Photo: David Hodges Collection*

Monaco Circuit

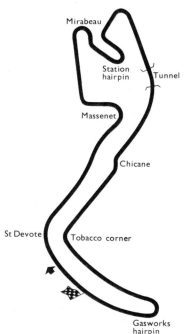

car since 1939 (Trintignant in Walker's Cooper). In 1959 Brabham won his first championship race in this race. Moss drove one of his greatest races to defeat the Ferrari team with an underpowered Lotus 18 in the 1961 GP, and in the following year McLaren gained for Cooper their only championship victory of the 1·5-litre Formula.

Graham Hill won in 1963, in 1964 and again in 1965, each time driving a BRM. The 1966 race, the first of the 3-litre Formula, also fell to a BRM, a 2-litre car driven by Stewart, ahead of only three other running cars. In 1967 Hulme's victory was overshadowed by the first fatal accident in the Grand Prix, when Bandini was trapped in his blazing Ferrari after clipping the curb in the chicane and crashing on the edge of the *quai*. The next two races fell to Graham Hill; in each he drove a Lotus 49B with untried mechanical novelties, in each he overcame these handicaps with tactical judgment and restraint—winning as slowly as possible. Nevertheless, in 1969 his winning speed was 80·18mph (129·04kph) for the first time.

The 1970 race was perhaps the most dramatic since 1933, lost, by Brabham, and won, by Rindt, at the last corner on the last lap, and notable for close racing further down the field. On the last lap Rindt broke the lap record and his speed for 80 laps was 81·84mph (131·70kph).

The only other races on this circuit have been supporting events at the Grand Prix meetings, since 1959 primarily for Formula Junior and Formula 3 cars. Lap record: Jochen Rindt (Lotus 49C); 84·56mph (136·09kph); 1min 23·1sec; 1970. DWH

Monte Carlo Rally
The Rallye Automobile Monte Carlo is one of the oldest and most famous of rallies. It was first held in 1911 when 23 intrepid crews left Paris, Berlin, Vienna or Brussels to drive down to Monaco in the middle of

January. The average speed required was 15mph (24kph) and they were allowed seven days for the journeys. The outright winner was Henri Rougier driving a Turcat Mery and so popular was his victory within France that the rally was run again the following year, when 87 competitors started from such places as Paris, Vienna, Berlin, Brussels, Geneva, Le Havre, Amsterdam, Boulogne, Turin and St Petersburg. The average speed required of the competitors remained the same and the winner was Beutler in a Berliet.

World War 1 then intervened but the idea of driving to the Riviera in the middle of winter had caught on and the rally began again in 1924. For the first time there was a starting point in the British Isles and the date was changed to March, but it was again a Frenchman, Jean Ledure at the wheel of a Bignan 2-litre saloon, who won the rally. The next year, the date reverted to January, where it has remained ever since, and for the first time bonus points were awarded for the more difficult starting points and a 50-mile (80km) mountain trial was instigated at the end of the event. This formula continued right through the remainder of the 1920s and into the heyday of the rally during the 1930s.

Originally, merely reaching Monaco from one of the starting points was test enough and it was not until 1931 that anyone got through from Athens, when Bignan made it with his Fiat. By the mid-1930s, however, cars were coming through unpenalized on the road sections, and even the mountain trial was not sufficient to determine the winner. Out of this situation grew the unsatisfactory method of deciding the winner by a 'wiggle-woggle' driving test. In 1936, for instance, Cristea and Zamfirescu won the rally by setting fastest time on this test in their Ford. In 1938, when no less than 61 of the 143 starters were unpenalized on the road section, Le Bègue, who had won the previous year in a Delahaye, lost the rally by making a technical error in the driving test.

World War 2 stopped the rally until 1949 and when it started again several things had changed. Firstly the number of entries was much greater — in 1953 it rose to a record 440 — and then the importance of the starting place was reduced almost to nothing by cancelling the start bonus and deciding the rally on a longer common route. There was also a tightening up of the regulations to prevent special cars and to restrict the rally to properly constructed touring cars. Perhaps most famous of the post-war competitors was Sydney Allard who won the rally in 1952 driving one of his own cars, a unique achievement.

Special stages had long been a part of the Monte Carlo but in 1961 came the factor of comparison and first three places that year went to Panhard who happened to have a production car which best suited the formula. The idea was to reduce the advantage of big powerful cars on the hill-climbs and stages and in that it was successful for a while, with Erik Carlsson in his 850cc Saab winning the rally in 1962 and 1963. By the end of 1965, in which year Timo Mäkinen earned everlasting fame by winning in a blizzard with a Mini Cooper, it became clear that the formula was not entirely satisfactory. After the 1966 event, when it gave a tremendous advantage to standard production cars and caused the great lighting controversy, it was dropped for good. The rally is at present run on a scratch basis with cars of all kinds competing on an equal basis.

The Monte Carlo may have fewer entries today by immediate post-war standards but because it has retained

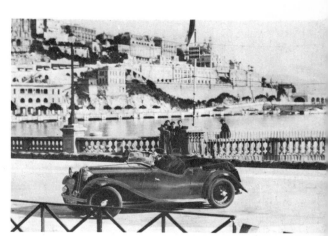

Monte Carlo Rally: S. H. Light (SS1) in the figure-of-eight test at the finish, 1934. *Photo: Autocar*

Monte Carlo Rally: Alfa Romeo and Dyna-Panhard, 1956. *Photo: Autosport*

Monte Carlo Rally: Michael Sutcliffe and Phil Crabtree (Ford Zephyr) in the Gorge de la Bourne, 1960. *Photo: Associated Press Ltd*

Monte Carlo Rally: Henri Greder and Jean Perramond (Opel GT 1900) in the Forêt de Lente, 1970. *Photo: Hugh W. Bishop*

its multiple starting points and its winter venue it is still high in public esteem as the senior rally of Europe and every year attracts the top rally teams and the associated publicity. JD

Monterey GP *see* Laguna Seca Raceway

Montjuich Circuit *see* Barcelona Circuits

Montlhéry Autodrome

Montlhéry Autodrome, conveniently situated on the Paris-Orléans main road about 15 miles (24km) from the capital, was completed in 1924, racing taking place there in October that year. The project was financed by M. Lamblin, a newspaper proprietor and owner of the radiator manufacturing company bearing his name. To this end he acquired a chateau and some 12,000 acres (5,000 hectares) of ground on which to build a banked speedway of concrete, like that at Brooklands in England but with a shorter lap distance and smoother but steeper bankings. Apart, however, from this banked autodrome, Montlhéry from the beginning had a series of road circuits, of varying distances, over which important long-distance races could be held.

The lap distance of the banked track, intended to be the fastest in the world, is 1·58 miles (2·5km) and under the two steep ferro-concrete bankings, connected by short straights, out of one of which the Paddock apron opens, lock-up garages were incorporated. Opening in October 1924 at a time when Brooklands was hampered by the newly-introduced silencer restrictions, Montlhéry got off to a good start, with such drivers as Parry Thomas and his Leyland Thomas, Ernest Eldridge and the giant chain-drive Fiat, Duray with a big 8-cylinder D'Aoust, various French small cars and a triumphant team of racing Austin Sevens taking part. From then on, Montlhéry was accepted as an important centre of speed. Innumerable records were attacked there, one advantage being that there were no noise restrictions to prevent night running. The first car to take a record on Montlhéry was a 2-litre 16-valve Bignan. Thereafter record bids came almost daily and many British drivers preferred Montlhéry to Brooklands for these attempts.

Four circuits were available at Montlhéry, embracing part of the banked track and two of road-course status, and if the entire road circuit and the banked section were used, the lap distance was a full 7·8 miles (12·553km). The first purely road circuit measured 4·7 miles (7·564km) to a lap, the second, from Les Biscornes to Deux Points corners, 5·7 miles (9·173km).

In the second season of activity at the Linas-Montlhéry track, its first full year of existence, the macadamized road course was used for a French Grand Prix, with part of the banked course having to be negotiated by the road-racing cars. The entire Montlhéry project is said to have cost the equivalent of £500,000 ($1,200,000), compared to the £150,000 ($360,000) which Brooklands involved, 17 years earlier.

Special arrangements were made to expedite traffic flowing from Paris to the Grand Prix, which covered a motorcycle race and a Touring Car Grand Prix in addition to the 621-mile (999·4km) Grand Prix proper, the competitors lapping the combined banking and artificial road circuit in a right-hand direction. The Grand Prix winner proved to be Robert Benoist's Delage, which averaged 69·7mph (112·17kph) to win from team-mate Wagner's Delage, watched by the President of the Republic. Montlhéry was well and truly established.

Winners of the Monte Carlo Rally

1911	Rougier (Paris)	*Turcat Mery*
1912	Beutler (Berlin)	*Berliet*
1924	Ledure (Glasgow)	*Bignan*
1925	Repusseau (Tunis)	*Renault*
1926	Bruce (John O'Groats)	*AC*
1927	Lefebvre-Despaux (Königsberg)	*Amilcar*
1928	Bignan (Bucharest)	*Fiat*
1929	Van Eijk (Stockholm)	*Graham-Paige*
1930	Petit (Jassy)	*Licorne*
1931	Healey (Stavanger)	*Invicta*
1932	Vasselle (Umea)	*Hotchkiss*
1933	Vasselle (Tallinn)	*Hotchkiss*
1934	Gas (Athens)	*Hotchkiss*
1935	La Haye (Stavanger)	*Renault*
1936	Zamfirescu (Athens)	*Ford*
1937	Le Begue (Stavanger)	*Delahaye*
1938	Bakker Schut (Athens)	*Ford*
1939	Paul (Athens)	*Delahaye*
	Trevoux	*Hotchkiss*
1949	Trevoux (Lisbon)	*Hotchkiss*
1950	Becquart (Lisbon)	*Hotchkiss*
1951	Trevoux (Lisbon)	*Delahaye*
1952	Allard (Glasgow)	*Allard*
1953	Gatsonides (Monte Carlo)	*Ford*
1954	Chiron (Monte Carlo)	*Lancia*
1955	Malling (Oslo)	*Sunbeam*
1956	Adams (Glasgow)	*Jaguar*
1958	Monraisse (Lisbon)	*Renault*
1959	Coltelloni (Paris)	*Citroën*
1960	Schock (Warsaw)	*Mercedes-Benz*
1961	Martin (Monte Carlo)	*Panhard*
1962	Carlsson (Oslo)	*Saab*
1963	Carlsson (Stockholm)	*Saab*
1964	Hopkirk (Minsk)	*Mini Cooper*
1965	Makinen (Stockholm)	*Mini Cooper*
1966	Toivonen (Oslo)	*Citroën*
1967	Aaltonen (Monte Carlo)	*Mini Cooper*
1968	Elford (Warsaw)	*Porsche*
1969	Waldegaard (Warsaw)	*Porsche*
1970	Waldegaard (Oslo)	*Porsche*
1971	O. Andersson (Marrakesh)	*Alpine-Renault*

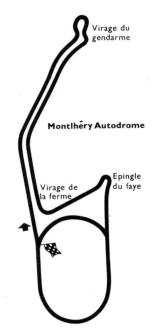

Montlhéry Autodrome

From then on, the Paris track drew countless record-breakers. Gwenda Stewart, and Douglas Hawkes, practically lived at Montlhéry and had lock-ups beneath the banking, from which their immaculately prepared racing machines emerged: the V-twin Morgan 3-wheeler, the slim Derby-Miller in which Gwenda had a nasty accident, but which she also drove with notable skill and courage, to establish a lap record of 145·94mph (234·86kph). The car with its centrifugal supercharger was prepared by her English mechanic, Fred Cann. This lap record went unchallenged for a long time but was ultimately broken by Raymond Sommer's 3-litre Alfa Romeo, with a speed of 148·4mph (238·8kph).

The fast French track brought record-breakers from England, notably George Eyston, who drove all manner of cars, from saloons to racing single-seaters, and John Cobb, who brought the 24-litre Napier-Railton over from Brooklands to try for the 24-hour record, only to have Freddie Dixon lose it in a skid which nearly took the big car over the top of the home banking to end up, after it had demolished much safety fencing, buried in the inner earth bank at the foot of the track. Motorcycles as well as cars were engaged on record bids at the track and thus in its first year the place was well established as both a record-breaking centre and a race circuit. The smoothness of the recently laid concrete, the absence of silencer restrictions, the high-speeds possible at the new track and unrestricted running twice round the clock were conducive to these attacks; and the success-ful ones earned excellent financial payments. It is impossible to list all the short- and long-distance and duration records established on the Montlhéry track. But night after night the Model-T Ford would sally forth to lay down George Eyston's red lanterns, used to mark the perimeter of the banked course when an all-night record attack was in the offing.

The leading French manufacturers took a significant part in onslaughts on records at Montlhéry. Voisin, Renault, Panhard-Levassor and Delage built special cars for the purpose and the Yacco oil people backed Citroën into running a series of incredible long-duration record attacks, of as much as 133 days. The attempts would be called off while a Grand Prix race was run at the track and thereafter resumed.

Apart from all the record-breaking for which Montlhéry is justly famous, there were many important races staged at the Paris circuit. The opening long-distance race was the Grand Prix de l'Ouverture of 1924 won by the Englishman, Jack Scales, driving a Talbot. The 1925 French GP has already been mentioned and that year the Grand Prix de l'Ouverture was a victory for George Duller, another driver from Britain, in a Talbot. The great French driver Albert Divo won the big Montlhéry race of 1926, called the Grand Prix du Salon, at the wheel of a Talbot. The French Grand Prix returned to the Paris autodrome in 1927 and was won by Robert Benoist, in a Delage. He also won the Grand Prix de l'Ouverture that year. Indeed, in 1927 there was much activity at Montlhéry: the Coupe de la Commission Sportive race was held there, won by André Boillot's Peugeot; there was a 24-hour sports-car race termed the Grand Prix de Paris, in which a 4½-litre Bentley shared by Frank Clement and George Duller proved the winner and then the ACF staged a Free-for-All race, won by Divo's Talbot, at 74·69mph (120·20kph).

The French Grand Prix was held again at Montlhéry from 1931 to 1937 (but in 1934 and again in 1935 this great series was replaced by short-distance races referred

Montlhéry: start of a light car race, c 1926; Salmson and two Amilcars. *Photo: Autocar*

Montlhéry: Caracciola's Mercedes-Benz and two Maseratis in 1931 French GP. *Photo: Autocar*

Montlhéry: Birkin's Maserati and Chiron's Bugatti in 1931 French GP. *Photo: Autocar*

Montlhéry: Mercedes-Benz and Auto Union in 1935 French GP. *Photo: Autocar*

to as the Grand Prix de France and of much lesser importance).

By 1937 the Bol d'Or long-distance race for small cars had found a new home at Montlhéry, being held there from 1937 to 1939, and again in 1954 and 1955. From 1947 onwards the Coupe du Salon and the Paris Grand Prix became notable annual races at Montlhéry. Various sports-car contests also took place there and British cars like Cooper and Lotus were successful; the Bentley Drivers' Club went to Montlhéry to indulge in 1-hour timed runs with their vintage cars, spurred on, perhaps, by a similar run undertaken in 1953 by T. H. Plowman, who averaged 106·9mph (172kph) for an hour from a flying start in a 1924 30/98 Vauxhall.

In recent years the Montlhéry Autodrome has been little used, apart from the annual Paris 1,000km sports car event. This was instituted in 1956, revived in 1960 and run annually until 1964 when two drivers and three officials were killed in an accident. The race was again revived in 1966 and has been run annually since. Other meetings still held include the Coupe du Salon, Prix de Paris and the AGACI 300, a rally-type series of stages totalling 300km and using the full road and track circuit. Lap record (road circuit): J. P. Beltoise and H. Pescarolo (Matra 650); 103·033mph (175·862kph); 2min 40·1sec; 1969. WB

Montseny Hill-Climb

The Montseny Championship climb is a long, winding road snaking its way up into the mountains inland from Barcelona, over the foothills of the Pyrenees. The start of the Carrera en Cuesta al Montseny is some 51km north-east of Barcelona and 109km south-west from the border post of Le Perthus. The course is 10·13 miles (16·3km) long, rising from 846ft (258m) to 3,746ft (1,142m) at the finish. The Real Automovil Club de Cataluña runs this well-organized event, opening the annual Championship. It is a slow and tortuous climb, and one of the trickiest in the series. Record: Peter Schetty (Ferrari 212E); 66·05mph (106·215kph); 9min 12·46sec; 1969. DCN

Mont Tremblant Circuit *see* St Jovite Circuit

Mont Ventoux Hill-Climb

This famous mountain climb and rally special stage is situated 37·28 miles (60km) north-east of Avignon, beyond Carpentras and Bédoin. It is the oldest surviving hill-climb in the world, and has been in use for competitions since 1902. The climb starts near Bédoin and runs through some fast curves through Ste Estève and on to the finish almost literally on the summit of the mountain. The road is 13·42 miles (21·6km) from start to finish, and rises from a height of 971ft (296m) to 6,217ft (1,895m). Record: Peter Schetty (Ferrari 212E); 80·46mph (129·492kph); 10min 00·5sec; 1969. DCN

Monza Autodrome

Home of Italian motor racing, Monza Autodrome lies in the attractive, wooded grounds of the Monza royal park, a few kilometres north-east of Milan. The original autodrome was built, reputedly in 100 days, and opened in 1922. In this form it offered two circuits, a 3·417-mile (5·5km) road course and a 2·796-mile (4·5km) banked track. These could be combined to produce a 6·214-mile (10km) course, and this was used for the Italian GP from 1922 until 1928, and from 1931 to 1933. The Florio combination road and track course, measuring 4·263

Above, Monza: Caracciola (Mercedes-Benz), Nuvolari (Alfa Romeo) and Varzi (Maserati) passing through the chicane in the 1934 Italian GP. *Photo: Daimler-Benz AG*

Above right, Monza: South Banking, 1955 Italian GP. *Photo: David Hodges Collection*

Below right, Monza: Neuhaus (Porsche 917) and Parkes (Ferrari 512) during the 1970 Monza 1,000km race. *Photo: Geoffrey Goddard*

miles (6·861km) was used in 1930 (Monza GP), and the Short Florio circuit—2·485 miles (4km)—in 1934 in an attempt to slow the Mercedes and Auto Unions. In 1935 and 1936 the Florio circuit had chicanes added to bring it up to 4·281 miles (6·890km) in length and in 1938 it was increased fractionally to 4·345 miles (6·993km).

During these years Monza was the home of every Italian GP apart from the 1937 event which was held at Leghorn, and it provided a fast course, blessed with generally good weather. A very bad accident occurred in 1928 when Ernesto Materassi's Talbot crashed into the crowd killing the driver and 20 spectators. In 1933 a series of crashes on oil in the South Curve took the lives of Borzacchini, Campari and Czaykowski during the heats of the Monza GP. Louis Zborowski died at Lesmo in a Mercedes in 1924 and Earl Howe had a miraculous escape in 1932 when he crashed into a tree.

The original banked circuit was demolished in 1939 and the rest of the parkland autodrome suffered badly

from the neglect and ravages of wartime. In 1948 the road circuit was rebuilt, again in 100 days, and the Monza Autodrome GP that year was won by Wimille in an Alfa Romeo, from the sister cars of Trossi and Sanesi. The new road course was 3·915 miles (6·3km) in length, and in 1955 a brand new concrete speed-bowl was constructed, half-sunk below ground level and half above it on concrete pillars. This crossed the road circuit via a bridge between the Serraglio Curve and Vialone, and combined with the road course to give a 6·214-mile (10km) lap once more. Indianapolis-like 500-mile races for the Two Worlds Trophy were run on this high-speed course in 1957 and 1958. The Italian GP used the combined circuits in 1955, 1956 and 1960: the banked track's bumpy condition led to a mass boycott of the 1960 event. The combined courses continued to be used for the Monza 1,000 kilometres race series until 1968 and the speed bowl was also the venue for numerous record attempts.

From 1955 the road circuit's lap length became 3·573

Monza Autodrome

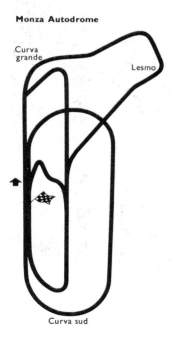

Curva grande

Lesmo

Curva sud

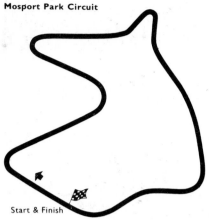

Ford); 113·34mph (184·73kph); 1min 18·1sec; 1969.
Can-Am: Dan Gurney (McLaren-Chevrolet);
113·492mph (192·64kph); 1min 18sec; 1970. ARB

Mosport Park Circuit

miles (5·75km), adopting the form it has today, and in
1959 a link road was built past the paddock and joining
the home straight to Vialone to form the Pista Junior,
widely used since then for FJ, F3 and minor national
events, some of them run under floodlights. Lap length
is 1·482 miles (2·385km), and in 1959 Brooks in a Ferrari
set an unofficial time of 56·8sec, 93·859mph (151·161kph),
in testing there.

Following von Trips' fatal accident entering the
Parabolica in 1961, in which a number of spectators also
died, safety precautions have been considerable, and
much of the circuit is now lined with Armco barriers and
high wire fences. The speed bowl has declined to a sad
degree and its future seems uncertain, but the road
circuit is one of the fastest in Europe, and one of the most
important. Lap record (long circuit): Jean-Pierre
Beltoise (Matra-Ford),1969 and Clay Regazzoni (Ferrari)
1970; 150·97mph (242·957kph); 1min 25·2sec. DCN

Moscow–St Petersburg Trial see
St Petersburg Races

Mosport Park Circuit

The rolling 2·46-mile (3·959km) Mosport circuit ranks
with the best North American road courses. Situated
among wooded hills near the shores of Lake Ontario,
Mosport is 60 miles (96km) east of Toronto, Ont., and
5 miles (8km) north of Bowmanville.

When Stirling Moss (he insists the circuit was named
after him, rather than being a contraction of motor sport)
won the 25 June 1961 Players 200 inaugural it stimulated
the idea of holding a championship series of professional
sports car races in the United States and Canada. Successful professional road races were being held on the
West Coast and much credit goes to the Canadians for
encouraging what, in 1966, became the Can-Am series.

Spectator viewing from hillsides within the circuit, and
on the outside of Moss Corner, a sweeping bend that
turns the track back to the start-finish line, is excellent. In
addition to Canadian club racing, Mosport holds the
Trans-Am, Formula A Continental, Can-Am and, on
alternate years, the Canadian Grand Prix.

As one of the three North American circuits that
stage both Can-Am and World Championship Formula
1 events, the comparative lap records are of interest.
Formula 1: Jackie Ickx and Jack Brabham (Brabham-

Mosport Park: 1967 Canadian GP. *Photo:
David Phipps*

Below right, Mugello: Alberto Rosselli's
Alfa Romeo GTA 1300, 1969 Mugello GP.
Photo: Autosport

Mugello Circuit

Mugello Circuit
This lengthy Italian road circuit takes in part of the
famous Mille Miglia route, and lies in the hills near
Mugello, between Bologna and Florence in Italy. In its
present form it tends towards roughness with some fast
and tricky sections interspersed by many slower corners,
and there is a considerable variation of both surface
condition and gradient.

The present lap distance is 41·135 miles (66·2km), and
this rugged course has survived several spates of 'close
the public road courses' movements because the
Florence Club had the foresight to register it as an autodrome. The course runs from the start near San Piero,
through the villages of Firenzuola and Santa Lucia. The
first Mugello race, in 1920, was won by Campari's Alfa
Romeo at a mere 37·8mph (60·83kph) over a distance
of 242 miles (389·5km). The race was run annually until
1925, and then from 1928 to 1929, before lapsing until
1955 when Maglioli won the 270-mile (434·5km) sports

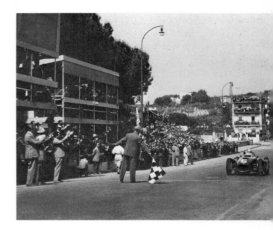

car race at the wheel of a Ferrari. Not until 1965 was the circuit revived, when a 329-mile (529·6km) sports car race was won by Casoni and Nicodemi in a Ferrari LM. In practice for the 1967 race Gunther Klass, a new Ferrari recruit, lost his life, and Mugello had claimed one of its rare victims. Like the Targa Florio course, Mugello has proved surprisingly safe.

Lap record: Nanni Galli (Lola T210); 83·34mph (134·128kph); 29min 36·8sec; 1970. DCN

Naples Circuit

The 2·548-mile (4·1km) circuit is situated in the suburbs of Naples, overlooking the famous bay, in the Posillipo district, from which the circuit takes its name. It has no flat section at all, either climbing or descending, and it twists and turns through the streets, edged by kerbstones, trees, concrete walls and houses. The original layout was a figure-of-eight, the joining of the two loops being at a wide cross-roads. In 1958 it was modified.

The first race in Naples was held in 1934 and was won by Tazio Nuvolari (Maserati) at 57·066mph (91·837kph). After that races were held in 1937 and 1939, in the latter year J. P. Wakefield (Maserati) being the winner at 63·662mph (102·454kph). Racing was resumed on the Posillipo circuit in 1948 and continued until 1962, alternating between Grand Prix events, sports car races and Formula Junior races.

The race was invariably run over 60 laps of the circuit, and in the heat of southern Italy it taxed the drivers' stamina to the maximum. Seldom was the winner seen to jump from his car after driving for more than two hours round the Posillipo circuit. He was usually so fatigued that he had to be lifted out of the cockpit, for in its twists and turns there was only one moment of respite on each lap, as the cars accelerated up the short pits straight, and even then the driver was changing gear.

In 1958 government restrictions in Italy, following the 1957 Mille Miglia accident, put a 2-litre limit on street racing and demanded the elimination of the short loop of the circuit, as it was considered too narrow and too dangerous. This began the demise of the Naples races. A Formula Junior race followed, won by Colin Davis (Taraschi) and in 1960 it was virtually a national sports car event. In 1961 and 1962 there was a revival, with Grand Prix events, the first won by G. Baghetti (Ferrari) and the second by W. Mairesse (Ferrari). However, the real glory of the Naples GP had gone, the 1960s being increasingly safety-conscious. Lap record: Mike Hawthorn (Ferrari 801); 73·02mph (117·515kph); 2min 5·6sec; 1957. DSJ

Left, Mugello: Nanni Galli (Lola T210) leads an Alfa Romeo 33 in the 1970 Mugello GP. *Photo: Autosport*

Right, Naples: Ascari (Lancia D50) winning the 1955 Naples GP. *Photo: Associated Press Ltd*

Below, Naples: Horace Gould (Ferrari) in the 1956 Naples GP. *Photo: Associated Press Ltd*

Right, Nassau Speed Week: Ferrari, Cobra, Ferrari, awaiting the start. *Photo: Roland Rose*

Nassau Speed Weeks

Nassau Speed Weeks were conceived by Captain Sherman Crise, a flamboyant promoter from the Pennsylvania Dutch country, and the Bahamas Ministry of Tourism. Windsor Field was the site from 1954 until 1957, the race moving to the 4·5-mile (7·24km) Oakes Field when Windsor was reinstated as New Providence Island's commercial airport. Granted FIA international status by the Royal Automobile Club, Nassau's traditional late November-early-December race dates consistently drew many international and US personalities. Located 200 miles (320km) east of Miami, the appeal of endless cocktail parties, Bay Street's tax-free bargains and the warm Caribbean waters, more than offset a rough circuit (lined with scrub pine course markers) and the arbitrary, rule-bending manner with which 'Red' Crise ran the event. Nassau regulars included De Portago; Peter Collins; Jo Bonnier; Innes Ireland (who could collect only half his winner's purse as he did not attend the victory dinner); Stirling Moss, who had a home in the island; Bruce McLaren, whose Elva-Olds won the 1965 Governors Trophy with a record 104·624mph (168·436kph) race average; the brothers Rodriguez and others of the Grand Prix circus. From the United States came Phil Hill, 1955 Nassau Trophy winner in a Ferrari; Chuck Daigh and Lance Reventlow, 1958 winners in the Buick-Scarab; Carroll Shelby; and multi-winner Dan Gurney; Indy veterans A. J. Foyt, 1963 winner of the 100-mile Governors Cup and the 250-miles Nassau Trophy; Lloyd Ruby; and Rodger Ward. But

the largest contingent were SCCA stalwarts such as Bob Grossman, Augie Pabst, Walt Hansgen, Charlie Kolb, Roger Penske, Jim Hall and Hap Sharp, whose Chaparral dominated the final years at Nassau.

A change in local government combined with a now flourishing tourist industry resulted in 1966 being the last of Nassau Speed Weeks, and Pedro Rodriguez the single internationalist on hand. In 1967 a GP of Volkswagens was held on nearby Freeport, but it was an unfortunate venture and appears to have finished motor racing in the Bahamas. ARB

New Zealand GP see Ardmore Circuit and Pukekohe Circuit

Norisring

The Norisring is a 2·45-mile (3·94km) circuit that runs round the gigantic Nazi rally stadium on the edge of the city of Nuremberg (Nürnberg) in Bavaria. To avoid confusion with the Nürburgring in Rhineland-Palatinate the circuit at Nuremberg is called after the ancient name of the city, which is Noris. The vast concrete Nazi tribune, holding 40,000 people, from where Hitler made his speeches, forms the main grandstand for the circuit, overlooking the wide starting area and the temporary pits. It runs in an anti-clockwise direction and there is a very fast long gentle curve to the right, away from the start, which ends in a hairpin to the left, then the road returns to the stadium on the other side of a wide grass verge, parallel to the outward leg. At the entrance to the stadium the course takes a sharp right corner followed immediately by a sharp left corner then runs behind the tribune to another left-hand hairpin. A fast left-hand bend returns it to the starting area. The whole circuit is flat.

Racing started on this circuit in 1947 with national motorcycle races which became international in 1952, by which time sports car races were being run as well as Formula 3. Activity expanded to saloon car events and GT races, until today the annual 200 miles race is for Groups 5, 6 and 7 sports/racing cars which can use all their speed on the long curve after the start, with lap times in the order of 1min 17sec, and an average speed of over 115mph (185kph). The annual meeting, which also includes motorcycle races and saloon car races, is organized by the Motorsport-Club Nürnberg affiliated to the ADAC and is one of the few remaining unspoilt amateur meetings in Europe, providing a weekend of motor sport for some 60,000 local people. Lap record: Jurgen Neuhaus (Porsche 917); 115·81mph (186·39kph); 1min 16·1sec; 1970. DSJ

Nürburgring

The Eifel Mountains area, west of the Rhine in Germany, is a countryside of great splendour. In 1925 the German government set in motion a vast undertaking to build a special motor road in the mountains in the form of a test-track with traffic going in a clockwise direction only. The idea was to give work to the unemployed in that part of Germany and to provide a testing ground and racing circuit for the growing German motor industry. It was completed in 1927 and as it was centred round the village of Nürburg, with its medieval castle overlooking the pits and paddock area, it was called the Nürburgring. The total length was 17·563 miles (28·265km), divided into two loops using the common pits area. The South Loop (or Südschleife) running down to the village of Mullenbach and back was 4·814 miles (7·747km) in

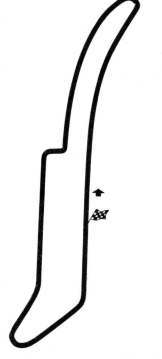
Norisring

length, and the main North Loop (Nordschleife) running down into the valley towards Adenau village and back up through the hills of Hohe-Acht was 14·17 miles (22·810km), and it is this loop that is principally used for motor racing. Officially there were 89 left-hand bends and 85 right-hand ones, while the highest point was 2,034ft (620m) above sea-level, at the pits area, and the lowest point 1,050ft (320m) at Breidscheid, near Adenau.

The German Grand Prix was held at the Nürburgring in 1927 over a distance of 316·53 miles (509·4km) and was won by Otto Merz with a Mercedes-Benz at an average speed of 63·38mph (102kph) in 4hr 59min 35·6sec. The Germans developed a sense of pride in their wonderful new mountain circuit. The tradition of the Nürburgring became such that crowds of 350,000 flocked to the races and continue to do so today. In 1932 and 1934 the German GP was increased to 354·37miles (570·3km) and in the latter year Hans Stuck won at 75·81mph (123kph) in 4hr 38min 19·1sec, but then it was reduced to 310·7 miles (500km). The Nürburgring was the scene of some mighty battles between the state-supported teams of Auto Union and Mercedes-Benz, though in 1935 Tazio Nuvolari beat them with a 3·8-litre Alfa Romeo in one of the classic races of the decade. In 1938 the German Grand Prix was won on the Nürburgring by the Englishman Richard Seaman, driving a Mercedes-Benz, and in 1939 Rudolf Caracciola won his fifth German GP on the famous circuit, having been victorious in 1928, 1931, 1932 and 1937, covering the 311·8 miles (501·8km) at the record speed of 82·77mph (133·2kph) in 1937, driving for 3hr 46min 00·0sec. Other events were held on the Nürburgring, notably the Eifelrennen (Eifel races) which acted as a warm-up event earlier in the year. Rallies and endurance runs also took place on the track and many German manufacturers used it for test purposes.

After clearing away the ravages of war the Nürburgring was back in the motor racing calendar in 1950, Alberto Ascari winning a shortened Grand Prix of 226·74 miles (364·9km) with a Ferrari, and it continued to be the scene of the German GP with breaks in 1959 and 1970. At all times the driver has to match his skill and wits against the Nürburgring itself, his direct human rivals being of secondary importance, and few can claim to have driven a full lap on the complete limit of their own and their cars' ability. In 1957 Fangio was credited with achieving this distinction during his famous race which he won for Maserati, and Stirling Moss was acclaimed in a similar way after winning in 1961 with a Lotus 18. The

Nürburgring: opening meeting, 1927; two stripped Hanomags in the front row, and behind them Mercedes-Benz 'S' and 'K' tourers. Photo: Neubauer Collection

Nürburgring: Muller testing an Auto Union at Pflanzgarten, 1938. *Photo: David Hodges Collection*

Above centre, Nürburgring: Fangio (Mercedes-Benz W196) and Moss (Maserati 250F) at Pflanzgarten during the 1954 German GP. *Photo: Motor*

Above right, Nürburgring: the 1968 German GP was held in the worst conditions for over thirty years. Graham Hill (Lotus-Ford), who finished 2nd, leads a group of cars through the murk. *Photo: Geoffrey Goddard*

Nürburgring: Le Mans-type start of the 1968 1,000km race; Porsche 908, Alfa Romeo 33 and Ford F3L in foreground. *Photo: David Hodges Collection*

Germans give such drivers the title of *Ringmeister*; it was also given to Caracciola for his five victories and to Ascari for his hat-trick of wins in 1950, 1951 and 1952. Fangio earned the title twice for he too achieved three victories in a row, in 1954, 1956 and 1957 (there was no race in 1955) all these races being for the German GP.

After the war the Nürburgring increased its activities and added the 1,000 kilometres sports car race to its annual fixtures in 1953. In 1966 America made its mark in Nürburgring history when the Chaparral 2D won the 1,000 kilometres race, driven by Phil Hill and Joakim Bonnier. The Eifelrennen continued to be held, quite often on the shorter South Loop and for small cars, such as Formula Junior and Formula 2, and motorcycle and bicycle races are regular features, as well as rallies, saloon car races and the incredible 84-Hour Marathon. Over the years various details have been changed, such

as the concrete banked hairpin at Karussell, the hump at Flugplatz has been removed and the chicane has been added before the start area. The last alteration was made in 1967, so that there are now officially 91 left-hand corners and the official length of the Northern Loop is 17·917 miles (28·835km).

When not in use for racing or testing the Nürburgring is open as a public road, though in one direction only, a small fee being charged to drive round it. It is administered by a full-time staff and run by a public company, Nürburgring GmbH, who hire it out to the clubs for them to hold their races and rallies. The Nürburgring has a tradition and grandeur all of its own, like the surrounding countryside, one that is respected the world over and accepted by all who go there. Lap record: Jackie Ickx (Brabham F1); 110·10mph (177·2kph); 7min 43·85sec; 1969. DSJ

Nürburgring

Metzgesfeld
Karussell
Pflanzgarten
Schwedenkreuz
Dottinger-Höhe
Flugplatz
Quiddelbacher- Höhe
Tiergarten
Hatzenbach

Ollon–Villars Hill-Climb

The Swiss hill-climb running from Ollon to Villars is one of the classic courses and scene of the annual Swiss Mountain GP which has attracted such drivers as Brabham, Clark and Siffert in the past. Jim Clark drove his Indianapolis Lotus there in the rain on one memorable occasion. The climb is off the Lausanne-Martigny N9 road, about 35 miles (56km) south-east from Lausanne itself, and measures 4·97 miles (8km) in length. It runs from 1,703ft (519m) to 3,878ft (1,182m) at the finish. Record: Peter Schetty (Ferrari 212E); 78·66mph (126·593kph); 3min 47·54sec; 1969. DCN

Olympic Park Circuit see Melbourne Motordrome

Ontario Motor Speedway

This 25·5 million dollar, multi-purpose racing complex opened on 6 September 1970 with a precedent breaking 500-mile race for Indianapolis cars. Located 40 miles (64km) east of Los Angeles, Ontario boasts of a 2·5-mile (4·023km) oval track with 9° banked turns (that are slightly faster than those at the Indianapolis Speedway) a 3·19 mile (5·134km) road course and a drag strip. In addition to the annual 'California Indy 500', major stock car and sports car races, a second U.S. Grand Prix and drag racing meets are planned to keep the complex busy on a year-round basis. A capacity crowd of 180,223 watched USAC veteran Jim McElreath, Coyote-Ford, win $150,000, covering the 500 miles with an average speed of 160·106mph (257·710kph). ARB

Oporto Circuit

The 4·603 mile (7·407km) Oporto circuit lay on the outskirts of the city, but nevertheless was a true street circuit, with kerbstones, brick walls and tram-lines (streetcar tracks). It began on a straight just before a large roundabout where the circuit turned left up the Avenida da Boávista for just over 1·24 miles (2km). Then it went left again, up a side street, and wiggled about over a hill and down the other side on a fast twisting descent to join the short, tram-lined straight. It was unusual in that it was raced anti-clockwise.

Ontario Motor Speedway

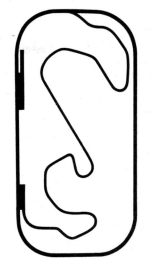

Below left, Oporto: Hawthorn (Ferrari) and Moss (Vanwall) in the 1958 Portugese Grand Prix. *Photo: Doug Nye Collection*

Below right, Oporto: Jim Clark (Lotus) in the 1960 Portuguese GP. *Photo: Bernard Cahier*

The first race held there was a sports car event in 1950, won by F. Bonetto in an Alfa-Romeo, and the following year it took the title of the Portuguese GP. As such it was continued until 1954 when it was called the Oporto GP, still for sports cars, and took the title of Portuguese GP again in 1955. In 1958 it achieved Formula 1 World Championship status, when it was won by Stirling Moss in a Vanwall. In 1960 another World Championship event was held at Oporto, won by Jack Brabham. This was the last race held on the circuit, as it did not meet with the more stringent safety requirements of the 1960s. Lap record: John Surtees (Lotus-Climax); 112·309mph (180·744kph); 2min 27·53sec; 1960. DSJ

Österreichring see Zeltweg

Oulton Park Circuit

This English road circuit, near Tarporley in Cheshire, was established by the Mid-Cheshire Motor Club. It was laid out originally to a roughly square plan, through the grounds of Oulton Hall, the foundations of which still protrude through the grass outside Old Hall Corner. The undulating circuit through the trees and past the lakes of the Park measured 1·504 miles (2·478km) to the lap. It was opened on 8 August 1953. Moss won the first International Gold Cup race there in 1954, averaging 83·48mph (134·35kph) in his Maserati; by that time an extension down by the large Lower Lake towards Island Bend had lengthened the course to 2·23 miles (3·579km). This extension was opened on 10 April 1954, and on 7 August that year yet another section was added, sweeping the course through Island Bend and into the slightly banked Esso Hairpin to complete a 2·761-mile (4·445km) circuit which was now one of the finest road courses in the country.

Rex Foster's promotion of the circuit brought some fine motor racing in all classes, and although its narrow access roads were hard put to cope with large crowds, the Gold Cup series and many club meetings attracted very good attendances. Moss won the Gold Cup five times, including his victory with the 4-wheel-drive Ferguson-Climax in 1961, and in 1965 the RAC TT was transferred to the circuit, but the event was in a state of sad decline

Oulton Park Circuit

Knicker brook

Druids

Cascades

Old hall corner

Esso hairpin

Lodge

Top, Oulton Park: Esso hairpin, with the lake in the background. *Photo: T. C. March*

Above, Oulton Park: start of the 1967 Gold Cup. *Photo: Doug Nye Collection*

by then, having no International importance whatsoever.

Oulton Park is a difficult and daunting circuit to drivers brought up on the open airfield courses of Britain, and its trees and lakes have claimed their victims. In 1969 the trees lining the Avenue were cleared as a safety measure, but it remains a circuit to teach the novice respect for his surroundings, and is one on which a driver may be proud to have done well. Lap record: Jackie Stewart (Matra-Cosworth Ford); 112·19mph (180·64kph); 1min 28·6sec; 1969. DCN

Pacific Raceways *see* Seattle International Raceways

Paris 1,000km *and* **Paris GP** *see* Montlhéry Circuit

Paris Races
From 1895 to 1903 the annual town-to-town races, usually starting from Paris, were the main motoring events in Europe. Organized by the Automobile Club de France (ACF) from 1896 onwards, they are included in the Club's list of Grands Prix, although the actual term Grand Prix was not employed until 1906. Although not a race, the Paris-Rouen Trial is included here as being the first motoring competition of any kind.

Paris-Rouen Trial The Paris-Rouen Trial of 1894, organized by the newspaper *Le Petit Journal* is generally regarded as the world's first motor competition. It was not quite the first to be arranged, for in 1887 another journal, *Le Vélocipède,* had proposed a short trial in the environs of Paris, but only one competitor turned up. Paris-Rouen was quite another matter; when the list closed on 30 April no less than 102 entries had been received. Many of these must have existed only in the

imaginations of their inventors, and a variety of weird motive powers were listed. These included a 'baricycle' moved by the weight of the passengers, 'multiple system of levers', 'combination of animate and mechanical motor', 'constant propulsion motor', and simply 'automatic'. When the competitors actually lined up along the Boulevard Maillot on 22 July there were only 21, and these were all powered either by steam or petrol. The route to Rouen covered 79 miles (126km), and 12 hours were allowed for the journey. In fact the leading car, a De Dion steam tractor, reached Rouen in approximately 6hr 48min, averaging 11·6mph (18·67kph). Second was a Peugeot driven by Lemaitre, and 3rd another Peugeot driven by Doriot. Only four cars out of the 21 failed to reach Rouen, and these were all steam driven. Although Count de Dion had finished 1st he was not awarded 1st prize as two men were needed to look after the vehicle. He therefore received 2nd prize; the 1st was awarded jointly to Peugeot and Panhard (prizes went to manufacturers not drivers).

The event was a remarkable demonstration of reliability, with a failure rate of less than 20%. Many later trials and races took a much heavier toll of cars, and the Paris-Rouen was a great tribute to the skill and understanding with which the drivers handled their machines.

Paris-Bordeaux-Paris No sooner was the Paris-Rouen Trial over than motorists decided that they and their machines were capable of a much more stringent test. Count de Dion and Baron de Zuylen de Nyevelt asked Pierre Giffard of *Le Petit Journal* if he would sponsor a larger event, but the paper's proprietors were afraid that any accidents would reflect badly on them, so Giffard had to decline. Baron de Zuylen and others then formed a committee which later led to the founding of the Automobile Club de France. They promptly began to organize their first event, a race from Paris to Bordeaux and back. In order to avoid charges of encouraging speeding, the committee said that the winning car must seat more than two passengers. The distance to be covered was 732 miles (1,178·0km). Forty-six cars were entered, but only 22 started, of which 15 had petrol engines, 6 steam, and one electric (Jeantaud's six-seater bus). The race proved the superiority of petrol over steam, and petrol cars took the first eight places. The first car home, and moral victor, was a Panhard driven by Emile Levassor at an average of 15mph (24·14kph), although because his car was a two-seater he was not awarded 1st prize. This went to Koechlin on a Peugeot. Only 9 of the 22 starters completed the course. An interesting entry, though it did not qualify, was André Michelin's Peugeot *l'Eclair*, which was equipped with pneumatic tyres.

Paris-Marseilles-Paris In November 1895 some members of the committee which had organized the Paris-Bordeaux-Paris event met to consider the formation of a permanent club, and on 12 November the Automobile Club de France was formed. Their first race was the major event of 1896, from Paris to Marseilles and back, a distance of 1,063 miles (1,711km) to be covered in ten daily stages. Twenty-three cars, 4 Leon Bollée tricars and 5 tricycles started, and this time there were only two steam vehicles in the contest, both De Dions. On the second day, when the cars were on the Auxerre to Dijon stage a tremendous storm brought down trees and made the roads very muddy. Several cars retired because of this, and a Léon Bollée was charged by an infuriated bull. Emile Levassor was thrown out of his Panhard after it had overturned, and received injuries from which he died the following spring. Only 16 of the starters reached Marseilles, but of these 14 made it back to Paris. The winner was Mayade's Panhard, at an average speed of 15·7mph (25·27kph), followed by Merkel and d'Hostingue, also on Panhards. The familiar makes of Panhard, Peugeot, and de Dion (tricycles) took the first six places, but the new firm of Delahaye made a good start with 7th and 10th places. Both steam cars retired.

Marseilles–Nice–La Turbie Although there were two Paris races in 1897, to Dieppe and to Trouville, the year's major event was the 145-mile (233·4km) Marseilles–Nice–La Turbie Race. Held in January at the height of the Riviera season, it attracted considerable attention from the fashionable holidaymakers in Nice, St Raphael, and other resorts. Although much shorter than the two previous races, the route involved steep hills and sharp corners. The winner was Comte de Chasseloup-Laubat in an 18hp De Dion steam brake, followed by Lemaitre on a Peugeot, and three Panhards.

Paris–Amsterdam–Paris This was the major event of 1898, and was the first motor race to cross an international frontier. The total mileage was 889, and the race was divided into six stages, which, with a rest day at Amsterdam, meant a seven-day event. For the first time there was a separate class for light cars (200 to 400kg), and also one for tourists who did not wish to drive at the excessive speeds of the faster cars. The tourists had a slightly longer route of 923 miles, and ten days to cover it in. Most cars, whether in the racing or touring classes, were still touring cars in conception, but the Paris–Amsterdam–Paris saw the appearance of the first cars built with the intention of racing. These were the streamlined 8hp Amédée Bollées, the fastest of which finished 3rd and 5th. Speeds were rising: Charron's winning Panhard averaged 32mph (51·50kph) over a 40-mile stretch, and his average over the whole race was 26·9mph (43·29kph). His team-mate Girardot was 2nd, while Giraud's Bollée finished in 3rd place. The light-car class was won by Corbière on a Decauville.

Tour de France Still searching for greater distance and variety of conditions, the ACF chose a circular route around France covering 1,350 miles (2,173kph) for their major event of 1899. The route included mountainous country in the Auvergne, and proved a very severe test of driver and car. At Le Mans, Charron broke a bearing between the gearbox and bevel drive on the sprocket shaft and was only able to travel in reverse. This he did for 25 miles. Forty-eight vehicles started the Tour, and 21 finished after seven days of motoring. The first four places were taken by Panhards, de Knyff being the winner at an average of 30·2mph (48·60kph).

The summer of 1899 brought a number of smaller races such as the Paris–St Malo, Paris–Trouville, Paris–Ostend and Paris–Biarritz. In the Paris–Trouville four racing cars competed on handicap against motorcyclists, cyclists, horses, and pedestrians. A horse won; Antony's Mors was the first car.

Paris–Toulouse–Paris Like 1897, 1900 was a year of consolidation in motor racing. The first Gordon Bennett Race attracted little attention and only five starters, and an unfortunate accident involving spectators in the Paris–Roubaix Race for tricycles led to a total ban on racing in France. This lasted less than a month, but served as a warning to the smaller clubs that safety precautions must be paramount. The year's longest race

Paris Races: Ernest Archdeacon's Serpollet steam bus, Paris–Rouen, 1894. *Photo: Museon di Rodo*

Right, Paris Races: Roger de Montais' steam car, Paris–Rouen, 1894. *Photo: Museon di Rodo*

Below, Paris Races: Avis' Amedée Bollée in the Tour de France, 1899. *Photo: Montagu Motor Museum*

Paris Races: Giraud's 12hp Panhard at the start of Paris–Berlin, 1901. *Photo: Montagu Motor Museum*

127

was the Paris–Toulouse–Paris, held over three days and
covering 837 miles (1,347kph). It was noteworthy for the
emergence of Mors as a threat to Panhard supremacy,
and for the appearance of the first British car in a Continental race, the 16hp Napier driven by S. F. Edge. The
Napier fell out, but the 24hp Mors cars finished 1st and
5th (Levegh and Antony), the winner's time being
40·2mph (64·70kph).

Paris–Berlin This, the major event of 1901, had the
largest entry list of any race up to that date, with a total
of 110 cars and 10 motorcycles actually starting from
Paris. The cars were divided into Heavy Cars (over
650kg), Light Cars (400–650kg), and Voiturettes (under
400kg). Some of the Heavy Cars were very heavy indeed,
the 60hp Mors turning the scales at 1,300kg. In all the
villages along the 687-mile route spectators had been
warned of the dangers of cars which could now travel at
a mile a minute, but nevertheless the local police bore
the final responsibility, as the organizers could not send
their officials everywhere. In fact there was only one
fatal accident, when a small boy was run over by Brasier's
Mors at Monchenot, near Reims. The winner was
Fournier on a Mors, with an average speed of 44·1mph
(70·97kph), followed by Girardot and de Knyff, both on
Panhards. Giraud's 12hp Panhard won the light car
class, and Louis Renault's 8hp Renault was the first of
the voiturettes. Renault in fact was faster than all the
light cars, and finished 8th overall.

Paris–Vienna The accident at Monchenot had strongly
reinforced the anti-motoring lobby in the Chamber of
Deputies, and apart from the government-sponsored
Circuit du Nord, only one race was held on French soil
in 1902. This was the first part of the most ambitious
international race yet held, from Paris to Vienna. The
actual racing distance (615 miles) was less than the Paris–
Berlin as the mileage through Switzerland was not
included in the racing distance, as the Swiss authorities
objected to motor racing in any form. The Austrian stage
included the ascent of the Arlberg Pass, which rose some
5,000ft (1,524m) in 10 miles (90·56km). The roads in this
district were very poor, with only boundary stones
between them and a drop of sometimes several hundred
feet. A total of 118 cars started from Paris, the first leaving
at 3.30am. This year the heavy cars were restricted to a
maximum weight of 1,000kg; the other classes were the
same as before. The Gordon Bennett Race was held
simultaneously, but ended at Innsbruck. This was won
by S. F. Edge's Napier after de Knyff's Panhard had
fallen out only 30 miles from Innsbruck. The Paris–
Vienna Race was won, surprisingly, by Marcel Renault's
16hp light car, which was 35 minutes ahead of Count
Zborowski's Mercedes. When speeds between all the
controls had been taken into account, 2nd place went to
Henri Farman's 70hp Panhard, 3rd to another light car,
Edmond's 24hp Darracq, and 4th to Zborowski.
Altogether 80 cars finished the course.

Paris–Madrid The Paris–Madrid Race of 1903 promised
to be the most ambitious motor race yet held; the course
covered 1,307km including the crossing of the
Guadarrama Mountains near Madrid, while the entry
list was the largest ever, at 216 cars and 59 motorcycles.
Of these, 179 cars actually started. To give an idea of the
numbers, the leading car of Louis Renault had reached
Tours, 135 miles from Paris, when the last motorcyclist
was being flagged off. The weight limit of 1,000kg for
heavy cars remained, and designers used every possible

Left, Paris Races: Maurice Farman's 70hp
Panhard in Paris–Vienna, 1902. *Photo:
Montagu Motor Museum*

Below, Paris Races: the *pesage* (weighing-in)
before the start of Paris–Madrid, 1903.
Photo: Montagu Motor Museum

Bottom, Paris Races: Henri Farman's 80hp
Panhard at the *pesage*, Paris–Madrid. *Photo:
T.A.S.O. Mathieson Collection*

means to keep within the limit and at the same time use enormous engines which were necessarily very heavy. Chassis frames and levers were drilled until they were almost skeletons, and seats were reduced to the absolute minimum with no thought for driver comfort.

The weather was very hot for the time of year, and the excitement of the racing drew a crowd estimated at three million for the 342-mile (550·4km) route to Bordeaux. The cars were faster than ever before, capable of 80mph in some cases, but without proportionate stopping power, and the crowds had little understanding of the speeds and dangers involved. The result was the worst series of accidents in any race up to that time. At least five drivers and mechanics were killed, as well as several spectators and numerous dogs and oxen. Among those who died was Marcel Renault. As a result of these accidents the race was stopped at Bordeaux; the cars were not even allowed to return home under their own power, but were towed behind horses to the station and put on a train for Paris. The leading driver at Bordeaux was Gabriel who had averaged 65·3mph (105·09kph) on his 70hp Mors. Behind him came Louis Renault on a 30hp Renault light car, and Salleron on another Mors. The voiturette class was won by Masson's 18hp Clement. Paris–Madrid was the last race held on unrestricted, open roads in Europe; the following year the Gordon Bennett Race became the premier event, and this took place on a circuit with crowd barriers and adequate policing. GNG

Pau Circuit

Two motor-racing circuits have been used bearing the name of this pleasant southern French town, one a fast triangular public road course east of the town and the other a round-the-houses affair in Pau itself.

The Grand Circuit Permanent de Pau belied its name in only being used once, for the 1930 French GP. It was based on the RN117 road, took in a level (grade) crossing and then swung abruptly north on to a straight ending in a tight little series of S-bends, heading back south

through a curving and very rough section to rejoin the RN117 at the hamlet of Ousse. It was 9·86 miles (15·875km) in length, and the 25-lap GP was won by Etancelin in a Bugatti at 90·38mph (145·447kph), from Birkin's stripped Bentley.

But in 1933 the round-the-houses circuit was established, running past the station and climbing into the small Parc Beaumont and measuring 1·715 miles (2·76km). The Pau GP was held there in 1933, and in 1935–9, recurring from 1947 to 1955 and from 1957 to date. Lehoux's Bugatti won the first event at 45·38mph (73·03kph), and in 1938 Dreyfus' Delahaye confounded the German teams by winning from the Lang and Caracciola Mercedes at 54·64mph (87·93kph). Fangio won for Maserati in 1949–50, and Ascari and Trintignant both scored double victories there. Behra had three consecutive victories in 1954–7 and Clark won his first F1 event there in 1961. The last F1 Pau GP was in 1963, also won by Clark at 61·62mph (99·17kph), and from 1964 to date the race has been an important F2 round. Lap record: Jochen Rindt (Lotus 59B); 78·06mph (125·9kph); 1min 18·9sec; 1969. DCN

Pedralbes Circuit see Barcelona Circuits

Penya Rhin Races see Barcelona Circuits

Pescara Circuit

The history of the Pescara circuit goes back to 1924, when Enzo Ferrari won the first Grand Prix with an Alfa Romeo at an average speed of 64·948mph (104·524kph). It was an outstanding circuit by reason of its length of 15·273 miles (25·579km) to the lap and its shape, which was roughly triangular, with one very long fast straight along the edge of the Adriatic coast of Italy, running south until it met the outskirts of the town. There it turned inland on a winding, climbing mountain section over the hills to the village of Capelle, where it turned right on to the third leg, which was a long and fast straight section, downhill until it met the coast road

Below, Pau: Jean Behra (Maserati 250F) in the 1956 Pau GP. Photo: Autosport

Bottom right, Pau: sports and racing cars are mingled in this Formula 2 race, c 1960. Photo: Bernard Cahier

Pau Circuit V.du lycée V. du parc beaumont V. de la gare

Pescara Circuit

at the village of Montesilvano and a sharp right-hand bend brought it on to the sea-level straight again. The start and finish and pit area were situated at the end of the coastal straight, just where the road entered the outskirts of the town of Pescara. Although very high speeds were obtained on the two straights, the average speed for a lap was not unduly high as the mountain section was fairly slow.

Apart from 1929 the Pescara Grand Prix was held every year until 1939, and from 1930 onwards a voiturette or small-car race was held before the main event. While the Grand Prix was the province of Italian cars and drivers, in 1933 the American driver Whitney Straight won the small-car race with an MG Magnette and the following year his team-mate H. C. Hamilton was the winner with a similar car. Meanwhile, such great names as Campari, Varzi, Nuvolari and Fagioli were inscribing their names on the winners' list of the Gran Premio Pescara. During the Fascist regime the race was known as the Coppa Acerbo, after Captain Tito Acerbo.

As speeds were getting high and the long coastal straight was narrow, ending in the pit area and the outskirts of the town, a chicane was introduced just before the pits in 1934, by building a short bypass road that turned the course right, left, left, and right back onto the straight, all the corners being rightangles. This lengthened the circuit to 16·031 miles (25·8km) and reduced the lap speed slightly, but not drastically. Before the chicane the fastest lap was held by Nuvolari, set up in 1932 with an Alfa Romeo, at 91·208mph (146·785kph) and by 1937 this figure had almost been reached on the modified circuit. In 1935 Seaman won the small-car race with his ERA and in 1936 he won it again with his old Delage car. During this time the giants of the Grand Prix world had really put Pescara on the racing map for the Mercedes-Benz and Auto Union teams supported the race and set standards of speed and a ferocity of battle that caused the Italians to shrink back. In 1937 Varzi (6-litre Auto Union) recorded the highest race average with 87·669mph (141·009kph) and the fastest lap at 90·887mph (146·268kph), and the German cars were reaching speeds of 180mph (288kph) on the straights, there being a timed flying kilometre stretch at the end of the downhill run at Montesilvano. In 1939 the Coppa Acerbo was reduced to a limit of 1·5 litres, and then World War 2 put a stop to racing.

The Automobile Club of Pescara was very strong and supported by the province and the community. The race was restarted in 1947, called once more the Pescara Grand Prix, though it did begin to suffer from changing times. In 1948 Ascari won with a Maserati at 83·388mph (134·020kph) for the 510km and his race time was 3hr 48min 19·4sec, a long time to be driving in the southern Italian sunshine. Fangio won in 1950 for Alfa Romeo and during this race he was timed at 192·839mph (310·344kph). Rosier in an unsupercharged Talbot did 166·935mph (268·656kph). Even so the fastest lap did not quite reach that of Varzi in 1937, Fangio's average being 90·516mph (145·671kph).

Costs were rising all the time and the race could not be held in 1951. In the following two years a 12-hour sports-car race was held, the second one being won by the two pipe-smoking Ferrari drivers Mike Hawthorn and Umberto Maglioli, which amused the Italians. When Grand Prix racing started on a new era in 1954, the Pescara Grand Prix was revived and Musso won with a 250F Maserati at 86·731mph (139·580kph). Bira in a similar car made fastest lap at 88·489mph (142·410kph) in a time of 10min 46·39sec.

In 1955 the race received another setback for after the fatal Le Mans accident the Italian government put a temporary ban on open-road racing, but in 1956 a sports car race was allowed, and in 1957 the Pescara Grand Prix returned in all its glory. A full GP was held, counting for the World Championship, and was dominated by Moss with a Vanwall, setting up new records during his winning drive. This was really the end for the Pescara circuit. In 1961 there was a final fling with a 4-hour sports car race, won by Bandini and Scarlatti in a Ferrari, and though a Formula Junior race was held later, the organizers of the Pescara circuit had to finally give in, a fact regretted by anyone who raced there. Lap record: Stirling Moss (Vanwall); 97·87mph (157·507kph); 9min 44·6sec; 1957. DSJ

Phoenix Park Circuit

The Phoenix Park circuit in Dublin was the site of the Irish Grand Prix from 1929 to 1931, and of numerous lesser events since. The circuit is about 4½ miles (7·25km) to the lap, with a 2-mile (3·219km) straight along one side; the width varies from 19 to 40ft (5·79 to 12·19m), as the route includes main and side roads. For the Irish Grand Prix two races were held, the Eireann Cup (un-

Pescara: Stirling Moss (Vanwall) winning the 1957 Pescara GP. Photo: Francis H. Rigg

limited) and the Saorstat Cup (1·5 litre), the winner of the Grand Prix being determined simply by the fastest times, no matter which race they were achieved in. The Saorstat Cup was held on a Friday, with the Eireann Cup on the following day. Both races were over a distance of 300 miles. In 1929 Boris Ivanowski with his 1750 Alfa Romeo won both races, so naturally took the Grand Prix. The team prize went to Lea-Francis, whose three cars were driven by S. C. H. Davis, W. H. Green, and J. W. Shaw. The 1930 Eireann Cup was won by Caracciola's Mercedes-Benz SSK, which also took the Grand Prix, with Victor Gillow's Riley, winner of the Saorstat Cup, in 2nd place.

In 1931 the Saorstat Cup winner, Norman Black (MG Montlhéry Midget) won the Grand Prix, while the Eireann Cup went to Sir Henry Birkin's Alfa Romeo with Giuseppe Campari's Maserati 2nd and Brian Lewis' Talbot 3rd. This was the last of the great international races at Phoenix Park; from 1932 onwards a series of shorter handicap races took place, but the entry lists were almost entirely of local or English drivers. The 1938 race gave C. S. Staniland's Multi Union its only road circuit victory. The handicap races were revived in 1951 and ran until 1959. In 1961 a Formula 1 and a Formula Junior race were held, and from 1962 onwards Formula Junior, Formula 3 and sports car races. Lap record: Chris Craft (Lola-Chevrolet); 89·37mph (143·89kph); 1min 51·6sec; 1968. GNG

Picardy Circuit

The small French circuit of Picardy, or Péronne as it was also known, after the nearby town, was in use from 1926 up to 1939 when the 14th Grand Prix of Picardy was held, won by Johnny Wakefield in a Maserati. It was of classical equilateral triangle form 6·068 miles (9·765km) in length with the start at a crossroads on the N37, just south of Péronne, not far from St Quentin, and it ran in a clockwise direction on typical narrow French roads. From the start it ran on a 2-mile (3·22km) straight to the village of Brie, turned right through the village and went to Mesnil, whence it returned to the start on a tree-lined straight. At the crossroads by the start there still stands a large monument erected in memory of Guy Bouriat and Louis Trintignant, elder brother of the well-known Maurice Trintignant. They were killed during the 1933 event, the latter during the practice and the former during the race, a Grand Prix that was won by Philippe Etancelin in a 2·3-litre Alfa Romeo at 85mph (136·79kph). In those days supporting races were held for voiturettes of 1,500cc capacity and later this category was used for the Picardy Grand Prix.

As the circuit consisted of public roads it is still possible to drive round it today, recalling ERAs, Maseratis, and Bugattis hurtling along the narrow undulating tree-lined roads at 140mph (224kph). DSJ

Pikes Peak

Popular on a regional basis, US hill-climbing is without a national championship series. The Sports Car Club of America includes hill-climbs in its solo events programme and regional organizers such as the Pennsylvania Hill Climb Asso., who run Giants Despair and Duryea Drive in eastern Pennsylvania, are active in many parts of America.

Each July the 5·2-mile (8·369km) private road up Mt Equinox in Vermont opens for a hill-climb; Chimney Rock, N.Car., is run regularly; and hill-climb groups are active on the West Coast. But only Pikes Peak, a 12·42-

miles (20km), dirt road that climbs through 154 turns to the clouds in the Rocky Mountains of Colorado, is known nationally. The first speed hill-climb was held here in 1916, when Rea Lentz made ftd (20min 55·6sec) in an aircraft-engined Romano Special.

It is said that the Unser family of Albuqurque, New Mexico, originally residents of Colorado Springs at the base of 14,110ft (4,301m) Pikes Peak, own the Hill. Bobby Unser, 1968 Indianapolis winner, has won Pikes Peak 11 times and holds records in Championship, Stock and the Sports Car class which was discontinued in 1967. The seven racing Unsers, including Uncle Louis, winner of nine climbs between 1934 and 1953 and Bobby's younger brother Al, winner in 1964 and 1965, have won Pikes Peak 26 times in its 47 years history.

In 1969 Mario Andretti acquired 30 points toward his USAC Championship total when he won the championship car class driving the Unser brothers' 5·4-litre front-engined Chevrolet dirt car. Until 1970, when a crowded calendar forced its withdrawal, Pikes Peak constituted a round in the US Auto Club Championship Trail. ARB

Pikes Peak Records

Championship Cars
1968 Bobby Unser (11min 54·90sec)   *Unser Chevrolet Special*

Stock Cars
1969 Bobby Unser (12min 40·05sec)   *Ford Torino*

Sports Cars
1964 Bobby Unser (13min 19sec)   *Lotus-Climax*

Pocono International Raceway

A 500-mile race for Indianapolis championship cars is scheduled to open a 2·5-mile (4km) tri-oval in the Pocono Mountains of eastern Pennsylvania on July 3, 1971. Located near Long Pond, about 85 miles (136km) from both New York and Philadelphia, Pocono International Raceway opened its 1·8-mile (2·9km) club course, three-quarter-mile (1·2km) oval and drag strip late in 1969. With Ontario and Indianapolis, Pocono becomes the third 500-mile event in the US Auto Club multi-million dollar Triple Crown. However, the 2·5-mile (4km), 60ft (18m) wide Pocono circuit, though the same length as the Speedway and Ontario, consists of three unequal straights. The first turn at PIR has a radius of 675ft (205·7m), and a 14° banking; the back straight is 3,055ft (931m); the second turn radius is 750ft (228·6m) with 8° banks followed by a short straight of 1,780ft

Pike's Peak: Jerry Unser Jr in the Offenhauser-powered Coniff Special. *Photo: Dr Vicente Alvarez*

(542·5m); the third turn radius is 800ft (243·8m) with 6° banks; the main straight being 3,740ft (1,140m). ARB

Pollsmoor Circuit see Cape Town Circuits

Portuguese GP see Oporto Circuit

Posillipo Circuit see Naples Circuit

Prescott Hill-Climb

The history of the Prescott hill-climb in Gloucestershire began in 1938. Tom Rolt, a founder member of the Vintage Sports Car Club, realized the potential of the driveway up to Prescott House, just north of Cheltenham, in 1937. The VSCC could not afford the initial outlay to develop the venue and so passed it on to the Bugatti Owners Club, who were looking for a suitable place for a hill-climb. Rolt, who lived near by, made the necessary introductions. In recognition of this, the Bugatti Owners Club allow the VSCC to hold an annual hill-climb meeting at Prescott.

Set in beautiful English countryside, the course winds its way up the wooded slopes, with two very sharp hairpin bends, a fast S, a deceptive left-hander and a never-ending right-hander which leads to the short finishing straight, the original length being 880yd (804·7m). In

Pocono International Raceway

Prescott: Pardon Hairpin with the new extension known as Ettore's Bend leading off to the right. *Photo: Studio 3*

1960 an extra loop of road was built cutting out the first hairpin but introducing another one further up the valley. It was known as Ettore's Bend, after Ettore Bugatti. This increased the length to 1,127yd (1,030·3m), but the VSCC by tradition still use the original 880yd course for their annual event.

In the time that it has been in operation, short compared to some venues, Prescott has built up an enviable reputation. The BOC have retained a pleasant and friendly atmosphere at the hill and the organization is devoid of too much professionalism. At the first meeting, on 15 May 1938, the ftd was set at 50·70 seconds by Arthur Baron in a Type 51 Bugatti, and by 1958 the record had been reduced to 41·00 seconds by David Boshier-Jones in a V-twin Cooper-JAP, a new era starting with the revised longer course. A new ftd was established at the opening of the 1,127yd course in June 1960 when David Boshier-Jones recorded 52·48sec, but this is now down to 46·01sec, set by Peter Lawson (BRM) in September 1968. DSJ

Prix de Paris see Montlhéry Circuit

Pukekohe Circuit
Completed a week before the 10th New Zealand Grand Prix, which was held in January 1963, Pukekohe, 35 miles (56km) south of Auckland, is administered by New Zealand International Grand Prix (Inc), and is the venue for the Grand Prix and the home circuit for Auckland-based car clubs. Built around the perimeter of

Pukekohe Circuit

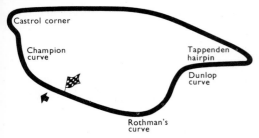

Castrol corner
Champion curve
Tappenden hairpin
Dunlop curve
Rothman's curve

a horse-racing track, the original 2·1773-mile (3·5035km) circuit — now used for the annual Benson & Hedges 500-mile production saloon car race, in which 40 starters are permitted, as well as some other events — has been supplemented by the faster 1·75-mile (2·816km) Grand Prix course, first used in 1967, and an 0·75-mile (1·207km) club circuit. Amenities include covered grandstands, hillside spectator terraces and a light aircraft landing strip. The short and long courses embody a flat-out straight with a slight curve in it to a hairpin from which there is a slight down gradient to a fast, bumpy left-hand curve, followed by a climbing right-hander and a descent to the start-finish line in the pit straight. The short course then swings right in a fast curve that is followed by comparatively tight left- and right-hand corners back to the main straight. The long course swings sharply left at the end of the pit straight and a short straight is followed by a right-hand loop and straight which culminates in a 90° turn into the main straight. Electric power poles that flank one side of the main straight are considered hazardous.

All Grands Prix held there have been under Tasman Formula rules, with the exception of the first 75-lap race which was won by John Surtees (Lola-Climax) at

85·3mph (137·28kph) from New Zealanders Angus Hyslop (Cooper-Climax) and Jim Palmer (Cooper-Climax). Average speeds in the Benson & Hedges 500, the other premier event on the Pukekohe calendar, have been about 65mph (104kph) in the years 1968–9 when the winning car was a 3·3-litre Vauxhall Victor. Lap record: Jochen Rindt (Lotus 49T); 58·9sec; 1969. PG

RAC Rally of Great Britain
The RAC Rally of Great Britain is one of the premier international events of Europe. As well as being one of the best organized, it is also one of the toughest and regularly attracts a bigger entry than even the Monte Carlo Rally. The story of the RAC Rally started in the early 1930s, when the RAC decided to run a rally which would base itself very much on the Monte Carlo. The first event was held in 1932. There were several starting places from which the entrants converged on some central point and then followed a common route to the finish. Along the way, they tackled several driving tests of a type similar to the infamous 'wiggle-woggle' of the Monte Carlo and these were laid out in convenient open spaces such as municipal car parks. The finish was normally at a seaside resort and before World War 2, such towns as Hastings, Torquay and Blackpool had all served as hosts to drivers who had tackled five days and one night of rallying.

Hill-climbs were added to the driving tests after a few years and by the time that the war was finished and the rally re-started again in 1951, it had grown to a full international. For the first two years there was no official classification and the class results were the most important. The driving tests still remained, though the number of hill-climbs and difficult road sections was on the increase. In 1957 the rally was cancelled and when it started again in 1958, there was a quiet gentleman called Jack Kemsley on the organizing committee. He turned out to be the father of the modern RAC Rally; the event which Gerry Burgess won with a Ford Zodiac in 1959, after much protest about roads closed by snow in Scotland, was the last of the classic type.

The driving tests were out and for the 1960 event,

Winners of the RAC Rally

Year	Driver	Car
1951	Ian Appleyard	Jaguar
1952	Goff Imhof	Cadillac-Allard
1953	Ian Appleyard	Jaguar
1954	Johnny Wallwork	Triumph TR2
1955	Jimmy Ray	Standard 8
1956	Lyndon Sims	Aston Martin
1957	Rally cancelled	
1958	Peter Harper	Sunbeam Rapier
1959	Gerry Burgess	Ford Zodiac
1960	Erik Carlsson	Saab 850
1961	Erik Carlsson	Saab 850
1962	Erik Carlsson	Saab 850
1963	Tom Trana	Volvo PV 544
1964	Tom Trana	Volvo PV 544
1965	Rauno Aaltonen	1275 Cooper S
1966	Bengt Söderström	Ford Cortina Lotus Mk I
1967	Rally cancelled	
1968	Simo Lampinen	Saab V-4
1969	Harry Kallström	Lancia Fulvia 1600
1970	Harry Kallström	Lancia Fulvia 1600

RAC Rally: Bo Ljungfeldt and Fergus Sager (Ford Cortina GT) on a special section in North Wales, 1964. *Photo: Francis Penn*

RAC Rally: Åke Andersson and Bo Thorszelius (Porsche 911S) on the Exton Park special section, 1970. *Photo: Hugh W. Bishop*

Left, Reims: start of the 1938 French GP, von Brauchitsch and Lang (Mercedes-Benz W154) on the front line. *Photo: David Hodges Collection*

Below left, Reims: Stuck (Auto Union) and Le Begue (Talbot) in Gueux village, 1939 French GP. *Photo: David Hodges Collection*

Bottom left, Reims: start of the 1958 French GP, Schell (BRM) leading Brooks (Vanwall), Hawthorn (Ferrari) and Collins (Ferrari). *Photo: David Hodges Collection*

Reims Circuit

Muizon

Bretelle nord

Bretelle sud

Thillois

Kemsley introduced special stages, though only a handful and at a lower average speed than is now common. A straightforward road section with navigation akin to national events was included and the rally of that year was won by Erik Carlsson, Stuart Turner and the small Saab. The following year, Kemsley got permission to use special stages in the forests. The road sections were no longer of importance and the only thing that counted was speed on the stages, which brought the rally into line with the traditional Scandinavian events and took it away from the Monte Carlo/Coupe des Alpes pattern. It is perhaps not surprising that a Scandinavian driver has won it every year since then, and indeed Erik Carlsson founded his great reputation on his three consecutive victories in this event.

Until 1958, the rally had alway been held in March but then it was changed to the second week of November, where it has remained ever since. The appearance of snow on this rally is no great surprise to anyone, but 1965 will long be remembered in that respect. Competitors in 1969 had the chance to prove how good they were in snow without spikes as the RAC Rally is one event that forbids the use of studded tyres. The rally has always been improving and is today sponsored by the *Daily Mirror*. Through its pages, plus the medium of television, international rallying has been brought into the homes of thousands of British people. JD

Rand 9-hour Race see Kyalami Circuit

Reims Circuit

Races on the circuit at Reims, in northern France, are run by the Automobile Club du Champagne, the cathedral city of Reims being the centre of the champagne industry. The circuit lies to the west of the city and is comprised of public roads in the form of a triangle run clockwise, the fastest leg being the downhill Route Nationale N31 which is the main Soissons to Reims road. It is an extremely fast circuit and up to 1951 it ran through the village of Gueux when it left the start, taking a right angle turn in the middle of the village and heading uphill to join the N31 at a crossroads. In the search for an ever faster circuit and to avoid the problems of racing through a village, it was altered in 1952 by the addition of a fast right-hand curve after the pits passing behind Gueux village, over the old Gueux to N31 road at right-angles, round a fast climbing right-hander, downhill to a left-hander and then to a hairpin to join the N31 at Muizon. Not only did this cut out the slow section in the village, but it also gave a much longer run along the main road, eastwards towards Reims with a very fast stretch down the hill to the hairpin at Thillois. There it turned right on to the undulating finishing straight, this last hairpin also being eased and banked to increase the lap speed, the aim being 125mph (200kph).

Racing started at Reims in 1925, with the Grand Prix of the Marne, named after the *département*, and the following year the Grand Prix was accompanied by a 12-hour touring car race. In 1932 the Grand Prix of the Automobile Club of France was held at Reims, won by Nuvolari (Alfa Romeo) at 92·297mph (148·538kph) and this event returned in 1938 and 1939. In the final race before the war Hermann Müller (Auto Union) raised the average speed to 105·249mph (169·381kph), all the while using the route through Gueux village. The Marne GP was reinstated in 1947, accompanied by a supporting race for 'Petites Cylindrées', won by 'B. Bira' with a Simca-Gordini, but that was the last time the original title for the Grand Prix was used. After that it was changed in various forms to the Grand Prix de Reims or the Grand Prix de France, as distinct from the Grand Prix de l'ACF which remained the premier race in France. The sports car race was revived in 1952, won by Stirling Moss in a C-type Jaguar. In subsequent 12-hour races the Reims circuit had the distinction of being the only one ever to have a curtain to keep the sun from the driver's eyes. As cars came down the hill to Thillois at sunrise the sun was dead centre in line with the road, so beyond the hairpin a bridge was built and vast velvet curtains were hung from it which blotted out the sun until it had risen quite high, the 12-hour races being run from midnight on Saturday to midday on Sunday.

In 1953 Mike Hawthorn won his memorable race against Fangio in the 40th Grand Prix de l'ACF and all the while the average speeds were rising. Peter Collins (Ferrari) won at 122·287mph (196·802kph) in 1956 and Luigi Musso (Ferrari) won the Reims GP in 1957 at 123·396mph (198·587kph), the magic 125mph (200kph) coming ever closer. It was achieved in 1958 when Hawthorn (Ferrari) won again, averaging 125·453mph (201·898kph), this time in the Grand Prix de l'ACF, and the following year Tony Brooks went even faster with a Ferrari, averaging 125·454mph (205·079kph). The speeds continued to rise and in 1960 Jack Brabham raised the race average to 131·801mph (212·113kph) and the lap record to 135·057mph (217·354kph). During the next five years GP races were limited to 1·5-litre cars so there was no further improvement, but in 1966 when the new 3-litre limit was introduced, Jack Brabham in his Brabham-Repco V-8 set an all-time race record of 135·058mph (220·315kph). Lorenzo Bandini made fastest lap at 141·435mph (227·618kph), though in practice he had gone round at 145·308mph (233·852kph). This was to be the last Formula 1 Grand Prix at Reims and the circuit began to lose status, running only Formula 2, Formula 3 and sports car events. In 1970 the club ran into financial as well as political difficulties and had problems over closing the roads, especially the Soissons–Reims road, so that the annual speed meeting had to be cancelled. Lap record: Paul Hawkins (Lola-Chevrolet); 142·32mph (229·04kph); 2min 10·5sec; 1967. DSJ

Rhodesian GP see Kumalo Circuit

Ricard-Castellet Circuit

Paul Ricard, a French liqueur manufacturer, financed this southern French circuit, built during 1969 and opened with a 2-litre Sports Car Championship qualifying round in April 1970. The circuit is about 20 minutes motoring from the village of Le Castellet, between Marseilles and Toulon, and offers three courses: 3·61 miles (5·81km), 2·02 miles (3·263km) and 1·36 miles (2·2km). Sited on a plateau the course is virtually level and rather featureless but has some good facilities. Reputed cost of the project is over one million francs. Brian Redman won the opening race at an average of 87·21mph (140·35kph) in his 2-litre Chevron-Cosworth B16. The initial lap record was set by Bonnier's Lola-Cosworth T210 at 90·03mph (145kph); 1min 21sec on the 2·02-mile circuit. The record for the 3·61-mile circuit is held by François Cevert (Tecno F2) at 106·46mph (172·290kph); 2min 1·4sec. DCN

Riverside International Raceway

Located 60 miles (96km) east of Los Angeles, in the shadow of the San Bernardino Mountains on the out-

Reims: Muizon Corner (exit to the RN31 straight leading to Thillois). Brabham-Climax following Cooper-Maserati in 1966 French GP. *Photo: David Hodges Collection*

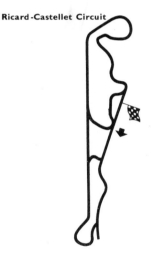

Ricard-Castellet Circuit

Right, Riverside: start of the 1962 Los Angeles Times GP. *Photo: Al Bochroch*

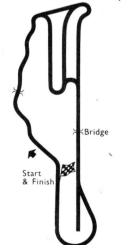

Riverside International Raceway

skirts of Riverside, this has been a major American road course since 1957. In 1958, before the Sports Car Club of America countenanced professional racing, the Riverside GP for sports cars was sanctioned by USAC. The initial race was won by Chuck Daigh in Lance Reventlow's Scarab with Dan Gurney, 2nd in a Ferrari.

Offering substantial purses and held each autumn when leading overseas drivers were in America for the United States GP, the professional sports car races at Riverside, with Laguna Seca and the Canadian tracks, were forerunners of the Can-Am series.

Following its financially disastrous introduction at Sebring in December 1959, Alec Ulmann brought the 1960 United States GP to Riverside, to fare no better in the California desert than among Florida's orange groves.

Phil Hill in a 3-litre Ferrari won the first Times GP in 1959 with an 89·05mph (143·31kph) average. Hap Sharp's Chevrolet-powered, automatic transmission Chaparral won in 1965 with a 102mph (164·2kph) average, the first entry to exceed 100mph (160kph). In 1969 Denny Hulme's winning McLaren averaged 120·8mph (194·4kph).

One of the most active US tracks, since 1963 Riverside has opened its season with a 500-mile stock car race (five times won by Dan Gurney) that was NASCAR's only major race over a road course and, until 1970, its single Grand National on the West Coast. Riverside has been the site of Trans-Am, Formula A-Continental, Can-Am, USAC road races for Indianapolis championship cars and until 1970, on alternate years, host for the SCCA, ARRC annual amateur run-offs.

As indicated on the circuit map, the length of the Riverside track can be varied for different events. Construction during summer of 1969 slightly altered the length of all three circuits.

While Riverside flourished under the management of former Los Angeles football star, Les Richter, the opening of nearby Ontario Speedway, the confusion that accompanied Riverside's acquisition by American Raceways and the reorganization which returned control to Richter, raises question as to its future.

Lap records: 2·62-mile (4·216km) circuit: Gurney (Plymouth Sedan); 111·087mph (178·741kph); 1min 24·25sec; 1970. NASCAR 2·54-mile (4·088km) circuit: Dan Gurney (Eagle-Ford); 118·515mph (190·728kph); 1min 15·95sec; 1969. USAC 3·3-mile (5·311km) circuit: Denis Hulme (McLaren-Chevrolet); 126·342mph (203·363kph); 1min 34·03sec; 1969. ARB

Road America Circuit

The park-like Road America circuit had its beginnings in 1950 when the Chicago Region of the SCCA sponsored sports car races on public highways in the Wisconsin hamlet of Elkhart Lake. After three successful years, a state law banning 'racing or speed events on public roads' resulted in local businessmen, headed by Clif Tufte, building the rolling 4-mile (6·437km) circuit, 2 miles (3·2km) east of Elkhart Lake. Famed Milwaukee beer, brewed 65 miles south of Elkhart Lake, and the circuit's refreshment stand specialities of grilled brat-wurst and fresh roasted corn, have made Road America as well known for its atmosphere of *Gemütlichkeit*, as for the quality of its racing. Shaded hillsides and a network of well-maintained trails enable spectators to move freely inside the course.

It is difficult to find an important American driver who has not raced at Elkhart Lake and Road America. After Jim Kimberley's Ferrari won the 1950 curtain-raiser, John Fitch drove a big blue and white Cunningham to victory in 1951. Fitch won again in 1952, leading Cunninghams home 1-2-3, with Phil Walters 2nd and Briggs Cunningham himself 3rd. Phil Hill, who was to win the first race over the closed course in 1955, finished 4th in 1952. The next decade saw the American stalwarts Carroll Shelby, Walt Hansgen, Roger Penske, Augie Pabst and Jim Hall winning major races at Road America.

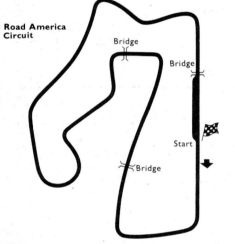

Road America Circuit

In addition to traditional club meets, Road America schedules Trans-Am, Formula A Continental and a late summer Can-Am. In the 1970 Can-Am Denis Hulme, after finishing first, was disqualified for accepting a push start on the circuit, his new team-mate, Peter Gethin, getting credit for the victory. Lap record: Denis Hulme (McLaren-Chevrolet); 112·150mph (180·480kph); 2min 8·4sec; 1969. ARB

Road Atlanta Circuit

A rolling 2·52-mile (4·056km), 11-turn circuit, located in Gainesville, Ga., Road Atlanta is the only major road racing course in the Southeastern United States, the heart of stock car racing. The Canadian-American Challenge Cup event of 13 September 1970, originally scheduled for Bridgehampton, was moved to Road Atlanta after the New York circuit failed to meet 1970 Can-Am safety and financial requirements. The inaugural race was won by Tony Dean's Porsche 908— the first of 20 consecutive Can-Am races not won by a Team McLaren entry. The winner's average speed 103·45mph (166·48kph). Beginning November 1970,

Opposite, Daytona International Speedway: Peter DaCosta (Porsche, No 6) and Roger Penske (Cooper Monaco, No 46) in the 1962 Daytona Continental. *Photo: Al Bochroch*

Roskilde Ring: two Ford Anglias and a Fiat-Abarth in a 1966 saloon car race. *Photo: Tuchsen Pressefoto*

Road Atlanta Circuit

Start & Finish

SCCA national amateur championships, the American Road Race of Champions, are staged at the Georgia circuit. Lap record: Pete Revson (Lola) and Peter Gethin (McLaren); 116·40mph (187·30kph) 1hr 18min 5sec; 1970. ARB

Roskilde Ring

Copenhagen's tiny Roskilde Ring was opened on 1 June 1956 and the main event in the inaugural meeting was won by Arthur Owen's Cooper-Climax. Lap length was a mere 0·404 miles (0·65km), and the banked loop of asphalt had large painted advertising signs on its surface which apparently made things slippery in the wet. It became the style at Roskilde to run events in a series of very short heats, winners being decided on aggregate times or on a points system.

International sports car races were held from 1957 to 1959. In 1960 the F2 Copenhagen GP was initiated, Brabham (Cooper) winning from Hill (Lotus) at 69·62mph (112·04kph), and George Lawton (who had come to Europe from New Zealand with Denny Hulme) was killed. Formula Junior events were inaugurated that same year for the Copenhagen Cup and the Copenhagen Junior GP, and these ran until 1963. In 1961 and 1962, F1 cars contested the GP, Moss and Brabham (both driving Lotus-Climaxes) winning at 70·21mph (113·00kph) and 70·49mph (113·44kph) respectively. In

1963 the GP was for FJ cars, Revson's Cooper winning, and from then until the circuit was closed in the late 1960s, international F3 events were run, winners including Ahrens (in 1965) when one of Roskilde's last major meetings was held. Although it had grown a little it was still ridiculously tight and tiny, and Danish motor racing soon centred on Djursland and the Jyllandsring. DCN

Rossfeld Hill-Climb

This wooded climb is near Hitler's notorious eyrie at Berchtesgaden in Bavaria, and it is short and tight with a difficult series of hairpins before the finish. The start is by the Gasthof Obersalzburg, and the climb runs up the mountainside for 3·66 miles (5·89km). The climb is difficult and can be dangerous, and it was here that Lodovico Scarfiotti lost his life in 1968. Record: Rolf Stommelen (Porsche Bergspyder); 73·15mph (118·2kph); 2min 59·37sec; 1967. DCN

Rouen-Les Essarts Circuit

Another of the medium-fast French road circuits, that at Essarts is laid out round a wooded valley, 7·45 miles

(12km) south from Rouen and 3·11 miles (5km) north of Elbeuf. It is formed from the RN138 and RN840, with a linking road on the western side running from the Nouveau Monde hairpin through Sanson to Gresil where it rejoins RN 138 to Rouen.

There was a short circuit through this valley between the wars, and in 1950 the Automobile Club Normand created a 3·17-mile (5·10km) circuit, climbing through Sanson and then turning right at the Virage de Beauval on to a straight connecting with the current pits and start-line area. The first meeting at this circuit was on 30 July 1950, Rosier's Talbot winning the main event; and in 1952 the French Grand Prix was held there, Alberto Ascari winning the 3-hour race at 80·14mph (128·97kph).

In 1955 the circuit was extended to its present length of 4·06 miles (6·542km), and the GP was again held there in 1957, 1962, 1964 and 1968. The Rouen Grand Prix has been held annually for sports, F1, FJ and recently F2 and F3 cars, and this narrow but difficult and testing course has seen some tremendous motor racing. It was here in 1957 that Fangio's Maserati flicked through the difficult downhill section to Nouveau Monde in a series of power-on drifts; and here that Dan Gurney scored two of his four World Championship-round wins, for Porsche and Brabham-Climax. The 1968 French GP was organized by the FFSA club and presented as the 'first' Grand Prix de France. It was run in a downpour. Ickx's Ferrari won at 100·45mph (161·662kph), while Schlesser crashed fatally on the downhill section to Nouveau Monde. Lap record: Tim Schenken (Brabham BT30); 121·143mph (194·960kph); 2min 0·8sec; 1970. DCN

St Jovite Circuit

Le Circuit Mont Tremblant–St Jovite in French-speaking Canada, 90 miles north of Montreal, was 1·5 miles (2·414km) long when Pedro Rodriguez's Ferrari won its first international event in September 1964. The course was lengthened to 2·65 miles (4·265km), and on 11 September 1966 the first Canadian-American Challenge Cup race ever held was run here. Located in Laurentian Mountain ski country, few race circuits have a more picturesque setting. As it is narrow, making passing difficult, and as several bumps can get the unwary airborne, some drivers consider St Jovite a tricky circuit.

In addition to the Can-Am, St Jovite is the site of Canadian club racing; Trans-Am Sedans; Formula A Continental and the Grand Prix of Canada on alternate years. Also, Indianapolis championship cars, though not scheduled regularly, have raced at St Jovite.

Lap records — (USAC): Al Unser (Lola-Ford 4wd); 99·69mph (160·43kph); 1min 35·7sec; 1968. (Can-Am): Hulme (McLaren-Chevrolet); 101·70mph (163·60kph); 1min 33·8sec; 1969. (F1): Clay Regazzoni (Ferrari 312B); 103·467mph (173·277kph); 1min 32·2sec; 1970. ARB

St Petersburg Races

There was very little motor sport in Tsarist Russia, and as nearly all of it centred on the old capital of St Petersburg (now Leningrad) it is convenient to consider all the events under this heading. The first recorded motor race in Russia took place in 1898 on a 25·849-mile (41·6km) circuit and was won by the Russian driver Mazi in a Panhard. His average speed was 14·91mph (24kph). Four years later the journal *Automobile* organized a race on a 39·77-mile (64km) route from Krasnoye Selo to Gatchina and back, won by Suromec in a Georges

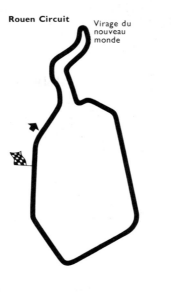

Rouen Circuit — Virage du nouveau monde

Top right, Rouen: the pits, 1952 French GP. *Photo: David Hodges Collection*

Right, Rouen: Nouveau Monde hairpin, 1952 French GP. *Photo: David Hodges Collection*

Below right, Rouen: curves between pits and Nouveau Monde, 1964 French GP. *Photo: Motor*

Opposite, Jarama Circuit: Jim Clark (Lotus), the winner, leading Jackie Stewart (Matra) in the 1967 Madrid GP. *Photo: Doug Nye*

St Jovite Circuit — Start & Finish

Richard at 27·79mph (44·78kph). In 1907 and 1908 the St Petersburg–Moscow Race was held. This was an incredibly punishing event of 438·25 miles (705·29km) over atrocious roads, won in 1907 by Duray in a Lorraine-Dietrich, and in 1908 by Hémery in a Benz, at the remarkable average speed of 52·4mph (82·72kph). There was no native automobile industry at that time so all the cars were foreign, as well as all the successful drivers.

During the years up to 1914 a number of long-distance trials were held, more in the nature of rallies than races, in which large German cars did best, although two British makes, Lagonda and Austin, achieved successes with smaller machines. The first race on an enclosed

circuit was the St Petersburg Grand Prix of 1914, held on a 19·88-mile (32km) course, Volchonka–Krasnoye Selo–Litchevo–Volchonka. The race covered seven laps, giving a distance of 139·19 miles (224km). Fourteen cars started, the winner being O. V. Šoll in a 15-litre Benz. His average speed was 77·05mph (124kph), and the fastest lap 85·75mph; (138kph). The outbreak of World War 1 prevented any further Grands Prix being held at St Petersburg, and after the Revolution of 1917 there was no motor sport in Russia for 20 years. VH

San Remo Rally see Italian Rally

San Sebastian Circuit

The 11·029-mile (17·6km) Lasarte circuit lay on the outskirts of the famous Spanish Atlantic coast resort of San Sebastian. Racing began there in 1923 with a series of events including voiturette races, a Touring Car Grand Prix and a Grand Prix proper of 277 miles (446km). This gave the GP Rolland-Pilain one of its few victories. The Grand Prix was held annually until 1928, the 1926 event being the European Grand Prix. In addition, the Spanish GP (a separate race) was held on the Lasarte circuit from 1926 to 1935. The Touring Car Grand Prix became a 12-hour event in 1925, and was held until 1929. Lap Record: Achille Varzi (Auto Union); 108·185mph (174·107kph); 5min 58sec; 1935. GNG

St Petersburg Races: start of the 1914 St Petersburg GP. Photo: Vladmir Havránek Collection

Sears Point Raceway

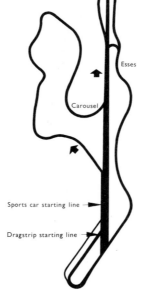

Seattle International Raceway

San Sebastian: André Dubonnet (Hispani-Suiza) in the 1923 Spanish Touring Car GP. Photo: José Rodriguez-Viña Collection

Savannah Grand Prize see American Grand Prize

Sears Point Raceway

Located 35 miles (56km) north of San Francisco, near Sonoma, on the edge of the California wine country. Opened early in 1969, the twisty, 2·52 mile Sears Point course had been the site of drag meets, stock car, Formula A Continental and Trans-Am racing. While the hilly circuit was considered tight, in 1970 Sears Point was scheduled to run one of the few USAC sanctioned 'Indy' championship car road races, as well as the final round in the 11 race Canadian-American Challenge Cup series for Group 7 sport cars. Claiming the circuit was losing money, its owners, a TV production organization, closed Sears Point in the summer of 1970, eliminating the final race in the Can-Am series. Lap record: Dan Gurney (Eagle-Ford); 92·523mph (148·895kph); 1min 37·0sec; 1970. ARB

Seattle International Raceways

A sharply rolling 2·25-mile (3·621km) road course and drag strip near Kent, Wash., 26 miles (41·84km) south of Seattle, opened in 1960 as Pacific Raceways. It is the site of SCCA club racing, Formula A Continental and Trans-Am events. Lap record (qualifying): Ron Grable (Lola-Chevrolet T190); 107·00mph (172·20kph); 1min 15·7sec; 1970. ARB

Sebring Circuit

American motor-racing promoters include former professional football players, race drivers and airline pilots. But only one, Sebring's Alex Ulmann, can be called an impresario. The 6-hour Sam Collier Memorial on 31 December 1950 was the first race over the flat, 5·2-mile (8·369km) combination of abandoned airport runways and country roads. Ulmann, who had used one of the Sebring airport warehouses to store surplus World War 2 aircraft parts, assumed responsibility for the first Sebring after Sam Collier was fatally injured at Watkins Glen in October 1950. The second Sebring, in March 1952, was the first to last 12 hours. But it was not until 1953, when the FIA introduced the Manufacturers' Championship, that the nondescript, central Florida retirement village began to play host to international motor racing.

Ulmann first became interested in automobiles as a small boy when he saw the start of the 1908 St Petersburg–Moscow Race. After the Revolution had driven the Ulmann family from Russia. Ulmann and his English-born wife Mary became active in the then budding Sports Car Club of America. But Ulmann was always internationally minded. After 1953, when John Fitch and Phil Walters won in the American-built Cunningham, no American car or team of American drivers were to win the Florida 12-Hour Grand Prix of Endurance until 1965, when the Texans Jim Hall and Hap Sharp survived a cloudburst to finish 1st in their Chevrolet-powered Chaparral. In 1954 Stirling Moss registered his only Sebring victory, teaming with American Bill Lloyd to bring their Osca home in front of the Rubirosa and Valenzano Lancia. This was to be a golden decade in American racing: the Mike Hawthorn and Phil Walters D-type Jaguar nosing out the Carroll Shelby and Phil Hill Ferrari in 1955; Fangio winning with Castellotti in 1956 in a Ferrari and again in 1957, teamed with Jean Behra in a Maserati. In 1958 Peter Collins and Phil Hill began the remarkable sequence that was to see Ferrari win six of the next seven races. Phil Hill and Olivier Gendebien were to win three Sebrings. Ford began to show its muscle in 1965 when the late Ken Miles and Bruce McLaren finished 2nd.

In 1966 Ford crushed the competition with Miles and Ruby, Hansgen and Donohue, and Scott and Revson sweeping the boards. Average speeds for the 12 hours had climbed from 62·83mph (101·12kph) for the Kulok and Gray 1952 winning Frazer Nash, until 1967 winners Mario Andretti and Bruce McLaren, 7-litre, Ford Mk 4, broke the 100mph (160kph) barrier with a 102·923mph (165·635kph) race average. In 1968 Jo Siffert and Hans Herrmann brought Porsche—and Herrmann who had shared the winning Porsche with Gendebien in 1960—their 2nd victory. Sebring ended the 1960s with one of its

Sebring: Cobra passing a ditched Abarth. Photo: Al Bochroch

Sebring Circuit

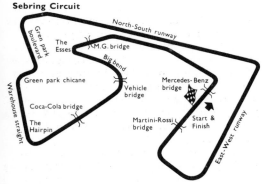

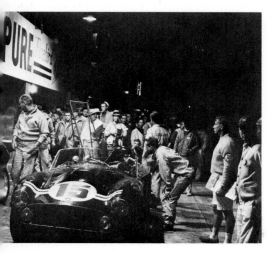

Sebring: Cobra pits at night; Dan Gurney in car, talking to Phill Hill. Photo: Al Bochroch

best races ever when Ickx and Oliver drove John Wyer's 5-litre Ford GT40 to a record-breaking win over the 3-litre Ferrari 312P of Chris Amon and Mario Andretti.

Although improvements have been made, the old bomber training base runways continue to deteriorate and Ulmann has announced plans to build eventually a new circuit six miles south of the village. Lap record: Jo Siffert (Porsche 917); 124·418mph (200·232kph); 2min 30·46sec; 1971. ARB

Sestrière Rally see Italian Rally

Shelsley Walsh Hill-Climb
Situated some 10 miles (16km) west of the city of Worcester, the hill used for sporting events climbs for 1,000yd (914·4m) from the orchard where the paddock is situated to the open fields at the top of the escarpment on Court House Farm which the owner, Mr Montague C. H. Taylor, first gave permission to the Midland Automobile Club to use in 1905. It was then little more than a bridlepath, but the club members could see its potential as a hill-climb, and after much labour in widening and clearing, the first Shelsley Walsh hill-climb was held on 12 August 1905. Still in use today, it is the oldest surviving speed hill-climb in the British Isles. It represents a particularly challenging event by reason of the speeds attainable between the corners in its short 1,000yd length, and the steepness of its gradient at the S-bend midway up the climb.

The start is already on an incline and the narrow road climbs sharply between banks, round the fast Kennel Bend, through the Crossing, and steeply up to the famous Shelsley-S. Well over 100mph (160kph) is attainable on this short straight and heavy braking is called for to negotiate the left-hand bend of the S. The right-hander is blind, and once out of it the road runs straight up and over the horizon, as much as 120mph (192kph) being reached across the finishing line.

From a sedate 77·6sec for the record in 1905, set up by E. M. C. Instone with a Daimler, the time has been reduced to 48·8sec in 1926 by B. H. Davenport (Spider), 38·77sec in 1937 by A. F. P. Fane (Frazer Nash) and down to the incredible 30·72sec by M. Brain with his Cooper-Chrysler, established in 1969. DSJ

Sierre–Montana–Crans Hill-Climb
This classic Swiss mountain course winds its way from the village of Sierre up to the finish just short of Montana. It is situated in Valais, 70·84 miles (114km) south-east of Lausanne and 26·72 miles (43km) from Martigny, quite near Brigue and the Col du Simplon. The road is 6·835 miles (11km) long, and rises from 1,936ft (590m) to 4,626ft (1,410m). The course was part of the 1968 Mountain Championship but not the 1969 series. Record: Gerhard Mitter (Porsche Bergspyder); 69·24mph (111·423kph); 5min 55·38sec; 1968. DCN

Silverstone Circuit
In the immediate post-World War 2 years the RAC examined many disused airfields in Britain in its quest for new racing circuits. These airfields were nearly all isolated from residential areas, and thus less likely to cause complaints about noise nuisance. The Northamptonshire airfield near Silverstone village seemed suitable, and the RAC devised a circuit there for the 1948 British GP. A 3·67-mile (5·896km) circuit was laid out, using both main runways and linking sections of perimeter road in a giant X-shape. Barriers in the centre

Silverstone Circuit

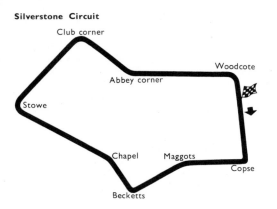

Snetterton Circuit

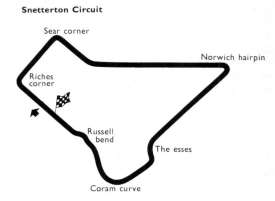

of the X saved drivers the unnerving sight of competitors approaching them, and the pits and start were established between Abbey Curve and Woodcote on today's circuit.

Villoresi won the first GP there in a Maserati at 72·28mph (116·32kph), and for 1949 the circuit was altered, using the perimeter road only and measuring exactly 3 miles to the lap (4·828km). The BRDC took over management of the circuit, farming the infield, and with help from the *Daily Express* initiated their International Trophy race in 1949, the first being won by Ascari in a Ferrari at 89·58mph (114·17kph). A club circuit was used taking in one of the longer runways in 1949–51, measuring 2·278 miles (3·67km), and this was shortened in 1952 to 1·608 miles (2·703km). The full circuit shrank to 2·889 miles (4·780km) in 1950–51 and settled at its present 2·9 miles (4·667km) in 1952.

In 1955 the British GP went to Aintree for the first time, returning to Silverstone in 1956, 1958 and 1960, then alternating between Silverstone and Brands Hatch from 1963 to date. The circuit became the home of production car racing under the BRDC's aegis, and became a 100mph (160kph) circuit early in the 1950s.

Many club race meetings were held regularly at the circuit, including historic car events organized by the Vintage Sports Car Club, and the 6-Hour Relay Race. Good pit and paddock facilities are available and the original scaffolding grandstands have survived to this day, Very large crowds have been claimed for almost every major meeting and although it is a typical airfield circuit, exposed, windy and bleak in bad weather, Silverstone has an air of history about it, lacking in the newer, and perhaps better-exploited circuits. It is also Britain's fastest motor-racing venue, with Stewart's 1969 lap record with his Matra-Cosworth Ford standing at 1min 21·3sec, 129·61mph (208·58kph). DCN

Right, Snetterton: production sports car race, 1960. Left to right, Marcos, Turner, Turner, Turner. *Photo: Michael Ware*

Left, Silverstone: Lola 70GTs, driven by Piper, Craft and Bonnier in the 1969 Martini Trophy. *Photo: London Art Tech*

Right below, Solitude: start of the 1961 Solitude GP. Ireland (Lotus) in the lead, followed by Herrmann (Porsche), McLaren (Cooper) and Gurney (Porsche). *Photo: Bernard Cahier*

Snetterton Circuit

This circuit lies in the flat East Anglian countryside some 18 miles (2·9km) south-west of Norwich. It was opened in October 1951, and was the brainchild of Oliver Sear. Lap length was 2·71 miles (4·361km) and it has remained virtually unchanged apart from the addition of a sharp S-bend before the pits. This corner, named after Jim Russell who runs a successful racing drivers' school there, was introduced in 1965 and has served to keep cars away from the pit line. The Lombank Trophy F1 race was held there from 1960 to 1964, the first and last events of the series both being won by Innes Ireland. The course is now one of the Grovewood Securities-controlled circuits (which include Brands Hatch, Mallory Park and Oulton Park). Lap Record: Reine Wissell (McLaren M10B); 117·26mph (188·711kph); 1min 23·2sec; 1970. DCN

Solitude Ring

The German Solitude Ring was laid out over a system of closed public roads, winding through the wooded

country around Schloss Solitude, just outside Stuttgart. It was first used in 1922 for motorcycle racing, and in 1923 the first mixed car and motorcycle meeting took place, Scholl (Aga), Salzer (Mercedes) and Cleer (Stoewer) winning their events. Cars continued to be raced on the narrow, winding 7·1-mile (11·5km) circuit until 1927, Otto Merz's Mercedes winning there in 1926 at a speed of 57·29mph (92·2kph). From 1928 until 1949, the narrow course was used for motorcycle events only, although Lang demonstrated a GP Mercedes-Benz in 1937 and described the course as being 'like a garden path'. Mercedes also used the course as a test track for some of their development models.

In 1949 Solitude was revived with another mixed car and motorcycle meeting, and the two Veritas single-seaters of Ulmen and Kling won their events. In 1950 Pietsch, Kurt Adolph and Kling won, again in Veritas cars, but from 1951 to 1955 the meeting was for motor-cycles only—the German GP often being held there. Continual development improved the circuit considerably and in 1956 cars raced there once more, Herrmann and Max Nathan winning in Porsches, the former averaging 92·03mph (148·1kph) in his event. A major FJ International was held there in 1959, won by Michael May in a Stanguellini at 85·94mph (138·5kph). Formula 1 came to the Solitude GP in 1961 when Ireland's Lotus-Climax again beat two Porsches, but in 1962 Gurney won for the Stuttgart company at 100·72mph (162·03kph). The Solitude race weekend had developed with the main F1 event supported by GT and FJ races. In 1965 the GP was for Formula 2 cars again. Chris Amon won in an MRP Lola-Cosworth at 104·08mph (167·53kph), but Solitude was finished. Stuttgart's traffic had increased and complaints of in-convenience from local people led to the authorities refusing to close the roads any more. DCN

South African GP *see* East London Circuit *and* Kyalami Circuit

Spa-Francorchamps Circuit
The Belgians love their motor racing, and almost every likely-looking hill in the country has been used at some time for a speed event. In 1924 a triangular circuit was used for the first time, using roads connecting the villages of Francorchamps, Malmédy and Stavelot, through the wooded hills of the Ardennes.

A 24-hour Touring Car Grand Prix was run in 1924 over this circuit, won by Springuel and Becquet sharing a Bignan and averaging 48·70mph (78·380kph). In 1925,

the first true Belgian GP was won by Antonio Ascari in an Alfa Romeo at 74·56mph (120·00kph). Team-mate Campari was an easy 2nd, and there were no other finishers. But although the Touring Car GP was held every year, together with major motorcycle events, the Belgian GP itself did not have its second running until 1930, and missed 1932, 1936 and 1938. During these years the circuit was steadily improved, although it was still in original form with quite sharp hairpins just beyond Eau Rouge and at Malmédy and Stavelot, in addition to the very sharp corner at La Source. In 1935 Caracciola scored one of his first great Mercedes victories in the Belgian GP, and during the German domination of the sport Hasse won for Auto Union in 1937, and Lang for Mercedes in 1939. But that latter race was a tragic one, as Dick Seaman was killed on the corner before La Source when his Mercedes hit a tree and caught fire. A small memorial stone marks the spot today, together with the Hollowell Memorial on the approach to Stavelot (in memory of Bill Hollowell, a works AJS rider who died there), and the circuit has a grim reputation as a challenge to both man and machine.

Nevertheless, it is a real motor-racing circuit in every possible sense of the term, and post-war modifications, bypassing the hairpin beyond Eau Rouge and providing wide and very fast curves at Malmédy and Stavelot, made it the fastest circuit in Europe. The Belgian GP was revived there in 1947, when Wimille won for Alfa Romeo, and since then it has only missed 1948, 1957, 1959 and 1969. The Touring Car GP was revived in 1948 as a 24-hour race, then lapsed again after 1953. In 1966 it was run once more, this first event of the new series being won by Ickx and Hahne in a works BMW 2000TI. Meanwhile the Spa GP for sports cars had been growing in importance, beginning in 1954 and eventually developing

Left, Spa: Peter Collins (Ferrari) leads the field in the 1956 Belgian GP. *Photo: Keystone Press Agency Ltd.*

Below, Spa: Phil Hill/Mike Spence Chaparral 2F in the 1967 1,000km race. *Photo: Doug Nye Collection*

Right, Spa: Tony Brooks (Vanwall) winner of the 1958 Belgian GP. *Photo: Doug Nye Collection*

Spa: a Lola T70 practising for the 1969 Spa 1,000km race. *Photo: Al Bochroch*

Stardust International Raceway

into the Francorchamps 1,000 kilometres race in 1966.

The circuit begins just south of Francorchamps village, and runs downhill into a valley head, across Eau Rouge and climbs along the side of a ridge before disappearing over the top at Les Combes and running downhill past some pleasant houses into the Burnenville corner, which sweeps right atop an earth embankment. The fast Malmédy corner is next, leading on to the curving Masta Straight which kinks through the hamlet of Masta itself before reaching the super-elevated curve bypassing Stavelot. From there a 'spooky' climbing section weaves back to La Source and the tribunes.

Spa-Francorchamps has seen its share of tragedy, with Archie Scott-Brown, Alan Stacey, Chris Bristow, Eric de Keyn, Wim Loos, Leon Dernier and Tony Hegbourne all crashing fatally there in recent years. Stirling Moss and Jackie Stewart were also badly injured at the circuit, and its unpredictable weather, with rain on one part of the circuit and not on another, has made it most unpopular with the drivers. The 1966 Belgian GP field was decimated on the opening lap by a sudden downpour at Burnenville. In 1965, when fuel shortage struck the field, Clark only knew he had won when he heard it on the public address system out at Stavelot.

The GPDA made basic requests for circuit safety precautions in 1969, and unfortunately this coincided with an internecine dispute in Belgian motor-racing promotion. A move was afoot for the GP to be taken to a new circuit south of Brussels, and while the clubs warred the GPDA took much of the blame for stopping a classic Grand Prix. But whatever the Belgian GP's future, with few exceptions it has taken a great racing driver to win at Spa, and Clark's four consecutive victories and Stewart's great but unlucky performances there bear witness to their ability. The present-day circuit is 8·76 miles (14·10km). Lap record: Pedro Rodriguez (Porsche 917); 160·51mph (258·320kph); 3min 16·5sec; 1970. DCN

Spanish GP see Jarama and Barcelona Circuits

Speedway Park Circuit
In 1968, forty-five thousand spectators, about 10 per cent of the population of Edmonton, Alberta, turned out to see the first Canadian-American Challenge Cup race held in Western Canada. In addition to a 2·53-mile (4·072km) road course, Speedway Park, located 10 miles (16km) from the city centre, contains an oval track and a drag strip. At Edmonton, the Can-Am 1969 becomes the Klondike 200, the race queen is Klondike Kate, and the winner is paid in bricks of solid gold. Lap record: Hulme (McLaren-Chevrolet); 108·688mph (174·943kph); 1min 23·7sec; 1969. ARB

Stardust Raceway
A combination 3-mile (4·8km) road circuit and drag strip built in the desert on the outskirts of Las Vegas, Nev., by the Stardust Hotel. The circuit closed in 1969 after a change in the hotel management. It was the site of the Can-Am in 1966 and 1967, when Surtees won in a Lola-Chevrolet; and in 1968, when victory went to Hulme in a McLaren-Chevrolet. Lap record: Bruce McLaren (McLaren-Chevrolet); 119·16mph (191·80kph); 1min 30·59sec; 1968. ARB

Surfers Paradise Circuit
Built on flat riverside marsh country a few miles inland from the Queensland Gold Coast resort of Surfers Paradise, the 2-mile (3·22km) Surfers Paradise circuit

Surfers Paradise Circuit

Lukey corner

Lucas corner

Castrol corner

brought a new era for Australian race promotion when it opened in 1966. Established by Keith Williams, a Queensland businessman, the plan originally called for a 2-mile Grand Prix circuit, an A-class drag-strip, a speedway dirt oval, a banked bitumen stock car oval, and an alternate 1·625-mile (2·615km) club circuit. The last two were due to be completed by the end of 1970, but meanwhile there had been some spectacular racing on both the main circuit and the drag-strip.

Three Tasman Cup rounds have been held at Surfers Paradise, as well as an annual 12-hour race for production touring cars and a 6-hour event for sports cars. Each year it holds a Speed Week, along the same lines as that at Nassau in the Bahamas; at the original Speed Week in 1966 the sports car race was run as a 12-hour event. Competitors in the race included Paul Hawkins and Jackie Epstein in a Ferrari 250LM and David Piper and Dick Attwood in a Ferrari P3/P4, and it was won by Jackie Stewart and Australian Greg Cusack in another 250LM. Surfers Paradise is fast, although not a specially good spectator circuit, and has acquired a reputation for phenomenal tyre wear on its rather abrasive surface. The track is classed as exceptionally safe, having had few serious accidents and no fatal injury. Lap record: Niel Allen (McLaren M10B); 104·66mph (168·43kph); 1min 8·8sec; 1970. TBF

Suzuka International Racing Course
This Japanese course was built during 1962 as a test ground for the Honda concern. It was designed by John Hugenholtz of Zandvoort fame and wove a lazy-eight pattern through hilly countryside some 93 miles (150km) west of Osaka and 31 miles south-west of Nagoya. The wide, well-surfaced track measured 3·73 miles (6·0km) in length and its first major race was the Japanese Grand Prix of 3–4 May 1963. This was won by Peter Warr's Lotus 23, from similar cars driven by Bill Knight and Arthur Owen.

Over 100,000 spectators saw that first event, dominated by invited European drivers, but the emphasis has now shifted to the Fuji circuit; Honda make greater use of Suzuka for testing production and occasionally competition cars and motorcycles. In 1969 a 1,000km race for sports cars was initiated, attracting strong support from factory teams. The current lap record (January 1971) stands to Kunimitsu Takahashi's 1969 Nissan Group 7 car at 2min 6·0sec, at 106·52mph (171·43kph). DCN

Swedish GP see Karlskoga Circuit

Swedish Rally
This is quite a new rally when compared with Monte Carlo or the Coupe des Alpes. It was a product of the

post-war era and was first held as an international event in 1950. The original formula for the event was a summer rally comprising an easy road section with the results being decided over a number of special stages over roads closed to the public. In this way, it differed greatly from the true road events and set the style for the Scandinavian type of rally.

Its original title was 'The Rally to the Midnight Sun' to underline the fact that in the middle of the Swedish summer it never really gets dark. In 1963 it made head-lines even outside Sweden by finishing in the mining town of Kiruna, north of the Arctic Circle, where there was a special stage organized deep in the heart of a mine. In 1965, because of the increasing difficulty of getting roads closed during summer and the damage done to the surfaces which are exclusively gravel, the date was changed to February and it became one of the few completely snowbound winter rallies.

In the last few years, the rally has become famous for fast snow and ice driving in the woods of central Sweden, with the added attraction of a special stage ploughed out on the surface of a frozen river. The most famous Swedish driver, Erik Carlsson, has had notoriously bad luck in his national event and only won it once, in 1959. Björn Waldegaard is the man with the most outstanding per-formance, having now won the rally three times running. It has never been won by anyone other than a Swedish driver. JD

Swiss GP *see* Berne Circuit

Targa Florio

Vincenzo Florio (1883–1958) was the youngest son of a prominent Sicilian mercantile family, and as such free of responsibility. His youthful enthusiasm for adventure focused on motor sport. Before the turn of the century he owned one of the first cars in Sicily, he spent some time in the company of the young Felice Nazzaro, took part in a few sporting events and, when thwarted in this by family opposition, became a patron of motor racing,

Swedish Rally: Tom Trana and Solve Andreasson (Saab) in the 1969 rally. *Photo: Autocar*

Winners of the Swedish Rally

1950	Cederbaum	BMW
1951	Bengtson	Lago-Talbot
1952	Persson	Porsche
1953	Nottorp	Porsche
1954	Hammarlund	Porsche
1955	Borgefors	Porsche
1956	Bengtsson	Volkswagen
1957	Jansson	Volvo
1958	Andersson	Volvo
1959	Carlsson	Saab
1960	Skogh	Saab
1961	Skogh	Saab
1962	Söderström	Mini Cooper
1963	Jansson	Porsche
1964	Trana	Volvo
1965	Trana	Volvo
1966	Andersson	Saab
1967	Söderström	Ford Cortina
1968	Waldegaard	Porsche
1969	Waldegaard	Porsche
1970	Waldegaard	Porsche
1971	Blomqvist	Saab V-4

Winners of the Targa Florio

'Great' Madonie

1906	A. Cagno	Itala
1907	F. Nazzaro	Fiat
1908	F. Trucco	Isotta Fraschini
1909	R. Ciuppa	SPA
1910	F. Cariolato	Franco
1911	E. Ceirano	SCAT

Tour of Sicily

1912	C. Snipe	SCAT
1913	F. Nazzaro	Nazzaro
1914	E. Ceirano	SCAT

continued

increasingly concentrating on the Targa Florio. This was announced in 1905 (after the first Coppa Florio had been run on the mainland). The Targa was jealously guarded by Florio and has survived many vicissitudes. In some aspects it is a relic of a past era; as a championship race, it has seldom been contested by all championship con-tenders. When run on the Madonie circuits, at least, it has always been a challenging test and, as befits the oldest-established race, one of the most romantic in the calendar.

Initially the 'Great' Madonie circuit was used; 92.48 miles (148.82km) to the lap, it started near the point where the road to Cerda left the main Messina-Palermo north coast road. Thence it ran through Cerda, wound and twisted up into the mountains from which the Madonie circuits take their name, through Caltavuturo and above 3,000ft (920m) to Castellana, to the highest point before Garaci. The return to the coast road was even more sinuous, down through Castelbuono, up and down lesser hills to Campofelice, and then along the easier final stretch to the start and finish point.

The roads were poor even by the standards of those used for early races further north on the Continent, and prospects for the first race must have seemed dubious. Of the 22 entries, ten came to the start on 9 May 1906, to race over three laps (277.41 miles; 446.42km). Cagno won in an Itala in 9hr 32min 23sec, at 29.07mph (46.78kph), from Graziani's Itala by some 33 minutes and four other finishers.

The 1907–11 races were run over the Grande Circuito. The first race having proved feasibility, 44 cars started in 1907, but only 13 in 1908. In 1909 the race-distance was cut to one lap because of the Messina earthquake disaster of late 1908, and contested by only 11 cars.

Partly because of three disappointing races, partly so that the benefits the race brought in its train should be more widely spread, the Targa Florio became the Giro di Sicilia until 1914. Unlike the Targa, this was run clock-wise, over 652 miles (1,049km) around the coast, Palermo-Messina-Catania-Syracuse-Gela-Agrigento-Marsala-Trapani-Palermo.

The 67.11-mile (108km) 'Medium' Madonie circuit was adopted for the 1919–30 races. This followed the Grande Circuito route through Caltavuturo almost into Castellana, then took the direct road through Petralia to rejoin the first circuit at Collesano. Here the race, and European racing, was revived in November 1919. The

Targo Florio

————— 'Great' Madonie
············· 'Medium' Madonie
– – – – 'Short' Madonie
————— Common Route

'Medium' Madonie		
1919	A. Boillot	Peugeot
1920	G. Meregalli	Nazzaro
1921	G. Masetti	Fiat
1922	G. Masetti	Mercedes
1923	U. Sivocci	Alfa Romeo
1924	C. Werner	Mercedes
1925	M. Costantini	Bugatti
1926	M. Costantini	Bugatti
1927	E. Materassi	Bugatti
1928	A. Divo	Bugatti
1929	A. Divo	Bugatti
1930	A. Varzi	Alfa Romeo
'Great' Madonie		
1931	T. Nuvolari	Alfa Romeo
'Short' Madonie		
1932	T. Nuvolari	Alfa Romeo
1933	A. Brivio	Alfa Romeo
1934	A. Varzi	Alfa Romeo
1935	A. Brivio	Alfa Romeo
1936	C. Magistri	Lancia
Palermo		
1937	F. Severi	Maserati
1938	G. Rocco	Maserati
1939	L. Villoresi	Maserati
1940	L. Villoresi	Maserati
Tour of Sicily		
1948	C. Biondetti and Troubetskoy	Ferrari
1949	C. Biondetti and Benedetti	Ferrari
1950	M. and F. Bornigia	Alfa Romeo
'Short' Madonie		
1951	F. Cortese	Frazer Nash
1952	F. Bonetto	Lancia
1953	U. Maglioli	Lancia
1954	P. Taruffi	Lancia
1955	S. Moss and P. Collins	Mercedes-Benz
1956	U. Maglioli and H. von Hanstein	Porsche
1958	L. Musso and O. Gendebien	Ferrari
1959	E. Barth and W. Seidel	Porsche
1960	J. Bonnier and H. Herrmann	Porsche
1961	W. von Trips and O. Gendebien	Ferrari
1962	W. Mairesse, R. Rodriguez and O. Gendebien	Ferrari
1963	J. Bonnier and C. M. Abate	Porsche
1964	A. Pucci and C. Davis	Porsche
1965	N. Vaccarella and L. Bandini	Ferrari
1966	W. Mairesse and H. Muller	Porsche
1967	P. Hawkins and R. Stommelen	Porsche
1968	V. Elford and U. Maglioli	Porsche
1969	G. Mitter and U. Schütze	Porsche
1970	J. Siffert and B. Redman	Porsche

Top, Targa Florio: Felice Nazzaro (Fiat) on his way to victory in 1907. *Photo: Cyril Posthumus Collection*

Centre above, Targa Florio: Count Masetti (Fiat) winner in 1921. *Photo: Cyril Posthumus Collection*

Centre below, Targa Florio: Ferdinand de Vizcaya (Bugatti) in 1925; the photo is inscribed by de Vizcaya to his friend Jules Goux ('Julot'). *Photo: Hugh Conway Collection*

Bottom, Targa Florio: Albert Divo (Delage) in 1926. *Photo: David Hodges Collection*

first driver to be sent off towards the mountains, and seasonal mud and snow, was Enzo Ferrari, who, together with two-thirds of the 24 starters, retired. André Boillot was the theatrical winner, spinning his 1914 Peugeot just short of the line, crossing it backwards, and was sent back to the point where he had spun to complete the race 'properly': at 34·19mph — (55·02kph) over four laps.

The race gained in general stature in the 1920s, when it was run over four laps (268·4 miles; 431·9km) until 1925, and then five laps (335·5 miles; 539·9km). In 1924 and 1925 the Coppa Florio was run concurrently. In 1931 the Grande Circuito was used for the last time — 4 laps, 369·91 miles (595·22km).

In 1932 the 44·74 mile (72km) 'Short' Madonie was devised. This left the old circuit at the crossroads outside Caltavuturo, reached its highest point of 1,930ft (588·26m), then dropped past Scillato, climbed through generally faster bends before descending again to Collesano, thence to Campofelice and the relief of the 5km near-straight along the Tyrrhenian Sea. The roads were still generally narrow — on the 'new' link some stretches were only about 12ft (3·6m) wide — steeply cambered, forever haphazardly patched, and for the most part still a succession of varying bends. The Piccolo Circuito was probably the best of the Madonie circuits, and Florio's own favourite.

Race distance dropped: eight laps in 1932, seven in 1933, six in 1934; and after Nuvolari had won at 49·27mph (79·29kph) in 1932 Madonie speeds did not increase until 1950. Then the 1936 event was run over two laps for 1·5-litre sports cars (Magistri winning in a Lancia Augusta), and the quite out of character 1937-40 events were run on the Palermo Favorita Park circuit, for 1·5-litre voiturettes (won by 6CM and 4CL Maseratis).

The 1948–50 Targa Florio races were incorporated in the 8th-10th Tours of Sicily. The course for these was longer (671 miles; 1,080km) than that used in 1912-14, from Gela in the south running inland to Enna, then turning back to Agrigento.

The Madonie roads were sufficiently repaired, and the start installations rebuilt for 1951 (for the second time, they had been destroyed by fire in 1923), and Vincenzo Florio resumed control of 'his' race. Through the 1950s fields grew larger, often including large-engined cars unsuited to the circuit, always including uncompetitive (cars and drivers) entries which would be ruinous to a characterless artificial circuit race, but became as much a part of the Madonie scenery as they were of the Mille Miglia. Coupled with these to contribute to the Targa atmosphere were tremendous local enthusiasm, a fair degree of chaos, and considerable freedom from the rigidities of latter-day 'mainstream' racing.

A new period opened in 1956, when for the first time the race was run over 10 laps (447 miles; 719km) and when Maglioli and von Hanstein with an RS gained a first Targa victory for Porsche at 56·37mph (90·72kph); from 1958 Porsche was to be the only company wholeheartedly to contest the race every year, their only serious rivals usually being Ferrari — but Ferrari sometimes ignored the event or made only token entries. (In 1957, the year of the accident which ended the Mille Miglia, the Targa Florio was a regularity trial.)

In 1958 and 1959 the distance was 14 laps — 626 miles (1,007km), but from 1960 to 1969 it reverted to 10 laps.

Siffert and Redman won the 1970 11-lap Targa Florio at 74·66mph (120·16kph), while their team-mate Leo Kinnunen put in the fastest lap in 33min 36sec, 79·89mph

Top left, Targa Florio: Peter Collins (Mercedes-Benz 300SLR) in 1955. *Photo: David Hodges Collection*

Left, Targa Florio: Paul Hawkins (Porsche 908), winner in 1967. *Photo: Geoffrey Goddard*

Right, Tatra Hill Climb: an Amilcar in a 1927 event. *Photo: Vladimir Havránek Collection*

(128·57kph). At the time it appeared that these speeds might well stand as all-time records for the Piccolo Madonie circuit, for officialdom seemed insistent that future races should not pass through Cerda, Collesano and Campofelice, a threat which appeared to be circumvented. If it should at some time come to pass, the Targa will lose part of its now almost unique character. However, it will never lose its history, in part already legendary, or the fact that it has been the longest-lived, and the last, of the great road races. DWH

Bottom left, Targa Florio: Brian Redman (Porsche 908/3), the 1970 winner, passing through Campofelice. *Photo: David Hodges Collection*

Teretonga Circuit

Tatra Hill-Climb

For a short time in the late 1920s the Tatra Hill-Climb was one of the best-known in Central Europe. It lay near Zakopane in the Polish Tatra mountains; the course ran from Lysa Polana to Wlosennica, a distance of 4·663 miles (7·504km). The height was 1,207ft (368m), and the maximum gradient 6%. Speed hill-climbs were held regularly from 1927 to 1931, and competitors included well-known names such as Stuck and Caracciola. Henryk Liefeldt of Poland set up the first record in 1927 with a speed of 41·06mph (66·079kph) in his Austro-Daimler, and the following year J. Ripper on a Bugatti raised it to 48·29mph (77·717kph). Hans Stuck set the ultimate record in 1930, with a speed of 52·11 (83·386kph) on an Austro-Daimler. Caracciola held the sports car record at 50·86mph (81·85kph) on an SSK Mercedes-Benz in 1931.

After 1931 speed meetings were no longer held, but the hill was included as a test in car and motorcycle rallies. VH

Teretonga Park Circuit

Situated on the outskirts of Invercargill, New Zealand's most southerly city, Teretonga Park has the distinction of being the permanent motor-racing circuit closest to Antarctica. Owned by the Southland Sports Car Club, it was opened in 1957 and replaced the Ryal Bush road circuit on which international races were held in 1956 and 1957, and won on each occasion by Peter Whitehead. The original circuit was 1·5 miles (2·414km) in length and extremely tight and twisty. It was extended by 176yd (160·9m) late in 1965, a series of S-bends being removed, and there was a dramatic increase in lap speeds henceforth. The circuit comprises a start-finish straight of about half a mile, a fast left-turning loop and a series of S-bends linked by short straights. The first international race, of 60 miles (96·6km), was held in 1958 and won by Ross Jensen (Maserati 250F). With the exception of 1967 when the race was excluded, a Tasman Championship race has been conducted annually at the circuit since 1964.

Virtually every international driver who has visited New Zealand has raced at Teretonga, the most successful being Bruce McLaren who, driving Cooper-Climaxes, won in 1959, 1962, 1963, 1964 and, in a BRM V-12, in 1968. Other Teretonga International winners have been Ian Burgess (Cooper Climax) in 1960; Jim Clark (Lotus) in 1965 and 1967; Jackie Stewart (BRM V-8) in 1967; Piers Courage (Brabham Ford V-8) in 1969; and Graham McRae (McLaren M10A Chevrolet) in 1970. Lap record: Jochen Rindt (Lotus-Ford 49BT); 99·48mph (160·1kph); 57·9sec; 1969. PG

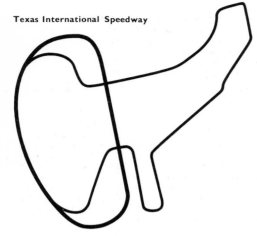

Texas International Speedway

Texas International Speedway

Located near Bryan, in central Texas, TIS combines a banked 2-mile (3·219km) and 3-mile (4·828km) road course. The road course was first raced in November 1969 with the season's final Can-Am, won by Bruce McLaren. In December 1969, NASCAR late model stock cars opened the oval; the 500-mile Grand National was won by Bobby Isaac's Dodge with a 144·277mph (232·121kph) race average.

TIS is part of American Raceways Inc, owners of Michigan International Speedway and part owners of Atlanta and Riverside Raceways. Early in 1970, ARI announced that the new Texas track would drop road racing to concentrate on stock and USAC championship car racing. Following the reorganization of ARI, TIR cancelled the majority of its 1970 race dates. Lap record: Denis Hulme (McLaren-Chevrolet); 115·016mph (185·130kph); 1min 33·9sec; 1969. ARB

Thompson Speedway

Located in the north east corner of Connecticut, 50 miles (80km) from Hartford, this 1·6-mile (2·575km) track was important in the early days of sports car racing in the United States. Opened in 1951 by George Weaver, who constructed the road course around the existing infield oval, Thompson was one of the first closed road racing circuits in the United States. Professional sports car races are occasionally held here. Lap record: Hobbs (Surtees TS-5); 96·96mph (156·05kph); 59·4sec; 1969. ARB

Thompson Speedway

Thousand Lakes Rally

The Finnish name for this rally is Jyväskylän Suurajot, which means quite literally the Grand Prix of Jyväskylä, a town in central Finland which has been host to the rally since its inception in 1951. The rally was created to provide the Finnish drivers with an international rally of their own so that they knew what to expect from the other European events. At first it was modelled on the Monte Carlo Rally and the first four in the series had many starting points, including one in Sweden. Initially it was just a touring event and the records show that the first rally had 26 starters and 26 finishers, and this despite a route of some 1,625 miles (2,600km).

It got its first foreign entries in 1954 and at the same time it dropped the multiple starting points, increased its special stages and became a classic Scandinavian event. Entries were still low and there were only 58 starters in 1957 when Erik Carlsson and Mario Pavoni won the rally in a Saab. This foreign victory created a lot of interest outside Finland and in 1959 the rally was given the status of a European Championship qualifier so that, for example, in 1965, 176 entries were received of which only 130 were allowed to start: the Finnish police were worried about having the roads for the special stages closed for too long a time to accommodate the bigger entry.

The Thousand Lakes is now invariably won by Finnish drivers who are practically alone in their mastery of the narrow switchback gravel roads that are used as special stages on the rally. For much of the time during the stages, the cars leap in the air only to land on the road again many yards later and it is this part of Finnish rallying that has occasioned the expression 'the Flying Finns'. JD

Thruxton Circuit

Situated in Hampshire, this is yet another of Britain's airfield perimeter circuits. It was first used by the Bristol Motor Car and Light Car Club in the early 1950s, and their 1953 meeting on a 2·76-mile (4·442km) circuit attracted quite a good national entry. Tony Rolt won the Formule Libre event in a Connaught, and also the F2 race from Horace Gould's Cooper-Bristol.

But the circuit was not very well developed and was used for motorcycle racing only until 1968, when the BARC made it their home circuit following the demise of Goodwood. The track was improved with the advice of Tony Brooks, and became a 2·356-mile (3·631km) undulating course with a good surface and some very difficult high-speed curves. There is no true straight and the nearly blind approaches to the club chicane and Campbell Corner are very tricky. One major international meeting has been the annual Wills Trophy F2 event, won three years in succession by Jochen Rindt in Brabham and Lotus cars. Thruxton also has a full club race programme, and is often used for test purposes, but

Thruxton Circuit

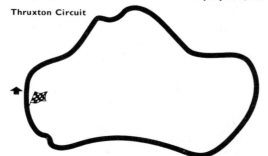

Thousand Lakes Rally: Simo Lampinen and John Davenport (Lancia Fulvia 1600) in 1970. Photo: Hugh W. Bishop

Winners of the Thousand Lakes Rally

1951	A. Karlsson	Austin Atlantic
1952	E. Elo	Peugeot 203
1953	V. Hietanen	Allard
1954	O. Kalpala	Dyna Panhard
1955	E. Elo	Peugeot 403
1956	O. Kalpala	DKW
1957	E. Carlsson	Saab 93
1958	O. Kalpala	Alfa Romeo
1959	G. Callbo	Volvo
1960	C-O. Bremer	Saab 96
1961	R. Aaltonen	Mercedes-Benz 220 SE
1962	P. Toivonen	Citröen
1963	S. Lampinen	Saab Sport
1964	S. Lampinen	Saab Sport
1965	T. Mäkinen	Mini Cooper S
1966	T. Mäkinen	Mini Cooper S
1967	T. Mäkinen	Mini Cooper S
1968	H. Mikkola	Ford Escort TC
1969	H. Mikkola	Ford Escort TC
1970	H. Mikkola	Ford Escort TC

unfortunately parts of the circuit pass close to a school at Kimpton village and injunctions have been sought against the noise.

The airfield itself is still active, and Chris Amon's aircraft business was based here for some time. Lap record: Peter Gethin and Frank Gardner (McLaren M10B); 115·24mph (185·46kph); 1min 13·6sec; 1970. DCN

Tour de Corse

The Tour de Corse Automobile is short in length but still it is one of the toughest events in the calendar and one which every rally driver would like to win. It lasts about twenty-four hours, during which time the route explores just about every road on the island of Corsica. For this reason it is nicknamed the Rallye des 10,000 Virages, for all the roads on Corsica are incredibly narrow and twisty.

It was held for the first time in 1956 when from 43 starters there were only 17 at the finish and this is a fairly normal retirement rate. The form of the rally has changed very little since François Siciliano founded it and though the route changes each year with the start alternating between Ajaccio and Bastia, the challenge remains much the same and it is very rare for any car to come through unpenalized. In fact some four years ago a prize was set up for any driver who could finish without penalties on the road sections — the closest man so far was Munari, who missed it by eight seconds in 1967. The classic date for the rally is the first weekend in November when even the mild-mannered Mediterranean can bring rain and snow to the island. In 1961 the rally had to be stopped midway because snow was blocking the road. The present trend in the rally is to set more special stages but that prize for finishing unpenalized has not yet been claimed. JD

Tour de France, 1899 see Paris Races

Tour de France Automobile

The Tour de France was created in 1951 by the Automobile Club of Nice with the help of the French journal, L'Equipe. Straightaway it established a formula for the event which is little changed today: a route of some 3,100 miles (5,000km) visited most of the famous racing circuits and hill-climbs of France and on each of these, a test was held. The rally was not run non-stop: it was not intended as an endurance event for the driver, and though some sections of the route did run through the night, the event was spaced out over a week and most nights spent in hotels.

In 1955 the Tour was not held following the tragedy at Le Mans but in the late 1950s it grew to be an important event with famous racing drivers participating and the prize money increasing with sponsorship from petrol companies such as Shell. In 1959, it used a foreign circuit for the first time: Spa-Francorchamps in Belgium; and in 1961 it went even further and the cars were all conveyed to Corsica for a hill-climb and a road race. By 1964, the money involved in the organization was enormous and it was no surprise when it was announced that the event had not sufficient sponsorship to be run in 1965. The event lapsed until 1969 when Bernard Consten, who had won the Touring category of this event some four times with his Jaguar, was elected president of the Fédération Française de Sport Automobile. This organization took over the event which is still run in conjunction with the Nice AC, and found sufficient sponsorship to revive it in all its old glory. JD

Winners of the Tour de Course

1956	Mme Thirion	Renault Dauphine
1957	Nicol	Alfa Romeo
1958	Feret	Renault Dauphine
1959	Orsini	Renault Dauphine
1960	Straehle	Porsche
1961	Trautmann	Citroën
1962	Orsini	Renault
1963	Trautmann	Citroën
1964	Vinatier	Renault Gordini
1965	Orsini	Renault Gordini
1966	Piot	Renault Gordini
1967	Munari	Lancia Fulvia
1968	Andruet	Alpine-Renault
1969	Larrousse	Porsche 911
1970	Darniche	Alpine-Renault

Winners of the Tourist Trophy

Isle of Man

1905	J. S. Napier Arrol-Johnston
1906	C. S. Rolls Rolls-Royce
1907	E. Courtis Rover
1908	W. Watson Hutton
1914	K. Lee Guinness Sunbeam
1922	J. Chassagne Sunbeam

Ards

1928	K. Don Lea-Francis
1929	R. Caracciola Mercedes-Benz
1930	T. Nuvolari Alfa Romeo
1931	N. Black MG
1932	T. Nuvolari MG
1934	C. J. P. Dodson MG
1935	F. W. Dixon Riley
1936	F. W. Dixon and C. J. P. Dobson Riley

Donington Park

1937	G. Comotti Darracq
1938	L. Gerard Delage

Dundrod

1950	S. Moss Jaguar
1951	S. Moss Jaguar
1953	P. Collins and P. C. Griffiths Aston Martin
1954	P. Armagnac and G. Loreau DB
1955	S. Moss and J. Fitch Mercedes-Benz

Goodwood

1958	S. Moss and C. A. S. Brooks Aston Martin
1959	S. Moss, C. Shelby and J. Fairman Aston Martin
1960	S. Moss Ferrari
1961	S. Moss Ferrari
1962	I. Ireland Ferrari
1963	G. Hill Ferrari
1964	G. Hill Ferrari

Oulton Park

1965	D. Hulme Brabham
1966	D. Hulme Lola
1967	A. de Adamich Alfa Romeo
1968	D. Hulme Lola
1969	T. Taylor Lola

Silverstone

1970	B. Muir Chevrolet

Winners of the Tour de France Automobile

1951	Pagnibon/Barraquet	Ferrari
1952	M et Mme Gignoux	Panhard DB
1953	Peron/Bertramnier	Osca
1954	Pollet/Gauthier	Gordini 2·7 litre
1956	De Portago/Nelson	Ferrari 250

(after this year there were separate classifications on scratch for GT and Touring cars)

	GT	Touring
1957	Gendebien/Bianchi Ferrari	Hebert/Lauga Alfa Romeo Giulietta
1958	Gendebien/Bianchi Ferrari	Hebert/Consten Alfa Romeo Giulietta
1959	Gendebien/Bianchi Ferrari	Ramos/Estager Jaguar 3·4
1960	Mairesse/Berger Ferrari	Consten/Renel Jaguar 3·8
1961	Mairesse/Berger Ferrari	Consten/Renel Jaguar 3·8
1962	Simon/Dupeyron Ferrari	Consten/Renel Jaguar 3·8
1963	Guichet/Behra Ferrari GTO	Consten/Renel Jaguar 3·8
1964	Bianchi/Berger Ferrari GTO	Procter/Cowan Ford Mustang
1969	Larrousse/Gelin Porsche 911R	Chasseuil/C. Barron Porsche 911
1970	Beltoise/Depailler/Todt Matra-Simca 650	Larrousse/Gelin Porsche 911S

Tourist Trophy

The Royal Automobile Club Tourist Trophy has a curiously checkered history, at times a race of international significance, at others little more than a domestic event. It is, however, Britain's oldest established motor race, first run in September 1905 on a 52-mile (83·69km) Isle of Man circuit — the longest ever used in Britain — which was free of the mainland restrictions on racing on public roads.

This had been used for the 1904 Gordon Bennett eliminating round. From the start just outside Douglas it climbed, then descended to Castletown in the south. Thence it ran almost due north, climbed to 680ft (207·26m), skirted St Johns, ran through Peel and north up the coast road. After Kirk Michael and Ballaugh, it swung through a large loop of minor roads back to Ramsey, then climbed from virtually sea-level to the Bungalow at 1,384ft (420·84m). The last 6 miles (9·6km) were in the main downhill off Snaefell.

The first TT was for touring cars, a principle to which the RAC long attempted to remain true, sometimes in the face of international trends. The main regulations governed fuel consumption (approximately 25·54mpg, weight, load (660lb; 299·37kg, to be made up of bodies or ballast) and proper touring bodywork; they required that duplicate cars be available for sale. Of the 46 final entries, 44 started, and by the narrow margin of 2min 9sec the 4-lap, 208-mile (334·7km), race went to Napier (Arrol-Johnston) from Northey (Rolls-Royce) and 16 other finishers.

In part to reduce the disruption of Island life a 40·25-mile (64·78km) circuit was used in 1906 and 1907 (this ran direct through Union Mills from Douglas to Ballacraine, while the most direct Ballaugh-Ramsey road cut out the northern loop). Regulations for 1906 were similar to those for 1905, and 'touring' suitability had to be demonstrated in pre-race trials. Nine of 29 starters finished and Rolls, dominant throughout, won for Rolls-Royce by almost 25 minutes. In 1907 there was the concurrent Heavy Touring Car race, wherein as well as a load, cars had to carry a screen to simulate a minimum height of 8ft (2·438m), and thus limousine frontal area, and average 16mpg. Only 2 of the 22 Trophy cars completed their set 6 laps, 240·5 miles (387km), several of the leading cars simply running out of fuel; the race went to Courtis' Rover at 28·8mph (46·35kph).

In 1908 the circuit length was reduced to 37·75 miles

Tourist Trophy: W. Watson (Hutton) and A. Lee Guinness (Darracq) in the 1908 Four Inch Race. *Photo: Autocar*

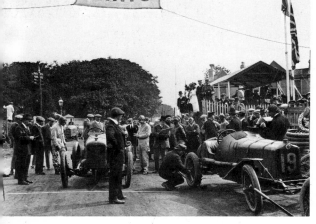

Tourist Trophy: Straker-Squire (centre) and Minerva (right) before the start, 1914. *Photo: Montagu Motor Museum*

Left, Tourist Trophy: the start in 1922; Bentley, Vauxhall and Sunbeam in the front row. *Photo: Motor*

Bottom, Tourist Trophy: Nuvolari (MG Magnette) passing through Newtownards in 1933. *Photo: Motor*

Right, Tourist Trophy: the start of the 1960 race at Goodwood. *Photo: Motor*

(60·77km), the direct Ballacraine-Creg Willey's-Kirk Michael road being substituted for the Peel-east coast stretch. This was the 'Four-Inch' race, the principal requirement apart from a minimum dry weight of 1,600lb (725·75kg) being an engine with not more than four cylinders, each with a diameter not exceeding 4in (101·6m). There were 36 starters, and two Darracqs were narrowly beaten by Watson's Hutton.

The next TT, in 1914, was run over two days with 8 laps, 300 miles (546·4km), on each, for cars with a maximum capacity of 3,310cc and minimum weight of 2,300lb (1,043·26kg). It was dominated by Sunbeam, Lee Guinness winning by some 10 minutes, at 56·44mph (90·83kph). Revived in 1922, the TT was run concurrently with a Trophy for 1·5-litre racing cars, which was just as well as only nine cars started in the 8-lap TT.

The 1928–36 TTs were run on the famous 13·6-mile (21·89km) Ards circuit in Northern Ireland, a rough triangle, Dundonald-Newtonwards-Comber, east of Belfast. The first leg, sinuous and hilly, led into the main square of Newtonwards; a fast stretch ran to Moate, then followed curves into Comber and a winding leg to the Dundonald hairpin, an S in the village, and the curve past the pits. From now on international regulations governed eligibility, and the RAC imposed their own handicap rules. In 1928, 44 cars were entered, and the Trophy went to Kaye Don (1·5-litre Lea Francis). J. Chambers' accident at Newtonwards in 1936 in which eight spectators were killed spelled the end of the Irish circuit.

Donington Park was used in 1937 and 1938, then the TT lapsed until 1950. West of Belfast, Dundrod was a true road circuit with, it transpired, the inherent dangers as well as attractions. The Dundrod lap was 7·42 miles (11·94km), winding and undulating, often narrow and between banks. The first of five Dundrod TTs was run in 1950, in foul weather; Moss drove his first Jaguar race, and won from Whitehead's similar XK 120. He repeated this victory with a C-type in 1951, and with Walker appeared set to do so in 1953 (there was no race in 1952), but tyre wear on the very abrasive road surfaces in effect cost them the race, which went to the Collins-Griffith Aston Martin at 81·71mph (131·50kph) for this longest of all TTs: 111 laps, 823·3 miles (1,325km). In 1954 the TT was truly international again and the 27-lap (in 94) advantage of the smallest cars was too great, so the Armagnac-Laureau 745cc DB-Panhard won, at 68·75mph (110·64kph) from the Hawthorn-Trintignant Monza Ferrari (86·08mph; 138·53kph). As a Championship qualifying event in 1955, the TT attracted its finest entry, an entry really too big and fast for Dundrod: a multiple accident once again left the TT homeless.

Seven TTs, the first in 1958, were run at Goodwood by the BARC, the first two under sports car regulations the next four, for GT cars.

The RAC took the TT back into their own hands in 1965, and organized five races at Oulton Park. International significance was scant, and for two years the tradition of the race was sacrificed to the fragility of sports-racing cars as it was decided on the aggregate of two parts. It was a Touring car event, and a round in the European Touring Car Challenge, in 1967 and 1970. DWH

Trento-Bondone Hill-Climb

One of the classic Italian mountain climbs, the Trento runs up from Montevideo to Vason. There are four extremely twisty sections with hairpin following hairpin up the mountainside. Its length is 10·75 miles (17·3km) and it climbs 4,596ft from the start at 1,207ft (368m) above sea-level to the finish at 5,803ft (1,768·8m). Record: Peter Schetty (Ferrari 212E); 58·76mph (94·564kph); 10min 58·6sec; 1969. DCN

Tripoli Circuit

The Mellaha circuit on the outskirts of the Libyan capital of Tripoli was opened in 1925, and the Tripoli GP was a relatively unimportant event in the calendar until 1933 when the 8·14-mile (13km) New Mellaha circuit was opened. In plan this was not much more than two parallel lines linked by oval turns at each end, and it proved to be the fastest of any of the Grand Prix road circuits. The 1933 race was won by Varzi in an Alfa Romeo; this result was one of the very few cases of a 'rigged' motor race, for a number of drivers held back to ensure Varzi's victory and share with him an agreed percentage of the winning lottery ticket in conjunction with the ticket holder. This race was also the occasion of Sir Henry Birkin's burn which resulted in his death a few weeks later. From 1935 to 1938 the German teams were triumphant at the Mellaha circuit, and they occupied the first three places in every Tripoli GP during this period. In 1939 and 1940 the Grand Prix was for 1·5-litre voiturettes, and was won by the small Mercedes-Benz W.165 (H. Lang) in 1939 and by Farina's Alfa Romeo 158 in 1940. Racing was not revived at Tripoli after the war. Lap record: Hans Stuck (Auto Union): 142·446mph (229·17kph); 3min 25·73sec; 1937. GNG

United States GP see Riverside International Raceway, Sebring Circuit and Watkins Glen Circuit

Vanderbilt Cup

In January 1904 W. K. Vanderbilt Jr presented a cup to the American Automobile Association for a race on Gordon Bennett lines, with teams from each country and races held in the country of the previous year's winner. Vanderbilt stipulated that the first two races should be held in the United States, but in fact the whole series took place there. From 1904 to 1909 the races were held on Long Island, the actual circuit being changed almost annually in order to find a course with a reasonable surface and not too near populous centres. Part of the 1904 course actually ran through New York City, at Queens, but the 1908 course was moved farther from the city, and included part of the Long Island Motor Parkway. The distance for all the Vanderbilt Cup races was approximately the same, at 280 to 300 miles (450 to 482km). Vast crowds flocked to the races, the 1906 event attracting over 250,000 spectators, and with only 16 policemen per mile to control them, conditions were not much better than in the notorious Paris–Madrid race. In the first four events racing had to be stopped after two or three cars had finished, because of crowds surging onto the track. The 1904 to 1908 races (none was held in 1907) saw the best sport, with top European cars and drivers such as Hémery's 80hp Darracq, Lancia's 130hp Fiat, and Duray's 130hp De Dietrich competing against local competition, some of it distinctly unusual, such as Walter Christie's fwd cars, the air-cooled Frayer-Miller, and the steam-driven White. European cars won the first three events, but in 1908 the Cup went to George Robertson's Locomobile in a race in which all the drivers were American.

From 1909 onwards the Vanderbilts were not so interesting, as they were open to production cars of 301 to 600ci (4,933 to 9,832cc) capacity. In 1910 the race moved to Savannah, Georgia, but its interest was eclipsed by that of the American Grand Prize which was for cars of unlimited capacity, and naturally attracted more spectacular machinery. From 1912 onwards the Vanderbilt moved around, being held on the same course as the Grand Prize, but over a smaller number of laps. The length remained at just under 300 miles, compared with over 400 miles (643km) for the Grand Prize.

In 1936 the name Vanderbilt Cup was revived for a 300-mile race at the Roosevelt Raceway, N.Y., to attract European cars and drivers to America. It was held to the prevailing 1,653·47lb (750kg) formula, and was won by Nuvolari's Alfa Romeo 12-cylinder car from Wimille's 4·7-litre Bugatti. The following year the German teams came over, Caracciola and Seaman driving for Mercedes-Benz, and Rosemeyer and von Delius for Auto Union. After Caracciola had retired, Rosemeyer won from Seaman, with Rex Mays in 3rd place on an Alfa Romeo which he had considerably modified, and which made 3rd fastest practice lap. GNG

Vila Real Circuit

Vila Real is a small town situated in the east of Portugal's port wine country, about 50 miles inland from Oporto. It stands on a spur of high ground and a fast 4·2-mile (6·925km) public road circuit is used to the north east of the town centre, around a valley head. This Circuito Internacional de Vila Real was first used for a national touring car race in 1931, won by Gaspar Sameiro's Ford. Racing continued until 1939, Victor Sameiro winning no less than six times.

After the war, sports car races were held from 1949

Vanderbilt Cup: George Robertson (Locomobile), the 1908 winner. *Photo: Peter Helck Collection*

Results of the Vanderbilt Cup

Long Island
1904	G. Heath	*Panhard*
1905	V. Hemery	*Darracq*
1906	L. Wagner	*Darracq*
1908	G. Robertson	*Locomobile*
1909	H. Grant	*Alco*
1910	H. Grant	*Alco*
Savannah		
1911	R. Mulford	*Lozier*
Milwaukee		
1912	R. de Palma	*Mercedes*
Santa Monica		
1914	R. de Palma	*Mercedes*
San Francisco		
1915	D. Resta	*Peugeot*
Santa Monica		
1916	D. Resta	*Peugeot*
Roosevelt Raceway		
1936	T. Nuvolari	*Alfa Romeo*
1937	B. Rosemeyer	*Auto Union*

Vila Real: Teddy Pilette (Lola T70), 1970 winner, on the ravine bridge. *Photo: Autosport*

to 1952. Lack of finance then stopped racing at Vila Real until 1958 when a non-championship Formula 1 race was held, won by Stirling Moss's Maserati 250F.

Not until 1966 was the course revived, this time for Formula 3 use, and in its present form with carefully graded corners in place of the original angular junctions. John Fenning won in a Brabham but the race was marred by the practice death of British independent, Tim Cash. In 1967 the late Chris Williams scored the first of his rare victories in a Brabham, and an additional sports and GT race was won by Mike de Udy's Lola T70 GT. He repeated the performance in 1968, Reine Wisell's Tecno winning the Formula 3 event. A 6-hour endurance race was instituted in 1969, won by the David Piper/Chris Craft Porsche 908 roadster, and in 1970 a 500km race was won by Pilette and Gosselin in a Lola-Chevrolet T70.

The circuit is quite fast—Chris Craft's 1970 record in a McLaren-Cosworth MC was 105·775mph (170·229kph), 2min 26·45sec—but includes many natural hazards, such as a single lane town section, a narrow bridge across the valley and two level (grade) crossings. DCN

Waimate Circuit

This 1·3-mile (2·092km) New Zealand circuit comprises streets of the South Island market town of Waimate and was the South Canterbury Car Club's Gold Star series road race from 1959 to 1966. This race was always known as the Waimate 50, the race from 1959 to 1963 being run over 50 laps, or about 70 miles (112km); subsequent races were run over a distance of 50·4 miles (81·11km). The course ran clockwise and was fairly bumpy, the start-finish straight being the longest and comprising a portion of the main street of the town. Most of the corners were right-angled and there was an artificial hairpin approach to the main straight.

The first race was run in a torrential downpour and hailstorm and was won narrowly by Bruce McLaren (Cooper-Climax) after Ross Jensen (Maserati 250F), who had established an early lead, spun off the course in the concluding laps.

The annual Waimate meeting was of national status only and, although it came each year towards the end of the New Zealand international series, there was never overseas participation. After the 1966 meeting the Motorsport Association of New Zealand refused to grant another permit, on the grounds that increased speeds had made the safety precautions for spectators inadequate. In 1967 the South Canterbury Car Club conducted the meeting on a round-the-houses circuit in the nearby city of Timaru, and since then has run its meetings on its own permanent circuit, the one-mile Timaru Motor Raceway situated north of the city. Lap record: Ian Dawson (Brabham-Climax); 70·06mph (112·75kph); 1min 6·8sec; 1966. PG

Warwick Farm Circuit

Twenty miles (32km) outside Sydney the Warwick Farm motor racing circuit is built around a horse racing track. Jointly owned by the Australian Automobile Racing Co, Ltd and the Australian Jockey Club, it was designed in 1959 and built in 1960. The designer was G. P. F. Sykes, a former assistant secretary of the British Automobile Racing Club and now secretary of the AARC. The circuit was originally conceived by the Australian Jockey Club as a means of bringing back the flagging horse-racing crowds.

Warwick Farm is exactly 2·25 miles (3·621km) long, of bitumen and hot mix construction. The first meeting

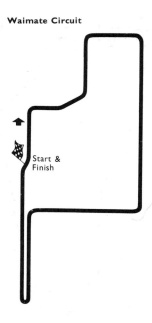

Waimate Circuit

Start & Finish

Warwick Farm Circuit

Creek corner

The Esses

Dunlop bridge

Shell bridge

Hume straight

Homestead corner

Northern crossing

Western crossing

Polo corner

Paddock bend

Leger corner

Start & Finish

Pit straight

Warwick Farm: Jackie Stewart (BRM), winner of the 1967 Australian GP. *Photo: Nigel Snowdon*

was held on 18 December 1960 in heavy rain. The lap record at the first meeting was taken by B. S. Stillwell (Cooper-Climax): 1min 54sec, 71·05mph (114·34kph). Recognized as the best designed race-course in Australia, Warwick Farm is marred only by the two prefabricated sections which are laid down across the horse-track for each meeting. Each crossing is placed just after a bend and creates an entirely different surface for the racing cars.

The Australian Automobile Racing Co is supported by a club formed under its articles to utilize the circuit. A small club circuit exists at the top end of the main track, and regular club meetings are held. A plan is afoot to build an even more spectacular short circuit incorporating the Warwick Farm S-bends and part of the main straight. Lap record: Neil Allen (McLaren-Chevrolet M10B); 94·63mph (152·26kph); 1min 25·7sec; 1970. TBF

Watkins Glen Circuit

The American road racing renaissance began at Watkins Glen on 2 October 1948, when Cameron Argetsinger, then a student at nearby Cornell University, convinced the village elders of this little resort on Lake Seneca, 250 miles (400km) from New York City, that automobile racing would bring them fame and fortune. More than 10 years had passed since the unsuccessful revival of the Vanderbilt Cup and the American public appeared to accept oval track racing as the Yankee standard. But pockets of road-racing enthusiasm survived. From the mid-1930s until the formation of the Sports Car Club of America in 1944, the Collier brothers, Charles Moran, George Rand, Briggs Cunningham and their friends raced an assortment of specials, some Bugattis and Alfa Romeos over estate and country roads, in the eastern U.S.

The 1948 Watkins Glen inaugural, eight laps over 6·6 miles of village streets and a combination of paved and unpaved country roads, was won by Frank Griswold's 2·9-litre Alfa Romeo coupé with a 63·7mph (102·52kph) average. Briggs Cunningham in a Buick-Mercedes special was 2nd and a supercharged MG TC, owned by Cunningham was 3rd. Where the course crossed railway tracks the arrangements with the New York Central RR were to flag down the train, not the race cars.

After there had been racing through the village for four years, lack of crowd control resulted in the death of a young spectator and the course moved to a 4·6-mile (7·403km) complex of public roads above the town.

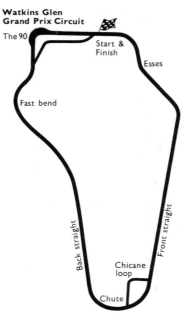

Watkins Glen Grand Prix Circuit

The 90

Start & Finish

Esses

Fast bend

Front straight

Back straight

Chicane loop

Chute

Top, Watkins Glen: Innes Ireland winning his first (and only) Grand Prix, and also the first of many GPs for Lotus. 1961. *Photo: Al Bochroch*

Centre, Watkins Glen: 1969 United States GP. *Photo: Al Bochroch*

Left, Watkins Glen: the Corvette Sting Ray pace car leads Can-Am and Group 5 cars in the 1970 Can-Am race. *Photo: Autosport*

SCCA 'Nationals' and the 1958, 1959 and 1960, Formule Libre races were the Glen's outstanding events. It was a fortunate generation of enthusiasts who watched drivers such as Walt Hansgen driving the Cunningham Jaguars, and giant-killer Bob Holbert, who was to become the first U.S. road racing champion in 1963. In Formule Libre, the victory of Jo Bonnier's Maserati over Dan Gurney's Ferrari and seeing the Stirling Moss Cooper-Climax finish ahead of Indianapolis veteran Eddie Johnson's Offenhauser-Midget, sharpened American interest in single-seater road racing.

In 1961, after false starts at Sebring and Riverside, the United States Grand Prix was successfully launched at Watkins Glen with Innes Ireland winning his only Grand Prix, and Colin Chapman earning the first of many *grandes épreuves* for Team Lotus. Graham Hill and Jimmy Clark each won three U.S. Grands Prix over the next six years, with Jackie Stewart victorious in 1968 and Jochen Rindt winning his first GP in 1969. Watkins Glen is not an especially good circuit for either drivers or spectators, but the magic of its name consistently draws the largest crowds in U.S. road racing. By guaranteeing $250,000 (paying $50,000 for a 1st, down to $6,000 for 24th) the 1969 and 1970 U.S. GP converted, at least for this event, those GP drivers who usually prefer to work on a starting money rather than a 'pay on performance' basis. The circuit is the property of a civic group, The Watkins Glen Grand Prix Corp., of which Cameron Argetsinger, who started it all, was executive director until he resigned early in 1970 to join Jim Hall as an officer of Chaparral cars. He was succeeded by Malcolm Currie.

Extensive circuit alterations are planned prior to running the 1971 U.S. GP. The track will be lengthened by approximately 1·3 miles, the pits moved and the entire course resurfaced.

Watkins Glen is the site of Trans-Am, International Manufacturers' Championship, Can-Am and the U.S. GP. Lap records (Can-Am): Denis Hulme (McLaren-Chevrolet); 132·27mph (212·81kph); 1min 02·60sec; 1969. (GP): Jackie Ickx (Ferrari 312B); 131·97mph (212·385kph); 1min 02·75sec; 1970. ARB

Wigram Circuit

Venue of the Lady Wigram International Trophy, the Wigram circuit, which is laid out on an operational Royal New Zealand Air Force station on the outskirts of Christchurch, has been used for one race meeting annually since 1949 (the base closes down for two days to allow this), with the exception of 1955 when there was no race because the airfield runways were being resurfaced. The inaugural 105-mile (169km) race was conducted by the Canterbury Car Club in 1949 and won by

Wigram Circuit

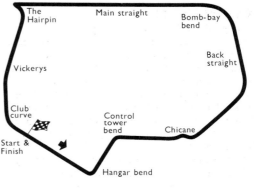

The Hairpin

Main straight

Bomb-bay bend

Vickerys

Back straight

Club curve

Control tower bend

Chicane

Start & Finish

Hangar bend

However, this was a makeshift arrangement and the first race over the present 2·3-mile (3·701km) closed course, during which the newly paved surface broke up badly, was held in the autumn of 1956.

George Constantine's D-type Jaguar won the first closed course event with a 71·4mph (114·91kph) race average. Thirteen years later Group 7 and Formula 1 machines were lapping the Glen at almost double Constantine's speed. From 1956, until Watkins Glen became the site of the U.S. Grand Prix in 1961, annual

Morrie Proctor in a Brooklands Riley, at 66·17mph (106·49kph). The trophy race has been on the international calendar since 1954. Over the years the races have varied in length from 50 to 150 miles (80·47 to 241·4km), but since 1964, when the circuit was slightly revised to make it 2·3 miles (3·701km) in length all races, which are included in the Tasman series, have been of 101·2 miles (162·8km). A predominantly left-turning circuit, Wigram is generally wide and comprises an interesting variety of fast and slow corners. The longest straight is about three-quarters of a mile (1·2km) where the Formula A/5000 cars reach speeds above 150mph. Lap record: Jochen Rindt (Lotus 49 Tas); 105·08mph (169·10kph); 1min 18·8sec; 1969. PG

World Cup Rally

Following on the success of the London to Sydney, the London *Daily Mirror* decided to promote a more ambitious marathon event to be tied to the World Cup football series. As the World Cup was held by England and the new contest was to be in Mexico, the rally became the London–Mexico or the World Cup Rally.

The number of works cars entered was much less than on the previous event to Australia, but this can largely be attributed to the short length of time between the announcement of the event and its starting date. As Mexico had to be reached before the football started, the cars left London on the third weekend of April 1970 and tackled a set of special stages in Europe, before taking ship from Lisbon to South America. At the end of these five stages, all held on classic rally roads of Yugoslavia, Italy, France and Portugal, the leaders were René Trautmann and Jean Pierre Hanrioud in a Citroën from Hannu Mikkola and Gunnar Palm in a Ford Escort. Highest placed of the works Triumph 2·5 PIs were Brian Culcheth and Johnstone Syer at 6th. The Citroëns were privately entered but received some works help and at Lisbon they were in a commanding situation with four cars in the first seven. Ninety-nine cars started from Wembley Stadium, and one week later at Lisbon there were 71 survivors.

The rally re-started some two weeks later in Rio de Janeiro, but the Citroëns did not stay long in the lead for Trautmann went out following an accident and the others suffered similar misfortunes or mechanical failure. At the end, only one was still in the running and that was crewed by Patrick Vanson, Olivier Turcat and Alain Leprince. The lead was taken over by the Mikkola Ford Escort, and it was a lead he was to hold to the finish. Of

Opposite, Kyalami Circuit: Ronnie Peterson (March 711), going out of picture, followed by Graham Hill (Brabham BT 33/4) and Rolf Stommelen (Surtees TS7) in the 1971 South African GP. *Photo: Motor Sport*

Results of the World Cup Rally

1	Hannu Mikkola	Ford Escort TC
2	Brian Culcheth	Triumph 2·5 PI
3	Rauno Aaltonen	Ford Escort TC
4	Paddy Hopkirk	Triumph 2·5 PI
5	Timo Mäkinen	Ford Escort TC
6	Tony Fall	Ford Escort TC

Left, World Cup Rally: an unusual rally car was the Rolls-Royce Silver Shadow of Bengry, Richards and Skeffington, seen here on the San Remo prime. *Photo: Hugh W. Bishop*

Right, Zandvoort: Stirling Moss (Vanwall) leads the field in the 1958 Dutch GP. *Photo: Autosport*

all the Fords his had the least mechanical trouble and he took full advantage of the fact. Rauno Aaltonen and Henry Liddon, also in a works Escort achieved some fast times in the first part of the South American section but later they suffered delays and the Culcheth Triumph passed them into 2nd place. For Fords, it was a magnificent rally as they took 1st, 3rd, 5th and 6th places overall as well as winning the manufacturer's team prize. In general, British cars dominated the event and from the point of view of publicity it proved even more of a success than its predecessor. JD

Zandvoort Circuit

There was motor racing through the streets of Zandvoort a pleasant little seaside town 7·45 miles (12km) from Haarlem, between the wars. During the occupation the Germans linked their emplacements in the sand-dunes with service roads. After World War 2, John Hugenholtz and the local KNAC (Royal Netherlands Automobile Club) built a motor race circuit through these sand dunes, using the old service roads as part of their foundation. Hugenholtz has since become an international consultant circuit designer, responsible for Suzuka and Jarama, but Zandvoort has been his most successful design.

The circuit is 2·6 miles (4·139km) in length, and the main straight runs parallel to the North Sea beach, just the other side of the sand-dunes behind the main grandstand. The 180° Tarzan corner at the end of this straight leads into a difficult twisty section through the Hunzerug corner behind the pits and out through a series of high-speed swerves on the back of the course before rejoining the main straight. A brave man in a Formula 1 car could just negotiate these curves flat at around 150mph (240kph), and speed through this section is critical for it determines entry speed to the straight. Wind direction at Zandvoort is also important, for if it blows down the straight behind the cars it will improve their lap times enormously. If it is against them times can suffer. Another Zandvoort phenomenon is the cross-wind off the dunes which can lay sand across the course, making it extremely slippery; but Zandvoort has a good safety record, and its rows of chicken wire fencing have proved capable of stopping cars from high speed with very little damage. However, two F2 drivers have lost their lives following accidents there, and Piers Courage was killed in the 1970 Dutch GP.

The first Zandvoort meeting was in 1948, organized by the BRDC, and featured a Formule Libre race won by the

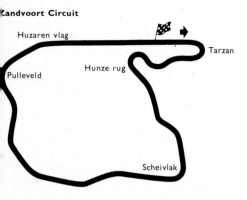

Zandvoort Circuit

Huzaren vlag

Pulleveld

Hunze rug

Tarzan

Scheivlak

Zeltweg (Österreichring): Rolf Stommelen (Brabham BT33) leading Emerson Fittipaldi (Lotus 49C) in the 1970 Austrian GP. *Photo: Motor*

Opposite, Le Mans: Willy Mairesse and 'Beurlys' (Ferrari P4) followed by Chris Irwin and Piet de Klerk (Lola-Aston Martin) on the Mulsanne Straight during the 1967 race. *Photo: Geoff Goddard*

Bira Maserati. The Dutch Grand Prix was instituted here in 1950, and it has been won four times by Jim Clark, and twice each by Rosier, Ascari, Brabham and Stewart. BRM's first major victory was at the 1959 event, and Clark had his great win on his first drive with the Lotus-Ford 49 in 1967. Lap record: Jackie Ickx (Ferrari 312B); 118·38mph (190·52kph); 1min 19·2sec; 1970. DCN

Zbraslav-Jíloviště Hill-Climb

The most famous speed hill-climb in Czechoslovakia was the Zbraslav-Jíloviště, near Prague, held almost annually from 1908 to 1931. The course was 5·6km long, with many curves and a maximum gradient of 8%. The first event of 1908, held during the Prague Motor Show, was won by the Mercedes works driver Otto Salzer, but the greatest period for the hill was during the 1920s. Drivers of international fame such as Carl Joerns of Opel, Divo, Merz, Stuck, Caracciola and Hieronymus took part, as well as local competitors such as George Lobkowicz, Josef Vermiřovsky, and especially Čeněk and Eliška Junek. In 1926 Eliška Junek made ftd with her Bugatti at 64·16mph (103·25kph), defeating Albert Divo on a Delage. It was the first time that the hill had been climbed at over 100kph. Another famous incident took place during the event's last year, 1931. Stuck and Caracciola, both driving Mercedes-Benz cars, recorded times only 0·1sec apart, Caracciola being the winner at a speed of 76·97mph (123·88kph). This stands as the ultimate record for the hill, as only part of the original course now exists. After the opening of the Brno circuit in 1930, interest in hill-climbs in Czechoslovakia dropped sharply, and Zbraslav-Jíloviště, like Brno-Soběšice, Ecce Homo, and other famous venues, was no longer used for motor sport. VH

Zeltweg Circuit

The Zeltweg airfield races first came to prominence in 1958 when von Trips' Porsche won a sports car event from the similar cars of Behra and Barth. The course was laid out along the runways and hard-standings of an operational military airfield, north of Graz and Klagenfurt and off the B17 Judenburg-Zeltweg road in Austria.

In 1959–60 Formula 2 races were held, won by Tony Marsh's Cooper and Moss's Porsche respectively, and in 1961 an F1 event won by Ireland's Lotus was run over

Zbraslav-Jiloviste: Caracciola (Mercedes-Benz SSKL) recording a speed of 76·98mph (123·88kph) in 1931. *Photo: Vladimir Havranek Collection*

a distance of 159 miles (255·9km). In 1963 the non-Championship Austrian GP was again held at Zeltweg and was won by Brabham's own Brabham-Climax. The following year the Austrian GP was a Championship round, and after many retirements caused by the rough concrete surface the race was won by Bandini's Ferrari V-6. This race saw Phil Hill's Cooper burn-out after running into the straw bale barriers marking out the course, and with generally poor facilities Zeltweg was not popular. But the organizing club were enthusiastic and pressed on with the only circuit they had, running a 198·8-mile (322km) sports car race from 1965 to 1967.

The 1·99-mile (3·2km) L-shaped circuit had deteriorated to a sad degree, but a new permanent course had long been projected in the hills above the airfield. This new circuit, known as the Österreichring, was opened in 1969 with two minor meetings preceding a full 1,000km event, won by the Siffert and Ahrens Porsche 917 at 115·780mph (186·33kph). It is 3·67 miles (5·911km) in length, and undulates through a series of fast and difficult swerves around a natural bowl in the hills above the plain of Zeltweg. Austria at last has a circuit well up to International standards. Lap record (Österreichring): Jackie Ickx and Clay Regazzoni (Ferrari 312B); 131·7mph (211·96kph); 1min 40·4sec; 1970. DCN

Zolder Circuit

The Belgian Omloop van Zolder (Circuit of Zolder) was built in the mid-1960s, and came into general use in 1965, when Jonathan Williams won an international F3 race in a Lucas Brabham at 90·97mph (146·314kph). In 1966 Brabham and Hulme dominated the first Limburg GP Formula 2 race with their Brabham-Hondas, Brabham winning at 94·83mph (152·609kph), and several important meetings were scheduled for the new circuit, including touring car and sports car meetings. International Formula 2 and 3 highlighted each season.

The circuit has a lap length of 2·6 miles (4·184km) and undulates gently through the sandy hills of the area. It lies just over 6 miles (10km) north-west of Hasselt and has become a popular and pleasant venue for motorcar, motorcycle and even bicycle racing. Lap record: Jochen Rindt (Lotus); 108·54mph (174·68kph); 1min 26·6sec; 1970. DCN

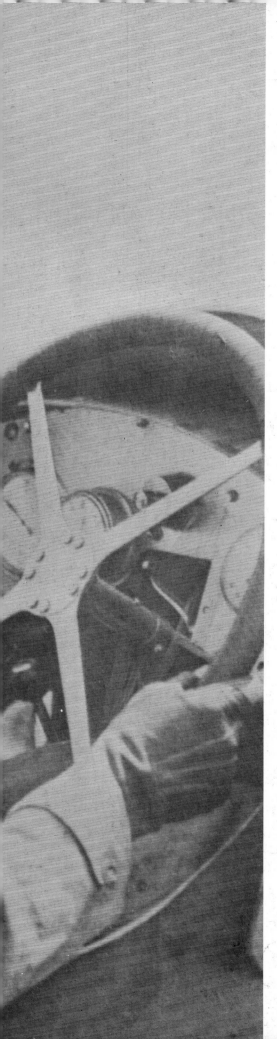

Drivers

Aaltonen, Rauno

Born in 1938 in Turku, Finland, Rauno Aaltonen was without doubt one of the finest rally drivers of the 1960s. At the age of 12 he started racing hydroplanes and was seven times champion of Finland and once champion of Scandinavia. At 16 he turned to motorcycles and raced an MV Agusta 125cc with which he won the Hedemora GP in 1957. He also motocrossed with a 500cc Matchless and a 250cc NSU and drove in speedway, in which he once represented Finland. His first rally was in 1956 with a Mercedes and the following year he bought a Saab 93. In 1961 he was Finnish champion driving both the Saab and a Mercedes and that year he also co-drove with Eugen Bohringer in the Polish, which they won, and the Liège–Sofia–Liège in which they were 4th.

In 1962 he drove a rhd Mini Cooper for the first time on the Monte Carlo and had an accident, his co-driver, Geoff Mabbs, saving him from burning to death. The same year he competed for the first time in the East African Safari Rally with a Mercedes. In 1963 he was fully accepted into the BMC works team and that year saw him very nearly win the Liège in a Healey 3000, only an accident stopping him on the last night. Undaunted, he came back the next year and won it outright in the same type of car. In 1965 he concentrated solely on European rallies in the Mini Cooper, for he had already won the Finnish championship for the second time the previous year. He won the Geneva, Czech, Polish, Three Cities and RAC Rallies and finished 2nd in the 1000 Lakes, which was sufficient to give him a clear win in the European championship. His victory in the RAC Rally was particularly notable as it was the first time that the rally had been won by a Mini Cooper, and it was also a very tough year with bad weather from start to finish.

In 1966 Aaltonen won the Tulip Rally and the Czech Rallies outright but missed some events in order to drive for Austin Healey in events like Sebring, Le Mans and the Targa Florio, where in company with Clive Baker he usually won the class with the little Sprite. Just to show that he had lost none of his touch, he won the Monte Carlo Rally in 1967 for BMC and then when they stopped rallying in the middle of that year he went to Lancia and took 3rd overall on the Tour de Corse in his first rally for them. His Lancia contract terminated in the middle of 1969 and he then drove for BMW in Corsica, finishing 6th, and drove a Datsun to 8th place in the RAC, helping them to win the team prize. In

Left, Pietro Bordino. *Photo: Cyril Posthumus Collection*

1970 he signed up with Ford and came very close to winning his favourite event, the Safari, for them with a Capri. With Henry Liddon, he was 3rd in the World Cup Rally. JD

Abecassis, George E.

This British driver, born in 1913, made a quiet entry into motor racing in 1935 with a modified sv Austin Seven which he drove at Brooklands and Donington Park. In 1938 and 1939 he drove a single seater 1·5-litre Alta with which he had a number of successes at Brooklands, Prescott, and the Crystal Palace.

After war service in the RAF, Abecassis joined with John Heath to form HW Motors Ltd of Walton-on-Thames, Surrey, builders of the HW-Alta and, later, HWM cars. During 1946 and 1947 Abecassis had a busy racing programme at home and abroad, driving his pre-war Alta, a Type 59 Bugatti, and a pre-war ERA fitted with Tecnauto ifs. He also drove a 1,100cc Cisitalia in the Caracalla race in Rome, and finished 2nd to Taruffi. The HWM team began racing in 1950, but Abecassis only drove occasionally for them because of business ties. However, he was a member of the Aston Martin sports car team, and among his successes was the 2- to 3-litre class at Le Mans in 1950 with Lance Macklin. In 1953 he was 2nd overall and 3-litre class winner at Sebring with Reg Parnell. From 1954 to 1956 Abecassis drove the HWM-Jaguar sports car in numerous events, winning at Snetterton, Castle Combe, and Oulton Park among other places, and in the 1955 Mille Miglia he drove a near-standard Austin Healey 100S into 11th place. However, the death of his partner John Heath in the race the following year, in the HWM-Jaguar, diminished Abecassis' interest in racing. In 1956 he married Angela Brown, daughter of Sir David Brown, and retired to run the HW Motors business full time. CP

Adamich, Andrea de

This Italian driver, born in 1941, began motor racing while studying law. He first made his name in an FJ Lola in 1963 and 1964, running one of Pedrazzini's early Novamotor engines in the latter season. He rallied with an Alfa Romeo Giulia TI Super, winning the Rally dei Fiori and Rally del Portagallo, and in 1965 he was Italian F3 Champion, driving his Lola-Novamotor Ford.

Autodelta signed him for their saloon car team, contesting the European Touring Car Championship, and he won at Monza and the Nürburgring, and was 5th in the Sebring event. Late that year his close friend, Bruno Deserti, was killed while testing a Ferrari at Monza and de Adamich thought of giving up racing. But he continued with a works Alfa Romeo GTA in 1966, winning his division in the European Touring Car Championship and also racing an F3 Brabham quite widely. He drove the Alfa Romeo T33 in long-distance events, showing considerable ability but suffering from the new design's unreliability. In 1967 he managed to share 5th place in the Nürburgring 1,000 kilometres, was 2nd in the Rossfeld hill-climb and won the touring car TT and Budapest GP in GTAs. These performances and his promise as an Italian driver brought him a Ferrari F1 drive in the Madrid GP at the end of the year, and he took part in the 1968 South African GP but crashed without injury. Practising for the Race of Champions at Brands Hatch his Ferrari went out of control over the bumps into Paddock Bend and he crashed heavily, receiving neck injuries.

This accident laid him low for much of the season, but he took 2nd place in an F2 Dino at the Rome GP in October. Andrea then dominated the winter Temporada Series in Argentina with the same car. John Surtees signed him for 1969 as one of his Formula A/5000 TS5 drivers and he did quite well in the class, adding 3rd place in the combined F1/5000 Oulton Park Gold Cup to 5th in the Monza 1,000 kilometres (with Gardner, Lola), 2nd in an Alfa T33 at Montlhéry and 3rd at Mugello with Vaccarella in Taylor's Lola. In 1970 he drove an F1 McLaren-Alfa without success; with the works T33/3 sports car he won at Buenos Aires, and had two 2nds and won the 1971 BOAC 1,000km with Pescarolo. His F1 car for 1971 was the Alfa-engined March 711. DCN

Ahrens, Karl Heinrich

'Kurt' Ahrens Jr is the son of a well-known German racing driver of the same name, and was born in 1940 near Hanover. Kurt Sr's post-war competition career naturally led to Kurt Jr's motor racing debut, and the pair of them offered strong opposition in the early days of Formula Junior. Kurt Jr's first race was in 1958, two days after passing his driving test, and he finished 18th. Shortly afterwards he was 2nd to his father (both in Formula Junior Coopers) at Solitude, and in 1960 he won the Australian FJ Championship, adding the German FJ title in 1961.

Ahrens continued to contest Formula Junior, 2 and 3 races after his father's retirement, and his Caltex-backed F2 Brabhams were always front-runners in 1967, 1968 and 1969, although he seldom completed a full season's programme. Away from the circuits he worked in his father's scrap-iron business. He joined the Porsche works team for a full season in 1969, won the Austrian 1,000 km with Siffert, and the Nürburgring 1,000 km with Elford in 1970 and then retired. DCN

Allison, Cliff

British driver, born in 1932. Cliff Allison's father was in the motor trade, and encouraged him in his first entry into motor racing, with a Mark 4 Cooper-Norton at Charterhall in 1952. He had to wait three years for a victory, but he usually performed creditably and finished well up against established drivers with later machines. In 1956 he joined Colin Chapman's Lotus team, and managed some good placings with the Lotus-Climax sports and Formula 2 cars in international events, catching the eye of Enzo Ferrari in so doing. As a result, he became in 1958 one of the first British drivers to race in the Italian team.

In 1959 Allison suffered a severe crash at Monaco with a Formula 2 car, and it was a year before he fully recovered his old form. When he was injured again during practice at Spa in 1961 while driving for the UDT Laystall team, he decided that the time had come to hang up his gloves.

Allison drove in a quick but unspectacular fashion, and impressed all with his style and ability. He achieved good placings rather than victories, and was at his best in long-distance events where his steady and unflurried approach bore the greatest dividends. DF

Amon, Christopher

Amon was born in Bulls, in New Zealand's North Island, in 1943. In 1961 his father bought him a 1956 1·5-litre Cooper-Climax, with which he was 2nd in his first race.

He learned a lot in 1962 driving a Maserati 250F, part-exchanged for the Cooper, and won two races. For

Rauno Aaltonen. *Photo: BMC Competitions News Service*

George Abecassis. *Photo: Autosport*

Andrea de Adamich. *Photo: Autosport*

Kurt Ahrens. *Photo: Porsche*

Cliff Allison. *Photo: Cyril Posthumus Collection*

Chris Amon. *Photo: Al Bochroch*

the 1963 Tasman Series he ran a 2·5-litre Cooper-Climax as part of Scuderia Veloce; Reg Parnell saw his talents in the New Zealand races and took him to Europe.

In 1963, at only 19, he was the youngest driver in Formula 1 but had a season of mixed fortunes with Parnell's Lolas, including crashing heavily at the Nürburgring and Monza. Parnell's death at the end of the year was a hard blow, but Tim Parnell carried on with the team, running BRM-engined Lotus 25s. Amon finished in the points just once, coming 5th in the Dutch GP. His Formula 1 fortunes sagged in 1965 and he failed to score a point, but his fellow New Zealander Bruce McLaren came to his rescue and he had a season of sports car racing with the works Elva-BMW and for Ford, driving a Shelby Cobra at Le Mans and having occasional GT40 outings. McLaren planned to run an F1 car for him in 1966 but engine problems meant his only GP that year was at Reims in a Cooper.

That season could have ended his career, but luckily he was signed as a Ford works driver, and shared the winning 7-litre Ford Mk II at Le Mans, with Bruce McLaren. He was 5th with Bruce in the Daytona 24 Hours and 5th with Ireland in a GT40 at Spa. In Group 7 events he was 2nd at Snetterton, Silverstone, Brands Hatch; and in the Can-Am Series, 2nd at Bridgehampton, 3rd at Mosport and St Jovite, driving as number two in the works McLaren team. He had proved his ability to handle really powerful cars, and was signed by Ferrari at the end of the year.

The season started well, Amon sharing the winning 330P4 Ferraris with Bandini at Daytona and Monza. Then Bandini was killed at Monaco, and Chris made his Italian F1 debut count by finishing 3rd after driving through the smoke and flames from his team-leader's accident. Parkes was injured at Spa where Amon, shaken yet again, was 3rd, and he was on his own for much of the year. He was 3rd in the British and German GPs, 4th in the Dutch, and 6th in the Canadian to finish 4th-equal in the World Championship, with Surtees.

At the start of 1968 Amon took a 2·4-litre Ferrari Dino V-6 to the Tasman Series, scored two 1sts and two 2nds and was runner-up to Clark in the Championship. But that was to be the high-spot of his year. Best F1 results were 2nd in the British GP after an epic duel with Jo Siffert, and the Oulton Park Gold Cup; and he was 4th in the South American GP. Amon's bad luck in Formula 1 was becoming legendary: he looked set for several victories before repeated failures put him out.

Amon was lucky, at last, in the Tasman Series at the start of 1969, winning four races and coming 3rd once to secure the title, and running Ferrari Dinos for himself and Derek Bell as a private entrant. Formula 1 was a total loss, however, with repeated failures leaving him with only 3rd place in the Dutch GP to score. He persevered all season with the Ferrari 312P G6 car and had some stirring battles with the Porsches, finishing 2nd at Sebring with Andretti. But at the end of the season Amon left Ferrari to join the March Engineering Company, in which he had an interest.

'Chrissie' scored two 2nds, one 3rd, one 4th, two 5ths and the fastest lap at Spa in the March, but moved to Matra for 1971, winning his Argentine début in the F1 V-12. DCN

Andersson, Ove

Ove Andersson was born in 1938 in Dannemora, near Uppsala in Sweden. His father was a farmer and Andersson learned to drive on tractors and later on

motorcycles before getting his driving licence at the age of 18. He then joined the army and served extra time with the United Nations force in Gaza in order to be able to buy a car when he returned to civilian life. He got that car, a Saab, and started rallying with it while pursuing his chosen profession of car repairer. He started by doing T-races and in 1962 out of seven events he won six and finished 2nd once. In 1963 he drove with BMC Sweden and entered his first international event, coming 5th in the Swedish Rally and winning his class.

In 1966, he joined Lancia and immediately began to have better luck finishing 3rd in the Monte Carlo, 3rd in the San Remo, 3rd in the Acropolis and 7th in the RAC Rally, this last performance being the first time a Lancia had finished the event. At the same time that he was driving for Lancia, he was driving a Ford in Sweden and although 'flu stopped him driving the Swedish Rally for them in 1967, he won the Gulf London Rally driving a Cortina Lotus. The same year he won the Spanish Rally outright. In 1968 he joined Ford, since when his fortunes have changed for the worse and his best results have been 2nd overall in the Tulip and 3rd — once more — in the San Remo Rally. In the London to Sydney he was paired with Roger Clark and they were leading at Bombay only to run into mechanical trouble with their Cortina Lotus in Australia. The following year he was a most convincing leader of the Acropolis Rally until the almost inevitable mechanical trouble claimed him as a victim and he had to retire. His best result in 1970 was 3rd in the Acropolis, but he began 1971 with victory in the Monte Carlo Rally. JD

Ove Andersson. *Photo: John Davenport*

Andretti, Mario

Mario Andretti, recognized by the American racing fraternity as the outstanding newcomer to USAC big car championship competition during the 1960s, migrated to the United States from Italy with his parents in 1959, when he was 19 years old. He had chosen auto-

Mario Andretti. *Photo: Indianapolis Motor Speedway*

Below right, Mario Andretti (left), with Roger McCluskey, at Mosport. *Photo: Al Bochroch*

Below, Luigi Arcangeli (right), behind him, with cap, is Alfieri Maserati. *Photo: Cyril Posthumus Collection*

mobile racing as a career while witnessing the 1954 Grand Prix of Monza and then had participated in what he describes as 'the Italian Government's Formula Junior training programme conceived by Count Giovanni Lurani.' Soon after the move to Nazareth, Pa., Mario started driving modified stock cars on the smaller tracks of that area; and, after reaching his 21st birthday, he began driving regularly on the URC sprint car and ARDC midget car circuits.

With the experience gained in three full seasons of such competition, during which time he attracted considerable attention despite his small stature, he advanced to the sprint-car and championship-car divisions of the United States Auto Club in 1964 to start his phenomenal record as a winning driver. By the end of the 1970 campaign, he had participated in 129 USAC big car championship races, won 31 of them and finished second on 24 other occasions. He also had won the national driving title three times (1965, 1966 and 1969) and had finished as runner-up for the crown in 1967 and 1968. In winning the title for the third time in 1969, he outpointed all rivals decisively on pavement as well as on the 1-mile dirt tracks; and he also found time to compete successfully in stock car and sports car events.

Mario's most important victory was scored at Indianapolis on 30 May 1969, when he drove his rear-engine (turbocharged Ford) STP Special to a new race record of 156·867mph (252·511kph) in the 53rd annual 500-mile event, ending three years of frustration at Indy since taking 3rd place as a 1965 rookie. Mechanical trouble had sent him to the sidelines in all three events although he had earned the No. 1 starting position twice with new qualifying records of 165·899mph (266·954kph) in 1966 and 168·982mph (271·933kph) in 1967. Even in 1969, he still seemed to be dogged by bad racing luck when his new car almost disintegrated as a broken rear hub sent it crashing against the outer retaining wall during practice. He sustained only minor

bruises and facial burns, however, and five days later he qualified for a starting position in a 1968 car which he had entered as a spare. After taking the lead for the third time on the 106th lap (of 200) he never was threatened during the remainder of the contest.

Seventeen of his other USAC championship car victories also were scored in races of more than 100 mile duration as follows: Indianapolis Raceway Park, 3; Trenton, N.J., 3; St Jovite, Canada, 2; Milwaukee, Wis., 2; Phoenix, Ariz., 2; Atlanta, Ga.; Hanford, Calif.; Langhorne, Pa.; Castle Rock, Col.; and Riverside, Calif. Among all active USAC drivers at the end of the 1970 campaign, on the basis of championship victories scored, he ranked second to A. J. Foyt, who earned his total of 41 over a period of 13 full seasons beginning in 1958.

To prove his versatility in other types of motor racing, he won the 1967 FIA-NASCAR 500-mile stock car race at Daytona Beach, Fla., and teamed with Bruce McLaren later in the same year to win the FIA 12-hour sports car race at Sebring, Fla. He won this event again in 1970, sharing a Ferrari 512S with Ignazio Giunti and Nino Vacarella. He started the 1971 season with impressive victories in the South African Grand Prix and the Questor, Calif., invitation race for Grand Prix Cars. AB

Andruet, Jean-Claude

Andruet was born in Paris in 1940 where he still practices his profession of advocate when rallying commitments allow. He started rallying in 1965 when he won the national novices title, and in the next two years had a number of successes at the wheel of his own Renault Gordini R8. During 1967 he was offered a works Alpine in which he won his category in seven events including the Coupe des Alpes and Rallye Mont Blanc. Together with his racing results in the Coupe Gordini these successes won him the Challenge Shell-Berre for 1967. The next year he stayed with Alpine officially and gained the rally championship of France, with wins in the Lyons-Charbonnières, the Ronde Cevenolle, the Mont Blanc and the Tour de Corse. His racing programme included Le Mans where he won the Index of Performance with J. P. Nicolas at the wheel of an Alpine 1000.

In 1968 and 1969 he had much less success, and his misfortunes caused him to be nicknamed 'le champion sortant' by his French colleagues. However, his luck changed dramatically in 1970; with victories in the Lyon-Charbonnières, Lorraine, Geneva, Polish, and Munich-Vienna-Budapest Rallies, and 2nd in the Tour de Course, Andruet was a clear winner in the European Rally Drivers' Championship. JD

Arcangeli, Luigi

Born in 1902, this talented driver from Forli, Italy began his racing career on bicycles, and then proceeded to motorcycles and cars. In his first year of racing, 1928, he drove a 2-litre Bugatti and a sports Itala, and in 1929 he joined the Scuderia Materassi, driving a 1·5-litre Talbot-Darracq in which he won the circuit of Cremona, defeating Nuvolari. His best year was 1930 when he joined the Maserati team and, among other successes, won the Rome GP in the new 2·5-litre car. He also drove a sports Alfa Romeo 1750 with considerable success that season. In 1931 he gained a place in the Alfa Romeo team, but was killed at Monza when practising for the Italian GP. In trying to out-do Campari's lap speed he crashed the big twin-engined 3·5-litre Tipo A Alfa Romeo on the Lesmo curve, at the same spot where in earlier years Zborowski and Sivocci had lost their lives. CP

Arnold, R. W.

Born in 1906, Billy Arnold, winner of the 1930 Indianapolis 500 race, was one of the first American drivers to be classified as a charger because of his unrestrained desire to run as fast as he could as long as he could with little regard for the strain on his equipment. Unlike his more experienced rivals of that era, who ran their races according to a plan, Arnold invariably charged to the front of the field at the earliest opportunity.

After two years of Indianapolis experience in cars owned by Mike Boyle, Arnold jumped at the opportunity in 1930 to drive a 151ci (2,474cc) Miller-Hartz fwd special entered by former AAA National Champion Harry Hartz, who had not recovered sufficiently from injuries sustained in a racing accident almost three years earlier to drive the car himself. Arnold qualified for the no 1 starting position, but former 500 winner Louis Meyer beat him into the first turn on the first lap of the race and managed to hold the lead for two laps. Then Arnold stormed into the lead and widened his margin steadily during the remaining 198 laps to average 100·448mph (161·573kph) for the full distance and win by more than four laps.

This also gave him the distinction of being the first driver to go the full distance without relief at a speed of better than 100mph (160kph), Peter DePaolo having relinquished the wheel briefly to another driver during his 1925 victory at 101·130mph (162·750kph).

Arnold also won two scheduled 200-mile (321·9km) races later in the season on the board track at Altoona, Pa.—one was cut to 116 miles (186·7km) because of rain —and finished the year as the AAA National driving champion.

Starting 18th at Indianapolis in 1931, because of his failure to qualify on the first day of time trials, Arnold took the lead on the seventh lap and remained in front until he crashed on the 163rd lap because of a broken axle. In 1932, he also led all but the first of the 58 laps he ran before crashing again, giving him a record of having led the field on 410 of the 420 laps driven at Indianapolis during the three-year period beginning in 1930. Arnold retired as a driver after his 1933 accident, worked several years for the Chrysler Corporation, served as a Lieutenant Colonel during World War 2 and then entered the real estate development and construction business in Oklahoma City, Okla., where he still lives. AB

Ascari, Alberto

Born in 1918, son of the famous Alfa Romeo driver, Antonio Ascari, Alberto was only 7 when his father was killed at Montlhéry. Determined, also, to be a racing driver, Alberto began to gain a reputation in 1937 by racing Bianchi motorcycles. In April 1940, Alberto Ascari was offered his first car drive by Enzo Ferrari in one of the new Type 815 two-seater 8-cylinder 1·5-litre Ferraris, the first cars of the make to be produced. The race was the Mille Miglia, and Ascari shared the wheel with the experienced Alfa Romeo driver Minozzi, who was his cousin. Their Ferrari led its class easily, but retired after 90 miles (145km) with a valve failure.

In 1947 he drove in a peculiar race for 22 of the little 046 Cisitalias held on Gezireh Island near Cairo, and driven by aces like Chiron, Taruffi, Lurani, Cortese, Tenni, Brivio and Serafini. Ascari received great acclaim by coming 2nd to Taruffi in his heat and 2nd to Cortese in the final by 13sec. As a result of this performance, he was invited to join the Scuderia Ambrosiana who were racing works Maseratis, and came under the wing of

Billy Arnold. *Photo: Indianapolis Motor Speedway*

Alberto Ascari: Principal Successes

1947	Circuit of Modena	Maserati A6G
1948	San Remo GP	Maserati 4CLT/48
	Coppa Acerbo (with Bracco)	Maserati A6G
1949	Buenos Aires GP	Maserati 4CLT/48
	Bari GP	Ferrari 166
	Coupe des Petites Cylindrées	Ferrari 166
	Swiss GP	Ferrari 125
	Italian GP	Ferrari 125
	Int Trophy, Silverstone	Ferrari 125
	Peron GP, BA	Ferrari 166
1950	Mar del Plata GP	Ferrari 166
	Modena GP	Ferrari 166
	Mons GP	Ferrari 166
	German GP	Ferrari 166
	Garda Circuit	Ferrari 166
	Rome GP	Ferrari 166
	Coupe des Petites Cylindrées	Ferrari 166
	Spanish GP	Ferrari 375
	Luxembourg GP	Ferrari 166
1951	Sestriere Rally (with Villoresi)	Lancia Aurelia
	San Remo GP	Ferrari 375
	German GP	Ferrari 375
	Italian GP	Ferrari 375
	Naples GP	Ferrari 166
	Monza GP	Ferrari 166
	Modena GP	Ferrari 500
1952	Syracuse GP	Ferrari 500
	Marseilles GP	Ferrari 500
	Belgian GP	Ferrari 500
	French GP	Ferrari 500
	British GP	Ferrari 500
	Dutch GP	Ferrari 500
	St Gaudens GP	Ferrari 500
	La Baule GP	Ferrari 500
	Italian GP	Ferrari 500
1953	Argentine GP	Ferrari 500
	Pau GP	Ferrari 500
	Bordeaux GP	Ferrari 500
	Dutch GP	Ferrari 500
	Belgian GP	Ferrari 500
	British GP	Ferrari 500
	Swiss GP	Ferrari 500
	Nürburgring 1,000km (with Farina)	Ferrari 375MM
1954	Mille Miglia	Lancia D24
1955	Naples GP	Lancia D50
	Turin GP	Lancia D50

their chief driver, Luigi Villoresi, who taught him a great deal. At Reims in July 1947, in the Grand Prix de la Marne, the tubular chassis 16-valve 4CLT Maserati made its debut in Ascari's hands. He raced many times in 1947, at Nice, Milan, Lyons, Lausanne, etc, in the racing Maseratis and was often among the leaders, but had constant mechanical troubles. However, he had one victory, in the Circuit of Modena, driving a new sports A6G Maserati with cycle-type wings, finishing in front of Villoresi's similar car, the race having been stopped at half distance due to an accident when Ascari was in the lead.

In 1948 Ascari and Villoresi appeared at San Remo with the improved 4CLT/48 Maseratis, and Ascari won the race in front of his tutor, after which the 4CLT/48 was popularly known as the San Remo Maserati. His only other 1948 victory was in the Pescara sports car GP after he had taken an A6G over from Bracco. In this year he was 2nd to Villoresi in the British GP at Silverstone, and it is pleasant from the point of view of tradition to record that he had one drive with the 158 Alfa Romeo team, finishing 3rd in the French GP at Reims behind his team-mates Wimille and Sanesi.

By 1949 Ascari, in his blue shirt and blue linen helmet, had become a force to be reckoned with. He began with a win in the Buenos Aires GP in a San Remo Maserati, after which both he and Villoresi transferred to Ferrari, and Ascari competed in Formula 1 and 2 events all over Europe, where he had 5 victories plus another win at Buenos Aires at the end of the season in the Peron GP.

In 1950 he had nine Ferrari victories and in 1951 six, but 1952 was his most successful year with twelve, and in this year he became World Champion when all the *grandes épreuves* were to the 2-litre formula, or Formula 2. He missed the first race of 1952, the Swiss GP as he was away qualifying at Indianapolis with the big 4·5 litre Ferrari, which suffered a wheel collapse in the 500, but for the other races he had a comparatively easy ride, Fangio, of the rival Maserati team, being out of racing

Alberto Ascari. *Photo: Geoffrey Goddard*

Above, Alberto Ascari (right), with Luigi Villoresi at Spa in 1953. *Photo: Associated Press Ltd.*

Left, Alberto Ascari, driving the 4·5-litre Ferrari to victory at San Remo, 1951. *Photo: David Hodges Collection*

for most of the season after a crash in the Monza GP in June.

In 1953 Ascari was again World Champion, backed up by his team-mates Hawthorn, Farina and Villoresi. This was a tougher year for him than 1952, with opposition from the Maseratis of Fangio and Gonzalez.

For 1954 Ascari signed to drive the new Lancia D50s in Grand Prix events, but the cars were not ready until the end of the season. He was 'loaned' to both Maserati (French GP) and Ferrari (Italian GP) but had no success in either race, and though he was fastest in practice when his Lancia made its debut at Barcelona, and he led the race in its initial stages, he had to retire with clutch trouble. His one big success in 1954 was a victory in the Mille Miglia for Lancia from Marzotto's Ferrari and Musso's Maserati.

In 1955 the Lancias were competitive, and Ascari led the Argentine GP until colliding with a fence after 20 laps. He won at Turin and Naples with the cars, and then at Monaco he lost control of his Lancia and it toppled into the harbour. Four days later, when still not recovered from a facial injury sustained at Monaco, he tried out a 3-litre sports Ferrari at Monza, without a helmet, and crashed fatally on the sweeping Vialone bend, for no apparent reason.

Ascari, a married man with two children, had abundant natural talent and a strong will. He was unaffected by very hot weather conditions, which were sufficient to lay out some of his competitors in the Argentine races, and he was unusual in not appearing to suffer from pre-race nerves. He was most relaxed when out in front of a race, and was unlike most drivers in that he did not give of his best when in 2nd place or further back, for the knowledge that he would have to find an opportunity to pass seemed to worry him. When in the lead he showed all his gifts, and it was well nigh impossible for anyone to catch him. PMAH

Ascari, Antonio

One of the great drivers of the early 1920s, Ascari, was born in 1888 and came from Casteldario, near Mantua, like Nuvolari. Ascari's father, a corn merchant, later moved to Milan, where Antonio started a motor business and workshop. Here, with his mechanic Sozzi, he prepared a modified 4·5-litre 1914 GP Fiat, Tipo S57/14B, with which he first came into prominence by winning the 1919 Parma to Berceto hill-climb and the Consuma Cup hill-climb, near Florence, although he

Richard Attwood. *Photo: Autosport*

Antonio Ascari. *Photo: Cyril Posthumus Collection*

crashed the car in the first lap of the 1919 Targa Florio when leading after covering only 30 miles (48km).

He became Alfa Romeo general agent for Lombardy, and it was at his suggestion that the successful 20/30 ES Sport was marketed. He won the 4·5-litre racing class with a 20/30hp in the 1920 Parma-Berceto event, and the same class in 1921 in an ES Sport. In 1923 he was 2nd in the same event in a 3-litre RL 'Targa Florio'. Then he won the 1923 Circuit of Cremona in the same or a similar car, finishing the season by coming 3rd in the Circuit of Mugello in an RLS sports car, which headed the touring class. However, his real fame came with his feats at the wheel of the P2 GP car, in particular winning the 1924 Italian GP and 1925 Belgian GP. Two narrowly missed victories must be mentioned, in the 1924 Targa Florio in a 3·6-litre RLTF racer and the 1924 French GP in a P2, when he suffered mechanical failures in both races when all set to win in the closing stages.

Immensely popular, Antonio Ascari was what the Italians call a *garibaldino* driver, who went flat out from the start with no thought of cool calculation. He met his death in a P2 in the 1925 French GP at Monthléry, when he refused to slacken speed while leading the race and a drizzle started falling. PMAH

Attwood, Richard

Attwood was born in Wolverhampton in 1940, joined Jaguar as a trade apprentice and made his race debut with a Triumph TR-3 in 1960. During the next two years he drove Cooper-Ford FJs, and in 1963 an FJ Lola in which he won the Monaco Junior GP. He had made a name as a very consistent driver, and in 1964 scored one 1st, three 2nds and one 3rd in Midland Racing Partnership's F2 Lolas. He was also in the original Ford GT team, and drove Tim Parnell's Lotus-BRMs in 1965 F1 events. He drove for Parnell's Tasman BRM team in 1966 and 1967, and after Mike Spence's death in 1968 he joined the official BRM team and gave them 2nd place and the lap record at Monaco in the greatest drive of his career. However he left the BRM team subsequently. In sports car racing 'Tatty Atty' has had consistent success at Kyalami, where he shared David Piper's winning car in the 9 Hours Race in 1965 (Ferrari), 1966 (Ferrari) and 1969 (Porsche). In 1970 he shared the Porsche with John Love as Piper was in hospital, but retired. DCN

Baghetti, Giancarlo

The elder son of a wealthy industrialist, Baghetti was born in Milan on Christmas Day, 1934. He entered the family business on leaving school at 18 but was already a motor racing enthusiast. Finances presented little problem, but Baghetti did not race until 1956. That year he entered a minor race at Monza with an Alfa Romeo 1900TI, but had to retire. In 1958 he finished an excellent 2nd in the Mille Miglia (being run as a rally for the first time), with his brother Marco navigating.

Baghetti went international in 1959 with a Fiat-Abarth 750, and had a works record run in a 1000 model at Monza, averaging 117mph (188·3kph) for 72 hours. He bought a Dagrada-Lancia Formula Junior for 1960, and scored three wins, three 2nds and two 3rds that year. These performances gained him an F1 Ferrari drive for FISA. At Syracuse he caused a sensation by beating the works F1 Porsches of Gurney and Bonnier. He won the 93-mile (149·67km) Naples GP and then reached his zenith, winning the French GP on his first *grande épreuve*. He was Italian National Champion for 1961.

In 1962 he was overshadowed in the Ferrari team by the improving Bandini, and when Ferrari cut back in 1963 he joined Phil Hill in the new ATS team. The team's troubles that year had their effect on Baghetti's reputation, and in 1964 he drove Centro-Sud BRMs with Maggs. The Italian's career was in rapid decline and nearly everything he drove broke under him. He scored some more minor successes, winning a Formula 3 race at Monza in a Branca in 1967. In 1968 he shared an Alfa T33 with Biscaldi to finish 6th in the Targa Florio, and that was his last international success. The final blow came in the *Daily Express* London–Sydney Marathon in December 1968, when Baghetti had his road book, documents and money stolen from his Lancia and had to retire as a consequence.

Giancarlo Baghetti's rise to fame was meteoric, and his sudden decline painful. Few were surprised to hear of his retirement after the Marathon, but many sympathized with the self-effacing and taciturn Milanese. DCN

Baker, Elzie W.
Born in 1919 and NASCAR Grand National champion in 1956 and 1957, Buck Baker now campaigns with a Pontiac Firebird in the Grand American series, leaving the GN sedans to his son, Buddy Baker, who started racing in 1959. Oldest of all active NASCAR drivers, with a career total of 46 GN victories, Baker three times won the Darlington Southern 500. ARB

Balls, Vernon
This British driver, who ran an Amilcar agency in London, raced almost exclusively in this make of car. He put a number of individualistically streamlined bodies on these chassis for Brooklands races, where he started his career in 1925. He developed these sv Amilcars into quite potent machines, entering three of them for the 1926 JCC 200 Miles Race, one of which was Cozette supercharged. Balls' supercharged Amilcar went well in 1927, lapping at nearly 95mph (152kph) in a Brooklands handicap lost only because Balls mistook the finishing line. It later went even faster, winning at the Easter meeting. Later that year Balls took over one of the dohc 6-cylinder Amilcars which he had tested at Montlhéry and finished 2nd in the 1,100cc class in the 200 Miles Race. He drove with considerable fire and, still Amilcar mounted, won his class in the 1928 200 Miles Race, in spite of engine maladies.

By 1929 Balls' Amilcar was regarded as fast enough for the Brooklands Lightning handicaps, one of which it lost by a narrow margin. By 1932 Balls had changed his allegiance to a team of ioe Crossley Tens modified to his own specification, with lowered chassis and long-distance equipment. They were unsuccessful. WB

Bandini, Lorenzo
Bandini was born to Italian parents in Barce, Cyrenaica, North Africa on 21 December 1936. The Bandinis moved back to Florence in 1939, where they spent the war years. Lorenzo's father died when he was 15, and he left home to become a motor mechanic in Milan. His employer, a Signor Freddi, was sympathetic to young Bandini's motor racing aspirations, but after five years' work 20-year old Bandini opened his own garage in Via Bardelli, Milan. He made his competition début in 1957, driving a borrowed Fiat 1100 in the Castell 'Arquato-Vernasca hill-climb, being 15th in class. Freddi loaned him a Fiat 1100, and later a Fiat 8V for more national events. Freddi eventually gave Bandini a Lancia Appia

Zagato, and with Ciali as co-driver Bandini won his class in the 1958 Mille Miglia.

From 1958 to 1960 he drove Volpini and Stanguellini FJ cars. He was in line for the FISA Ferrari drive in 1961 but when Baghetti was chosen Guglielmo Dei, patron of Scuderia Centro-Sud, bought him an F1 Cooper-Maserati. He was 3rd behind Clark and Bonnier in his first Formula 1 appearance at Pau, and 3rd at Naples, making his Championship début as Spa, where his engine failed. He shared a sports Ferrari with veteran Giorgio Scarlatti to win the Pescara GP and underlined his promise of the previous year. Then Ferrari signed him as reserve driver. He had several good placings, including 2nd in the Targa Florio (with his friend Baghetti) and at Naples, before finishing a brilliant 3rd in his first works Championship appearance at Monaco. He won at Enna and was 2nd in a 250GTO at Nassau to end the season.

Ferrari ran a two-car team in 1963, and Dei a red BRM V8 for Bandini. He drove this car extremely quickly and aggressively, practising faster than the works cars at the Nürburgring. Ferrari then took Bandini on as number two to Surtees; he finishing 5th in a Ferrari V-6 in the United States and South African GPs and 3rd (to Surtees) in the Rand GP. He won Le Mans with Scarfiotti and had a very good all-round season.

He had now won a permanent place in the Ferrari team, and won the car-breaking Austrian GP at Zeltweg airfield in a Formula 1 V-6. He was 3rd in the German

Giancarlo Baghetti. *Photo: Gösta C. Zwilling*

Below, Lorenzo Bandini. *Photo: Autosport*

Bottom, The Ferrari team for the 1967 Daytona 24 Hours; left to right, Lorenzo Bandini, Mike Parkes, Chris Amon and Ludovico Scarfiotti. *Photo: Daytona Speedway Press Department*

Woolf Barnato (right), with Sir Henry Birkin, at Le Mans in 1929. Photo: T. A. S. O. Mathieson Collection

Edgar Barth. Photo: Gösta C. Zwilling

Jean Behra. Photo: Autosport

GP, 5th in the British and (with a new V-8) 3rd in the Italian GP. With a flat-12 he was also 3rd in Mexico. Several sports car successes were added to this impressive list and for 1965 Bandini was again number two to Surtees, although he made it obvious he did not like the arrangement. He hated racing in the rain, however, and was always outshone by his English team leader in such conditions. He finished 6th in the World Championship that year, but the rift between himself and Surtees had widened throughout the year and as an Italian driver in an Italian team he was very conscious of his responsibilities. In 1966 he drove an interim 2·4-litre V-6 car into 2nd place at Monaco, was 3rd in the wet at Spa and became team leader when Surtees left the team before the French GP. At Reims Bandini led for 31 laps before his throttle cable parted and let Brabham through to win. He scored only twice more, with 6th place in the Dutch and German GPs.

In the meantime Bandini had married Margherita Freddi—daughter of his old sponsor—and the 1967 season started well for him. He won both the Daytona 24 Hours and Monza 1,000 kilometres, sharing a works 330P4 with Amon, and was a fighting 2nd to Gurney's Eagle in the Race of Champions. Ferrari entered the Championship at Monaco, Bandini's favourite circuit, and he qualified as 2nd fastest to Brabham. He was chasing the leader (Denis Hulme) hard in the race when he began to tire noticeably in the latter half. On lap 82 his Ferrari mounted the bales on the chicane exit, overturned and caught fire. Rescuers were slow to release the fearfully injured driver, and three days later he died from his burns and internal injuries. DCN

Barnato, Woolf

'Babe' Barnato's racing apprenticeship was served at Brooklands, where he was seen first with large Locomobile, Mercedes and Austro-Daimler cars. His family had made their fortunes in diamond mining in South Africa, and he could afford to apply a debonair attitude to the sport. His large, tanned and smiling figure became inseparably associated with the Bentley sports-racing team in the late 1920s, when he became one of the leading lights of the 'Bentley Boys'. He could be not only socially gregarious but also generous, and for a time he assisted in financing the ailing Bentley company.

His high spirits masked considerable dedication and driving skill—sufficient to enable him to secure three consecutive victories in the gruelling Le Mans race, before his interests turned to other fields. Since 1948 the Woolf Barnato Trophy has been presented annually by the SCCA for outstanding contribution to the club. DF

Barth, Edgar

Born in 1917, this German driver started his career in motor sport with the DKW team in the Tourist Trophy of 1937. After World War 2 he took part in numerous motorcycle races until changing to four wheels. In 1952 he drove a Formula 2 car of the Rennkollektiv Johannisthal (DAMW). His first race was at Rostock and he finished 4th. His first victory was at Leipzig and more followed which brought him the East German championship for 1952 and 1953. In 1954 he drove the new 1·5-litre EMW sports car, but he had no chance of international competition. One of his outstanding victories was a class win in the 1955 Eifelrennen.

At the end of the 1956 season EMW (or AWE as it was called at that time) gave up racing. Barth moved from East to West Germany and began to drive for

Porsche, started in the Nürburbring 1,000 kilometres race and gained a 1·5-litre class win together with Umberto Maglioli. An overall victory in the 1959 Targa Florio together with Seidel in a 1500 RSK was the biggest success of his career to that date and at the end of the season Barth was European Hill-climb Champion. In 1959 and 1960 he took part in an NSU tourer in the Argentinian Gran Premio de la Republica. He drove the Formula 2 Porsche in the 1960 season. But the peak of his career came in 1963 and 1964, when he was again European Hill-climb Champion. Edgar Barth died in 1965. HON

Behra, Jean

France's top driver of the 1950s, born in Nice in 1921, Behra served his speed apprenticeship on two wheels, first as a cycling champion, then as French motorcycling Champion three years running. An admirer of fellow-Niçois René Dreyfus, Behra aspired to race cars, achieving his ambition with a 4-litre Talbot in the 1949 Coupe du Salon at Montlhéry, finishing 6th. He then finished third overall and won his class in the 1950 Monte Carlo Rally with Quinlin in a 1,100cc Simca, and next drove in the Le Mans 24 Hours itself, sharing a Simca with another racing motorcyclist, Roger Loyer. They retired, but a month later Behra won the 1·5-litre racing class of the Mont Ventoux hill-climb in a borrowed 1·5-litre 4-cylinder Maserati. In 1951 Amédée Gordini gave him his first Formula 2 drive at Sables d'Olonne, the 'new boy' getting home 3rd and setting fastest lap. At Cadours he won his heat, finished 3rd overall, and shared fastest lap with team-mate Trintignant.

Obviously Gordini had discovered a promising driver in the lean, wiry Behra. He stayed with the French team until 1954, putting up many gallant performances. In 1952 he won at Aix-les-Bains with the new 2-litre 6-cylinder F2 Gordini, was 3rd at Pau and Berne, then beat the works Ferraris of Ascari, Farina and Villoresi fair and square to win the Reims GP.

His indomitable spirit endeared him greatly to the French. At Pau in 1953 he cut a tyre valve in too close contact with a Ferrari and crashed, suffering spinal and arm injuries, yet he was quickly back in the fray, though ill-rewarded by frequent retirements with the brittle Gordinis. In the 3-litre sports car, however, he performed brilliantly in the Tour de France, winning almost every speed test and placing 2nd overall. In 1954 Behra with his distinctive checkered helmet beat the Ferraris again to win the Pau GP, and also won at Cadours and Montlhéry.

Then he joined the Maserati team in 1955. The greater reliability of the Italian cars immediately told, for Behra scored two F1 wins at Pau and Bordeaux, and four sports car wins at Bari, Monza, Oporto and the Nürburgring. Then he crashed badly in the TT at Dundrod, Northern Ireland, losing an ear and gaining a British plastic substitute—and also the Guild of Motoring Writers' award of their 'Driver of the Year' title.

There were several high placings in 1956 but no victories in World Championship events. He shared the Maserati victory in the Nürburgring 1,000 kilometres with Moss, Taruffi and Schell, and the Paris 1,000 kilometres with Rosier. In 1957 Behra won at Sebring with Fangio, and the Swedish sports car GP with Moss; then won BRM their first GP victory at Caen, following it up by leading their 1-2-3 success in the BRDC Silverstone race. Back in a Maserati he won at Modena and in the Moroccan GP at Casablanca.

Left, Jean Behra in the 1955 aerodynamic Formula I Maserati. *Photo: Planet News*

Right, Jean-Pierre Beltoise. *Photo: Doug Nye Collection*

Jean Behra: Principal Successes

Year	Event	Car
1952	Aix les-Bains GP (F2)	Gordini 2-litre
	Reims GP (F2)	Gordini 2-litre
1954	Pau GP	Gordini 2-litre
	Circuit of Cadours	Gordini 2-litre
	Coupe du Salon	Gordini sports
1955	Pau GP	Maserati 250F
	Bordeaux GP	Maserati 250F
	Bari GP	Maserati 300S
	Supercortemaggiore GP, Monza	Maserati 300S
	Oporto GP, Portugal	Maserati 300S
	Nürburgring 500km	Maserati 150S
1956	Nürburgring 1,000km, with Moss, Taruffi, Schell	Maserati 300S
	Paris 1,000km with Rosier	Maserati 300S
	Bari GP	Maserati 200S
	Rome GP	Maserati 300S
1957	Caen GP	BRM
	International Trophy	BRM
	Modena GP	Maserati 250F
	Moroccan GP, Casablanca	Maserati 250F
	Sebring 12-Hours, with Fangio	Maserati 450S
	Swedish GP with Moss	Maserati 450S
1958	Coupe de Vitesse, Reims	Porsche RSK
	Rheinland Cup, Nürburgring	Porsche RSK
	Berlin GP, AVUS	Porsche RSK
	Mont Ventoux Hill-Climb	Porsche RSK
1959	Aintree 200-Miles race	Ferrari Dino 246

Then Maserati withdrew from racing, and Behra signed with BRM for 1958 GPs and with Porsche for sports car events. It was a season of mixed fortunes: his best result was 3rd in the Dutch GP. The sports Porsches served him better, with wins at Reims, AVUS and Nürburgring and in two hill-climbs as well, plus some good placings in Championship events.

Not surprisingly, Behra left BRM in 1959 and joined Ferrari, opening his season well with victory in the Aintree '200'. He shared 2nd at Sebring and 3rd in the Nürburgring 1,000 kilometres, but had little luck with Ferraris elsewhere. Privately he evolved a special single-seater F2 Behra-Porsche, built in Modena to Colotti designs: Hans Herrmann drove it to 2nd place at Reims, but Behra himself had little success with it. Unduly nervous and 'edgy' that season, his career with Ferrari ended explosively with the French GP at Reims, when he resigned after quarrelling with team manager Tavoni. A fortnight later he drove an RSK Porsche to 2nd place in the Auvergne 2 Hours race, and a week after that, driving the same car at the AVUS in the 1959 Berlin sports car race, Behra spun at the top of the wet, slippery concrete banking, struck a concrete block, was flung out, hit a flagpole in mid-air, and was killed instantly. CP

Bell, Derek

British driver, born in Pinner, Middlesex in 1941. Bell's stepfather Bernard Hender, known as 'The Colonel', offered to finance him if he did well. In 1964 he had his first race in a 1,498cc Lotus 7 shared with a friend, John Enfold, and he won a Goodwood handicap event in pouring rain. He scored several other good places that season and acquired a Lotus 31 F3 for 1965, finishing 3rd in his first Formule Libre race.

Bell also drove Cuff Miller's Marcos GT with some success, and his stepfather backed him by buying a Lotus 41 F3 for the 1966 season. Bell had a full Continental season with this car and proved very fast, but had his fair share of incidents and unreliability from the car. De Sanctis and BWA offered him drives in Italy for 1967 but he joined Westbury and Daghorn in the Felday Formula 3 team instead, driving Brabham BT21s. He scored nine 1sts, and moved on to an F2 Brabham BT23C for 1968, running under the 'Church Farm Racing Team' banner.

Late in 1968 Ferrari gave him an F2 test drive, and although he was put out in a crash at the start of the Lottery GP (his first race in the works Dinos), he was signed on. His first Formula 1 appearance was in the Oulton Park Gold Cup, and he later took part in the Italian GP. But 1969 was to be a year in the doldrums. He drove the 4wd McLaren M9A in the British GP, but

Derek Bell, at Brands Hatch, January 1967. *Photo: E. Gerry Stream*

shone in Tom Wheatcrofts' F2 Brabham in 1970 with one 1st, two 2nds and three 3rds. For 1971 JW gave him a Porsche drive, he joined William's March F2 team and Tom sponsored an F1 March seat. DCN

Beltoise, Jean-Pierre Maurice Georges

Beltoise was born in Paris in 1937, and followed Nuvolari and Surtees in becoming a successful racing motorcyclist before moving on to cars. He began racing motorcycles after completing his military service and between 1961 and 1964 won 11 French Championships.

Beltoise won the Index of Energy at Le Mans in 1963, sharing a René-Bonnet with Bobrowski. In 1964 he was critically injured in a bad accident early on in the Reims 12 Hours. He suffered leg and arm injuries which have left him with a badly scarred body, a slight limp and a weak arm, but in 1965 he was back after six months' treatment. Bonnet had been acquired by Matra so in 1965 the French aerospace company entered Formula 3 racing. Beltoise was given a place in the team, but was put out by a broken throttle linkage at La Châtre and crashed at Clermont because his arm was still too weak to steer through left-hand corners. Then came Reims, and he started the race with fear in his heart. He spun at Muizon, then began to be pushed by his friend Roby Weber's Alpine. Beltoise suddenly found he wanted to win, to settle the account, and he slipstreamed his way to score Matra's first international success.

This decided Matra to continue their programme, and Beltoise repaid them with a victory in the F3 Monaco race in 1966, then dominated the Argentine Temporada series at the start of 1967, winning all four races. Matra ran their first Formula 2 cars in 1966 with Beltoise as their team leader, and he won the German GP class (and was 8th overall), came 2nd at the Bugatti circuit after leading Clark and Hulme, and was 3rd at Reims. The following season he finished 2nd at Crystal Palace, Enna and Vallelunga, and 3rd at Zolder and Langenlebarn, before Matra entered him in a ballasted F2 car in the United States and Mexican GPs: the game little Frenchman finished 7th both times. At the start of 1968 his overweight F2 finished 6th in the South Africa GP, and the team then ran it in the F1 feature event at Cape Town's Killarney circuit where he gained Matra their first 'F1' victory.

Later that season Matra's new F1 V-12 was unveiled; Beltoise scored one 2nd, two 5ths and a 6th place in World Championship events before the engine was withdrawn at the end of the season for further development. He achieved three Formula 2 victories that season, winning the European F2 Championship, and joined Tyrrell's F1 team for 1969 as number two to Stewart. He drove hard and fast all season, ending the year with 2nd place in the French GP, two 3rds, a 4th, one 5th and one 6th place to finish 5th in the World Championship. Beltoise and his compatriots persevered all year with the poorly-handling Matra V-12 sports cars and he won the Paris 1,000 kilometres, a shortened event, with Pescarolo. He scored two 2nds and two 3rds in Formula 2 and entered the 1970s as Matra's premier driver in F1 sports. He notched two 3rds, a 4th, two 5ths and 6th in F1, but his career was marred in 1971 by Giunti's fatal crash at Buenos Aires and subsequent charges of manslaughter.

Jean-Pierre Beltoise is a French hero, for he has tremendous courage and has overcome injury and personal tragedy more than once. His first wife, Elaine, was killed in a road accident, and for a while Beltoise's driving was extremely erratic. He has since remarried and has emerged as a fast and competent driver. DCN

Benjafield, J. D.

'Doc' Benjafield achieved fame as one of the 'Bentley Boys', the team that brought a string of successes to Britain in the Le Mans races of the late 1920s. He was a bacteriologist, and although of more sober aspect and quieter humour than some of the others, fitted into the team very well.

He first came into prominence at Brooklands, where his red 3-litre Bentley and Salmson cars were consistent competitors. He also raced Alfa Romeo, Aston Martin, Bugatti, De Dion Bouton, MG and Panhard-Levassor cars. The Brooklands Racing Drivers Club is said to have evolved from the informal dinner parties which he gave for his motoring friends.

Benjafield co-drove to victory with Sammy Davis in the 1927 Le Mans, running his own car as one of the works team, despite Davis' damaging involvement in a multiple accident at White House corner early in the race. During the next few years he had fairly consistent bad luck, which caused his retirement in several major events, and his failure to win by a narrow margin in others. Although he purchased an ERA in 1936, he withdrew from racing shortly afterwards. DF

Benoist, Robert

Born in 1895, Benoist began his motor-racing career in 1921 on long-distance rallies in France and on cyclecars. In 1922 he had a 1st place in a 1,100cc Salmson in the 200 miles race at Brooklands, and others in Provence and in Spain. Success continued the next year with the Salmson in the cyclecar Grand Prix in Italy, at Boulogne, Sitges, Le Mans, San Sebastian and in the GP of France.

In 1924 Benoist became a Delage works driver and had many victories in their special hill-climb car, and then transferred to the racing team which brought him a 3rd place at the GP of Europe at Lyons in the 2-litre car. In 1925 he continued with Delage and in the French Grand Prix drove an excellent race, leading after Ascari tragically lost his life in the leading Alfa Romeo, until

Divo took over the car to win when his own car failed. A few weeks later Benoist came 2nd to Divo in the Delage at San Sebastian.

The following year was not so successful for Delage as the new 1·5-litre car was not yet right. Severe overheating of the cockpit occurred from a badly positioned exhaust. The cars were not ready for the French GP but started in the Euorpean GP at San Sebastian in conditions of extreme heat. The leading Delage was driven by Benoist, Morel, Wagner, Thomas and Sénéchal in a series of driver changes. A week later he managed a 3rd place in the Formula Libre Spanish GP in the 1925 2-litre car, and then a short while later he shared 3rd place with Dubonnet in the first British GP at Brooklands, once more with the 1·5-litre car, still troubled with overheating of the drivers. In 1927 he and the 1·5-litre Delage swept all before them, winning the World Championship for Delage, GPs in France, Spain, Italy and Britain, and a Légion d'Honneur for himself.

Delage gave up racing at the end of 1927, but Benoist managed to get a drive for the first time with Bugatti at the end of the season at San Sebastian; the car arrived at the last minute and he had no time to practice but achieved a 2nd to Chiron in another Bugatti.

Later, Benoist had some success in sports-car racing, winning the 1929 Spa 24-hour race in an Alfa Romeo, and driving a Chrysler at Le Mans, then going into virtual retirement. He began again in 1934 as a member of the Bugatti team, along with Wimille and Dreyfus, later replaced by Taruffi, and later still by Williams. He had a few places in the 3·3-litre Type 59 Bugatti, and then shared in the successes in the 3·3-litre Type 57G Bugatti 'tank' cars at the 1936 French GP, although unplaced himself. He ran at Marne again in the 'tank' and then in 1937 shared a magnificent victory with Wimille in the car at Le Mans. This was a suitable moment for him to end his active racing career.

Benoist managed the Paris showroom of the Bugatti works in the Avenue Montaigne for several years before World War 2. During the war with the rank of captain he was an active member of the French Resistance, making many trips between Britain and Occupied France. Arrested in Paris by the Gestapo, he was sent to Buchenwald where he was executed with many others on 12 September 1944. HGC

J. D. Benjafield. *Photo: Montagu Motor Museum*

Above, Robert Benoist, in 1923 Salmson at Brooklands. *Photo: Montagu Motor Museum*

Below, Robert Benoist (right) with Louis Chiron, after 1928 San Sebastian GP. *Photo: Hugh Conway Collection*

Below left, Robert Benoist (left), with Attilio Marinoni, winners of the 1929 Spa-24 Hour race. *Photo: Hugh Conway Collection*

Bertram, Oliver

Among those drivers whose names will for ever be linked with Brooklands is Oliver Bertram. Born in 1910, he started his career in 1929, while still at Cambridge, driving cars of all types and sizes in Brooklands speed trials, and in hill-climbs, during the next three years. His big opportunity came in 1933 when he acquired the 10·5-litre Delage with which John Cobb had been so successful. With this car he quickly showed his mastery of the track by lapping easily at over 130mph (208kph), winning two races, and being placed in three others, including 2nd place in the Gold Star Handicap at the Whitsun Meeting.

Bertram's successes with the Delage continued in 1934, including 3rd places in the Gold Star Handicap and Brooklands Championship races, which, with a 1st and a 2nd, gave him 3rd place in the BRDC Track Star results for the year. In 1935 he was nominated to drive the Barnato-Hassan Special, and with this car, and the Delage, had a splendid season breaking the lap record at 142·7mph (229·6kph) at the BARC August Meeting and finishing joint 1st for the BRDC Track Star. He lost the lap record to Cobb in October the same year.

The 1936 season was disappointing due largely to mechanical troubles, but Bertram had the satisfaction of winning the Brooklands 500 Kilometres race, sharing the driving of Cobb's Napier-Railton. Both 1937 and 1938 were successful years for he won, or was placed, in numerous races driving both the Barnato-Hassan and Bowler-Hofman Specials, winning the BRDC Track Star for the second time in 1938.

Bertram, who had no interest in road racing, was one of the only three drivers ever to lap Brooklands at over 140mph (224kph) and will always be remembered for his masterful driving of all types of cars, the Barnato-Hassan in particular. TASOM

Bianchi, Lucien

Lucien Bianchi was born in Milan in 1934, elder son of an Alfa Romeo mechanic. The family moved to Belgium while Lucien was still quite young, and after World War 2 his father became racing mechanic to Johnny Claes, one of the leading Belgian drivers at the time. Lucien helped his father work on the competition cars, and began rallying at the age of 18.

In 1955 he started his international career, going with Claes on the Liège-Rome-Liège Rally. Tragically, Claes was a delicate and sick man and he was taken ill during the event. Will-power and Bianchi's support brought the team 3rd place overall, but Claes was hospitalized and died shortly afterwards. Bianchi took to circuit racing, although his services as a handy navigator and second driver were in great demand among the rally fraternity. In 1957 he was 7th overall and won his class at Le Mans in a 2-litre Ferrari (with Harris), and scored the first of three successive victories in the Tour de France (with Gendebien).

Bianchi drove regularly for the Equipe National Belge (ENB), nearly always in sports Ferraris, until 1960 when ENB ran Cooper, Lotus and Emeryson Formula 1 machines and he scored 4th place in the South African GP and 5th in the Belgian. He won the Liège in 1961 in a Citroën DS19; and the Sebring 12 Hours in 1962, sharing a Ferrari with Bonnier. His Belgian GP drive in a Lola in 1963 was notable for several separate accidents, but the friendly little sandy-haired Italian excelled in long-distance events, coming 2nd at Daytona (with Piper), 4th in the Nürburgring 1,000 kilometres and 5th

in the Paris 1,000 kilometres (both with Langlois van Ophem) in 1964. His brother Mauro drove for Alpine and the pair won the Nürburgring 500 kilometres in 1965. He drove saloons and rally cars whenever possible, and was 2nd in the Paris 1,000 kilometres in 1967 (with 'Beurlys'). Lucien also drove USAC track cars in America, where he became a close friend of Mario Andretti, but failed to qualify for the Indianapolis 500.

In 1968 the ailing Cooper concern gave him a Formula 1 seat and he acquitted himself well, finishing 3rd at Monaco and 6th at Spa in the uncompetitive BRM-engined cars. Driving Alfa Romeo T33s he was 6th at Daytona and 3rd in the Targa Florio, and then joined the JW GT40 team in place of the injured Brian Redman. He won the Watkins Glen 6 Hours (with Ickx), and then his team-mate broke an arm in the Canadian GP meeting. So Bianchi was teamed with Pedro Rodriguez for the postponed Le Mans 24 Hours, and after the demise of the Porsches they won handsomely. John Wyer described Bianchi as '. . . a most intelligent driver', and his abilities were reserved for Autodelta in 1969.

He drove a Citroën in the London–Sydney Marathon and was cheated of a certain win when he was struck by a non-competing car a few miles from Sydney.

Back at Le Mans for the test weekend in April 1969 his T33/3 slowed at the end of the Mulsanne Straight, then suddenly veered into the trees and exploded. Lucien Bianchi was killed instantly, leaving a widow and three children. Tragically, Mme Bianchi lost her life soon afterwards in a riding accident. DCN

Bignotti, George

Bignotti was born in 1918 and began as a successful midget builder and mechanic in his native San Francisco. Bignotti machines have gone on to win more than 50 USAC championship races, including four Indianapolis 500s and five USAC national championships. Bignotti was Foyt's chief mechanic when he won the 500 in 1961 and 1964, and he was in charge of Graham Hill's Lola when the English driver won at the Speedway in 1966. In 1970 Bignotti designed and helped to build the P. J. Colt in which Al Unser won the 500 and nine other Championship Trail races to earn the USAC 'big car' title, acquiring a new season record of 5,130 points. Equally at home with sports cars, Bignotti was chief mechanic for Jackie Stewart and Parnelli Jones in the John Mecom Jr Can-Am Lolas. ARB

'Bira, B.'

This pseudonym hid the identity of Prince Birabongse Bhanuban, of Thailand (formerly Siam), born in 1914 and educated at Eton and Cambridge. He started racing in 1935 when he was living in London with his cousin Prince Chula Chakrabongse and studying sculpture, subsequently exhibiting at the Royal Academy. Bira began racing at Brooklands with a Riley Imp and then an MG Magnette. Then Chula bought him an ERA (R2B, christened 'Romulus') for his 21st birthday. He was 2nd in his first race with the car, the 1,500cc event at Dieppe, won by Fairfield's ERA. Also in 1935 he was 2nd in the Prix de Berne Voiturette race behind Seaman's ERA.

Then followed four years of very successful racing by The White Mouse Stable run by Prince Chula with Bira as the sole driver. The main successes were obtained with B-type ERA cars named 'Romulus', 'Remus' and the C-type 'Hanuman': 'Romulus' won easily the most races. An ex-Whitney Straight 8CM 2·9-litre Maserati

Oliver Bertram. *Photo: Montagu Motor Museum*

Lucien Bianchi. *Photo: Autosport*

B. Bira. *Photo: Fox Photos Ltd*

Left, B. Bira in his BMW 328. Photo: World Wide Photos

Above, Sir Henry Birkin. Photo: Cyril Posthumus Collection

Right, Sir Henry Birkin (left), with W. O. Bentley at the 1929 Tourist Trophy. Photo: Montagu Motor Museum

was also used, mainly for Brooklands racing and fast circuits, and Chula bought 1·5-litre Delages from Seaman and Capt. Davis, but these were not successful after being fitted with ifs. A sports Delahaye was also added to the stable, and other cars Bira raced were a 750cc works sv single-seater Austin, a works sports 328 BMW (3rd in the 1937 TT), HRG, Aston Martin and Alfa Romeo machines, the last-named a 6C 2500 shared with Sommer which retired at Le Mans in 1939.

Bira was a very fast and neat driver who used his head and he looked curiously expressionless at the wheel in a blue linen helmet and dark goggles, or else gave a calm, collected and studious appearance in a blue crash helmet and a visor, wearing spectacles beneath the visor. He won the BRDC Road Racing Gold Star in 1936, 1937 and 1938, and raced under blue and yellow Siamese colours in 1939.

In 1946 the Stable was active again, gaining a 6th at Chimay with the Maserati and at Geneva with 'Romulus', and winning the Ulster Trophy with 'Hanuman', now converted to B-type specification after a crash at Reims in 1939. In 1947 'Bira' acquired a new 4CL 1·5-litre Maserati, in which he won at Chimay. At Berne he drove borrowed Maseratis from the Scuderia Milan and the Scuderia Platé, but retired. However, he had great success with the little single-seater Simca-Gordinis, beating Wimille and Sommer in similar machines, and besides winning in Switzerland, France and the Isle of Man, he was 2nd in the Coupe de Lyon to a 2-litre Martin/BMW. He drove the 2·9 Maserati twice at Shelsley, making 3rd ftd on one occasion, but he retired 'Hanuman' in the Ulster Trophy, his last ERA drive.

In 1948 he won at Zandvoort in a new 4CLT/48 San Remo Maserati. Towards the end of the year the Chula-Bira racing partnership was dissolved.

In 1949 Bira had a very active year racing his San Remo Maserati with the Scuderia Platé, being 2nd to Fangio's similar car in the Argentine Mar del Plata GP as well as at Albi and the Grand Prix de Roussillon at Perpignan, where, however, he beat Fangio in the second heat. He led the British GP before retiring; won a Silverstone International Trophy heat; won the Swedish Summer GP; was 2nd in the Grand Prix de France to Chiron's Talbot; was 3rd to Villoresi's Ferrari and de Graffenried's 4CLT/48 at Zandvoort; and 3rd to Ascari's Ferrari and Etancelin's Talbot in the Grand Prix d'Europe at Monza.

The 1950 season was a poor one for the San Remo

Maseratis generally, and with the Platé team 'Bira' only achieved a victory at a Goodwood meeting and a 4th at Berne. In 1951 he had a 4·5-litre V-12 Osca engine put into his Maserati, but only won a short race at Goodwood.

'Luck seemed to have deserted me long ago in racing' he wrote in 1952, and in 1952/3 he flew to Bangkok and back in his Miles Gemini light aircraft with his Argentinian bride, spending some months in his native land. In 1954, with a new 250F Maserati he resumed the life of a professional racing driver, his record in Formula 1 including a 1st at Chimay, 2nd at Rouen and Pescara and 4th in the French GP and at Caen. He shared a works DB3 Aston Martin with Peter Collins at Le Mans but crashed.

In 1955 he had his last big victory in the New Zealand GP at Ardmore, and his last successful race was in England, where he was 3rd to the similar 250Fs of Peter Collins and Salvadori in the International Trophy at Silverstone. Later in the year he sold his 250F to Horace Gould and retired from racing for good.

In 1970 he was resident in Thailand, running an airline. PMAH

Birkin, Sir Henry

'Tim' Birkin was born in 1896, and took part in his first race at Brooklands in 1921, when his streamlined DFP finished 2nd in a handicap event. Apart from a sand race meeting at Skegness in 1924 he was not seen again in competition until 1927 when he ran a 3-litre Bentley at Brooklands, following this with a 4·5-litre of the same make in 1928. He was 5th at Le Mans with Chassagne, 5th in the TT, and 5th in the Boillot Cup, making fastest time in the latter two races, both of which were handicap events. In 1929 he achieved his first Le Mans victory, sharing with Barnato a Speed Six Bentley which led from start to finish, and in which Birkin made the fastest lap.

In 1930 the Hon. Dorothy Paget bought the team of supercharged 4·5-litre Bentleys, Birkin's 'brain-child'. With one of these cars Birkin retired at Le Mans and in the Brooklands Double Twelve, but finished 4th in the Irish GP. He ran a stripped 'blower 4½' in the French GP and finished 2nd. With a single seater supercharged car he took the Brooklands lap record at 135.53mph (218·15kph) from Kaye Don's V-12 Sunbeam, only to lose it to Don a few weeks later.

At the end of the year Dorothy Paget sold the team of 4·5-litre supercharged Bentleys, and as Bentley Motors had already withdrawn from racing, Birkin had to look elsewhere for a car for 1931. He purchased a Maserati and an Alfa Romeo, the former for Grand Prix events and the latter for sports car events. With the Alfa he won the Irish GP and (with Earl Howe) Le Mans, while in the Maserati he finished 4th in the French GP with Eyston. In England he was still driving the single seater Bentley which he had bought from the Paget stable, and with it re-took the Brooklands lap record at 137·96mph (222kph). With the Maserati he won the Brooklands Mountain Championship.

Birkin had a disappointing season in 1932, retiring at Le Mans and the Brooklands 1,000 Miles Race. His best major race was 3rd at Spa in the 24 Hour Sports Car Race. In 1933 he purchased a new 3-litre Maserati with Bernard Rubin, and raced it for the first time in the Tripoli GP. After fighting for the lead with Nuvolari and Varzi he finished in 3rd place. During the race his arm was burned on the Maserati's exhaust pipe, the burn turned septic, and three weeks later he died in a London hospital. TASOM

Bjørnstadt, Eugen

The only Norwegian driver to gain international fame in pre-World War 2 racing, Eugen Bjørnstadt from Oslo began racing with a Bugatti, changed to a 2·3-litre Monza Alfa Romeo, then to a British ERA. Most of his racing was confined to the northern countries, and his name first appeared in 1931, when he placed 4th in the Finnish GP. He brought the 2·3 Alfa in 1933, and finished 2nd in its first race, the Swedish Winter GP on frozen Lake Ramen, all cars being equipped with tyre spikes. A fiery and enterprising driver, Bjørnstadt then won the Lwow GP in Poland, beating two similar Alfas, and was disappointed when his car gave trouble in the first Norwegian GP, held in 1934 at Lillehammer. In the second, run on the frozen lake at Bogstad early in 1935, he again had trouble, but he won his national race on his third attempt in 1936, when it took place at Gjersjøen.

The Alfa by then had been converted to a single-seater, and with it he won the Swedish Winter GP on Lake Ramen, repeating his success in 1937 on Lake Flaten, ahead of Ian Connell's ERA. He followed up with two further victories at Västerås and Brunnsviken in Sweden, then himself acquired an ERA which he took to Italy for the Turin voiturette GP on the Valentino street circuit. His fierce driving technique, acquired by racing on ice with spikes, astonished the Italians, and despite little practice and the presence of 13 Maseratis on their home ground, plus two other ERAs, the Norwegian in his red car won the race.

The Norwegian then took his faithful old Alfa Romeo across the Atlantic to the Vanderbilt Cup race on Long Island, New York. Starting from the last row, he worked up to 8th place by 200 miles, then had to retire with engine trouble. Before the start Bjørnstadt had announced it would be his last race, and he kept his word and retired. CP

Böhringer, Eugen

It is unusual to find rally champions emerging at 37 years of age but that is precisely what Böhringer managed to do. He was born in Stuttgart in 1923 and learnt to drive his father's tractor before graduating to motorcycles. At the end of World War 2 he was languishing in a Russian prison camp and it was not until the late 1950s that he got back from Siberia to Stuttgart. He spent two

seasons driving Porsches and Alfa Romeos in hill-climbs and circuit races and then in 1960 came the offer of a works drive for the Mercedes factory in rallies.

His first event was the Monte Carlo in which he finished 2nd overall to team-mate Walter Schock who went on to win the European Championship title of that year. Böhringer's only other outing for the team was on the Coupe des Alpes where he was one of six drivers to win a coupe for an unpenalized performance. In the Tulip Rally, he was fourth overall and won his class, a performance he was to repeat a few weeks later in the Acropolis Rally. For the Polish Rally he took with him a young Finnish driver, Rauno Aaltonen, and between them they won the event which put Böhringer in the running for the European Championship, but in the RAC rally, again accompanied by Aaltonen, his car left the road and broke the transmisson regaining it.

For Böhringer his third season with Mercedes proved most successful, for in 1962 he started in eight championship events, had seven class victories, three outright wins in the Acropolis, the Polish and the Liège–Sofia–Liège, and two 2nd places, of which one was the Monte Carlo Rally. His only retirement of the year came in the RAC Rally when he crashed with the European Championship already won.

In 1963, Mercedes were already beginning to reduce their participation in competition but they gave Böhringer one of their new 230SL sports cars for the Liège–Sofia–Liège and the diminutive, balding German became one of the very few people to have won this event twice. In the same year, he won the Acropolis outright with a Mercedes 300SE and also won the touring category on the Lyons–Charbonnières with a similar car.

Being such a small quiet man in charge of such large cars Eugen Böhringer has become one of the legends of rallying despite only competing seriously for a period of just over four years in international events. He has now retired and with his wife, Luise, runs an hotel among the vineyards to the south of Stuttgart.

Before retiring, Böhringer had one last epic outing— this time at the wheel of a Porsche 904—in the Monte Carlo Rally of 1965 when with a very unsuitable car, he finished 2nd overall. JD

Boillot, André

André Boillot has always suffered by comparison with his elder brother Georges, but nevertheless he had considerable success in long distance events with Peugeot cars. His first, and greatest, success came in the 1919 Targa Florio when he drove a 1914 2·5-litre

Eugen Bohringer, in the Porsche 904 with which he finished 2nd in the 1965 Monte Carlo Rally. *Photo: John Davenport*

171

Boillot, Georges

At the peak of his career Georges Boillot, who was born in 1885 represented the 'spirit of France in motor racing', as a contemporary report put it. He worked on the competition side of the Peugeot organization throughout his racing years, starting with the 'rival' Lion-Peugeot concern and changing to the big Peugeots when the two companies fused. In his first event, the 1908 Sicilian Cup, he retired his single-cylinder Lion early in the race. His placings in the two big French voiturette races of that year were 4th in the ACF's Grand Prix and 12th in the Coupe. He retired again in the 1909 Sicilian Cup, and in the Catalan race he fought a spirited duel with Jules Goux before overturning his car on a corner. Misfiring spoilt his chances in the Coupe des Voiturettes, but his single-cylinder machine put in the fastest lap at 55mph (88·51kph), though he came in 4th behind Giuppone and Goux, the latter using one of the odd twins. In 1909 also came Boillot's first victory in the obscure Normandie Cup at Caen, and in 1910 he had better luck in Sicily, winning the voiturette section at 34·85mph (56·09kph), a speed which outstripped all the competitors in the Targa Florio proper. Once again Goux came 1st in the Catalan Cup, Boillot taking 2nd place. In the Coupe des Voiturettes he was given the fearsome 65 × 260mm V-4 Lion-Peugeot, which proved a real handful, though he and Goux fought it out for fastest lap, and Boillot finished 4th in what turned out to be Hispano-Suiza's race. He drove a V-4 again in the 1911 Coupe de l'Auto, and took 2nd place, only 1min 11sec behind Bablot on the Delage: a fastest lap at 57mph (91·73kph), however, could not compensate for a voracious tyre consumption, which explains why this was the old Lion's last racing season.

Both Boillot and Goux drove Peugeots in record attempts at Brooklands, and Boillot also did well in hill-climbs, with ftd at Mont Ventoux on a single in 1910. At that year's Gaillon event he drove both the twin and the V-4, but was still defeated by Goux on the smaller car. The year 1912 saw the emergence of the work of his friends Zucarelli, Henry, and Goux in the shape of the dohc 7·6-litre GP Peugeot, and Boillot drove a magnificent Grand Prix to win from the immense and archaic Fiats, even if the car in its original form was little faster than the sv 3-litre Sunbeams running in the parallel Coupe de l'Auto, In the GP de France which Goux won, Boillot was eliminated by a seizure. He achieved a formidable double in 1913: his 3-litre car won the Coupe de l'Auto after Goux's tank started to leak; and the 5,654cc GP version took him to victory at Amiens.

Georges Boillot's last race was undoubtedly his greatest, for at Lyons in 1914 he took on the 4·5-litre Mercedes and fought them right through the Grand Prix, almost to the bitter end. The German cars were undoubtedly faster, and what Boillot gained by his 4-wheel brakes he lost owing to defects of handling occasioned by the mounting of the spare wheels in the cars' tails. That he got as far as he did on driving alone was a tribute to his skill, for neither Goux nor Rigal on the other Peugeots could match the Germans. He was shot down over the Western Front in 1916, but his brother André carried on the Peugeot racing tradition after World War 1. MCS

Coupe de l'Auto Peugeot to victory against formidable opposition and despite leaving the road six times. He never won the Targa again, but was 3rd in 1925, and won the Coppa Florio in 1922 and 1925. He also won the Touring Car Grand Prix in 1923 and 1925, and the Belgian 24 Hour Race in 1926, with Louis Rigal. All these successes were achieved with sleeve valve Peugeots, and he drove a specially-built 2·5-litre version to victory in the 1927 Coupe de la Commission Sportive at Montlhéry. In 1931 Peugeot built a small sports car, the 201X, powered by half a Type 35 Bugatti engine. With this car Boillot took the 1·5-litre 24 Hour record, but during testing in 1932 he was killed, and Peugeot proceeded no further with the car. MCS

Top, André Boillot. *Photo: Cyril Posthumus Collection*

Above, Georges Boillot. *Photo: T. A. S. O. Mathieson Collection*

Bondurant, Robert

A former helicopter pilot, Bob Bondurant was born in Evanston, Ill., in 1933 and now lives in California, where he began racing with a Morgan in 1957. After driving Corvettes to a West Coast championship he turned to Cobras in 1963, joining Carroll Shelby as a works driver the following year. With Gurney he was 4th in his Cobra coupé at Le Mans in 1964 and with Ginther, in a Ford GT-40, he was 3rd overall and 1st GT at Daytona in 1965. Bondurant also registered 1st GT with Jo Schlesser at Sebring, with Allen Grant at Monza, at the Nürburgring with Neerpasch, and with Schlesser again at Reims. Bondurant's consistent performance in traditional sports car endurance races, plus his class victories in the Sierra–Montana, Rossfeld and Freiburg hill-climbs, helped Cobra capture its 1964 U.S. title and beat Ferrari for the 1965 International Manufacturers' GT championship.

Bondurant raced a 2-litre Formula 1 BRM for Bernard White in the 1965 Grand Prix championship, finishing 4th at Monaco, 9th at Brands Hatch and 7th in the Italian GP at Monza. He switched to Ferrari for the 1965 United States GP, finishing 9th, and later drove an F1 Eagle for Dan Gurney. His best race in 1966 was a 4th at the Nürburgring with Paul Hawkins in a Porsche Carrerra 6. Bondurant was seriously injured in June 1967 when his McLaren-Chevrolet crashed during the Watkins Glen U.S. Road Racing championship.

Bondurant, who owns a West Coast racing drivers school, returned to competition in 1970; after several DNFs his Lola placed 2nd in the Road America Can-Am. ARB

Bonetto, Felice

Although he only came to the fore internationally after World War 2, this Italian driver, born in 1903, first raced cars in 1933 with a 2·3-litre Monza Alfa Romeo after a spell of motorcycle racing. His first success came in the 3-litre sports class on the Monte Ceneri hill-climb in Switzerland, and then, driving in very select company, he took 3rd place both in his heat and the final of the Monza GP, the race which cost the lives of Campari, Borzacchini and Czaykowski.

After showing such promise Bonetto made few further appearances before the war. Not until 1946 did his name reappear in the lists, when he took a Fiat to 3rd place at Mantua. The following year he drove the new 1,100cc Cisitalia monoposto to 1st places at Asti and Vigevano, then switched to a sports 3-litre Delage to win the Circuit of Florence at Cascine. Two more Cisitalia wins at Vercelli and Mantua came in 1948, also distinguished 2nd places in the Bari GP, ahead of Varzi, and in the Aosta–Great St Bernard hill-climb, behind *Bergmeister* Hans Stuck.

For 1949 the tough, cheerful, pipe-smoking Felice Bonetto joined Ferrari, his score totalling three 2nds (Mille Miglia, Monza GP, Naples GP), a 4th (Marseilles GP) and a 5th (San Remo GP). His versatility was well demonstrated in two very mixed seasons of racing in 1950 and 1951. Driving the big 4·5-litre V-12 Alfa Romeo sports car he gained his first big victory outside Italy in the 1950 Circuit of Oporto in Portugal. He also drove a Maserati-Milan F1 car, a 1,100cc Osca, and a sports Alfa. With a touring Alfa he won the 2-litre production class of the 1951 Circuit of Sicily. Sharing a Type 158 Alfa Romeo with Farina he finished 3rd in the Italian GP.

In 1952, Bonetto won the Targa Florio outright with a Lancia and was 2nd in the Circuit of Sicily. The 'try anything' Bonetto also dabbled in Formula 3, driving a rear-engined Volpini-Gilera 500 in the Vetturetta GP

Felice Bonetto in a Maserati 250F at Silverstone. *Photo: Cyril Posthumus Collection*

at Chieti and having a 16sec lead when the car broke down.

Lancia introduced their D24 V-6 sports-racing cars in 1953. Bonetto drove one to victory in the GP of Portugal at Lisbon; to 2nd place in the Autodrome GP at Monza; and to 3rd place in the Mille Miglia. Six weeks later, in his fourth Carrera Panamericana, Bonetto won the first leg with his Lancia, was 2nd in stages 2 and 3, and on the 4th stage from Mexico City to Leon he braked very fiercely entering the village of Silao, left the road, and was killed when he struck a lamp standard.

Bonetto was 51 when he died. His devil-may-care attitude, and spectacular, sometimes erratic driving methods earned him much popularity with his countrymen, who called him 'Il Pirata'—the pirate. CP

Bonnier, Joakim

Bonnier is the son of a Swedish professor of genetics and was born in Stockholm on 31 January 1930. He studied at Stockholm, Paris and Oxford before being apprenticed in his uncle's publishing house, Bonniers Förlag AB.

His natural love of cars led to his first competitive appearance in a rally in 1948, and he specialized in off-road rallying for five seasons. In the meantime he had joined the navy, being commissioned as a lieutenant, and in 1953 he started ice racing. He ran a 3·5 Alfa Romeo Disco Volante in these events and between 1953 and 1955 became uncrowned 'king of the ice'. Alfa Romeo awarded him their Swedish distributorship in 1954, and he commenced circuit racing with their products, winning the 1955 Stockholm GP and a touring car event at Oulton Park.

Bonnier gained many more Alfa Romeo touring and GT car victories in 1956, and also ran a 1·5-litre Maserati in single-seater events. He was in the works Maserati Formula 1 team in 1958, later moving to BRM, but mechanical failures dogged him although he managed to win the Naples GP and a Formule Libre at Watkins Glen (on Maseratis), and set fastest time at the Freiburg hill-climb in a 1·5-litre Borgward. He was also 2nd at Syracuse, Caen and the Berlin GP.

Maserati ran a car in the Tasman races that winter, but he signed exclusively for BRM in 1959, scoring their first World Championship win at Zandvoort in the

Dutch GP—his only victory in a major event to that date. He had several Ferrari sports car drives that season, and although 1960 was an unhappy year with the BRMs he did well in Formula 2 and sports-racing works Porsches, winning at Clermont-Ferrand and the Modena and German GPs, and sharing the Targa Florio victory with Hans Herrmann. He was 2nd in the Aintree 200 and Nürburgring 1,000 kilometres and in the Cape and South African Formula 2 GPs during the winter.

Bonnier ran a Cooper-Climax in the Tasman series, winning at Teretonga and Levin and returned to Europe as a Porsche Formula 1 works driver, team-mate to Dan Gurney. He was 2nd at Pau in a Lotus, and repeated the result in the Targa Florio, Mosport sports car race and Modena GPs. He was 5th in the British GP and 3rd in the Rand, Natal and South African GPs at the end of the season. In 1962 the 4-cylinder Porsches were replaced by flat-8s and although Gurney's car won the French GP the Porsches were heavy and unreliable. Bonnier was a depressed driver that season, and when Porsche withdrew at the end of the year he joined Rob Walker, driving a Cooper-Climax, and on occasion showed very good form in it, although real success eluded him still. However, he won the Targa Florio, with Carlo Abate.

Walker ran a Brabham-Climax in 1964 and the Swede came 6th in the Austrian GP, in addition to 5th at Monaco and 2nd at Snetterton in the Cooper. In long-distance races he won the Reims 12 Hours (Ferrari 275LM/P with G. Hill); was 2nd at Le Mans (330P with Hill); and 5th in the Nürburgring 1,000 kilometres (Porsche 904/8 with Ginther). Walker had a two-car Brabham team in 1965 with Siffert and Bonnier pushing each other along and both drivers improving considerably. Bonnier just missed the points with 7th places in the Monaco, British, German, and Italian GPs and was 8th in the American event. Driving works Porsches with Hill and Rindt he was placed 4th in the Targa Florio and 3rd in the Nürburgring 1,000 kilometres.

For 1966 Bonnier became an entrant in his own right, running a 3-litre Cooper-Maserati. He crashed at Spa in the rain and came 6th at Mexico City to retain his graded driver status. He still went well in big sports cars, and won at the Nürburgring, sharing the Chaparral 2D with Phil Hill. He retained the Cooper for 1967,

finished 5th in the German GP and 6th at Watkins Glen. He ran the McLaren-BRM M5A in 1968, finishing 6th at Monza, and went well in a works Honda in Mexico to come 5th. He showed tremendous form in his own Ecurie Bonnier McLaren Group 7 and Lola GT Group 4 cars, and won at Anderstorp, was 2nd at Silverstone, Karlskoga and Oulton, and 3rd at Mount Fuji, Japan. In 1969 he bought a Lotus 49 Formula 1 car but wrote it off at Oulton, escaping with slight injuries. He also crashed Filipinetti's Lola at Brands Hatch and was severely concussed in a rare accident. Sharing a Lola with Herbert Muller he was 2nd in the Austrian 1,000 kilometres and 5th at Spa, and he won the Prix de Paris single-handed and was 2nd at Snetterton and Thruxton. Bonnier virtually disappeared from F1 in 1970 but scored five points, two 2nds and two 3rds in various sports events.

Jo Bonnier has been Chairman of the Grand Prix Drivers' Association since 1962, and lives in Lausanne where he runs an art gallery. DCN

Bordino, Pietro

Described by H. O. D. Segrave as 'the finest road race driver in the world', the Italian Pietro Bordino, born in 1890, was an immensely fast and determined performer in factory Fiat cars. He started at 14 as a racing mechanic in 1904, riding with Vincenzo Lancia, Nazzaro and DePalma, then drove a Fiat himself for the first time in the 1908 Chateau Thierry hill-climb in France, winning outright. In 1910 he scored again in a Modena sprint meeting, and in 1911 made a fruitless visit to Britain with the huge airship-engined 300hp Fiat built for record breaking. After lapping Brooklands at considerable speed, which FIAT later claimed set a new 'mile record' without quoting any specific figures, Bordino took the car to Saltburn sands in Yorkshire, only to bog down in the soft sands, having to be hauled out.

Rejoining the Fiat team after World War 1, he made fastest lap at 96·31mph (155kph) in the first Italian GP on the Montichiari circuit, Brescia, in 1921 with his 3-litre straight-8 Fiat, but retired with a broken oil pipe after leading from lap 1 to 14. Early in 1922 he took one of the 3-litre cars to America for several speedway races in California with varying success. He retired from the

Left, Jo Bonnier. *Photo: Gosta C. Zwilling*

Above, Jo Bonnier, in Rob Walker's Brabham-Climax in the 1965 Dutch GP. *Photo: Doug Nye Collection*

Beverly Hills 250 miles after making fastest lap at 115·9mph (186·5kph); won the first heat and came 4th in the final of the Beverly Hills 50-mile race; finished 5th in the Fresno 150 miles; won the Cotati 50 miles race at Santa Rosa at 114·5mph (184·3kph), and retired from the 100 miles race at the same course.

Back in Europe, Bordino put up an electrifying performance in the French GP at Strasbourg, leading in the 2-litre 6-cylinder Fiat from lap 2 until 2 laps from the finish, when his rear axle broke. Two months later the new Monza track outside Milan was opened, the inaugural events proving a sensational 'Bordino benefit': he won the Voiturette GP at 83·25mph (133·98kph), leading a Fiat 1-2-3-4 formation, and won the Italian GP for 2-litre cars at 86·89mph (139·83kph), setting the fastest lap in both. He was less successful in 1923, although he again took the lead in the French Grand Prix at Tours until supercharger trouble halted him on lap 11.

In 1924 the fiery Bordino kept a little 1·5 litre blown Fiat in 3rd place in the Targa Florio, behind a 2-litre Mercedes and a 4·5-litre Alfa Romeo until heat exhaustion stopped him; Felice Nazzaro took over but overturned the car, despite which the gallant pair eventually brought it home 4th. In the French GP at Lyons Bordino took the lead as usual, but on lap 10 his Fiat's brakes failed; he retrieved the lead on lap 11, but had to give up. Late that year he took one of the GP cars to the United States, running at Culver City in December without success. Fitted with a single-seater body, the Fiat then ran in the Culver City 250 miles in March 1925, finishing 6th; won a 25-mile heat at the same track in April; then went on to Indianapolis for the 500 miles Race. It could not match the pace of the lighter Duesenbergs and Millers, and during the race Bordino damaged his hand and had to be relieved by Mourre, the pair doing well to take 10th place.

In 1927 Bordino and Fiat made a surprise return to racing with a very advanced 1·5-litre 12-cylinder car, the Tipo 806. It was too new for the long-distance Italian GP, but ran instead in the supporting GP of Milan for Formule Libre cars. In wet, slippery conditions, Bordino outstripped all rivals, winning the 50km heat at 92·89mph (149·49kph) and the 50km final at 93·6mph (150·63kph), leaving bigger-engined P2 Alfa Romeo and Bugatti opposition well behind.

With Fiat's final and irrevocable withdrawal from racing, Bordino changed to a 2·3-litre Type 35 Bugatti. He finished 7th in the 3-litre class of the 1928 Mille Miglia after much trouble en route, then in practice for the Circuit of Alessandria race had to swerve at high speed to avoid a dog on the circuit. The dog jammed the steering, and the Bugatti went out of control, ending up in the River Tanaro, and the hapless Bordino was drowned. Thereafter the Alessandria race was called the Coppa Pietro Bordino in memory of one of Italy's greatest drivers. CP

Borzacchini, Baconin Mario Umberto

Born in Terni in 1899, the slightly built Borzacchini began his career by racing motorcycles and then a 1,100cc Salmson. With the Salmson he won several hill-climbs, and had class successes in 1926 in the Florence-Cascine Circuit, the Coppa Ciano, the Coppa Acerbo, the Padua Circuit and Tripoli GP and the Targa Florio in 1926–7. Until 1931 he raced Maseratis, winning the 1,500cc class in the Coppa Ciano at Montenero and the Coppa Pistoiese in 1927. In 1928 he had a class victory at

Mugello and an outright win in the Coppa Etna, and then his 1929 Maserati successes included 2nd place at Alessandria to Varzi's P2 Alfa, and at Tripoli to Brilli-Peri's Talbot at the wheel of a 1929 'Monza' 1,700cc model. At Cremona he covered 10 kilometres at 152·9mph (246·10kph) in the W4 two-engined 'Sedici Cilindri' 4-litre Maserati, the fastest speed ever recorded on the road at that time, and an international record. In 1930 with the same 16-cylinder Maserati he won the Tripoli GP, but a bid in the Indianapolis 500 in the same car minus its blowers was a failure.

In 1931 Borzacchini went to drive Alfa Romeos for the Scuderia Ferrari, where he became a close friend of Nuvolari, and the pair were so inseparable they were called the 'fratellini'. His only 1931 victory was at Avellino with a Monza Alfa. However, he was 2nd in a 1750 to Nuvolari's 2·3 Alfa in the Targa Florio; and 2nd in Monza Alfas in the Monza GP; in the Italian GP with Minoia; in the French GP with Campari; and in the Belgian GP with Nuvolari. He only missed winning the Ulster TT by 5sec in a sports 2·3 in which he put up the fastest and record lap.

In 1932 Borzacchini was 2nd in a P3 to Nuvolari's similar car in the French GP and 2nd in a Monza to Nuvolari's Monza in the Targa Florio. He shared a Monza with Marinoni and Caracciola to come 3rd in the Italian GP, and again in a P3 he was 2nd to Nuvolari in the Coppa Ciano and 3rd in the German GP. His biggest victory came in this year, driving a sports 2·3 Alfa in the Mille Miglia.

In 1933 he was 2nd in the Monaco GP in a 2·6 Monza Alfa and made ftd in the Mont Cenis hill-climb in a 2·3 Monza before being tragically killed in an 8C 3000 Maserati in a multiple accident in the Monza GP. A memorial to him was unveiled at Terni in the spring of 1935. PMAH

Baconin Borzacchini. *Photo: Cyril Posthumus Collection*

Bottoms, Alfred J.

Alf Bottoms was one of the very few drivers who graduated successfully from British speedway to four wheels. A well-known Wembley rider, he entered the 500 racing scene in 1950 with the Coward and Lang special, to which he had fitted a revised rear suspension. His exuberant driving style did not always pay off, and he suffered more than his share of mechanical failure, but he took two major internationals in his first season, driving a JBS. The following year started well, with a lighter tubular-frame JBS, and Bottoms' driving was showing consistency as well as skill and daring. However, in practice for the 1951 Luxembourg GP meeting, he collided with a car parked down an escape road, and received fatal injuries. DF

Boyer, Joseph, Jr

Joe Boyer, one of the wealthiest race drivers of his era, gained most of his fame as a member of the Frontenac and Duesenberg teams during the 9-year period beginning in 1916. He was born in 1890, the son of a prominent Detroit industrialist, and became a professional chiefly because of the thrills he experienced in competition against first-class opponents, rather than for the prize money involved; and he invariably was a contender for the lead in every race as long as his equipment held together. Too often, however, he failed to go the scheduled distance because of mechanical trouble.

He began to attract attention in 1916 for Frontenac, taking 2nd place in a 112·5-mile (181km) race on the board track at Uniontown, Pa., in May and defeating

Joe Boyer. *Photo: T. A. S. O. Mathieson Collection*

National Champion Earl Cooper and others in a special three-heat match race on the same course six weeks later. He then served as a volunteer private in the United States Army until the end of World War 1.

After being eliminated by mechanical trouble on several occasions in 1919, he gained a victory in a 225-mile (362km) race at Uniontown. He then changed his tactics for one of the major events of the season on another board track at Cincinnati, Ohio. The distance was 250 miles (402km) and Boyer finished strongly to win at an average speed of 101·69mph (163·64kph) after allowing team-mate Arthur Chevrolet to set the early pace. Making his second start at Indianapolis the following year, he charged to the front on four occasions and led the field for a total of 93 laps, but wrecked his car with eight laps to go.

During his first season as a member of the Duesenberg team, 1921, he also had made a fine showing in the French Grand Prix at Le Mans, a race won by team-mate Jimmy Murphy. Boyer was running 2nd on the 18th lap of the 30-lap race when he was eliminated by a broken connecting rod.

In 1924 at Indianapolis, when his Duesenberg developed trouble after he had taken the early lead, he relieved team-mate L. L. Corum on the 109th lap and charged from 4th place to take the lead on the 177th lap and win at a record-breaking speed of 98·23mph (158·09kph). It was the first of Duesenberg's three Indianapolis victories and the first 500 triumph for any car powered by a supercharged engine. Three months later, Boyer was injured fatally when he crashed during a race on the board track at Altoona, Pa. AB

Brabazon of Tara, Lord see Moore-Brabazon, J. T. C.

Brabham, John Arthur

The first Australian ever to become World Champion, and the first racing driver to win the championship in a car of his own manufacture, Jack Brabham was born in a Sydney suburb in 1926. He had contact with cars, trucks and mechanical things from the age of six. First apprenticed as a fitter and turner, he became a trainee motor mechanic and learned automotive engineering at night school before joining the Royal Australian Air Force. After discharge in 1946, he was talked into building a speedway midget car by an American friend Johnny Schonberg. After winning Australian speedway titles in 1948, 1949, 1950 and 1951 he had his first taste of road racing in a hill-climb with the speedway car. He won the 1953 Australian hill-climb title, and then bought a Mark IV Cooper-JAP. In 1953 he bought a Cooper-Bristol, the famous Redex Special, and finished 2nd in the New Zealand GP, and 4th in the 1955 New Zealand GP.

Brabham went to England in 1955 and began driving Peter Whitehead's Cooper-Alta. The machine was very unreliable, and a meeting with John Cooper persuaded him to build his own car at the Cooper works. This was the start of a long and successful association with Cooper, and he joined the works team in 1957. His first Grande Epreuve victory was the 1959 Monaco GP, and in that year he also won the British GP and the World Championship. In 1960 he won the Dutch, Belgian, French, British and Portuguese GPs to take the title again, and he also drove for Cooper in 1961, winning the New Zealand and Brussels GPs in a Cooper-Climax 2·5 litre, and finishing 9th at Indianapolis in a 2·7-litre car. This was the beginning of the movement away from the traditional Indy

Above, Jack Brabham, 1970. *Photo: Geoffrey Goddard*

Below, Jack Brabham, in the Cooper-Alta, 1955. *Photo: Geoffrey Goddard*

Jack Brabham: Principal Successes

1958	New Zealand GP	Cooper-Climax 2·2
	Nürburgring 1,000km (with Moss)	Aston Martin DBR-I
1959	Monaco GP	Cooper-Climax 2·5
	British GP	Cooper-Climax 2·5
	Daily Express Trophy, Silverstone	Cooper-Climax 2·5
1960	New Zealand GP	Cooper-Climax 2·5
	Belgian GP	Cooper-Climax 2·5
	Dutch GP	Cooper-Climax 2·5
	French GP	Cooper-Climax 2·5
	British GP	Cooper-Climax 2·5
	Portuguese GP	Cooper-Climax 2·5
1961	New Zealand GP	Cooper-Climax 2·5
	Brussels GP	Cooper-Climax 2·5
1963	Australian GP	Brabham-Climax BT4
	Solitude GP	Brabham-Climax BT7
	Austrian GP	Brabham-Climax BT7
1964	Aintree 200	Brabham-Climax BT11
	Daily Express Trophy, Silverstone	Brabham-Climax BT11
1966	French GP	Brabham-Repco BT20
	British GP	Brabham-Repco BT20
	Dutch GP	Brabham-Repco BT20
	German GP	Brabham-Repco BT20
	Sunday Mirror F2 Trophy, Goodwood	Brabham-Honda BT18
	Pau GP, F2	Brabham-Honda BT18
	Juan Jover Trophy, Barcelona	Brabham-Honda BT18
	Zolder GP, F2	Brabham-Honda BT18
	Reims GP, F2	Brabham-Honda BT18
	Karlskoga GP, F2	Brabham-Honda BT18
	Keimola GP, F2	Brabham-Honda BT18
	Ile de France GP, Montlhéry F2	Brabham-Honda BT18
	Albi GP, F2	Brabham-Honda BT18
1967	French GP	Brabham-Repco BT24
	Canadian GP	Brabham-Repco BT24
1970	South African GP	Brabham-Ford BT33

Charles Brackenbury. *Photo: courtesy Dudley Gahagan*

roadster towards the European style rear-engined car.

At the end of 1961 Brabham left Cooper to build and race his own cars, driving a Lotus-Climax in 1962 until his own Brabham-Climax was ready. Its first appearance was at the German GP where Brabham retired, but he was 2nd in the Mexican GP at the end of 1962. In 1963 he won the Australian, Solitude and Austrian GPs, and in 1964 he was 3rd in the French GP at Rouen, a race which gave Dan Gurney his first Championship victory — and the first Championship victory for a Brabham car. It was not until 1966 that Jack himself had a Championship victory in one of his own cars, but his win in the French GP that year was followed in rapid succession by the British, Dutch and German GPs, to give him the Drivers' Championship for the third time, and the double honour of the Manufacturers' Championship as well. For this achievement he was awarded the OBE in 1966. Denny Hulme took the Drivers' Championship for 1967 on a Brabham car, but Jack's luck was out in 1968, his best position being 5th in the German GP. This decline in fortune was due to the troublesome 4-ohc Repco engine, and for 1969 Brabham turned to the growing number of manufacturers using the Cosworth-Ford engine. He won the Silverstone International Trophy, a non-championship race, but during the season had several retirements and absences due to injury. However, he had a better end to the year, with 2nd in the Canadian GP, 4th in the United States GP and 3rd in the Mexican GP. He started the 1970 season well, winning the South African GP in his new monocoque BT33, and seemed certain to win the Monaco and British GPs, but in both races last lap troubles (an error at Monaco, running out of fuel at Brands Hatch) held him down to 2nd place. He was 3rd in the French GP, and 4th in the 1970 Drivers' Championship. The Mexican GP, in which he retired, was his last race, for immediately after it the 44-year-old Brabham announced his retirement from racing. He had taken part in a total of 127 Championship races, more than any other driver, and had won 14 Championships, a total exceeded only by three other great drivers — Clark, Fangio and Moss. TBF

Brackenbury, Charles

This British driver, born in 1907, started his career at Brooklands riding motorcycles. In 1929 he switched to cars, his first success being a 3rd place, in a BNC, at the August Meeting the same year. From 1930 to 1939 he was a regular competitor in Brooklands events, obtaining many successes both with his own Bugatti and with other makes, including winning the Gold Star Handicap in both 1933 and 1935. He also drove at Le Mans in 1935, as a member of the Aston Martin team. He finished third, with Charles Martin, and won the Rudge Whitworth Cup. He drove for Lagonda in 1937, with Hindmarsh, and in 1939 with Arthur Dobson finishing 3rd.

In addition to driving for factory teams Brackenbury was associated very closely, for a number of years, with Charles Martin, acting in various capacities from team manager to reserve driver. He also drove for Freddie Dixon's Riley team on several occasions, and for the Riley factory in the International Trophy of 1936. After World War 2 he was in the Aston Martin team in 1949 and 1950, finishing 3rd in the Belgian 24-hour race in the former year, with Johnson as co-driver. He continued to drive in long-distance events up to 1954, one of the last races being the Hyères 12 hours in which he finished 6th in the Aston Martin which he shared with Nigel Mann. He died in 1959. TASOM

Brandon, Eric

A close friend of the Cooper family, this British driver had the second Cooper 500 to be built. He was a safe rather than spectacular driver, and could be relied upon to finish well up rather than either win or cause damage to himself or the motor. Nevertheless, his consistency had much to do with the establishment of Cooper supremacy in the 500 class, and in 1952 he also drove the works Cooper-Bristol. Only occasionally was he seen at the wheel of other cars, such as the Halseylec which he drove in sports-car races in 1955. DF

Brauchitsch, Manfred von

This German driver, born in 1905, was a member of the famous Mercedes-Benz team from 1934 to 1939, and nephew of Field Marshal von Brauchitsch. Manfred von Brauchitsch came to the fore in motor racing in 1932 winning the Avus GP in a privately entered 7-litre Mercedes-Benz fitted with special streamlined bodywork; he averaged no less than 120·7mph (194·2kph), defeating a field containing Caracciola, Fagioli, Stuck, Divo, Williams and Dreyfus, and attracting works attention. He had, in fact, done well the previous year with a

Eric Brandon, victor of the 500cc class at Silverstone in 1951. *Photo: Geoffrey Goddard*

Manfred von Brauchitsch, after finishing 2nd in the 1937 German GP. *Photo: Cyril Posthumus Collection*

Mercedes SSK, scoring two 3rds in the Eifelrennen and Avusrennen, the cumulative result being a contract to drive the new Mercedes-Benz all-independently sprung straight-8 GP car in 1934, alongside Caracciola and Fagioli.

At first all looked well, for Brauchitsch won the new Mercedes its first race, the 1934 Eifelrennen at the Nürburgring. Then the troubles which earned Brauchitsch the nickname *Pechvogel* ('unlucky bird') began. While practising for the German GP at Nürburg, he crashed badly, his injuries virtually ending his season. With two masters like Caracciola and Fagioli in the team, 1935 proved a year of places and no victories for Brauchitsch, who was a good driver but without that genius that makes a star. His greatest disappointment was losing the German GP on the last lap under pressure from Nuvolari in his older Alfa Romeo; a rear tyre on the Mercedes burst only 8 kilometres from the finish, and the unfortunate Brauchitsch, race leader for the last ten laps, finished a miserable 5th.

Then 1936 was a bad year for Mercedes and an atrocious one for the red-helmeted Brauchitsch, with five retirements and one 7th place, but 1937 was better for him with a fine victory in the Monaco GP, albeit in defiance of team manager Neubauer's orders to let Caracciola past. A heat win at AVUS, four 2nds in the German, Pescara, Masaryk and Donington GPs and two 3rds in the Eifel and Swiss GPs finished his season, and when 1938 brought Brauchitsch another victory in the French GP at Reims it looked as if the *Pechvogel* tag no longer applied. But there was further calamity in the German GP, which he lost for the second time: he was in the lead when his car caught fire at the pits during refuelling. Then he was disqualified from the Coppa Ciano at Leghorn after taking the checkered flag as he had been push-started after a spin, Lang inheriting his victory.

The next year brought little comfort. His team-mate Lang was obviously faster and more mechanically sympathetic, facts which the proud Brauchitsch found galling. He finished 2nd at Pau and 3rd at Spa and Berne, each time behind Lang, and in his last race for Mercedes, the Yugoslav GP at Belgrade, held on the day war broke out, Brauchitsch led for 16 laps at meteoric pace, then spun his chances of a last victory away, Nuvolari getting through to win. After the war Brauchitsch made a desultory but unsuccessful effort to resume racing with an AFM and a Veritas; there was a proposal that he should drive a 3-litre Maserati in the Argentine Temporada series, but this fell through, and eventually he moved to East Germany, taking up a post in the Ministry of Sport. CP

Brilli-Peri, Count Gastone

This sporting and forceful Italian aristocrat, born in 1893, began racing in 1920 and had minor successes in Diatto, Steyr and FIAT cars, being 2nd in a Fiat in the 1922 Parma–Berceto hill-climb, and 1st in 1923. He sprang into prominence in 1925 as a works driver for Alfa Romeo in the P2 GP team, his victory in the Italian GP giving Alfa Romeo the World Championship. From 1926 until 1929 he was seen at the wheel of a P2 as an independent, though he drove a works supercharged 1,750cc Alfa sports car in the 1929 Targa Florio and finished 3rd. He also drove Talbot-Darracqs for the Scuderia Materassi. With the P2 he was 2nd in the 1926 and 1929 Rome GPs, and in 1929 won the Tunis GP and the Circuit of Cremona, after which he sold the car back

Count Brilli-Peri (right), with Giuseppe Campari. *Photo: Montagu Motor Museum*

Marquis Antonio Brivio, at Monaco in 1937. *Photo: Cyril Posthumus Collection*

to the factory. With an 8-cylinder 1·5-litre GP Talbot-Darracq he won the 1929 GP of Tripoli, but was killed in one of these cars in 1930 when practising on the same Mellaha circuit. PMAH

Brivio, Marquis Antonio

Born in Biella, Italy, 'Tonino' Brivio began racing with an 1,100cc supercharged Derby in 1927, and the next year bought a 1·5-litre Talbot-Darracq with which he joined the Scuderia Materassi. In 1932 and 1933 he drove Alfa Romeo sports cars, finishing 2nd (with Trossi) in the 1932 Mille Miglia, and winning the Belgian 24 Hour Race the same year, with Siena as his co-driver. He won the Targa Florio in 1933 and 1935, and in a 2·6-litre Monza Alfa he won the 1933 Swedish Summer GP. In 1934 he joined the Bugatti team, and in a Type 59 finished 2nd and made fastest lap in the Belgian GP. From October 1934 until his retirement in 1937 Brivio drove for the Scuderia Ferrari, his greatest success being victory in the 1936 Mille Miglia (with Ongaro) in a 2900A Alfa Romeo. In the 1960s Brivio put in a regular appearance at vintage car events in Italy. PMAH

Brooks, C. A. S.

Some drivers become masters by sheer hard work; others seem gifted with a natural genius at the wheel which, with development and experience, makes them stars. Moss, Fangio, Clark and Stewart are examples of the latter, and Tony Brooks, now retired from racing, is another. Slight in build, quiet and serious-minded, he did not readily suggest the traditional racing driver, but his record shows him to be a master; one, moreover, whose smooth skill in a car gained the warm approval of Fangio himself.

Parental interest in sporting motorcars set 20-year-old Tony, a dental student from Dukinfield, Staffordshire, on the road to fame via a secondhand Healey Silverstone which he raced at Goodwood, Snetterton and elsewhere in 1952.

His first single-seater drive was in Riseley-Prichard's F2 Connaught in August 1955, when he came 4th at Crystal Palace behind Hawthorn, Schell and Salvadori, all in F1 cars. By then John Wyer had signed him up for Aston Martin. He took 3rd place in his first race for them, the Goodwood Nine Hours, with Peter Collins as his no 1. At Aintree he drove a works Connaught sports, placing 2nd to Chapman's Lotus. Three weeks later this

Tony Brooks, after winning the 1958 Belgian GP. *Photo: Autosport*

remarkable young man, who had never raced abroad nor driven a Formula 1 car, won a Continental Grand Prix.

This was his famous 1955 Syracuse GP victory, the first by a British car since 1924, and Brooks, a late nomination by the Connaught works, won the 240-mile (384km) race hands down, defeating Maserati and Gordini works cars, and breaking Marimon's 1954 lap record three times. It was the first tangible sign of Britain's coming domination in motor racing, and Brooks played a vital part in furthering that domination. BRM signed him in 1956, a fruitless move bringing him a 2nd place in the Aintree 200 and an unpleasant accident in the British GP at Silverstone. He won the Goodwood Trophy for Aston Martin, however, won at Oulton with a Mercedes-Benz 300SL, and took the Rob Walker F2 Cooper to 2nd place behind Moss in the Gold Cup race and to a victory at Brands Hatch.

The next season, 1957, was a Brooks year. He left BRM and joined Vanwall, was 2nd to Fangio at Monaco, and although weakened by a crash at Le Mans he shared the winning car in the British/European GP at Aintree with Stirling Moss. For Aston Martin he scored another historic victory in the Nürburgring 1,000 kilometres—the first major British win at this classic circuit—and won two races at Spa, and with Rob Walker's F2 Cooper he took the Lavant Cup at Goodwood. Brooks was now one of the world's top six drivers. In 1958 he carried off three classics, the Belgian, German and Italian GPs, with a Vanwall; shared a TT victory for Aston Martin with Moss; and won the F2 class of the Aintree 200.

He married an Italian girl in 1958 and went 'all Italian' for 1959, signing with Ferrari for GP and sports car racing. He won the French and German GPs, coming 2nd overall in the World Championship. By 1960 racing was beginning to pall with Brooks. He joined the Yeoman Credit team, driving rear-engined Coopers, and a 4th at Monaco and two 5ths in the Portuguese and British GPs were his score. In 1961 he went back to BRM to drive their Coventry Climax rear-engined 1·5-litre F1 cars, but Brooks, an extremely fast driver, missed the power of the old 2·5-litre front-engined Vanwalls and Ferraris. However, he managed a 3rd in the United States GP, 4th in the Italian, and fastest lap in the British GP at Aintree. By then a family man, with a garage business in Weybridge to run and his dental profession in the background, Tony Brooks decided to retire from racing. He is still to be seen at the circuits occasionally, however, writing for a Sunday newspaper and sometimes broadcasting. CP

Bruce-Brown, D.

This American driver, born in 1890, was without question a 'natural', but one whose career came to an untimely end. As an 18-year-old schoolboy, he bluffed his way into the driving seat of a 90hp Fiat at the 1908 speed trials on Ormonde Beach, Daytona, and broke W. K. Vanderbilt Jr's 1904 mile record of 92·30mph (148·54kph) by 3sec. That same year he was the fastest amateur at the Shingle hill-climb promoted by the Yale University motor club, and he won the event outright the following year, driving a massive 120hp Benz. He also drove this car at Ormonde Beach in 1909, running 2nd to Oldfield's 200hp Blitzen Benz over the mile, and beating DePalma's Fiat in the Dewar Trophy, contested in three 1-mile heats, and also in a 10-mile open race.

By 1910 Bruce-Brown won international fame by his

victory in the American Grand Prize at Savannah in a factory-entered 120hp Benz—by a mere 1·42sec from team-mate Hémery. In 1911 Bruce-Brown joined the FIAT team, finished 3rd in the first Indianapolis 500 Miles race, then scored his second Grand Prize victory at Savannah ahead of a Benz and a Mercedes. He drove a National in the 1912 Indianapolis 500 but retired with valve trouble, then went to Europe for the 1912 French Grand Prix at Dieppe, driving in the team of 14·1-litre Fiats with DePalma and Wagner.

In the two-day, 956-mile (1,538·5km) race he leapt into the lead from the very start, outpacing Europe's finest racing men and duelling fiercely with the great Boillot; he set the fastest lap and won the first day's race by over 2 minutes from Boillot (Peugeot) and FIAT colleague Wagner. On the second day the young American's luck deserted him; a petrol pipe broke after four laps, and after repairing it out on the circuit near Eu he took on petrol away from the pits, thereby incurring disqualification. He pressed on to the finish, crossing the line third, though technically a non-finisher. Four months later, on 1 October 1912, this brilliant American driver was killed while practising for his third American Grand Prize, at Milwaukee, Wis.; his Fiat burst a tyre and overturned, throwing Bruce-Brown out on to the road to instantaneous death. CP

Bryan, James Ernest

This American racing driver, born in 1927, was one of the sport's greatest dirt-track performers and gained additional renown by scoring impressive victories at Indianapolis and Monza.

After five years of competition in sprint-car and midget-car events on the nation's smaller tracks, Jimmy Bryan was placed 6th as a rookie at Indianapolis in 1952 and then became a regular contender on the big car championship circuit the following year. He won the national big car championship three times—in 1954, 1956 and 1957—and finished second in the final standing in 1955. At one stage during this four-year period he won seven consecutive dirt track championship events.

Tony Brooks (centre), with Olivier Gendebien and Stirling Moss, before trying out the proposed Jurby circuit in the Isle of Man, 1969. *Photo: Ford Motor Co Ltd*

David Bruce-Brown (left). *Photo: T. A. S. O. Mathieson Collection*

Bryan also finished 2nd once and 3rd once at Indy before winning the 500 in 1958 at an average speed of 133·791mph (215·242kph) in a lay-down engine Salih.

He won the first Monza 500 in 1957, averaging 160·067mph (257·611kph) for a two-lap margin over his nearest challenger; and came 2nd to Jim Rathmann in the second Monza 'race of two worlds' a year later.

Three weeks after failing to complete the 1960 Indianapolis race because of fuel pump trouble, he suffered fatal injuries in a racing accident at the Langhorne, Pa., track. AB

Bucknum, Ronald

Ronnie Bucknum was born in California in 1936. Following the 1962 and 1963 West Coast seasons in which he drove Austin Healeys and Porsches to more than 50 victories and was five times a Divisional champion, he joined the Honda works team. He drove Formula 1 for the Japanese builders in 1964, 1965 and 1966, his best finish being a 5th in the 1965 Mexican GP.

Bucknum also drove sports cars for Ford, finishing 3rd in the 1966 Le Mans. In 1968 he captured the inaugural 250-mile (402km) Indy car race at Michigan International Speedway and in 1969 raced Chevrolet Camaros for Roger Penske in the Trans-Am series in which he won at Mid-Ohio and Kent. Bucknum qualified 26th for the 1970 Indianapolis 500 but was eliminated by an accident on his 162nd lap. Co-driving a Ferrari 512-S with Sam Posey, he finished 4th in the 1970 Le Mans. ARB

Bueb, Ivor Leon

Ivor Bueb was a cheerful Londoner born in 1923 who looked most unlike the popular idea of a racing driver. Behind the wheel, however, he could display the real 'tiger' quality which sets apart the top-liners from the merely skilful. He was highly popular with the racing fraternity, and when 'Ivor the Driver' lost his life he was sadly missed.

As an impecunious mechanic he started his career with a primitive Iota 500, graduating to a Cooper, via a season with Arnott in 1953 that was not very fruitful. Some very good drives with the Formula 3 cars in 1954 earned a place in the Cooper works team for 1955, and in that year he also showed his versatility with his driving of the winning Jaguar in the tragic Le Mans. He continued to drive Coopers in 1956, and for 1957 turned to Lotus, as well as winning again at Le Mans for Jaguars. He also tried his hand in Formula 1 racing in Connaught and Maserati cars. In 1958 he drove Lotus and Lister-Jaguar sports cars with some success, and became a member of the works Lister team for 1959. Ironically it was in a Cooper, the make with which he had made his name, that he was killed that year in a Formula 2 race at Clermont-Ferrand. DF

Bugatti, Ettore

Ettore Bugatti, born in Milan on 15 September 1881, was the youngest son of Carlo Bugatti, artist and furniture designer, and brother to Rembrandt Bugatti who later distinguished himself as an animal sculptor. Ettore soon found himself turning to the mechanical arts, and this, coupled to a love of speed and racing (in those early days on power-driven tricycles) led to his setting out to produce, at the age of 19, a car of his own design and manufacture. With only a short apprenticeship at an engineering works in Milan he acquired a proficiency with tools and this coupled to a natural ability to visualize

Jimmy Bryan. *Photo: Indianapolis Motor Speedway*

Ivor Bueb, after winning at Le Mans with Ron Flockhart, 1957. *Photo: Associated Press Ltd.*

and to draw enabled him to design the whole chassis and engine of a 4-cylinder 90 × 120mm 4-wheel vehicle with gearbox and chain drive. Exhibited at a trade fair at Milan in 1901, it won a gold medal and its design was immediately sold to Baron de Dietrich from Niederbronn in Alsace — this being a period when the dawn of the motor age encouraged such development.

It is clear that this early and remarkable success as a creative designer, undisciplined by formal engineering education, coloured the whole of Ettore Bugatti's subsequent career, and fed a natural egoism. Clearly highly intelligent, with strong spatial abilities, he was quick to pick up design concepts or features which could be appreciated visually. Conversely the study of his work shows no ready appreciation of scientific or thermodynamic principles, which explains a too-long retention of techniques demonstrably unsatisfactory.

Under the sponsorship of Baron de Dietrich he moved just before his 21st birthday to Niederbronn to produce a series of large cars known as De Dietrich-Bugatti, manufactured in parallel with other De Dietrich versions. The latter achieved greater fame in the races and trials of the first few years of the century, although Bugatti's designs attracted attention in the technical press of the day, and had some success in competition, including in the hands of Bugatti himself.

In 1904 Bugatti moved to Strasbourg and joined Emil Mathis, designing the Hermes for him, another large 4-cylinder overhead valve car with chain drive. Then in 1906 he moved to Cologne as Chief Engineer of the Deutz Company, the producers of the original Otto engine, and made two designs for them, a large chain-driven ohv-engined chassis, and a smaller one with for the first time a classic layout with bevel-gear rear axle and separate gearbox. This was a good design, with an excellent engine layout: the valves were in the head and operated by a single overhead camshaft (a feature Bugatti claimed later to have originated), with curved or arcuate cam followers operating the valve stems.

Bugatti evidently found the confines of an industrial organization not to his liking, because in 1908 he produced a car design of his own in his own home and eventually severed his connection with Deutz in 1909. This 'private venture' was a small 62 × 100mm 4-cylinder car. It was this chassis design which inspired him to launch out on his own, and in 1910, with help from banking friends, he started to produce the little chassis, now enlarged to 65 × 100mm and 1,400cc at Molsheim, to the west of Strasbourg. This car, the first real Bugatti, was shown at the 1910 Paris Automobile Show and caused some comment. Five cars were produced in 1910 of which, remarkably, two still survive (one each in England and in Czechoslovakia). Production got under way in 1911, and such was the performance and quality of the little car that its future was assured.

Although it seems certain that its conception owes at least something to the 1908 Isotta Fraschini, detail design of this car shows Bugatti's flair and originality: certainly his next important design conception did not come until 1922–3 when the 8-cylinder GP model arrived on the scene. The chassis had half elliptic springs, front and back, a gearbox separate from the engine and a three-quarter floating rear axle with straight bevel reduction. In 1913 an improvement was made which was to remain until 1940 — the use of reversed quarter elliptic springs at the rear, the springs being in tension on the drive, convenient from the body mounting point of view in having a full width, strong chassis extended well earwards. The gear box had four speeds and reverse and was of interesting conception in having the constant mesh gears at the output end, which in practice reduced the inertia of the speed changing gears, resulting in a delightfully quick and light gear change.

The engine itself had a 3-bearing crank in an aluminium crankcase, and a monobloc cylinder with integral head, originally with two valves per cylinder, and in late 1914 and then after the war four valves per cylinder. Bore and stroke were originally 65×100mm, soon moved to 66×100mm, after the war to 68 and finally 69×100mm.

The unusual feature of the engine was the valve operation from an overhead camshaft, curved or banana-shaped tappets acting between the cams and the valves, a feature originally used in the Deutz design but, in the case of the little car, dispensing with the rollers on the ends of the tappets which were employed on the earlier design. The clutch was of the multi-plate, cast-iron and steel-disc type which characterized all subsequent Bugatti designs until 1934.

In 1911 Bugatti produced a complete chassis design which he licensed to Robert Peugeot, for production as the Baby Peugeot. From the performance car point of view more significant at this time was the production of three or four racing chassis of 5 litres (100×160mm) which do not appear to have a type number in the series which Bugatti now established (the 8-valve car was Type 13, 15, 17, depending on the chassis length). As one of the first prospective customers was the aviator Roland Garros, the model is usually called the 'Garros', or Black Bess after the surviving chassis in Britain. This car had a 3-bearing crank, and two inlet valves and one exhaust operated from an overhead camshaft, using fingers or levers between cam and valve. The 4-speed box was integral with the final drive, the transmission to the rear axle being by chain. Although one chassis was fitted at one time with a two-seat coach body the car was really intended for racing and had some success in the hands of Bugatti himself in hill-climbs, at Mont Ventoux in particular.

A chassis was entered in the Indianapolis 500 in 1914, Friderich being the driver, and in this case fitted with a normal rear axle. The car ran well for some distance until a bearing in this axle failed. Another chassis went to the United States in 1915 and was unsuccessful in the 500-mile race, suffering engine bearing trouble. The original chassis eventually arrived in Britain after the war and had several successes in hill-climbs and at Brooklands before an honourable retirement.

In July 1914 Bugatti designed a new cylinder block with four valves per cylinder for the 8-valve chassis, with the intention of entering the Coupe des Voiturettes of that year, but although the chassis were prepared, the race was cancelled by the crisis; the cars were salvaged after the war.

Bugatti began again at Molsheim in 1919 and raced as often as his finances would permit. The 1914 short-chassis Type 13 cars entered and won the 1920 Voiturette race at Le Mans, and were much noted in the press of the day. Then in 1921 a sensational success was achieved with a team of five of the cars, now with roller-bearing crankshaft, and dimensions 69×100mm (1,496cc), in the Voiturette GP at Brescia, the cars taking the first four places at a remarkable 72mph (115·87kph). The resulting Brescia model was widely sold in touring and racing form. They established Bugatti once and for all as a producer of racing cars that anyone could buy, and started a long period of success for the make.

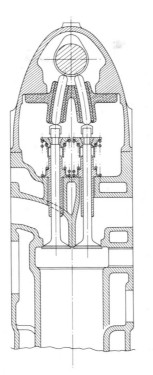

Above, Cross section of 1920 16-valve Bugatti engine, showing banana-shaped tappets. *Hugh Conway Collection*

Above right, Ettore Bugatti at the wheel of a 5-litre Bugatti at Mont Ventoux, 1912. *Photo: Hugh Conway Collection*

Right, Engine of 1906 Deutz, designed by Ettore Bugatti. This had curved tappets and exposed valves. *Photo: Hugh Conway Collection*

Below, Ettore Bugatti in 1922. *Photo: Hugh Conway Collection*

Below right, Bugatti Type 30 engine, on test-bed. *Photo: Hugh Conway Collection*

At this time Bugatti was working on an 8-cylinder engine of 2 litres, which became the Grand Prix formula in 1922. This had a crank mounted on three separate ball-bearings, with two 4-cylinder blocks, with a bore and stroke of 60 × 88mm. Twin inlet and single exhaust valves were used again, as on the Garros model (and a wartime design of aero engine). The camshaft was bevel-driven and in a cambox above the blocks. The big-end bearings were plain and lubricated by jets, a weakness which plagued Bugatti's designs and no doubt forced him to go to the more complicated and expensive roller-bearing solution for the later GP car. The Brescia type multi-disc wet clutch was used, as were the chassis frame, gearbox and rear axle on these early cars, although these were soon reinforced.

Bugatti produced a batch of 8-cylinder racing models for the 1922 French GP at Strasbourg, fitted with long-tailed single-seat bodies; they ran well enough, Friderich achieving 2nd place. The same chassis, re-bodied, ran the next year at Indianapolis but failed through big-end trouble. One chassis, owned by Count Zborowski, then came to England and was often seen at Brooklands.

In 1923 the 8-cylinder racing model went through a further stage of its development, first by the addition of roller-bearing connecting rods, with split caps, to eliminate the oiling weakness of the original jet-lubricated big ends, and then by installing the engine in a remarkable short chassis (of 2m wheelbase), with a 3-speed gearbox built into the rear axle, and a tank body, aerofoil in section in elevation by rectangular in plan. Three of the cars ran in the 1923 Grand Prix of the Automobile Club de France and created a great deal of interest, as did the similarly streamlined and even more bizarre cars designed by Bugatti's friend Voisin. In the race the poor roadholding of the Bugattis handicapped them, and only Friderich finished, in 3rd place to Segrave and Divo in Sunbeams. These 'tanks' did not compete again in serious racing, but the way was now prepared for Bugatti's tour-de-force, the famous Type 35 which was ready for the French GP at Lyons in 1924.

He reverted to a more straightforward layout, probably stimulated by the aesthetics of the Fiats and Delages of 1923, and now produced one of the finest looking racing cars of all time. The chassis frame was new, and waisted front and rear to follow the streamlined contour of the two-seater body. The rear axle and gearbox were adapted from the production models; the front axle was a fine piece of work, tubular in section, the springs passing through holes in the axle, and the ends being forged down after machining of the hollow central section. Really well-worked-out cable-operated 4-wheel brakes were new, and the sensational feature was the cast alloy 8-spoke wheels with integral brake drums. The body form was dominated by a small size horse-shoe radiator of what is now considered the classic Bugatti profile. The engine was similar to that of the year before but the crank was new, being fully built-up with five main ball- or roller-bearings, and one-piece, lightened connecting rods, with rollers at the large ends. Speeds of up to 6,000rpm were possible.

Although the car showed promise and was the subject of much favourable comment its performance in the race was marred by continual tyre trouble, all five cars entered suffering from continuous failure of unvulcanized covers. The car performed better with a 2nd place at the Spanish GP a few weeks later, with different tyres, but its future was already ensured with 20 or 30 cars ordered from the factory.

Ettore Bugatti, Jules Goux and Señor Rezola, President of the Real Auto Club of Guipuzcoa, at San Sebastian in 1926. *Photo: Fotocar*

Ettore Bugatti with his son Jean, c 1936. *Photo: Hugh Conway Collection*

Various engine versions were soon seen, with a few 1,100cc (51·3 × 66mm) cars, 1,500cc (60 × 66m) and 2,300cc (60 × 100mm) to supplement the standard 2-litre (60 × 88mm). Reluctant at first to adopt supercharging, which required more than a design flair to evolve, Bugatti now had the Italian designer Moglia produce a Roots blower design for him which he added to the 2-litre car (Type 35C) and 2·3-litre (Type 35B), although initially intended for the Type 39 1,500cc formula version.

From 1927 to 1931 the Type 35B and its stable mates dominated the racing scene, helped by blown (37A) and unblown (37) 4-cylinder versions, achieved by adapting the plain-bearing 69 × 100mm engine produced originally to replace the Brescia touring model.

By 1931 the 35B was beginning to age and a more powerful version was needed. This was produced with some encouragement from Bugatti's elder son Jean, by copying the twin-ohc inclined-valve layout of the Miller fwd engine, the new cylinder block and drive arrangement adapting directly on to the roller-bearing crankcase, and blower, with minimum alteration to the manifolding. This new car, known as the Type 51, made its debut in 1931 and was instantly successful, the extra power being obtained without detriment to roadholding and braking. Apart from a few details, the only change made to the car was the use of well-base one-piece cast wheels in place of the earlier detachable rim type. At this time a batch of 4·9-litre Type 54 racing cars was produced, with a twin camshaft engine in a traditional chassis with leaf springs, and too heavy to handle well. These cars had a few successes but were no match for the large Alfa Romeos of the day, let alone the Auto Unions and Mercedes soon to appear.

By 1933 it was clear that a new more powerful car was needed and a version of the contemporary 8-cylinder touring car, known as the Type 59, was designed. This was virtually new from stem to stern, originally of 2·8-litres but soon 3·3. The layout was as before but with

greater wheelbase and track, and remarkable piano-
re wheels, and for the first time on a Bugatti an outside
haust pipe. A batch of eight or nine cars was made and
tered in various events in 1933 and 1934, with little
ccess. Then they were sold off to private owners, one
ing retained for sports car racing in the hands of
imille, while the factory produced a few 3·3-litre 'tank'
odels with all-enveloping bodies, known as Type
G. These were most successful, winning the French
P in 1936 and the Le Mans 24-Hour Race in 1937 and
38.

The final car was a 4·7-litre single-seater with a special
in-cam engine known as the 50B, but World War 2
me before any notable success could be recorded.
gatti died in 1947. HGC

uzzetta, Joseph

orn 1936 in Brooklyn, N.Y., and now a resident of
mithtown, Long Island, Joe Buzzetta began racing
ile in Germany with the US Army. Primarily a
rsche driver, he was Sports Car Club of America 'F'
odified champion in 1962, 'E' modified title-holder in
63 and in 1967 finished in a tie with California Porsche
ot Scooter Patrick for the under 2-litre US Road
acing Championship. Buzzetta has frequently driven
orks Porsches in the United States and Europe. He
n the Nürburgring 1,000 kilometres with Udo Schutz
1967 (Porsche's first outright victory in the 1,000
lometres) and earned class victories in a world cham-
onship events at Bridgehampton, Daytona and
bring. ARB

agno, Alessandro

orn in 1883, Cagno was noted for his precise, delicate
ay of handling the early monster racing cars, and the
telligence he applied to his racing. He joined FIAT in
01 and drove for them until 1906. He had a number of
ll-climb successes, and was 3rd in the 1905 Gordon
nnett Race. From 1906 to 1908 he was the leading
iver for Itala, winning the first Targa Florio of 1906,
d the 1907 Coppa della Velocita. He drove for Itala
the Grand Prix and in the major American races, but
d little success.

After 1908 Cagno's interest turned to aviation, and
art from an unsuccessful drive for FIAT in the 1914
rand Prix, he was not seen on the circuits again until
23 when he made a come-back, winning the Italian
oiturette GP in a 1·5-litre Fiat with Wittig super-
arger. This was the world's first road race victory for a
percharged car. In the same year Cagno took a touring
at to Russia for the Leningrad-Tiflis-Moscow trial,
d made best performance. One of the few survivors of
e heroic age. Cagno was living quietly in retirement in
urin in 1970. CP

ampari, Cavaliere Giuseppe

orn in Fanfulla, near Milan, in 1892, Campari joined
e ALFA firm as a test driver in his teens. He was soon
iving their racing cars, and finished 4th in the 1914
oppa Florio in a 40/60hp Alfa. After World War 1 he
ill drove the big Alfas for the new Alfa Romeo com-
ny, and gave the firm its first racing victory in 1920 at
ugello with a 40/60hp. He later drove the 3-litre RLTF
orts car, and had many successes with the P2 Grand
rix cars, including winning the European GP at Lyons
1924. Until 1930 he drove his own P2 as an independ-
t, while driving works sports cars for Alfa Romeo.
uccesses in this period included winning the Coppa

Alessandro Cagno, at Mont Ventoux in 1905.
Photo: T. A. S. O. Mathieson Collection

Giuseppe Campari. Photo: Cyril Posthumus
Posthumus

Sir Malcolm Campbell in Bluebird, 1935.
Photo: Montagu Motor Museum

Acerbo in 1928 and 1929, and 2nd in the 1929 European
GP in the P2, and victory in the 1928 Mille Miglia (with
Ramponi) in a 1750 Alfa sports car. In 1931 he won the
Italian GP with Nuvolari in a Monza Alfa, and the
Coppa Acerbo in the twin-engined Tipo A Alfa, and
was 2nd in the Mille Miglia with Marinoni. He also
drove Maseratis on occasion, finishing 2nd in the
Eireann Cup at Phoenix Park in a sports 2·5-litre. He
won the 1933 French GP in a 8C 3000 Maserati, and was
driving an Alfa P3 in the Monza GP when the car
skidded on an oil patch and Campari was killed. In
addition to motor racing he had a life-long love of opera
(his wife was the well-known singer Lina Cavalleri) and
he could probably have made a great success in this
field if he had not chosen to be a racing driver. PMAH

Campbell, Sir Malcolm

Malcolm Campbell was born in England in 1885 into
an affluent family, but received little early encouragement in his passion for speed. He progressed from
racing bicycles in Germany to motorcycle trials, achieving three consecutive 'golds' in the London-Edinburgh
trials of 1906, 1907 and 1908. In 1910, following the
failure of an aircraft he had built, he took to the Brooklands motor track. His first racing cars were called The
Flapper after a racehorse, and were equally unsuccessful.
The name Bluebird was adopted after he had seen
Maeterlinck's play of that name in 1912, and he regarded
the name as lucky, even after he had finished a race with
only the nearside wheels remaining on his 1906 10·5-litre
Darracq. Before World War 1, in addition to his Darracqs, he raced Lion Peugeot, Renault, Schneider,
Sunbeam, Charron and Grégoire cars.

After service with the Royal Flying Corps, Captain
Campbell returned to Brooklands with a 7·6-litre 1912
GP Peugeot and a 2·6-litre Talbot. During the next six
years he drove Talbots of 1·5, 1·8, 3·8 and 4·5-litres (the
last with an ex-Lambert engine), Italas, a Star, a 1·5-litre
Austro-Daimler, a 5-litre Sunbeam, a Fiat, Ballot and
Chryslers, with much success.

In 1923 he persuaded Coatalen to sell him K. Lee
Guinness' old V-12 350hp Sunbeam for the Fanø
speed trials in Denmark, but the timing gear was inadequate and no records were taken. The 1924 sortie to
Fanø brought further disappointment, but this merely
acted as a spur, and the record was taken with 146·16mph
(235·30kph) at Pendine in Wales. This was raised to
150·87mph (242·81kph) in March 1925, but the limitations of the car were apparent: the first Napier-Campbell
Bluebird had been started that winter. This car, with
502bhp, reached 174·88mph (287·93kph) in 1927 at
Pendine.

Racing activities were continued, with an old 1·5-litre
Talbot and various Bugattis, joined by an 8-cylinder
GP Delage in 1928. That year the Bluebird, boasting
900bhp from its Napier Sprint Lion motor, reached
206·96mph (333kph) at Daytona, but this record was
soon broken by Keech and then Segrave. In 1931
Campbell was again successful, with a new car designed
by Reid Railton, built by Thomson and Taylor's and
bodied by Gurney Nutting around a 1,450bhp Napier
Schneider Trophy engine. This car earned a knighthood
for its sponsor and driver with a two-way average of
246·09mph (396·04kph) and in 1932 reached 253·97mph
(408·71kph). A Rolls-Royce 'R' engine was then fitted,
giving 2,350bhp and 272·46mph (438·40kph) in 1933 —
still at Daytona, despite the bumps on the beach.

Finally, the 1935 version of this car achieved Campbell's last ambition —averaging over 300mph (480kph) at Utah. He had by now curtailed his racing activities, and later diverted his drive and determination with almost equal success to the water speed record. Fired by a strong spirit of adventure, he travelled widely and indulged in such pastimes as looking for treasure on Cocos Island. His strength of purpose and courage was boundless—even in the illness from which he died early in 1949. DF

Cannon, John

A Canadian citizen, born in London in 1937, Cannon started racing sports cars in Quebec in 1960 and acquired an outstanding record in Canadian Formula car competition. He finished 4th behind Surtees, McLaren and Amon, in the first Can-Am at St Jovite in September 1966 and surprised the racing world by driving his overage McLaren Mk II to victory over Denny Hulme in the rain-swept Monterey Can-Am at Laguna Seca, Calif., in October 1968. In 1969 Cannon won Formula A Continental championship races at Riverside, Sears Point and Mosport. He opened the 1970 season by driving his McLaren-Chevy Formula A single-seater to victories at Riverside and Kent; he won again at Road America and with 2nd place finishes at St Jovite, Donnybrooke and Mid-Ohio, became the 1970 Continental champion. ARB

Caracciola, Rudolf

This German driver, born in 1901, started racing in 1922 with a Fafnir, winning his class at the AVUS, and finishing 4th in a race at the Opel track. The following year he began the season by winning a race at the Berlin Stadium, in an Ego, but soon after joined Mercedes, with whom he was to remain for the remainder of his career except for a short period in 1932–3. During the rest of that season he competed in numerous sprint events and rallies, making ftd in the Solitude, Pforzheim and Krahberg hill-climbs.

In 1924, with the latest 1·5-litre supercharged Mercedes, Caracciola had a most successful year obtaining class victories in numerous hill-climbs and speed trials. He also won the Circuits of the Teutoburgerwald and Eifel. He was equally successful in 1925 winning the Circuit of the Teutoburgerwald for the second year in succession. The following year Caracciola scored his first major victory by winning the German Grand Prix at the AVUS. He also won the touring car classes of the Circuit of the Teutoburgerwald and was a member of the Mercedes team that took part in the 12-hour Touring Grand Prix at San Sebastian where he co-drove with Kuhnle, the pair finishing 7th. In 1927 the Nürburgring opened, Caracciola winning the sports car race at the Inaugural Meeting, following this up by victories in the Circuits of Buckower-Dreieck and the Teutoburgerwald, the latter for the third time. He had his usual successes in hill-climbs, recording victories at Baden-Baden, Schauinsland-Freiburg and Klausen, and in speed trials at Baden-Baden, Freiburg and Antwerp.

In 1928 he won the German Grand Prix, at the Nürburgring, with Werner, made ftd in seven hill-climbs, and again made ftd in the speed trials at Antwerp. The following year he finished 3rd in the first Monaco GP and won the Tourist Trophy race in Ulster, giving an example in the latter event of his uncanny ability to drive fast under bad weather conditions. He also had five hill-climb and speed trial successes, finishing off the season by winning a long-distance event at the Nürburg-

ring for unsupercharged touring cars.

Caracciola competed in the Mille Miglia for the first time in 1930, and with Werner as co-driver finished 6th. The pair also took part in the 24-hour race at Le Mans but were overwhelmed by the might of the two Bentley teams. Caracciola had his revenge, however, a few weeks later when he won the Irish GP, and towards the end of the season finished 2nd in his heat in the Monza GP. He also won the European Mountain Championship. In 1931 he scored an outstanding victory in the Mille Miglia, following this up with wins in the Eifel, German and AVUS Grands Prix and again became European Mountain Champion.

With the withdrawal of Daimler-Benz from racing at the end of 1931, Caracciola accepted an offer to join Alfa Romeo, with whom he had a very successful season, finishing 2nd at Monaco and the AVUS; 1st in the Eifel and Lwów GPs; 3rd in the Italian and French GPs; 2nd in the Coppa Acerbo at Pescara; and 1st in the German and Monza GPs. He also won the European Mountain Championship for the third time.

Disaster struck, however, in 1933 for in practice for the Monaco GP Caracciola crashed and fractured his thigh. Only after months of treatment, and great suffering both physical and mental, his wife having been killed during the winter in a skiing accident, was he pronounced fit for the opening of the 1934 season, a season of great importance to him for Daimler-Benz had re-entered racing on the introduction of a new Grand Prix formula, with cars of revolutionary design. Although not really fully recovered, Caracciola carried out tests the new Mercedes, and took his place in the team for the French GP, where all three cars retired. He did better in the German GP, finishing 2nd. Sharing the driving with Fagioli, he won the Italian GP, was 2nd in the Spanish GP at San Sebastian but retired in the Swiss and Czechoslovak GPs.

His health now greatly improved, Caracciola had a highly successful season in 1935, winning the Grands Prix of Tripoli, Eifel, France, Belgium, Switzerland and Spain and finishing 2nd in the Penya Rhin GP. These successes made him Champion of Europe. In 1936, due to the inferior road holding of the Grand Prix Mercedes of that year, Caracciola was less successful but even so he won the Grands Prix of Monaco and Tunis and was 2nd in the Penya Rhin GP.

With the introduction of a new GP model in 1937, Mercedes-Benz reestablished their domination in Grand Prix racing. Caracciola won the AVUS, German, Swiss, Italian and Czechoslovak GPs; finished 2nd in the Eifel, Monaco and Donington GPs: becoming European Champion for the second time. A new formula came into force in 1938 but Caracciola continued his successful way winning the Coppa Acerbo and the Swiss GP; finished 2nd in the Grands Prix of Pau, France and Germany; and 3rd in the Grands Prix of Tripoli and Italy, again becoming European Champion. He also broke the flying mile and kilometre records at over 267mph (430kph) in the 5 to 8-litre class.

In 1939 Caracciola began the season with another successful attack on the mile and kilometre records, this time in the 3-litre class. He then took 2nd place in the Tripoli GP, confined to 1·5-litre cars, following this with a 3rd in the Eifel GP; a 1st in the German GP for the 5th time, and a 2nd in the Swiss GP at Berne.

After hostilities were over, Caracciola endeavoured to take a Mercedes to Indianapolis in 1946 but red tape prevented him doing so and he accepted an offer to drive

John Cannon. *Photo: Al Bochroch*

Rudolf Caracciola (left), with Manfred von Brauchitsch and Hermann Lang. *Photo: Mercedes-Benz Photodienst*

Rudolf Caracciola, c 1951. *Photo: Montagu Motor Museum*

Rudolf Caracciola: Principal Successe

1923	27km race, Berlin Stadium	Ego
1924	Teutoburger-wald Circuit	Mercedes 1·5-litre
1924	Eifel Circuit, Nideggen	Mercedes 1·5-litre
1925	Teutoburger-wald Circuit	Mercedes 1·5-litre

Year	Race	Car
1926	Teutoburger-wald Circuit	Mercedes K
1926	German GP, AVUS	Mercedes K
1927	360-kilometre sports car race, Nürburgring	Mercedes-Benz S
1927	Buckow-Dreiecks Circuit (sports classes)	Mercedes-Benz S
1927	Teutoburger-wald Circuit	Mercedes-Benz S
1928	German GP, Nürburgring (with Werner)	Mercedes-Benz SS
1929	Tourist Trophy	Mercedes-Benz SS
1930	Irish GP	Mercedes-Benz SSK
1931	Mille Miglia	Mercedes-Benz SSKL
1931	Eifel GP, Nürburgring	Mercedes-Benz SSKL
1931	German GP	Mercedes-Benz SSK
1931	AVUS GP	Mercedes-Benz SSKL
1932	Eifel GP	Alfa Romeo Tipo P3
1932	Lemberg GP	Alfa Romeo Tipo P3
1932	German GP	Alfa Romeo Tipo P3
1932	Monza GP	Alfa Romeo Tipo P3
1934	Italian GP, with Fagioli	Mercedes-Benz W25
1935	Tripoli GP	Mercedes-Benz M25
1935	AVUS GP	Mercedes-Benz M25
1935	Eifel GP	Mercedes-Benz M25
1935	French GP	Mercedes-Benz M25
1935	Penya Rhin GP	Mercedes-Benz M25
1935	Belgian GP	Mercedes-Benz M25
1935	Swiss GP	Mercedes-Benz M25
1935	Spanish GP	Mercedes-Benz M25
1936	Monaco GP	Mercedes-Benz W25E
1936	Tunisian GP	Mercedes-Benz W25E
1937	AVUS GP	Mercedes-Benz W125
1937	German GP	Mercedes-Benz W125
1937	Swiss GP	Mercedes-Benz W125
1937	Italian GP	Mercedes-Benz W125
1937	Czechoslovak GP	Mercedes-Benz W125
1938	Swiss GP	Mercedes-Benz W154
1938	Coppa Acerbo	Mercedes-Benz W154
1939	German GP	Mercedes-Benz W163

Below, Eugenio Castellotti. Photo: Autosport

Below right, Erik Carlsson (left), with Torsten Aman. Photo: SAAB

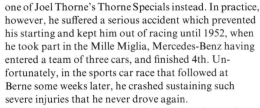

one of Joel Thorne's Thorne Specials instead. In practice, however, he suffered a serious accident which prevented his starting and kept him out of racing until 1952, when he took part in the Mille Miglia, Mercedes-Benz having entered a team of three cars, and finished 4th. Unfortunately, in the sports car race that followed at Berne some weeks later, he crashed sustaining such severe injuries that he never drove again.

Over the years motor racing has produced a number of famous drivers and among these there is a small coterie, whose members stand out as the great champions, and it is to this select band that Caracciola belongs. Certainly in wet weather conditions he had no equal, his uncanny skill on slippery roads being a byword and earning him the title of *Regenmeister*. Greatly admired and respected his untimely death in 1959 was universally mourned. TASOM

Carlsson, Erik

Like his brother-in-law Stirling Moss, Erik Carlsson has never been formally acknowledged as champion in his branch of motor sport, but there is no doubt that this Swede is the best known and best liked rally driver, and his victories in the major rallies have been unequalled. Carlsson was born in 1929 in Trollhättan. To start with, it was British motorcycles that took Carlsson's fancy, but having completed his military service, he started to take an interest in cars and competed in small rallies with cars as diverse as VWs and an Austin A40 Somerset.

His first big event was the Swedish Rally in 1953 when he went as co-driver to his employer in a Volvo 444. In 1954 he bought a Saab 92 and had his first success towards the end of that year when he won his class in an event in western Sweden. His continuing success with this car brought him some degree of works support, but it was not until he officially joined SAAB as a test driver in 1957 that he had a full works prepared car. That same year he won outright the Finnish Thousand Lakes Rally, having already competed in his first foreign event, the 1957 Tulip Rally.

In 1958, he was Swedish ice race champion in the up to 1,000cc class, a title he was to win another four times. He took 2nd place in the Adriatic Rally that year and in 1959, and he also won the Swedish and German rallies in 1959. In 1960 came his first big European victory outside Scandinavia, which was to set him on the road to fame and fortune: he won the RAC Rally with a

bespectacled motoring journalist called Stuart Turner sitting next to him. The astonishingly newsworthy aspects of this large Swede beating all comers in a little red car powered by an 850cc 2-stroke engine were quickly seized upon by the press and when he repeated his RAC victory the following year, the legend of Erik Carlsson was born.

Also in 1961 he won the Acropolis Rally and finished a praiseworthy 4th overall in the Monte Carlo behind the winning Panhards, driving in an estate car because that was the only Saab with a 4-speed gearbox at that time. The following year he took Gunnar Haggbom as his co-driver and made a determined attack on the European Championship which despite a third victory in the RAC Rally, he lost to Eugen Böhringer by just two points. In the course of trying to secure the title, he won the Monte Carlo outright, finished 2nd in the Geneva and the Acropolis, and 3rd in the Swedish and the 1,000 Lakes Rally. He also found time to take in the East African Safari where, in company with Walter Karlsson he finished 6th overall.

In 1963, still with his tiny Saab, he won the Monte Carlo for the second time, took 2nd place in the Swedish and 3rd overall in the RAC Rally that he had won so often. His most amazing performances that year were a 2nd place on the Liège–Sofia–Liège with one of the smallest capacity cars in the event, and the 92-minute lead that he had established on the East African Safari before crashing into an anteater and retiring.

At the beginning of 1964, he married Pat Moss who at that time had just left Ford to drive for SAAB, and in the same month he took 3rd place on the Monte Carlo and then went straight to Italy where he won outright the San Remo Rally with Pat taking 2nd place overall. In the East African Safari he was 2nd overall, a position he also occupied in the Polish and Geneva rallies as well as repeating his incredible 2nd place in the Liège–Sofia–Liège. That year also saw him fulfil an ambition by winning a Coupe in the Coupe des Alpes at his fourth attempt.

Since his marriage, Carlsson's active participation in rallies has declined though he still works for SAAB, giving lectures and demonstrations around the world. JD

Castellotti, Eugenio

Castellotti was born in Milan in 1930, and but for a nameless benefactor would never have had enough money to start motor racing. He was bought a sports Ferrari when only 20 and he began racing it in local Italian events in 1950. He came to prominence by winning the Portuguese sports car GP in 1952, and that same season was 2nd to Marzotto at Monaco and 3rd at Bari. He won the first of his three Italian Mountain Championships in a Lancia D24 in 1953, and that same season saw him win the Messina night race (with Musitelli) and come 3rd in both the Coppa Inter-Europa and (with Luoni) in the Carrera Panamericana.

Castellotti had an enormous will to win, but his heart tended to rule his head. Time and again he led early in races before breaking his car or losing time through stops to change worn tyres, and he led the might of both Jaguar and Mercedes in the 1955 Le Mans 24 Hours before retiring. That was a good season for him, with 2nd places in Lancias at Monaco and Pau, and in a sports Ferrari in the Dolomite Gold Cup at Belluna. He was 3rd in the Italian GP, the Targa Florio (with Manzon) and the Swedish GP. His heart pushed him into an early lead in the Mille Miglia, charging past the winning Moss/

Jenkinson Mercedes-Benz an embarrassingly short time after the start. Jenkinson vividly recalls following the wildly sliding 4-cylinder Ferrari, and Moss backing off slightly to avoid the accident which seemed inevitable. The Ferrari needed a complete tyre change at the first depot, and the British pair went by and never saw him again.

The following year Castellotti reached his zenith, winning the Mille Miglia after an astonishingly fast drive through pouring rain. He shared Ferraris with Fangio to win the Sebring 12 Hours, finished 2nd in the Nürburgring 1,000 kilometres and 3rd in the Supercortemaggiore GP at Monza. He won the Rouen GP in a sports Ferrari and the Shell GP at Imola in an OSCA.

Early in 1957 Castellotti shared both 1st and 3rd places in the Buenos Aires 1,000 kilometres, but on his return to Europe he crashed in the Esses at Modena while testing a Lancia-Ferrari in the rain. His car nosed into a concrete barrier, and the handsome, mercurial Italian catapulted to his death. DCN

Caters, Baron Pierre de

Baron Pierre de Caters, born in 1875, was one of the best-known Belgian sportsmen at the turn of the century. From 1900 onwards his name was closely linked with motorcars, motorboat racing, and the beginnings of aviation. He drove many makes of car in competition, including Bolide, Mors, Jenatzy-Electromobile, Wilford, Mercedes, Itala, Germain, and Pipe. In 1901 he took part in the Semaine de Nice, which consisted of a race (Nice–Salon–Nice), a speed trial on the Promenade des Anglais, and a hill-climb at La Turbie. Driving a 24hp Mors, de Caters was 3rd in the race, and took part in the other competitions though he did not figure very high in the results. In 1902 he was again driving a Mors, this time a 60hp car; he finished last in the heavy-car class in the Circuit du Nord, but he reached 18th place in the Paris-Vienna Race out of 80 finishers. On 29 July 1902, also on his 60hp Mors, he broke the world record for the flying kilometre (afterwards known as the Land Speed Record) at Ostend, with a speed of 75·10mph (120·806kph). He also donated the Coupe Baron de Caters, for the record for the standing start kilometre.

In 1903 he left Mors for Mercedes, and on a 90hp car he broke the kilometre record again with a speed of 97·257mph (156·521kph) at Nieuwpoort (Nieuport), Belgium. This was in May 1904, and a month later he drove a Mercedes in the Gordon Bennett race on the

Taunus circuit. He finished 4th. In the 1905 Gordon Bennett Race he could manage no higher than 9th place, and was 6th in the same year's Circuit des Ardennes. In 1906 he drove an Itala, finishing 5th in the Targa Florio, but in the Grand Prix none of the Itala team lasted more than half distance on the first day's racing, so neither de Caters nor his team-mates found themselves in the final. He drove a Pipe in the 1907 Kaiserpreis, but returned to Mercedes for the Circuit des Ardennes, in which he achieved his greatest triumph, by winning the Grand Prix car class with a 120hp car. At the beginning of 1908 de Caters abandoned motor racing in order to concentrate on aviation. He was the first man to fly a heavier-than-air machine in Belgium (1908), and also in Germany, Poland, Greece and Turkey (1909). He died in 1944. GdeB

Chapman, Anthony Colin Bruce

Chapman was born in Richmond, Surrey, on 19 May 1928. He showed an early flair for mechanics and an enthusiasm for wheeled transport, and studied engineering at University College, London. In early 1946 he and fellow student Colin Dare began buying and selling second-hand cars, a business which folded up when the petrol ration was cancelled in 1947.

Modifications and alterations had been made to several of the old cars in stock, and one — PK 3493, a 1930 Austin Seven fabric saloon — formed the basis of his first trials special, the Lotus Mark 1. This and subsequent specials were built in North London. Late in 1948 Chapman was awarded his BSc(Eng), and after receiving basic flying training in the University Air Squadron, joined the RAF. His service delayed production of the Mark 2 and he finally decided to abandon his RAF career in late 1949, going to work for a constructional engineering company.

He drove his specials widely in trials and 750 Motor Club events, and in 1951 joined brothers Michael and Nigel Allen in building a trio of new specials. The 1951 season was a great one for the embryo Lotus, the Allens helping Chapman run his Mark 3 which proved extremely successful. Mike Lawson, who had bought the Mark 2 trials car from him, ordered a replacement and on 1 January 1952 Colin Chapman founded the Lotus Engineering Company in premises owned by his father in North London.

Chapman split his time between working for the British Aluminium Company and as a part-time director of Lotus, with partner Michael Allen working full-time.

Left, Eugenio Castellotti (right), with Stirling Moss at Monaco, 1956. *Photo: Autosport*

Centre, Baron Pierre de Caters in his 60hp Mors, setting a new kilometre record (29·80sec), July 28th 1902. *Photo: courtesy Baron Guy de Caters*

Above, Baron Pierre de Caters. *Photo: courtesy Baron Guy de Caters*

Colin Chapman, in the Lotus Mark 2 trials car, 1949. *Photo: Shell*

Right above, One of the most successful Chapman designs was the monocoque Lotus 25: Jim Clark at the wheel. *Photo: Autosport*

Colin Chapman, with Graham Hill. *Photo: Doug Nye Collection*

Louis Charavel ('Sabipa'). *Photo: Cyril Posthumus Collection*

Allen withdrew from the partnership in early 1953, and Chapman was working so hard he had no time to drive the first eight Mark 6 production models which were to make Lotus' name.

With these cars Chapman proved his ability to produce reliable lightweight frame structures and efficient suspension systems, and with assistance from Peter Ross and 'Mac' Mackintosh — both de Havilland Aircraft employees from Hatfield — the little company progressed well. Mike Costin, another de Havilland engineer, joined the little team and with Chapman freed to race his own car more publicity came Lotus' way from a number of decisive victories in 1172 Formula Mark 6s. Frank Costin produced the aerodynamic body design for the Mark 8, Chapman's first incursion into the 1,500cc sports car class. By 1954 his company was well-established as a sports-racing car constructor, and Chapman himself as a designer/driver of exceptional ability. He drove at Le Mans in 1955, reversing his Mark 9 out of the sand at Arnage and being disqualified; and in 1956, retired with big-end failure.

Chapman's genius for chassis and suspension design was put to good use by Vanwall in their 1956 cars. He produced his first Lotus single-seater design in 1957, for Formula 2. At the same time the all-fibreglass Elite was in the melting pot, a road/track design which really established Chapman's name as an original thinker and a trend-setter in terms of lightweight car construction.

In June 1959 Chapman moved Lotus into a new factory at Cheshunt, and in 1960 produced his first rear-engined single-seater design, the Mark 18. From this stemmed the FJ and F1 cars up to the Type 24 and in 1962 Chapman himself rang the changes by introducing the monocoque Type 25 at the Dutch GP. While this car and its derivatives won the World Championship in 1963 and 1965 Chapman became more involved in the running of what was now the Lotus Group, producing road and track cars in series-production quantities.

First Len Terry and then Maurice Phillippe were taken on as designers working on Formula 1 and Indianapolis cars; one of the subsidiaries, Lotus Components, had its own design staff working on customer minor formula machines. In 1966 Chapman moved his group into spacious new premises on Hethel Airfield, near Wymondham in Norfolk, and lives with his wife and family in a large house on the other side of the site. He is an enthusiastic private pilot, and when day-to-day business commitments permit still keeps a close watch on Lotus designs. As a team manager he has something of a

reputation for being ruthless and often unsympathetic with his drivers; but the will to win and the will for Lotus to succeed seems a prime motive force. His nine-season association with Jim Clark resulted in a record number of Grand Prix wins, two World Championship titles and victory in the Indianapolis 500. Graham Hill gave the Phillippe-designed, Chapman-inspired Lotus 49 the world title in 1968 and Jochen Rindt became the first posthumous Champion with the Lotus 72 in 1970. Chapman's story is the story of Lotus; it is one of the great success stories of recent years. DCN

Charavel, Louis (Sabipa)

Charavel, or Sabipa as he was usually called, was born in the South of France in 1890, and started racing in 1920 when he finished 4th in the Cyclecar GP at Le Mans in a Weler. The following year he bought a Bugatti which he drove in minor events for the next four years. In 1925 he drove in the 12 Hour Touring Car GP at San Sebastian, winning the 1,500cc class single handed. He was a member of the Bugatti works team in the 1926 Italian GP at Monza which he won, and in the 1927 Targa Florio he had a lucky escape when he skidded in avoiding a large boulder in the road, and ended up in a garden 50 feet below, quite unhurt. He had another lucky escape in the 1930 French GP at Pau when he overturned and was thrown out into the road, to be narrowly missed by Birkin's Bentley which was following close behind. During this period he was mostly to be seen at the wheel of Bugatti cars, although for the 1928 Le Mans race he drove an Itala, finishing 8th. His last appearances in competition were at Le Mans in 1932 and 1933, when he drove an Alfa Romeo with Mme Siko; they finished 4th in 1932.

Charavel acquired his pseudonym of Sabipa when in response to a journalist's question he answered, in Provençal dialect 'Sabe pas' (I don't know). TASOM

Charron, Fernand

Charron was perhaps the first great name in motor racing. Born in France in 1866, like so many of his contemporaries he started as a racing cyclist, riding Clément bicycles (he married Adolphe Clément's daughter) and winning 116 1st prizes in eight years. He first took the tiller of a Panhard in the Marseilles–Nice–La Turbie, 1897, but was eliminated almost at the start by a spectacular incident in which the car turned a somersault. In 1898 he supported two major races and won both, despite burner troubles in the Marseilles–Nice; in the longer Paris–Amsterdam–Paris a combination of good driving and better luck with tyres than Girardot, his closest rival, earned him his laurels. He came first in the Paris–Bordeaux in spite of lying only 8th at Angoulême. He was the hero of the marathon Tour de France: at the end of the second stage he was leading despite two broken springs, and he was still 2nd three stages later, but transmission disorders at Le Mans forced him to continue for some 25 miles (40km) in reverse before even he gave up the unequal struggle. A 3rd place in the Nice–Marseilles followed in 1900, but his final victory, in the first of the Gordon Bennett series, was a fairly empty one: the only other finisher was his team-mate, the faithful Girardot, but even on this occasion he had an adventurous time, for a St Bernard dog became wedged in his steering gear.

In 1901 Charron joined forces with Girardot and Voigt, another Panhard driver, to form the C.G.V. company, although he still drove for Panhard in the Paris–Berlin, coming in 6th. This marked his official retirement: unlike Girardot, he did not drive the new marque apart from an abortive outing in the 1902 Circuit des Ardennes. Nor did the C.G.V. prosper as a racing car, and Charron subsequently sold out, going for a while to Clément-Bayard, his father-in-law's concern. His last manufacturing venture was the Alda, also seen on the circuits in the immediate pre-World War 1 period. He died in 1928. MCS

Chevrolet, Gaston

Gaston Chevrolet was born in France in 1892 and joined his older brothers (Louis and Arthur) in America as a young man. His promising career as a race driver ended abruptly in California only six months after he had added his name to the exclusive list of Indianapolis 500-mile winners. That was an objective which neither of his brothers had been able to attain, although both of them contributed more to the success of the sport than Gaston, as car builders as well as drivers.

Gaston attracted attention to himself as a driver for the first time in 1917. He finished well in four races that year, including a 250-mile (402km) event on the Cincinnati board track, 30 May 1917, when he came third behind Louis Chevrolet and Ira Vail (Indianapolis was not run that year because of World War 1). Later in the same season, however, he participated in one or more races not sanctioned by the American Automobile Association and their Contest Board suspended him for a period of 12 months.

Louis Chevrolet. *Photo: Indianapolis Motor Speedway*

Opposite, Monaco Circuit: Lorenzo Bandini (Ferrari) passing the harbour during the 1965 Monaco GP. *Photo: Geoff Goddard*

Left below, Gaston Chevrolet, in the Monroe-Frontenac which he drove to victory at Indianapolis in 1920. *Photo: Indianapolis Motor Speedway*

Below, Gaston Chevrolet. *Photo: Indianapolis Motor Speedway*

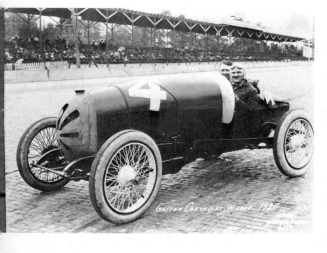

He was reinstated in time to drive in the 1919 Indianapolis event and finished 10th in a 4-cylinder Frontenac designed and built by brother Louis. Three important victories followed in rapid order on the board tracks, two at Sheepshead Bay, N.Y., and one at Uniontown, Pa.

His impressive Indianapolis victory came on 31 May 1920, in a Monroe Special, which actually was one of the new 3-litre Frontenacs under the Monroe name. His nearest challenger, René Thomas of France in a Ballot, trailed by more than six minutes at the finish; and Gaston's car was the first to go the full 500 miles and win without a tyre change.

Gaston Chevrolet died as the result of injuries sustained in a flaming crash with another car driven by Eddie O'Donnell, also injured fatally, during a board track race at Beverly Hills, Calif., on 26 November of the same year. AB

Chevrolet, Louis

Louis Chevrolet, born in Switzerland in 1878, came to the United States in 1900 by way of Montreal after serving his automotive apprenticeship with De Dion, Bouton et Cie in France. After working two years for the New York agency of the same company, he joined the staff of E. Rand Hollander, New York importer of European cars, and drove a 1905 Fiat in his first race. William C. Durant persuaded him to become a member of the Buick racing team three years later and Chevrolet won recognition in 1909 as one of America's leading road course drivers.

His victories that year included the 395-mile (635·7km) Cobe Trophy event at Crown Point, Ind. at 49·3mph (79·34kph), and a 200-mile speedway event at Atlanta, Ga., at 74mph (119·09kph). He also won several shorter races at the Indianapolis Motor Speedway during the season and led the field most of the way in the 1910 Vanderbilt Cup race at New York before his car was wrecked because of a broken steering knuckle, with eight laps to go.

In 1911, Durant contracted with Chevrolet to design the first of the Chevrolet passenger cars, which ultimately became the best-selling car in the world for the General Motors Corporation. The association, however, lasted only a little more than two years. Then, after a violent argument with Durant—and longing for a return to active competition on the race track—Chevrolet formed his own company in 1914 to build a series of 4-cylinder and 8-cylinder cars under the Frontenac name. The Frontenacs provided most of the principal opposition for the Duesenbergs and Millers from 1916 until the early 1920s. Louis himself drove them to many victories on the board tracks at Uniontown, Pa., Chicago; Cincinnati, Ohio; and Sheepshead Bay, N.Y. It was his younger brother Gaston and Tommy Milton, however, who scored the two most important Frontenac victories by winning the 1920 and 1921 Indianapolis 500-mile races, respectively. Louis drove in the Indianapolis 500 four times, being sidelined by mechanical trouble on three occasions and finishing 7th in 1919 for his best Indy performance.

For 12 years, beginning in 1922, Louis manufactured and sold special cylinder heads of his own design for use by the drivers of the popular Fronty-Ford race cars which dominated the sport on the small dirt tracks throughout the United States. He also did some design work on marine and aircraft engines during the 1930s and was in demand as a consulting engineer until shortly before his death in 1941. AB

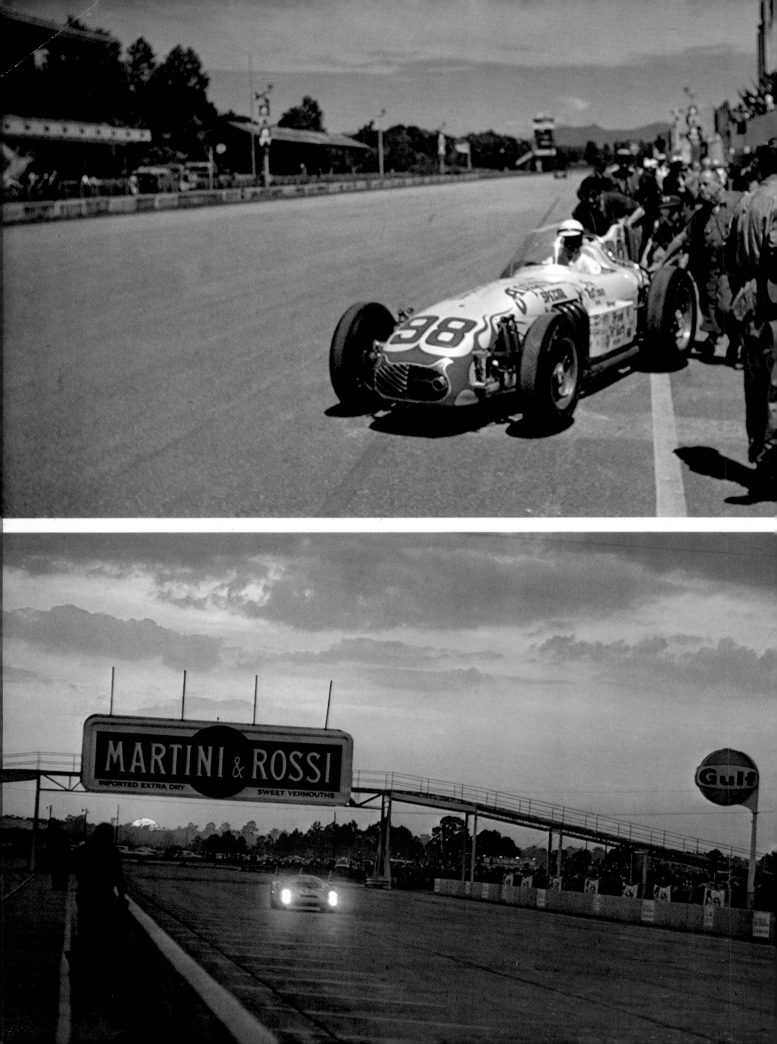

Chiron, Louis

Chiron, born in 1900 in Monaco of French parents, became an army driver at the end of World War 1. He was personal driver to Marshal Foch in 1919. He started his racing career on Bugattis, under the eye of Ernest Friderich, the ex-Bugatti driver who ran the make's agency at Nice, initially on a Brescia and then in 1926 a Type 35: in early 1927 he obtained the first 2·3-litre supercharged Type 35B which left the factory. Later that year he ran for the first time at Brooklands in a Bugatti in the British GP, finishing 4th.

In 1928 he did outstandingly well with his supercharged Bugatti (2·3- and 2-litre) winning the Grand Prix at Rome, Marne, Spain and Italy. The following year he won the German and Spanish GPs, and then, deserting Bugatti temporarily, he took a 1·5-litre Delage to Indianapolis but without success. In 1930 he won the European and Lyons GPs missing victory by seconds from Dreyfus at Monaco, all for Bugatti.

In 1930 he had had some success for Bugatti with the 16-cylinder Type 45, and in 1932–3 he had several wins in hill-climbs in the 4-wheel drive Type 53 Bugatti. He won at Monaco in a Type 51 Bugatti in 1931, and shared a win with Varzi at the French GP that year. In 1933 he joined the Scuderia Ferrari to drive an Alfa Romeo. In that year he won at Brno in Czechoslovakia and at San Sebastian with the Alfa Romeo. The next year he had places with the same make at Monaco, Alessandria, Tripoli, Nürburg, and won the GP of the Automobile Club de France at Montlhéry against new German competition, but Auto Union and Mercedes were soon to be the masters.

He continued with Alfa Romeo in 1936 with little or no success, and then in 1937 transferred to Talbot to compete in sports car races, this giving him a win in the French GP. Although he tried a Delahaye at Le Mans in 1938, his racing career was in the doldrums and he retired to his native Monaco.

In 1946 he took up the wheel again in a Talbot at the Nice Grand Prix but was soon in trouble; shortly afterwards the same occurred in the Belgian GP. In 1947 he drove for Maserati without success at Berne and in the Italian GP., and then won the French GP at Montlhéry in a Talbot. In 1948 he had a remarkable 2nd place in the Talbot at Monaco, and repeated his win for Talbot in 1949 at Reims.

In 1950 he drove a Maserati (Monaco, 3rd), and again in 1951 without success. His last race was at Monaco in 1956 when he drove a Lancia V-8 into 6th place. Two years earlier he won the Monte Carlo Rally in a Lancia Aurelia. After retirement from active competition he was asked by Prince Rainier of Monaco to become *Commissaire Général* of the Grand Prix and Rally associated with the Principality.

Colourful and dashing in his youth, Chiron had a reputation for elegant and polished driving which persisted throughout his career. HGC

Claes, Johnny

This popular and charming Belgian became as well-known in motor racing as he was in jazz spheres, where he ran a band called 'Johnny Claes and his Clay Pigeons'. He was born in London in 1917 of a Scottish mother and Belgian father, and took up motor racing in 1948 with a Veritas and Louis Rosier's Talbot which he borrowed for the GP des Frontières at Chimay finishing 3rd. In 1950 he scored HWMs first Continental F2 win in the same event, breaking the lap record for the

Louis Chiron (right), with, from the right, Achille Varzi, Albert Divo, Guy Bouriat and Ernest Friderich, at Monaco in 1931. *Photo: Hugh Conway Collection*

Louis Chiron, at Silverstone in 1953. *Photo: Central Press Photos Ltd*

Louis Chiron: Principle Successes

1926	Comminges GP	Bugatti Type 35
1928	Italian GP	Bugatti Type 35
	Spanish GP	Bugatti Type 35
	Antibes GP	Bugatti Type 35
	Marne GP	Bugatti Type 35
	Rome GP	Bugatti Type 35
	San Sebastian GP	Bugatti Type 35
1929	German GP	Bugatti Type 35
	Spanish GP	Bugatti Type 35
1930	Lyons GP	Bugatti Type 35
	Belgian GP	Bugatti Type 35
1931	Monaco GP	Bugatti Type 51
	French GP (with Varzi)	Bugatti Type 51
	Czechoslovak GP	Bugatti Type 51
1932	Dieppe GP	Bugatti Type 51
	Czechoslovak GP	Bugatti Type 51
	Nice Circuit	Bugatti Type 51
1933	Spanish GP	Alfa Romeo P3
	Marseilles GP	Alfa Romeo P3
	Czechoslovak GP	Alfa Romeo P3
	Spa 24-Hours, (with Chinetti)	Alfa Romeo 2·3-litre sports
1934	French GP	Alfa Romeo P3
	Marne GP	Alfa Romeo P3
1935	Lorraine GP	Alfa Romeo P3
1937	French GP	Talbot 4-litre
1947	French GP	Talbot 4·5-litre
	Comminges GP	Talbot 4·5-litre
1949	GP de France	Talbot 4·5-litre

Chimay course, and became Belgian Champion that year. In 1951 he won again at Chimay, in a Simca, but a greater achievement was his victory in the Liège–Rome–Liège Rally without the loss of a single mark, in a privately-entered Jaguar XK 120. His co-driver was Jacques Ickx, father of GP driver Jacky Ickx. In 1953 he won this gruelling rally again, this time in a Lancia Aurelia, driving for 52 hours without relief after his co-driver Trasenster had been taken ill. He was elected Driver of the Year by the Guild of Motoring Writers.

He also drove Talbot, Gordini F2, Connaught and Porsche cars, winning the 1,500cc class at Le Mans in 1954 with the latter, and in the 1955 Liège–Rome–Liège he finished 3rd with Lucien Bianchi as co-driver, despite being ill and running a high temperature. It was his last event; his health deteriorated and in February 1956 he died of tuberculosis. He was only 39. CP

Clark, James

The Scotsman Jim Clark was one of those drivers whose ability set the standard in their time and whose skill and results became the targets not only for their contemporaries, but for succeeding generations. He was born in Kilmany, Fifeshire, on 14 March 1936, the only son of a well-to-do Scottish sheep farmer. In 1942 the family moved to Duns, Berwickshire, and took over Edington Mains farm where Clark had his earliest experience of driving, playing around with the tractors and then driving his father's Austin Seven at the age of nine. An Alvis Speed Twenty was revived in 1946 and the boy was allowed to drive it around the farm. His first contact with someone involved in motor sport was in 1948 when his eldest sister married a local farmer, Alec Calder, who raced a Brooklands Riley 9 and had a 3-litre Bentley at the time. Clark saw his first motor race at Brands Hatch while in the area visiting relatives, and was thrilled by the sight of Farina's Thinwall Special at Charterhall.

He passed his driving test at 17 and was given the family Sunbeam-Talbot when his father replaced it with a Rover. He wanted to try competition driving, and Jock McBain, a local garage owner, persuaded him to enter a Berwick & DMC driving test meeting at nearby Winfield. It seems he won it, but was not a club member and so never heard any more about it. He took part in a number of minor rallies and driving test meetings, and in 1955 ran an Austin-Healey in the Scottish Rally with Billy Potts. In June 1956 he had his first race, driving his

Opposite top, Monza Autodrome: Troy Ruttmann in Agajanian's Indy Roadster in the 1958 'Race of Two Worlds'. *Photo: Al Bochroch*

Opposite bottom, Sebring Circuit: Sunset during the 12-Hour Race, 1964. *Photo: Al Bochroch*

friend Ian Scott-Watson's DKW Sonderklasse at Crimond despite parental opposition, and finished 8th. He scored several class victories in his own Sunbeam and Scott-Watson's DKW. Then, late in 1957, Scott-Watson traded in the DKW for a Porsche 1600S and with this car Jimmy Clark began to make his name — pushed, guided and cajoled the whole time by Scott-Watson.

Clark had two victories, two 2nds and a 3rd in the Porsche, and began racing regularly in 1958. As the only son of the family, his parents put pressure on him to stop, and he was torn between his new-found sport and his responsibilities to the farm. The Border Reivers team (named after the old Scottish border plunderers and rustlers), was re-formed in 1958 and the founders, under Jock McBain, asked Clark to drive their ex-Scott-Brown, Henry Taylor Jaguar D. He ended the season with 12 victories in 20 events entered, and was 8th in the Spa Cup race in which Scott-Brown was killed — a race which left him a hatred of Spa ever after. Scott-Watson bought a Lotus Elite later that year and Clark raced it at Brand's Hatch against Colin Chapman, collided with a back-marker and lost the race. Chapman had already been impressed by the young Scot's prowess while sampling an F2 Lotus at Brands Hatch, but in 1959 he really made his name in the Border Reivers' ex-Halford Lister-Jaguar. He achieved 12 1sts and four 2nds in the car, and had great success with an Elite which the Reivers bought after running it for Lotus at Le Mans; Clark and Sir John Whitmore drove the car into 2nd place in class there.

Clark's first single-seater race was at Brands Hatch on 26 December 1959, when he drove an FJ Gemini entered by Graham Warner, against whose Elite he had been racing for most of the season. Meanwhile Reg Parnell, who knew McBain, fixed an F1 Aston Martin trial for Clark early in 1960 and signed him on for that season. But the front-engined Astons were too late in appearing and Clark was released from his contract to drive for Lotus in F2 and FJ. The Lotus 18 had just been released, and Clark scored nine firsts and three seconds during that first of his eight full seasons with Team Lotus. Chapman upgraded him to the Formula 1 team at the Dutch GP, in which he finished 5th, and he shared the FJ Championship that season with team-mate Trevor Taylor. He shared 3rd place at Le Mans with Salvadori in the Reivers' Aston Martin DBR1/300, and in 1961 began his historic, winning career in Formula 1, scoring at Pau and in the Rand, Natal and South African GPs at the end of the season.

He was a professional racing driver now, utterly absorbed in the job in hand and showing a rare degree of skill for one so young (he was 25). But his career was marred by his fatal collision with von Trips' Ferrari at Monza in 1961, an experience of which he was to talk little, although it had obviously affected him deeply. His F1 debut at Spa had affected him similarly, for this was the 1960 race in which his team-mate Alan Stacey, and Chris Bristow were killed. These tragedies intensified his dislike of Spa-Francorchamps. But his inate ability and enthusiasm kept him going, and once in the cockpit his mind put these thoughts behind him, and fused man and car in a way seldom seen before, or since.

In 1962 Chapman introduced his monocoque Lotus 25, and Clark won his first Grande Epreuve in it, at Spa. The season produced a running battle with Graham Hill's BRM for the Championship, resolved in the final round at East London when Jim's Lotus-Climax failed

after establishing a commanding lead. But in 1963 luck, reliability and his own unique abilities stood by him, and he won six Grandes Epreuves, four of them consecutively, to gain the World Championship crown he so richly deserved. He was an inquisitive, curious driver, anxious to know what other cars were like to drive, and appeared in large and small saloons, sports cars and

Top, Jim Clark, after winning the 1966 United States GP. *Photo: Al Bochroch*

Above, Jim Clark winning the 1967 Italian GP in a Lotus 49. *Photo: Doug Nye Collection*

even NASCAR stockers, satisfying this curiosity. In some cases these were once only drives, and he did not repeat the experiment, having satisfied himself that he now knew what racing a Galaxie or a NASCAR machine was all about. A major feature of leading British race meetings at this time was the supporting programme with Clark at the wheel of a Lotus-Cortina or Lotus 30 sports car — always giving of his best and setting the standard for the rest of the field.

Chapman built a Ford V-8-powered Indianapolis car in 1963, and Jim shook the American track-racing establishment by finishing 2nd in a car they looked upon as a joke. He was *the* star racing driver of the time, and although he lost his title to Surtees in the last Championship round of 1964 he was still the man to beat, and the man the people came to see. Yet despite the publicity he remained a modest, quietly-spoken Border farmer, uncomfortable yet capable in the limelight; friendly and unassuming out of it.

He regained the World Championship title in 1965, won the Indianapolis 500 at his third attempt and went into the 1966 F1 season with a basically obsolete car (a 2-litre Lotus-Climax) while the H-16 Lotus-BRM 43 was being prepared. He scratched hard all season, and his drive against Brabham in that year's Dutch GP was a model: he turned his opponent's misfortune (an oily track) to his own advantage, and fought all the way to the finish, despite suffering a mechanical failure on the way. When the BRM-engined car appeared he confirmed all that people knew of his abilities of high-speed car control and mechanical sympathy, lapping Monza at incredibly high speed after a stop and winning the US GP with a collapsed rear suspension.

In 1967 the Cosworth-Ford V-8-powered Lotus 49 appeared at the Dutch GP, Clark winning with it first time out. He ran Hulme very close for the Championship that year, and again was always the man to watch, the driver to beat.

In the meantime he had run into tax problems under the British system, and moved to Paris, seldom appearing in the United Kingdom apart from such major events as the British GP. Edington Mains was still his farm, and was managed for him, but Clark had been the complete professional racing driver for several seasons.

He was a natural, capable of adapting himself entirely to conditions whether rainy or dry, oily or windy. He never had an off-day, and his lap times were always indicative of his car's optimum performance, whatever trim or state of preparation it was in. Several times he experienced failures which could easily have been fatal to a lesser man, but his special qualities of reflex and car control always got him out of trouble. Clark was an equally formidable opponent, whatever the circuit or class he happened to be driving in at the time. While he won at the super-fast circuits like Spa and Monza, he did equally well at Pau and shot away from the field at Monaco — although this was his unlucky circuit, and he never finished there. He was at his best in the face of adversity, and led the 1962 Nürburgring 1,000 kilometres for many laps in a tiny Lotus 23 before a combination of failing brakes and exhaust fumes in the cockpit put him off into the bushes.

At the beginning of 1968 he won the South African GP to notch his 25th Grande Epreuve victory, one more than Fangio's record total. This included five victories in the British GP, and four consecutive successes in the Belgian GP at Spa — positive proof that here was one of those very special drivers, a man who raced not only against

Jim Clark: Principle Successes

Year	Event	Car
1960	*Motor Racing* FJ Championship (Shared with Trev Taylor)	Lotus-Ford 18
1961	Pau GP	Lotus-Climax 18
	Rand GP	
	Natal GP	Lotus-Climax 21
	South African GP	
1962	Belgian GP	
	British GP	
	United States GP	
	Mexican GP	Lotus-Climax 25
	Gold Cup, Oulton Park	
	Rand GP	
	Lombank Trophy	Lotus-Climax 24
	Aintree '200'	
1963	Belgian GP	
	Dutch GP	
	French GP	
	British GP	
	Italian GP	
	Mexican GP	
	South African GP	
	Pau GP	Lotus-Climax 25
	Imola GP	
	Daily Express Trophy, Silverstone	
	Swedish GP	
	Gold Cup, Oulton Park	
	Milwaukee '200'	Lotus-Ford 29
	British Empire Trophy Oulton Park	Lotus-Ford 23
	Snetterton 3hr	
	Riverside GP	
1964	Belgian GP	
	Dutch GP	Lotus-Climax 25
	News of the World Trophy	
	British GP	Lotus-Climax 33
	Solitude GP	
	Pau GP F2	
	Eifelrennen F2	Lotus-Ford 32
	Guards Trophy F2	
	Brands Hatch F2	
1965	South African GP	
	Belgian GP	
	French GP	
	British GP	
	Dutch GP	Lotus-Climax 33
	German GP	
	Syracuse GP	
	Goodwood F1	
	Indianapolis '500'	Lotus-Ford 38
	Pau GP	
	Crystal Palace F2	Lotus-Ford 35
	Rouen F2	
	Brands Hatch F2	
	Tasman Championship	Lotus-Climax 32B
1966	United States GP	Lotus-BRM 43
	Warwick Farm	Lotus-Climax 35
1967	Dutch GP	
	British GP	
	United States GP	Lotus-Ford 49
	Mexican GP	
	Madrid GP	
	Tasman Championship	Lotus-Climax 39
	Barcelona F2	
	Madrid F2	Lotus-Ford 48
	Keimola F2	
1968	Tasman Championship	Lotus-Ford 49
	South African GP	Lotus-Ford 49

Jim Clark, with Graham Hill. *Photo: Doug Nye Collection*

Jim Clark talks to Dean Delamont, Head of the RAC Motor Sport Division (right). *Photo: Lynton Money*

others, but also against his personal feelings of disquiet and distrust for a circuit he thought dangerous.

After the Lotus 49's promising showing in 1967, the 1968 season was to have been Jim's year: few people could foresee anyone seriously challenging his third World title. On 6 April 1968, Jim Clark was racing his uncompetitive Lotus 48 in the opening-round of the European F2 Championship at Hockenheim. He was lying 8th on lap five of the first heat, finding the going difficult with wide tyres on a wet surface. He seemed to be in some engine trouble and had waved two cars past on the previous lap when the Lotus slid broadside off the long right-hand return sweep out in the woods, took down some saplings and hit a stout tree side-on at very high speed. It broke in two and Clark was taken from the crushed cockpit section to Heidelberg Hospital, but was already beyond saving. The wreckage was too badly mangled to give any firm clue to the cause of the accident, and although many reasons have been put forward, including tyre failure (refuted by Firestone), suspension breakage (refuted by Lotus), engine cut-out, children crossing the track and simple driver error, it seems that nobody will ever know for sure what caused the World Champion's death. The most probable explanation is that the offside rear tyre lost pressure and left the rim, putting the car into a broadside.

The racing world was literally stunned by the news, refusing to believe such a tragedy possible — doubly tragic because Jim had had no chance of success in this unimportant, little event. But he was gone, a champion in his prime, one of the greatest seen in the sport. DCN

Clark, Roger

Born in 1939, Roger Clark is one of the best-known and most successful British rally drivers of the 1960s. His first rally was at the wheel of a Ford Thames van navigated by the same man, Jim Porter, with whom he rallies today. While still working for his father, he entered more rallies and in 1961 he became East Midlands champion. Soon after that he acquired a Mini Cooper and started entering bigger events. In 1963 he entered the Tulip Rally and the same year he very nearly won the Scottish Rally, which led the Reliant team to give him his first works drive in the Coupe des Alpes, in a Sabre Six, where he finished and won the category.

In 1964, he changed the Mini Cooper for a Cortina GT and promptly won the Welsh, Scottish and Gulf London rallies, triumphing over the official Ford works entries. The Rover team became interested and for 1965 gave him a place in their team, which he rapidly justified by finishing 6th overall on one of the toughest Monte Carlo Rallies ever and winning the Group 1 category. He drove in the Acropolis, Coupe des Alpes and RAC rallies for Rover, but then Ford lent him a car for the Tulip Rally. Although he failed to finish, Ford seemed to be pleased, for in 1966 they gave him a full contract with the team.

His first rally for them was the Monte Carlo where he finished a steady 4th to the three works Mini Coopers only to be disqualified in the great lighting fiasco of 1966. In Sweden his car broke down but in the Acropolis he finished 2nd to his team-mate, Bengt Söderström.

For Fords, 1967 was a quiet year as they changed from rallying the Cortina to the Escort, but Clark did win the Scottish and also travelled to Canada where he won the Shell 4000. Towards the end of the year he spent a lot of time testing the Escort and when this car came on the rally scene, he rapidly won the Circuit of Ireland, the Tulip Rally, the Acropolis Rally and the Scottish with it. At the end of 1968 he drove in the London to Sydney with Ove Andersson in a Cortina Lotus and they were leading at Bombay but had trouble with the axle in Australia. In 1969 he won the Circuit of Ireland again and finished 2nd in the Acropolis after a very rare excursion cost him the lead. He also came 6th in a very snowy RAC Rally. In the Monte Carlo in 1970 he was 5th overall and best Touring car, and at home he won the Circuit of Ireland once more. JD

Frank Clement, after finishing 2nd in the 1922 Tourist Trophy in a 3-litre Bentley. *Photo: Cyril Posthumus Collection*

Left below, Victims of the 1966 lighting disqualification in the Monte Carlo Rally: left to right, Paddy Hopkirk, Timo Makinen, Rosemary Smith and Roger Clark. *Photo: Central Press Photos Ltd*

Below, Roger Clark. *Photo: Hugh W. Bishop*

Right below, John Cobb, in the TT Vauxhall, c 1927. *Photo: Montagu Motor Museum*

Clement, Francis C.

This British driver was born in 1886. Before joining Bentley Motors, where he was to achieve fame as one of the immortal 'Bentley Boys', Frank Clement had been with Vauxhall, Napier and Star as road tester. In 1914 while preparing for the Tourist Trophy in the Isle of Man as a member of the Star team, he met W. O. Bentley, the private entrant of a DFP. 'W. O.', as he was known, must have been impressed by Clement's driving during the race for he engaged him in 1921 as competition and test driver.

In 1922 Bentley Motors entered a team of three cars for the TT and Clement, in a brilliant piece of driving under appalling weather conditions, finished 3rd. In 1923 he partnered Duff in the first 24-hour race at Le Mans, in which they finished joint 4th. He was teamed with Duff again at Le Mans in 1924, and the pair won a magnificent victory, but in 1925 they failed to finish due to a broken valve.

In 1927, in the Essex 6-Hour race, Clement led for nearly two hours before retiring with engine trouble, but later in the race he relieved Birkin in another Bentley, eventually finishing 3rd. At Le Mans, driving the prototype $4\frac{1}{2}$-litre he led the race until 9.30 in the evening when, with Callingham his co-driver at the wheel, the car was involved in the famous White House crash. Clement had the satisfaction, however, of making fastest lap. Later in the year he won the 24-hour Grand Prix de Paris, recording the $4\frac{1}{2}$-litre's first victory.

He was 4th at Le Mans with Chassagne in 1929 and at the end of the season won the Brooklands 500 Miles race with Jack Barclay.

Clement's last year of competition was 1930 and it was fitting that he should win the Double-Twelve race partnered by Barnato. At Le Mans, after many disappointments in previous years, he finished 2nd with Watney as co-driver, thus bringing to a close a long and successful career in which he had had more than his share of bad luck. Clement died in 1970. TASOM

Cobb, John Rhodes

John Rhodes Cobb holds for all time the Brooklands outer-circuit lap record. This British racing driver was born in 1899, and was by profession a fur broker. Big cars were Cobb's speciality. He lived close to Brooklands Track as a young man and became fascinated by the sort of racing conducted there. Serving his racing apprenticeship in Warde's old but fast 10-litre ohc 1911 Fiat, Cobb won his first race in this venerable car at a 1925

West Essex MC meeting. The following year, after several places in short races in this Fiat, he drove Parry Thomas' giant Liberty aero-engined racer 'Babs' on its first Brooklands appearance. After this Cobb continued to gain experience with cars such as Thomas's Leyland Thomas, Howey's Ballot and a TT Vauxhall. He also won a Lightning handicap in the Fiat and on another occasion survived when that ancient car elected to lap with its steering tie-rod hanging free.

In 1929 Cobb bought the 10·5-litre V-12 Delage and began a career which went from strength to strength. This big, quiet, shy man gained many successes in the Delage, including the Brooklands standing-start lap record at 112·93mph (181·65kph) and the Class A hour record at 112·8mph (181·5kph). He also raised the absolute top record to 132·11 (212·62kph) and eventually to 133·16 (214·30) and 133·88mph (215·43kph) with this car, before selling it to Oliver Bertram. Cobb drove many other cars: the Brooklands Riley in the TT, Alfa Romeo, the single-seater Talbot 105 in the 500 Miles Race, and so on. But it was the really big-engined cars which appealed to him and caused him to have the Napier Railton track car, powered by a 450hp Lion aero engine, built for him by Thomson & Taylor at Brooklands. With this car Cobb, aided as appropriate by other drivers, took innumerable records, not only at Brooklands but at Montlhéry and on the Utah salt flats. These included the fastest-ever flying and standing start kilometre at Brooklands, at 151·97 (244·51) and 88·5mph (142·43kph) respectively; the hour record at 152·7mph (245·7kph); and the 24-hour record at 150·6mph (242·4kph). He also realized another of the ambitions behind the commissioning of this car — winning the BRDC 500 Miles and later the 500 kilometres races.

Craving something even faster, Cobb had Reid Railton design for him the highly unconventional Railton twin-engined record car, powered by two non-supercharged Napier Lion engines. It was with this car that Cobb broke the Land Speed Record at 350·20mph (563·6kph) in 1938, raised this to 369·70mph (594·9kph) in 1939, on the eve of World War 2, and went out again to Utah in 1947 to become the first man to exceed 400mph (643kph) on land, in the course of taking the absolute car speed record to 394·19mph (634·44kph). It was while trying for the World Water Speed Record that John Cobb lost his life, at Loch Ness in 1952 in his jet-engined craft *Crusader*. WB

Collins, Peter

It was natural that this British driver, born in 1931, should grow up surrounded by cars as his father, Patrick, ran a large motor dealership in Kidderminster. When Peter Collins was only 17 he had his first racing car, a 500cc Formula 3 Cooper-Norton, and he made his debut with it in 1949. He immediately displayed his class, winning at Goodwood and Silverstone (this in a 100-mile event), and in 1950 he branched out into hill-climbing with Cooper-JAP twins.

Despite his youth he was readily accepted into the rough-and-tumble world of 500cc Formula 3, and he teamed up with Frank Aiken, Alf Bottoms and R. M. Dryden to race Bottoms' JBS-Nortons. But in 1951 Bottoms was killed at Luxembourg and Dryden at Castle Combe, tragedies which hastened Collins' move from the 500s. John Heath asked him to join Moss and Macklin in his HWM F2s and Collins took the opportunity to enter Grand Prix racing. Reg Parnell was convinced of Collins' promise and introduced him to John Wyer, team manager for Aston Martin, who signed him on for 1952. Teamed with Pat Griffith he won the Goodwood 9 Hours and, in 1953, the Northern Ireland RAC TT at Dundrod. That year he was 2nd, again with Griffith, in the Goodwood 9 Hours, and Tony Vandervell signed him for the 4·5-litre Thinwall Special Ferrari he was running under Formule Libre. Collins fought the car to many memorable successes, and his 1954 season culminated in the Italian GP, driving the original 2·2-litre Vanwall and finishing in 7th place.

His Formule Libre performances in the Thinwall Special had often overshadowed the V-16 BRMs, and for 1955 he was in the Owen Organization camp, initially with their experimental 250F Maserati and later with the first 2·5-litre BRMs. He led the field for the opening laps on the new car's first appearance at Oulton Park, and his talents were also recognized by Mercedes when they teamed him with Moss in the Targa Florio: their winning drive secured the Constructors' Championship.

Collins' extrovert and playful character made him immensely popular, and his friendship with Mike Hawthorn produced many a practical joke. He joined Ferrari in 1956, and spent the season developing his essentially smooth style under team-leader Fangio's tuition. Now he was fulfilling all his promise, winning the Belgian and French GPs and challenging Fangio for the World title. The Italian GP was the decider, but Fangio retired early on and Musso refused to surrender

John Cobb in the Napier-Railton. *Photo: William Boddy Collection*

John Cobb. *Photo: William Boddy Collection*

Peter Collins in a 1,200cc Cooper at a sprint meeting in 1950 in which he made joint ftd with Duncan Hamilton (ERA). *Photo: Francis Penn*

Count Carlo Conelli. *Photo: Cyril Posthumus Collection*

Earl Cooper. *Photo: Indianapolis Motor Speedway*

his car in this his home race. Moss's Maserati was leading and had set fastest lap, then Collins swept into the pits for a tyre-check, leapt from the cockpit and waved Fangio in. Fangio finished 2nd to secure the title, made possible by Collin's selfless sportsmanship.

In 1957 Hawthorn returned to Ferrari to join Collins, and the highlights of the team's season were Collins's two victories at Syracuse and Naples. Ferrari were fully competitive again in 1958, and Collins fulfilled an ambition by winning the British GP at Silverstone, adding to his International Trophy victory there earlier in the season. At the Nürburgring Collins and Hawthorn were chasing Tony Brooks' leading Vanwall hard when, after 10 laps, Collins attempted to pass the green car at Pflanzgarten. He lost control, the car hit the bank and threw its driver out against a tree. Collins was flown to hospital by helicopter, but nothing could be done for him. DCN

Conelli, Count Carlo Alberto

Count 'Caberto' Conelli was one of Italy's leading amateur drivers in the 1920s, and had his first big success when he made ftd at the Aosta-Great St Bernard hill-climb of 1920 at the wheel of a Diatto-Bugatti. He drove this car and a Ballot up to 1924, and in 1925 was invited to join the Sunbeam-Talbot-Darracq team. In his first drive for them, the Grand Prix de Provence at Miramas, he was 2nd, as he was also in the Grand Prix de l'Ouverture at Montlhéry. In this event he was following Duller near the finishing line and pulled out to pass, only to skid and overturn, crossing the finishing line upside down and in 2nd place. Fortunately he was only slightly hurt, but he must be the only driver on record to finish 2nd on his head.

Conelli had little success in 1926, but joined the Bugatti team in 1927. With them he came 2nd in the 1927 Targa Florio, and 3rd in this event in 1928 and 1930. He also had a number of other successes including victory in the 1931 Belgian GP at Spa, with Williams. At the end of the 1931 season Conelli retired from competition. TASOM

Cook, Humphrey W.

Cook was born in 1893. His name as a driver is associated mainly with Brooklands, where his racing spanned the years from 1914 to 1937. However, he achieved a notable run of successes in sprints, and raced also on a wide variety of circuits. From 1920 his black and red E-type

Left above, Peter Collins in a Ferrari before the 1955 British GP at Silverstone. *Photo: Keystone Press Agency Ltd*

Above, Peter Collins in Milan, August 1956. *Photo: Publifoto, Milan*

Right above, Humphrey Cook (far right), with, right to left, Bernard Rubin, J. D. Benjafield, Woolf Barnato, Frank Clement and Sir Henry Birkin. *Photo: Cyril Posthumus Collection*

30/98 Vauxhall (known as 'Rouge et Noir') achieved many good placings, being lightened for the 1921 season and streamlined for 1922. In that year he also raced a 1919 8-cylinder 5,104cc Ballot. For 1923 he purchased one of the 1922 TT Vauxhalls, which was named 'Rouge et Noir II', and this car also was successful. In 1925 he suggested to Amherst Villiers that it be supercharged, thus forming the genesis of Mays' very successful Vauxhall Villiers sprint car. He crashed the works Aston Martin in the 1925 JCC 200 Miles race, possibly because of a steering failure, and also used the very slim 'Razor Blade' version, which might have been thought ill-suited to his substantial build. In the late 1920s he raced Bentleys, and then drove again for the Aston Martin team in 1931.

Of a quiet and reserved disposition, Cook showed his patriotism and enthusiasm most memorably in the form of the £75,000 which he provided to set up the ERA concern. His judgment was vindicated by the position the ERA quickly gained as Britain's most successful racing car of the 1930s. The first appearance of an ERA was Cook's entry in the 1934 BRDC British Empire Trophy, and he also obtained the make's first victory, in a Brooklands Mountain Handicap with the 1,100cc model. He subsequently raced ERAs at Donington, the Isle of Man, the Nürburgring, Dieppe and Albi. DF

Cooper, Earl

Earl Cooper, born in 1886, first driver to win the United States national championship three times, became a consistent winner for the famous Stutz team in 1913 after five years of only moderate success with other makes of cars on the California dirt tracks. His contemporaries regarded him as a master of racing strategy and he made no secret of the fact that he believed the stamina of his cars was of even more importance than their speed.

Unlike many other stars of his era, he passed up frequent opportunities to drive in lucrative exhibition and match races in order to concentrate his efforts on the major championship events.

His most important victories while winning the 1913 championship included the 445-mile (716km) Santa Monica, Calif., road race at 73·8mph (118·77kph) and the Corona, Calif., 301-mile road race at 74·7mph (120·22kph). He also won races of 200 miles (320km) and 250 miles (400km) on the Tacoma, Wash., track.

After a disappointing 1914 season, which included his

first appearance at Indianapolis, where he failed to finish, Cooper won the national driving title again for Stutz the following year. His 1915 performance included victories in the 305-mile (490km) Point Loma road race at San Diego, Calif., at 65·05mph (104·69kph), the 301-mile Elgin, Ill. road race at 74·98mph (120·67kph) and the inaugural 500-mile race at the short-lived Twin Cities Speedway near Minneapolis, Minn., at 86·35mph (138·97kph), and 4th place at Indy.

When Stutz discontinued their racing programme in 1916, Cooper purchased one of the cars and won the 1917 driving title without factory help. With Indianapolis suspending operations for the duration of World War 1, the 250-mile race on the new board track at Chicago became the year's premier event and Cooper won it at a speed of 103·15mph (166·08kph).

He announced his retirement at the end of the season, but was persuaded to resume his driving career at Fresno, Calif., in 1921 as a replacement for Joe Thomas, who had suffered a broken arm in practice. Cooper won the race and joined the Durant team for the 1922 and 1923 seasons. Then, with financial help from the Studebaker Corporation, Cooper designed and built a Miller-powered Studebaker Special which he drove to 2nd place at Indianapolis in 1924. Later in the season, in the same car, he won again at Fresno.

In 1925, Cooper drove a Miller Special at an average speed of 121·6mph (195·7kph) to outdistance his challengers in a 250-mile (400km) board track race at Charlotte, N.Car., and agreed to drive a new fwd Miller Special in 1926. With it, he qualified for the pole position at Indianapolis but failed to finish because of transmission trouble. One month later the car performed perfectly in a 200-mile (320km) race on the Rockingham, N.H. board track as he scored what was to be his last important victory.

His racing career, however, still was not finished. The Marmon Motor Car Company commissioned him to build a Miller-powered Marmon Special for the 1927 European Grand Prix at Monza, and he came 3rd in that event with Peter Kreis as co-driver.

He subsequently was associated for approximately 20 years with the Union Oil Company as a consultant engineer and also served with distinction as a senior race official for the AAA Contest Board until a few years before his death in 1965. AB

Cortese, Franco

'Franchino' Cortese was born in 1903 at Oggebio, in the Novara district, between Milan and Turin. He began racing in 1926 with an Itala, and came 3rd in the 140-mile (225km) Leghorn Cup sports car race in 1927 and 1928 behind Alfa Romeo and Maserati opposition. In 1930 he began driving Alfa Romeos for the Scuderia Ferrari, finishing 4th in the Mille Miglia with ex-motorcyclist Pietro Ghersi, and 2nd with Ivanowski in the Spa 24-hour race, in 1,750cc models. In 1932 he came 2nd at Le Mans in an 8C 2·3 Alfa Romeo with Guidotti; and finished 2nd in the 1933 Mille Miglia in an 8C 2·3 Monza Alfa Romeo with Zagato sports bodywork, sharing with Castelbarco.

In 1934 began his remarkable domination of the Targa Abruzzo sports car race on the Pescara circuit, always driving 6C 2300 Alfa Romeos. In the 24-hour races of 1934 and 1935 he was partnered by Francesco Severi, then he won driving solo in 1937, and was partnered by Ghersi to win in 1938, these last two races being of only six hours duration. He also started driving single-seaters in 1937, being 3rd in the Pescara Circuit Voiturette Race and 2nd in the Tripoli Voiturette Race in a 6CM Maserati 1·5-litre, sandwiched at Tripoli between the similar cars of Dreyfus and Severi. As well as two victories with a 6CM in 1938, on the Varese Circuit and at Modena, Cortese also had a 2nd place in the Targa Florio which was held on a small circuit in the Favorita Park, Palermo.

At the end of the year he went to South Africa with the Scuderia Ambrosiana, and in January 1939, with his 6CM was 2nd in the South African GP to Villoresi's 6CM, and won the Grosvenor GP from Peter Aitken's ERA R11B. Later in the year he was 2nd in the Coppa Ciano at Montenero to Farina's 158 Alfa Romeo driving a new works 16-valve 4CL Maserati.

In 1946 Cortese won at Modena in a sports Lancia, and in 1947 he won a race for leading Italian drivers in Egypt, all driving D46 Cisitalias. In that year he drove the first product of the new Ferrari Company, a 1·5-litre V-12 Type 125, in a sports car race at Piacenza in May, but had fuel-pump trouble when leading two laps from the end. He gained two victories with a 125 in 1947, and was 2nd in the Coppa Acerbo for sports cars.

He drove a Type 166 V-12 2-litre sports Ferrari in 1948, but 1949 was a better year with his privately owned 2-litre V-12 Formula 2 short-chassis car. In this he came 3rd in the Rome GP, 2nd at Bari, and 3rd in the Czech GP at Brno. In 1950 he won the Naples GP in Count Lurani's Ferrari.

In 1951 came his best known victory, when he won the Targa Florio on the Short Madonie Circuit in his Le Mans Frazer Nash from a Ferrari and a Maserati. In that year he also campaigned with his short-chassis 1949 Formula 2 Ferrari fitted with a special engine with stub exhausts. In 1953 he retired the Frazer Nash in the Targa Florio, and in the following years had two places with Ferraris in sports car races, a 3rd to two other Ferraris in the Bari 3-hour Race in 1954 in a 500 Mondial, and what appears to be his last recorded success, 2nd in the 1956 2-litre sports car race on the Reggio Calabria Circuit in southern Italy to Cerini's Ferrari, after 30 years in the sport. PMAH

Corum, Lora L.

This American racing driver and engineer, born in 1895, was associated with Louis and Arthur Chevrolet in the development of Frontenac cylinder heads for Ford engines which powered many inexpensive race cars on the half-mile dirt track during the early 1920s. 'Slim' Corum made his debut in major racing circles at Indianapolis in 1922. On that occasion he drove one of Chevrolet's Monroe Specials in the 500 but was eliminated on the 170th lap because of mechanical trouble. One year later he attracted national attention by driving the Barber-Warnock Fronty-Ford Special to 5th place in the 500 in competition with many cars of greater horsepower.

He joined the Duesenberg team for the 1924 Indianapolis race, qualifying and starting the 8-cylinder Duesenberg which Joe Boyer drove to victory. Corum drove the first 107 laps of the race and Boyer the last 93 laps, coming from behind to win.

Corum remained with the Duesenberg company for several years, before joining the engineering staff of the Stutz company in 1930, when he drove a Stutz Special to 10th place at Indianapolis. He also worked as an engineer for the Allison Division of General Motors until shortly before his death in 1949. AB

Franco Cortese. *Photo: Cyril Posthumus Collection*

Lora L. Corum. *Photo: Indianapolis Motor Speedway*

Costantini, Meo

This Italian driver was a member of a distinguished Venetian family. He acted as an official works driver for Ettore Bugatti from 1924. Costantini's worth was shown in 1925 in the Targa Florio, which he won for Bugatti in resounding style, following it up with successes in the 1·5-litre class in the French Grand Prix and at Monza in the Italian GP. In 1926 he repeated his Targa Florio victory and then won the San Sebastian and the Italian Grand Prix for Bugatti.

W. F. Bradley has written of his ability, especially in the difficult conditions of the Targa Florio. 'He knew with unfailing accuracy at exactly what speed and in what manner each and every turn could be negotiated; the more difficult the road conditions the more he drew away from his rivals by reason of his absolute and mathematical precision.'

Costantini retired from active racing at the end of 1926, because of failing health, and became Bugatti's team manager. He saw them win the Targa Florio three more times. In 1931 as racing manager he led Bugatti's new team of Type 51 racers into the forefront; he remained with the company until 1935, when he returned to his native Italy. He died in 1940. HGC

Courage, Piers Raymond

Courage was born on 27 May 1942, son of one of the heads of John Courage, the English brewery concern. He was educated at Eton, and developed a keen interest in motoring and motor sport while there. After leaving school he was articled to a firm of accountants, and his competition career began in 1962, driving a Lotus 7 in a BRSCC meeting at Brands Hatch. He raced at most of Britain's leading club circuits that season and gained two places. In 1963 Courage bought a Merlyn-Climax Mk 4 sports racer and had a number of minor successes with it, turning professional in 1964. He formed Anglo-Swiss Racing with Jonathan Williams and Charlie Graemiger from Lausanne, and the team raced a pair of F3 Brabham-Fords all over Europe. Successes were few, with only a 3rd at Reims and a 2nd at Zandvoort, and as yet Courage seemed just another club driver.

At the end of the 1964 season he returned to England, and Charles Lucas invited him to join his newly-formed

Above, Meo Costantini (centre), with the Bugatti team at San Sebastian in 1924. *Photo: Fotocar*

Above right, Piers Courage. *Photo: Autosport*

Below, Meo Costantini. *Photo: T. A. S. O. Mathieson Collection*

'C. Lucas Engineering'. F3 Brabham team in 1965. Courage accepted and made his mark that year, winning international Silverstone and Rouen events, coming 2nd at Goodwood and Reims and 3rd in the Monza Lottery, in addition to scoring several minor successes. Lucas ran the works Lotus 41 F3 team in 1966, and Courage was the team's most successful driver, winning at Pau, Rouen, Brands Hatch and Albi.

That was a good season and BRM took Courage and Chris Irwin to the Tasman Championship, giving them three drives each with a view to settling an F1 contract on their results. Piers was very fast but erratic and had a number of incidents, while Irwin was smooth but slightly slower — he finished, however, and got more F1 drives that season, Courage only appearing in the South African and Monaco GPs and retiring from both. He ran an F2 McLaren-Cosworth for John Coombs, coming 2nd at Zandvoort and 3rd at Hockenheim, and early in 1968 took this car to the Tasman Championship with Saccone Gin sponsorship. This was his second chance and he took advantage of it with some very fast and competent performances, winning the final round in torrential rain at Longford in addition to one 2nd and three 3rd places. Tim Parnell signed him for his private BRM in F1 racing; Frank Williams bought an F2 Brabham-Cosworth for Courage to contest the European Championship. He was 4th in the Italian GP and 6th in the French with the hardly competitive BRM V-12, and took one 1st, one 2nd and three 3rd places in Formula 2.

Williams ran a modified F1 Brabham BT24 in the 1969 Tasman Championship, powered by a 2·5-litre Cosworth V-8, and in this Courage had one victory, a 2nd and a 3rd place to finish 3rd in the standings behind Amon and Rindt. Meanwhile an F1 Brabham-Cosworth Ford BT26 was being built up. Courage did well with this, finishing 2nd in the Monaco and American GPs, and 5th in the British and Italian. He also won the F2 round at Enna, and scored five 3rd places in Williams' F2 Brabham-Cosworths.

In 1970 Williams ran the works De Tomaso-Cosworth Ford F1 cars for Courage. The De Tomaso was initially a slight disappointment for it was a very heavy car, but Piers had some success with Autodelta, including winning one of the Temporada sports car rounds in the Argentine.

He was always very competitive indeed with the 3-litre Alfa Romeo T33/3s, sharing usually with De Adamich, but the cars were unreliable.

In Formula 1 Piers and the De Tomaso became more and more in tune, taking third place in both heats of the International Trophy at Silverstone and then running seventh for many laps at Monaco before hitting trouble and finishing too far behind to be classified. In the Dutch GP at Zandvoort Courage was lying seventh and gaining on Regazzoni's Ferrari when the red De Tomaso went missing on lap 23. The car had crashed through the chicken wire on the curving back section of the course, tipping a bridge parapet and bursting into flame. There was no helping poor Piers, apparently already dead from impact injuries. DCN

Cowan, Andrew

Andrew Cowan was born in 1936 at Duns in Berwickshire, where he now lives and farms as his father did before him. He started rallying in 1959 with a Sunbeam Rapier and had considerable success in local events. He entered his first international event in 1961 when he won the Scottish Rally, a performance he was to repeat the following year with works assistance, but still in a Rapier. In 1963 he won the private entrants award in the Tulip Rally, and in 1964 on the Tour de France he drove an Alan Mann prepared Ford Mustang with Peter Proctor and won the Touring category outright.

He has been very successful in the Monte Carlo Rally, winning his class in 1967 and 1968 with a Hillman Imp. In the Scottish Rally he won his class in 1968 and 1969, when he also took 2nd place overall. Undoubtedly his best-known result was 1st place in the London to Sydney Marathon driving a Hillman Hunter with Colin Malkin and Brian Coyle. As a result of this victory he also drove a Hunter in the Southern Cross Rally in Australia in 1969 and won that too. He signed a contract with BLMC at the end of 1969 to drive Triumphs and was best Triumph in the RAC Rally that year. JD

Cummings, William

'Wild Bill' Cummings was born in 1914. This American driver was a product of the half-mile dirt tracks in Indiana and surrounding states. He moved up to AAA championship competition in 1930 and — beginning that year — drove in nine consecutive Indianapolis 500 races.

His 1934 victory at Indianapolis at a record-breaking speed of 104·863mph (168·805kph) was scored with the first winning car there since 1920 to be powered by a 4-cylinder engine, a 220ci (3,605cc) Miller which was the forerunner of the reliable Offenhauser units. He also won the National AAA driving championship the same year.

In other appearances at Indianapolis, Cummings finished 3rd in 1935, 5th in 1930, 6th in 1937 and won the pole position in the starting line up twice with superb qualifying performances. As one of the pre-race favourites in 1936, he also suffered the embarrassing experience of failing to get away from the starting line because of a faulty clutch.

Cumming's racing record also includes a 7th-place finish in the 1936 International event on the road course at Roosevelt Raceway, N.Y., and victories in 100-mile AAA championship races on dirt tracks at Syracuse, N.Y., twice; Langhorne, Pa.; Ascot, Calif., twice; and Detroit, Mich. He was killed in a highway accident near Indianapolis in 1939 when he lost control of his car on a wet surface and crashed into a bridge abutment. AB

Andrew Cowan. *Photo: BMC*

Bill Cummings. *Photo: Indianapolis Motor Speedway*

Below, Briggs Cunningham, at Le Mans in 1960. *Photo: Al Bochroch*

Below right, Briggs Cunningham in a 2-litre 'Birdcage' Maserati. *Photo: Al Bochroch*

Cunningham, Briggs Swift

Born in Cincinnati, Ohio, in 1907, Cunningham has had major careers as an auto racing driver-patron and as an internationally known salt water sailor. Before World War 2, he raced six metre boats as a US team member and in 1958 captained the victorious *Columbia* in the America Cup races against Great Britain. While attending Yale University, Cunningham met Ralph DePalma, winner of the 1915 Indianapolis 500, and became interested in automobile racing and engineering. With Charles Chayne, then chief engineer for Buick, Cunningham built the Bu-Merc, a Mercedes-Buick hybrid that Miles Collier drove at the New York World's Fair race in December 1940 and in which Cunningham finished 2nd at the 1948 Watkins Glen inaugural.

Urged by Miles and Sam Collier to mount a Le Mans challenge, Cunningham and Phil Walters drove a Cadillac Special, known affectionately by the French as 'Le Monstre', to 11th in the 1950 Le Mans. Another Cunningham entry, a stock Cadillac coupé driven by the Collier brothers, finished 10th. Cunningham returned in 1951 with three C-2R's, powered by 5·4 Chrysler engines. Only Fitch and Walters, who finished 18th, completed the 24 hours, although they had run as high as 2nd place as late as 8 am. Cunningham and Bill Spear drove a 5·5-litre Chrysler-engined-Cunningham-C-4R to 4th place in the 1952 Le Mans race and in 1953 Walters and Fitch averaged 104·039mph (167·464kph) for the 24 hours to finish 3rd. Two other Cunninghams finished in the first ten in 1953; Briggs and Bill Spear 7th and Charles Moran and John Bennett 10th. In 1954 Spear and Sherwood Johnson brought a C-4R home 3rd with Briggs and Bennett 5th. Also in 1954 Cunningham won the SCCA 'F' modified championship, driving an Osca.

Production of Cunningham cars stopped in 1955 but Briggs carried American colours to Le Mans again in the 1960s with teams of Corvettes, Maseratis and Jaguars. Among many drivers who raced cars entered by Cunningham and prepared by his adviser and head mechanic, Alfred Momo, were Stirling Moss, Walt Hansgen, Augie Pabst and Bruce McLaren. John Fitch and Bob Grossman brought a Cunningham-entered Corvette home 8th in the 1960 Le Mans race, to win GT honours.

In 1965 Cunningham opened one of the finest automobile museums in the United States. More than 80 thoroughbred cars, many with racing pedigrees, grace Cunningham's collection at Costa Mesa, Calif. ARB

Czaykowski, Count Stanislas

Of Polish origin but living in Paris, Count Czaykowski was a wealthy enthusiast who had the means to buy the best cars he needed. He always drove Bugattis, first coming to notice in the 1929 Comminges GP where he finished 4th. In 1931 he bought one of the first Type 51 Bugattis sold to a private owner, and was runner-up at Dieppe, Lorraine and Comminges, as well as scoring class wins at Dieppe, Comminges and Nimes in 1932. In 1933 Czaykowski acquired one of the difficult but very fast 4·9-litre Type 54 Bugattis. At the AVUS track he set up a new world hour record at 132·87mph (213·8kph), and broke several distance records as well. In the subsequent AVUS GP he was beaten by a mere ⅕th sec. by the great Varzi. At Brooklands he won the British Empire Trophy race from Kaye Don. After two wins in the 2-litre Bugatti (Dieppe and La Baule) he took the Type 54 to Monza and was killed in the final when the car spun off an oily section of the track and exploded. CP

Davis, Sydney Charles Houghton

'Sammy' Davis was born in London in 1887. His career as a racing driver now tends to be overshadowed by his exploits with the pen, but he displayed equal ability and versatility behind the wheel. After an apprenticeship at Daimler's, he took to journalism as a career, starting in motor sport at the same time by racing a Douglas motor-cycle and competing in trials with Cummikar and Pilot cycle-cars. As a devoted Brooklands *habitué*, his reward came when he was invited to join S. F. Edge's AC team in 1921. This was followed in 1922 with ten world and 22 national class records for Aston Martin—and on his youthful build was modelled the slender single-seater Aston known as 'Razor Blade'. In 1925 he just failed to win at Le Mans with a twin-cam Sunbeam, and the next year crashed while attempting to take the lead in his first race with the Bentley team. He crashed again in 1927, but with co-driver Benjafield nursed the crippled car to a famous victory.

In 1928 Davis raced in the fwd Alvis team at Le Mans, and with a works Riley in the Tourist Trophy. He was an 'eternal second' in 1929—in the Double-Twelve and the 500 at Brooklands, and at Phoenix Park with the Lea-Francis team—and in 1930 he gained enough placings to earn a BRDC track-racing Gold Star.

Always eager to drive different cars, Davis' career was interrupted in 1931 when an Invicta took charge at a wet Easter Brooklands meeting. The resultant inactivity merely increased his output of writing: his book *Motor*

Count Czaykowski, after winning the 1931 Moroccan GP. *Photo: Hugh Conway Collection*

Joe Dawson. *Photo: Indianapolis Motor Speedway*

Racing became a classic and an inspiration to countless schoolboys. He was well known for very many years for his regular contributions to *The Autocar*, in his own name, under the pseudonym 'Casque', and as Sports Editor. He was also an accomplished artist, and tended to illustrate his books with his own line drawings.

Davis drove with his head, and was regarded as safe and responsible, if a little unlucky, while at the same time having the ability to motor very quickly indeed when required. He had no more than his fair share of accidents, but the ones he did have became famous because he wrote about them so well. His best per-formances were in long-distance sports-car events, but besides racing and record runs, Davis participated with success in hill-climbs, rallies and veteran car events. The 1897 Léon Bollée tri-car, purchased in the early 1930s for 300 francs and christened Beelzebub, took part in numerous Brighton runs. In pre-World War 2 Monte Carlo rallies, Daimler, Armstrong-Siddeley, Railton, Talbot and Wolseley were the makes he drove. As well as competing, Davis played an important part on the organizational side, sitting on various club committees, and doing much work in the furtherance of the sport he loved. DF

Dawson, Joe

Joe Dawson was born in Indianapolis in 1889 and was only 21 years old when he was selected as a member of the Marmon racing team under the guidance of Ray Harroun in 1910. He scored three major victories during that season.

His first success was recorded in the 200-mile (321km) Cobe trophy race on 1 July at the Indianapolis Motor Speedway, which had not yet inaugurated its annual 500 events. In November of that year he also won a 200-mile race at the Atlanta Motordrome and the 200-mile Savannah Trophy Race on the 17·3-mile (27·84km) road course at Savannah, Ga.

In one other important race that year, the Vanderbilt Cup event on the Long Island Motor Parkway, he made an unscheduled stop to report a serious accident at a distant point on the course and still finished only 26 seconds behind the winner, Harry Grant in an Alco.

Dawson came 5th in the first Indy 500 on 30 May 1911, a race which Harroun won as captain of the Marmon team. The Marmon Company, however, decided to rest on its laurels following that victory and it announced its immediate withdrawal from all racing activity.

Dawson then joined the National Motor Vehicle Company's racing team a few weeks before the 1912 Indianapolis race and won it at a record-breaking speed of 78·72mph (126·69kph) when Ralph DePalma's faster Mercedes was eliminated because of a broken connecting rod while leading the field by more than five laps with only two laps to go. National, like Marmon, also dis-continued its racing programme; thereafter Dawson competed only a sporadically until he retired following a 1914 racing accident in which he sustained serious back injuries.

Dawson continued his close association with the sport until his death in 1947, however, serving as a member of the Contest Board of the American Auto-mobile Association and as its Eastern Zone Supervisor of racing. AB

Delius, Ernst von

This small, cheery, determined German driver, born in 1910, called *Kleiner* ('little one') by his intimates,

S. C. H. Davis (centre), with left, his son, Colin, and right, Don Parker; Aintree, October 1954. *Photo: Charles Dunn*

raduated to the Auto Union GP team in 1936 after
acing Dixi, Alfa Romeo, Zoller, Röhr, BMW and
RA cars.

As a new recruit to the Auto Union team containing
tuck, Rosemeyer and Varzi, Delius had little chance to
nine, and his best performance in 1936 was 2nd at
escara. Early in 1937 he and Rosemeyer went out to
outh Africa for the Springbok series, and with the aid
f a 2min 6sec start over his meteoric team-mate in the
irosvenor GP, run at Cape Town on a handicap basis,
Delius scored his one outright victory for Auto Union,
veraging 80·37mph (129·34kph) to Rosemeyer's
0·5mph (129·55kph).

A plucky driver in the difficult rear-engined cars, he
id extremely well on returning to Europe to score 3rd
t Tripoli, and 2nd in the ultra-high-speed AVUS GP,
nly 2 seconds behind winner Lang and pressing hard
espite the fact that his Auto Union was of open-
vheeled road-racing type while Lang's Mercedes was
ully streamlined. Then Delius went to the United States
vith Rosemeyer for the Vanderbilt Cup, finishing 4th,
nd returned to Europe for the 1937 German GP. There
is temerity involved him in a horrific 210kph crash
vhile duelling with Seaman along the finishing straight.
he Auto Union leapt a hump-backed bridge, landed
skew and tore off-course, taking Seaman's Mercedes
vith it. Seaman survived but the Auto Union careered
hrough a wire fence, bounced nose over tail twice, and
nded up in the Coblenz road; von Delius died in
iospital the following morning. CP

Ernst von Delius (right), with Bernd
Rosemeyer. *Photo: Cyril Posthumus Collection*

DePalma, Ralph

Ralph DePalma, who came to the United States from
taly with his parents in 1893, when only 10 years old,
arned universal recognition as one of the all-time great
lrivers of the annals of American automobile racing.
His record at Indianapolis, alone, is tremendously
mpressive. He gained even greater honours in the
iation's early road races, however, and enjoyed almost
qual success on the dirt and board tracks, as well as on
he sand at Daytona Beach, Fla.

In his 10 races at Indianapolis, where he drove seven
lifferent makes of cars (Simplex, Mercedes, Mercer,
Packard, Ballot, Duesenberg and Miller) he always ran
vith the leaders. Although his only Indy victory was
cored with a Mercedes in 1915 at an average speed of
19·84mph (144·58kph), a record not broken until 1922,
ie finished 7th or better on five other occasions and still
iolds the distinction of having led the 500 for more laps
han any other participant (613). In 1912 he was far
ahead of the field with only two laps to go when a broken
:onnecting rod prevented him from finishing at the
vheel of an earlier model Mercedes; and in 1921 he was
eading the race in a Ballot at 275 miles when he experi-
:nced a similar misfortune.

DePalma also drove for Sunbeam and FIAT in other
mportant races; and the car in which he gained his
:arly experience on dirt tracks in the New York area
Juring the 1908 season was an Allen-Kingston. He made
iis first appearance in a race of major importance later
n the same year, coming 9th for FIAT in the Savannah
Grand Prix won by Louis Wagner. DePalma continued
:o drive for FIAT with moderate success for two more
years before changing to Simplex for the inaugural 500
at Indianapolis in 1911, where he was placed 6th. By the
:nd of that year, however, he was driving the Mercedes
which carried him to many important triumphs, beginning in 1912. Following his heart-breaking defeat at

Below, Ralph DePalma. *Photo: Indianapolis
Motor Speedway*

Below right, Ralph DePalma in a 1914 GP
Vauxhall. *Photo: T. A. S. O. Mathieson
Collection*

Indianapolis, he won the 305-mile (490·8km) and 254-
mile (408·8km) road races at Elgin, Ill., as well as the
299-mile (481·2km) Vanderbilt Cup Classic with an
average speed of 68·97mph (110·99kph) at Milwaukee,
Wis., to capture his first national driving title. Two days
later, challenging Caleb Bragg's Fiat for victory on the
last lap of the 410-mile (659·8km) American Grand Prix
over the same course, DePalma was injured critically
when his car overturned.

He resumed his racing career in 1913 as captain of the
Mercer team in time to win again at Elgin, but the
DePalma-Mercer association lasted only a few months
before Ralph resigned in anger when factory officials,
without his approval, appointed Barney Oldfield to the
team. Lacking a suitable car for the start of the 1914
season, DePalma rebuilt the wrecked Mercedes, which
had been in storage, and scored another Vanderbilt
Cup victory at Santa Monica, Calif., by averaging
75·49mph (121·48kph) for the 294 miles (473·1km) to
finish 80 seconds ahead of Oldfield's Mercer.

Still driving the ageing Mercedes, DePalma qualified
for a starting position again at Indianapolis, but withdrew on the morning of the race because he was not
satisfied with the car's performance in practice. From
Indy, he headed for Europe to compete in a French
Grand Prix for the second time. In 1912, while driving
for FIAT, he had been disqualified when running 8th —
because of his unfamiliarity with refuelling regulations
— and this time he again failed to go the distance as a
member of the Vauxhall team because of mechanical
trouble. Immediately after the event, however, he
travelled to Germany and took delivery of a new
Mercedes only a few days before the outbreak of World
War 1. Back in America, he drove it to two victories in
important road races at Elgin to clinch his second
national driving title. He also won with it at Indianapolis
the following year and drove it to additional victories
in 1916 at Minneapolis, Minn., Des Moines, Iowa, and
Kansas City, Mo. before joining the engineering staff of
the Packard Motor Car Company. At Packard he worked
on the development of the famous Liberty engine and,
eventually, he helped design and build the 905ci
(14,830cc) Packard V-12 which he used to set a new
measured mile record of 149·87mph (241·21kph) at
Daytona Beach, Fla., in 1919.

He signed with Ballot in 1920, winning another
important road race at Elgin and scoring several
victories at shorter distances on the board speedways
before crossing the ocean for his third French Grand

Peter DePaolo. *Photo: Indianapolis Motor Speedway*

Albert Divo. *Photo: Cyril Posthumus Collection*

Freddie Dixon, 1935. *Photo: T. A. S. O. Mathieson Collection*

Prix in 1921 for a 2nd-place finish behind Jimmy Murphy's Duesenberg. DePalma continued to be a formidable competitor for Duesenberg, Packard and Miller in major American races for four more years with moderate success before beginning to devote most of his time to exhibition races on the smaller tracks, while also making a number of speed and endurance stock car runs for Chrysler. When the critical economic conditions of the early 1930s caused even such appearances to become unprofitable, he joined the Mobil Oil Company as a consulting engineer and remained active in that capacity until shortly before his death in 1956. AB

DePaolo, Peter

Peter DePaolo, nephew of one of auto racing's outstanding pioneer drivers, was born in the United States in 1898 and began his association with the sport immediately after World War 1 as riding mechanic for his uncle Ralph DePalma. It was 1922, however, before DePaolo made his first competitive appearance as a driver in one of Louis Chevrolet's Frontenacs; and he announced his retirement before the end of the season after wrecking the car on three different race tracks. He then spent the next 18 months as owner and operator of a service station in California, but resumed his racing career when he received an invitation to join the Duesenberg factory team for the 1924 Indianapolis event, in which he was placed 6th.

Gaining experience and confidence with each additional race, he became almost unbeatable in 1925 and finished the year as the national driving champion. His most important victories were scored at Indianapolis and on the board tracks at Fresno, Calif., Altoona, Pa., Laurel, Md., and Rockingham, N.H. His Indy triumph was particularly noteworthy because he averaged 101·13mph (162·75kph) to top the 100mph mark for the first time despite the handicap of blistered hands which caused him to relinquish the wheel to a relief driver (Norman Batten) for approximately 20 laps. During the season he also drove an Alfa Romeo in the Italian Grand Prix and came 5th.

DePaolo started the 1926 campaign with another Duesenberg victory in the 300-mile (480km) inaugural race on the Miami Beach, Fla., board speedway. In his quest for a second national championship he was outpointed by Harry Hartz and Frank Lockhart, but he won the crown again in 1927 while driving for Harry Miller. He missed most of the 1928 schedule because of critical injuries sustained in practice at Indianapolis as the result of a broken steering arm and, after being eliminated early at Indianapolis in 1929 and 1930, he 'retired' again to accept a position with the Chrysler Corporation.

Harry Miller, however, lured him back to racing with a new fwd car for the 1934 Grand Prix of Tripoli on the Mellaha circuit, where DePaolo finished 6th. He then went to Barcelona to drive a Maserati in the Grand Prix of Penya Rhin, but was seriously injured in a practice crash which caused him to abandon any other plans he may have had to continue his racing career after returning to America.

He worked for various automotive companies in subsequent years and, since 1966, has been the factory agent for the American Rubber and Plastics Company at the Ford Motor Company. AB

Divo, Albert

Albert Divo was born near Paris around 1895, and was apprenticed to an automobile works, acting as a mechanic in pre-World War 1 motorboat races at Monte Carlo. During the war he became a pilot. He began racing in 1919 for Sunbeam and then Talbot as mechanic to Réné Thomas, being given the wheel when Thomas left Talbot to drive for Delage in 1922, and managing a 2nd place in the voiturette race in the Isle of Man TT. In 1923 he was 2nd in the French GP for Sunbeam, and 1st for them at Sitges, Spain.

In 1924 he joined Delage and drove the hill-climb Delage cars to win in many sprint events in France; in main events he was 2nd in the European GP at Lyons, and 4th at San Sebastian. The following year he had an even longer list of successes in hill-climbs and sprints, and a win in the Spanish GP at San Sebastian. In 1926 he returned to Talbot but the new 1·5-litre cars were not completely ready; they ran in the British GP at Brooklands but all failed mechanically although Divo had a good race. In 1927 he again drove for Talbot but the car failed once more in the French GP, only one finishing. He then transferred to Delage for the Spanish and British GPs but was unplaced in both. At the end of the year both Talbot and Delage withdrew from racing.

Divo then transferred to Bugatti with immediate success in the 1928 Targa Florio, but had no luck in Spain. The French GP that year at Comminges was a fiasco with insufficient entries. The next year he again won the Targa Florio for Bugatti and was 4th in the Fuel Consumption French GP. He drove a Type 43 Bugatti in the TT in Ulster but was unplaced.

In 1930 he managed a 3rd for Bugatti at Spa but little else and then in 1931 he drove one of the new Type 51 twin-cam cars, but again without success.

Divo now dropped out of GP racing until the beginning of sports car racing saw him driving a Delahaye in 1936 (4th at Marseilles, but unplaced in the GP of the Automobile Club de France at Montlhéry. The following year he joined Chiron in the Talbot team and came in 3rd to Chiron winning at Montlhéry, followed by a 2nd place at the Marne GP a few weeks later. In 1939 he drove a Delahaye at Le Mans but by now his age was telling and he withdrew from racing. During World War 2 he worked for the truck firm of Latil and died, unnoticed, in Paris in November 1966. HGC

Dixon, Frederick W.

Born in Yorkshire in 1892, Freddie Dixon came to car racing from motorcycles, with which he had gained a great reputation for toughness and mechanical ingenuity. He saw the potential of the Riley engine with its twin high camshafts, short pushrods and hemispherical head, and with multi carburettors he obtained phenomenal results. His first racing car was a Riley Nine which he stripped, lightened, and fitted with a long tailed body, and entered for the 1932 Ulster TT. He astonished everyone by leading the race for four hours, when he touched a curb at Quarry Corner, and the little black Riley leapt a hedge and ended up in a garden.

With a specially streamlined single-seater Riley he took class records at Brooklands, and in 1933 he won the Mannin Beg. In 1934 he produced the famous aluminium Rileys, clean, offset single seaters with long tails. He won the 500 Mile Race at Brooklands, came 3rd at Le Mans with Cyril Paul, and in 1935 won the Ulster TT outright, and headed a 1-2-3 Riley victory in the British Empire Trophy race. In 1936 he won the TT a second time, and also the 500-Mile Race. The appearance of the ERAs ended Dixon's Riley era, but he tuned Tony Rolt's ex-Bira ERA 'Remus' with very successful

eddie Dixon in one of the aluminium
leys. *Photo: Cyril Posthumus Collection*

thur Dobson. *Photo: Cyril Posthumus
llection*

low, Kaye Don in a Crouch, c 1923.
oto: *Montagu Motor Museum*

low right, Kaye Don in the Sunbeam
ger. *Photo: William Boddy Collection*

results, and at the outbreak of war was planning a
revolutionary Land Speed Record car with 4-wheel
drive and a swash-plate engine. After World War 2
Dixon worked with Rolt on the Ferguson transmission
system. He died in 1956. CP

Dobson, Arthur

Arthur Dobson was one of the band of British amateur
drivers who enjoyed racing at Brooklands and Donington before World War 2 and who, by his dashing
character and driving style lent interest to the preceed-
ings. He appeared with a Bugatti in 1934, a 2·3 he shared
with Charlie Martin in 1935. He drove Fairfield's
1,100cc ERA in the 1936 International Trophy Race
but by 1937 had become a customer for a new ERA, a
2-litre car painted white, with which he gained a number
of notable successes, including winning the Invitation
Race for ERA at Brooklands in 1938, at 72·35mph
(116·44kph). For a time in 1937 he had held the Campbell circuit lap record with a 1·5-litre ERA at 73·13mph
(117·69kph). In 1939 he held this lap record in the 2-litre
class with his bigger ERA, at 75·57mph (121·62kph),
until this was taken from him by Raymond Mays.

Dobson was one of the faster pre-war ERA drivers
and he drove these cars and a sports Riley with distinction at the Crystal Palace, where he won two sports car
races, and at Donington Park, where he was twice 2nd
in the Nuffield Trophy Race in the ERA. Poor health
ended his racing career but he remains actively interested
in fast cars. WB

Don, Kaye

This British driver started in the sport with motorcycle
trials in 1912, but he was best known for his exploits
with cars at Brooklands. He achieved fame in the early
1920s for his courageous handling of the Wolseley
Viper, and sprang into real prominence with a marvellous
1928 season, using three special works Sunbeams (Cub,
Tiger and Tigress) and a 2·3-litre Bugatti. With one of the
4 litre V12 Sunbeams, he was the first to achieve a
130mph (209kph) lap of the Outer Circuit. He also won
a sensational Tourist Trophy at Ards, after an epic duel
between his Lea-Francis and Leon Cushman's Alvis.

Another excellent season followed in 1929, when his
forceful driving enabled him to retain the British
Championship, and great interest attended his attempt
on the Land Speed Record in 1930, with a special 24-
litre car built under Louis Coatalen at Sunbeam's. This
car, christened the 'Silver Bullet', ran at Daytona but
was sold after disappointing trials.

Don followed the steps of Segrave in taking to the
water, breaking this speed record twice in 1930 with his
'Miss England', sponsored by Lord Wakefield. He was

less fortunate in the International Trophy which he
contested with the American, Gar Wood.

In 1931 he raised the Brooklands lap record to
137·58mph(221·43kph) with the V-12 Sunbeam Tigress.
For the next three years he raced a 4·9-litre Bugatti,
known as Tiger II and painted red, as were all his vehicles.
Although modified to improve the handling, the car
proved unreliable and never as fast as Tiger I.
Although naturally cheerful, Don took his racing much
more seriously than was common in Britain in the inter-
war years, and this professionalism was not always fully
appreciated by others in the sport. He retired from active
participation in 1934, after a road accident in the Isle of
Man which led to the death of his mechanic K. Taylor
and a subsequent conviction for manslaughter. DF

Donohue, Mark

Born in Summit, N.J., in 1937, Donohue graduated
from Brown University as mechanical engineer 1959.
He drove a Corvette to a hill-climb victory in his first
event. He earned the 1961 Sports Car Club of America
'E' production national championship in an Elva
Courier after a year-long struggle with Peter Revson's
Morgan. In 1965 Donohue won the SCCA championship
in his Formula 'C' Lotus 20B and 'B' production in a
Mustang. Walt Hansgen introduced Mark to profes-
sional racing; first as his co-driver in John Mecom's
Ferrari, then as a member of Team Ford. Donohue and
Hansgen opened 1966 with a 3rd at the Daytona 24
Hours and a 2nd at Sebring.

Following Hansgen's fatal crash during the Le Mans
trials, Donohue began driving for car-dealer Roger
Penske, a former sports car champion. Donohue won
the 1967 and 1968 US Road Racing championship in
Penske's Group 7 Lola-Chevrolets. In the 1966 Can-Am
Donohue won Mosport, finishing 2nd in total points
for the six race series. Donohue twice brought the Trans-
American Sedan manufacturers' championship to
Chevrolet. Driving Penske Z-28 Camaros he won 10 of
13 Trans-Ams in 1968 and six of 12 in 1969. Chuck
Parsons teamed with Donohue to win the February
1969 Daytona 24 Hours, in spite of their Lola coupé
spending over 2 hours in the pits. Penske withdrew from
the Can-Am in 1969 and entered Donohue in the
Indianapolis 500 where Mark earned 'Rookie of the
Year' honours, qualifying Penske's 4-wheel drive Lola-
Offenhauser 4th and finished 7th.

In the 1970 '500' Donohue qualified the Penske Sunoco

Special Lola-Ford, at 168·911mph, for 5th on the grid. He finished 2nd, on the same lap with winner Al Unser, winning $86,440. In the Trans-Am series Penske switched to American Motors where Donohue won Bridgehampton, Road America and St Jovite. Donohue and team-mate Peter Revson brought the Penske AMC Javelins home second to the works Ford-Mustangs. Donohue entered the final three Continental races in a Lola T192-Chevrolet, winning Mosport and Sebring and finishing 3rd at Mid-Ohio. He is a director of the proposed Chesapeake International Raceway, which he designed. He lives in Media, Pa. with his wife and two sons. ARB

Dreyfus, René

René Dreyfus was born in Nice in 1905, the son of a wealthy linen merchant. He began racing with a small Mathis in 1925, but then became a Bugatti enthusiast, first racing a Brescia and then a 35B. He joined Ernest Friderich in his Bugatti agency at Nice, and encouraged by Friderich was 8th in the 1928 Targa Florio and had his first big victory in 1929 at Dieppe in the 37A, with which he also came 5th in the Monaco GP. For 1930 at Monaco, Friderich secured for him a works prepared 2·3 Type 35B, on which Dreyfus won in an all-Bugatti finish from Chiron and Bouriat and established his name, defeating the official works team. An additional fuel tank enabled him to run non-stop.

A two-year period with the works Maserati team brought him little but bad luck, and he was less successful than the other team driver, Fagioli, showing only a 2nd place in a Maserati 1-2-3 in the Prix Royal of Rome at Littorio in 1931 and a lap record at the AVUS with the 'Sedici Cilindri' at 130·87mph (210·61kph) in 1932. In 1933 he joined the works Bugatti team and in a Type 51 was 3rd in the Belgian GP to Nuvolari's Maserati and Varzi's Bugatti, and 3rd at Monaco to Varzi (Bugatti) and Borzacchini (Alfa Romeo). In 1934 he was 3rd at Monaco behind Moll and Chiron's P3 Alfas in a 2·8-litre Type 59 Bugatti. In the Swiss GP in a 3·3-litre Type 59 he was 3rd behind the Auto Unions and 4th at Vichy, and he won the Belgian GP from Brivio's Bugatti and Sommer's Maserati at Spa.

In 1935, now a married man, he joined the Ferrari

Mark Donohue. *Photo: Professionals in Motion Inc*

Left below, René Dreyfus, 1928. *Photo: Hugh Conway Collection*

Right below, René Dreyfus, admiring a Type 35 Bugatti at Bridgehampton. *Photo: Al Bochroch*

Alfa Romeo team, won the Dieppe and Marne GPs an was 2nd in the Italian GP sharing a 3·8-litre P3 with Nuvolari and splitting the Auto Unions. He was 3rd a Nice, behind team-mates Nuvolari and Chiron. In 1936 he was 3rd in the Coppa Ciano in an 8C-35 from team-mates Nuvolari and Brivio and 4th in the Italian GP at Monza in a 12C-36. In this year he went to Talbo to help them develop their sports cars, and was 3rd in Marne GP for unsupercharged sports cars behind the Bugattis of Wimille and Benoist.

In 1937 he signed to drive Delahaye sports cars, but also had a highly successful season with a 6CM 1·5-litre Maserati voiturette, winning at Tripoli and Florenc and coming 2nd at Péronne and Turin. For Delahaye he was 3rd at the Pau GP sports car race behind Wimill Bugatti and Sommer's Talbot, and 3rd at Le Mans wit Stoffel.

In 1938 in a 12-cylinder GP 4·5-litre Delahaye he ha a great victory at Pau, beating Lang's Mercedes, and h won the Cork GP from the 'Bira' Maserati and Louis Gerard's Delage, and became Champion of France.

He joined the French army in 1939, and while on leave in 1940 came 10th at Indianapolis in an 8CTF Maserati with René Le Bègue. As France fell to the Germans while he was in the United States, he stayed there and opened a restaurant in New Jersey. In 1941 h tried to join the American army after Pearl Harbor, an was accepted in 1942, taking part in the Salerno landin in 1944. In 1945 he opened a restaurant, Le Gourmet, New York, but sold it in 1952 after the death of his seco wife and returned to France. Here he drove a 4·1-litre Ferrari at Le Mans with 'Heldé', but retired after 4 hou with clutch trouble. In January 1953, with brother Maurice and sister Suzanne he opened his famous Le Chanteclair Restaurant at 18 East 49 Street, New York which flourishes today. PMAH

Dubonnet, André

This French driver was born in 1897 and made his deb in 1921, when he scored a splendid victory in the Coup Georges Boillot at Boulogne in a Hispano-Suiza. The quality of his driving soon had its reward for, when Ingibert crashed his Duesenberg during practice for the Grand Prix a month later, on Charles Faroux's recom-

mendation Dubonnet was offered his place in the Duesenberg team. Numerous eyebrows were raised at this surprise choice, but Dubonnet confounded his critics by finishing 4th in the GP after a fine exhibition of driving.

In 1922 he crashed in the Coupe Georges Boillot, run in appalling weather conditions, and was lucky to escape unhurt, but made up for this by winning the Gran Premio d'Autumno at Monza, defeating a large field of cars in his Hispano Suiza, which had been modified to his own ideas.

Dubonnet won the Grand Prix Tourismo Guipuzcoa at San Sebastian in 1923, and in 1924 took part in the Targa Florio and Coppa Florio races in Sicily. The Hispano-Suiza with its long wheelbase was not the ideal car for this winding mountain circuit but Dubonnet, pitted against the finest drivers in Europe, and against no fewer than six works teams, gave a magnificent exhibition of driving ability by finishing 6th in the Targa and 5th in the Coppa.

With the introduction of the Type 35 Bugatti, Dubonnet had found the ideal machine and in 1926 finished 5th in the Targa Florio. As a result of these efforts as an independent, Bugatti invited him to drive in the Grand Prix d'Alsace, and a few weeks later he acted as a reserve driver to the Delage team in the British GP at Brooklands. In both these races he was successful, winning the former and taking 3rd place, with Benoist, in the latter. In 1927 he joined the Bugatti team and finished 6th in the Targa Florio, 2nd in the San Sebastian GP. In 1928, after winning the Bugatti GP at Le Mans, he retired from active competition. During the period he was racing, Dubonnet was undoubtedly France's leading amateur driver, quite capable of holding his own with the best professionals.

In later years Dubonnet designed a successful independent front-wheel suspension, which was adopted by both General Motors and by Alfa Romeo, who used it on their racing cars. He also produced two prototype cars incorporating a number of advanced ideas. TASOM

Duff, John

Although he drove a number of different makes, John Duff will always be remembered as the first British driver

Above, André Dubonnet. *Photo: Cyril Posthumus Collection 1921*

Above right, George Duller in a supercharged Austin Seven, 1925. *Photo: Montagu Motor Museum*

Below, John Duff in the Elcar Miller in which he finished 10th at Indianapolis in 1926. *Photo: Indianapolis Motor Speedway*

Below right, George Duller with a supercharged Austin Seven, 1932. *Photo: William Boddy Collection*

to win the Le Mans 24 Hour Race. He first drove at Le Mans in the inaugural race of 1923, when with Frank Clement he finished 4th in a 3-litre Bentley. The following year he and Clement won the race at a speed of 53·7mph (86·4kph). Encouraged by this success, Bentley Motors entered two cars for Le Mans in 1925, with Duff and Clement driving No 2, but engine trouble put them out after thirteen hours. In September 1925 Duff made two successful record attempts at Montlhéry with Bentleys, the 1,000 miles with Dr. Benjafield, and the 24 hours with Woolf Barnato.

In 1926 Duff went to America where he drove an Elcar Miller at Indianapolis. He was in 10th place when rain caused the race to be stopped at 400 miles. He remained in America to drive four races on the board tracks at Altoona, Pa, Atlantic City, N.J., Charlotte, N.Car, and Rockingham, N.H. His best performance was at Altoona where he finished 3rd. Unfortunately at Rockingham he crashed badly, and was so seriously injured that he never raced again. He died in 1958. TASOM

Duller, George

A British driver who made his name as a steeplechase jockey before he so much as saw a racing car. He turned to motor racing and was very much one of the Parry Thomas era. He also persuaded his wife to race occasionally. Duller drove a number of different cars,

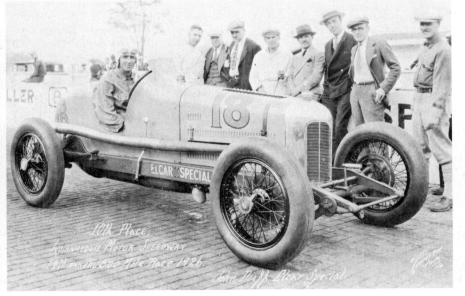

including the Marlborough Thomas, but he is mainly remembered for his exploits with a Grand Prix Bugatti. Before this he had driven a Silver Hawk for Capt Macklin, an Ansaldo, a pre-1914 Sunbeam, and other machines at Brooklands in the 1920s. Apart from his participation in the shorter races, Duller covered the greatest distance in the 1927 Essex MC Six-Hour Sports Car Race at Brooklands, driving a dohc 3-litre Sunbeam. From that the versatile Duller went over to record breaking with a Riley Nine. He also took his place in the 'invincible' Talbot-Darracq team, winning the 1925 Grand Prix de l'Ouverture at Montlhéry in one of these 1·5-litre cars from which the supercharger had purposely been removed; drove a supercharged Darracq into 2nd place in the 1924 200 Miles Race of the JCC; and shared with Frank Clement the 4½-litre Bentley which won the 1927 Paris sports car 24-hour race at Montlhéry, at 52·1mph (83·85kph). Duller was also associated with Gwenda Stewart and her road-racing Derby-Maserati. WB

Duray, Arthur

Arthur Duray was born in 1881 in New York of Belgian parentage, though he assumed French nationality later in life. He began his long racing career in 1902 with Gobron-Brilliés, but had little success with them. However he put up the fastest flying start kilometre time to date (in effect the World Land Speed Record) at Ostend in 1903 with a speed of 83·47mph (134·33kph), and improved this figure a few months later to 84·73mph (136·36kph). In 1904 Duray moved to Darracq; he led the field on the first lap of the Circuit des Ardennes, then dropped back to finish only 6th. His best performance that year was 4th in the Coppa Florio, and for 1905 he moved on to de Dietrich. The 1905 season was not particularly distinguished, but in 1906 he achieved his first victory, winning the Circuit des Ardennes at 65.8mph (105·9kph). His 3rd place in the Vanderbilt Cup the same year was made memorable by his splendid gesture in retrieving both his mechanic and a spare rim when man and component all but went overboard on a corner. In 1907 and 1908 he continued to drive for de Dietrich, but although he led the 1907 Grand Prix for a while he had no victories.

During the 'interregnum' of Grand Prix racing Duray drove an Excelsior voiturette in 1911, and a 3-litre Alcyon in the 1912 Coupe de l'Auto, and drove for Delage in the 1913 Grand Prix de France and 1914 French Grand Prix. He also returned to record breaking with the immense 28·4-litre Fiat S76 with which he covered a flying kilometre at Ostend at 132·37mph (213·01kph). It was not recognised as an official record as he never did a return run. In 1914 Duray drove a Coupe de l'Auto Peugeot at Indianapolis, and finished in 2nd place.

After World War 1 Duray moved on to touring cars, driving a Voisin in the 1922 Touring Car Grand Prix in which he finished 2nd. From 1924 to 1928 he drove Excelsior and Ariès touring cars at Boulogne and Le Mans with no great success, but 1927 saw a final victory in the voiturette race at Boulogne in a 6-cylinder 1,100cc supercharged Amilcar. His last major race was the 1928 Boillot Cup in which he drove an Ariès into 7th place. Duray died in 1954. MCS

Eaton, George

Eaton was born in Toronto in 1945, youngest of four brothers whose family own Canada's largest chain of department stores. He first raced in 1965 and soon

Arthur Duray, 1907 French GP. *Photo: T. A. S. O. Mathieson Collection*

George Eaton. *Photo: Al Bochroch*

Opposite, Nürburgring: Jack Brabham (Brabham BT24) and Chris Amon (Ferrari) in the 1967 German GP. *Photo: Geoff Goddard*

S. F. Edge (right), with John Weller and John Portwine, founders of AC Cars Ltd, at Brooklands, c 1922. *Photo: Montagu Motor Museum*

gained Dominion-wide attention driving a Cobra and McLaren Mk 3. Following good performances in the 1968 Can-Am, young Eaton finished 5th in the 1969 series, winning $51,300. He joined the BRM Formula 1 team in October 1969 at Watkins Glen and drove both F1 and Can-Am for BRM in 1970. A 13th in the French GP at Clermont-Ferrand in F1 and a 3rd at the St Jovite Can-Am in the BRM Group 7, P154, were his best 1970 finishes. ARB

Edge, Selwyn Francis

S. F. Edge's motor-racing career was brief (1899–1904), but he won Britain her first major victory on the Continent, and was perhaps the greatest of that generation of super-publicists that dominated the British motoring scene in the early years of the 20th century.

His first race was the 1899 Paris–Bordeaux on a De Dion tricycle, but he had to retire. Meanwhile his Motor Power Co. had taken over the agency for the new Napier car, and Edge devoted the next thirteen years to promoting the make; and, from 1904 onwards, the 6-cylinder engine with which Napiers were to become increasingly identified. Their 16hp 4-cylinder car was used by Edge to contest the Paris–Toulouse–Paris that year, but he once again retired.

In 1901 came that large and expensive mistake, the 50hp of over 17 litres' capacity. Edge tried hard with this one, but was disqualified from the Gordon Bennett Cup because he did not use British tyres (which failed to stand the weight), retiring in the Paris–Bordeaux and Paris–Berlin alike. A timed kilometre between Chartres and Ablis at 69mph (111·04kph) and a class win at Gaillon were his sole rewards.

A more modest 30hp was Montague Napier's contribution to the 1902 season, and Edge drove this in the Gordon Bennett Cup, run concurrently with the Paris–Vienna. It was not a particularly fast car, but it outlasted the French challengers and Edge won the Cup for Great Britain. On the strength of his victory, Edge was offered a place in the 1903 British team without having to run in the Eliminating Trials, but in the Irish race his 80hp Napier finished last and was then disqualified. After 1904 he acted as non-driving captain to the Napier team. A 6-cylinder Napier racer made its first appearance in 1905, and with the opening of Brooklands Motor Course in 1907 Edge's Napiers settled down to two successful seasons the first of these alone recording 12 wins. Further, Edge himself used a stripped 6-cylinder touring model to cover 1,582 miles in 24 hours at Brooklands, his average being 65·91mph (106·08kph).

In 1908 it looked as if the make was going to return to major events when Edge entered a team of cars for the French GP, but the ACF barred their Rudge-Whitworth wire wheels, and he withdrew them in a fit of pique. Soon afterwards Napier gave up racing altogether, and after his breach with the company in 1913 Edge abandoned the motor trade (by agreement) until 1921, when he took over the direction of the AC company at Thames Ditton, Surrey.

Once again Edge devoted himself to an energetic publicity campaign, but he did not race himself. In July 1922, however, he sought to break his 1907 24-Hour record at Brooklands. As racing at night was now forbidden, the attempt had to be made in two 12-hour stages, and Edge chose a 30/40hp 6-cylinder Spyker; AC unfortunately, had as yet nothing suitable. He beat the old Napier's performance comfortably with a speed of 74·27mph (119·52kph).

S. F. Edge in the 30hp Napier, winner of the 1902 Gordon Bennett Cup. *Photo: Veteran Car Club of Great Britain*

Opposite, Rouen-Les Essarts Circuit: Pedro Rodriguez (BRM) leads John Surtees (Honda) in the 1968 French GP. *Photo: Geoff Goddard*

The collapse of AC Cars Ltd in 1929 was a severe blow from which he never really recovered. Edge's last appearance on a racing car was at the opening of the Campbell Circuit at Brooklands in 1937, when he drove Earp's 1903 Gordon Bennett Trials Napier on the track. He died in 1940. MCS

Elford, Victor

This British driver was born in Peckham, London, in 1935. He served a five-year apprenticeship with the South Eastern Gas Board, and became a sales engineer, later moving on to sell life insurance. Vic Elford's competition career began in the late 1950s, in minor club rallies organized by the Sevenoaks & District MC. David Seigle-Morris was an active member of that club and Elford joined him as rally navigator.

In 1961 he began racing Minis, but rallying was still his speciality, and he was lent a rally-prepared DKW for 1962 on the condition that he would pay for any damage he caused. He did well in this car in the Tulip Rally, and he became a member of the Standard-Triumph works team until 1964, when he started a three-year contract with Ford of Dagenham. He was an extremely fast rally driver, but inclined to overdo things occasionally. Huschke von Hanstein of Porsche lent him a car for the Tour de Corse, and he joined their works team in 1967. He proved his ability as a racing driver that season by dominating the 2-litre British saloon car class in a

Vic Elford. *Photo: Peter Roderick Ltd*

Porsche 911, entered by Porsche Cars (GB), and he won the 1968 Monte Carlo Rally with David Stone.

Porsche gave the ambitious Elford a drive at Le Mans in 1967; he shared a 906 with the Dutchman Ben Pon. He was in their regular long-distance team in 1968, and shared the winning car at Daytona with Neerpasch, Siffert, Stommelen and Herrmann. He and Neerpasch were 2nd at Sebring, and 3rd at Brands Hatch in the BOAC 500. He won the Nürburgring 1,000 kilometres, sharing a new Porsche 908 3-litre car with Siffert, and drove brilliantly to make up lost time and win the Targa Florio (with Maglioli).

Elford's single-seater début was made in the Eifel-rennen Formula 2 race, driving a Protos-Cosworth, and Colin Crabbe's Antique Automobiles organization gave him a Formula 1 drive in 1969, initially with an obsolete Cooper-Maserati and later with the McLaren-Ford M7B. He underlined his versatility (having taken part in the Daytona 500 stock car race early that year) by going very well in the McLaren, finishing 5th in the French GP and 6th in the British. Near disaster struck when he crashed into the wreckage of Andretti's German GP accident, destroying the McLaren and ending up in hospital with a badly fractured arm. This effectively laid him low for the rest of the season but he had already come 2nd in the BOAC 500 (with Attwood) and Targa Florio (with Maglioli again), and 3rd in the Francor-champs and Nürburgring 1,000 kilometres (with Ahrens).

Elford retired from rallying after the 1969 Monte Carlo event to concentrate on circuit racing. In 1970 Vic won the Nürburgring 1000km for Porsche Salzburg, the 500km for Chevron, four minor victories, and four long-distance placings. He also drove the AVS Shadow and Chaparral in Can-Am. DCN

Etancelin, Philippe

Born in Rouen in 1896, Etancelin, or 'Phi Phi' to his friends, began his career in 1926 competing in hill-climbs and speed trials in north-west and central France with his Bugatti.

In 1927 he scored his first big victory, winning the Grand Prix de la Marne at Reims, following this up with 3rd place in the Coupe Florio in Brittany.

He did not race in 1928 but in 1929 he competed in events all over France, winning the Prix de Conseil Général at Antibes, the Grand Prix de la Marne for the second time, the Grand Prix de Comminges and the Grand Prix de La Baule.

In 1930 he won the Algerian GP, and returning to France he finished 3rd in the Lyons GP and won the Circuit de Dauphiné at Grenoble. He also won the French GP at Pau.

In 1931 the Type 51 Bugatti was introduced and a number of independents rushed to buy it. Not so Etancelin who decided to wait, having heard of the new Alfa Romeo that was due to appear. He therefore started the season, with his old Bugatti, in the Tunis GP where he was forced to retire. He won the Circuit of Esterel Plage at St Raphael and was 2nd in the Casablanca GP. The *grandes epreuves* in 1931 were 10-hour races requiring two drivers. For these events Etancelin teamed up with his old friend and rival Marcel Lehoux. At Monza they made a brilliant showing in the latter's Bugatti in the early stages of the Italian GP but were forced to retire, and the same fate overtook them in the French GP at Monthléry. Shortly after Etancelin took delivery of the new Alfa Romeo he had ordered and finished 4th with it at Reims. The remainder of the season was a triumph for he won, in succession, the Dieppe GP, the Circuit de Dauphiné, and the Comminges GP.

In 1932 Etancelin, again driving an Alfa Romeo, competed in eight Grands Prix in France and North Africa, winning at Picardy.

The next season Etancelin, still faithful to Alfa Romeo, won the GP of Picardy for the second time. After a terrific battle with Campari (Maserati) in the French Grand Prix at Monthléry he finished 2nd, and 2nd also at Nîmes. He returned to winning form at Reims, beating Wimille by 1/5th of a second.

A new Grand Prix formula was introduced in 1934 and to comply with it Etancelin bought the latest 3-litre Maserati. With this car he finished 2nd at Casablanca; retired at Monaco after harrying the Ferrari Alfa Romeos for over half the race; came 2nd in the GP of Montreux; and for the first time took part in the 24-hour race at Le Mans where, partnered by Chinetti in an Alfa Romeo, he finished 1st. He retired in the French GP where the new Mercedes-Benz and Auto Unions created a sensation, but soundly trounced the Ferrari and Alfa Romeo at Dieppe where he scored a magnificent victory. He was 2nd at Nice.

Realizing that the independent had little chance of success, Etancelin joined the Scuderia Sub-Alpina in 1935 but as his new 3·7-litre Maserati was not ready, drove his 3-litre in the opening race at Pau. At Monaco, however, with the new car, he fought a terrific duel with Caracciola (Mercedes-Benz) for 2nd place but, having 'seen off' his rival his brakes began to fade and he could only finish 4th. At Tunis he was 3rd but at Tripoli, the AVUS and the Eifelrennen his car was outclassed by the Mercedes-Benz and Auto Union teams, and in the Grand Prix of Penya Rhin he retired. For the Grand Prix de la Marne he was entrusted with the new V-8 4·4-litre Maserati, but having finished 2nd in his heat was forced to retire in the final. Reverting to the 3·7-litre for the German Grand Prix he was, as at the AVUS and Eifelrennen, outclassed by the opposition. The 1936

season began well for Etancelin for he won the Grand Prix of Pau on the V-8 Maserati but his bad luck returned for he failed to finish at Monaco, Tripoli and Tunis taking no further part in racing that year.

With the advent of sports car racing in France, and the domination of Grand Prix racing by the German teams, Etancelin went into temporary retirement. He did not appear again until 1938 when he joined the Talbot team partnering Chinetti at Le Mans, but the pair did not finish. In the French GP he had no better luck, but remained with the Talbot team in 1939 finishing 3rd at Pau and 4th in the French GP at Reims.

After World War 2 Etancelin, as full of enthusiasm as in his younger days, drove an Alfa Romeo in the first post war race to be held in France, the Coupe des Prisonniers in the Bois de Boulogne. He showed his old fire until his car could stand the pace no longer. It was not until 1948, however, that he was able to obtain one of the new Talbots, but with this he was 2nd in the Albi GP.

In 1949 he had a successful season, winning the Grand Prix de Paris, at Monthléry, and finishing 2nd in the Grands Prix of Marseille, of Europe at Monza, and Czechoslovakia.

The next year was disappointing for Etancelin took part in all the leading races but his best performance was 4th in the Grands Prix de Penya Rhin and Pescara. But 1951 was slightly better with a 2nd at Zandvoort, a 3rd at Pescara, and a 5th at Pau and in the Grand Prix de Paris.

With the greater number of races in 1952 being for Formula 2, Etancelin did not compete in so many events as in previous years but he was 3rd in the 200 miles race at Boreham and 5th in the Ulster Trophy. There were even fewer Formula 1 races in 1953 but he managed to finish 3rd in the Rouen GP and shared the wheel of a Talbot with Levegh in the 12-Hour Grand Prix of Casablanca, the pair finishing 3rd. At the end of the season he retired.

Undoubtedly Etancelin will rank as one of the best

Below left, Philippe Etancelin has a wheel changed on his Talbot-Lago during the 1951 Dutch GP in which he finished 2nd. *Photo: John Schaepman*

Below, Philippe Etancelin at Silverstone, 1951. *Photo: A. R. Smith*

drivers that France has ever produced and will always be remembered for his very fast and forceful driving, sparing his car nothing, his one determination being to obtain the lead and remain there until the end of the race. When the pioneer custom of wearing a cloth cap back to front had long since passed out of general use Etancelin clung to his, which made him easily distinguishable. Even after crash helmets became obligatory he managed to combine both. TASOM

Eyston, Capt. George Edward Thomas

Few living men have established more records, with more types of car, than this versatile Briton, born in 1897. He has held the Land Speed Record three times— 312·2mph (502·4kph) in 1937, 345·5mph (556·6kph) and 357·5mph (575·3kph) in 1938; the World 1-Hour four times—130·72 miles (210·33km) in 1932, 133·01 miles (214·02km) in 1934, 159·30 miles (256·3km) in 1935, and 162·53 miles (261·55km) in 1936; the World 12 Hours three times—143·98mph (231·653kph) in 1935, 149·02mph (239·83kph) in 1936, and 163·68mph (263·43kph) in 1937; the World 24 Hour twice—140·52mph (226·13kph) in 1935, and 149·19mph (240·14kph) in 1936; the World 48 Hour twice—116mph (186·7kph) in 1934, and 136·34mph (219·46kph) in 1936. His diesel records include the flying start kilometre at 128·70mph (207·1kph) in 1934, and at 158·67mph (225·41kph) in 1936.

From 1926 to 1954, Eyston took literally hundreds of records at Brooklands, Montlhéry, Pendine and the Utah salt flats with cars ranging in size from an unsupercharged 750cc MG Midget to the mammoth 73-litre, 4,500bhp *Thunderbolt*, which had three axles, eight wheels, and weighed nearly 7 tons. His other record cars include Bugatti, Riley, Alfa Romeo, Sunbeam, Singer, Panhard et Levassor, Hotchkiss, Delage, Bentley, the diesel-powered *Black Magic* and *Flying Spray*, and the 25-litre *Speed of the Wind*.

Eyston raced motorcycles under an assumed name while still a schoolboy. After a most distinguished World War 1 career he rode twice in the motorcycle Belgian GP, then took up car racing in 1923, mainly with Aston Martins. In his first year he was lapping Brooklands at over 100mph (160kph), and came 4th in the 200 Miles despite constant plug trouble, equalling Joyce's fastest lap. After his marriage in 1924 he turned to hydroplane racing for a time, with considerable success. By 1926 he was back in motor racing to gain many awards with various Bugattis until 1929, when he drove Alfa Romeo, Lea-Francis, Maserati and Riley cars with similar success. From 1933 to 1935 he raced MGs, with an occasional return to Alfa, before deciding to concentrate on record-breaking. He was also seen occasionally with OM, 2-litre GP Sunbeams, and the ingenious Halford Special.

Although Eyston is not considered primarily a racing driver, he had many achievements on the track including 2nd (with Ivanowski) in the 1929 Spa 24 Hours; 2nd in the 1932 Ulster TT; 1st in the 1934 British Empire Trophy; 2nd in the 1930 Saorstat Cup; 1st in the 1927 La Baule GP; 2nd in the 200 Miles of 1928. Many lesser Brooklands awards included the Gold Vase and Founders' Gold Cup of 1927. The 1932 British Empire Trophy brought a classic duel with Cobb, Eyston's 8-litre Panhard finishing just 1/5sec behind the V-12 Delage, which won at an average of 126·36mph (203·4kph) in the first (and fastest) of the entire series. In the Brooklands 500 Miles, Eyston's car led on four occasions only to

retire—in 1929, 1932, 1933 and 1934. He has driven in almost every classic race, in places as far apart as Czechoslovakia and North Africa.

Eyston won the *Light Car* Trophy in 1927, gained his Brooklands 120mph badge in 1929, won the BRDC Gold Star in 1931, the 130mph badge in 1932, was awarded the AIACR Gold Medal in 1935, and the Segrave Trophy in 1936.

A skilled and qualified engineer, Eyston has always worked in close co-operation with the designers of his record cars. He was responsible for the successful Powerplus supercharger. When *Thunderbolt* broke its clutch on its first appearance in 1937, in less than two weeks Eyston designed a new one, fitted it, and took the Land Speed Record at the Bonneville Salt Flats Utah. He then had the car lightened considerably, converting from leaf to coil springs, and raised the record again in August 1938. Immediately he began converting to ice cooling, blanking off the air intake and removing the tail fin to reduce drag. When Cobb beat his record in September, Eyston was able to regain it the following day by adding 12mph (19·31kph) to his own earlier speed.

When Gardner's car retired from record-breaking in 1952, Eyston persuaded MG to build one of similar shape on an MGA chassis, with unsupercharged TF engine bored out to 1,500cc. With this, in 1954, he averaged 120·74mph (194·26kph) for 12 hours. This was his last drive. He then directed all subsequent MG record attempts at Utah including the last, in 1959.

Eyston has also achieved much in other spheres; he has sculled with distinction, reached Olympic standard as a yachtsman, and held a pilot's licence until the age of 70. He was involved in the planning of the Normandy landings in 1944, and was awarded the OBE in January 1948. He is a Knight of the Sovereign Order of Malta, and a Chevalier of the Légion d'Honneur. FWMCC

Fagioli, Luigi

This Italian driver, born in 1898, whose long career began in 1925, first came into prominence in 1926 by his victory in the 1,100cc class of the Premio Perugina del Turismo, and until the end of 1929 when he joined Maserati, he confined his activities to this class, always driving a Salmson. In 1927 he came 2nd in the Targa

Capt George Eyston in the MG EX120 750cc record car, 1931. *Photo: F. Wilson McComb Collection*

Capt George Eyston. *Photo: F. Wilson McComb Collection*

Florio, the Coppa Perugina and the Circuit of Pescara, then in 1928 he had a splendid season, winning no fewer than eleven events, these including the circuits of Caserta, Modena, Mugello, Rimini, the Targa Abruzzo, Senigallia and the Coppa Principe di Piemonte. The remaining victories were in hill-climbs.

In 1929 Fagioli was 2nd in the Tripoli GP; 1st in the circuit of Pozzo, and 2nd in the Three Provinces circuit —in this last event he drove a Maserati. In 1930 he was a member of the official Maserati team, and among other successes he won the circuits of Principe di Piemonte and Montenero, and the Coppa Castelli Romani.

Fagioli remained with Maserati in 1931, scoring a brilliant victory in the Monza GP. He also won the 1,100cc class of the Three Provinces circuit in his Salmson, for the second year in succession.

In 1932 he became No 1 driver for Maserati and was entrusted with the 4-litre 16-cylinder car, originally built in 1929 and now considerably modified, for races for which it was suitable such as the Rome GP run over the Littorio Autodrome where he scored an easy victory both in his heat and in the final. In the Italian Grand Prix at Monza he was 2nd in the 16-cylinder, only poor pit work robbing him of victory. He also won his heat and was 2nd in the final of the Monza GP.

Fagioli started the 1933 season with Maserati, retiring at Tunis, Monaco and Tripoli, and then left to join the Scuderia Ferrari where his luck changed, for Alfa Romeo had just released a number of the famous monoposto cars to this organization. In succession he now won the Grands Prix of Pescara, Comminges, Marseilles and Italy, finishing the season with 2nd places in the Grands Prix of Czechoslovakia and Spain. This highly successful year, despite the disappointing start, brought Fagioli to the attention of Alfred Neubauer, the Mercedes-Benz team manager, on the look out for a possible substitute for Caracciola if the latter, after his severe accident at Monaco in 1933, was unable to stand the strain of a long season of racing. Fagioli was, therefore, engaged for 1934, and found himself as no 2 driver in the best organized and most experienced racing team in the world, with a new car of somewhat revolutionary design.

The Eifelrennen, at the Nürburgring, was the Mercedes-Benz team's first race, and from the start Fagioli found himself subject to team discipline, and team orders, which he was expected to obey. During the race he had to play second fiddle to von Brauchitsch, his team-mate, a good but rather inexperienced driver, not in the same class as himself. Infuriated at not being permitted to pass von Brauchitsch he left his car out on the circuit, returning to the pits on foot.

Despite this inauspicious start to the season Fagioli finished 2nd in the German GP, won the Coppa Acerbo at Pescara, the Italian GP with Caracciola, the Spanish GP at San Sebastian and was 2nd in the Swiss GP, retiring in the French GP at Monthléry. In 1935 he again drove for Mercedes, having another successful season and winning at Monaco, the AVUS and at Barcelona; 2nd with von Brauchitsch in the Belgian GP after being called into the pits for disobeying team orders, his car being taken over for the remainder of the race by his team-mate.

In spite of his disagreements with authority, Fagioli remained with Mercedes-Benz in 1936, taking 3rd place at Tripoli and 4th at Berne. Because of the inferior road holding of the 1936 Mercedes-Benz, the racing programme was considerably curtailed, the team taking part in fewer races than in the two previous years.

In 1937 Fagioli left Mercedes-Benz and joined Auto Union, for whom he was 5th at Tripoli. Because of illness he was unable to take part in the Eifelrennen, nor in the German and Monaco Grands Prix, but was fit in time to finish 4th at Pescara. He did not race in either 1938 or 1939.

After World War 2 Fagioli returned to racing, joining the Alfa Romeo team in 1950. He had a successful season, finishing 2nd in the European GP at Silverstone, the Swiss GP, the Belgian GP and the French GP, and 3rd in the Coppa Acerbo at Pescara and in the Italian GP. In his own Osca he won the 1,100cc class in the Mille Miglia, was 2nd in the 1,100cc class in the Circuit of Garda and 3rd in the Formula 2 race at Naples. He remained with Alfa Romeo in 1951 but drove only once, when he shared the winning car with Fangio in the European Grand Prix at Reims. In 1952 he was 3rd in the Mille Miglia in a Lancia, winning the 2-litre class but, during practice for the sports car race at Monaco, he crashed, dying several weeks later as a result of his injuries.

Luigi Fagioli, the 'Old Abruzzi Robber' as he was affectionately known to his many friends, was perhaps too much of an individualist to make an ideal team driver; even so he must rank as one of the greatest drivers ever produced by that country of fine drivers, Italy, and his magnificent record speaks for itself. TASOM

Luigi Fagioli. *Photo: Cyril Posthumus Collection*

Fairman, John Eric George

Jack Fairman was a driver of exceptional versatility. He was born in 1913, his career spanned a considerable period, and he earned a reputation as one who could be relied upon to go quickly without taking unnecessary risks. He was widely respected also as a test driver, where his engineering knowledge and experience of a variety of cars stood him in good stead. Tall, good-looking and debonair, he brought to the circuits a touch of the pre-war English amateur driver. He maintained an amateur outlook while serving as a member of works teams, acting at the same time as managing director of a precision tool business.

Fairman bought a Type 35C Bugatti with his demobilization gratuity, and raced this in 1947 and 1948. In 1949 he was co-driver with Stallebrass in an Aston Martin at Spa; drove his own 6-cylinder Riley in smaller events; and was a member of the HRG team at Le Mans. In 1950 he had some drives in Tony Rolt's 3·4-litre Alfa Romeo, and in 1951 he joined the works Jaguar team, co-driving with Stirling Moss in the C-type which led at Le Mans until put out by engine failure. In the smaller sports class he also drove a 2-litre Frazer Nash.

In 1952 he continued to drive Jaguars, and also drove Allards in many events, though plagued with mechanical troubles. In both 1953 and 1954 he drove in the Bristol team at Le Mans, continuing to drive Jaguars and HWMs in other events, and a Borgward in the saloon class. The following year he was instrumental in the development of the Connaught GP car, in which he held the lap record at Silverstone for a time. Once again he competed at Le Mans as a member of the Bristol team, finishing 9th with Tommy Wisdom, and in 1956 continued to drive for Connaught and Jaguar. He became a member of the Ecurie Ecosse team for the next two years, competing in both the Monza 500 races.

For 1959 and 1960 he drove for Aston Martin with considerable success, also using Coopers in single-seat racing. From this time on his energies were directed more towards testing than racing, doing 'Track Tests'

Jack Fairman. *Photo: Pace*

for *Autosport*, and helping in the development of the Ferguson and the projected Serenissima V-8. He was entered to drive a Buick-engined car at Indianapolis in 1962, but failed to start after another driver had crashed the car in practice. DF

Fall, Tony

One of Britain's best young rally drivers is Tony Fall who was born in Bradford, Yorkshire, in 1940. In 1962 he joined the Bradford firm of Ian Appleyard, himself a famous rally driver of the 1950s, and worked as a car salesman. In 1964 he started rallying with a Cooper S under the firm's name and gained a lot of success on local events. In 1965 he entered the Alpine Rally and won a coveted *coupe* for an unpenalized run. This brought him to the attention of BMC who gave him a works Mini Cooper to drive in the Three Cities Rally in which he was 2nd overall. The following year he was given more works Minis to drive and won the Circuit of Ireland and the Scottish Rallies, and on the Continent he won the Polish Rally outright and was second touring car in the Geneva Rally.

In 1967 he was 3rd in Poland and with a BMC 1800 he won the Three Cities Rally outright. He also co-drove an MGB in the Nürburgring 84 Hours with Andrew Hedges and Julien Vernaeve and they finished 2nd overall. In 1968, BMC did very little rallying but Fall was given an 1800 for the London to Sydney and despite mechanical trouble made it to the finish. He had also started to drive for Lancia for whom he won the TAP Rally in Portugal. He drove for them in the 1969 Monte Carlo but crashed and then did quite a lot of racing for them which included winning the Nürburgring 84 Hours. He also had a magnificent drive on the RAC Rally where he finished 3rd overall. In 1970, he started to drive for Ford, his principal signing being for the World Cup Rally where he took footballer Jimmy Greaves as co-driver; they finished 6th. In late 1969, he had gone to South America to reconnoitre for the Ford team and as part of the exercise entered the Rally of the Incas with an Escort T/C and won it outright. JD

Fangio, Juan Manuel

Fangio was born in Balcarce, a small town in the interior of the Province of Buenos Aires, on 24 June 1911. In his early school days young Juan Manuel played football and due to an unusual way he had of kicking the ball he was nicknamed 'Chueco' (bow-legs), a name that has stuck throughout his life among his close friends. While still at school he began to be fascinated by the motorcar, and at the age of 11 he managed to get an old Panhard started on his own, excited but fearful lest his parents should find out. When he was 17 he had the chance to ride as mechanic with a friend in a local race, which he took without hesitation even though it was liable to bring parental rage down upon his head, for his father did not encourage his interest in cars. This was in 1928 and his enthusiasm for racing was fired, but it was not until 1934 that Fangio was able to drive his own car in a race. This was a Model T Ford, rebuilt by himself, which was followed by Ford V-8 powered cars. By the summer of 1939 he had driven in about a dozen events without conspicuous success, when the people of Balcarce clubbed together to buy him a car in which he could compete in the Gran Premio Nacional long-distance road race. They intended to buy a Ford, but there was no suitable car available, so they brought a brand-new 1940 model Chevrolet coupé. Fangio won one leg of the 1939 Gran

Tony Fall. *Photo: BMC*

Juan Manuel Fangio: Principal Siccesses

1940	Gran Premio del Norte, Argentina	Chevrolet
1941	Getulio Vargas GP	Chevrolet
1942	Mar y Siera GP	Chevrolet
	Mar del Plata GP	Chevrolet
	Rosario GP	Chevrolet
1947	Spring GP	Chevrolet
	Prix Doble Vita	Chevrolet
1948	Vuelta de Pringles GP	Chevrolet
	Ontono GP	Chevrolet
1949	Albi GP	Maserati 4CLT/48
	Mar del Plata GP	Maserati 4CLT/48
	Marseilles GP	Maserati 4CLT/48
	Monza Autodrome GP	Maserati 4CLT/48
	GP de Roussillon, Perpignan	Maserati 4CLT/48
	Pau GP	Maserati 4CLT/48
	San Remo GP	Maserati 4CLT/48
1950	Belgian GP	Alfa Romeo 158
	French GP	Alfa Romeo 158
	Monaco GP	Alfa Romeo 158
	GP des Nations, Geneva	Alfa Romeo 158
	Pau GP	Maserati 4CLT/48
	Pescara GP	Alfa Romeo 158
	San Remo GP	Alfa Romeo 158
1951	French GP	Alfa Romeo 159
	Spanish GP	Alfa Romeo 159
	Swiss GP	Alfa Romeo 159
	Bari GP	Alfa Romeo 159
1952	Argentine GP	Ferrari
	Buenos Aires GP	Ferrari
1953	Italian GP	Maserati A6GCM
	Modena GP	Maserati A6GCM
	Carrera Panamericana	Lancia D24
1954	Argentine GP	Maserati 250F
	Belgian GP	Maserati 250F
	French GP	Mercedes-Benz W196
	German GP	Mercedes-Benz W196
	Swiss GP	Mercedes-Benz W196
	Italian GP	Mercedes-Benz W196

continued

Premio, as well as the Argentine 1,000 kilometre race. In 1940 he won the 5,900-mile (9,495km) Gran Premio del Norte outright, and was Argentine National Champion in 1940 and 1941. He continued to race Chevrolets, coupés in road events and single-seaters on the track, until 1948 when he visited Europe, bringing back with him a Maserati 4CLT. In January 1949 he won the Mar del Plata GP from Bira, and followed this up with European victories at Albi, Marseilles, Monza, Perpignan, Pau, and San Remo GPs. He was 38 years old in this, his first full European season.

As a result of his performances with the Maserati, Fangio was signed up by Alfa Romeo for 1950. He had a very successful season with the Tipo 158, and came 2nd to Farina in the World Championship. In an Alfa Romeo saloon he was 3rd in the Mille Miglia. Fangio drove for Alfa again in 1951, and clinched the Championship soundly with 31 out of a possible 36 points. Alfa Romeo withdrew from GP racing in 1952, and Fangio found himself without a car. He drove a Ferrari in South American Formule Libre events, winning three, and drove a V-16 BRM at Albi and in Ulster, retiring on both occasions. In the Monza GP he crashed in a Maserati, sustaining injuries which put him out of racing for the rest of the season. In 1953 he won the Italian and Modena GPs, and was 2nd in the British, French and German GPs, all in Maseratis. He was also 2nd in the Mille Miglia in an Alfa Romeo Disco Volante coupé, despite driving for a considerable distance with only one front wheel responding to the steering. He drove a Maserati again in 1954, winning the Argentine and Belgian GPs, before joining Mercedes-Benz to win four GPs, and become World Champion for the second time. In 1955 he won his third Championship, driving exclusively for Mercedes-Benz. In sports car races he was 2nd in both the Mille Miglia and the Targa Florio (with Kling) in a 300SLR, on each occasion yielding first place to Stirling Moss.

Mercedes-Benz withdrew from racing at the end of 1955 and as in 1952 Fangio was without the cars and company which had served him so well. Undaunted, he turned to Ferrari and in the 2·5-litre Lancia-Ferrari he took his fourth World Championship. He returned to Maserati in 1957, his last full season, winning four GPs and the Championship for the fifth time in the ageing Tipo 250F, and the Sebring 12 Hours (for the 2nd time) in a Tipo 450S. In 1958 he won the Buenos Aires GP and after finishing 4th in the French GP the 47-year-old Champion announced his retirement. Although he was beaten on occasions during his last two years, by drivers young enough to be his sons, in superior cars, he was never really out-driven in a Grand Prix car. He had remarkable stamina and unlimited powers of concentration, being able to combat conditions of heat, rain or cold that proved to be too much for many younger men. He also had a remarkable ability to deal with mechanical difficulties, able to nurse an ailing car to the finish when others would either give up or break the car completely. If a circuit had a very fast corner that most people thought could be taken almost flat out, the story would soon get round that Fangio *could* take it flat out, and sure enough when the time came he would show that the story was true, his ability to drive on the limit of tyre adhesion, and sometimes beyond it, being uncanny and showing a remarkable sensitivity.

He had a shy and retiring nature when not racing, speaking his native Spanish quietly, and though he speaks only a little Italian and no other European

Above left, Juan Manuel Fangio in a Chevrolet Special, 1947. *Photo: Dr Vicentè Alvarez*

Above, Juan Manuel Fangio at Indianapolis. *Photo: Indianapolis Motor Speedway*

Left, Juan Manuel Fangio driving his Maserati 250F to victory in the 1957 German GP. *Photo: Motor*

Bottom, Juan Manuel Fangio. *Photo: David Hodges Collection*

1955	Argentine GP	Mercedes-Benz W196
	Belgian GP	Mercedes-Benz W196
	Dutch GP	Mercedes-Benz W196
	Italian GP	Mercedes-Benz W196
	Buenos Aires GP	Mercedes-Benz W196 (3-litre)
	Eifelrennen (Sports cars)	Mercedes-Benz 300SLR
	Venezuela GP (Sports cars)	Maserati 300S
1956	Argentine GP with Musso	Lancia-Ferrari 801
	Mendoza GP	Lancia-Ferrari 801
	British GP	Lancia-Ferrari 801
	German GP	Lancia-Ferrari 801
	Syracuse GP	Lancia-Ferrari 801
	Sebring 12-Hours, with Castellotti	Ferrari 860
1957	Argentine GP	Maserati 250F
	Buenos Aires GP	Maserati 250F
	French GP	Maserati 250F
	German GP	Maserati 250F
	Monaco GP	Maserati 250F
	Portuguese GP (Sports cars)	Maserati 300S
	Cuban GP (Sports cars)	Maserati 300S
	Sebring 12-Hours, with Behra	Maserati 450S
1958	Buenos Aires GP	Maserati 250F

language, he always seemed to be at home no matter where he was, from Portugal to Sweden, or England to Sicily. He was quite content to avoid unnecessary publicity, winning races being the only publicity he enjoyed. Out of a racing car he was a gentle man, quiet and relaxed, but at the wheel he was a ruthless tiger, giving way to nobody and fighting hard all the time, but nonetheless driving with a spirit of fairness that was an example to all. In his home country he was a national hero, the welcoming demonstrations on his return each winter during the height of his career being almost unbelievable to European eyes. In spite of shunning publicity he had a magnetic personality, and still has even in his retirement. This makes itself felt wherever he goes and even today his appearance at a race track, wearing a quiet dark suit, will occasion an outbreak of applause from motor racing enthusiasts in any European country. One World Champion driver of today, who was a schoolboy when Fangio was racing, drove out to a prize-giving function with 'the old maestro' and was visibly impressed by the simple fact of having been driven by the great Fangio. He is still very much in touch with the world-wide racing scene and is very appreciative of the talents of today's premier drivers, even though conditions are very different from those when he was at the top. Similarly he retains his interest in the mechanical progress of racing cars, and his keen eyes are as bright as ever they were, especially when he is in the pits at a modern race meeting. DSJ

Farina, Guiseppe

Farina was born in 1906 in Turin, son of the eldest of the coachbuilding brothers, and nephew of Pinin Farina. He owned and drove his first car, a twin-cylinder Temperino, at the age of 9, and while studying law at Turin University he bought a second-hand Alfa Romeo 1500. He ran it in the Aosta-Grand St Bernard hill-climb against his father who finished 4th — he finished in hospital with broken bones and a wrecked car. A fine sportsman, Farina, or 'Nino' as he was usually called, centred his energies on motor racing, running private Maseratis and Alfas in 1933 and 1934 and his fiery performances and obvious enthusiasm impressed Tazio Nuvolari, who became his friend and mentor.

Under Nuvolari's guidance Farina developed into a fast and stylish driver, but was hardly the most sporting of competitors and was given to displays of temperament which sometimes affected his judgment and his driving. During 1935 he drove a Maserati with few successes, and then joined the Scuderia Ferrari Alfa Romeo team for 1936. He was 2nd to team-mate Brivio's car in the Mille Miglia, driving without lights through the night, and scored some minor placings in other events; 1937 was better and included a win at Naples, and 2nd at Turin and Milan. The Alfa Romeo works re-entered motor racing in 1938 and Farina was one of their drivers, chasing the German cars throughout the season and ending the year as Italian Champion. He retained the title in 1939, driving the Alfettas. Italian motor racing continued into 1940 and he finished 2nd at Brescia and won at Tripoli.

After World War 2 Farina soon returned in a works Alfetta, winning the GP des Nations at Geneva in 1946. He drove Maseratis in 1948, winning at Monaco, Geneva, Garda and Mar del Plata, and his distinctive straight-armed style (developed from Nuvolari's stance) was seen in Ferraris and Maseratis in 1949. Alfa Romeo had lost Trossi and Wimille and in 1950 they set up their famous 'Three Fs' team with Farina, Fangio and Fagioli. Farina had a splendid year, winning at Silverstone, Monza and Berne, and winning the World Championship title instituted that year.

In the 1951 season Farina remained with Alfa Romeo, and drove Maseratis occasionally. Alfa withdrew in 1952, and Farina joined Ascari and Villoresi in the Ferrari team. He was not very happy as junior member to Ascari and had a checkered season as a result, punctuated by several spins and crashes. He came 2nd to Ascari in the Championship, and settled down more in 1953, which included a brilliant tigerish drive in the German GP to win after losing a front wheel. He became team leader in 1954 when Ascari went to Lancia but he crashed badly in a 4·9-litre Ferrari when leading the Mille Miglia. He recovered from his injuries in time for the Monza 1,000 kilometres race, but while practising his 3-litre Ferrari a rear universal joint broke, and the driveshaft punctured a fuel tank and flooded the cockpit with burning petrol. Farina jumped clear but was badly burned. His determination forced him back into racing in the Argentine in 1955 when, despite his need for painkilling injections, he finished 2nd. He was later 3rd in the Belgian GP, but full recovery from his injuries was a

Giuseppe Farina at Silverstone, 1951. *Photo: A. R. Smith*

Giuseppe Farina: Principal Successes

1934	Masaryk Voiturette GP	Maserati 4C
1937	Naples GP	Alfa Romeo 12C-36
1939	Antwerp GP	Alfa Romeo 158
	Coppa Ciano	Alfa Romeo 158
	Prix de Berne	Alfa Romeo 158
1940	Tripoli GP	Alfa Romeo 158
1946	GP des Nations, Geneva	Alfa Romeo 158
1948	Monaco GP	Maserati 4CLT/48
	GP des Nations, Geneva	Maserati 4CLT/48
	Mar del Plata GP	Maserati 4CLT/48
	Circuit of Garda	Ferrari 125
1949	Lausanne GP	Maserati 4CLT/48
	Rosario GP	Ferrari 125
1950	British GP	Alfa Romeo 158
	Italian GP	Alfa Romeo 158
	Swiss GP	Alfa Romeo 158
	Bari GP	Alfa Romeo 158
	International Trophy, Silverstone	Alfa Romeo 158
1951	Belgian GP	Alfa Romeo 159
	Paris GP	Alfa Romeo 159
	Ulster Trophy	Alfa Romeo 159
	Goodwood Trophy	Alfa Romeo 159
1952	Monza GP	Ferrari 500
	Naples GP	Ferrari 500
1953	German GP	Ferrari 500
	Naples GP	Ferrari 500
	Rouen GP	Ferrari 625
	Buenos Aires GP	Ferrari 625
	Nürburgring 1,000km, with Ascari	Ferrari 375MM
	Spa 24 Hours, with Hawthorn	Ferrari 375MM
	Casablanca 12 Hours, with Scotti	Ferrari 375MM
1954	Syracuse GP	Ferrari 625
	Agadir GP (Sports cars)	Ferrari 375 Plus
	Buenos Aires 1,000km, with Maglioli	Ferrari 375MM

slow process and he was forced to retire from the sport he loved so much.

He had survived untold accidents in his 16 years of active race driving, including collisions which killed Marcel Lehoux at Deauville and Lazlo Hartmann at Tripoli, but when his head won over his heart he was unbeatable. After his retirement he was involved with Jaguar's Italian distribution, and then returned to Alfa Romeo in a similar post. He still appeared around the circuits and made two abortive sorties to Indianapolis, with a Ferrari-engined Kurtis in 1956 and a Kurtis-Offenhauser in 1957. American driver Keith Andrews crashed fatally while testing the latter car and the Italian Doctor of Law officially retired then. In 1966, while driving a Lotus Cortina to the French GP, Farina hit a telegraph pole on an icy road, and was killed. DCN

Ferrari, Enzo

The name Ferrari is almost synonymous with all that is best in motor racing. Enzo Ferrari himself is an autocratic yet often genial and kindly Italian, who lives simply and whose life has been intimately connected with motor sport for over 50 years.

He was born in 1898, the son of a structural engineer, whose small workshop produced sheds and gangways for the railway, and as a child he wanted to be an opera singer, a sports writer or a racing driver. But these ambitions had to wait for World War 1, from which he was invalided into a hospital for incurables. His fragile health improved and after the Armistice he took a job with a firm converting second-hand vans into sports cars. Young Ferrari also did some test driving for CMN (Costruzioni Meccaniche Nazionali), and finished 9th for them in the 1919 Targa Florio.

The following year he joined Alfa Romeo, the start of a long and fruitful association. He was 2nd in the 1920 Targa Florio driving an Alfa Romeo 20/30, and 2nd again in the 1921 Circuit of Mugello. In 1923 Ferrari won the Circuit of Ravenna and for his performance in that event he was presented with a Prancing Horse shield by the parents of Francesco Baracca, an Italian fighter ace who had been killed at the end of the war. The following season he won the Coppa Acerbo at Pescara and the Circuit of Polesine, but his health prevented him racing as often as he liked.

His talents as an organizer and administrator were put to good use in this period, and he attracted several of FIAT's best technical brains to Alfa Romeo when the other company's racing programme began to contract. In the late 1920s Alfa's own programme followed FIAT's, and in December 1929 Ferrari left to run quasi-works cars under his own name. Scuderia Ferrari was established in his home town of Modena, using the Baracca shield as its emblem and preparing its own and private entrants' Alfa Romeos for racing. In 1938 Alfa Romeo terminated their arrangement with Ferrari in an attempt to take on the might of Germany as a fully-fledged works team, and the severance agreement stipulated that Ferrari should not re-form his Scuderia for four years.

But then came the outbreak of World War 2, despite which Ferrari raced the first cars of his own manufacture at Brescia in 1940, under the name of Auto Avio Costruzioni. They were designed by Massimino and built by Enrico Nardi, incorporating many FIAT components, and were known as the Tipo 815s. Both retired.

Once racing activities ceased, Ferrari worked for a small aero engine firm in Rome and then set up a machine

tool concern to support the ball-bearing industry. It was Italian government policy to decentralize industrial settlement, and Ferrari moved out from Modena to nearby Maranello.

In 1947 the first car appeared with 'Ferrari' as the maker's name, and a Colombo-designed 1·5-litre V-12 made the marque's racing debut at Piacenza in May that year. Since then Ferraris have won the World Championship in 1952–3, 1956, 1958, 1961 and 1964. The Mille Miglia fell to them eight times and Le Mans nine, to say nothing of many other classic and lesser events around the World. Enzo Ferrari ruled his kingdom with an iron hand, working longer hours than many a younger man would entertain, and remaining personally involved in every branch of his company's activities.

His only son, Dino, was born in 1931, but suffered from indifferent health and died in 1956 leaving his father a more detached and sombre character, without an heir. Ferrari has had some of the world's greatest drivers racing for him, but for many years has not watched his cars competing. He makes a regular appearance at Monza during practice for the Italian GP and maybe the 1,000 kilometres, but never attends on race day.

Ford attempted to buy a controlling interest in Ferrari in 1967, but FIAT's backing was increased until at the end of the decade they took over a major interest. Enzo Ferrari remains at its head, still building his cars to carry the Prancing Horse emblem. DCN

Fitch, John C.

Born in 1917 in Indianapolis, Ind., this former World War 2 flyer was exposed to motor racing as a child by his stepfather, George Spinder, sales manager of Stutz. After his release as a prisoner of war, Fitch bought an MG TC and set up a foreign car repair shop in White Plains, New York. Fitch's first race, in June 1949, in which he finished 5th, was through the streets of Bridgehampton. Fitch raced an XK 120 Jaguar in the first Sebring event, 31 December 1950, and in March 1951, joined a group of Americans in Argentina in the General Peron Grand Prix for sports cars, which he won driving a Cadillac-Allard. Briggs Cunningham invited Fitch to

Enzo Ferrari winning the 1923 Circuit of Savio in an Alfa Romeo RLTF. *Photo: Alfa Romeo SpA*

Enzo Ferrari. *Photo: Shell Photographic Service*

Enzo Ferrari, 1970. *Photo: Geoffrey Goddard*

share a C-2 at Le Mans with Phil Walters, their Cunningham running 2nd overall at the 18th hour only to have engine trouble set them back to an 18th place finish. Fitch won at Elkhart Lake in 1950 and in 1951 became the Sports Car Club of America's first national champion. Uhlenhaut of Mercedes invited Fitch to test a 300SL at the Nürburgring and in October 1952, Neubauer asked Fitch to join Mercedes-Benz in the Pan American Road Race in which he finished 4th, only to be disqualified for a procedural violation. On his return from Le Mans Fitch continued driving for Cunningham, registering victories at Elkhart Lake and in the Seneca Cup race at Watkins Glen in a new C-type with none other than Jaguar managing director, Sir William Lyons, looking on. Phil Walters and John Fitch won the 1953 Sebring 12 Hours in a Cunningham and in June Fitch drove the new C-5R to 3rd place at Le Mans. Fitch crashed the Cunningham at the Reims 12 Hours but a week later ran in the Alpine Rally for Rootes.

In 1954 Fitch joined Baron de Graffenried as a technical director for the 20th Century-Fox film of Hans Ruesch's novel, *The Racer*. Fitch became a member of the Mercedes-Benz sports car team for 1955. His first event was the Italian Mille Miglia, in which his 300SL production coupé was 1st in the GT and 5th overall. In June Fitch was to drive a SLR with Pierre Levegh at Le Mans, but Mercedes withdrew following the pit-straight disaster in which Levegh and 82 spectators were killed. In the autumn of 1955, Team Mercedes journeyed to Dundrod, Northern Ireland, where, with his partner doing most of the driving, Fitch and Stirling Moss won the Tourist Trophy.

Following Mercedes' withdrawal from racing Fitch became Team Manager for General Motors' Sebring Corvette effort in 1956 and in 1957 worked with Corvette designer Zora Arkus-Duntov, on the 4·6-litre Sebring Super-Sport. For several years Fitch served as manager of the Lime Rock race course near his home in Connecticut and opened a shop in Falls Village. In 1960 he began producing the Fitch Corvair Sprint, a Corvair Monza Coupé modified to give additional performance and comfort and in 1968 made similar modifications to the Pontiac Firebird. ARB

Fittipaldi, Emerson

Fittipaldi, born in 1946, brought Brazil into the international motor racing scene in 1969, when he burst upon English club racing, rocketed straight to the top and made his Formula 1 debut as third member of the works Lotus team in 1970. He had a motor racing background, for his father Wilson Fittipaldi was a Brazilian journalist who followed Fangio's European career in 1950 and who raced motorcycles until a bad crash in 1952.

Emerson was allowed to start racing 50cc bikes at the age of 15, while acting as mechanic to his brother Wilson's racing karts. Emerson was given his own kart at the age of 17, and in 1965 won the São Paulo Kart Championship. This earned him a works-backed Renault 850 Dauphine Gordini with which he won the Brazilian Group 2 Novices Saloon Car Championship. Successes in saloon car racing and Formula Vee followed in 1966 and 1967, and in the latter year he won the Brazilian F. Vee Championship.

That same year he was second to Carlos Pace in the national GT Championship, driving a Karmann Ghia VW with a 2-litre Porsche engine, and won the kart title with his own Minikart. With backing from the distributor the brothers built and raced a 2-litre Porsche-based Fittipaldi GT in national events, showing tremendous speed but suffering transmission troubles. Brazilian motor sport was in a decline at this time, however, with returns from kart racing topping those from the cars and in March 1969 Emerson travelled to England and bought a Merlyn Formula Ford.

Merlyn introduced him to engine specialist Denny Rowland and the latter provided Ford engines for Emerson's Merlyn Mk 11A. He scored a string of successes in the car and Jim Russell, head of the Snetterton racing driver's school, offered him an F3 drive in a new Lotus 59. He was 5th, 3rd and then 1st in his first three races with the car, and then went on to seven more major victories and clinched the Lombank F3 Championship.

He had quickly proved himself a driver of tremendous ability, and Lotus Components signed him on for an F2 drive in 1970. That season he was not outstandingly successful in the class, but his potential was still very evident. When Piers Courage was tragically killed in the Dutch GP, entrant Frank Williams was looking for a new driver to take over his De Tomaso F1. He approached Fittipaldi, and Lotus reacted quickly to sign him on as part of the F1 team. His first race was in the British GP driving a Lotus-Cosworth 49C in which he finished 8th after a heady race, and in the next round—the German GP at Hockenheim—he drove the same car into a good 4th place. His car failed in the Austrian GP and he crashed the new Lotus 72 in practice for the Italian GP at Monza, just before team-leader Jochen Rindt was killed in a similar incident. However, in the penultimate race of the season, the U.S. GP at Watkins Glen, he justified Lotus' hopes for him by winning, despite a poor start which left him in eighth place at the end of the first lap. DCN

Flaherty, George Francis Patrick

Pat Flaherty, born in 1926, started driving race cars in his native California immediately after World War 2 and finished 10th in his first Indianapolis race as a 1950 rookie. Later that season, however, the Contest Board of the American Automobile Association suspended him for two years for driving in unsanctioned stock car events.

Following his re-instatement, he crashed in the 1953 Indianapolis race and also was involved in another accident in the 500 the following year while driving relief for Jim Rathmann. He finished 10th again in the 1955 Indianapolis event and scored his first major AAA

Emerson Fittipaldi. *Photo: Autosport*

Ron Flockhart, after winning at Le Mans in 1957 with Ivor Bueb. *Photo: Associated Press*

Below left, Pat Flaherty. *Photo: Indianapolis Motor Speedway*

Below, Pat Flaherty, after winning the 1956 Indianapolis 500 in a John Zink Special. *Photo: Indianapolis Motor Speedway*

Below right, George Follmer. *Photo: Al Bochroch Collection*

victory in a 250-miler later that season at Milwaukee, Wis.

In 1956 he won the first Indianapolis event sanctioned by the United States Auto Club, which had been formed to succeed to the AAA Contest Board as the major sanctioning body of auto racing in America, leading the field for all the last 125 laps of the 200-lap race. One week later he won again at Milwaukee and appeared destined to become USAC's first national driving champion until he suffered severe injuries in a dirt track event at Springfield, Ill.

Flaherty did not race again until August 1958, when he made a comeback by winning a 200-mile USAC stock car race at Milwaukee. He returned to Indianapolis the following spring and came from behind three times to take the lead before hitting the wall on the 163rd lap while running 4th.

He announced his retirement in 1961, after several practice laps at Indianapolis, and became a tavern owner in Chicago, where he still lives. AB

Flockhart, William Ronald

Born in Edinburgh in 1924, Flockhart began with motorcycle racing, and drove an MG TV and a JP-Vincent from 1949 to 1951, he then progressed to ERAs, and in 1954 he was signed by BRM with whom he remained until 1960. He had little success and several accidents with BRMs, his only victory being in the 1959 Lady Wigram Trophy. However he had a much better time in sports car racing, winning Le Mans twice with D-type Jaguars, in 1956 with Ninian Sanderson and in 1957 with Ivor Bueb. He also had several wins with a Lotus-Climax in 1957. In 1960 he drove sports and F2 Coopers, finishing 2nd in the Frontières GP at Chimay in one of the latter, and then in 1961 he turned to aviation, making an attempt on the Australia–England solo record. While practising for a second attempt, in April 1962, he was killed. FWMcC

Follmer, George

Born in 1934, this American driver, after success in Sports Car Club of America club racing won the 1965 United States Road Racing Championship driving a Lotus-Porsche of his own design. One of the growing number of road racers to invade oval track racing, Follmer won the 1969 Phoenix 150 in a rear-engined Chevy powered car, the first Championship Trail victory for Chevrolet. At Indianapolis he qualified 27, left the race on lap 27 and finished 27th. Follmer also qualified

for Indy in 1970 but his Hawk-Ford broke on the 18th
lap. After being a member of the Javelin Trans-Am
works team he joined Ford in 1969 and won at Bridgehampton. In 1970, with one 1st and three 2nds, Follmer
helped team-mate Parnelli Jones bring Ford the Trans-
Am championship. In the Can-Am series, where his
best finish had been a 2nd at Stardust in 1968, Follmer
drove the experimental AVS Shadow its first time out
at Mosport in June 1970 where it qualified 6th but failed
to last. Follmer was a late starter in the 1970 Continental
series where he brought Ford their first Formula A wins,
his Lotus-70 being first at the St Jovite and Mid-Ohio
Circuits. ARB

Fontes, Luis

This wealthy amateur British driver of Spanish ex-
traction who was born in 1914 leapt from obscurity to
international fame in just one season— 1935 —when he
won the 250-mile International Trophy race at Brooklands on Jubilee Day, driving a 2·3-litre Alfa Romeo
Monza in expert style and heading F. W. Dixon and E.
R. Hall home. Before this surprise victory Fontes had
raced an MG Midget and a 4·5-litre Invicta with little
success.

His Brooklands victory precipitated a wave of success
for the bespectacled Fontes, whose interests were
divided equally between cars and flying. A week later he
won the unlimited class in the Southport 50 miles sand
race, finishing 2nd overall with the Invicta. A fortnight
after that he came 3rd with his three-year-old Alfa
Romeo to two 3·3-litre GP Bugattis in the Mannin
Moar race at Douglas, Isle of Man. Two weeks later he
and John S. Hindmarsh scored a striking British victory
at Le Mans with a 4·5-litre Lagonda. A week following
that signal triumph Fontes made fastest lap in the
County Down Trophy race at Bangor, Northern Ireland,
but had to retire, and a fortnight later he won the Limerick
GP outright, catching Fairfield's ERA from the
scratch mark to win by a bare 200 yards. And on his last
drive with the Alfa Monza, he came 2nd in the Phoenix
Park Trophy handicap race, Dublin, averaging 90·96mph
(146·39kph) to the winning MG's 69·94mph
(112·55kph).

On the debit side, he had little success with a Squire at
Brooklands, and after 1935 he gave up racing. He lost
his life while flying in the RAF during World War 2. CP

Fournier, Henri

Born in 1871, the Frenchman Fournier was first seen on
motorcycles, riding a De Dion tricycle in the Paris–
Toulouse–Paris, 1900. By 1901 he had graduated to the
wheel of a Mors, and pulled off an impressive double,
winning both the Paris–Bordeaux and the Paris–Berlin
by a comfortable margin and at record speeds. Armed
with a formidable reputation, he wintered in America,
collecting numerous sprint awards and doing the fastest
fs mile yet recorded in the Western Hemisphere, in
51·8sec. He also sponsored the unsuccessful Searchmont
car, but was back in Europe in 1902 to race an express
train during the Paris–Vienna, and to cover the first leg
of this marathon at a cracking 71mph (114·26kph).
Unfortunately this was too much for the Mors' gearbox and he was soon out. A brief change of allegiance to
Clément, one of whose voiturettes he drove in the Circuit
des Ardennes, was equally unsuccessful, and an attempt
to launch another season in America failed to attract
sufficient backing.

Meanwhile Fournier had gone into the motor trade in

Above, Luis Fontes at Brooklands, 1935.
Photo: Cyril Posthumus Collection

Above right, Henri Fournier, 1911. *Photo: T. A. S. O. Mathieson Collection*

Below, Luis Fontes (left) with John Hindmarsh, after winning at Le Mans in 1935. *Photo: Cyril Posthumus Collection*

A. J. Foyt. *Photo: Indianapolis Motor Speedway*

France, where he acted as selling agent for the new
Hotchkiss car (his brother Achille drove for them). He
was not destined to race again untill 1907, by which
time he was selling Italas. He had little success with these
his best result being 8th in the 1907 Kaiserpreis, although
he continued to represent Itala in Paris until 1914. He
died five years later. MCS

Foyt, Anthony Joseph, Jr.

A. J. Foyt, born in 1935, a three-time Indianapolis 500
winner and the only driver in racing history to capture
the national championship five times, began to attract
attention in midget-car and sprint-car competition during
the 1957 season. He failed to finish his first Indianapolis
race the following year, but was one of the USAC contingent making the trip to Italy for the Monza race a few
weeks later and was placed 6th as a relief driver for
Maurice Trintignant.

By mid-season of 1959 he had established himself as a
formidable contender in all types of racing and, from
that time until June 1966, he earned a starting position
in each of 87 consecutive championship events on the
USAC schedule for a record of consistency never approached by any other American driver. By the end of the
1970 campaign he had driven in 187 USAC big car
championship events and emerged victorious 42 times
while also finishing 2nd or 3rd on 36 occasions. In addition he has done most of the engine work on his own
championship cars since the start of the 1967 season.

Blessed with exceptional strength and stamina, 'A.J.'
won four of the last five 1960 USAC 100-mile championship races on the one-mile dirt tracks to secure his first
national title, despite his failure to earn any points at
Indianapolis that year because of clutch trouble. He was
again champion in 1961 and also won the 500 for the
first time with an Offenhauser-powered roadster at an
average speed of 139·13mph (224·15kph). A new 'Offy'
of similar design, the last of this type to win a 500-mile
race, carried him to his second Indy victory at a record-
breaking speed of 147·35mph (237·18kph) in 1964 and
he won the race for the third time in 1967 by setting
another new record of 151·207mph (243·311kph) with a
turbocharged V-8 Ford rear-engine car. His prize money
for those three Indianapolis races alone totalled
$443,152 ($117,975 in 1961, $153,650 in 1964, and
$171,527 in 1967). He was also placed in the first ten at
Indianapolis on four other occasions and was the
fastest qualifier twice. His average speed of 161·233mph
(259·455kph) for the 1965 pole position was a new record

and he won the No. 1 starting spot again in 1969 with a speed of 170·568mph (274·513kph). This was a record for piston-engine cars but not quite as fast as Joe Leonard's 171·559mph (276·094kph) in a 1968 turbine car.

Foyt earned his other national driving championships in 1963, 1964 and 1967; and was runner-up for the crown in 1962 and 1965. Although particularly outstanding at Indianapolis and in the 100-mile dirt track events, he also won a total of nine USAC championship races of more than 100 miles duration at such tracks as Trenton, N.J., Phoenix, Ariz., Castle Rock, Colo., and Hanford, Calif.

He has been almost equally successful in USAC stock-car racing since he became interested in that aspect of the sport during the 1962 season. He won the USAC title for Ford in 1968 and has ranked among the top eight in the final point standing on six other occasions during the last eight years. Eight of his many USAC stock car victories were scored in events of 200 miles or more at Indianapolis Raceway Park, Dover, Del., Langhorne, Pa., Hanford, Calif. and Milwaukee, Wis.

Foyt's impressive record also includes important accomplishments in events other than those sanctioned by USAC. He won the Nassau Trophy and Governor's Cup sports car races in the 1963 Nassau Speed Week, the FIA-NASCAR 1964 and 1965 Firecracker 400 races at Daytona Beach, Fla., the FIA-NASCAR 1964 and 1971 Atlanta, Ga., 500-mile events; the 1971 NASCAR 500 at Ontario, Calif., and teamed with Dan Gurney on a Ford GT40 to win at Le Mans in 1967. AB

Frame, Frederick

Fred Frame, who was born in 1894, started his racing career only three years before the onset of the 1930s economic depression, which caused almost all American tracks except the Indianapolis Motor Speedway to suspend operations. He won the 500 in 1932 and earned championship points (12th place or better) on four of his other six Indianapolis appearances.

Frame scored his victory at the wheel of an 8-cylinder Miller-Hartz Special by averaging 104·144mph (167·666kph), after the early leaders had eliminated themselves. Billy Arnold and Bob Carey both crashed while running in 1st place, setting the stage for an exciting duel between Frame and Wilbur Shaw, until a broken axle also forced Shaw to the sidelines.

Frame had finished 2nd the previous year in a Duesenberg and, in 1933, he was one of the early leaders before going to the sidelines because of valve trouble. He retired as a driver in 1938 and died in 1962. AB

Above left, A. J. Foyt, at Nassau with Stirling Moss. Photo: Al Bochroch

Above, Fernand Gabriel, 1913. Photo: T. A. S. O. Mathieson Collection

Fred Frame. Photo: Indianapolis Motor Speedway

Frère, Paul

Born in 1917, Paul Frère is a leading Belgian journalist who achieved great success as an amateur driver between 1948 and 1960. His debut was in the 1948 Spa 24 Hour race when he drove a 1936 MG PB with Jacques Swaters, and finished 4th in class. Over the next few years he drove Dyna-Panhard, Jaguar, and Oldsmobile cars, winning the 1952 Production Car Race at Spa in one of the latter. He was given an HWM F2 drive in 1952, winning at Chimay and finishing 5th in the European GP at Spa, and 2nd in the 1953 Eifelrennen. He drove a Porsche at Le Mans with von Frankenberg in 1954, winning the class, and also drove Aston Martin sports and Gordini F1 cars. He drove for Jaguar in 1956, winning his class in a 2·4-litre saloon in the Production Car Race, and finishing 2nd with Mike Hawthorn in a D-type in the Reims 12 Hours. This event brought him victory in 1957 and 1958, with Olivier Gendebien as co-driver, both times in Ferraris. At the beginning of 1960 he returned to single seaters for the first time since 1956, and won the South African GP in an F2 Cooper-Climax. Later that year he ran his last race, sharing Gendebien's winning works Ferrari at Le Mans. At the age of 43 Frère retired to concentrate on journalism. DCN

Gabriel, Fernand

Gabriel was one of the leading early French drivers and had a long career, but he only won one major event, the famous Paris–Madrid race of 1903. His career began in 1899 when he won the voiturette class of the Tour de France on a 5hp Decauville. He almost won the 1902 Circuit des Ardennes, a broken chain on his big Mors allowing Jarrott to take the lead on the last lap; Gabriel finished 2nd. He recorded ftd at that year's Château-Thierry hill-climb, and in 1903 won Paris–Madrid on a 70hp Mors. He covered the 342 miles to Bordeaux (where the race was stopped) at an average speed of 65·3mph (105·09kph). He was 4th for Mors in the 1903 Gordon Bennett Race, but in 1904 he transferred to De Dietrich with whom he remained for four seasons. The 12·8-litre Turcat-Méry-designed cars were old-fashioned, and for his first two seasons with the firm Gabriel had little success, just failing to make the French Gordon Bennett team in both years. In 1906 he was 5th in the Circuit des Ardennes, while his 1907 record included 4th in the Grand Prix and in the Coppa della Velocita, and 6th in the Targa Florio. In 1908 he drove for Clément-Bayard, but finished only 12th in the Grand Prix.

From 1911 to 1914 he drove a variety of undistinguished cars such as FIF, the 2-stroke Côte, and Th. Schneider, and his best result in these years was a touring car victory at Gaillon hill-climb for the latter make. After World War 1 Gabriel drove for Ariès in touring car events, finishing 5th in the two seater class in the 1923 Touring Car Grand Prix at Lyons. He was killed during an RAF air raid on Paris in 1943. MCS

Gardner, Lt Col A. T. G.

Born in 1889, this British driver started racing at Brooklands in 1924 with an Austin Seven; he also drove Salmsons and a supercharged Amilcar. He raced a C-type MG in 1931, and was the first to lap the Outer Circuit at over 100mph (160kph) in a 750cc car. He abandoned road racing after a crash in the 1932 TT which aggravated an old wartime wound in his right leg and hip. In 1934 he finished 3rd in the Brooklands 500 Miles with Behjafield in an MG K3. Goldie Gardner bought

Above left, Lt Col Goldie Gardner (left), at
Daytona with Sir Malcolm Campbell, 1935.
Photo: Montagu Motor Museum

Above, Lt Col Goldie Gardner. Photo: F.
Wilson McComb Collection

the ex-Horton offset single-seater K3 and in 1935 lapped the Outer Circuit at Brooklands at over 120mph (190kph). The next year with the same car rebodied he established the Outer Circuit record for 1,100cc of 124·4mph (200·2kph) which was never beaten. In 1937 he took various Class G records at almost 150mph (240kph) at Montlhéry and Frankfurt.

With a new MG record car based on Eyston's Magic Magnette he achieved 186·6mph (300·3kph) at Frankfurt in 1938, gaining the BRDC Gold Star and Segrave Trophy. In 1939, he covered the flying start kilometre at 203·54mph (327·56kph) on the Dessau autobahn; the engine was then bored out to 1,106cc for further records in Class F.

Goldie Gardner achieved 159·15mph (256·18kph) at Jabbeke in Belgium in 1946 with a 6-cylinder 750cc engine which had been built in 1939 and stored during World War 2. Using only four cylinders of the same unit he then took 500cc records in 1947 at 118·043mph (189·965kph). He then fitted a 4-cylinder Jaguar engine in 1948 for 2,000cc records at 176·6mph (284·2kph); for this he was awarded his second BRDC Gold Star. Next Goldie Gardner fitted another 6-cylinder MG engine with three cylinders inoperative for 500cc records at 154·91mph (149·22kph). In 1949 the colonel was given the OBE and received a bar to his Gold Star.

Using only two cylinders of the 1949 MG engine, he achieved 121·048mph (194·73kph) on 500cc at Jabbeke in 1950. By this time the Gardner-MG held records in six of the ten international classes, from 350cc to 1,500cc with the MG, and 2,000cc with the Jaguar unit.

A supercharged MG TD engine was installed in this same car in 1951 for 1,500cc records class on the Bonneville Salt Flats, Utah, which included 137·4 miles (221·1km) in one hour. In 1952 two different engines were used: a modified Wolseley unit for 2,000cc records at up to 148·72mph (239·33kph), and another MG TD engine for 1,500cc records at up to 189·5mph (305kph). With the latter, 220mph (354kph) was expected, but wet salt caused severe wheel-slip.

Goldie Gardner was 63 at the time of this, his last record attempt. A long illness followed and he died in August 1958. FWMcC

Gardner, Frank

Frank Gardner was born in Sydney, Australia, in 1931, and after showing proficiency in several sports such as swimming, rowing and boxing, took up motor racing in 1953 when he won a 25 mile race at Mount Druitt in his Jaguar XK 120. He moved to Europe in the late 1950s, and in 1961 helped Ron Tauranac and Peter Wilkins to

Below, Frank Gardner. Photo: Autosport

Below right, Camille du Gast in a 1903 30hp
De Dietrich. Photo: Montagu Motor Museum

build the original FJ Brabham. In 1962 and 1963 he drove an FJ Brabham and a Lotus Elite sports with success, winning the Index of Thermal Efficiency at Le Mans in the latter in 1962. In 1964 he joined the John Willment team, driving F2 Lotus and Brabham single seaters, Cortina saloons and Cobra GTs. He drove an F1 Brabham-BRM without great success in 1965, and also drove a Brabham-Climax in the Tasman Series, taking three 2nd places.

In 1966 Gardner continued to drive Brabham F2s and was also seen in a Ford GT with Sir John Whitmore, while in 1967 he dominated the British Saloon Car Championship in a Ford Falcon. He won this Championship again in 1968, in a Ford Escort, and also drove Alec Mildren's 2·5-litre Alfa Romeo-engined Brabham in Tasman events. In 1969 he continued to drive Alan Mann Escorts in saloon car events, and also had some victories in a Lola GT in Europe and South Africa. In 1970 he dominated the British saloon car scene in a Boss Mustang, and developed the F5000 Lola T190 into a race-winner.

Gardner is now an extremely experienced driver, equally fast in saloons, GTs, sports and single seater cars. DCN

Gast, Camille du

Though Camille du Gast's racing career was brief and without laurels, she deserves her place in history as the first woman to compete in *grandes épreuves*, and this at a time when to motor at all was not considered womanly. The wife of a Paris store director, she raced under her maiden name, and was first seen at the wheel of a 20hp Panhard in the 1901 Paris–Berlin race. Accompanied by the Prince du Sagan as mechanic, she finished 33rd against more powerful opposition. For the Paris–Madrid in 1903 she entered a 30hp De Dietrich, the smaller of the two types of racer fielded by Lunéville, but still a *grande voiture* of 5·7 litres' capacity. What is more, she was lying 6th in the race and might have figured prominently in the result had she not stopped to render first aid to Stead, her seriously injured teammate. Nor did the carnage of 'the race to death' deter her, for she was provisionally given a place in the 1904 Benz racing team, only to lose it when women were specifically barred from racing that year. Thereafter she turned to racing motorboats and competed in the Algiers–Toulon event. In later life she was active in charities, especially those for the prevention of cruelty to animals. She died in 1942. MCS

Gendebien, Olivier

One of Belgium's greatest racing drivers, Olivier Gendebien, born in 1924 is a wealthy and patrician character who served as a paratrooper towards the end of World War 2, and then spent some years working in the Congo. While there, his driving over the rough roads of the country impressed Charles Fraikin who asked him if he would be interested in rallying on his return to Europe.

Back home he made his competition debut in a minor race with an old Veritas, but retired. Later in 1952 he won on a production sports car race at Spa in Jerry d'Hendecourt's Jaguar XK 120, and shared Fraikin's Jaguar Mk VII in that year's Liège-Rome-Liège Rally. The following year the pair were 2nd in the Liège and Gendebien won at Spa with a 2-litre Ferrari MM. In 1954 he was 2nd yet again in the Liège rally with a B20 GT Lancia, won his class in the Tour de France with an Alfa SS, and entered his first Mille Miglia in an XK 120. He bought himself a Mercedes 300SL for the 1955 season, and was 2nd to Fitch's works car in the Mille Miglia GT section before gaining three big victories in the Stella-Alpine, the Liège-Rome-Liège Rally (with Stasse) and the Dolomite Cup. He won the last event in pouring rain from Castellotti's poorly-managed works Ferrari. A week later Gendebien was invited to Modena and signed on as a Ferrari works driver. His first event for them was the Aosta-Grand St Bernard hill-climb in which he came 2nd to Maglioli.

He was given a full season in 1956, finishing 2nd in the Buenos Aires 1,000 kilometres (with Phil Hill), 3rd in the Giro di Sicilia and 5th in the Mille Miglia — winning the GT class in both these events. He was 2nd in the Nürburgring 1,000 kilometres (with de Portago) and 3rd at Le Mans (with Trintignant), and scored twice in the World Championship with 5th places in the Argentine and French GPs. The 1957 season brought him a string of long-distance and sports car successes, including winning the Tour de France with Bianchi. In 1958 he won at Le Mans, scored his second consecutive Reims 12 Hours victory with Frère, won the Targa Florio and his second successive Tour de France.

The elegant Belgian was indisputably one of the greatest long-distance drivers, his rally background and sensitivity in wet weather making him a consistent and safe driver, while he also had great mechanical sympathy.

In 1960 he won Le Mans again, with Frère, and then achieved further great successes there in 1961–2. with Phil Hill. This remarkable total of four Le Mans

Bob Gerard (left) with Baron de Graffenried at Silverstone in 1949. *Photo: Associated Press*

Below left, Olivier Gendebien, with the Ferrari in which he won the 1958 Tour de France with Lucien Bianchi. *Photo: M. L. Rosenthal*

Below, Olivier Gendebien. *Photo: David Phipps*

Below right, Bob Gerard in an ERA, 1949. *Photo: Cyril Posthumus Collection*

24 Hours victories were added to three consecutive wins in the Tour de France, three in the Targa Florio, one in the Nürburgring 1,000 kilometres, two in the Reims 12 Hours, and three consecutive 1sts at Sebring. In his rare non-Ferrari appearances he won at Sebring and was 3rd in the 1960 Targa Florio, sharing a Porsche with Herrmann. His best Formula 1 finish was 3rd in the Belgian GP that year, at the wheel of a Yeoman Credit Cooper. His last F1 race was the 1961 Belgian GP, driving a yellow-painted Ferrari V-6. He retired after his 1962 Le Mans victory. DCN

Gerard, Frederick Robert

The British driver Bob Gerard was born in 1914 and came from a family of noted Riley-fanciers. His competition debut was with a Riley Nine in the 1933 Land's End Trial. He graduated through sprint events to Brooklands and Donington, where he was racing a well-tuned Sprite in 1937. After World War 2, it was a natural progression from Riley to ERA, and by 1948 he had three of them. He preferred road racing to sprints, and although his overall victories were restricted to the smaller events, he gave the Italian teams a run for their money in Grand Prix racing for several seasons with his apparently outdated cars. This was despite the handicap of very short sight — there can have been few bespectacled drivers who achieved such a reputation. In part this was due to his cool, skilful and strategic driving, and in part to his meticulous pre-race preparation and pit-work, which set a new standard for the amateur driver.

From 1950 onwards he drove Cooper 500s and a Frazer Nash in sports events, and from 1952 he became a force to be feared in Formula 2 with a Cooper-Bristol, while still using an ERA in Formule Libre events. To ease himself towards retirement, he used a small sports Turner, but he was still winning races with this car in 1960. Even when he did finally retire, having achieved the distinction of having a bend at his home circuit (Mallory Park, near Leicester) named after him, he continued to participate most actively in the sport by running quasi-works teams in F2. DF

Ginther, Paul Richard

Richie Ginther was born in Los Angeles in 1930 and moved to Santa Monica where he met Phil Hill. His first competition was in 1951 driving a Ford-engined MG TC in Southern California's Sandberg Hill-climb. Following two years of military service as an Air Force

Richie Ginther (Ferrari) passing the station at Monaco in 1960. *Photo: Bernard Cahier*

Richie Ginther. *Photo: Autosport*

Léonce Girardot, 1905. *Photo: Cyril Posthumus Collection*

mechanic, Ginther rode with Phil Hill in the 1953 and 1954 Mexican Road Races. They crashed the first year, but Phil Hill drove Alan Guiberson's 4·5 Ferrari to a 2nd-place finish in 1954. While working as an automobile mechanic, Ginther raced an Aston Martin DB3S, a 4·9 Ferrari and, with considerable success, a Porsche Spyder for California Porsche distributor Johnny von Neuman.

Ginther's first European race was Le Mans in 1957, which his 2-litre Ferrari failed to finish. After campaigning successfully in West Coast racing and finishing 2nd in the 1960 Argentine 1,000 kilometres, he was invited to join Ferrari. In 1960 Ginther drove the first rear-engined Formula 1 Ferrari to 6th place at Monaco in his Grand Prix debut, and was 2nd to Phil Hill in the Italian GP at Monza. Now a regular member of the Ferrari Formula 1 works team and chief Ferrari test driver, Ginther was 2nd to Moss at Monaco and with 3rds at Spa and Aintree finished 5th in World Championship point standings. During 1960 he drove Ferrari sports cars to a 2nd at Sebring with Von Trips and a 3rd at the Nürburgring with Gendebien. Ginther left Ferrari and drove for BRM in 1962, 1963 and 1964. He was 2nd to Graham Hill at Monaco in 1963 and 1964; 2nd at Monza in 1962 and 1963; 3rd in the French GP at Rouen in 1962 and 3rd in the German GP in 1963. Ginther shared the Rover-BRM Turbine at Le Mans with Graham Hill and completed the 1963 GP season tied for 2nd place in driver's points with his BRM team-mate. Among Ginther's 1963 honours was the *Road & Track* Trophy awarded annually to America's outstanding international driver. Ginther's BRM was the only GP car to complete every championship Formula 1 event in 1964; however, he moved to Honda in 1965. In the 1965 Daytona 24 Hours Ginther and Bob Bondurant finished 3rd driving a Ford GT40. Ginther's first year in the Japanese car produced two 6ths and a 7th-place finish before winning his first and only GP at Mexico in the final event of 1965. His last Formula 1 race was the 1966 Mexican GP in which his Honda finished 4th. Ginther was competition manager for the 1969 Porsche Can-Am team that finished 4th in the series. ARB

Girardot, Léonce

Born in 1864, Girardot was nicknamed 'the Eternal Second', and indeed the Frenchman scored seven 2nd places in six racing seasons, these tending to obscure his three victories. His first appearance was in the Paris–Dieppe, 1897, in which his Panhard finished well down the list, but in 1898 he was unlucky to finish 2nd behind Charron in the Paris–Amsterdam–Paris at 26·6mph (42·81kph), as he had been among the leaders the whole way, and actually in 1st place at Amsterdam. In 1899 there were two more 2nd places (Nice–Castellane–Nice and the Tour de France) and a 3rd in the Paris–Bordeaux; by contrast, his two victories (Paris–Ostend and Paris–Boulogne) were relatively minor ones, both fought very closely against Levegh in a Mors. A 5th place in the 1900 Circuit du Sud-Ouest was followed by 2nd and last place in the Gordon Bennett Cup, which he won in 1901, though this time he was the sole survivor, and his 10th position in the concurrent Paris–Bordeaux indicates a fairly unimpressive performance. His 2nd place in the Grand Prix de Pau was gained at a no more than respectable 36mph (57·94kph) after he had hit a heap of stones, though in Paris–Berlin he managed to come in 2nd ahead of de Knyff after another long-drawn-out battle.

In 1901 Girardot, who had been in partnership with Charron selling Panhards in Paris, joined his team-mate and Voigt in the CGV venture. He drove one of the firm's first racers in the Paris–Vienna (and the parallel Third Gordon Bennett Cup), but was out with a split fuel tank within the first 145km, and in the Circuit des Ardennes he could manage no better than 5th. His 1903 season was a little better, for he scored his final 2nd place in the Belgian race at 51·3mph (82·56kph), after retiring in the Paris–Madrid. CGV did not race in 1904, but Girardot turned up once more in the 1905 French Gordon Bennett Trials on the Auvergne circuit, only to be eliminated by a near-fatal crash. After his resignation from the CGV concern he tried his luck with another make, the GEM petrol-electric. When this failed, he, like Henri Fournier, became an importer, handling Knight-Daimlers in France. He died in 1922. MCS

Giraud-Cabantous, Yves

Yves Giraud-Cabantous was a works driver, driver/manufacturer, and independent driver during his 30 years of racing. He joined the Salmson company as a mechanic after being demobilized from the French Air Force, and drove his first speed event, the Argenteuil hill-climb, in March 1925. By 1927 he had won his first race, the Grand Prix des Frontières at Chimay, Belgium, driving an 1,100cc supercharged Salmson, and in 1929 he won the Gaillon hill-climb and scored one of the rare victories for the twin-supercharged straight-8 Salmson voiturette in the Marne GP at Reims.

By 1930 he had become a manufacturer, his 1,100cc Ruby-engined Caban cars making a remarkable debut in the Bol d'Or 24-Hour race at St Germain, Cabantous himself winning the race, with Roger Labric 3rd in another Caban. Two years later the Cabantous/Labric/Caban combination were runners-up in the Rudge Whitworth Biennial Cup at Le Mans, but in the 1933 Bol d'Or Cabantous was involved in a five-car multiple crash, getting his damaged car back to the pits, repairing it, and still finishing 7th. With the Cabans getting old, he drove a Bugatti now and then, and in 1937 amazed the French by rebuilding two of the famous 1925 1,100cc 'Tank' type Chenard-Walckers and running them in the Bol d'Or. His wisdom was borne out when the two cars finished 1st and 2nd, the famous weight-lifter Rigoulot heading Cabantous home. He drove one at Le Mans a month later, but had to retire. In 1938 his machine there was a 3·5-litre Delahaye, with which he and Serraud finished runners-up to a similar car.

The war years past, 'G-C' joined Paul Vallée's Ecurie France, scoring three notable victories in 1947 in the Frontières GP, the Coupe du Salon at Montlhéry, and the San Remo GP—the first French victory in an Italian race for many years. As a good engineer as well as driver, he also test-drove the infamous CTA-Arsenal, France's abortive 'national' Grand Prix car in 1947, covering 10 laps of the Montlhéry *piste de vitesse* at an average of 134·84mph (216·96kph), with a fastest lap at 145·4mph (234·6kph). With the CTA unfit for racing, Cabantous acquired an F1 Lago-Talbot for 1948, won the Grand Prix de Paris, was 2nd at Pau and 3rd in the Coupe du Salon, and became French Champion.

Pleased with the Talbot's rugged characteristics, he raced it all over Europe during the next five years, gaining innumerable good placings. He visited Silverstone in 1950, coming 4th behind three Alfa Romeos in the GP of Europe, then Ulster in 1951, and Charterhall in Scotland in 1952. Ever versatile, in 1949 he took part a long-distance record attempt at Montlhéry with an [I]AP-Diesel, setting new figures up to 12 hours, and in [19]52 he drove for the HWM team in several French [ra]ces. A sage, steady driver with keen mechanical sense, [h]e scored two 4ths, three 5ths and a 6th in 1952–3 at a [ti]me when the British cars were neither fast nor notably [re]liable. He shared a 4·5-litre sports Talbot with Rosier [in] the 1953 Reims 12 Hours, the pair coming 2nd, and [d]rove 750cc Panhard-engined VPs at Le Mans without [su]ccess in 1954 and 1955, his last year of racing. CP

[G]odin de Beaufort, Count Carel

[T]his last scion of an ancient Dutch aristocratic family, [M]aster of Maaren and Maarsbergen, was born in 1936. He [w]as large in stature, a big-hearted, generous and popular [m]an.

[H]e began racing sports Porsches in the late 1950s and [c]ontinued with the make throughout his racing career. [A]n early success was winning the 1,500cc class at Le [M]ans in 1957, sharing a Porsche RS with American, Ed [H]ugus. In 1958 the wealthy and enthusiastic amateur [sh]ared the class-winning Porsche in the Nürburgring [1,]000 kilometres and in 1959 repeated the performance [in] the Sebring 12 Hours. His driving was spectacular in [m]ore ways than one: he crashed over the towering [A]VUS North Wall on one occasion, bounding down [in]to the paddock and driving back on to the course with [h]is battered Porsche.

His driving tactics initially brought him much criticism, [b]ut his engaging personality off the track more than [m]ade up for this. He ran a pair of ex-works F1 Porsches [in] 1962 and 1963; his driving settled down to be fast [a]nd competent, and made the best of outdated machinery. [H]is Ecurie Maarsbergen cars scored points in the 1962 [a]nd 1963 World Championships, and had a splendid [r]ecord of reliability. They entered their fourth F1 season [in] 1964, and De Beaufort planned to replace them with [a]n F2 Brabham, specially modified to accommodate his [h]uge frame. But it was not to be, for he crashed fatally [a]t Bergwerk while practising for the German GP — [t]rying, as ever, to set a competitive time in his obsolete [c]ar. DCN

[G]oldsmith, Paul

[T]his former motorcycle champion, born in 1923, drove [a] Pontiac to win the last stock car race on Daytona [B]each in 1958. USAC stock car champion in 1962 and [19]63, he qualified for the Indianapolis 500 from 1958 to [19]63 inclusive; a 3rd in 1960 was the best of his six [fi]nishes. Goldsmith retired in 1969 after winning nine [N]ASCAR Grand Nationals and in 1970 was general [m]anager of Nichels Eng., in charge of the Dodge [C]harger driven by Charles Glotzbach. ARB

[G]onzalez, José Froilan

[O]ne of the colourful and talented Argentinian drivers [w]hose arrival in Europe after World War 2 had such a [m]arked effect on GP racing, Froilan Gonzalez (known [a]s 'Pepe' or 'Il Cabezon' — the Pampas Bull) was second [o]nly to his friend and compatriot Fangio in his feats over [h]ere. Plump, chubby-faced and impassive of mien, he [d]rove his earlier European races with more courage [t]han finesse, crouched in the cockpit, hauling at the [w]heel and proceeding with great slides, but his lap times [s]howed Gonzalez to be very fast indeed.

After racing extensively in local Argentine events, he [c]ame to Europe in 1950 to drive one of the blue and [y]ellow Scuderia Argentina 4CLT/48 Maseratis when

Above, Yves Giraud-Cabantous (right) with a Caban at Le Mans in 1932. *Photo: courtesy Yves Giraud-Cabantous*

Below, Yves Giraud-Cabantous, 1952. *Photo: courtesy Yves Giraud Cabantous*

Above right, Froilan Gonzalez. *Photo: Rodolfo Mailander*

Count Carel Godin de Beaufort. *Photo: Auto-Visie*

Paul Goldsmith. *Photo: Al Bochroch Collection*

Fangio had been taken on by Alfa Romeo. His first success came in the Albi GP when he won the 2nd heat and was classified 2nd overall.

Gonzalez really came to the fore in 1951, firstly when he astonished the racing world by twice defeating the resuscitated team of 1939 3-litre supercharged GP Mercedes-Benz at Buenos Aires, driving a 2-litre Ferrari. In Europe he drove a 4·5-litre Talbot in the Paris GP, coming 2nd, and in the Swiss GP, where he retired. But then he got his chance with Ferrari when their No 3 driver Taruffi went sick before the French GP at Reims. Driving their latest 4·5-litre unblown V-12, he was lying 2nd when Ascari took over, finishing in that position, then went with the team to Silverstone for the British GP. In a superb drive Gonzalez won the race outright, breaking the long chain of Alfa Romeo victories, and at the Nürburgring in the German GP he was 3rd. Next he won the Pescara GP in Italy, and wound up his season with 2nd places at Bari, Monza, Barcelona and Modena, the last a Formula 2 race.

Naturally Gonzalez was in demand in 1952. He signed with Maserati for F2, scoring 2nds in the Italian and Modena GPs; with a 2-litre Ferrari he ran 2nd to Fangio at Buenos Aires and Piriapolis, in Uruguay, and won at Gavea; with Tony Vandervell's 4·5-litre Thinwall Special he won the Richmond Trophy at the Easter Goodwood; and with BRM he drove the difficult 1·5-litre 16-cylinder cars with much fire but little success at Silverstone and Albi, apart from fastest lap in the latter race, then led the BRM 1-2-3 success in the *Daily Graphic* Trophy race at Goodwood in September, and also won the Woodcote Cup race the same day.

His 1953 season brought four 3rds with F2 Maseratis in the Argentine, Naples, Dutch and French GPs, 2nd place with a BRM in the Albi F1 GP, and an unpleasant crash at Lisbon in a Lancia. With the advent of the 2·5-litre Formula 1 in 1954 he joined Ferrari and had a splendid season in the face of strong Mercedes-Benz and Maserati opposition. He won the Bordeaux and Bari GPs and the BRDC International Trophy at Silverstone; won the British GP a second time, defeating the Mercedes; and was 2nd in the German and Swiss GPs. In sports car racing he won Le Mans with Trintignant in a 4·9-litre Ferrari, the supporting sports car race at the BRDC Silverstone, and the Portuguese GP at Lisbon.

Then came misfortune when he crashed at Dundrod, Northern Ireland, in practice for the TT race in a 3-litre Ferrari. He was seriously hurt, and only resumed racing on a limited scale in 1955 in his own country. In the Argentine GP, held in tremendous heat, he showed

typical Gonzalez spirit by duelling fiercely with Ascari's Lancia, finally getting the lead only to have to pull in for relief. Resuming later he chased Fangio's leading Mercedes hard but again had to hand over, finally sharing a hard-fought 2nd place with Trintignant and Farina.

His last major placing was 3rd with Behra in the 1956 Buenos Aires 1,000km sports car race with a 3-litre Maserati. In July that year Tony Vandervell hired Gonzalez for £1000 to drive one of his Vanwalls in the British GP at his favourite Silverstone, but a last-minute change of wheel sizes brought the anti-climax of broken transmission on the starting line. Thereafter Gonzalez contented himself with local appearances, chiefly with a Chevrolet-engined Ferrari in national events, and devoting his time to his motor business. CP

Goux, Jules

Goux, born in 1885, was one of Peugeot's great drivers and the complement of Georges Boillot: he was considered to be Boillot's superior in long-distance events, but like Boillot he became expert in handling the very awkward and often towering Lion-Peugeot voiturettes which preceded the Henry-designed GP machinery. Trained as an engineer at the Arts et Métiers in Paris, he worked as Peugeot's chief tester before driving for the firm. In the 1907 Coupe des Voiturettes he finished 3rd, behind the all-conquering Sizaire-Naudin singles. It was the same story in the 1908 ACF voiturette race, though in that year's Coupe he managed to beat the third member of the Sizaire team, Lebouc, by 3sec to take his customary 3rd position. He was given a twin for the 1909 event, which brought him up to 2nd behind his

Above left, Froilan Gonzalez (Ferrari 553 Squalo) in the 1954 French GP. *Photo: Motor*

Left, Froilan Gonzalez (centre), with Alberto Ascari (right) *Photo: N. W. Newbatt*

Above right, Jules Goux in a Lion-Peugeot, 1909. *Photo: Montagu Motor Museum*

Right, Jules Goux in a Peugeot, 1913 French GP. *Photo: T. A. S. O. Mathieson Collection*

José Gonzalez: Principal Successes

1951	President Peron GP, Buenos Aires	Ferrari 166
	Eva Peron GP, Buenos Aires	Ferrari 166
	British GP	Ferrari 375
	Pescara GP	Ferrari 375
1952	Richmond Trophy, Goodwood	Thinwall Special
	Circuit of Gavea, Rio de Janeiro	Ferrari 2-litre
	Daily Graphic Trophy, Goodwood	BRM V-16
	Woodcote Cup, Goodwood	BRM V-16
1954	Bordeau GP	Ferrari 625
	Daily Express International Trophy, Silverstone	Ferrari 625
	Daily Express Sports Car Race, Silverstone	Ferrari 375 Plus
	Le Mans 24-Hours Race, with Trintignant	Ferrari 375 Plus
	British GP	Ferrari 625
	Bari GP	Ferrari 625
	Portugese GP	Ferrari 375 Plus

team-mate Guippone on the still-faster single, but he managed a couple of wins as the tide turned for Lion-Peugeot, in the Sicilian Cup event over the Madonie circuit, and in the Spanish Catalan Cup sponsored by Alfonso XIII.

In 1910 his Coupe des Voiturettes car was still the 2-cylinder machine, which was more manageable than Boillot's V-4; but a jumped sprocket, a broken shock absorber and constant tyre changes told their own story and it is a tribute to Goux's driving that he achieved 2nd place behind Zucarelli's Hispano-Suiza. In the Sicilian race he could manage no better than 3rd, but he won a second Sicilian Cup.

The last year of the complex Lion-Peugeots was 1911 and he retired his V-4 in the Coupe de l'Auto. Meanwhile Goux, in association with Zucarelli and Boillot, had persuaded Peugeot to set up a racing department, the results of which were the brilliant Henry designs first seen in 1912. That year the firm elected to concentrate their efforts on the Grand Prix, and thus Goux had no car for the Coupe de l'Auto, as well as retiring in the big race. He did, however, manage a victory in the 1912 Coupe de la Sarthe at Le Mans, and took the GP car to Indianapolis in 1913 to win the 500 at 75·93mph. Both in the Coupe de l'Auto and in the Grand Prix he finished 2nd behind Boillot, his average in the latter race being 71·8mph (115·55kph). He drove without success in the 1914 French GP, eclipsed by Boillot's one-man battle against the might of Mercedes. Goux campaigned with a 1914 4·5-litre GP car (with American-made Premier block) in the 1919 Indianapolis 500, but Peugeot's 1920 Indianapolis car was a flop, and he got nowhere with it.

At this point Peugeot withdrew from GP racing for

good, and Goux transferred his allegiance (along with Henry) to Ballot, taking 3rd place in the 1921 French GP, and scoring a win in the Italian race for that unlucky make. A crash ended his chances in the 1922 French GP, but he drove his 2-litre dohc machine brilliantly to take 2nd place in the Targa Florio. He was entered to drive the cuff-valve Rolland-Pilain in the 1922 French race, but it did not start, and he retired his Ballot in the 1924 Targa Florio. It seemed that he was now to be relegated to safe race-losers, as his drives on the Schmid (formerly Rolland-Pilain) achieved nothing. In 1925, however, Goux joined the Bugatti works team; though the cars were slower than the contemporary Alfa Romeos and Delages he drove his Type 35 into 5th place in the French GP, and also finished 4th in the touring-car event behind his three team-mates on a road-equipped version. Though oil-pump trouble eliminated him from the 1926 Italian GP, and his entry for Indianapolis failed to start, he finished 2nd at San Sebastian and Milan and won two races. Of these, the French GP was an empty victory on the windswept expanses of Miramas, for only three Bugattis started, and Goux's was the sole finisher, but in the European GP, held in Spain that year, he was up against full opposition. He was also in the 1927 team, but one of his scheduled appearances was in the French race, from which Bugatti scratched, and his only recorded performance was a 3rd in the Touring-Car GP. After this he retired from the circuits, though even in the late 1950s he was still using a Bugatti as his personal car, and worked for that firm as late as 1955. He died in 1965. MCS

Graffenried, Baron Emanuel de

A cheery, popular Swiss driver from Fribourg, 'Toulo' or 'Barney' de Graffenried was an energetic member of the International racing circus both before and after World War 2. He began well by winning the 1·5-litre sports class of the national Prix de Bremgarten at Berne in 1936 with a far from new 6-cylinder Alfa Romeo, and next season went into partnership with an American, John du Puy. Their cars were a Type 6C Maserati and an earlier 4-cylinder model with Tecnauto ifs fitted, which gave them much useful experience on French, Italian, Swiss and British circuits.

He won his class in the Prix de Bremgarten in 1938 and 1939 with the 6C Maserati, which he also drove in the La Turbie hill-climb, running 2nd to Sommer's 3-litre Alfa Romeo in the absence of a 1·5-litre class. For 1946 de Graffenried had a new 4-cylinder, 16-valve Maserati and teamed up with compatriots Kautz and Basadonna to form Ecurie Autosport. His share of success was a victory in the Maloja hill-climb, and the honours of first Swiss finisher (5th) in the Grand Prix des Nations at Geneva. The Maserati was less reliable in long races, but de Graffenried did well once again before his own countrymen to come 3rd at Lausanne in 1947, and to win the Circuit of Erlen, in eastern Switzerland, and finish 2nd to Farina in the GP des Nations in 1948. A 3rd at Monaco was another indication that de Graffenried was one of the better *Maseratisti* of the day.

By 1949 he had acquired a 4CLT/48 San Remo Maserati, with which he scored his greatest victory, the British GP at Silverstone. He won again at Erlen, and took creditable 2nds at Pau, Jersey, and in the Dutch and Swedish GPs. By 1950 the San Remo Maserati was getting rather tired, but he nursed it to more good placings, notably two 3rds in the Douglas, Isle of Man, and Jersey races. That same year Alfa Romeo paid de Graffenried signal honour as the premier Swiss driver by

Baron de Graffenried, 1954. *Photo: Dr Vicente Alvarez*

Andy Granatelli. *Photo: Al Bochroch Collection*

offering him a drive in their famous team of 158·1159 F1 cars in the Geneva GP. He finished 2nd to team-mate Fangio—and no one could do much better than that. Alfas offered him further drives in 1951, and he came 5th for them in the Swiss GP and 6th in the Spanish.

Formula 2 took over in 1952–3, so de Graffenried drove a Maserati-Platé (a shortened, unsupercharged 4CLT/48) to score three 3rds at Silverstone, Aix-les-Bains and Cadours. Then in 1953 with a new F2 Maserati he enjoyed his best season of all. He won the Syracuse GP after all the Ferraris retired; won two races at Goodwood; the Eifelrennen at the Nürburgring; and the Freiburg and Ollon-Villars hill-climbs. At Silverstone in the BRDC/*Daily Express* race he won his heat, but jumped the start in the final. Although he slowed at once he·was penalized 1 minute, and was so disgusted that he withdrew from the race.

For his 1954 racing the Baron went further afield: to South America, taking his 1953 F2 Maserati with 2·5-litre engine installed, and also a 2-litre sports Maserati. The single-seater brought a modest 8th in the Argentine GP, but the sports car won him two Brazilian races—the Rio de Janeiro GP on the sinuous 'Devil's Springboard' mountain circuit at Gavea, and the São Paulo GP at Interlagos. In his last season, 1955, he signed off with a satisfying 2nd in the Lisbon GP with a 3-litre sports Maserati, and a 3rd in the GP of Venezuela at Caracas in a 3-litre Ferrari. His son Leo keeps the family name in racing today with a Mini-Cooper. CP

Granatelli, Anthony

Born in Texas in 1923 and reared in Chicago, Andy Granatelli has been involved with motor racing as builder, promoter, driver, mechanic and car owner. With his brothers, Vincent and Joseph, he built speed equipment, promoted night racing at Soldier Field, Chicago, drove hot rods in the Midwest and, in 1948, crashed while trying to qualify for Indianapolis. Granatelli first entered the 500 in 1946 with a Mercury-powered Miller Special, which the Granatelli brothers drove from Chicago to Indianapolis. But it was not until Andretti won the 1969 classic that a Granatelli entry reached victory lane.

Granatelli's repeated attempts to rejuvenate the popular Novi V-8 earned him a considerable following and in 1965 Bobby Unser drove the Ferguson 4wd Novi to the first Indianapolis race lap over 160mph (256kph). The controversial STP Turbines came within minutes of bringing victory to Granatelli in 1966 and 1967. A broken gear box stopped Parnelli Jones five miles from the finish line in 1967 and, in 1968 (after qualifying three smaller Pratt & Whitney Lotus-STP Turbocars), fuel-pump shaft failure eliminated both Joe Leonard, who was leading after 480 miles (272km) and Art Pollard. Leonard's 1968, four-lap qualifying mark of 171·559mph (276·094kph) still stands as an Indianapolis record. After 23 barren years, in 1969 Granatelli entries won eleven races (9 Andretti—2 Pollard) on USAC Championship Trail.

In 1970 Granatelli entered Grand Prix racing with Ford-powered March Formula 1 machines for Jo Siffert, Chris Amon and, in selected events, Mario Andretti. Also a new STP-March Group 7 sports car was driven by Chris Amon in the three final 1970 Can-Am races. Now a major industrialist, Granatelli brings to American racing the fortunate combination of substantial funds, a flamboyant news-making personality and a keen love of motor racing. ARB

Gregory, Masten

Gregory was born in Kansas City, Mo., in 1932, and first raced at Caddo Mills, Tex., November 1952. Influenced by his brother-in-law, Dale Duncan, who drove an Allard, Gregory bought one of these cars, but soon changed to a C-type Jaguar in which he won his first race at Golden Gate Park, San Francisco, in 1953. Late that summer at Floyd Bennett Airfield, New York, Gregory approached Henry Wessel, owner of an almost new C-type Jaguar, inquiring as to its price, explaining that his own had just caught fire. The transaction was completed on the spot and Gregory raced it that afternoon. Failing to finish the 1954 Argentine 1,000 kilometres in his Jaguar, Gregory bought the winning 4·5 Ferrari and campaigned with it in Europe. Co-driving with Biondetti, he was 4th in the Reims 12 hours; 3rd at Lisbon and winner of sports car features at Aintree and Nassau.

Gregory's first year in Formula 1, 1957, was his best. His Maserati was 4th at Pau, 3rd at Monaco and 4th at Pescara and Monza. He completed every race he started and tied for 4th place in World Championship point standings. In 1959 Gregory was 3rd in the Dutch GP at Zandvoort and 2nd at Lisbon but his habit of bailing-out of rapidly moving, accident-bound cars, while calling for skill and courage, is said to have made it difficult for the spectacled, articulate Missourian to get first-class rides. In 1961, co-driving a Type 61 Maserati with Lloyd 'Lucky' Casner, the American airlines pilot who promoted the Camoradi USA racing team that was to have relied on public support, Gregory won the Nürburgring 1,000 kilometres. He captured the 1963 Players 200 at Mosport and, with Jochen Rindt, was a surprise winner of the 1965 Le Mans, driving the North American Racing Team 250 LM Ferrari entered by three-time Le Mans winner Luigi Chinetti. Gregory passed his Indy drivers test in 1963 but did not make the starting grid until 1965, when he qualified 31st and on race day electrified the crowd by moving up to 5th by the 43rd lap, before he dropped out with mechanical failure. A 5th at Laguna Seca in 1966 has been Gregory's best Can-Am finish. In 1970 Gregory and Toine Hezemans (Alfa Romeo T-33) completed 247 laps, one less than the winning Ferrari, to finish 3rd in the Sebring 12-hour Race. ARB

Grossman, Robert

Born in Philadelphia in 1923, and now a foreign car dealer in Nyack, N.Y., Bob Grossman studied singing and sang professionally before turning to motor racing. He drove an Alfa Romeo to the Sports Car Club of America 'G' production national championship in 1958, captured the 'C' production title with a Ferrari coupé in 1959, and finished 1961 in a three-way tie for SCCA 'A' production honours. For six years running (1959–64) Grossman finished in the top 10 at Le Mans; a 5th in 1959 with local stonemason Tavano co-driving a stock Ferrari convertible, was his best finish. Grossman and Don Yenko drove a Camaro to 10th overall and 1st in class in the 1969 Sebring 12 hours. ARB

Guinness, Sir Algernon Lee

A British driver who drove Darracqs very effectively in the early days. He came 3rd in the TT race of 1906 and was 2nd in this race in 1908, driving a 'four-inch' Darracq. At Brooklands and on Saltburn sands, Yorkshire, Guinness drove the fearsome V-8 200hp Darracq, which was little more than a bare chassis, two bucket seats and a 22,518cc engine. On this car Guinness covered 440yd (402·3m) at Brooklands in 1907 at 115·4mph (185·7kph). Still active after World War 1, Sir Algernon won a very wet 1·5-litre TT race in the Isle of Man in 1922, averaging 53·3mph (85·78kph) for 226 miles (363·7km) in a 16-valve Talbot-Darracq, keeping ahead of team-mate Albert Divo. He adopted a back-to-front cap, securely tied on.

In later years Sir Algernon acted in an official capacity in motor racing and took a very prominent interest in the affairs of the British Motor Cycle Racing Club. He died in 1954. WB

Guinness, Kenelm Lee

An early insight into motor racing was obtained by K. Lee Guinness when he went as riding mechanic to his brother Algernon Guinness, who owned the 200hp Darracq and other fast cars of this make. The younger brother then became a racing driver in his own right, winning the 600-mile Isle of Man TT for Sunbeam in 1914, bring the 3·3-litre Wolverhampton car home ahead of the challenging Minervas. Guinness had made his own sparking plugs, using mica insulators, for racing engines and they were so successful that he founded the famous KLG sparking plug factory at the Robin Hill works at Putney Vale. He had been a works driver in Louis Coatalen's Sunbeam team since 1913 and resumed this position after World War 1, as an STD team driver. Lee Guinness was particularly successful with the 1·5-litre Talbot-Darracq voiturettes, on which he finished 2nd in the 1921 Grand Prix des Voiturettes at Le Mans and in that year's JCC 200 Miles Race at Brooklands. In 1922 Guinness followed this up by winning three 1·5-litre races in a row for Talbot-Darracq, the JCC 200, at Le Mans and in the Penya Rhin Grand Prix. Guinness took the Talbot-Darracq and Sunbeam cars and drivers to their distant race engagements in his yacht *Ocean River*.

Apart from road racing, Lee Guinness drove various Sunbeams in Brooklands races, and with the 350hp V-12 single-seater established the last Land Speed Record to be made at the track, with a two-way speed of 133·75mph (215·18kph) over the kilometre. Guinness also won with the big Sunbeam at the 1922 Brooklands Duke of York Royal Meeting, lapping at 122·67mph (197·41kph). He then proceeded to win the 1924 200 Miles Race in a supercharged Darracq. Then, during the 1924 San Sebastian Grand Prix, Guinness' Sunbeam crashed, killing the riding mechanic and seriously injuring the

Sir Algernon Lee Guinness (left). *Photo: Montagu Motor Museum*

driver. Guinness never really recovered from this accident, although he acted in an official capacity in America during Segrave's 200mph (320kph) Land Speed Record and at Phoenix Park, Dublin in 1929. He died in 1937. WB

Gurney, Daniel Sexton

Dan Gurney was born in Port Jefferson, New York, in 1931. Gurney's parents—his father was a professional singer—moved to Southern California near Riverside Raceway in 1948. Following military service in Korea, Gurney drove his first sports car race in a TR2 at Torrey Pines, California in 1955. After driving a Porsche Speedster and Corvette, Dan moved up to a short wheelbase 4·9 Ferrari and was soon ranked among the best of Southern Californian drivers. In 1957 he ran 2nd to Carroll Shelby at Riverside and won over a distinguished field at Palm Springs.

Gurney made his first trip to Europe in 1958, where he and fellow Californian Bruce Kessler, who crashed in the rain, drove a 3-litre Ferrari at Le Mans. Two weeks later Gurney raced a Ferrari coupé with the Belgian André Pilette in the Reims 12 Hours, where they failed to finish. Gurney returned to Europe in 1959 to drive sports cars for Ferrari but was given works Formula 1 rides by mid-season. His Ferrari was 2nd in the 1959 German Grand Prix at the AVUS and although Phil Hill and Gendebien, then Ferrari's top sports car pair, replaced Gurney and his co-driver Chuck Daigh, Gurney was credited with sharing the winning Ferrari in the 1959 Sebring. Gurney drove a factory Formula 1 BRM without success in 1960 and with Stirling Moss brought a Maserati home 1st in the 1960 Nürburgring 1,000 kilometres.

The tall Californian became a member of the Porsche team in 1961 with 2nds at Reims, Monza and Watkins Glen enabling him to score second highest points in the 1961 World Drivers' Championship, the best finish of his career. In sports cars Dan and Jo Bonnier earned a 2nd for Porsche in the 1961 Targa Florio. In 1962 Gurney won the French GP at Rouen for his first and Porsche's only Grand Prix. Gurney's Lotus-Ford captured the inaugural Daytona Continental in 1962 and in May he drove his first Indianapolis 500. After trying John Zink's Trackburner, an experimental turbine, Dan switched to one of Mickey Thompson's Buick-powered rear-engined cars. He qualified 8th but dropped out on lap 93 with transmission failure. Supporting the claim that he is the most versatile of American drivers, Gurney won the Riverside 500-mile stock car race in 1963, and in 1964, 1965, 1966 and 1968, driving a Ford sedan.

After his 1962 Indy debut Gurney was so convinced that a well-designed rear-engined machine could win the 500 that he paid for Colin Chapman's 1963 Indianapolis trip, when Gurney introduced the brilliant English designer to the Speedway's mysteries and, perhaps of more importance, to key Ford Motor Co personnel. Driving a works Formula 1 Brabham-Climax in 1963 Dan earned a 2nd at Zandvoort and a 3rd at Spa. At Indianapolis Gurney did much to assure proponents of Indy's traditional heavy, solid-axle, front-engined roadsters that the supposedly fragile rear-engined monocoque design was sturdy, when he crashed his Lotus-Ford into the wall, walked away unhurt, and qualified the Team-Lotus 'mule' the following day. He finished the 1963 Indy in 7th place and was 3rd in the USAC Milwaukee 200. Gurney won both the GP of France and Mexico in 1964, his second Rouen victory again being the first-ever GP for a new make, this time for Brabham. He qualified his Lotus-Ford at 154·487mph (248·541kph), 6th on the 1964 Indy grid, but was withdrawn as a safety measure after 110 laps when team-mate Jim Clark had tyre failure.

Dan Gurney and Carroll Shelby founded All-American Racers in 1964; Gurney acquired sole ownership of this racing car manufacturing firm in 1967. Anglo-American Racers, formed in 1965 to handle Gurney's Formula 1 engine-building programme and Gurney-Weslake cylinder heads, moved from Rye, Sussex, to Ashford, Kent, where it closed in 1968 when Gurney abandoned Formula 1 racing.

Gurney continued to drive for Jack Brabham in 1965, registering 3rds in the French GP at Clermont-Ferrand, the Nürburgring and Monza, plus a 2nd in the United States GP at Watkins Glen, and finishing 4th in driver point standings. Gurney was sidelined with timing gear failure in the 1965 Indy after 42 laps. After again winning the Riverside 500 NASCAR Grand National, Gurney teamed with Jerry Grant in a Ford Mk II to finish 2nd in the 1966 Daytona 24 Hours. At Sebring Gurney and Grant were well in the lead when Gurney ran out of fuel on the final lap within 200 yards of the finish and was disqualified for pushing his Mk II over the line. Gurney's AAR Eagle-Ford was damaged in the 1966 Indianapolis first lap melée and he was unable to restart. His Lola-Ford won the Bridgehampton Can-Am, the only non-Chevrolet engine victory in the first four years of the Canadian American Challenge Cup.

Gurney did not win the 1967 Riverside 500 stock car race but his Eagle captured the Formula 1 'Race of Champions' at Brands Hatch and went on to win the Belgium GP at Spa; the first American to win a Grand Prix in an American car since Jimmy Murphy's Duesenberg took the French GP at Le Mans in 1921. In sports cars he teamed with A. J. Foyt to set a record 135·48mph

Above, Dan Gurney at Indianapolis in 1968, after finishing 2nd in an Olsonite Eagle. *Photo: Al Bochroch*

Above right, Albert Guyot in a Schmid, 1924. *Photo: Hugh Conway Collection*

Mike Hailwood. *Photo: Patrick Benjafield*

Albert Guyot in a Delage, 1913 French GP. *Photo: T. A. S. O. Mathieson Collection*

(218·03kph) average to bring Ford their second Le Mans victory and he survived a driving rain to finish 3rd in the Canadian GP at Mosport. At Indianapolis he set a new one-mile lap qualifying record of 167·942mph (270·263kph) only to have Andretti top his four lap average, relegating Gurney to the middle of the front row. He briefly led the 1967 500 but was eliminated by engine failure after 160 laps. Gurney wound up his 1967 season winning the Rex Mays 300 Championship car race at Riverside, becoming the first driver to win championship races in all four major categories: Formula 1, Sports cars, Stock cars and Indianapolis cars.

After winning his fifth Motor Trend 500 stock car race to begin 1968, Gurney's 166·512mph (268·023kph) 4-lap qualifying average was fifth fastest at Indianapolis. Gurney brought his AAR-Eagle stock-block Ford home 2nd with Gurney-built Eagles also finishing 1st and 4th. Gurney also won Indy car races at Mosport and Riverside in 1968, but had little success in Can-Am and Grand Prix racing. He dropped Formula 1 in 1969, concentrating on Indianapolis, Can-Am and occasional drives for Ford in the Trans-Am series. Gurney won $67,723 in the 1969 Indianapolis, again finishing 2nd, and he drove Indy cars on road courses to win 100-mile heats at Indianapolis Raceway Park and Donnybrooke.

Ford's long association with Gurney ended in 1970 when he became responsible for a two-car team of Plymouth Barracudas for himself and his young protégé, Swede Savage, in the Trans-American Sedan series. Dan won the 1970 Indy car race on the Sears Point road course in his Eagle-Ford but changed to a turbocharged Offenhauser for the 500 in which he finished 3rd, winning $59,000.

Following Indianapolis Gurney joined Team McLaren, driving both Formula 1 and the McLaren M8D-Chevrolet that his friend, the late Bruce McLaren, had planned to drive in the 1970 Can-Am series. In F1 Dan gathered a 6th in the French GP at Clermont-Ferrand and did not finish at Zandvoort and Brands Hatch. But in the Can-Am series Gurney won the first two races at Mosport and St Jovite and was ninth at Watkins Glen. However a conflict over Team McLaren and Gurney oil company commitments resulted in Dan's departure. His replacement, Peter Gethin, finished second to Denny Hulme in the next Can-Am at Edmonton. In September Gurney qualified second in the Ontario 500 and was leading before his retirement on the 99th lap. Dan Gurney announced his retirement as a race driver following the 4 Oct 1970 Riverside

Trans-Am, in which his Plymouth sedan finished fifth. Gurney plans to stay in racing as a constructor and team-manager. In 1971 Indy veteran Bobby Unser and Swede Savage, who won the November 1970 Phoenix 150 in Gurney's AAR Eagle stock-block Ford for his first auto racing victory, are campaigning Gurney AAR Eagles on USAC's Championship Trail. ARB

Guyot, Albert

This burly, cheerful Frenchman came from Orleans where he had a motor business. His first race was in a Minerva in the 1907 Kaiserpreis, and the following year he won the GP des Voiturettes on a single-cylinder Delage. He continued to drive for Delage up to 1914, coming 2nd in the GP de la Sarthe in 1913 and 3rd at Indianapolis in 1914. He also drove a Sunbeam in the 1913 Indy race, finishing 4th. After World War 1 he drove a Ballot at Indy in 1919 (finishing 5th), and a Duesenberg in the French GP in 1921 (finishing 6th), and won the 1921 Corsican GP in a Bignan. He drove for Rolland-Pilain in 1922 and 1923, winning the 1923 San Sebastian GP, and then turned manufacturer with his sleeve-valve Guyot Speciale racing car. He did not have much success with these cars, and in 1926 retired from racing. CP

Hailwood, Michael

Born in 1941, Mike Hailwood began racing motorcycles at the age of 17, and had a brief drive with a Lotus-Climax at Aintree in 1960. He remained in the motor-cycle world until 1968, winning nine World Championships before his retirement, but during this period he also drove cars, mainly for Reg Parnell whose Lotus-BRM he campaigned in a number of events. After his retirement from motorcycling Mike turned to long distance sports car racing, co-driving Eddie Nelson's Springbok Championship-winning Ford GT40 in late 1967, and driving Mirage M2 and GT40 cars during 1969. He also drove a works-backed Lola F5000 single-seater, coming 3rd in the Guards European F5000 Championship. He drove in F5000 events again in 1970, and also shared a JW Porsche 917 at Le Mans with David Hobbs. DCN

Hall, James E.

Jim Hall was born in Abilene, Tex., in 1935, and since 1953 has helped his brother Charles to manage the family oil business. He enrolled at the California Institute of Technology to study geology but changed courses and graduated as a mechanical engineer. In 1954 he drove his first race in an Austin Healey at Fort Sumner, N.Mex. Later he drove Ferraris, a 'Birdcage' Maserati, and a Lister-Chevrolet. With the last-named, Hall began his experiments with sports car engineering. Previously in his own words, 'I had just taken the cars as they came from the manufacturer, and played driver. If something didn't work right I just figured it was the manufacturer's fault'. He had no great success with the Lister-Chevrolet, and in 1961 commissioned Troutman and Barnes of Culver City, Calif., to build a front-engined, spaceframe sports car which he christened the Chaparral. For Hall's career with this car and its successors, see page 392.

In 1960 Hall bought a Formula 2 Lotus in which he installed a 2·5-litre Coventry-Climax engine so that he had something quite close to a 2·5-litre F1 Lotus. With this car he finished 7th in the 1960 US Grand Prix at Riverside. In 1961 and 1962 he raced a 1·5-litre F2 Lotus, and in 1963 went to Europe where he drove the second Lotus-BRM car (Innes Ireland had the first) in the British Racing Partnership. Hall drove in every Grand Prix race that season except for the South African; his best performance was 5th at the Nürburgring. BRP gave up racing after 1963 and in any case Hall found the Grand Prix scene uncongenial, so he concentrated on the Chaparral project from 1964 onwards. A severe accident at the Stardust Raceway in November 1968 resulted in nine weeks in hospital, and Hall has not driven Chaparral cars in a race since. However, in 1970 he mounted a two-car assault on the Trans-Am series with Chevrolet Camaros for himself and SCCA veteran Ed Leslie. GNG/ARB

Hamilton, J. Duncan

Born in Eire in 1920, Hamilton conformed to type by learning on Austin Sevens before the war, and was an enthusiastic habitué of Brooklands. After demobilization from the Fleet Air Arm, he purchased an R-type MG and a 35B Bugatti for sprints and hill-climbs, following this in 1948 with a 6C Maserati, which had some success in races. A class win with a Healey Silverstone at the venue which had given the name to the car earned Hamilton works drives at Le Mans with the Nash-Healeys, which performed creditably in achieving 4th place in 1950 and 6th in 1951. This was the year when he acquired a GP Talbot Lago, and in the storm-ridden British GP he really sprang into the limelight by running 2nd to Parnell ahead of all the Continental 'names'. Works drives in Formula 2 with HWM came in 1952, and with Jaguars in sports racing, but the HWM was now quick enough against international competition and this was one of Jaguar's unlucky years. They made

up for it in 1953, when Hamilton (partnered by Rolt) won at Le Mans with the C-type, and the same partnership ran a close 2nd with the D-type Jaguar in the 1954 race.

Hamilton's own well-tuned C-type also achieved many good results, before being replaced with a D-type for 1955. He joined the Ferrari team in 1956 after a disagreement with the team manager of Jaguars, but achieved little success, and resorted to 'privateering' with his own Jaguars in 1957. A painful crash in the 3-litre Jaguar in the 1958 Le Mans, and the deaths of many of his closest friends, took away much of his pleasure in racing and the burly and colourful Hamilton announced early in 1959 that he was to hang up his gloves. DF

Hanks, Samuel, Jr

Sam Hanks, born in 1914 and one of America's busiest race drivers for the first 12 years after World War 2, campaigned successfully in three different divisions of the sport after gaining his early experience during the six seasons before the war years.

He won the Pacific Coast midget championship in 1937 and again in 1946; the National midget championship in 1941 and 1949; the Pacific Coast stock car championship in 1956; and the National big car championship title in 1953. He also earned ranking among the top ten big car championship drivers during four other seasons and finished high in the national stock car point standings three times (2nd in 1954, 5th in 1956 and 3rd in 1957).

Hanks earned his 1953 big car crown by winning two of the 11 events on the championship schedule, coming 3rd at Indianapolis and 5th or better on six other occasions.

During his career, he drove in 12 of the annual Indianapolis events, also finishing 3rd in 1952 and 2nd in 1956 before finally winning the 500 in 1957 by setting a new race record of 135·600mph (218·300kph) in the Belond Exhaust Special with its Offenhauser engine mounted in a horizontal position instead of the conventional vertical manner.

He announced his immediate retirement as a driver while being interviewed in Victory Lane at the end of that contest. Since then, however, he has maintained a close association with racing by serving as a member of the Indianapolis Motor Speedway staff on a part-time basis during May of each year and doing public relations work for the Monroe Auto Equipment Company, the Raybestos Company and the new Ontario (Calif.) Motor Speedway. His home is in Pacific Palisades near Los Angeles, Calif. AB

Jim Hall (left), with Roger Penske at Daytona. *Photo: Albert Bochroch*

Jim Hall. *Photo: Al Bochroch Collection*

Below left, Duncan Hamilton with a Jaguar D-type, 1955. *Photo: Jaguar Cars Ltd*

Below centre, Sam Hanks, after winning the 1957 Indianapolis 500 in a horizontal-engined Salih Offenhauser. *Photo: Indianapolis Motor Speedway*

Below, Sam Hanks. *Photo: Indianapolis Motor Speedway*

Hansgen, Walter

This American racing driver was born in 1919 and was introduced to cars as a boy in his father's Westfield, N.J., repair shop. Hansgen began racing an XK 120 Jaguar in SCCA club events in 1951. His first international race was Sebring in 1952, in which Hansgen and Randy Pearsall placed their MG TD 10th overall. Hansgen's 1953 Jag Special, a cross between a C-type and Cunningham C-3, won SCCA nationals at Cumberland and Watkins Glen, but Ferraris began beating the special. In 1956, at Cumberland, Hansgen drove a D-type Jaguar to victory over the Cunningham team of new D-types driven by John Fitch, Sherwood Johnson and John Gordon Bennett. Two weeks later Briggs Cunningham asked Hansgen to race for him and for the next four years the Cunningham-entered, Alfred Momo-prepared Jaguars brought Hansgen the SCCA 'C' modified title. Hansgen made his first trip to England in 1958, winning a sedan race at Silverstone and sports car and Formule Libre races at Snetterton.

At Bridgehampton, where 'Hansgen's Bend' honours him for being the first to take the fast downhill right-hander after the pits without backing-off, Hansgen won the 1963 FIA Manufacturers Double 500 in Cunningham's Cooper-Buick. Hansgen's 'King of the Bridge' sobriquet was earned in 1964 when in spite of a 10-minute pit stop he bought John Mecom's Scarab a victory over the Ferrari of Pedro Rodriguez.

After qualifying 10th for the 1964 Indianapolis 500, Hansgen's MG-Liquid Suspension Special ran as high as 2nd until mechanical troubles resulted in a 13th place finish. Hansgen, and his protegé Mark Donohue, drove a Ford Mark II to 3rd place in the 1966 Daytona 24 Hours and finished 2nd at Sebring.

The quiet, stocky, grey-haired veteran, now a member of the Ford team, went from Sebring to Le Mans for spring practice and carburation tests. Heavy rains had left the Sarthe circuit treacherous for the big, 427ci (6,997·28cc), Mark IIs with their wide tyres, and drivers had been alerted to the danger of aquaplaning. After achieving laps of 3min 46sec, Hansgen failed to make the fast right-hander after the pits and crashed in the escape road. He was flown at once to the US Army Hospital at Orleans, where he died five days later. ARB

Hanstein, Baron Fritz Huschke von

Born in 1911, Huschke von Hanstein started motor sport with motorcycles, in 1929 in Hamburg. Triumph, FN, Ardie, BSA, Norton and BMW were the makes he rode up to 1933. In 1934 he began 4-wheel competitions in a Hanomag in the second German 2,000 kilometres trial. In the following years he specialized in long-distance rallies like the Liège-Rome-Liège, the Morocco and others, and in the various German cross-country trials, driving Hanomags. Hanstein drove an Adler in long-distance races such as the Le Mans and Spa. In 1938 he took the German hill-climb championship in the 2-litre sports car class in a BMW 328. His outstanding success was overall victory in the shortened 1940 Mille Miglia with Bäumer in a works-entered BMW 328.

After World War 2 he drove a 750cc Condor racer, a Monopoletta Formula 2 car and a Volkswagen Special in the 1,100cc sports car class. He was a member of the record teams of Volkswagen in 1950 and Porsche in 1951. In a Porsche he returned to long-distance races including Le Mans, Sebring, the Carrera Panamericana, and the Targa Florio, which he won, with Maglioli, in 1956, as well as the Liège-Rome-Liège Rally. Until 1968

Above, Walt Hansgen. *Photo: Al Bochroch*

Above right, Baron Fritz von Hanstein (left) with Les Leston. *Photo: Geoffrey Goddard*

Peter Harper. *Photo: Hugh W. Bishop*

he was Porsche's racing manager and now acts as public relations manager for the VW-Porsche Vertriebs-gesellschaft. HON

Harper, Peter

For many years the name of Peter Harper has been synonymous with the success of Rootes' cars, firstly in rallies with a Sunbeam Rapier and more recently in rallycross with an Imp. This British driver was born in 1921, but it was not until 1947 that he started in motor sport by competing in the London to Blackpool rally with a 2-litre Sunbeam-Talbot. In the ensuing years he participated more and more in rallies with the Sunbeam-Talbots until in 1954 he ventured on to the continent for the first time, driving in the Monte Carlo, the Coupes des Alpes and the Tulip.

In 1956 came his first outing as a full works driver when he went to the Mille Miglia with a new Sunbeam Rapier and won his class. In 1958, the Mk 1 Rapier terminated its career with Harper finishing 5th overall in the Monte Carlo, and in March he took the first of the Mk 2 Rapiers to an outright victory in the RAC Rally. The same year he won his class in the Coupe des Alpes, plus a Coupe for an unpenalized run. The number of times at this period that he won the award for the highest placed British car on the Monte Carlo is legendary, and so is his association with Raymond Baxter of the BBC, with whom he brought the thrills of rallying straight into people's homes.

When the Rapier was no longer capable of beating its rivals Peter Harper persevered and right through 1962 and 1963 he was winning his classes in race meetings in England and in rallies abroad. By 1964, however, the Rapier was so obviously outclassed that Harper made one of his rare changes of allegiance and drove a Falcon for Ford of America in the Monte Carlo. The following year he was back, again powered by Ford, but in a Sunbeam Tiger with which he finished 4th overall. In a similar car, he won the GT category on the Coupe des Alpes in 1966 but was disqualified when the scrutineers found that the exhaust manifold was too *small*.

Harper has competed twice at Le Mans in a Sunbeam Alpine and won the Index of Thermal Efficiency. In 1966 he drove a Cobra at Le Mans and a 275 LM Ferrari in the Nürburgring 1,000 kilometres. Since then he has done very little rallying and most of his competition activity has been taken up with the new sport of rallycross. The first year that the TV championships were held he tied for 1st place in his Hillman Imp, and the following year, 1969, he won the championship easily. In 1970 he finished 2nd overall. JD

Harroun, Ray

Born in 1879, American racing driver and engineer Harroun, winner of the first Indianapolis 500-mile race on 30 May 1911, drove in competition for the first time on the Harlem dirt track at Chicago in 1905. When plans for construction of the Indianapolis Motor Speedway were announced, he moved to Indianapolis in 1908 to join the Marmon Company as an engineer and race driver; and he participated in the inaugural events at Indy beginning on 19 August 1909. After winning several handicap and free-for-all races at shorter distances, he finished 3rd behind two members of the Buick team in the featured 100-mile trophy race and also enjoyed considerable success three months later on the new two-mile dirt course at Atlanta, Ga., where he finished 1st or 2nd five times during the five-day programme.

Harroun started the 1910 season with two important victories on the new Playa del Rey board track in California and earned the national driving championship for the year with additional triumphs at Atlanta and Indianapolis. His chief victory at Atlanta was scored in a 200-mile race and his impressive Indianapolis performance during a 10-race programme included four victories, two 2nd places and three 3rd places. The most important Indianapolis race he won during that 1910 campaign was the 200-mile Wheeler-Schebler trophy event at a speed of 71·06mph (114·36kph) against the National, Buick, Jackson and Pope-Hartford teams.

Although Harroun had announced his retirement before the start of the 1911 season, Howard Marmon finally persuaded him to make one more competitive appearance in the inaugural 500 at the wheel of a distinctive new streamlined single-seater Marmon 6 with a piston displacement of 447ci. All other race entries were of conventional design, with provisions for a riding mechanic, and many of the cars were powered by larger engines close to the maximum limit of 600ci. Harroun's rivals attempted to have the car disqualified, contending that he might be a hazard on the course without a riding mechanic to keep him informed of cars approaching from behind, but Ray won permission to compete after designing and installing what is believed to be the first rear-view mirror ever used on a car.

During the first 100 miles he closed in on the leaders relentlessly, moving from 28th to 5th place behind David Bruce-Brown (Fiat), Ralph Mulford (Lozier), Ralph DePalma (Simplex) and Johnny Aitken (National). After a brief rest, while relief driver Cyrus Patschke was moving the Marmon up to 2nd place, Harroun took the wheel again and finished strongly to defeat Mulford by 1min and 43sec at an average speed of 74·59mph (120·04kph) with Bruce-Brown 3rd. After two more years with Marmon, which had discontinued racing after the Indianapolis triumph, Harroun contracted to design and build two race cars in 1914 for the Maxwell Company. One, driven by Teddy Tetzlaff at Indianapolis, was eliminated early by mechanical trouble. The other, relying on a special carburettor patented by Harroun, completed the full 500 miles on 30 gallons of kerosene (paraffin) for 9th place with Willie Carlson driving.

After World War 1, Harroun was associated with various automotive accessory companies as a design engineer; and in later years he remained active as a consulting engineer until shortly before his death in 1968. At 82 years of age he participated in the Speedway's 1961 golden jubilee ceremonies by lapping the track in his original Marmon Wasp, and the car is on permanent display at the Indianapolis Speedway museum. AB

Hartz, Harry

Hartz, born in 1896 and one of America's outstanding drivers at the peak of the board track era in the 1920s, also enjoyed a great deal of success as a car owner after recovering from critical injuries sustained in a racing accident.

His first association with racing was as a riding mechanic for Eddie Hearne for three years, beginning in 1919. Duesenberg then signed Hartz as a driver at the start of the 1922 season and he scored his first important victory on 16 April of that year in a 150-mile race on the San Carlos, Calif., board track. Six weeks later he finished 2nd to Jimmy Murphy for Duesenberg in the Indianapolis 500 and he was also among the leaders in several other events during the remainder of the season before severing his connection with Duesenberg to drive Miller-engined cars for various private owners.

He finished 4th or better at Indy for five straight years, running 2nd again in 1923 behind Tommy Milton and 2nd to Frank Lockhart in 1926. Hartz outdrove Lockhart during the remainder of the season, however, to win the national AAA driving title by a wide margin. He started in 19 othe 24 championship events, winning five times and finishing 2nd seven times. His most important victory was scored on the Atlantic City, N.J., board track when he covered 300 miles at an average speed of 134·091mph (215·742kph), the fastest performance for that distance on any track in the world.

Hartz was injured seriously while driving a Miller in a 1927 board track race at Rockingham, N.J. Three years later, however, he built two Miller-powered fwd cars which Billy Arnold and Fred Frame drove to Indianapolis victories in 1930 and 1932, respectively.

Later in the 1930s, Hartz also established several stock-car endurance records for DeSoto, Chrysler, Chevrolet and Studebaker. Since World War 2, he has served annually as an official for the 500-mile race and also worked as a member of the Chrysler-Plymouth sales staff in Indianapolis. AB

Harvey, Major Cyril Maurice

This British driver raced an AC in competitions before World War 1 and took some records at Brooklands with a Silver Hawk in 1920 before joining Alvis in 1921, where he became chief competition driver and service manager. In 1921 he drove an sv 10/30hp in the Coupe des Voiturettes at Le Mans, retiring with a holed sump after lying 4th behind the Talbot-Darracq team. His big

Ray Harroun. Photo: Indianapolis Motor Speedway

Harry Hartz. Photo: Indianapolis Motor Speedway

Major C. M. Harvey in the Alvis with which he won the 1923 JCC 200-Mile Race. Photo: T. A. S. O. Mathieson Collection

victory came in 1923 when he drove an ohv racing 12/50 in the Brooklands 200 Miles with remarkable consistency to win at the record speed of 93·29mph (150·13kph) from Cushman's Brescia Bugatti and Joyce's AC. In 1924 Harvey was competing nearly every weekend for Alvis in sprints and reliability trials throughout the country and won many awards. He came 8th in the Brooklands 200 Miles race and established a series of class records there with a single-seater Alvis.

In 1925 he made 2nd ftd at Shelsley Walsh, 0·4sec slower than Segrave's blown GP 2-litre Sunbeam, driving the new 1·5-litre Alvis fwd sprint car running unblown, and in a 12/50 four-seater was 3rd in the Georges Boillot Cup at Boulogne to a Chenard-Walcker and an Ariès. In 1927, driving a 12/50, he was 4th on distance in the Essex 6 Hours Race at Brooklands, and won the JCC 4 Hours Sporting Car Race at the same venue.

In the class handicap 230-mile (370km) Georges Boillot Cup Eliminating Race at Boulogne, Harvey won in a 12/50 Alvis from Ariès, Salmson, Bugatti and Lorraine-Dietrich cars, only the 3-litre Ariès putting up a faster average. In 1928, driving an unblown 4-cylinder fwd Alvis with H. W. Purdy at Le Mans, he won the 1·5-litre class and was 6th overall. He also drove the straight-8 fwd Alvis in 1929 and 1930, though with no great success.

After Alvis retired from racing in 1930, Harvey drove Riley, Frazer Nash and Aston Martin cars. In the 1931 TT he won his class with an Aston Martin, and in the 1932 Brooklands 1,000 Miles Race he led at half distance at the end of the first day driving a Riley with R. M. V. Sutton, but retired on the second day. Harvey's health was affected by his service in World War 1, and he died in 1935. PMAH

Hawkes, Gwenda

This British lady driver was among the most talented of her sex and insisted on her cars being turned out in immaculate condition. Her early association with speed came in 1922, when, as Mrs Janson, she attacked a 'Double-Twelve'-hour record at Brooklands on a 249cc Trump-JAP motorcycle, afterwards teaming up with Lt Col. Stewart on long-distance record attempts at Montlhéry on various motorcycles. As Mrs Stewart, Gwenda drove all manner of cars and motorcycles, operating from an under-banking depot at the French track. She was assisted by Douglas Hawkes and they did much fast work with Morgan 3-wheelers, in one of which Mrs Stewart was timed at 118mph (189·9kph) at Arpajon. It was with the narrow single-seater Derby-Miller, tuned by the English mechanic Fred Cann that Gwenda Hawkes—she married Douglas Hawkes in 1937—that she accomplished her most notable records, these including the ladies' lap records at Brooklands and Montlhéry, respectively at 135·95mph (218·78kph) and fractionally under 149mph (239·8kph). This was a light car, difficult to handle, so these high speeds were all the more credit to Gwenda Hawkes, who survived a nasty accident in the car at Montlhéry, when it went out of control at a speed of about 150mph (240kph). WB

Hawkins, Robert Paul

Born in 1937 in Melbourne, Australia, Hawkins was a tough, fast and totally professional driver, and a colourful character. His first race was in 1958, when he spun a borrowed Healey 100S out of the lead at Phillip Island, Melbourne.

He competed in several club events before deciding to come to Europe, arriving in England in early 1960. He got a job with John Sprinzel, and raced his Sebring Sprites that year. In 1961 he won a works Healey drive at Le Mans, then joined Ian Walker in 1962 as Formula Junior team chief mechanic and driver. He continued with Walker in 1963, surviving a number of spectacular FJ accidents. In 1964 he joined the Willment team, having driven for them in South Africa that winter, scoring several successes. In 1965 he raced Dickie Stoop's private Formula 1 Lotus-Climax, surviving a plunge into the harbour at Monaco, and in 1966 he combined occasional works Porsche and Ford drives with Jackie Epstein's old Ferrari 275LM in some events. Hawkins drove for Porsche, Ferrari and JW Automotive in 1967, and campaigned with his own GT40, Epstein's Lola GT and Lotus saloons as well. JW Automotive signed him on for 1968 in their GT40s, while he continued to race his own car widely, going racing very professionally and sharing premises with David Piper.

For 1969 he bought a Lola-Chevrolet GT, had several fine drives in it and then spun into a tree while making up time in the TT at Oulton Park. The car caught fire and rescuers could do nothing to save him. DCN

Hawthorn, John Michael

Britain's first World Champion driver, Hawthorn was born on 10 April 1929 at Mexborough in Yorkshire. Two years later his father, Leslie, bought the TT Garage in Farnham, Surrey, and the family moved south. Leslie Hawthorn was a keen motorcycle racer and tuner and at Farnham was handily placed for racing and testing at Brooklands. In 1950 the Hawthorns went motor racing, running a pair of Rileys, an 1100cc Imp and a 1500cc Sprite, in the Brighton Speed Trials. Mike, as he was universally known—then only 21—won the smaller class, while his father was 2nd in his. In 1951 Leslie damaged his back and could not drive, so Mike ran both the 1,100 and 1,500cc cars in England and Ireland, winning the Ulster and Leinster Trophy races in the Sprite. He also won the *Motor Sport* Brooklands Memorial Trophy that year for consistent successes at Goodwood club meetings.

In 1952 Formula 2 temporarily assumed the mantle of premier racing class from Formula 1 and an old friend of the Hawthorns, Bob Chase, bought a new Cooper-Bristol for Hawthorn to drive. In his first race—at the Goodwood Easter meeting—he won two preliminaries and was 2nd to Gonzales' 4·5-litre Thinwall Special in the main event. That year Hawthorn's performances at home and abroad in the Cooper added to his stature, he drove for BRM and Vandervell (in the Thinwall Special) and won a Coupe des Alpes in the Alpine Rally driving a works Sunbeam.

Ferrari offered him a works drive for 1953, but Hawthorn was slow in accepting—hoping that a competitive British car would appear. He had crashed badly in the Cooper during tests at Modena in late 1952, and made his mind up while recuperating in the London Clinic and signed for Ferrari. Highlight of the season was a last-minute victory over Fangio in the French GP at Reims—the first Englishman to win that race since Segrave in 1923. The following season Hawthorn was burned badly about the legs at Syracuse early in the race, and was then the victim of a petty campaign because he missed military service—service from which a kidney ailment exempted him anyway. Final blow to his buoyant spirit came when his father crashed his Lancia on the way

Gwenda Hawkes (Mrs Stewart), 1934.
Photo: Montagu Motor Museum

Paul Hawkins. *Photo: Autosport*

Mike Hawthorn: Principal Successes

Year	Event	Car
1951	Leinster Trophy	*Riley-Sprite*
	Ulster Handicap	*Riley-Sprite*
1952	Chichester Cup, Goodwood	*Cooper-Bristol*
	Lavant Cup, Goodwood	*Cooper-Bristol*
	Daily Mail Trophy, Boreham	*Cooper-Bristol*
	Ibsley formule libre	*Cooper-Bristol*
	Turnberry F2	*Connaught*
1953	French GP	*Ferrari 500*
	Pescara GP	*Ferrari 500*
	Daily Express Trophy,	*Ferrari 500*
	Ulster Trophy	*Ferrari 500*
	Spa 24-Hours, with Farina	*Ferrari 375MM*
1954	Spanish GP	*Ferrari 553*
	Supercortemaggiore GP with Maglioli	*Ferrari 750*
1955	Le Mans 24 Hours, with Bueb	*Jaguar D-type*
	Sebring 12 Hours, with Walters	*Jaguar D-type*
	International Trophy, Crystal Palace	*Maserati 250F*
1956	Supercortemaggiore GP with Collins	*Ferrari Testa*
1958	French GP	*Ferrari Dino 246*
	Glover Trophy, Goodwood	*Ferrari Dino 246*

home from Goodwood, and was killed.

The need to manage the Farnham garage led to Hawthorn to sign with Vanwall for 1955 Grands Prix, but the new car needed development and he returned to Ferrari later in the year. Tragic climax of the year came when he won Le Mans in a Jaguar, shared with Ivor Bueb, and was involved in the disastrous accident to Levegh's Mercedes 300SLR. 'Hawthorn est coupable' was typical of the subjective headlines in the Continental press and not until some months later was he rightly exonerated.

But motor racing was still Hawthorn's only real love, and his essentially cheerful character again helped him through a difficult period to come back with a great fighting drive against the Mercedes team in the TT at Dundrod. Sharing his Jaguar D-Type with Desmond Titterington he was 2nd near the finish when a hard-driven crank broke. Jaguar retained his services in 1956 and in order to honour this contract Hawthorn went to BRM for Formula 1, only to suffer recurrent failures and accidents in the new 2·5-litre cars. His unhappy season was sufficient to convince him of Ferrari's efficiency and he rejoined the Italian team for the 1957 season.

As the frustrations of the British teams dropped away behind him, and bitter memories of his past treatment faded, the old Hawthorn re-emerged as a truly great

Above left, Mike Hawthorn, with 'Nino' Farina at Monza, 1953. *Photo: Autosport*

Above, Mike Hawthorn. *Photo: Associated Press Ltd*

Above right, Mike Hawthorn, after learning of the death of his team-mate Luigi Musso in the 1958 French GP. On his right, Olivier Gendebien. *Photo: Al Bochroch*

Below left, Mike Hawthorn. *Photo: Autosport*

Below, George Heath in a Panhard, 1908 French GP. *Photo: T. A. S. O. Mathieson Collection*

driver on the track, and a great character away from it. In 1958, remaining with the Ferrari team, he again won the French GP and with 2nd places in the Belgian, British, Italian, Portuguese and Moroccan GPs secured the World Championship by a single point from Stirling Moss. But even this ultimate triumph was to be clouded by tragedy, for Musso had died at Reims; Lewis-Evans crashed fatally in Morocco; and Hawthorn's great friend, Peter Collins, killed only yards ahead of him at the Nürburgring.

His was a bitter victory and he announced his retirement at the end of the season. His essential enthusiasm survived, however, and he wrote the Carlotti motor racing boys' stories in addition to spending many spare hours restoring a 1931 Alfa Romeo 2300 and the famous old 1·5-litre Riley Sprite.

But one rainy morning in January 1959, Hawthorn lost control of his Jaguar 3·4 when driving quickly downhill into Guildford. The car jack-knifed round a small tree, and the 29-year old World Champion was killed instantly. DCN

Heath, George

George Heath was a native of Long Island, N.Y., who preferred to live in Paris, where it is believed that he ran a tailor's shop. He was first seen at the wheel of a Panhard in the Paris–Amsterdam–Paris, 1898, finishing 13th, and he never drove any other make of car in competition. He achieved little until 1904 when he had two victories in the Ardennes race, when a slow 4th lap was compensated by a brilliant last circuit in which he beat Teste's sister car by less than a minute, and in the Vanderbilt Cup on his native territory, in which his Panhard and Albert Clément's Clément-Bayard were the sole finishers.

The 1905 Panhards were not fast enough to make the French Gordon Bennett team, and though Heath's was the best of the three his 41·6mph (66·95kph) in the eliminating trial was no match for the Brasiers of Théry and Caillois. He was 2nd in the 1905 Vanderbilt Cup but although he drove for Panhard in the Grands Prix of 1906 to 1908 he achieved no further success. MCS

Heath, John B.

As the main activator, with his partner George Abecassis, in the praiseworthy HWM Formula 2 venture which helped to put Britain back on the racing map, John Heath did far more for the sport than his actual competition record suggests. Born in 1914, he was a neat, methodical driver who began racing in 1946 with the

supercharged 2-litre sports Alta, scoring successes at Elstree, Prescott, Gransden and Bo'ness, and took a very creditable 2nd place on his first Continental foray, the 1947 Grand Prix des Frontières at Chimay, Belgium, behind a Delahaye. He drove the new Grand Prix Alta occasionally without success, and in 1948 began development of the HW-Alta, using an unsupercharged 2-litre Alta engine in a new frame, carrying full-width aerodynamic bodywork. In this form he drove the car to 4th place in the 1948 Stockholm F2 GP; and at Spa in the 24 Hours race he and Abecassis led their class until the latter crashed at 55 laps.

For 1949 Heath scrapped the aerodynamic body and fitted an open-wheeled two-seater type, won the Manx Cup race at Douglas, Isle of Man, then scored an outstanding 2nd place in the French Grand Prix for sports cars at Comminges. Business at HW Motors at Walton, in Surrey, and the running of the F2 team kept Heath out of the cockpit much of the time thereafter, but he was always ready to stand in at short notice and drove with skill and mechanical sympathy. When the F2 HWM became out of date he and Abecassis evolved the HWM-Jaguar for sports car racing, and after many months away from racing he elected to drive it in the 1956 Mille Miglia. Heavy rain. slippery roads and massed crowds made it a particularly arduous race; Heath crashed at Ravenna and succumbed to his injuries. CP

Hémery, Victor

Hémery, born in 1876 has been described as Louis Wagner's master, though he will go down in history as one of the most difficult personalities to grace the circuits. He was no respecter of rules or persons, which makes it all the more remarkable that he survived in the autocratic Alexandre Darracq's employ until 1907, since Darracq expected his drivers to win, and blamed them (not the cars) if they failed. A former seaman and a native of Brest, he was first seen at the wheel of a Darracq *voiture legère* in the 1902 Circuit des Ardennes. In 1904 came his promotion to major events, though he ran in the British rather than the French Gordon Bennett Trials, at the wheel of one of the unfortunate 100hp Weir-built Darracqs. Being Hémery, he ignored controls, but the cars were lacking in brakes and preparation alike. He did better in light-car events, now more or less a Darracq preserve, coming 2nd in this category of the Circuit des Ardennes and 1st in the Coppa Florio. In 1905 he drove a big Darracq and achieved 109·65mph (176·48kph) over the flying kilometre at Arles-Salon (in effect a World's Land Speed Record, though no such title as yet existed). His 8th in the French Gordon

Above right, John Heath (centre), with Duncan Hamilton and Stirling Moss, 1953. *Photo: Maxwell Boyd*

Above, John Heath. *Photo: Cyril Posthumus Collection*

Victor Hémery in a Lorraine-Dietrich, 1912 French GP. *Photo: T. A. S. O. Mathieson Collection*

Bennett Trials failed to earn him a place in the ACF's team, but the season brought his first big win on the American Vanderbilt Cup, marred by abusive treatment of the photographers after the race was over. Even worse were his displays at temperament during the 1906 Florida Speed Meet. He first threatened to withdraw the entire Darracq team after his *voiture legère* had been declared overweight, and then jumped the start of a race. A lot of trans-Atlantic cabling ended in his personal disqualification from the meeting.

Hémery moved on to Benz, for whom he scored a 2nd place in the 1907 Coppa Florio at 62·5mph (100·58kph), though he retired in the Kaiserpreis. Benz did not support the Grand Prix, so he drove a Mercedes instead and finished only 10th. However, 1908 started well with a victory for Benz in the St Petersburg-Moscow, and continued with a gallant near-victory in the Grand Prix, where he finished 2nd to Lautenschlager's Mercedes, despite tyre trouble and an injury which deprived him of the sight of one eye. At Savannah he was 2nd in a closely fought American Grand Prize. There was virtually no racing in 1909, but Benz produced the immense 21·5-litre Blitzen machine, in which Hémery did a mile in 31·2sec at Brussels, and later in the year recorded 125·95mph (202·68kph) at Brooklands.

In 1911 Hémery once again tried his luck in the American Grand Prize, turning in a record lap at 81·5mph (131·16kph), but he had lost much time earlier in the race and subsequently retired. That year's Grand Prix de France was not much of an event, but Hémery won with a 10·5-litre sports Fiat. There was a resurgence of interest in 1912 in big events and his Grand Prix machine at Dieppe was a close relation of the big Benz, the 15-litre chain-driven Lorraine-Dietrich. Engine troubles put paid to his chances and to those of Hanriot on the sister car, but he took some international class records at Brooklands.

Victor Hémery made a comeback in 1922 and 1923 with Rolland-Pilains in the French Grands Prix, but the cars were not winners. In later years he ran a garage business, and died by his own hand in 1950. MCS

Herrmann, Hans

Hans Herrmann was born near Stuttgart in 1928, and with few exceptions has spent his long racing career with the two Stuttgart makes, Mercedes-Benz and Porsche.

He began driving in 1953, sharing a Porsche with Bauer in the Mille Miglia in which they won their class. After other successes in racing and hill climbing during 1953 and 1954 Herrmann was invited to join the Mercedes-Benz team and finished 3rd in the 1955 Swiss GP. In a Porsche he was 3rd in the Carrera Panamericana. After Mercedes-Benz retired from racing, Herrmann returned to Porsche full time, and among other successes were victory in the Rheinland Cup and the Solitude GP, and 3rd place in the 1956 Mille Miglia and 1958 Le Mans race. He drove BRP's BRM in the German GP at AVUS in 1959, but crashed and miraculously escaped with only slight injuries. Since then he has driven both sports and F2 Porsches with great success and reliability. For instance, in 1967 he finished in the first six in nine out of the ten long-distance Championship races, and in 1968 managed to repeat the performance in eight of the eleven rounds, including sharing the victories at Daytona, Sebring and the Paris 1,000 kilometre race. In the mid-1960s Herrmann had a spell with Fiat-Abarth cars, winning the Nürburgring 500 kilometres with Pilette in 1963 and alone in 1964, and also did well in the European Hill-Climb Championship. 'Hansl' retired after winning Le Mans (with Attwood) in a Salzburg Porsche 917K in 1970. DCN

Hill, Norman Graham

Born at Hampstead, London, 15 February 1929, Hill was educated locally and at Hendon Technical College, before taking a five-year apprenticeship with Smiths. They gave him further training in the Midlands, and while there he bought a motorcycle and rode it in a few rallies and scrambles. He was riding it home to London one night when he had a serious accident, breaking his hip and leaving his left leg shorter than his right. Nonetheless he was called up in 1950 and did his National Service as an engine room artificer in HMS *Swiftsure* before rejoining Smiths on discharge. He was an enthusiastic oarsman, having been introduced to rowing by his cousin, and stroked the London Rowing Club's first eight to victory in the Grand Challenge Cup at Henley in 1953. That year he bought his first car, drove it first and passed his test (without instruction) later.

In the rowing off season Graham saw an advertisement for the Universal Motor Racing Club based at Brands Hatch, joined, paid an extra £1 and did four laps in a Cooper. He was gripped with determination to get into motor racing, and took every Wednesday off from Smiths to help prepare the Club's single car. He left Smiths in 1954, living on national assistance and help from his mother and taking a bus to Westerham in Kent every day to prepare two cars belonging to a would-be racing drivers' school proprietor. He had his first race in one of these F3 Coopers at Brands Hatch in April 1954, finishing 2nd in his heat and 4th in the final. He became the school's chief instructor but left after a disagreement with the management. In August that year he was stranded at Brands Hatch after the Bank Holiday meeting, and hitched a lift back to London on the Lotus van with Colin Chapman and Mike Costin. He talked himself into a job as a Lotus mechanic, working for Dick Steed and, in 1955, for Dan Margulies, who was racing a C-type Jaguar.

He was offering his services as mechanic in return for an occasional drive, and appeared in Lotus cars belonging to Jack Richards and Peter Lumsden, among others. Chapman held a Lotus test-day for prospective customers at Brands Hatch at the end of the season, and Hill

Graham Hill: Principal Successes

Year	Event	Car
1957	Christmas Trophy, Brands Hatch	Lotus 11
1958	Christmas Trophy, Brands Hatch	Lotus 15
	Silver City Trophy, Brands Hatch	Lotus 16
1959	Farningham Trophy, Brands Hatch	Lotus 17
1961	Christmas Trophy, Brands Hatch	Ferrari TR/61
	Oulton Park Trophy	Jaguar E-type
1962	Dutch GP	BRM V-8
	German GP	BRM V-8
	Italian GP	BRM V-8
	South African GP	BRM V-8
	Glover Trophy, Goodwood	BRM V-8
	International Trophy, Silverstone	BRM V-8
1963	Monaco GP	BRM V-8
	United States GP	BRM V-8
	Tourist Trophy	Ferrari 250GTO
1964	Monaco GP	BRM V-8
	United States GP	BRM V-8
	Reims 12 Hours, with Bonnier	Ferrari 250LM
	Tourist Trophy	Ferrari 330P
	Paris 1,000km, with Bonnier	Ferrari 330P
	Longford GP	Brabham-Climax BT 11A
	Rand GP	Brabham-Climax BT 11A
1965	Monaco GP	BRM V-8
	United States GP	BRM V-8
	New Zealand GP	Brabham-Climax BT 11A
	International Trophy, Snetterton	Brabham-Cosworth BT 16
1966	Indianapolis 500	Lola-Ford T90
	New Zealand GP	BRM V-8
	Australian GP	BRM V-8
1968	Spanish GP	Lotus-Ford 49
	Monaco GP	Lotus-Ford 49B
	Mexican GP	Lotus-Ford 49B
1969	Monaco GP	Lotus-Ford 49B
	Albi F2	Lotus-Ford 59B

Above right, Graham Hill, with Raymond Mays. Photo: Autosport

Above centre, Graham Hill (BRM) in the 1964 French GP in which he finished 2nd. Photo: Doug Nye Collection

Below centre, Graham Hill in the Lola-Ford in which he won the Indianapolis 500 in 1966. Photo: Indianapolis Motor Speedway

Right, Graham Hill, with Colin Chapman before the start of the 1967 South African GP. Photo: Alton Berns

Left, Graham Hill at Watkins Glen, 1967.
Photo: Autosport

Above, Phil Hill, 1961. *Photo: Bahamas News Bureau*

managed to put in some laps right at the end of the day, setting second-fastest time overall.

Hill was now recognized as something more than just a good mechanic, and though he continued as a Lotus employee he drove Allison's works car to 1st and 2nd places at Brands Hatch in 1956, and had a number of drives in other people's cars during 1957. He felt Lotus held little future for him, and left to join Speedwell Conversions, later to become its chairman. Lotus entered Formula 1 in 1958 and Graham was invited back, making his World Championship debut at Monaco, retiring when placed 4th. The F1 Lotus 16s of 1958 and 1959 was extremely fragile and broke time after time. Hill quickly made himself a reputation as a 'tinkerer' and after two unsuccessful seasons he left. BRM needed a good development driver, and Hill's engineering knowledge was put to good use when they signed him for 1960.

BRM had just produced their first rear-engined car, and although it handled badly he did his best for them, leading the British GP until he hit an oil patch and spun off tantalizingly few laps from the finish. In the 1961 season the interim Climax-powered cars struggled along until the promising new 1·5-litre V-8 engine was unveiled at Monza. Hill was 13th in the World Championship after his fourth GP season, and seemed just another good driver hamstrung by his machines.

But the 1962 season saw the British V-8s dominant, and Hill's precise style, and the way he worked so hard to learn the circuit and set his car up, began to pay off. He won the Dutch GP to give BRM their second Championship victory, and went on to take the German, Italian and South African GPs. Clark had run him close for the World title, but when the Lotus retired at East London the crown was his after nine long years of endeavour.

Hill seemed a fixture at BRM by this time, and he stayed with them for four more seasons, scoring three consecutive victories both at Monaco and in the United States, nurturing the young Jackie Stewart in his first Formula 1 season and always working hard to achieve a perfectly set-up car, or a perfect line through a corner. He is not a natural driver, a Clark or a Stewart, but has the application and concentration to make himself, and his car, do what he wants it to do. Meantime Hill was amassing a long string of successes in sports and GT races, whether 10-lap supporting events or 1,000km-plus endurance events, at the wheel of Porsches, Jaguars, Ferraris and Fords.

Philip T. Hill: Principal Successes

Year	Event	Car
1956	Swedish GP (Sports cars), with Trintignant	Ferrari 290MM
	Messina 5 Hours	Ferrari Testa Rossa
1957	Venezuelan GP (Sports cars), with Collins	Ferrari 412MI
1958	Le Mans 24 Hours, with Gendebien	Ferrari 250 Testa Rossa
	Sebring 12 Hours, with Collins	Ferrari 250 Testa Rossa
	Buenos Aires 1,000km, with Collins	Ferrari 250 Testa Rossa
1959	Sebring 12 Hours, with Gendebien	Ferrari 250 Testa Rossa
1960	Italian GP	Ferrari Dino 256
	Buenos Aires 1,000km, with Allison	Ferrari 250 Testa Rossa
1961	Italian GP	Ferrari 156
	Belgian GP	Ferrari 156
	Le Mans 24 Hours, with Gendebien	Ferrari 250 Testa Rossa
	Sebring 12 Hours, with Gendebien	Ferrari 250 Testa Rossa
1962	Le Mans 24 Hours, with Gendebien	Ferrari 350 TR/LM
	Nürburgring 1,000km, with Gendebien	Ferrari 246/SP
1964	Daytona 2,000km, with P. Rodriguez	Ferrari 330GT
1966	Nürburgring 1,000km, with Bonnier	Chaparral 2D
1967	BOAC 6 Hours, Brands Hatch, with Spence	Chaparral 2E

He practised a Mickey Thompson-entered car at Indianapolis in 1963, and won there in 1966 driving a Lola-Ford. From the proceeds he bought himself a twin-engined aircraft, having learned to fly shortly beforehand, and he flew himself to race meetings in many parts of the world.

Then, late in 1966, came the surprise announcement that Graham Hill was rejoining Lotus. The BRM H-16 was being troublesome and Lotus would be running the new Cosworth-Ford V-8 engine in 1967 and looked promising. So Hill teamed with Jim Clark, and this formidable pair showed a clean pair of heels in most of the GPs, while they lasted. Hill in particular had a heart-breaking series of mechanical failures, but after Clark's tragic death in April 1968, he became team leader and took the Gold Leaf Team Lotus colours to victory in the Spanish, Monaco and Mexican GPs and secured an immensely popular second World Championship.

In 1969 Hill won at Monaco for the 5th time in seven years, emphasizing his fantastic powers of concentration and mechanical sympathy. His car was destroyed at Barcelona after an aerofoil failure, and he could not compete with Stewart's Matra for the rest of the year. At Watkins Glen he spun and restarted without being able to refasten his seat belts. A tyre was deflating, which caused his spin, and he lost control again, this time hitting a bank and being thrown out. Both Hill's legs sustained serious injuries, and he was in hospital for some months. This accident prompted a wave of public sympathy in Britain seldom equalled for any sporting personality, and against doctor's orders he was driving again in the South African Grand Prix in March 1970. He could hardly walk, but he could drive, and finished 6th on his first appearance in Rob Walker's private Lotus-Ford 49C.

Graham Hill's career is a remarkable story of single-mindedness, courage and hard work reaping their reward, of a driver who is one of the best ambassadors the sport has ever had. DCN

Hill, Philip T.

This American driver was born in 1927 in Miami, Fla., and brought up in Santa Monica, Calif., where his father was the city postmaster. Hill stopped racing in 1967, but remains active in motor sports as a racing commentator on American television. Although Phil Hill won the world driving championship in 1961, it is his record in the classic sports car endurance races that is outstanding.

As with many Americans of his generation, Phil's first sports car was an MG TC. In 1950, with Ritchie Ginther as his crew chief, Phil Hill won the first race over the tree-lined 1·8-mile (2·897km) Pebble Beach course (Monterey Peninsula, Calif.). He finished 6th in the 1952, 2,000-mile (3,219km) Carrera Panamericana Mexico, driving a 2·5-litre Ferrari that his sponsor had bought from Alberto Ascari. Phil's first Le Mans was 1954, in which the Wacker and Hill Osca dropped out while leading its class. After being put out by an accident during the 1953 Mexican road race, Hill, with Ginther as a passenger, finished 2nd in 1954, 24 minutes behind Umberto Maglioli. The 1955 Sebring saw Hill and Carroll Shelby's 3-litre Ferrari Monza finish a disputed 2nd to the D-type Jaguar of Mike Hawthorn and Phil Walter.

With the help of Luigi Chinetti, Ferrari's man in America, Hill began his long association with the Ferrari factory. The first of Hill's many rides with Oliver Gendebien was in January 1956 in Buenos Aires, where they finished 2nd to the Moss and Menditeguy Maserati. At Buenos Aires, Hill was invited to join the Ferrari works team in Europe. When Hill reported for the 1956 Nürburgring 1,000 kilometres, he found it difficult to believe he was part of a team that included Fangio, Musso, Castellotti and Collins in Formula 1, and de Portago, Gendebien, Paul Frère and Trintignant for sports cars.

Hill and Gendebian won at Le Mans in 1958 and 1961. With Peter Collins, Hill captured the Sebring 12 hours in 1958 and, with Gendebien, in 1959 and 1961. In 1960, following a 3rd at Monte Carlo, Hill won at Monza, the first American to win a Grand Prix since Jimmy Murphy captured the French GP in a Duesenberg in 1921. His victory in the 1961 Italian GP, following 3rd place finishes at Monte Carlo and the Nürburgring, a 1st at Spa and 2nds at Zandvoort and Aintree, made Phil Hill the only American to have held the world drivers title. But the Monza crash that killed Wolfgang von Trips, Hill's team-mate, rival and friend, took the edge off the American's triumph.

Relations between the dictatorial Commendatore Ferrari and the irascible world champion deteriorated and Hill left Ferrari at the end of 1962 (after he and

Phil Hill (right) with Olivier Gendebian after they had won at Le Mans in 1958. *Photo: Al Bochroch*

Below, Phil Hill at Sebring. *Photo: Al Bochroch*

Right, Phil Hill (Ferrari) in the 1959 French GP in which he finished 2nd. *Photo: Al Bochroch*

Gendebien had won their 3rd Le Mans and the Nürburgring 1,000 kilometres) to join former Ferrari engineer, Carlo Chiti and ex-Ferrari team manager Romolo Tavani at ATS. While the ATS project floundered, Hill won the 1964 Daytona 2,000 kilometres with Pedro Rodriguez and in 1966 began driving for the gifted Texan, Jim Hall. Bonnier and Hill drove the radical Chaparral to win the 1966 Nürburgring 1,000 kilometres; Hill piloted the winged Chaparral in the 1966 Can-Am series, where he won once, finishing the season 4th in total points. On 30 July 1967, Mike Spence and Phil Hill won a keenly fought battle over the Jackie Stewart and Chris Amon Ferrari to win the BOAC Six Hours at Brands Hatch for what may be the former Yankee champion's final victory.

Besides his TV work, Hill's activities include restoring vintage cars and collecting classical-music records. ARB

Hobbs, David Wishart

Born in Leamington Spa in 1939, David Hobbs is the son of the inventor of the Hobbs Meccamatic automatic transmission, and began racing cars fitted with this device in order to prove its value. His first race was at Snetterton in 1959 driving an automatic Morris Oxford,

David Hobbs. *Photo: courtesy David Hobbs*

and the following season Hobbs scored four wins on an automatic Jaguar XK 140 before moving on to an automatic Lotus Elite for 1961 with which he scored fourteen wins. In 1962 he shared the Index-winning Team Elite car at Le Mans with Frank Gardner, and won his first single seater race at Oulton Park in an MRP Cooper-Ford FJ. In 1963 he finished 4th in the National *Express & Star* Championship for FJ cars in a Lola, and also drove the prophetic Lola-Ford GT at Le Mans.

Between 1963 and 1967 Hobbs drove a wide variety of cars including Lotus-Cortina saloons, Porsche 904 and Lola-Chevrolet T70 sports cars, F2 Lola-BMW and Merlyn, and F1 BRMs. In 1968 he signed with JW Automotive, and won the Monza 1,000 kilometres, coming 2nd in the Watkins Glen 6-Hours, both in GT40s with Paul Hawkins. Also in 1968 he drove a Ford Falcon in the British Saloon Car Championship, and won the Nürburgring 6 Hours with Hahne in a BMW 2002 saloon. In 1969 he shared a JW GT40 with Hailwood to finish 3rd at Le Mans, and took in a full F5000 season in a Surtees TS5. In this he won the Dublin GP at Mondello Park, and in America finished only one point behind Formula A Champion Adamowicz. DCN

Holbert, Robert

Bob Holbert was born in 1922 in Warrington, Pa., near Philadelphia, where he owns Porsche and Volkswagen dealerships. He began racing an MG TD in 1952, winning his first event at Thompson the following year. Holbert started racing Porsches in 1957 and was a Sports Car Club of America national champion in 1958, 1960, 1961 and 1962. Sharing a Porsche with Masten Gregory, Holbert was 1st in the under 2 litres and 5th overall in the 1961 Le Mans. Driving Cobra-Fords for Carroll Shelby, while running his Porsche on shorter circuits, brought Holbert the 1963 US Road Racing Championship. Holbert and Ken Miles, with whom he shared 'best Porsche driver in America' honours, finished 1st in GT and 2nd overall in the 1963 Road America 500 to secure Holbert's USRRC title. Holbert and Dave McDonald drove a Cobra Daytona Coupé to 1st in GT and 4th overall in the 1964 Sebring. Two months later Holbert retired. ARB

Hopkirk, Paddy

Perhaps the best known rally driver of them all, Paddy Hopkirk was born in Belfast, Northern Ireland, in 1933.

On leaving Dublin university he exchanged his old Austin Seven for a Volkswagen and in 1955 he won the Hewison Trophy for the Irish Championship. The same year, Ken Richardson of Standard Triumph offered him the chance of a drive in one of their cars and this finally came to fruition when Hopkirk drove a Standard Ten in the RAC Rally of 1956. He broke the sump in Yorkshire, but not before making a very favourable impression. In 1957 he drove for them again, finishing 3rd overall in the Tulip Rally in a Standard Ten and 2nd in his class in the Coupe des Alpes in a TR3 and winning the first of many Coupes in that event.

In 1958 he won the Circuit of Ireland with a TR3 but at the end of that year he moved to the Rootes team, for whom he drove a Rapier for four years. He won another Coupe in the 1959 Coupe des Alpes and finished 3rd overall. This put him in line for a silver Coupe, thought he did not win one until 1965. In 1961 and 1962 he won the Circuit of Ireland, finished 3rd in both the Monte Carlo and the Coupe des Alpes and made his only appearance in the East African Safari.

At the beginning of 1963 he fell into Stuart Turner's net and joined BMC, finishing 6th for them in the Monte Carlo in his first drive in a Mini Cooper. In the Tulip Rally he was 2nd overall; he was 1st on handicap in the Tour de France with the first 1071 Cooper S; won his class with an MGB at Le Mans; and briefly had a Healey 3000 in which he finished 4th overall in the RAC Rally. After that auspicious start, it was no surprise when he won the Monte Carlo Rally in 1964 with a Cooper S and went on to win the Austrian Alpine in a Healey 3000, and his class in both the Spa 24-hour race and at Le Mans. In 1965, he won the Circuit of Ireland yet again, this time with a Cooper S, and collected his silver Coupe in the Coupes des Alpes. The next year, he was disqualified along with the rest of the BMC team in the Monte Carlo lighting squabble and then won the Acropolis Rally, only to have that laurel taken away following a protest concerning servicing in a forbidden zone. However, a few weeks previously he had won the Austrian Alpine for the second time with a Cooper S.

A vintage year for Hopkirk followed in 1967 when he won several major rallies just at the time that the pundits were saying that the Cooper S was finished as a rally car. He came 2nd on the San Remo Rally with the car close to collapse, went home to win the Circuit of Ireland for the 5th time, avenged his disappointment the previous year by winning the Acropolis Rally and then won the Coupe des Alpes in fine style.

The following year BMC did very little in the way of rallying. However, Hopkirk drove a BMC 1800 for them on the London to Sydney Marathon and finished 2nd. Since then he has driven Triumphs for the same team, now known as BLMC. Clutch trouble robbed him of a good place in the 1969 RAC Rally, and a gearbox stopped him on the last test of the Austrian Alpine. In the World Cup Rally his luck was a little better and he finished 4th overall.

As well as rallying, Hopkirk has driven BMC cars in races all over the world, at Sebring, the Targa Florio and in Australia, as well as founding a most successful motor accessory business. JD

Horn, Eylard Theodore

Ted Horn, born in 1910, one of the world's most consistent racing drivers, accomplished a feat unequalled by any other participant in the sport by reigning as the American champion for three consecutive years. Although particularly outstanding on dirt tracks, he also attained the enviable record of finishing 4th or better in nine consecutive Indianapolis 500s, where he invariably was a strong contender although never a winner.

Horn gained his early racing experience on the dirt tracks of California, beginning in 1931, and began a series of appearances in other sections of the United States two years later. After visiting Indianapolis for the first time as a spectator in 1934, he participated in his first 500 a year later as a member of the factory-sponsored Ford V-8 team but failed to finish because of mechanical trouble. He ran with the leaders all of the way, however, in all of his nine other Indianapolis events, driving Miller-powered cars six times before moving on to the ageing Maserati which had carried Wilbur Shaw to two victories.

With the resumption of racing in America after World War 2, Ted won his first national title in 1946 by a margin of more than 750 points. He retained the crown in 1947 by winning three of the ten events on the schedule and finishing 6th or better in all but one of the other

Paddy Hopkirk. *Photo: BMC Competitions News Service*

Ted Horn. *Photo: Indianapolis Motor Speedway*

Earl Howe, with Sir Henry Birkin at Le Mans in 1932. *Photo: Motor*

seven. He won again in 1948, leading the field home twice and being placed 4th or better in eight of the other ten championship races before being injured fatally in a racing accident at Duquoin, Ill., late in the season when his car crashed because of a broken spindle.

Horn did almost all of his own mechanical work, except at Indianapolis. He owned and maintained the cars he drove in championship and sprint-car competition on other tracks after borrowing enough money to purchase his own car in 1936. AB

Howe, Earl

Born in 1884, Edward Richard Assheton, Viscount Curzon, took up racing seriously in 1928, entering the Essex 6 hours race at Brooklands and the RAC Tourist Trophy with a Bugatti. He brought to the sport an immense enthusiasm, which allied to common-sense approach and determination in adversity, his very considerable skill and the general balance of his character added a new dimension to the concept of the English gentleman racing driver. Although he was able to finance his participation in the sport from his private means, there was nothing amateurish about his preparation and driving.

He also drove in the next eight Tourist Trophy races, usually finishing well despite various troubles, at the wheel of Bugatti, Mercedes-Benz, Alfa Romeo, Talbot and Lagonda cars. In 1930 he had several good placings with Mercedes-Benz and Talbot cars, while 1931 was an extremely good year in which he won at Le Mans (with Birkin in an Alfa Romeo) and also made good use of the 1·5-litre GP Delage that he had purchased from Malcolm Campbell. In 1932 he drove the notorious 4·9-litre Bugatti, amongst other cars, and though gaining a run of successes with Alfa Romeos and his own Delage, Bugatti and Mercedes-Benz, tried his hand with MGs as well in 1933. In 1935 he achieved a succession of high placings in major events with the Delage and a Type 59 Bugatti, while in 1936 he sold the Delage to Dick Seaman and took over Benjafield's ERA instead. Driving as usual in long-distance sports-car races with the Hon Brian Lewis, he also had some high placings that year as a member of the Fox and Nicholls Lagonda team. In the two remaining years before the War he continued to campaign the ERA with good results, driving other cars as opportunity presented, such as the Lagonda V-12 with which he lapped Brooklands at 108·27mph (174·24kph) in 1938.

Lord Howe worked tirelessly after the War in the cause of motor sport, speaking in the House of Lords on numerous occasions and serving on a large number of Committees, in addition to acting as President of the British Racing Drivers' Club. He died in 1964. DF

Hulme, Dennis Clive

Born in 1936, son of a World War 2 Victoria Cross winner, New Zealander Dennis Clive Hulme (pronounced Hull-m) came up very much the same way as Jack Brabham, with a similarly casual but determined outlook. Hulme worked in a garage after leaving school and started competition with an MG TF in local car club events in the Te Puke district in the Bay of Plenty. Soon with parental help he bought a 2-litre Cooper-Climax. This was at a stage in Australasian racing when two-year-old 'works' formula cars were very much the best equipment, and in 1959 Hulme was selected with George Lawton for the 'Driver To Europe' scholarship set up by the New Zealand International Grand Prix

Left, Denny Hulme in a Brabham-Repco BT20, 1967. *Photo: David Phipps*

Left below, Denny Hulme at Indianapolis. *Photo: Indianapolis Motor Speedway*

Right, Jacky Ickx. *Photo: Autosport*

earned him the 1967 World Championship. It was in 1967 that Hulme joined fellow-New Zealander Bruce McLaren, to drive in the Can-Am series. In his first season he won three out of six races, and in 1968 he became Can-Am Champion and also won the Italian and Canadian GPs in a Formula 1 McLaren. In 1969 he won the Mexican GP and five Can-Am events, and was 2nd in the 1970 South African GP. In practice for the Indianapolis 500 race Hulme crashed and suffered severe burns to his hands, and did not return to racing until the Watkins Glen Can-Am in June. However, in the rest of the season he won six Can-Am races to take the Johnson Wax Championship for the second time. TBF

Dennis Clive Hulme: Principal

1965	Tourist Trophy	Brabham-Climax BT8
1966	Tourist Trophy	Lola T70
1967	Monaco GP	Brabham-Repco BT20
	German GP	Brabham-Repco BT20
	Road America	McLaren-Chevrolet M8
	Chevron GP, Bridge-hampton	McLaren-Chevrolet M8
	Players 200, Mosport	McLaren-Chevrolet M8
1968	Italian GP	McLaren-Ford M7A
	Canadian GP	McLaren-Ford M7A
	Daily Express Trophy, Silverstone	McLaren-Ford M7A
	Tourist Trophy	Lola T70
	Players Trophy	Lola T70
	Martini 300, Silverstone	Lola T70
	Road America	McLaren-Chevrolet M8A
	Klondike 200, Edmonton	McLaren-Chevrolet M8A
	Stardust GP	McLaren-Chevrolet M8A
1969	Mexican GP	McLaren-Ford M7A
	Labatt 50, St Jovite	McLaren-Chevrolet M8B
	Klondike 200, Edmonton	McLaren-Chevrolet M8B
	Buckeye Cup, Lexington	McLaren-Chevrolet M8B
	Inver House Trophy, Bridge-hampton	McLaren-Chevrolet M8B
	Los Angeles Times GP, Riverside	McLaren-Chevrolet M8B
1970	Watkins Glen	McLaren-Chevrolet M8D
	Klondike 200, Edmonton	McLaren-Chevrolet M8D
	Buckeye Cup, Lexington	McLaren-Chevrolet M8D
	Minneapolis Tribune Trophy, Donney-brooke	McLaren-Chevrolet M8D
	Monterey Castrol GP, Laguna Seca	McLaren-Chevrolet M8D
	Los Angeles Times GP, Riverside	McLaren-Chevrolet M8D

Ickx, Jacques-Bernard

'Jacky' Ickx, born in Belgium in 1945, comes from a motor racing family. His father is one of the foremost French-language motoring journalists and his elder brother Pascal used to race motorcycles quite successfully. But this involvement left young Jacky uninterested: he saw his first race — the Belgian GP at Spa — when he was 13 and was bored stiff. But there was not much else to do on long Sundays at the family home in Braine l'Alleud and so he started running a motorcycle in local trials at the age of 16. He was good, and the Belgian Zündapp importer offered him a trials motorcycle for the winter and a road-racer for the summer. He was not yet 17, but soon Suzuki were interested in him and entered him in the Belgian GP on a 50cc machine. His entry was disallowed — he was too young.

But the young Belgian already had three national motorcycling titles to his credit, and then his Zündapp entrant — also a BMW distributor — lent him a BMW 700 coupé for a hill-climb season. He turned it over in his first event, gained a lot of TV publicity and ended up with a Ford of Belgium Cortina drive. He was 18.

Then came a spell in the Army where he was a tank instructor. In 1965 he won the Spa 24-hour touring car race with Langlois van Ophem, sharing a BMW 1800. The next year he repeated the performance, sharing an 1800 TI with Hahne, and was an impressive 2nd at Zolder in a Lotus-Cortina. Ken Tyrrell was impressed by young

Association — the scholarship which had sent Bruce McLaren to Europe in 1958.

Hulme started in 1960 by buying a Formula Junior Cooper-BMC to tour the Continent. Lawton was killed in his Cooper at Roskilde Ring, and Hulme took his place in a Cooper at Snetterton in his first Formula 1 race — his last for some years. Hulme went back to New Zealand in a 2·5-litre Cooper-Climax for 1961, then later that year returned to the Continental Formula Junior circus, his best result a 2nd at Messina. With fellow New Zealander Angus Hyslop, Hulme finished 4th in the general classification at Le Mans in 1961 in the only works 850cc Abarth to finish. In 1962 he had occasional drives in Ken Tyrell's Formula Junior Coopers, but took Australian Gavin Youl's place as Brabham FJ driver when Youl retired after an accident. In 1963 the quiet New Zealander won seven of the fourteen FJ races in which he started in the works car, and joined Brabham in a 2·5-litre Brabham-Climax for the 1964 Tasman Cup series. He had occasional drives in Formula 1 in 1964 and 1965, but still spent most time in Formula 2. It was not until 1966 that Hulme won a full works drive, for Brabham. He was 2nd in the British GP and had several 3rd placings, as well as many successes in the F2 Brabham-Honda. He finished 2nd with Ken Miles at Le Mans in a Ford GT40, but for his first Grand Epreuve victory he had to wait until Monaco in 1967. Victory in the German GP and other good placings

Ickx's cool, cerebral approach in the Budapest GP, and gave him a Matra F3 drive when he left the Army. His car often broke under the strain, but he was 2nd at Zandvoort and did well elsewhere. In 1967 he was Stewart's team-mate in the Tyrrell F2 Matras, and drove the JW Gulf Mirages. He scored three victories and two 3rds in F2 that season, excelling when Stewart was elsewhere and winning the European F2 Championship. Ickx also got his F2 Matra on to the front row of the German GP grid and led many F1 stars before retiring. He backed this up with four wins in the Mirages, and in September made his F1 debut in the Italian GP, driving a Cooper-Maserati and finishing 6th.

Ferrari signed on the meteoric young driver for 1968. He won the French GP at Rouen after an exemplary wet-weather drive; was 3rd in the Belgian, British and Italian GPs; and 4th in the Dutch and German. He also scored four victories in the JW Gulf GT40s, and won the Coupe de Spa against negligible opposition in a Ford Mustang. His driving was fast and fearless but he only really showed his best form when he was number one, a trait very marked in his days with Tyrrell. He broke a leg practising for the Canadian GP but recovered very quickly and, under his father's guidance, signed with Brabham to run Gulf-backed Cosworth-powered cars in 1969.

He had a good season, winning the German and Canadian GPs (the latter after a do-or-die attempt to pass Stewart had pushed the champion off the road); was 2nd in the British and Mexican; 3rd in the French; and 5th in the Dutch. He set fastest laps at the Nürburring, Mosport and Mexico City and was 2nd in the World Championship. He had two victories for JW (sharing with Oliver) and drove a brilliantly-judged final stint to win narrowly at Le Mans. Ickx also won the non-Championship Oulton Park Gold Cup F1 race, and won at Imola in a JW Mirage M2. In 1970 Ickx, with his 312B Ferrari, won the Austrian, Canadian and Mexican GPs. Politics sickened him and he resigned from the GPDA after continual disagreements. This great driver stayed with Ferrari for 1971. DCN

Ikusawa, Tetsu

Ikusawa came to England in 1966, learning race driving at the Motor Racing Stables school at Brands Hatch and running his own F3 Lotus 41. He had little success but showed promise, and raced a Porsche Carrera 6 back in Japan during the winter, his results benefiting enormously from his European experience.

Above left, Jacky Ickx in an F2 Matra at Oulton Park, 1967. *Photo: Nick Loudon*

Above, Jacky Ickx. *Photo: Autosport*

Opposite, Silverstone Circuit: Lorenzo Bandini (BRM) leads Jo Bonnier (Cooper) and Richie Ginther (BRM) in the 1963 British GP. *Photo: Geoff Goddard*

Below, Innes Ireland. *Photo: Autosport*

Innes Ireland. *Photo: Autosport*

Tetsu Ikusawa. *Photo Autosport*

He returned to the MRS in 1967, bought an F3 Brabham and scored a number of victories with this and a tuned Honda S800 coupé, including three firsts in one Brands Hatch meeting in July. A new F3 Brabham was acquired in 1968 and Tetsu won the Martini Trophy F3 event at Silverstone, was 2nd at Zandvoort and 3rd at Reims. This earned him a place in the Porsche works team for the Watkins Glen 6 Hours, and he shared the 6th place Porsche 908 with Attwood and Herrmann. He had raced a Porsche 910 of the Taki Racing Team back home earlier that year and Porsche seemed pleased with his performances.

But for 1969 he returned to Formula 3 with a private Lotus 59, winning at Mallory Park, and coming 2nd in two Silverstone races and 3rd at Keimola and Albi. This encouraged him to buy an F2 Lotus 69 for 1970, and his fast 'elbows-out' style was well-suited to the faster slipstreaming circuits. Nonetheless, his only notable placing was 2nd to Regazzoni's Tecno in the Jim Clark Trophy at Hockenheim. He drove the 'Mitsubishi Colt' —really an F2 Brabham BT30—in the JAF Grand Prix at Fuji but had trouble and has never really fulfilled his early promise. DCN

Ireland, Robert McGregor Innes

Ireland was born in 1930 in Kirkcudbright, Scotland, the son of a veterinary surgeon. He and his elder brother Alan, excelled at school athletics and Innes developed a mechanical flair at an early age. He was riding a 1928 Rudge motorcycle when just 15, and he became apprenticed to Rolls-Royce's aero engine division in Glasgow at 18. An engine blew up on the bed there, and Innes rapidly transferred to Rolls' car division in London.

His first motor race was at Boreham in 1952, driving a 4½-litre Bentley into 4th place. In 1953 he joined the Army and was commissioned in the Parachute Regiment. On his discharge he rejoined Rolls-Royce and then entered a garage partnership near Aldershot, specializing in Rolls-Bentley servicing. He returned to racing in 1955, and in 1956 Major Rupert Robinson—a friend of his brother's—backed him in buying a Lotus 11. He won the Brooklands Memorial Trophy with the car in 1957 and co-drove a works 1500 with Cliff Allison in the Swedish GP, finishing 9th. He drove for Ecurie Ecosse among others in 1958 and scored 15 victories that season, joining Team Lotus in 1959 and finishing 4th in his GP début at Zandvoort. The Lotus suffered from unreliability, but in 1960 in the new rear-engined Mark 18 Ireland beat Moss at Goodwood and Silverstone and finished 2nd in the Dutch GP. In 1961 he got off to a bad start with an accident in the tunnel at Monaco, but five weeks later he returned at Spa, only to have the engine break. After winning the non-Championship races at Zeltweg and Solitude, he scored a 'double first' at the US GP at Watkins Glen. This was not only Ireland's first victory in a Championship event, but also the first such success for a works Lotus.

Ireland's place was taken by Jim Clark in the works Lotus team of 1962, and the extrovert Scot found himself driving for UDT Laystall. He had a sad Formula 1 season, but excelled in the team's Lotus 19 sports cars and won the TT for them in a Ferrari 250GTO. In 1963 the team lost its backing to become simply BRP (British Racing Partnership), and he scored some early season success in their Lotus 24s. He crashed badly in mid-season, driving a Team Rosebud Lotus-Ferrari at Kent Wash., and smashed a hip. He returned at Snetterton in early 1964, winning a wet race after a memorable drive,

and went on to finish 12th with Maggs and Spence in the World Championship series, driving a monocoque BRP-BRM V-8. His career was well-punctuated with various accidents but Ireland was a popular member of the regular Formula 1 'circus'. He drove a Parnell Lotus-BRM in 1965 which was hardly competitive, and made his last GP appearance in Bernard White's 2-litre BRM at the 1966 Mexican GP.

Innes Ireland reached the zenith of his driving career in 1961, but never quite managed to reproduce such scintillating form thereafter. He was sports editor of *Autocar* magazine until April 1970. DCN

Isaac, V. Robert

Bobby Isaac who was born in 1934, won the NASCAR 1970 Grand National driving championship with 11 victories, finishing in the first ten 38 times in 47 starts. He won $121,470 and brought his nine-year career total to 32 GN wins. On 24 November 1970 Isaac set a new closed-course Land Speed Record of 201·104mph (323·706kph) in his Dodge at Talladega. ARB

Ivanowski, Boris

Ivanowski was reputed to be an ex-officer of the Russian Imperial Guard, and it is certain that he was resident in Paris after World War 1. He began racing with small French sports cars, being 2nd in the 1924 24 hour Bol d'Or race in the forest of St Germain in an 1,100cc EHP and 3rd in the 1,100cc Boulogne Light Car and Voiturette GP in 1926 in a Ratier.

He became best known at the wheel of works-prepared 1,500 and 1,750cc Alfa Romeo sports cars. In 1928, in a blown 1,500cc, he won the Georges Boillot Cup sports car handicap at Boulogne; the 6-hour Circuit des Routes Pavées, near Lille, and the Spa 24-hour race, partnered by Marinoni. In 1929 in a 1,500cc Alfa Romeo he was 4th in the Double-Twelve race at Brooklands with W. E. Dunkley, and 2nd at Spa with George Eyston. In a 1,750cc he was 4th in the Brooklands 6 Hours, sharing with Dr J. D. Benjafield. At Phoenix Park, Dublin, he won the 300-mile Saorstat Cup in a 1,500cc Alfa Romeo and the 300-mile Eireann Cup for bigger cars in a 1,750cc model, to become victor of the Irish GP on aggregate.

In 1930 Ivanowski won the 2-litre class in the Brooklands Double-Twelve sharing a 1,750cc Alfa Romeo with Eyston, and came 2nd in the Spa 24-hour race in a 1,750cc with Cortese.

In 1931 Ivanowski did some intensive racing with a big 38/250hp Mercedes SSK, which he shared with the Frenchman Henri Stoffel. With this car they came 5th in the 10-hour Italian GP at Monza, and 2nd to the Howe and Birkin 2·3 Alfa Romeo at Le Mans, after Ivanowski had put up the fastest lap.

After this the name of Ivanowski ceased to appear in the motor racing results, but he was almost certainly the most successful Russian-born driver in the annals of the sport. PMAH

Jarrott, Charles

Like S. F. Edge and others, Charles Jarrott, born in 1877, started his career as a racing cyclist and was still active in this field as late as 1898. He had, however, already been attracted to the motor vehicle, and drove a Bollée in the Motor Car Club's Coventry-Birmingham run in the spring of 1897. For three years he raced tricycles, and drove the prototype Napier-engined Panhard in the 1,000 Miles Trial of 1900, but was never in the running for an award. His first serious race was the Paris-Berlin,

Above, Boris Ivanowski. *Photo: Cyril Posthumus Collection*

Above right, Charles Jarrott with his mechanic Cecil Bianchi, in a 1904 Wolseley. *Photo: Veteran Car Club of Great Britain*

Opposite, Spa—Francorchamps Circuit: The start of the 1965 Belgian GP. Graham Hill's BRM in the lead. *Photo: Motor Sport*

1901, in which he drove Panhard No 13—duly painted green to cancel out the effects of the unlucky number. He finished 10th, but did better in 1902, when he drove his 40hp car into 2nd place in the Circuit de Nord alcohol race, and struggled through to 11th in the 1,000kg class of the Paris–Vienna, despite troubles with a distorted frame. He was given the wheel of one of the first 13,672cc 70hp cars for the Circuit des Ardennes, which he won in fine style. By 1903 he was actively engaged in the motor trade, handling Oldsmobile and the French-built De Dietrich; he drove for the latter make in two of the year's big races, finishing 3rd in the Paris–Madrid at 58·2mph (93·66kph), but retiring in the Ardennes. In the Gordon Bennett Cup he switched to Napier, crashing in the early stages. In 1904, incidentally, he hedged his bets for the Gordon Bennett, competing in both British and French eliminating trials (on the former in a Wolseley, and on the latter in a de Dietrich). He was accepted for the British team, and brought the Wolseley home in 12th place at Homburg.

Like his great rival S. F. Edge, however, he found that it was impossible to combine active racing with the promotion of several makes of motor car, and he retired from major events in 1905, while still supporting sprints. In 1906 he set a London–Monte Carlo record of 37½ hours on a 40hp Crossley, which was promptly beaten by another of the great pioneer propagandists, the Hon. C. S. Rolls, on a 20hp Rolls-Royce. Jarrott, after a certain amount of mutual recrimination in the columns of the weekly press, retrieved his record, again with a Crossley, in 1907. His firm, Charles Jarrott and Letts Ltd, was acquired by Crossley in 1910, but Jarrott remained in the motor trade under his own name, for several years longer. During World War 1 he served as Director of Mechanical Transport to the Royal Flying Corps. He died in 1944. MCS

Jenatzy, Camille

The 'Red Devil', so nicknamed on account of his red hair and beard, was a Belgian, born in 1868, who trained as a civil engineer, and also did his share of cycle racing. Unlike most drivers of his generation, he approached competitions via manufacture, and not the other way round. In fact the World's Land Speed Record ultimately stems from Jenatzy's rivalry with Charles Jeantaud, a competitor of his in the 1898 Paris Motor Cab Trials. Both men built sprint cars to promote sales of their cabs

243

and from late 1898 to the spring of 1899 the kilometre record was under constant attack. Jenatzy had already made ftd at Chanteloup, a hill short enough for a battery-electric's endurance, and his first successful flying start kilometre came on 17 January 1899, when he recorded 41·4mph (66·63kph) at Achères. When de Chasseloup-Laubat's Jeantaud raised this to 43·69mph (70·31kph) on the same day, Jenatzy replied with 49·92mph (80·34kph), only to be beaten again. Finally Jenatzy produced what was perhaps the world's first aerodynamic car, the cigar-shaped *La Jamais Contente* with electric motors geared direct to the back axle, large-section pneumatic tyres and tiller steering, and pushed the record up to 65·79mph (105·83kph), well out of the reach of de Chasseloup-Laubat and his slightly modified tourers.

Meanwhile Jenatzy had been tackling long-distance races, running a Mors in the Tour de France and the Paris–St Malo. In the latter he came 7th, but his 9th place in the French marathon sounds more impressive when it is realized that he drove non-stop through the night at one stage to make up for endless mechanical troubles. In 1901 he brought out the Jenatzy petrol-electric, a Mercedes-like vehicle anticipating later Lohner-Porsche experiments, which suffered from too much weight and made little impression either at Deauville or at Gaillon. Jenatzy drove a later version with conventional transmission in the 1902 Circuit des Ardennes, but crashed it into a pinewood.

He continued to experiment with cars and with a patent magnetic clutch (used by Pipe and Rochet-Schneider among others), but transfered his allegiance to Mercedes in 1903, finishing 11th (and 14th in general classification) in the Paris–Madrid. That year also he won the Irish Gordon Bennett Race after a steady and consistent drive which belied his reputation, and thus earned himself a Mercedes in the 1904 race at Homburg. This gained him a 2nd place at 52·8mph (84·97kph), but though he held this position throughout the contest rumour told of a phenomenal avoidance with a loco-motive at Wehrheim level-crossing on the second lap, and this incident is said to have so shaken him that his driving was never quite the same again. He retired his Pipe in that year's Circuit des Ardennes, and thereafter a slow decline set in. He retired in the 1905 Gordon Bennett and Vanderbilt Cup races, but finished 5th in the latter in 1906.

For the 1907 Circuit des Ardennes Jenatzy had a faster machine in the shape of a Pipe once more, and in the early stages he lay 2nd to Hautvast in a sister car, but both retired, leaving the field clear for the Minervas.

By 1908 Jenatzy was back with Mors for the Grand Prix, but that firm was on the downgrade and a 16th

Left above, Camille Jenatzy in a 120hp Mercedes which he drove in the 1905 Gordon Bennett race. *Photo: Cyril Posthumus Collection*

Above, Camille Jenatzy, 1904. *Photo. T. A. S. O. Mathieson Collection*

Right above, Parnelli Jones (centre), with Ed Leslie and Dan Gurney. *Photo: Al Bochroch Collection*

Parnelli Jones. *Photo: Al Bochroch Collection*

at 58·8mph (91·41kph) placed Jenatzy and his car alike as has-beens. In 1909 and 1910 he drove a 180hp Mercedes based on the 1908 Grand Prix winner in sprints and hill-climbs, doing well at Brussels, though at Gaillon in 1910 he had to give best to that other vast German machine, Fritz Erle's Benz. Jenatzy always insisted that he would die in a Mercedes, and he did, after being shot in mistake for a wild boar on his estate in 1913. MCS

Jones, Parnelli

Born in 1933, this American driver is regarded by the racing fraternity as one of the outstanding Indianapolis drivers of the last decade. He entered the 500 for the first time in 1961 with nine years of experience in stock-car and sprint-car competition. On five of his seven appearances at Indy he led the field at some stage of the race and he was the first driver to qualify at better than 150mph (240kph) when he won the pole position in 1962.

One year later he raised that record to 151·153mph (243·285kph) and also set a new record of 143·137mph (230·361kph) to win the race in an Offenhauser-powered entry. A fuel tank explosion, during a pit stop while leading the field again in 1964, ended his chances of winning two consecutive races, but he finished 2nd in 1965 with a Ford-engined car and was within three laps of a decisive victory in 1967 when his turbine-powered STP Special was sidelined by a drive shaft bearing failure.

Jones also won important USAC championship car races at Milwaukee, Wis., Phoenix, Ariz. and Trenton, N.J. while campaigning successfully in two other divisions of the USAC programme. He earned the national sprint-car title in 1961 and 1962, as well as the national stock-car championship in 1964.

He announced his retirement as a driver of national championship cars before the 1968 Indianapolis race, but scored several victories in stock-car events during the remainder of the season and appeared in a few races of that type in 1969—as well as in some Trans-Am events—while devoting increasing attention to his business enterprises. In 1970 he won five Trans-Am events to bring Ford Mustang the 1970 Trans-Am Championship. He owns and operates one of the largest Firestone stores in California; and he is co-owner of a prosperous Ford dealership. AB

Junek, Elizabeth

Elizabeth Junek was born in 1900 and first came into prominence by her driving in the Targa Florio of 1927, although she had in fact started her career three years earlier during the season of 1924. Both she, and her husband Čenek, a banker in Prague, were enthusiastic

Bugatti fans and owned a number of cars of this make with which they competed in the leading events in their native Czechoslovakia.

Between 1924 and 1926 Madame Junek raced successfully in such events as the Zbraslav-Jiloviště and Brno-Sobesice hill-climbs to mention only two of the many in which she took part, but in 1926 she ventured further afield, competing in the Klausen hill-climb in Switzerland.

In 1927, however, she and her husband decided to enter for the Targa Florio, something much more ambitious than either had tackled previously. Their original plan was for Madame Junek to drive the first three laps, her husband relieving her for the fourth, while she took over again for the fifth and final round.

To thoroughly prepare for this task the Juneks came to Sicily one month before the race and, not only did Madame Junek drive a lap (sometimes more than one) of 67 miles (107·83km) each day during this period but she and her husband found time to complete a lap on foot in order to memorize the many hundreds of corners. In the actual race Madame Junek completed the first lap in 4th place immediately behind the official Bugatti team of Minoia, Dubonnet and Materassi. Unfortunately on the second round trouble developed in the steering of her Bugatti necessitating her withdrawal. Later in the year she finished 2nd in the Circuit of Praded and won the 3,000cc class in the German Grand Prix over the newly opened Nürburgring.

If Elizabeth Junek's driving had aroused widespread interest, and much favourable comment in Sicily in 1927, in 1928 she caused a sensation. Fourth at the end of the first lap she led the field consisting of such drivers as Divo, Campari, Materassi, Minoia, Conelli and Nuvolari on the second, falling back to 2nd place on the third and fourth laps and finally finishing 5th having been forced to slow in the final round because of mechanical trouble. Her performance that day will for ever be remembered by those who were fortunate enough to be present, and only the worst of luck prevented her from finishing in the first three.

Tragedy was to follow for two months later her husband was killed in the German Grand Prix and out of respect for his memory Madame Junek gave up competitive driving.

Over the years there have been many fine lady drivers but it is generally accepted that Elizabeth Junek has never had, nor is likely to have, an equal. In recent years she has paid several visits to England as guest of the Bugatti Owners' Club, and in 1969 she drove Bernard Kain's Type 35B with considerable verve at Oulton Park. TASOM

Left above, Elizabeth Junek (Bugatti Type 35) at Brno-Soběšice Hill-Climb, 1927. *Photo: Vladimir Havranek Collection*

Above, Elizabeth Junek, 1932. *Photo: Hugh Conway Collection*

Right above, Elizabeth Junek, with Francisco d'Amico at the 1928 Targa Florio. *Photo: Hugh Conway Collection*

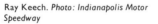

Ray Keech. *Photo: Indianapolis Motor Speedway*

Kallström, Harry

Harry Kallström was born in Södertälje, Sweden, in 1939. His father was a well-known rally driver and was the first man to win the Swedish T-race championship in 1952 driving a Volkswagen. The family business was concerned with timber lorries and that is how the young Kallström got his first experience of driving. He started rallying in 1958 when he took his father's old rally car on an event in which his father was entered and beat him. At his second event he won the junior class and finished 3rd overall which earned him the nickname of Sputnik for his quick rise to fame. He was champion of T-race in Sweden in 1959 and 1963 with a VW and in 1963 also finished 2nd in the RAC Rally.

In 1964 he transferred to a BMC Sweden Mini Cooper, won the T championship again and was also Scandinavian champion that year. 1966 was his last year with BMC, who were closing down their Swedish competition department, and he managed to finish 2nd again in the RAC Rally of that year. In 1967 he started to drive for Renault and among his achievements was winning a Coupe des Alpes in a Gordini. In 1968 he joined the Lancia team, for whom he still drives, and immediately began to have a big success. In his first event he was given a minute wrong on a special stage and lost the outright victory by one second to Pat Moss.

The following year he became European Champion after winning the prototype section of the Monte Carlo Rally and finishing 2nd on scratch. In the Swedish Rally he finished 4th and then he won the San Remo Rally. He finished 2nd in the Austrian Alpine Trial and went on to win the Spanish and the RAC Rallies as well as co-driving the winning car in the Nürburgring 84 Hours. In 1970 he won the RAC Ralley, and was 2nd in the San Remo-Sestriere and Moldau Rallies. JD

Kawai, Minoru

Born in 1942, Kawai was the leading Toyota driver in Japanese Group 7 racing. He began his career in 1965 with the Toyota S800 saloon, with which he had several class victories. He won the 1969 'Can-Jap-Am' Fuji 200 race for Toyota, and led in the early stages of that year's Japanese GP. His 5-litre V-8 Toyota G7 was the only one capable of challenging the 6-litre Nissan R382s, and he was faster there than team-mate Vic Elford. He was killed in August 1970, while testing a new Group 7 Toyota. DCN

Keech, Ray

This American racing driver, born in 1898, whose early racing experience had been limited to competition in minor events on the smaller tracks of Pennsylvania and neighbouring states, flashed to prominence in 1928 by setting a new world land speed record for the measured mile on the sand at Daytona Beach, Fla.

Driving J. W. White's unique Triplex Special on 22 April, Keech averaged 207·552mph (333·983kph) for the two-way run to erase the former mark of 206·956mph (333·064kph) set 8 weeks earlier by Malcolm Campbell of England in a Napier-powered car. Campbell's performance had broken the record of 203·79mph (327·94kph) set in 1927 by H. O. D. Segrave in a Sunbeam Special.

Keech's successful record run resulted in an opportunity for him to drive at Indianapolis for the first time on 30 May of the same year and he finished 4th behind Lou Meyer. Later in the season he scored three important championship victories, one on the Rockingham board speedway and two on the one-mile dirt tracks at Detroit, Mich., and Syracuse. N.Y.

He then won the 1929 Indianapolis 500-mile race in a 1·5-litre Miller-powered Simplex Special by a margin of more than six minutes over Lou Meyer, but was injured fatally two weeks later in a racing accident on the Altoona, Pa., board speedway. AB

Kling, Karl

Like many drivers, this German, born at Glissen in 1910, started his career in motor sports in the long-distance and cross country trials of the 1930s. He was a member of the Mercedes-Benz team. After World War 2 he started racing: his first victory was at Hockenheim in 1947 in the 2-litre BMW 328 racing coupé which had been the winning car in the 1940 Mille Miglia. His next car was a Veritas and in 1948 and 1949 he was German Champion in the 2-litre sports car class. The Formula 2 Veritas-Meteor was the next step. In 1950 he averaged 126·6mph (203·8kph) on the Grenzlandring. In the Argentine excursion by the three Mercedes-Benz pre-war racers in 1951 he took a 2nd place in the Gran Premio Evita Peron behind Gonzales (Ferrari). In 1952 he gained a 2nd place in the Milla Miglia, and victories in the Berne Grand Prix and the Carrera Panamericana, all in the new Mercedes-Benz 300 SL.

After an interlude with Alfa Romeo without notable success he joined the new Mercedes GP team in 1954. His debut in the new car was a 2nd place after Fangio at Reims and he achieved 5th place in the World Championship of 1954. When Mercedes-Benz withdrew from racing Karl Kling remained with the firm, as competition manager for a time, and is still with them today. HON

Kitano, Moto

Born in 1941, Kitano is one of the Nissan group's works drivers. Kitano has been regarded by visiting teams as one of the best drivers the Japanese have, and he won the 1968 Japanese GP at the wheel of a Nissan R381. In 1971 he won the All Japan Suzuka 300km Race in a Datsun 240Z. DCN

Knyff, René de

One of the greatest figures in the pioneer days of motor racing, the Chevalier René de Knyff, born in 1864 in Belgium, was more than a talented, calculating driver: he became first President of the Commission Sportive of the AC de France from its creation in 1899 until 1926, and President of the Commission Sportive International (CSI) from 1922 until 1946, thus contributing experience, enthusiasm, wisdom and totally impartial judgment to the organizational side of motor sport for many years.

To many, indeed, the large, imposing, heavily-bearded

René de Knyff in an 80hp Panhard at the *pesage* before the start of Paris–Madrid, 1903. *Photo: T. A. S. O. Mathieson Collection*

Karl Kling (left), with J. M. Fangio after they had finished 2nd in the 1955 Targa Florio. *Photo: Peter Miller*

Robert Laly, 1927. *Photo: Cyril Posthumus Collection*

de Knyff was the doyen of the 'heroic age'. He always raced Panhard-Levassors, being a director of the Company, and after a quiet start in 1897 with 4th position in the Marseilles–Nice–La Turbie race, 5th in the Paris–Dieppe and 6th in the Paris–Trouville, he scored his first victory in 1898 in the 358-mile (576km) Paris–Bordeaux event. In 1899 he gained outright victory in the Tour de France; de Knyff averaged 30·2mph (48·60kph) in his 16hp Panhard, leading by almost 5 hours. That same year he won Belgium's first race, the Spa–Bastogne–Spa, and finished 2nd in the Paris–Bordeaux.

More successes came in 1900: the 125-mile (201·2km) Nice–Marseille–Nice and the 209-mile (336·4km) Circuit de Sud-Ouest based on Pau, when he just crossed the finishing line before stopping with a seized engine. He was 3rd in the classic 1901 Paris–Berlin race, and competed in the first four Gordon Bennett Cup races, retiring when leading the 1902 event which eventually fell to the British Napier, and coming 2nd to Jenatzy's Mercedes in 1903. That was de Knyff's last race, as he devoted his very considerable energies thereafter to organization work with the CSI. He died in 1954. CP

Kurosawa, Motoharu

Born in 1941, Kurosawa is one of Japan's leading racing drivers, contracted to the Nissan-Datsun works team. He has driven saloon cars (Datsun Fairlady), GTs (Datsun 240Z) and Group 6 sports/racing cars (Nissan R380 and R382) with considerable success since 1965, when he turned from motorcycle to car racing. He shared the Japanese GP-winning 6-litre Nissan R382 with Y. Sunako at Fuji in 1969. DCN

Laly, Robert

Born in France in 1887, Laly spent many years as a mechanic before he had an opportunity to drive. This came in 1924 when he joined the Ariès company, and from then until his retirement in 1930 he drove only for Ariès, in sports and touring car events all over France, and in Belgium and Spain as well. He competed regularly at Le Mans but never had much success there, but he won the 3-litre class in the Spanish Touring Car GP at San Sebastian in 1924, and in the 1926 Circuit des Routes Pavées. His most successful season was 1927, when he won the Coupe Florio at St Brieuc and the Georges Biollot Cup at Boulogne outright. He was in the lead at Le Mans until the 23rd hour when they retired. In 1928 he won the sports car class of the 4 Heures de Bourgogne, coming 2nd overall. Some 1,100cc class wins at Spa and Pau in 1929 and 1930 marked the end of his career; for he retired after the 1930 season. TASOM

Lambert, Percy

A well-liked British driver of the pre-1914 days who, with his brother Harold, was a regular competitor at Brooklands. Percy Lambert drove the 20hp Austin 'Pearley III' at Brooklands in 1911 and he then turned to driving Talbots for Lord Shrewsbury and Talbot, in sand races, speed trials and on the Track. Lambert's most notable performance was taking the World 1-hour record to 103·84mph (167·16kph) the first time a car had exceeded 100 miles (160kph) in the hour, and this with a side-valve engine of 25hp. It was when attempting to regain this record from Peugeot in 1913 that the Talbot overturned on the Member's banking at Brooklands and Percy Lambert was fatally injured, in 1913, after he had lapped at well over 114mph (183kph). In addition to Austins and Talbots, Lambert also drove Singers at Brooklands. WB

Lampinen, Simo

Simo Lampinen was born in Porvoo, Finland in 1943. His parents ran a factory for skis and it was only natural that the young man should take to skiing as his first sport. By the age of 13, he was a junior ski-jump champion. However, when he was almost 15 he contracted polio and the next few years were spent in and out of hospitals, one of which was in Nottingham where he learned to speak English. On returning to Finland, he learned to drive both cars and motorcycles despite having very little movement in his feet. At one time he used to drive his Jaguar into Helsinki every day for treatment, and it was in this car that he drove his first rally in 1960 just three years after falling ill.

Motor sport gave him an interest that he could find in no other sport and he bought himself a Saab in which he drove many small rallies, though his first 1000 Lakes was in 1961 with the faithful Jaguar. So good did he become that Saab offered him a contract in 1962 and in 1963 and 1964 he was Finnish champion, winning the 1000 Lakes in both years. He continued to drive for Saab in Scandinavia and finished 2nd in the Swedish Rally no less than three times, in 1966, 1967 and 1969. In 1965, he signed a Triumph contract and drove a Spitfire in the Monte, Tulip and Alpine and a 2000 in the RAC and Welsh rallies as well as the 1966 Monte. When Triumph stopped rallying, he drove a DAF in the 1967 Tulip, winning the class. However, his main interest was still with Saab, for whom he won the RAC Rally in 1968 and the Scottish Rally in 1969. At the beginning of 1970 he signed a contract with Lancia for whom he won the TAP Ralley and Rally of the Thousand Minutes, and finished 3rd in the Thousand Lakes. JD

Lancia, Vincenzo

Lancia, born in 1881, the son of an Italian soup manufacturer, was apprenticed to the Ceirano brothers in pre-FIAT days. Though nominally a book-keeper, he soon progressed to the workshops and became FIAT's chief tester, in which capacity he backed Felice Nazzaro in early races, and won the Padua-Vicenza-Treviso-Padua race in 1900. When Nazzaro moved on to work for Vincenzo Florio, Lancia stayed in Turin, and in 1902 he took 2nd place behind Florio's Panhard in the Padua-Riunione race. He first appeared outside Italy at the wheel of a Fiat in the 1903 Paris-Madrid race, but retired without distinguishing himself. In 1904 he beat

Nazzaro's Panhard in the Milan Speed Trials, as well as winning the Coppa Florio at 72mph (115·87kph) over the very fast Brescia circuit, and taking the honours in the Consuma Cup hill-climb.

Abroad, the Fiats had yet to find their form, as Lancia's 8th place in the Gordon Bennett and a 12th in the Circuit des Ardennes showed. However, 1905 saw Lancia with a really fast car, with which he could win if he did not break it first. His best performance was 3rd in the Coppa Florio, but he led the Gordon Bennett race for the first two circuits, making fastest lap at 52·6mph (84·65kph), before his Fiat succumbed to the strain. Only a minor scrape with the fwd Christie deprived him of the lead in the Vanderbilt Cup. In spite of this he managed 4th place. Once again in 1906 his only victory was in a long-distance rally, the 2,485-mile Coppa d'Oro, but he finished 2nd in the Vanderbilt, and set a cracking pace in the early stages of the Grand Prix. Though lying 9th at the end of the first day's racing, he managed to take 5th place. A leaking fuel tank eliminated him from the Targa Florio, which he nearly won, in 1907, setting yet another fastest lap at 34mph and finishing close behind Nazzaro. A 6th place in the Kaiserpreis was

Top, Percy Lambert in a Vauxhall, 1912 French GP. *Photo: T. A. S. O. Mathieson Collection*

Left above, Simo Lampinen with his wife Mirja. *Photo: Top-Foto*

Vincenzo Lancia in a Fiat, 1907 Kaiserpreis. *Photo: T. A. S. O. Mathieson Collection*

counterbalanced by a victory in his heat (Nazzaro won the other) and another fastest circuit. For two laps of the Grand Prix he duelled with Arthur Duray's Lorraine-Dietrich for first place, only to retire through clutch trouble and misfiring. Tyre trouble robbed him of victory in the 1908 Targa Florio (he finished 2nd), and his Fiat was never in the running in the Grand Prix, but his last appearance on the fast triangular circuit used for the Coppa Florio was magnificent. The usual troubles held him down to 5th place, but he made fastest lap, with a speed of 82·3mph (132·45kph).

Lancia set up on his own as a manufacturer, and pressure of business caused him to stop driving for FIAT after 1908. Though he entered his own products in minor Italian speed trials until 1910–11, he never returned seriously to the sport, devoting the rest of his life (he died in 1937) to the evolution of magnificent fast tourers of advanced design. It has been said with some justice that the Lancia factory never made a bad car. MCS

Lang, Hermann

Few drivers had such a meteoric rise to fame as Lang, born in 1909, the young Mercedes racing mechanic who looked after Fagioli's car in 1934, and then got his chance to race. He came to Mercedes with a sporting background, however, having raced motorcycles since 1928 with considerable success, specializing in sidecar hill-climbing events and becoming German Champion of the class in 1931. This undoubtedly assisted his transfer from the pits to the cockpit, and in his first car race, the Eifelrennen of 1935, he finished 5th despite a spin in the rain. For a newcomer to the powerful German cars this was impressive, and after three more races that season 'for experience' his ability to go very fast, revealed during an illicit lap or two at Tripoli in 1936, earned him a rebuke from team manager Neubauer for taking the curve past the pits flat out.

In the German GP he actually led lap 1 but broke his little finger during gear-changing; he still finished 7th, driving another car, and by 1937 was a fully fledged member of the team. Tripoli brought this short, stocky, quiet German his first Grand Prix victory in 1937; and he followed swiftly with another at AVUS, averaging a fantastic 162·61mph (261·72kph) in a fully streamlined Mercedes, and backed it up with two 2nd places in the Swiss and Italian GPs. He scored two more victories in 1938, at Tripoli and Leghorn, when his team-mate von Brauchitsch was disqualified. In 1939 Hermann Lang was at his peak, the fastest and most tigerish GP driver on the circuits. He scored seven outright victories, comprising: his third Tripoli GP in a row with the new 1·5-litre V-8 Mercedes voiturette, the Pau, Eifel, Belgian and Swiss GPs, and the Vienna and Grossglockner hill-climbs, which gained him extra honours as German Hill-climb Champion.

Lang was the only member of the Mercedes-Benz GP team to make a successful come back after World War 2, although much of his old fire had gone after long years of inactivity. Nonetheless he won the very first post-war German event, the Ruhestein hill-climb in 1946, driving the same BMW which had won the 1940 'substitute' Mille Miglia at Brescia. He also raced an F2 Veritas, scoring a 2nd at Solitude in 1950 and retiring from the 1950 German GP. He very happily returned to racing a 1939 3-litre GP Mercedes in the 1951 Argentine Temporada, but age of men and machines told and he could only finish 2nd to Gonzalez' 2-litre Ferrari in one race, and 3rd in the other.

When Mercedes took up sports car racing with the 300 SL in 1952 Lang joined the team, came second at Berne, won the Le Mans 24 Hours race with Fritz Riess, won the Jubilee sports car race at the Nürburgring, and was runner-up to team-mate Kling in the Pan American Road Race in Mexico.

Two drives with Maseratis in 1953 perhaps brought it home to Lang that his best days were over, but he managed a 5th in the Swiss GP, and with Mercedes' return to GP fields in 1954 with the new W196 he drove his last classic, the German GP. He worked up to 2nd place behind Fangio by lap 5, then got involved in a duel with team-mate Kling, spun off, stalled his engine, and could not restart. He retired from the race, and from racing, after an outstanding career, but is still at the Untertürkheim works and available to drive one of their carefully cherished historic racing cars. CP

Larrousse, Gérard

Born in France in 1940, Larrousse entered rallying in 1962, and by 1966 was driving regularly for the French NSU importers, his successes including the Rallye de Lorraine in 1966. The following year he drove for Alpine, winning eight rallies during the year, and also driving in events such as the Targa Florio and Le Mans. In 1968 he won the Neige et Glace and Lorraine rallies, and drove the Alpine V-8 in a number of races, although never finishing very high in this slow car. In 1969 he moved to Porsche with whom he had a very successful season in rallying and racing. 2nd overall in the Monte Carlo rally in a 911 was followed by victory in the Tour de France and the Tour de Corse, and 2nd overall (with Herrmann) in a 908 in the Le Mans 24 Hour race. In 1970 he repeated his 2nd place in the Monte and led the the first few laps in the Targa Florio, and was 2nd again at Le Mans, this time sharing a Porsche 917L with Willy Kauhsen. JD/DCN

Laurent, Claude

Laurent was born in 1935 in Orleans, France, and made his competition debut with a Renault 4CV at the Orleans circuit. He drove this car and a 2CV Dagonnet Citroën in various events, but his first good result was a class win in the 1956 Sestrieres Rally in a Dyna Panhard. In 1960 he won his class at Le Mans in a Lotus Elite, and in 1962 and 1963 drove DKWs in rallies with considerable success. He won the Mont Blanc rally in 1964 in a Citroen DS19, and in 1965 bought a Lotus Elan which was very fast but unreliable. However he won four French events in it in 1965 and 1966.

In 1965 Laurent was offered a works car by DAF, and it is with this make that he has become firmly associated, though he has still driven his own BMW or Porsche on occasions. His record with the little DAF is amazing; in 1965 alone he covered 93,200 miles (150,000km) in the course of competing in 25 rallies, and won his class eight times. In 1966 he won his class six times in sixteen events, and in 1967 nine times in seventeen events. One of his best results was in the 1969 Acropolis Rally when he finished 3rd overall, while the same year he was 5th overall in the Tulip Rally. With a Porsche 911T he was 2nd in his class at Le Mans in 1968 and 3rd in class in 1969. JD

Lautenschlager, Christian

Lautenschlager was born in 1877 of poor parents and served his apprenticeship with a locksmith before spending his early working years in Switzerland. Thence he proceeded to a cycle factory in Chemnitz, Germany,

Hermann Lang. *Photo: Fumagalli*

Christian Lautenschlager. *Photo: T. A. S. O. Mathieson Collection*

joining the Daimler Motoren-Gesellschaft in 1900, and achieving the position of foreman-inspector. He acted as Salzer's mechanic in the 1906 Circuit des Ardennes, and won his first major race, the 1908 French GP. Though Hémery's eye injuries probably lost Benz the event to Mercedes, Lautenschlager's driving was steady and devoid of any element of risk, especially on corners: a good thing, for at the end of the race his pit had no spare tyres left. Mercedes returned to racing in 1913 with some big chain-driven 6-cylinder cars, but these ran only in the Grand Prix de France, in which Lautenschlager finished 6th. The factory's 1914 French GP machines, however, were far more effective, and he drove another well-calculated race at Lyons, steadily wearing down the lead established by Georges Boillot on the Peugeot. Once again he had won in France amid icy silence and the sounds of *Deutschland über Alles*.

Though he drove in the works team after World War 1, he never fully recovered his form. A 10th place (and 2nd in class) in the 1922 Targa Florio on a 4·9-litre front-wheel-braked version of his 1914 winner was a modest showing; at Indianapolis in 1923 he crashed into a wall; and in the 1924 Targa the best he could attain on a 2-litre unblown car was 10th place. For the rest of his life he continued to work for Daimler-Benz at Unter-türkheim. He died in 1954. MCS

Lehoux, Marcel

Born of French parents in Algeria in 1892, Lehoux began racing in 1924, winning the Casablanca GP in a Bugatti in his first season. During the next five years he confined his racing mainly to North Africa, winning the Algerian GP in 1928 and 1929, and the Tunisian GP in 1928. He came to Europe for selected races, including the Spanish Touring Car GP at San Sebastian which he won in 1927, and the GP de Provence at Miramas in which he won his heat in 1926 and was 2nd in 1927.

In 1931 he and Etancelin teamed up while the latter was waiting for his Alfa Romeo, and although they retired from the Italian and French GPs, Lehoux won the Geneva and La Marne GPs, and was 2nd in the Circuit de Dauphiné. During 1932 and 1933 Lehoux stuck to his Bugatti Type 51, although the enlarged Monza Alfa Romeo was appreciably faster, and had several victories including the Pau GP in a snowstorm. He also won the tragic Monza GP in which Campari, Czaykowski and Borzacchini lost their lives.

Lehoux joined the Scuderia Ferrari in 1934, but his best performance was 2nd at Dieppe. In 1935 he went independent again, driving a Maserati, but he had a poor season with little chance of success against the works teams, especially those from Germany. In 1936 he joined the ERA team for voiturette events, and bought a Lagonda for sports car races. In the Deauville GP he was driving a 2-litre ERA when he was killed in a collision with Farina's Alfa Romeo. TASOM

Leiningen, Prince Hermann zu

Prince Leiningen, who was born in 1901, began motor racing in 1927 with a 1·5-litre Bugatti, gaining a class victory in the Baden-Baden flat race and hill-climb for touring cars. At the same event in 1928 he achieved four class victories, two in the racing car class in his Bugatti and two in the sports car class in an Amilcar. Freiburg, Hohe Wurzel, Kesselberg, Regensburg, were all events in which he finished 1st or 2nd. For 1929 he changed to a Mercedes SSK and took 2nd places at Zbraslav-Jiloviste, Baden-Baden, Kesselberg, Freiburg,

Marcel Lehoux, 1933. *Photo: Cyril Posthumus Collection*

The Hon Brian Lewis. *Photo: Cyril Posthumus Collection*

Stuart Lewis-Evans in the Vanwall, 1957 Italian GP. *Photo: John Ross*

Prince Hermann zu Leiningen, 1934 French GP. *Photo: Cyril Posthumus Collection*

St Moritz and Gaisberg. In 1930–32 he had further successes in a Bugatti. He then joined the Auto Union team. His outstanding success was in the 1934 Italian Grand Prix when he finished 2nd with Stuck behind Caracciola and Fagioli. He withdrew from racing at the end of 1934, but took up the sport again in 1951, and with Count Berckheim won the Travemünde and Wiesbaden rallies in a Porsche. HON

Lewis, Hon, Brian Edmund

Brian Lewis (later to become Lord Essendon) was one of the most consistent and reliable drivers of his day, participating in a large number of major events throughout the world in the space of a few years. He was born in 1903. His motoring career began with an AV monocar, which was followed by a series of Frazer Nashes, starting with a rare Ruby-engined model and culminating in 'The Slug', which he raced at Brooklands in 1927. At this period he also became so involved with Bugattis that he was known as 'Bug' Lewis, a nickname which remained even after he had joined the works Talbot team.

Although seldom in the running for outright victory, these cars were extremely efficient and reliable, and Lewis achieved a long run of good placings, which he backed up with similar results in other cars. Several successes were achieved with Alfa Romeos, and other makes raced included Delage, Riley, Maserati, Singer, Lagonda and ERA. Apart from his remarkable three consecutive wins in the Isle of Man Mannin Moar races, his list of victories is not impressive, but during 1931, for instance (when he won a BRDC track-racing Gold Star at Brooklands), he achieved no less than eight 2nd or 3rd places. He became known as one who always finished, come what may, be it a Brooklands handicap or a Le Mans 24-hour race (in which he was 3rd twice).

His career ran parallel to that of Earl Howe, with whom he shared cars in several long-distance races, and like Howe he later played a part in the organizational side of motor racing. DF

Lewis-Evans, Stuart

Born in 1930, Lewis-Evans was the son of a garage owner in Beckenham, near London, who was well-known himself in 500 racing at the time when his son was competing. He started at Brands Hatch with a Cooper, and soon made a mark. His driving was both forceful and consistent. After nearly five years of consistent placings in the 500 class he earned his reward with a place in the Connaught Grand Prix team. In 1957 he also drove for Ferrari in sports car races, finishing 5th at Le Mans. For 1958 he was driving works Aston Martins in sports car races and a Formula 2 Cooper for the British Racing Partnership. Following Connaught's withdrawal, he was recruited to the Formula 1 Vanwall team in 1957, and was somewhat unlucky not to record an outright victory. At the end of the 1958 season he crashed in the Morocco GP, and died some time later of the burns he had sustained.

Lewis-Evans was of very small but wiry build, and had a quiet and even-tempered manner which masked a determined approach to the sport he had espoused. DF

Lobkowicz, Prince Georg-Kristian

After the Juneks, the name of G. K. Lobkowicz who was born in 1901 is one of the greatest among Czech racing drivers. He began racing in 1924 with an Austro-Daimler, and his first successes were gained a few years later with a

Bugatti. In particular, he scored many victories at hill-climbs such as Zbraslav-Jíloviště and Brno-Soběšice (Czechoslovakia); Gaisberg, Semmering, and Pötschen Pass (Austria); Tatra (Poland) and so on. In 1930 he entered the Masaryk Grand Prix, but had to retire with ignition trouble. The next year Lobkowicz was 4th in this race, behind Chiron, Stuck, and von Morgen. Other successes encouraged him to buy a Bugatti Type 54, the hard-to-handle 4·9-litre car which later claimed the life of Czaykowski. While driving this car at the AVUS track in April 1932, Lobkowicz crashed fatally. There were two curious incidents concerning his death. At the exact moment of the accident, the stopwatch in his pit came to a standstill, while his death on that day had been foretold by a fashionable soothsayer, Erik Hanussen, who had also foretold von Brauchitsch's victory in the same event. VH

Lockhart, Frank

This American racing driver and engineer, born in 1902, whose brief but meteoric racing career was due in part to his development of a patented intercooler to cool the compressed air in supercharged engines, flashed to prominence at Indianapolis in 1926. During the two previous years he had attracted some attention on California tracks by making an excellent showing in his own Fronty-Ford in competition against Duesenbergs and Millers. He had made the trip to Indianapolis only with the hope of a chance to drive relief for Bennett Hill; but the illness of Peter Kreis resulted in the selection of Lockhart for a starting position in a Miller Special.

Driving brilliantly, Frank took the lead on the 60th lap and was approximately five miles in front of his nearest challenger when race officials terminated the event at 400 miles because of rain. He also scored important victories on the board tracks at Charlotte, N.Car., and Fresno, Calif., later in the year while experimenting with various types of intercoolers. Using one of his own design on a new Miller Special, he returned to Indianapolis in 1927 and broke the qualifying record by almost 7mph with an average speed of 120·1mph (193·3kph) to win the pole position. He also led the race for the first 91 laps and regained command after a pit stop, before being eliminated by a broken connecting rod on the 119th lap. Also in 1927 he modified a 91ci (1,491cc) Miller, extracting 252bhp. This car recorded a two-way flying mile in his hands at 164·85mph (265·29kph), and was timed at 171mph (275·19kph).

After further victories later in the season on the board tracks at Altoona, Pa., and Rockingham, N.H., and a one-lap record of 147·7mph (237·7kph) on the boards at Atlantic City, N.J., Lockhart obtained financial assistance from various companies for an assault on the world's land speed record in a Miller-powered car of distinctive design to be called the Stutz Blackhawk. His first attempt to break Sir Malcolm Campbell's mark of 206·956mph (332·990kph) at Daytona Beach on a blustery February day in 1928 ended in failure when a gust of wind caused him to swerve into the sea. Two months later, after Ray Keach had erased Campbell's record with an average of 207·552mph (333·983kph), Lockhart tried again in the Blackhawk and crashed to his death when a tyre failure flipped the car end-over-end while travelling at an estimated speed of better than 210mph (338kph). AB

Lurani, Count Giovanni

Count 'Johnny' Lurani, 'with his perpetual 20-year-old

Above, Prince Georg-Kristian Lobkowicz. *Photo: Erwin Tragatsch Collection*

Right above, Count Johnny Lurani, with George Eyston at the start of the 1933 Mille Miglia in which they won their class. *Photo: Cyril Posthumus Collection*

Below, Frank Lockhart. *Photo: Indianapolis Motor Speedway*

Bruce McLaren: Principal Successes

1958	Nürburgring (F2)	Cooper-Climax 1·5-litre
1959	United States GP	Cooper-Climax 2·5-litre
	Teretonga Trophy	Cooper-Climax 2·5-litre
	Dunedin GP	Cooper-Climax 2·5-litre
1960	Argentine GP	Cooper-Climax 2·5-litre
1962	Teretonga Trophy	Cooper-Climax 2·5-litre
	Australian GP	Cooper-Climax 2·5-litre
	Lavant Cup, Goodwood	Cooper-Climax 2·5-litre
	Monaco GP	Cooper-Climax 1·5-litre
	Reims GP	Cooper-Climax 1·5-litre
1963	Lady Wigram Trophy	Cooper-Climax 2·5-litre
	Teretonga Trophy	Cooper-Climax 2·5-litre
	Longford	Cooper-Climax 2·5-litre
	Sandown Park	Cooper-Climax 2·5-litre
1964	New Zealand GP	Cooper-Climax 2·5-litre

continued

air' as Achille Varzi once put it, was born in 1905 and began racing in 1925 with a Salmson. He drove a Ruby-engined Derby in his first road race at Alessandria in 1927.

He took part in nine Mille Miglia races, winning his class in 1933 (MG Magnette, with Eyston), 1948 (Healey) and 1952 (Porsche 356, with Count Berckheim). He finished second in his class three times (once with C. Penn Hughes in an MG Magnette in 1934) and was third on one occasion, in 1949, in a Bristol shared with H. J. Aldington. His class wins in hill-climbs, often at record speed, include events at Freiburg (twice), Klausen, La Turbie, Biella, Kesselberg (three times), Trieste, Rome, Brunate, Varese, Gurnigel, Geneva and Stelvio (three times), mostly on Maseratis, but also Alfa Romeos. He was captain of the Maserati team in South Africa in 1937/8, coming 3rd in the 1937 Johannesburg GP and in the 1938 Capetown GP. Also on Maseratis he was 3rd in the 1,500cc class in the 1938 Tripoli GP, and 2nd overall in the 1937 Targa Florio in the Favorita Park, Palermo. In 1938 he broke his hip practising in a Maserati at the Crystal Palace meeting.

He broke more than 30 class records driving his own cars, Nibbio I and Nibbio II, and also Abarths, from 1935 to 1956. Nibbio I was the first 500cc car to exceed 100mph (in 1935), and the first to exceed this speed with a 250cc supercharged engine (in 1947).

In 1951 Count Lurani was 12th at Le Mans in a 2-litre Lancia shared with Bracco, but he retired in the 1953 race in a 2-litre Fiat. His last event was the 1953 Alpine Rally in which he won a Coupe des Alpes as a member of the Lancia team. During his career he drove in over 160 events in 8 different countries.

A Doctor of Engineering, as well as author and journalist, he edited *Auto Italiana* until 1961, and since then has edited *Autorama*. He was the instigator of Formula Junior racing in 1957, is Vice-President of the Guild of Motoring Writers and an honorary member of the BRDC. He now has a collection of vintage cars with which he still competes in vintage events. PMAH

McLaren, Bruce

McLaren was born in New Zealand in 1937 and started to serve his motoring apprenticeship at the age of 13 with an Austin Seven, progressing through a Ford 10 special and an Austin-Healey to Cooper-Climax sports and racing cars. He travelled to Britain in 1958 as the first driver under the 'Driver-to-Europe' scheme sponsored by the New Zealand Grand Prix Drivers' Association, and attached himself to the Cooper factory, competing at first in Formula 2 events. With his victory at Sebring in

1959, he became the youngest driver ever to achieve a victory in a championship Grand Prix.

In 1960 he was 2nd in the World Championship, and 3rd in 1962, but Cooper fortunes were on the wane, although he remained loyal to them up to the end of 1965. However, with the development of his own Group 7 sports-racing cars, Bruce achieved the limelight again, winning the Can-Am Championship in 1967 and 1969—his team-mate Hulme being successful in the intervening year.

Possibly the three years in childhood that he spent immobilized with Perthes' disease contributed towards the unruffled and philosophical demeanour with which he faced triumph and disaster alike. He had been called 'the driver who never made a mistake', and certainly from 1960 onwards he had very few off the road excursions. Although regarded even more highly as a development engineer than as a driver, his great skill and calm at the wheel was universally acknowledged by his fellow drivers. The designs of his cars were attributed to others, and his modesty concealed the large contributions he made in their development; the quality of his preparation and organization became a byword among other teams. Reserved by nature, he was one of the most popular drivers, always cheerful and prepared to answer questions frankly. As a test driver he really excelled, and it was tragically ironic that he should have met his death during private testing at Goodwood, driving an M8D Group 7 car on 2 June 1970. He had already received several awards in recognition of his efforts in Grand Prix racing, the Indianapolis 500 and the Can-Am series, and was due to be honoured with the Segrave Trophy by the RAC. DF

	Lady Wigram Trophy	Cooper-Climax 2·5-litre
	Teretonga Trophy	Cooper-Climax 2·5-litre
	BARC Trophy, Aintree	Cooper-Climax sports
	BRDC Trophy, Silverstone	Cooper-Climax sports
	Guards Trophy, Brands Hatch	Cooper-Oldsmobile sports
	Mosport	Cooper-Oldsmobile sports
1965	Australian GP	Cooper-Climax 2·5-litre
	Daily Express Trophy, Silverstone	McLaren-Oldsmobile sports
	Governors' Trophy, Nassau	McLaren-Oldsmobile sports
1966	Le Mans 24-Hours with Amon	Ford GT40 Mk2
	Labatt Trophy, St Jovite	McLaren-Chevrolet M1B
	Mosport	McLaren-Chevrolet M1B
	Pepsi Cola Trophy, St Jovite	McLaren-Chevrolet M1B
1967	Sebring 12-Hours, with Andretti	Ford GT40 Mk4
	Los Angeles Times GP	McLaren-Chevrolet M6A
	Monterey GP, Laguna Seca	McLaren-Chevrolet M6A
1968	Race of Champions, Brands Hatch	McLaren-Ford M7A
	Belgian GP	McLaren-Ford M7A
	Los Angeles Times GP, Riverside	McLaren-Chevrolet M8A
	Teretonga International	BRM P126
1969	Race of Champions, Brands Hatch	McLaren-Ford M7C
	Labatt Trophy, Mosport	McLaren-Chevrolet M8B
	Watkins Glen	McLaren-Chevrolet M8B
	Road America, Elkhart Lake	McLaren-Chevrolet M8B
	Michigan International	McLaren-Chevrolet M8B
	Monterey-Castrol GP, Laguna Seca	McLaren-Chevrolet M8B
	Texas International	McLaren-Chevrolet M8B

Above left, Bruce McLaren at Watkins Glen. *Photo: Al Bochroch*

Above right, Count Aymo Maggi. *Photo: courtesy Countess Maggi*

Left, Bruce McLaren (centre) with Stirling Moss and Denny Hulme, after receiving the Johnson Wax Trophy from Moss at the conclusion of the 1969 Can-Am season. *Photo: AHD Associates*

Maggi, Count Aymo

This Italian aristocrat was born in 1903. He started racing in 1921, on motorcycles, changing over to cars the following year. His first victory of note was the 1923 Pontedecimo–Giovi hill-climb, in a Chiribiri. In 1924 he won the 1,500cc class of the Circuit del Garda, finishing 4th in the general classification. During 1925 he competed in most of the leading Italian events, with his Bugatti, winning the Circuit del Garda outright.

In 1926, with a new Type 35 Grand Prix Bugatti, Maggi began the season well by winning the Rome GP, defeating the official Alfa Romeo team of P2 Grand Prix cars in the process. He followed this up with two victories in Sicily in the Coppa Vinci, at Messina, and the Coppa Etna at Catania. These successes did not go unnoticed by the Bugatti factory, and he was invited to drive in the Grand Prix d'Alsace, a race confined to cyclecars of 1,100cc in which Bugatti had entered three special cars to be driven by Dubonnet, de Vizcaya and Maggi. The winner was Dubonnet, hard pressed throughout the race by Maggi, who finished a close 2nd having been flagged to slow down twice by team manager Costantini. Returning to Italy, Maggi finished 3rd in the Circuit of Pescara winding up a highly successful season by winning the Circuit of Garda for the second time.

He took part in the first Mille Miglia, with Alfieri Maserati as co-driver, the pair winning the unlimited class and finishing 6th in the general classification with their Isotta Fraschini.

In 1928, driving a Maserati, he was 2nd in the Circuit of Pozzo, winning the 1,500cc class, but failed to finish in the Mille Miglia.

Maggi took little part in racing in 1929 but in 1930 drove an Alfa Romeo in the Mille Miglia, partnered by Mazzotti, and in the Targa Florio. He was 3rd in the Circuit of Montenero, and finished the season by driving a Maserati in the San Sebastian GP, taking 2nd place behind his team-mate Varzi. This was his last race, for he retired from serious competition at the end of the year.

Apart from his renown as a racing driver, Count Maggi did a great deal for Italian racing. It was largely due to his efforts that the Mille Miglia was first organized. He died in 1961. TASOM

Maggs, Anthony Francis O'Connell

Tony Maggs was born in Pretoria, South Africa, in 1937. His first race was in an Austin-Healey at Cape Town in 1958, and the following year he came to Europe where he had some success in club events with a Lotus 11. He then bought a Tojeiro-Jaguar with which he returned to South Africa and drove to several victories in the winter of 1959–60. Back in Europe in 1960 Maggs showed great promise in a Cooper F2 and Merlyn FJ, and also shared an Aston Martin DB4GT with Jim Clark in the Paris 1,000 kilometres. In 1961 he had eight wins with Ken Tyrrell's Cooper FJ team and tied with Jo Siffert as European Formula Junior Champion. Also in 1961 he made his Formula 1 debut in a Lotus 18 at Aintree and drove in the German GP at the Nürburgring. For 1962 he signed as number two driver to Bruce McLaren in the works Cooper F1 team, and finished 2nd in the French GP and 3rd in the South African GP. In 1963 he was again 2nd in the French GP and 5th at Monaco, but the Cooper chassis was becoming increasingly uncompetitive. He drove Scuderia Centro-Sud BRMs in 1964, coming 4th in the Austrian GP and 6th in the German, and also raced F2 Lolas. In 1965 he stayed mainly in South Africa, driving a Willment-entered Brabham-Ford. During a local meeting at Pietermaritzburg he crashed this car, and a young boy standing in a prohibited area was killed. This tragedy made Maggs abandon motor racing. DCN

Maglioli, Umberto

Born in Biella, Maglioli was one of the better Italian sports car drivers, with a long and distinguished career on the hills and race circuits. His early performances with Fiat and Lancia cars brought him a contract with Lancia in 1951, and he was 2nd in that year's Mille Miglia. In 1953 he won the Targa Florio for Lancia, and shared the winning sports Ferrari at Pescara with Hawthorn. For the next year he moved from one manufacturer to another for occasional drives, winning hill-climbs with both Lancia and Ferrari cars. His greatest victory came in 1954 when he won the Carrera Panamericana in a Lancia D24. After Lancia's withdrawal from racing Maglioli stayed with Ferrari for two years, scoring a number of hill-climb and race successes. In 1956 he won the Targa Florio for the second time, on this occasion sharing a Porsche with von Hanstein, and thereafter he divided his drives between Porsche and Ferrari. He won at Sebring in 1964 in a Ferrari shared with Parkes, and in 1965 was 3rd in the Targa and 5th in the Nürburgring 1,000 kilometres, both in works Porsches with Linge. Just as his first great victory was in the Targa, so most of his recent successes have been in this gruelling event: 5th in a Porsche Carrera 6 in 1966, first (with Vic Elford) in a Porsche 907 in 1968 and 2nd with Elford in 1969. He also drove a privately-entered Ford GT40 with Nino Vaccarella during the 1967 season, and in 1970 drove an Autodelta Alfa Romeo in the Targa, but retired early on. DCN

Mairesse, Willy

'Pure tiger' is a phrase which describes this Belgian driver most aptly. Only son of a timber merchant, he was born in Momignies in 1928 and developed a fascination for fast cars at an early age. His parents opposed his sporting aspirations but he made his début in the 1953 Liège–Rome–Liège Rally, co-driving a Porsche 1500 with a Dr Missone. They retired after a hair-raising series of misadventures, but Willy was back next year to finish 26th in a blown Peugeot 203. In 1955 he won the Huy 12 Hours in the same car and this success prompted him to buy a Mercedes 300SL for a programme of rallies and minor speed events. He won the Liège Rally in 1956 and won again at Huy, his lurid style and glowering countenance already making their mark. In 1957 he gained the sponsored drives he so much wanted, but

Umberto Maglioli. *Photo: Autosport*

Willy Mairesse, after winning the 1965 Spa GP. *Photo: Daniel Paris*

Left below, Willy Mairesse (Ferrari 156) in the 1962 Brussels GP. *Photo: David Hodges Collection*

Below, Willy Mairesse, 1962. *Photo: David Phipps*

crashed the Belgian national team (ENB) Ferraris three times, smashed a borrowed 300SL at Huy and his own in the Liège–Rome–Liège.

ENB were not pleased, but Jacques Swaters, Belgian Ferrari distributor, helped him buy a Berlinetta for 1958 with which he had several successes. In 1959 he had a quiet year apart from finishing 2nd to Gendebien's works Ferrari in the Tour de France, a performance which worried the Belgian champion considerably. Ferrari offered Mairesse a works drive in 1960 and he did well in sports car events and made his first Formula 1 appearance. This drive heightened the rivalry between Mairesse and Gendebien, but when Willy fought his way to victory in the Tour de France his place was assured in the 1961 works team. He had another good, if often spectacular season and was offered the post of chief tester on Ginther's departure at the end of the year.

Mairesse had an unquenchable will to win and triggered the first-lap accident at Monaco in 1962, then suffered bad burns in a high-speed collision with Trevor Taylor's Lotus at Spa. He showed no after-effects on his return at Monza and was retained as tester for 1963. He crashed at Silverstone; won the Spa GT race and Nürburgring 1,000 kilometres; then suffered burns on scar tissue at Le Mans. On his return for the German GP his car landed askew after a bump and he was in hospital again with serious injuries.

The indomitable little Belgian's Formula 1 career was finished, but after a lengthy recovery he returned to sports car racing with much success. He seemed a new driver, much smoother and restrained than before, but as his confidence returned so did his reputation for over-stepping the limit. He crashed heavily at Spa in an ENB Ferrari, and then failed to close his GT40's door properly, leaving the line at Le Mans in 1968. The door flew open on the straight and pitched the car into the trees and Mairesse back into hospital.

After that he could no longer get the drives he so badly needed to satisfy his competitive instincts. He knew little else but motor racing, and with this denied to him frustration and eventually despair took over. Willy Mairesse took his own life at Ostend, early in September 1969. DCN

Mäkinen, Timo

Mäkinen was born in 1938 in Helsinki and since his rallying career started in 1960, he has become the epitome of the ultra-fast special stage driver. His results are usually spectacular though they are often outnumbered by his retirements. For Mäkinen to crash is almost un-heard of despite his fast times, and both behind the wheel and explaining his exploits in his own brand of 'Finn-glish', he is a good ambassador for his firm and for his country.

Mäkinen started driving while working for his father, Antero Mäkinen, who owns a transport fleet which delivers newspapers to all parts of Finland. During this period, the young Mäkinen got plenty of experience of driving plus a large number of fines for speeding. In 1960, he started driving in rallies and ice races with a variety of cars which ranged from Volvos and Saabs to one exalted occasion when he ice-raced a D-type Jaguar. His ability to control anything capable of movement led him to receive the support of the BMC agent in Helsinki for whom he eventually went to work as a car salesman. His first proper works drive came at the end of 1962 when Stuart Turner imported a lot of talent from the northern countries to drive his Mini Coopers, in an attempt to

Timo Mäkinen. Photo: Ford Motor Company

Timo Mäkinen, 1970. Photo: John Davenport

Robert Manzon. Photo: Cyril Posthumus Collection

stop Erik Carlsson winning the RAC Rally yet again. Partnered by John Steadman, Mäkinen let others set the pace in these unfamiliar surroundings and finished, winning his class.

In 1963 he joined the BMC team and his first assignment was the Monte Carlo, where he took Miss Christabel Carlisle in a Healey 3000 and won his class. For almost the whole year, he drove Healeys, retiring in the Coupe des Alpes with Mike Wood when a wheel fell off, and retiring in the Liège-Sofia-Liège with Geoff Mabbs when they hit a bus. In the RAC Rally he was more successful, coming 5th overall and once more winning his class. Once during the year he drove a Mini Cooper and also had his initiation into Continental racing when he competed in the Tour de France for the first time.

One of the big problems that Mäkinen seemed to suffer at this time was the lack of a regular co-driver. In 1964 he was to solve this problem, though in the first part of the year he drove with Patrick Vanson in the Monte Carlo in a 1,071cc Cooper S and finished 4th, and with Tony Ambrose in the new 1,275cc Cooper S he won the Tulip Rally outright. In the Liège-Sofia-Liège he drove with Don Barrow and they retired their Healey 3000 after having six punctures in one section. When Barrow fell ill before the Tour de France, Mäkinen was teamed at the last moment with Paul Easter who had previously driven rallies himself. They got on so well that it became a regular pairing for the rest of Mäkinen's years at BMC.

Nineteen sixty-five will always be remembered as the year that the Monte Carlo Rally was nearly wiped out by a blizzard. It was also the year that Mäkinen won it with the most incredible display of driving in adverse conditions likely to be seen. The same year he won Finland's own Thousand Lakes Rally in a Cooper S, and went on to win it three years in succession. In the 1965 RAC Rally he very nearly became the only man ever to win that event in a Healey 3000, but an icy patch in Wales caused him to lose time and he had to be content with 2nd place. In 1966, he was again fastest car on the Monte Carlo Rally, only to have his victory taken away as a result of the disqualification caused by the lighting dispute. The following year, he hit a rock that had fallen into the road during the Monte Carlo but later in the year completed his hat-trick of Thousand Lakes victories even though the rally career of the Mini Cooper was nearly over.

BMC virtually closed down their competitions department in 1968. By the end of the year, Mäkinen was driving a private Ford Escort T/C in the RAC Rally, which he led until mechanical failure caused him to retire. At this time, he was turning his attentions to powerboat racing; in 1968 he was Finnish offshore champion, and in 1969 he won the Round Britain race. Some thought that his rally career was over but for the latter half of 1969 he signed a contract for Lancia and drove in the Coupe des Alpes, Corsican, and RAC rallies for them, but only finished in Corsica, where he drove an open prototype much against his will. In 1970 Stuart Turner went to Fords as competition manager so that it was no surprise to find Mäkinen there too. He finished 7th in the 1970 Monte Carlo, despite losing a wheel, was 2nd in the Thousand Lakes and won the Finnish Snow Rally, all in Escort Twin Cams. JD

Manzon, Robert

A member of the Gordini team which so valiantly carried French colours around the European circuits on a shoestring budget, Robert Manzon was first spotted by Amedée Gordini in mid-1948. This followed a successful season and a half as private owner of a 1,100cc Cisitalia with which he scored two 2nds at Angoulême and Comminges, and chased the Simca-Gordinis hard at Reims and Nîmes in 1947, and at Perpignan and Geneva in 1948. His first race with a Formula 2 Simca-Gordini was the Circuit of the Ramparts at Angoulême, where he made fastest lap and led the final until his transmission broke.

In 1949 Manzon was 2nd to Sommer at Lausanne, won his heat at his favourite Angoulême, and was 2nd in the final to his No 1, Trintignant, and won the Bol d'Or 24 Hours race, driving a production Simca coupé with special engine. In 1950 he had a 1,100cc class victory in the sports car races preceding the German GP at Nürburgring; outright F2 wins at Périgueux and Mettet; another victory at Mont Ventoux; a 2nd to Sommer's Ferrari at Roubaix; and an outstanding 4th in the 300-mile (480km) Swiss Formula 1 GP at Berne with his little Wade-supercharged 1·5 Simca, behind two 158 Alfa Romeos and a 12-cylinder Ferrari. With the same car he actually lay 3rd in the Penya Rhin F1 GP before he blew up.

The fragility of the highly stressed Simca-Gordinis undoubtedly lost their drivers other victories, and Manzon only managed one in 1951, at Mettet, reinforced by three 2nds at Rouen, Sables d'Olonne and Cadours. The next season brought the new 2-litre 6-cylinder F2 Gordini, with which he won his heat at Silverstone but retired in the final, scored a notable 3rd to two works Ferraris in the Belgian GP at Spa, and won his third Mont Ventoux hill-climb. With sports Gordinis he won the 2-litre Prix de Monte Carlo on the famous street circuit, and the Coupe du Salon at Montlhéry, but after a disheartening 1953 season he left Gordini and contracted to drive one of Louis Rosier's private Ferraris in 1954. These were naturally slower than the works cars, but Manzon came 2nd to Gonzalez' factory Ferrari in the Bordeaux GP, and scored a very creditable 3rd in the French GP behind the sensational new F1 Mercedes-Benz cars.

He also drove Lancia sports cars, but returned to Gordini in 1955, only to suffer a series of retirements, generally through the car's weakest point—transmission. His best placing that season was in fact in a works sports Ferrari, when he came 3rd, co-driving with Castellotti, in the Targa Florio which was dominated by two 300 SLR Mercedes. Undaunted, Manzon returned to the fray in 1956, being rewarded by two outstanding victories in Italy, one with the old 6-cylinder F1 Gordini in the Naples GP, the other with the 2-litre sports Gordini in the Pescara GP, where he beat Maserati, Ferrari and Osca opposition to win the 225-mile (360km) race by a mere half second from Taruffi. He also put up a gallant fight with the dated F1 car in the Monaco GP, lying 3rd, then retiring 3 laps from the finish with the almost inevitable transmission breakage. Hard racing elsewhere produced only three 6th places at Goodwood, Syracuse and Monza, so after ten years of very varied racing and some pleasing successes, Robert Manzon retired. CP

March, Earl of see Richmond, Duke of

Marimon, Onofre

Known to his countrymen as 'Pinocco', Onofre Marimon, born in 1924 in Argentina, was a protégé of Fangio, who frequently raced against his father, Dimingo Marimon, in South American long-distance stock car road races. Onofre drove his first races in home-built 'Meccanica

'Nacional' specials, winning a race at Mar del Plata in 1950, and getting caught up in the fever to go racing in Europe. He got there in 1951, sharing a 4·5-litre sports Talbot with Gonzalez at Le Mans, but being comparatively slow after his mercurial team-mate. Nevertheless he kept the car in the running, the pair lying 4th to three Jaguars when the Talbot broke down.

Marimon drove again at Le Mans in 1953, with Fangio himself as his team-mate in a works Alfa Romeo, but the car blew up early and Onofre never got a drive. That same year, however, he had been signed by Maserati in their F2 team, and had a season full of dramatic experiences if not victories.

With Fangio going to Mercedes and Gonzalez to Ferrari in 1954, Marimon found himself virtual no 1 in the Maserati team, driving the new 250F 2·5-litre car. He put up several good fights against more experienced drivers, duelled with Hawthorn at Syracuse, where he made fastest lap, made fastest lap at Bari, won the Rome GP at Castel Fusano, and was 3rd in the British GP. He shared a sports Maserati with Fangio in the Supercortemaggiore GP at Monza, the two working up to 2nd place but retiring only 7 laps from the end of the 6¼-hour race.

Perhaps because he tried too hard to emulate his brilliant compatriots too soon in his career, this highly promising young Argentinian lost his life while practising at the Nürburgring for the 1954 German GP. He failed to take a turn and his Maserati plunged straight on through a hedge and somersaulted down a steep slope, Marimon being killed instantly. CP

Maserati Brothers, The

The illustrious *fratelli* Maserati who contributed so much to motor racing history were six in number, sons of Rodolfo Maserati, an engine driver from Voghera, and his wife Carolina, née Losi. In order of age, the brothers were Carlo, Bindo, Alfieri, Mario, Ettore and Ernesto; Mario withdrew from the motoring scene early on to become an artist. Carlo, the eldest, built the Carcano motorcycle for its sponsor the Marchese Carcano, racing it successfully in pioneer Italian inter-town events in 1899–1900. Next he joined the growing FIAT concern at Turin, becoming head tester, then left to work for Bianchi as tester and driver. He came 9th in the 1907 Coppa Florio at Brescia, and 16th in the second Kaiserpreis eliminating race, then joined the new Junior company as designer/tester/driver. His future looked highly promising, but unfortunately he was taken seriously ill in 1910 and died.

Meanwhile Bindo and Alfieri Maserati had joined Isotta-Fraschini in Milan, and while Bindo stayed steadfastly on the mechanics' side of racing through most of his career, Alfieri strongly aspired to race, and did so in 1908 with one of the beautiful little 1·2-litre ohc Isotta-Fraschinis in the Grand Prix des Voiturettes at Dieppe. The car was not so fast as its specification suggested, and he could only manage 14th place. After a spell in Isotta-Fraschini's subsidiary factory in Argentina, Alfieri and Ettore returned to Italy and set up a small workshop at Pontevecchio, Bologna. There they repaired cars and began manufacturing Maserati sparking plugs, which were first used in World War 1 aircraft engines and subsequently in cars.

In 1922 Alfieri built a special racing car with shortened Isotta chassis and one half of an Hispano-Suiza V-8 ohc aero-engine on a special crankcase. He scored several notable victories with this car, including the Circuit of

Onofre Marimon. *Photo: Alfa Romeo SpA*

Alfieri Maserati (from a painting by his brother Mario). *Photo: Cyril Posthumus Collection*

1929 Maserati 16-cylinder, with which Borzacchini set a new Class C record (152.9mph) at Cremona. *Photo: Cyril Posthumus Collection*

Mugello in 1922. He also prepared and raced a much-modified 3-litre Diatto, winning the 3-litre class of the 1922 Autumn GP at Monza and some hill-climbs. In 1924 he modified a 2-litre 4-cylinder sports Diatto for racing, and drove it in the San Sebastian GP in Spain, working up to 3rd place when his engine let him down. The Diatto Company then commissioned him to build an out-and-out 2-litre straight-8 GP car, but delays meant the car was not completed until the Italian GP late in the 1925 season. Sheared blower bolts put it out of the race and when, shortly after, the Diatto concern found itself in financial trouble, the Maserati brothers inherited the GP car, presumably in lieu of payment. The little works at Pontevecchio was now established as the Officine Alfieri Maserati, and the brothers set about reducing the Diatto's engine capacity to 1·5 litres to meet the 1926–7 GP rules. With other modifications, the car emerged in 1926 as the first Maserati, its radiator bearing the now famous Neptune's trident motif, symbol of Bologna for centuries, and forthwith ran in the Targa Florio with Alfieri driving. He finished 9th overall and won the 1,500cc class, and by now the youngest brother, Ernesto, had taken to racing as well, driving the car to 1st places in the Bologna sprints and the Collina hill-climb in 1926, and winning the 1·5-litre class of the Tripoli GP in North Africa in 1927.

But the new make suffered a setback that year when Alfieri crashed at Messina, suffering a loin injury; he recovered to race again, but in 1932 had to undergo a further operation from which, tragically, he died. Officine Maserati thus lost its founder and chief inspiration, but Bindo, Ettore and Ernesto rallied and the little Bologna factory moved on to further glories. By then they had risen to Grand Prix winners, with straight victories in 1930 alone in the Tripoli, Rome, Monza and San Sebastian GPs and the Ciano and Acerbo Cup races. The ferocious 16-cylinder Maserati, winner at Tripoli, had also furthered the name with a new Class C record at Cremona in 1929 at 152·9mph (246kph), and Ernesto Maserati's Rome GP victory in 1931.

For 1933 a new 3-litre Maserati appeared, with which Nuvolari won the Nice and Belgian GPs and the Ciano Cup, while Campari won the French GP. The appearance in 1934 of the German Formula cars forced the Maseratis gradually into the 1·5-litre voiturette class, where they

scored countless victories up to 1939. By then, however, Officine Alfieri Maserati had been taken over by the Orsi industrial group headed by Comm. Adolfo Orsi and his son Omer, and the famous brothers were virtually employees, albeit very privileged ones. The works were transferred from Bologna to Modena, and a new 16-valve voiturette and a 3-litre 8-cylinder GP car were developed.

In 1948 the brothers left the company bearing their name to found the Osca concern (Officine Speciallizate Costruzione Automobili) back in Bologna. Osca itself has now been absorbed by Meccanica Voghera, makers of the MV motorcycle, and Bindo, Ettore and Ernesto Maserati have retired. CP

Masetti, Count Giulio

Count Masetti was born in Florence in 1895 and began his racing career in 1919 with a 1914 GP Fiat. With this car he scored numerous successes in Italian hill-climbs and races, his most notable victory being in the 1921 Targa Florio. Later he bought another pre-war GP car, a 1914 Mercedes, with which he won the 1922 Targa Florio against very stiff opposition which included the official Mercedes team with brand new cars. This success earned him a works Ballot drive at Strasbourg in 1922, but he was forced to retire in this race.

In 1923 Masetti joined Alfa Romeo for whom he won the Circuit of Mugello and came 2nd in the 1924 Targa and Coppa Florio races which were run concurrently. He also drove briefly for Mercedes, and in 1925 he joined the Sunbeam-Talbot-Darracq team, with whom he was 3rd in the French GP, 2nd in the Brooklands 200 Mile Race, and made ftd and a new record at Klausen hill-climb. He remained with STD in 1926, but was released temporarily to drive a Delage in the Targa Florio. It was considered highly probable that Masetti would repeat his successes of 1921 and 1922, but on the first lap, due to mechanical failure, the Count crashed and was killed. TASOM

Materassi, Emilio

Born in Italy in 1889, Materassi began driving in 1919 and took part in races and hill-climbs for five years without scoring any notable successes. By 1923, however, he had completed a car which was to bring him many victories. This was an Itala chassis into which he put half of a Hispano-Suiza V-8 aero engine. With this he competed from 1923 to the end of 1926, during which period he won nine races and took innumerable 2nd and 3rd places.

At the end of 1926 Ettore Bugatti appointed Materassi as Number One driver in the Bugatti team for 1927. The Italian quickly proved worthy of 'le Patron's' choice, for within a few weeks of the opening of the season he had won the Tripoli GP and the Targa Florio. Later in the year he won the San Sebastian GP and the Circuits of Bologna and Montenero. At the end of 1927 Materassi left Bugatti to form his own Scuderia, the first of its kind, and bought the team of three 8-cylinder 1·5-litre Talbots that had been raced without much success during 1926 and 1927. Materassi carried out minor modifications during the winter of 1927 so that the cars were fully prepared for the 1928 season. He won the 1·5-litre class of the Coupe Pietro Bordino, and went on to win the Circuits of Mugello and Montenero outright, and take class wins in the Circuit of Pescara and Rome GP. His 'Number Two', Arcangeli, won the Circuit of Cremona, Materassi being 2nd. Alas, during the European GP at Monza he crashed inexplicably on the 18th lap, swerving into the crowd, killing himself and 22 spectators. TASOM

Mathieson, T. A. S. O.

Born in Glasgow in 1908, 'Taso' Mathieson began racing at Brooklands in a one-make Lagonda meeting in 1930, and had his first victory at the track in the Norfolk Senior Mountain Handicap in 1932, driving a blown 2·3-litre OM. He had three other wins in 1932 and 1933 with Bugattis, and set a new Mountain Circuit lap record for 2-litre cars at 72·15mph (116·11kph). Indifferent health kept him out of racing from 1934, and his Bugatti was driven on several occasions by Chris Staniland. By 1938, however, 'Taso' was back, taking 3rd place at Chimay with a Bugatti Type 57S. He drove at Le Mans in 1938 and 1939, in a 4-litre Talbot with F. E. Clifford in 1938 and a 4·5-litre Talbot with Luigi Chinetti in 1939, but in both events mechanical trouble eliminated them.

After the war 'Taso' became the first Briton to race again on the Continent, acquiring an ex-Birkin 3-litre Maserati which he drove during the 1946 season. In 1950 he bought a 2-litre Le Mans Frazer Nash with which he scored a class victory at Le Mans that year (with Dickie Stoop). In the 1951 Targa Florio he was 3rd in the Frazer Nash when the fan belt broke. He was 2nd at Senigallia and 4th at Oporto, and in 1952 he bought the ex-Baird 2·3-litre Ferrari which he drove to 6th place in the Targa Florio, winning the 3-litre class. In 1953 he drove a 2-litre sports Maserati with which he won his class at Roubaix and Bressuire. His last race was at Brands Hatch in 1955 with a San Remo Maserati, after which he concentrated on writing and building up his magnificent collection of photographs. He is the author of a number of authoritative books, including 'Grand Prix Racing 1906–1914'. CP

Matich, Frank

Born in 1935, Matich represents Australia in the International Grand Prix Drivers Association. One of Australia's most successful drivers, he has received several offers to race overseas, but apart from one sortie in America in his own car, he has remained on the Australasian circuits. Matich began racing in 1954 and since then has become five times Australian sports car champion — all but once in a car of his own design and manufacture. In early years he held the Australian GT title in a D-type Jaguar, the Australian Formula Junior title and several state titles in both classes. He has also been sports car champion six times in New South Wales, five times in Victoria, and four times in Queensland, and three times South Pacific sports car champion.

Matich rose to international prominence in 1964 when he won pole position on nearly every grid in the Tasman Series of races against some of the world's top drivers. However, mechanical faults in his Brabham Climax prevented him finishing prominently in the actual races. He returned to monoposto racing in 1970 and won the New Zealand Grand Prix — and came 2nd in the Tasman Series to New Zealander Graham Lawrence (Ferrari) after a series of mechanical breakdowns. Matich was driving a McLaren F5000 — and has now become a director of McLaren's manufacturers, the Trojan Group in Australia.

One of Australia's most prolific car designers, he pioneered V-8 sports car racing in the South Pacific region — working first on the basic design of a Lotus 19 sports car and then on his own designs. He has built eight Matich SR sports cars: two of them are raced in the United States, another in New Zealand and the rest in Australia. All except one have been designed to take large 5-litre V-8 engines. Since building the SR cars Matich has been virtually unchallenged in Australian sports car racing. Australia's first professional driver, he now runs a (Aus.) $500,000 tyre and wheel firm in Sydney — as well as his (Aus.) $80,000 a year motor-racing programme. TBF

Mayer, Timothy

Tim Mayer was born in Dalton, Pa., in 1938, the brother of Teddy Mayer of McLaren Cars and nephew of the former Governor of Pennsylvania, William Scranton. He began racing with an Austin-Healey at Marlboro in 1959 and in 1960 drove the first Lotus 18 Formula Junior in the United States. After graduating from Yale with a degree in English literature, the tall, slender Pennsylvanian won the 1962 Formula Junior title in a Cooper and was awarded the Kimberly Cup as the SCCA's 'Most Improved Driver'. After driving the ex-Roger Penske Cooper Monaco and getting his first championship Formula 1 ride in the US Grand Prix at Watkins Glen, young Mayer joined Ken Tyrrell's Cooper Formula Junior team.

Mayer died in Longford, Australia, when his 2·5-litre Cooper-Climax became airborne and crashed while practising for the final race in the 1964 Tasman championship — which had already been won by the team of Bruce McLaren and Tim Mayer. ARB

Mays, Raymond

British driver, born in 1899. While at Cambridge, Mays purchased a Hillman sports which was named 'Quicksilver' and tuned with the help of Kensington Moir and Miles Thomas until it was the equal of Bedford's similar works car in sprint events. For 1922 a Brescia Bugatti was acquired from B. S. Marshall. This car was extensively modified by Mays' friend Amherst Villiers, and proved so successful that Bugatti himself expressed an interest, supplying a new model for 1924. Both cars were then run, and called 'Cordon Rouge' and 'Cordon Bleu' by kind permission of the wine producers, Messrs. G. H. Mumm. Use of alcohol fuel, lubrication modifications and lightweight engine parts enabled nearly 7,000rpm to be obtained, and between 1921 and 1924 Mays' resolute and radical approach to sprints and hill-climbs earned him some 250 awards.

In 1925 Mays signed for AC under S. F. Edge, but achieved little success, mainly because of engine troubles consequent to supercharging experiments. Another lean

Above, Frank Matich. *Photo: M & M Engravings Pty Ltd*

Right above, Raymond Mays, with the TT Vauxhall, c. 1928. *Photo: Montagu Motor Museum*

Below, Tim Mayer, *Photo: Moss Photo-Service Inc.*

Raymond Mays in an ERA at Brooklands, 1934. *Photo: Cyril Posthumus Collection*

year followed in 1926, although marked by Mays' first meeting with Peter Berthon. He drove for Mercedes-Benz (Britain) in 1927, achieving some success with the 4-cylinder Targa Florio car, but none with the dangerous 8-cylinder 2-litre model with which he was also entrusted.

Mays' long and successful association with the Villiers modified ex-1922 TT Vauxhall began in 1928. This car pioneered the use of twin rear wheels at Shelsley Walsh in 1929, and in 1930 (when re-named the 'Villiers Supercharge') was giving nearly 300bhp at 6,000rpm. The 'White Invicta', belonging to the India Tyre Co., was first used in that year, ably backing up the Villiers in sprint events, and also proving successful in racing. Both cars were sold to Humphrey Cook, and for 1933 the 'White Riley' appeared, prepared with the help of Peter Berthon and Victor Riley, and equipped with a Jamieson designed supercharger and crankshaft. This car supplied the inspiration for the ERA, and from 1934 Mays' fortunes were tied up with this concern, which was based literally in his backyard.

When he left in 1939, Mays took with him the famous Zoller-blown R4D, with which he achieved many more successes until his retirement from the active list. On occasion he drove other vehicles, including a single-seater GP Talbot at Reims, and the first post-war Thinwall Special. In 1949 he was preparing a new sprint special, with tubular frame, 2-litre ERA engine and chain drive, but this project was submerged in the BRM plans.

Throughout his career Mays displayed a gentlemanly demeanour, linked with a passionate determination and enthusiasm for the sport which earned him many friends. His greatest driving achievements were unquestionably his fantastic run of successes in hill-climbs

nd sprints, especially at Shelsley Walsh, where the 'Old Man' became something of a legend in his time. He will be remembered also for his faith and perseverance in the ambitious BRM project, surmounting many difficulties which had deterred others. His enthusiasm remained undiminished in later years, his interests including a projected mini-car (the Tici) in 1967. DF

Mays, Rex

This American racing driver, born in 1915, was one of the first of the 'chargers' to appear at Indianapolis: Mays usually drove his cars at full throttle as long as they remained in running condition; and he gained many honours in American races despite his failure to complete the full distance on numerous occasions. Some of the records he established on American one-mile dirt tracks remained unbroken for several years and he still is the only driver to have won the no 1 starting position at Indy four times on the basis of his superior performances in the official time trials.

After gaining his early racing experience in modified stock cars on California tracks, he drove in twelve consecutive Indianapolis races beginning in 1934. He led the field on one or more occasions in nine of those races and finished second twice: behind Wilbur Shaw in 1940 and behind Mauri Rose in 1941. Usually he drove Miller-powered cars, but he drove a Thorne Engineering Special in 1939, an Alfa Romeo in 1938 and a Novi fwd Special in 1949.

He was the third man in racing history to win two consecutive national driving championships, accomplishing that objective in 1940 and 1941 to duplicate the earlier achievements of Tommy Milton and Louis Meyer.

Mays also drove in both International road races at Roosevelt Raceway, New York, and was the first American driver to finish the 1937 event, being placed 3rd behind Bernd Rosemeyer's Auto Union and Dick Seaman's Mercedes-Benz in the same Alfa Romeo that Tazio Nuvolari had driven to victory the previous year. He was the only driver to finish in a non-German car in a Grand Prix race in 1937.

In his last full season of championship competition, 1948, Mays came 3rd in the national ranking. Late in the 1949 campaign he was injured fatally in a racing accident on a dirt track at Del Mar, Calif. AB

Meregalli, Guido

This Italian driver was chiefly noted as the winner in a 6-cylinder Nazzaro of the extremely gruelling Targa Florio race of 1920, run over 275 miles of the Madonie circuit in Sicily in appalling conditions of rain, wind and roads that were a sea of mud in many places. Meregalli averaged 31·8mph (51·18kph) to win from Enzo Ferrari's Alfa Romeo by more than 7 minutes in a race lasting over 8 hours. Meregalli's other claim to fame was his 'hat-trick' of victories in the Circuit of Garda road race, run around the boundaries of Lake Salo, north of Brescia. He won in 1922, 1923 and 1924, each time driving a 2-litre Diatto. Further successes included class victories in the Consuma hill-climb of 1919 and the Parma-Poggio di Berceto of 1920 with a Nazzaro, and class victories at Mugello and Parma-Poggio in 1922 with a Diatto.

Driving a Diatto in the 1922 Italian GP at the newly opened Monza track, Meregalli overturned but pluckily resumed the race, only to retire later. In the subsequent Coppa Florio in Sicily he again overturned his Diatto, suffering a broken arm and other injuries while his

Above, Rex Mays. *Photo: Indianapolis Motor Speedway*

Right above, Guido Meregalli with a Nazzaro before the 1920 Targa Florio. *Photo: T. A. S. O. Mathieson Collection*

Otto Merz. *Photo: Cyril Posthumus Collection*

mechanic Giuseppe Gioacchino was killed; the pair were moved to a safer spot off-course by H. O. D. Segrave, driving a Sunbeam in the race. CP

Merz, Otto

Merz was born in Cannstatt in Germany in 1889 and had an unusual and most exciting career. Going to Mercedes (Daimler Motoren Gesellschaft) as a mechanic in 1906 he acted in this capacity to Willy Poege, a Mercedes driver of the period, until 1912 when he became chauffeur to the Archduke Ferdinand of Austria. On that fatal day, 28 June 1914, when the Archduke and Duchess were assassinated in the streets of Sarajevo, it was Merz driving the second car in the procession who rushed to his master's assistance and carried the dying man into a nearby house.

After the assassination Merz returned to Mercedes and, at the conclusion of World War 1 entered their racing department. His initial successes were in local hill-climbs. Then in 1924 he obtained two outstanding victories by making ftd in both the Solitude and Klausen hill-climbs. In 1925 he won the Circuit of Solitude, a victory he repeated the following year.

At this time, however, because of the grave economic situation in Germany, Mercedes considerably curtailed their racing programme. Nevertheless, Merz, partnered by Caracciola, in a single car entry took part in the 12-hour Sports Car Race at San Sebastian, and in the same event the following year when Mercedes entered a full team of three cars. In neither of these events did he obtain any outstanding success. In 1927 he won the German GP on the newly opened Nürburgring and was 2nd in the same race the following year. He took part in the TT in Ulster in 1929 with Caracciola on a sister car. It was in this event that he gave a demonstration of his legendary strength (it was said he could drive a 6in nail into a board with his bare hand) when he tore off a damaged front wing from his car. During 1930 and 1931 Merz competed in a number of events, partnering Caracciola in the French GP of the latter year, and also finishing 5th in the German GP at the Nürburgring. But in 1932 Mercedes temporarily abandoned racing and his activities were confined to experimental and test driving.

In 1933 he was entered for the AVUS race with a new aerodynamically streamlined SSKL, but when practising a few days before the race he overturned and was killed instantly. TASOM

Meyer, Louis

Meyer, born in 1904, first three-time winner of the Indianapolis 500-mile race, has remained actively connected with the sport in the United States as a builder of

LOUIS MEYER, Driver
Alden Sampson, Mech.
In SAMPSON SPECIAL
Indianapolis Motor Speedway 1930

Louis Meyer at the wheel of the 16-cylinder Sampson Special which he drove into 4th place at Indianapolis in 1930. Photo: Indianapolis Motor Speedway

Opposite, Targa Florio: The Ford GT40 driven by Bob Bondurant and Sir John Whitmore passing through Collesano in 1965. Photo: Geoff Goddard

Louis Meyer. Photo: Indianapolis Motor Speedway

Hannu Mikkola. Photo: Autosport

racing engines since retiring as a driver in 1939 after twelve full seasons of outstanding accomplishments on board, dirt and paved speedways. Unlike most of his contemporaries, the first important race in which he participated was the 1927 Indianapolis event and he captured the national championship twice before making his first appearance on the dirt tracks where young drivers usually gained their early experience.

An unusual chain of circumstances contributed to Meyer's quick rise to fame. He had worked as a mechanic for veteran race driver Frank Elliott in 1926 and arrangements had been made for him to drive that same car at Indy in 1927, with Elliott behind the wheel of a new fwd entry. But Wilbur Shaw, destined to become the second three-time 500 winner, was also looking for a car and had sufficient financial backing to purchase the older car from Elliott. Meyer had to be content with acting as Shaw's mechanic and driving 40 laps in a relief role for a share of the 4th-place prize money.

One year later the tables were reversed. Alden Sampson purchased a car intended for Shaw and put Meyer in the cockpit. Pacing himself well, and moving up steadily from his no 13 starting position, Meyer finished strongly to win at an average speed of 99·482mph (160·103kph). He also won a 200-mile race on the boards at Altoona, Pa., and was placed well in other events on the year's schedule to capture his first national title.

He performed consistently again in 1929, winning a pair of 200-mile races at Altoona and coming second to Ray Keech at Indianapolis for enough championship points to retain his national crown. It was only the second time in racing history for any driver to win that honour in consecutive years.

The board track era was nearing its close and the start of the financial depression of the 1930s was at hand. The annual schedule of major races was sharply curtailed and Meyer's only major victories of the next three years were scored in 100-mile races on dirt tracks at Detroit and Altoona. Mechanical troubles caused his early elimination twice at Indianapolis. Then, in 1933, he led the field for all of the last 71 laps and won the 500 for the second

time with a record-breaking average speed of 104·162mph (167·703kph). At the end of the season he was crowned national champion for the third time and he continued to race with distinction for six more years.

His third 500 victory came in 1936, when all cars were limited to 37·5 gallons of fuel for the race. Seven exhausted their supply during the late stages of the contest but Meyer again paced himself well. Starting in the next to-last row of the 33-car field, he advanced steadily and was never threatened after surging into the lead with 54 laps still to go. His average speed of 109·069mph (175·514kph) again was a new race record.

After wrecking his car at Indianapolis in 1939 while battling Wilbur Shaw for first place with only four laps to go, Meyer retired as a driver and turned his attention to engine development. At the conclusion of World War 2 he went into partnership with Dale Drake and formed the Meyer-Drake Engineering Company to purchase the plant in which Fred Offenhauser (successor to Harry Miller several years earlier) had been building the dependable 4-cylinder non-supercharged Offenhauser racing engines. The 'Offies' powered every winning car at Indianapolis for 18 consecutive years, beginning with 1947. The partnership was disbanded during the summer of 1964 because of Meyer's decision to accept an attractive offer from the Ford Motor Car Company. For the next five years he supervised the assembly—and worked on the development—of Ford's special V-8 racing engines, both turbocharged and non-turbocharged; and four of the Indianapolis winning cars during that period were powered by such units. AB

Mikkola, Hannu

Born in 1942 in Joensuu, Finland, Hannu Mikkola is the typical modern rally driver whose speciality is extremely fast driving over special stages. He started rally driving in 1963 when, just before going up to university, he bought a second-hand Volvo, entered a rally, and finished 4th overall. This participation in events with the Volvo continued through 1964 but in 1965 he concentrated more on his studies. In 1966, he started again and came second in the Finnish championship and was offered a drive for the Finnish importer of Volvo. He entered abroad for the first time in the Monte Carlo 1967 with Lancia and was lying 6th when his co-driver lost the road book and they had to retire. In 1968, while continuing to drive for Volvo at home, he drove for Datsun in the Monte Carlo where he finished 9th and later that year he was given a Ford Escort to drive in Finland after very nearly beating the Ford works team in Austria. On his first time in an Escort T/C, he won the 1,000 Lakes Rally and 1969 saw his full acceptance into the Ford team. During that year he won the Austrian Alpine and the 1,000 Lakes but in other events success escaped him. In 1970 he retired from the Monte Carlo with mechanical failure, but he came back to win the Arctic Rally in Finland which, combined with a 2nd overall, put him into the lead in the Finnish championship. In May he won the punishing World Cup Rally, and in August the Thousand Lakes, both with Gunnar Palm as co-driver. JD

Miles, Kenneth

Born in Sutton Coldfield, near Birmingham, Ken Miles served as a sergeant in a British armoured regiment before migrating to Southern California in 1952. After racing MG TDs and MG specials, including his legendary 'Flying Shingle', Miles became one of America's most successful Porsche drivers. He made important contri-

butions to Carroll Shelby's Cobra programme and in February 1965, with Indy veteran Lloyd Ruby, won the Daytona 2,000 kilometres, bringing the Ford GT40 its first victory. A month later Miles teamed with the late Bruce McLaren to finish 2nd at Sebring. In February 1966 Miles and Ruby repeated their Daytona win. Only in 1966 it was for 24 hours in the big Ford Mk II. One month later the same pair won at Sebring again, driving the Shelby entered experimental Ford roadster. At Le Mans, Miles was in the lead after 24 hours when the whim of having the Miles-Hulme and McLaren-Amon Mk II's finish two abreast backfired. Miles and Denny Hulme were deprived of their victory champagne when officials ruled the McLaren-Amon car the winner as it had started farther back on the grid and consequently had covered a greater distance. Miles was killed at Riverside Raceway on 17 August 1966 while testing one of the new Ford J cars. A sardonic, yet surprisingly gentle man, this lean, hawk-nosed Englishman played an important part in the development of American road racing. ARB

Miller, Capt. Alistair

This British driver was one of the most versatile Brooklands performers. Born in 1893, he was the son of Sir George Miller and succeeded to the title during his racing career. Miller bought the two 1914 Grand Prix Opels after World War 1 and ran them at Brooklands, Segrave gaining experience in them. With a used car motor business to run, Miller also contrived to do a great deal of racing. In 1921–2 he held the post of Competitions Manager to the Wolseley Motor Company and for them evolved the two Wolseley Moth 10hp single-seaters and the two-seater racing Wolseley Ten for the 1922 JCC 200 Miles Race. He broke records innumerable, over very long distances with the small Wolseleys and also with a Wolseley Fifteen two-seater for which two different sizes of ohc engine were available, enabling records to be taken in different International classes. For the fastest Brooklands racing of all. Miller had constructed the 11-litre Wolseley Viper two-seater, with a Hispano-Suiza V-8 aero-engine in an elderly shaft-drive Napier chassis. In this seemingly fearsome but actually quite docile car he made his name at Brooklands' Bank Holiday meetings and ran the giant in occasional sprints.

Miller also did very well at Brooklands in a 5-litre Indianapolis Sunbeam and it was he who resurrected the pre-1914 200hp Benz four-seater and ran this venerable motorcar successfully at the Track. But Miller would handle any car which came his way and from early appearances with a war-time Crossley he graduated to Buick, Bianchi, Alvis, Riley, Napier, and many other makes of cars. For a time Miller lived at Brooklands, in the premises later used by Parry Thomas. His best achievements were with the Wolseleys, but he assisted Thomas with record runs in his Leyland, did some very occasional long-distance and road racing, in Riley Nine and other cars, and had as great a knowledge of what was required to drive successfully at Brooklands as any man. WB

Milton, Thomas W.

Tommy Milton, born in 1893, combined a tremendous competitive spirit with exceptional skill and courage to become one of the greatest of all American racing drivers during the boom years of the sport after World War 1.

Despite the handicap of total blindness in one eye, he was the first driver to win the national championship for

Ken Miles (right), with Graham Hill. Photo: Al Bochroch

Alistair Miller. Photo: Montagu Motor Museum

Opposite, Targa Florio: The Alpine-Renault driven by Thomas and Guilhaudin, passing through Campofelice in 1966. Photo: Geoff Goddard

Tommy Milton. Photo: Indianapolis Motor Speedway

two consecutive years and the first to win two Indianapolis 500-mile races. He set a record of 156·046mph (251·170kph) for the measured mile at Daytona Beach, Fla., in 1920 and performed with equal success on dirt tracks, board tracks, paved tracks, oval courses and road courses for Mercer, Frontenac, Duesenberg and Miller. He was also an automotive engineer of considerable ability, a designer and builder of race cars, and one of the nation's outstanding racing officials.

Tommy, born without sight in his left eye, managed to pass the required tests early in his career by memorizing the standard eye charts used at that time; and was permitted to continue his racing activities when more modern examination methods revealed the defect during the early 1920s. He began to attract attention on dirt tracks in 1914 while driving a Mercer as a salaried member of Alex Sloan's barnstorming exhibition group, but was dropped from the tour 18 months later for refusing to run as instructed in these events which were planned so that the better-known drivers won.

He became a member of the Duesenberg team in 1916, missed the 500 because his car was not finished in time to participate, and then started to make a name for himself on other tracks. When the car finally was delivered three weeks later, he wrecked it on the board track at Des Moines, Iowa, when team-mate Wilbur D'Alene's car lost a wheel immediately in front of him. He finished 4th behind Ralph DePalma, however, in a 150-mile race at Minneapolis, Minn., on 4 July; 3rd behind Dario Resta in a race of similar length on the boards at Omaha, Nebr., two weeks later; and 2nd to Eddie Rickenbacker in a 300-mile race at Tacoma, Wash., on 5 August. At the end of the season, although still without a major victory, he was placed 7th among American drivers.

Milton started the 1919 campaign as captain of the Duesenberg team, when racing was resumed after World War 1, and scored his first important triumph in the 301-mile Elgin, Ill., road race, averaging 73·9mph (118·93kph) to finish more than 24 minutes in front of his nearest challenger. One week later, however, he was burned severely in a crash on the Uniontown, Pa., board speedway and was unable to race again until February 1920. While recuperating, he helped design and build a twin-engine Duesenberg car which he drove to a new record of 156·046mph (251·170kph) on the sand at Daytona Beach on 27 April. A broken connecting rod ended his chances of winning at Indianapolis, but he was victorious in three races of more than 200 miles' duration—two at Uniontown and one at Tacoma—while driving consistently on other tracks to win his first national championship.

In 1921 he led the field home at Indianapolis for the first time in a Frontenac at an average speed of 89·62mph (144·23kph), won again at Tacoma over the 250-miles route and was highly enough placed in other events to retain his national crown. During the remainder of his racing career Milton drove Miller Specials, except for his appearance in the 1925 Italian Grand Prix for Duesenberg. On that occasion, after leading at the halfway mark, he lost 20 minutes while repairing a broken oil line and had to be content with 4th place.

He averaged 90·95mph (146·37kph) to score his second Indy victory in 1923 at the wheel of an HCS Miller Special and won further races of more than 200 miles duration as follows: Beverly Hills, Calif., in 1922; Charlotte, N.Car., twice, in 1924; Charlotte again and Culver City, Calif., in 1925.

Retiring as a race driver, he started work in 1926 on Cliff Durant's $150,000 fwd Miller-powered Detroit Special for the 1927 Indianapolis race. When Durant was too ill to drive it, Milton qualified the car and drove it to 8th place with the help of relief drivers, despite frequent pit stops due to overheating problems.

Tommy then joined the staff of the Packard Motor Car Company as a consulting engineer in charge of customer relations, formed the Milton engineering company and served as president of the Hercules Drop Forge Company until shortly before his death in 1962. He ruled as chief steward of the Indianapolis 500-miles race for four years, setting a pattern which has been followed by his successors, and he also served with distinction for several years as a member of the AAA Contest Board. AB

Mitter, Gerhard Karl

This German driver was born in Schönlinde (now Krásná Lípa) in the Sudetenland, in 1935, and made his competition début in 1952, racing motorcycles. He was good, even at 17, and in 1955 he won the European Junior Championship as a solo rider.

He was a sound engineer, and his motorcycle experience taught him the intricacies of 2-stroke tuning. He developed his own tuning shop at Böblingen, working mainly with 3-cylinder DKW engines and later moving on to road Porsche preparation. In 1959 he ran his own Mitter-DKW FJ car, coming 3rd in the Eifelrennen behind the Stanguellinis of von Trips and May, and in 1960 he won the FJ Championship, despite some reliability problems with his highly-stressed little engines. He had proved their value at the Gaisberg hill-climb in 1959, when his car trounced the works Porsche RSKs in pouring rain. Mitter continued to race in FJ in 1961 and 1962, and the following year Godin de Beaufort gave him an F1 Porsche drive in the German GP. He finished 4th, and was 6th with Koch in the 1964 Reims 12 Hours (Porsche 904), and in 1965, came 2nd in the Targa Florio (with Davis), then gained one victory, four 2nds, a 3rd and a 4th in the European Mountain Championship

Tommy Milton in the twin-engined Duesenberg Land Speed Record car, 1920. Photo: Indianapolis Motor Speedway

Gerhard Mitter. Photo: Porsche

Guy Moll. Photo: T. A. S. O. Mathieson Collection

rounds—all for Porsche. He drove an F1 Lotus-Climax in the German GP, but he was to have much more success with sports cars, and particularly in the Mountain Championship, which he won for Porsche in 1966, 1967 and 1968.

Important placings in 1966 included victories at Hockenheim and in the Austrian GP, and 4th in the Monza 1,000 kilometres. In the 1967 season he ran an F2 Brabham BT23 with little success. He still drove for Porsche when his tuning and preparation business permitted. That year he was 3rd at Sebring and Monza, and 4th in the Nürburgring 1,000 kilometres, and he won at Mugello (with Schutz). In 1968 he came 2nd in the BOAC 500 and Spa 1,000 kilometres, and won seven of the eight rounds of the Mountain Championship. At last his big sports car victory came in 1969 when he and Schutz took the Targa Florio for Porsche; he also took a 3rd at Brands Hatch and 5th at Sebring. He had been signed by BMW to drive their F2 cars, but left the team after a disagreement, only to return for the 1969 German GP. He knew the circuit well, but during Friday afternoon practice his car suffered a suspension failure, and left the road after the Flugplatz. Gerhard Mitter died on his way to hospital. DCN

Moll, Guy

Moll, son of a Spanish mother and French father, started his career by racing a sports Lorraine-Dietrich in his homeland of Algeria. His talent must have been noticed by his fellow Algerian, Marcel Lehoux, for he drove Lehoux's Bugatti in his first European race, the GP of Marseilles at Miramas in 1932, and finished 3rd behind the Alfas of the aces Sommer and Nuvolari. In 1933 he drove a Bugatti in the Pau GP (run in a snow-storm) and finished 2nd behind Lehoux and in front of Etancelin's Alfa Romeo. By June 1933, Moll had acquired an Alfa Romeo Monza, in which he came 3rd behind Nuvolari and Etancelin, also Monza-mounted, in the Nîmes GP. Then came a succession of 3rd places at Nice, Comminges and Miramas, with a 2nd in the Monza GP.

In 1934 Moll drove for the Scuderia Ferrari, and in a 2·9B Monoposto P3 won the Monaco GP and finished 2nd to Varzi and in front of Chiron on similar cars, only one-fifth of a second behind the winner. In a special streamlined 3·2-litre P3 he won the track race at the AVUS. In a 2·9B P3 he took 3rd place, sharing with Trossi, in the French GP, and was 2nd to Varzi's P3 in the Coppa Ciano, beating Nuvolari's Maserati in 3rd place. While fighting for the lead with Fagioli's Mercedes in a P3 in the Coppa Acerbo, Moll was killed in an unexplained accident when passing Henne's Mercedes. His career was very short and meteoric, but Ferrari said he was the only driver who could be compared with Nuvolari and Moss. He was buried in the Maison-Carrée cemetery in Algiers. PMAH

Momberger, August

This German driver was born in 1905. The flat races and hill-climbs at Darmstadt and Bad Homburg in 1923— two minor events—were his first racing successes, in a 1·5-litre supercharged Mercedes. He then changed to the small supercharged NSU, driving the 1·3-litre in 1924 and the 1·5-litre in 1925. His major success at this period was his overall victory in the 1925 Taunus Race. During his time as an engineer with Steyr he drove the Steyr 5-litre in the Krähberg hill-climb of 1926, winning the sports car class. In 1927 he could be seen in a Bugatti litre and gained hill-climb victories. The next change [wa]s in 1929 to a Mercedes SSK. He achieved 3rd places [in] the German and the Monza GPs and victories in a [nu]mber of hill-climbs that year. After an interval of a [fe]w years he joined the Auto Union team for 1934. In [th]e Avusrennen he finished 3rd behind Moll and Varzi [in] their Alfas, and in the Swiss Grand Prix came in 2nd [be]hind Stuck. It was Momberger's only season with [Au]to Union and he retired from active racing at the end [of] 1934. He died in 1970. HON

[M]oore-Brabazon, J. T. C.

[Bo]rn in 1884, Lord Brabazon of Tara served his motoring [ap]prenticeship as the Hon C. S. Rolls' mechanic on the [Iri]sh Fortnight of 1903, later driving a 90hp Mors in [sp]rints in 1905. In 1907 he handled Minervas both in the [Ka]iserpreis and in the Circuit des Ardennes. Though he [re]tired in the German event, he scored a double in [Be]lgium, winning the big race after the Pipes faded away, [an]d taking 2nd place in the Coupe Liedekerke behind [Th]érier on a similar car: this time it was the Métallurgique [te]am that failed to stand the pace. His last motor-racing [se]ason was 1908 and in both his big events he was [un]successful. Valve trouble eliminated his Métallurgique [fr]om the TT, and Brabazon himself later described the [6-]cylinder Austin racer as 'not really a racing car at all, [bu]t a very fast tourer', which explains why he could [ma]nage nothing better than 18th in the Grand Prix, [th]ough he was at least ahead of Resta on a sister car. [He] continued his active interest in motoring to the end, [an]d in his 80th year he not only drove a 300SL Mercedes-[Be]nz at 115mph, but also took a 1904 Thornycroft [th]rough the London-Brighton Run. He died in 1964. MCS

[M]oser, Silvio

[On]e of the smallest drivers in stature, Silvio Moser is [kn]own universally as 'Big Silv'. He was born in Zurich in [19]41, and began racing an XK 120 Jaguar at the age of [?]. The following year he drove an FJ Lotus 20 to victory [at] the Halle-Saale-Schleife circuit, but concentrated on [hil]l-climbing. With a borrowed Brabham FJ he made [?]st at the Mittholz-Kandersteg hill-climb in 1962, and in [19]63 he bought this car and took it to the Temporada [se]ries where he was extremely successful, becoming [Te]mporada Champion.

[The] Brabham was fitted with a 998cc engine for the [ne]w Formula 3, and with it Moser scored wins in five [ev]ents in 1964, during which year he also drove for de [Sa]nctis, Abarth and Alfa Romeo. In 1965 he bought a [ne]w Brabham chassis with Formula 3 and Formula 2 [en]gines, but apart from one F3 win and ftd at two hill-[cli]mbs he had a disappointing season. He won some [he]ats in the 1966 Temporada, but lost his title to Charles [C]richton-Stuart.

[In] 1968 Moser entered Formula 1 with a Brabham-[R]epco V8, his best place being 5th in the Dutch GP. The [fol]lowing season he drove an ex-works Brabham BT24 [wi]th Cosworth DFV engine, and raced in most of the [Gr]and Prix series; his best place was 6th in the United [St]ates GP. In 1970 he retained his old Cosworth engine, [bu]t mounted it in a new chassis built by Vittorio Bellasi. [Un]fortunately the newly-introduced qualifying system [pr]oved very hard on Moser, and he seldom managed to [ge]t a start. DCN

[M]oss, Pat

[Al]though now officially Pat Carlsson, the lady rally [dr]iver whom it is normal to find ahead of the boys is best

Top, J. T. C. Moore-Brabazon, at the wheel of the Minerva he drove in the 1907 Kaiserpreis. *Photo: Cyril Posthumus Collection*

Above, J. T. C. Moore-Brabazon at Brooklands in the 1920s. *Photo: Montagu Motor Museum*

Right above, J. T. C. Moore-Brabazon in the 1908 Grand Prix Austin. *Photo: T. A. S. O. Mathieson Collection*

Silvio Moser. *Photo: Bill Gavin*

known as Pat Moss. She was born in Thames Ditton, Surrey, and most of her early days were spent idolising her elder brother Stirling. Before she took up driving she had a most successful career in show jumping, and in 1952 Ken Gregory, Stirling's racing manager, persuaded her to go on a small rally with him. Pat navigated, and got lost on the way to the start. Despite this, she soon acquired a Morris Minor convertible and entered a number of small rallies, although her main interest at this time was still show jumping. In 1954 she progressed to a Triumph TR2 and more challenging events, and in March 1955 she was offered a works MG TF for the RAC Rally. Success in this event led to a works MG Magnette, followed by an Austin Westminster in 1956 and a Morris Minor 1000 in 1957. In 1958 BMC team manager Marcus Chambers allowed her to branch out into Riley 1·5s and Austin Healey 3000s, and with these she and Ann Wisdom won the European Ladies Championship. In 1959 they tied for 1st place with Erik Carlsson, and in 1960 won the Liège-Rome-Liège outright in an Austin Healey. It was the first time that a feminine crew had won a major international event, and the Liège was reckoned to be the toughest of them all. In 1961 she continued to drive for BMC, but also acquired a Saab and had many successes with both makes. She finished 3rd in the 1962 East African Safari in the Saab, despite hitting an antelope. That year she also won the Tulip and German Rallies.

After six years with BMC, Pat left to join Ford in 1963, and won the ladies prize on the Tulip and Acropolis Rallies. An injury to her knee kept her out of the Coupe des Alpes, but not out of church, for on 9 July she was married to Erik Carlsson. She changed again to work for Saab which was her husband's company, and with

Pat Moss with Liz Nyström, 1964 Monte Carlo Rally.
Photo: John Davenport Collection

co-driver Liz Nyström she had many successes with Saabs up to the end of 1967. She then took up an offer from Lancia, and driving a Fulvia won the 1968 Sestrieres Rally. She was 6th and highest placed Lancia in the 1969 Monte Carlo Rally. Since the birth of her baby, Susan, early in 1970 Pat has taken part in only a few rallies. JD

Moss, Stirling Craufurd

Whether Stirling Moss came to the fore because of the post-war boom in motor racing, or whether he was partly the cause of the boom, is debatable, but it is undeniable that in the 1950s his name became a household word, and everybody's idea of the complete racing driver. His own personal firm of Stirling Moss Ltd was run as a full-time business to promote his name wherever possible. Behind all this high-pressure publicity there was a truly remarkable young man who excelled at almost anything he tried, and his prowess with a racing car put him among the great drivers of all time.

Stirling Moss was born in London on 17 September 1929. Both his parents had motoring backgrounds, his father Alfred having driven at Brooklands and at Indianapolis where he finished 14th in 1924 in a Fronty-Ford, and his mother Aileen drove a Marendaz and other cars in trials of the 1930s, and won the Ladies Expert Trial in 1935 and 1936. Stirling began racing in the post-war Formula 3 boom in 1948, at the early age of 18. In his first season he scored ten class victories in British hill-climbs and races with his Cooper-JAP, and immediately attracted attention with the way in which he used the engine and gearbox as in a motorcycle, although he had never ridden one. In 1949 he drove a 996cc Cooper-JAP as well as the 497cc F3 car, and scored seven wins as well as his first foreign victory in the 500cc race at Zandvoort. He branched out into larger cars in 1950, driving the 2-litre HWM as well as the Jaguar XK 120 in which he scored his first major victory, in the Tourist Trophy. He was awarded the first of his ten Gold Stars by the British Racing Drivers' Club, becoming British Champion while still only 20.

During the next three years Moss drove a wide variety of cars, including HWM, Formula 3 Kieft, Jaguar and

Year	Event	Car
1950	Tourist Trophy	Jaguar XK 120
1951	Tourist Trophy	Jaguar C-type
	British Empire Trophy, IoM	Frazer Nash Le Mans
	Lavant Cup, Goodwood	HWM
	Madgwick Cup, Goodwood	HWM
	Wakefield Trophy Dublin	HWM
1952	Reims Sports Car Race	Jaguar C-type
	Boreham Sports Car Race	Jaguar C-type
	Alpine Rally, 2-litre class (Coupe des Alpes)	Sunbeam Talbot 90
1953	Reims 12-Hours, with P. Whitehead	Jaguar C-type
	London Trophy, Crystal Palace	Cooper-Alta
1954	Sebring 12-Hours, with Lloyd	OSCA 1·5-litre
	Aintree 200	Maserati 250F
	Gold Cup, Oulton Park	Maserati 250F
	Daily Telegraph Trophy, Aintree	Maserati 250F
	Goodwood Trophy	Maserati 250F
1955	Gold Cup, Oulton Park	Maserati 250F
	British GP	Mercedes-Benz W196
	Targa Florio, with Collins	Mercedes-Benz 300SLR
	Mille Miglia, with Jenkinson	Mercedes-Benz 300SLR
	Tourist Trophy, with Fitch	Mercedes-Benz 300SLR
	Governor's Cup, Lisbon	Porsche Spyder
1956	Aintree 200	Maserati 250F
	Richmond Trophy, Goodwood	Maserati 250F
	Italian GP	Maserati 250F
	Monaco GP	Maserati 250F
	Australian GP	Maserati 250F
	New Zealand GP	Maserati 250F
	Buenos Aires 1,000km, with Menditeguy	Maserati 300S
	Venezuelan GP	Maserati 300S
	Bari GP	Maserati 300S
	Nassau Trophy	Maserati 300S
	Australian TT	Maserati 300S
	Nürburgring 1,000km, with Behra, Taruffi, Schell	Maserati 300S
	British Empire Trophy	Cooper-Climax
	Daily Express Trophy, Silverstone	Vanwall
	Daily Herald Trophy, Oulton Park	Aston Martin DB3S
	Ardmore Handicap	Porsche Spyder
	Goodwood Trophy	Aston Martin DB3S
	BRDC Trophy, Silverstone	Maserati 300S

continued

Frazer Nash sports cars, and the ill-fated G-type ERA with which, through no fault of his own, he had little success. In 1952, 1953 and 1954 he won Coupes des Alpes in the Alpine Rally, these three successive achievements winning him one of the only two Coupes des Alpes en Or ever awarded. His patriotic determination to drive British cars delayed his rise to fame, for Enzo Ferrari offered to make him World Champion by 1953 if only he would drive for him. In 1954 Moss swallowed his patriotism and drove a Maserati 250F, joining the works team by mid-season. So well did he demonstrate his skill that Alfred Neubauer signed him up to drive for Mercedes-Benz as number two driver to Fangio. During 1955 Moss really developed as a Grand Prix driver, learning more in that one season than all others put together. He was at his best when he had the backing of Mercedes-Benz, their technical ability being capable of staying well ahead of Stirling's driving ability. With Maserati and Vanwall he achieved great things, but his enthusiasm for experimentation occasionally let him down, as it did in later years with Cooper and Lotus cars. At the wheel of Mercedes-Benz sports and GP cars in 1955 he won the Mille Miglia, Targa Florio, Tourist Trophy and British GP, and was 2nd in the Belgian, Dutch and Buenos Aires GPs, in the Swedish sports car GP and the Eifelrennen. He was 2nd to Fangio in the World Championship. There were no Mercedes-Benz works cars for him to drive in 1956, but he had many successes with sports and GP Maseratis, being again runner-up for the Driver's Championship. He reached this position again in 1957, 1958 and 1961, being 3rd in 1959 and 1960. During his rising years he was always

Stirling Moss, with Charles Cooper, at Silverstone in 1948.
Photo: Reuter

57	British GP, with Brooks	Vanwall
	Italian GP	Vanwall
	Pescara GP	Vanwall
	Swedish GP, with Behra	Maserati 450S
	Nassau Trophy	Ferrari 290MM
58	Argentine GP	Cooper-Climax 2-litre
	Caen GP	Cooper-Climax 2-litre
	Aintree 200	Cooper-Climax 2-litre
	Melbourne GP	Cooper-Climax 2-litre
	Dutch GP	Vanwall
	Portuguese GP	Vanwall
	Moroccan GP	Vanwall
	Nürburgring 1,000km, with Brabham	Aston Martin DBR-1
	Tourist Trophy, with Brooks	Aston Martin DBR-1
	Circuit of Vila Real	Maserati 300S
	Kannonloppet	Maserati 300S
	Cuban GP	Ferrari 412MI
	Silverstone Sports Car Race	Lister-Jaguar
	British Empire Trophy	Aston Martin DBR-2
	Sussex Trophy	Aston Martin DBR-1
59	New Zealand GP	Cooper-Climax 2-litre
	Italian GP	Cooper-Climax 2·5-litre
	Portuguese GP	Cooper-Climax 2·5-litre
	Rouen GP (F2)	Cooper-Borgward 1·5-litre
	Syracuse GP (F2)	Cooper-Borgward 1·5-litre
	Gold Cup, Oulton Park	Cooper-Climax 2·5-litre
	Roskilde Ring	Cooper-Monaco
	Kannonloppet	Cooper-Monaco
	Nürburgring 1,000km, with Fairman	Aston Martin DBR-1
	Tourist Trophy, with Shelby and Fairman	Aston Martin DBR-1
	Governor's Trophy, Nassau	Aston Martin DBR-2
	Rouen Sports Car Race	Maserati 60
60	Monaco GP	Lotus-Climax 18
	United States GP	Lotus-Climax 18
	Watkins Glen Formule Libre	Lotus-Climax 18
	Gold Cup, Oulton Park	Lotus-Climax 18
	Pacific GP, Laguna Seca	Lotus-Climax 19
	Kannonloppet	Lotus-Climax 19
	Cape GP	Porsche F2
	South African GP	Porsche F2
	Tourist Trophy	Ferrari 250GT Berlinetta
	Nürburgring 1,000km, with Gurney	Maserati 61
	Cuban GP	Maserati 61
61	German GP	Lotus-Climax 18
	Monaco GP	Lotus-Climax 18
	Modena GP	Lotus-Climax 18
	Roskilde Ring	Lotus-Climax 18
	Kannonloppet	Lotus-Climax 18
	Silver City Trophy, Brands Hatch	Lotus-Climax 18

continued

behind Fangio, and although Moss was undoubtedly number one driver after the Argentinian's retirement he lost the championship because of mechanical misfortunes and a tendency to make unnecessary experiments with his cars when he could beat all the opposition with a perfectly standard vehicle.

He began to drive for Vanwall in 1956, and in the following year he achieved his patriotic ambition of winning the British GP (at Aintree) in a British car. He also drove the Vanwall to victory at Pescara, and in the Italian GP that year. He won the Dutch and Moroccan GPs for Vanwall in 1958, and in 1959 he also began a string of successes in the Formula 1 Cooper-Climax. He began to drive for Lotus in 1960, and after winning the Monaco GP and coming 4th in the Dutch, he had a bad crash while practising for the Belgian GP, breaking both legs and his nose, and crushing the ninth vertebra. His attitude to physical recovery was like his attitude to racing, demanding 100% effort and concentration, and fifty days after the Spa crash he was back in racing, winning the Karlskoga sports car GP in a brand-new, untried Lotus-Climax. He had an excellend end of season period in America with Lotus Formula 1 and sports cars, winning Grands Prix at Watkins Glen and Riverside, and sports car races at Laguna Seca and Riverside. His last full season was 1961, and he had magnificent victories in the German and Monaco GPs, driving the privately-owned 4-cylinder Lotus to victory over the works V-6 Ferraris, and winning at Modena in a Lotus, and the Tourist Trophy in a Ferrari. He also gave the 4wd Ferguson its first victory in the Oulton Park Gold Cup, setting a new lap record in the process.

In 1962 he had three victories in New Zealand and Australia, and at the Goodwood Easter Meeting he drove a 1·5-litre V-8 Lotus in the Glover Trophy. After trouble with the car had delayed him at the pits he was driving as hard as he could go to make up for lost time when he crashed for reasons that have never been fully explained. This time it was the end of his career as a racing driver, for his brain was damaged, and he lost all the sharp edges of sight, judgment, concentration and skill that put him above everyone else. His physical recovery from the accident was typical Moss, but he could not regain his original mental reactions. Rather than trying to race again and proving mediocre he accepted early retirement at the age of 31.

Not only was he the fastest driver in his day, but also the most perfect; one of his rivals once summed it up by saying 'we get one corner exactly right in ten, Stirling gets all of them right, and on every lap'. Being 100% professional he endeavoured to race on every possible occasion, considering that when he was not in a racing car he was not earning money. As an individual he was a remarkable man, well above the average in eyesight, reflexes and judgment, and was always on top of his form, unlike some of his rivals who had off days. Moss was never known to put up a mediocre performance with a racing car, whether he was leading or in last position due to some mechanical fault. He always considered that he earned money through people paying to see him drive, and therefore it was up to him to give them value for money at all times, which is a refreshing outlook compared with that of some racing drivers. The only man to whom he admitted inferiority was Fangio, but

Stirling Moss driving the Ferguson to victory in the Oulton Park Gold Cup, 1961. *Photo: T. C. March*

Stirling Moss in a Mercedes-Benz W196 at Aintree, 1955. *Photo: Geoffrey Goddard*

only then in a single-seater GP car. His special ability was that he could make any car do what he wanted it to do, whereas most racing drivers adapt themselves to what the car fundamentally wants to do when cornering. From the first racing car he drove, a Cooper-JAP, to the last, a Lotus-Climax V-8, Moss was always the master of his machine. In 1953, in Jaguar sports cars, he was quick to see the value of the disc brake, and in the 1955 Mercedes-Benz GP car he exploited the road holding beyond the imagination of the designer. In their sports car, with hydraulically-operated air-brake, he soon found a method of using it for improved cornering, which the designers had not anticipated but could appreciate, seeing the use of aerodynamics to aid cornering ten years before most people. In the small rear-engined Cooper-Climax cars Moss led the 1959–1960 revolution in racing car design, and in 1961 in Lotus cars he showed that he was the finest driver extant by beating rivals in cars far more powerful than his. To Stirling Moss the impossible did not exist, and even if he did not always achieve the impossible, he never jibbed at trying.

The Stirling Moss of today is a hard-working business executive, applying all his energies to keeping Stirling Moss Ltd a successful company. He lives in the centre of London's West End, but travels widely wherever business interests take him. He attends the Can-Am series in his capacity as PR adviser to Johnson's Wax, and also does vehicle evaluation for Chrysler Australia. DSJ GNG

	Aspern Airfield	Lotus-Climax 18
	International Trophy, Silverstone	Cooper-Climax 2·5-litre
	British Empire Trophy, Silverstone	Cooper-Climax 2·5-litre
	Lavant Cup, Goodwood	Cooper-Climax 2·5-litre
	Gold Cup, Oulton Park	Ferguson-Climax
	Pacific GP, Laguna Seca	Lotus-Climax 19
	Players 200, Mosport	Lotus-Climax 19
	Sussex Trophy, Goodwood	Lotus-Climax 19
	BRDC, Silverstone	Lotus-Climax 19
	Tourist Trophy	Ferrari 250GT Berlinetta
	Nassau Tourist Trophy	Ferrari 250GT Berlinetta
	Warwick Farm International	Lotus-Climax 18
1962	New Zealand GP	Lotus-Climax 18
	Lady Wigram Trophy, Christchurch	Lotus-Climax 18
	Warwick Farm International	Lotus-Climax 18
	Daytona 3-Hours (Touring Class)	Ferrari 250GT Berlinetta

Motschenbacher, Lothar

Motschenbacher migrated to the United States from his native Germany (where he had been apprenticed to Mercedes-Benz) in 1958 when he was 19. He began racing Formula Juniors on the West Coast, at one point winning thirteen consecutive events. He moved up to a Ford-Cobra in 1965 and from 1966 has been a regular Can-Am campaigner. Motschenbacher's 1970 Can-Am record of one 2nd, three 3rds, one 6th and one 5th, earned $81,000 for second place in the series. In 1967 Motschenbacher won the Tim Mayer award, designed to aid the career of a promising driver. He has been American agent for McLaren Cars and lives in Beverly Hills, Calif. ARB

Mulford, Ralph

Mulford, born in 1885 and one of America's outstanding pioneer racing drivers, gained his early fame as a member of the Lozier team. After spending six years with that company, assembling marine and automotive engines, he was teamed with Harry Michener in 1907 for one of the 24-hour races which were so popular in America during the first decade of the 20th century. They won decisively

Left above, Stirling Moss at Sebring, with Dan Gurney and Graham Hill. *Photo: Al Bochroch*

Above, Stirling Moss at Monterey, 1969. *Photo: Al Bochroch*

Below, Lothar Motschenbacher. *Photo: Al Bochroch*

on the 1-mile Point Breeze dirt track at Philadelphia, Pa. and Mulford then teamed with other drivers, including Harry Cobe and Cyrus Patschke, to win similar events at Brighton Beach, N.Y., and other tracks during the next three years.

In 1911, Mulford won the national driving championship despite the handicap of not participating in some important events on the calendar because his religious convictions did not allow him to race on Sundays. He finished second to Ray Harroun in the inaugural Indianapolis 500-mile race that year; came 2nd to Erwin Bergdoll's big Benz in a 200-mile road race at Philadelphia; finished among the leaders in several other events; and made sure of the title by winning the 291-mile (468·3km) Vanderbilt Cup Race in a Lozier on a road course at Savannah, Ga., at an average speed of 74·21mph (119·43kph). It was the last race in which a Lozier team participated. Mulford was placed 10th or better in five other Indianapolis races and scored several victories on the board tracks, including the 300-mile inaugural race at Des Moines, Iowa in a Duesenberg. He also drove with distinction for Knox, Mercedes, Peugeot and Frontenac during a racing career which spanned approximately 20 years. He now lives in retirement at his home in New Jersey. AB

Munari, Sandro

Sandro Munari was born in 1940, the son of a farmer in Cavarzere, a small town not far from Venice. Toward the end of 1964 he became the owner of an 850 Abarth, but his first try in it came to an end two kilometres up the Agordo–Nevegal hill-climb when the gear change broke. He started to drive in rallies with the car but results seemed difficult to achieve. In 1965 he took up the job of co-driver with Cavallari, who was an official driver for the Jolly Club's Alfa Romeo GTAs, and together they won the Sardinian Rally, San Martino di Castrozza and several other Italian rallies in addition to being well placed in foreign events like the Semperit Rally in Austria.

Like many people before him, Munari was not content to be a co-driver and when he heard that Lancia were looking for drivers he asked for a car and was accepted. He competed in several internationals, including the Thousand Lakes, with a Lancia Flavia and showed himself to be very quick on special stages. In the Monte Carlo in 1966 he was lying 2nd but on the final mountain circuit a moment's inattention cost him his good place. The rest of the year was a tale of mechanical woe, but 1967 dawned with a 5th overall in the Monte Carlo and he went on to win every rally in Italy and become Italian champion. However, the real high point of the year came when he won outright the Tour de Corse after a fantastic drive in the rain against much faster and more experienced opposition.

That same year he had also made quite a name for himself in Italian racing, winning his class with a Lancia Fulvia at the Nürburgring and at Mugello. However, at the beginning of 1968, he was involved in an accident on the run-in of the Monte Carlo Rally in which his co-driver, Luciano Lombardini, was killed and he himself seriously injured. This meant that he was out of rallying for almost one year but in 1969 he made a spectacular come-back by winning the Sestriere and going on to win the Italian championship for the second time. He also had a very good drive at Mugello, where he finished 5th in a 1600 Fulvia. Generally his luck has not been of the best, and 1970 has started with retirements in the Monte

Ralph Mulford. *Photo: Indianapolis Motor Speedway*

Sandro Munari. *Photo: John Davenport*

Jimmy Murphy. *Photo: Indianapolis Motor Speedway*

Luigi Musso. *Photo: Geoffrey Goddard*

Carlo, Swedish, Italian and Safari Rallies, though in the last of these he was leading just before half-way. JD

Murphy, James

Jimmy Murphy, born in 1895 and forced to earn his own living after being orphaned at an early age, found employment at a California garage frequented by prominent members of the American racing fraternity. As soon as he became 21 years old, he accepted an invitation to become riding mechanic for Eddie O'Donnell of the Duesenberg team in 1916 and he also rode in many races with Tommy Milton, Duesenberg team captain, before being elevated to the rank of driver for a 1919 Labor Day race on the Altoona, Pa., board speedway.

Although involved in an accident on that occasion, Duesenberg made another car available to Murphy for the 250-mile (400km) inaugural event at the Beverly Hills, Calif., board track five months later and he defeated a field of veterans with an average speed of 103mph (165·8kph). After he had finished 4th at Indianapolis in 1920 and won a 200-mile board track race later in the season at Fresno, Calif., the Duesenberg brothers selected him as their No. 1 driver for the 1921 French Grand Prix at Le Mans.

Driving the first American car ever equipped with hydraulic 4-wheel brakes, Murphy averaged 78·22mph (125·88kph) to win against a field of the best cars and drivers from two continents and become the first American to score a major victory in Europe. After returning to the United States, however, Murphy was impressed by the performance of the Harry Miller racing engines and he purchased the Le Mans car from Duesenberg in order to enter it as a Murphy Special with a Miller engine at Indianapolis in 1922. He won impressively with an average speed of 94·48mph (152·05kph), breaking Ralph DePalma's existing record, set in 1915, by almost 5mph; he also registered important victories in board track races of more than 200 miles (320km) duration at Beverly Hills, Uniontown, Pa., and Tacoma, Wash. to earn the 1922 national driving championship.

As captain of the newly-formed team of six Durant Specials with Miller engines, Murphy started the 1923 season with additional victories on the Beverly Hills and Fresno board tracks. He then finished 3rd at Indianapolis and accepted an invitation from Harry Miller to drive a new Miller Special in the Italian Grand Prix at Monza in September, being placed 3rd. The championship races he missed in the United States because of that trip, however, made it impossible for him to retain his national driving title, although he was second to Eddie Hearne in the final point standing.

He regained the crown in 1924 by scoring three board track victories and placing well in most of the other events, including Indianapolis, where he finished 3rd again. Late in the season, with the title already assured, he was injured fatally at Syracuse, N.Y., while challenging Phil Shafer for first place in a 100-mile dirt track championship contest. AB

Musso, Luigi

Luigi Musso was born in Rome in 1924, the youngest of three sons of an Italian diplomat. His brother Giuseppe raced Alfa Romeo saloons with some success, and Luigi followed him into the sport in 1950. From this early stage a considerable rivalry grew between the aristocratic Roman and Eugenio Castellotti, the 'commoner' from the north.

Money was not a problem to Musso, and as he slowly gained experience his name began to appear in the results. In 1953 he won the Perugina Cup in a sports Maserati, and in 1954 he raced both Formula and sports cars, winning the Naples, Pescara and Senigallia GPs (in F1 and sports Maseratis), finishing 2nd in the Spanish GP and Targa Florio, and 3rd in the long-distance Tour of Calabria and the Mille Miglia. In 1955 he shared the winning Maserati with Behra in the Supercortemaggiore GP, and was second in the Bari, Caserta and Naples sports car races, and in the Syracuse GP. He completed a good season with 3rd places in the Giro di Sicilia and Dutch GP, and was champion Italian driver for Maserati.

At the beginning of 1956 Musso scored the only World Championship victory of his career, sharing the Argentine GP-winning Lancia-Ferrari with Fangio. He also won the 1-hour Rome GP in the OSCA, was 2nd at Sebring (with Schell) and Syracuse; 3rd in the Shell GP at Imola (being beaten by Castellotti in a similar OSCA); and 3rd again in the Mille Miglia. Musso was generally the smoother of the two, but Castellotti could be much quicker on his day. In 1957 the Roman won the non-championship Marne GP at Reims and the Buenos Aires 1,000 kilometres, and scored a long string of 2nd places to underline his ability: with Ferraris he was 2nd in the European GP, French GP, Modena F2 GP, Syracuse GP and Venezuelan GP (with Hawthorn); and he was 3rd in the Buenos Aires GP (with Collins) and 2nd—in a Maserati—in the Bordeaux GP.

After the death of his team-mate, but arch-rival, Castellotti, Musso was driving not so much for himself as for Italy. He was intensely patriotic and was now the last Italian driver left in top-class motor racing. In 1958 he was driving harder than ever, but retained his essential consistency to win the Syracuse GP (at last) and the Targa Florio (with Gendebien). He was also 2nd in the Argentine and Monaco Championship GPs, and in the non-championship Buenos Aires race, and he shared the 3rd-place Ferrari with Mike Hawthorn and Phil Hill in the Monza 500 Miles.

Musso went to the French GP at Reims determined to do well after his long series of second places, but crashed at 150mph on the long Gueux curve while chasing Hawthorn, and was killed. Luigi Musso was a brilliant shot, fencer and horseman, as well as a fast and competent racing driver. DCN

Nazzaro, Felice

Born in 1881, the son of an Italian coal-merchant, Felice Nazzaro served his apprenticeship with the FIAT company. His skill as a driver and mechanic was soon recognized, and his first major race was the Vicenza–Padua (1900) in which he came 3rd. The following year he won the Giro d'Italia on one of the firm's first 4-cylinder cars. Nazzaro's expertise in dealing with influential and difficult customers led to his employment as Vincenzo Florio's chauffeur, and while in Florio's service he took part in various Italian events. In 1904 he drove a Panhard into 5th place in the first Coppa Florio, but in 1905 FIAT were seriously involved in racing, and with Vincenzo Lancia, Nazzaro became the spearhead of the works team.

A friendly rivalry was soon established between the two drivers: Lancia's showier performances led to record laps, but he was something of a car-breaker, whereas Nazzaro could be relied upon to finish. This in fact happened in the Gordon Bennett race over the Auvergne Circuit, where Nazzaro finished 2nd after

Lancia's retirement, but in the Coppa Florio Nazzaro was 6th, three places behind his team-mate. Nazzaro's best 1906 performance was 2nd in the Grand Prix. However, 1907, was a golden year for manufacturer and driver alike. Despite the complications of three different classes of vehicle for the three major events (the Targa Florio, the Grand Prix and the Kaiserpreis), Nazzaro won all three, with his heat in the German race thrown in for good measure. The 1908 season started poorly with retirement in the Targa Florio (which Trucco's Isotta Fraschini won) and the Fiats also faded in the Grand Prix. But Nazzaro had his revenge on Trucco (now at the wheel of a Lorraine-Dietrich) in the Coppa Florio, which he won at the impressive speed of 74·1mph 119·25kph) on a car which was in poor shape at the end. He was robbed of another certain victory in the American Grand Prize at Savannah when a tyre burst on the final lap, in spite of which misfortune he still finished 3rd.

With the virtual cessation of major events, Nazzaro raced only once in 1910, leading the American Grand Prize for a while despite damage sustained in a skid. A chain broke and he retired on the 19th lap. Then, like Lancia, he sought to capitalize on his personal reputation by building cars. Unlike Lancia, he drove them himself on the circuits, but also (unlike his former team-mate) he was none too successful, despite a couple of impressive performances: a win in the 1913 Targa Florio, a good hour ahead of his nearest rival, the Aquila-Italiana of Marsaglia; and a repeat performance in the 1914 Coppa Florio. He also tried his luck in the 1913 French GP at the wheel of a rotary-valve Itala, but retired with a broken rear spring. In the 1914 race his machine was a 4·5-litre sohc Nazzaro, but the make was never prominent and he retired again.

Felice Nazzaro disposed of his business interests in 1916, and had nothing to do with subsequent Nazzaro cars. In 1921 he and Pietro Bordino performed the opening ceremony at the Monza Autodrome, and 1922 saw him back with FIAT and winning his second French GP at Strasbourg on a 2-litre car. Triumph, however, was mixed with tragedy for rear-end failures eliminated both his team-mates, one of whom, Felice's nephew Biagio, was fatally injured in the ensuing crash. For the time being Nazzaro continued to race, finishing 2nd in the Italian GP. He retired in the 1923 French race at Tours with supercharger trouble, but the blown Fiats were up to the mark in time for the Italian GP at Monza, in which he came in 2nd behind Carlo Salamano's sister car. This was almost his last race, though in 1924 he took over Bordino's car in the Coppa Florio and crashed it, and retired with plug trouble in the French

Left above, Felice Nazzaro in an Itala, 1913 French GP. *Photo: T. A. S. O. Mathieson Collection*

Above, Felice Nazzaro in a Fiat, 1922 French GP. *Photo: Cyril Posthumus Collection*

Alfred Neubauer at the 1935 Monaco GP. *Photo: Mercedes-Benz Photodienst*

Alfred Neubauer, 1965. *Photo: Cyril Posthumus Collection*

GP. He was appointed head of FIAT's competition department in 1925, and continued to work for them until his death in 1940. He was last seen in competition at the wheel of a 6-cylinder Tipo 525SS sports car in the 1929 Alpine Trial. MCS

Neerpasch, Jochen

Jochen Neerpasch was born in Krefeld, Germany, in 1939 and made his competition motoring debut with a Borgward in 1960. He quickly showed promise, driving saloon, GT and single-seater cars and was given a great chance in 1964 when he was offered a Cobra Daytona GT drive for the Shelby team at Le Mans. He turned in a good performance, although the car failed, and also appeared in a Lotus F3 on occasions. He took his car to the Argentine Temporada and crashed heavily, but returned to Europe still with a reputation as a rising star.

In 1965 he shared the 2nd-place Ford Mustang with Roy Pierpoint in the Nürburgring 6-Hour event, and in 1966 he shared a Porsche 906 with Gerhard Koch to win the Circuit of Mugello race. Partnering Michel Weber in a similar car he won his class in the Monza 1,000 kilometres, and finished the season 2nd in the German GT Championship.

Neerpasch was in the Porsche works team in 1967, winning the Nürburgring 84-Hour Marathon; sharing 910s with Vic Elford for 3rd places in the Targa Florio and Nürburgring 1,000 kilometres; and partnering Rolf Stommelen in another 910 to finish 6th in the Le Mans 24 Hours. He and Hans Herrmann were 4th in the BOAC 500 (really a 6-hour race) with an 8-cylinder prototype, and he and Stommelen were 2nd at Mugello in a similar car.

The 1968 season started off well with Neerpasch sharing the winning Porsche 907 at Daytona, and he was then 2nd at Sebring, 3rd at Brands Hatch (both with Elford), 2nd at Monza (with Stommelen), 4th in the Targa Florio (with Herrmann) and 4th again at the Nürburgring (with Joe Buzzetta). He shared with Elford again at Monza but had an enormous accident at Malmédy, spinning along the road so fast that Hobbs' JW GT40 could not accelerate past him. He returned in time for Le Mans, where he partnered Stommelen to 3rd place and then retired at the end of his best season to become competitions manager for Ford of Germany. DCN

Neubauer, Alfred

Alfred Neubauer is unique in motor racing history, not as a racing driver, although he began his career as one, but as team manager for Mercedes-Benz from 1926 to 1955. He brought new techniques to the art of running a professional racing team, and with his vast build, his necklace of stopwatches, his bull-like voice and 'sergeant-major' discipline concealing a warm heart and ready wit, Neubauer became a legendary figure in the Grand Prix world.

Born in 1891, after serving in the Imperial Army in World War 1, he joined Austro-Daimler of Wiener-Neustadt as a test driver. He was a member of their three-car team of 'Sascha' voiturette models in the 1922 Targa Florio, bringing the only surviving car home in 19th place. He joined Mercedes in 1923, the year in which Dr Ferdinand Porsche became their designer, and again drove in the Targa Florio in 1924, this time with a 2-litre 4-cylinder Mercedes with which he took a modest 15th place and 3rd in class. At the Semmering hill-climb that year he was 5th, and he drove in the Mercedes team of 2-litre 8-cylinder cars in the Italian GP.

Neubauer gave up racing and took up team management in 1926, the year in which Mercedes and Benz combined forces. Without any doubt his shrewdness in team tactics and organization played as vital a part in Mercedes-Benz' magnificent racing record as did their drivers. He directed team policy during their intensively active racing period from 1934 to 1939, when they won 34 Grands Prix; when they resumed racing in the sports car class in 1952, and won Le Mans, the Carrera Panamericana and other events, Neubauer was again the king-pin; and in 1954–5, when the sensational W196 with desmodromic valves and fuel injection swept the board in GP racing, and the 300 SLR won the Sports Car Championship, it was Neubauer again who managed the team, deciding when, where and how they would race. He was a master psychologist and a great talent-spotter too, giving mechanic Lang his chance to race, inviting Dick Seaman to join the team, and securing the services of top men like Fangio, Moss and Collins after the war. When Mercedes-Benz withdrew from racing after 1955, Neubauer remained their authority on racing, with particular charge of the racing exhibits in the Untertürkheim museum. He has now retired, and lives quietly at Aldingen, near Stuttgart. CP

Nicolas, Jean-Pierre

Quite often in motor sport, the sons of famous fathers rise to the top and Nicolas is a good example of this. He was born in Marseilles in 1945, the son of Georges Nicolas who now owns a big Renault garage but used to race for that company before World War 2. The young Nicolas started out in 1963 driving a Renault Dauphine 1093 with his father as co-driver, and among their successes was a victory in the Rallye Mistral. Next year he was driving a Gordini and won the same event before the French Army claimed him for national service.

On his return in 1966, he received some help from the factory and rewarded them by winning the Tour de Madere, and also a Coupes des Alpes for an unpenalized run in the event of the same name. In 1967, he won the Critérium Jean Behra with an Alpine, won the Touring category in the Tour de Corse with a Gordini, and was leading the TAP Rally with the same kind of car, only to retire with mechanical failure 50 kilometres from the end. The following year he was an official driver for the Alpine factory and started off by coming 2nd in the Neige et Glace and then won the Ronde des Maures. He went back to a Gordini to win the difficult Morrocan Rally; also in a Gordini he took a very good 7th overall in the Spanish Rally.

The year 1969 was rather unlucky for Nicolas as a broken spark plug cost him the 1st place in the Rallye Mediterranée (part of the Monte Carlo Rally). However, he did finish the Moroccan Rally, the only Renault driver to do so, and in 1970 he proved equally consistent, being the only team driver to finish both the Monte Carlo and the Swedish rallies for Alpine. He was 2nd in the Geneva, and won the Spanish RACE Rally. JD

Nowicki, Zbigniew

One of the few men to win the East African Safari twice, 'Nick' Nowicki was born in 1928 and works in East Africa for Marshals, the Peugeot distributors. He has competed in every single one of the Safari series and has failed to finish only twice. In 1962 he was 2nd overall with a Peugeot 404 and won the rally the following year, when only seven cars finished because the weather was

so bad. Again it was a bad year for rain in 1968 when he won for the second time and again there were only seven finishers. In 1968 too he was East African Rally champion and has since then finished the Safari twice, but never higher than 10th place. JD

Nuvolari, Tazio Giorgio

In 1964, some 25 years after he had attained the peak of his career and a decade after his death, a well-known motor-racing writer was still describing Nuvolari as one of the greatest drivers in the history of motor racing. Perhaps the main reason for Nuvolari's impact was his uniqueness, for this Italian's style of driving was unlike that of the other great drivers before or since. Partly this was due to the age he lived in, the sort of cars he drove, and the circumstances of his career.

Nuvolari came from a landowning family and was born in 1892 at Casteldario, about 15 miles (24km) from Mantua, hence his later title of 'Il Mantovano Volante' or 'The Flying Mantuan'. He spent his youth at nearby Ronchesana where his father, Arturo, who went in for cycle racing, managed the property of Tazio's uncle, Giuseppe. Giuseppe Nuvolari had become a highly successful racing cyclist and spent some time racing abroad in Spain, Germany and at the Crystal Palace in England, as well as in Italy. On giving up cycle racing he started a motor business as Bianchi agent for Mantua, in which young Tazio joined him. Tazio was small and wiry and had already suffered the first of many broken bones by falling off a horse.

Because of the war, Nuvolari was nearly 30 before he had the chance to race. He started on motorcycles in 1920, and his first car race was the Circuit of Garda in 1921, in which he came 4th behind the Bugattis of Silvani and Costantini and the Ansaldo of Lotti, the most successful Ansaldo driver of the time. Nuvolari's basically touring Ansaldo was similar to Lotti's. In 1922 he was 2nd at Garda in the Ansaldo behind Meregalli's Diatto, and in front of the well-known Nando Minoia's OM, which was a good performance. In 1923 Nuvolari raced in Spain with a 1·5-litre Chiribiri and came 5th in the Penya Rhin GP at Villafranca, and 4th in a race on the track at Sitges. He also put up fastest lap at Garda. In 1923 his name began to be noticed in motorcycle racing, for at Rapallo, foreshadowing future achievements, he put up a notable performance on an unsuitable machine by gaining 3rd place on a horizontally-opposed twin-cylinder Fongri. His first motorcycling victory was at Parma in 1923 on a Garelli, and he had further successes in this year on Nortons and Indians. In 1924 he became 500cc Champion of Italy on Nortons, and from 1925 to 1927 riding Bianchis, he concentrated solely on motorcycle racing. He also raced cars in 1924, gaining his first victory driving a 2-litre Bianchi, and he won the 1·5-litre class at the Circuits of Savio and Polesine on a Chiribiri.

In 1925 he was given a trial on a P2 Alfa Romeo at Monza, but crashed badly due to a seized gearbox. Just a week later, heavily bandaged, he was lifted on to his Bianchi motorcycle and won the Grand Prix des Nations in pouring rain.

In 1927 Nuvolari founded a Type 35 Bugatti stable with his faithful mechanic, Decimo Compagnoni, Achille Varzi, Cesare Pastore and others, selling some of his land at Ronchesana to obtain the finance. He had five outright victories with the Bugattis, but Varzi left the team and acquired a P2 Alfa Romeo. It was in 1929, at Leghorn, that Nuvolari first drove an Alfa Romeo, a

Tazio Nuvolari at San Sebastian, 1933. *Photo: Fotocar*

Tazio Nuvolari. *Photo: Cyril Posthumus Collection*

Tazio Giorgio Nuvolari: Principal Successes

Year	Event	Car
1924	Circuit of Tigullio, Genoa	Bianchi 2-litre
1927	Prix Royal of Rome	Bugatti Type 35
	Circuit of Garda	Bugatti Type 35
1928	Tripoli GP	Bugatti Type 35
	Circuit of Pozzo	Bugatti Type 35
	Circuit of Alexandria	Bugatti Type 35
1930	Mille Miglia, with Guidotti	Alfa Romeo 1750
	Tourist Trophy	Alfa Romeo 1750
1931	Italian GP, with Campari	Alfa Romeo Monza 2·3
	Targa Florio	Alfa Romeo Monza 2·3
	Coppa Ciano	Alfa Romeo Monza 2·3

continued

Year	Race	Car
1932	Monza GP	Alfa Romeo Monza 2·3
	Targo Florio	Alfa Romeo Monza 2·3
	Italian GP, with Campari	Alfa Romeo 2·6B P3
	Avellino Circuit	Alfa Romeo 2·6B P3
	Coppa Ciano	Alfa Romeo 2·6B P3
	Coppa Acerbo	Alfa Romeo 2·6B P3
1933	Tunis GP	Alfa Romeo Monza 2·6
	Eifelrennen	Alfa Romeo Monza 2·6
	Bordino GP	Alfa Romeo Monza 2·6
	Nîmes GP	Alfa Romeo Monza 2·6
	Le Mans 24 Hours, with Sommer	Alfa Romeo 8C 2300
	Mille Miglia, with Campari	Alfa Romeo 8C 2300
	Belgian GP	Maserati 8CM 2·9
	Coppa Ciano	Maserati 8CM 2·9
	Nice GP	Maserati 8CM 2·9
	Tourist Trophy	MG K3 Magnette
1934	Circuit of Modena	Maserati Type 34 6C
	Circuit of Naples	Maserati Type 34 6C
1935	Pau GP	Alfa Romeo 2·9B P3
	Bergamo Cup	Alfa Romeo 2·9B P3
	Biella Circuit	Alfa Romeo 3·2B P3
	Turin GP	Alfa Romeo 3·5B P3
	Coppa Ciano	Alfa Romeo 3·5B P3
	Nice GP	Alfa Romeo 3·5B P3
	Modena Circuit	Alfa Romeo 3·5B P3
	German GP	Alfa Romeo 3·8B P3
1936	Penya Rhin GP	Alfa Romeo 12C-36
	Vanderbilt Cup	Alfa Romeo 12C-36
	Circuit of Milan	Alfa Romeo 12C-36
	Circuit of Modena	Alfa Romeo 12C-36
	Hungarian GP	Alfa Romeo 8C-35
	Coppa Ciano	Alfa Romeo 8C-35
1937	Milan GP	Alfa Romeo 12C-36
1938	Italian GP	Auto Union Type D
	Donington GP	Auto Union Type D
1939	Yugoslav GP	Auto Union Type D
1946	Albi GP	Maserati 4CL

Tazio Nuvolari at Silverstone, 1950. *Photo: Geoffrey Goddard*

supercharged 1,750cc sports car, in which he came 2nd to Varzi's P2 in the Coppa Ciano, driving in a plaster corset after breaking two ribs in an accident on his Bianchi motorcycle, also at Leghorn, the previous weekend. He also had a 2nd place in the Monza GP in 1929 driving a Talbot-Darracq.

His last motorcycling season was 1930, when his greatest years began, during which he mainly drove for Alfa Romeo with the Scuderia Ferrari. His change to Maseratis in 1933 was occasioned by his disappointment after having had numerous transmission failures on Monza Alfa Romeos. He also had a brief period with the Bugatti team in 1934, his best performance being 3rd in the Spanish GP at San Sebastian with a Type 59.

His successes speak for themselves, but what is so extraordinary is that his driving did not conform to the accepted standards of the top-flight drivers of his day, or any day. He gave an impression of immense vitality in the cockpit, almost dancing from side to side, pulling faces, and jiggling the wheel. He liked to sit rather high up, and well back from the steering wheel. He took his corners like a slalom skier, flinging the car into a slide and going round in a 4-wheel drift with little or no use of the brakes, yet with the car perfectly placed for a straight line exit, accelerating hard. He is credited with being the instigator of the 4-wheel drift. He finished in 5th place in the 1934 Italian GP in a Maserati with literally no brakes at all. The mechanics had drained even the hydraulic fluid for the brakes to make the car light enough for the weighing-in, and had forgotten to top up the reserve reservoir afterwards. On a very twisty circuit at Monza, with many chicanes, Nuvolari drove for much of the 4¾ hour race, using the gearbox to slow down.

Prince Chula once described the odd clothes 'Nivola' wore when driving a Maserati at the Grand Prix des Nations at Geneva in 1946: a dark red leather windcap over his brown hatchet face, a yellow high-necked pull-over over which he wore a leather waistcoat, then bright blue overall trousers and white sand shoes. Each time he approached a corner he would turn down the tiny aero-screen in front of him, only to put it up again when he had straightened out. His yellow shirt bore the mono-gram 'TN' and the little tortoise emblem originally given to him by Gabriele d'Annunzio, the soldier-airman-poet as the symbol of prudence and slowness. The crowd loved his antics and his dress, of course, which was in direct contrast to his more conventional rival Varzi, immaculate in both his dress and his driving.

In anybody else but Nuvolari, his pecularities in the cockpit would have got him nowhere, yet Nuvolari triumphed in every aspect of the sport, not only Grand Prix races, but long-distance sports car events like Le Mans, the Mille Miglia, the TT and the Targa Florio, and in track races, sprints, hill-climbs and 200mph (320kph) record attempts. Few other champions have been so versatile. Above all Nuvolari was immensely courageous and quite indomitable, he was never dis-couraged if he started a race in an inferior car, for he would still fight whether for 1st, 7th or 17th place.

His most famous victory against the odds was in the 1935 German GP on the Nürburgring where he drove an outmoded 3·8-litre-engined P3 Alfa Romeo, far less powerful than his German rivals. After being as low as 6th in the race, after all his team-mates had retired, he gradually overhauled all the opposition to take the lead. Delayed by a long pit stop when the handle of the re-fuelling pump broke, he was gaining 16sec per lap on the leader von Brauchitsch's Mercedes, and when Brau-

Right, Tazio Nuvolari. *Photo: George Monkhouse*

chitsch retired with a puncture, Nuvolari swept past to win from all the string of silver Auto Unions and Mercedes with a lead of 2min 14·4sec over the Auto Union in 2nd place. In 1936 Nuvolari beat the German cars in the Hungarian GP, the Penya Rhin GP and the Milan GP, but most remarkable was the Coppa Ciano at Leghorn, where the circuit was just to the Maestro's liking. After his own 12C-36 Alfa Romeo had retired, he took over Pintacuda's 8C-35, caught up the Auto Union team, who were in the lead, and pressed them really hard. With the crowd nearly crying with excitement Nuvolari overhauled the Auto Unions one by one and took the lead himself. He gave them such a battering that their brakes, which had not been relined since they contested the German GP the previous weekend, started to fail, with the result that they were passed by Nuvolari's team-mate Brivio and Dreyfus, giving Alfa Romeo a 1-2-3 victory, with the best Auto Union in 4th place.

His courage was shown on the Lucca-Altopascio autostrada when taking records with the Bimotore Alfa Romeo in 1935. On the outward run the big car was struck by a sidewind after passing under an arch, and Nuvolari fought the car for nearly 200yd, leaving great black marks on the road. On the return run he was going even faster and skidded again at the same spot at around 200mph (320kph), but fortunately not to such a great extent.

That he was not without nerves, though, was shown in practice for the Pau GP in 1938. His Type 308 Alfa Romeo suddenly burst into flames on the straight, and he had to steer it off the road into some bushes. Nuvolari suffered burns to his arms, leg and temple, and was so shaken that he swore never to race an Alfa Romeo again.

and even to give up racing, but only the former vow was kept, for he was soon driving Auto Unions, and showing himself as one of the few drivers capable of mastering those difficult cars.

By nature Nuvolari was generous, but he could be brusque in speech. He had his sadnesses. Both his sons died in their teens, and when the Maestro returned to racing after World War 2, though he had lost none of his skill, he soon suffered from an incurable ailment in which it was dangerous for him to inhale petrol and exhaust fumes, and had to wear a special mask over his nose and mouth against them. In the Marseilles GP in 1946 he led the race in his Scuderia Milano 4CL Maserati from Sommer before he retired with a broken valve. At Albi he won from Louveau and Raph's Maseratis, but collapsed after the race. In the Milan GP in the Parco Sempione he had to retire after driving with one hand holding a blood-soaked handkerchief to his mouth. He was 2nd in the Mille Miglia in 1947 in a 1,100cc Cisitalia after leading at Bologna, then being delayed by ignition trouble due to rain. In the same year he won the 1·5-litre class at Forli and Parma in a 125 Ferrari, and was 3rd overall in a Cistalia in the Circuit of the Lido, Venice. In 1948 he retired at half distance when leading the Mille Miglia in a Ferrari whose chassis gave out.

He drove his last race at the age of 58, the Circuit of Monte Pellegrino, in which he was 1st in the 1·5-litre class in a Cisitalia, and died at his home in Mantua on 11 August 1953, soon after his 61st birthday. PMAH

Oldfield, Berna Eli

Barney Oldfield, a brilliant showman and able driver born in 1877, made his name synonymous with automobile racing in the United States before such other American pioneer drivers as Ralph DePalma and Ray Harroun had ever driven in competition. As a picturesque and fearless cigar-chewing competitor, Barney became the favourite of race fans throughout the nation by scoring a series of impressive victories with Henry Ford's famous 999, beginning in 1902. During the early years of his career, he also won frequently with the Winton Bullet, the Peerless Green Dragon and the fwd Christie.

Until the Indianapolis Motor Speedway was built in 1909, Oldfield devoted most of his time to 'barnstorming' tours of the nation's smaller dirt tracks as the top driver of an exhibition troupe which entertained thousands of spectators almost daily with a programme of short-distance 'contests' run according to plan. During the inaugural programme at Indianapolis, however, he set several records in a Benz and established further records on other courses in 1910, including an American record of 131·724mph (211·936kph) for the measured mile at Daytona Beach, Fla., in the same car.

At the time of the first Indianapolis 500-mile race in 1911, Oldfield was under suspension by the Contest Board of the American Automobile Association for participating in unsanctioned events; and it was late in 1912 before he was eligible again for championship competition. A suitable car was not available immediately, but David Bruce-Brown of the FIAT team was injured fatally a few days before the annual Grand Prix at Milwaukee, Wis., and his car was repaired in time for Oldfield to drive it to 4th place.

Apparently unaware of the bitter rivalry between DePalma and Oldfield, officials of the Mercer Company signed Oldfield in 1913 as a member of the Mercer racing team captained by DePalma. The latter's angry reaction was to resign from the team instantly and Oldfield was

then assigned the car intended originally for DePalma, driving it to 2nd place behind Earl Cooper's Stutz in a 445-mile road race at Santa Monica, Calif. Oldfield, however, continued to devote most of his time to a series of lucrative personal appearances in match races against other cars and drivers as well as exhibition events in which he raced his car against one of the early aircraft flown by the stunt pilot Lincoln Beachey. In a period of only 12 months, Barney moved from Mercer to Maxwell to Stutz, limiting his actual competitive appearances to only the most important championship events on the schedule.

His 1914 record included 2nd place in a Mercer behind DePalma's Mercedes in the 295-mile Vanderbilt Cup Race; 2nd place in a Maxwell behind Eddie Pullen's Mercer in the 301-mile Corona, Calif., road race; and 5th place for Stutz at Indianapolis, where he was the first American entry to finish. Oldfield also drove a Maxwell to victory in the 300-mile road race at Venice, Calif., in 1915 and, one year later, on his second and final Indianapolis appearance, came 5th again in a Delage.

Too old for military service in 1917, Oldfield continued his exhibition tour and drove in competition on some of the board tracks with the widely publicized 'Golden Submarine', a unique Miller-engined car with the cockpit enclosed. He retired as a driver in 1918 to form the Oldfield Tire & Rubber Company, which he sold to Firestone four years later. After losing almost all of a fortune estimated at more than one million dollars in the 1929 market crash, Oldfield became active in automotive circles as a consulting engineer. He died in 1946. AB

Oliver, Keith Jack

A British driver who was born in 1942 and has lived most of his life in Romford, Essex. He began his career with Minis before buying an early Marcos which he raced for two seasons until it was destroyed in a crash at Snetterton.

Oliver came to prominence through his driving of two Lotus Elans, entered by DR Fabrications. He also scored several successes with their Mustang, and led the Ilford 500 at Brands Hatch in 1965 for most of the way before his co-driver crashed, in an E-Type Jaguar. He acquired a new Formula 3 Brabham for 1966 and after only three races he was offered a works-backed Lotus F3 drive. He was always competitive, and although he had little real success he continued to show promise. In 1967 he drove the Lotus Components' F2 car, and became a full-time professional driver in the middle of the season. He won the Formula 2 class in the Spring Cup race at Oulton Park, then again in the German Grand Prix class.

Following Jim Clark's death in April 1968, Oliver became No 2 to Graham Hill in the F1 Lotus team. He scored his first World Championship points by finishing 5th in the Belgian GP, and was lucky to escape unhurt from a massive high-speed crash in practice for the French GP at Rouen. Best placing of the season was 3rd in the Mexican GP, and he was also third in the Oulton Park Gold Cup. He raced a privately-entered F2 Lotus 48 without success that season, although he managed some respectable placings in the Argentine Temporada with what was by then an obsolete machine.

For the 1969 season Oliver joined BRM as No 2 to Surtees, and signed with JW Automotive for long-distance events. He had a sorry year in Formula 1, his delicate BRM finishing in the points only once: 6th in the Mexican GP. Oliver's long-distance performances were a revelation, however, for he was teamed with Jacky

Barney Oldfield. *Photo: Indianapolis Motor Speedway*

Barney Oldfield with a model of his projected Land Speed Record car. *Photo: Montagu Motor Museum*

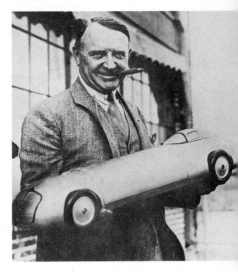

Jackie Oliver. *Photo: Autosport*

271

Ickx in a Ford GT40 and won at Sebring and Le Mans. Late that year he drove the Autocoast Ti-22 Can-Am car and was set for several good finishes only to have the experimental car break under him. In 1970 he was 2nd at Mosport, crashed badly at St Jovite and with a new car re-named the Norris Industries Ti-22 was 2nd at Laguna Seca and Riverside to take 3rd place in the Can-Am Trophy with $50,800 prize money. For 1971 Jack returned to JW, sharing Rodriguez's Porsche and winning at Daytona. DCN

Orrenius, Carl

Born in 1936 the son of a Swedish manufacturer, Orrenius is now a works driver for SAAB. His first event was in a five-year-old Saab 92 when during his military service in 1956 a friend encouraged him to enter a small rally. He won his first event in 1957 and in 1960

Top, Jackie Oliver (right), with Colin Chapman. Photo: David Phipps

Left above, Jackie Oliver in the 1970 Norris Industries Ti-22. Photo: Norris Industries

Left below, Carl Orrenius (right), with Lars Persson. Photo: Saab

Below, Mike Parkes, 1969. Photo: Autosport

Right below, Mike Parkes drives the Fry-Climax at Silverstone, 1959. Photo: Bruce Edwards

he drove in his first overseas rally, when he came 2nd overall in the Tulip Rally. After that first taste of success he rallied less often until in 1966 he started again and was offered a works Saab for the Swedish Rally where he helped that make win the team prize.

In 1967 he won his class in the Swedish Championship. Abroad he won the Norwegian Winter Rally, finished 3rd in the Scottish Rally and 4th in the Gulf London Rally. The following year he won the Norwegian event again, came 3rd in the Gulf and was an excellent 2nd in the RAC Rally. In 1969 he won the Finnish Hankirallyt —unsual—for a non-Finn, and came 3rd in the Austrian Alpine and 2nd once again in the RAC Rally. JD

Parkes, Michael Johnson

This British driver is the elder son of John Joseph Parkes, Chairman and Managing Director of Alvis Ltd, and was born in Richmond, Surrey on 24 September 1931. He was educated at Haileybury College, where Stirling Moss was two years his senior, and joined the Rootes Group as a trainee when he left in 1949.

Parkes' racing début was in 1952, driving a 1933 MG PB at Silverstone. After four seasons with MG and Frazer Nash cars he bought a Lotus 11 in 1957, and was works team reserve driver at Le Mans. He helped David Fry build and develop the Fry-Climax rear-engined Formula 2 car for Stuart Lewis-Evans in 1958, and after the latter's death Parkes raced the car with some success.

In 1961 Parkes beat Moss in a Ferrari 250GT at Snetterton and Goodwood, attracting Ferrari's attention and being given a trial drive at the Le Mans test weekend. He lapped faster than the works drivers and drove a 3-litre TR with Mairesse in the 24 Hours, finishing 2nd. Parkes also raced Formula Juniors Geminis and altogether had fourteen wins and eight 2nds that season, including six victories in six races one weekend. In 1962 he drove for Equipe Endeavour and Maranello Concessionaires and made his first Formula I appearance in a Bowmaker Cooper at Mallory Park, finishing 4th.

Parkes left Rootes at the end of the year, joining Ferrari as a development engineer and reserve driver, and was 3rd at Le Mans (with Maglioli) and 2nd in the TT and Coppa Inter-Europa. In 1964 Parkes won the Sebring 12 Hours (with Maglioli again) and the Spa GP. He was 2nd at the Nürburgring and underlined his prowess as a long-distance specialist. He crashed while testing to cut short his season, but in 1965 won the Monza 1,000 kilometres for Ferrari and was 2nd at the Nürburgring (both with Guichet) and Reims (with Surtees). In 1966

Parkes joined Scarfiotti in the 3-litre V-12 cars: a special chassis being built to accomodate his 6ft 4in frame. He debuted at Reims in the French GP and finished an excellent 2nd, repeating the performance at Monza to make a Ferrari one-two in the Italian GP. He won the Monza 1,000 kilometres with Surtees, the Spa 1,000 kilometres with Scarfiotti and the Paris 1,000 kilometres with Piper, and began 1967 with high hopes. He was 2nd with Scarfiotti at Daytona, Monza and Le Mans, and 5th with his 1966 car in the Dutch GP. But at Spa he crashed badly on the opening lap of the Belgian GP and was taken to hospital with severe leg injuries.

Mike Parkes recovered and continued his duties as development engineer although his racing career seemed finished. However, he returned to co-drive Piper's Lola GT with Attwood in the 1969 Paris 1,000 kilometres and slowly played himself back into driving regularly. He was 4th at Daytona (with Sam Posey) in a Ferrari 312P early in 1970 and then 6th at Sebring (with Parsons) in the same machine. Driving for Filipinetti he was placed 6th in the Targa and 4th at Nürburgring and continued with the Swiss team in 1971. DCN

Parnell, Reginald

Born in 1911 and maturing through years of experience from a rather wild young driver in the mid-1930s to a father-figure in British racing in the mid-1950s, Reg Parnell—or 'Uncle Reg' to the many who valued his ready help and advice—was one of the most popular British drivers in the 1946–56 period. Stocky, fair-haired and cheerful, he came from Derby, and first raced at nearby Donington Park road circuit. In 1935 he drove a very fast offset single-seater 1,087cc MG Magnette, and scored victories at Donington and Brooklands.

In 1939, Parnell acquired the big 4·9-litre Bugatti-engined BHW single-seater, a car which taught him a lot, and with which he practically cornered Donington club races. He also began development of a new 2-stage blown 1·5-litre racing car with air strut suspension and De Dion rear axle, called the Challenger. After World War 2 the Challenger was fitted with a Delage engine and sold, while Reg himself raced the ex-Johnny Wakefield 1939 4CL Maserati.

Early in 1947 he took the original 1934 ERA to Sweden, winning both races at Rommehed and Vallentuna; next he won the Jersey Road Race with the Maserati and was 3rd at Nîmes. He then bought one of the E-type ERAs, and looked like winning at Ulster when the De Dion tube broke. The award of the BRDC Gold Star to Parnell for 1947 came as some compensation. In 1948 he drove the Maserati and the E-type, his best result being 3rd at Jersey and at Zandvoort in the former. Then he sold the E-type and secured a 4CLT/48 'San Remo' Maserati, which he drove to 5th place in the Italian GP, then started a precedent by winning at the first Goodwood meeting. He won so regularly at the Sussex track thereafter that he was dubbed 'The Emperor of Goodwood'. In the Penya Rhin GP he ran a strong 2nd to Villoresi's works car, and his overall 1948 performances again won him the BRDC Gold Star.

That San Remo Maserati worked extremely hard during the next few years. It gained him seven more Goodwood victories, heat wins at Zandvoort in 1949 and at Silverstone in 1950, a first at Douglas, Isle of Man, and diverse placings elsewhere. By then his services were sought by others. Alfa Romeo offered him their fourth car for the 1950 GP of Europe at Silverstone; he accepted with delight and came a model 3rd. Aston Martin signed

Above, Reg Parnell at Goodwood, 1954. *Photo: Central Press Photos*

Right above, Reg Parnell after his final victory at Ardmore in 1957. On his left, Peter Whitehead. *Photo: Associated Press*

Chuck Parsons. *Photo: Indianapolis Motor Speedway*

him on and he won the 3-litre class of the 1950 TT for them. He gained the trouble-fraught BRM organization their first victories, two on one wet day, at Goodwood in 1950, and a hard-won 5th in an oven-hot car in the 1951 British GP. And he drove Vandervell's 4·5-litre Thinwall Ferrari; 'won' the sensational 1951 International Trophy race at Silverstone which was stopped by an incredibly savage storm; ran 2nd to Farina's works Alfa 158 both at Dundrod and Goodwood; won at Winfield, Scotland; and was 4th in the French GP the same year.

Parnell's 1952 season was punctuated by class victories at Silverstone and Boreham with Aston Martins, but in the Goodwood Nine Hours his car caught fire while re-fuelling; team manager John Wyer was put in hospital with burns, so Parnell took over team direction and clinched an Aston Martin victory. More 1sts, a 2nd place at Sebring with George Abecassis, a 2nd in the TT with Eric Thompson came in 1953. In 1954 Parnell also raced a private 2·5-litre F1 Ferrari, winning at Goodwood, Snetterton and Crystal Palace. It was the mixture as before in 1955, with a further spate of Parnell/Aston Martin wins, notably in the *Daily Express* Silverstone, the *Daily Herald* Oulton Park, and Charterhall.

Late that year he went to New Zealand with a new single-seater Aston Martin, but a 2nd place at Dunedin was his sole reward. Back in Europe, now aged 45, the indefatigable Parnell won his heat and his class in the 1956 British Empire Trophy race, and was 3rd in the Spa sports car GP. He scored a final victory in the 1957 New Zealand GP at Ardmore, then retired to become Aston Martin's team manager, a task which he performed so effectively that the make scored many more victories, culminating in the 1959 World Sports Car Championship. On their withdrawal from racing in 1960, Parnell managed the Yeoman Credit and then the Bowmaker F1 teams, with John Surtees and Roy Salvadori among his drivers. It was cruel that 'Uncle Reg', epitome of sturdiness and endurance, should have died suddenly after an operation in January 1964, when he was only 53. His son Tim has carried the name Parnell on in racing, and is currently team manager for BRM. CP

Parsons, Charles

'Chuck' Parsons was born in the Blue Ridge mountains of Kentucky in 1927. A childhood accident left him with a pronounced limp. In 1947 he moved to Carmel, Calif. After watching the final meet at Pebble Beach in 1956, he became interested in motor racing and began by driving an Austin-Healey. After racing a Porsche, 'Birdcage' Maserati, Lotus 23B twin-cam and a Cobra, Chuck attracted national attention in 1965 driving a Mk 10 Genie-Chevrolet. With sponsorship help from auto dealer John Hilton, Parsons won the 1966, eight-race, US Road Racing championship, switching from the Genie to a McLaren-Chevrolet late in the season. He won that year's final USRRC, the gruelling Road America 500, without relief. Teamed with Mark Donohue in Roger Penske's Lola-Coupé, Parsons won the 1969 Daytona 24 Hours, in spite of spending over two hours in the pits.

Parsons' 1969 Can-Am record shows one 2nd; three 3rds; three 5ths; one 6th and one 7th; the most consistent of all American drivers, and good for $77,000 for 3rd overall in the eleven-race series. In 1970 Parsons' was placed 3rd in the Continental Formula A series opener at Riverside; his best Can-Am finish was a 4th at Mid-Ohio and he finished 6th in the Sebring 12 Hours co-driving a Ferrari 312P with Mike Parkes. ARB

Parsons, John

Johnnie Parsons, born in 1918, who was one of the outstanding young American drivers to gain national recognition following World War 2, started his racing career on the midget circuit in California and moved up to the AAA big car championship division late in the 1948 season.

In 1949, which was his first full year in such top-flight competition, he won the opening event on the schedule at Arlington Downs, Tex.; finished 2nd to Bill Holland at Indianapolis; and led the field home in four events on other tracks to secure the national driving title.

In his second Indianapolis race one year later, he ran at the head of the pack most of the way and won the rain-shortened event by averaging 124·002mph (199·603kph) for the 345 miles (555·2kph) completed before officials red-flagged the participants because of a wet track. Parsons also was in the starting line-up at Indianapolis for each of the next eight 500 events before retiring as a driver prior to the 1959 event. He finished 10th in 1952, 4th in 1956 and 12th in 1958, but was put out by mechanical trouble on five occasions.

His record on tracks other than Indianapolis shows a total of 10 victories in races of 100 miles or more.

Following his retirement as an active driver, Parsons worked for several years as a member of the Champion Spark Plug Company's highway safety team and also promoted midget races for two seasons in California, where he now makes his home. AB

Patrick, Merlin

'Scooter' Patrick of Manhattan Beach, Calif., was born in 1932 and began racing in a Mercedes 300SL in 1956. Patrick first drove a Porsche at Palm Springs in 1959 and was soon asked to race for the California Porsche agent, Otto Zipper. He drove a Porsche 906 to the under 2-litre US Road Racing Championship in 1966 and tied with Joe Buzzetta for the USRRC under 2-litre title in 1967. In 1968 Patrick won the Sports Car Club of America 'B' modified crown in a Porsche 911H and in 1969 drove an Alfa Romeo Type 33 to capture again the SCCA 'B' modified championship. In 1967 Patrick and Gerhard Mitter drove a works Porsche 910 prototype to 3rd overall and 1st under 2 litres in the Sebring 12 Hours, then in 1968 Patrick joined Joe Buzzetta as a member of the Porsche team at Le Mans. ARB

Pearson, David G.

This American driver, born in 1934, was Grand National

Above, Roger Penske. Photo: Professionals in Motion Inc

Right above, Roger Penske in the Zerex Special, 1962. Photo: Al Bochroch

Henri Pescarolo. Photo: Doug Nye Collection
David Pearson. Photo: Ford Motor Company

champion in 1966, 1968 and 1969; Lee Petty was the only other NASCAR driver who achieved the championship three times. Pearson's career total of 58 GN victories is second only to Richard Petty's 119. Driving Fords for Holman-Moody, Pearson won $118,842 in 1968 and $183,700 in 1969, contributing substantially to the Ford Motor Co's victories in the 1968 and 1969 GN munufacturers' championship. ARB

Penske, Roger

Penske, born in 1937, graduated from Lehigh University and the Sports Car Club of America's Marlboro Driving School in the spring of 1958. After owning MG's, Jaguars and Corvettes, Penske bought a Porsche from Bob Holbert and soon attracted national attention. He won the national SCCA 'F' Sports racing title in 1960 and in 1961 teamed with Bob Holbert to earn the Sebring Index of Performance, finishing 5th overall. One of America's first sports car drivers to acquire substantial industry support, Penske won the 1961, 1962 and 1963 'D' sports racing category in cars known as 'Telar' and 'Zerex Specials': i.e. a Birdcage Maserati, Cooper Monaco and a Formula 1 Cooper which Penske rebuilt into a controversial but winning sports car. In 1962 he won Riverside and Laguna Seca and in 1963 Penske and Augie Pabst captured the GT class at Sebring in a Ferrari. In 1964 Roger joined Jim Hall, bringing a Chaparral home 2nd at the Riverside International Raceway and winning Laguna Seca. Penske left his job as sales engineer in 1964 to become a Philadelphia automobile dealer.

In 1966 Penske retained Mark Donohue to drive his Lola-Chevrolet, finishing 2nd in the initial Can-Am series. Penske's Group 7 Lola and McLaren Chevrolets were driven to US Road Racing Championships by Mark Donohue in 1967 and 1968. Besides his Can-Am programme, in 1967 Penske entered Chevrolet Camaros in the Trans-Am sedan championship. In 1968 Donohue drove Penske McLaren-Chevrolets to 3rd in the Can-Am series. Although for three years the highest standing US Can-Am entry, in 1969 Penske withdrew from the Group 7 series to concentrate on Trans-Am sedans and Indianapolis 500. In February 1969 Donohue and Chuck Parsons won the Daytona 24 hours in Penske's Lola coupé. Penske Camaros, with Donohue registering most of the victories, won Trans-Am championships for Chevrolet Division of General Motors in 1968 and

969. In 1970, Penske, a Chevrolet dealer, switched to American Motors Trans-Am Javelins, driven by Mark Donohue and Peter Revson.

Penske's 1969 Speedway debut saw Mark Donohue qualify Penske's 4wd Offenhauser-powered Lola 4th and finished 7th. The highpoint of the 1970 season was the 2nd place by the Penske-entered, Donohue-driven Ford-powered Sunoco Special at Indianapolis.

Known for his attention to detail and meticulous preparation, Penske is referred to as America's Alfred Neubauer. ARB

Pescarolo, Henri

Pescarolo is the son of one of France's leading physicians, and was born on 25 September 1942. He studied medicine, but was torn between his vocation and his enthusiasm for motor racing. Pescarolo learned basic race driving at the AGACI school, after navigating for his father in an amateur rally for doctors in 1964. He drove a Lotus in the Ford Jeunesse scheme to foster young French drivers, and dominated his class.

Matra Sports were really getting under way at that time, and the bearded young medical student was offered third place in their F3 team, with Beltoise and Jassaud. But it was to be a season of disappointment, for his car was not ready until Clermont in June, and then Beltoise raced it. 'Pesca's' first race was in the Coupe du Salon at Montlhéry, but the car was badly prepared, and the throttle linkage broke. The 1967 season saw Pescarolo became *the* man to beat in Formula 3, and he started very well by leading all the established stars home at Monaco, winning from Jaussaud and Bell. His driving was fast and smooth, and he scored four more major victories, two 2nds and two 3rds in Formula 3, backing them with a win at Montlhéry in the Matra-Ford coupé.

Matra promoted him to the F2 team in 1968, and he put up several excellent performances in support of Beltoise, winning at Albi and coming 2nd five times and 3rd once in major internationals. He also stirred French hearts at Le Mans, forcing the Matra V-12 coupé he was sharing with Servoz-Gavin up into 2nd place at one point before it failed near the end of the race.

The 1969 season started badly when he crashed in the Matra 640 V-12 prototype coupé on the Mulsanne Straight at Le Mans during private high-speed testing in April. Henri escaped but suffered serious injuries which laid him low for most of the season. He was back in the cockpit in August, however, and won the Formula 2 class in the German GP after a really good drive. He was scarred and battered, and despite his even temperament and innate skill he seemed to have lost his old touch. In October that year he shared the Matra 650 G6 car with Beltoise to score a popular home win in the Paris 1,000 kilometres, and ended a near-disastrous season on a high note. Early in 1970 he and Beltoise shared the winning Matra in the Buenos Aires 1,000 kilometres, and Pescarolo moved into Formula 1 as number two driver of the Matra-Simca V-12s but was not very successful. For 1971 he drove F1/F2 Marches for Frank Williams. DCN

Petillo, Kelly

Born in 1902, Petillo, a California truck driver, gained his early racing experience on the smaller tracks in that area and finished 12th on his first Indianapolis 500 appearance in 1932.

Two years later he managed to lead the field for the

Above, Kay Petre with the supercharged Austin. *Photo: Fox Photos Ltd*

Below, Kelly Petillo. *Photo: Ted Wilson*

Lee Petty. *Photo: Plymouth*

first six laps of the 500 and finished 11th; and he reached the pinnacle of his career in 1935 by winning at Indianapolis and also capturing the AAA National driving championship with additional victories to his credit in 100-mile events at St Paul, Minn., and Langhorne, Pa. In the late stages of the Indianapolis race, Wilbur Shaw was closing fast and Petillo's victory definitely was in serious jeopardy with 23 laps remaining, but a sudden shower caused officials to display the yellow flag making it mandatory for all contestants to maintain their relative positions. Despite this opportunity to complete the race at reduced speed, Petillo still averaged 106·240mph (170·960kph) for a new race record.

Petillo failed to finish any of his four subsequent Indy races, however, and was among the veteran drivers who did not resume their racing careers after the four-year interruption during World War 2. He died in 1970. AB

Petre, Kay

Little Kay Petre, dark-haired and attractive, was one of Brooklands' idols. She began racing quietly in sports cars but showed real talent and graduated to fast cars. She drove an ERA in a long-distance race, was taken into the Austin team to drive their sv single-seater, but her most courageous feat was racing the old 10·5-litre V-12 Delage. In this car she was vanquished by only one other lady driver (Gwenda Hawkes) and by a very narrow margin, for Mrs Petre lapped Brooklands at 134·75mph (216·78kph) in 1935. WB

Petty, Lee

Lee Petty of Randleman, N.C., is the patriarch of the premier family of stock car racing. He was born in 1915 and before retiring in 1963 he had won a total of 54 NASCAR Grand Nationals, including the first Daytona 500 in 1959, and, with David Pearson, is a record three-time winner of the NASCAR Grand National driving championship. The senior Petty manages a factory-backed team of Petty-Blue Plymouths, his son Maurice is crew-chief, and his son Richard and, in 1970, Pete Hamilton, were the drivers. Hamilton, a former NASCAR 'Rookie of the Year' earned $131,406 in 1970, his Petty-Plymouth winning the Daytona 500 and two Grand Nationals at Talladega. ARB

Petty, Richard L.

Born in 1937, the son of former stock car champion Lee Petty, Richard began racing in 1958 and by the end of 1970 had reached a record career total of 119 NASCAR Grand Nationals. He has twice (1964 and 1967) been Grand National champion; captured the Daytona 500 in 1964 and 1966; won a record 27 GNs in one season and, in 1969, became the only NASCAR regular to have won the Riverside 500 stock car road race. Richard Petty was NASCAR top money winner in 1970, earning $138,969 from 18 victories in 40 starts. ARB

Pietsch, Paul

Starting his racing career in 1932 when 21 years old with an ex-von Morgen 2·3-litre Type 35B Bugatti, German amateur driver Paul Pietsch from Neustadt in the Black Forest made third fastest time in only his second event, the Kesselberg hill-climb. In his fourth, the Würgau climb, he was 2nd, and then he took the plunge and ran in the German GP at the Nürburgring. A ruptured radiator put him out on the opening lap, but he took over Lewy's similar Bugatti, only to overturn it on the South Curve after climbing from 9th to 5th place.

Undaunted, Pietsch continued hill-climbing, scoring two victories at Riesengebirge and Litoměřice (Leitmeritz), and then he acquired a 2·3-litre 'Monza' Alfa Romeo for 1933.

This brought him many successes, including an ice race in Sweden and numerous German hill-climbs. He went road racing beyond Germany to Tunis, North Africa, Italy, France and Czechoslovakia. His successes in 1933 and 1934 culminated in an offer to drive for Auto Union in 1935. Pietsch accepted, coming 6th in his first race with the unwieldy 16-cylinder rear-engined car, the Eifelrennen. His best placing for Auto Union was 3rd with Rosemeyer in the 1935 Italian GP, and he did not race again until 1937, on his own behalf with a white-painted 3·7 Maserati, which was far too slow for the opposition.

Pietsch left the ultra-expensive, tense, GP world for voiturette racing with a works-supported 1·5-litre Maserati in 1938. He won his heat at de Berne but retired in the final, and was 2nd at Pescara. In 1939 he won the 1,500cc class of the Vienna hill-climb, and was 2nd in class on the Grossglockner, but his greatest feat that attenuated season was in nearly winning the German GP with a works 3-litre 8CTF Maserati. With Lang's retirement on lap 2 Pietsch moved into the lead, only to suffer plug and brake troubles which pushed him back to 3rd place at the finish.

World War 2 over, Pietsch set about establishing a new German motoring journal, *Das Auto, Motor und Sport,* and a publishing business, but found time to join in the German racing renaissance in the next few years, securing German National Championships in 1950 and 1951 with Veritas and Maserati cars. In 1951 he was honoured by Alfa Romeo in being offered the wheel of a Type 159 GP car for the German GP. He had scarcely two laps' practice with the very fast car, but lay well up in the race until he spun, and crashed. In his last season, 1952, he drove Veritas sports and racing cars, winning a sports car event at the Nürburgring. After a serious accident at the AVUS, Pietsch retired, and since then has devoted his time to his publishing concern, Motor-buch Verlag of Stuttgart. CP

Piot, Jean-François

Perhaps the only Frenchman ever to drive regularly for a British works team, Jean-François Piot was born in 1938 and is now a member of the Ford rally team. His occupation is that of a garage owner in Paris and for many years he ran a Renault agency. With the idea of furthering his own sales he started rallying in 1962 with a Renault Dauphine and later changed to a Gordini R8 and an Alpine 1100 as these cars became available. By 1967, his successes in French rallies had led to a regular works drive for Renault: with Jean Vinatier and Gerard Larrousse he became one of the 'three musketeers' who were so successful in the blue cars of Renault. In 1967, he finished 7th overall in the Monte Carlo and then went to Sweden, where he astonished the locals by finishing 11th, a feat equalled by few non-Scandinavians. He then won the San Remo Rally and the Three Cities Rally, and came in 7th in the Danube Rally which put him 2nd overall in the European Championship.

The next year, Renault started campaigning with the Alpine outside France and Piot came 2nd in Spain, 3rd in Germany and 5th in Czechoslovakia—all in a car which at that time was very fragile. For 1969, he was signed by Ford and rewarded them by finishing 4th in the Monte Carlo and winning the Touring car category

Paul Pietsch. *Photo: Cyril Posthumus Collection*

Jean-Francois Piot. *Photo: John Davenport Collection*

David Piper. *Photo: Porsche*

with an Escort T/C. He drove an Escort mainly in French rallies and won the Criterium de Touraine and the Criterium Jean Behra, but could only manage 6th overall in the French Championship. However, towards the end of the year, Ford Germany gave him a Capri to drive and he finished 6th in the Tour de France and an excellent 3rd in the Tour de Corse. JD

Piper, David

Born in 1931, David Piper is an independent entrant who has conducted his racing as a successful business for many years, and became one of the most experienced and widely-travelled of all drivers. On one of his earliest trips abroad, in 1955, he won the Leinster Trophy in Ireland in a Lotus 6, and the following year he and Bob Hicks raced a pair of Lotus 11s on the Continent, driving the cars on the road with their tools, baggage and spares in the passenger seats, and taking part in many events. By 1958 Piper was living as a professional racing driver, and in 1960 he went to the Tasman Series, where he was 2nd to Jack Brabham in the Wigram Trophy, driving a F2 Lotus 16. In 1961 he followed a full Continental FJ season with a Lotus 20, but his real *forte* was long-distance sports car racing, and in 1962 he bought a Ferrari GTO with which he won the Kyalami 9-Hours. He has since won this race five times, with Ferrari and (in 1969) Porsche cars. From 1964 to 1969 he drove Ferrari sports cars in a wide variety of events in Europe, America and Africa, winning the 1965 Angola GP and 1966 Paris 1,000 kilometres race and achieving several other good placings. This long Ferrari association led to occasional works drives; in 1969 he shared the 312P with Pedro Rodriguez to finish 2nd at Spa, and was also in the works team at Le Mans. Meanwhile he had bought a Lola-Chevrolet as there was no comparable Ferrari available. Alain de Cadenet teamed him with Chris Craft in his Porsche 908 for a number of races, and later in 1969 Piper became one of the first private entrants to run a Porsche 917. In mid-1970 David crashed while filming with actor Steve MacQueen at Le Mans. As a result of this accident he subsequently lost a leg, but continued as an entrant. DCN

Porsche, Ferdinand

Ferdinand Porsche will go down to history as the man who created the two outstanding rear-engined cars of the 1930s: the Grand Prix Auto Union and the Volkswagen. He was, however, of the generation of Ettore Bugatti and Laurence Pomeroy the elder, having been born in Reichenberg (now Liberec), Northern Bohemia, in 1875. The son of a tinsmith, he was experimenting with electricity by the time he was fifteen, and in 1893 he was apprenticed to the Bela Egger company in Vienna, rising to headship of the test department by 1897. His first contact with the new locomotion came when he was engaged by the coachbuilder Jacob Lohner to design electric cars. The Lohner-Porsche system involved the use of hub-mounted electric motors, initially at the front, though 4-wheel drive was also tried, without much success. Porsche himself won the 1900 Semmering hill-climb on a curious tandem-seated car with torpedo nose. Until 1918 he continued to work on this system, trying petrol-electric vehicles based on Panhard and Mercedes chassis in 1902. The latter in 28hp form was quite fast, winning the 1,000kg class at Exelberg, but it was nearly 3 minutes slower up La Turbie than conventional gear-driven cars, and though Porsche was still toying with a *mixte* racer as late as 1907, his move to Austro- (Österreichisches) Daimler at Wiener-Neustadt two years previously had channelled his interests towards serious racing.

In 1910, he designed the famous 5·7-litre Prince Henry with its 86bhp ohc 4-cylinder engine. The chain drive was hardly progressive, and the lubrication system crude, but Porsche had devoted himself meticulously to the evolution of a rally winner: such details as headlamp brackets and wing retaining nuts were streamlined in to match Ernest Neumann-Neander's wind-cheating tulip-shaped bodywork, and Porsche insisted on procuring supplies of German petrol for preliminary tests in Austria.

The new cars swept the board, the designer (who was accompanied by his wife) winning the premier award. Some 200 of this model were sold between 1911 and 1914, though for subsequent Austrian Alpine Trials Porsche favoured smaller and simpler sv machines, 2·2-litre engines being used in 1911, and 3·6-litre units in 1912. On both occasions Porsche (in the best Austro-German tradition) captained his team, collecting the team prize in the former year. Austro-Daimler failed to win it in 1912, but one of the four cars to come through without loss of marks was Porsche's.

At this juncture the firm's increasing preoccupation with aero-engines and commercial vehicles caused the abandonment of competition work, though immediately after World War 1 Porsche was back with the ADV-type, an advanced 4·4-litre ohc six in which light alloys were liberally used. This one was no sports car, but the little 1,100cc 4-cylinder Sascha of 1922 was a full-blooded competition machine with front-wheel brakes, 4-speed gearbox and cantilever rear springing, which proved capable of 87mph (140kph) and had an excellent season on the circuits. Unfortunately for Porsche, Camillo Castiglioni, who now controlled the destinies of Austro-Daimler, objected to the high cost of a racing programme and Porsche's predilection for interesting new models (yet another 2·5-litre ohc six was on the stocks), and by 1923 both the racing voiturette and its designer had been dropped.

Porsche's next move in that strange game of musical chairs affected by German designers took him to Mercedes, where he perfected the 2-litre 4-cylinder Targa Florio cars of 1924, and evolved an interesting 2-litre dohc straight-8 GP machine with dry-sump lubrication and a crankshaft with nine roller bearings. There was mention of 8,000rpm, but Porsche was still considered mainly as an engine man, and though the eights eventually won at the AVUS and Solitude in 1926, their handling was terrible. The same also went for the first of the big supercharged ohc sporting sixes he evolved for Mercedes, the 6,240cc Model K of 1925, but its successors were far better, despite immense weight and brakes that never matched up to the rest of the car. The 6·8-litre Model S offered 180bhp with blower engaged by 1927, and the legendary 7,069cc SS of 1928 had a long and distinguished competition record. This unit in its fiercest form, as fitted to the short and specially lightened SSKL sports-racing cars, developed around 300bhp and was still racing to good purpose in 1931, though by this time Porsche had moved on once more.

Alongside the big supercharged cars Daimler-Benz were developing a line of stodgy sv sixes and eights which were not to Porsche's liking, though just before his departure from that company in 1929 he had propounded a GP car with 3-litre dohc straight-8 engine, rear-axle gearbox, and swing-axle rear suspension.

Ferdinand Porsche (Austro-Daimler) in the the 1909 Prince Henry Trial. *Photo: Neubauer Collection*

There followed a second spell in Vienna with Steyr, for which firm he evolved an excellent medium-powered light-alloy push-rod 6-cylinder engine and a magnificent companion straight-8. Neither was sporting in character, and in any case after the Austrian bank crash Steyr had no money to spend on an all-out development programme. He therefore decided to go free-lance, and by the end of 1930 he had set up a design bureau in Stuttgart.

As yet the Porsche Bureau was unable to devote much of its energies to sports or racing cars: such things were hardly viable in the depths of the Depression, and between 1931 and 1933 he was working on a design which was eventually to bear fruit as the KdF or Volkswagen in 1938. Initial studies were conducted for the Zündapp motorcycle firm, but they dropped out when

Ferdinand Porsche (right) with Alfred Neubauer and his mechanic; 1924 Targa Florio. *Photo: T. A. S. O. Mathieson Collection*

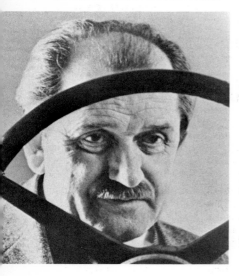

Ferdinand Porsche's best-known design of the 1920s was the S-series Mercedes-Benz. This is an SSK at Phoenix Park. *Photo: Montagu Motor Museum*

Ferdinand Porsche, c 1950. *Photo: Porsche*

Marquis de Portago (right), 1957 Cuban GP. *Photo: Autosport*

strous 6 × 4 streamliner with 44-litre inverted V-12 aero-engine with which Daimler-Benz were planning an attack on the World Land Speed Record. The car still exists in the factory museum at Stuttgart.

By VE-Day Porsche was operating from Gmünd in Austria, but before the end of 1945 he had been imprisoned by the French, and was not released until 1947, though while in captivity in France he had advised on the new 4CV Renault. His bureau, however, was still very active under the direction of his son Ferry, and was retained by Piero Dusio's Cisitalia firm to evolve a 4 × 4 GP car with flat-12 engine. This was the work of Ferry Porsche, Hruschka, Rabe and Carlo Abarth, thought it had the older Porsche's blessing. The same was true of the first of the VW-based Porsche sports cars which left Gmünd in 1948, even if these derived directly from his pre-war efforts. By this time Porsche was a sick man, though he lived to see the firm which bore his name move back to Stuttgart. When he celebrated his 75th birthday in September 1950 some 300 Porsches had been made and sold, and owners from all over Germany gathered to do homage to the veteran designer. He suffered a stroke in 1951, and died in January 1952, weakened by his two years of captivity. In his funeral oration the West German Minister of Transport said: 'We are burying with him the heroic epoch of the motor car'—but in fact the only make to bear his name has enjoyed a more successful competition record than any of the models he actually designed. MCS

Portago, Alfonso Cabeza de Vaca de

The 17th Marquis de Portago and Count of Mejorada, born in 1928, was a Spanish aristocrat who became a great all-round sportsman. As a horseman he rode twice in the British Grand National at Aintree and won the French amateur jockey championship three times. He was an Olympic class bobsleigher (breaking the Cresta Run record), an Olympic class swimmer, a crack shot and a most accomplished polo player.

'Fon' began motor racing with a private black and yellow Ferrari sports in 1954, winning at Metz and in the Governor's Trophy at Nassau. In 1955 he bought his way into the Ferrari team, and quickly proved he had ability to back his wealth. He won again in the Bahamas, beating Phil Hill, and was 2nd to Fangio's Maserati in the 213-mile (342·8km) Venezuelan GP at Caracas. The following year he won the Tour de France (with Nelson, the friend who taught him bobsleighing), beat Hill's sister car again at Oporto, and was 2nd in the Swedish GP (with Hawthorn and Hamilton) and at Karlskoga (behind Carlsson's Ferrari). He was also 3rd in the Nürburgring 1,000 Kilometres (with Hill and Gendebien), and in the Nassau Trophy.

The Commendatore also gave him some GP drives, and after Collins had crashed his own car in the 1956 British GP, he took over de Portago's to achieve a shared 2nd place. Early in 1957 de Portago shared with Gonzales to take 5th place in the Argentine GP and was 3rd (with Collins and Castelotti) in the Buenos Aires 1,000 kilometres. Back in Europe he won the Coupe de Vitesse at Montlhéry in a sports Ferrari, and then took part in the Mille Miglia sharing his big Ferrari with Nelson. The pair were lying 3rd 120km from the finish when the car careered into the roadside spectators, killing both occupants and ten bystanders. It is probable that a tyre burst, but this accident led the Italian government to ban the Mille Miglia, and cost the life of a great all-rounder. DCN

their 2-wheeler sales started to pick up, so Porsche then worked in conjunction with NSU. He also found time to design some advanced touring cars for Wanderer of Chemnitz, using a development of the 6-cylinder Type XXX Steyr engine, and was even invited to the USSR in 1932 with the object of settling there and evolving a people's car project. Porsche, however, declined. More important, his work for Zündapp and NSU brought him into the forefront of chassis design through the creation of an efficient system of torsion-bar suspension. During the 1930s the Porsche Bureau worked for German, French, Swedish, Austrian and Italian manufacturers, and Porsche's trailing-arm ifs was adopted on later versions of the 1·5-litre ERA racing voiturettes in Britain.

In 1933 came the debut of the P-wagen, a vehicle sponsored by the Auto Union concern which embraced Porsche's former client Wanderer as well as Audi, DKW and Horch. This advanced aerodynamic GP car was designed round the 750kg formula due to come into force in 1934, and featured all-round independent springing, a rear-mounted V-16 engine and 5-speed gearbox, a tubular ladder-type frame, and fuel tanks located between power unit and driver, thus ensuring that weight distribution was unaffected by the amount of fuel on board. This was in effect an anticipation of 1960s GP practice, but the result was exceedingly tricky to drive, and only the former racing motorcyclist Bernd Rosemeyer ever truly mastered it. Porsche's first GP Auto Unions ran to 4·4-litres and 295bhp, but by the time the Formula had worked itself out he was getting 520bhp from 6·1-litres. He remained as technical chief of Auto Union's racing department until the end of 1937, and his attention to detail prevented the emergence of a *Rennleiter* or racing manager of the stamp of Alfred Neubauer in the Auto Union camp. Thereafter he was increasingly preoccupied with work on the Volkswagen, and the later 3-litre Auto Unions were designed by Eberan von Eberhorst. Porsche, however, found time to produce two vastly different competition cars in 1939. The first of these was an aerodynamic coupé version of the VW using a 40bhp 1·5-litre air-cooled flat-4 engine; three prototypes were built for the Berlin–Rome Rally scheduled for September, but war intervened. World War 2 also interfered with his second project, a mon-

Posey, Samuel

Sam Posey was born in New York in 1944. A graduate of the Rhode Island School of Design, Posey's first race was in Formula Vee in 1965 at Lime Rock near his Sharon, Conn., home. Sam finished 3rd in the 1967 US Road Racing Championship and in 1969 won Formula A races at Laguna Seca and Lime Rock, finishing 3rd in the thirteen-race Continental series. Substituting for Peter Revson, who was in Indianapolis, Posey won the Lime Rock Trans-Am in a Shelby Ford-Mustang. He also ran Indy cars on road courses in 1969, driving Andy Granatelli's 4wd Plymouth to a 5th at Indianapolis Raceway Park and 3rd at Kent. In 1970 Posey shared the 4th place Ferrari 512 in the Daytona 24 Hours with Mike Parkes and finished 4th, in a Ferrari, at Le Mans with Ronnie Bucknum. Posey drove a factory-backed Dodge Challenger in the Trans-Am series in which Dodge finished third, behind Mustang and Javelin. ARB

Sam Posey. Photo: Al Bochroch Collection

Rathmann, Richard ('Jim')

This American racing driver, unwilling to wait until reaching the required age of 21 years before driving in his first race (he was born in 1928), borrowed the birth certificate of his brother Jim in 1946 to convince officials of his eligibility; and he has operated under Jim's name in all of his competition, business and social activities since that time. When the older of the Rathmann brothers also became interested in racing a few years later, he registered as Dick Rathmann and the two have proceeded with their careers on that basis.

'Jim' by far the more successful of the brothers, gained his early experience with hot rods and modified stock cars before making his first appearance at Indianapolis in 1949. He drove at Indy in 14 of the next 15 races, leading the field at some stage of six of the events and finishing second three times before winning in 1960 with a record-breaking average speed of 138·767mph (223·311kph) in the Offenhauser-powered Ken-Paul Special. He was also runner-up for the national driving championship in 1957.

In his only international appearance, Rathmann won the 500-mile Race of Two Worlds at Monza in 1958 at the wheel of the Offenhauser-powered Zink Leader Card Special by averaging 166·722mph (268·333kph) to surpass Jimmy Bryan's 1957 record on the same track by more than 6mph.

Rathmann became a successful Cadillac-Chevrolet dealer at Melbourne, Fla., in 1961 and he has devoted all of his attention to that business since retiring as a race driver after the 1963 Indy event, in which he finished 5th. AB

'Jim' Rathmann. Photo: Indianapolis Motor Speedway.

Redman, Brian

Born in 1937 at Burnley, Lancashire, Brian Redman had his first motor race at Rufforth in 1959 in an unlikely sounding supercharged Morris Minor Traveller. Between 1959 and 1965 he competed widely in the lower echelons of motor sport, winning over 50 awards in races, sprints, hill-climbs and rallies. In 1965 he drove an E-type Jaguar for Charles Bridges, scoring 13 wins out of 15 starts, and the next year Bridges bought a Lola-Chevrolet T70 Group 7 car with which Redman put up some fine performances. He drove an F2 Lola-Cosworth during the 1967 season, but most of his successes were with sports cars. He was 6th in the Spa 1,000 Kilometres with Peter Sutcliffe in a Ford GT40, and also 6th in the Paris 1,000 Kilometres with Richard Attwood in a Ferrari 275LM. At Kyalami in November Redman and

Brian Redman. Photo: Autosport

Jackie Ickx won the 9 Hour race in a JW Mirage, and Brian joined the JW Automotive team for 1968, also signing with Cooper for a Formula 1 drive. He had little luck with the uncompetitive Cooper-BRM V-12, although 3rd in the Spanish GP was creditable, but with the GT40s he won the BOAC 500 at Brands Hatch and the Spa 1,000 Kilometres, sharing with Ickx. He crashed in the Cooper in the Belgian GP, but recovered in time to drive in South Africa at the end of the year, and in 1969 signed with Gulf-JW. With Jo Siffert he won the BOAC 500, Spa, Monza and Nürburgring 1,000 kilometres, and Watkins Glen 6 Hours. In this excellent season he also had some successes in Sid Taylor's Lola-Chevrolet T70, and drove the prototype Chevron B16 to victory single handed in the Nürburgring 500 kilometre race.

In 1970 Brian shared a JW Porsche 917 again, winning three Championship events, and the Imola 500km. He also raced the works Chevrons, winning the 2-litre Sports Car Championship and retired to South Africa at the end of the season, where he races Chevron sports and single-seaters. DCN

Regazzoni, Gianclaudio

'Clay' Regazzoni, born in 1940, came up the hard way through the tough competition of Formula 3 and Formula 2, and finally moved into the top echelon of the sport in 1970 with some fine Formula 1 Ferrari drives.

His father runs a body shop in Mendrisio in the Italian-speaking part of Switzerland. Regazzoni junior began his competition career in 1963 with an Austin-Healey Sprite sports car. He participated in hill-climbs and minor speed events, took a race driving course at Montlhéry, and contested further minor events with a Cooper Mini in 1964. He had some success and bought an F3 De Tomaso for the 1965 season but had a lot of trouble with it. He was advised to try a Brabham by fellow Swiss Silvio Moser, and he borrowed Moser's own car to complete another course at Montlhéry.

He continued to race Brabham F3s, and was 2nd to Ernesto Brambilla's similar car at Vallelunga in 1966. Tecno were impressed and the Pederzanis invited him to join their team in 1967. He drove the forward-cockpit car in the Argentine Temporada with no success, but when the team corrected their mistakes his Tecno-Ford became extremely competitive, winning at Jarama at the end of the season and coming 2nd at Hockenheim.

In 1968 Tecno entered Formula 2 with a car very similar to their successful F3 design and Regazzoni finished 3rd at Crystal Palace for their best class result of the season. In Formula 3 he made many enemies by a do-or-die last lap effort to win the European Championship event at Hockenheim, his battered car crossing the line first with a trail of other people's wreckage behind it.

Nonetheless here was a driver of considerable ability, even though his will to win often seemed to overcome any sense of self-preservation, and in 1969 Ferrari took him on to their F2 team strength. The ancient Dinos were uncompetitive, however, and were withdrawn before the end of the season, Regazzoni returning to Tecno. In 1970 he justified their faith by giving them their first F2 win at Hockenheim, and with a new car he scored again at Ricard-Castellet. He drove the 512S sports Ferrari at Le Mans, being involved in the multiple accident which eliminated three of the Italian cars, and then made his Formula 1 debut as number two to Jackie Ickx in the Dutch GP.

Here a new Regazzoni emerged, a driver who tempered his speed with a consistency and control belying his past record. He was 4th in the Dutch GP then 4th again in the British GP at Brands Hatch. He led the Austrian GP before moving over to let Ickx through in an unusual display of team tactics, finishing 2nd, and then made a cleverly timed break in the slip-streaming Italian GP at Monza to score another popular win for Ferrari.

Regazzoni is a thrusting, determined driver, who matured in 1970 to show skill and restraint deemed beyond him in his earlier years. Occasionally his fire broke through, as in a desperate attempt to pass Hulme in the closing stages of the British GP, but otherwise Ferrari have adopted a remarkable talent. DCN

Resta, Dario

To the present generation of motor racing enthusiasts the name of Resta means very little, but 50 years ago he was world famous and regarded, justifiably, as one of the greatest drivers. Resta was born in Italy in 1884. When 2 years of age, he came to London, with his parents, where he was brought up. On leaving school he entered the motor industry, spending several years in the trade before opening his own premises in the West End of London.

When Brooklands opened in 1907 Resta took part in the Inaugural Meeting driving a Mercedes for a client, F. R. Fry. In the Montagu Cup race he finished 3rd, having mistaken a signal when leading and doing an extra lap which cost him 1st place. He made amends, however, at the August Meeting by winning the Prix de France Cup, again driving Fry's Mercedes. His skill was recognized when Resta was invited to drive one of the Austins in the 1908 French GP at Dieppe. Here he had the misfortune to crash twice in practice, the second accident landing him in jail, whence he was only rescued in time for the *pésage* by the intervention of Fry his Brooklands sponsor. In the race itself the Austins were outclassed, Resta finishing 19th.

From 1909 to 1911 he did little racing, but in 1912 he became a member of the newly-formed Sunbeam team. In the Coupe de L'Auto, run concurrently with the French GP at Dieppe, he led from the 8th lap (4th in the Grand Prix) until the last, when his team-mate Rigal passed him to win. Resta had to be content with 2nd place in the Coupe and 4th in the Grand Prix. Later in the year, in company with Crossman and Coatalen he was successful in attacking long-distance records at Brooklands.

In 1913 he again drove in the Sunbeam team, finishing 6th in the French GP at Amiens. In the autumn with Chassagne and Lee Guinness he broke long-distance records at Brooklands. In 1914 the Sunbeam team took part in two big races, the Tourist Trophy and the French GP at Lyons. In the former Resta was out of luck, being forced to retire on the first lap of the two-day race, but in the Grand Prix, in spite of insufficient practice, he drove brilliantly to finish 5th. Returning to Britain he drove the 9-litre 12-cylinder Sunbeam in the Saltburn speed trials to make ftd, and at the Brooklands August Meeting, in the same car, won a race at the fastest speed of the day.

Leaving for America in the autumn, on a protracted business trip, he was approached, in New York, by the Peugeot Importation Company to drive one of their cars in the leading races in America in 1915. The circuit for both the Grand Prize, and the Vanderbilt Cup, was in the Exposition Grounds in San Francisco. In the

Clay Regazzoni. *Photo: Geoffrey Goddard*

Dario Resta, 1908. *Photo: T. A. S. O. Mathieson Collection*

Below, Dario Resta at Indianapolis, 1923. *Photo: T. A. S. O. Mathieson Collection*

Right below, Dario Resta at Brooklands in the GP Sunbeam, 1924. *Photo: Montagu Motor Museum*

former, run under appalling weather conditions with the roads awash, Resta easily defeated the pick of the finest drivers in America and, to show that this was no flash in the pan, he repeated the performance in the Vanderbilt Cup a week later. Resta was a sensation and, after taking second place in the Indianapolis 500 Miles, he continued his victorious progress, winning twice at Chicago and Sheepshead Bay. At the end of the season he was 2nd in the National Championship, with $37,700 in prize money.

In 1916 Resta renewed his contract with Peugeot, and was even more successful with victories at Indianapolis Chicago (twice), Omaha, and in the Vanderbilt Cup, at Santa Monica, for the second time. His victories gave him the National Championship with 4,100 points, the greatest number recorded up to that time and $44,400 in prize money.

Resta was hailed as 'The Speed King of America'. He was the only foreign driver ever to win the National Championship, and the only British driver (he had been naturalized) ever to win the Vanderbilt Cup and the Grand Prize.

With America's entry into World War 1 there was little racing in 1917. He competed in only one event; in 1918 there was still less. Resta, now driving his own Resta Special, competed in two meetings, at Sheepshead Bay and at Chicago, both consisting of sprint races. In the former he obtained two 2nds and a 3rd, and in the latter a 2nd and a 3rd. Business activities curtailed his racing in 1919, for he had been negotiating to become the Sunbeam Motor Car Company's agent in America. He took part in two meetings, at Sheepshead Bay and Tacoma, again driving his own car but had no success. During the next two years he did not race at all but confined his activities to business.

In 1923 Resta made a return to racing driving a Durant Miller Special in a 250-mile (400km) race at the Beverley Hills Speedway, Los Angeles, finishing 8th, and for the Packard team at Indianapolis, where he retired after 88 laps. Soon after this he returned to Britain and rejoined the Sunbeam team which was now part of the Sunbeam Talbot-Darracq group. In the autumn a combined team made a trip to Spain to take part in the Grand Prix de Penya Rhin, a voiturette race over a road circuit near Barcelona, and the two races at the Inaugural Meeting of the new Tarremar Speedway, Sitges. In the Penya Rhin event Resta was 3rd in a Talbot-Darracq; in the 2-litre race at the speedway his Sunbeam gave him trouble, forcing him to retire. In the voiturette race,

however, again driving his Talbot-Darracq, he led from
start to finish, his first victory since the Vanderbilt Cup
1916. Resta remained with Sunbeams in 1924 being
largely responsible for the preparation and testing of the
new Grand Prix car. With the prototype GP car he made
d at the Aston Clinton hill-climb, which he followed
two weeks later by repeating the feat at South Harting,
beating the record for both hills by a substantial margin.

With Kenelm Lee Guinness, he took part in the Swiss
Voiturette GP and finished 2nd, in a Talbot-Darracq, to
his team-mate. Soon after this he set out again for his
last big race, the Grand Prix of Europe, at Lyons. The
Sunbeam team were out of luck, however, for all three
cars suffered from mysterious misfiring during the race
and Resta was flagged off before completing the full
distance.

On 3 September he who had driven in so many races,
and broken so many records, met with a fatal accident
while attacking records at Brooklands. A security bolt
broke puncturing a rear tyre. The Sunbeam crashed
through the fence on the Railway Straight, killing Resta
and seriously injuring his mechanic Perkins. TASOM

Revson, Peter

Following success in American Formula Junior racing,
Revson moved to England in 1963 to gain international
experience. He won at the Roskilde Ring near Copenhagen and in 1964 got his first Formula 1 ride in a Team
Parnell Lotus-BRM at Oulton Park. Revson then drove
works Lotus F2 and F3, winning F3 at Monaco and
setting a new F2 lap record at Enna. Returning to the
United States, Revson and Skip Scott drove a Ford
GT40 to class victories at Sebring, Monza and Spa to
help Ford obtain the 1966 Manufacturers' World
Championship. In the Trans-Am series Revson has
driven factory-supported Cougars, Mustangs and
Javelins. In the 1969 Indianapolis 500, he moved his
Brabham-Repco V-8 from 33rd, last on the grid, to a
5th place finish. Two months later he drove the Repco
at Indianapolis Raceway Park road course to win the
USAC race for Championship (Indy) cars. Revson
opened 1970 by driving film star Steve McQueen's
Porsche 908 to a brilliant 2nd place finish in the Sebring
12 Hours. While McQueen himself drove well, it was
Revson who enabled the 908 to finish on the same lap as
the record breaking Ferrari. The young New Yorker
qualified a McLaren-Offy at Indianapolis in 16th place
but was sidelined early with ignition failure. He drove
the L & M Lola-Chevy to a 2nd and two 3rds in the 1970
Can-Am series to win $40,850 and his McLaren-Offy
finished 5th in the Ontario 500. In 1971 Revson is driving
the Can-Am series and major USAC races for Team
McLaren. ARB

Richmond, Duke of

Frederick Charles Gordon-Lennox, 9th Duke of Richmond and Gordon, was born in 1904. After leaving
Oxford, the Earl of March, as he was then, joined
Bentley Motors as an apprentice 'serving his time', and
considered the years spent with that famous firm as the
best part of his education.

His first long-distance event was the JCC High Speed
Trial in 1929 in which he completed the course, gaining
a Premier Award. In 1930 he joined the Austin team,
partnering Arthur Waite in the Brooklands Double-
Twelve-Hour race in which they finished 7th. Later in
1970, with Sammy Davis as co-driver, he scored his first
big success by winning the Brooklands 500 Miles race.

Peter Revson. Photo: Professionals in Motion Inc

Louis Rigal at Montlhéry in a 2·5-litre Peugeot, 1927. Photo: T. A. S. O. Mathieson Collection

In 1931 he formed his own team of MG Midgets and,
partnered by Chris Staniland, won the Double-Twelve
at Brooklands. In the Irish GP and the TT he confined
his activities to organizing the team and did not drive.
In 1932 he drove one of the new single-seater Austins in
the first British Empire Trophy meeting, winning the
South African Trophy in heat 1. From then on, apart
from occasional appearances, the Duke confined his
motor racing activities to team organization and official
duties in connection with motor sport, acting in various
capacities from marshal to steward up to 1939. After
World War 2, when both Brooklands and Donington
were no more, the Duke made available the Goodwood
circuit on his estate. In addition to his record as a driver,
the Duke has done a great deal in the service of motor
sport. TASOM

Rigal, Louis

This French driver began his racing career in 1922 when
he drove a Panhard in the speed trials and hill-climb at
the Boulogne meeting. During 1923 and 1924, he drove
for Ariès, competing in all the leading sports car races in
Europe and taking 2nd place in the Gran Premio Turismo
Guipuzcoa at San Sebastian in the latter year. In 1925 he
drove for Ariès at Le Mans, and at Boulogne; in the
remaining races he drove for Peugeot, taking part in the
Targa Florio and finishing 3rd in the Touring Grand
Prix at Monthléry. He was 2nd in Gran Premio Turismo
Guipuzcoa at San Sebastian, now a 12-hour event, being
the only competitor to drive single-handed.

In 1926 and 1927 he drove only for Peugeot. The
former year was a successful one for he gained his first
victory, in the 24-hour Belgian GP with Boillot as co-
driver. With Serre he was 5th in the 24-hour race at
Monza. Earlier in the year at Le Mans, where he had
co-driven with Boillot, the pair had had the misfortune
to be disqualified, when lying 2nd, due to the breaking of
the windscreen mounting near the end of the race.

He began the season well in 1927 by winning the
Circuit d'Esterel Plage (sports cars) at St Raphael and,
with Serre once again as co-driver, finished 2nd at San
Sebastian. Rigal drove for Ariès in 1929, taking part in
the leading sports car events including Le Mans, the
Belgian 24-hour race, the French GP at Comminges,
and the Georges Boillot Cup, but did not have any
great success.

Leaving Ariès at the end of the 1929 season, Rigal
joined Alfa Romeo and took 2nd place in his first race,
the Circuit de Cap d'Antibes, following this up by
finishing 3rd in the Belgian 24-hour race with Zehender
as co-driver. He also took part in the first Monaco GP,
finishing 9th. Towards the end of the season he scored a
fine victory in the 12-hour Spanish GP at San Sebastian,
again with Zehender as co-driver, and another in the
sports car categories of the Circuit des Routes Pavées, at
Lille, to round off a successful year.

In 1930 Rigal partnered Brisson in a Stutz at Le
Mans, the pair failing to finish, and in 1931 in the French
GP, a 10-hour event, he was co-driver to Ferrand in a
Peugeot.

Rigal's last two races were at Le Mans in 1937, when
he finished 11th with Porthault, and 1938, when he
retired with mechanical trouble. In both events his car
was a Darl'mat Peugeot. TASOM

Riley, Peter

Riley was born in Birmingham in 1931. While at Cambridge studying engineering he bought a Healey Silver-

Left, Peter Riley (left) and Tony Nash at Monte Carlo in 1963. *Photo: UPI*

Right, Jochen Rindt at Le Mans after his victory in the 1965 24 Hour Race. *Photo: Al Bochroch*

Opposite, Jochen Rindt winning the 1970 Dutch GP in a Lotus 72. *Photo: Geoffrey Goddard*

Jochen Rindt: Principal Successes

Year	Event	Car
1964	Crystal Palace (F2)	Brabham-Ford BT10
1965	Le Mans 24-Hours, with Gregory	Ferrari 275LM
	Reims (F2)	Brabham-Ford BT16
	Prix du Tyrol	Abarth 2000
1966	Eifelrennen (F2)	Brabham-Ford BT18
	Motor Show 200, Brands Hatch (F2)	Brabham-Ford BT18
	Sebring 4-Hours	Alfa Romeo Giulia 1300 TI
1967	Snetterton (F2)	Brabham-Ford BT23
	Silverstone (F2)	Brabham-Ford BT23
	Pau GP (F2)	Brabham-Ford BT23
	Eifelrennen (F2)	Brabham-Ford BT23
	Reims GP (F2)	Brabham-Ford BT23
	Rouen GP (F2)	Brabham-Ford BT23
	Langenlebarn (F2)	Brabham-Ford BT23
	Brands Hatch (F2)	Brabham-Ford BT23
	Hameenlinna (F2)	Brabham-Ford BT23
1968	Thruxton (F2)	Brabham-Ford BT23C
	Zolder (F2)	Brabham-Ford BT23C
	Crystal Palace (F2)	Brabham-Ford BT23C
	Hockenheim (F2)	Brabham-Ford BT23C
	Langenlebarn (F2)	Brabham-Ford BT23C
	Enna (F2)	Brabham-Ford BT23C
1969	United States GP	Lotus-Ford 49
	Lady Wigram Trophy, Christchurch	Lotus-Ford 49T
	Warwick Farm International 100	Lotus-Ford 49T
	Thruxton (F2)	Lotus-Ford 59B
	Pau GP (F2)	Lotus-Ford 59B
	Zolder (F2)	Lotus-Ford 59B
	Langenlebarn (F2)	Lotus-Ford 59B
1970	Monaco GP	Lotus-Ford 49C
	Dutch GP	Lotus-Ford 72
	French GP	Lotus-Ford 72
	British GP	Lotus-Ford 72
	German GP	Lotus-Ford 72
	Thruxton (F2)	Lotus-Ford 69
	Eifelrennen (F2)	Lotus-Ford 69

stone and during 1949 started competing in university events with it. In 1950 he completed with a 4½-litre Bentley in the Bugatti Owners Welsh Rally and came 2nd overall. The following year he took part in more difficult events by entering his Healey Silverstone in the Liège–Rome–Liège, winning his class and finishing 8th overall. Between then and 1958 he competed in a variety of international and national rallies, first with the Healey and later with Austin Healeys.

At the beginning of 1959 he entered the Ford works team and finished 3rd overall for them in the Tulip Rally—driving a car prepared by the press department. In the Coupe des Alpes he drove a Mk 2 Zodiac and was among the select few to win a coupe. For the Liège–Rome–Liège he drove a Healey 3000 with the Rev Rupert Jones and they won the GT category which led BMC to offer him a contract.

In 1960 he found himself paired with Tony Ambrose and in an Austin 105 they came 2nd in their class in the Tulip Rally. With an MGA he was 2nd in his class in the German Rally, and in a Healey 3000 again for the RAC Rally he took 2nd in class. In 1961, he drove a Mini in the Tulip Rally and won his class, and took a Healey 3000 on the Acropolis Rally where he finished 3rd overall and won the GT category. He also drove a Healey 3000 in the Swedish Rally—one of the few Englishmen to have driven there—and finished 12th overall and 2nd GT car.

The following year he drove an MG Midget in the Monte Carlo and won the class. In 1963 he joined Fords for the second time and in his first outing drove a Mk 3 Zodiac in the Monte Carlo. Later he drove a Cortina GT, a Rover 2000 and a Sunbeam Tiger. Since 1965 Riley has concentrated on building up his motor accessory business. JD

Rindt, Karl Jochen

Rindt was born in Germany in 1942 of Austrian and German parentage. His parents died under Allied bombing in 1943 and he was taken to Graz in Austria where he was brought up by his grand-parents. He took his place in the family spice importing business on leaving school, but his interest in motor sport found expression in 1962 when he took to racing a Simca Montlhéry saloon. He raced an uncompetitive Formula Junior Cooper in 1963 and did surprisingly well, and Ford of Austria backed his F2 Brabham-Cosworth in 1964. He made his mark in two F2 events in England

that Whitsun, finishing 2nd at Mallory Park and winning at Crystal Palace, London, against top-class opposition. He was later 3rd at Clermont, but he had made his mark and joined McLaren in the F1 Cooper team for 1965.

The Coopers were uncompetitive but Rindt managed 4th place in the German GP and 6th in the American. In Formula 2 he started a long association with Roy Winkelmann's private Brabham team, winning at Reims and taking 3rds at Pau and Vallelunga. He was already something of a national hero in Austria, and won the Prix du Tyrol at Innsbruck in an Abarth 2000. The Rindt driving style was distinctive, apparently reckless but in fact consistent and very fast. He shared a works Porsche 8 with Bonnier in the Nürburgring 1,000 Kilometres to finish 3rd, and then won Le Mans, sharing a NART Ferrari 275LM with Masten Gregory, after the Fords and works Ferraris had broken.

McLaren left Cooper at the end of the season, and Rindt became temporary No 1 until Surtees joined from Ferrari. The Cooper-Maseratis were heavy but dependable, and Rindt was 2nd at Spa (after an excellent fighting drive in the wet); 2nd in the American GP; 3rd in the German; 4th in the French and Italian; and 5th in the British races. Brabham-Hondas dominated Formula 2 that season, but Rindt won the Eifelrennen and the last race of the 1-litre class at Brands Hatch, beating Brabham. He also won the Sebring 4-Hour saloon car race for Alfa Romeo.

In 1967 the Coopers were outclassed and Jochen managed to score only two 4th places in the Belgian and Italian GPs. But meantime he established himself at the top of Formula 2, taking his Winkelmann Brabham to no less than nine 1st and four 2nd places. The Austrian's reputation as a fearless driver grew after he crashed while trying to qualify an Eagle at Indianapolis. He stepped out of the burning car as it came to rest and his heart-rate was perfectly normal in the compulsory medical examination which followed. In the 500 he was classified 24th after retiring, and frankly described Indianapolis as 'a place for making money, no more...'

On expiry of his three-year Cooper contract, Jochen became number two to Jack Brabham in the works Formula 1 team, but the Repco V-8 engine had reached the end of its development with twin ohc to each bank and was most unreliable, giving the Austrian an unhappy season. He scored once, finishing 3rd in the German GP. Consolation came in Formula 2, for he won six major events in the Winkelmann Brabhams.

Jochen Rindt. *Photo: Geoffrey Goddard*

Brands Hatch Race of Champions, and then gave the revolutionary new Lotus 72 an inauspicious début in the Spanish GP at Jarama. In private practice there, a front brake became separated from its shaft, although Jochen managed to control it, and in the race itself the engine only lasted 10 laps.

Jochen had another unhappy meeting with the 72 in the Silverstone International Trophy, and while the car was being redesigned Gold Leaf Team Lotus fielded a pair of 49Cs at Monaco. The closing stages of that race saw Rindt at his courageous best, literally hurling the old car round the Monte Carlo streets in pursuit of Jack Brabham, who slid off on the final corner to let Jochen through to a magnificent and classic second Grande Epreuve victory.

He retired in the Belgian GP—again in the 49C—and then the revised 72 fulfilled its promise in the Dutch GP, Jochen taking pole position on the grid, the lead from lap 3 on and holding it to the finish. This victory was horribly overshadowed by the death of Piers Courage, one of Rindt's closest friends, but he continued to drive the 72 with undiminished verve, winning luckily in the French and British GPs, and worthily in the German GP at Hockenheim. He hit trouble in the Austrian, but went to Monza for the Italian GP ready to clinch his World Championship title.

Practice was held on Friday and Saturday, September 4–5, and half an hour into the Saturday session Rindt's Lotus veered sharp left under heavy braking into the Parabolica, dived under the Armco crash barriers and bounced back onto the track, its front end torn away. Jochen Rindt was lifted clear by officials, but if he was not already dead there was no hope of his surviving terrible chest injuries. Officially he died in the ambulance on the way to a Milan hospital.

Jochen's loss on the eve of what seemed a certain World Championship victory stunned the racing world, and when Fittipaldi's Lotus 72 beat the Ferraris in the US GP his points lead in the title was secured. Karl-Jochen Rindt became motor racing's first posthumous World Champion.

During this last season Jochen had run the works Formula 2 Lotus team in conjunction with Bernie Ecclestone, and although they had troubles with the Lotus 69s he continued his winning ways in the class, retaining his formidable standing in F2. But after the loss of Piers Courage, Jochen would almost certainly have retired at the end of the season had he won the Championship. It was cruel irony, that fate robbed him of his ambition at the last moment, and took the life of a great racing driver. DCN

At the end of the year Rindt signed with Team Lotus as joint number one with Graham Hill. His first outings were in the Tasman Series, in which his score read one rolled, two 1sts and two 2nds, and his forceful but perhaps not-too-thoughtful approach made him Stewart's greatest rival in F1. Not until the British GP did his Lotus finish a race, and then he was delayed to finish 4th. He had crashed heavily in the Spanish GP following an aerofoil collapse, but quickly recovered from a broken jaw and concussion, although he had some vision and balance problems for some time afterwards. He was 2nd in the Italian GP after Stewart outplanned him, and 3rd in the Canadian; then at Watkins Glen he scored his long-awaited first championship round victory in the United States GP. He was 2nd in the non-championship Formula 1 races at Silverstone and Oulton Park, and scored four F2 victories in Lotus 59Bs run by the Winkelmann organization. Early in the season his outspokenness had led to some problems with Colin Chapman, differences which were patched up at the German GP and which preluded his winning drive in the American GP.

Following Graham Hill's US GP accident, Jochen became team leader in the Lotus equipe and began the 1970 season as number one with John Miles in support. He was a comfortable second in his Lotus 49C in the

Roberts, Floyd

This American driver, born in 1901, was one of the two Indianapolis 500 mile race winners to suffer fatal injuries on the track where they had gained their greatest fame (the other was Bill Vukovich). He first attracted attention as a driver on the smaller tracks of California in the mid-1920s. Unable to win consistently, however, he left the sport for three years before returning to competition in 1930 against such contemporaries as Wilbur Shaw and Rex Mays.

Roberts made his first start at Indianapolis in 1935, finishing 4th, but the following year he was one of seven 'victims' of the 37·5-gallon (141·95-litre) fuel limit imposed by AAA regulations. He was running 5th and improving his position steadily when he ran out of fuel with 17 laps to go.

oyd Roberts. Photo: Indianapolis Motor
Speedway

A poor-handling chassis prevented him from being a serious threat in 1937; but he established a new race record of 117·200mph (188·500kph) for an impressive victory the following year, when he also set a new record in the time trials by averaging 125·681mph (202·332kph) for the 10-lap distance which prevailed for six years beginning in 1933. He also won the 1938 AAA national driving title.

His fatal accident occurred on the 107th lap of the 1939 Indianapolis race when he was unable to avoid a car which spun out of control immediately in front of him on the No 2 turn. The Roberts car flipped over the wall and he died from a broken neck. AB

Robertson, George

George Robertson was born in 1884 and though he was racing in amateur events as early as 1903–4, he was truly a second-generation automobilist, for his father ran one of New York's first big garages, and George was brought up on Mors, Panhard and the like. He did not emerge in a major event until 1905, when he handled the fwd Christie racer in the Vanderbilt Cup Eliminating Trials: despite a dismal performance it was selected for the American team. Robertson, however, was not, Christie electing to drive his own machine. He was also unlucky in the 1906 Trials; his Apperson proved extremely fast in practice, but a day or two before the race Robertson crashed it into a telegraph pole. In 1907, however, he rose to prominence in a variety of cars. He drove the Christie to good purpose at Ormond Beach and Daytona Beach, though his usual sprint car was the ex-Shepard 1906 GP Hotchkiss, in which he managed a mile in 52sec. In the Lowell 250 he won his first major victory for Locomobile.

The 1908 events included three of the fashionable 24-hour grinds at Brighton Beach, N.Y., in which Robertson handled Simplex as well as Locomobile. The former make scored him his victory, though he took a 5th place on one of the Mercedes-based cars. The Locomobile gave him two other victories, one in the Fairmount Park 200 (Philadelphia) at 50mph (80·47kph), and the other in the Vanderbilt Cup, at 64·3mph (103·48kph) at the wheel of the legendary 'Old No. 16'. With this victory he became the first American to win the nation's top road race on an American car.

The 1909 season was an excellent one for George Robertson and the big chain-driven Simplexes that were now almost his staple, though he did score a 2nd in the Indian Trophy and a 3rd in the Cobe Trophy for Locomobile. He won at Lowell, at 54·2mph (87·23kph); Fairmount Park, at 55·4mph (89·16kph); and Brighton Beach (where he vanquished DePalma and his Fiat). However, at the August Brighton Beach ground he switched to a vast 4-cylinder Houpt-Rockwell. This proved too heavy for even the burly Robertson to crank, and was withdrawn when the pit staff tired of pushing it.

In 1910 he successfully attacked records with his Simplex on the new Playa del Rey board track; there was also a final Brighton Beach victory. In March he was back at Ormond Beach and Daytona Beach with the fwd Christie, recording 120mph (193·1kph) over the mile. Robertson was appointed to captain the Benz team for the 1910 Vanderbilt Cup (last of the series to be staged on Long Island), but crashed with near-fatal results while showing the course to a newspaper reporter and never raced again.

Robertson went to France with the American Expeditionary Force in 1917, in charge of road transport.

In 1921 he served as Duesenberg's team manager during their successful assault on the French GP. When George Vanderbilt staged a new Vanderbilt Cup at the Roosevelt Raceway in 1936 and attracted the 750kg Formula cars to the United States, Robertson was the circuit manager. He gave a fast demonstration lap in his 1908 winner, 'Old No. 16'. Robertson died in 1955. MCS

Robson, George

American racing driver, born in 1907. Robson, eliminated early because of mechanical trouble on his only two previous Indianapolis appearances, won the first 500-mile race after World War 2 at an average speed of 114·820mph (184·830kph) at the wheel of an eight-year-old 6-cylinder Thorne Engineering Special.

Robson still was a comparatively unknown driver at that time, except in his home state of California, and his car was only the second to win at Indy with a 6-cylinder engine. All except two of the entries in that 1946 race were of pre-World War 2 vintage and his car proved to be the best in the field as 24 of the 33 starters failed to go the distance.

Robson, starting 15th, improved his position steadily as most of the favourites experienced mechanical trouble or were involved in accidents during the first 200 miles of the race. His only serious challenger during the remainder of the contest was Jimmy Jackson, who trailed by 34sec at the finish with Ted Horn more than 11 minutes farther back in 3rd place.

Three months later, Robson was killed in a racing accident on the dirt track at Atlanta, Ga. AB

Rodriguez, Pedro

Pedro Rodriguez was born in Mexico City on 18 January, 1940, one of a family of four children and son of a prosperous contractor. Pedro's competition career began at the age of 12, when he raced a 125cc Adler motor-cycle, scoring instant success and taking in many speed events in his early teens. He was racing a Jaguar XK 120 at 15, and in these exploits was joined by his younger brother, Ricardo. At first these activities were without parental knowledge, but later father Rodriguez helped his sons purchase and run a series of cars and motor-cycles. Pedro left school and studied business administration at university, and later started a Mercedes and Rootes dealership in Mexico City.

The Rodriguez brothers' exploits brought them drives for the North American Racing Team, and Pedro

Below, George Robson. Photo: Indianapolis Motor Speedway

Right, Pedro Rodriguez (Lotus-Climax) at Silverstone, 1965. Photo: E. Gerry Stream

drove a Ferrari for them at Sebring in 1957—he was 17; his younger brother raced a Porsche in the same event.

In 1960 Ricardo was 2nd at Le Mans, sharing a works Ferrari with André Pilette. Ricardo was in the works Formula 1 team in 1961. Pedro shared a car with him at Le Mans and the pair were fighting hard in 2nd place when a piston broke. The brothers were 3rd at Sebring and won the Paris 1,000 kilometres at Montlhéry, a performance repeated in 1962. But at the end of that year Ricardo crashed at Mexico City and died of his injuries. This must have been a tremendous blow to Pedro and his career seemed in the balance. Motor racing was in his blood, however, and he continued in 1963, sharing 3rd place at Sebring with Graham Hill (in a Ferrari) and winning the Daytona Continental for NART. In 1964 he drove Ferraris, mainly for NART, winning the Daytona Continental once more, and the Canadian Sports Car GP, coming 2nd in the Paris 1,000 Kilometres (with Schlesser), and 3rd in the Bahaman TT at Nassau. In 1965 he shared the Reims 12 Hours—winning Ferrari 375P with Guichet and came 3rd in the Canadian Sports Car GP at Mosport.

The following season Rodriguez's career was at a low ebb, with only 3rd place in the Nürburgring 1,000 Kilometres (sharing a Dino with Ginther) and 4th in the Daytona 24 Hours (Ferrari 365P with Andretti) to show.

In 1967, however, he began racing much more seriously. He was given a single drive by Cooper in the South African GP at the start of the year, and won. His intelligent approach to that race impressed Roy Salvadori and he signed a Cooper contract for the rest of the year, while he retained his sports car drives and also ran an F2 Protos-Cosworth for Ron Harris. He was 5th in the Monaco and British GPs and 6th in the French. In long-distance races his only good finish of the season was 3rd

at Daytona (with Guichet in a Ferrari 330P3/4).

The taciturn little Mexican joined BRM in 1968, and achieved 2nd place in the Belgian GP, 3rd in the Dutch and Canadian, 4th in the Mexican and 6th in the German, all with a generally uncompetitive car. He was also a fighting 2nd in the Race of Champions, but had a lean year in long-distance events until JW Automotive signed him to drive their GT40 at Le Mans. Sharing with Lucien Bianchi, he won. In 1969 he was in the Parnell BRM team, but their inadequate engines could not do him justice: he was released from his contract and drove for Ferrari at the end of the season, finishing 5th in the United States GP. He upheld Ferrari long-distance honour, sharing 2nd place at Spa with Piper after driving most of the way, then went to Matra at the end of the year, finishing 4th at Watkins Glen (with Servoz-Gavin) and 2nd in the Paris 1,000 Kilometres (a shortened event) with Redman. In 1970 he won the Belgian GP for BRM and had an excellent season in sports car racing, winning four major events in JW Automotive Porsche 917s and staying with both teams for 1971. DCN

Rodriguez, Ricardo

Ricardo, born in 1942, was the younger brother of Pedro Rodriguez and his early career followed a parallel path. He went to motorcycle races with his brother and began riding at a very early age, scoring many successes when only 13. The brothers raced a Jaguar XK120 while still in their early teens, and when Pedro got his first NART drive at Riverside in 1957, Ricardo came along with a Porsche. In 1958 Pedro drove at Le Mans, but Ricardo's application was turned down on the grounds that he was too young.

But he was already experienced, having been Mexican motorcycle champion at 14. The brothers began racing

Left, Pedro Rodriguez at United States GP, 1969. *Photo: Al Bochroch*

Top, Pedro Rodriguez, 1970. *Photo: Autosport*

Above, Pedro Rodriguez in the winning Porsche 917 which he shared with Leo Kinnunen, BOAC 1,000km 1970. *Photo: Gulf Oil*

Ricardo Rodriguez. *Photo: Bahamas News Bureau*

sports Ferraris together in long-distance events with considerable success, including consecutive wins in the Paris 1,000 Kilometres in 1961 and 1962. Ricardo was the faster and more flamboyant of the pair, and he was included in the Ferrari Formula 1 team in 1962. There he established a reputation for very fast if rather wild and erratic driving, and had a number of incidents from which he escaped unharmed. But he became the first Mexican driver ever to score Championship points, picking up four during the season. He was already married at 20, and late that year the first Mexican GP was organized at Mexico City. Ferrari were not interested in this non-Championship event, but Ricardo got a drive in Rob Walker's Lotus-Climax 24. He was one of the first drivers to go out for practice on the new track, and crashed into the rails at the top of the banking, dying shortly afterwards. The nation mourned for him and the President of Mexico walked at his funeral. DCN

Rolls, The Hon. Charles Stewart

Rolls, born in 1877, will chiefly be remembered as a pioneer publicist of the motorcar and as one of the founders of Rolls-Royce, but with the Hon John Scott-Montagu he shared the honour of being the first British driver to race on the Continent, driving a Panhard in the Paris-Ostend and Paris-Boulogne in 1899. In the former event he was 2nd in the tourist class; he was 5th in the Paris-Boulogne. After acting as S. F. Edge's mechanic in the Paris-Toulouse-Paris (1900) he drove a Mors into 18th place in Paris-Berlin in 1901. From 1902 onward he was an energetic supporter of sprints, driving a succession of Mors cars, though at Brighton in 1905 he made an unsuccessful appearance on the 26·4-litre 4-cylinder Dufaux. Despite his growing involvement with Royce, he drove a Wolseley in the 1905 Gordon Bennett Cup, making the best British performance (8th). His 20hp Rolls-Royce retired on the 1st lap of the TT, but Rolls's ensuing recriminations were redeemed by his victory in 1906, when he beat the faster Arrol-Johnstons, his average being 39·3mph (63·25kph). In the same year he joined in the unauthorized sport of attacks on the Monte Carlo-London record, averaging 27·3mph (43·94kph) as far as Boulogne on a Rolls-Royce.

Tony Rolt talking to Duncan Hamilton after their victory at Le Mans in 1953. *Photo: Keith Duerden*

Tony Rolt in the ERA-Delage. *Photo: Geoffrey Goddard*

Left below, The Hon C. S. Rolls in a 1901 60hp Mors. *Photo: Montagu Motor Museum*

Below, Mauri Rose. *Photo: Indianapolis Motor Speedway*

Though his sales promotion tour of the United States in the winter of 1906-07 included another Rolls-Royce victory at the Empire City Track, N.Y., and he was one of the team who took the first Silver Ghost through its officially-observed 15,000-mile trial, thereafter aviation claimed most of his time until his fatal crash in 1910. MCS

Rolt, Anthony Peter Roylance

Tony Rolt, born in 1918, belonged to the generation of pre-World War 2 British amateur drivers, starting racing in 1936. In 1938, driving an ERA, he had a very good season with a number of high placings, and in 1939 he won the British Empire Trophy at Donington Park. He also drove the ill-fated E-type ERA. After distinguished war service in the Army, he resumed competition with a large Alfa Romeo, converted from the fearsome Bi-motore project of the pre-war years. He also acquired a 1·5-litre straight-8 Delage from R. P. R. Habershon, and after the original engine was damaged installed the ERA unit from P. D. C. Walker's crashed E-type GP1. For two years this unlikely special proved a strong and reliable contender in minor races; Rolt also ran Nash-Healey, Jaguar, Connaught and HWM cars in other classes with some good results. He shared the winning Jaguar at Le Mans with Duncan Hamilton in 1953, and with the same co-driver was 2nd in 1954, and 2nd also in the 1954 Reims 12-Hour Race.

For 1953 he drove Connaughts, and had an excellent season in the Formula 2 class. Pressures of business led to a reduction in the number of events he drove in thereafter, though his enthusiasm for the sports was undiminished, as was seen in the development work which led to the successful Ferguson P99 racing car, with which he was closely connected. DF

Rose, Mauri

This American racing driver and automotive engineer, born in 1906, compiled an outstanding record in competition despite the fact that he spent almost his entire racing career as a part-time driver because of his duties with the various automotive companies for whom he has worked since 1930.

He gained his early racing experience, beginning in 1927, on the half-mile dirt tracks of Indiana and Ohio and the last of the half-mile board speedways at Woodbridge, N.J., Bridgeville, Pa., and Akron, Ohio. He moved up to the one-mile dirt tracks in 1932 and drove at Indianapolis for the first time the following year, participating in 15 consecutive 500-mile events before retiring as a driver. Even at Indianapolis, where most contenders find it necessary to spend the entire month of May in preparation, Rose usually practised one weekend, qualified for a starting position on the next weekend, and then worked at his regular job until the day before the race. His most important victories on the one-mile dirt tracks were scored in 100-mile championship races at Syracuse, N.Y., Detroit, Mich., Milwaukee, Wis., and Langhorne, Pa.

The dates of his association with manufacturing companies, usually as a development engineer, are as follows: Hupmobile, 1930-4; Chevrolet Division of General Motors, 1934-7; Allison Division of General Motors, 1937-45; Studebaker, 1945-51; Chevrolet again, 1952-69; and Hurst Performance Products since May 1969.

Mauri's record was particularly impressive at Indianapolis, where he led the field home for the first time in 1941. When ignition trouble caused the early elimination of the supercharged Maserati in which he had earned the No. 1 starting position that year he climbed into an Offenhauser-powered team car and charged from 14th place to win at an average speed of 115·117mph (185·331kph). He drove one of Lou Moore's fwd Blue Crown Spark Plug Specials to victory in 1947 and won again in the same car in 1948 with a record-breaking average speed of 119·814mph (192·826kph). He also led at some stage of four other Indianapolis races, finishing 2nd in 1934, 4th in 1936, 3rd in 1940 and 3rd again in 1950. His retirement in 1951 followed an accident in which he escaped injury when his car overturned while he was running with the leaders.

After finishing 4th in the 500 in 1936, he earned sufficient championship points in his rare appearances on other tracks to capture the national driving title that year. Late in the same season he also gained the distinction of being the first American to finish the inaugural Roosevelt Raceway (New York) International road race in competition with Europe's best cars and drivers. Despite the handicap of transmission trouble, which forced him to run in high gear continuously, he came 6th in an Offenhauser-powered Lou Moore entry. AB

Rosemeyer, Bernd

This German, born in 1909 in Lingen, burst upon the Grand Prix racing scene in 1935, and in three short seasons established himself as one of the world's greatest drivers. He never raced any car other than the 16-cylinder rear-engined Auto Union, yet he would fling these difficult, tail-heavy, oversteering machines around with astonishing abandon. Like many other stars, he graduated from two-wheeled racing, being a successful member of the Auto Union group's DKW motorcycle team until he badgered his way into the car racing side as a 'junior' in 1935.

His first race, the Avusrennen, brought the anti-climax of retirement, but his second put him firmly on the road to fame. It was the Eifelrennen at his favourite Nürburgring, and with the other team cars in trouble he made a meteoric spurt, passed the great Caracciola, and led the race. A mile from the finish and the wily Caracciola caught him again, but the German public had a new idol in the irrepressible Rosemeyer. Like Lang, his contemporary in the rival Mercedes camp, Rosemeyer then ran several races mainly to gain experience, yet at the end of the season he won his first big race, the Masaryk GP on the long, rugged Brno circuit in Czechoslovakia.

Rosemeyer had a highly successful year in 1936, aided by Mercedes' mechanical ailments and Alfa Romeo's lack of speed. He won the Eifelrennen in grim, misty conditions which gained him the nickname *Nebelmeister* or 'mist master'; he won the German GP, the Acerbo Cup at Pescara, and the Swiss and Italian GPs; and achieved ftd in the Freiburg hill-climb for good measure. Yet perhaps his greatest year was 1937, when he fought virtually on his own for Auto Union against the highly effective W125 Mercedes, and still beat them in the Eifelrennen, the Vanderbilt Cup race, the Acerbo Cup, and the Donington GP.

The 50,000 or so British spectators who thrilled to Rosemeyer's masterly driving on the narrow Donington circuit in October 1937 watched the last victory of this great driver. Three months later, on a gusty January day on the Frankfurt–Darmstadt autobahn, he died in a pointless record attempt. Caracciola had just set up a new Class B flying kilometre record at over 268mph (430kph) in a Mercedes, and Rosemeyer in an ultra-streamlined

Auto Union set out to beat it. At maximum speed the car suddenly lurched, a tyre flew off, and the car smashed against a concrete bridge. Bernd Rosemeyer was flung out and killed instantly. CP

Rosier, Louis

This French driver, born in 1905, was renowned for his calm consistency and 'hasten slowly' approach to racind. Rosier's temperament particularly suited the kind of car with which he was most successful: the 4·5-litre, unsupercharged Lago-Talbot, which gained on rugged reliability and good fuel consumption what it lost in sheer speed. He came from the hilly Puy de Dôme district in the heart of the Auvergne, where as a young man he successfully raced motorcycles in local events. In 1928, when 23, he bought an 1,100cc supercharged SCAP sports car which he drove in hill-climbs in between establishing his garage business in Clermont-Ferrand. His competition début with the Talbot make came in 1938, when he drove a 4-litre sporting model in the La Turbie hill-climb, Le Mans and elsewhere, but success eluded him until World War 2 was over.

In 1947, when Rosier was 42, the successes began with the Albi GP when the faster but more fragile blown cars dropped out one by one and the 'ponderous, ancient' Talbot, well-prepared by Rosier himself, went through to win. Elsewhere its reliability took it to a place, as at Chimay, Strasbourg and the first post-war French GP, where Rosier finished 4th. In 1948 he took delivery of the first of the 4·5-litre single-seater Lago-Talbots, finishing in the first four in five major Grands Prix and winning the Grand Prix du Salon. In 1949, with Alfa Romeo withdrawing for a year, the Maseratis getting old, and the blown Ferraris fast but thirsty, Rosier and the Talbot came into their own, his greatest victory being the Belgian GP at Spa which, with other high placings, collectively made him Champion of France—a title he went on to win four years in succession.

The faithful Lago-Talbots served him well until 1951, his victories including the Dutch and Albi GPs, plus a 2nd in the Argentine 500 Miles race at Rafaela in 1950, and the Dutch and Bordeaux GPs in 1951. In addition, a GP Talbot was rebuilt as a sports car for Le Mans, 1950, a race ideally suited to Rosier's temperament and stamina. Driving 20 of the 24 hours, with his son Jean-Claude relieving for the other four, Louis Rosier scored France's last great victory in her great long-distance classic. In 1952 he acquired two Ferraris, a 4·5-litre F1 car and a 2-litre F2 car, clocking two victories with both: the Albi GP in 1952 and 1953 with the big car; and Cadours 1952, and Sables d'Olonnes 1953 with the small. His last fling for Talbot came in the 1953 Carrera Pan Americana in Mexico, where he finished 5th.

Changing formulas in 1954 brought another change in machines for Rosier; he bought a 250F F1 Maserati and a sports Ferrari, racing in places as far afield as Dakar, Agadir, Charterhall in Scotland and Castle Combe, but wins came more rarely now. His last major success was as co-driver to Jean Behra in the rain-soaked Paris 1,000 Kilometres race at Montlhéry in June, 1956, driving a 3-litre sports Maserati. For a driver so sage and steady, who never crashed, Rosier's end was tragic. Again in pouring rain at Montlhéry, the track he knew so well, his sports Ferrari spun on braking at Ascari curve during the Coupe du Salon in October 1956. Unfortunately the car caught a bank and over-turned, Rosier suffering severe head injuries. Three weeks later he died, aged 51. In recognition of his

Bernd Rosemeyer at Donington, 1937.
Photo: Cyril Posthumus Collection

Louis Rosier in an F2 Ferrari at Silverstone.
Photo: Cyril Posthumus Collection

Louis Rosier. *Photo: C. & R. Nockolds Ltd*

services to the sport and his example to French youth, Rosier was posthumously awarded the French Order of the Nation. CP

Rougier, Henri

Born in 1876, Rougier made his name on the Turcat-Méry, a make he subsequently represented in Paris. His famous racer *La Tarasque,* so named after the legendary monster whose teeth were painted on its pointed nose, was first seen in the Paris–Madrid, where he finished 9th in the *grande voiture* category and 11th in general classification, and that October he also set up a new record at the Mont Ventoux Hill-climb in the snow. A further ftd followed at this venue in 1904, but meanwhile his Turcat-Méry had shown a good turn of speed in the French Gordon Bennett Trials, and a 3rd place at 75·5mph (121·51kph) on the fast Mazagran circuit led to his participation in the race proper at Homburg. This time he finished 3rd again, at 46·8mph (75·32kph).

He turned to De Dietrich in 1904 and shared in the general triumph of that make that was the Circuit des Ardennes, finishing 3rd behind Duray's sister car and Hanriot's Darracq. He drove without success in the 1907 Kaiserpreis and the 1907 and 1908 Grands Prix, but finished 3rd in the very rapid Coppa della Velocita.

The virtual abandonment of racing after 1908 led Rougier to turn to flying, and he did well with a Voisin biplane. His only subsequent motoring appearances in pre-World War 1 years were in the Monte Carlo Rallies of 1911 and 1912, in which he drove Turcat-Méry cars. He won on the former occasion, Rougier was back at the wheel of a sports Turcat-Méry for the 1921 Corsican GP, in which he finished 2nd, but in latter years he drove for Gabriel Voisin, handling one of that designer's aerodynamic-bodied C3 4-litres in the 1922 Touring Car GP, which he won. He also made ftd at La Turbie on a Voisin, and drove one of the odd 6-cylinder GP machines in the French and Italian Grands Prix of 1923. At this point Voisin transferred his interests from racing to long-distance record work, and Rougier retired from the scene, though he continued to sell Voisin and Steyr cars in the 1930s, and was engaged in the food business in Marseilles at the time of his death in 1956. MCS

Ruby Lloyd

Born in 1928 and one of the more versatile Indianapolis regulars, this quiet Texan has won seven USAC Championship races and has repeatedly led the Indianapolis 500, only to be side-lined by mechanical failure. In the 1965 Daytona Continental Ruby and Ken Miles brought the Ford GT40 its first victory. The veteran pair then drove a Ford Mk II and the open Ford XI to world championship victories at Daytona and Sebring in 1966, and in 1967 Ruby teamed with A. J. Foyt in a Ford Mk II to finish 2nd at Sebring. Ruby began racing midgets in 1946, joined USAC in 1957 and had his best Indy finish, a 3rd, in 1964. He missed most of the 1966 season recuperating from back injuries received in a private plane crash. In September 1970 Ruby's 177·567mph (285·811kph) four-lap qualifying average in a turbo-charged Offenhauser Mongoose earned the pole position in the inaugural California 500 at Ontario Speedway. ARB

Ruesch, Hans

A wealthy and versatile Swiss amateur from Zurich who drove a wide variety of cars between 1932 and 1953, Hans Ruesch was best known for his successes with the

Henri Rougier, 1905. *Photo: T. A. S. O. Mathieson Collection*

Lloyd Ruby. *Photo: USAC*

Below, Hans Ruesch at Donington, 1936. *Photo: Cyril Posthumus Collection*

Right below, Troy Ruttman and S. C. Agajanian, owner of the car in which Ruttman won the Indianapolis 500 in 1952. *Photo: Indianapolis Motor Speedway*

big 3·8-litre 8-cylinder Alfa Romeo which he purchased from the Scuderia Ferrari in 1936, and which subsequently passed into the hands of Dennis Poore. Ruesch won the 1936 Donington GP with Richard Seaman co-driving the Alfa, finished 2nd in the Mountain Championship at Brooklands that year, and won this event outright the following year. He also scored several easy victories on the Continent against negligible opposition. Ruesch also ran his big red car in the South African series of races early in 1937, scoring two 4ths and a 5th against heavy handicaps and the Auto Union team. In his last drive with the Alfa at Crystal Palace in 1939, Ruesch came up against 'Bira' and his ERA, a combination better suited to the sinuous London circuit. Ruesch nonetheless won the first heat of the Sydenham Trophy.

Although many of his successes have been in comparatively easy races, and some have resulted from protests against other competitors, there can be no question of Ruesch's undoubted driving skill. Apart from the big Alfa he drove a 1·5-litre Maserati in voiturette events, finishing 2nd in the 1935 Eifelrennen and 3rd in 1936 at Albi and Pescara. He also set up world Class D records at Montlhéry with a 3-litre GP Maserati in 1933 and 1934.

After 1939 Ruesch stayed out of racing but made a surprise return in 1953 with a 4·1-litre Mille Miglia sports Ferrari, and showed he still retained his old skill by finishing 3rd in both heat and final of the British Empire Trophy race at Douglas, Isle of Man. After a long career the Swiss finally gave up racing and took up writing instead. CP

Ruttman, Troy

The American Ruttman, born in 1930 and the youngest driver ever to win an Indianapolis 500-mile race, accomplished that objective in 1952 by setting a new race record of 128·922mph (207·433kph) in the Offenhauser-powered Agajanian Special. He was only 22 years old at the time, having gained acceptance as a rookie at Indianapolis in 1949 by falsifying his birth certificate. He also drove in 11 other Indy events during the period from 1949 until his retirement after the 1964 race, but finished 10th or better on only one other occasion, when he was placed 4th in 1954. He led the field, however, at some stage of the 1957, 1960 and 1961 events.

After his 1952 victory, Ruttman also won a 200-mile championship race at Raleigh, N.Car., and appeared to be headed for the national driving title when he was

Above, Troy Ruttman. *Photo: Indianapolis Motor Speedway*

Right above, Lodovico Scarfiotti (far right), with other members of the 1963 Ferrari team at Le Mans. Right to left, Bandini, Parkes, Mairesse and Surtees. *Photo: Autosport*

Below, Roy Salvadori. *Photo: Autosport*

Roy Salvadori with Raymond Mays. *Photo: A. Hollister*

Lodovico Scarfiotti. *Photo: Manfred Kistermann*

injured critically in a sprint car race at Cedar Rapids, Iowa.

He was one of the select group of USAC drivers to invade Italy for the two Monza 500-mile races, finishing 2nd to Jimmy Bryan in 1957, and 10th in 1958. AB

Sabipa see Charavel, Louis

Salvadori, Roy Francesco

Roy Salvadori was born in 1922 to Italian parents in Dovercourt, Essex. In 1947 he entered his first race, the Grand Prix des Frontières at Chimay, Belgium, in a 2·9-litre Alfa Romeo. He finished 5th and decided to go professional. In the early 1950s he drove works and private Maserati, Frazer Nash, Jaguar, Ferrari and Connaught cars and joined the Aston Martin team in 1953. His professional approach brought him drives in a wide variety of cars, and in 1956 he had 10 wins, four 2nds and two 3rds, mainly in F2 Coopers. In 1958 he was 2nd in the German GP and 3rd in the British, in a Cooper, but he was even more effective in big sports cars, winning at Le Mans in 1959 in an Aston Martin with Carroll Shelby. In 1960 he shared a similar car with Jim Clark to finish 3rd. He joined John Surtees in Yeoman Credit F1 Coopers for 1961 and had some success in the Tasman Series, despite a bad accident.

In 1963 he raced saloon, GT and sports cars for Tommy Atkins with some success, and he won the Coppa Inter-Europa at Monza in an Aston Martin DB4GT (the wildly enthusiastic crowd thought he was an unknown Italian). Early in 1964 he helped develop the Ford GT40 prototypes, and raced a Cobra before retiring at the end of the season. He was Cooper F1 team manager in 1966 and 1967, and is now a director of Thomson & Taylor at Cobham, Surrey. DCN

Scarfiotti, Lodovico

Scarfiotti was born in Turin on 18 October 1933, son of a cement manufacturer and grandson of the first president of FIAT. He began his competition career with a Fiat 500, and moved on to OSCA sports and FJ models. He won his class in the 1956 and 1957 Mille Miglias, and raced extensively in club events just for the fun of it.

In 1962 his first big victory at Lake Garda in an Abarth won him a works Ferrari drive at Le Mans, deputizing for the injured Mairesse. He had found his niche, and although his car failed after 17 hours, Ferrari signed him on as their European Mountain Championship contender. He won four consecutive Championship rounds and the title. In 1963 the gentlemanly Italian shared the Sebring 12 Hours victory with Surtees, and scored again at Le Mans, sharing with Bandini. He was also 2nd in the Targa Florio (sharing with Bandini and Mairesse). Ferrari were impressed and gave him an F1 drive in the Dutch GP where he finished 6th. But at Reims, practising for the French GP, he crashed heavily into a telegraph pole. As a result he was out of action for some time and said he would not drive Formula 1 again.

But Scarfiotti was back in the Ferrari sports car team in 1964, winning the Nürburgring 1,000 kilometres with Vaccarella, coming 2nd at Sebring and in the Canadian Sports Car GP and 3rd in the Reims 12 Hours. The following year again won the Nürburgring 1,000 kilometres (with Surtees), was 2nd in the Monza 1,000 kilometres and made a late entry in the Mountain Championship with a Dino 206S, winning four consecutive rounds once more to secure his second title.

Scarfiotti was one of those rare drivers who was

equally good in almost any car, and he combined the sprint ability necessary even for the long Continental hill-climbs with the sense of pace and consistency for long-distance events. A combination of these characteristics predicted a useful Grand Prix driver, and he was back in the Ferrari F1 team in 1966, as third driver in the Italian GP. Bandini and Parkes supported him admirably, and he won his greatest-ever race: an Italian driving an Italian car to win the Italian GP for the first time since 1952. He shared the Spa 1,000km victory with Parkes that year, was 2nd in the Mountain Championship and had a few outings in a Tyrrell F2 Matra. In 1967 he scored just one victory, a staged dead-heat with Parkes in the Syracuse GP, and shared the 2nd-place Ferraris at Daytona, Monza and Le Mans also with Parkes. But his spell at Ferrari ended that year, for he left after a disagreement and signed for Porsche and Cooper-BRM.

He was 4th in the Spanish and Monaco GPs with the underpowered but reasonably reliable Coopers, and 2nd for Porsche in the BOAC 500 at Brands Hatch. He set second fastest time in the opening European Mountain Championship climb at Montseny, and on 8 June 1968, was practising his Porsche Bergspyder at Rossfeld, Germany. The car went straight on at a corner, hit a tree and Italy lost one of its greatest all-rounders. DCN

Scaron, José

With a racing career extending over 30 years, and notable talent and endurance, the Frenchman José Scaron garnered a great number of successes. He was an Amilcar dealer in Le Havre, and raced a car of this make, one of the very fast 1,100cc 6-cylinder supercharged voiturettes, which he prepared meticulously, scoring numerous class successes in races all over Europe and in North Africa between 1928 and 1934. They included La Baule, three times; Tunis, three times; Dieppe twice; Monza twice; also Reims, Boulogne, Comminges, Casablanca, Rome, Dauphine, Oran and Pescara. In 1933 he tried a 1·5-litre Bugatti without success, but won the La Vallette and Chanteloup hill-climbs with his Amilcar. In 1934 he essayed GP racing with a 2·3 Monza Alfa Romeo, scoring places at Dieppe and Vichy, plus another Amilcar win at Chanteloup.

With the demise of the old Amilcar make, Scaron secured a Simca agency, and in 1938 he switched to sports car racing, sharing a 1,100cc Simca-Fiat with Amédée Gordini at Le Mans. They led the 1,100cc class until the car broke down on the second day, but at Le

ans 1939 the Gordini and Scaron combination won
e Rudge Whitworth Cup and the 1,100cc class out-
ght. Scaron also showed his versatility by winning his
ass in the 1939 Monte Carlo Rally with a Simca, and
ter World War 2 cheerfully took up racing single-
eaters, both in the *Petites Cylindrées* (1,100cc) category
nd also in GPs with a 4-litre Talbot. He won at Nice and
t Cloud with a Simca in 1946 and, was 2nd to 'Bira' at
eims in 1947. With the Talbot he was 6th at Albi, 7th
t Comminges and 9th at Strasbourg in 1947. The
ollowing year this remarkably tough Frenchman won
oth the Bol d'Or and the 1,500cc class of the Belgian 24
ours, with Pierre Veyron.

In 1949 Scaron came 3rd in the ACF Grand Prix at
omminges, his Simca the first 1,500 home, and in 1950
e and co-driver Pascal won the 1·5-litre class of the
Monte Carlo Rally with a 1·2-litre Simca saloon. His
nal triumph was another Bol d'Or victory for Simca in
951, for although he tried again at Le Mans the following
ear his car retired early in the race, after which Scaron
imself retired from racing. CP

chell, Harry

rought up in France by American parents, Harry
chell was exposed to motor racing from childhood.
is mother won the Monte Carlo Rally Coupe des
ames in 1929, his father and mother finished 2nd in the
936 Monte Carlo, and Laury Schell supported Ecurie
leu Talbots and Delahayes that raced in pre-World
ar 2 Europe. In 1940 Harry Schell came to Indianapolis
ith his friends, French champion René Dreyfus, and
uigi Chinetti who had twice won Le Mans for Alfa
omeo and was to bring Ferrari their first 24 hours
ictory in 1949. Schell's Indy entry, the Lucy O'Reilly
chell Maserati Special, qualified 31st and finished 10th,

Jo Schlesser. *Photo: Central Press Photos Ltd*

Left below, Harry Schell (right), with C. A.
Vandervell (left) and M de Peyrinhoff,
President of the FIA in 1956. *Photo: Cyril
Posthumus Collection*

Left bottom, Harry Schell in a Gordini F2
(left). *Photo: F. C. Taylor*

Below, Harry Schell. *Photo: Vic Blackman*

but only René Dreyfus, who drove in relief of René Le
Begue, made the race.

In the 1950s Schell proceeded from a 1,100cc Osca to
driving his own and works Formula 1 cars. In 1954 his
Maserati was 2nd in the Rome Grand Prix and 3rd at
Aintree. Schnell won Castle Combe and Snetterton for
Vanwall in 1955 and in August 1956 captured the GP of
Caen in a Maserati. He had 2nds at Pau and Silverstone
in 1957 and in May 1958 brought BRM a 2nd in the
Dutch GP at Zandvoort.

In sports cars Schell won the 1956 Nürburgring 1,000
Kilometres, in which he teamed with Moss, Taruffi and
Behra. His Sebring record shows a 2nd with Musso in
1956; 2nd with Moss 1957; and in 1958 his Porsche was
1st in the under 2 litres and 3rd overall.

In December 1959 Schell's Cooper astounded the
factory teams by earning the pole position in the first
United States GP at Sebring; he is said to have found a
short-cut that saved several seconds.

An urbane, civilized man, Harry Schell belonged to a
more relaxed era in motor racing. His practical jokes
enlivened many race meets and his interest in the Paris
bistro, *L'Action Automobile*, made it a popular rendez-
vous for international race fans. Schell was killed while
practising in the wet, in a Cooper-Climax at Silverstone
in May 1960. ARB

Schlesser, Jo

Jo Schlesser, born in 1928, came from Madagascar, and
his competition career began in 1954 when he took part
in a number of local races and rallies. He had some minor
success there, and in 1957 made the headlines when he
spent a holiday taking part in the Liège-Rome-Liège
Rally, sharing a Mercedes with Claude Storez and
finishing 2nd overall. He rallied in a 250GT Ferrari in
1958 but crashed it badly on the Tour de France. In
1959 he started racing the rebuilt 250GT and entering
single-seater events in a Cooper.

Schlesser left his job with a computer company in
Madagascar and moved to France that year, racing
widely in Europe. In 1961 he was given a works Ferrari
drive at Le Mans, but he crashed heavily in the test
weekend and missed the rest of the season. He returned
to Madagascar on his recovery but in 1962 a friend
sponsored him and bought one of the earliest Formula
Junior Brabhams. The stocky, jovial and popular
Schlesser returned to Europe and became French FJ
Champion, repeating the performance in 1963. Aston
Martin entrusted him with one of their DB4GTs and
he gave them a win at Montlhéry. Ecurie Ford France
backed his racing and he won the Critérium des Cevennes
Rally in a Ford Falcon—a most unlikely vehicle for the
tight, twisting lanes of the Cevennes. In 1964 he drove a
Formula 2 Brabham, Shelby Cobras and GT40 proto-
types, and in 1965 came 2nd at Daytona, 4th at Sebring
and 5th at Reims in Cobras.

Schlesser became number two to Beltoise in the 1966
Matra Formula 2 team, and he was 2nd at Albi and 3rd
in the German GP F2 section. Ecurie Ford France ran
F2 Matras for him in 1967, resulting in 3rd places at
Rouen, Brands Hatch and Oulton, and his long-distance
partnership with ex-Rugby player Guy Ligier won the
Reims 12 Hours in a Ford GT Mk II. The pair raced
Ecurie Inter Sports McLaren F2s in 1968, Schlesser's
fast and exuberant driving giving him 2nd place at
Monza.

Schlesser seemed to be on the verge of real success
when Honda decided to race their brand-new RA302

Lou Schneider. *Photo: Indianapolis Motor Speedway*

Archie Scott-Brown in a Lister-Bristol. *Photo: Geoffrey Goddard*

Opposite, Thousand Lakes Rally: The Volvo 122S shared by Lauri Koskinen and Jouko Leino. *Photo: Hugh Bishop*

Richard Seaman. *Photo: Downton's News Service*

V-8 air-cooled car in the French GP at Rouen, and asked him to drive it. On the second lap his Honda's engine cut out on the difficult downhill section to Nouveau Monde, the car went out of control in the rain and crashed. Schlesser's death shocked the motor racing world, for here was a true enthusiast, a genuine character and a driver who never gave up. DCN

Schneider, Louis

Born in 1899, Schneider, a member of the Indianapolis Police Department's motorcycle squadron when he started his racing career on American mid-western half-mile dirt tracks during the 1920s, gained most of his racing fame during six Indianapolis 500 races beginning in 1927.

Mechanical trouble ended his chances on the 136th lap of his first Indianapolis appearance, but he finished 11th in 1928, 3rd in 1930 and won in 1931 with a Miller-powered Bowes Seal Fast Special after several favourites had been eliminated by mechanical trouble and racing accidents.

Although he failed to score any other major victory on the AAA circuit during the remainder of the season, which was curtailed sharply because of economic conditions, Schneider picked up sufficient points to finish the year as National champion. He was eliminated at Indianapolis in 1932, after running 125 laps, and he retired as a driver after his car stalled on the first lap of the 1933 race. He died of tuberculosis in 1942. AB

Scott-Brown, William Archie

Archie Scott-Brown was unique in British motor racing. A Scot, born in Paisley in 1927, who lived in Cambridge, he was deceptively frail in build, and was born with an unformed right hand and part-crippled leg, yet he overcame these physical handicaps by sheer courage and determination. He started racing in 1951 with an MG TD which he drove in local sprints, scoring several class victories, then graduated to a ferocious JAP twin cylinder-engined Tojeiro Special owned by his friend Brian Lister. With this Scott-Brown won his first Silverstone race.

These displays of manual dexterity plus his immense enthusiasm and flair for racing encouraged Lister to enter Scott-Brown seriously for races, but the latter's disability at first prevented him from breaking into major events. The organizers of the 1954 British Empire Trophy race at Oulton Park would not accept his entry, but eventually he secured an unrestricted licence: ironically, he won that very same race the following year with a Lister-Bristol, and again in 1957 with a Lister-Jaguar. The races he won between 1954 and 1958 form a very long list, and included numerous events at Snetterton, his local circuit, and others at Oulton Park, Silverstone, Crystal Palace, Brands Hatch, Charterhall in Scotland, Goodwood, Aintree, Ibsley, and elsewhere.

He drove for Brian Lister throughout his career, with MG, Bristol, Maserati and Jaguar-engined sports cars, but late in 1955 he also signed with Connaught to drive in Formula 1. He won three times at Brands Hatch with their 'Syracuse' model; was 2nd to Moss's Vanwall in the 1956 BRDC Silverstone after a tremendous duel with his eternal rival Roy Salvadori. Besides driving Listers and Connaughts, he also found time in 1956 to win races with a 1,100cc sports Elva and a DKW saloon.

For 1957 Brian Lister had a new car built around a Jaguar D-type engine, a very powerful combination which took Scott-Brown to more impressive victories. He also

drove a D-type Jaguar in the Swedish sports car GP for the Scottish Ecurie Ecosse, and in 1958 he took a Lister Jaguar with 3·8-litre engine out to New Zealand, winning the Lady Wigram race at Christchurch and the Inver-cargill race at Teretonga. He also went to Florida for the Sebring 12 Hours with a Cunningham-entered 3-litre Lister-Jaguar, but a rival Ferrari collided with him in the first hour, forcing him out. In the British Empire Trophy race at Oulton Park he finished 3rd to Moss and Brooks in Aston Martins, and he won at Aintree. In the Spa GP on 18 May in very wet condition Scott-Brown went off the road. His car caught fire and this pluckiest of drivers, trapped inside, lost his life in a cruel parallel to the tragic end of Dick Seaman at a nearby point on the same circuit, in the same sort of weather 18 years before. Archie's name is perpetuated motor racing in the Scott-Brown Memorial Trophy meeting, held regularly at his 'home circuit', Snetterto in Norfolk. CP

Seaman, Richard

Dick Seaman, born in 1913 in Sussex, was an excellent example of the wealthy amateur racing driver who turned professional and was ultimately accepted as a works driver in the fabulous pre-war Mercedes-Benz Grand Prix team.

This British driver was educated at Rugby and Cambridge and began his motoring career with an MG Magna which he ran in trials from 1931 onwards. This was changed for a 2-litre Bugatti which he raced at Brooklands and Donington without success in 1933. While at Cambridge Seaman had become very friendly with the rich American enthusiast, Whitney Straight, and when Straight left to form a motor racing compan Seaman acquired from him an MG Magnette and, afte leaving Cambridge at the beginning of 1934, began to race this car on a semi-professional basis. The MG wo its class in the Inter-Varsity Speed Trials, was driven without success in a long-distance Brooklands race, an then taken to the Continent, where Seaman won the Prix de Berne. That year, 1934, Seaman raced at Brno and in South Africa, and came 2nd in the Nuffield Trophy Race at Donington. Whitney Straight gave up racing after this but Seaman decided to go on, and to make motor racing his career. To this end he purchased 1·5-litre ERA, painted in his colours of black and silver With it he undertook a busy season of Continental racing, taking a most professional interest in the startir and bonus money he was offered. But the ERA was in frequent mechanical trouble and, discontented with the service offered by ERA Ltd, Seaman, encouraged by h technical adviser, Guilio Ramponi, embarked on a remarkably courageous programme. He purchased Ea Howe's ancient 1927 1·5-litre straight-eight Delage, which Ramponi meticulously rebuilt and lightened and modified. With this apparently outdated racing car Seaman set out to beat the full weight of the official ERA team. By his skilful driving and the fact that the black Delage could often run non-stop through a voiturette race in which the highly supercharged ERAs had to refuel, this gamble succeeded. Whereas in 1935 Seaman had won three races in ERAs, had retired twic and had not started in other races, with the old Delage he took four 1st places, in spite of crashing while going well in two others. Indeed, the carefully-rebuilt, comparatively light-stressed car retired only once, from a long-distance race, and that was on its last appearance, in 1937. Already, in 1936, Dick Seaman had started to

drive cars other than the Delage voiturette. He won the British Empire Trophy Race at Donington in a 3-litre Maserati; shared a sports 4·5-litre Lagonda with Freddie de Clifford in the Spa 24-hour race; handled Maseratis on the Continent, sharing Trossi's at the Nürburgring, and experienced the Ulster TT in a 2-litre Aston Martin Finally, in that year, he won the Donington Grand Prix with a 3·8-litre Alfa Romeo co-driven with Hans Ruesch. It was the little Delage that had taken young Seaman to fame, for in it he won the Isle of Man, at Pescara, at Berne, and in the 200 Miles Race at Donington, all impeccable victories, three of them on consecutive weekends; 1936 closed with Seaman losing the BRDC Gold Star to 'Bira' by a single point.

These performances drew the attention of Herr Neubauer to the skill and determination of Seaman and he was invited to become a member of the Mercedes-Benz Grand Prix team. In spite of early crashes which put him in hospital, Seaman soon mastered the technique of handling these very powerful, oversteering cars. He became a popular and valued member of the German team. His first place for them was in the American Vanderbilt Cup race, in which he was 2nd. That year he crashed at the Nürburgring and again in the 1937 season, retiring from the Donington Grand Prix. But the following year he won on the Germans' home ground, the Nürburgring followed this up with 2nd place in the Swiss Grand Prix, had a break by driving a 328 BMW in the TT, then came in 3rd at Donington, after he had retired at Monza, Seaman was now living in Ambach and he married the daughter of the head of the BMW company. As the war clouds gathered, Seaman found himself in an unenviable position, but he was advised to remain with the German team for diplomatic reasons. This he did and the 1939 season opened with retirement from the Eifelrennen Grand Prix. Seaman then started in one of the 3-litre Mercedes-Benz in the Belgian Grand Prix at Spa, and had taken the lead on the wet track, at an average speed of 94·19mph (151·58kph) when, 13 laps from the finish, he skidded into a tree, receiving injuries from which he died in hospital. He is buried at Putney, London. Among the wreaths at his funeral was one from Adolf Hitler. WB

Segrave, Henry O'Neal de Hane

The greatest British racing driver of the 1920s, Segrave, was outstanding as the only British winner in a British car of any Continental Grand Prix for 32 years. He won two, in fact: the French GP in 1923 and the San Sebastian GP in 1924, both with Sunbeams.

Born in Baltimore, Md. in 1896, of an Irish father and American mother, Segrave's interest in motor racing was kindled by a wartime visit to Sheepshead Bay, Long Island. With the return of peace he lost little time. He acquired a 1914 GP Opel, won three races at Brooklands in 1920, and the following year joined the Sunbeam-Talbot-Darracq racing team. He drove in the 1921 Grand Prix at Le Mans in a 3-litre Talbot, finishing 9th after 14 punctures and numerous other troubles; came 3rd in the Grand Prix des Voiturettes at the same course in a 1·5-litre Talbot-Darracq; then with the same car won the 200 Miles Races at Brooklands. But for a broken contact-breaker he could have won the 1922 TT in the Isle of Man, having led for five of the eight laps by an ever-increasing margin. He retired, too, in the 1922 Grand Prix at Strasbourg, but won four races at Brooklands; was 2nd in the Coppa Florio in Sicily after numerous adventures; 3rd in the 200 Miles race and the GP des

Voiturettes at Le Mans; and 4th at Penya Rhin, Spain.

In 1923 Segrave won his famous victory in the French Grand Prix at Tours. At that time of far fewer races this was the blue riband of motor racing, and opposition came from FIAT, Bugatti, Voisin and Rolland-Pilain. Segrave, worried by clutch slip, did not move up until the second half of the race, but when Salamano's Fiat broke down he took the lead with only two of the 35 laps to go, and the British green Sunbeam won the Grand Prix for the first time ever. He went on to win the Boulogne GP for voiturettes with a Talbot-Darracq.

By 1924 Sunbeam had supercharged their GP cars, and Segrave was a favourite for the Grand Prix at Lyons. He led impressively for the first 64km, after which maddening ignition trouble set him back to 5th place, with fastest lap as his sole consolation. But he won the 386-miles (621km) San Sebastian GP on the Lasarte circuit in Spain; it was in this race that he pioneered the wearing of a crash helmet in racing. In 1925 Segrave won the 200 Miles race again, also the 313-miles (503km) Grand Prix de Provence at Miramas, near Marseilles, both in Talbots; won the Shelsley Walsh and Kop hill-climbs, three races on Southport sands, and the Black-pool speed trials, all with a 2-litre Sunbeam.

A change of GP Formula from 2 to 1·5-litres in 1926 ended the Sunbeams' works careers, and Segrave drove the new 8-cylinder 1,500cc Talbot. It was woefully unready for the British GP at Brooklands, but he made fastest lap before retiring with brake and supercharger troubles; then scored his third 200 Miles Race victory, and was 2nd in the Grand Prix du Salon at Montlhéry.

It was at Southport, two months later, that Segrave was launched on his remarkable record-breaking career, driving a new 4-litre Sunbeam with V-12 engine using two 2-litre GP cylinder blocks. After much supercharger trouble he got in two-way runs through the flying kilo-

Sir Henry Segrave, 1926. *Photo: Montagu Motor Museum*

Opposite top, Watkins Glen: The start of the 1962 U.S. GP. *Photo: Al Bochroch*

Opposite bottom, Zweltweg Circuit: Graham Hill (BRM, No 3) and Jo Siffert (Brabham, No 20) in the 1965 Austrian GP. *Photo: Geoff Goddard*

Sir Henry Segrave in the 1923 French GP-winning Sunbeam. *Photo: Hugh Conway Collection*

metre which averaged 152·33mph (245·15kph), breaking the current World Land Speed Record by 1·53mph (2·46kph). This new record lasted only six weeks, when Parry Thomas in the 27-litre 'Babs' raised it to 169·29mph (272·44kph). That gave Sunbeams, and Segrave, a new target to aim for — 200mph (320kph) on land — and a new car, the '1,000hp' Sunbeam, was planned, using two 22·4-litre Sunbeam World War 1 aero-engines. Meantime, between Talbot engagements, Segrave also drove the versatile 4-litre V-12 Sunbeam in races and hill-climbs during 1926, winning a hectic speed trial at Boulogne at no less than 140·6mph (226·3kph). That was Segrave's last full racing season.

In March 1927 Segrave went to Daytona, Fla., with the huge red 1,000hp Sunbeam, and broke the land speed record at 203·79mph (327·94kph). While in the United States he bought two racing motor boats, and from then his interest in motor racing waned. His last race was with a 3-litre sports Sunbeam in the 1927 Essex Six Hours race at Brooklands, when he was disqualified for refuelling away from the pits. In 1928 his 203·79mph (327·94kph) record fell, first to Malcolm Campbell's Bluebird and then to the American White Triplex, and Segrave forthwith set out to retrieve it with a new car, the 930hp Napier-engined Irving Special, or 'Golden Arrow'. In March 1929, in two slick runs, he successfully raised it to 231·44mph (372·46kph). He also won the International Championship for racing boats at Miami with his new 'Miss England', and on his return to England was knighted for his services to British prestige. On 13 June 1930, Sir Henry Segrave lost his life just after setting a new water speed record on Windermere in the Lake District. His boat, 'Miss England II', was believed to have struck a floating branch which ruptured a step and caused it to capsize. CP

Sénéchal, Robert

Born in France in 1892, Sénéchal started racing in 1921 in a cyclecar of his own manufacture. During the next four years he continued to compete with these cars in hill-climbs and races throughout France, winning the Bol d'Or in 1924 and again in 1926. In 1925 he came to an agreement with Chenard-Walcker to construct the cyclecars bearing his name and, in addition to driving his own cars, he also competed in Chenard-Walckers in sports car events.

When attending a race meeting at San Sebastian in 1926, where he intended competing in the Touring GP, an opportunity presented itself which he was not slow to take. At one point during the Grand Prix of Europe the Delage team were in serious trouble due to the furnace-like heat of the cockpits of their new GP car, and to the extreme temperature of the day. As a result the team drivers were forced to stop, one after another, for medical attention. Seeing the situation, Sénéchal hurried to the Delage pits and offered himself as relief driver. His offer accepted, he set off without any previous experience of these cars, keeping Bourlier's going not far behind the leader, Goux (Bugatti), until Bourlier himself was able to retake the wheel. Between the two of them the Delage finished 2nd and, in spite of a protest which at first went against them, they were finally awarded 2nd place. Two weeks later Sénéchal, now an official driver in the Delage team, shared the wheel of the winning car, with Wagner, in the British GP at Brooklands.

During the next few years Sénéchal continued to race fairly extensively, winning the 24-hour Belgian GP in 1927, and in 1930 purchased one of the 1,500cc GP Delages. With this he took part in the French GP at Pau, and in the French and Italian GPs of 1931. He also competed with Delage cars in touring car events such as the Circuit des Routes Pavées, and in record attempts.

Besides his interest in the competitive side of motoring sport, Sénéchal found time to assist in the organization and running of the Motorcycle Club de France, of which he became President. In 1970 he was also Vice-President of the Fédération Motorcycliste de France and President of l'Amicale des Coureurs Automobile de France. TASOM

Servoz-Gavin, Georges

French driver born in Grenoble on 18 January 1942, son of a local café owner. He loved skiing, but also had a predilection for night-life. In 1963 he took a race driving course at Magny-Cours, was pronounced 'too wild' and ran out of money. Still intent on motor sport, the handsome young socialite began navigating in rallies, sharing Ogier's Citroën in the 1964 Monte Carlo and Piot's Renault in the Alpine Rally.

He bought himself an old Volvo which he ran in local events, and was selected by his club to run one of the Jeunesse Ford Lotus 7s in a scheme to help aspiring French drivers. 'Johnny', as Servoz-Gavin is generally known, set his heart on an F3 car, and ordered a new Brabham for 1965, joining the Continental circus and living in a tent because he had spent all his money on the car. He was 7th in his first race, at La Châtre, but showed promise, improving to finish 3rd in his last race of the season at Albi. He had two victories in minor events, was 4th in the French F3 Championship and won a place in the works Matra team for 1966. He did well, winning at Le Mans (Formula 3 on the Bugatti circuit). But in 1967 he was overshadowed by Jaussaud, Beltoise and Pescarolo and at the end of the year he realized what was happening, took a firm grip on himself and finished 4th in the Madrid GP at the end of the year, driving an F2 car against the F1s and heading Ickx's similar car before it retired.

That year he deputized for the injured Stewart in the 1968 Monaco GP. He led for three laps until an apparent brush with the chicane broke the Matra's suspension. He drove a Cooper in the French GP and was then 2nd in Tyrrell's second car in the Italian. He fought hard in the closing stages of the European F2 Championship, snatching the title from Hahne in the final round at Vallelunga. He drove Tyrrell's 4-wheel-drive Matra MS84 at the end of the season, coming 6th in the Canadian GP with the uncompetitive car, and was 4th in the Watkins Glen 6 Hours sharing a Matra 650 with Rodriguez. In the middle of the 1970 season, Servoz-Gavin announced his retirement from motor racing. DCN

Robert Sénéchal. *Photo: Cyril Posthumus Collection*

Below, Johnny Servoz-Gavin. *Photo: Autosport*

Left below, Johnny Servoz-Gavin in a Matra MS7. *Photo: Matra*

Sharp, James R.

'Hap' Sharp, of Midland, Tex., an oil-well drilling contractor by profession, teamed with his fellow-townsman Jim Hall as a driver and business associate in the early days of Chaparral cars. Sharp was 5th in the 1964 US Road Racing Championship and 3rd in the 1965 series. During 1965, his most successful year, Sharp's Chaparral won feature races at Bridgehampton, Riverside, Stardust, Nassau and, with Jim Hall, the Sebring 12 Hours. Driving a Corvette, Sharp and Dave Morgan won the GT class and were 6th overall in the 1958 Sebring. Sharp, also a former speedboat champion, no longer races regularly. ARB

Shaw, Wilbur

Shaw, born in 1903, one of the great drivers of the 1930s, also contributed more than any other individual to the growth of the sport in the United States during the decade after World War 2 through his promotional activities.

As a teenager living in Indianapolis, he began to idolize the participants in the annual 500-miles races; and realized his ambition to compete in that world-renowned event for the first time in 1927, after three seasons of successful campaigning on the unsanctioned half-mile dirt tracks of Indiana, Illinois and Ohio. He attracted considerable attention by finishing 4th and he was also placed among the leaders in all of the first three 100-miles AAA championship races of the summer programme on the one-mile dirt tracks.

His outlook on life never had been brighter as he travelled to Milwaukee, Wis., for what he hoped would be his first AAA victory—and learned by telephone that his wife of only a year had died in childbirth. Stunned and disoriented by the tragic news, although he attempted to continue his racing career later in the season, he found it impossible to compete successfully in AAA championship races and returned to the half-mile tracks following his early elimination at Indianapolis in 1928.

In the spring of 1929, after he had emerged from this period of mental anguish and remarried, he set his eyes again on Indianapolis but was refused permission to compete in any AAA event until after the 500 because of his half-mile track activities. Then, again in good standing, he won six of the first seven 100-mile AAA dirt track races in which he participated. Except in 1933, however, when he drove an Offenhauser-powered Mallory Special to 2nd place, his efforts at Indianapolis were unproductive until 1933. On three occasions he was eliminated early because of mechanical trouble; and, as a member of the Duesenberg team in 1931, he crashed over the outer retaining wall when involved in a multiple-car

Wilbur Shaw. Photo: Indianapolis Motor Speedway

Left, Wilbur Shaw in the Gilmore-Offenhauser in which he won the Indianapolis 500 in 1937. Photo: Indianapolis Motor Speedway

Right, Wilbur Shaw in the Maserati 8CTF (Boyle Special) in which he won the Indianapolis 500 in 1939 and 1940. This photo taken in 1941. Photo: Charles Lytle

accident. Undaunted, despite minor cuts and bruises, he walked back to the pits and rejoined the race as a relief driver for Jimmy Gleason in another Duesenberg which finished 6th.

With AAA racing activity at its lowest ebb in the history of the sport, because of the economic depression, Shaw decided in 1935 to concentrate on winning the one big annual purse at Indianapolis during the remaining years of his driving career. For two more seasons he did make occasional appearances elsewhere, including both of the international road races on the Roosevelt, New York, course, where his best finish was 8th place in 1937 with a two-year old Alfa Romeo. His Indianapolis record, however, was phenomenal as he won three times and finished second twice during a six-year period beginning in 1935.

Driving his Offenhauser-powered Shaw Gilmore Special, he broke the race record by more than 10 minutes to win in 1937 at a speed of 113·58mph (182·83kph). After boosting his speed in the same car a full 2mph the following year, but finishing 2nd behind Floyd Roberts, he drove Mike Boyle's 183ci (2,998·83cc) supercharged 8-cylinder Maserati to his other 500 victories in 1939 and 1940 at speeds of 115·035 (185·131) and 114·277mph (183·921kph), respectively. Headed for an unprecedented fourth 500 victory—and his third in a row with the Boyle entry—he hit the wall in 1941 when the right rear wheel collapsed while he was leading the field with only 49 laps to go.

With the outbreak of World War 2, Shaw headed the Firestone Tyre and Rubber Company's aircraft division and worried about the future of the 500 as the speedway and installations began to show signs of increasing deterioration during more than four years of idleness. When hostilities ended, however, Shaw persuaded Anton Hulman, a prominent Hoosier businessman and sportsman (see Indianapolis Motor Speedway) to assume the financial responsibility for restoring the important race to its traditional position on the international schedule.

As president and general manager of the track for the new owner, Shaw played an important part in building up interest in the 500 to a new high level. Attendance increased each year and he persuaded many new car owners and sponsors to participate as the prize money also grew steadily.

Of equal importance, he stimulated interest in the sport throughout the entire nation by visiting every other important race track and making thousands of press, tv and radio interviews and appearances before his death while flying as a passenger in a private aircraft which crashed on 30 October 1954. AB

Shelby, Carroll

Born in Leesburg, Tex., in 1923, son of a rural mail carrier, Shelby drove an MG TC to victory in his first race in May 1952 at Norman, Okla. After winning drives in XK 120 Jaguar and Cadillac Allard, Shelby joined Phil Hill, Masten Gregory and Bob Said as an American team entry in the January 1954 Argentine 1,000 Kilometres. In Buenos Aires, Carroll met John Wyer, who was to become his team manager at Aston Martin and later an associate of Shelby's in his Cobra and Ford ventures. Shelby first raced in England at Aintree early in 1954 where his Aston Martin DB3 finished 2nd to Duncan Hamilton's C-type Jaguar. In August 1954, Shelby, Donald Healey, Capt George Eyston and Roy Jackson-Moore set more than 70 Land Speed records for Austin-Healey on the Bonneville Salt Flats. Phil Hill and Shelby, in a 3-litre Ferrari, finished a disputed 2nd to the Hawthorn and Walters D-type Jaguar at Sebring 1955, and the tall, casual, Texan, with his striped farmer's coveralls, was a frequent winner in SCCA nationals.

Shelby was injured at Riverside in September 1957 during practice, but recovered by November to win a classic contest with Gurney, Gregory and Hansgen at the same circuit. In the October 1956 Cuban GP, Shelby, driving John Edgar's 4·9 Ferrari, finished 2nd to Juan Manuel Fangio. In the Cuban GP in January 1958, in which Fidel Castro engineered a propaganda coup by kidnapping Fangio, Shelby was in 3rd place behind Moss and Gregory when an accident caused the race to be terminated. Shelby's Formula 1 experience, limited to the Syracuse GP in 1955, three 1958 rides in a Centro Sud 250F Maserati and the front-engined Aston Martin, obsolete before it was raced, was uniformly dismal. Shelby said that winning the 1959 Le Mans, in the Aston Martin DBR1/300 with Roy Salvadori, was the highpoint of his racing career. His last season as a driver was 1960. He won sports car races at Riverside in April and at Castle Rock, Colo., in June, but recurrent chest pains were diagnosed as angina pectoris and Shelby decided to concentrate on his dream of building an American sports car (*see also* Cobra). ARB

Siffert, Josef

This slightly-built Swiss has come to the top through sheer hard work and determination. Known as Jo or Seppi, Siffert was born in Fribourg, on 7 July 1936, son of a motor dealer, Alois Siffert. Money was short, but he started racing in 1957 with a Gilera 125 motorcycle.

He turned to cars in 1960 with a FJ Lotus 18, and also drove a Stanguellini, finishing 2nd to Colin Davis in a heat at Messina. But he liked the Lotus and bought a later Mark 20 model for 1961. He leapt to prominence that year by scoring seven wins and many more placings, and became joint European Formula Junior Champion with Tony Maggs. He acquired a FJ Lotus 22 for 1962 and a 4-cylinder Formula 1 Lotus 21 both to be run under national Scuderia Filipinetti colours. He scored three Formula Junior victories, and was 6th in the Brussels GP using the FJ car with a 1·5-litre Cosworth push-rod engine installed. He was 7th in his true F1 début at Pau, and was faster in practice than works drivers Bonnier, Maggs and Taylor at Monaco, only to be rejected by the seeding system there.

Filipinetti ran a Lotus-BRM 24 for Siffert in 1963, and he won the Syracuse GP and was 2nd at Imola before going fully independent and breaking with the team. Siffert was now a motor trader in his own right with a

garage at Granges-Paccot just outside Fribourg. He bought a new Brabham-BRM for the 1964 season; there were problems with the car but he managed a good 4th place in the German GP. Rob Walker handled his entries for the American races at the end of the season and Siffert joined Bonnier's Brabham-Climax in the team, taking a brilliant 3rd place behind Hill and Surtees in the United States GP. He also beat Clark and Ireland at Enna, and Walker ran a two-car team for 1965 with Siffert and Bonnier driving. Retaining the BRM V-8-engined car, Seppi was 6th in the Monaco and French GPs and 4th at Mexico City, and he beat Clark again in the Mediterranean GP at Enna.

Siffert was an accepted part of the GP 'circus' now, and Walker bought him a new Cooper-Maserati V-12 for the start of the 3-litre Formula in 1966. The car was heavy, underpowered and initially ill-handling, and the year's best result was 4th in the American GP. Siffert was 2nd in the non-championship South African GP early in the year, but that was in the Brabham-BRM.

He drove a Porsche 906 in sports car events in 1966, and Porsche and Ferraris in 1967. Among several good places, 2nd at Spa and Reims (with Piper) were his best.

Walker bought him a new Lotus 49B for 1968 but Siffert wrote it off first time out at Brands Hatch. An ex-Tasman chassis replaced it and he won the British GP, was 5th at Watkins Glen, 6th at Mexico City and set fastest lap in the British, Canadian and Mexican events. He also won at Daytona, Sebring, the Nürburgring and Zeltweg in works Porsches and had achieved a great reputation for spectacular, fast and fearless driving.

Formula 1 performances were not so good in 1969, with only 2nd, 3rd and 4th places to show in the Dutch, Monaco and South African GPs. Porsche took their Championship, however, with the partnership of Siffert and Brian Redman winning at Brands Hatch, Spa, the Nürburgring and Watkins Glen, and Siffert and Ahrens winning the Österreichring 1,000 Kilometres. He also drove BMWs in Formula 2, his best finish being 2nd in the Eifelrennen. The year 1970 saw Jo buying a March F1 drive and having a dreadful season. He scored three major wins for Gulf-JW Porsche, won at Rouen for BMW and joined BRM for 1971. DCN

Singh, Joginder

The most successful Asian rally driver, Joginder Singh was born in Kericho, Kenya. For many years he worked with the AA of East Africa, during which time he rallied a VW with his brother Jaswant. His first Safari was in 1959 when he finished 7th overall, but it was not until 1965, when he had bought the ex-Tom Trana Volvo PV 544, that he won the Safari as well as the Uganda Rally and the Tanganyika 1000 to become the East African Rally champion. He drove with Volvo in the Swedish Rally of 1966 and had also competed twice in the Austrian Alpine Rally with a Porsche. He was East African champion again in 1969 and now drives for Datsun, with which make of car he was 2nd overall in the 1970 Safari. JD

Sivocci, Ugo

This Italian driver was a former racing cyclist who drove for Alfa Romeo in the early 1920s, and scored his greatest success for them in the 1923 Targa Florio. He began driving in this event in 1913, when he finished 6th in a De Vecchi, and was leading in 1914, also in a De Vecchi, when he crashed. He drove for CMN in the 1919 Targa (finished 7th) and during his time with this firm persuaded

Carroll Shelby. *Photo: Autosport*

Jo Siffert. *Photo: Autosport*

Jo Siffert, in Brian Redman's pit during the Spa 1,000km, 1970. *Photo: Nigel Snowdon*

nzo Ferrari to join him. When Ferrari went to Alfa vocci followed him, and drove a 20/30 ES sport in ill-climbs and races in 1921 and 1922, winning the 4·5-tre touring car class of the 1921 Targa, and coming 4th verall.

Sivocci was the first to drive an RL Alfa Romeo in ompetitions, finishing 4th overall in the Autumn GP at Monza in 1923. It was in a special RLTF model that he on the 1923 Targa Florio. In September 1923 he was ractising for the Italian GP in a P1 Alfa at Monza when e was killed at the Curva del Vialone, a bend destined claim the lives of Luigi Arcangeli in 1931 and Alberto scari in 1955 — all practice accidents. PMAH

lotemaker, Rob

ow famous for his anti-skid school in Holland, Rob otemaker was born in Djakarta, Indonesia in 1929. He arted rallies and racing just as a hobby but it soon rned into much more than that. After training as a lot in Canada, he returned to Holland where he has riven mainly for the Alfa Romeo, BMW and DKW nporters. He drove in rallies for the Triumph team in)64 and 1965, in the Monte Carlo, Alpine, Tour de rance and the RAC Rally. In 1966 he drove a Citroën the Monte Carlo but since then has rallied in BMWs, inning his class twice in the Tulip Rally and also in the)69 Monte Carlo, In Holland he has raced Alfa Romeo TAs, and with this car won the Dutch Touring car ampionship in 1967 and 1968. JD

ommer, Raymond

orn in 1906, the son of a rich French felt manufacturer, is racing driver was so full of courage, determination d enthusiasm on the track that his countrymen nick-amed him 'Coeur de Lion'. He enjoyed working on his rs and was famous for the 'box of beautiful shining ols' he always had with him. Rather than retire he ould work on a car to get it going again, and carry on hen he had lost all chance of a victory or a place. He was so very helpful to up and coming drivers.

In 1931 he had a class win in the Belgian 24-hour race riving a big Chrysler with Delmar, but first became mous in 1932 when he shared an 8C 2300 Alfa Romeo ith Chinetti at Le Mans, drove for 21 hours as his co-river was unwell, and won the race against the works lfa team. Later in the year he drove his 2·3 Monza Alfa omeo in the Marseilles GP at Miramas and achieved e apparently impossible by winning against Nuvolari a 2·6-litre P3 Monoposto Alfa Romeo, thanks to a iscalculation in Nuvolari's pit, followed by a burst re. In 1933 Sommer again won at Le Mans in an 8C ³00 Alfa Romeo, by a mere 10sec, and his partner was uvolari. He also drove a Monza Alfa in this year, and n a Maserati stable in partnership with Freddy ehender. In 1934 he was 3rd to two Type 59 Bugattis in e Belgian GP driving a 2·9 Maserati. In 1935 he quired a 3·2-litre P3 Monoposto Alfa Romeo and at the Ferrari team in the Comminges GP and was 3rd Dreyfus and Chiron's Ferrari Alfas in the Marne GP. 1936 he was 4th in the Vanderbilt Cup, New York, in ·9B P3 which he sold to Joel Thorne, and won the orts car French GP with his great friend Wimille in a reamlined Bugatti, then the Belgian 24-hour Race with everi in an 8C 2900 Alfa Romeo. In 1937 he won two orts car races at Marseilles and Tunis in Talbots. He ove the outclassed Scuderia Ferrari Alfas in 1937 rands Prix, and the equally outclassed Alfa Corse cars 1938, managing a 4th at Tripoli in a Type 308 behind

Ugo Sivocci before the 1922 Targa Florio.
Photo: T. A. S. O. Mathieson Collection

Rob Slotemaker. *Photo: Gösta C. Zwilling*

Raymond Sommer. *Photo: Cyril Posthumus Collection*

George Souders. *Photo: Indianapolis Motor Speedway*

three Mercedes in the latter year. In the 8C 2900 Alfa coupé he drove with Biondetti at Le Mans in 1938, he insisted on driving in a straw hat which he gaily waved as he passed the stands in the lead on the first lap. Unfor-tunately the car broke down with a 100-mile (160km) lead after over 18 hours. In 1939 Sommer was 2nd to his team-mate Farina in a works sports 412 Alfa Romeo in the Antwerp GP, and he had quite a good season with his private Type 308 Alfa Romeo, including a victory in the Circuit des Remparts at Angoulême, and breaking the Montlhéry track lap record.

It is said Sommer served as a private soldier in the war, and at the end was one of those responsible for getting Dr Porsche released from prison at Dijon. He was 2nd in the very first post-war race in a single-seater Talbot to Wimille's Bugatti in the Bois de Boulogne in Paris in 1945. The next year was probably his best, with five victories, including beating the 158 Alfas at St Cloud, giving him the Championship of France, which he had also won in 1937 and 1939. He also made fastest lap in a 4CL Maserati running against the 158s at Berne. He was ill in 1947 after inadvertently swallowing methanol at Pau, but continued his successes, in 1948 and 1949 Formula 1 races, actually mixing with the 158 Alfas with his big Talbot, and beating Fangio's Maserati in a heat at Albi. In 1950 he was seen at the wheel of a 16-cylinder BRM, just as he had been associated with two almost equally recalcitrant French cars, the SEFAC before the war and the CTA-Arsenal after. He was certainly not above racing 500cc cars, which he did with some success, and then was tragically killed in a minor race driving an 1,100cc Cooper at Gardours in the Haute Garonne GP in 1950. It was thought a wheel-bearing had seized. PMAH

Souders, George

Souders, born in 1903, gained his early racing experience on the dirt tracks in the mid-western and south-western areas of the United States, and flashed to almost instant fame in 1927 by winning the first India-napolis 500 miles race in which he participated.

Driving a privately-owned Duesenberg entered by William White, Souders maintained a steady pace and gradually improved his position as his better known rivals were eliminated because of mechanical trouble and accidents. He advanced to 2nd place when a broken connecting rod put out Frank Lockhart, the favourite; and took the lead on the 150th lap when Peter DePaolo, driving relief for Bob McDonough, found it necessary to reduce speed because of supercharger trouble.

Souders also came 3rd at Indianapolis in a Miller-powered car the following year. Later in the season, how-ever, he suffered serious injuries in a racing accident at Detroit and never drove in competition again. For many years he operated a garage and service station in Lafayette, Ind., where he is living now in retirement. AB

Spence, Michael Henderson

This British driver was born in 1936 in Croydon, Surrey, the elder son of a sliding-door engineer. In 1957 he began rallying his father's Turner 950, and with parental support he bought a second-hand AC Ace-Bristol for 1958. Spence made his racing début at Goodwood, D finishing 4th in a BARC Members' Handicap, and retained the car for 1959, racing widely in home club events.

An FJ Cooper-Austin was acquired for 1960 in which Spence scored three victories, three 2nds and set three

lap records; he also had two unsuccessful Formula 2 drives in a 1·5 Cooper-Climax that season. In 1961 he raced an FJ Emeryson-Ford, and the Ace, and made his first Formula 1 appearance in an Emeryson-Climax, retiring at Solitude and finishing 2nd to Tony Marsh's BRM at Brands Hatch. In 1962 he ran his own FJ Lotus-Ford 22 under Ian Walker's team banner, working for his uncle's Coburn Engineering company at Peasmarsh in Surrey during the day and preparing his car long into the night. He achieved one win, seven 2nds and four 3rd places in 22 starts with the car, and won a three-year Lotus contract beginning in 1963.

That year the Lotus 27 FJ needed a lot of development but Spence drove well and stood in for the injured Trevor Taylor in the Italian GP. In 1964 he shared the 3rd-place Formula 1 Lotus with Peter Arundell at Syracuse and raced widely in Formula 2. Arundell crashed badly at Reims and Spence found himself in the Formula 1 team in his place. He had a good 1965 F1 season, including a win in the non-championship Race of Champions at Brands Hatch, and also won the non-championship South African GP for Lotus in early 1966. When Arundell returned to the works team, Spence signed to drive Tim Parnell's Lotus-BRM, taking some good places with the uncompetitive car. In 1967 he persevered with the Parnell team's H16 BRM, consistently nursing the car to the finish. He also teamed up with Phil Hill in

Left above, Mike Spence (right) in the Emeryson FJ, at Silverstone in 1961. *Photo: Michael Ware*

Above, Mike Spence, after winning his first Formula 1 race, the 1965 Race of Champions at Brands Hatch. *Photo: A. R. F. Cooke*

Below, John Sprinzel. *Photo: Hugh W. Bishop*

Left below, Mike Spence. *Photo: Norman Reich*

Below, Jackie Stewart at Monaco during his BRM days. *Photo: Geoffrey Goddard*

the Chaparral 2F for long-distance races, and won the BOAC 500 at Brands Hatch at the end of the season. Then came the Can-Am series and a series of good driv in an obsolete McLaren.

Spence was selected for the BRM works team in 196 his analytical approach greatly helping their test programme. Then Jim Clark was killed and Lotus offered him a drive at Indianapolis in the Lotus 56 turbine car. He accepted readily and passed his 'rookie tests easily when the track opened for qualifying on 1 May. Three days later he set the then second-fastest la ever at Indianapolis at 169·555mph (272·88kph), and later that afternoon took out team-mate Greg Weld's c for a few shake-down laps. He had got up to a lap in 163·1mph when he lost control and hit the wall in turn one. Damage was not severe, but the right front wheel folded back and hit the driver; he died in hospital 4½ hours later. DCN

Sprinzel, John

John Sprinzel was born in Berlin in 1930 but shortly afterwards his family moved to London where he studi economics and became a pilot with the RAF in 1948/9 His first rally was the RAC in 1955, for which auspicio event he borrowed his mother's Austin A30, drew number one and managed to finish. He was so taken w the sport that he bought a TR 2 and had such success that he was offered a works drive with the BMC team. rallied an A35 through 1957 and 1958 and during that time founded the firm of Speedwell, whose main busine was to tune cars of that type. He also raced the A35 an narrowly missed winning the Touring Car Championship.

In 1958 he got one of the first Austin Healey Sprites and won the London Rally and his class in the Alpine Rally. During the next two years, he carried on with th Sprite and in 1960 was 3rd overall in the Liège-Sofia–Liège and 2nd overall in the RAC Rally, results which put him 6th overall in the European Championship. H also won the BTRDA Gold Star and the RAC Rally championships.

Since then he has concentrated mainly on running hi own garage business under the name of John Sprinzel Racing, but on many occasions has taken time off to drive in works teams such as Triumph, Ford, Porsche, Datsun, Peugeot and Saab. In the 1964 Safari he drove to a magnificent 4th overall in a Mercedes 190 and in 1969 he was a member of the winning Datsun team.

As well as driving himself he has co-driven on occasic with Erik Carlsson (Portuguese Rally) and Hans Walt (RAC Rally) and has also written on rallying, for the *Daily Mirror* and BLMC's *High Road* magazine. For three years he has also been World of Sport commentate for rallycross and other motoring sports on British independent television. His most recent achievement h been to organize the *Daily Mirror* World Cup Rally as secretary of the event. JD

Stewart, John Young

The Scotsman Jackie Stewart continues in the traditior of Fangio, Moss and Clark, setting the standard for Grand Prix driving in his time. He was born on 11 June 1939, younger son of the Dumbarton Jaguar dealer. Hi brother, Jimmy, raced for Ecurie Ecosse and the works Aston Martin team in the mid-1950s, but retired after a bad crash at Le Mans. He returned to the Dumbuck Garage business, where 15-year old Jackie had recently started work as a mechanic.

Jackie Stewart: Principal Successes

Year	Event	Car
1964	Snetterton (F2)	Lotus-Ford 32
	Oulton Park	Cooper Monaco
	Marlboro' 12-Hours	Lotus-Cortina
1965	Italian GP	BRM V-8
	International Trophy, Silverstone	BRM V-8
1966	Monaco GP	BRM V-8
	Tasman Championship	
	Christchurch	BRM V-8
	Invercargill	BRM V-8
	Sandown Park	BRM V-8
	Longford	BRM V-8
	Mount Fuji	Lola-Ford
	Surfers' Paradise 12-Hours, with Buchanan	Ferrari 275LM
1967	New Zealand GP	BRM V-8
	Australian GP	BRM V-8
	Karlskoga (F2)	Matra-Ford
	Enna (F2)	Matra-Ford
	Oulton Park (F2)	Matra-Ford
	Albi (F2)	Matra-Ford
1968	Dutch GP	Matra-Ford MS 10
	United States GP	Matra-Ford MS 10
	German GP	Matra-Ford MS 10
	Oulton Park Gold Cup	Matra-Ford MS 10
	Barcelona (F2)	Matra-Ford
	Pau (F2)	Matra-Ford
	Reims (F2)	Matra-Ford
1969	South African GP	Matra-Ford MS 80
	Spanish GP	Matra-Ford MS 80
	Dutch GP	Matra-Ford MS 80
	French GP	Matra-Ford MS 80
	British GP	Matra-Ford MS 80
	Italian GP	Matra-Ford MS 80
	Race of Champions, Brands Hatch	Matra-Ford MS 80
	Eifelrennen (F2)	Matra-Ford
	Jarama (F2)	Matra-Ford
1970	Spanish GP	March-Ford 701
	Race of Champions, Brands Hatch	March-Ford 701
	Crystal Palace (F2)	Brabham-Ford BT30

Below, Jackie Stewart at Monaco during his BRM days. Photo: Geoffrey Goddard

Right, Jackie Stewart, 1969. Photo: Geoffrey Goddard

Jackie had watched his brother racing, but took up clay-pigeon shooting as his sport. He had reached Olympic standard before turning his interests towards motor racing. One of Dumbuck Garage's wealthy patrons, Barry Filer, took Jackie along as mechanic to some meetings, then gave him drives in a Marcos, an Aston Martin DB4GT, an AC Ace and the garage's own Jaguar E demonstrator. A test session at Oulton Park early in 1962 revealed Stewart's rare ability, and from that day forward he determined to become a professional racing driver.

Ecurie Ecosse gave him some drives in their Tojeiro coupés and an old Cooper Monaco in which he showed tremendous promise, enough for the Goodwood track manager Robin McKay to mention his prowess to Ken Tyrrell, who was at that time planning his Cooper-BMC F3 team for 1964. Stewart bettered Bruce McLaren's times round Goodwood in a pre-season test session with the cars, and Tyrrell signed him on the spot. That first F3 season was a Stewart triumph, for he won every race he entered except two, and the beginning of his meteoric rise. He was given a Ron Harris-Team Lotus F2 drive at Clermont, finishing 2nd to Hulme, and later won for the team at Snetterton. He did a few practice laps in Clark's F1 Lotus-Climax at Brands Hatch before the British GP and deputized for Jimmy, who had slipped a disc, in the Rand GP at the end of the year, winning the second heat after shearing both drive shafts in the first.

Many offers had come his way, and he accepted that from BRM, entering his first full Formula 1 season in 1965. His Championship début was in the South African GP in which he finished 6th and scored a point; he set the joint perpetual Goodwood lap record with Clark in the Easter Monday meeting there; then won the international Trophy at Silverstone; was 3rd at Monaco; and 2nd at Spa, Clermont-Ferrand and Zandvoort, trailing his compatriot Clark and underlining his latent ability in no uncertain manner. At Monza he won his first Grande Epreuve, and ended the year 3rd in the World Championship standings.

Stewart was making his mark. In 1966 he won the Tasman Championship and the Monaco GP, then led for many laps at Indianapolis before a scavenge pump broke. But at Spa the Belgian GP field ran into rain on the opening lap and he crashed badly at Masta, breaking a shoulder and cracking a rib—an accident which put him back two years, and made him the great protagonist of racing in safety.

He was back for the Dutch GP but the H-16 BRM was slow in developing and the 2-litre V-8s he and Hill were driving had little chance against the still-nimble 3-litre Repco Brabhams. However, he had driven for Tyrrell's F2 Cooper team in 1965. Tyrrell had been approached by Matra, who were interested in entering Formula 2 in 1966. Stewart tested an F3 chassis with an F2 engine installed at Goodwood late that year, and the Tyrrell Racing Organization ran two Matra-Cosworths in the 1966 season.

The connection with Tyrrell and Matra in F2 continued through 1967 while Stewart became team-leader at BRM after Hill had moved to Lotus. The H-16s never fulfilled their promise and although Stewart was 2nd at Spa his only other good placing was 3rd with a V-8 in the French GP. At the end of the year the combination of Matra, Cosworth, Dunlop and Stewart began to succeed in Formula 2, and he won at Karlskoga, Enna and Albi and in the F2 section of the Oulton Park Gold Cup race.

Stewart's career reached a cross-roads at the end of the season, for a deal with Ferrari collapsed and BRM seemed destined to make little improvement in 1968. Tyrrell was keen to enter Formula 1 ever since seeing the Cosworth V-8 engine's successful first competitive run in the Dutch GP, and a deal was concluded with Matra, Dunlop and the Elf fuel company whereby they would back Tyrrell and Stewart racing under the Equipe Matra International banner, using Cosworth engines in special Matra chassis.

The experiment would have been a great success but for a minor accident in an F2 race at Jarama which broke a bone in Stewart's wrist and put him out of the Spanish and Monaco GPs, and the Indianapolis 500. He reappeared at Spa, racing with his wrist supported by a plastic cast, and would have won but for running out of fuel on the last but one lap. He did win the Dutch, German and United States GPs and was in the running for the Championship when a fuel blockage slowed him in Mexico. The year's performance had been enough to prove the combination's value and in 1969 the Matra-Cosworth and Stewart swept all before them, winning the South African, Spanish, Dutch, French, British and Italian GPs to secure his first, long-awaited World Championship title.

In 1970 he struggled manfully with the Tyrrell March, winning the Spanish GP and (luckily) the Race of Champions. In F2 he scored one 1st and one 2nd in Coombs' Brabham and also won the JAF GP in Japan. He drove the Chaparral 2H at Watkins Glen and signed with Goodyear and Lola for 1971, in addition to his Tyrrell ties.

Stewart has concentrated on single-seaters in recent years, and in common with most leading drivers his dislike for Le Mans is well known, although he shared the Rover-BRM gas turbine car there in 1965. But he is a natural sportsman, and excels at anything he turns his mind to. His confidence and skill is obvious from his record; he also has great determination, evident during

1968 when he was driving with his damaged scaphoid. He finished 6th in the British GP, utterly exhausted after forcing himself to endure the pain of his damaged wrist, jolted over every bump at Brands Hatch. He won in pouring rain at the Nürburgring, still wearing his plaster-cast in a brilliant drive which would have been impossible had it been dry—his narrow Dunlop wet-weather tyres lightened the steering and relieved the load on his wrist.

Stewart lives at Begnins, near Geneva, with his wife and two young children. DCN

Stommelen, Rolf-Johann

Stommelen was born in Siegen in 1943, and in 1970 became the first German driver to compete regularly in Formula 1 races since the death of von Trips. His father owns a garage in Cologne, and Rolf began racing with Porsche in 1964 as a private entrant. He was fast and fearless from the very beginning, characteristics which have sometimes got him into trouble.

In 1965 he ran a private Porsche 904GTS and scored two 2nd places in internationals, one at Solitude and the other in the Prix du Tyrol at Innsbruck, where he was beaten by Rindt's Abarth 2000. The following season was an arid one, but in 1967 the youthful Stommelen's promise was recognized by Porsche and he was given a number of works drives. In one of these he shared the 1967 Targa Florio victory with Hawkins, and then

shared the 6th-place 910 with Neerpasch at Le Mans. The same pair were 2nd to Schutz and Mitter at Mugello. Stommelen excelled in the Mountain Championship rounds, winning four of them and coming 2nd in two to become runner-up to Mitter for the title. In 1968 he shared the winning cars at Daytona and in the Paris 1,000km; he was 2nd in the Monza and Nurbürgring 1,000km; and 3rd at Spa and Le Mans. He crashed heavily at Rossfeld in the meeting where Scarfiotti was killed, but was 2nd in the climbs at Sierre and Mont Ventoux and 3rd at Montseny, Cesana, Schauinsland and Gaisberg.

In 1969 he became one of Porsche's fastest drivers, setting a new unofficial Le Mans lap record in practice at 143·76mph (231·3kph) with an early Porsche 917. During the season he was 2nd at the Nürburgring, 3rd at Sebring and in the Targa, 4th at Spa and 6th at Brands Hatch. He was given a Lotus 59 F2 drive in the German GP and put up a sterling performance in his first single-seater race (he finished with the car on fire). The Porsche works officially withdrew from racing at the end of the season, but Stommelen ran his own F2 March team in 1970 with backing from Eifelland Caravans, was backed in an F1 Brabham-Cosworth Ford BT33 by *Auto, Motor und Sport*, and joined Autodelta for long-distance racing. He scored a 3rd and two 5ths in F1, and ran a Surtees-Cosworth in 1971. DCN

Jackie Stewart (Matra-Ford MS80) at Nürburgring, 1969. *Photo: Geoffrey Goddard*

Rolf Stommelen. *Photo: Autosport*

Straight, Whitney Willard

Born in 1912, Straight was an exception to a prevailing tradition, in as much as he was an American who raced in Britain and Europe when such drivers were unknown outside Indianapolis and were then mostly professionals. Straight first took up racing as a sport while he was an undergraduate at Cambridge, creating much interest by flying himself down to Brooklands after sitting for an examination at the University. He quit studies and made a profession of motor racing, forming for the purpose Whitney Straight Limited and buying a couple of 2·9-litre Maseratis and two MG Magnettes. That was in 1934, after Straight had established his reputation as a driver the previous year by breaking Birkin's Mountain circuit lap record at Brooklands in a 2·6-litre Maserati in the course of winning the Mountain Championship Race at 73·64mph (118·51kph).

Straight was a millionaire but intended to make his motor racing pay. He took on Giulio Ramponi as his head mechanic and used a chauffeur-driven 8-litre Bentley saloon and a de Havilland Moth aircraft for attending races. Those who drove for Straight included Marcel Lehoux, Buddy Featherstonehaugh, H. C. Hamilton and Dick Seaman, the latter a pupil of Straight's, who started with one of the MGs and later based his career on the business lines adopted by Straight. Straight's successes included winning the 1934 Prix de Berne in an MG, and in the same year he was 2nd in the Nuffield Trophy Race, 3rd at Pescara, 5th in the Masaryk GP and the East London GP. He followed this up by winning with a single-seater Maserati the International Trophy Race at Brooklands, the Donington Park Trophy and the South African Grand Prix, and he made ftd at the Mont Ventoux and Shelsley Walsh hill-climbs and broke his own Mountain circuit lap record at Brooklands in again winning the Mountain Championship. He was also 3rd at Comminges and 2nd in the Empire Trophy Race but in 1935 forsook motor racing for commerce. He became Managing Director of BOAC after a brilliant war-time RAF career, and joined Rolls-Royce Ltd in 1955. WB

Hans Stuck: Principal Successes

Year	Event	Car
1931	Lwow GP	Mercedes-Benz SSK
	Rio de Janeiro GP	Mercedes-Benz SSK
1934	German GP	Auto Union A-type
	Swiss GP	Auto Union A-type
	Masaryk GP	Auto Union A-type
1935	Italian GP	Auto Union A-type
1939	Bucharest GP	Auto Union D-type
1951	Grenzlandring-rennen (F2)	AFM
1960	Hockenheim 12-Hours with S. Greger (Touring)	BMW 700

Between 1925 and 1963, Hans Stuck achieved over 400 1st places in International hill-climbs. These include: *Germany*—Freiburg, Kesselberg, Rossfeld, Semmering, Grossglockner; *Switzerland*—Ollons-Villars, Klausen, Arlberg, Maloja, Albis, Bernina, Sierre-Montana, Klosters-Davos; *Italy*—Aosta-Great St Bernard, Stelvio, Sella Nevea, Trento-Bondone, Susa-Moncenisio; *France*—La Turbie, Mont Ventoux; *England*—Shelsley Walsh; *Czechoslovakia*—Zbraslav-Jiloviste; *Poland*—Tatra; *Rumania*—Feleac.

Cars driven: *Austro-Daimler, Mercedes-Benz, Auto Union, Cisitalia, AFM, BMW.*

Left, Whitney Straight (centre) with Brian Lewis (left), after winning the 1934 JCC International Trophy Race. *Photo: Cyril Posthumus Collection*

Right, Hans Stuck. *Photo: Cyril Posthumus Collection*

Stuck, Hans

Hans Stuck of Grainau, Austria, born in 1900, can claim one of the longest and most successful careers in motor racing and hill-climbing, spanning 39 years from 1924 to 1963. The father of this tall, cheerful, immensely fit and capable man came from Freiburg, famous speed hill-climb venue in south-west Germany, where many of Stuck's successes were scored. Stuck began with a Dürkopp in 1924, gaining swift success in local climbs, then graduating to Austro-Daimler cars, first a sports car in 1927, then a special 3-litre 6-cylinder short wheelbase Austro-Daimler to tackle the racing classes.

Stuck's record book soon attained formidable proportions: seven fastest times of day in 1927, 14 in 1928, 9 in 1929 and 12 in 1930, the year he came to Britain and set a new Shelsley Walsh record with the white Austro-Daimler. In 1931 Stuck moved to Mercedes, driving the huge SSK sports cars in races as well as hill-climbs and scoring 17 victories in two years. These included the Lwów GP in Poland and the Rio de Janeiro GP in Brazil, his first road race successes, both gained in 1931. In 1934 came the great German racing renaissance; Stuck contracting to drive the sensational 16-cylinder rear-engined Auto Union. He set three new world records at around 134mph (215kph) at the AVUS in March, and then came the first Grands Prix. He was 2nd in the Eifelrennen, and won the German GP. He followed up with further victories in the Swiss and Czech GPs and won four hill-climbs at Freiburg, Kesselberg, Mont Ventoux and Feldberg. That year, not surprisingly, Stuck was Champion of Germany.

In 1935 his sole victory was the Italian GP, and thereafter he had several disappointments: in 1936 he was pipped at the post in the Tripoli GP by his team-mate Varzi, and had a crash at Monza; in 1937 he went to South America, only to be beaten on the unending corners of the Gavea circuit at Rio de Janeiro by Pintacuda's more agile Alfa. But he came 3rd in the 1938 German GP, and won a very poorly supported Bucharest GP in 1939. In compensation there were his unending hill-climb successes: La Turbie in 1936, 1937, 1938

Far left, Hans Stuck, with a C-type Auto Union. Photo: Montagu Motor Museum

Left, John Surtees in the Tyrell Cooper-Austin, 1960. Photo: Reuter

John Surtees: Principal Successes

Year	Event	Car
1961	Lombank Trophy, Snetterton (F2)	Cooper-Climax
	Glover Trophy, Goodwood (F2)	Cooper-Climax
1962	Longford	Cooper-Climax
	Mallory Park 2,000 Guineas	Lola-Climax V-8
1963	New Zealand GP	Lola-Climax 4
	Sebring 12-Hours, with Scarfiotti	Ferrari 250P
	Nürburgring 1,000km, with Mairesse	Ferrari 250P
	German GP	Ferrari 156
	Mediterranean GP	Ferrari 156
	Rand GP	Ferrari 156
1964	German GP	Ferrari 158
	Italian GP	Ferrari 158
	Syracuse GP	Ferrari 158
1965	Nürburgring 1,000km, with Scarfiotti	Ferrari 330P/2
	Gold Cup, Oulton Park (F2)	Lola-Ford
	St Jovite	Lola-Chevrolet T70
	Players 200, Mosport	Lola-Chevrolet T70
	Guards Trophy, Brands Hatch	Lola-Chevrolet T70
1966	Belgian GP	Ferrari 312
	Monza 1,000km, with Parkes	Ferrari 330P/3
	Syracuse GP	Ferrari 312
	Guards Trophy, Brands Hatch	Lola-Chevrolet T70 Mk2
	Players Quebec, St Jovite	Lola-Chevrolet T70 Mk2
	Los Angles Times GP, Riverside	Lola-Chevrolet T70 Mk2
	Stardust GP, Las Vegas	Lola-Chevrolet T70 Mk2
	Mexican GP	Cooper-Maserati
1967	Italian GP	Honda R 301
	Guards Trophy, Mallory Park (F2)	Lola-Ford
	Zolder (F2)	Lola-Ford
	Stardust GP, Las Vegas	Lola-Chevrolet T70 Mk 3B

and 1939; Freiburg in 1935 and 1937; Kesselberg, Feldberg and Taunus in 1935; and the Grossglockner and Maloja in 1938. Stuck the versatile also broke the 1-hour water speed record with an Auto Union-engined boat, and was appointed to drive the Porsche-designed, 6-wheeled, aero-engined Mercedes-Benz land speed record car, but World War 2 put paid to this interesting project.

With the return of peace, Stuck acquired one of the first 1,100cc monoposto Cisitalias—a switch from 600-plus bhp to about 60 which the *Bergmeister* found 'amusing'. A victory at Hockenheim in 1947 heralded several more in races and hill-climbs, including the 1948 Aosta-Great St Bernard hill-climb. Then he took to a Formula 2 AFM fitted, first with a BMW engine, then with a special Küchen-designed V-8, and enjoyed more successes, notably in the 1950 Monza GP when his noted ability for getting off the line quickly took him to a heat win against the Ferraris; in the 1951 Grenzlandring race which he won outright; and in the usual hill-climbs. In 1957 he joined BMW as demonstrator and racing driver, fielding their V-8 507 sports model extensively in Continental hill-climbs and scoring 22 victories. As late as 1960, at the age of 60, this remarkable man won the Hockenheim 12 hours touring car race in a BMW 700, with Sepp Greger co-driving; and in the Ascari Trophy 12 hours at Monza they were again 1st in class, only to suffer disqualification for a technical breach of rules. In 1963, *Bergmeister* Stuck decided at last to retire from racing, having driven in over 700 speed events, and scored 427 1st places ranging from classic Grands Prix to hill-climb class victories. His son has now taken up racing where Stuck left off—in the BMW team. CP

Surtees, John

Born in 1934 and brought up in an atmosphere of motor-cycling competition, this British driver received early encouragement from both his parents, while at the same time being taught to make his own decisions and to work hard for what he wished to achieve. On leaving school he was apprenticed to Vincent's, the motorcycle en-

gineers, and his first successful racing machine was a 500cc Vincent 'Grey Flash' which he raced in 1951. Following this with a long run of victories on Norton machines, he earned a place in the Norton works team in 1955. In 1956 he transferred to the Italian MV concern, winning for them seven World Championships up to 1960—four in the 500cc and three in the 350cc class—and also assisting in their mechanical development.

Surtees took trials with Vanwall and with Parnell's Aston Martin team in 1959, and for 1960, when motor-cycling commitments permitted, drove a Tyrrell Cooper-Austin in Formula Junior, his own Cooper-Climax in Formula 2, and a works Lotus in Formula 1. In 1961 he joined Parnell's Yeoman Credit Cooper team, his best placing in the Grands Prix being a 2nd in the wet at the Nürburgring. He also drove the unwieldy rear-engined Vanwall. For 1962 he brought the Lola Formula 1 car that he had commissioned under Bowmaker's, who had taken over the Yeoman Credit team. This car was promising rather than successful, but Surtees did sufficiently well for Enzo Ferrari to repeat for 1963 the offer he had made a year earlier, and this time 'Big John' accepted. He rapidly enhanced his reputation both as driver and as development engineer, and his devotion to work, both at the wheel and behind the scenes, earned

John Surtees, passengering his father at Brands Hatch, c 1952. Photo: Photosurveys

the ultimate dividend in the form of the 1964 World Drivers' Championship.

Meanwhile he continued his association with Lolas, racing and assisting in the development of the T70 Group 7 sports car, but suffered a very serious crash through a suspension breakage at Mosport in 1964. His concentration and will-power facilitated a near-miraculous recovery, and his first event in convalescence was the 1965 Nürburgring 1,000 kilometres race which he won.

The Ferrari team manager's temperament was not always the perfect foil for Surtees' analytical approach, and the end came in 1966 when Surtees precipitately left, driving Cooper-Maserati and Matra for the rest of the season, and winning the Can-Am Group 7 series for Lola.

For the next two years he devoted his attention to developing the Honda Formula 1 car into a race-winner. He was supplied with Japanese mechanics, but worked under the handicap of having no established liaison with the factory design staff. His perseverance was rewarded with a GP victory at Monza in 1967, after an epic duel with Brabham. The car was developed still further during 1968, but could not quite match the rival makes which had started with a weight advantage. Then Honda produced a lighter air-cooled V-8 which was not given to Surtees to develop. The car was destroyed and its

John Surtees (centre), receiving the 1966 Johnson's Wax Can-Am Trophy from Samuel C. Johnson, president of Johnson's Wax. Left, Stirling Moss, racing director. *Photo: S. C. Johnson & Son Inc*

Left, John Surtees in the 1967 Honda V-12 at Brands Hatch. *Photo: Evan Selwyn-Smith*

Below, Bob Sweikert. *Photo: Indianapolis Motor Speedway*

Right, Bob Sweikert in the John Zink Special (Kurtis-Offenhauser) in which he won the Indianapolis 500 in 1955. *Photo: Indianapolis Motor Speedway*

driver, Jo Schlesser, killed on its debut at Rouen. Although Surtees finished 2nd in this race and led at Monza, and a second V-8 car was built, Honda withdrew at the end of that season.

For 1969 Surtees joined the BRM team, helping to develop the P153 V-12, but this was not an altogether successful car, and his highest placing was but 3rd in the United States GP. By this time he was devoting more time to his own business interests, which included construction of the 'Team Surtees' TS5 Formula 5000 car, developed in his workshops at Colnbrook, near Slough and at Edenbridge. In 1970 he raced his private Formula 1 McLaren to keep his hand in while his own design, the TS7 was being prepared. His best result with this car was 5th in the Canadian GP. DF

Sweikert, Robert

Bob Sweikert, born in 1926, one of America's most daring race drivers of the 1950s, crashed to his death in 1956 while at the peak of his racing career. One year earlier he had won the Indianapolis 500 miles race, as well as the national big car and Midwest sprint car championships; and he again was a strong contender for both titles, after finishing 6th at Indy, when he was injured fatally in an accident on the half-mile track at Salem, Ind.

Sweikert, who gained his early experience in midget and sprint car races in California, tried without success to win starting positions at Indianapolis in 1950 and 1951. On both occasions his average speed in the time trials was too slow. Mechanical trouble ended his hopes of finishing well in each of the next two Indianapolis events and he was flagged in 14th position behind Bill Vukovich in 1954.

One year later, when Vukovich crashed while leading the field at Indianapolis in quest of a third straight 500 victory, Sweikert was in position to battle with four other rivals for the no 1 position. He gained and then lost the lead twice, but came from behind again on the 160th lap and gradually increased his margin during the last 100 miles to finish with an average speed of 128·209mph (206·314kph).

He clinched the national driving title that season by finishing 4th or better in seven of the other nine championship events on the schedule. In 1956 he drove a D-type Jaguar at Sebring, and partnered by Jack Ensley, finished 3rd. AB

Szisz, François

The name of François Szisz, or Ferenc in his native Hungary, will live forever in motor racing history as the winner of the first French Grand Prix of all with a big,

red-painted 90hp Renault. This short, stocky and capable man born in 1873 came to France in 1900 and joined Renault Frères in their thriving Billancourt factory, first as a riding mechanic with Louis Renault, then as chief tester and racing driver. His mechanical skill and calm temperament helped to develop a deliberate, machine-like style of driving, totally in sympathy with the big, powerful, intractable racing cars of the time.

He drove the new 12·9-litre 90hp Renault in the Auvergne eliminating tests for the 1905 Gordon Bennett Cup, and was unfortunate to miss a place in the three-car French team owing to tyre troubles and overheating in the curious Renault cooling system of that year. As one of the first five finishers, however, he won a starting place in the Vanderbilt Cup race, held in October 1905 on Long Island. After lying 2nd on laps 2 and 3, Szisz had to cope with the same overheating troubles which plagued him in the Auvergne, eventually finishing 5th.

Then came the 1906 Grand Prix, successor to the controversial Gordon Bennett series, and Szisz drove one of three Renaults, now with conventional cooling and detachable wheel rims which cured the tyre problem. The race was over 770 miles (1,240km), split into two one-day runs of 385 miles on the fast Sarthe circuit outside Le Mans. In scorching summer heat Szisz won the first day's race by 25 minutes and the second by 32 minutes—a complete triumph for Renault, for France, and for the quiet, unassuming Szisz, who averaged an impressive 61·3mph (98·65kph) inclusive of all stops for tyres and vital fluids.

Driving basically the same 90hp Renault, Szisz emphasized its growing obsolescence by finishing 2nd in the 1907 Grand Prix and retiring after lying 3rd in the 1908 race. His last drive for Renault was in the 1908 American Grand Prize, when he climbed from 4th to 2nd place by lap 3, but retired on lap 7 with a broken wheel bearing. The unpronounceable name of Szisz then departed from racing, and it was thought he had retired until, in 1914, he reappeared for the Grand Prix at Lyons at the wheel of an Alda. Though driving with skill and remarkable consistency, Szisz never got higher than 17th and retired after 11 laps for a most unusual reason—he was struck by a passing Opel while changing a punctured wheel, suffering arm injuries. Despite this, eighteen days later, Szisz won a lesser French road race—the Circuit of Anjou held near Rochefort. Driving a 12-litre Lorraine-Dietrich, he covered the distance of 222 miles (357·3km) in 3hr 31min 6sec, over 27 minutes faster than

the second finisher, and averaging 65mph (104·6kph) on a course which he declared was as difficult as that for the 1914 Grand Prix. With that pleasing little victory Szisz retired from racing. He died at Tiszaszentimre, Hungary in June 1970, at the age of 97. CP

Takahashi, Kunimitsu

Born in 1940, Takahashi made his name as a World Championship-class racing motorcyclist with the Honda team. He was the first Japanese rider to win a major European Grand Prix race while with them, and when Soichiro Honda decided to withdraw his support, Takahashi turned to 4-wheel racing.

He joined Kurosawa in the Datsun-Nissan works team in 1965, and has driven Datsun Bluebird and Fairlady saloons as well as Nissan R380 Group 7 cars. He won the 1970 Fuji 1,000km in a Datsun 240Z. DCN

Taruffi, Piero

Taruffi, born in 1906, is from a Roman family and received much encouragement from his father, Dr Pompeo Taruffi. While a 17-year-old schoolboy he won the 1923 Rome–Viterbo reliability trial in the family Fiat 501S, and until 1930 was a successful racing motorcyclist on AJS, Panther, Guzzi and Norton machines. His first chance in car racing came from his friend Lelio Pellegrini whose 2·3 Bugatti he shared in the 1930 Mille Miglia to finish 40th. He then won the Tunis–Tripoli trial with Pellegrini's 1750 Alfa Romeo, and in 1931 was 8th in the Circuit of Montenero in his Model 65 2-litre Itala. His showing with the Itala, and a 112mph (180·2kph) lap at Monza on his Norton, determined Enzo Ferrari to give him a trial for the Scuderia Ferrari. In the Coppa Frigo hill-climb (Bolsena–Montefiascone), his 2·3 Alfa made ftd and beat Biondetti's 2-litre Bugatti by 17sec. In 1932 he was 2nd in the Spa 24-hour race with D'Ippolito in a 2·3 sports Alfa, and 2nd in the Rome GP between Fagioli's 16-cylinder Maserati and two Type 51 Bugattis, driving a Monza Alfa. He did not have a Ferrari car for the 1933 Mille Miglia, but came 3rd with Pellegrini in the latter's 2·3 Alfa. In a Ferrari Monza Alfa, Taruffi came 3rd in the 1933 Eifelrennen at the Nürburgring. Meanwhile he was still racing motorcycles, and was asked to leave the Ferrari car team after beating the Ferrari motorcycle team's best rider, Aldrighetti on a Rudge, with his Norton at Montenero.

Taruffi then purchased an 8C 3000 Maserati with the help of friends, and was 3rd in the Coppa Acerbo behind Fagioli (P3 Alfa) and Nuvolari (Maserati). In 1934 he was driving works Maseratis, but crashed badly at Tripoli in the big 16-cylinder W5. In 1935 he drove for Bugatti and won a 3rd at Turin, but his Type 59 crashed at the Nürburgring after a mechanical failure. Although Taruffi rode in his last motorcycle race in 1937, he was racing manager for Gilera up to World War 2, his car racing being mainly with the Scuderia Ambrosiana (Maserati) and Piero Dusio's Scuderio Torino (Alfa Romeo and Maserati). In 1936 he drove Earl Howe's Type 51 Bugatti at Brooklands and was 2nd in the Mountain Championship to Straight's Maserati, and was 2nd in the Grosvenor GP in South Africa in his old 3-litre Maserati. In 1937 he was 2nd in the Cape Town GP in an Ambrosiana 6C Maserati 1·5-litre. Then in 1938 he was 2nd in the Grosvenor GP to Earl Howe's ERA. In 1939 he won at Cape Town in Earl Howe's ERA and gained places with 1·5-litre Maseratis in Italian races.

In 1947 Taruffi had many successes in Italy with

Left, François Szisz, 1907. *Photo: T. A. S. O. Mathieson Collection*

Below, Piero Taruffi. *Photo: Montagu Motor Museum*

Piero Taruffi (right), with Raymond Mays.
Photo: Autosport

Henry Taylor. *Photo: Autosport*

Below, Trevor Taylor. *Photo: Autosport*

Centre, Henry Taylor (Lotus FJ) at
Snetterton, 1961. *Photo: Brian Bane*

Right, Trevor Taylor (right), with Gerhard
Mitter. *Photo: Bernard Cahier*

Dusio's 1,100cc Cisitalia single-seaters and was Italian 1,500cc Champion, repeating this Cisitalia driving less successfully in 1948, interspersed with a 4th place in the Monza GP in the 158 Alfa Romeo team. In 1949 Cisitalia successes made him Italian Formula 2 Champion, and he was 2nd in the Rome GP in a Formula 2 Ferrari. In 1951 he was an official Ferrari works driver, winning the Carrera Panamericana, gaining GP places, and finishing 3rd in a Brands Hatch 500cc race in a Cooper-Norton. In 1952 he was 3rd in the World Championship with his Ferrari placings, though he had an outright victory in the Ulster Trophy with Vandervell's Thinwall Special Ferrari.

For Taruffi 1953 was an unsuccessful year of many retirements with sports Lancias, but in 1954 he won the Targa Florio and Giro di Sicilia with these cars. In 1955 he was racing Ferraris again, but also drove in the Mercedes-Benz GP team, being 2nd in the Italian GP and 4th in the British. Then 1956 was a Maserati year, with places in sports car events, though he drove a Vanwall in the Italian GP, but retired.

In 1957 Taruffi had a fine victory in a Ferrari in his 14th Mille Miglia, the last to be held, and this was the culmination of a long, successful and varied career. From 1948 to 1957 he had gained world's records almost annually in his own unusual twin-boom Tarf cars with Guzzi, Gilera or Maserati engines. PMAH

Taylor, Henry C.

This British driver, born in 1932, first raced in 1954 at Brands Hatch, in a Formula 3 Cooper-Vincent Mk IV 500. He won the JAP Championship in 1955-6 and the 1956 Clubman's Championship with 15 victories to his credit. He had several sports car successes in this period, and raced widely in F2 Coopers. He joined the Yeoman-Credit Cooper Formula 1 team in 1960, and took 4th place in the French GP and 7th in the Dutch. He also raced Cooper and Lotus FJs with some success, notably at Monaco (a Ken Tyrrell entry) and Silverstone. He signed with UDT-Laystall for the 1961 season, and finished 2nd in the Lombank Trophy, 10th in the French GP and 11th in the Italian. He crashed badly in pouring rain in the British GP at Aintree and had to be cut free from the wreck. He also scored one 1st and three 3rd places in the team's Lotus 19 sports cars that year.

His Aintree accident prompted retirement from Formula 1, and Taylor concentrated on rallying, driving for the Ford works team. His first outing for Ford was the Monte Carlo Rally, with Brian Melia in an Anglia.

They struck a rock on the Turini, breaking a rear spring, but the pair still finished and were the best Ford entry. In the Acropolis Rally, again in an Anglia, they came 10th overall and 2nd in class; in the RAC Rally they were 6th overall. Taylor was the first man to drive a Cortina in a rally, the 1963 Monte Carlo, but a blocked road section put paid to his chances. In the Acropolis Rally he was 4th, and in the Coupe des Alpes he came 2nd in the Touring class and won a Coupe des Alpes. He was also one of the first to rally with a Lotus-Cortina and finished 4th in the Liège–Sofia–Liège with such a car.

He continued to rally for Fords until the beginning of 1966 when he was offered, and accepted, the job of team manager. It was under his direction that the Lotus-Cortina reached its zenith both in rallies and on the track. In 1967 he was responsible for the conception and appearance of the Escort Twin Cam as a competition car. Since the middle of 1969, Taylor has worked for Fords Advanced Vehicles Operation which in May 1970 produced the BDA Escort with its four valves per cylinder. DCN/JD

Taylor, Trevor Patrick

Taylor was born in Sheffield, Yorkshire, in 1936 and began racing with a Triumph TR2 at Aintree in 1954. He had three seasons in Formula 3, from 1956 to 1958, driving Erskine-Staride, and Cooper-Norton cars, and won the British F3 Championship in 1958. Taylor's family invested in an F2 Cooper for 1959, and an FJ Lotus 18 for 1960, which was entered by the works. He scored four major victories with this car, and shared the British FJ Championship with Jim Clark. He also had some F2 Lotus drives that year, and in 1961 he had his first Formula 1 race, at Zandvoort where he finished 13th. He was also British FJ Champion in 1961.

In 1962 and 1963 Taylor drove in Formula 1 events for Team Lotus, winning the Natal GP in 1962 but also having two bad accidents. He drove for BRP in 1964 F1 events without great success, and also raced saloon cars in the United States and Great Britain, and won his class in a sports car race at Laguna Seca in a Brabham-BRM. In 1965 he was out of F1 but drove a Lotus 30 Group 7 car for JCB, his best result being 2nd at Silverstone. From 1966 to 1969 he drove mainly saloon cars for Team Broadspeed, as did his sister Anita, but in 1969 he had a regular Formula 5000 drive in a Surtees TS5, scoring four major victories and challenging Peter Gethin very strongly for the European F5000 Championship. DCN

Therier, Jean-Luc

Born in 1944, Jean-Luc Therier is the most important of
the new French rally drivers. He made a name for himself in the Coupe Gordini of 1966, which was a series of
circuit races for amateurs driving the Renault Gordini
R8. He finished 3rd overall and the next year turned his
attention to rallies, winning the Jeanne d'Arc Rally and
finishing 4th in the Rallye de l'Ouest. He also won the
Chinetti Trophy for his circuit performances, and consequently drove for the first time at Le Mans. In 1968 he
was given a factory Gordini with which he won his class
many times and also impressed with his performance
on the Lyons-Charbonnières, where he set fastest time
on several of the tests. At Le Mans he drove an Alpine
1300 with Bernard Tramont and they won their class.

In 1969 he surprised the establishment by finishing
7th overall in the Monte Carlo in a Group 1 Renault-
Gordini, beating much more powerful cars. He went on
to win the category in the Rallye de Lorraine and to win
outright the Andernach–Nürburgring Rally. The following year he was taken into the Alpine team but broke
down on the Monte Carlo and then won the Italian
Rally from the reigning European Champion, Harry
Kallström. Later in 1970 Therier won the Acropolis
Rally. JD

Théry, Léon

At his peak this French driver, born in 1878, was compared to Felice Nazzaro, and like Nazzaro he was a
thoroughly competent mechanic. As early as 1899 Théry
drove a Decauville Voiturelle in the Paris-Bordeaux.
He continued to campaign with the make until 1903,
though his best placings were 5th in class in the Paris-
Bordeaux, 1901, and a 6th in his category in the Paris-
Madrid, 1903. He retired in the 1902 Circuit des
Ardennes as the result of an incident which earned him
the nickname *mort aux vaches,* but by 1904 he had
transferred his allegiance to Richard-Brasier and his
exploits on their cars resulted in a new name — the
Chronometer. His fastest lap at Mazagran during the
French Gordon Bennett Trials was his 2nd (50min
28·4sec), but his slowest was exactly 1 hour, a small
variation over a lap distance of more than 55 miles. He
repeated this performance with an even smaller discrepancy in the race proper at Homburg, when on a
79·5-mile (127·94km) lap over a hilly course the difference between his fastest and slowest times was just over 3min.
Nor was this consistency won at the cost of speed, for he
won the Cup as he had won the eliminating trials, and in
the former he recorded the fastest circuit as well, at
55·3mph (89·00kph), although his winning average was
appreciably down on the trials: Mazagran had been a
flat course.

Though the 1905 cars were now plain Brasiers and a
little more powerful. Théry's contribution was a repeat
of 1904. The daunting Auvergne circuit at Clermont-
Ferrand caused a certain amount of variation, but
nobody else had the same combination of speed and
consistency, and Théry won once more. In the race
proper, he was once again more than a match for Lancia's
fiery manipulation of his Fiat, and an 8min discrepancy
between laps showed Léon Théry at his best. Unfortunately, like many a driver, he tried his luck in industry.
The projected Théry car never saw the light of day, and
in 1908 he was back in the Brasier team in time for the
French Grand Prix. Both driver and car had, however,
passed their peaks: this was his last appearance, and he
died in 1909 of tuberculosis. MCS

Léon Théry, 1905. Photo: T. A. S. O.
Mathieson Collection

Parry Thomas. Photo: William Boddy
Collection

Parry Thomas in the 1925 1·8-litre Thomas
Special. Photo: William Boddy Collection

Thomas, John Godfrey Parry

Parry Thomas was the greatest Brooklands driver of
them all. He was a talented Welsh engineer who patented
electrical transmission systems and designed the technically advanced Leyland Eight luxury car for Leyland
Ltd of which company he was Chief Engineer. When
Leyland decided not to proceed with production of this
fine chassis Parry Thomas left them and took up the
building and racing of cars as his full-time occupation.
Before he left Leyland he had raced a stripped Leyland
Eight at Brooklands with some success and he now went
to live inside the track, taking on Ken Taylor as his
engineer and further developing the speed potential of
the Leyland Eight, which he endowed with his own
conception of streamlined body. He also built a sister
car for J. E. P. Howey. He won many Brooklands races
with the big Leyland-Thomas cars, and broke the
Brooklands lap record in 1924 and 1925, leaving it at
129·36mph (208·20kph). In 1926 Thomas set the standing-
start lap record at 110·19mph (177·34kph). He also broke
a very large number of World and International Class
records with the Leyland-Thomas, including the hour
record, after Dunlop had provided tyres which would
last 60 minutes on this fast and heavy car. Thomas had
previously taken this coveted record with a pause to
change all four wheels and he had also experimented
with flooding part of the track to cool the covers, and
had waited for a wet day for the same reason. He tested
tyres for manufacturers, bursting covers by deliberately
skidding the Leyland.

One of the star attractions at Bank Holiday meetings,
Thomas was very popular with other drivers and his
mechanics. He won the famous match race against
Eldridge's much bigger Fiat but crashed his first
Leyland Thomas at the Boulogne Speed Trials.

In contrast to the big Leyland, Thomas built a slim
1·8-litre 4-cylinder Thomas Special, which he drove in
the 1925 *News of the World* 100-Mile Handicap, winning
at 98·23mph (158·09kph). He also raced the Marlborough
Thomas in speed trials and in the Junior Car Club 200
Miles Race. Later he turned to long distance racing,
designing and building two very low and technically
advanced straight-8 Thomas Specials, known as the
'flat-irons', in 1926, with supercharged 1·5-litre engines.
He took over Count Zborowski's Higham Special and
tuned its 400hp Liberty aero engine, using this giant
two-seater for short races at Brooklands and for attacks
on short distance records. He then took 'Babs', as the
car was now called to Pendine sands and broke the Land
Speed Record twice, taking it to 171·02mph (275·23kph).
It was while trying to regain this record in 1927 in the
old chain-drive car that Thomas was killed when it
overturned. WB

Thomas, René

Born in France in 1886, René Thomas' racing career
spanned 22 years in which he drove a wide variety of
cars, yet his outright victories were few. He began
driving in 1906, with a Lacoste et Battmann voiturette,
and in the succeeding three years drove Prima, Delage,
and Le Gui voiturettes. In 1911 he rejoined Delage and
finished 2nd for them in the Coupe de l'Auto. He drove
for Peugeot without any great success in 1912, and
handled one of the unspectacular GP Th. Schneiders in
1913. Again he returned to Delage for 1914, and accompanied Guyot to Indianapolis with two of the 1913 GP
cars. The race was a triumph for Thomas who won at the
record speed of 82·47mph (132·72kph) against powerful

opposition from Georges Boillot and Jules Goux on Peugeots, and the best American drivers.

Thomas served in the French Air Force in World War 1, and joined Ballot in 1919 as *Chef du Service Course*. He took a 4·9-litre Ballot to the 1919 Indianapolis race, but could do no better than 10th, while in the Targa Florio he left the road after a terrific battle with André Boillot (Peugeot). In 1920 he again took a Ballot team to Indianapolis and finished 2nd, while in this year he also drove a Silver Hawk in the GP des Voiturettes at Le Mans (fin. 7th), and broke records at Gaillon hill-climb in the 350hp Sunbeam. He drove for Sunbeam-Talbot-Darracq in 1921 and although he had bad luck with the larger cars he won the Coupe Internationale des Voiturettes, this being his second major victory. For the rest of his career he drove for Delage, taking the Land Speed Record in 1924 with the 10·5-litre V-12 car, and driving this and the 2-litre V-12 at hill-climbs all over Europe. He was 3rd in the 1925 San Sebastian GP, and with the introduction of the 1,500cc formula in 1926 he retired from racing, although he continued to act as team manager until 1928. He was made a Chevalier of the Legion of Honour in 1934. TASOM

Titterington, J. Desmond

Born in Ireland in 1928, Desmond Titterington had a remarkable career which in five years took him from minor Irish events to a place in the works teams of Jaguar, Connaught and Mercedes-Benz. He began racing in 1951 in a 17-year old Fiat Balilla, then bought a new Allard J2 in which he had many hill-climb successes and won the 1952 Leinster Trophy and 1953 Phoenix Park (Dublin) race. He had several successes with a works Triumph TR2, then joined Ecurie Ecosse in 1954. In 1955 he had works drives with Jaguar as well as Ecurie Ecosse and was one of the winning team in the 1955 Silverstone Touring Car Race. He finished 1st on scratch and 2nd on handicap in the Ulster Trophy, and had other successes at Charterhall, Goodwood, Snetterton and Aintree. Then he and Mike Hawthorn were chosen to challenge the entire Mercedes-Benz team, with a lone Jaguar, in the 1955 TT. They led for more than half the race, then fell back and retired.

A week later Titterington had his first Formula 1 race with a Vanwall at Oulton Park, and finished a remarkable 3rd behind Moss and Hawthorn. Offers came from Ferrari and Mercedes-Benz; he took up the latter, shared a 300SLR with John Fitch to come 4th in the Targa Florio, and then Mercedes retired from racing. In 1956 he drove a works Connaught in Formula 1 and Jaguars in sports car events, but had no important victories, and retired at the end of the year. He also had some rallying successes, being twice runner-up in the Circuit of Ireland (1955 and 1956), and twice 3rd in class in the Coupe des Alpes (1951 and 1958). FWMcC

Titus, Jerry

Born in the Long Island, N.Y., village of Bridgehampton in 1928, Jerry Titus moved to California in 1961 after an early career as a jazz musician and technical writer for motoring magazines. He began racing Formula Juniors in 1960 and in 1965 his Mustang won the Pacific Coast 'B' production championship. Before he became a full-time professional race driver Titus successfully combined writing and driving, becoming editor of the *Sports Car Graphic* magazine and in 1966 winning the Sports Car Club of America 'D' production title in a Porsche 911. In 1966 and 1967 Titus led Carroll Shelby's Ford-

René Thomas. *Photo: Cyril Posthumus Collection*

Desmond Titterington. *Photo: Wilson McComb Collection*

Jerry Titus, 1968. *Photo: Al Bochroch Collection*

Pauli Toivonen. *Photo: John Davenport*

Mustangs to the Trans-American Sedan championship, and in 1968 Titus joined Canadian Terry Godsall in mounting a Pontiac Firebird Trans-Am challenge. On 5 August 1970 he died from injuries received on 19 July 19 1970 while practising for the Road America Trans-Am at Elkhart Lake, Wis. ARB

Toivonen, Pauli

Pauli Toivonen is one of the largest and most amusing men who have won the European Rally Championship. He was born in Helsinki, Finland, in 1931 and his early interests were in athletics and playing in dance bands. His relationship with the automobile started when he became a car salesman in the town of Jyväskylä which every year is the home of Finland's Thousand Lakes Rally. In 1954, Toivonen decided that he could sell more cars if he had a reputation as a rally driver and he entered himself in a Volkswagen 1200. Much to his surprise, he won his class and finished 10th overall. From that moment, spiked tyres began to play a more important part in his life than spiked running shoes.

During the next four years he drove several types of car in Finnish rallies, then in 1959 bought a Simca Monthléry with which he managed to net 2nd place in the Finnish championship. For 1960 came the offer of a Citroën supplied by the factory, but he had a rather disappointing year. The following year he stayed with Citroën and went outside Finland and Scandinavia for the first time to the Monte Carlo, where he was 4th on scratch but finished nowhere in the general classification because of the handicap. He won his class in the Swedish Rally and came second in the Thousand Lakes, which ensured the Finnish championship title for him. In his 3rd year for Citroën, he started by crashing in the Monte Carlo, but went on to come 3rd in the Finnish Hanki-rallyt and he won both the Norwegian events, the Viking and the Winter Rally. In Greece, he won his class in the Acropolis Rally.

In 1963, he was again driving for Citroën and his results included finishing 2nd on the Monte Carlo, and winning the Hankirallyt. He drove VWs without much success in 1964, and in 1965 drove a Porsche 904. The 1966 season brought some confusions for Toivonen: he was credited with winning the Monte Carlo with a Citroën, but not before four other cars had been disqualified by the organizers. For the rest of the year he drove for the Renault factory in a Gordini, unfortunately with little success.

In 1967 he signed for Lancia but his bad luck dogged him despite the change and he had retirements in the Monte Carlo and the Acropolis through minor mechanical failures.

At last in 1968 he seemed to make all the right decisions and his contract with Porsche led him to more victories in one year than most men can count in a lifetime. He started the year by finishing 2nd in the Monte Carlo to Vic Elford, and he then won the San Remo, both German rallies, the Danube Rally, the Spanish Rally and the Geneva Rally. His only mistakes were in Greece, where the car fell off a broken jack and he took 3rd overall, and in the Thousand Lakes where he crashed. These victories were ample to give him the undisputed European title.

Since then, Toivonen has driven in the Monte Carlo and the Acropolis rallies for Porsche in 1969, retiring on the first and winning the other. He now works for the Porsche and Chrysler agents in his homeland as sales director. JD

Opposite, Mario Andretti: *Photo: Geoff Goddard*

Tracy, Joe

One of the first American racing drivers to win international standing, Joe Tracy was born in Co. Waterford, Ireland, in 1873, emigrating to the United States at the age of 19. He trained as a steam engineer, acquiring his experience in a steam-powered electric light plant in New York. He drove Panhard and Richard Brasier cars in 1903 and his first major long-distance event, the first of the Vanderbilt series, was a failure, his Royal Tourist suffering from too high an axle ratio and expiring ignominiously on its second lap. This race did, however, see the beginning of a successful partnership with his riding mechanic, Al Poole. The Peerless did not start at Daytona in 1905, but Tracy did better in the 100-mile event at Havana, Cuba, where he drove Gould Brokaw's 1904 racing Renault into 2nd place. He was also selected by the ACA to take part in the Gordon Bennett Races over the Auvergne Circuit on a vast 17·7-litre (1,080·117ci) Locomobile of Mercedes-like aspect. This was a brute to drive (the mechanic had a hand-operated auxiliary clutch lever) and Tracy's chances were wrecked when he slipped second gear on the run from Le Havre to Clermont-Ferrand — his retirement was almost a foregone conclusion. Back in the United States he finished 2nd in the Vanderbilt Cup Eliminating Race at 55·8mph (89·80kph), improving his average to 56·9mph (91·57kph) in the race proper to take 3rd place behind a Darracq and a Panhard — the best showing so far in an international event by an American driver or car.

He was again at the wheel of a Locomobile for the 1906 Vanderbilt, winning the eliminator from Thomas and Pope-Toledo by playing a waiting game, this despite persistent radiator leaks which Poole stopped with chewing-gum. It was said that at points on the course the spectators added their cast-off gum as well. A fearsome appetite for tyres spoiled his chances in the Cup itself, only two of his laps being free from tyre changes: on one of these he circulated at 67·6mph (108·79kph), fastest lap of the day. A 10th place was disappointing, and a wild skid on the course injured a boy spectator: it was probably this accident which persuaded Tracy to abandon racing and become a consultant to the Locomobile company. He also worked for Craig-Toledo and Matheson, and during World War 1 undertook researches into fuel economy for the US Government's Bureau of Oil Consumption.

During the latter part of a full career as a consulting engineer Tracy became a pioneer of the antique-car movement and an energetic old-car hunter, and in his last years he undertook restoration jobs for the Long Island Automotive Museum, driving to and from his work in a vintage Model-A Ford. He died in 1959. MCS

Trana, Tom

Born in Kristinehamn, Sweden in 1937, Trana established himself in the mid-1960s as one of the fastest men on loose surfaces in the world. Both his father and mother were keen on motor sport, his father on motorcycles and his mother with cars. In 1956, he obtained his first car licence and bought an old Volvo which he rebuilt and drove in circuit races. By 1958 he was well known in Sweden and won his class in most of the bigger rallies and races. In 1959, he finished 2nd to Volvo's top driver, Gunnar Andersson, in the Swedish racing championship and also won two international saloon car races. The next year he beat Andersson for this same championship and was officially given a Volvo to drive, with which he repeated his success in 1961 and 1962,

while at the same time becoming Swedish ice race champion in 1961 and rally champion in 1962.

Trana's first trip abroad was for the RAC Rally in 1962 at the invitation of BMC for whom he drove a Mini Cooper and led the rally until retiring in Scotland. The following year Volvo sent him back and he made no mistake, winning the RAC Rally outright. For 1964, Volvo gave him a fairly full season abroad during which he finished well up in the Monte Carlo, and won the Swedish Rally, the Acropolis and the RAC Rally for the second time to become European Champion. The following year he won the Swedish Rally and in 1966 he was Swedish Rally champion once again. However, Volvo were closing their competition activities and in 1967 he joined SAAB for whom he now rallies, as well as doing most of their test and development driving. He has never seemed quite so much at home with the fwd Saab as he did in the more conventional Volvo, but he won the Norwegian Autumn Rally for them in 1967, finished 2nd in that event in 1968, and was also 2nd in the Swedish Rally that year. In 1968 he was Swedish Rally champion in Group 2 but since then has competed less and less in rallies. JD

Trautmann, Claudine

Born in Paris in 1931, Claudine Trautmann is one of the most successful of women rally drivers and since rallying with her husband René has shown that she is an excellent co-driver as well. Her first rally was in 1957 with a Simca when she finished 4th overall and first Touring car in the Rallye du Mont Blanc. This she considers her 'mascot' rally as she has won the Coupe des Dames on it eleven times; her *bête noire* is the Alpine which she has started five times with a female co-driver and never finished, though more recently she has finished twice with her husband. In 1960 she was given a drive with Citroën for whom she won the Coupe des Dames in almost every French event on the calendar. This was the first of nine championships of France that she was to win, four times with Citroën and five with Lancia whom she joined in 1964.

With Citroën, she drove five times on the Liège–Sofia Liège and finished three times, but only won the Coupe des Dames twice: the other occasion was in 1960 when Pat Moss won outright. She has won the Paris–St Raphael Rally for women drivers five times and always in a Lancia, but in a different model on each occasion: Flavia Coupé, 1964; Flavia Zagato, 1965; Fulvia Coupé 1967; Fulvia Coupé 1400, 1968; and Fulvia Zagato 1600 1969. JD

Trautmann, René

Born in Marseille in 1927, René Trautmann is perhaps the most famous of French rallymen. Although by profession he is a photographer, he started rallying in 1956 as a co-driver in a Peugeot 203 with a friend. Finding that he liked the sport, he started driving himself in a Renault 4CV and later in a Citroën. The latter firm eventually offered him a works car for 1960 when he was second in both the French and European championships. That year he won the Tulip Rally and was one of the few people ever to get out of Yugoslavia unpenalized on the Liège–Sofia–Liège. At this time he was hill-climbing with a Ferrari. When Citroën did not have a car for a rally, he would often borrow one: for example, the Alfa Romeo in which he won the Rally du Limousin in 1960. In 1963 he was Champion of France in rallies and at one time or another he has won practically every event held

Tom Trana. *Photo: SAAB*

in France with the exception of the Monte Carlo.

His most remarkable achievements include winning a Coupe des Alpes no less than six times—in 1960, 1962, 1963, 1965, 1968 and 1969—for which he has gained two Coupes d'Argent, a rare award in itself. He has also won the Tour de Corse twice, in 1961 and 1963. Like many drivers, he sets these achievements aside and looks on his performances in the Liège-Sofia-Liège as his best, for in that rally he started and failed to finish five times but was nearly always leading when he retired.

In 1964 he joined Lancia and in his first year won the Lyons-Charbonnières for them and followed it up by winning the Coupe des Alpes outright the following year. Since then his second Coupe d'Argent on the Alpine has been won with the Lancia Fulvia. JD

Trintignant, Maurice

Trintignant is a driver who bridged the years between the loss of the truly great Frenchmen like Wimille and Sommer, and the rise of the new generation, young men such as Beltoise, Pescarolo and Servoz-Gavin. He was born in Sainte Cécile-les-Vignes (Vaucluse) on 30 October 1917, the youngest of five sons of Fernand Trintignant, a prosperous vineyard owner.

Maurice rode as mechanic with his brothers Réné and Louis while a schoolboy, but the latter was killed at Péronne in 1933, while driving a 2·3-litre blown Bugatti. The youngest Trintignant was badly shocked by the tragedy, but in 1938 he bought back the Bugatti and made his own driving debut in the Pau GP. He raced occasionally before the outbreak of World War 2, and won the Grand Prix des Frontières at Chimay. In 1945 his Bugatti was on the grid for the Coupe de la Libération in the Bois de Bologne; fuel starvation put him out of this first post-war motor race and gave him his nickname. The fault was caused by rat droppings ('les petoules') left in the tank during the car's long lay-up, and Wimille dubbed Trintignant 'Le Petoulet' on the spot.

In 1946 Trintignant continued racing the old Bugatti, then replaced it with an Amilcar for 1947, with which he won at Avignon. He drove a Delage and later that year joined the Simca-Gordini team. In 1948 he won at Perpignan and Montlhéry, and then crashed badly at Berne in the meeting which took the lives of Varzi, Kautz and Tenni. Trintignant raced private Ferraris with Rosier in 1952, but still drove regularly for Gordini, winning at Albi, Angoulême, Cadours, Chimay and Geneva, sharing his class victory at Le Mans with Schell, then scoring again at the Nürburgring. Ferrari signed the dapper little Frenchman for 1954, and he gained four Formula victories, in addition to sharing the winning Le Mans car with Gonzalez. He was retained by Maranello for 1955, winning at Monaco and in the Messina 10 Hours (with Castelotti). The following year Vanwall signed him although agreeing to his Bugatti retainer for their return, and he also drove Ferrari sports cars. It was not a good year, for he had little success with the British team. The Bugatti 251 only appeared once (at Reims) before being withdrawn.

Next season he was with BRM and Ferrari. In 1958 he drove for Rob Walker, winning at Monaco once more, this time in Walker's 1·96-litre Cooper-Climax. That season he also won at Pau and was 3rd in the German GP, and raced the dark-blue cars again the following year, scoring a 2nd, 3rd and two 4ths in Championship rounds, winning at Pau in an F2 Cooper-Borgward, and driving very well for Aston Martin.

In 1960 he appeared in Walker Coopers, Porsches,

the F1 Aston Martin (11th in the British GP), and later entered his own F2 Cooper with which he had considerable success. The 1961 season was an unhappy one with Scuderia Serenissima, and in 1962 he was back with Walker, but had a series of accidents (none of them his fault) and no success, apart from an early third victory at Pau. The 46-year old French champion had no regular F1 seat in 1963, although he drove for both Walker and Parnell on occasion, and in 1964 he ran an ex-Hill/Centro Sud spaceframe BRM, painted pale blue. He scored with 5th place in the German GP to end a long and honourable Formula 1 career.

In 1959 Trintignant was elected mayor of Vergèze (Gard). A wine from his vineyards is known as 'Le Petoulet'. DCN

Trips, Wolfgang Graf Berghe von

Born in 1928, this German count started his career in motor sport with a privately entered Porsche and after a short period he was chosen for his international debut, the Mille Miglia of 1954 in which he won the 1,300cc GT class together with Hampel. The next remarkable steps led via the 1956 Le Mans (Porsche) to membership of the Mercedes-Benz team and the 300SL sports car which he drove in the Tourist Trophy and at Kristianstad in Sweden and at other events in 1955. In 1956 he was again at Le Mans with a Porsche and won the 1,500cc class with von Frankenberg. Later in 1956 he joined the Ferrari team and in 1957 started in his first Grand Prix in Argentina. That year brought a 2nd place in the Mille Miglia in a Ferrari and several starts in hill-climbs for Porsche. During 1958 he continued with Porsche. He was still a member of the Ferrari team, but had bad luck during 1958 and 1959 in Formula 1. However, with Porsche he gained the European Hill-climb championship in 1958. In 1959 he tried the Porsche Formula 2 in Monte Carlo, and won at Sebring on a Porsche Spyder in the 2-litre class with Bonnie. In 1960 he was active again for Ferrari, winning the Formula 2 race on the Solitude circuit.

His most successful, and tragically his last year in motor racing was 1961. He gained his first victory in a Grand Prix, the Dutch GP, and also won the British GP. He led in the World Championship before the Italian Grand Prix at Monza, where he came off the road after a crash with Clark's Lotus and was killed. He was the first German driver to win a Grand Prix since 1939. HON

Left, Maurice Trintignant in a Bugatti Type 251 at Reims, 1956. *Photo: Geoffrey Goddard*

Above, Maurice Trintignant. *Photo: Autosport*

Opposite, Lorenzo Bandini. *Photo: Geoff Goddard*

Wolfgang von Trips. *Photo: Brian Foley*

Trossi, Count Carlo Felice

This Italian aristocrat, known as 'Didi' possessed a
love of things English. His hobbies included speedboats,
aircraft and cars. He was a good business man, an
engineer, and was described by Ferrari as a great racing
driver. In 1932 he was President of the Scuderia Ferrari,
and came 2nd in an 8C 2300 Alfa Romeo shared with
his friend the Marquis 'Tonino' Brivio in his very first
race, the Mille Miglia. In 1933 he drove a 2·6-litre Monza
Alfa Romeo and made ftd at Gaisberg, came 2nd to
Nuvolari at Alessandria 3min ahead of Brivio's Monza
in pouring rain, and won at Florence and in the Targa
Abruzzo. At Monaco in 1934, Trossi's 2·9B P3 Monoposto Alfa set a new lap record, and with a similar car he
duelled with Etancelin's monoposto Maserati to win the
Montreux round-the-houses race. This duel was repeated in the Vichy GP with Trossi again the victor,
finally finishing 5sec in front of Straight's Maserati. He
won the race through the streets of his native Biella in
front of Varzi's similar P3.

In 1935 again he showed his skill at round-the-houses
racing at Biella, where he set up a lap record and passed
Nuvolari on a similar 3·2-litre P3 Alfa to his own, but
retired while in the lead because of illness. In the Coppa
Ciano he was 3rd to team-mates Nuvolari and Brivio,
all on 3·2-litre P3s. During 1935 he built an experimental
GP racing car with 16-cylinder supercharged 2-stroke
air-cooled radial engine mounted in the nose and driving
the front wheels. It was never raced. By 1936 Trossi had
given up presidency of the Scuderia Ferrari, coming 6th
in the Vanderbilt Cup in the United States in a Maserati,
and scoring no less than five victories in 1·5-litre races on
Maseratis, though he was 2nd to Seaman's Delage in the
voiturette race at Pescara. In 1937 he won the Naples
voiturette race in a 6C Maserati, and back driving for
the Scuderia Ferrari in a 12-cylinder Alfa Romeo he was

3rd at Turin and won at Genoa. In 1938 he drove a
360bhp 8CTF Maserati and made fastest lap at Tripoli
against the might of the Germans before retiring. In
1940 he drove a works 1·5-litre 158 Alfa Romeo voiturette at Tripoli and finished 3rd behind team-mates
Farina and Biondetti.

In the post-war years he was a member of the all-
conquering 158 Alfa GP team, and his 1946 record
included a 2nd in the Swiss GP, 6th at Turin and a win
in the Milan GP. In 1947 he was 3rd in the Swiss GP,
3rd at Spa and won the Italian GP. In 1948 he won the
Grand Prix d'Europe at Berne and was 2nd to Wimille
in the Monza GP. This was his last race, for he died of
cancer in a Milan clinic in 1949. PMAH

Tullius, Robert

Born in 1935 in Rochester, N.Y., and now living in Falls
Church, Bob Tullius runs Group 44, one of America's
few professional club racing teams. Best known as the
driver of the Triumph TR4 with the reversed number 44,
Tullius started racing at Marlboro in 1961. He won the
SCCA national 'E' production title in 1962, the 'D'
national championship in 1963 and 1964, and Northeast
division 'D' honours in 1965. He was invited to join
the Triumph team at Le Mans in 1964 and, with Dr
Richard Thompson, drove the Howmet Turbine there in
1968. Driving a Dodge Dart, Tullius won the first race in
the Trans-American sedan series at Sebring in March
1966; drove the only American sedan to ever win the
Marlboro 12 Hours; and opened the 1967 Trans-Am
championship with a victory over the Detroit factory
teams at Daytona. ARB

Turner, Stuart

The most famed backroom boy of modern rallying is
Stuart Turner who has been co-driver, journalist and one
of the most successful team managers of the 1960s.
Born in the English Midlands in 1933, Turner trained as
an accountant and perhaps it was this acquaintance with
the manipulation of figures that made him such a successful co-driver in British events. For many years he
rallied with Ron Goldbourne and then John Sprinzel,
during which time he was *Autosport* champion navigator
three years running. He accompanied Goldbourne in one
of the first works Triumph TRs on the Tulip Rally in
1958 and in the years that followed he built up a formidable knowledge of foreign events with a variety of drivers.
In 1960 he moved to London where he took the job of
rallies editor of *Motoring News* and established the pen-
name of Verglas. He arranged to take part in the Coupe
des Alpes with Erik Carlsson but a broken piston on the
way to scrutineering ended that rally prematurely. However, with the same car and driver, he won the RAC
Rally that November. By the end of 1961, he had received an offer to go to BMC as their competitions
manager and he started work for them at the beginning
of 1962.

For both Turner and BMC, this was to be a golden
era, with Minis winning the Monte Carlo three times and
being disqualified once, and in other internationals,
outright victory seldom eluded them. As well as proving
a success at developing cars such as the Cooper S, Turner
was also responsible for the rise to fame—and fortune—
of many of the famous names in rallying today, both
drivers and co-drivers.

However, even success can become boring and after
BMC won the Monte Carlo in 1967 he left to accept a
new challenge with a job at Castrol. After spending some

Left below, Count Trossi (left). *Photo: Cyril Posthumus Collection*

Left bottom, 1935 Trossi-Monaco 16-cylinder GP car. *Photo: Museo dell'Automobile, Turin.*

Below, Count Trossi, 1934. *Photo: Montagu Motor Museum*

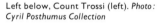

time out of the public eye while he studied the new world of advertising and promotion, he emerged to start a programme of involvement with competition at club level which has re-established the company's position among motor sporting enthusiasts. Direct contact with the sport was rare but at the end of 1968, Turner was involved via Castrol with the running of the London to Sydney Marathon and it was only a few months after that event had finished that it was announced that he had accepted an offer to go to Fords as competition manager. Success was a little slower in coming than it had been at BMC, but in May 1970 his genius for organization carried Fords to victory in the longest rally of them all, the World Cup. JD

Tyrrell, R. Kenneth

Born in 1924, Ken Tyrrell is a director of Tyrrell Bros Ltd, timber merchants from whose yard near Ripley, in Surrey, he operates his Formula 1 racing team. He had his first race in 1952, driving an F3 Cooper-Norton 500, and his cars soon became a familiar sight, carrying Tyrrell's axe-head insignia. He raced in F3 from 1952–7 with some success, and formed an F2 Cooper-Climax team with Alan Brown and Cecil Libowitz in 1958.

Such drivers as Brabham, McLaren, Ireland, Gregory, Flockhart and Lucas drove the partnership's cars, and in 1960 Ken retired from active driving to run a works-backed Cooper FJ team. Henry Taylor and Keith Ballisat drove for him, and the timber merchant soon established a reputation for talent-spotting. He gave Surtees his first car race at Goodwood (where he finished 2nd to Clark), and in 1961 the Tyrrell Racing Team ran FJ Cooper-BMCs and Mini-Cooper saloons for the works. John Love and Tony Maggs notched 13 wins, ten 2nds, and seven 3rds in International FJ, and continued in 1962 to seven 1sts, nine 2nds and five 3rds. Ken

Ken Tyrrell (right), with Jackie Stewart and the 1970 Tyrrell-Ford Formula 1 car. *Photo: Tyrrell Racing Organization*

managed the works Cooper F1 team briefly while John Cooper himself was recovering from a road accident.

The Cooper FJs were outpaced in 1963, but the Tyrrell Racing Organization soldiered on with cars for Procter and Love. Ken was impressed by Jackie Stewart's prowess in a private test session at Goodwood, and signed him on with Warwick Banks for the 1964 Cooper-BMC F3 team. These two were 1st and 2nd in the *Express & Star* F3 Championship, and scored 13 1sts, and six 2nd places during the year.

Tyrrell moved up into Formula 2 in 1965, running Cooper chassis with Cosworth and BRM 1-litre engines, but success was limited. Then Matra Sports approached him with a proposition to run their Formula 2 team, since he had both the organization ability and experience, and the driver they badly needed. Tyrrell and Stewart accepted, and this Matra F2 association developed into the Dunlop Matra-Elf F1 project of 1968. Ken had seen Jim Clark's Dutch GP win in 1967, marking the victorious début of the Cosworth-Ford V-8 engine, and he placed an order as soon as he returned home to Ockham. He did not know how he was going to use the engines or in what chassis, but Matra soon agreed to build special chassis and Stewart signed with him to drive them. Sponsorship came from Elf and Dunlop—with whom Tyrrell has had a long association—and in 1968 the Stewart/Matra combination won the Dutch GP (scene of the original 'spark' the previous year), the German and the United States GP, and nearly the World Championship.

In 1969 there was no holding Stewart in the Tyrrell quasi-works Matra, but for 1970 Matra wanted to run their own V-12 engines while Ken and Jackie wanted to retain the Cosworth-Ford DFV. So March chassis were ordered, and despite early development problems the Scot won the Race of Champions and the Spanish GP.

During 1970 Tyrrell unveiled his own Tyrrell-Ford GP car, and Stewart led the Canadian and US GPs with it, continuing with the car for 1971, and backed by François Cevert. DCN

Unser, Al

Born in 1939, Al Unser, followed the pattern set by other members of this American racing family (his father, two uncles and two brothers) and started his career as a driver in modified stock cars on tracks near his home in Albuquerque, N. Mex., and in the 1960 Pikes Peak Hill-Climb event, finished 2nd. He was runner up again at Pike's Peak in 1962 and he won the 1964 event over that challenging course to break his brother Bobby's long string of victories there.

Al began to attract National attention in 1965, competing in 13 USAC big car championship events with more than average success. He continued to show steady improvement during each of the next two seasons, finishing as high as 2nd in seven races of 100 miles or more in length before scoring his first major USAC championship victory at Nazareth, Pa., on 13 July 1968. Four other victories followed in rapid order that season as he moved up to No 3 ranking in the final National point standing.

Despite a broken leg sustained in a non-competitive motorcycle accident early in 1969, which put him out of action for about two months, he won five major USAC events during the last half of the campaign for runner-up honours behind Mario Andretti in the final standing.

One of Al's 2nd places in 1967 was scored at Indianapolis—on his third 500 appearance—and he was

making a strong bid for 1st place there the following year when he hit the wall on the 42nd lap.

After attending the 1969 Indianapolis event as a spectator, because of his broken leg, Unser dominated the action there during the entire month of May in 1970. He turned in the fastest practice laps consistently, earned the no. 1 starting position with a four-lap average speed of 170·221mph (273·932kph) and led the field on Race Day for all but 10 of the required 200 laps, relinquishing 1st place only briefly on the first two of his mandatory pit stops for fuel.

He finished at an average of 155·749mph (250·576kph), falling 1·118mph (1·799kph) short of Mario Andretti's 1969 record, but collecting $271,697.72 as his share of auto racing's first million-dollar purse ($1,000,002.22). By his victory, he also joined his older brother Bobby as the first winning brother combination at Indianapolis.

He completed the 1970 season as USAC National Champion, winning 10 of the 18 scheduled events and was placed second or third five times.

Unser also has been active in stock car racing for the last three years with considerable success. He finished 4th and was named 'Rookie of the Year' in the 1968 Daytona Beach (NASCAR) 500-mile race; and came 5th, 4th and 8th, respectively, in USAC's national stock car championship standing beginning in 1967. AB

Unser, Robert William

A member of a prominent racing family, Bobby Unser was born in 1934 and gained his early experience in competition on the challenging Pike's Peak hill-climb course in Colorado. He scored the first of his nine victories in the championship-car division of this annual event in 1956, but did not begin to attract national attention until his first appearance at Indianapolis in 1963.

Two years later he was running with the leaders consistently in USAC championship events, finishing 2nd twice and 5th or better six other times. Continuing to improve steadily, he won his first two championship races in 1967 and was placed in the top ten on twelve other occasions for 3rd-place ranking in the national point standing for the year.

Unser then won four of the first five USAC championship races on the 1968 schedule, including the Indianapolis 500-mile event in a turbocharged Offenhauser car at a record-breaking speed of 152·882mph (246·033kph), and finished the season as national champion by a margin of 11 points over Mario Andretti.

His only 1969 victory was scored in a 150-mile race at

Left, Al Unser, in the Johnny Lightning Special (Colt-Ford) in which he won the Indianapolis 500 in 1970. *Photo: Indianapolis Motor Speedway*

Above, Al Unser. *Photo: Indianapolis Motor Speedway*

Right, Bobby Unser, with the Leader Card Special he drove at Indianapolis in 1969. *Photo: Indianapolis Motor Speedway*

William K. Vanderbilt (Mors 70hp) before the start of the Paris–Madrid, 1903. *Photo: T. A. S. O. Mathieson Collection*

Langhorne, Pa., but he was placed high in many other events and finished the campaign as the nation's 3rd-ranked driver behind Andretti and his younger brother Al Unser. He also scored championship points in 10 of 18 races in 1970 for second place in the final standing. AB

Vanderbilt, William Kissam

'Willie K' (born in 1878) is perhaps best remembered as a race patron, and was in effect the American Vincenzo Florio. Of millionaire stock, Vanderbilt was brought up against a background of horse-racing, and took the helm of high-powered motorboats in later years. In September 1900 he was one of a small group of enthusiasts who formed the National Automobile Racing Association, staging a modest hill-climb at Newport which he himself won on a 24hp Cannstatt-Daimler. Even if his time of 8min 54sec over the 5 miles scarcely merited the title Champion of America, it was a beginning. Vanderbilt came to Europe in 1902 for a full season. In April 1902 he recorded 65·79mph (105·87kph) over the kilometre at Achères, the fastest time to date by a petrol car, later improving this to 67·78mph (109·08kph)

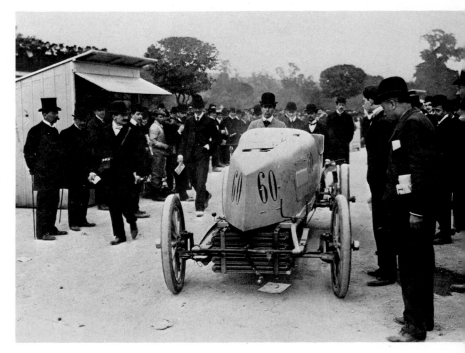

at Ablis, and raising it again in May to 69·94mph (111·10kph).

Willie K staged his second and last European season in 1903, competing unsuccessfully in the Paris–Madrid, and the Circuit des Ardennes. In 1904 came the start of the Vanderbilt Cup races on Long Island, which initiated America into the European style of racing, and, more important, bred a whole generation of fast luxury cars in the European idiom (Locomobile, Simplex). Vanderbilt, however, had not finished with competitive motoring, for that January he took his 90hp Mercedes to the Ormond-Daytona Speed Trials and recorded 92·3mph (148·54kph) over the mile, just beating Henry Ford's 91·37mph (147·04kph), attained on the frozen Lake St Clair with the bizarre 999. Later in the meeting, Vanderbilt improved his speed to 96·77mph (155·73kph), and subsequently to an unofficial 102·85mph (165·58kph): had this been recognized it would have been the first time an automobile had been timed at over 100mph. He was back at Ormond Beach in 1905, but by this time the Mercedes was no match for the 6-cylinder Napier and the best Vanderbilt could do was 3rd in the Dewar Trophy.

Even after the Vanderbilt Cup moved away from Long Island, Willie K retained his interest in the race. When at home, he invariably acted as starter, and though as a sportsman he declined to compete for his own trophy, he sponsored other drivers (in 1908 his entry was the Mercedes driven by the German-American Luttgen) and delighted in making a fast 'inspection lap' of the course before the race proper. He died in 1944. MCS

Varzi, Achille

Achille Varzi's stature as a driver is shown by the fact that he was Nuvolari's greatest rival, and he only lacked that touch of eccentric genius, which somehow made Nuvolari different from all the other great drivers before or since, to prevent him being considered the equal of 'Il Mantovano Volante'.

Born in 1904, Varzi was the son of a wealthy textile manufacturer, and came from Galliate, near Milan. He took up motorcycle racing, and was able to afford the best machines, starting with Garellis and then going on to British Sunbeams. He and Nuvolari were motorcycle racing stars at about the same period but, strangely enough, seldom came up against each other on the track.

The two rivals started their serious motor racing in partnership, in a stable of Type 35 Bugattis. In his first car race, in 1928, at Tripoli, Varzi was 3rd after a pit stop, and Nuvolari won. At Alessandria Varzi was 2nd to Nuvolari and, feeling his style was being cramped, Varzi left the stable and bought a P2 Alfa Romeo, coming 2nd in front of Nuvolari's Bugatti in the Italian GP. With this very competitive car he had victories in 1929 at Alessandria, Rome, Montenero and Monza. In 1930 he sold his car to the Alfa Romeo works, who modified it, and Varzi then drove it as a works entry to win at Alessandria and followed this with a great victory in the Targa Florio.

Nuvolari was also signed up with Alfa Romeo at this time, so Varzi went over to Maserati to avoid the inevitable complications. He had a better 1930 than Nuvolari, winning the Monza GP, the Spanish GP and the Coppa Acerbo in an 8C 2500 on top of his Alfa Romeo victories, compared with Nuvolari's two sports car wins in the Mille Miglia and the TT — in which Varzi was 3rd. Having been declared Italian Champion for 1930, in

Achille Varzi, Tunisian GP 1931. *Photo: Hugh Conway Collection*

1931 Varzi signed with Bugatti and in a Type 51 had three victories, at Tunis, Alessandria and the French GP, sharing in the last-named race with Chiron. In 1932 he had only one victory, at Tunis, but in 1933 he beat Nuvolari's Alfa Romeo at Monaco and Tripoli, and had a victory at the AVUS.

In 1934 he took the wise course of returning to the Scuderia Ferrari, as the Monoposto Alfas were very competitive, and Nuvolari had taken a period away from the Scuderia to drive Maseratis and Bugattis. Varzi reaped the benefit and won seven races in a P3, and the Mille Miglia in a road-equipped Monza Alfa with his faithful mechanic Amedeo Bignami, who was to Varzi as Compagnoni was to Nuvolari. Nuvolari was 2nd in the Mille Miglia in a non-Ferrari Alfa, and for the second time Varzi was declared Italian Champion.

In 1935 Nuvolari returned to the Scuderia Ferrari, so Varzi went to Auto Union. He soon mastered the unorthodox cars and won his first race in one, the Tunis GP. Only tyre trouble prevented his winning at Tripoli and also at the AVUS, where he was 2nd, but he won the Coppa Acerbo quite easily. In 1936 he was 2nd to Caracciola in a wet Monza GP and won at Tripoli after setting a record lap at 141·29mph (227·34kph). At Tunis in 1936 he had his first crash, caused by a sudden sidewind striking his Auto Union at 180mph (288kph). Varzi was unhurt after an end-over-end accident, but did not have any more outright victories that year. He was 3rd in the Hungarian GP behind Nuvolari's Alfa and Rosemeyer's Auto Union, and Nuvolari beat him in the Milan GP in the Sempione Park by 9sec. In the Coppa Acerbo he was 3rd, and he came 2nd in the Swiss GP behind Rosemeyer.

Half of 1937 had gone by before Varzi did any racing. Some said he suffered an affair of the heart, and it was a surprise when he appeared in the San Remo GP for voiturettes with a 6CM Maserati and won both his heat and the final. His last appearance for Auto Union, and his only one for them in 1937, was the Italian GP at Leghorn, where he was a lowly 6th. He drove only once in 1938, a new 3-litre Maserati at Tripoli, but retired early

317

in the race. Now it was being said his health was bad, and he was resorting to drugs.

He did not return to racing until 1946, when he was in the 158 Alfa Romeo team. These cars were so superior to the opposition that victories could be divided among the team members, and Varzi had his share. He also had two successful forays to South America for the Argentine Temporada series in 1947 with a pre-war Type 308 Alfa Romeo, and in 1948 with a pre-war 12C-312 enlarged to 4·6 litres. He was very popular with the Argentinians, and planned to live in their country on retirement, but in practice for the 1948 European GP at Berne his Type 158 skidded in the wet at about 110mph (176kph) near the Jordenrampe curve and overturned, and Varzi was killed.

The courageous Varzi, immaculate both in his dress and his driving, had a droll sense of humour despite an unsmiling exterior. He was a great driver and formed in the Argentine the Scuderia Achille Varzi which set Fangio on the road to fame. Fangio, who said he owed much to Varzi, was invariably accompanied during his racing career by Varzi's old friend and mechanic, Amedeo Bignami. PMAH

Veyron, Pierre

This French driver was born in 1903 and started racing in 1930 with an EHP in which he finished 2nd in the 1,500cc class in the Touring Grand Prix of Oran. In 1931 he acquired a Type 37A Bugatti and, besides winning the 1,500cc class of the Geneva GP, finished 2nd in the Grands Prix of Tunis and Comminges.

For the next four years Veyron confined his activities mainly to the 1,500cc or voiturette class, and in 1932 changed his Bugatti for an 8-cylinder Maserati with which he won the Grands Prix of Casablanca, Lorraine and Comminges, and finished 2nd at Tunis, Oran and Nice, and at Brno in the Czechoslovak GP. In 1933 he drove one of the latest Type 51A Bugattis, and with this car won the voiturette races at the AVUS, the Grands Prix of Lwow, Poland, and of Albi; finished 2nd in the Grand Prix de La Baule; and 3rd in the Grands Prix of the Eifel and Dieppe. He was invited to join the Bugatti team in 1934, as a driver for voiturette races, and won at the AVUS and Albi, taking 2nd place in the Prix de Berne. He also drove a Type 51 Bugatti in the Grands Prix of Albi (unlimited class race) in which he came 3rd.

In 1935 Veyron had another successful season, winning the Grands Prix of Lorraine and Albi for the third year in succession, and the Grand Prix des Frontières (2nd in general classification). He was 2nd in the Czechoslovak GP and 3rd at Dieppe. For the most part the races in France in 1936 were confined to sports cars and Veyron became a full member of the Bugatti team for these races. He finished 6th in the French GP, a 1,000 kilometre event at Montlhéry, partnered by W. Williams, and 4th in the Grand Prix de la Marne. He was 2nd at Albi, a race by then confined to voiturettes.

Between 1937, and his retirement from racing in 1953, Veyron competed only at Le Mans, where he finished 1st in 1939 with Wimille as co-driver. The pair scored an outstanding victory at record speed, but in all the other years he failed to finish. He died in 1970. TASOM

Villoresi, Emilio

'Mimi' Villoresi was rather overshadowed by his brother Luigi, but nevertheless had an ample share of the family talent. He is believed to have gained experience driving sports Fiats, particularly in the Mille Miglia,

then in 1937 he began driving Scuderia Ferrari GP Alfa Romeos, which were dominant in the smaller Italian races, finishing 3rd at Naples and Genoa in an 8C-35 behind his team-mates.

In 1938 he won the 1·5-litre Coppa Ciano race at Leghorn in a Type 158 Alfetta, the first appearance of these cars. In the Coppa Acerbo his 158 suffered plug troubles, but he won the 1·5-litre race preceding the Italian GP at Monza, duelling with his brother's Maserati as he had done at Leghorn until Luigi retired.

In 1939 at Tripoli his 158 was 3rd to Lang and Caracciola's 1·5-litre Mercedes. Much development work went into the 158 after this defeat, and whilst testing one of the new cars Emilio Villoresi, the most successful pre-war Alfetta driver, was killed at Monza in July 1939. PMAH

Pierre Veyron. *Photo: Cyril Posthumus Collection*

Emilio Villoresi. *Photo: Cyril Posthumus Collection*

Luigi Villoresi (right), at Silverstone in 1949 with Alberto Ascari. *Photo: A. R. Smith*

Luigi Villoresi: Principal Successes

1937	Masaryk Voiturette GP	Maserati 6CM
1938	Albi GP,	Maserati 6CM
	Pescara GP	Maserati 6CM
	Circuit of Lucca	Maserati 6CM
1939	South African GP	Maserati 4CL
	Targa Florio	Maserati 4CL
	Circuit of Abazzia	Maserati 4CL
1940	Targa Florio	Maserati 4CL
1946	Nice GP	Maserati 4CL
	Circuit of Voghera	Maserati 4CL
1947	Buenos Aires GP	Maserati 4CL
	Mar del Plata GP	Maserati 4CL
	Nîmes GP	Maserati 4CL
	Nice GP	Maserati 4CL
	Strasbourg GP	Maserati 4CL
	Lausanne GP	Maserati 4CL
1949	1st Buenos Aires GP	Maserati 4CL
	2nd Buenos Aires GP	Maserati 4CL
	Comminges GP	Maserati 4CLT/48
	Albi GP	Maserati 4CLT/48
	British GP	Maserati 4CLT/48
	Penya Rhin GP	Maserati 4CLT/48
	Naples GP	Osca 1,100cc
1949	Interlagos GP	Maserati 4CLT/48
	Circuit of Gavea	Maserati 4CLT/48
	Brussels GP	Ferrari 166
	Luxembourg GP	Ferrari 166
	Rome GP	Ferrari 166
	Circuit of Garda	Ferrari 166
	Dutch GP	Ferrari 125
1950	Buenos Aires GP	Ferrari 166
	Rosario GP	Ferrari 166
	Marseilles GP	Ferrari 166
	Circuit of Erlen	Ferrari 166
	Autodrome GP, Monza	Ferrari 3-litre

continued

Villoresi, Luigi

An Italian driver, born in 1909, with a highly impressive record of successes in a 25-year racing career, 'Gigi' Villoresi drove Maserati, Osca, Ferrari and Lancia cars, racing as far afield as South Africa, Brazil, Argentina and the United States as well as all over Europe. Born in Milan, he and his elder brother Emilio began racing in 1931 with tuned sports Fiats, then turned to Maserati voiturettes in 1936. Both brothers had a certain reputation for wild driving in their youth, but Luigi won his first major race, the Brno GP for voiturettes, in 1937, and by 1938 his talents were moving him up into Grand Prix spheres. He drove a works 3-litre 8CTF Maserati in the Coppa Acerbo at Pescara, a favourite circuit of his, and to everyone's surprise set the fastest lap against German opposition. He drove the same car in the Donington GP.

Emilio, by then an Alfa Romeo works driver in the new Type 158 voiturette team, was most unfortunately killed while practising at Monza early in 1939, by which time Luigi was Maserati's No. 1, racing the famous 16-valve 4CL. Villoresi epitomized the ebullient Italian driver of pre-World War 2 days, with victories at Albi, Pescara, Lucca, Palermo, in South Africa and elsewhere to his credit. He emerged from the war white-haired after a long spell as a prisoner of war, returning happily to racing, and in 1946–8 vied with Farina as Italy's fastest driver. He took a 3-litre 8CL Maserati to Indianapolis, in 1946, coming 7th, and with 4CL and then 4CLT/48 1·5-litre supercharged Maseratis he scored numerous victories, including the first post-war British GP at Silverstone in 1948.

Villoresi taught the wiles of his craft to Alberto Ascari, who combined them with his own inherent ability to become World Champion twice, a title which eluded his teacher although Villoresi was Italian Champion in 1947 and 1948. In 1949 both Villoresi and Ascari joined Ferrari, winning numerous races and remaining faithful to the 'Prancing Horse' stable until 1954 when they both signed with Lancia. The following year Ascari was killed and with Lancia's withdrawal from racing shortly afterwards, Villoresi returned to driving Maseratis. But by then his greatest days were over. He had suffered two serious crashes at Geneva, one in 1948, the other in 1950, had crashed again in the 1954 Mille Miglia, and when, in the 1956 Due Giornate meeting at Rome he had a fourth serious accident in a 2-litre sports Maserati, his family begged him to give up racing. With over 50 victories to his credit and by then 47 years of age, Villoresi did so. Activities since his retirement have included running an Innocenti agency. CP

Vinatier, Jean

Jean Vinatier was born in Paris in 1932 and started his race and rally career at the age of 16 by participating in the slow race at Rue Lepic. More seriously, in 1953 he started racing a Panhard Monopole, with which he won at Pau and Clermont, and then transferred to a DB with which he won his class at the Nürburgring and Rouen. He won his class in the Liège-Sofia-Liège and in 1961 won the class with an Abarth in the Tour de France. By 1964, he was getting works drives and won the Tour de Corse that year in a factory Gordini. The following year he was accepted into the Renault team for whom he won the Lyons-Charbonnières and finished 6th in the Alpine and 3rd in Corsica. That year also saw him at the wheel of an Alpine-Renault for the first time when he did some hill-climbs with it and broke the outright record at Mont d'Or.

1951	Syracuse GP	Ferrari 375
	Pau GP	Ferrari 375
	Circuit of Genoa	Ferrari 166
1951	Mille Miglia	Ferrari 340 America
	Coppa Inter-Europa, Monza	Ferrari 212
	Marseilles GP	Ferrari 166
	Circuit of Senigallia	Ferrari 340
1952	Turin GP	Ferrari 375
	Circuit of Sables d'Olonne	Ferrari 500
	Daily Mail Trophy, Boreham	Ferrari 375
	Circuit of Modena	Ferrari 500
1953	Autodromo GP, Monza	Ferrari 3-litre
	Circuit of Sicily	Ferrari 340MM
1954	Oporto GP	Lancia D24

Bill Vukovitch. Photo: Indianapolis Motor Speedway

In 1966 he finished 2nd in the Lyons-Charbonnières with an Alpine and was 2nd on index at Le Mans with Mauro Bianchi in a similar car. He also won the class with a Gordini at the Spa 24-hour race for touring cars. The following year, he was 2nd in the Danube Rally and 4th in the Tour de Corse, and also won the Circuit of Casablanca as well as widening his experience by driving in the 1,000 Lakes Rally in Finland.

The year 1968 was important for he won the Alpine Rally outright as well as the Critérium des Cevennes, the Rallye de Vercors and the Czech Rally. He was also 5th overall in the San Remo Rally and 3rd GT car in the Monte Carlo. The same year he drove a 3-litre Alpine at Le Mans. In 1969, he went even better and won the Alpine Rally a second time, was 3rd in the Monte Carlo and won many French events to give him the French championship. In 1970 he was 2nd in the Acropolis and 3rd in the Italian Rally. JD

Vukovich, William

Bill Vukovich, an American racing driver, born in 1918, whose outstanding racing accomplishments are linked almost entirely with the Indianapolis Motor Speedway, set his eyes on the 500 after winning the 1950 AAA midget car championship. His first Indy appearance the following year was made in a car of inferior quality and it lasted only 29 laps, but he earned championship points in five other big car events on other tracks during the season to merit a new Offenhauser-powered roadster for 1952.

After qualifying second fastest at 138·212mph, he took the lead on the seventh lap and engaged in a tremendous three-way battle with Jack McGrath and Troy Ruttman for more than 300 miles (480km) before gaining what appeared to be an insurmountable advantage. With nine laps to go, however, a steering pin broke and forced his elimination as Ruttman went on to win. Later in the season Vukovich scored victories in 100-mile races at Detroit, Mich., and Denver, Colo.; but, with the start of the 1953 season, he concentrated all of his attention on Indianapolis.

He won the pole position with a speed of 138·392mph (222·72kph) and led the field for all but five laps, while making a pit stop for fuel and tyres, to finish more than three and a half minutes in front at 128·74mph (207·16kph) going the full distance on a terribly hot day when most of his rivals used relief drivers.

Although relegated to 19th starting position because his car was not ready on the first day of trials, he won again in 1954 at a record-breaking speed of 130·84mph (210·56kph); and one year later, in quest of an unprecedented third straight 500 victory, he was well in the lead when a three-car accident developed immediately in front of him. With no time to reduce speed, he crashed over the wall in flames and was killed instantly, the other drivers involved escaping without serious injury. AB

Wagner, Louis

This French driver, born in 1882, joined the Darracq team in 1903, a year after Victor Hémery, and won the voiturette section of the Circuit des Ardennes that season, as well as finishing 3rd of the voiturettes in the Paris-Madrid and 28th in general classification. In 1905 he won his second voiturette race in the Ardennes. Darracq did not have a good year in 1906. Wagner was 8th in the Circuit des Ardennes, a state of affairs which was redeemed by his performance in the Vanderbilt Cup. He led throughout and finished 3½min quicker than

Lancia on the Fiat. Like Hémery, he had had enough of Alexandre Darracq by 1907, and when that gentleman explained his retirement in the Targa Florio (caused by a half-shaft failure) as 'running out of road', Wagner moved on to FIAT, in time to take 5th place in the Kaiserpreis and work up to 2nd in the Grand Prix before retiring.

Wagner's second American victory came in November 1908 at Savannah, where he won the Grand Prize from Hémery's Benz and Nazzaro on a sister Fiat. Unfortunately he retired once more in the 1909 and 1911 races, and his 2nd place in the 1912 Grand Prix marked the swansong of the giants. Wagner was by now working for the Hanriot aircraft firm and aviation engaged much of his time, but he emerged in 1914 to drive for Mercedes in the Grand Prix at Lyons, finishing 2nd behind Lautenschlager at 65·3mph (105·09kph).

In 1921 he was to have driven a Fiat at Indianapolis, but this entry never materialized, and his only run for his old employers was in the Italian GP, where his repeated tyre changes brought some hostility from the crowd. In spite of this he came in 2nd at 86·9mph (139·85kph). Like Hémery, he was persuaded to try his luck with the 2-litre Rolland-Pilain in the 1922 event, but the cars retired.

Wagner joined Alfa Romeo in 1924, taking 9th place in the Targa Florio behind his team-mates Masetti and Campari, after collecting a soldier on his bonnet. By mid-1925 he was driving for Delage, taking an excellent 2nd place on the 2-litre V-12 in the French GP at Montlhéry at an average speed of 68·7mph (110·56). He also found time to take 2nd place in the Targa and Coppa Florio on a sleeve-valve Peugeot, and drive an Ariès into 6th place at Le Mans. In 1926 he drove a sleeve-valve Peugeot in this event and retired; he was down to 6th place in the Targa Florio, but could still rate 2nd in the Coppa.

In 1927, he drove a 1·5-litre straight-8 Talbot but endless mechanical troubles dogged his one appearance in the French GP, though he broke the lap record at 78·5mph (126·33kph). This was his last racing season. He remained a superb and 'delicate' driver almost to the end, and despite the loss of a leg he was able to drive an old friend, the 1911 Coupe de l'Auto Delage, in 1953. In latter years he was instructor-supervisor at the Montlhéry Autodrome. Wagner died in 1960. MCS

Waldegård, Björn

Perhaps the most successful rally driver of the late 1960s is Waldegård, whose names is often spelt Walde-

Left, Louis Wagner. *Photo: Cyril Posthumus Collection*

Above, Björn Waldegård. *Photo: John Davenport*

Peter Walker at Donington, 1937. *Photo: Cyril Posthumus Collection*

gaard abroad. Born in 1943 in Rö, Sweden, Waldegård is the son of a farmer.

For many years he drove his own car in T-races (a type of small rally in Sweden with short, tough special stages) and rallies and then he was offered a car by Scania-Vabis, the Volkswagen importers in Sweden. With this he was very successful, although it was considerably slower than some of the opposition. This was set right when Scania gave him a Porsche for the 1968 Swedish Rally which he and Helmer won in convincing style, just 27 minutes ahead of the next crew. During that year, Waldegård won nearly every event in Sweden, both T-race and rally, winning the championship in the former category and coming third in the rally section. In 1969, though not severing his connections with Scania, he started to drive for the Porsche factory and won the Monte Carlo for them and followed it up with his second victory in Sweden.

The 1970 season was even better for Waldegård, for in a factory Porsche he repeated his victories in both the Monte Carlo and the Swedish rallies and added the Austrian Alpine to his laurels. In the Targa Florio he made a sensational debut in racing driving a JW Porsche 908 with Richard Attwood: they finished a remarkable 5th overall. JD

Walker, Peter D. C.

A daring and highly competent British driver, born in 1913, Peter Walker in pre-World War 2 days was nicknamed 'Skidder' for his spectacular method of broadside cornering with the B-type 1·5-litre ERA he often shared with its owner, his friend Peter Whitehead. There was much controversy as to the benefits of the method, Richard Seaman for one dismissing it, yet Walker's performances suggested that it had considerable value with the older, high-built ERA, but not with lower, better suspended cars; certainly he dropped it after the war. He first raced in 1935 with Whitehead's 1,100cc Alta, then scored two 2nds in Brooklands Mountain races in 1936 with the ERA. He and Whitehead subsequently shared several successes in this car.

After the war Walker drove the Whitehead ERA at the 1948 Prescott International meeting; on a slippery hill in heavy rain he made ftd, nearly 1½ seconds faster than anyone else, Mays and Gerard in ERAs included, in a performance described by *The Motor* as 'staggering'. In 1949 he had further hill-climb successes, and also drove the E-type ERA, a car with which no driver gained much glory, though Walker managed two 2nds at Goodwood.

In 1950 he was signed up by Jaguar and BRM; with an XK 120 he won the over 3-litre sports car race at

verstone, and drove for BRM in the Penya Rhin GP
Spain, working the fragile 16-cylinder car up to 4th
ace before losing all his gearbox oil and retiring. In
51, the old partnership, Whitehead and Walker,
red its greatest success—victory at Le Mans with a
orks XK 120C Jaguar. Walker also finished 2nd to
am-mate Moss in the Dundrod, Northern Ireland, TT.
s second BRM drive came in that memorable British
P at Silverstone, when Parnell and Walker finished
n and 7th respectively, after immensely plucky drives
ring which their legs and feet were seriously burnt by
rnace-like heat in the cockpits.

Walker drove for Jaguar until 1954, winning his class
the 1952 Goodwood 9 Hours, and coming 2nd at Le
ans and 4th in the TT in 1953, each time co-driving
th Stirling Moss. In 1952 he also set up new sports car
ords on Shelsley Walsh and Prescott hills with an
X 120C, and went to Italy to drive Whitehead's V-12
rrari in the Monza F2 GP, coming a highly creditable
n.

Walker joined the Aston Martin team in 1955, sharing
ne Goodwood 9 Hours victory with Dennis Poore in
DB3S, the same pair bringing home the first British
r in the Dundrod TT, 4th behind the triumphant
ercedes trio. Luck was not with him in his last season,
56: the Aston Martin he and Salvadori shared in the
irburgring 1,000 Kilometres broke its De Dion tube on
e last lap when well up; at Le Mans they were holding
n place after 13 hours when Walker crashed during
avy rain on the very fast, slippery bend past the pits.
e suffered bruises, a broken finger and concussion,
d, with 14 enterprising years of racing behind him,
alker gave up competitive motoring. CP

alker, R. R. C.

ivate entrants in the costly world of Grand Prix
cing are rare nowadays, and none has figured so
ominently or consistently since the mid-1950s as Rob
alker of Nunney, Somerset. He is a Scot, born in 1917,
e great-great-grandson of the Johnnie Walker of
orld-wide whisky fame, and has been a tremendous
thusiast for motor racing ever since he was taken as a
y to the Boulogne races in 1924. His competition
reer began in 1934, when he drove a supercharged TT
a-Francis in the Lewes speed trials, and thereafter he
ok part in many inter-Varsity and club trials, sprints
d hill-climbs, his cars including Austin Sevens, the old
at iron' Thomas Special and two Delahayes. His debut
circuit racing came in an unfortunate year, 1939, with
r imminent, but he found time to win a Mountain
ce at Brooklands and finish 3rd in another, and to
me 8th at Le Mans with Ian Connell co-driving, all in
3·5-litre Delahaye, before joining the Fleet Air Arm for
r years.

When peace returned, family affairs prevented him
cing seriously, but he ran in innumerable speed trials
d hill-climbs right up to 1957, driving such cars as the
elahaye, Delage, Connaught, Cooper, and a 300SL
ercedes-Benz and scoring numerous class victories.
eantime he had started the RRC Walker Racing Team,
sed at his Pippbrook Garage in Dorking, Surrey, and
onsored a succession of first-class drivers, including
olt, Parnell, Collins, Peter Walker, Salvadori, Brooks,
oss, Trintignant, Brabham, Bonnier, Siffert and
raham Hill. His cars ranged from a GP Delage with
type ERA engine fitted, to F2 and F1 Connaughts, F1
d F2 Coopers, F1 Lotus and Brabhams, an F1 Cooper-
aserati, a Lotus 49 and a Lotus 72.

Rob Walker watching Alf Francis fitting the
carburettors to the 1959 Cooper-BRM.
Photo: Ruck Press Services

Rob Walker. *Photo: Cyril Posthumus
Collection*

Walker team cars have always been painted in St
Andrew's blue, and such is the respect with which race
organizers the world over hold him that not one ever
tried to make him switch to British green when that was
customary. In preparation and turn-out his cars were the
equal of the best factory teams, as were the pits, with Rob
himself wielding the watches and his wife Betty the lap
chart. The apparent antithesis of the forbidding Neubauer
as a team manager, Walker's courteous affability cloaks
a very professional efficiency, and the team's successes
vindicate this.

Prepared by that great mechanic Alf Francis, Walker
Coopers driven by Stirling Moss won the 1958 Argentine
GP (the first World Championship race won by a private
owner) and the 1959 GPs of Italy, Portugal and New
Zealand. In Walker Lotuses, Moss won the Monaco and
United States GPs in 1960 and the Monaco and German
GPs in 1961, and the Frenchman Trintignant won the
1958 Monaco GP. All these classic victories were gained
against opposition from the cream of the GP teams, and
many lesser F1 and F2 wins also fell to the Walker team.
In recent years, rocketing costs made it seem improbable
that they could continue in exotic GP fields, but from
1966 to 1969 they were co-sponsored by Jack Durlacher,
the team's Lotus 49 winning the 1968 British GP at
Brands Hatch, driven by Jo Siffert. In 1970 the Brooke-
Bond Oxo Group took on sponsorship, thus guaranteeing
continued operation of Walker's famous team, and in
1971 they jointly reached agreement with John Surtees
to run the Formula 1 Surtees car.

Besides Formula 1, which is Walker's main interest,
he writes Grand Prix race reports for an American
monthly journal, and also keeps a collection of historic
cars. It is well for motor racing, both currently and
historically, that there are such enthusiasts as Rob
Walker. CP

Wallard, Lee

American racing driver, born 1911. Lee Wallard raced
for 15 years on the smaller tracks in the eastern part of

the United States before moving up to the AAA big car championship division in 1948, and established himself quickly as one of the nation's most consistent performers. He finished 6th in the 1948 national standing, 8th in 1949, 12th in 1950, and was leading in points—after winning the 1951 Indianapolis race—when forced to retire from racing by severe burns sustained in a racing accident.

He attracted considerable attention as a 1948 rookie at Indianapolis by driving the underpowered Iddings Special (only 233ci—3,785cc) to 7th place and finished 6th in 1950 after being eliminated early in 1949 because of mechanical trouble.

In 1951 at Indianapolis, he proved his superiority early in an exciting battle for first place, surging from behind on four occasions during the first 200 miles and leading the field for the remainder of the race to win at an average speed of 126·244mph (203·166kph) for a new record.

Wallard's tragic accident took place at Reading, in a sprint car race four days later. After many months of gradual recuperation, he joined the Champion Spark Plug Company's highway safety team, making almost daily talks to the driver training classes of the nation's high schools. He died of a heart ailment in 1963 at his home in Florida. AB

Ward, Rodger

American racing driver born in 1921. Known throughout the United States as auto racing's goodwill ambassador because of his hundreds of personal appearances to stimulate interest in the sport, Ward began his professional driving career after serving as a P-38 Lightning pilot and instructor in the United States Air Force for the duration of World War 2.

With five years of experience on the nation's smaller tracks in stock-car and midget-car events, he came to Indianapolis in 1951 for the first of his appearances in fifteen of the annual 500-mile speed classics. Mechanical trouble prevented him from going the full distance in seven of his first eight Indy events and he finished no better than 8th on the other occasion. In 1959, however, he began a long and profitable association with car owner Bob Wilke and crew chief A. J. Watson.

He set a new race record of 135·857mph (218·691kph) in an Offenhauser-powered car to win at Indianapolis that year and repeated the performance in 1962 when he became the first 140mph (225·3kph) winner at a speed of 140·293mph (225·78kph). He also finished 2nd at Indy

Lee Wallard. *Photo: Indianapolis Motor Speedway*

Christian Werner. *Photo: Cyril Posthumus Collection*

Below, Rodger Ward. *Photo: Indianapolis Motor Speedway*

Left, Rodger Ward, in the Leader Card Special (Watson-Offenhauser) in which he won the Indianapolis 500 in 1962. *Photo: Indianapolis Motor Speedway*

in 1960, 3rd in 1961, 4th in 1963, and 2nd with a Ford-engined car in 1964 for one of the outstanding six-year performances in speedway history.

Ward was almost equally successful on other tracks, winning the 1959 and 1962 national driving titles and scoring a total of 26 big car championship victories before announcing his retirement from open-cockpit racing in 1966. Since then he has made some appearanc in stock-car races, a division of the sport in which he was the 1951 national champion; but he has devoted most of his time to his various business interests, as we as public relations work for the Ontario, Calif., speedway. AB

Werner, Christian

Born in Stuttgart in 1892, Werner during his comparatively short racing career drove only for Daimler Motorer Gesellschaft, but his magnificent victory, against the cream of the world's best drivers and cars, in the Targa and Coppa Florio races (run concurrently) in 1924 stamped him as a driver of real class. By the nature of h employment in the experimental and racing departmen of Mercedes he did not have the opportunity that independent drivers had of competing in many races, and when Mercedes curtailed their racing programme in 1925, because of the economic conditions in German his opportunities became fewer. Nevertheless Werner competed in many hill-climbs and speed trials in Germar between 1923 and 1928, amassing an impressive numbe of fastest times of day, including the famous Freiburg hill-climb which he won in 1925 and 1926.

In 1927 he won the Inaugural Race (racing car class) at the Nürburgring and was 2nd in the German GP a month later over the same circuit. He won this event th following year, however, in partnership with Caracciol He did little racing in 1929 but in 1930 he partnered Caracciola in the Mille Miglia, the pair finishing 6th, and again in the Grand Prix d'Endurance at Le Mans, where they put up a spirited fight until overwhelmed by the all-powerful Bentley teams of 4½-litre supercharged and 6½-litre unsupercharged cars. By nature a quiet and reserved man, Werner was greatly respected by all. He died in 1932. TASOM

Wharton, Kenneth

This British driver's name first appeared in the motorin press in 1936, with a 3rd and a 4th in an Austin Seven special at Donington Park. Not until after World War with a garage business established in Smethwick, did Wharton's passion for the sport blossom in several different directions. By 1948 he had built an MG J4-engined sprint car, a BSA-engined 500 single-seater, an a trials special (KHA 1) which won the RAC Trials Championship in two successive years. This machine, with Ford 10 engine in a modified Austin Seven frame, caused much rethinking among those with whom the V-8 machines were then fashionable, and really set the style for the modern trials special.

Wharton was also successful with Fords in rallies, winning the Tulip three times and the Lisbon in 1950. I that year he took to the hills with a Cooper-JAP 1,000c and to the circuits with a 500-engined version. Just in time for the Trials Championship, a new special was built (PHA 1) with Austin A40 engine, which was as successful as its predecessor.

In 1951 he achieved his first hill-climb championship with a Cooper-JAP 1100, and used a Kieft and a Coope Norton in the 500 class. His first works drives came in

52, with the unfortunate V-16 BRM and in F2 with
almost equally unsuccessful single-seater Frazer
sh. He also drove a Le Mans Frazer Nash, and one or
events for the Ecurie Ecosse with a Cooper-Bristol.
hill-climbs Wharton made up for his disappointing
cings in circuit racing, setting the pattern for the next
years with fastest times of the day with the Cooper
nearly every event entered—and often backing up
h second fastest in the 2-litre ERA. It was not until
55 that he relinquished his hold on the RAC Hill-
mb Championship.

Wharton had better results with the old BRM in 1953,
d many good races with the F2 Cooper-Bristol, and
1954 his range of activities extended to long-distance
ing for Jaguar and F1 drives in the Owen Maserati
OF. In the Vanwall team for 1955, he started by crash-
g badly at Silverstone, and then again in the Tourist
ophy with the fibreglass-bodied sports Frazer Nash.
s immense enthusiasm was quite undiminished, but this
s another unsuccessful season, apart from an hour run
th an MGA at Montlhéry.

Freelancing again in 1956, Wharton won, as was
coming his habit, his class in the saloon car race at the
ily Express Silverstone meeting with an apparently
suitable car (Austin A95), and also drove Alfa Romeos,
aseratis and Ferraris. He was leading a sports car race
Ardmore, New Zealand, on 12th January, 1957, when
made one of his rare errors of judgment, the results of
nich proved fatal. The sport mourned the loss of the
rceful, versatile and courageous driver, whose grim-
ss at the wheel was matched by his humour
sewhere. DF

Left, Ken Wharton in the V-16 BRM at
Goodwood, 1954. *Photo: Louis Klementaski*

Above, Ken Wharton. *Photo: Autosport*

Right, Peter Whitehead (right), with Ian
Stewart in the Jaguar which they drove into
4th place at Le Mans, 1953. *Photo: Keith
Duerden*

Left, Sir John Whitmore in a Cortina Lotus,
1966. *Photo: Alan Mann Racing Ltd*

Below, Sir John Whitmore. *Photo: Alan
Mann Racing Ltd*

Whitmore, Sir John

Born in 1937, Sir John Whitmore was one of the leading
drivers in European saloon car racing during the 1960s,
and was also seen in America and South Africa. He
began racing with a Lotus 6 in 1958, and in 1959 he
scored 12 victories in 15 starts in national and international events, driving a Lotus Elite. That year he shared
an Elite at Le Mans with Jim Clark. He ran an FJ Lola
and F2 Cooper in 1960, and in 1961 was included in the
BMC works team at Sebring where he was 2nd in class
with an MGA. He also made his mark in saloon car
racing that year, winning the British Saloon Car Championship in a works Mini-Cooper. He was runner-up for
this Championship in 1962, and also drove a Lotus Elan
for the Stirling Moss Automobile Racing Team. In 1963
he joined the works Lotus-Cortina team, for which he
drove with great success for three years. In 1966 he drove
for Alan Mann, in a Lotus-Cortina in saloon car events,
and a Ford GT 40 in sports car events. He also drove the
first Ford Falcon to race in Britain. After the 1966 season
he retired from racing, sold his family estate at Orsett in
Suffolk, and now lives in Switzerland. DCN

Whitehead, Peter Neild

Whitehead, born in 1915, was one of the last of the truly
amateur British drivers and travelled far and wide during
his 20 years of racing. With interests in wool and farming,
he had the means to buy the best available cars and he
raced for pleasure, not profit.

Beginning in 1934 he graduated via an ex-Victor
Gillow Riley Nine and a 1,100cc supercharged Alta (in
which he finished 3rd at Limerick and won the Dancer's
End hill-climb in 1935) to a B-type ERA by 1936. He
raced this car extensively in the British Isles and in
Europe; took it out to Australia in 1938, winning the
Australian GP on the then new (and largely unsurfaced)
Mount Panorama circuit at Bathurst, New South Wales.

After World War 2, Whitehead brought out his
beloved black ERA again, winning a Prescott hill-climb
in 1946, but he also fell for the deceptive good looks of
the E-type ERA and raced it without success at Turin late
that season and at Jersey in 1947. After that he reverted
to his 1936 B-type, finishing 2nd in the British Empire
Trophy at Douglas, Isle of Man. In 1948 he was seriously
injured in an air crash at Croydon aerodrome when en
route to Milan to arrange for a new car, but in 1949 he
bought a Formula 1 V-12 supercharged 1·5-litre Ferrari,
with which he won the Czech GP and finished 3rd in the
French GP.

In 1950 Whitehead won the Jersey Road Race and the Ulster Trophy at Dundrod with the Ferrari, and ran 3rd to two Alfa Romeos in the BRDC Silverstone. He also took to sports car racing that year, coming 2nd in an XK 120 Jaguar to Stirling Moss's similar car in the first post-war TT at Dundrod. The following year he and Peter Walker shared a works XK 120C Jaguar at Le Mans, scoring a glorious victory for Britain.

He drove an F2 Alta in 1952 and a Cooper-Alta in 1953 while with D-type Jaguars he won the Reims 12 Hours race with Moss in 1953 and with Wharton in 1954, and also the 1953 Hyères 12 Hours in the South of France with Tom Cole co-driving. In 1954 Whitehead had a new Jaguar-engined sports Cooper constructed, and also acquired a special 3-litre-engined single-seater Ferrari, both of which brought him successes.

Whitehead also bought a 3-litre sports Maserati that year, winning the Leinster Trophy scratch race and setting a new lap record. His last great drive was at Le Mans in 1958, when he and his half-brother Graham Whitehead shared an Aston Martin DB3S to 2nd place overall. Three months later, competing in the Tour de France with Graham in a sports Jaguar, Peter Whitehead was killed when the car crashed down a ravine near Lasalle. CP

Wilcox, Howard

Wilcox, born in 1889, earned an important niche in the annals of American racing history despite the fact that his business interests in Indianapolis prevented him from participating in the sport on a full-time professional basis. All of the race cars he drove, except the Peugeots, were built by Indianapolis automotive companies: Stutz, National, Fox, Premier and HCS (Harry C. Stutz).

His principal interest was the annual Indianapolis 500-mile race and his record of having participated with distinction in all of the first eleven Indy classics was an accomplishment unequalled by any other driver.

'Howdy's' early victories in other parts of the country included one on the boards at Playa del Rey, Calif., and on the dirt at Sioux City, Iowa. He was also a formidable contender on road courses as indicated by his 2nd-place finishes behind Dario Resta in the 300-mile Vanderbilt Cup event and the 402-mile American Grand Prize in 1915 at San Francisco.

His association with Peugeot originated when the managers of a few American speedways, faced with a shortage of entries because American industry was involved in producing World War 1 material, formed their own racing teams in order to keep the sport alive as long as possible. Wilcox was selected as a member of the Indianapolis Motor Speedway team, which was formed by the Speedway's purchase of Premier and Peugeot race cars late in 1915, and he won the 1919 Indianapolis 500 with a Speedway-owned Peugeot at a speed of 88·05mph (141·70kph). He was also a member of the Peugeot factory team at Indianapolis in 1920.

Wilcox was the fastest qualifier for the 1915 Indianapolis race with a Stutz, led the field at some stage of four Indianapolis races and, as a relief driver, helped Tom Milton win the 1923 500 in an HCS Special. He died as the result of a racing accident at Altoona, Pa., in 1924. AB

Williams, William

William Grover-Williams was born in 1903 at Montrouge near Paris, his father being English and his mother

Above, Howard Wilcox. Photo: Indianapolis Motor Speedway

Right, William Williams at Montlhéry, 1927. Photo: Autocar

Jean-Pierre Wimille: Principal Successes

Year	Race	Car
1932	Oran GP	Bugatti Type 51
	Lorraine GP	Alfa Romeo Monza
1934	Algerian GP	Bugatti Type 59
1936	French GP, with Sommer (Sports Cars)	Bugatti Type 57G
	Comminges GP (Sports Cars)	Bugatti Type 57G
	Marne GP (Sports Cars)	Bugatti Type 57G
	Deauville GP	Bugatti Type 59
1937	Le Mans 24-Hour Race, with Benoist	Bugatti Type 57G
	Marne GP (Sports Cars)	Bugatti Type 57G
	Pau GP (Sports Cars)	Bugatti Type 57G
	Bone GP (Sports Cars)	Bugatti Type 57G
1939	Le Mans 24-Hour Race, with Veyron	Bugatti Type 57C
	Coupe de Paris	Bugatti 4·7-litre
	Luxembourg GP	Bugatti 4·7-litre
1945	Coupe des Prisonniers	Bugatti 4·7-litre
1946	Burgundy GP	Alfa Romeo 8C-308
	Coupe de Paris	Alfa Romeo 8C-308
	Perpignan GP	Alfa Romeo 8C-308
1947	Belgian GP	Alfa Romeo 158
	Swiss GP	Alfa Romeo 158
	Coupe de Paris	Simca-Gordini
1948	French GP	Alfa Romeo 158
	Italian GP	Alfa Romeo 158
	Monza GP	Alfa Romeo 158
	Valentino GP	Alfa Romeo 158
	Rosario GP	Simca-Gordini

French. Brought up in France in comfortable circumstances, married to a Frenchwoman and living most of his life in France, apart from trips to England to see relatives, he remained English only in name and character.

In 1926, at the age of 23, Grover-Williams took up motor sport, initially entering the Monte Carlo Rally in a Hispano-Suiza. In 1926, too, he bought his first Bugatti and started a long and successful career with the type, always driving under the name Williams, and confusing everyone, more or less, as to his real name. In that year he made best times at Mont-Agel, La Turbie and Ester and was 2nd at Miramas behind Segrave in a Talbot. In 1927 he forsook his Bugatti for a Talbot but returned in a Type 35C in 1928 to win the French GP at Comminges, and then in 1929 won the first Monaco Grand Prix. He won the French Grand Prix that year as well, but crashed in the Italian.

These achievements were followed by a poor year in 1930, with an unsuccessful run in the Targa Florio. Success came again with a 1st in the Belgian Grand Prix at Spa in 1931, driving with Conelli; 1st at La Baule three years in succession in 1931–3; and 2nd at Dieppe 1932. Following another quiet spell he was then asked to join the official Bugatti works team for 1934, but had bad luck and few successes until 1936. Then he was 6th with Veyron in a 57S 'tank' in the French Grand Prix, and shared in the driving of the world one-hour record in one of these cars.

At the outbreak of World War 2 he volunteered in Paris for the British Army and became one of Colonel Maurice Buckmaster's special service men. Several times landed in occupied France, he was arrested eventually on 2 August 1943, at the house of Robert Benoist and finally shot by the Gestapo. Benoist himself was arrested later. HGC

Wimille, Jean-Pierre

Wimille, born in Paris in 1908, was destined to develop into one of France's finest Grand Prix drivers. He made his début in Grand Prix racing in the French GP at Pau in 1930, in a Bugatti, where he failed to finish. In early 1931 he was 2nd in the Monte Carlo Rally and then he was seen among the giants sharing a Type 51 Bugatti with Gaupillat in the Italian GP and coming in 4th.

He continued in 1931 with the Bugatti in the French G

ght, Jean-Pierre Wimille (left), with
né Dreyfus at Molsheim, c 1934. Photo:
gh Conway Collection

r right, Jean-Pierre Wimille in the 3-litre
gatti at Cork, 1938. Photo: Cork Examiner

but retired; 1932 was not a great year for him with a
2·3-litre Monza Alfa Romeo, although he won the
Lorraine GP in it. He entered for several hill-climbs, and
drove the Type 54 4·9-litre Bugatti. In 1933 he completely
deserted Bugatti for Alfa Romeo, and managed a 2nd
place at the Marne GP, a 3rd at Brno in Czechoslovakia,
and a 5th at San Sebastian.

Wimille returned to Bugatti in 1934 as a works driver
in a 3·3-litre Type 59, retiring in the French GP, and
having little real chance to show his mettle although he
won the Algiers GP at the end of the season. Next year
he ran in the Belgian GP keeping the Bugatti up among
the Mercedes until the car failed; he managed a 2nd at
Tunis but retired again at Monza, although he kept
going for a 4th at San Sebastian. He continued to try in
the Type 59, in 1936, being among the tail-enders at
Monaco, 3rd at Tunis, and then achieving a splendid
win with Sommer in the 'Tank' Type 57G Bugatti in the
French GP at Montlhéry. He repeated this win at
Marne and Comminges and won at Deauville in the
Type 59 and drove a lone Bugatti against the German
giants at the Nürburgring, but retired, a performance he
repeated in the Swiss GP shortly afterwards. In October
1936 he drove the 4·7-litre single-seat Bugatti to a 2nd
place in the Vanderbilt Cup in the United States, the first
time a European-entered Bugatti had been seen there for
many years.

In 1937 Wimille was the sole works representative for
Bugatti, driving various versions of the car with 3·3- or
4·7-litre engines. He won at Pau and shared the victory
that year at Le Mans with Benoist in the Type 57G
'Tank' and once again at Marne. In 1938 he turned up
with the new 3-litre single-seater Bugatti at Cork, but
although very fast, it suffered mechanical trouble. The
car failed again in the French GP at Reims, and Wimille
threw his hand in, deserting to Alfa Romeo, although it

did not bring him much luck. However, having shared a
victory with Veyron at Le Mans in the Bugatti Tank with
supercharged Type 57C engine he was then persuaded
by Jean Bugatti to take the single-seat Bugatti to Prescott
Hill-climb in Gloucestershire at the end of the summer,
in 1939, and achieved 2nd fastest time on the unfamiliar
course.

War now came and during it he served in the French
Air Force and later with the Resistance.

Soon after the war ended racing began again in France.
Wimille won the Coupe des Prisonniers in the Bois de
Boulogne in Paris in the 4·7-litre single-seat Bugatti,
then in 1946 returned to Alfa Romeo for a 3rd in the
Geneva GP and a 2nd at Turin, showing his potential by
fastest times in both events—and that of these new
1·5-litre cars.

In 1947 his successes continued in the Swiss and
European GPs; established firmly in the Alfa Romeo
team and now free to drive as he pleased he beat his
team-mates Varzi and Trossi in both events but tactfully
did not do so at Monza. The following year he again
drove for Alfa Romeo and occasionally for his native
France in a Simca-Gordini, showing incomparable form
by winning the French, Italian and Monza GPs and
conceding 2nd place to the Italian Trossi at the Swiss
GP at Berne only as homage to Varzi who had lost his
life in practice in that event.

And then unhappily in January 1949, practising for
the Buenos Aires GP in a Gordini, Wimille was evidently
blinded by the sun, ran off the road, hit a tree, and died
shortly afterwards.

Wimille was rated as a driver of exceptional quality
with an extraordinary ability to cover ground with no
apparent effort, in any weather and on all circuits; the
great Fangio described him as the world's top driver of
his time. HGC

Yarborough, Caleb

American racing driver, born in 1939. Cale's best year was 1968 when his Mercury won at four NASCAR superspeedways. His 194·015mph (312·228kph) qualifying mark for the 1970 Daytona 500 is a track record, and his 183·295mph (299·48kph) race average, established while winning one of the two, 125-mile, 1970 Daytona 500 qualifying heats, is a closed course world record race average. After winning 13 stock car Grand Nationals, including the 1968 Daytona 500, Yarborough, who had raced at Indianapolis in 1966 (28th) and 1967 (17th), switched to Indianapolis championship cars in 1971. ARB

Yarbrough, LeeRoy

This American driver, born in 1938, rewrote the NASCAR record book in 1969 driving factory-supported Ford and Mercury sedans entered by former NASCAR champion Junior Johnson, himself 50 times a Grand National winner. LeeRoy captured an unprecedented seven superspeedway Grand Nationals, including the Daytona 500, to earn an all-time stock car record of $200,000. In 1970 the quiet Southerner won the Charlotte 500 to bring his career total to 14 GNs. In single-seaters Yarbrough qualified for Indianapolis for the third time, finishing 19th; and was leading the California 500 when his engine blew nine laps from the finish. ARB

Zanelli, Juan

Zanelli came from Chile, but lived much of his time in Italy, Spain and France. He began racing in 1926 with a Fiat, then acquired a Bugatti, winning that unique event, the Bugatti Grand Prix, (organized by Bugattis for Bugattis only at Le Mans, with a Bugatti as first prize) both in 1929 and 1930. As an amateur he also scored two notable 2nds in the 1929 Marne GP (behind Etancelin) and the 1930 Bordino Cup at Alessandria (behind Varzi), and was 3rd in the French GP at Pau. In 1931 Zanelli gave further evidence of his considerable skill by driving a new Spanish 3-litre car, the straight-8 unsupercharged Nacional Pescara, in European hill-climbs, breaking the record at Kesselberg outright and beating Caracciola, scoring class 2nds at Shelsley Walsh and Rabassada (Spain) and a 3rd at Mont Ventoux. The cumulative points he scored established the small Chilean as 1931 European Mountain Champion, to the astonishment of Continentals accustomed to seeing their hill-climb events dominated by local stars such as Stuck and Caracciola.

Zanelli drove a 2·3-litre Alfa Romeo in numerous races during 1933, winning the Penya Rhin GP at Barcelona, and coming 6th in the 500 Miles race at Brooklands, winning the 2-3-litre class. By 1934 this car was becoming unreliable, but he ran in several hill-climbs with the Nacional Pescara, now wearing a single-seater body, beating Count Trossi's monoposto Alfa in the 3-litre class at La Turbie in 1934. In 1935 he won the Val de Guech climb outright, was 2nd at La Turbie, Kesselberg and Alpilles, and 3rd on the Grossglockner. By 1936 the Spanish car was getting old and Zanelli's last success with it was a class 3rd at La Turbie. He raced a monoposto Maserati occasionally that season, then retired from the sport. CP

Zasada, Sobieslaw

Born in Krakow, Poland in 1930, where he lives at present and runs his own garage business, Sobieslaw Zasada started rallying after World War 2 and such was the reputation that he gained that he was one of the

Cale Yarborough. *Photo: Ford Motor Company*

LeeRoy Yarbrough. *Photo: Ford Motor Company*

Below, Juan Zanelli. *Photo: Cyril Posthumus Collection*

Right, Sobieslaw Zasada with his Steyr-Puch, 1965. *Photo: John Davenport*

first drivers behind the Iron Curtain to get one of the BMC Minis at the beginning of the 1960s. In partners with his wife, he competed in many events in Poland a Czechoslovakia. In 1964 he formed an accord with the Austrian firm of Steyr-Puch and started driving in the little 650cc-engined car based on the Fiat 500 body. H was immediately successful, winning the Polish Rally from Erik Carlsson's Saab; the following year he was 2nd to Aaltonen's Mini Cooper in that rally and won class in Greece, Monte Carlo and the RAC Rally.

By choosing his rallies with care and by driving with great deal of verve in a small car, he won the Europea Championship in 1966, a performance he was to repea the following year, but this time driving a Porsche. In 1967 he travelled to South America and won the Gran Premio d'Argentina with a works Porsche and in 1968 he finished the London to Sydney in a similar car. 196 saw him driving the Safari in a works Porsche in which he came 6th overall and finished 1st on the road. In the 1970 Safari he led most of the way in a Porsche until the sump broke, and also in 1970 he had his first drive in a Ford Escort in the World Cup Rally. JD

Zborowski, Count Louis Vorow

Born in England in 1895, of a Polish father, Count Eliot Zborowski, and an American mother, Count Zborowski was a legendary figure, as a result of his liking for giant racing cars, of which his Chitty-Chitty-Bang-Bangs enlivened Brooklands when it reopened after World War 1. But he was in fact a serious-minded racing driver, able to indulge his whims on account of very considerable personal wealth, and accepted into the Mercedes works team. Zborowski was in many way the prince of the fairy tale. Living at Higham, near Canterbury, after the death of his mother, with little to distract him from his hobbies, he employed Capt (later Lt Col) Clive Gallop as his engineer and for the 1921 season they evolved Chitty I out of a pre-war chain-driven Mercedes chassis powered by a 23-litre Maybach aero engine. This car stole the headlines and was a sensation at Brooklands, where it was also very successful.

Chitty won its first race, at the 1921 Easter Brookland Meeting, a 100mph Short Handicap, at 100·75mph

Above, Count Louis Zborowski in Chitty-Chitty-Bang-Bang I, at Brooklands, 1921.
Photo: *William Boddy Collection*

Right, Count Louis Zborowski (left), with S. C. H. Davis in the Miller at Lyons, 1924.
Photo: *T. A. S. O. Mathieson Collection*

(162·08kph). It then won the Lightning Short Handicap the same day and was 2nd in a sprint race. This was the commencement of an auspicious career for this famous car, but in 1922 it burst a tyre on the banking in practice and left the Track backwards, chopping some fingers from the hand of an official who had slipped into a ditch to avoid it. Zborowski escaped unhurt but that virtually ended his association with the car. He had built Chitty II, a similar car with an 18·8-litre Benz aero engine, at the end of 1921 but this ran only at that year's Autumn Meeting at Brooklands, although it was used thereafter for some sensational Continental tours, with Chitty III, a shaft-drive Mercedes aero-engined monster, following in its wake as a baggage wagon, these two giants penetrating far into the Sahara desert.

At this time Zborowski raced a 1914 Grand Prix Mercedes, winner of the last pre-war French Grand Prix, a 5-litre Ballot, and ancient Blitzen Benz until even he decided it was too dangerous to go on running this 200hp chain-drive monster, and won a race with Chitty III.

Anxious to do some long-distance racing, the Count drove a Salmson in the 1,100cc class of the 1924 JCC 200 Miles Race and in 1923 took a team of straight-8 Type 30 Bugattis to Indianapolis. Nothing much came of this American interlude, except that Zborowski returned to England with the latest 2-litre straight-8 Miller racing car. He tried it on Brooklands without much success, except for one club meeting where it performed well. Wishing to get into road racing, Zborowski gave financial support to the Aston Martin Company, then run by Lionel Martin and Robert Bamford, which resulted in his driving Aston Martins of various kinds at Brooklands, in the 200 Miles Race and abroad. He sent Gallop to France to acquire drawings for a twin-cam 16-valve cylinder head for the 1·5-litre Aston Martin engine, after experiments with the Robb single-cam 16-valve head and the Benson twin-ohc 8-valve head had proved abortive. Although outclassed on swept volume, Zborowski and Gallop did quite well with the Aston Martins in Spain where he was called *el eterno segundo,* as he finished 2nd in the Penya Rhin light car race in 1922 and 1923 (on Aston Martin), and at Sitges on the Miller in 1923. In the same year he was 3rd in the 1·5-litre class at Sitges in an Aston Martin, and in 1924 Zborowski took S. C. H. Davis with him in the French GP at Lyons, for a wild ride in the unsuitable Miller.

The previous year Zborowski had persuaded Gallop to construct for him at the Canterbury estate, where Zborowski had his racing-car workshops and 7in-gauge model railway, a new two-seater in the Chitty image, powered by a 27-litre Liberty V-12 aero engine, the largest-engined car to race at Brooklands. The Rubery Owen chassis frame was deliberately made in primitive fashion, as Zborowski disliked the idea of a modern lattice-braced frame, and the car had stub axles from a 1908 Mercedes and the gearbox from the old 200hp Benz. For road use Zborowski had a beautiful Hispano-Suiza two-seater and his American wife used an Eric Campbell. By the latter part of 1924 Count Zborowski had been given a place in the Mercedes works team and it was while driving one of their current dangerous 2-litre straight-8 cars that he was killed, when he skidded into a tree at Monza during the Italian Grand Prix. His riding mechanic, Martin, escaped. Thus was cut short the promising career of this mercurial driver, whose name is inevitably linked with his Chitty-Chitty-Bang-Bangs but who had the making of a good racing driver. Legend has it that when he was killed Louis Zborowski was wearing the same cuff-links which had killed his father, Count Eliot Zborowski, by catching his sleeve in the hand-throttle of his Mercedes at the La Turbie hill-climb of 1903. After the Count's death Parry Thomas acquired the Higham Special or 'Babs' as the Liberty-engined car had been named, and died at the wheel of it in 1927. WB

Zehender, Geofredo

'Freddie' Zehender was born in Italy in 1901 and started racing in the late 1920s. Co-driving with Ledure in a Chrysler, he took part in the 1928 24-hour races at Le Mans and Spa, retiring in the former but finishing 3rd in the latter. He was 4th in the San Sebastian GP later in the year and 3rd in the Circuit des Routes Pavées. He drove for the Alfa Romeo sports car team in 1929 and was 3rd with Rigal in the Belgian GP, 3rd in the 12-hour race at San Sebastian with Varzi and 1st in the Circuit des Routes Pavées.

In 1930 Zehender drove a Bugatti, without achieving any good placings, and was 3rd in the 24-hour race at Spa with Canavesi, in an Alfa Romeo, and 5th in an Imperia in the European GP run over the same circuit. He again drove for Alfa Romeo in 1931, but this time in the Grand Prix team, the *grandes épreuves* being 10-hour races requiring two drivers. He won the Circuit d'Esterel Plage, St Raphael (sports car race), and was 3rd in the Circuit de Dauphiné He also won the Circuit des Routes Pavées for the second time. In addition to these races he acted as co-driver to Prince Djordjadze, in the latter's Mercedes-Benz, in the Belgian 24-hour race, which they won, and in the Brooklands 500 Miles where they failed to finish.

In 1932 Zehender drove a 'Monza' Alfa Romeo as an independent, winning the Grand Prix de Comminges and finishing 2nd at Oran, but otherwise he had a rather disappointing year.

The new 3-litre 8CM Maserati was introduced in 1933, and Zehender drove one of these in most of the French and Italian races. It was a notoriously difficult car to drive in its initial form and he had another disappointing year, being 3rd at Tunis and in the Italian GP at Monza, with retirements in the Grands Prix of France, La Marne,

Goffredo Zehender. *Photo: Cyril Posthumus Collection*

Nice, Comminges, Marseilles and Belgium.

After driving in the 1934 French and La Marne Grands Prix, where he retired, Zehender teamed up with Count Villapadierna for the rest of the season and came 2nd at Dieppe in the second heat and 5th at Nice. Earlier in the season he shared the wheel of a Bugatti at Le Mans with Brunet, but the pair failed to finish. He drove a Maserati again in 1935, finishing 3rd in the French GP at Monthléry against the full strength of Mercedes-Benz, Auto Union and Alfa Romeo. In 1936, with Brunet, he was 3rd in the French GP, a sports car event of 1,000 kilometres, and in 1937 joined Mercedes-Benz as a reserve driver. He was 5th at Monaco in one of the few races in which he drove.

With the introduction of the new formula in 1938, Maserati produced a new model. Zehender joined the team and took part in the Coppa Ciano and the Italian GP but failed to finish in either event. From 1939 onwards he took little active part in racing. He died in 1958. TASOM

Cars

Abarth (I)

Carlo Abarth came to Turin in 1947, acting as one of the Porsche project engineers involved with Dusio in the ill-fated GP Cisitalia programme. When Cisitalia failed he stayed on in Turin, forming his own company. Initially this specialized in producing exhaust systems and tuning bits for FIAT, Lancia and Alfa Romeo products, and to publicize these items a series of racing and record cars were built. The racers used many Cisitalia pieces and appeared in 1950; Abarth record cars ran throughout the 1950s, specializing in the longer distances and employing Fiat and Alfa Romeo engines mounted in invariably good-looking coupé cars, designed by leading Turin stylists.

The Abarth 1100 sports cars continued until 1955 when FIAT released their 600 model, and the company based later variants on it, slowly growing in capacity until 850cc was reached. Twin overhead camshafts were used in the Abarth engines and these handsome but very expensive Zagato coupés were raced widely in the late 1950s. In 1960 Abarth introduced their 2000 model using the large Fiat engine as its basis, and during the early 1960s Abarth's Bialbero competition saloons were virtually unbeatable on the Continent. They produced a Mono-mille model for road work and eventually had their 2-litre coupés homologated as Group 4 sports cars. Meanwhile a special range of rear-engined and mid-engined sports-racing cars had been produced, hill-climbed and raced with great success by Herrmann, Schetty and Merzario, among others.

Other Abarth models included the Abarth-Simca, various tuned Fiat variants and special bodies for Porsche Carreras, while the smaller-capacity sports cars established an enviable record in the Nürburgring 500 kilometres race, winning it from 1960-64 and in 1966. In 1968 an Abarth F1 car was developed using the company's own V-8 3-litre engine, but it never appeared because of the inadequacy of its rumoured 320bhp output. A V-8 engine also appeared in a sports-racing chassis, and in 1968 the company produced a number of 2-litre sports-racing models using the dohc Fiat-based engine, still mounted behind the rear-axle line. In 1969 the engine took up a more normal mid-position in some very nicely-built wedge-shaped cars, and with one of these Merzario scored the make's first really major long-distance sports car win at Mugello. Abarths contested the 2-litre sports Championship in 1970, but were overshadowed by the British opposition, apart from a 1-2-3 win again at Mugello. DCN

ABC (GB)

The ABC was one of the most successful air-cooled light cars of the 1920s, over 1,500 being made between 1920 and 1927. It was powered by a 1,203cc flat-twin engine

Left, 1903 De Dietrich 45hp Paris–Madrid car. Lorraine Barrow at the wheel. *Photo: Montagu Motor Museum*

Left above, 1965 Abarth 1000 coupé in the Targa Florio. *Photo: Geoffrey Goddard*

Above, 1922 ABC 200 Mile Race car; E. C. Gordon England at the wheel. *Photo: T. A. S. O. Mathieson Collection*

Left, 1970 Abarth 2000 spyder driven by Leo Kinnunen at Mugello. *Photo: Autosport*

developing 30bhp, and had a 4-speed gearbox and shaft drive. ABCs with special racing bodies ran in the JCC 200 Mile Races at Brooklands in 1921, 1922, and 1923, but were handicapped by having to run in the 1·5-litre class, as their engines were slightly too large for the 1,100cc class. Even so, one finished 6th in 1922. E. C. Gordon England overcame the problem in 1923 by fitting a Bristol Cherub aero engine of 1,076cc, and this car finished 4th in its class. It was driven by S. J. Bassett as Gordon England was at the wheel of one of the first of the racing Austin Sevens which were to bring him so much fame in later years. GNG

AC (GB)

A Fivet-engined 4-cylinder AC ran in the RAC Light Car Trials of 1914, but serious competition work began in 1921 with the arrival of S. F. Edge at Thames Ditton, Surrey, the company's home. For that year's 200 Miles Race at Brooklands the company entered three more or less standard 1,496cc cars with sv Anzani engines, and another three very special machines using 42bhp ohc units derived from John Weller's advanced 2-litre Six, first seen at Olympia in 1919. Both types (and indeed, all ACs up to 1932) had the infelicitous 3-speed transaxle, the ohc racers being differential-less as well. The latter all retired, though Stead's sv model came in 8th. Later in the year Harry Hawker went after records with an ohc single-seater, achieving 105·14mph (169·26kph) over the flying mile, but Joyce and Kaye Don failed to attain 100 miles in the hour, 94 being their best in 1921. The

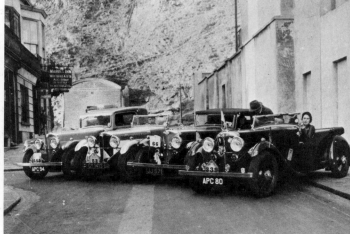

Left, 1970 Abarth 2000 coupé driven by Tondelli at Hameenlinna. *Photo: Autosport*

Left below, 1922 AC 200 Mile Race car. B. A. Davey at the wheel. *Photo: Montagu Motor Museum*

Right below, 1933 AC team for the RAC Hastings Rally. *Photo: Montagu Motor Museum*

following spring Joyce achieved his objective — the first ,500cc car so to do, with a speed of 101·39mph 163·14kph).

More records followed in 1923, though a prentice effort in 1921 with a 6-cylinder AC came to nothing, and he ohc cars also failed in the 1922 Brooklands 200. They eventually found their form in 1923, when AC won a 3rd place behind a 12/50 Alvis and a Bugatti. The 1924 race saw another unsuccessful car with blown Anzani engine, and in 1925 came AC's last serious racing car, a supercharged 12-valve ohc machine which turned out to be an expensive mistake, despite all Raymond Mays's endeavours. It was timed over the half-mile at 116mph 186·7kph, but its engine was eventually purchased by Sir Henry Birkin for use in a motorboat.

AC attacked long-distance records again in 1925, when Gillett undertook a solo drive at Montlhéry to take the World 24-Hour Record on a 2-litre Six at 82·58mph (132·90kph). In 1926 the Bruce and Brunell 2-litre became the first British car to win the Monte Carlo Rally. Mrs Bruce followed this up with a 6th place in 1927 and a 5th in 1928. In 1927 both Bruces set up a further series of records at Montlhéry, covering 15,000 miles (24,140km) at 68·01mph (109·46kph).

Financial difficulties in 1929 led to a reorganization under the Hurlock brothers, and with the 1933 Ace series ACs acquired conventionally-located 4-speed gearboxes. That year Kitty Brunell won the RAC Torquay Rally outright, other 2-litres being placed 4th, 6th and 7th. The cars also did well in the 1934 event.

Early post-war ACs were fast tourers, but at the 1953 Earls Court Show the company exhibited a new and advanced Ace, consisting of the faithful old 2-litre engine, now developing 85bhp, in an all-independently-sprung ladder-type frame designed by John Tojeiro. By 1956 this model could be had with the 1,971cc, 105bhp Bristol unit, and was doing well in club racing in the hands of Ken Rudd and others. There were victories at Gosport, Brunton, Snetterton, Goodwood, Mallory Park and Brighton in 1957, when ACs also ran in the Reims 12-Hour Race and the Mille Miglia, took the 2-litre honours at Le Mans, and won the *Autosport* 3-Hour Series Production Race at Snetterton at an average speed of 78·05mph (125·61kph). The cars were still prominent in minor events in 1958, but more important were a 2nd place in class at Pau, and 8th and 9th places at Le Mans.

By this time the AC and Bristol engines were no longer competitive, but in 1961 the American driver Carroll Shelby installed an American Ford V-8 engine, and the result reached both circuit and catalogue as the Cobra (see page 404). MCS

Ader (F)

Clement Ader had been a pioneer of telephones (sucessful and aviation (unsuccessful) when he built his first V-twin light cars in 1900. Two 12hp 1,566cc cars ran in the light-car class of the 1902 Paris-Vienna race, and one finished. For 1903 Ader built a Í6hp V-4 of 1,809cc, and by the simple expedient of mounting two engines together, a 32hp V-8 of 3,618cc. No fewer than seven Aders ran in the Paris-Madrid race, one V-twin, three V-4s, and three V-8s. The V-4s, which ran in the voiturette class, were in fact faster than the V-8s, whose weight of 1,433lb (650kg) took them into the *voiture légère* class. Birnbaum's V-4 averaged 40·5mph (65·18kph) between Paris and Bordeaux, where the race was stopped, and all seven cars finished. Three V-4s ran

in the 1903 Circuit des Ardennes, but the make did not figure in sporting events after that, and all production ended in 1907. GNG

Adler (D)

This German make was first seen in serious competition in 1903 when Edmund Rumpler (then their designer) and Teves supported local races, and a low-built 4·1-litre aiv 4-cylinder racer with tubular frame, said to be capable of 50mph (80·47kph), appeared in the 1904 Frankfurter Rennen. Adlers competed unsuccessfully in both the Kaiserpreis and the Circuit des Ardennes in 1907, and their only other pre-war racing appearance was in 1914, when a team of 3·3-litre ioe cars with well-streamlined bodies, based on the 15/40PS fast tourer, ran in the TT. All three retired.

Adler supported the 1928 and 1929 Alpine Trials, but did not return to serious competition until the introduction of Röhr's fwd range in 1932. The original 1·5-litre Trumpf averaged an impressive 51·57mph (83kph) in the 1933 ADAC 2,000km Trial. In the Alpine event Adlers took the 2-litre team award in 1933, 1934 and 1936: 1934 was an especially good year, as the 3-litre rwd 6-cylinder Diplomats tied in their class with the Roesch Talbots, and the 995cc Trumpf-Juniors were placed 3rd in the 1,100cc category. The cars were in evidence in rallies throughout Europe, with wins in Portugal, Rumania and Yugoslavia in 1936.

The fwd cars were also raced. Wins in Irish events such as the Bray Round The Houses Race (1934) and the Leinster Trophy (1935), led to better things, when Adler's experience with record work on a lightened and streamlined Junior was applied to the 1,645cc *Rennlimousin*, a high-geared lightweight on which first-class aerodynamics were made to compensate for a modest 55bhp. A 1·5-litre prototype averaged 76·86mph (123·70kph) for four days at Avus in November 1935, and in 1936 another car did 24 hours at 99·79mph (160·59kph). Unstreamlined two-seaters were still being used in that year's Swedish Winter touring-car GP (in which a multiple accident eliminated the entire Adler team), but later in the season the new saloons scored their first triumph, a 1-2-3 win in the 2-litre class of the Belgian 24-Hour Race at Spa, after the solitary Aston Martin had retired. In 1937 the Orssich/Sauerwein car finished 6th at Le Mans, and Adlers were 6th and 7th in 1938, annexing the Biennial Cup as well.

An even more efficient streamliner with 1,500cc engine was prepared for the 1939 race, but for once the traditional reliability was absent, the Adler challenge lasting only 45 minutes. As their 2·5-litre 6-cylinder entry had crashed in practice, this was a sad last appearance. MCS

1958 AC Ace at Le Mans. *Photo: Geoffrey Goddard*

Above, 1914 Adler in the Tourist Trophy. *Photo: Montagu Motor Museum*

Left below, 1903 Ader 32hp V-8 at the start of Paris–Madrid. *Photo: T. A. S. O. Mathieson Collection*

Below, 1938 Adler coupé at Le Mans. *Photo: Motor*

Aero (CS)

This aircraft factory at Prague-Vysocany began car manufacture in 1929. In 1931 they introduced their first sports model, the Aero 600 with a 662cc 2-cylinder 2-stroke engine developing 16bhp. Maximum speed was 60mph (96kph), and with one of these cars Bohumil Turek won the under 2-litre class of the ADAC 10,000km Trial in 1931. The next sports model was the Aero 1000 with a 998cc 20bhp engine and 68mph (110kph) maximum speed. One of these cars, again driven by Turek, finished 3rd in the under 1,500cc class in the 1933 Monte Carlo Rally, and won its class in the 1934 Czech Thousand Miles Rally. In 1934 came the Aero 30, also with the 998cc 2-cylinder engine, but with a longer wheelbase and lower appearance, followed by the 4-cylinder 2-litre Aero 50, with a 48bhp engine and 100mph (160kph) maximum speed. A special car with two 662cc engines was built for the Czech Thousand Miles Rally, and was also used for racing. A later twin-engined model used two 750cc engines, but was not sold to the public.

During World War 2 a prototype known as the Aero Pony was built, but production never started. The Aero cars should not be confused with the post-war Aero Minor, which was a development of the Jawa. VH

Aero Minor see Jawa

AFM (D)

AFM was one of the small German makes which appeared after World War 2; the initials stood for Alex von Falkenhausen, Munich, formerly an engineer with BMW. He used the famous 6-cylinder BMW engine of the pre-war Type 328 as the basis of his designs. A 1·5-litre — with stroke reduced to 75mm — as well as a 2-litre version were available and were seen in various sports car competitions, mainly in German national events. Another version had a FIAT 1,100cc engine. In 1949 a GP version was launched and, driven by Hans Stuck, it achieved 7th place at the Monza GP that year. A year later the car appeared with a new V-8 2-litre engine of Küchen design featuring four overhead camshafts. The car was fast but not very reliable. In the 1951 Grenzlandring Race Hans Stuck won the Formula 2 class with an average speed of 128·2mph (206·3kph). Finances did not allow further development and this was the end of AFM. HON

Aga (D)

From 1921 Aga cars appeared in national sports car meetings. A new Aga design took part in the Targa Florio of 1924. The engine was a 1,495cc 4-cylinder ohc unit developing 50bhp at 5,000rpm and with a maximum speed of 90mph (144kph). One of these cars finished 2nd in the 1·5-litre class driven by Scholl. In the Zbraslav-Jíloviště hill-climb of 1924 Loge in his Aga finished 2nd to Caracciola's Mercedes. This type was Aga's only venture into motor sport and was produced only during 1924 and 1925. HON

Alco (US)

The Alco was a high-quality car produced from 1905 to 1913 by a subsidiary of the American Locomotive Company, the cars being of Berliet design built under licence. The 54hp 580ci (9,505cc) chain-drive model was campaigned actively for a few years, the leading driver being Harry Grant. He won the Vanderbilt Cup in 1909 and 1910, the latter by only 25 seconds from Joe Dawson's

Marmon. Alcos also took part in other famous events such as the American Grand Prize at Savannah and elsewhere, and the Elgin races. Grant finished 2nd in the 1911 Elgin Trophy, and B. Taylor was 3rd in the Grand Prize at Santa Monica Calif. in 1914, a year after the company had ceased to make cars. GNG

Alcyon (F)

This motorcycle manufacturer tried hard in voiturette racing before World War 1, but remained an also-ran. Between 1906 and 1910 they competed in several events, but their best result was Cissac's 4th place in the 1907 Coupe de l'Auto. In 1911 Barriaux drove a 3-litre 4-cylinder with push- and pull-rod actuation for the valves in the GP de France as well as in the classic light-car event, but was again unsuccessful, and even at Gaillon, he had to be content with 2nd place in the racing category behind a Lion-Peugeot.

The 1912 16-valve 3-litre was unfortunate enough to coincide with Coatalen's sv Coupe de l'Auto Sunbeam, hence Duray's 6th place at Dieppe, and Barriaux had to retire from the GP de France when he was in 2nd place. Most Alcyons of the Vintage era were copies of the Sima-Violet, but Giroux had one or two local successes in the Lyons area with tuned versions of the 1922-3 2-litre 4-cylinder model, which he called Alcyon-GLs. MCS

Alda (F)

The Alda was made by Fernand Charron after he had left the company bearing his own name. The touring cars used either poppet valves or Henriod rotary valves, but for his competition cars Charron kept to the former.

Above, 1935 Aero 30 coupé. *Drawing: Jiry Nejedly*

Below, 1924 Aga Targa Florio model at Solitude. *Photo: Neubauer Collection*

Below, 1908 Alcyon Grand Prix des Voiturettes car. Barriaux at the wheel. *Photo: Montagu Motor Museum*

Bottom, 1914 Alda Grand Prix car. François Szisz at the wheel. *Photo: T. A. S. O. Mathieson Collection*

Three cars were entered for the 1913 Coupe de l'Auto; they had 4-cylinder engines developed from those of the 15hp touring cars, but with stroke reduced from 140mm to 132mm to bring them within the 3-litre limit. They had dashboard radiators and double transverse rear springs. In the race, Tabuteau finished in 6th place, and Petit retired. For the 1914 Grand Prix, Alda entered three cars, with engines enlarged to 4·5 litres capacity, and the transverse springs replaced by large cantilevers. They were driven by Szisz, Pietro, and Tabuteau, who made the fastest lap of the three at 60·42mph (97·23kph). All three retired, Szisz lasting just over half distance into his 11th lap. Alda cars were made until 1922, but took no part in competitions after World War 1. GNG

Alexis (GB)

The Alexis Formula Junior appeared in 1961 and achieved early success, particularly in the hands of Peter Proctor. Designed and developed by Alec Francis and Bill Harris, the Birmingham-built cars outgrew a 'poor man's Lotus' image, and a small but steady production rate was achieved over the next few years. An interesting development was the 1965 Formula 3 Alexis-DAF, used by the Dutch firm to exhibit the reserves of their belt transmission system. In this year also Paul Hawkins achieved a Formula 2 victory for the make at the Nürburgring.

Up to this time trials machines were also available, but were dropped when the cheaper Cannon effectively cornered this market. In 1967 a Formula Ford design was introduced, marketed at first by the Jim Russell organization and known as the Russell-Alexis. Allan Taylor was in charge of production. In 1968 the Mark 14 FF cars of Dave Walker and Maurice Harness scored some victories. Ian Ashley, Peter Clanford and Dave Morgan were among the more successful 1969 drivers, when the Mark 15 FF car was in production and the wedge-shaped Mark 17 Formula 3 car introduced. Productions in 1970 included the Mark 18 FF and Mark 19 F3 cars, and successes continued particularly in the FF class, with a series of victories by Ken Bailey and Dick Barker. The firm moved to new premises at Coleshill towards the end of the year. DF

Alfa Romeo (I)

ALFA (Sta Anonima Lombarda Fabbrica Automobili) began making cars in 1910 at Portello, on the outskirts of Milan, in a factory formerly occupied by the Italian branch of the French Darracq firm, which had discontinued production as their small cars proved underpowered for Italian conditions. Thus the new ALFA or Alfa cars were all fairly big and powerful and were designed by Giuseppe Merosi, formerly of FIAT and Bianchi. Racing commenced in 1911 in the Targa Florio, but the first competition success was in 1913 when Franchini came second to Marsaglia's Aquila-Italiana in the 33-mile (53km) Parma-Poggio de Berceto hill-climb driving a 40/60hp Alfa, which had a 4-cylinder 100mm × 160mm push-rod ohv 6,082cc engine developing 73bhp at 2,000rpm. In the 1914 Coppa Florio race over 277 miles in Sicily, Franchini and Giuseppe Campari in 40/60 Alfas came 3rd and 4th behind a Nazzaro and an SCAT.

In 1914 Merosi designed a dohc 4·5-litre 100mm × 143mm 88bhp Grand Prix Alfa with 4 cylinders, 16 valves, 8 plugs, twin carburettors and dry sump lubrication, but it was not raced until after World War 1, and never took part in a GP.

1961 Alexis Formula Junior at Silverstone. P. Proctor at the wheel. *Photo: Michael Ware*

1920 Alfa Romeo Type ES Sport in the Targa Florio. Campari at the wheel. *Photo: T. A. S. O. Mathieson Collection*

In 1915 ALFA became part of Nicola Romeo's industrial combine, and racing recommenced in 1919 with the pre-war models now called Alfa Romeos. In 1920 came the first big victory when Campari on an 82bhp twin-carburettor special racing version of the 40/60 won the 230-mile (370km) Mugello Circuit race over the Futa Pass near Florence. Later in the year Enzo Ferrari was 2nd in the Targa Florio, driving an sv 4,084cc 100mm × 130mm 20/30hp Alfa Romeo.

Several minor successes were obtained with a new version of the 20/30hp known as the ES Sport, with a 67bhp bigger bore 4,250cc 102mm × 130mm engine, and in 1921 Campari again won at Mugello and was 3rd in the Targa Florio with his 40/60hp racer. He narrowly missed winning the Gran Premio Gentleman (260 miles; 418·4km) at Brescia in the 1914 GP car, but retired when in the lead on the penultimate lap with a radiator leak. Baroness Maria Avanzo was 3rd in a 20/30hp ES Sport.

In 1922 Merosi introduced his most famous design, the push-rod ohv 6-cylinder 3-litre 76mm × 110mm RL in touring, sports and racing form, and a racing 3·1-litre 78 × 110mm version won the 1923 Targa Florio driven by Ugo Sivocci. This year saw the now famous green *quadrifoglio*, or four-leaf clover, painted on works Alfa Romeo racing cars.

The RL Targa Florio, or TF, type racing cars (in 80mm × 120mm 3,620cc 112mph (180kph) form they developed 125bhp at 3,800rpm) and the RLS and RLSS sports cars gained many successes in important Italian races and hill-climbs, and the fame of their drivers—Ascari, Campari, Sivocci and Ferrari—began to spread abroad, but it was in 1924 that the name of Alfa Romeo first became truly world-famous in motor racing.

This was after one of the most talented designers in the world, Vittorio Jano, had joined Alfa Romeo from FIAT. Using an abandoned 1923 6-cylinder GP design of Merosi's as a test bed for supercharging experiments, in a few short months Jano produced the 8-cylinder dohc 2-litre 61mm × 85mm supercharged roller-bearing P2 GP Alfa Romeo, which won the very first *grande épreuve* in which it took part, the 1924 French GP at Lyons, the victorious driver being Giuseppe Campari. The P2 team was opposed by immensely strong opposition from Sunbeam, FIAT, Delage and Bugatti.

This was in August, when the cars, fitted with single carburettor engines, produced 134bhp at 5,200rpm. By October, when Antonio Ascari won the Italian GP at

Left above, 1924 Alfa Romeo P2. *Photo: Alfa Romeo Spa*

Right above, 1929 Alfa Romeo 1750 team at San Sebastian Sports Car GP. *Photo: Fotocar*

Below, 1932 Alfa Romeo Monza. *Photo: Montagu Motor Museum*

Left below, 1925 Alfa Romeo P2 at Montlhéry. Count Brilli-Peri at the wheel. *Photo: Montagu Motor Museum*

Right below, 1934 Alfa Romeo P3 in the Mannin Moar. Hon Brian Lewis at the wheel. *Photo: Montagu Motor Museum*

Monza, which was not strongly contested, two Memini carburettors had been fitted increasing the output to 145bhp at 5,500rpm. For 1925, 155bhp at 5,500rpm was achieved, thanks to the use of a special racing fuel called Elcosine developed by the Werner brothers of Turin, composed of petrol with 44% ethyl alcohol and a small percentage of ether. In 1925 Ascari was victorious in the Grand Prix d'Europe at Spa, a race in which the V-12 Delage opposition retired, but the whole team was withdrawn despite being in the lead in the French GP at Montlhéry when Ascari ran off the road and was killed. Count Gaston Brilli-Peri won the 1925 Italian GP for Alfa Romeo in his P2, at the same time gaining the title of World Champion for Alfa Romeo. After this a laurel wreath was added as a surround to the radiator badge of all Alfa Romeos.

The P2s (six of which were built) continued to have successes in Italian *formule libre* events and Continental hill-climbs up to the end of the 1929 season as private entries in the hands of such notabilities as Campari, Varzi and Brilli-Peri. The amateur, Gino Ginaldi, won the 1925 Coppa Acerbo at Pescara in an RLTF Alfa Romeo, and in 1926 Willy Cleer, a German Alfa Romeo agent, was 3rd in the German GP at Avus in a sports RLSS 22/90hp.

The years 1927 to 1930 saw a pre-eminence in racing achieved by dohc versions of Jano's production 6-cylinder 1,500cc and 1,750cc sports cars, commencing with a victory by Enzo Ferrari in the 1927 Circuit of

Above, 1935 Alfa Romeo Bimotore. Austin Dobson at the wheel. *Photo: Montagu Motor Museum*

Right above, 1935 Alfa Romeo 8C-35 at a post-war hill-climb at Rest-and-be-Thankful with Dennis Poore at the wheel. *Photo: W. Henderson*

Below, 1937 Alfa Romeo 12C-37 in the Swiss GP at Berne. Farina at the wheel. *Photo: Klementaski Studio*

Below right, 1938 Alfa Romeo 158 in the Milan GP at Monza. Emilio Villoresi at the wheel. *Photo: T. A. S. O. Mathieson Collection*

Modena race in an unblown 62mm × 82mm 1500. In 1928 a host of events fell to blown 1500 Alfas, including the Mille Miglia (Campari and Ramponi); the Georges Boillot Cup at Boulogne (Ivanowski); the Essex 6-Hour Race at Brooklands (Ramponi); and the Belgian 24-Hour Race at Spa (Ivanowski and Marinoni).

In 1929 the 1,750cc (65mm × 88mm) version of the 1·5-litre car began to overshadow it, though a blown 1·5-litre won the JCC Double-Twelve Hour Race at Brooklands (Ramponi) and the Saorstat Cup in Phoenix Park, Dublin, (Ivanowski). Supercharged 1750 cars won the Eireann Cup and Irish GP (Ivanowski); the Mille Miglia (Campari and Ramponi); and the Belgian 24-Hour Race at Spa (Marinoni and Ghersi).

The last major racing year for the 6C 1750 was 1930, main victories being in the Mille Miglia (Nuvolari and Guidotti), the TT (Nuvolari) and the Belgian 24-Hour Race (Marinoni and Ghersi).

The most a 1750 ever developed, in a special fixed head competition version of the engine, was 102bhp at 5,000rpm, and the car was successful, not because it was extremely fast—105mph (169kph) was its absolute maximum—but because of its reliability, superb roadholding, and the outstanding ability of its drivers.

In 1930 Alfa Romeo revived three of the old P2s, increasing the bore from 61mm to 61·5mm to bring the capacity from 1,987cc to 2,006cc, and incorporating various 6C 1750 parts in the chassis, including a 1750 radiator. The engines developed 175bhp at 5,500rpm and

Varzi won the 1930 Targa Florio with one of these cars and broke the lap record. A good P2 was capable of 140mph (225kph).

Four Type A 12-cylinder 3,504cc racing cars were built in 1931, developing 230bhp at 5,200rpm, each fitted with two special fixed head 1750 supercharged engines side by side, with two gearboxes and twin propellor shafts. Maximum speed approached 150mph (240kph), and Campari won the 1931 Coppa Acerbo road race over 188 miles (301·6km) in one of these monsters.

Another of Jano's great designs came in 1931, the supercharged 8C 2300 sports car whose 65mm × 88mm 2,336cc dohc engine developed 142bhp at 5,000rpm in standard form. For competitions 155bhp at 5,200rpm was available in 1931, increased between 1932 and 1934 from 160bhp to 180bhp at 5,400rpm. The first of four consecutive Le Mans wins for the 8C 2300 was achieved in 1931 by Lord Howe and Sir Henry Birkin, and also in 1931 Tazio Nuvolari won the Targa Florio on an 8C 2300. The Italian GP at Monza in May, which was also the European GP, brought the début of the GP version of the 8C 2300, known as the Monza. This produced 165bhp at 5,400rpm, and one of these cars driven by Campari and Nuvolari proceeded to win the Italian GP, breaking Ascari's P2 lap record set up in 1924 in the process. Also in this year, a private owner, Philippe Etancelin, won three French races with his Monza: the Dieppe GP, the Comminges GP at St Gaudens and the Dauphiné Circuit at Grenoble against Bugatti opposition.

to do the best he could with Monzas, which he bored out to 2,556cc, 68mm × 88mm, so they produced 180bhp at 5,600rpm with a maximum speed of over 130mph (209kph). With opposition from Bugatti and Maserati, the latter often with slightly bigger engines, Ferrari had a harder row to hoe than in 1932, but in August the works relented and returned the P3s to the circuits. Their victories recommenced and were shared among Nuvolari, Fagioli and Chiron.

Once more the sports cars were victorious at Le Mans, Spa and in the Mille Miglia; notably successful private owners in Monzas were Etancelin, Brian Lewis and Guy Moll.

The peak years were 1932 and 1933, and with the

Left, 1947 Alfa Romeo 158. J.-P. Wimille at the wheel. *Photo: Montagu Motor Museum*

Far left below, 1953 Alfa Romeo Disco Volante coupé at the finish of the Mille Miglia. Fangio at the wheel. *Photo: Rodolfo Mailander*

Left below, 1953 Alfa Romeo 1900TI in the Coppa Dolomiti Rally. *Photo: Rodolfo Mailander*

Perhaps Jano looked upon the Monza as a compromise GP car as it had a close affinity with the 8C 2300 sports model, and in 1932 he produced a true GP car in the immortal Type B Monoposto, which almost immediately was known colloquially as the P3. This had a fixed head twin-supercharged version of the plain bearing 8-cylinder engine of 2,654cc, 65mm × 110mm, developing 215bhp at 5,600rpm in a slim single-seater chassis, and a maximum speed of over 140mph (225kph). An unusual feature was a split propellor shaft in the form of a V, with the differential at the base attached to the back of the gearbox so that it was sprung weight, and consequently a very light back axle incorporating a crownwheel and pinion for each shaft, the half-shafts being mere stubs. Alfa Romeo had a great year in 1932 as the P3 was virtually unbeatable in the GP field, with drivers of the calibre of Nuvolari and Caracciola, and the Monza was often capable of winning a GP in which the P3s were not present. The 8C 2300 was generally the fastest car in sports car races, winning Le Mans (Sommer and Chinetti), the Mille Miglia (Borzacchini and Bignami) and the Belgian 24-Hour Race at Spa (Brivio and Siena).

A blow fell in 1933, the year Alfa Romeo was nationalized, when it was announced the works were withdrawing from racing. Since 1930 Enzo Ferrari's Scuderia Ferrari had been responsible for Alfa Romeo's racing programme, but from 1933 the Scuderia was more autonomous than it had been in the past, and the prancing horse Scuderia badge replaced the quadrifoglio on the official Alfa Romeo team cars. The 'withdrawal', in fact, really amounted to the retirement of the P3s, and Ferrari had

coming of the German Mercedes and Auto Unions a decline started in 1934. For this year the P3s were given wider cockpits to comply with formula regulations, and the engines were enlarged to 2,905cc, 68mm × 100mm, to produce 255bhp at 5,400rpm. Notable P3 successes were in the French GP at Montlhéry (Chiron) and the Monaco GP (Moll); Varzi won the Targa Florio in a P3, and the Mille Miglia went to a 2·6-litre Monza driven by Varzi and Bignami. Le Mans was won by Chinetti and Etancelin in an 8C 2300 sports car. Moll (now a Scuderia Ferrari driver) won the Avusrennen in an annual streamlined P3 with a 71mm × 100mm 265bhp 3·2-litre engine. A new unsupercharged 6-cylinder 2·3-litre sports car was produced, and an example won the 24-hour Targa Abruzzo race at Pescara (Cortese and Severi).

For 1935 reversed quarter elliptic rear springs were introduced to replace the former semi-elliptics on the P3 and Dubonnet ifs was also available. With such a car, fitted with a 3,822cc 78mm × 100mm engine developing 330bhp at 5,400rpm, Nuvolari defeated the Mercedes and Auto Unions at the Nürburgring in the German GP. A 2·9-litre P3 made into a two-seater won the Mille Miglia, and, as a purely Scuderia Ferrari venture, two *Bimotore* cars were built for track racing and records. Designed by Luigi Bazzi, they each had P3 engines fore and aft of the driver's seat.

The 3·8-litre engine in an independently sprung chassis formed the Type C 8C-35 GP car; a similar car in appearance had a 4,064cc, 70mm × 88mm, V-12 engine producing 370bhp at 5,800rpm and was called the 12C-36. Maximum speeds were quoted as 170mph

(274kph) and 180mph (290kph) respectively. In a 12C-36 Nuvolari beat the Mercedes and Auto Unions in the 188-mile Spanish Penya Rhin GP of 1936, and also in the 1936 Hungarian GP at Budapest, and he won the Milan GP in the Sempione Park by 9sec from Varzi's Auto Union in the same year. Another 1936 victory by Nuvolari and the 12C-36 was in the Vanderbilt Cup on the Roosevelt Raceway, Long Island, New York.

In 1936 that outstanding sports racing car the 8C 2300 was replaced by a virtually road-going 8C-35, with a smaller 2·9-litre P3 engine slightly detuned to give 220bhp, the car being called the 2900A. Only six were built, and victories in 1936 included the Mille Miglia (Brivio and Ongaro) and the Sao Paulo GP in Brazil (Pintacuda).

In 1937 Nuvolari in a 12C-36 managed to beat Hasse's Auto Union in winning the Circuit of Milan race in the Sempione Park, and in the Rio de Janeiro GP Pintacuda on an 8C-35 won by 8sec from Stuck's Auto Union. But in the Grandes Epreuves Nuvolari's 4th place in the German GP in a 12C-36 was the best effort. An independently sprung 105bhp 6C 2300 won the Mille Miglia (Pintacuda and Mambelli) and Còrtese on a non-independent 6C 2300 won the Targa Abruzzo (now a 6-hour race) for the third time running, there having been no event there in 1936.

A new GP car, the low-chassis 12C-37 whose 4,495cc 72mm × 92mm engine produced 430bhp at 5,800rpm was introduced in August 1937, but it was not a success, and was the reason for Jano leaving Alfa Romeo and going to Lancia.

Three GP models were produced for the 3-litre formula of 1938–9: the 8-cylinder Type 308, with a 2,991cc 69mm × 100mm version of the evergreen P3 engine, producing 295bhp at 6,000rpm; the 12-cylinder Type 312 with a 2,995cc 66mm × 73mm engine producing 350bhp at 6,500rpm; and the 16-cylinder Type 316, with a 2,958cc 58mm × 70mm twin-crankshaft engine producing 440bhp at 7,500rpm. All had similar chassis, with the usual GP Alfa Romeo independent suspension system of trailing links with coil springs in hydraulic dampers at the front, and swing axles with a transverse leaf spring below the axle housing at the rear, with the gearbox integral with the rear axle. However, these new cars had tubular chassis instead of the channel frames of the 8C-35 and 12C-36. Not one of these cars was fast enough to beat the Germans, the 308 scoring the only race wins, these being the 1938 Rio de Janeiro GP (Pintacuda) and the 1939 Circuit des Remparts at Angoulême (Sommer). The 308 was destined to have several post-war victories in 1946–9 by Sommer (holder of the Montlhéry track lap record with his 308) in France, and by various Italian and indigenous drivers in South American events. A Type 316 came 2nd in the 1938 Italian GP thanks to the determination of Farina, who kept going when most of the Mercedes and Auto Unions fell out, but its main claim to fame is that the engine of the almost invincible 8-cylinder Type 158 voiturette was virtually half that of a Type 316.

From 1938 the Scuderia Ferrari no longer controlled Alfa Romeo racing, which passed to an organization known as Alfa Corse, and the quadrifoglio replaced the Scuderia Ferrari prancing horse on the cars.

The 1938 Mille Miglia went to a 'production' version of the 2900A known as the 2900B (Biondetti and Stefani), and Cortese yet again won the Targa Abruzzo, now with an independently sprung 6C 2300B. In 1939 this race went to Aldrighetti and Rangoni with a larger version of

Cortese's 1938 car, the 6C 2500; and a 110bhp 72mm × 100mm 2500 also won the 1939 Tobruk-Tripoli race (Boratti and Sanesi) and was 2nd to a BMW in the 1940 Mille Miglia (Farina and Mambelli). The first post-war Mille Miglia, in 1947, was won by Biondetti and Romano with a 2900B running unblown. An unsupercharged version of the 12-cylinder GP engine developing 220bhp at 5,500rpm in what was virtually a 2900A chassis was named the Type 412, and these sports racing cars won the 1938 Belgian 24-Hour Race (Pintacuda and Severi) and the 1939 Antwerp GP (Farina).

Once some initial plug troubles had been overcome, the 158 cars had several voiturette wins in 1938–40, all in Italian organized events except for the 1939 Prix de Berne over the Swiss Bremgarten circuit (Farina). Designed by Gioacchino Colombo, the 158 (1,500cc and 8 cylinders) originally developed 190bhp at 6,500rpm, increased to 225bhp at 7,500rpm in 1939 when a roller bearing crankshaft was fitted. The usual Alfa Romeo swing axle system was employed at the rear, with trailing link ifs utilizing a transverse leaf spring.

As Formula 1 GP contenders, these cars were virtually unbeatable from 1946 to 1948 and from 1950 to 1951 when they had to bow to the 4·5-litre unsupercharged Ferraris. They were not raced in 1949, after the deaths of drivers Wimille and Count Trossi. The 58mm × 70mm, 1,479cc, cylinder dimensions were retained throughout the years, but in 1951 '159' form the engine developed 404bhp at 10,500rpm with over 30lb boost, necessitating needle roller bearing big-ends. The 159 in its final 200mph form, as the 159A, had a De Dion rear axle.

After 1951 Alfa Romeo retired from GP racing, but made two attempts to regain their pre-war reputation as makers of world-beating sports racing cars. The first attempt was with the Disco Volante (Flying Saucer), which in its most powerful form had a 6-carburettor 6-cylinder engine of 3,576cc, 88mm × 98mm, developing 260bhp at 6,700rpm. This design showed promise, and Fangio drove one to 2nd place in the 1953 Mille Miglia. The cars failed at Le Mans and Spa, and the only victory was by Fangio in the 1953 GP of Supercortemaggiore at Mercano, after which Alfa Romeo never ran them again.

The second attempt to gain world sports car honours was with the Type 33, designed by Satta and Busso. It was announced in January 1967, by Autodelta, the organization under Ing. Carlo Chiti founded in 1964 to develop and race sports prototype, GT and touring Alfa Romeos. The Type 33 originally had a 250bhp 1,995cc, 78mm × 52·2mm, V-8 engine, later stretched to 2,460cc, 78mm × 64·4mm. A Type 33 won the 1968 Mugello race (Vaccarella, Bianchi and Galli).

The original large diameter tube chassis was aban-

doned in 1969, and for 1970 the Type 33-3 had a conventional riveted duralumin platform chassis. The mid-engine was a 3-litre V-8 with 4 valves per cylinder said to develop around 400bhp and rev up to 9,500rpm, with a useful range as low as 5,800rpm. The cars showed both reliability and speed early in 1970, when a 5-speed Type 33-3 won a race in the South American Temporada series (Piers Courage).

A 2·5-litre Type 33 V-8 engine had been raced in a Brabham single-seater chassis in the 1968 Tasman races. Also in that year Cooper were experimenting with a 3-litre version in a single-seater chassis for Formula 1 racing, but this project was abandoned. For 1970 a 420bhp V-8 engine of 3 litres was being fitted into a Formula 1 M7 McLaren chassis for De Adamich to drive at Monaco, with the promise of a new M14 chassis being available in July 1970, also destined to house a V-8 Alfa Romeo engine.

The Autodelta team drivers for 1970 were announced as Piers Courage and Andrea De Adamich; Nanni Galli and Rolf Stommelen; and Masten Gregory and Toine Hezemans.

With their production 1,300cc Giulietta, Alfa Romeo won the 1,300cc class of the FIA Grand Touring Championships in 1961, and Autodelta gained successes with various models, several with the 1,570cc, 78mm × 82mm, Giulia GTZ producing 130bhp, and the GTZ2, 160bhp coupés, but more with the Giulia GTA, an 115bhp lightweight Bertone coupé. To these cars fell the Transamerican Championships in 1966, the European Touring Car Challenge Cup in 1966 and 1967 and the Touring Class of the European Mountain Championship in 1967. A GTA driven by De Adamich won the 1967 TT at Oulton Park for Group 2 saloons. PMAH

Alfa Romeo in America: Alfa Romeo have been active in Sports Car Club of America racing since 1957 when Templeton Briggs, Bob Grossman and Chuck Stoddard captured three consecutive national championships. Scooter Patrick drove a Type 33 to win the 1969 B sports racing (modified) title; Horst Kwech, 1966, and Victor Provenzano, 1967 and 1970, were SCCA B sedan champions and Harry Theodoracopulos Jr won the 1969 C sedan honors in a GTA. In professional road racing Alfa Romeo GTA sedans won under 2-litre Trans-American honors in 1966 and 1970, and Alfa Romeo engines have powered a variety of Formula cars. Car classifications for 1971 show various Alfa Romeo models competing in five SCCA production classes. ARB

Allard (GB)

Sydney Allard had already gained experience on Morgans before he launched his first Allard Special in 1936. This was a rebuild of a 1934 3,622cc Ford V-8 with divided-axle ifs and a body from a GP Bugatti which fitted where it touched. It had an excellent career in trials in the hands, first of its creator and then of Guy Warburton, scoring 19 best performances, 11 runners-up cups, 5 special cups, 15 first-class awards and 25 team prizes in four seasons. The success of this one-off persuaded Allard to go into limited production in 1937, though the first Allards were primarily 'trials irons', either with the Ford engine or with the 4·4-litre V-12 Lincoln-Zephyr. Hutchison tried his Lincoln-engined machine in the 3-Hour Sports Car Race at Brooklands, but could manage no better than 9th. The Allards continued their impressive performances in trials and sprints in 1939, a domination of trials being accompanied by a new sports-car record at Poole, ftd for Allard him-

self at Backwell, and two wins in the big sports-car class at Prescott, where he motored spectacularly backwards off the course, giving the name to Allard's Gap.

Post-war models, such as the L-type four-seater and M-type drophead coupé, were more civilized, though Allards continued to do well in trials until the swing towards smaller machinery based on the 1,172cc Ford Ten; and in 1947 Imhof won the Lisbon Rally, but the Allard challenge in the Alpine Trial ended in a disastrous crash for Potter in one of the 1940 models. In 1948, however, Potter came 2nd in his class and won a Coupe des Alpes, and Allard had devised a new special for sprints and hill-climbs. This utilized a good many standard chassis parts and was crowned by the 1946-type Allard grille, but the engine was a 3·7-litre air-cooled V-8 Steyr designed for military work, which gave 165bhp and 97mph (156·11kph) on the level. This car really came into its own in 1949, when its builder won the British Hill-Climb Championship, with a 2nd place at Bo'ness, and fastest times of day at Bouley Bay, Craig-antlet and Prescott—the times in the last two cases (73·4 and 44·26sec) were both new course records. In rallies, Potter once again won his class in the Alpine and drove a M-type into 4th place in the Monte Carlo; Imhof scored his second victory in the Lisbon event.

At the 1949 London Show Allard exhibited a new lightweight sports car, the J2 with De Dion back axle, sold on the home market with either the regular V-8 or the 4,375cc Ardun-Mercury ohv unit, the work of Zora Arkus-Duntov, later to be responsible for the development of Chevrolet's Corvette. J2s were also exported engineless to America, where enthusiasts were quick to adapt them to something far more powerful, the 5,420cc V-8 Cadillac, developing over 160bhp. The result was first seen early in 1950 at Palm Beach, where Cole made a good impression before retiring, and was raced energetically during the season, Cole winning at Bridge-hampton and taking 2nd place in the Heart Trophy, while Richter won at Santa Ana and Goldschmidt at Watkins Glen. Also in 1950 the Allard/Cole partnership

1950 Allard J2 at Goodwood. *Photo: Autosport*

1953 Allard J2 duelling with a pre-war Ford Ten tourer. *Photo: Richmond Pike*

1953 Allard J2R at Le Mans. *Photo: Rodolfo Mailander*

scored an impressive 3rd place at Le Mans, averaging 87·75mph (141·22kph). The Steyr-Allard's best performances during the season were fastest at Craigantlet and 2nd fastest at Shelsley Walsh, where it set a new overall record for unsupercharged cars in 38·05sec.

Allard's subsequent competition career was a valiant struggle against those rising stars, Jaguar and Aston Martin. The Cadillac-engined cars could not be sold in Britain because of the dollar crisis, though the works raced them: Sydney Allard had set a new sports-car

record at Brighton in 1950, and in 1951 he tried a new bi American unit of like capacity, the hemi-head Chrysler. A crash, however, eliminated him from the Mille Miglia Though the Steyr-Allard set another new record at Craigantlet, the marque's great successes were in the New World, where a good season started at Buenos Aires, with Fitch's victory at 56·77mph (91·36kph) from Wacker's car with Hydramatic transmission. Armstrong was 2nd at Palm Springs, and Pollack won at Pebble Beach, using a Cadillac unit bored out to 6 litres. Cole's Chrysler-Allard took the honours at Bridgehampton with a speed of 86·9mph (139·85kph), with Goldschmidt' Cadillac-J2 3rd, and Pollack scored another win at Reno though the best the cars from Clapham could do at Watkins Glen amounted to 5th and 6th places. Even worse was 1952; the cars lost their dominance in America there was another retirement at Le Mans, and an unimpressive showing in the 9 Hours of Goodwood. None the less Sydney Allard won the Monte Carlo Rally on a P-type saloon with the 4·4-litre engine; Jackson won the London MC's Little Rally, and Imhof's J2 annexed its class in the RAC event.

The company made its last serious racing bid in 1953, with some improved aerodynamic JR-type two-seaters: these used Cadillac engines said to give 300bhp, but both Allard and Duntov retired at Le Mans, and a year later even touring Allards were being made only in penny numbers.

The firm's last road-going car, the Allardette, was in fact a slightly modified version of Ford's 105E-series Anglia which competed in some rallies, but in 1961 Allard produced his first dragster in the American idiom This used a 5·75-litre Chrysler engine giving 450bhp, and a 2-speed box. Its first appearance at Brighton that September was inauspicious, but it marked the advent of a new branch of the sport in the United Kingdom. MCS

Alpine (F)

The Société des Automobiles Alpine was founded in 1955 by Jean Redélé, and has always had very close ties with Renault. Redélé's first Alpine was a coupé based on the Renault 750, which he entered in rallies and races from 1952, and eventually put into production at Dieppe in 1955 as the A106 Mille Miles (after a class victory in the Italian Mille Miglia). This was continued until 1960, with tuned Dauphine 904cc and 998cc engines. The A108, Dauphine-based with a fibreglass body, appeared in 1957, and its most notable variant, the Berlinette Tour de France, in 1961. This had an Alpine backbone-type chassis, and 845/998cc Renault engines; it became prominent at least in French races and rallies, competitive within its classes.

Alpine tended to concentrate on French events, and their cars first ran at Le Mans in 1963 (three retired); in the following year they finished 17-20-25, the 1,147cc-engined car of Lageneste and Morrogh winning the Index of Thermal Efficiency. In the 1964 Reims 12 Hours Alpines finished 18-19-20, thoroughly beating their Matra rivals.

When the first Alpine single-seaters appeared in 1964, they were welcomed as the first French 'open-wheel' cars since the Gordinis. In the F2 and F3 cars the Brabham pattern, and the guiding hand of Tauranac, was obvious in the make-up of chassis and running gear; their Renault engines were developed by, respectively, Gordini (whose twin-ohc version initially gave a claimed 110bhp at 8,500 rpm) and Mignotet, and drove through a Hewland gearbox in the F2 car and a Renault R8 box in the F3

r. Several Alpines ran in the first race of the 1,000cc formula 2, at Pau, where Rosinski placed one 4th, but it soon became apparent that the Renault engine was outpowered by Ford-based units, and the F2 cars were in effect sidelined.

Alpine continued with the F3 cars, although these done only in French races, Grandsire winning the 1964 national championship, and their best placings in top-class international company were a 2nd at Reims and a d at Monaco. In 1965 Matras became the French pace-tters, and the best Alpine showings in leading events were again a 2nd (Mauro Bianchi at Pau) and two 3rds. eber won two races in 1966 (Magny-Cours and Montlhéry), and some good lesser placings, but in 1967 Alpine's only victory was at Montlhéry (Depailler).

During this year Alpine F1 aspirations were effectively quashed when the French government favoured Matra. Alpine persevered with F3, with revised cars in 1968, andicapped by lack of resources and the Renault ngine. New cars, A330/360, came in 1969; once again ood placings in French events (and a 1st-place tie at Montlhéry) were the sum of their achievements. After Alpine had turned away from racing, one of the 1969 ars was raced privately with a Ford engine. The only ther Alpine single-seaters have been Formule France ars.

The sports car effort was more rewarding, when from 1964 to 1969 Alpine raced the A210/A220 cars in events which suited them. The original spaceframe of the A210 as designed by Terry, and clothed with an aerodynamic ody which went some way to compensate for power eficiencies. Various Gordini-developed Renault en-nes were used, at first 998cc, 1,150cc and 1,300cc, from 967 1·5 litres and the 3-litre V-8. Inevitably the Alpine ffort was greatest at Le Mans, and results good: A210s ere 9-10-12-13 in 1967, taking the 1·3- and 1·5-litre roup 6 classes, and 8-9-10-11 in 1968, taking the In-exes of Performance and Thermal Efficiency. The car nat finished 8th was a 3-litre A220, the prototype of which was first raced in the 1967 Paris 1,000 Kilometres 6th). The V-8 soon developed reliability, but never the ower to challenge for outright honours, even a secon-ary event like the Paris 1,000 (4th and 6th in 1969). At Le Mans in 1969 all three 3-litre Alpines were outclassed, nd retired. The 1300 placed 12th won the Index of erformance. The best showings for Alpines outside rance were in the Monza 1,000 kilometres, where a -litre A211 finished 3rd in 1968, and an A220 6th in 1969.

At the end of 1969 Alpine withdrew from racing, to oncentrate on rallies. In this field they worked to make ne Renault-Gordini really competitive in classes, ationally and internationally, and to bring Alpines to ne fore in outright competition. Results began to show 1967—3rd in the Spanish and 5th in the Alpine after ading convincingly—and two events, the Coupe des lps and the Czech, fell to Alpine coupés in 1968. In 969 they were run with 1,300cc (1300S), 1,440cc and ,600cc engines, and thus had adequate power to cope ith, for example, the Porsches. Highlight of the year as a 1-2-3-6 in the Coupe des Alpes; Alpines were also st and 2nd in the Three Cities, and 3rd in the Monte arlo. The Alpines became respected for their speed, but ained a reputation for fragility; this was not substan-ated by their performance in the first 'rough' event which ney contested in their extended 1970 rally programme, when Alpines were 1st and 3rd in the notoriously rugged talian Rally and was quite discredited when an A110 on the Acropolis Rally, and lesser events such as the

1963 Alpine Le Mans coupé. *Photo: Autosport*

1967 Alpine A210 coupé at Le Mans. *Photo: Doug Nye Collection*

1970 Alpine A110 coupé driven by Jean Vinatier in the Lyon–Charbonnières Rally. *Photo: David Hodges Collection*

Tour de Corse fell to Alpines. Early in 1970 any slight coyness about the Renault association, which might have lingered, was dispelled by the announcement that Alpine was to be responsible for the entire Regie Renault competition programme. The parent company must have been delighted to see the team from their Dieppe subsidiary come within two points of the manufacturers' championship (26 against Porsche's 28 points). This confirmed Alpine as an international force in at least this branch of motor sport. The 1971 season started well with Ove Andersson's win in the Monte Carlo Rally. DWH

343

Alta (GB)

The prototype Alta was built by Geoffrey Taylor at Kingston upon Thames, Surrey, in 1928. Even the en-engine—a twin-ohc, aluminium block, 1,074cc 4-cylinder said to have been inspired by the contemporary Norton—was made by hand. This car, in spite of its low build, was used successfully in classic trials as well as speed events, and by 1931 had attracted sufficient notice to warrant production on a small scale at Fuller's Way, Surbiton, in a works constructed by Taylor for the purpose. The engine gave 49bhp at 5,200rpm, or 76bhp with a Roots-type blower, in which form the car could reach (intermittently) 110mph (176kph) at 6,400rpm. These early models earned some reputation for being temperamental under stress, yet that of Briault completed the 300-mile British Empire Trophy race at Brooklands in 1934.

In 1935 a 1,486cc offset single-seater, with chain-driven camshafts, was built for A. J. Cormack, who held the 1,100cc Brooklands Mountain circuit lap record with

the earlier model. Shortly afterwards the 1,960cc model was also announced. Improved, lighter versions with independent coil suspension on all wheels were introduced in 1937, and Philip Jucker's 1·5-litre car was timed at 144mph (231·7kph). A variety of well-known drivers of the time handled these cars, and immediately before and after World War 2 quite considerable successes were listed, mainly in sprints, hill-climbs and the shorter type of event. The leading driver was George Abecassis, who took the Prescott record in 1938 and held several class records, and Lady Mary Grosvenor was also frequently victorious. A 3-litre V-8 GP was planned, using two 1·5-litre blocks, but was never made.

In 1948 the new 1·5-litre GP car was ready, with 'square' stroke/bore ratio, and suspension by rubber blocks in compression. On paper the initial figures of 230bhp to propel 1,344lb (610kg) appeared promising, but development was very slow, partly because of Abecassis' increasing commitment with HWM. Geoffrey Crossley's car took class records at Montlhéry in 1949.

1928 Alta prototype in the Land's End Tri Photo: Montagu Motor Museum

Opposite, Jim Clark. Photo: Geoff Goddard

Far left, 1939 Alta 2-litre sports car at Prescott. Photo: Guy Griffiths

Left, Alta 1,496cc supercharged F1 car at Silverstone, 1951, in the British GP. Joe Kelly at the wheel. Photo: Geoff Goddard

Joe Kelly's 1950 model sported 2-stage supercharging. Although a regular and persistent competitor, his results were inconsistent.

For 1951 a Formula 2 model with new engine was produced, and the last Alta completed was Peter Whitehead's 1952 version, with dual twin-choke Weber carburettors and twin-plug head, enabling 150bhp to be turned out at 6,000rpm. A new GP car was made to the 2·5-litre formula, but was never finished. Instead the firm concentrated on the supply of these engines to makers of lighter and better-handling machines, including HWM and Connaught. One of the 1951 Formula 2 models was rebuilt as a Jaguar-engined sports car and achieved a new lease of useful competition life in the hands of Phil Scragg. DF

Alvis (GB)

T. G. John Ltd, of Coventry, was founded in March 1919, and their first car, the 10/30hp Alvis with a 4-cylinder 30bhp 1,460cc 65mm × 110mm sv engine, was produced in 1920. In May 1920, a 10/30 driven by its designer, G. P. H. de Freville, won a silver medal in the MCC London–Edinburgh Trial, and later in the month H. G. Evans's 10/30 made ftd at the Cardiff Motor Club's Rhiwbina hill-climb. T. G. John himself also drove in competitions, gaining a place on formula at Style Kop hill-climb in 1921, and a gold medal in the MCC London–Exeter Trial in 1922.

In 1921 a 10/30 racing car driven by the works driver, Major C. M. Harvey, won the only two car races, both handicaps, at a motorcycle meeting at Brooklands in July and, after considerable weight reduction, ran in the 1921 Coupe Internationale des Voiturettes at Le Mans. A stone cracked the sump when Harvey lay 4th behind the three victorious Talbot-Darracqs, and the car retired.

No racing was indulged in in 1922, but a number of successes were obtained in trials and speed hill-climbs by the 10/30 and the 11/40 (later called the 12/40) with a 1,598cc 68mm × 110mm sv engine producing 40bhp in sports form.

In 1923 came the famous 12/50hp Alvis with a 4-cylinder 1,496cc 68mm × 103mm push-rod ohv engine producing 50bhp. During the summer Harvey, often accompanied to the venues by Capt. G. T. Smith-Clarke, chief engineer and designer of what was now the Alvis Car and Engineering Co, won many sprint successes with a special 12/50, registered HP 6161, known as 'Racing Car No 1'. This had a much drilled chassis and even the foot pedals, handbrake and spring shackles were drilled. Dry-sump lubrication was featured and special close-ratio gears, and the weight of this bare chassis plus bolster tank was around 1,700lb (771·107kg). For the 1923 Brooklands 200 Miles Race in October, Smith-Clarke evolved two 12/50 racing cars with streamlined bodies, light differential-less back axles, and 53bhp engines with dry sumps, lightened connecting rods and a 6:2 compression ratio replacing the standard 5:3 to 1. Harvey achieved Alvis's greatest racing success in winning this race, finishing over 3 minutes ahead of Cushman's Brescia Bugatti and averaging 93·29mph (150·13kph), with a fuel consumption of just under 24mpg, breaking class records in the process by between 4 and 5mph.

Two special 12/50 two-seater racing cars were built for the 1924 Brooklands 200, plus a single-seater for racing and records there. Lower, shorter and lighter than the 1923 cars, weighing 1,232lb (558·82kg), their engines, with a 6·6 to 1 compression ratio, high-lift camshaft and

1922 Alvis 12/40 two-seater. *Photo: Montagu Motor Museum*

Opposite, Juan Fangio. *Photo: Geoff Goddard*

very light connecting rods, were said to produce 70bhp at 4,500rpm. There were just two brakes, on the transmission and rear axle. The two-seater cars did not produce their designed speed in the race, though both finished, driven by Harvey and Frank Halford. One car, chassis no. 2929, later achieved great fame in supercharged form in Australia on the Maroubra Speedway, Sydney, driven by Gordon P. Garlick, who was killed in the car there in January 1927.

Smith-Clarke and his chief designer, W. M. Dunn, were not only pioneers of fwd in England, but were also among the pioneers of supercharging in the early 1920s. In a search for still more lightness, Dunn designed a fwd sprint car, very small, very low, with a duralumin chassis and semi-monocoque body, weighing only 1,064lb (682·62kg). Its 12/50 engine, with a Roots-type Alvis supercharger, developed 100bhp. A De Dion type front axle was employed, as on the American Miller, but the fwd Alvis appeared at Kop hill-climb in March 1925, two months before the fwd Miller first appeared at Indianapolis. Running unblown at a wet Shelsley Walsh in 1925, a sprint fwd driven by Harvey clocked 54·2sec, won its class, and made 2nd ftd to the 53·8sec of Segrave's supercharged 2-litre GP Sunbeam. The 1925 supercharged fwd Alvis could lap Brooklands at 104mph (167·4kph), and two cars in the 200 Miles Race split the Darracqs, but later retired because of brake deficiencies. Also in 1925, Harvey came 3rd in a four-seater 12/50 sports car in the Georges Boillot Cup at Boulogne, gaining the team award for Alvis with R. M. V. Sutton, who finished 6th on a similar car. At Brooklands, H. W. Purdy won the Essex Open 100 Miles Handicap at 86·77mph (139·64kph) in his private 12/50.

For 1926 Alvis entered the GP lists with an advanced fwd supercharged 1,497cc 55mm × 78·75mm straight-8 developing around 110bhp. Horizontal valves were featured and similar suspension to that on the 1925 fwd cars. Two GP cars ran in the 1926 Brooklands 200 Miles Race but Harvey's car crashed when in 4th place and the Earl of Cottenham retired.

For 1927 the GP cars were redesigned with a dohc engine producing about 125bhp in a chassis with ifs in

which the driver was seated centrally. Again they ran in the Brooklands 200 (Harvey and George Duller) but both retired, Duller at half distance when 2nd in the 1·5-litre class to Campbell's winning 8-cylinder Bugatti. This year 12/50s proved the most successful British 1·5-litre sports cars in racing, winning the Essex 6 Hours Race at Brooklands (S. C. H. Davis); the JCC 4 Hours Sporting Car Race at Brooklands (Harvey); and the Georges Boillot Cup Eliminating Race at Boulogne (Harvey).

For 1928 Alvis produced an all independently sprung fwd production sports car with a 4-cylinder, sohc 1,482cc 68mm × 102mm engine, developing 75bhp in supercharged form. Two unblown cars ran at Le Mans (Harvey/Purdy, and Davis/Urquhart-Dykes) finishing 6th and 9th, with the Harvey/Purdy car winning the 1·5-litre class. With a blown fwd, Leon Cushman was 2nd in the TT, 13sec behind Kaye Don's Lea-Francis. Mr and Mrs Urquhart-Dykes took the 12-hour 1·5-litre class record from a blown Lea-Francis at Brooklands at 81·38mph (130·97kph) in their 12/50, and Harvey and Willday took 500-mile, 6-hour and 1,000km Class F records at the track with a single-seater fwd.

Left, 1924 Alvis 12/50 single-seater at Brooklands. C. M. Harvey at the wheel. *Photo: T. A. S. O. Mathieson Collection*

Right, 1925 Alvis fwd cars at the start of the JCC 200-Mile Race. *Photo: T. A. S. O. Mathieson Collection*

1930 Alvis FA straight-8 sports cars in the Tourist Trophy. *Photo: Montagu Motor Museum*

A straight-8 sports/racing car, also all independently sprung, was announced for 1929 with a 1,491cc 55mm × 78·5mm supercharged roller-bearing engine of 125bhp. A single-seater version averaged 95·24mph (153·27kph) for 1,000 miles (Harvey and Cushman) at Brooklands to take Class F records, and in 1930 Cyril Paul in a straight-8 fwd was 4th behind the 1,750cc Alfa Romeos in the TT and won the 1·5-litre class.

Alvis did not race officially after 1930, when fwd production ceased, but gave some help to private owners. In 1932 Ivan Waller on a 6-cylinder 2,148cc Silver Eagle won the Senior Race at Phoenix Park, Dublin, and in 1933 Frank Hallam in a straight-8 fwd won the 50-mile Canada Trophy race at Brooklands at 102·48mph (169·93kph). In 1938 Michael May in his Silver Eagle, with a 2,511cc Speed 20 block, won the 75-mile Irish GP handicap at Phoenix Park at 88·03mph (141·67kph), and he had many Brooklands successes with this car, which could lap at 113·97mph (183·41kph). In 1939 the Irishman C. E. Robb won the 154-mile Leinster Trophy race at 64·16mph (103·26kph) in his 12/50. Brooklands successes were also achieved by Charles Follett (12/50, Speed 20), Philip Fotheringham-Parker (Silver Eagle)

and Anthony Powys-Lybbe (12/50); but most notable, perhaps, was Charles Dunham, who lapped at 116·64mph (187·76kph) in his fabric-bodied single-seater Speed 20 and at 110·43mph (177·65kph) in his 4-cylinder 1,842cc 12/70hp of 1938/9.

After World War 2 the 12/70 was 6th in a race at Brussels in 1946, driven by F. R. ('Lofty') England; was 3rd in the 1948 Manx Cup (Leslie Johnson); and, fitted with the engine out of the Speed 20, won the 1951 Manx Cup driven by Dunham's son, Gerry, in the last significant Alvis victory. PMAH

Amédée Bollée (F)

After building a number of steam vehicles in conjunction with his father, Amédée Bollée *fils* turned to the petrol engine, and completed his first car in 1896. This was a *vis-à-vis* with 2-cylinder horizontal engine, and belt drive. It ran in the Paris-Marseilles-Paris race, with its builder at the wheel, but was written off when it crashed into a tree which had fallen across the road. In 1897 a two-seater Amédée Bollée was 4th in its class in the Paris-Dieppe race. This was strictly a touring car, like all its competitors at that time, but for 1898 Bollée prepared four 8hp cars which were probably the first machines in the world intentionally designed and built for racing. They had torpedo-shaped bodies sharply pointed at front and rear. They were entered for the Paris-Amsterdam-Paris Race, and at Amsterdam the first three places were taken by these cars, driven by Giraud, Girardot, and Bollée himself. However, a series of accidents on the return journey prevented them from doing better than 3rd (Giraud) and 5th (Loysel). Later that year Loysel won the Paris-Biarritz race, and Giraud made ftd for petrol-engined cars at Chanteloup hill-climb.

For the Tour de France in 1899 Bollée built a new racing car with horizontal 20hp engine whose four cylinders were cast *en bloc*, a very advanced feature for that time. On test this car was said to have achieved over 60mph (96kph), which, if true, would have made it the fastest petrol-engined car in the world. (Jenatzy's electric, *La Jamais Contente*, had reached 65·75mph (105·81kph), in April 1899.) Four of these cars ran in the Tour de France, but only one finished, Castelnau's which was 5th. The Paris-Amsterdam successes had resulted in a number of orders for the 8hp torpedo, but the 20hp cars were too radical to appeal to the ordinary motorist, and none too reliable either. Amédée Bollée preferred to concentrate on touring cars, and no more racing machines were made. GNG

America (E)

America cars were designed by Manuel Pazos, a versatile engineer who did valuable work in the fields of valveless engines, internally sprung wheels, and, more especially, synchromesh gearboxes. The first America of 1917 was a large car with 4-cylinder valveless engine, but the best-known model was the Type B, a light car with 1,100cc 4-cylinder engine which did well in hill-climbs and rallies in the period 1918 to 1922. From this was developed the Type C, a racing car available in single- or two-seater form. Made in 1922 it was the fastest America car, but valve troubles prevented it from achieving great success. JRV

Amilcar (F)

Salmson's great rival in the small sports-car market, the original Amilcar had a 903cc 4-cylinder sv engine, a 3-speed gearbox, and a differential-less back axle. In one

1922 America Type C racing car. *Photo: Manuel Pazos*

1925 Amilcar CGS sports car at a VSCC Prescott Hill-Climb in the 1960s. *Photo: Montagu Motor Museum*

of these André Morel won the first Bol d'Or race at 37·54mph (60·41kph) in 1922, though the works team (Fardeau, Morel, and Mestivier) had to be content with 4th and 5th places in the Coupe Internationale des Voiturettes behind the all-conquering Salmsons. The same state of affairs prevailed in the 1923 Cyclecar GP, and Amilcar concentrated their efforts on hill-climbs and minor events, scoring 102 first places in 1924 alone, though they annexed the 1,100cc class in the Targa Florio and the Belgian 24-Hour Race. The later production 4 CGS two-seaters with 1,100cc engines did very well in club events, especially between 1926 and 1928, but by the end of 1925 Amilcar had an answer to Petit's twin-cam Salmson in the shape of their own racing 1100, a dohc 6-cylinder from which 83bhp were extracted at 6,000rpm with the aid of a supercharger (production models were credited with only 62bhp). This was eventually worked up to 108bhp, and proved more than an answer to the later Salmson straight-8.

The factory claimed 74 wins in 1926, when Morel won the Italian Voiturette GP at 82·6mph (132·93kph). He was also successful in the GP de Provence, and in the JCC 200 at Brooklands, Amilcars made a clean sweep of

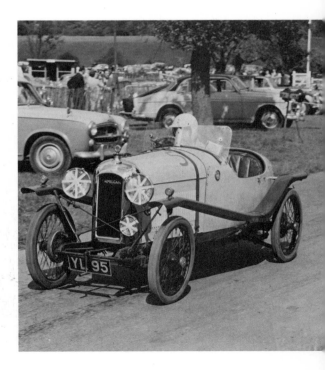

the 1,100cc category, Martin leading the class home in 4th overall position at 66·65mph (107·26kph), followed by Duray in 5th place and Morel in 7th. A 4-cylinder car was placed 11th. In 1927 Morel and Duray were 1st and 2nd in the GP de Provence, and there were further 1,100cc class honours at Lasarte, Boulogne, the Swiss GP, Monza, the 200, and at Chimay, while a super-charged 7CV saloon driven by Lefèvre and Despeaux won the Monte Carlo Rally.

By 1928 a 1,270cc version of the engine was produced to bring the model into the 1·5-litre class, and the wins continued: 1st and 2nd for Morel and Zampieri in the Rome race; the 1,100cc class victory at Juan-les-Pins for Moriceau; 2nd and 3rd places at Algiers; and 3rd places at Boulogne, Tunis, and in the Eifelrennen. José Scaron was Amilcar's star in 1929, when he won the Dieppe GP at 61·84mph (99·52kph), and the make repeated its 1928 success at Algiers, Treffel was 2nd in the Picardie GP, and Bartsch won in the Eifelrennen. At Comminges, Scaron was 2nd behind a similar car driven by Danoman, but an attempt by Moriceau at Indianapolis with the 1,270cc six was a failure. In 1930 Scaron won the 1,100cc class at Comminges, averaging 71·75mph (115·47kph), was 1st at Dieppe, and 2nd in the Monza Voiturette GP, and though thereafter Amilcar abandoned their sporting machines in favour of small luxury saloons, the sixes continued to race.

The only big win in 1931 was once again Scaron's, in the Tunis GP, but Arco was 2nd at Masaryk and in the German Voiturette GP at the Nürburgring, and 3rd in the Monza voiturette race. The cars, however, were back on form in 1932 with an outright win for Scaron at 73·68mph (118·58kph) in the Pescara race, not to mention a class victory at Nîmes. There were 2nds for Dourel and Druck respectively in the Comminges and Picardy voiturette events; a new 1,100cc record at La Turbie; and a ftd at Gaillon; and surprisingly the Martin and Bodoignet 6-cylinder won its class at Le Mans. Even in 1934 the de Gavardie brothers could manage 12th in this race, plus the class honours in the Belgian 24-Hour, and one of them won the Bol d'Or at 44·37mph (71·30kph).

By this time these basically 1925 cars were nearing the end of their effective life—apart from Grignard's 3rd place in the 1936 Bol d'Or. However, the 1935 Circuit d'Orléans saw the first appearance of a new sports car. This 2,350cc Pégase used a Grillot-designed ohv 4-cylinder engine in place of the 12CV Delahaye unit found on its touring counterparts; the chassis had in-dependent front suspension. Mestivier won his class at this first outing; he was beaten by an SS Jaguar in the 1936 Marne race, but again defeated the 2·5-litre opposition in the 1937 Circuit of Lorraine and the 1938 Paris 12-Hour. The cars did less well at Le Mans, where Mmes Roux and Rouault ran as late as 1938.

The last of the Amilcars was the strictly touring 1,185cc fwd Compound financed by Hotchkiss, and the make vanished into the world of vintage competitions, though not before Flahault had finished 3rd in the 1946 Burgundy GP. MCS

Ansaldo (I)

Launched in 1920 by the great Italian munitions and aircraft concern, and surviving until absorption by FIAT in 1931, Ansaldo was never a vigorous racing make. Nevertheless the sporting single-ohc 4-cylinder 4CS model with 1,980cc 72·5mm × 120mm, engine was a lively and inviting car in the early 1920s to Italians short of racing machines. One such was Tazio Nuvolari himself, who drove his second car race, the 1921 Circuit of Garda, in an Ansaldo, and came 2nd in the 2-litre class to another Ansaldo exponent, Corrado Lotti. The latter also won the first Montenero Cup race at Leghorn, the 2-litre class of the Mugello race in 1921, and the Consuma and Susa-Moncenisio hill-climbs in 1922.

Many other Italians scored hill-climb and road race successes with Ansaldos right up to 1930, notably G. Platè, winner at Cagliari, Sardinia, in 1922; Marinoni who won the 2-litre classes at Mugello, Consuma and Susa-Moncenisio in 1923 and Biella-Oropa and Trento-Bondone in 1928; Lazzaroni, 1st in the 1923 Criterium of Rome and the 2-litre class of the Targa Abruzzo race at Pescara in 1925; and Bacchetti, who won this same category in 1926. By then Bugatti, Diatto and O.M. were largely eclipsing Ansaldo performances in the 2-litre class, but the make continued to appear in competitions until its demise. CP

Apollo (D)

The chief designer of this make, Karl Slevogt, drove the cars in numerous races with considerable success. The first was gained by him in the 1910 Ostend Week when he won the 12·43-mile (20km) race as well as the Circuit d'Ostend in the 1·6-litre class. His car was a Type B with a 4-cylinder ohv engine of 995cc developing 12bhp at 2,400rpm. Between 1910 and 1913 this model, with capacity and output slightly increased, was among the

1927 Amilcar CGSs sports car in an Ilkley Club Trial. *Photo: Montagu Motor Museum*

Below, 1927 Amilcar CGSs racing car with Eldridge radiator cowl. *Photo: Montagu Motor Museum*

Right below, 1927 Amilcar 1100 6-cylinder racing car at Montlhéry. André Morel at the wheel. *Photo: T. A. S. O. Mathieson Collection*

most successful German cars in international competitions. Besides Slevogt the most notable driver was Baron de Vizcaya.

After World War 1 the small Apollo appeared in a much improved version as the 4/20 PS. There was a swing axle at the front, the first German car featuring this innovation. The system combined a transverse leaf spring with a pneumatic damper. The engine was also improved, the overhead valves being operated by four push-rods and rockers. The capacity was 1,030cc and the output of competition versions reached 25bhp. This model appeared at some events in 1924 with an open streamlined body, raced by Slevogt himself: as when he was overall winner of the Gabelbach hill-climb. Production of Apollo cars ceased in 1925. HON

Apperson (US)

Apperson of Kokomo, Ind., made great play with their Jackrabbit of 1907, a hefty chain-driven 4-cylinder raceabout guaranteed to do 75mph (120kph), and in pre-1914 days they raced similar machines. Lyttle was 4th in the Briarcliff Trophy in 1908, but was seriously injured in a crash at Long Island the following year. Harding carried on the good work with a 3rd at Fairmount Park, Philadelphia and a good showing in the Vanderbilt Cup before he retired. Thereafter Appersons failed to distinguish themselves in major events. Hanshue ran in the 1910 Vanderbilt Cup, and Lyttle in the 1911 Indianapolis 500, and as late as 1914 Goode supported both the Grand Prize and the Vanderbilt Cup. His Apperson was the last chain-driven car to enter for a big American race. MCS

Aquila Italiana (I)

The Aquila Italiana was the work of the enterprising Ing. G. C. Cappa (later of FIAT and Itala), and his design of 1906 prescribed several advanced features, including a monobloc cylinder casting, a crankshaft running in ball bearings, and liberal use of aluminium. Production and other problems delayed the Aquila's appearance until 1908–09, by which time Cappa had also introduced aluminium pistons, probably the world's first in a car. These featured in the 1912 4·2-litre 82mm × 132mm Aquila six, a fine car which attained 60bhp at the then high crankshaft speed of 3,600rpm.

Driven by Marsaglia the car took 2nd place in the 1913 Targa Florio, then scored an outright victory in the Parma Poggio di Berceto hill-climb and class 1sts at the Mont Ventoux and Gaillon hill-climbs in France. Aquila's other driver, Beria d'Argentina, scored a class win in the Vercelli flying kilometre sprints with a smaller 12/15 4-cylinder car fitted with very advanced, stream-

1924 Apollo 4/20PS sports car. *Photo: Neubauer Collection*

1913 Aquila Italiana 12/15hp. Beria d'Argentina at the wheel. *Photo: G. N. Georgano Collection*

1908 Ariès GP des Voiturettes car. *Photo: Montagu Motor Museum*

lined aluminium bodywork, and drove it in more spartan form to other class victories at Parma-Poggio and Mont Ventoux. Rounding off an excellent 1913 season for Aquila, Cav. Vincenzo Florio accompanied by Marsaglia won the Sport Club of Sicily's speed/fuel consumption Cup race around the famous Targa Florio circuit.

Another Parma-Poggio hill-climb victory came in 1914, this time for a new driver, Bartolomeo Costantini, later of Bugatti fame. Aquila also took 3rd place and a class victory in the gruelling 3,100-mile (4,989km) Tour de France, and Marsaglia achieved a 1st in the Circuit of Tuscany. That year Aquila entered for the French GP with three advanced single-ohc, hemispherical-headed sixes, novel for the 'funnel' air intakes to their exhaust pipes aimed to provide a velocity discharge of the gases, featured later by Mercedes in 1923 and by Vanwall in 1958. Unfortunately the full team was not ready and only Costantini took part, retiring after 10 laps.

Aquila disappeared after 1917, but the 1912 sixes were still raced after World War 1, being particularly successful in hill-climbs. CP

Ariès (F)

The Ariès hovered on the fringe of French competition motoring for nearly a quarter of a century without achieving any outstanding fame. In 1908, some single-cylinder machines contested both the Coupe des Voiturettes and the Grand Prix des Voiturettes without success. The Ariès' greatest impact came in the 1920s, with the ohc sports cars. Three 1,100cc machines ran in the 1923

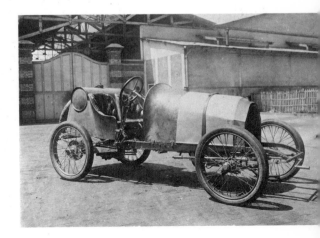

1925 Ariès 3-litre (front row right) at Boulogne. *Photo: Montagu Motor Museum*

Grand Prix de Tourisme, and Forest finished 2nd in the Circuit des Routes Pavées. There was another try in the 1924 touring-car race, when Gabriel drove in the team, but the cars were too thirsty; that year the Gabriel/ Lapierre 1100 managed 11th at Le Mans. The fast 4-cylinder 3-litre was in evidence in 1925: this was eventually persuaded to give 96bhp. Wagner and Flohot were 6th at Le Mans, but Lalaurie scored another 2nd place in the Circuit des Routes Pavées and in the Boillot Cup at Boulogne Laly was 2nd and Rigal 7th. Two 3-litres (Laly/Chassagne, and Flohot/Duray) went to Le Mans in 1926 along with some 1,100cc cars, but they failed to finish, though Laly once again came 2nd in the Paved Roads race, which he did again for Ariès for the third time in succession in 1927. This was perhaps the make's best year, for Laly won the Boillot Cup at 68·76mph (110·66kph) (ably backed by Duray's 1,100cc machine in 4th place), and he and Chassagne finished 2nd and won their class in the Belgian 24-Hour Race at Spa, an 1100 also collecting its class honours. This partnership was, however, unlucky at Le Mans, where a seized camshaft drive put them out of the running when comfortably in the lead, leaving the badly damaged Bentley of Davis/ Benjafield to take the chequered flag. Ariès were still racing in 1928, with entries for Le Mans and the Boillot Cup, but class wins at Le Touquet and the Circuit des Routes Pavées represented the limit of success. MCS

Arnolt-Bristol

This make used a 2-litre Bristol engine and two-seater sports car body built by Bertone of Italy for the car dealer S. H. (Wacky) Arnolt of Chicago, Ill., and was introduced to United States racing in 1954. Fred Wacker, Arnolt-Bristol, and Ted Boynton, Frazer Nash, tied for the 1954 Sports Car Club of America 'E' modified national championship. Arnolt-Bristols were Sebring class winners in 1955 and 1956, and Ralph Durbin and Max Goldman won the under 2-litre Grand Touring honours at Sebring in 1960. The last Arnolt-Bristols were sold in 1964 after 340 cars had been produced in 10 years. ARB

Arnott (GB)

The Arnott 500, devised by George Thornton, followed the usual rear-engined layout found in the first Formula 3,

but had suspension by torsion bars. Some dozen were built at Miss Daphne Arnott's North London works, but no major successes were achieved, despite work on a desmodromic-valve JAP engine, and one or two record attempts. Fibreglass bodies were supplied by Automobile Plastics.

In 1954 a sports model was introduced, with an A30 engine for road use or a 1,100cc Coventry-Climax for competition. This model featured cross-linked rear suspension. The cars were unlucky in competition, and although alternative engines (including blown Ford Ten and Lea-Francis) were tried by private owners, once again no notable wins were recorded. Manufacture ceased in 1957. DF

Arrol-Johnston (GB)

Traditionally a most unsporting car, this Scottish make emerged from the dogcart era in 1905 by entering two large 3·8-litre flat-twins with conventional shaft-driven chassis for the first TT of all. The car's designer, J. S. Napier, won at 33·9mph (54·56kph) (and, significantly) 31·1mpg, Roberts taking 4th place. The cars had no further success as tourers or racers, though they ran again in the 1906 event. Four-cylinder models, still with wire wheels, supported both light and heavy categories in 1907. In the 1908 Four-Inch event they ran some 4·1-litre ioe cars said to give 60bhp, but all three, driven by Resta, Moss, and Roberts, retired. Some stolid near-touring Arrol-Johnstons were entered for the 1911 and 1912 Coupe de l'Auto races in France: in the former year these were only tuned 2·6-litre 15·9hp models with dashboard radiators, but in 1912 they tried harder with 5-speed boxes, frontal V-radiators, and (in the case of two of the team) side-chain drive. These were finished in tartan. Though Wyse came in 5th, their overall performance was less good than in 1911, when all three cars were slow but regular. MCS

Right below, 1955 Arnott 1,100cc sports car. *Photo: G. N. Georgano*

Right bottom, 1912 Arrol-Johnston Coupe de l'Auto car. *Photo: Montagu Motor Museum*

AS (F/E)

The AS light car was an international product, with chassis and engines made in Paris, and bodies in Bilbao, where all tuning for the competition models was done. The engine was an 1,100cc sv unit. AS light cars took part in a number of races, including the Circulo Motorista of the Peña Mataró (Barcelona), in which they finished 2nd; the 1925 Circuito de Levante (3rd and 5th); and the 1925 San Sebastian Cyclecar Grand Prix (6th in class). Production of AS cars ran from 1923 to 1926. JRV

Aston Martin (GB)

Robert Bamford's and Lionel Martin's hybrid (consisting of a Coventry-Simplex engine in an Isotta Fraschini voiturette chassis) was running in 1914, but the true Aston Martin was not seen until 1919, when Addis won a gold in the London–Edinburgh Trial on a production prototype with 40bhp 1·5-litre sv unit. Both Martin and Kensington Moir were winning races at Brooklands by 1921, when the first true racing Aston made its appearance in the 200 Miles Race. This had a Robb-designed single-ohc unit and was not a success, though Zborowski managed 10th place: he was beaten by Marshall in the sv machine, 'Bunny', which came in 9th. In 1922 'Bunny' went on to take ten world and 22 class records. Aston Martins also gained thirteen 1st places in hill-climbs and sprints, and there was a new racing model, this time with fwb and a dohc 54bhp unit designed by Gremillon, formerly of Peugeot. This was not a great success. In the former race, however, 'Bunny' redeemed the honour of Aston Martin by taking 2nd place at 86·35mph (138·97kph), between two Talbot-Darracqs. Another record car appeared, 'Razor Blade', which used the twin-cam 16-valve engine and an incredibly narrow single-seater body only 18in (46cm) wide. It failed to attain 100 miles in the hour ahead of AC, though Halford lapped Brooklands at 99·81mph (160·63kph). The

Benson-designed 8-valve dohc engine appeared in 1924, but finance was the main problem, and the one car entered for the 1925 Brooklands 200 crashed on the first lap.

A reorganization in 1927 brought a new generation of single-cam 1·5-litres designed by A. C. Bertelli, which lasted until 1936. The first competition engines gave 63bhp, and were installed in low worm-drive chassis. Neither of the two cars entered for Le Mans in 1928 finished the course, but thereafter (with the exception of 1929 and 1930) the make was to be represented without interruption at the Sarthe Circuit until 1964 — an unrivalled record. A 5th place in the Double-Twelve at Brooklands was Aston Martin's best in 1929, but they improved on this in 1930, when Bertelli finished 4th at 73·76mph (118·7kph), though the cars were less successful in the Saorstat Cup at Phoenix Park. A team of improved machines with 70bhp engines appeared in 1931, and in the Double-Twelve they managed 6th place and a class victory in face of a virtual MG 'landslide'. There was another class victory in the TT, and the Bertelli/Harvey car was 5th at Le Mans, where the former driver won the Biennial Cup in 1932, though his was not the best Aston in the race — Newsome and Widengren were ahead of him in 5th place again.

In 1934 guise the works cars were really prototypes of the legendary 'Ulster' model; weight (always a problem) was down to 1,960lb (890kg) and on 80bhp 110mph (176kph) was available. Results were patchy: a 3rd place at Phoenix Park; wholesale retirements at Le Mans (though two private entries finished 10th and 11th); and 3rd, 6th and 7th places plus the Team Prize in the TT, after Bertelli had repainted his machines in the red of his native Italy. There were also two Glacier Cups in the Alpine.

The 1935 season started well, with the privately-owned Ulster of Clarke/Faulkner winning the 1,500cc category

1921 Aston Martin 200-Mile Race car, 'Bunny'. B. S. Marshall at the wheel. *Photo: Montagu Motor Museum*

of the Mille Miglia at 56·16mph (90·38kph). A 12th place at Le Mans was a disappointment, but TT placings (4th, 5th and 11th) were just as good as in 1934, and the Lurani/Strazza car not only took class honours in the Targa Abruzzo, but also came in 3rd overall. In 1936 came the new and rapid 2-litre, still an ohc four—competition versions had dry-sump lubrication. It was unable to show its paces at Le Mans, since this event was cancelled, and both Seaman and Phipps retired in the TT. On the credit side the Headlam/Wood 1·5-litre won its class in the Belgian 24-Hour Race at Spa. There were no works cars in 1937, but at Le Mans the 1·5-litre of Skeffington/Murton-Neale took 5th place, and the 2-litre driven by Morris-Goodall and Hichens was 11th and won the Rudge-Whitworth Cup. Another 2-litre was driven to victory in the 1938 Leinster Trophy by Horsfall, and in the Bol d'Or Polledry finished 2nd, winning the 1·5-litre class in an Ulster. Contet won this event outright in 1939, when Hichens took 12th place at Le Mans in his 2-litre, and a single-seater version of the current Speed Model appeared at Brooklands, driven by R. G. Sutherland, Aston Martin's chief.

The company did not recommence serious production until the arrival of David Brown in 1947, but Horsfall's pre-war 2-litre won its class in the 1946 Belgian GP, and by 1948 Claude Hill's new push-rod 4-cylinder engine had been installed in another of these chassis for Rolt and Pilette to drive at Spa. An all-new car was handled by Horsfall and Johnson, and the Aston Martins not only led their class, but the whole race, against an opposition that included Delage and Ferrari. The works car won at 72·07mph (115·98kph). In 1949 a full works team was entered for Le Mans, all the cars being streamlined saloons. Those of Maréchal/Macklin and Haines/Jones were 2-litres, but the Johnson/Brackenbury car was powered by the 2·6-litre dohc 6-cylinder 123bhp engine designed by W. O. Bentley for David Brown's other recent acquisition, Lagonda. A crash eliminated one of the fours, and the six retired, but the remaining works DB1 came in 7th, and a private entry was 11th. At Spa the 2·6-litre redeemed itself with a 3rd place at 76·5mph (123·11kph), closely followed by Horsfall's old 1936 car, now with push-rod engine.

Serious racing started in 1950, with the famous team of DB2 saloons (VMF 63, VMF 64 and VMF 65). These were managed by John Wyer, and did well at Le Mans, where Abecassis and Macklin were 5th (winning the Index of Performance) and Parnell and Brackenbury 6th.

In 1952 a new sports-racer was brought out, the DB3, designed by Eberan von Eberhorst. This started life with the 2·6-litre engine in 140bhp form, though it was enlarged during the season to 2·9 litres; other features included a new tubular frame, a 5-speed gearbox, and a De Dion back axle. The DB2s were, however, used for the Mille Miglia, Wisdom and Parnell coming 1st and 2nd in their class, and finishing 12th and 13th in general classification, so that the first serious appearance of the DB3s was in the Production Car event at Silverstone, where they finished 2nd, 3rd and 4th. The DB2s turned out again for the Prix de Berne, where the new 300SL Mercedes-Benz cars were too much for them, though they took 4th and 5th places behind the Germans. Le Mans was a disaster, but the Nine Hours Race at Goodwood was some compensation, despite a spectacular fire at the pits which eliminated the Parnell/Thompson 2·9. Collins and Griffith went on to win in a 2·6-litre at 75·42mph (121·37kph) after the Salvadori/Baird Ferrari had expired.

Above, 1930 Aston Martin International in a 1938 trial. *Photo: Montagu Motor Museum*

Left above, 1922 Aston Martin, 'Razor Blade'. In front of the car, Clive Gallop, and by the cockpit Count Zborowski. *Photo: Montagu Motor Museum*

Left below, 1922 Aston Martin French GP car. H. Kensington Moir at the wheel. *Photo: Hugh Conway Collection*

Apart from another total collapse at Le Mans, 1953 was better: a 2nd place and class victory at Sebring for Parnell and Abecassis: a 5th place for the Parnell and Klementaski car in the Mille Miglia; and an outright win at 73·96mph (119·03kph) for Parnell in the British Trophy Race in the Isle of Man, using the more elegant 150bhp DB3S version. The works DB3S Astons scored a processional win (headed by Parnell) in the *Daily Express* Silverstone race, and there was a second victory in the Goodwood Nine Hours for Parnell and Thompson (after their clutch had failed), Collins and Griffith being 2nd. These two cars reversed their positions in the TT. Only DB3S models were fielded in 1954, when disc brakes were being tried, as well as a new 4·5-litre V-12 Lagonda; all this was too much for Aston Martin. The sole bright spots were a 1-2-3 victory in a later International Sports Car Race at Silverstone, and Beauman's victory on a privately-entered DB3 in the Dutch sports-car GP at Zandvoort.

A 7th place and a class victory in the Monte Carlo Rally for the Gatsonides and Becquart DB2/4 formed an unusual start to 1955, but Parnell was 3rd in the British Empire Trophy Race at Oulton Park, and the make was back on form in the *Daily Express* Silverstone, where Parnell and Salvadori were 1st and 2nd. There was a 2nd place in the Hyères 12-Hour Race for Gaze and McKay, a 1-2-3 finish at Aintree, a 4th place in the TT, another win (for Walker and Poore this time) in the Goodwood Nine Hours, and a victory plus record lap in the *Daily Herald* sports-car race at Oulton Park. Paul Frère won the Belgian Production Sports Car Race at 107·9mph (173·6kph), and 1955 was Aston Martin's best Le Mans so far, with Collins and Frère coming 2nd at 105·4mph (169·6kph). The 2·9-litre engines were giving 230bhp by this time, and the DB3S had another season in front of it, though during 1956 the company brought out a new design, the DBR. This featured a new twin-cam 2,493cc 6-cylinder engine with dry-sump lubrication, a light, multi-tubular frame, Girling disc brakes, and a 5-speed gearbox in unit with the De Dion rear end.

The DBR was first seen at Le Mans that season, but meanwhile the older types soldiered on, with a 4th place at Sebring; a win for Moss at Goodwood in April; a victory for Salvadori (ahead of Moss) in the *Daily Express* Silverstone at 94·79mph (152·54kph); a 2nd for Parnell in the production-car event at Spa; a 3rd for Whitehead at Chimay; and a 2nd for Moss at Rouen.

1949 Aston Martin DB1 saloon at Le Mans.
Photo: Motor

1952 Aston Martin DB3 at Goodwood.
Photo: Klementaski Studio

1958 Aston Martin DBR2 at Silverstone.
Stuart Lewis-Evans at the wheel. *Photo:*
J. H. Horsman

1959 Aston Martin GP car at a 1970 VSCC
Silverstone meeting. Neil Corner at the
wheel. *Photo: Montagu Motor Museum*

Brooks and Parnell drove the new DBR 1/250 at Le Mans
but retired, though the Moss/Collins DB3S finished 2nd.
Sims won the 1956 RAC Rally on a secondhand 2·6-litre
DB2 saloon. DBRs in 1957 ran with 3-litre and 3·7-litre
engines, but they retired at Le Mans, leaving a privately
owned DB3S to take 11th place. The 3-litre, however, did
well elsewhere, for Brooks won the Belgian sports-car
race at 103·97mph (167·3kph), and Salvadori was 2nd.
Even better was Brooks's victory at 82·39mph
(132·59kph) in the Nürburgring 1,000 Kilometres, and
Salvadori capped the season by winning the *Daily*
Express Silverstone race. Units of 3·9 litres appeared at
Oulton Park in 1958, where Moss and Brooks were 1st
and 2nd in the British Empire Trophy Race. Frère and
Shelby had to be content with 2nd and 3rd places behind
a Lister-Jaguar at Spa, but the Moss/Brabham Aston
achieved a second victory at the Nürburgring, and the
3-litres took 1st, 2nd and 3rd places in the TT, now staged
at Goodwood. Le Mans was once again unfortunate, for
all the DBRs retired, leaving the Whiteheads to finish a
creditable 2nd in a DB3S.

Aston Martin's competition zenith came in 1959, for
in that year David Brown became the only British manufacturer ever to win the Sports Car Constructors'
Championship. Further, Moss won an International GT
race at Silverstone, averaging 86·94mph (139·91kph) on
one of the new 3·7-litre DB4 saloons. At the Nürburgring
there was a third successive victory, the laurels going to
the sole works entry, driven by Moss and Fairman.
Aston Martins (Salvadori/Shelby, and Trintignant/
Frère) were 1st and 2nd at Le Mans: the winner's average
was 112·5mph (181kph). First and 4th places in the TT
secured the Championship, and at this point the firm
announced their retirement from racing.

Meanwhile, there had been a brief involvement with
Formula 1. As early as 1956 a 2·9-litre single-seater had
been tried in New Zealand, where Parnell had taken 4th
place in the Lady Wigram Trophy, but in 1959 there was
a team of GP Astons. These were 2·5-litre sixes based on
the DBR series, with similar suspension and transmission
the twin-cam engines were credited with an optimistic
280bhp at 8,250rpm. Salvadori opened the season promisingly with a 2nd place in the International Trophy at
Silverstone, averaging 102·38mph (164·83kph) to the
102·73mph (165·35kph) of Brabham's victorious Cooper
—but there was no encouraging sequel. The cars both
retired in the Dutch GP, and when they finished, they
did so low down the list—6th in the British GP, 10th in
the Italian GP, and 6th and 8th in the Portuguese GP. In
1960 they were modified to conform to the 3-litre Tasman
Formula, and achieved a measure of success in Australia
Davison was 2nd in the 1960 Australian GP.

Not that the make vanished immediately from Le
Mans. Two 3-litre DBRs (Clark/Salvadori, and Baillie/
Fairman) finished 3rd and 9th in 1960, when Fairman
also won at Rouen. In 1961 no fewer than five Aston
Martins turned up at Le Mans, three of these being relatively stock DB4 GTs and the other two the DBRs once
more. None finished, but in 1962 there was a new works
prototype, the 4-litre 212 coupé with De Dion back axle,
which Hill and Ginther worked up to 2nd place before
retiring. An improved version, the 215 with 360bhp
engine, was seen in 1963, but this one did not last long.
and Aston Martin's only major success during the season
was Salvadori's victory with a DB4 in the Coppa Europa
at Monza. A solitary Aston made no impression in the
1964 race, and thereafter the company concentrated on
superb fast tourers, with only a single brief renaissance.

...t the end of 1966 they announced a new 5-litre 4ohc V-8 ...ngine with dry-sump lubrication, which was fitted to ...e 1967 Le Mans Lolas. Both entries retired early in the ...ace, and Lola switched to the less expensive Chevrolet ...nit, but by 1970 production Aston Martins had 8-...ylinder engines. MCS

Astra see Nathan

ATS (I)

...utomobili Turismo e Sport was formed by Count ...olpi, who financed the Scuderia Serenissima, Giorgio ...illi and Jaime Ortiz Patino in 1962, with Carlo Chiti as ...esigner (Volpi soon withdrew, otherwise its make name ...night have been Serenissima). A factory was built at ...ologna, and a handful of cars made.

A Formula 1 car was completed late in 1962. Rear-...ngined, it was outwardly unusual, with a shallow body, ...eep screen, and hump over the enclosed engine, but by ...ontemporary standards there was nothing novel in the ...rudely-made tubular frame. The engine was a 90° 4-ohc ...-8 (66mm × 54·6mm, 1,494cc, 190bhp at 10,000rpm). ...eam drives were Phil Hill and Baghetti, and the manager ...as Tavoni, who temperamentally was hardly suited to ...he company atmosphere of crisis and dissent. They had ... miserable 1963 season, the cars running only in the ...elgian, Dutch and Italian GPs (at Monza they were at ...east classified, 11th and 15th). Then the promoters ...arted company.

The F1 project was resurrected in 1964 by Alf Francis ...nd Vic Derrington, and a 'Francis-Derrington ATS' was

built around some existing components (substantially redesigned, with a stiffer frame and engine producing 200bhp at 10,500rpm). This ran briefly in the Italian GP, driven by Carbral; thereafter no more was seen of it.

A few GT coupés, with rear-mounted twin-ohc 2·5-litre V-8s, appeared early in 1964; in competition they were unsuccessful, as was the attempt to revive the design as a Serenissima in 1965. ATS V-8 engines spasmodically turned up in later years, e.g. in 995cc form in the Swiss GB-ATS spyder in 1969, and — notably unsuccessfully — in 3-litre form as a GP engine in 1966.

In August 1968 a Serenissima Group 6 coupé appeared, based on an old Group 7 McLaren M1B chassis and using the 285bhp V-8 engine and Colotti-Francis transmission. Jonathan Williams was 2nd to Siffert in the Enna Cup in this car, and in 1969 the open Mk 168 variant appeared at Norisring, again driven by Williams. It was unsuccessful. In 1970 Moreno Baldi purchased some of the hardware of the original (liquidated) company, and began modest efforts to revive ATS. DWH

Auburn (US)

Made in the Indiana town from which they took their name, Auburn cars first appeared in 1900, but made no impact on the sporting world until Erret Lobban Cord became general manager in 1924. He introduced a new range powered by 4·5-litre straight-8 Lycoming engines, and available in striking dual colour schemes. In 1927 this 8-88 model, in sedan and roadster form, took a number of long-distance records at Salem, N.H., and Atlantic City, N.J., board tracks. These included 1,000 miles (1,609km) at 72mph (116·68kph), and 15,000 miles (24,140km) at 61·4mph (98·81kph). In 1928 came the 8-90 speedster, a boat-tail two-seater capable of 108mph (174kph). This car broke the stock-car record for Pike's Peak hill-climb. Power of the Eight was up to 100bhp by 1932, when it was joined by the 160bhp 6·8-litre V-12. This model also broke many International and US speed records, covering the flying mile at 118·32mph (190·33kph), and averaging 109·33mph (175·95kph) for 500 miles (804·7km).

The final Auburn speedster was the 851 of 1935, with 4·6-litre straight-8 Lycoming engine and Schwitzer-Cummins supercharger which boosted power to 150bhp. This car and its very similar successor, the 852 of 1936, took more than 70 speed records with Ab Jenkins at the wheel. At one time in 1935, Auburns held all US stock-car records up to 24 hours and 15,000 miles (24·140km). However, this did not sell enough cars, and the company closed its doors early in 1937.

Auburns were seldom raced, although a much-modified 8-cylinder car ran in the 1930 Indianapolis 500 under the name of Trexler Special. It crashed, and the sponsors tried again in 1932, but the car was insufficiently fast to qualify. GNG

Audi (D)

After Dr August Horch broke away from the firm that bore his name in 1909, the new Audis made down the road from his original factory took on the competition mantle of Horch. Very successful was the 3,563cc ioe 4-cylinder Alpensieger, which gave 40bhp in sports form and wore lightweight tulip-form aluminium tourer bodywork. One clean sheet was scored in the 1911 Austrian Alpine Trial, but two cars were penalty-free in 1912. In 1913 and 1914 the cars won the team event, tying with Hansa in the latter year. The post-1918 cars failed to distinguish themselves even in touring events. MCS

Below, 1963 ATS Formula 1 car; Phil Hill at the wheel. *Photo: Geoffrey Goddard*

Bottom, 1970 ATS-Cosworth 1-litre spyder at Mugello; Moreno Baldi at the wheel. *Photo: Autosport*

Austin (GB)

Herbert Austin was no stranger to racing when he built four 100hp cars for the 1908 French GP; he had designed and driven the 30hp Wolseley in the 1902 Paris–Vienna Race. Three of the big Austins ran in the French GP and two finished. Though well down the list, they were the only British finishers. Some production 25/30hp Austins had already been seen in hill-climbs and trials. A modified version, Thompson's famous 'Pobble', raced regularly at Brooklands until 1912 and eventually lapped at 91mph (146·45kph). Modified Austin 20 models included Lambert's 'Pearley III', Scriven's amazing four-seater 'Sergeant Murphy' (which lapped at 94·99mph—152·87kph) and the 'Black Maria' of Austin's son-in-law, Capt Arthur Waite. These sired a production sports version of the Austin 20. Years later, in 1934, the Yacco Oil Co's Austin 20 maintained 84·07mph (135·29kph) for 12 days at Montlhéry.

Like Lagonda, Austin entered touring cars in the Russian International Tours of 1910–1911. A 40hp car with Vitesse sporting four-seater body won the 1910 St Petersburg Automobile Club trophy with Harold Kendall at the wheel, and in 1911 a new 40hp car known as the Defiance had a clean sheet in the Czar's Cup trial, until eliminated in a crash only a few miles from the finish. A 20hp tourer driven by Kendall and Vernon Austin won a silver plaque in the 1914 Austrian Alpine Trial.

In July 1922 Austin announced his Seven, and a week later a prototype took a modest 3rd in class at Shelsley Walsh. The car that was to revolutionize British motoring was no ideal sports machine with its unpredictable roadholding and indescribable brakes. But it was well made, long lasting, and has been called 'the finest Meccano set ever produced'. Tuners could not resist the challenge, and for the next 17 years the racing history of Austin is the story of the Seven.

It saw the Class H flying start mile raised from 84·29mph (135·65kph)—Waite's Austin, 1925—to 130·51mph (210·02kph)—Kohlrausch's MG. 1935, and divides into roughly four phrases: from 1923 to 1926, the unblown sv Sevens and Gordon England's remarkable racing achievements; from 1925 to 1930, the blown sv cars including the Ulster, culminating in the Double-Twelve victory; from 1930 to 1935, the running battle with MG which brought the 'Rubber Duck' single-seaters and the hiring of Murray Jamieson; from 1936 to 1939, the development of the Jamieson dohc single-seaters to unrivalled eminence in short-distance events.

Waite won a Brooklands handicap in March 1923 with a rebodied Seven; further modified, it was taken to far-off Monza for the Cyclecar GP in April. The first British

car to race there, it won at 55·86mph (89·90kph). Austi[n] was then approached by the clear-thinking young Gordo[n] England, who soon made a Seven lap Brooklands at ov[er] 70mph (112kph). Further modified, it took 750cc recor[ds] at up to 79·62mph (128·13kph). Rebodied as a two-seater, it came 2nd in the 1,100cc class of the 200 Miles [at] an average of 76·84mph (123·66kph), touching 85mph (136·79kph) at times and setting a series of new long-distance records—this with an unsupercharged sv two-seater of 747cc.

Austin's Sports Seven of 1924 had a high and ugly bod[y,] slightly advanced ignition, and did something over 50mph. Gordon England's 'Brooklands Super-Sports' was low, purposeful and sold with a 75mph guarantee. England won the new 750cc class of the 200 Miles at 75·61mph (121·69kph), with one con-rod in the sump, and headed a 1-2-3-4 Austin victory at Montlhéry. He won repeatedly at Brooklands, lapping at well over 80mp[h] (128kph). He took 21 records at Montlhéry, up to 600k[m] at 79·32mph (127·65kph), and lapped at 84·1mph (135·35kph). Later, England did very little racing, but won the 750cc class of the 200 Miles yet again in 1925 an[d] 1926.

Left above, 1914 Audi in Austrian Alpine Trial. August Horch at the wheel. *Photo: Neubauer Collection*

Below, 1908 Austin Grand Prix car. *Photo: Wilson McComb Collection*

Below centre, 1911 Austin 20, 'Pearley III'. *Photo: Montagu Motor Museum*

Bottom, 1914 Austin 20 Austrian Alpine Trial tourer. *Photo: Autocar*

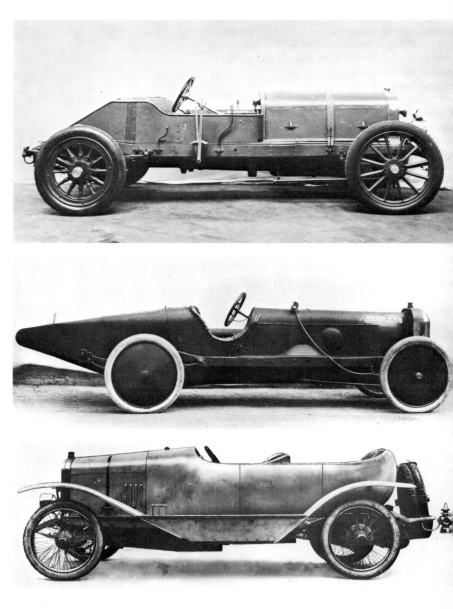

His amazing record brought mixed reactions at the Austin works, where the racing shop experimented with supercharging from 1925 to 1930 in a vain attempt to achieve the world's first Class H 100mph (160kph). Their much-lowered supercharged cars scored some successes in 1925. Depper lapped Brooklands at 85·43mph (137·49kph), and Duller won a 50-mile event with a 775cc version at no less than 89·9mph (144·68kph). With a blown single-seater Waite took short-distance records on several occasions. With an unblown car Zubiaga won the 1925 Spanish Cyclecar GP, the cyclecar class of the 1926 French Grand Prix des Voiturettes, and took 3rd in the 1,100cc class of the 1926 Targa Florio. Although England was out of racing, his cars were raced successfully by Samuelson and others. Waite finished 1926 with a batch of Class H records including 83·66 miles (134·64km) in the hour, then sailed to Australia, where he won the Australian GP in 1928. The original supercharged Seven was sold and later reappeared as 'Slippery Anne', driven by Coldicutt.

During 1927 and 1928 the private owners were prominent, especially Boyd-Carpenter, Chase, Dingle, Hendy, Walter and Spero. No 750cc car finished the 1927 200 Miles in the time limit, but Spero won the class at 79·95mph (96·48kph) in 1928 with 'Mrs Jo-Jo' (England's 924/5/6 car rebuilt). Boyd-Carpenter, Chase and Parker did successful record runs at Montlhéry, including 12hr at 62·53mph (100·63kph) in 1927 and 24hr at 65·98mph (106·19kph) in 1928. Dingle won the 750cc class of the 1928 6 Hours, 2nd overall.

Strangely, the origins of the famous Ulster, with dropped front axle and optional Cozette supercharger, are clouded by controversy; even its introduction is variously dated as 1928, 1929 or 1930. Actually, Austin built very few genuine sports cars for sale to the public, leaving that field open to dozens of specialist coachbuilders. Works cars certainly appeared in 1929 at Southport and the Irish GP. For the TT, Austin asked Gordon England to manage the team. He did so to good effect. The four supercharged Sevens led for most of the race and finished 3rd, 4th, 16th and 19th. In the first Brooklands 500 Miles, Holbrook won the 1,100cc class at an excellent 80·25mph (129·15kph), 6th overall.

Waite now returned from Australia (where Dickson was 3rd in the 1930 GP), and with the Earl of March won the 750cc class of the Brooklands Double-Twelve. Mis-flagging denied him 2nd place in the Irish GP and he crashed in the TT. Out of racing himself, he prepared a car for the Brooklands 500 Miles, which Davis and March won outright at 83·41mph (134·24kph). Then Davis and Goodacre took a crop of Class H records including 89·08mph (143·36kph) for the flying start kilometre. In January 1931 the same car was sent to Daytona, where Campbell tried for 100mph but fell short by 6mph. One week later, Eyston's MG achieved 103·13mph (166·05kph) at Montlhéry.

With a new record car, the 'Yellow Canary', Cushman managed the first Class H 100mph (160kph) in England. Goodacre and Trevisan were 2nd in the 1,100cc class of the Mille Miglia. Dickson won the 200-mile (321·9km) Phillip Island race in Australia. But MG brought out a new 750cc model which overwhelmed the Austins in the Double-Twelve, the Irish GP and (in supercharged form) the TT. Austin replied with the 'Rubber Duck' single-seaters, which won the Relay Race at 81·77mph (131·59kph), but the whole team retired from the 500 Miles.

The 'Ducks' appeared seldom in 1932, plagued by

cracked cylinder heads, but Austin successes included the 750cc class of the British Empire Trophy at 92·51mph (148·88kph) and 2nd in the 1,500cc race of the Avusrennen. A young employee of Amherst Villiers, T. Murray Jamieson, was seen at Brooklands with a much-modified Ulster. Austin hired him to sort out their own cars.

Jamieson's first modifications to the 'Rubber Ducks' met with limited success: the team prize in the 1933 International Trophy, a class 2nd at AVUS, and 4th in the Relay Race. His new record car took some Class H records at Montlhéry without reaching 120mph (193kph), and MG soon won them back again.

In 1934 Driscoll took one Class H record at Southport. The engine was then fitted to a neat single-seater sprint car which Driscoll drove to such good effect that in 1935 another was built for Dodson, and both fitted with tubular front axles. Goodacre also came into the picture,

1929 Austin Seven Ulster sports car. *Photo: Wilson McComb Collection*

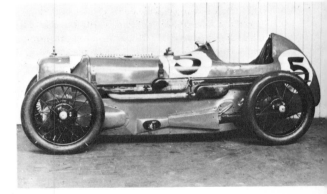

Centre, 1933 Austin Seven 'Rubber Duck' racing car. *Photo: Wilson McComb Collection*

1936 Austin Seven twin-ohc racing car. Bert Hadley at the wheel. *Photo: Wilson McComb Collection*

and the three specialized in hill-climbs and racing at Southport or on the Mountain Circuit, where the class record took a lot of punishment. A private Austin team won the 1934 Relay Race at 84·65mph (136·23kph). Each Austin record attempt was countered by an MG one, Kohlrausch setting the flying start mile to 130·51mph in 1935. Four sports Sevens ran at Le Mans and two finished, at the tail of the field. Then came good news: the MG racing department had been closed down.

Meanwhile Jamieson had been working hard. His dohc single-seaters at last appeared in 1936. They were exceptionally pretty little cars giving 116bhp at 8,500rpm from the 744cc engine, robustly designed to achieve 12,000rpm eventually. Weight was under 1,120lb (508kg), and 121mph (194·7kph) was attained in initial tests. Consumption of sprint fuel was about 4mpg with a Roots-type supercharger giving around 20psi. They cost £3,000 apiece, and Herbert Austin said their main objective was to beat MG's flying start mile figure. Drivers were chosen from Dodson, Driscoll, Goodacre and Baumer. Bert Hadley, an Austin apprentice, was training in mud trials with the 'Grasshoppers''. Kay Petre was to drive an sv car.

The first year, 1936, brought many failures through fuel starvation and burned pistons. The sv cars scored at the June Shelsley Walsh meeting and Craigantlet hill-climb, the dohc at Freiburg hill-climb and the Eifel-rennen. Driscoll set the Mountain Circuit class record at 77·02mph (123·95kph), never beaten, but a crash at Backwell hill-climb in July put car and driver out of action. Dodson took some Class H records, lapping the Outer Circuit at 121·2mph (195kph). There was talk of giving up, and Jamieson left to join ERA. But in 1937 they won at Donington (the Junior Trophy and four races on Coronation Day), Crystal Palace (Crystal Palace Trophy and Imperial Trophy) and Brooklands (Relay Race at a record 105·63mph (170·05kph) average). They won at Shelsley Walsh (750cc class and team prize, June and September) and Craigantlet (ftd and record). Baumer made 3rd ftd with a 750cc record at Freiburg, and ftd with an 1,100cc record at Dreifaltigkeits. Hadley made ftd at Bristol Speed Trials and put the Campbell Circuit class record up to 69·87mph (112·44kph), never beaten. There were no 750cc finishers in the 500 Miles, and Kay Petre was injured in a practice crash. Sports Austins came 2nd in the Donington 12 Hours, but retired from the TT and Le Mans.

In 1938 Goodacre left and in came Buckley, trained, like Hadley, with the 'Grasshoppers'. The team concentrated on Donington, winning the British Empire Trophy (no longer held at Brooklands), 2nd place in the Nuffield Trophy, and two handicaps at the Coronation Trophy meeting. They ran occasionally at Crystal Palace and Brooklands without much success. They did well at Shelsley Walsh (2nd ftd twice and team prize in September), Prescott (750cc class and record, twice) and Craigantlet (ftd). But not a single new international Class H record was set up, by Austin or any other make.

Dodson also left in 1939, so Hadley usually played lone wolf. At Shelsley Walsh he made 4th ftd, at Prescott 5th ftd and a new 750cc record, backed up by Buckley. At Donington he was 2nd in the Crystal Palace Cup, and on his last appearance won the Imperial Trophy. Again there were no new international Class H records; indeed, Austin never did regain the flying start mile, pushed above 140mph (225kph) in 1936. In January 1939, however, Van Riet's Seven won a 100-mile handicap held before the South African GP.

After World War 2 the amateur tuners came into their own again, just as in the 'twenties. Dowson and Issigonis scored many successes with the Lightweight Special, built before the war from Austin Seven components. The 750 Motor Club popularized racing with cars cleverly rebuilt by Birkett, Mallock, French, Colin Chapman and others who made good use of 'the finest Meccano set'. It formed the basis of the first Lotus and some early 500cc cars.

The original post-war Austin A40 made some appearances in international rallies and several record attempts, as did the A90 at Indianapolis. As so often before, it was someone outside the Austin organization who made use of Austin components to produce a good sports car when, in 1952, Donald Healey designed the Austin-Healey. After 1954, Austin entries in rallies were made by the new Competitions Department of BMC, and private owners achieved some racing successes with the A35 and new-style A40. The sporting career of the Austin Mini is dealt with under BMC. In the mid-1960s the Longbridge factory again had ambitions to design a sports car and extensive development work was done behind closed doors, but the project was not successful. FWMcC

Austin-Healey (GB)

The first Austin-Healey records were established at Jabbeke, Belgium, before the make really came into existence, the prototype covering the flying start kilometre at 117·7mph (179·7kph) (and mile at 110·9mph (178·4kph). A few days later it was announced at the 1952 Motor Show in London that Donald Healey's new sports car would be built by Austin. It featured a 4-cylinder 2,660cc Austin A90 engine, many Austin chassis components, and a particularly handsome two-seater body. Production began in May 1953 with 3-speed gearbox and overdrive, replaced two years later by a 4-speed box with optional overdrive. In September 1956 came the 100-Six, using BMC's 2,639cc 6-cylinder engine to give 102bhp, raised to 117bhp a year later with a new cylinder head. July 1959 brought the 3000 model with 2,912cc engine and 124bhp, later raised to 132bhp with three carburettors, then reduced to 130bhp with two carburettors. Rallying experience dictated chassis changes in the Mk III, the last Austin-Healey, built from early 1964 to the end of 1967.

From late 1957 all Austin-Healeys were built at Abingdon. All the earlier cars were built at Longbridge except the first 20 and two special 4-cylinder models, the 100M (110bhp) and 100S (with 132bhp and disc brakes, the fastest production Austin-Healey.

The 948cc Sprite, based on Austin A35 components, was also built at Abingdon from its announcement in May 1958. Three years later came the Mk II with re-styled body, no longer frog-eyed, to which disc front brakes and a 1,098cc engine were added in October 1962. The Mk III (March 1964) featured semi-elliptic rear springs and other changes. The Mk IV (October 1966) had further body changes and a 1,275cc engine.

Early Austin-Healey entries in rallies brought some success, but from 1958 to 1965 the make became established as an outstanding rally contender, as Sprite or 'big Healey', in the hands of private owners and those who drove professionally for BMC (see p. 375). The rebodied 995cc Sebring Sprite, developed by John Sprinzel in the early 1960s, was equally at home in rallies or races.

But the racing history is less consistent. In 1953 the 100M prototypes retired from the Mille Miglia but

1953 Austin-Healey 100 at Le Mans, followed by an Osca and a Porsche. *Photo: Rodolfo Mailander*

1953 Austin-Healey 100 at Brunton Hill-Climb. *Photo: Charles Dunn*

nished 2nd and 3rd in class at Le Mans, and 8th overall n the Goodwood 9 Hours. At Utah a modified car overed the flying start mile at 142·6mph (229·5kph) and veraged 122·91mph (197·72kph) for 12hr; a standard 00 maintained 104mph (167·4kph) for 24hr. In 1954 the 00S appeared at Sebring to finish 3rd overall despite a roken valve rocker. Another was 5th in class at 73mph 117·48kph) in the Mille Miglia, but Healey then withrew his entries from Le Mans and other races in protest gainst increased specialization. Two works cars were ntered, however, for the Pan-American Road Race, but oth retired. Private 100 models finished 2nd to 6th verall in a Swedish race. The 1953 record car was taken o Utah again to average 132·47mph (213·11kph) for 2hr and 132·29mph (212·84kph) for 24hr, and a supercharged version covered the fs mile at 192·62mph 310·03kph).

Several series-production classes were announced for 955, so the works Austin-Healeys returned to racing. They came 1-2-3 in class at Sebring (the Moss and Macklin car 6th overall) and took a class 1-2 in the Mille Miglia. After the 1955 Le Mans crash came an unsuccessul period, but private Austin Healey 100 models gained 1st and 3rd overall at Hockenheim, and a 100S an verall 3rd in Sweden.

In 1956 the 100S was 3rd in class at Sebring, 2nd in the price class' of the Mille Miglia, and 8th overall in the Reims 12 Hours. Two private 100S models gained a class 1st and 2nd in the *Autosport* production sports car championship. At Utah the new 100-Six, with slightly streamlined body and the later six-port head, covered 00 miles at 153·14mph (246·46kph). The 1954 supercharged record car did a timed run at 203·06mph 326·20kph).

Three cars similar to the Utah 100-Six ran in the 1957 Sebring 12 Hours, one finishing 2nd in class. In the Mille Miglia a 100-Six, again with the later cylinder head, won he price class. One of the Abingdon record cars, EX179, was fitted with a prototype Sprite engine and taken to Utah. Unsupercharged, it averaged 118·13mph 190·15kph) for 12hr, then it took records at speeds up o 142·08mph (228·63kph) in supercharged form.

While the 100-Six, Sprite and 3000 went on to achieve great things in international rallies the Warwick factory continued to build a few more specialized cars for longdistance races. Three 100-Six cars won the team prize at Sebring in 1958, and a private Sprite won the Leinster Trophy.

With the 3-litre car under way, Warwick concentrated on the Sprite for 1959, gaining a class 1-2-3 at Sebring to win the team prize, and a class 6th in the Targa Florio. Private Sprites won the Pietermaritzburg, South Africa, 6 Hours on index, and a class in the Coupe du Salon; they were also 1-2-3 in class for the *Autosport* championship and won the team trophy. A 100-Six was 3rd in class and 4th overall in the Silverstone GT race. The new 3000 scored a class win in the Oulton Park Gold Cup, and came 3rd overall in the *Autosport* championship. Though raced successfully by some private owners, the big Healey was always more of a rally car, and always outpaced by 3-litre Ferraris in international races. At Utah, EX179 reappeared disguised as EX219, but still with Sprite engine. This supercharged 948cc unit propelled it through 15 records, including 146·95 miles (236·48km) in one hour and 138·75mph (223·28kph) for 12hr—faster than the 1954 record car with unblown 2,660cc engine.

In the new 4-hour Sebring race of 1960, Moss drove the works Sprite to finish 2nd overall to an Abarth. In the

Top, c 1960 Austin-Healey Sprite I Speedwell coupé at Goodwood. John Venner-Packe at the wheel. *Photo: Autosport*

Above, 1961 Austin-Healey Sebring Sprite followed by a Sprite Mk I at Sebring. *Photo: Wilson McComb Collection*

12 Hours the Sprite won its class again; the big Healey came 2nd and 3rd in class. At Le Mans the lone 3-litre retired, but the Sprite won its class at 85·6mph 137·76kph). Two big Healeys and a Sprite ran in the TT, and the Sprite at Nürburgring also, winning its class in the 500 kilometres. Another Sprite class win came in the Nassau TT. Many lesser races were won by Adams, Hawkins, Sprinzel, Gaston and Jackson. With a streamlined Speedwell Sprite, Graham Hill covered the flying start kilometre at 132·2mph (212·7kph) at Jabbeke.

Two separate Sprite teams appeared for the Sebring 4 Hours in 1961, one entered by Healey, one by Sprinzel, with a star-studded list of drivers in Hansgen, McLaren, Stirling Moss, Leavens, Pat Moss and Cunningham. They finished in that order, Hansgen 2nd overall—again to an Abarth. In the 12 Hours the Sprites took a class 2nd and 3rd behind a Lola. Other class awards of 1961 were 2nd in the Mille Miglia; 1-2-3 in the Brands Hatch GT race; 3rd in the Claremont 6 Hours GT race; and 2nd and 3rd in the Aintree GT race. At Le Mans all three cars (two Sprites and a 3000) retired, but Sprites won the La Chartre GT race outright, and finished 3rd, 4th and 7th in the Nürburgring 500 kilometres.

Throughout 1962/3/4 the works Sprites were in the doldrums. Moss, Rodriguez, Ireland and McQueen

drove at Sebring in 1962, but no awards were won. Le Mans brought only another retirement. Private cars did better, Olthoff's big Healey taking 1st in the Leinster Trophy and 2nd in the Rand 6 Hours, with a class 2nd for a Sprite in the Nürburgring 1,000 kilometres. In 1963 the Sprites again failed to complete 12hr at Sebring or 24hr at Le Mans, though two big Healeys finished at Sebring, 4th and 5th in class behind the Ferraris. A class 2nd went to the Sprites in the Nürburgring 1,000 kilometres and the Silverstone GT race, and a class 3rd in the Brands Hatch GT race. In 1964 the works Sprite retired yet again at Sebring, but having completed the minimum distance was officially awarded the class prize. It finished at Le Mans, but retired from the Targa Florio. Sprites took a class 3rd in the Nürburgring 1,000, always their favourite, and a class victory at Nassau.

Next year brought better results. In the heavy Sebring rain of 1965, the big Healey won its class and the Sprites were 1st and 2nd in class. The big and small Healeys were both 2nd in class in the Targa Florio. In the Brands Hatch 1,000 miles, the Sprite came 2nd overall to an MGB, the big Healey 4th. At Nürburgring the Sprite took a class victory in the 1,000km race, and a 2nd place in the 500km event. At Le Mans, the works Sprite at last won its class again, 12th overall at 96·48mph (155·27kph).

Top, 1959 Austin-Healey 3000 at Silverstone. John Gott at the wheel. *Photo: Wilson McComb Collection*

Above, 1967 Austin-Healey Sprite coupé in the Targa Florio. *Photo: Geoffrey Goddard*

Opposite, Dan Gurney. *Photo: Geoff Goddard*

In 1966 the Sprites won their class in the Daytona 24 Hours, the Sebring 3 Hours, the Sebring 12 Hours and the Nürburgring 1,000 kilometres. They were 2nd in class at Mugello and 4th overall in the Nürburgring 500. At Le Mans, however, neither Sprite finished.

Two classes were won at Sebring in 1967, and at Le Mans the Sprite came 15th overall at 100·9mph (162·3kph) to win the *Motor* Trophy as the best (and only) British finisher. The results for 1968 were almost identical: a class victory at Sebring and a repeat performance at Le Mans; 15th overall at 94·73mph (152·45kph) to win the *Motor* Trophy again. The inevitable class win was gained in the Nürburgring 1,000 kilometres, and another at Mugello. In 1969, a class 1-2- at Sebring brought Austin-Healey's official competition record to a close. FWMCC

Austin-Healey in America: America's first look at the Austin-Healey was in 1953 when Donald Healey and his drivers, George Eyston, Bill Spear, John Gordon Benett and Jackie Cooper, drove two stock roadsters to a series of international records at Bonneville, Utah; Dick Kincheloe won the SCCA D production national championship for Austin-Healey in 1954 with Fred Moore, Dr Dick Thompson and Fred Spross earning similar successes in 1957, 1958 and 1959. Introduction of the Sprite resulted in a road racing rarity, one-marque events with Sprites making-up entire H production fields. In 1963, one of America's few successful woman drivers, pink-suited Donna Mae Mims, drove her pink Sprite to a national championship. Sprite honours in 1970 were won by Dennis Daly. ARB

Austro-Daimler (A)

The first Vienna-built racers were seen in 1901, and were identical to the unfortunate 24hp Cannstatt-Daimlers of 1899. Also entirely German in design were the 90hp ioe racing cars of 1904, these being 'extra' Mercedes made in Austria in conformity with the Gordon Bennett rules. Braun was 5th and Wilhelm Werner 11th, but the black-and-yellow crypto-Mercedes did less well in the last Gordon Bennett of 1905, and the replacement of Paul Daimler by Ferdinand Porsche at Wiener-Neustadt was not immediately fruitful. Porsche, Fischer and Boos-Waldeck handled the works team of three 6·5-litre chain-driven cars in the 1909 Prince Henry Trials, but though these merely proved reliable, 1910 was very different. This time Porsche entered some brilliant 5·7-litre ohc 5-bearing fours, designed to do 88mph (142kph) on 86bhp, and capable of running up to 2,300 rpm. The Neumann-Neander tulip-shaped bodies were aimed at circumventing the regulations, but streamlining was intelligently applied, and these *Austrian* Daimlers (as they were still known) swept the board, Porsche, Fischer and Hamburger taking the first three places. Two other cars finished in the first ten, and the make won nine of the twelve cups for which they were eligible.

With the demise of the Prince Henry Trials, Porsche turned his attention to the Austrian Alpine event, running a team of more modest 2·2-litre sv models in 1911; these had shaft drive in place of the side chains of the original 'Prince Henry' cars. None the less, they were capable of 60mph and took the first five places and the team prize. In 1912 the Alpine Austro-Daimlers were 3·6-litre 14-32PS models, and two teams were entered, Porsche being one of the four unpenalized drivers.

The famous Saschas with short-stroke twin-ohc 4-cylinder engines and 4-wheel brakes appeared in 1922. Four 1,100cc versions ran in the Targa Florio, Alfred

Neubauer winning his class at 34·6mph (55·68kph). One of these cars was timed over the kilometre at 89mph (143·23kph), and Austro-Daimler claimed 43 wins that year. Versions of the Sascha were also made with 1,500cc and 2-litre engines, one of the latter doing extremely well at Brooklands in 1926. As early as 1922 Malcolm Campbell had driven the smaller type at Saltburn, Yorkshire.

The departure of Porsche and the advent of a new ohc six, the 2,540cc ADM, occurred in 1923. This started life as a fast tourer, but had grown up by 1926–7 into the 3-litre 12/100PS (19/100 in England), which could lap Brooklands at over 100mph (160kph). Though a racing version was seen at Brooklands in 1926, and 1928 saw Mason and Paul finish 3rd and 4th in the TT, the 6-cylinder Austro-Daimler was at its best in rallies and hill-climbs. In 1927 there were numerous victories in Germany, Austria, Hungary and Poland (where Austro-Daimler won the Polnische Tourenfahrt); Liefeld won the little-known Polish GP as late as 1930.

The ADMs had dominated the 1924 Alpine Trials, where they took the first six places and the team prize, and even in 1930 the make could claim five clean runs and ftd on the Josefsberg. In 1931 there were three Coupes des Glaciers. There was only one in 1932, but surprisingly one of the ponderous 4·6-litre Alpine 8s had won the ADAC's 10,000km Trial in 1931. The hill-climb scene was dominated by Hans Stuck whose special sprint car was based on the 12/100PS. What started with 120/130bhp ended up with the later 3·6-litre Bergmeister engine boosted to 200bhp, and Stuck won the Swiss hill-climb title in 1928, the Austrian title in 1929, and the European one in 1931, when his successes included fastest times of day at Gaisberg and Kesselberg. In 1930 he broke the record at Shelsley Walsh with a time of 42·3sec. which was to stand until 1933. MCS

Autocoast (US)

The Autocoast Ti-22 were two Chevrolet-powered Group 7 cars designed and built by Peter Bryant in Costa Mesa.

Opposite, Graham Hill. *Photo: Geoff Goddard*

Top, 1912 Austro-Daimler in the Austrian Alpine Trial. *Photo: Autocar*

Right, 1928 Austro-Daimler ADMR at Semmering Hill-Climb, 1929. Hans Stuck at the wheel. *Photo: T. A. S. O. Mathieson Collection*

Below, 1922 Austro-Daimler Sascha 1·5-litre racing car. *Photo: Montagu Motor Museum*

1969 Autocoast Ti-22 Can-Am car. Jackie Oliver at the wheel. *Photo: Richard George Photographics*

Calif. They represent the first use of strong, lightweight titanium (Ti-22 is the atomic symbol and atomic weight of titanium) in a racing car chassis. The Autocoast's debut was at the Monterey Can-Am in October 1969 when Jackie Oliver finished 13th. He was 2nd at Mosport in 1970, having led Gurney's McLaren for 16 laps, but the car was destroyed in a crash at St Jovite in June. A second, lighter and stronger car was built with fresh finance from Norris Industries, and ran in the last two Can-Am races of 1970 under the name Norris Industries Ti-22 Mk 2. Oliver finished 2nd and made fastest lap at Laguna Seca, and was 2nd again at Riverside his three 2nd places earning him $50,800. ARB

Autodynamics (US)

One of America's largest race car builders, Autodynamics Corp, Marblehead, Mass., headed by Ray Caldwell, has produced over 1,000 competition machines since 1964. Driving one of his own cars, Caldwell earned the 1964 national Formula Vee championship and was named Sports Car Club of America 'Rookie Of The Year.' In 1967 Caldwell built the D-7, a Can-Am car for Sam Posey, that with its De Dion rear axle, solid-beam front axle and chassis-mounted wing, ran contrary to then current Group 7 design. In 1969 an Autodynamic's D-9 Formula Ford, driven by Skip Barber, was national champion. Autodynamics-prepared Dodge Challengers were driven by Sam Posey (who severed his relationship with Autodynamics at the end of the 1970 Trans-Am season) to 4th place in the 11 race 1970 Trans-Am series. ARB

Auto Union (D)

Auto Union of Zwickau, Saxony, go down in history as the first make successfully to race rear-engined Grand Prix cars. The engine-behind-driver layout is commonplace today, but in 1934 it was highly revolutionary and even a series of race victories did not convince the world that its designer, Dr Ferdinand Porsche, was on the right track. It took 21 years after the last Auto Union raced before rear-engined Grand Prix cars became the rule rather than the exception.

Auto Union was founded in 1932 by the fusion of Horch, Audi, DKW and Wanderer, and with encouragement from the new Hitler regime, they decided to take up Grand Prix racing in time for the 750kg Formula of 1934, acquiring the remarkable P-Wagen design which Porsche had produced independently a year earlier. This specified a large, robust, 45° V-16 supercharged engine of

1967 Autodynamics Caldwell D-7 Can-Am car. Sam Posey at the wheel. *Photo: Al Bochroch*

1971 Autodynamics Caldwell D-13 Formula Vee. *Photo: Autodynamics Corp*

4·4 litres, with a single central ohc operating all the valves the inlets directly, the exhausts by push-rods. Mounted ahead of the rear axle and behind the driver's cockpit, it drove the rear wheels through a 5-speed gearbox and initially gave about 295bhp at 4,500rpm.

The chassis was of steel tubing with ample cross bracing, ladder fashion, and suspension was independent all round, with torsion bars and trailing links at the front, and a transverse leaf spring and swing axles at the rear. The radiator was in the nose, water circulating via the frame tubes, the fuel tank was between the driver's seat and the engine, and the body was of light alloy with doped fabric side panels.

The Auto Union made a sensational debut early in 1934 when no 1 driver Hans Stuck attacked world records at the AVUS track, averaging 134·9mph (217kph) for the hour, and also setting new 100 miles and 200km figures. Then the new team from Zwickau went racing. They came 3rd in their first event, the 1934 AVUS GP; 2nd in their second, the Eifelrennen; retired in their third, the French GP; and won their fourth, the German GP. They won the Swiss and Czech GPs too, Stuck the driver each time, to round off a fine season for so revolutionary a car.

Yet their success did not send the opposition rushing to copy them, as happened in 1960–61. The rival Mercedes-Benz and Alfa Romeo kept their engines in the traditional place, and a less successful 1935 season for Auto Union left the issue in doubt. Undoubtedly the tremendous power at the rear, transmitted through swing axles, could produce uncontrollable oversteer unless very carefully used, and driving an Auto Union was a tricky business. The design had been tidied up for 1935, when it was called the B type; the engine was improved and enlarged to 4·9 litres, giving 370bhp; short vertical exhaust stubs replaced the tail pipes, the transverse leaf rear springing was changed to torsion bars; and the doped fabric body sides gave way to light alloy sheeting. Despite all this, the cars could not match the Mercedes that year; Stuck won the Italian GP when the rival team retired, while in their absence Varzi won the Tunis GP and the Coppa Acerbo, and sensational 'new boy' Bernd Rosemeyer won the Czech GP.

The 1936 season was infinitely better. Rosemeyer swept all before him, winning the Eifel, German, Pescara, Swiss and Italian GPs and the European Championship; Varzi added the Tripoli GP to Auto Union's score. The cars were now C types, with 6·1-litre 520bhp engines and in 1937 Rosemeyer fought valiantly against much improved Mercedes to win the Eifel, Pescara and Donington GPs and the Vanderbilt Cup in the U.S. Hasse won the Belgian GP and von Delius the Grosvenor GP in South Africa.

That season marked the end of the 750kg GP Formula, replaced in 1938 with a top capacity limit on supercharged cars of 3 litres. Dr Porsche had left the team by then, but Feuereissen, von Eberhorst and Werner evolved a new D type Auto Union with a 12 cylinder three-camshaft supercharged 3-litre engine giving about 400bhp at 7,000rpm. The transmission and chassis were much as before, but De Dion type rear suspension was used and the driver was set further back with fuel tanks on each side of him, all of which made an easier handling, more controllable car.

However, the tragic death of Rosemeyer in a record attempt early in 1938 was a demoralizing blow which set the team back by months. The first 1938 Auto Union was an ugly 'compromise' shape based on the 1937 car, but in mid-season a handsome new body was evolved and this, plus the coming of Tazio Nuvolari, revitalized the team.

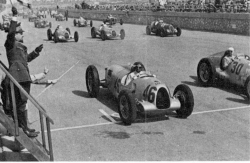

Baker Electric (US)

The Baker Motor Vehicle Company of Cleveland, Ohio was one of the most important producers of electric cars in the United States, and, like similar firms, concentrated on light two-seater runabouts and staid broughams for city work. However, in 1902 and 1903, they sponsored two dramatic torpedo-like racing cars. The first was actually built by the Electric Vehicle Company of Hartford, Conn., to W. C. Baker's design. It had the appearance of a submarine, with two seats in tandem under a conning tower with tiny mica windows, and was powered by a 12hp Elwell-Parker motor driving by chain to the rear axle. The batteries were distributed throughout the vehicle, some in front of the driver, some between him and the motor, and others behind the rear axle. It was a large car, over 18ft (5·5m) long, and weighing 3,000lb (1,360·8kg). At Staten Island in June 1902, Baker and C. E. Denzer covered a mile in 47sec before crashing into the crowd and killing a spectator.

This car was shown at the Crystal Palace, London, in February 1903, but later in the year another racing car was built, called the Torpedo Kid. This was of generally similar appearance, but was lighter, and carried only one person in an open cockpit. In September 1903 it broke 2 to 10 mile records at Cleveland, but in a race for electric cars it crashed after colliding with a Waverley. GNG

Ballot (F)

Ballot built proprietary engines before World War 1, and their racing cars preceded anything the general public could buy by a good couple of years. In 1919 they had secured the services of Ernest Henry, formerly of Peugeot, and for Indianapolis that year he produced a classic dohc 4·9-litre straight-8. René Thomas did a lap at 104·2mph (167·7kph), but Ballot's best performance was Guyot's 4th place. By the latter part of the season the cars had fwb, but they achieved nothing in the Targa Florio (the only other major race in 1919), even if Thomas broke the course records at Gaillon that autumn.

Some smaller cars (with fwb from the start) were produced for the new 3-litre GP formula of 1920, these giving 107bhp as against the 125/130 of the 1919 type. There was still no Grand Prix, so the cars ran at Indianapolis, where Thomas was 2nd, De Palma 5th, and Chassagne 7th. A full team of Ballots also turned up at Gaillon, but even the 4·9s stood no chance against the 350bhp Sunbeam. The year 1921 was rather mixed. At Indianapolis DePalma's 3-litre retired, but not before he had taken $20,000 in lap prizes to add to the $11,300 he

Above, 1939 Auto Union D-type on the Grossglockner Hill-Climb. H. P. Muller at the wheel. *Photo: Montagu Motor Museum*

Top right, 1934 Auto Union A-type. *Photo: Montagu Motor Museum*

Right centre, 1936 Auto Union C-type at the start of the Tripoli GP. Bernd Rosemeyer at the wheel. *Photo: Cyril Posthumus Collection*

Right, 1938 Auto Union D-type in the Swiss GP. Nuvolari at the wheel. *Photo: Cyril Posthumus Collection*

Right below, 1921 Ballot 3-litre at the Targa Florio. Jules Goux at the wheel. *Photo: Montagu Motor Museum*

The Italian won the Italian and Donington GPs at the end of that season, and in 1939, when two-stage supercharging was adopted, Muller won the French GP and Nuvolari the last pre-war GP of all, at Belgrade, Yugoslavia.

That was Auto Union's last racing appearance, although the design for a 12-cylinder 1,500cc car to meet the anticipated 1940 1·5-litre Formula was well advanced when war ended it all. In 1945 the factory passed into the Russian Zone and apart from a C-type chassis in the Munich museum no Auto Union racing car has since been seen in the West. Besides Grands Prix, Auto Union took part in many spectacular record attempts in 1934-8, clothing high-boost versions of their GP machines in aerodynamic all-enveloping bodywork which taught many useful lessons in streamlining, besides boosting the ever-hungry prestige machine of the Third Reich. Rosemeyer averaged 253·7mph (408·3kph) on the Frankfurt-Darmstadt autobahn late in 1937, but when he lost his life three months later in attempting to regain the record from Mercedes-Benz, Auto Union abandoned record activities. CP

AWE see EMW

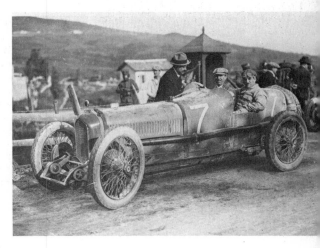

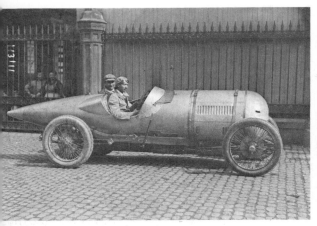

had won in 1920. In the French GP he finished 2nd behind Murphy's Duesenberg, and Goux on the 2-litre was 3rd. Goux made ftd at Gaillon and won the Italian GP at 90·4mph (145·48kph).

Ballot gave up major events at this juncture, but the 2-litre was developed into an excellent if expensive sports model, the 2LS. The Goux and Decrose 2LS took 2nd place in the 1922 Targa Florio, Foresti finishing 3rd on a similar machine. Another 2-litre was 3rd at San Sebastian in 1923, and as late as 1925 Debuck and Decrose's Ballot expired almost on the finishing line of the Belgian 24-Hour Race at Spa. This humiliation was avenged by a win in the Spanish Touring Car GP at 61mph (98·17kph).

By this time the firm was making the 2LTS, a sohc 2-litre 4-cylinder tourer, and the straight-8s that followed these were both heavy and unreliable. Grosse won the 2-litre class of the Paris–Nice with one of the former models in 1927, and in 1933, over a year after the last Ballots had left the Paris factory, an eight-year-old car took 3rd place in this event. MCS

Bandini (I)

Bandini were best known for their little 750cc sports cars, used in Italian Formula 3 racing during the 1950s. The company was one of the many tuning Fiat models, and work with the Fiat 500 developed into the building of these specialist two-seaters with many Bandini-made parts.

Eventually only such components as the front suspension and transmission casings remained of FIAT manufacture, while Bandini produced a high-revving little 749cc dohc 4-cylinder engine, measuring 59 × 63·5mm, which was mounted in the nose of a conventional tubular chassis. The cars were sold in two-seater form, and for F3 use the mudguards were simply unbolted and a cover fitted over the passenger seat. DCN

Barnato-Hassan see Bentley

Beardmore (GB)

Production of this Scottish-built car began in 1920, but the first sports model appeared three years later. The 11hp sports had a 1,656cc single-ohc engine developing 30bhp. More exciting was the 12.8hp Super Sports with capacity enlarged to 1,960cc, and higher compression ratio, giving a speed of 70mph (112kph). These cars were successful in hill-climbs and sand racing all over the British Isles; the leading driver was Cyril Paul who used a special works car with 1,988cc engine and lightweight body. With this car he broke the Shelsley Walsh record in 1925, lowering it to 50·5sec. This was faster than either Raymond Mays' Brescia Bugatti or Humphrey Cook's TT Vauxhall.

Sports Beardmores were not listed after 1924, although production of the touring cars continued until 1929, and of taxicabs until 1967. GNG

Beattie (GB)

After spending the 1968 season preparing Tim Schenken's successful Formula Ford Merlyn, Charles Beattie, in

Far left, 1922 Ballot 2-litre GP car at the *pesage* for the French GP at Strasbourg. Jules Goux at the wheel. *Photo: T. A. S. O. Mathieson Collection*

Left centre, 1956 Bandini 750cc at a 1957 SCCA meeting at Fort Worth, Texas. *Photo: Autosport*

Above, 1970 Beattie Formula Ford. *Photo: Autosport*

Left below, 1923 Beardmore 2-litre at Shelsley Walsh. Cyril Paul at the wheel. *Photo: Montagu Motor Museum*

Below, 1913 Bédélia cyclecar at the Amiens Cyclecar GP. Bourbeau at the wheel. *Photo: T. A. S. O. Mathieson Collection*

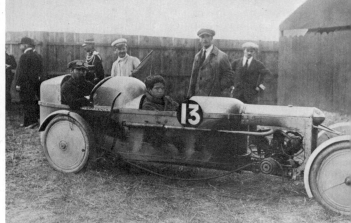

partnership with New Zealander Bruce Smith, designed and built his own cars for 1969. A number of Formula Ford cars and a prototype F100 model were turned out, as well as a monocoque conversion of a Lola T142 F5000 car, built for Irishman Lingard Goulding, and known as the Beattie P1100. For 1971 Goulding asked Beattie to build him an all-new F5000 car. DF

Bédélia (F)

With the British GN the Bedelia was one of the few cyclecars which was specifically built in sporting form, and which achieved many competition successes. The first Bédélia appeared in 1910; it was powered by a transversely-mounted V-twin engine, with chain drive to a countershaft about half way down the chassis, from which drive was taken to the rear wheels by belts. Steering was by the outdated centre-pivot system in which the whole front axle turned with the wheels. It seated two in tandem, the driver occupying the rear seat.

Two special Bédélias ran in the cyclecar races of 1913; they had larger engines of 1,055cc, and needed two men to drive them. The driver proper, at the rear, looked after steering, braking, and the horn, while the man in front, who lay on a kind of hammock, coped with gear changing. These racing Bédélias dispensed with the countershaft, having direct belt drive from the crankshaft to the rear wheels. Bourbeau and Bonville won the 1913 Cyclecar Grand Prix at Amiens at an average of 41·2mph (66·30kph), but came no higher than 10th in the Le Mans event three weeks later.

Bédélias did well at hill-climbs such as Gaillon, and at Brooklands H. Jones took the one hour record for under 1,100cc cars at 45·29mph (77·88kph). The Bédélia survived World War 1, and was made until 1925, but the later cars did not figure in competitions. GNG

Begg (NZ)

Manufactured by George Begg, of Drummond, Southland, the Begg is the only production racing car constructed in any quantity in New Zealand. Begg 1,600cc spaceframe cars, generally powered by Ford twin-cam engines, have enjoyed considerable success in recent years in the New Zealand Racing Cars and Specials Championship series. More recently, the Chevrolet-powered Formula A/5000 Begg FM2 has appeared, the latest version being a monocoque with the engine located by a tubular outrigger rear section. Begg FM2s were driven in the New Zealand section of the Tasman Championship in 1970 by the American Pierre Phillips and former New Zealand speedway rider Geoff Mardon without much success, but have performed quite well in club and national events. Graham McRae scored a notable success when he won the final round of the 1970 Motorsport Association New Zealand Gold Star in an FM2 at Timaru Motor Raceway in February 1970. Based on the McLaren CanAm Group 7 car, a Begg Chevrolet holds the New Zealand speed record. It was set by Lawrence Brownlie at 177·9mph (286·3kph) in May 1969. PG

Bellasi (I)

One of the minor Italian F3 constructors, Bellasi were notable only for the extreme spideriness of some of their offerings until 1970, when the Swiss independent Silvio Moser ordered a Cosworth-Ford powered F1 car from them. They set to and produced a workmanlike aluminium monocoque tub, using the V-8 engine from the Brabham BT24 which Moser had driven in World

Championship events during 1969. A front tubular subframe carried radiator and front suspension; the suspension geometry itself was conventional. DCN

1970 Bellasi-Ford Formula 1 at Zandvoort. Silvio Moser at the wheel. *Photo: David Phipps*

Bentley (GB)

W. O. Bentley's 80 × 149mm ohc 4-cylinder 3-litre was exhibited at the 1919 London Show, but it was not until 1921 that the cars began to reach the public, and that May Frank Clement took Ex. 1, the first of the line, to Brooklands, winning a race at 72·5mph (116·68kph). In 1922 some nearly standard chassis with hc pistons and flat radiators were prepared for Indianapolis and the TT (the modifications were said to cost £25 per car). Hawkes did well to finish 13th in the Indianapolis 500, but in the Isle of Man, Clement was 2nd at 55·21mph (88·86kph), followed by 'W.O.' himself in 4th place and Hawkes in 6th. It was W.O.'s last race as a driver, though he was to act as Birkin's mechanic in the 1929 TT. In 1923 the 3-litre, Duff's car, appeared at Le Mans, still with rwb only, being a private entry with works support. Duff came in 4th behind two Chenard-Walckers and a Bignan, but was back at Le Mans in 1924, winning at 53·78mph (86·55kph). The first works team (Duff/Clement, and Benjafield/Moir) contested the 1925 race, but both cars retired, and the same misfortune attended their 1926 entry, which included a 9ft (274cm) chassis 'Green Label' driven by Gallop/Thistlethwayte, S. C. H. Davis was unfortunate enough to crash his car 20 minutes before the end of the race, giving the Lorraine-Dietrichs a 1-2-3 victory.

Meanwhile in 1925 a special single-seater had been attacking World and International Class records at Montlhéry, eventually taking the World 12-Hour title at 100·96mph (162·40kph) in 1926. The next year was Bentley's *annus mirabilis* at Le Mans, when a multiple crash eliminated both Callingham on the first of the 4½-litres and Duller on a 3-litre, and nearly eliminated 'Old No. 7', the other 3-litre driven by Davis and Benjafield. The damaged car was nursed through to victory after the principal opposition, the Laly/Chassagne Ariès, succumbed to mechanical troubles. There was also a 3rd place for the Birkin brothers in the Essex Six-Hour Race at Brooklands, and a first victory for the 4½-litre in the hands of Clement and Duller in the Grand Prix de Paris at Montlhéry.

By 1928 the 3-litre was outmoded, and the works entered three '4½'s at Le Mans, which offered 110bhp plus as against the earlier model's 88bhp. As much as 250bhp was subsequently extracted from the 4½-litre unit. The cars were entrusted to Clement/Benjafield,

1922 Bentley in the Tourist Trophy. *Photo: Montagu Motor Museum*

73·63mph (118·50kph). Both a works 6-cylinder and Birkin's new supercharged 182bhp 4½-litre were among the Bentleys in the TT, but Kidston crashed the Speed Six, and none of the others was among the leaders. Nor did Birkin's car achieve anything in the BRDC 500 at Brooklands, though Clement and Barclay drove an excellent race in an unsupercharged 4½-litre to win at 107·32mph (172·73kph), and the 6½-litre was 2nd at 109·4mph (176kph). The Barnato/Dunfee Speed Six also took the Six-Hour Race, now under BARC sponsorship, at 75·88mph (122·12kph), and Kidston drove the same car ('Old No. 1') into 2nd place in the Irish GP at Phoenix Park after Birkin's supercharged 4½-litre had broken up the Mercedes opposition.

The 1930 season was the last for the works team. The Speed Sixes of Barnato/Clement and Davis/Clive Dunfee finished 1st and 2nd in the Double-Twelve after Birkin's supercharged 4½-litre, now under the sponsorship of the Hon. Dorothy Paget, had faded out. At Le Mans the official Speed Sixes were joined by the Birkin/Paget team, and Birkin once again obliged by forcing the pace, setting a new lap record at 89·69mph (144·34kph). He retired, but Barnato's and Kidston's 6-cylinder car disposed of Caracciola's Mercedes-Benz which was out by the early hours of the morning, leaving the Bentley to win at 75·88mph (122·12kph). Its sister car, driven by Clement and Watney, averaged 73·73mph (118·66kph) to take 2nd place. Blown cars contested the Irish GP, which furnished Caracciola with his revenge, though Birkin was 4th. Alfa-Romeo dominated the TT at Bentley's expense, but Birkin pulled off an amazing 2nd place, at 88·5mph (142·43kph), in the French GP at Pau, beating Bugattis of less than half the supercharged car's weight. Three of these, including Birkin's single-seater, contested the Brooklands 500, Benjafield and Hall finishing 2nd at 112·12mph (180·43kph). The 1931 event was also a Bentley victory, for 'Old No. 1' at 118·39mph (190·54kph). Birkin continued to race the single-seater '4½', taking the Brooklands lap record at 137·96mph (222kph) in 1931; it did not run there after 1932. Some very fast specials were, however, built, notably the Barnato-Hassan of 1934, which started life with a 6½-litre engine, changed in 1935 for an 8-litre unit, in which form Bertram took the lap record at 142·6mph (229·5kph). Other Brooklands machines were Marker's Bentley-Jackson, and the Pacey-Hassan, which started life as a 4½-litre, but ended up with a bored-out and supercharged 3-litre under its bonnet.

Another remarkable Bentley was Forrest Lycett's special 8-litre. This road-going machine recorded a standing-start mile at 93·4mph (150·31kph), and a flying-start mile at 134·755mph (216·788kph), both when 20 years old.

The acquisition of Bentley Motors by Rolls-Royce resulted in 'The Silent Sports Car', a push-rod 3½-litre based on the 20/25hp Rolls-Royce, but even this raced, E. R. Hall persuading Derby to back his entry for the 1934 TT. His tuned lightweight version came in 2nd behind Dodson's MG at 78mph (125·53kph), and in 1935 he repeated the process. Even with 152bhp he could not defeat his handicap, and this time he lost to a Riley, as he did once more in 1936, though he now had the benefit of a 163bhp 4¼-litre engine. His average speed of 80·81mph (130·05kph) was a record for the Ards Circuit. In 1939 the special overdrive-equipped aerodynamic saloon evolved by Walter Sleator made two successful attacks on the unofficial 'saloon car hour', its second one being done at 114·63mph (184·55kph) in the

Above, 1930 Bentley team in the Tourist Trophy. Beyond the Bentleys are four Alfa Romeos and two OMs. *Photo: Montagu Motor Museum*

Left top, 1930 Bentley 6½-litre at Le Mans. *Photo: Montagu Motor Museum*

Left centre, 1929 Bentley 4½-litre at Le Mans. *Photo: Montagu Motor Museum*

Left, 1929 Bentley 4½-litre in the Brooklands 500-Mile Race. *Photo: Montagu Motor Museum*

1931 Bentley 4½-litre supercharged single-seater. *Photo: Montagu Motor Museum*

Birkin/Chassagne, and Barnato/Rubin, the last pair winning, against Stutz and Chrysler opposition, at 69·11mph (111·23kph). Birkin and Chassagne were 5th.

In 1929 came the 6,597cc 6-cylinder Speed Six (derived from a model current since the 1925 London Show) which offered 200bhp and only once succumbed to mechanical failure, in that year's Double-Twelve at Brooklands, during its racing career. This British event was the make's first race of the season, and the Davis/Gunter 4½-litre only just lost on handicap to Ramponi's 1,500cc Alfa-Romeo. At Le Mans the company ran the Barnato/Birkin Speed Six and four 4½-litres (Clement/Chassagne, Kidston/Jack Dunfee, Benjafield/d'Erlanger, and Howe/Rubin). The result was a triumph for Bentley, with the 6-cylinder car leading three 4½-litres home at

hands of G. E. T. Eyston. Nor was the story over, for H. S. F. Hay ran this machine at Le Mans in 1949, coming in 6th at 73·56mph (118·39kph). He tried again in 1950 but could only manage 14th place, though Hall in the 1936 TT car was 8th. Hay's final effort was in 1951 — a 23rd place is understandable when it is considered that the car had done 92,000 miles.

Bentleys are still seen in action wherever Vintage cars race, and an indication of the performance available was given at Montlhéry in 1960, when Gerald Crozier averaged 120·62mph (194·13kph) in a Speed Six for 100 miles. MCS

Benz (D)

This great pioneer *marque* was almost a byword for plodding reliability; Karl Benz himself disapproved strongly of racing. Inevitably, however, the French agent Emile Roger entered one of the early belt-driven cars for the Paris–Rouen Trials of 1894, and was classified 5th, though he finished 14th in time. The following year he ran his machine under his own name. Muller entered a Benz in the *Chicago Times-Herald* competition in America. This 3hp machine turned up on both occasions, being the sole survivor out of two contestants in the first abortive run-off, and one of only two finishers in the second. Two Benz cars ran in the 1897 Marseilles–Nice–La Turbie race, but by this time others had achieved equal reliability and a lot more speed, and the make's next victory was Fritz Held's in Berlin-Leipzig, achieved on a 16hp 'racing model' with huge frontal V-radiator: replicas were catalogued in London at 750 guineas. Thereafter competitions were ignored until the arrival of Marius Barbarou's unfortunate Parsifal with front-mounted vertical engine and shaft drive in 1902. These big fours had 40hp and started with aiv, though 'modern' T-head units were later used. Barbarou drove one of his Parsifals in the Paris–Madrid without any success, though he finished, and also took 2nd place in his class at the Semmering hill-climb. Once again there were rumours of a Benz entry in the 1904 Gordon Bennett Eliminating Trials, but neither trials nor car materialized.

In 1907 came dual-ignition ioe engines of 8 litres' capacity (8·9 litres where the rules permitted): this 60hp was a favourite of Prince Henry of Prussia himself and won Fritz Erle the Herkomer Trophy. In this, the make's first racing season, Benz secured the services of Victor Hémery, but their record was patchy. All their three entries (driven by Erle, Spamann and de Bojano) finished in the Targa Florio, but their best placing was 15th, and in the Kaiserpreis only Hémery got through to the final, to retire early on without distinguishing himself. The cars did, however, find their form in the Coppa Florio, where Hémery came in 2nd at 62·5mph (100·58kph) and his team-mate Hanriot was 3rd at 60·9mph (98·01kph).

By 1908 Benz were heavily committed to racing, with some 155 × 165mm ohv racers with ht magneto ignition rated at 120hp. Hémery started the season well by winning the 438-mile (705km) St Petersburg–Moscow grind over appalling roads at an average speed of 51·4mph (82·72kph), and in the French Grand Prix only tyre troubles and an eye injury lost him the race to Lautenschlager's Mercedes. He finished 2nd at 67·5mph (108·63kph), closely followed by Hanriot in 3rd place. Erle was a creditable 7th. In America Bergdoll had already driven his 60hp to victory in the Florida 100, and Hémery clinched this by finishing 2nd in the Grand Prize at Savannah with his Grand Prix car at 64·9mph (104·45kph). Hanriot, who had been timed at 100mph

1899 Benz, winner of the Frankfurt–Cologne Trial. Fritz Held at the wheel. *Photo: Daimler-Benz AG*

1900 Benz 16hp racing model. *Photo: Montagu Motor Museum*

1903 Benz 40hp Paris–Madrid racing car. Marius Barbarou at the wheel. *Photo: Daimler-Benz AG*

(160kph) during the race, came 3rd once more, though Erle retired. For the Prince Henry Trials Benz used some similar cars with engines of 6·6 litres capacity (7,479cc in the case of Erle's machine). These engines developed 100bhp, and were said to turn at 2,000rpm — quite a speed in view of the 180mm piston stroke.

Despite the abandonment of serious racing in Europe in 1909 Benz continued to campaign with their big cars in America, where David Bruce-Brown set a new amateur record for the mile at 109mph (175·4kph) and Barney Oldfield did a standing-start mile in 43sec. These later Benz chain-driven racers were enlarged to 15,095cc and were virtually prototypes for the 1912 GP Lorraine-Dietrichs. The firm's efforts in the Prince Henry Trials were not notably successful, but late in the year there

Above, 1908 Benz Grand Prix car. Hanriot
at the wheel. *Photo: T. A. S. O. Mathieson
Collection*

Right, 1910 Benz at Savannah. D. Bruce-
Brown (the winner) at the wheel. *Photo:
T. A. S. O. Mathieson Collection*

appeared a formidable monster, the 21,504cc ohv 4-
cylinder Blitzen Benz racer with cowled radiator and
chain drive, said to develop 200bhp. At Semmering in
September it could manage no better than 3rd ftd, but in
October Hémery covered a standing-start kilometre in a
record 31·2sec, and a month later he did a flying-start
kilometre at Brooklands at 125·95mph (202·68kph).

Successes in America came in 1910. Barney Oldfield
recorded a flying-start mile at 131·72mph (211·93kph) on
the 21·5-litre car, and all the three 150hp cars entered for
the Grand Prize at Savannah distinguished themselves.
Haupt led in the early stages before crashing, and Bruce-
Brown only just beat Hémery to win at 70·55mph
(113·54kph). For the Prince Henry Trials the works
entered some 7,271cc 16-valve ohv cars with elaborate
streamlining and cowled radiators, said to be capable of
3,000rpm. They were certainly the fastest machines in
the event, with a speed of 85·8mph (138·08kph) over the
timed sprint, as against the 80mph (128·75kph) of the
victorious Austro-Daimlers, but though there were seven
Benz in the top twenty, Erle's 5th place was their best. A
good showing in the 1912 Austrian Alpine Trial concluded their serious interest in this type of event.

In 1911 Bob Burman did an unrecognized flying-start
mile at Daytona Beach at 140·865mph (226·708kph) on
the 200hp cars, and a similar machine was used by Heim
to make ftd in the Riesrennen. At Brooklands Hornsted
was achieving a measure of success with a 5·7-litre car
which recorded 103·759mph (166·994kph) over the half
mile, and Bergdoll's 150hp won at Fairmount Park in
Philadelphia. Hearne took 2nd place in the Grand Prize
at 74mph (119·09kph) but on this occasion engine
trouble eliminated Hémery's car. Both the 150hp and

the 200hp were in evidence in 1912, Bergdoll scoring 2nds
in the Elgin Trophy and the Grand Prize. Hornsted
campaigned his example, known to Brooklands habi-
tués as the 'Big Benz', to some purpose there, as well as
winning an event for unlimited racing cars on Saltburn
Sands, Yorkshire, at 90·93mph (146·34kph). Erle made
ftd at Gaillon on the monstrous Blitzen, rocketing up the
hill at a scarcely-controllable 101mph (162·5kph), and he
followed this up the ensuing year with ftd at Limonest.
Benz were still doing well in Russia and took the last two
pre-war St Petersburg Grands Prix, Suvorin driving a
7·3-litre sv shaft-drive 4-cylinder to victory in 1913, and
Scholl's 150hp winning in 1914. Meanwhile Hornsted
had taken one of the 200hp cars back to Britain and tried
hard for the World Hour Record, being defeated by the
Benz's tyre consumption. He did, however, take numerous records, starting with the World standing-start
kilometre at 73·47mph (118·24kph) late in 1913 and
ending with an official flying-start mile at 124·1mph
(199·8kph)—slower than Burman's 1911 performance.

Few German makers could afford serious competition
work in the immediate post World War 1 years, though a
competition version of the 1,570cc ohc 6/18 PS model
won the first race at the AVUS track in 1921. The huge
pre-war Benz machines were still seen, Hornsted driving
a 200hp at Brooklands in 1921, and two of them were
racing there in 1922, in which year Hörner used one at
home to make ftd at Semmering. For 1923, however,
Mannheim made a final bid for Grand Prix honours with
an advanced design from the drawing-board of Edmund
Rumpler. Its dohc 2-litre 6-cylinder engine, which
developed 80bhp, was situated behind the driver, and
crowned by a crescent-shaped radiator. The gearbox had

Below, 1911 Benz 27hp at Brooklands.
Photo: Montagu Motor Museum

Right, 1923 Benz *Tropfenwagen*. *Photo:
Montagu Motor Museum*

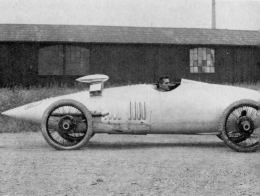

nly three forward speeds, but there were 4-wheel brakes those at the rear were inboard) and swing-axle irs. The Benz *Tropfenwagen* appeared only once in a major ace—the Grand Prix de l'Europe at Monza. Drivers 'ere Walb, Minoia and Hörner, and the two latter nished 4th and 5th. At least one of these cars ran with oad equipment as a sports model, and Walb (later Auto Union's competitions manager) ran a 2-litre Benz in ninor events in 1924, winning at Freiburg. Two years ter the firm merged with Mercedes, and the last Benz ar to race seriously was the veteran four-seater Blitzen. s late as 1930 Cyril Paul lapped Brooklands in it at 15·82mph (186·43kph). MCS

erkeley (GB)
Designed by Laurie Bond of 3-wheeler fame, the Berkeley as an attempt to make a sports car in a lower size and rice than any other on the British market at the time. he first model, which appeared in 1956, had a 322cc ritish Anzani 2-cylinder 2-stroke engine driving the ont wheels by chains. Later Berkeleys used the 492cc -cylinder Excelsior and 692cc 2-cylinder 4-stroke Royal nfield. The latter gave 50bhp at 6,250rpm, and a speed f over 90mph (144kph). The 492cc model won its class a 12-hour Race at Monza in 1959, defeating several barths, and also won its class in the 1959 Mille Miglia. his was after the Mille Miglia had ceased to be a road ace. Berkeleys did quite well in club racing in Britain, nd were raced widely in the United States between 1958 nd 1961, winning the SCCA J production class in 1959 Edward Wright) and I sports racing class in 1958 (Sam Moses), 1960 and 1961 (P. Jeffrey). Production ceased in 961. GNG

erliet (F)
lthough their American cousins, the Alcos, were uccessfully raced, Berliets were seldom seen on the rcuits. Their brief sally into racing followed a class ictory by Bablot, their Marseilles agent, in the 1905 oupe des Pyrénées. In 1906 he drove a 6·3-litre 4-ylinder chain-drive car into 3rd place in the Targa Florio ehind two Italas, and he was 2nd in the TT on one of the naller 3·8-litre machines. Favre took 2nd ftd at the Mont entoux Hill-climb. Rigal and Porporato drove Berliets the 1907 Targa Florio, but both retired, and only one f the three cars entered in the St Petersburg–Moscow ace of 1908 finished the course. The cars did well in aly that year, Porporato's 4th place in the Targa Florio eing followed up in September with an outright win at 5·3mph (105·09kph) in the Targa Bologna. Beutler won ne 1912 Monte Carlo Rally, and one of the 4·4-litre 25hp ars did well at Brooklands in the immediate pre World Var 1 period under the nickname of 'Whistling Rufus'. An abortive appearance at Le Mans in 1923 marked the nd of Berliet's interest in competitions. MCS

erta (RA)
reste Berta made his name with a number of national ngle-seater cars powered by FIAT-based engines, which ere raced in his native Argentina in the late 1960s. For e 1970 Temporada, he obtained sponsorship from the ational newspaper *La Razon* to build a sports car ompetitive with the imported works machines from urope. The result was a neatly-made spaceframe Group car, wide and low, with an ex-Alan Mann Cosworth-ord V-8 engine installed. Named the Berta LR, this ar had a chequered career, being severely damaged both private testing and in one of the two Temporada

events, although it proved very competitive indeed in the hands of Luis di Palma and his rather wild team-mate, Carlos Marincovich. The team brought the car to Europe for the Nürburgring 1,000km race at the end of May 1970, and it went quite well until a water-hose popped off and ended its run. In 1971 a Berta-engined car was rumoured. DCN

Bertelli (GB)
A. C. Bertelli was the designer of the 1½-litre Enfield-Allday, and drove one of these cars in the Brooklands 200 Mile Race and other events in 1922. For 1923 he entered a team of three cars in the 200-Mile Race, under his own name. These had chassis of Enfield-Allday design, but the engines were of the Burt McCollum single-sleeve type, designed by Bertelli, and financed by Woolf Barnato in whose premises at Lingfield, Surrey, they were built. The 4-cylinder units had a capacity of 1,498cc. The exhaust pipes entered the body behind the driver, and emerged from the apex of the tail, as in the 1922 Grand Prix Bugattis. They were driven by Bertelli himself, Woolf Barnato, and J. C. Douglas. Barnato managed to finish, although a long way behind the winners, but his team-mates retired.
In 1924 Douglas raced a modified Bertelli with conventional exhaust system, under the name Larubia. Bertelli later designed a single-ohc 1·5-litre sports car which became the 1927 Aston Martin. GNG

BF (D)
The first success of this make was in the 1924 Avusrennen when a BF car driven by its constructor Fiedler took 1st place in the 1-litre class. Fiedler had experimented with 2-stroke engines for a few years before this success. Subsequently he laid down a small series of cars using his 3-cylinder 2-stroke engine of 1,026cc. It developed 28bhp at 3,800rpm, and maximum speed is said to have been 75mph (120kph).
A 6-cylinder engine was developed, based on the 3-cylinder; capacity was 2,050cc, output 35bhp and maximum speed about 80mph (129kph). A specially developed 4-cylinder model took part in the 1926 Avus-rennen—the first German Grand Prix—but retired after it had made very good times in practice. HON

Bianchi (I)
The Bianchi is the least sporting of the major Italian makes, though the Maserati brothers figure prominently in the story, and Tazio Nuvolari raced the Milanese firm's motorcycles to good purpose in the 1920s. Some 8-litre cars with oversquare 4-cylinder engines supported the 1907 Kaiserpreis, in which Tommaselli finished 18th and Carlo Maserati 23rd. The latter's 9th place was the make's best showing in the Coppa Florio, and none of the five machines entered for the Herkomer Trophy finished in the running.
In the early 1920s their 2-litre ohv Tipo 20 figured in minor Italian events, and there was even a project to build true racers for the 1922 Italian GP, though these never materialized. In 1923 Bianchis once again took 1st and 2nd places in their category of the Touring Car GP at the same track, and 1924 brought two minor wins, at Melfiore (for Ernesto Maserati) and in the Circuit of Tigullio; this latter was Nuvolari's first victory in a 4-wheeler. A Bianchi did quite well in the 1925 fuel-consumption race at Monza, and as late as 1927 Nuvolari drove one in the first Mille Miglia, taking 5th in his category. For a few more years the smaller S4 and S5 ohv

1924 BF 3-cylinder racing car. Designer Fiedler at the wheel. *Photo: Neubauer Collection*

1924 Bianchi 2-litre at Brooklands. Alistair Miller at the wheel. *Photo: Motor*

4-cylinder models appeared in touring and sports car events such as the Giro di Sicilia and the Mille Miglia, but with only modest success. In the 1930 Italian Coppa delle Alpi Frigo had to be content with 3rd place in the 1·5-litre section behind an Alfa Romeo and a Fiat. A team of police drivers turned up for the 1931 Mille Miglia in sports S5s, but Bianchi's best placing was 43rd. In the 1933 event the 'over 1,100cc Utility class' might have been tailored for the model, and Marinelli and Tragella duly captured it: their average speed of 52·23mph (84·06kph) was lower than that of the stock Fiat Balillas in the smallest category, and by 1934 Lancia's Augusta had shut the S5 and S9 out of even this sector of competition. MCS

Bignan (F)

The Bignan's effective life amounted to little more than eight years, but during that period the company fielded an astonishing variety of competition cars. Their entries for the 1920 Grand Prix des Voiturettes at Le Mans were hardly inspiring, as they used 1,400cc T-head 4-cylinder units said to give 27bhp. These, however, worked well

1924 Bignan 2-litre sports. *Photo: Montagu Motor Museum*

enough to let Nougué finish 2nd and Delauney 3rd behind a Bugatti. In 1921 came a 16-valve 3-litre ohc sports car with fwb and low, streamlined four-seater bodywork which could attain 100mph (160kph) on 96bhp, and gave Guyot a win in the Grand Prix de Corse. However, it was not produced in series, the standard big Bignans being fairly ordinary 2·9-litre and 3·5-litre affairs. For 1922 the company fitted a Causan-designed 2-litre unit with desmodromic valve gear, from which 70bhp was extracted; this car retired in the Grand Prix de Tourisme, though Gros took 3rd place (and the class honours) in the Belgian GP. De Marne also drove a Bignan into 4th place in the Bol d'Or; but the firm's 1100s were in fact one hundred per cent Salmson, except that the radiators were without the Cross of St Andrew.

The *desmodromique* had gone by 1923, replaced by another ohc 16-valve unit giving 75bhp from 2 litres, and Chenard-Walcker-type front-wheel and transmission brakes were now provided. This was the most successful of the competition Bignans, and in the first Le Mans 24 Hour Race Gros and de Tornaco finished 3rd and de Marne and Martin 4th. Martin also won the San Sebastian Touring-Car GP at 56·5mph (90·93kph), Matthys's car repeating this success in 1924, when the factory tried their luck with a 3-litre six. This offered 124bhp, but it retired both at Le Mans and at Spa, though at the former venue the de Tornaco and Barthelemy 2-litre came 10th and in the Belgian race another 4-cylinder (Springuel and Becquet) won at 48·7mph (78·38kph), with a second Bignan in 3rd place. Ledure also won the Monte Carlo Rally on a standard 2-litre saloon.

By 1925 the 2-litre was giving 80bhp, and Clause won the Marne GP; there was also a victory at Comminges though the make could do no better than 14th at Le Mans. Lowered chassis and 85bhp engines featured in 1926, when Clause was 2nd at Comminges and 4th in the German GP at Avus (where he averaged 81mph (130·36kph)), and Gautier finished 3rd in the Marne GP. The Bignan faded out when leading the field in the Monza 24 Hours, and attempts to keep things going with tank bodies and superchargers in 1927 were of no avail. The cars retired at Reims and the Nürburgring, and the 2-litre's final success was 3rd place in the touring-car race at San Sebastian for Clause and Gros. MCS

Birel (I)

Ernesto Brambilla built the original Birel F3 car in 1966/7, a conventional spaceframe model looking markedly like a Brabham and using a modified Ford engine with many Novamotor parts. Brambilla scored a number of successes with the car, including a very high-speed win in the 1967 Fina GP at Monza, and his exploits earned him a drive for Ferrari in 1968. His younger brother, Vittorio, began racing the updated Birel and he was also quite competitive with this interesting car. DCN

Bluebird (GB)

The name Bluebird was first used by Malcolm Campbell in 1912 for his 1906 Darracq which he was racing at Brooklands at the time. Between the wars it was applied to the series of Land Speed Record contenders driven by Campbell, and after World War 2 to another LSR car built by his son Donald. The various Bluebirds can be classified as follows:
(1) 1927 Napier-Campbell with 23·9-litre 12-cylinder Napier-Lion engine developing 500bhp. The cylinders were arranged in three banks of four. The car had a conventional chassis, Perrot-type front wheel brakes and a

was set slightly ahead of the other, so the 1935 Bluebird actually had a shorter wheelbase on one side than on the other. With this car Campbell achieved 276·82mph (445·53kph) at Daytona in March 1935 and 301·13mph (484·65kph) at Bonneville in August 1935. This was the last LSR attempt by Sir Malcolm Campbell who then turned his attention to the Water Speed Record.
(7) The gas turbine car built in 1956–9 for Donald Campbell. This used a Bristol Proteus gas turbine developing over 4,000bhp, driving all four wheels through two David Brown gearboxes. The body was built by Motor Panels Ltd of Coventry, and the car was assembled in their works. It was 30ft (9·144m) long and 8ft (2·4384m) wide, with 52in (1·3208m) wheels. In its first attempt on the record at Utah in September 1960 it crashed, but was re-built as Bluebird II. A new attempt was made at Lake Eyre, Australia, and after many vicissitudes a speed of 403·1mph (648·8kph) was achieved in July 1964. The car is on display at the Montagu Motor Museum, Beaulieu, Hampshire. GNG

Blue Crown see Indianapolis Cars

BMC (GB)
When the British Motor Corporation was formed in 1952, Austin were almost inactive in motor sport and Morris completely so. MG were giving surreptitious and unapproved assistance to some selected drivers. Donald Healey was applying his considerable experience to the design of the Healey 100, soon to become the first Austin-Healey. In late 1954 the MG chief, John Thornley, gained permission to reopen the Abingdon competitions department, closed since 1935. It was soon renamed the BMC Competitions Department, with Marcus Chambers as manager. The new department was to concentrate on rallies, using any suitable BMC model. Racing and record attempts were, with a few exceptions, left to MG's development department and the Donald Healey Motor Co at Warwick.

British prestige in rallying was low at the time: from 1955 to 1961 inclusive, only five championship rallies were won by British cars and crews. BMC's first season brought a few minor awards with largely unsuitable cars like the MG TF and Austin A90. In 1956 a privately-owned Austin A30 won the Tulip Rally with little works assistance. Team cars gained rather more class awards, and Nancy Mitchell won the ladies' European rally championship driving MGAs and Magnettes. She re-

constant-mesh gearbox. It set a new record of 174·88mph (281·43kph) at Pendine in February 1927.
(2) 1928 Napier-Campbell; the same car as above, but with a 950bhp Napier engine and new body, the result of wind-tunnel research, with wheel fairings and a large tail-fin. Surface radiators were mounted on each side of the tail, so that the front could be fully streamlined. This car achieved 206·96mph (333kph) at Daytona, Fla., in February 1928, a record beaten two months later by the Triplex Special's 207·55mph (333·98kph).
(3) A modified version of the above, with frontal radiator, taken to Verneuk Pan, South Africa, in 1930, but failed to beat the Golden Arrow's 231·44mph (372·46kph).
(4) A completely new car built in 1931 with 1,450bhp supercharged Napier-Lion engine as evolved for the Schneider Trophy seaplane, offset transmission and Gurney Nutting body. It reached 246·09mph (396kph) at Daytona in February 1931 and 253·97mph (408·71kph) in 1932, both of these being new records.
(5) 1933 version of above, with 2,500bhp Rolls-Royce 'R' engine whose weight/power ratio was only 11oz per horsepower. The chassis was lengthened, giving an overall length of 27ft (8·230m). This car achieved 272·556mph (438·59kph).
(6) 1935 version of above. Although using the same engine, the car was completely rebuilt by Thompson & Taylor, with much lower lines than the previous car, and servo-powered air-flaps. To provide maximum traction Reid Railton designed a rear axle in which two bevels on the propeller shaft each drove a crown wheel with its own axle shaft attached to it. To provide clearance, one shaft

Top, 1927 Bluebird (Napier-Campbell 23·9-litre). *Photo: Montagu Motor Museum*

Above, 1964 Bluebird at Lake Eyre, Australia. *Photo: Montagu Motor Museum*

Below, 1928 Bluebird at Brooklands. *Photo: Montagu Motor Museum*

Right below, BMC: two Austin A35s at Barnby Moor during the 1957 Monte Carlo Rally. *Photo: Associated Press Ltd.*

Above, BMC: Austin-Healey 3000s in the 1961 Alpine Rally; the Shepherd/Gott car leads that of the Morley twins. *Photo: Motor*

Left, BMC: c 1964 Mini-Cooper S in a Swedish Rally. *Photo: Pe O Eriksson*

Above, BMC: 1969 Mini-Coopers at Brands Hatch driven by Spice and Rhodes. *Photo: Autosport*

Left, BMC: 1970 British Leyland Maxi (Rosemary Smith, Alice Watson and Ginette de Rolland) approaching Trieste in the World Cup Rally. *Photo: British Leyland*

peated this success in 1957. With a BMC-prepared Austin A35, a Cambridge University team averaged 74·90mph (120·54kph) for seven days at Montlhéry. Two significant occurrences were the addition to the BMC rally team of Pat Moss (who had been training since 1954 with an MG TF and other cars), and the transfer to Abingdon of Austin-Healey 100-Six production, replacing that of the Riley 1·5.

In 1958 the new Austin-Healey Sprite was announced based on the Austin A35 and also built at Abingdon, and the dohc version of the MGA appeared later in the year. There was now a wide choice of promising cars, all of which the team used together with the Minor 1000. Pat Moss and Ann Wisdom made full use of them to win the ladies' championship, their greatest achievement being 4th overall in the 4-day Liège–Rome–Liège or 'Marathon' with the 100-Six, which also took the team prize. In the Alpine, the 100-Six finished 2nd in category and Sprites were 1-2-3 in class. A 100-Six driven by the Cambridge team averaged 97·13mph (156·32kph) for 10,000 miles at Montlhéry.

The summer of 1959 brought the more powerful Austin-Healey 3000 and the original Mini-Minor to join the new-type Austin A40. The 'big Healey' was 2nd overall in the German Rally and 4th in the RAC, with the Sprite 2nd in the RAC and 2nd in category in the Alpine. Many class and team awards were claimed with the two Healey models and the Austin A40. By 1960 the team was ready for its first big successes: 1st and 3rd in the Marathon, 2nd in the Alpine, and 2nd and 3rd in the RAC Rally. The Morley brothers and the Moss and Wisdom partnership used the big Healey, and Sprinzel was prominent with the Sprite. As 'Ecurie Safety Fast', the BMC team won awards in almost every event entered. The girls won their second ladies' championship and were elected Drivers of the Year by the Guild of Motoring Writers. Almost unnoticed, the new Mini-Minor won its first few class awards in international rallies.

A slightly leaner year followed in 1961. The big Healey won the Alpine driven by the Morleys, who gained the only Coupe des Alpes awarded. It was 2nd in the RAC and 3rd in the Acropolis Rally. Again a host of awards was won with the two Healey models, but this was the last year the team used the Sprite. With extensive experience of the BMC A-type engine in Formula Junior, John Cooper was developing the Mini-Minor, and the 997cc Mini-Cooper was announced in September. John Whitmore won the BRSCC saloon racing championship with his Mini-Minor. In October, Marcus Chambers handed over the BMC Competitions Department to Stuart Turner, a skilful rally co-driver and strategist.

Now the new Mini-Cooper began to challenge the supremacy of the successful 'big Healey', winning the 1962 Tulip, Swedish, German and Routes du Nord rallies. To the Austin-Healey went the Alpine, and 2nd and 3rd in the RAC. In all, 18 major awards were won with the Mini and 12 with the Healey. The new MGB was announced in October, and John Love won the saloon racing championship with a Surbiton-tuned Mini-Cooper. During the year, Turner hired Hopkirk, Mäkinen and Aaltonen. Ann Wisdom married in March, and Pat Moss left the team (having won the ladies' championship for the third time) at the end of 1962.

As the new team settled down with each other and the new 1,071cc Mini-Cooper S (announced in April 1963), there came another thin year relieved by some major achievements. Mäkinen's Healey won the GT category of the Monte Carlo. No outright winner was declared for

BMC: Timo Makinen, Mini-Cooper S, in the 1965 Swedish Rally. *Photo: Rolf Sundh*

BMC: 1971 Mini Clubman 4wd in Lydden Hill Rallycross. Brian Chatfield at the wheel. *Photo: Autosport*

the Alpine, but the Touring category went to Aaltonen's Mini, and these cars also took the team prize and other awards. In the 10-day Tour de France, Hopkirk's Mini startled the European motoring world by finishing 1st on index and 3rd on scratch. The big Healey continued to win its class, plus 2nd in category on the Tulip, decided by a curious handicap system. Privately-entered Sprites won the Circuit of Ireland and the International Police Rally. The new 'hot Minis' were prominent in racing.

Things started with a bang in 1964 when Hopkirk's Mini won the Monte Carlo outright, BMC took the team prize, and the Morleys' MGB won the GT category. After that, the department's demands for special parts enjoyed a better response within BMC. The new 1,275cc version of the Mini-Cooper S won the Tulip Rally on its first outing, and came 4th in the Touring category of the Alpine. The big Healey at last won the Marathon—the last one held as a road event—and also the Austrian Alpine, together with the GT category of the Tulip, a category 2nd in the Alpine, and 2nd overall in the RAC. Private Minis won the Welsh and Silvretta Mountain rallies. Warwick Banks took the European saloon racing championship with a Mini, and Jackie Stewart the *Express and Star* Formula 3 championship with a BMC-powered Cooper. The year ended with six out-right and 55 class victories in international rallies, 51 in international races, and ten individual championships.

In 1965 rally organizers began to favour the very strict requirements of Group 2 regulations, which left the much-developed Healey almost high and dry in the GT category with little chance of outright victories. However, the BMC competition department found that with the right crews and efficient organization, the standard Mini-Cooper S could still be a rally winner if dismantled and carefully reassembled with painstaking attention to detail. The BMC team now consisted of the Morleys (who specialized in driving the Healey), Hopkirk, Mäkinen and Aaltonen as drivers of really exceptional ability, and three brilliant co-drivers in Ambrose, Liddon and Easter. Behind them lay the department's ten years of experience in international rallying. It was to pay great dividends in the next two years, with a record of successes unapproached by any other manufacturer so far.

In near-impossible weather conditions, Mäkinen fought through to win the 1965 Monte Carlo, his Mini the only unpenalized car on arrival. The BMC Minis also won the Circuit, the Geneva, the Czechoslovak, the Polish, the Finnish 1,000 Lakes, the Three Cities and the RAC Rally; in the Tulip they made best performance but were classified 3rd on the 'class improvement' handi-cap. Private owners won the Basco-Navarrais, the Flowers and Perfumes, the RAC Rally, the Lorraine, the Austrian Gold Cup, the Bodensee, the Saragossa, the Armagnac and the Portuguese rallies. The big Healey took a category 2nd in the Alpine, 3rd in the Geneva, 4th in the Tulip, and 2nd overall in the RAC on its very last appearance. Aaltonen, Ambrose and Mäkinen occupied the first three places in the rally championship; it was the first time the championship had been won with a British car, seven of the 13 events in the series going to either Aaltonen or Mäkinen. BMC cars won a total of 17 international rallies in the year, with a total of 116 major awards in rallies and races of international status. By the end of the year the team's supremacy unchallengeable.

But 1966 started with an unpleasant setback. The BMC Minis finished 1st, 2nd and 3rd overall to perform an incredible two-way hat-trick in the Monte Carlo Rally. The organizers stripped the cars to the last nut and bolt,

failed to find any mechanical component that infringed the strict Group 2 regulations, then disqualified all three because the headlamp dipping system was non-standard. World-wide publicity brought little consolation to the drivers.

However, they went on to win the Circuit, the Tulip (now run on a scratch basis), the Austrian Alpine, the Scottish, the Czechoslovak, the Polish, the 1,000 Lakes and the Three Cities rallies. Hopkirk won the Acropolis, but a much-disputed penalty dropped him to 3rd place. The team were also 3rd on the Alpine, and 2nd on the Geneva and RAC rallies. A complicated subdivision into categories spoiled the rally championships, but BMC won six of the 14 events in the series, a total of 15 inter-national rallies, and 106 major awards. International races brought the total up to 165, with particular success by Minis in New Zealand and Australia, where one 500-mile saloon race produced the astonishing sight of Minis filling the first 10 places. The Austin-Healey did not appear at all; in fact the Morley brothers retired before the 1966 season opened.

In 1967 the team faced several problems. Constant bickering with rally organizers was upsetting both them and their competitors. The Mini needed major redevelop-ment to face the challenge of the dohc Lotus Cortina, and it was not forthcoming; instead, the department was pressed to use the somewhat unwieldy BMC 1800. Stuart Turner left early in the year and his successor, Peter Browning, placed more emphasis on racing and record attempts.

Revenge was enjoyed at Monte Carlo when Aaltonen's Mini won the 1967 event; it was, Hopkirk and Aaltonen agreed, 'his turn anyway'. BMC won the Circuit, the Acropolis (another revenge), the Danube with an 1800, the 1,000 Lakes and the Alpine. No outright winner was declared for the Tulip Rally, but they finished 1-2-4 in category and took the team prize. They were 2nd in the Rally dei Fiori, and 3rd in the Swedish and Geneva rallies. Private owners brought the total of international rally victories up to 10. A works Mini came 2nd in the 84-hour Nürburgring 'Marathon' that had replaced the old Liège–Rome–Liège road event, and Minis won the usual collection of races in New Zealand and Australia. A BMC 1800 took an impressive array of class E records at Monza, averaging 92·80mph (149·35kph) for seven days and covering 25,000km at 92·78mph (149·32kph).

Within the camp, however, it was known that the mechanics had to work miracles to get the ageing Minis to the finish of an event. Experiments with crossflow heads and fuel injection could only bring results in Group 6, and no effective chassis development was being done. In 1968 the new dohc Ford Escort came into prominence, and for the first time since 1959, the BMC team won not a single international rally. They finished 3-4-5 in the Monte Carlo, 2nd in the Scottish, 3rd in the Tulip, 4th in the 1,000 Lakes and RAC, and 5th in the Acropolis. All the 1800s retired from the Safari Rally, but one car finished 2nd in the London–Sydney Mara-thon.

The Leyland take-over of BMC came in May 1968, and at the end of the season Mäkinen and Aaltonen left the team, together with all the co-drivers. The department continued its existence under the new name of British Leyland Competitions Department, with a drastically reduced programme of activities concentrating on the more publicized events such as rallycross and the World Cup Rally, until it was closed down completely in the summer of 1970. FWMcC

BMW (D)

One of the first notable BMW competition successes was gained with the 3/15PS, which was a development of the Dixi, a licence production of the Austin Seven. A team of three cars won a class victory in the 1929 Austrian Alpine Trial. The first real BMW to be successful in competitions appeared in 1934, the Type 315/1. It was based on the 315 and in common they had the 1,490cc 6-cylinder engine but the 315/1 had three carburettors and an output of 40bhp compared with the 34bhp of the standard version. The Type 319/1 (based on the 319) supplemented the 315/1 in 1935; engine capacity became 1,910cc and output 55bhp. Both models were very successful in competitions and achieved a great number of class victories in the 1·5- and 2-litre class. It was the advent of the 315/1 — and its capture of the team prize in the 1934 Austrian Alpine Trial — that led to the cooperation between BMW and Frazer Nash. The Type 326 with its famous 1,971cc engine of 66 × 96mm had its début at the 1936 Berlin Motor Show. This engine was also used in a sports version and Ernst Henne — famous for his world records on BMW motorcycles — won the 1936 Eifel-rennen at the Nürburgring with this car, which from 1937 was made in two-seater sports form as the Type 328. The 50bhp of the 326 was increased to 80bhp which enabled the car to do 100mph (160kph). The overhead valves, set at 90°, were operated by cross-push-rods. The 2-litre sports car class became a BMW preserve in the following years. The Tourist Trophy, the Bucharest Grand Prix, the AVUS, the Grand Prix des Frontières, the Francorchamps 24 Hours, the German Grand Prix, the Tobruk–Benghazi–Tripoli, Le Mans and the Mille Miglia are simply the most significant events appearing on the list of BMW victories up to 1939. In 1940 BMW gained an overall victory in the abbreviated Mille Miglia with a streamlined coupé version of the 328 driven by Baron von Hanstein and Bäumer, at an average speed of 103·5mph (166·6kph); this car was the ultimate pre-war development of the 328. The output was about 130bhp at 5,000rpm and the maximum speed was 125mph (200kph). It was at this stage that development of the 328 engine was taken up after World War 2, for example by Frazer Nash to whom BMW handed all construction details in 1945.

The end of the war brought nationalization of the BMW plant in Eisenach (see EMW). Original BMW 328 cars and several BMW derivations (Veritas, AFM, Monopol and a number of one-offs) appeared and were dominant in sports car and Formula 2 races for a few years. Production of cars was begun in the Munich works in 1952. A series of 6- and 8-cylinder prestige cars offered no successor to the pre-war sports cars and precipitated a crisis for the company. Only the Type 507 with a V-8 engine of 3·2 litres and 150bhp was a true sports car in appearance and performance. During 1959 and 1960 it competed in the GT class in various hill-climbs and gained a number of successes, very often driven by Hans Stuck, notably at Freiburg, the Swiss Hill-Climb Grand Prix, Gaisberg and Rossfeld.

BMW abandoned the big models and after an interlude with the Isetta and the Type 600 launched the 700 in 1959. The rear engine was an air-cooled opposed twin of 697cc which in the sports version developed 40bhp. It took part successfully in touring car events. The Type 700 RS was a special works version using certain 700 components. It had a tubular spaceframe and a shortened wheelbase, and the engine was placed ahead of the rear axle instead of behind and developed 70bhp at 8,000rpm.

Above, 1940 BMW Type 328 Mille Miglia coupé. *Photo: BMW*

Right, 1940 BMW Type 328 Mille Miglia, photographed in 1965. *Photo: H-O Neubauer*

Above, 1970 BMW 2002 TI saloon at Helsinki. Kauko Eriksson at the wheel. *Photo: Top-Foto*

Right, 1968 BMW Monti Hill-Climb car with Lola T120 chassis. Dieter Quester at the wheel. *Photo: Autosport*

Next BMW developed a range of touring cars, starting with the Type 1500, followed by the 1800, which appeared in various versions and designations. In 1964 the 1800 TI scored its first victory in a touring car event at Trier, driven by Hubert Hahne, who became synonymous with further BMW successes. The 2002, introduced in 1968 and developing over 200bhp in the works-prepared versions, brought BMW their greatest post-war successes in international competition and was a true touring car compared with the Porsches and Alfa Romeos, its main rivals in touring car races.

In 1966 a prototype BMW single-seater made its debut in the Aldrans hill-climb near Innsbruck. It used a 2-litre 4-cylinder engine with a special cylinder head designed by Ludwig Apfelbeck. This used 16 valves (two inlet and two exhausts per cylinder) disposed radially in the combustion chambers and operated by a complex mechanism from two overhead camshafts. Its output was around 260bhp at 8,000rpm and it was mounted in an ex-F1 Brabham chassis.

This engine was reduced to 1·6-litres for the new Formula 2 starting on 1 January 1967, and with an output of about 225bhp it was used in Lola T100 chassis raced by John Surtees' Lola Racing team. The engine was tall, heavy and unreliable, and after making an unsuccessful debut at Snetterton, best results of the year were Surtees' second and Hahne's fourth places in the Eifelrennen.

The 2-litre engine was used in a spaceframe Lola Group 7 chassis for the European Mountain Championship—driven by Quester—and at the beginning of 1969 the Munich company began running their own Formula 2 works team. They used developed Lola chassis initially before Len Terry-designed and Dornier-built monocoques became available. The Apfelbeck layout had been replaced by two-by-two exhaust and inlet valves in a new head design, and the 64 × 89mm, 1,596cc M20 unit produced some 225bhp at 10,300rpm. A two and sometimes three car team was fielded, with special streamlined bodies being used on faster circuits such as Reims and Vienna but results were still meagre with only two second places and a fifth in the entire series. Mitter crashed fatally during practice for the German GP probably due to a suspension failure, and the year ended miserably.

For 1970 the team continued development of their Dornier-built chassis and signed Ickx, Siffert, and BMW regulars Hahne and Quester to drive them. Development engineer Dieter Basche also proved himself a capable pilot, and Hahne won the second Hockenheim race, Siffert won at Rouen, Ickx at Salzburg and Tulln-Langenlebarn, and Quester at the final Hockenheim meeting and Neubiberg, after which the BMW directors announced their withdrawal from racing and the laying-up of their four cars and 12 engines. BMW's final fling with the single-seaters came in the Formule Libre Macau GP, when Quester won easily with a 2-litre model.

Ickx's Salzburg victory marked the introduction of a new engine with crossflow cylinder head and the valves repositioned yet again, inlets and exhausts now facing each other side-by-side. Three plugs per cylinder were retained, and mid-range power output was raised by some 7bhp although it dropped off after 9,000rpm in contrast to the earlier top-endy units. Sadly this unit's full potential went unrealised. HON/DCN

BNC (F)

The original BNC light cars were developed from the Jack Muller cyclecars, and went into production at the works of Bollack, Netter et Cie of Levallois in 1923. The

1969 BMW 2002TI in Welsh Rally, driven by Roy Fidler and Barry Hughes. Photo: Hugh W. Bishop

Right, 1970 BMW Formula 2 at Thruxton. Jacky Ickx at the wheel. Photo: Doug Nye

Below, 1970 BMW Formula 2 streamlined version, Dieter Quester at the wheel. Photo: Studio Wörner

sports model used an ohv Ruby engine of 1,095cc, and took part in rallies such as the Paris–Pyrenées–Paris and Tour de France, as well as the Boulogne Light Car Grand Prix where Bucciali (later to build his own cars under the name Buc) finished 3rd. In 1925 came a new BNC with 1,100cc SCAP engine, and this model established the make as a serious rival to the Amilcar CGSs. Alternative engines were the 1,088cc Ruby DS and 1,097cc Ruby K, the latter giving 60bhp and a speed of 100mph

1935 BNC 996cc (Duval/Treunet) passing Delaroche's wrecked Riley at Le Mans. *Photo: Autocar*

(160kph). At the end of 1925 a BNC was catalogued with a supercharger, a vertically-mounted Cozette; it was probably the first supercharged car to be sold to the public in France. The supercharged short-chassis model became known as the Montlhéry, the unsupercharged short-chassis the Monza, and the long-chassis the Miramas. For 1927 a new car with sloping radiator was introduced, and this Model 527 became the best-known BNC. They achieved many sporting successes, including 1st and 2nd in the 1927 Bol d'Or (Mme Violette Morris and Lefevre-Despaux), and 2nd in the 1927 24-Hour Sports Car Race at Montlhéry, behind Clement and Duller's Bentley (Doré and Pousse). Doré and Treunet were 7th at Le Mans in 1928, the firm's best performance in that event. For the 1929 Le Mans race they entered two 1,100cc cars, of which one was a Lombard in disguise, and a four-seater car with 1,500cc Meadows 4ED engine; all retired. A few Meadows-engined cars were sold to the public.

Production of BNCs ended in 1931, but parts were taken over by the Garage Siréjols who assembled a few cars for several years, and supported an active sporting programme. Thus BNCs ran at Le Mans each year from 1931 to 1935, albeit without great success, and also in the Bol d'Or (3rd in 1932, 2nd in 1935). André Siréjols was still racing a supercharged BNC in vintage events in 1970. GNG

Bobsy (US)

Bobsy Cars of Medina, Ohio, began production in 1962. Jerry Mong is the manager. The firm makes the Bobsy, Vanguard and Vega, Formula Vee and sports racing cars. Charles Dietrich won the 1963 Sports Car Club of America 'G' modified honours driving a Bobsy-II, powered by a 1,100cc Holbay-Ford. A Bobsy-Saab and Bobsy-Osca won SCCA 'H' modified championships in 1965 and John Igleheart's Bobsy-Ford led the 1967 'H'

modified category. In Formula Vee a Bobsy captured the 1965 SCCA Central Division title. ARB

Bolide (F)

Bolide cars had large horizontal engines of 2 or 4 cylinders, and belt or chain drive. Although they were high machines, with vast vertical radiators, they took part in many of the town-to-town races between 1899 and 1901. The chief drivers were Lefèbvre, by whose company the cars were built, and Champrobert, although Jenatzy drove one in the initial Gordon Bennett race of 1900. They were never very successful, the highest placing being Champrobert's 6th position in the Paris–St Malo race of 1899. Most of the racing was done with the 15hp 2-cylinder car, whose capacity was 5,304cc, but in 1900 and 1901 Lefebvre drove a vast 4-cylinder machine known variously as a 30hp or a 40hp, with a capacity of 11,692cc. After 1902, Bolides had vertical proprietary engines by De Dion, Aster, or Tony Huber, and the 16hp car that Floiret entered for the Paris–Madrid in 1903 was one of these. Early Bolides were made in Belgium by M. Snoeck of Ensival. Jenatzy covered a flying kilometre at 63mph (101·39kph) in a Snoeck in 1900. GNG

Bolster (GB)

The original Bolster special, known as Bloody Mary, was built in 1929 by John and Richard Bolster whilst they were still at school. An ash frame was made, to which various cyclecar running parts were grafted, and a front-mounted 760cc JAP engine. This was replaced first by a 981cc sv, and then by one, and later two 981cc KTOR ohv units, coupled one behind the other. With only 784lb (356kg) to propel, John was extremely successful in sprint events both before and after World War 2, taking some fastest times of day and numerous class awards, albeit mostly sideways. Richard Bolster, who was killed during the war, also made a less successful ut more conventional special, while John spent from 1937 to 1939 fruitlessly attempting to perfect a fearsome machine with no less than four V-twin engines. DF

Bond (GB)

The first Bond 500 was a very small and simple design, which achieved some good results in shorter events where the lack of suspension was less of a disadvantage. Laurie Bond's C-type production model, with suspension by friction discs with rubber couplings and front-mounted JAP engine, was heavier and not competitive with the contemporary Coopers. In 1961 the Lancashire firm offered a front-drive Formula Junior model, but this did not make a mark on the circuits. DF

Borgward (D)

Though the Hansas which preceded this make had been in production since 1906, their only competition success had been the team prize in the 1914 Austrian Alpine Trial. Carl Borgward was, however, responsible for the first new touring-car design to come out of Germany after 1945, the 1500 of 1949. In 1950 a 66bhp streamliner based on this model took 12 international class records at Montlhéry, including 1,000 miles at 107·3mph (172·7kph). Further Class F records fell in 1952 on a later 1·5-litre, and in 1953 a special car based on their 1800D diesel saloon added 14 more in Class E to the score.

The first stirrings in the competition car field were seen at the 1951 Frankfurt Show, where the company displayed a 135bhp dohc 1,500cc prototype with 5-speed gearbox, but conventional push-rods and a hemispherical head were used by Karl Brandt for the first of his *Rennsports,* which had coil-and-wishbone ifs and a De Dion back axle. The engine was giving 100bhp by 1952, but throughout its racing career Borgward were always handicapped by lack of money, lack of time to spare from their production car programme, and excess weight. The 1952 season was promising, with a victory at 121·54mph (195·56kph) at Grenzlandring, and a class win at the AVUS.

A new engine with Isabella block (touring-car components were always liberally used in racing Borgwards) and designed from scratch for fuel-injection was installed for the 1954 season, when Bechem won the Eifelrennen, and he and Hammernick were unlucky to be eliminated by crashes when they were leading the Porsche opposition in the Carrera Panamericana. There was a 1,600cc class victory in the 1955 Mille Miglia, but otherwise Brandt used this season to develop a new twin-cam wet-liner 5-bearing unit said to give 150bhp at 7,200rpm. By the end of its career it had been worked up to 172bhp, but 1956 was a bad year, and a lightweight car with space-frame built in 1957 was never duplicated. Herrmann's 2nd place in the 1957 European Mountain Championships was followed by a better season in 1958. At the Nürburg-ring in April transmission trouble eliminated the *Rennsports,* but at the German GP meeting later in the year the Porsches had a hard fight, Borgwards taking 2nd, 4th and 6th places. In the Freiburg hill-climb, however, Bonnier put up a brilliant performance, his time of 7min 32·6sec being an absolute record, beating both Hans Stuck's pre-war time with the Auto Union, and Zeller's record on a BMW motorcycle. In spite of this, the cars from Bremen still failed to win the Mountain Championship, though they took 2nd and 3rd place behind von Trips's Porsche.

The 90mph (144kph) Isabella TS distinguished itself in saloon-car racing, with class victories at Spa and in the Gran Premio Argentino in 1957, and in 1956 Reg Parnell had won his category of the Production Touring Car Race at the *Daily Express* International Trophy Meeting at Silverstone. Later the One-Point-Five Rileys got the better of the German cars until W. B. Blydenstein managed to extract more power. His personal Isabella UUV 75 had a long and distinguished record in saloon-car racing. With output raised from 75 to 84bhp the car's career culminated in a victory in the 1961 Spa Touring-Car Race at 93mph (149·67kph), beating Riley, Alfa Romeo and Volvo in the process. Borgward engines were also used by Revis and Cooper in England. MCS

Bowin (AUS)

The Bowin is the brainchild of Australian designer John Joyce who worked for five years in England as project engineer for Team Lotus and later as design engineer for Lotus components. Joyce was in charge of the team which produced the very successful Lotus Europa sports car. Returning to Sydney in 1968, Joyce began his Bowin project, designing his first monocoque construction car for Queensland driver Glynn Scott who raced it with a Cosworth FVA 1,600cc engine. The car features independent suspension, wheels of Joyce's own design and weighs only 810lb (367·4kg). The rolling chassis cost (Aus.) $12,000 to produce. Only three F2 cars have been built—two with monocoque frames and one with a spaceframe. The rest are Formula Ford cars.

The Bowin Formula Ford is of spaceframe design, based on the Formula 2 car. But it is so light it must carry 14lb (6·35kg) of ballast to bring it up to the minimum weight for the class of 882lb (400kg). The original Formula Ford cost $8,000 to design and construct, but rolling chassis are now selling for $3,500. TBF

Brabham (GB)

Jack Brabham's Motor Racing Developments Ltd is Europe's largest builder of formula racing cars. The cars have achieved long lists of victories all over the world, and have always reflected the sound engineering talent of Brabham and his partner Ron Tauranac. In the late 1950s Brabham persuaded Tauranac, who had worked on Jack's first real racing car, a Cooper Mark IV, in Australia, to join him in Britain. Their first car was a Formula Junior machine of 1961, called an MRD after Motor Racing Developments. By the time that Formula Junior came to an end in 1963, Brabham had built 32 cars for the Formula which had been dominated by his products, leading drivers being Denny Hulme and Frank Gardner. Brabham's first Formula 1 car, powered by a Coventry-Climax V-8 engine, appeared late in 1962. It was of spaceframe construction, with conventional suspension and 6-speed Colotti gearbox. It made its début in the German GP and retired after about two-thirds of the race. The 1963 and 1964 seasons were ones of continuous development of the spaceframe construction, and the cars came to be regarded as conventional but superb in handling. Their successes included the Australian, Solitude and Austrian GPs in 1963, all with Jack Brabham at the wheel, Aintree and Silverstone *Daily Express* Trophy (Brabham), Mediterranean GP (Siffert) and Mexican GP (Gurney) in 1964. At the same time the factory was producing and selling all over the world fine Formula 2 and 3 cars, the F3 cars dominating the 1965 season. They also built 12 BT8 sports cars with 2-litre Coventry-Climax engines; with one of these Denny Hulme won the 1965 TT.

For 1966 Brabham turned to a relatively cheap

1948 Bond 500 at Altcar sprint meeting. *Photo: G. N. Georgano Collection*

1958 Borgward *Rennsport* at Gaisberg hill-climb. Joakim Bonnier at the wheel. *Photo: Martin Pfundner*

1968 Bowin P3 Formula 2 car at Lakeside. Leo Geoghegan at the wheel. *Photo: Peter Geran*

Left, 1961 Brabham MRD Formula Junior prototype. *Photo: Doug Nye Collection*

Below, 1962 Brabham-Climax BT3 Formula I at Oulton Park Gold Cup. Jack Brabham at the wheel. *Photo: John F. Whitmore*

Above, 1966 Brabham-Repco BT20 Formula I at Brands Hatch. Jack Brabham at the wheel. *Photo: Autosport*

Left, 1969 Brabham-Ford BT30X Formula 2/3 on test at Silverstone. Tim Schenken at the wheel. *Photo: Nigel Snowdon*

above, 1963 Brabham-Climax BT8 sports
t Brands Hatch. Frank Gardner at the
heel. *Photo: Patrick Benjafield*

ight, 1970 Brabham-Ford BT33 Formula I
t Brands Hatch. Jack Brabham at the
heel. *Photo: Autosport*

development of the General Motors aluminium V-8 block using single-ohc heads. Designed by the brilliant Australian Phil Irving within the Repco Group, the Repco engine in the uncomplicated and proven 1965 spaceframe chassis with outboard suspension was an instant success, not only on reliability but also on weight and handling. It won Jack Brabham his third World Championship, in 1966, as well as the Manufacturers' Championship, a unique achievement. In 1967 Denny Hulme won the Drivers' Championship for himself and the Manufacturers' Championship again for Brabham. In his Formula 2 cars Brabham had an extremely successful 1966 season using untried Honda engines. He and Hulme won 12 of the 15 races, and two others were won by the Winkelmann Racing Team Brabham-Cosworth driven by Jochen Rindt. The 1968 Formula 1 cars used the Type 860 Repco engine with four overhead camshafts and four valves per cylinder, but they had a lot of mechanical trouble, and their best placings were 3rd and 5th in the German GP (Rindt and Brabham). A Brabham F2 chassis with 2·5-litre Alfa Romeo engine won the 1968 Australian Championship for the Mildren Team and driver Kevin Bartlett. In 1969 Brabham turned to the Cosworth-Ford engine for his Formula 1 cars, and ran a two-car team for himself and Jackie Ickx. Ickx won the German and Canadian GPs, and although Brabham had only a fair season, the make finished 2nd in the Manufacturers' Championship. In Formula 2 Brabhams were not so successful in 1968 and 1969 as they had been in previous years, and their Formula 3 cars met stiff opposition from Matra and Tecno.

Through all this Brabham had stuck to spaceframe construction for all his cars, and it attracted buyers because the frames were easier to repair after an accident than a monocoque, particularly in countries away from the home factory. He did produce a monocoque in 1968 for Indianapolis, but his F1 cars did not go that way until 1970 with the BT33. With this car Jack Brabham won the South African GP and finished 2nd at Monaco and Brands Hatch. The spaceframe design was continued in 1970 with the F2 BT30 in which Derek Bell finished 2nd in the F2 Drivers' Championship. TBF

Branca *see* Moretti

Brasier *see* Georges Richard

Brawner (US)
Clint Brawner began building midgets in his hometown of Phoenix, Ariz., in the mid-1930s. In 1953 he became chief mechanic for Al Dean and for almost fourteen years Dean Van Line Specials were among the most successful on the USAC Championship Trail. Although nineteen Brawner cars have qualified for the Indianapolis 500 and

Brawner-prepared cars won six USAC National Drivers championships and over 50 individual USAC championship races, it was not until Andretti captured Indy in 1969 that a Brawner machine entered victory lane there. One of the first chief mechanics to adapt the monocoque rear-engined principle, the original Brawner-Hawk rear-engined cars were based on Brabham designs. In 1970 Clint Brawner and his colleague, Jim McGee, ended their six-year association with Mario Andretti to work with the Indianapolis veteran, Roger McCluskey. ARB

Briham *see* Elden

Bristol (GB)
The Bristol Aeroplane Co's 1,971cc 6-cylinder luxury tourer, introduced in 1947, was based on the pre-war BMW, and its chief claim to fame was that the company supplied their engine to specialist constructors, notably Frazer Nash, Cooper, Lister, and AC. The American Arnolt was a joint effort with bodies made by Bertone in Italy. In competition form the Bristol unit was worked up from the 85bhp of the original 400 series to the 130bhp of the later BS 4s.

Designed primarily as fast tourers, the earlier Bristols did, however, figure in competition. The make's first victory came in the 1948 Polish Rally by the Czechs Dobry and Treybal, who had optimistically opened an agency in Prague. They followed this up by taking 3rd place in the 1949 Monte Carlo and winning the 1950 Czechoslovak event; meanwhile, in 1949, 400s had run in the Mille Miglia, the Alpine and the Targa Florio. Only in the first of these was there modest success: a 3rd place in the 2-litre touring category for Lurani and Aldington. However, Lurani, now partnered by Cortese, went on to win the touring-car class of the Coppa Toscana. Bristol 401s were 3rd and 4th in the big-car class of the 1951 RAC Rally; Sleigh and Porter won their class in the 1952 Tulip; and the Banks and Porter car came 2nd overall in this event the following year.

At the end of 1952 Bristols purchased the Bristol-powered Formula 2 G-type ERA, and used this as the

Right, 1953 Bristol 450 coupé. *Photo: Bristol Aeroplane Co*

basis for three aerodynamic sports-racing coupés, the 3-carburettor 450s with tubular frames and De Dion back axles. The team's debut at Le Mans in 1953 was disastrous, but they went on to win their class in the Reims 12 Hours, and also took some International Class Records at Montlhéry, including 200 miles at 125·87mph (202·6kph). The Bristols turned up for both these French races in 1954, finishing in line ahead on both occasions (7th, 8th and 9th at Le Mans, and 10th, 11th and 12th at Reims) and taking the 2-litre honours on the former occasion. In 1955 the cars ran as open two-seaters with tail fins, and their performance at Le Mans was almost a repeat of 1954. Thereafter Bristols became heavier and more expensive, disappearing even from rallies. MCS

BRM (GB)

Automobile Developments Ltd was formed by Raymond Mays and Peter Berthon from funds raised by the British Motor Racing Research Trust. Their first car (Type 15) was supposed to be racing in 1949, but was not completed until December of that year. Two-stage centrifugal superchargers, built by Rolls-Royce, fed Berthon's ambitiously-designed 135° V-16 engine of 1,496cc swept volume, driving to a 5-speed gearbox in unit with a ZF limited-slip differential. The next year was dogged by many problems: numerous testing difficulties, driveshaft failure on the car's debut in Sommer's hands at Silverstone, overheating at Barcelona. Reg Parnell won an unimportant race at Goodwood and gave some heart to the many supporters who had faith in the enterprise.

During 1951 a few placings were achieved, but rectification of some of the problems only served to reveal others, notably the poor handling (possibly caused by deflection of the front suspension arms supporting the Lock-heed air struts), and the lack of sufficient engine torque for Grand Prix type circuits. The engine was achieving most of its designed revs, made an ecstatic noise, and pushed out around 450bhp, but this alone was not enough. Disc brakes were fitted for 1952, but following the withdrawal of the Alfa Romeo works team most Grand Prix organizers took to Formula 2, and the BRM suffered an untimely relegation to inconsequential Formule Libre events. Three cars had been built.

A disillusioned Trust sold out at the end of 1952 to Alfred Owen, one of the foremost of the original sponsors, who built one more car—the shorter, lighter 1954 Mark 2 version. (One of the original cars was also converted.) Performances in 1953 flattered to deceive, but during 1954 and 1955 only six victories were recorded out of eleven starts in Formule Libre races, mostly of little importance. The cars were never really reliable, and the torque and handling problems remained to the end.

In 1955 the Type 25 was built for the 2·5-litre formula, contrasting in its simple 4-cylinder engine with the complexity of the earlier car. The De Dion rear-axle layout, with integral gearbox and final drive, was retained with transverse leaf suspension. The disc brakes tended to grab at inopportune moments, and the turbo-cooled transmission brake was not altogether a success. This car was not popular with drivers, and although Behra won at Caen, Brooks, Collins, Fairman, Flockhart, Mackay Fraser, Hawthorn, Leston, Salvadori, Schell and Trintignant all tried before Bonnier notched up the marque's first Championship win at Zandvoort in 1959—a triumph of perseverance for the sponsors and developers. The car now had different brakes, a smaller frontal area, and coil suspension at each wheel. The end of the year saw tests at Monza with the rear-engined Project 48.

Left below, 1953 BRM V-16 at Goodwood. Fangio at the wheel. *Photo: J. C. Green*

Left bottom, 1957 BRM Type 25, 2·5-litre. Harry Schell at the wheel. *Photo: Doug Nye Collection*

Below, 1961 BRM-Climax 1·5-litre. Jack Fairman at the wheel. *Photo: Doug Nye Collection*

Bottom, 1966 BRM Type 83, 3-litre H-16. *Photo: Doug Nye Collection*

bove, 1970 BRM P153 3-litre V-8 at
rands Hatch. Jackie Oliver at the wheel.
noto: Autosport

ght, 1970 BRM P154 7·5-litre Can-Am at
dmonton. George Eaton at the wheel.
noto: Autosport

963 BRP 1·5-litre V-8 at Zandvoort. Innes
eland at the wheel. *Photo: Autosport*

The 1960 season proved to be yet another unlucky one, and although Dan Gurney and Graham Hill managed some high placings, no further victories were recorded. The 1·5-litre car for 1961 was originally equipped with the 4-cylinder Coventry-Climax engine, and had a power/weight ratio inferior to its rivals. BRMs own motor first appeared at Monza, and the following year the 1,498cc V-8 powered the lighter Type 56 to the marque's *annus mirabilis*, becoming World Champions; Graham Hill also took the Drivers' Championship with victories in the Dutch, German, Italian and US Grands Prix.

During 1963, 1964 and 1965 both Hill and BRM held their heads high, with 2nd place in the Championships. Hill scored an amazing double hat-trick of victories in these years in the Monaco and American GPs. A new crank enabled over 11,000rpm to be used, and in 1964 fuel injection was pioneered, the V-8 giving nearly 200bhp. Engines were sold to BRP, Gilby, Parnell, Scirocco and Siffert. A duralumin semi-monocoque developed by Tony Rudd was used in 1963, and handled rather better than the full monocoque introduced in 1964. Stewart joined the team in 1965 and won at Monza.

In 1963 a modified GP chassis was used as the basis for the gas-turbine Rover-BRM two-seater which finished an unofficial 7th at Le Mans, covering 2,592·5 miles (4,172·19km) in the 24 hours. A sleek coupé, prepared for the 1964 race, was entered in 1965, but dirt in the compressor caused a power loss, and Jackie Stewart and Graham Hill finished no higher than 10th.

For the 3-litre formula introduced in 1966 great things were expected of the P83, with H16 engine based on the cylinder blocks of the old 1·5-litre V-8. Unfortunately the cars suffered continual breakages in both engines and transmissions, and for two years almost the only relief was a run of victories in the Tasman series with a 2-litre version of the V-8. Len Terry came to the rescue with the P126 60° V-12 design, developed later at the team's Bourne headquarters as the P133. They made an auspicious works debut in the 1968 South African GP, when Mike Spence and Pedro Rodriguez finished 1st and 2nd, but Spence was killed soon after and Rodriguez commenced a long sequence of ill luck. By this time the 2-litre V-8, which had proved such a useful standby engine not only for the works but also for other works teams and for many private entrants, was too old to be competitive. Relief from the doldrums was afforded by Peter Lawson, who took the RAC Hill-Climb Championship with the

experimental 4wd car built in 1964. In doing so he followed a tradition of using BRMs on hills initiated by Tony Marsh, who had made use of one of the stubby and manoeuvrable 2·5-litre cars in taking this Championship in earlier years.

John Surtees and Jackie Oliver were the 'new boys' in the team in 1969, campaigning with the V-12 P138 and P139 cars throughout the season with no success, although the 4-valve-per-cylinder engines were turning out some 450bhp at 10,000rpm. Although Oliver's luck during 1970 grew worse and worse, Rodriguez returned to the team and took the Belgian GP with the improved P153, sponsored by the Yardley cosmetics firm. He and Oliver were 4th and 5th in the Austrian GP. The P160 for 1971 was 4in wider than its predecessor, and had inboard rear brakes.

Although selling engines and old works cars quite freely to selected private buyers and rival organizations, BRM remained unique among British racing-car manufacturers in never offering new vehicles for sale. Furthermore, they had from the beginning concentrated on Formula 1, and so there was much speculation when the P154 'Can-Am' car, designed by Tony Southgate, was announced. It was a conventional monocoque design, with Chevrolet 7·5-litre engine and Newland transmission, and first appeared at Mosport in 1970 in the hands of team driver George Eaton. His best 1970 place was 3rd at St Jovite. DF

BRP (GB)

The British Racing Partnership cars were originally built in 1963 for Formula 1, with BRM V-8 engines. Innes Ireland scored a victory for the monocoque design in the *Daily Mirror* Trophy race at Snetterton in March 1964, but thereafter the cars were plagued with minor troubles and accidents, and the highest placings achieved by team drivers Ireland and Trevor Taylor in Grands Prix were a couple of 5ths. Tony Robinson designed a new monocoque for the 1965 Indianapolis, with a Ford V-8 engine, but the cars of both Masten Gregory and Johnny Boyd retired. Plans for a range of other models came to naught, but there was still hope in 1966, when Carl Williams started at Indianapolis and John Willment placed an entry in the Italian GP for a car rebuilt by Paul Emery with a Tecalemit fuel-injected Godiva V-8 engine giving 312bhp. When these attempts failed the make was allowed to die, although one car was still racing in Australia and New Zealand in 1970. DF

Buc (F)

The first cars built by the Bucciali brothers were racing cars powered by vertical twin and V-4 2-stroke engines, which they made for their own use. They raced them at the Boulogne Grand Prix des Voiturettes in 1922 and 1923, finishing 3rd in the former year, and in hill-climbs. In 1924 they went into production with the AB5, a conventional light car with 4-cylinder SCAP engine of 1·6 litres capacity. Sporting models of this were built and raced, and it was followed in 1926 by the AB6, with specially-built 1,489cc single-ohc engine. This car developed 70bhp, and had a maximum speed of 105mph (169kph). Only one was made, which was raced in a number of French events, and in the San Sebastian Grand Prix of 1927, where it finished 8th.

From 1928 to 1933 the brothers built a number of fwd cars with 6-, 8-, 12-, and 16-cylinder engines, but though some were of dramatic appearance, none was a sports car. In 1928 de Maleplane drove a car entered under the name Bucciali in the National Trophy Race at Boulogne, finishing 6th. In fact, it was a 1·5-litre sleeve-valve Guyot Spéciale renamed. GNG

Buckler (GB)

Buckler's speciality was the construction of chassis to special builders' requirements: as a result, the number of Bucklers raced under other names probably exceeded those which admitted their parentage. Frames were built for several of the early 500 racers, including the second Smith special with Norton engine. Other engines ranged from Morris 10 to Lincoln Zephyr V-12, and from 1947 onwards a Ford 10-engined kit-built car was available, suitable for and successful in the 1172 Formula. The heyday of the Buckler was from 1952 to 1959, when no less than six different standard models were on offer at the same time, and an impressive list of British trials, sprint and racing successes were being recorded by W. A. Liddell, W. G. Marriott, M. C. Parrott, G. Tapp, C. Waddup and many others, including Derek Buckler himself. DF

Bugatti (D;F)

Ettore Bugatti achieved some sporting successes, including hill-climbs, with cars of his own design before setting up as an independent manufacturer at Molsheim, near Strasbourg, in 1910, but his first noteworthy result was Friderich's 2nd place in the 1911 GP de France in the diminutive 1·4-litre Bugatti Type 13. In 1914, Friderich drove a 5-litre 'Garros' model Bugatti at Indianapolis but retired with axle trouble after 425 miles when well placed.

Racing was resumed after World War 1 by the entry of three cars in the Voiturette GP at Le Mans, in 1920.

Left, 1926 Buc AB6 at Montlhéry. *Photo: Autosport*

Above, 1961 Buckler 1172cc at Silverstone. M. Fielden at the wheel. Photo: Michael Ware

Below, 1911 Bugatti Type 13 at the start of the Grand Prix de France. Friderich at the wheel. *Photo: Hugh Conway Collection*

Bottom, 1914 Bugatti Type 13 at the 1920 GP des Voiturettes at Le Mans. Friderich at the wheel. *Photo: Hugh Conway Collection*

These were 16-valve, 1·4-litre Type 13 cars, originally prepared for a similar event in August 1914, cancelled because of the war. Friderich won the event after the withdrawal of de Vizcaya in one of the cars, Baccoli in the third car being 5th. If this win caused much favourable comment, the victory at Brescia in 1921 in similar cars caused a sensation, Friderich again coming 1st, at 72mph (115·87kph) with team-mates 2nd, 3rd and 4th.

In 1922, the new 8-cylinder 2-litre car was entered for the French GP at Strasbourg. Nazzaro on a Fiat came i

1st but Bugattis were 2nd, 3rd, and 4th, albeit some way behind the leader. A short while later the same cars ran at Monza but de Vizcaya could only manage a 3rd place. The next year saw the appearance of the strange 2-litre 'tank' Bugattis at the French GP at Tours, no match for the more refined and less unorthodox Sunbeams and Fiats. Friderich did well to manage a 3rd place at 70·8mph (113·94kph) compared with Segrave's Sunbeam at 75·3mph (121·18kph).

A few months before the Tours GP the 1922 cars, re-bodied with single-seater coachwork, ran at Indianapolis; engine failure caused the withdrawal of four cars, only the fifth, that of Prince de Cystria, managing to keep going to finish 9th.

Meanwhile Bugatti was having many successes in short-distance races and hill-climbs with the Type 13 Brescia models. Raymond Mays had many outstanding wins in hill-climbs in England with his two sprint cars, Cordon Rouge and Cordon Bleu.

It was at Lyons for the French GP of 1924 that Bugatti produced his sensational Type 35 aluminium wheel car of unquestionably fine appearance and remarkable performance shortly to be demonstrated. In the event he was dogged by continued tyre trouble; although the car showed its promise he could only manage 7th place (Chassagne) and 8th (Friderich) to the winning Alfa

Romeo of Campari. Later that summer the car ran again and Costantini came in 2nd to Segrave's Sunbeam at San Sebastian. In 1925 the car began to show its form, winning the Rome GP (Masetti), leading brilliantly in Sicily in the Targa Florio (Costantini) — the first of five wins there in succession — and in 1·5-litre form it won the Italian Voiturette GP.

Next year the Bugatti swept all before it, although there was less opposition as Sunbeam, Fiat and Alfa Romeo had withdrawn from racing. In this year too Bugatti at last abandoned a stand against supercharging and introduced blown 1·5- and 2-litre versions (the 35B 2·3-litre car came in 1927). In 1926 the car won the European Championship with successes at Rome; in the Targa Florio; in the French GP; the European event at San Sebastian; at Monza for the Italian and Milan GPs; back to San Sebastian for the Spanish GP; and a 2nd at Brooklands in the British GP.

In 1927 again the Targa Florio and the Rome and the San Sebastian GPs; it was in this year that the Delage 1·5-litre car was insuperable with Benoist winning all the major GPs. At the end of the year Delage gave up racing. For the next three years racing was somewhat in the doldrums, and the Bugatti 35B had matters more or less its own way, with outstanding wins in the new round-the-houses race at Monaco, and in the French GP.

Below, 1923 Bugatti Type 30 prepared for Indianapolis. Pierre de Vizcaya at the wheel. *Photo: Hugh Conway Collection*

Right below, 1926 Bugatti 1,100cc in the GP d'Alsace; the winner, André Dubonnet at the wheel. *Photo: Hugh Conway Collection*

Bottom, 1931 Bugatti Type 53 4wd car. *Photo: Hugh Conway Collection*

Right bottom, 1932 Bugatti Type 55 at Lewes Speed Trials. *Photo: Autocar*

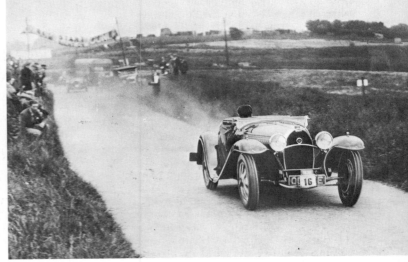

It was clear by 1931 that the 35B needed more power and the new twin-ohc version, Type 51, appeared in April 1931. It made a good start with wins that year at Monaco (Chiron), Montlhéry (Chiron and Varzi), Spa (Williams and Conelli), Tunis (Varzi), Morocco (Czaykowski) and Czechoslovakia (Chiron). Similar successes were recorded in 1932 and 1933 but after this the model itself was eclipsed by the more powerful Alfa Romeos and Maseratis, to be put in the shade in turn by the German titans.

At this time Bugatti also produced a few 4·9-litre Type 54 cars, which were difficult to handle and never very successful: the most notable results were 1st and 2nd places (Varzi and Czaykowski) at AVUS in 1933; and Czaykowski and Kaye Don at Brooklands British Empire Trophy race in that year. Czaykowski was killed later at Monza in his car.

In 1930–31 Bugatti produced a 16-cylinder racing chassis, the engine having two geared banks of 8 cylinders and the model being known as Type 45. It was never properly developed but was tried out on one or two occasions by Chiron (e.g. ftd at Klausen, and Bernina Pass, both in Switzerland, 1930).

In 1931–2 Bugatti designed a 4-wheel-drive racing car, building two prototypes. These cars had the 4·9-litre supercharged engine from the Type 54, and suffered in not having constant velocity joints in the front transmission — this affecting steering — and no doubt would have benefited from more modern developments as produced by Ferguson. Notwithstanding the poor handling the cars had several successes in hill-climbs (1932 La Turbie, Wimille; Klausen, Chiron; 1933 Wimille repeated his win at La Turbie; 1934, Dreyfus won there, and in 1935 Benoist at Château Thierry — all fastest times of the day).

The final racing car produced in quantity was the 3·3-litre Type 59, which first appeared in 2·8-litre form at San Sebastian in 1933. These most beautiful cars, perhaps the last 'real' racing cars of classic appearance, had a few wins in 1934 (Dreyfus at Spa, and Wimille at Algiers) and some places (Monaco, Dreyfus 3rd; Spain, Nuvolari 3rd), but the expense of the team was too much for Molsheim and the cars were sold off to private owners in England at the end of the year.

In 1935 Benoist drove a few laps in a new version of the Type 59, with a new twin-ohc engine of 4·7-litres (known as the 50B), and a pair of more normal sports Type 57 models ran in the Ulster TT (Lord Howe, 3rd). Wimille himself had a few places in a Type 59 which had been

Left, 1934 Bugatti Type 59. *Photo: Hugh Conway Collection*

Above, 1938 Bugatti 3-litre GP car. Jean-Pierre Wimille at the wheel. *Photo: Hugh Conway Collection*

retained by the works. In 1936 Wimille also drove a 4·7-litre single-seater (2nd place in the American GP), and shared in the driving of the 57G 'tank' cars which first appeared at the French Grand Prix. A team of three cars was built, Wimille and Sommer winning. In 1937 one of the cars won the 24-hour race at Le Mans (Wimille and Benoist), and then the final success was in 1939, just before World War 2, when Wimille won again at Le Mans with Veyron as co-driver, this time with a modified 'tank' using a 3·3-litre engine from the Type 57C touring car.

Wimille turned up again that year in the 4·7-litre single-seater at La Turbie and Prescott, and six years later drove it again in the Bois de Boulogne in the 1945 'Coupe des Prisonniers' — the last occasion when a Bugatti was entered by the factory in a race, if no account is taken of an abortive attempt to produce a car (Type 251) in 1956 long after Bugatti himself had left the scene.

Since then Bugattis have been seen only in vintage or historic racing, the earlier 35 and 51 models gladdening many a heart and eye with their performance, appearance and sound. HGC

Buick (US)

The original flat-twin ohv Buick was quite a performer, and was already participating in minor events in 1905. In 1906 it set a new record at Eagle Rock hill-climb as well as winning at Mount Washington. By 1908 Bob Burman was driving for Buick, taking 2nd place in the Savannah light-car event on a 4-cylinder model. Buick took stock-car racing seriously in 1909, their 'circus' running to 15 cars and a staff of 40; Lewis Strang and the brothers Louis and Arthur Chevrolet were among the team. Victories included the Cobe Trophy and the Atlanta 200 (Louis Chevrolet), New Orleans (Burman), and a 100-mile stock-car event at Ormond-Daytona (Strang). Here also Burman raced his Buick against an early biplane and won, and the Chevrolets came 3rd in the 6th Brighton Beach 24. The inaugural meeting at Indianapolis that year was almost a Buick benefit, with a 1-2-3 victory in a 5-mile sprint — and a win for Burman in the 250-mile event.

Louis Chevrolet won a stock-car event at the Brickyard in 1910, in which year Buick campaigned with a special racer, the 4-cylinder 'Bug' of over 550ci (9 litre) capacity. This added more awards to the company's score, as well as being timed at nearly 106mph (170kph) at Indianapolis. In England, the small 144ci (2·7-litre) 15/18hp cars (sold as Bedford-Buicks) did well at Brooklands, a special race being staged for the make in

912. One of these won a Gold Medal in that year's Russian Reliability Trials. By contrast neither of the two cars entered for the 1913 Coupe de l'Auto finished, and Buick did not return to racing in any form till the period of the Junk Formula at Indianapolis, when 6-cylinder and straight-8 engines were found in some of the specials fielded between 1930 and 1933.

In 1940 there was another curious Buick-based special, Briggs Cunningham's Bu-Merc, *alias* a 320ci (5·2-litre) Century 8 masquerading as an 'SSK' Mercedes-Benz. This one took 2nd place at Watkins Glen in 1948, but more exciting and even uglier were Max Balchowsky's stark 'Old Yallers' using 326ci (5,350cc) Buick V-8 engines with fuel injection. Hauser won at Santa Barbara in 1957 on one of these, and they continued to race to some purpose in America until 1960, Balchowsky himself finishing 2nd (behind a Ferrari) at Palm Springs in 1958. In 1962 Mickey Thompson sought to apply the small 215ci (3·5-litre) V-8 unit to the Cooper-like cars he had entered for Indianapolis, but though output was boosted from 185bhp to some 330, only one car (Gurney's) qualified, and that retired with transmission disorders. MCS

BWA (I)

This Italian F3 manufacturer came to the fore in May 1965 when Giacomo Russo won a minor F3 race at Barcelona in Spain in one of their cars. Massimo Natili and Enzo Corti raced BWA-Fords later in the season, winning at Vallelunga, but no major success came their way. Several chassis were sold in 1966, and Channel Islander Boley Pittard drove a works car in Italian events, with Corti, and came 2nd at Mugello and Monza. The cars were never really competitive in the face of Brabham, Matra and even De Sanctis and Tecno opposition, but Chris Craft drove four races with them in 1967. During 1968 the monocoque BWAs were still raced in private hands, Corti taking several good places in international European events. But the manufacturer had run short of money, and faded from the scene, having seldom ventured outside Italy and building only a limited number of chassis. DCN

Caban (F)

Between 1926 and 1932 the racing driver Yves Giraud-Cabantous built a number of small sports and racing cars powered by Ruby engines, under the name Caban.

The earliest Cabans used the 30bhp Ruby Type OC engine, but from 1928 onwards the 38bhp Type OS was employed; some cars of 1931 and 1932 employed the still more powerful Type K developing 43bhp. Racing Cabans of 1931-2 used the K engine with Cozette supercharger giving 60bhp and 105mph (168kph). Capacity of all these engines was 1,097cc. A total of 19 sports and racing Cabans were built, and many successes were achieved in races and hill-climbs. The most notable were Giraud-Cabantous' victory in the 1930 Bol d'Or, with Roger Labric in 3rd place (Cabans took the first four places in their class), 2nd in the 1930 Circuit de Dieppe (Just Vernet), 1st in the 1931 Circuit de Torvilliers (Giraud-Cabantous), 2nd in class in the 1931 Le Mans race (Vernet and Vallon), and 2nd in class in the French GP in 1931 (Georges Monneret) and 1932 (Cabantous). In 1933 lack of capital forced Giraud-Cabantous to abandon car production, but he continued to have a very successful racing career for many years. GNG

Caldwell see Autodynamics

Calthorpe (GB)

G. W. Hands of the Calthorpe concern drove his 2·8-litre 16-20hp with distinction in the 1908 Irish Trials, but more ambitious was an entry in that year's Four-Inch TT. The Calthorpes had short-stroke 4-cylinder Alpha engines, and Porter's car finished 4th at 47mph (75·64kph). Even braver was support for the 1909 Coupe des Voiturettes with a team of round-radiatored 1,775cc cars (still Alpha-engined fours) which managed 8th and 9th places in the heyday of the grotesque Lion-Peugeots. Hands was racing his cars at Brooklands in 1910, when the company tried again in the French light-car race, this time using long-stroke (65 × 170mm) sv 4-cylinder units of their own manufacture, which gave 30bhp as against the 22bhp of the older type. All the team retired, but their 1911 successors had 2,848cc units and could do 80mph (128kph), and used 4-speed overdrive gearboxes. Burgess's 6th place was nothing spectacular, nevertheless a Calthorpe was 3rd in the hill-climb run in conjunction with the Coupe des Voitures Légères.

The 1912 Coupe de l'Auto Calthorpes were the last of their line, but even on 68bhp they had no success. A promising small car appeared in 1913, the 1,094cc sv 4-cylinder Minor, which managed a flying mile at Brooklands in standard trim, won a 6-hour event at 51·75mph

Left, 1931 Caban, winner of the 1,100cc at Le Mans, driven by Vernet and Vallon. *Photo: courtesy Yves Giraud-Cabantous*

Right, 1912 Calthorpe Coupe de l'Auto car. Burgess at the wheel. *Photo: Montagu Motor Museum*

(83·28kph), and also collected the cyclecar class on formula at Shelsley Walsh. A tuned version (surprisingly with 2-speed gearbox) was prepared for Burgess to drive in the 1914 Cyclecar GP, but this event, scheduled for September, had of course to be cancelled. This led the way to the 1,260cc Sporting Four of 1919, which was guaranteed to do 60mph (96kph) and had some success in sprints. In 1921 there was a works-prepared racer with the same engine boosted to give 30bhp at 4,000rpm in a new chassis with ultra-narrow single-seater bodywork. It had a long career in the hands of Whale, who won several races at Brooklands between 1924 and 1926, and persuaded it to lap at over 84mph (135kph). In 1927 a Meadows engine replaced the original Calthorpe unit. MCS

Camen (I)

The Camen was an unconventional Italian 1,100cc racing car from Naples, which first appeared in 1927 when Mario Esposito scored two class victories in the Naples and Avellino sprint meetings, beating Salmson and Amilcar opposition. Two Camens were built, having supercharged 1,036cc V-4 two-stroke engines and ifs by Lancia-like vertical coil springs. Both ran in the 1928 Targa Florio, Sirignano lying second in the 1,100cc class only to retire on the last lap. That the car was very quick off the mark was shown by Esposito, who secured class victories in the Sorrento hill-climb both in 1928 and 1929, and in the Agnano hill-climbs of 1928 and 1930. He also demonstrated that a blown 2-stroke can last out a road race by finishing 3rd to Fagioli's Salmson and a Fiat in the 152·2 miles (245km) Prince of Piedmont Cup race at Avellino in 1928. A Camen driven by Jossa gained an 1,100 class victory as late as 1931, in the Autumn Cup sprints at Naples. CP

Cannon (GB)

Mike Cannon, operating from his Kentish home, constructed such a large number of trials specials that he virtually killed his own market. Design was based on a simple tubular framework, usually with Ford 10 sv engine and mechanical parts, but with several special features, such as the separate 'fiddle' handbrakes to each rear wheel. In the hands of such protagonists as multiple champion Rex Chappell, the Cannons and Cannon derivatives took the main British trials awards through most of the 1950s and 1960s. From time to time Cannon also made special GT models of original design, but eventually he decided that the construction of trailers was more remunerative than cars. DF

Cannstatt-Daimler see Daimler (D)

Case (US)

The J. I. Case Company of Racine, Wis., were old-established makers of threshing machines and agricultural machinery who built cars from 1910 to 1927. For a few years they pursued an active racing programme, entering teams in many dirt-track events in the upper Middle West and Southern Canada from 1910 to 1916, and running cars at Indianapolis in 1911, 1912, and 1913. The 1911 entries were conventional 4-cylinder cars with artillery wheels and bolster tanks, but for 1912 Case prepared two beautifully streamlined machines with cowled radiators, pointed tails and wire wheels. None of the Case entries in 1911 or 1912 finished, but undaunted, they entered three cars in 1913. These returned to conventionally stark appearance, and two of them had chain drive. The third was a 6-cylinder car with shaft-drive. This and one of the 4-cylinder cars retired, but the other 4-cylinder car driven by Louis Disbrow, finished in 8th place.

Eddie Hearne drove a Case in the 1915 Vanderbilt Cup, but did not finish, and apart from this Case's racing activities were confined to the dirt tracks. Here they used a variety of vehicles from stripped stock chassis to the monster Jay-Eye-See (JIC), which was actually a re-bodied 200hp Fiat, usually driven by Louis Disbrow. GNG

CD see Panhard

Cegga (CH)

The name of this small concern is derived from those of the brothers *C*laude *E*t *G*eorges *G*achnang, and *A*igle where the cars are made. The Gachnangs specialize in all-round independent suspension and tubular chassis or spaceframes in which are installed engines by well-known makers. Their first car was the Cegga-Bristol, with tuned 1,971cc engine giving 130bhp at 5,750rpm, in a tubular frame and two-seater coupé body designed and built at Aigle. Driven by Georges Gachnang and André Wicky, it finished 22nd at Le Mans in 1960. Next came the Cegga-Ferrari, a sports car with 3-litre V-12 engine and irs which ran twice in the Nürburgring 1,000 kilometres, and once in the Pescara 4-Hour Race, as well as in Swiss hill-climbs. For 1962 they built a Formula 1 racing car, the 1·5-litre Cegga-Maserati, using a 5-speed gearbox from a Maserati Tipo 63 sports car. More successful in hill-climbs than in racing, it was followed by a 2-litre Cegga-Maserati which broke the record for the Lens-Crans hill in 1964, and a 3-litre Cegga-Ferrari racing car. GNG

Left, 1964 Cannon trials car driven by Geoff Newton. *Photo: Motor Sport*

Below, 1912 Case. Louis Disbrow at the wheel. *Photo: Indianapolis Motor Speedway*

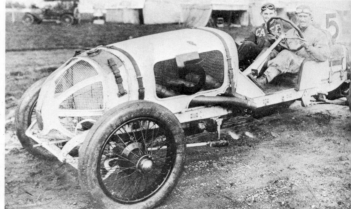

1924 Ceirano in the Coppa Nissena, Sicily. Ignoto at the wheel. *Photo: T. A. S. O. Mathieson Collection*

Right, 1903 CGV 30hp racing car. Fernand Charron at the wheel. *Photo: G. N. Georgano Collection*

Right below, 1905 CGV 100hp Gordon Bennett racing car. Léonce Girardot at the wheel. *Photo: T. A. S. O. Mathieson Collection*

Ceirano (I)

Giovanni Ceirano, the most active of the famous pioneer motoring family from Cuneo, established the *marca* Ceirano in 1919. Its first notable product was the sturdy, slow-revving, 80 × 130mm sv 4-cylinder CS model, which developed into the CS2 competition car with a 78mph (125kph) maximum in sports form. This car, and a faster CS2H with engine enlarged to 85 × 130mm, launched Ceirano into racing with many successes. They won the 3-litre class at Mugello, 1921, Garda, Cagliari, Venezia Giulia and Mugello in 1922, won the first two places in the 1,721 miles (2,770km) Alpine Cup contest that year, and won the 3-litre class of this difficult event two years later. They also shone in early post-World War 1 hill-climbs, prominent Ceirano drivers of the time including Ernesto Ceirano (son of Giovanni), Saccomani, Cattaneo, Pagani, and Boggio.

The introduction in 1924 of the lively 1·5-litre 4-cylinder N150 sporting model with independent front suspension ensured a continuation of Ceirano successes in Italy for the next few years, until the arrival of the much faster twin-ohc 1,500cc Alfa Romeo in 1928. Apart from many hill-climb successes, prominent 1,500cc class race wins by the N150 or 'Ceiranina' included the Montenero Cup 1925; the Rome and Alessandria Touring GPs in 1926, in both of which they scored 1-2-3; the Sila Cup at Cosenza; the sports and racing categories at Cascine; and the Targa Abruzzo at Pescara in 1926, with further local victories accruing right up to 1930, when the make was merged with FIAT. CP

CGV (F)

This make, the ancestor of the Charron, was created by three distinguished Panhard drivers, Charron, Girardot and Voigt, and in its earlier manifestations was hard to distinguish from a Panhard. In 1901 Audineau drove a 16hp light car in both the Paris-Bordeaux and the Paris-Berlin, with equal lack of success, but in 1902 a big 9·9-litre racer was chosen for the French Gordon Bennett team. Girardot retired after less than 90 miles; his reputation as the 'eternal second' took a downward turn, since his best achievement that year was 5th in the Circuit des Ardennes, though 1903 was a little better. CGV engines now boasted moiv, and in the Belgian race

Girardot actually finished 2nd; Voigt was 7th in the Paris–Madrid. For the 1905 Gordon Bennett Trials Girardot came up with a low-built 12·9-litre affair, now shaft-driven, and with radiators at each end of its engine to cope with the mountainous Clermont-Ferrand circuit. It crashed spectacularly on the third lap and that was the end of the firm's competition career. MCS

Chadwick (US)

In 1907 the Chadwick company, of Pottstown, Pa., introduced the Great Six, an enormous touring car with 11·2-litre 6-cylinder engine. The cylinders were cast in pairs, each pair surrounded by a copper water-jacket. This Great Six was also made as short-wheelbase runabout, very successful in hill-climbs when driven by

Above, 1910 Chadwick Great Six, winner of the 1910 Fairmount Park race. Len Zengle at the wheel. *Photo: Montagu Motor Museum*

Right, Chamberlain Special in 8-cylinder form, c 1938. *Photo: Ian Fraser*

works driver Willy Haupt as well as by private entrants. In an attempt to improve on its 60mph (96kph) top speed, Haupt suggested the use of three carburettors which, with other tuning, boosted the speed to 85mph (136kph). Further development was limited by the valve area, which could not be increased because of the water-jackets. Haupt then tried a compressor which forced the mixture into the cylinders at a greater pressure than that of the atmosphere. First one, then three compressors were used, driven by leather belts at six times engine speed. This was the world's first supercharger, although this word was not used at the time. It gave the Chadwick a superiority over most of its rivals in hill-climbs when short bursts of power were required, but was not very successful in racing.

Haupt drove a supercharged car in the 1908 Vander-bilt Cup, and for a while led the field, but fell back later, and was only in 10th place when the race was stopped. In the Savannah Grand Prize a month later he retired on the 4th lap. The supercharger was never employed on cars sold to the public. In 1909 a Chadwick broke the world record for 10 miles, in 8min 23sec, beating a 200hp Benz, and the following year Len Zengle won the Fairmount Park Race in Philadelphia, setting a new record for the course. After 1910 financial troubles bedevilled the company, and they could no longer support racing. All production ended in 1916. GNG

Chamberlain Specials (AUS)

The two Chamberlain Specials were built on a hobby basis by the proprietors of a company which subsequently went on to produce an incredible variety of items, ranging from tractors to original-equipment car pistons and naval torpedoes before it was eventually taken over by Repco.

The most famous Chamberlain Special started life in 1929 as a tube-chassis sprint car powered by a hybrid engine consisting of two Model 18 Norton barrels on a Harley crankcase, chain-driving the front wheels. In 1934, the car crashed at a hill-climb in Victoria and its designer-driver, Robert Chamberlain, broke his leg. The wreck was then taken over by his brother, William, who further developed the car and installed a 1,100cc 2-stroke Jamieson engine. Eventually, the Chamberlain ended up with an immensely complicated 8-cylinder 2-stroke engine in which an upper crankshaft was employed to actuate pistons that opened and closed the inlet and exhaust ports, leaving the lower crank and pistons to drive the vehicle. In effect, the engine had opposed

piston crowns, but the top pistons provided little driving effort. Chain drive connected the two cranks. The engine was supercharged with a 1·5-litre Roots blower, had eight spark plugs, eight coils, two distributors, four sets of points and could deliver 64,000 sparks a minute.

No complete horsepower figures were ever obtained for the 1,100cc engine, but it was dynomometer run at 4,500rpm at which speed it delivered 84hp at the wheels. The engine would rev reliably to 8,000rpm.

The Chamberlain was used only for sprint work and was capable of covering the standing quarter mile in 17sec with wheelspin for the entire distance. The car had its last competition run in the early 1950s and is still in the Chamberlain family.

The other Chamberlain Special was designed and built by Robert Chamberlain not long after he recovered from the crash in the original car. It was intended for use with a 2-litre Chamberlain-designed engine mounted amid-ships, but instead was equipped with a Ford 85A V-8 in 1938. After the war James Hawker (son of aviator Harry Hawker) completed the car which is now owned by another member of the Hawker family. TBF

Chaparral (US)

In 1961 Jim Hall commissioned Troutman and Barnes of Culver City, Calif., to build a front-engined, spaceframe sports car which he christened the Chaparral after a West Texas bird familiarly known as the road runner. Troutman and Barnes built six of these cars, powered by Chevrolet engines, two for Hall, two for Harry Heuer, one for Dick Troutman (raced by Skip Hudson), and one for Phil Scragg in England. Hall won the 1962 Road America 500 race with one of his cars, and also a number of sprint events. In 1962, with James 'Hap' Sharp, Hall incorporated Chaparral Cars at Midland, Tex., where a private 2-mile test track, Rattlesnake Raceway, was built. Here they made what Hall considers the first real Chaparral, a rear-engined semi-monocoque car with fibreglass construction and Oldsmobile engine. Later, a Chevrolet engine was fitted, and in this form Hall raced it for the first time at Riverside in October 1963. Its first victory was at Pensacola in April 1964, and a month later it won again at Laguna Seca when it was fitted with Hall's tradition-shattering automatic transmission. Although he broke his arm in a crash at Mosport and missed the last three races, Hall won the 1964 US Road Racing Championship. On 27 March 1965 Hall and Sharp won the Sebring 12 Hours, their Chevrolet-powered Chaparral being the first American car and driver victory at

Sebring since that of Walters and Fitch in a Cunningham C4-R in 1953. The 1965 season was very successful, the drivers being Hall, Sharp, and Ron Hisson; they ran in 21 races and won 16 of them.

For 1966 Hall built a Chaparral coupé for European racing. This 2D was powered by a 327ci (5,360cc) Chevrolet engine, and with it Joakim Bonnier and Phil Hill won the 1966 Nürburgring 1,000 kilometres Race. Chaparral's second overseas victory was that of Hill and Mike Spence in a 2F coupé at the Brands Hatch 500 Miles Race in 1967. The 2F was generally similar to the 2D but had a 427ci (7-litre) engine and an aerofoil. This aerofoil, which shook the racing world, was first seen on the Chaparral 2E at the Bridgehampton Can-Am race in September 1966. Elevated 54in (1·3716m) above the ground, the driver-actuated wing was supported by two vertical struts attached to the rear suspension, not the chassis. The wing concept, soon adopted by the world's leading formula and sports car constructors, became universal until banned by the FIA in 1969. In the 1966 Can-Am series the Chaparral 2Es took one 1st, three 2nds, and a 4th place. At Monterey, Hill was 1st and Hall 2nd. A smaller, aluminium-skinned car, the 2G, ran in the 1967 Can-Am races, and finished 5th in the series. For 1968 Hall abandoned European races as he had no

engine suitable for the 3-litre Group 6 Formula, and concentrated on the Can-Ams. He ran a 2G with wider tyres than on the 1967 car, and fuel injection for the 7-litre Chevrolet engine. He had one 2nd and one 3rd place, but in the last race of the season a bad accident involving Lothar Motschenbacher's McLaren sent Hall to hospital for nine weeks. The 2G was destroyed, and for the 1969 season Hall designed a completely new car, the 2H, with narrow track and no aerofoil. John Surtees drove it in the Can-Am series, but his best result was 4th at Edmonton.

In 1970 Jim Hall sprang another surprise to rival that of automatic transmission on the 1964 cars, or the aerofoils in 1966. The Chaparral 2J which first appeared at Watkins Glen in July had a ground-effect system which sucked the car towards the road in order to improve adhesion. A 45bhp 2-cylinder 2-stroke Snowmobile engine drove two rear-facing fans which sucked air from beneath the car; skirts made of Lexan, a thermoplastic material, formed a seal with the track, providing the principle of a hovercraft in reverse. With this car, powered by a 465ci (7·6-litres) engine, Jackie Stewart made the fastest lap at Watkins Glen and Vic Elford was consistently fastest in practice in other Can-Am races. The ground-effect system was banned by the FIA in December 1970. GNG/ARB

Left below, 1961 Chaparral built by Troutman and Barnes. Photo: Bernard Cahier

Right below, 1967 Chaparral 2F coupé, driven in the Targa Florio by Phil Hill and Hap Sharp. Photo: Geoffrey Goddard

Left bottom, 1967 Chaparral 2G. Jim Hall at the wheel. Photo: Griswold-Eshleman Co

Right bottom, 1970 Chaparral 2J. Photo: Goodyear Aerospace Corp

Chenard-Walcker (F)

Although founded in 1901, the Chenard-Walcker company did not enter serious competitions until 1922. That year saw the first of the inspired, Touté-designed ohc sports cars with 2-litre and 3-litre 4-cylinder engines and the curious combination of Hallot servo brakes on the front and a transmission brake taking care of the rear end. In 3-litre form 80/90bhp were available, and the breed's first success was a 3rd place in the 1922 Boillot Cup at Boulogne. In 1923, however, Lagache and Leonard's 3-litre won the first Le Mans 24-Hour Race at 57·21mph (82·07kph), Bachmann and Dauvergne clinching it with a 2nd place. They also won the Circuit des Routes Pavées in 1924; Sénéchal's 3-litre averaged 54·4mph (87·55kph), and Pisart's 2-litre was 2nd. They fielded four cars at Le Mans—a 3-litre, two 2-litres with lightweight 'tank' bodywork, and a new 4-litre straight-8 developing 130bhp, which was the fastest machine in the race and warded off the 3-litre Bentley for 20 hours before retiring. The small Chenards came in 4th and 5th.

In 1925 the 8-cylinder was endowed with conventional brakes, but it was still not reliable enough to stay the course at Le Mans, though Lagache and Leonard subsequently took the Belgian 24-Hour Race at Spa. Even more interesting, however, were some new tank-bodied 1,100cc sports-racers. These marked a reversion to push-rod ohv, there were only two main bearings, and back axles were innocent of differentials. They were surprisingly fast on 55bhp, Montlhéry lap speeds being quoted as 96mph unblown and 107mph (172·2kph) in supercharged form. A 10th place (and 1st in class) for Glaszmann and de Zuniga at Le Mans earned Chenard-Walcker the Biennial and Triennial Cups, while Lagache went on to win the Boillot Cup outright at 63·5mph (102·19kph). The firm concentrated on the 'tanks' in 1926, and had an excellent season: 1st and 2nd at San Sebastian; the 1,100cc class of the Belgian 24-hour event; and a triumph at Boulogne, where the three works cars (Lagache, Leonard and de Zuniga) were the sole finishers in the Boillot Cup.

The alliance with Delahaye in 1927 killed off all sporting enthusiasm, and Touté moved to Ariès, but the 'tanks' were revived in 1937. They failed at Le Mans and a 5th place in the small-car category of the French GP was only to be expected when they were competing against modern 1500s, however Rigoulot and Giraud-Cabantous did finish 1st and 2nd in that year's Bol d'Or. MCS

1924 Chenard-Walcker 3-litre at the pits, Le Mans. *Photo: Autocar*

Chevrolet (US)

Curiously enough, though the make's name was chosen on the strength of Louis Chevrolet's racing prowess, the cars he built for racing were not Chevrolets but Frontenacs, and had no connection with the vehicles that bore his name. Though a car with a 6-cylinder Chevrolet engine ran at Indianapolis in 1930, the make made little impact in racing until 1940, when Fangio won a 5,900-mile (9,495km) marathon from Buenos Aires to Lima and back on a stripped 6-cylinder coupé, averaging 53·6mph (86·26kph). The future world champion continued to campaign with his Chevrolets until 1942, winning the GP Getulio Vargas, the Argentinian Thousand, and the Sea and Mountain event. Then he was back at the wheel in 1947 with more successes in local races. Chevrolets' post-war competition history, except for some brief participation in NASCAR in the 60s, is divided between three distinct cars, the Corvette, the Corvair and the Camaro. MCS

Corvette

America's only current production sports car had its beginning as a project of a sort that rarely finds its way into production: a General Motors Styling show car. Harley Earl was Styling chief then, and the Corvette was his brainchild, even if he drew heavily upon the then popular Jaguar XK-120 for the conception—using its 102in (2,591mm) wheelbase and choosing an in-line 6-cylinder Chevrolet engine of size comparable to the Jaguar's. An unveiling of the Corvette styling mock-up to GM executives set Ed Cole, then Chevrolet chief engineer, off on an enthusiastic project to engineer it into a roadgoing reality. This began in June 1952; the car was shown to the public at the New York Automobile Show in January 1953 before the engineering work was complete.

The first Corvette was mechanically anything but exciting, with its 150-bhp 6-cylinder and 2-speed automatic transmission; but it was a beginning and there was a very interested engineer at Chevrolet—one Zora Arkus-Duntov—who was determined to make it better, even to make it raceworthy. His chance came with the 1956 model—restyled and more handsome, with roll-up windows replacing the side curtains, but more importantly to be available with a 3-speed, close-ratio manual gearbox to go with the V-8 engine it had acquired in 1955—and he took a modified one to Daytona Beach in December 1955 to put a two-way average speed of 150mph (240kph) in the record book.

The 1956–57 Corvette small-block, 265ci V-8, as developed by Zora Akus-Duntov, became the workhorse of U.S. road racing. Given lightweight heads, and frequently enlarged to as much as 494ci, it is the standard Can-Am engine. At 305ci it powers the majority of Formula A single-seaters and the Camaro Trans-Am sedan.

In 1957 the fruits of Duntov's special project—fuel injection—became available on the Corvette, and so did a 4-speed manual gearbox, the first on an American car in many years. Also in 1957 there was the SS model with spaceframe, De Dion rear axle and a 315bhp fuel injection engine. It retired at Sebring (where a stock Corvette finished 12th). Duntov had intended to run the cars at Le Mans, but General Motors lost interest at this point. The Corvette was, however, beginning to make an impression in SCCA racing, with victories at Fort Worth, Riverside, and the Governor's Trophy at Nassau. From 1956, when Dr Dick Thompson earned SCCA C production honours, until 1971 Corvettes won 19 national SCCA championships. In B production, Jim

960 Chevrolet Corvettes, entered by
Briggs Cunningham, at Le Mans. *Photo: Al Bochroch*

Below, 1968 Chevrolet Corvette, driven at
Le Mans by Umberto Maglioli and Henri
Greder. *Photo: Geoffrey Goddard*

Right below, 1969 Chevrolet Corvette on
the Clermont-Ferrand circuit during the
Tour de France. *Photo: John Davenport*

Jeffords (1958–59), Dr Thompson (1957–61) and Don
Yenko (1962–63) each took multiple national titles.
Apart from a face-lift in 1958, when quad headlights and
some unsightly styling bulges were added, and a tail-lift
in 1961 when a new rear end (quite unrelated to the
front) was adopted, Corvette remained much the same
car through 1962. By that year the maximum power
available from the production line had worked itself up

to 360bhp (from the fuel-injection 327 engine) and with
appropriate gearing the car could accelerate from rest to
60mph (96kph) in 5·9sec — a far cry from the 11·0sec
figure of the original Powerglide six.

Corvettes did well in SCCA races in 1959 and 1960,
and in the latter year Briggs Cuningham took two to Le
Mans where they finished 8th and 10th. The Johnson
and Morgan Corvette came 9th at Sebring in 1961 and

they raced again at Le Mans in 1962, only to retire.

But the chassis had not kept pace with the engine and the old live axle had trouble delivering all that power to the road. Arkus-Duntov, however, had been busy with his staff on an all-new chassis for the new Corvette which was to appear as the 1963 Corvette Sting Ray—a name derived from a Styling show car.

The 1963 model was the high point in the Corvette story: more compact outside, roomier inside, better looking, and it had independent rear suspension. Even though it did not have disc brakes—there was a complex self-compensating all-drum system available for competition work—the 1963 was truly an up-to-date sports car. In 1963 Corvettes took 3rd and 4th places in the Governor's Trophy at Nassau, and in 1964 Roger Penske won the Nassau TT from Ferrari and Cobra opposition. Corvettes earned honours at Sebring in 1966, 1968 and 1970.

Except for the introduction of a larger-block (and heavier) engine in 1965, a 396ci (6,489cc) unit that grew later to 427ci (6,997cc) and most recently to 454ci (7,440cc) and disc brakes in 1965, the Sting Ray remained the same car through 1967. Fuel injection dropped by the wayside as cubic inches proved the cheaper way of getting power, and the Gran Sport Corvette—a lightened racing version—was never campaigned by Chevrolet because GM decided to abstain from racing. However, Corvette engines, rebuilt and tuned by such experts as Traco (Jim Travers and Frank Coon) or by individual teams such as McLaren and Chaparral, have dominated Can-Am racing, powering all but two of the winning cars between 1966 and 1970.

In 1968 a brand-new body was laid over the existing Sting Ray's ladder frame. The new envelope allowed the use of wider wheels and tyres, but it also restricted interior and luggage space while being bulkier on the outside and heavier. As of 1971 this configuration remains in production, selling in quantities of about 30,000 annually, and is available with engines of 350ci (5,735cc) and 454ci (7,440cc) in power ratings from 300 to 390bhp. RW/ARB

Corvair

Many of the 1·4 million Corvairs sold between 1960 and 1969 were bought by automobile enthusiasts. Only a few were raced but in the mid-1960s the Corvair became one of the most popular rally cars in America, helping the Chevrolet Division of General Motors to win the 1967 SCCA Manufacture Rally Championship. Yenko Stingers, Corvairs modified by Chevrolet dealer, Don Yenko, participated in SCCA club racing. Jerry Thompson's Stinger won national D production honours in 1967. ARB

Camaro

Chevrolet Camaros have had successes in both U.S. oval track and road racing. They won the NASCAR Grand Touring division (changed to Grand American in 1970) in 1969 with 23 victories in 35 races, and repeated the success as 1970 Grand American champions with Tiny Lund, a former Daytona 500 winner, earning the title. Running as Sunoco Specials, Roger Penske Camaros won the 1968 and 1969 Trans-American championship for the Chevrolet Division of General Motors. In 1968 Dick Lang was national A sedan champion, and Bill Petree's Camaro took the big sedan title in 1969. ARB

Chevron (GB)

Derek Bennett of Salford, Lancashire, produced specials for the 750 and 1172 formulas, Midget speedway racing

and Formula Junior, before introducing the first Chevron model in 1965. This was a Clubman's car, with 1,500cc Ford engine, and was outstandingly successful in the hands of Bennett and Brian Classick. A further seven replicas were built during 1966, and in their class they achieved a long run of successes, spread over several years.

In 1966 the first GT car was introduced from new premises at Bolton, with twin-cam Ford engine and Hewland HD5 gearbox. Digby Martland won at Oulton Park on the car's debut, and John Lepp was successful with a similar car. The basis of the model was a fully triangulated spaceframe, with monocoque sills and bulkheads, independent suspension all round, and a sleek fibreglass body by Specialised Mouldings. Further versions were built with BMW and BRM 2-litre engines for Derek Bennett and Brian Redman. By 1967 production of the very successful B6 type was well under way, and the following year came homologation in Group 4 with the BMW engine. Other motors used included the Cosworth FVA (later very popular) and the FPF Coventry-Climax 4-cylinder. Updated versions were the B8 of 1968 and the B16 in 1969, both of which were immediately successful in Group 6 racing, with Ford twin-cam or BMW power units, the output of the latter having been raised in stages from 180 to 230bhp. Variations on the theme included a B12 car with V-8 Repco engine.

With some 90 GT cars completed by 1970, and most of them racing, the successes achieved were too numerous to mention. Brian Redman, with a B16, won the ADAC 500 kilometres at the Nürburgring in September 1969. They were virtually unbeatable in their class except by the occasional Porsche, and were campaigned with successfully by, among others, John Bridges, John

Below, 1966 Chevron B2 Clubman's car at Oulton Park. Don Hill at the wheel. *Photo: Autosport*

Bottom, 1968 Chevron B8 coupé at Oulton Park. John Bridges at the wheel. *Photo: F. E. Hall*

Burton, T. Croker, Peter Gethin, D. Jesson, George Silverwood, Chris Skeaping, Barry Smith, T. Stock, Andrew Mylius, A. Rollinson, P. Taggart and Trevor Twaites, in addition to those already mentioned. In order to remain competitive in 1970 in international events, a lighter open version, the B19 was also developed. With this car, Redman and Attwood won the 1970 Springbok Championship with six South African victories in a row.

Meanwhile, Bennett had in 1967 introduced his first Formula 3 design, the B7 raced by Peter Gethin, and in 1968 fifteen production B9 Formula 3 cars were sold, although at first they suffered from various shortcomings which limited the successes achieved. The B9b was an improved version with a stiffer chassis, the B10 was the Formula 2 car, and B14 was allocated to the Formula B version for SCCA racing. For 1969 an improved Formula 3 car was announced, the B15 with new monocoque centre cockpit section and revised tubular spaceframe, at a price of £1,775 less engine but with Hewland Mk 6 gearbox. This model won major European races in the hands of Reine Wisell (Snetterton, Pau and Brands Hatch), Peter Hanson (Hockenheim) and A. Rollinson (Silverstone), with backing from Howden Ganley, Barry Maskell, G. Pianta, Richard Scott and many others.

Derivatives included the B15b Formula B version, corresponding B17 and B17b models for 1970, and the B17c for Formula 2. The B18 was the company's first full monocoque production, available also in Formula 3, Formula 'B' or Formula 2 guise. DF

Chiribiri (I)

Founded in 1913 by Antonio Chiribiri, who worked with Bernardi and Isotta-Fraschini, and was a pioneer of aluminium welding, the Italian make Chiribiri came into prominence in the early 1920s, marketing a range of lively touring and sports cars, and racing in the voiturette class. Always up against the factory Fiats, Chiribiris nonetheless amassed several creditable victories. The works racing cars followed current GP fashion in having 4-cylinder, twin-ohc, 65 × 112mm engines, and handsome two-seat bodies with wedge tails and distinctive fairings over the front dumbirons. They were driven by Chiribiri's son Amedeo, who raced as 'Deo', Ramassoto, and the Englishman Jack Scales, who lived in Turin and formerly worked with FIAT as tester/driver. Scales scored the first success with the new car in the 1922 Aosta-Great St Bernard hill-climb, and in the subsequent Penya Rhin GP in Spain Ramassoto came 3rd to two Talbot-Darracqs while 'Deo' made fastest lap.

In 1923 two new men joined the team, Tazio Nuvolari and Marconcini. The former was 5th in the Penya Rhin GP, and won the 1,500cc classes in the Savio and Polesine Circuits in 1924; Marconcini gained numerous hill-climb successes plus class victories in the Belfiore, Cremona, Pescara and Montenero road races in 1924. 'Deo' took the 1·5-litre class in two important 1923 hill-climbs, Parma Poggio di Berceto and Susa-Moncenisio, and in 1925 G. Platé acquired one of the cars, finishing 2nd in the Tripoli and Rome GPs, winning the 1·5-litre class of the Targa Florio, and collecting other firsts at Savio and Messina that year, and at Tripoli (1·5-litre class) in 1926.

Another car went to Serboli, who did very well with it with three hill-climb 1sts and the 1·5-litre class of the Garda race in 1925, class victories at Pozzo, Savio and Terni in 1926, and at Trento-Bondone in 1928. Serboli's car featured in a spectacular fire at Monza during the 1926 Italian GP, but was repaired in time for the Milan

Top, 1969 Chevron B15 Formula 3 car. Photo: F. E. Hall

Centre, 1969 Chevron B17 coupé. Brian Redman at the wheel. Photo: Derek Bennett Engineering Co Ltd

Right, 1923 Chiribiri 1·5-litre racing car. Jack Scales at the wheel. Photo: Cyril Posthumus Collection

GP a week later, when it finished 2nd to Costantini's Bugatti. Another successful Chiribiri exponent was Valpreda, winner of the 1,500cc class of the Montenero and Ligure Piemontese road races in 1926, and Alessandria and Montenero in 1927. The company itself, badly hit economically in the stormy 1920s, virtually ceased business in 1928. CP

Chitty-Chitty-Bang-Bang (GB)

The Chitty-Chitty-Bang-Bangs were built at Higham, near Canterbury in Kent, the home of Count Louis Vorow Zborowski, for the express purpose of taking part in the fastest Brooklands handicap races and for long-distance touring. The recipe was to install World War 1 aviation engines in high-geared pre-war chain-drive chassis. Chitty I appeared in 1921, Clive Gallop having aided Zborowski in its construction. This was the second of the aero-engined giant racing cars to appear after the war—but unlike the 350hp Sunbeam, it had a two-seater body. Although limited by the tyres then available, it provided the Count with many Brooklands successes but crashed badly in 1922 when a tyre burst and was not raced

again by its original owner. Before this the Chitty, which had a 23-litre Maybach ohv 6-cylinder engine in a Mercedes chassis, had lapped at 113·45mph (182·58kph). It was eventually broken up.

Chitty II with 18·8-litre Benz engine, and four-seater body was completed late in 1921 but ran at only one Brooklands meeting, its best lap speed being at 108·27mph (174·21kph). After this it was used by the Count for touring, including venturing into the Sahara Desert. It is still in existence. Chitty III was a shaft-drive Mercedes chassis into which the Count put a 6-cylinder ohc 14·7-litre aero-engine of the same make. It had Westinghouse 4-wheel brakes, lapped Brooklands at 112·68mph (181·33kph) and was also used on the road, notably as baggage-wagon to Chitty II. WB

Christie (US)

John Walter Christie, (1867–1944) was an American engineer who anticipated the BMC Mini layout of transverse engine and front wheel drive by some 55 years. Apart from basic layout, Christie's cars were as different from the Mini as can be imagined, for they were mostly enormous racing cars of up to 19 litres capacity. The wheels were driven directly from each end of the crankshaft, which took the place of a front axle. There was no differential, and cornering was achieved with the inside wheel clutch slipping. Instead of a conventional frontal radiator, the Christies had what amounted to an enormous cooling blanket wrapped around the bonnet behind the engine, and extending as far back as the dash.

The first two cars of 1904 and 1905 had in-line 4-cylinder engines of 40 and 60bhp; the latter won a 50-mile race at the Ormond-Daytona Speed Carnival in 1905. Later in that year came the 'Double Ender', with two 60bhp engines, one driving the front wheels, and the other behind the driver powering the rear wheels. It covered a mile in 38sec (99mph; 159·33kph), but on the whole did not perform well. With the rear engine removed, this car became Christie's entry for the 1905 Vanderbilt Cup, in which race it collided with Lancia's Fiat, and withdrew. The 1906 Christie had a V-4 engine of 13 litres capacity. It covered a mile at Ormond Beach in 35·2sec, achieving ftd, and came 2nd to Marriott's Stanley 'Wogglebug' in a 30-mile race. The 1907 V-4 car built for the French Grand Prix was Christie's largest at 19 litres (185 × 185mm), and was also the largest-engined car ever to compete in a Grand Prix. It retired on the fourth lap with a stuck exhaust valve.

Christie entered no more important races, but from 1907 to 1910 he toured the United States giving demon-

strations on dirt track circuits, and entering a few local races. One of his drivers on these occasions was Barney Oldfield. One further V-4 racing car was built, making six in all, as well as a road-going two-seater, a tourer, and a taxicab. Christie afterwards built a number of fwd fire engines, and high speed tanks. GNG

Chrysler (US)

From its inception the 201ci (3·3-litre) 6-cylinder Chrysler with hydraulic fwb was something of a performer, and in its first year — 1924 — Ralph DePalma used one to win the Mount Wilson hill-climb. In 1925 the make won a 1,000-mile stock-car speed trial at Culver City. Malcolm Campbell also raced a streamlined racing model at Brooklands, lapping at close on 100mph (160kph), and Stoffel and Desvaux drove a Chrysler at Le Mans: they were placed 7th, but failed to qualify. Chryslers were back at Le Mans in 1928 with four roadsters, and the best of these (Stoffel and Rossignol) came in 3rd at 64·56mph (103·90kph), with another Chrysler in 4th place. The big 309ci (5·1-litre) Imperial of De Vere and Mangin also took 2nd place in the Belgian 24-hour event, with smaller cars of the same make 3rd and 6th, and in 1929 two Chryslers (Stoffel and Benoist, and De Vere and Mangin) were 6th and 7th at Le Mans. Raymond Sommer drove a 282ci (4·6-litre) straight-8 in 1931, retiring at Le Mans (as did de Corte on an immense 385ci (6·3-litre) CG-type), but winning his class at Spa. In the same year the biggest eights took some official American stock-car records. More records fell to a CV-type 8-cylinder of the ill-starred Airflow series in 1934: it did 95·7mph (154·01kph) over the mile.

Thereafter the name Chrysler disappeared from

929 Chrysler at Le Mans. Henri Stoffel at the wheel. *Photo: Autocar*

Right, 1946 Cisitalia 1100 driven by Franco Cortese in the Brezzi Cup, Turin. *Photo: Cyril Posthumus Collection*

Right below, 1948 Cisitalia flat-12 GP car. *Photo: Porsche*

serious competition until the appearance of the effective 160bhp hemi-head ohv 331ci (5·4-litre) V-8 in 1951. This engine was used by Allard and Cunningham, and in the 1951 Carrera Panamericana Chryslers came in 3rd and 4th, Indianapolis driver Troy Ruttmann occupying the latter position. In 1952 and 1953 they had to give best to the Lincolns, but there was a surprising entry of a car (Frère and Milhoux) in the 1953 Mille Miglia, which beat the Mk VII Jaguars in the biggest touring category. In 1954 a 331ci (5·4-litre) New Yorker model was timed for 24 hours at 118·18mph (190·23kph). With the coming of the 354ci (5·8-litre) 300 series in 1955 Chrysler moved into NASCAR racing, winning that year's Grand National at 92·05mph (148·14kph). The 300s won 21 races in 1956; though they were only 4th in placing as a make, they had taken the largest number of events, and the year's star driver, Buck Baker, was a Chrysler man. Subsequent stock-car racing by the Corporation has been done mainly on Plymouths and Dodges, but for three seasons (1956-7-8) Alsbury's Imperial (the biggest Chrysler model, since 1955 a make in its own right) was outright winner of the Mobilgas Economy Run. MCS

Cisitalia (I)

Produced by Piero Dusio to Dante Giacosa's designs, the Cisitalia was an essay in cheap light-car racing which anticipated Britain's more successful Formula 3 movement. As might have been expected in 1946, Dusio chose the 1,100cc category and based his single-seater on the well-established 3-bearing ohv Fiat engine, endowed with magneto ignition and tuned to develop 60bhp. This lived in an advanced multi-tubular spaceframe with transverse ifs, and for £1,000 the amateur could buy a 110mph (176kph) performance. Forty of them did, in the make's first season, when an impressive line-up of drivers (Nuvolari, Chiron, Sommer, Taruffi, Cortese, and Biondetti) faced a field of Simcas and Fiats in the Coppa Brezzi at Turin, which Dusio himself won. Nuvolari took a 2nd place at Mantua, and in 1947 there were some impressive victories: Bonetto was first at Asti and Taruffi at Vercelli, and the cars took the first four places in the 1,100cc race at Comminges. Loyer ran his Cisitalia in the GP proper, finishing 4th.

A curious aspect of the 1947 scene was Dusio's attempt to popularize one-class racing. He formed a Cisitalia 'circus' of 16 drivers (including Lurani, Brivio, Taruffi and the as yet little-known Alberto Ascari) which was prepared to perform to order at meetings, and did so in Cairo, though there were no other takers for this enter-

tainment, and the idea died. Cisitalia's beautiful and much-admired 1,100cc sports cars also raced, Nuvolari finishing 2nd in the year's Mille Miglia, with sister models in 3rd and 4th places, and the make had won Taruffi the national championship by the end of the season. The cars for 1948 were improved, with twin-carburettor 70bhp engines, while 1,200cc units became available to meet both the increased size and performance of Amédeé Gordini's creations and a dwindling interest in the 1,100cc category. Cisitalias finished 2nd and 3rd at Bari. Taruffi won the 1,100cc event at Berne; in the sports-car field he

was 2nd in the Targa Florio, and challenged strongly in the early stages of the Mille Miglia, only to retire. Meanwhile Ferry Porsche had created a Formula 1 1·5-litre car which sounds like a blueprint for the 1970s, with rear-mounted flat-12 engine, 5-speed gearbox, and 4-wheel drive.

Output was said to be 300bhp, but by the time the car was complete the money had run out and Dusio had transferred operations to Argentina. Though he was back in Italy making sports cars by 1952, the GP projects did not survive this upheaval, and Cisitalias ceased to be a force in competition. The prototype Porsche 360 never came under starter's orders anywhere and now reposes in the Porsche factory museum at Stuttgart. MCS

Citroën (F)

Founded in 1919, this make was seldom seen in competition in the first decade of its existence, though a B-type two-seater, driven by Chassagne, won its class in the 1923 Circuit des Routes Pavées. However, 1931 saw the first of the famous 'Rosalies' sponsored by the Yacco Oil concern, which tried for long-distance records at Montlhéry.

Rosalie I was a 2·5-litre sv 6-cylinder with single-seater bodywork with which Marchand and his crew took 14 world records, including 9 days at 67·3mph (108·31kph). Rosalie II, also a six, circulated for 54 days in 1932 and established records for distances of up to 100,000km. Petite Rosalie (1933) was a 1,453cc 8CV 4-cylinder which ground on for 300,000km and 133 days, averaging 58mph (93·34kph) and setting up 296 records. Another 6-cylinder, Rosalie V, kept the 8CV company for 80,000km, and a slightly over-bored 15CV ('Rosalie-Spido') ran for 20,000km at 81·97mph (131·92kph). The last of the rwd 6-cylinder record cars, Rosalie VI, was out in 1934, taking seven more records, all at over 95mph (153kph). With the advent of the fwd Citroën (the famous *traction avant*), a stock 7CV coupé (Rosalie VII), running without wings, moved in on Class E (1,501–2,000cc), covering 10,000 miles (16,090km) at 69·1mph (111·04kph). This was the end of the Rosalie story, apart from Rosalie IX, a standard 7CV saloon which was subjected to an endurance test at Montlhéry in 1937. No records were claimed.

The *traction* did little in competition before World War 2, though François Lecot set himself the task of

1933 Citroën 'Petite Rosalie' record car.
Photo: William Boddy Collection

driving 400,000km in 12 months on a 'II *Legère*'; his marathon included the 1936 Monte Carlo Rally.

There were some early post-war successes won with the aid of proprietary 4-speed gearboxes, notably 1st and 2nd places in the 2-litre class of the 1947 Alpine Rally, and Gautruche's Coupes des Alpes in the 1948 and 1949 events. He also finished 4th in the 1950 Monte Carlo, in which year Ton's 15CV was placed 6th in the Tulip. But Citroën's first major rally victory was that of Seibert and Bolz on a secondhand 15CV in the 1953 Sestrière event. In 1952 Vinatier set up some international Class J (350cc) records on a linered-down 2CV special, but Citroën did not enter competitions seriously until 1959,

Left, c 1951 Citroën 15CV, winner of the 1953 Sestrieres Rally. *Photo: Sedgwick and Marshall Collection*

Below, 1959 Citroën DS19, the original works rally car, in the 1970 Ronde Cevenolle. *Photo: Michel Morelli*

when the works-entered DS19 of Coltelloni and Alexandre won the Monte Carlo Rally; the Marang/Badoche car was 4th; and the make annexed the Manufacturers' Team Prize. At the end of a good season Coltelloni was European Rally Champion. René Trautmann won the 1960 Tulip, and Citroëns also finished 2nd and 4th in the East African Safari. In 1961 there were victories for Bianchi/Harris in Liège-Sofia-Liège and for Trautmann/ Ogier in the Tour de Corse.

Victories in 1962 included the Norwegian Winter event, the Lyons-Charbonnières, the Alpine and the Thousand Lakes; and four of the 18 unpenalized cars in the Liège-Sofia-Liège were DSs, resulting in a class win and another team award. Toivonen was 1962 Scandinavian Rally Champion in a Citroën. The Finnish and Norwegian Winter rallies, the Lyons-Charbonnières and the Alpine fell to Citroën in 1963, along with team awards in the Monte Carlo and the Liège-Sofia-Liège, but 1964 was less impressive, despite a 2nd place (Ogier and Groll) in the Acropolis and a 7th (Verrier and Coltelloni) in the Spa-Sofia-Liège. Citroën won at Monte Carlo again in 1966, drivers being Toivonen and Mikander; the other 2·2-litre DS21s came in 4th, 7th and 9th. Mlles Pointet and Fougeray took the Coupe des Dames.

By 1967 the Citroëns were beginning to be outpaced, in spite of which Ogier and Mlle Pointet were 6th in the Italian Flowers Rally, and the Bohnicek and Pfisterer car well placed in the Austrian Alpine. Citroëns also finished 5th and 6th in the Canadian Shell event, and the cars won their class in the Alpine, but the appearance of some unsuccessful lightweight prototypes in the Tour de Corse indicated the trend. Placings in 1968 were low: all the Citroëns entered for the Alpine retired, and 19th in the Monte Carlo and 11th at San Remo were hardly encouraging, even if Lucien Bianchi nearly won the London-Sydney Marathon, being eliminated by a crash a mere 100 miles from the finish. Neyret and Terramorsi came in 9th. The lightweights were again in evidence in 1969, when Citroëns were 9th and 10th in the Alpine and won a 1-2-3 victory in the Rallye du Maroc, in which their only 'works' opponents were Renault. In the 1970 Monte Carlo Rally they won their category of Group 2, but there were no Citroëns in the first ten places. The cars challenged strongly in the World Cup Rally, but their best placing was 7th (Vanson/Turcat/Leprince). MCS

Clément-Bayard (F)

Adolphe Clément left Clément et Cie to form his own firm in 1903. By the end of that year a low-built and streamlined light racer had been seen at the Dourdan Speed Trials, and in 1904 his racing coverage embraced all categories. The team's star driver was Clément's 19-year-old son Albert. The 30hp light cars were beaten by the Darracqs in the Circuit des Ardennes, but in the voiturette class the positions were reversed, and Hanriot also won the light racing category of the Ostend Speed Trials. For the French Gordon Bennett Trials Clément-Bayard actually tried two types of racer, both T-headers with 4-cylinder engines, though the small 11·3-litre had shaft drive, while its bigger sister ran to 16·3-litres, side chains, and 100bhp. Neither was successful, though Albert Clément subsequently drove one of the smaller models into 2nd place in the Vanderbilt Cup at 51·9mph (83·52kph). The 1905 racers had Talbot-type radiators, well-streamlined bodies and shaft drive, but these 12·9-litre machines achieved nothing, though they had a better season in 1906. In the Grand Prix, Albert Clément lay 2nd at the end of the first day's sport, and finished 3rd

Top, 1904 Clément-Bayard 80hp Gordon Bennett car. Albert Clément at the wheel. *Photo: Montagu Motor Museum*

Above, 1908 Clément-Bayard 135hp GP car. Victor Rigal at the wheel. *Photo: Montagu Motor Museum*

overall: he was also 4th in the Vanderbilt Cup and 6th in the Circuit des Ardennes, in which the team finished intact. In the latter part of 1906 Clément-Bayard built a vast 18·3-litre T-head 6-cylinder racer with chain drive, said to give 160bhp at 1,200rpm. It never contested a major race, but turned up regularly for sprints and hill-climbs, winning the unlimited class at Evreux in 1907, and the same category at Gaillon as late as 1908. Clément-Bayard's best 1907 placing was Alézy's 5th in the Coppa della Velocita at Brescia. Albert Clément was killed practising for the Grand Prix, and his team-mates Garcet and Shepard came in 8th and 9th.

Last of the racing cars were some advanced 13·9-litre machines with ohc and hemispherical heads which ran in the 1908 Grand Prix. They were probably the fastest cars in the race, for Rigal's 4th was the best French placing, and his average of 63·6mph (102·35kph) took in 19 tyre changes. Hautvast used one of these to make ftd at Ostend, but thereafter Clément-Bayard lost interest in the sport. MCS

Cobra and Shelby-GT (US)

Jim and Dick Hall, partners in Shelby's Dallas Sports car business, purchased his interest and Carroll settled in California as a racing tyre distributor and proprietor of a high-performance driving school. In September of 1961, after failing to interest General Motors into letting him use their lightweight V-8, Shelby received two 221ci (3,622cc) Ford engines, which he promptly shipped to AC Cars in England. Shelby had discussed the idea of a simple, lightweight, inexpensive Anglo-American sports car with Charles Hurlock of AC, and the Cobra, then designated CSX001, was completed in February 1962. Donald Frey of Ford liked what he saw and Shelby began receiving 260ci (4,261cc) high-performance versions of the original 221ci (3,622cc) engine. In June 1962, Shelby moved to the old Scarab plant in Los Angeles and what first was the 'Shelby AC Cobra' then 'AC Cobra' and finally 'Ford Cobra' went into production. After 75 cars had been made with the 260ci (4,261cc) engine, Ford began supplying 289ci (4,736cc) units. Before Cobra production stopped Shelby was using 427ci (6,997cc) engines and had moved to a giant plant near the Los Angeles airport. The competition version used aluminium cylinder heads as opposed to cast iron for the road version, and a variety of differential ratio options. Power output was 490bhp at 6,500rpm. In January 1963 Shelby Cobra's won their first race when David Mac-Donald and Ken Miles finished 1st and 2nd at Riverside. From 1963 until 1969 Cobras dominated SCCA 'A' production racing. But Shelby was after bigger game. In 1964 Cobra topped US road racing standings and came close to winning the FIA manufacturers' championship, scoring 78·3 points to Ferrari's 84·6. The Cobra Daytona coupé, designed by young Peter Brock, (originally hired by Shelby to run his driver's school) won the international GT championship in 1965 and the 289ci (4,736cc) Cobra engine had been used in a high-performance version of the Sunbeam Alpine sports car known as the Tiger. But the Cobra was beginning to be overshadowed by Ford's more sophisticated GT-40 and Mk II programme, in which Shelby was to play an important part.

Following the success of the Ford Motor Company's Mustang, Shelby phased-out the Cobra racing programme by turning it over to private entrants and in 1965 began building the Shelby GT-350, a highly tuned and lightened version of the Mustang, with improved handling. Jerry Titus, who was to help bring Ford-Mustang the 1966 and 1967 Trans-Am sedan championship, won the 1965 American Road Race of Champions, the SCCA national run-offs, at Daytona, and Ken Miles,

who had helped Shelby develop the Cobra, became part of the Ford GT programme. Late in 1965 Dan Gurney and Carroll Shelby formed All American Racers, their primary aim being to mount an American Formula 1 and Indianapolis challenge. Shelby acted as team manager when Ford Mark IIs won at Le Mans in 1966 and devoted much of the remaining year to developing the Trans-Am Mustang. In 1967 Shelby introduced the GT-500, using the Ford 428ci (7,014cc) engine. Shelby withdrew from All American Racers in 1968 and Ford assumed manufacturing responsibilities for the Shelby-GT line, which they discontinued early in 1970 after producing 14,810 Shelby-GT units. Shelby entered two Ken Wallis designed turbines in the 1968 Indianapolis 500 but they proved non-competitive and were withdrawn before the close of qualifying.

Early in 1970 Shelby cut his racing ties to devote himself to other business interests. Carroll Shelby's contributions to racing were many, but what he will probably be best remembered for are the 1,140 fierce, no-nonsense Cobras, an American dream come true. ARB

Coldwell (GB)

In 1969 W. D. C. Needham introduced the rear-engined Coldwell GT coupé, designed for Mini components and manufactured by Coldwell Engineering and Racing of Sheffield for club racing. By mid-1970 three had been made, and open models were offered also for the F100 formula and for Group 6. DF

Condor (D)

José Jungbecker of Aachen was the sponsor of this small racing car. The 743cc BMW R75 motorcycle engine was used, later versions—in accordance with the new Formula 3 regulations—had a reduced capacity of 500cc. Huschke von Hanstein was one of the Condor drivers. In 1949 he won at the Grenzlandring with the 750cc version at a speed of 83·6mph (134·54kph). A year later Dilthey won in the Formula 3 class at 87·5mph (142·82kph). HON

Connaught (GB)

The first of the Connaughts, the L-type sports two-seater of 1949, utilized a 1,767cc 4-cylinder push-rod Lea-Francis engine in a chassis which soon acquired ifs, but it ran only in club events in the hands of its sponsors, Rodney Clarke and Kenneth McAlpine. However, in 1950 came a Formula 2 single-seater, the A-type, powered by a 1,960cc unit of similar type which developed 135bhp. This was mated to a 4-speed Wilson preselector gearbox with quick-change spur gears mounted behind the bevel

Left, 1963 Cobra sports at Silverstone in 1968. Nick Granville-Smith at the wheel. *Photo: Doug Nye Collection*

Below, 1965 Cobra Daytona coupé in the Spa 500km race. Bob Bondurant at the wheel. *Photo: Daniel Paris*

Above, 1952 Connaught A-type Formula 2 car, at Silverstone, 1956. B. Holt at the wheel. *Photo: T. C. March*

Right, 1954 Connaught B-type with streamlined body, at Silverstone. Kenneth McAlpine at the wheel. *Photo: T. C. March*

Below, 1954 Connaught ALSR-type sports car at Silverstone in 1955. Les Leston at the wheel. *Photo: T. C. March*

Below, 1954 Connaught B-type with standard body. *Photo: Keith Dannatt*

Right below, 1957 Connaught B-type with 'toothpaste tube' body, at Goodwood. Stuart Lewis-Evans at the wheel. *Photo: Geoffrey Goddard*

box; suspension was by wishbones and torsion bars all round, and cast elektron wheels were fitted. The car appeared only once during its first season, when McAlpine collected a 2nd and a 5th at Castle Combe. De Dion back axles featured in 1951, but as yet only minor events were supported, places being gained at Goodwood, Boreham and Ibsley.

With the upgrading of Formula 2 in 1952, serious works racing began. Four cars finished in the British GP at Silverstone and there was also a 1-2-3 victory in a race at Charterhall. Hilborn-Travers fuel injection was tried in 1953 and output went up to 165bhp. In the *Daily Express* Trophy at Silverstone, Salvadori took 2nd place behind Hawthorn's works Ferrari, while Rolt was 3rd, and there were other wins and places at Goodwood, Silverstone, Oulton Park, Thruxton, Ibsley and the Crystal Palace. The cars did less well on the Continent, even though the works Connaughts were supported by Claes's privately-owned machine. It is not surprising that 1954 was an interregnum, the A-types turning out unsuccessfully for the British GP while the B-type was under development. The only new car to race was the ALSR-type sports model with 1,484cc Lea-Francis-type engine; it finished 10th in the TT, but failed to satisfy its owner, John Coombs, who put the power unit into a Lotus. Connaught 1·5-litre engines also went into two sports-racing Coopers, while in 1955 the ALSR won its class in the Goodwood 9 Hours' Race. A second example with tail-fins, said to be capable of 146mph (235kph), ran at Le Mans that year, but retired; shortly afterwards it was destroyed in an accident which killed W. T. Smith, its driver, during the Dundrod TT.

The B-type was first seen in late 1954, and featured a 2,470cc dohc 4-cylinder Alta engine (initially with SU fuel injection but later with Weber carburettors) which developed 240bhp at 6,400rpm. The tubular ladder-type frame was new, but the gearbox, suspension and final drive were inherited from the A-type, and by the time it reached the circuits it had disc brakes and magnesium alloy wheels as well. Full-width aerodynamic bodywork with a tail-fin was used in early days. This car cost £15,000 to develop, and was raced for three seasons on a shoestring: it was hoped that sales to private owners would finance the team, and several were sold, though the customers preferred conventional bodywork resembling that of the A-types. At home 1955 was a poor year, with several retirements, and only Parnell's 4th place at Oulton Park was a consolation. Two cars were, however, sent to Syracuse for Brooks and Leston to drive, and the miracle happened. Tony Brooks defeated the works Maseratis at an average speed of 99·05mph (159·41kph) and broke the lap record as well.

Only open-wheel bodies were used in 1956, when Connaught tried to cram as many events as possible into a difficult season. In the Richmond Trophy at Goodwood Leston was 3rd behind a pair of Maseratis; and the 2nd and 3rd places of Scott-Brown and Titterington in the *Daily Express* race were the consequences of heavy retirements among the faster cars. Fairman took 4th place in the British GP; he was also 5th in the Italian GP, two places behind his team-mate, Ron Flockhart. Leslie Marr put a 3,442cc twin-ohc Jaguar engine in his B-type and raced it in New Zealand, finishing 3rd in the Lady Wigram Trophy and 4th in the Grand Prix, and Patsy Burt set a new ladies' record (25·45sec) at Brighton Speed Trials.

Two new cars were built in 1957, though a third prototype, the rear-engined 'D', was never made. One of these machines was a B-type with a dart-shaped body, nicknamed the 'Toothpaste Tube', but the C-type had a spaceframe, strut-type front suspension, and inboard rear brakes. At Syracuse Bueb was 5th (the other two Connaughts retired); in the Richmond Formula 1 race at Goodwood Lewis-Evans and Fairman were 1st and 2nd, but this was the works team's last success. Third and 5th represented their best against Maserati and Gordini opposition at Pau, Lewis-Evans retired at Naples, and drove the 'Toothpaste Tube' into 4th place at Monaco. At this juncture the finances ran out, and that October the Connaughts and their spare parts came under the hammer at the little factory at Send. The C-type, which had not yet run, was eventually completed, and Bob Said retired it in the 1959 United States GP. Lately, Connaughts have run in Historic Races in Britain. MCS

Conrero (I)

Virgilio Conrero's Turin tuning establishment has had a long association with competitive motoring, mainly in the sports and GT classes, modifying FIAT and Alfa Romeo products. When Formula Junior was recognized internationally in 1959, Conrero produced an attractive little single-seater with a front-mounted engine and a body shape evolved by Giovanni Michelotti. All-independent suspension was used with swinging links and coil-spring damper units, and the centre cockpit was made possible by a very low transmission line, leading to drop gears behind the differential. A choice of Fiat 1100 or linereddown Peugeot 203 engines was offered, but the cars achieved little major success.

Conrero are still thriving as one of Italy's leading speed equipment and tuning companies. DCN

Cooper (GB)

Charles Cooper of Surbiton in Surrey had served a full apprenticeship in motor sport as mechanic and manager to Kaye Don between the wars. In 1946 he built the first Cooper 500 cars for his son John and Eric Brandon. These featured both front and rear suspension by courtesy of the front ends of the Fiat Topolino, with rear-mounted JAP engines of speedway type. Both were very successful, and for 1948 a batch of 12 Mark 2 versions was laid down, with the since-famous alloy wheels. Stirling Moss and Peter Collins were among the early race-winners.

Improved designs were brought out each year, and the cars were seldom headed in national or international competition. Even between 1951 and 1954, when com-

petition was most active, they won 64 out of 78 major races, their successful drivers including J. Brise, Alan Brown, Ivor Bueb, Ian Burgess, Ken Carter, J. Coombs, Bob Gerard, D. Gray, Les Leston, Stuart Lewis-Evans, André Loens, Jim Russell, George Wicken and Bill Whitehouse. Milestones included the adoption of a tubular frame with the Mark 6 in 1952 and Palmer-HRG disc brakes on the 1955 Mark 9, but the transverse-leaf suspension layout remained the same throughout. Virtually every conceivable 500 engine was used at some time, but latterly the 'double-knocker' twin-ohc Norton predominated in the results.

With little modification, about 100 cars were fitted with V-twin engines, the most useful of which was the JAP. Ken Wharton, who had completed a 1,000-mile rally in 1950 with a front-mounted MG-engined Cooper, took the RAC hill-climb championship with these cars from 1951 to 1954, Tony Marsh and David Boshier-Jones following this up with three years each as champions on the hills. These cars also showed well in the shorter F2 and Formule Libre races, where their exceptional power-weight ratio could overcome the handicap of engines with less capacity and reliability than their rivals.

Further sports models were constructed, including the MG-engined JOY 500 of Cliff Davis, with bodywork styled on a Superleggera Ferrari, which won many races.

In 1952 the 2-litre Cooper-Bristol was introduced, featuring a front engine in a box-section frame, with a tubular superstructure supporting the body. Mike Hawthorn made a name for himself and the model with his driving of Bob Chase's car, and other successes were gained by Alan Brown, Bob Gerard, Rodney Nuckey and Ken Wharton, among others. Stirling Moss's original Cooper-Alta was an unlucky car partly designed by John Cooper of the *Autocar* staff, no relation of his namesake, but its replacement was based on the later tubular Cooper-Bristol frame. A few sports versions were also made. In 1954 the Cooper-Jaguar was introduced, and Peter Whitehead's car, lighter and with better road-holding than the contemporary D-type Jaguar, won the Irish Wakefield Trophy race.

In 1955 a new rear-engined centre-seat sports model was introduced, with 1,098 or 1,460cc ohc Coventry-Climax engines. The cut-off tail was said to be featured for expediency in transporting, but was found to be aerodynamically efficient on the principles expounded by Professor Kamm. Jack Brabham used a single-seat version with Bristol engine for his entry into GP racing. Class victories were recorded in the Sebring 9 Hours and

1952 Cooper-MG sports car. Jack Sears at the wheel. *Photo: Guy Griffiths*

Left below, 1952 Cooper-Bristol Formula 2 driven by Ken Wharton (left), with Ron Flockhart's A-type Connaught. *Photo: T. C. March*

Below, 1951 Cooper-JAP Formula 3 car at Brands Hatch. B. C. Ecclestone at the wheel. *Photo: Sport & General*

Goodwood 12 Hours races, and the works drivers Ivor
Bueb and Jim Russell achieved a number of good
placings in smaller events.

Formula 2 cars were made to similar specifications,
and these were the leaders in the category in 1957 and
1958 in the hands of Brabham, Bruce McLaren and Roy
Salvadori. The 1958 model discarded transverse leaf
suspension for the first time. In 1959 the Cooper-
Borgward cars run by the British Racing Partnership
won all 19 major races in the class.

The make gained a rapid foothold in Formula 1 when
Rob Walker's entries of Stirling Moss and Maurice
Trintignant defeated the conventional front-engined
cars in the 1958 Argentine and Monaco Grand Prix, and
Jack Brabham set the seal on Cooper's success and set
the rear-engined trend for the future with the World
Championship in 1959, backed by McLaren and Salvadori. He underlined it with another Championship in
1960, a decisive one with six victories in *grandes épreuves*
for the Type 60. An interesting Formula 1 special was the
Cooper-Castellotti with 4-cylinder Super Squalo Ferrari
engine, and a portent of things to come might be seen in
J. T. Atkins' Cooper-Maserati.

The spaceframe Cooper Monaco was introduced in
1958, at first with 2·7 Coventry-Climax engine, and this
was the car to beat in sports car racing. As late as 1963
Roy Salvadori scored several major wins, and this model
was also developed by Carroll Shelby, retailer of the AC
Cobra models, as the basis of his King Cobra V-8-
engined sports racing car.

In 1960 the Mark 1 Formula Junior was made, being
superseded by the Mark 2 at the end of the year. John
Surtees, newly weaned from two wheels, was one of the
more successful drivers of these cars, whose BMC
engines did not always perform as well as the Fords.
The 1961 model, with coil rear suspension and fibreglass
body, performed better and gave some wins to John
Love, Tony Maggs and John Rhodes.

British Grand Prix racing suffered a setback in 1961 in
having no engine immediately available that was competitive with the Italians, and Cooper had a lean year.
At Indianapolis, however, Brabham's basically Grand
Prix car caused amusement among the establishment
before the start, but troubled looks after it had finished
9th. Following Brabham's departure to build his own
cars, Bruce McLaren was upgraded to no 1 driver for
1962, and victories at Spa and at Reims earned 3rd place
in the drivers' and constructors' championships.

Ken Tyrrell took over the management of the Formula
3 team for 1963, using the T66 and the same team of
McLaren and Maggs, but this was another poor year.

Top, 1954 Cooper-Bristol sports car driven
by Archie Scott-Brown leads Tony Brooks'
Frazer Nash at Goodwood. *Photo: Autosport*

Above, 1955 Cooper-Climax at Brunton
Hill-Climb. Patsy Burt at the wheel. *Photo:
A. Hollister*

Left, 1961 Cooper-Climax Indianapolis car.
Jack Brabham at the wheel. *Photo:
Indianapolis Motor Speedway*

Right, 1966 Cooper-Maserati Type 81
emerging from the tunnel at Monaco.
Jochen Rindt at the wheel. *Photo: Michael
R. Hewitt*

In Formula Junior the BMC hydrolastic suspension
was employed, but the works cars were seldom in the
picture. Roger Penske in the United States was doing
well with the Cooper-based Zerex special, later to form
the genesis of the line of McLaren sports-racing cars.

In 1964 came the meteoric rise to fame of Jacky
Stewart at the wheel of the T72 Formula 3 model.
Though the T73 Formula 1 car was of similar design,
McLaren and ex-World Champion Phil Hill achieved
little of note. The sports cars were now dropped, and the
semi-monocoque Formula 2 model did not perform well.

In the following year the Formula 1 team was strengthened by backing from the Chipstead Motors group and
by the recruitment of the up-and-coming Jochen Rindt,

but once again a disappointing season ensued, and this time there was no dominance of any subsidiary formula to compensate. A determined effort to recover was made in 1966, with a new monocoque designed by Tony Robinson, and V-12 engines developed specially by Maserati for the project following the non-materialization of the 16-cylinder Coventry-Climax. Drivers during the year included Bonnier, Ginther, Ligier, Rindt and Surtees. However, the cars still had an uncompetitive power-to-weight ratio, and difficult handling, and only did well by skilful driving or by default of others. The new T83 car in Formula 3 was even less successful.

New Maserati engines were tried for 1967 without sufficient improvement, although Pedro Rodriguez achieved an unexpected victory in the South African GP. In 1968 the cars were improved again, this time with BRM V-12 engines, but the team was beset with driver troubles, starting with the loss of Ludovico Scarfiotti. By this time it was only in hill-climbs that Coopers were at all competitive in major events.

A last effort was made in 1969 with the early announcement of the T90 full-length monocoque for Formula 5000, with the Vegantune Chevrolet engine as standard, but this car was not as successful as later and lighter designs in the class. Insufficient sponsorship could be found to develop the Formula 1 car, now trying Alfa Romeo engines, and except for the badges on high-performance British Leyland Minis, the Cooper name faded quietly from the scene. DF

Cornelian (US)

The Cornelian was one of the most advanced racing cars of its day, but because only one car was built, it has been largely neglected by historians. It was developed from a production light car of 1914, made by Blood Brothers Machine Company, of Allegan, Mich., which had the unusual features of frameless monocoque construction, and independent suspension all round by transverse leaf springs, two at the front, and three at the rear. The engine was a 1,688cc 4-cylinder Sterling, giving 18bhp in the production car. A stripped stock two-seater driven by Cap Kennedy finished 7th in a 100-mile race at Kalamazoo against competition from monsters such as Burman's Peugeot and de Palma's Mercedes. For the 1915 Indianapolis race Howard Blood and Louis Chevrolet prepared a racing model with engine enlarged to 1,883cc, larger valves and aluminium pistons, which increased power to about 35bhp. It had a streamlined body with built-in windscreen formed around the scuttle cowling. With Chevrolet at the wheel, the Cornelian was in 12th position at one point, but retired after 77 laps with a broken valve. It never appeared again at Indianapolis, but was driven by Roscoe Dunning at dirt track meetings for several years afterwards. GNG

Corre, La Licorne (F)

The first Corres were Renault-like voiturettes with shaft drive and 634cc single-cylinder De Dion engines, and supported the appropriate class of the big events in 1901; a 3rd in this category in the Paris–Berlin represented their best performance, though 1902 was somewhat better. That year's cars ran to 864cc, and there was a 4th in the Circuit du Nord, plus a victory in the voiturette class of the Ardennes race, thanks to the absence of all the big names. They had progressed to 2·5-litre aiv twins by 1903, when the cars ran both as voiturettes and *voitures légères*, Corre himself finishing 5th in the smallest class of the Circuit des Ardennes. By 1906 they had moved up to the 1,000kg class with a shaft-drive 10·6-litre 4-cylinder, innocent of bodywork, but d'Hespel broke his gearbox on the first lap of the Ardennes race, and Collomb's 17th place in the 1907 GP was hardly impressive. This car also ran, without success, in the 1911 Grand Prix de France, but by this time voiturette racing was once again in fashion, and Corre supported this category in 1907, 1908 and 1910, the 1907 cars (which achieved nothing) being the first to race under the La Licorne name. Collomb was 5th in the 1908 Coupe de l'Auto, and 1910 saw two period freaks, a 100 × 250mm single driven by Delpierre and a 100 × 300mm (2,350cc) machine entrusted to Collomb, who came in 5th in that year's race.

The firm was planning a return to the sport in 1914, but unlike many of the Coupe de l'Auto projects of that year the La Licorne emerged with a vengeance in 1920. It had a very long-stroke 1·4-litre push-rod unit with four separate cylinders, the work of Causan, which developed

Left, 1915 Cornelian at Indianapolis. Louis Chevrolet at the wheel, with his brothers Arthur and Gaston at right, behind the car. *Photo: Indianapolis Motor Speedway*

Below, 1920 (Corre) La Licorne at Le Mans. Collomb at the wheel. *Photo: T. A. S. O. Mathieson Collection*

47bhp. In its first operational season it ran well at Gaillon, but retired in the Coupe Internationale des Voiturettes. What is more, Collomb tried again in the 1921, 1922 and 1923 races, though his only success was in the 1,500cc category of the 1921 voiturette event at Boulogne, and not in the Coupe.

Latterly La Licorne concentrated on sports-car events, using 2-litre and later 1·5-litre cars. Though they supported all the first four Le Mans 24-Hour Races, their best placings were 8th and 9th in 1925. One of the old Causan-designed machines could still show a good turn of speed in the 1928 National Trophy at Boulogne, though it retired. In this year Petit took 6th place in the Monte Carlo Rally, following it up with an outright win in 1930. Vallon's 1,100cc 'sports car' (one of the popular 905cc 5CV sv models) took 2nd place in the 1931 Bol d'Or, and in 1932 he and Galoczy took 1st and 2nd places in general classification, though both were beaten on speed by Sandford with one of his 3-wheelers. MCS

Costin-Nathan see Nathan

Cosworth (GB)
Designed by Robin Herd, this 1969 Formula 1 project by the well-known engine firm was never fully developed. It was powered by a Cosworth-Ford DFV Series 9 engine and several notable features were incorporated, including 4-wheel drive. However it was found that the added weight and complication was not justified by the performance. DF

Côte (F)
This firm ran 3-litre 2-stroke 4-cylinder cars in the 1911 and 1912 Coupe de l'Auto Races, without much success, though in the former year they were the sole representatives of valveless units after the Koechlins non-started. De Vere was 10th in 1911 and 8th and last in 1912, though he also took 7th place in that season's Grand Prix de France. More interesting was Gabriel's appearance in the 1912 Côte team. The cars had overdrive gearboxes and Riley detachable wheels. MCS

Cottin-Desgouttes (F)
Like its fellow Lyonnaise make, La Buire, the Cottin-Desgouttes was seen either in hill-climbs or fuel consumption races. As early as 1908 the company claimed ten places in hill-climbs and another five in sprints, but though Lord Carbery raced one at Brooklands in 1911, his 10·6-litre 4-cylinder sv sprint machine (now owned by John Goddard) is more typical of the firm's interests at the time. In 1924 three 3-litre 4-cylinder ohv cars with dry-sump lubrication and triple ignition (two magnetos and a coil) were prepared for the Grand Prix de Tourisme. Lacharnay, Colas and Rost took the first three places in the four-seater category, the first-mentioned averaging 55·8mph (89·80kph), and the firm repeated their success in 1925, Lacharnay again being the team's best performer. L. G. Hornsted brought a 3,921cc 6-cylinder ohv sports model to Brooklands that year, but raced only once. MCS

Cox (GB)
Announced for 1967, the Cox GTM featured a mid-engine position for the Mini power unit, in a semi-monocoque steel chassis unit, a layout which appeared promising to the club racer in the GT coupé class. This promise was fulfilled by one or two drivers, notably Howard Heerey, who took over production for 1969. By 1970 some 50 kits had been supplied. DF

Left top, 1927 Cozette 1,100cc racing car. *Photo: Montagu Motor Museum*

Right top, 1912 Côte Coupe de l'Auto car. De Vere at the wheel. *Photo: Montagu Motor Museum*

Above, 1924 Cottin-Desgouttes in the Touring Car GP, Lacharnay at the wheel, followed by Dauvêrgne's Peugeot. *Photo: Autocar*

Cozette (F)
Built by René Cozette of supercharger fame, this little racing car had a 4-cylinder 2-stroke engine, with eight pistons and two crankshafts in a vertically-opposed layout similar to that of the pre-World War 1 Gobron-Brilliés. Dimensions were 56mm × 55·8mm × 2, giving a swept volume of 1,100cc. A large Cozette supercharger was mounted vertically ahead of the cylinder block. The engine and prop-shaft were tilted slightly towards the rear, and the body was of the classic single-seater racing car design of the period. The car was built in 1927, and entered in the 1928 French Grand Prix, but did not start. With it, Prince Cantacuzene broke records at Montlhéry. Later, René Cozette was killed in it when the steering failed at nearly 120mph (193kph). GNG

Crespelle (F)
The first Crespelle was made in 1906, and the early models made a feature of long-stroke single-cylinder engines such as De Dion (100 × 280mm) and Aster (106 × 192mm). Three Aster-engined cars ran in the 1909 Coupe des Voiturettes, but all retired, while no better fortune attended d'Avaray's De Dion-engined Crespelle in the 1909 Catalan Cup. Another long-stroke single-cylinder car whose exhaust rockers and tappet rods projected through the top of the bonnet ran in the 1912 Grand Prix de France, but again retired. Despite this discouraging record on the circuits, Crespelles did well in hill-climbs, winning their class at Gaillon five times

between 1906 and 1912, and at least once at Mont Ventoux. Their 1912 Mont Ventoux car had a 4-cylinder T-head Janvier engine of 3 litres, and with this car Crespelle entered in the 1913 Coupe de la Sarthe, holding the lead for five laps before retiring with timing gear trouble. Production of touring Crespelles continued until 1923. GNG

Crosley (US)

The Crosley light car was made in Cincinnati, Ohio, from 1939 to 1952. Pre-World War 2 cars used air-cooled 2-cylinder engines and were quite unsporting, but in 1946 the company introduced a 726cc 4-cylinder water-cooled engine with single overhead camshaft. This was used to power the Hotshot sports two-seater which competed successfully in the smallest class, at the time, of SCCA racing for several years. Fritz Koster and Ralph Deshon won the Index of Performance at the first Sebring

Top, 1911 Crespelle at Gaillon. d'Avaray at the wheel. *Photo: Montagu Motor Museum*

Above, 1961 Crosslé-Ford Formula Junior at Kirkistown. John Crosslé at the wheel. *Photo: Brian Foley*

Left, 1964 Crosslé-Ford 1·6-litre sports car, in Dunboyne village. Charles Eyre-Maunsell at the wheel. *Photo: Brian Foley*

Below, c 1966 Crosslé-Ford 4·7-litre V-8 racing car. *Photo: Brian Foley*

12-Hour Race in December 1950, and Briggs Cunningham entered a Hotshot at Le Mans in 1951. It failed to finish, but lapped at 74mph (119·09kph), the speed of the winning Alfa Romeo 17 years earlier. ARB

Crosslé (GB)

John Crosslé built his first car in 1957, and with this and subsequent one-offs won the Ford Championship of Ireland in 1958, 1959 and 1960. From 1959 he was building replicas of the spaceframe 1,172cc Ford-engined car for his friends, and in 1961 he set up near Belfast as a full-time racing car constructor.

The first single-seater was a Formula Junior machine made in 1961, but this rear-engined vehicle was more successful when converted to 1,172 specification, winning the championship race at Kirkistown in 1962. A similar car in Davidson's hands won the Ford points championship in 1961, 1962 and 1963. In 1963, when Crosslé's products finished in the first three places in the Kirkistown race, Crosslé introduced his first sports model, with frame of round and square section tubing and his own fibreglass bodywork. Charles Eyre-Maunsell took the 1964 Irish Sports Car Championship in Class D with this machine. Most cars which were raced in Ireland were equipped with Lotus-Ford engines, whereas those used abroad were more successful in the 2-litre BMW-powered variety. One of these, converted to a GT car, was used successfully by John Green as late as 1969. Ford V-8 engines were employed in both sports and single-seaters, and Brian Nelson's Daimler V-8-engined car was also well known.

Crosslé subsequently concentrated on single-seaters, constructing on average some two dozen a year. The 12F of 1967, with Crosslé's own wheels, 5-speed Hewland gearbox and tubular spaceframe, won the 1968 SCCA Formula B Championship in the hands of Roger Barr. Its successors were the 14F in 1968 and the 18F for 1970, used by Brian Nelson that year in winning the Leinster Trophy. The 16F model, developed in conjunction with C. T. Wooler Ltd, was also very successful, being used by Gerry Birrell to win the 1969 European Formula Ford Championship. The 17F was a Formula 3 car and the 19F a Formula 2 version.

The later fibreglass bodies were supplied by Brian Faloon and Co. of Belfast, but all design and mechanical construction work was carried out on Crosslé's own premises, and the cars were noted for their sound engineering and meticulous finish. DF

Crosslëy (GB)

Crossley of Manchester scratched their 1905 TT entry,

and the firm made its first serious impression when Charles Jarrott set the fashion for record runs between London and the French Riviera in 1906, with an outward trip at 24·2mph (38·95kph). Despite the censorious attitude of the press, he improved on this time in 1907, but it was not until the 1910–13 period that Crossleys started to make a name in hill-climbs and sprints, largely in the hands of Hubert Woods, their designer, and Cecil Bianchi. These more or less stock sv machines were fast and powerful — the 4·5-litre 20 gave 62bhp at 2,000rpm — and their successes were numerous, for instance at Saltburn in 1910; Ironbridge, Saltburn and Cornist Hall in 1911; and at Rivington Pike, Aston Clinton, Caerphilly and Shelsley Walsh in 1912, when Woods's 20 actually beat two Coupe de l'Auto Sunbeams in a scratch event. Once again they tried in the 1914 TT with lightly-tuned tourers, but had no success. In the early 1920s, Leon Cushman ran a pair of the 3·8-litre sv 20/70hp sports models at Brooklands achieving lap speeds of 95–100mph (152–160kph). Crossley's last competition cars were a team of very special Tens linered down to bring them into the 1,100cc category, which Vernon Balls ran unsuccessfully in both the British Empire Trophy Race and the TT in 1932. MCS

Crouch (GB)

The Crouch light car began as a 3-wheeler in 1912, but a 4-wheeler was made in 1913, and in the early 1920s a number of racing versions ran at Brooklands. A car with rear-mounted 1,090cc V-twin engine and chain drive was driven by J. Cocker to several victories in 1921, and was entered for that year's 200 Miles Race, but did not start. The following year two Crouches were entered, one with rear engine, driven by J. W. Tollady, and the other a new front-engined car, still a V-twin, driven by Pressland. They both retired. Tollady's car was a sprightly performer in handicap races, lapping at over 82mph (132kph), and winning several times during the 1922 season. It finished 5th in its class in the 1923 200 Miles Race, in which event a new Crouch with 4-cylinder 1·5-litre Anzani engine was driven by Alfred Moss, Stirling's father. He retired after 29 laps. This model was offered for sale as the Super Sports, with boat-tail body, and a top speed of 70mph (112kph). Production lasted until 1926; touring Crouches were made until 1928. GNG

CTA Arsenal (F)

The CTA-Arsenal of 1947 emanated from the Government-controlled Centre d'Etudes Techniques de l'Automobile et du Cycle, and was an attempt to produce a French Formula 1 contender. Designed by Albert Lory,

who had been responsible for the 1926 GP Delage, it was a 1,482cc V-8 with 4ohc and hemispherical heads, with independent suspension (by torsion bars) all round and 2LS hydraulic brakes. The engine was said to give 266bhp at 7,500rpm, and good weight distribution was assured by dividing the fuel between five tanks. Sommer entered one in the 1947 French GP, but it broke a half-shaft on the start-line, and though both CTAs turned up for practice in 1948, they were withdrawn. In 1951 Antoine Lago was 'caretaking' the cars at Suresnes, and there was talk of putting a CTA engine into a Talbot chassis. Automobiles Talbot, however, were already short of cash, and preferred to use what little was available on their well-tried 4·5-litre sports-racers. MCS

Cummins (US)

In 1930 the Cummins Diesel Company was a small one whose main business was making engines for private yachts. As this trade was disastrously hit by the Depression, president Clessie Cummins turned to demonstrating the practicability of the diesel engine in motorcars. The first Cummins racing car used a 360ci (5,899cc) 85bhp 4-cylinder Model U engine in a chassis derived from that of the Model A Duesenberg. With this car Cummins set a world record for diesel-engined cars at Daytona, with a speed of 100·75mph (162·06kph), in 1931. For that year's Indianapolis race the same car was entered, driven by Dave Evans who completed the 500 miles without a stop, finishing 13th at an average speed of 86·17mph (138·67kph). The following summer Cummins toured Europe in this car, and while in England took it to Brooklands where he lapped at 74·63mph (120·11kph). Lower gearing fitted for touring purposes accounted for the lower speed.

1932 Crossley Ten sports car in a West Hants Trial. *Photo: Montagu Motor Museum*

1931 Cummins Indianapolis car, with luggage trunk fitted for touring. Clessie Cummins at the wheel. *Photo: Cummins Engine Company*

Far left, 1923 Crouch V-twin at Brooklands. Ian Parker at the wheel. *Photo: Montagu Motor Museum*

Left, 1947 CTA-Arsenal 1·5-litre GP car. *Photo: Cyril Posthumus Collection*

1952 Cummins Indianapolis car. Fred Agabashian at the wheel. *Photo: Indianapolis Motor Speedway*

Daf (NL)

The Dutch small car and heavy commercial manufacturer took a great interest in racing and rallying in the mid-1960s, beginning an F3 programme in 1965. The competition department, under Rob Koch, brought Brabham chassis and had them lengthened to accommodate standard Cosworth F3 engines and their own Variomatic belt-drive automatic transmission. Later their own special chassis were built. Eventually they bought Tecno frames and used Holbay power units. Drivers included Mike Beckwith and Gijs van Lennep, and the cars achieved some notable performances, especially in very wet conditions. The Variomatic system allowed the engines to work at almost peak revs constantly, and consequently the sound of an approaching F3 DAF was unmistakeable. The small power deficit eventually became a marked disadvantage in this competitive class, and the team withdrew at the close of the 1968 season having completed some useful development. The leading DAF exponent in rallying was Claude Laurent, who covered 93,200 miles (150,000km) in the course of 25 rallies in 1965. He was 3rd in the Acropolis Rally and 5th in the Tulip, both in 1969. DCN

Later Cummins-engined entries at Indianapolis were in 1934, when two cars ran, of which one finished 12th and the other retired; 1950, when one car ran, and retired with defective supercharger; and 1952, when a car was driven by Fred Agabashian. In the qualifying trials he broke the track record at 139mph (223·7kph), but retired in the race with clogged turbocharger intake. GNG

Cunningham (US)

In 1950 Briggs Cunningham entered two Cadillacs, a stock coupé and a special-bodied open two-seater, 'Le Monstre', at Le Mans, and in 1951 he returned with two sports cars of his own design, built at Palm Beach, Fla. They had 331ci (5·4-litre) Chrysler V-8 engines, tubular frames and De Dion rear axles. The Fitch and Walters car ran as high as 2nd place for a while, but finished only 18th. Cunningham and Bill Spear drove a C-4R into 4th place at Le Mans in 1952, and in 1953 Walters and Fitch finished 3rd. Two other Cunninghams finished in the first ten in 1953: Cunningham and Spear 7th, and Moran and Bennett 10th. The Cunningham's first, and only major, victory was at the Sebring 12 Hours Race in March 1953 (Walters and Fitch). In 1954 Cunninghams were 3rd and 5th at Le Mans (Spear and Johnson, and Cunningham and Bennett). All these cars had used the Chrysler V-8 engine, but in 1955 Briggs built the C-6R powered by a 182ci (3-litre) 4-cylinder Meyer-Drake-Offenhauser engine. It ran at Le Mans but retired at about half distance. GNG

Dagrada (I)

Dagrada were the first of the Formula Junior manufacturers to offer a Lancia Appia V-4 engine, and their cars were tubby-looking front-engined vehicles with a very short wheelbase. The transmission line was offset from the angled engine to pass along the right side of the cockpit. Twin Weber carburettors fed from either side of the block, demanding a large bulge in the bodywork on the right-hand side. Independent suspension was by links and coil-springs at the front and a transverse leaf at the rear. Giancarlo Baghetti was one of Dagrada's leading drivers, but as the British makes began to dominate the Formula with their Ford engines and advanced chassis design, so Dagrada production ceased. DCN

Daihatsu (J)

Daihatsu's only notable contribution to motor sport has been their P5 Group 6 prototype released in early 1967. This car, showing some similarity to the Porsche Carrera 6, was a mid-engined fibreglass bodied two-seat coupé, weighing some 540kg and being powered by a 1,261cc dohc four valves per cylinder engine, fuel injected and driving through a 5-speed transaxle. The car was introduced under a veil of secrecy and contested the up to 1,300 and 2-litre classes in national events with works drivers Yoshida and Fukusawa. DCN

Left, 1952 Cunningham C3 coupé. *Photo: Ozzie Lyons*

Right, 1953 Cunningham C5R at the start of the Le Mans 24-Hour Race. *Photo: Rodolfo Mailander*

Daimler (D)

The first competition in which Daimler cars took part was a joint event in 1898, a car and bicycle trial in the Tyrolean Alps. Two chain-drive type Daimlers took part, driven by Wilhelm Bauer and Wilhelm Werner. Designed by Maybach, the new 24hp Daimler Phönix appeared for the 1899 season and was entered for the Nice Week by Emile Jellinek. He won the Nice-Castellane hill-climb in the touring car class for which he used his pseudonym 'Monsieur Mercédès' for the first time. The first Semmering hill-climb of 1899 — not really a race in this year but a club run — brought out Jellinek again and another Daimler driven by Gyulai. For 1900 a two-seater Phönix racing car appeared at the Nice-La Turbie hill-climb, in which Wilhelm Bauer so tragically died, while Stead won in the touring car class. Bauer's accident made it clear that this short-wheelbased, high car was not suitable for

gh-speed competition driving and led to the development of the later models. Nevertheless, this car had an ove average performance. The engine was a 4-cylinder 5-litre developing about 24hp and good for a maximum peed of 55mph (88kph). It had two more victories to its edit: Ritter von Stern won the second Semmering ill-climb and the Salzberg-Linz-Vienna long-distance ial. From the 1901 Nice Week onwards the name Mercedes was used for all Daimler private cars. HON

aimler (GB)

s early as October 1897 Henry Sturmey drove a 2-ylinder Coventry-Daimler from John O'Groats to ands End at a running average of 10mph (16kph), and 1899 the make won three gold medals in the ACGBI ichmond Trials. The Hon. John Scott-Montagu's 3-litre -cylinder was also the first all-British combination of river and car to race on the Continent, even if a 3rd place the tourist class of Paris–Ostend (1899) was nothing gnificant in itself. Stead won his class in a hill-climb as ar away as Turin, but Daimler's great years started in 904 and extended to 1908. This was the heydey of their ast L-head 4-cylinder type with side-chain drive and the amous fluted radiator. All of these were big: the 36hp f 1904 ran to 5·7 litres, but the 58s seen in sprints and ill-climbs in 1908 disposed of a formidable 10,431cc. here was a good start in 1904 when Instone made 2nd d behind a Gordon Bennett Napier at Sunrising, and here were six major fastest times of day in 1905. Occa-ionally, as at Blackpool in 1906, other makes, such as Darracq, beat them, but the Daimlers were cars to be eckoned with even in America, where there were two laces at Brighton Beach in 1905, and several victories, ncluding Atlantic City and Wilkes Barre, the following eason. The works also supported the Herkomer Trophy rials in 1905 and 1906. On their second appearance Mrs Manville and Lord Montagu won gold medals. The cars vere seen in the 1906 Italian Coppa d'Oro, and a team of hree, run as de Lucas after the Daimler Co's Italian cences, were driven by Ison, Hémery and Le Blon in the 907 Targa Florio. These all finished, a better fate than ttended the special 8-litres built for the Kaiserpreis. Only Ison reached the final, surviving one lap.

In 1909 came the Knight double-sleeve-valve engine, tandardized for all models in 1910, and Daimler's nterest in competitions—not to mention their frequent weekly win' advertisements—faded away. Not that the leeve-valvers were necessarily slow: there were, for nstance, class victories at Beaulieu and Pendine in 1909.

In the later 1930s there were works Daimler entries for he bigger British rallies, their 1939 crop including Crouch's 2·5-litre 'Dolphin' sports tourer, which took a rd in class in the Scottish event. This design's successor, he short-stroke Century, made a brief impression in aloon-car racing in 1954, when Parnell headed his class n the International Touring Car event at Silverstone, veraging 73·74mph (118·67kph) to the 75·55mph 121·59kph) of the fastest Mk VII Jaguar. A true sports Daimler appeared in 1959, the Turner-designed 2,548cc hv V-8 SP 250, but despite an output of 140bhp and a naximum speed of over 120mhp (190kph) its impact at ome was confined to club racing. There were, however, uccesses abroad including a class victory in the 1960 SCCA championships in the United States and a victory n the New South Wales Sports Car Championship at Catalina Park as late as 1963. This engine has also been applied to sprint cars since 1962, the outstanding instance eing Peter Westbury's Felday. MCS

DAMW (D)

This was a combine (Deutsches Amt für Material—und Warenprüfung) backed by the East German government. Three types of cars were developed in 1951: 1·5- and 2-litre sports cars and a Formula 2 racing car. Chassis of these types were identical, as was the 2-litre engine layout. This was based on the pre-war BMW 328, bore and stroke being 66 × 96mm. Output was about 125bhp. The 1·5-litre engine differed only in having a bore and stroke of 66 × 73mm and had an output of about 105bhp. A 1·5-litre car scored a remarkable victory in the 1952 Avus-rennen, when Rosenhammer won his class with an average speed of 105mph (169kph), ahead of Glöckler in a Porsche. At the end of the 1952 season this combine was transferred to EMW. HON

Daren (GB)

The prototype Daren GT, designed, built and raced by John Green, was outstandingly successful in British Club events, starting with victories in the car's first three races. However, with the lifting of the minimum weight regulations for 1969, Green had to produce a new design, and the Daren Mark 2 was a Group 6 sports car design, based on a composite steel and aluminium central monocoque section. During the next two years eight of this model were produced at the Leighton Buzzard works, those of Peter and Jeremy Richardson achieving some success in their classes in Continental hill-climbs and races, and the Lucas Formula 3-engined car of Martin Raymond making quite a mark in British Club racing, including 21 victories from 25 starts. An improved Mark 3 version appeared in 1971 built for Daren in the Palliser works at Clapham, London. DF

Below, 1960 Daimler SP250 sports car at Silverstone in 1963. The Hon Basil Fielding at the wheel. *Photo: Michael Ware*

Right, 1968 Daren GT coupé. *Photo: Autosport*

Right below, 1970 Daren Mk 2 at Mondello Park, Dublin. Arthur Collier at the wheel. *Photo: Brian Foley*

Darmont-Morgan (F)

The Darmont was the French-built Morgan 3-wheeler. As early as 1920 the cars did well at the Gaillon hill-climb, other class victories being scored in the early Vintage years at La Turbie, Mont Agel, Laffrey, Mont Ventoux and Val Suzon. The make achieved a 1-2-3 victory in the 1921 Paris–Nice Trial: interestingly enough not only Darmont, but also Sandford, later a rival 3-wheeler manufacturer, was driving in the team on this occasion. Like their English counterparts, Darmonts went after international class records: Poiret won a new class title on a 668cc single-seater in 1922, in the Bois de Boulogne, and a year later Darmont, Dhome and Pierpoint took still more records. In 1927 Dhome covered a mile at Arpajon at 90·41mph (145·50kph), and a 500cc version managed 71·57mph (115·18kph). A Darmont finished 2nd in the cyclecar (i.e. 3-wheeler) category of the 1927 Bol d'Or, but by 1929 the more sophisticated Sandfords were predominant. MCS

Darracq, Talbot (ii) (F)

This make's competition career spans 57 years, though Alexandre Darracq's debut was inauspicious, as the huge 50hp chain-drive 4-cylinder car built in 1900 never came under starter's orders. Darracq tried again the following year in the voiturette class with 1,884cc twins and 3,770cc fours which did well from the start. Henry Farman's class win in Pau-Peyrehorade was followed by a 1-2-3 victory in the Nice–Salon–Nice, where the best Darracq averaged 29·9mph (48·12kph) to the 36mph (57·94kph) of the outright winner, Werner's Mercedes. The cars were, however, beaten by Giraud's Panhard in the Paris–Bordeaux, though they filled the next three places. The 4-cylinder machines were already over-engined, but in 1902 Darracq moved up to the *voiture legère* category with 5·9 litres and a nominal 24hp. Marcellin not only won his class in the Circuit du Nord, but also finished 5th overall, and in the Paris–Vienna the Darracqs proved very fast, being beaten only by Marcel Renault's Renault (which deprived them of a class victory) and Farman's big Panhard. There was compensation in that Guillaume's voiturette beat the Renault opposition. The 1903 light cars had heavily-drilled pressed-steel frames which were necessary as the new T-head engines ran to nearly 5·7 litres, and even the voiturettes had 3·8-litre units, hence a virtual absence of bodywork.

As light-car racing went into temporary eclipse, Darracq moved up into the heavy category with some 11,259cc ioe 4-cylinder cars for the 1904 Gordon Bennett Cup, which ran in their true colours in the French

Opposite top, from left to right, Brian Redman, Piers Courage and Richard Attwood. *Photo: Geoff Goddard*

Opposite bottom, left, Carroll Shelby and right, Phil Hill. *Photo: Geoff Goddard*

Left, 1905 Darracq 80hp Gordon Bennett racing car. *Photo: Montagu Motor Museum*

Right, 1905 Weir-Darracq 100hp in the English Eliminating Trials for the Gordon Bennett Race. A. Lee Guinness at the wheel. *Photo: Montagu Motor Museum*

eliminating trials at Mazagran, but turned up in the British trials as Weirs, and wore the white of Germany a Opels. In spite of this ambitious programme, only one Darracq (von Opel's Rüsselsheim-built car) appeared a Homburg, and this did not survive a single lap. Darracq 1905 racers were lighter 9·9-litre cars with full ohv and 3-speed gearboxes in unit with their differential-less bac axles. Success again eluded them in the Gordon Bennett Trials, but Hémery won the Circuit des Ardennes at 61·6mph (99·14kph) and the Vanderbilt Cup at almost exactly the same speed. During the year, too, the company completed a new sprint car with 22,518cc ohv V-8 engine, which recorded 109mph (175·4kph) at Arles-Salon, and was later persuaded to do over 117mph (188·3kph).

Best performances during the 1906 racing season wer Hémery's 2nd place in the Circuit des Ardennes and Algernon Guinness's 3rd place in the TT; 1907 was not much better, possibly because Alexandre Darracq, un-like de Turckheim of Lorraine-Dietrich, was not adept a keeping his drivers happy. The best they could do in the Grand Prix were 5th and 6th places, though Demogeot took 2nd place in the Coppa Velocita at Brescia and ther was a win in the relatively unimportant Coupe de la Commission Sportive. There were no GP cars in 1908, when a team of excellent 5-litre ohv machines contested the 'Four-Inch' TT. Guinness was 2nd, George 3rd, and Rawlinson 7th. After this the only event supported by Darracq until 1920 was the 1914 Austrian Alpine Trial, in which a works team failed to distinguish itself.

By 1920 the firm had been incorporated into the STD combine, and the cars switched identities confusingly; latterly Suresnes' racing cars were Talbots (pronounced as in French) when they raced in their homeland, and th twin ohc 3-litre 'Talbot-Darracq' that raced at Indiana-polis in 1921 was in fact a Sunbeam. As a general rule, however, nothing over 1,500cc wore the Talbot-Darracq label during this period. Between 1921 and 1925 there was a brilliant series of twin-ohc 1·5-litre 4-cylinder cars with differential-less back axles which 'never lost a race' except when attempts were made to run them in sports-car events. In 1921 there were 1-2-3 victories both in the Coupe Internationale des Voiturettes at Le Mans and in the 200 Miles Race at Brooklands, Segrave winning the British event at 88·8mph (142·91kph). There were victories in 1922 in the Isle of Man International 1,500cc Race (Algernon Guinness's swansong); the 200 Miles Race; the Le Mans voiturette race (1-2-3 again, but against weak opposition); and at Penya Rhin in Spain.

The original 56bhp 16-valvers were replaced in 1923

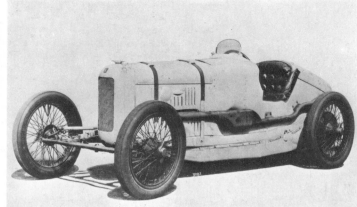

y new Bertarione-designed 8-valve cars with 70bhp ngines, and the triumphal procession went on. Segrave on at Boulogne, despite running into a telegraph pole; ivo and Moriceau led the field home in the voiturette vent at Le Mans; and Resta was victorious at Sitges. utput was boosted to 100bhp with the aid of super-hargers in 1924, when the Grand Prix de l'Ouverture aw the usual procession at Montlhéry; in the Swiss GP e winner was Guinness; and Duller collected the urels in the 200 at Brooklands, which Talbot had voided in 1923, presumably because of the advent of the upercharged Fiats. The organizers banned superchargers both the Grand Prix de Provence and the Grand Prix e l'Ouverture in 1925, but this did not stop the cars, hich came in 1-2-3 on the former occasion, and 1-2-4 on e latter. Segrave and Masetti were 1st and 2nd in the 00 Miles Race, although the cars blotted their copybook understandably) in the Grand Prix de Tourisme, shed-ng their road equipment, and a curious hybrid using the win-cam engine in a stock 10CV DC-type chassis was nsuccessful at Le Mans.

Last of STD's racing Talbots were the magnificent 5 × 75·5mm 1·5-litre straight-8s of 1926, which were ever fully developed, as money was running out. Front xle failures eliminated the whole team from that year's ritish GP at Brooklands, though Segrave won yet nother 200 at 75·5mph (121·51kph), and there was a 2-3 victory in the Grand Prix du Salon at Montlhéry gainst a poor entry. They did little better in 1927 even if ivo managed to lap faster than Benoist's Delage in the rly stages of the French GP. During the 1928–30 riod they raced in Italian colours, scoring six class ctories in 1928, and two 1sts and a 2nd in 1929—the

Left, 1922 Talbot 200-Mile Race car. *Photo: Montagu Motor Museum*

Right, 1925 Talbot 1·5-litre record car. *Photo: Montagu Motor Museum*

Opposite, Jackie Stewart. *Photo: Geoff Goddard*

Left, 1927 Talbot straight-8 at Montlhéry. Williams at the wheel. *Photo: Autocar*

Right, 1948 Lago-Talbot 4·5-litre at Monaco. Etancelin at the wheel. *Photo: J. Dognibene*

latter fell to Nuvolari in the Monza GP.

In the declining years of STD, Suresnes did little, though a Talbot finished 3rd in the 1928 Monte Carlo Rally, and the Schells (of Delahaye fame) collected 4th place in the 1933 event. However, in 1936 came the Lago régime, with brilliant new cross-push-rod 4-litre sports cars designed by Becchia, which could exceed 130mph (209kph) on 165bhp, and used Wilson preselective gear-boxes. These fine cars took some time to reach their form and though one of them put up a record lap in the French Sports-Car GP at Montlhéry the first season's results were modest: 3rd places in the Marne and Comminges races. The cars dominated the second French GP for sports cars in 1937, Chiron leading home his team-mates Comotti (2nd) Divo (3rd) and Sommer (5th). Sommer spearheaded a 1-2-3 victory at Miramas, averaging 112·74mph (181·36kph), and Comotti and Le Bègue were 1st and 2nd in the TT at Donington Park. If 1938 was a less inspiring year, Talbot increased the capacity of their engines to 4·5 litres, and the Le Bègue and Morel car won the Paris 12 Hours. The former driver, partnered on this occasion by Carrière, took a creditable 5th place in the Mille Miglia behind three Alfa Romeos and the new V-12 Delahaye. The Talbots did less well at Le Mans, though the 4-litre coupé of Prenant/Morel managed 3rd place, while in the same year a pair of stripped 4·5-litre two-seaters made a brave, if pathetic showing against the might of Mercedes-Benz and Auto Union in the French GP at Reims. Some new low-chassis monoposti were ready by 1939, and though a promised blown 3-litre V-16 engine never materialized, the cars finished 3rd at both Pau and Reims thanks to German and Italian retirements.

1948 Lago-Talbot saloon in the Alpine Rally. *Photo: Junior, Nice*

1952 Lago-Talbot 4·5-litre at Le Mans. Pierre Levegh at the wheel. *Photo: Rodolfo Mailander*

c 1918 David cyclecar. Juan Andreu at the wheel. *Photo: David, SA*

After World War 2 both the sports and racing machines emerged under the name of Lago-Talbot. The racing cars acquired a new lease of life, largely due to a modest fuel consumption which allowed them to dispense with the pit-stops so needful to the blown 1·5-litre Italian contenders. In 1947 Rosier won at Albi, Chiron won the French GP and finished 2nd at Nîmes, and Comminges was a Talbot procession with the big cars in the first three places. A new engine with twin high-set camshafts (used in the faster sports models since 1946) was introduced for 1948, and output went up from around 195bhp to 280bhp. Its effect was almost immediate. The new model's first season saw Rosier's win the Coupe du Salon, and 2nd places at Monte Carlo, Comminges and Albi. But 1949 was even better — the French GP (Chiron), the Coupe du Salon (Sommer), the Paris GP (Etancelin), and the Belgian GP (a non-stop performance by Rosier at 96·82mph (155·81kph)). The Talbots continued winning in 1950, Albi, Zandvoort and Paris all standing to their credit, and a new star — Juan Manuel Fangio — won the Rafaele 500 Miles in Argentina at 109·8mph (176·7kph). However, 1951 brought a decline, with only two victories (the Dutch and Bordeaux GPs) and four 2nd places, and 1952 marked the end of the road as far as Formula 1 was concerned, with scarcely-noticed wins in the Finnish and Australian Grands Prix, though Whiteford won the latter for the second time in 1953.

Sports-car racing, however, continued to claim Lago's attention. Rosier had won at Le Mans in 1950 in what amounted to a road-equipped Grand Prix car, and though 1951 was a lean year for Suresnes, Pierre Levegh would undoubtedly have won again in 1952, had he not insisted on driving the whole 24 hours without relief. Talbot tried hard in 1953 with new lightweight aerodynamic cars said to give 247bhp, but though they continued to enter as late as 1957, success never came their way again. In the last two seasons Lago was reduced to using 2·5-litre 6-cylinder Maserati engines, and 1957 was a tragedy: one car did not start and the other stalled on the line, never to recommence. Two years later Simca were in control at Suresnes and a great line of competition cars was dead. MCS

Dastle (GB)

Dastle cars were made by Geoffrey Rumble at West Horsley and Ripley, Surrey. The first model was a 250cc special of 1959, and this was followed by a Formule Libre Ford-engined car. The production Type 3 came out in 1967 as a midget racer for the Spedeworth formula, with full triangulated spaceframe, fibreglass body, and Ford running parts. The Type 4 was a simplified version with beam axles, of which only two were made, and the Type 5 a lightweight wedge-bodied design with Mini wheels. Type 6 was a prototype Formula Ford car, and Type 7, with 1300 Ford or British Leyland engine, the successor to the Type 3 in the midget racer class. For some time Dastle held a monopoly in this class, which was popular not only with the impecunious youngsters but also with evergreen semi-retireds such as Paul Emery. For 1971 a new RAC-affiliated Midget Auto Racing Club was formed. DF

Datsun see Nissan

David (E)

The David was the original Spanish cyclecar, and first appeared in 1914 after several years of experiments with powered 'soap-box cars'. Originally a JAP engine was fitted, but later power units included V-twin MAG or 4-cylinder Ballot or Hispano-Suiza engines. The maker always stressed that their chassis was more important than the engine; it was an armoured wood frame, and had ifs by transverse leaf springs. Final drive was by belts, and a patent gearbox gave 16 positions. A very wide track gave great stability. The most powerful Davids had a speed of over 80mph (128kph), and the make figured frequently in sporting results between 191 and 1923. In the 1921 Trofeo Armangue Davids took 1 out of 12 places, including the first five. They also did we in the Barcelona–Madrid–Barcelona Rally, the Vuelta Cataluña, the Rabassada hill-climb and other events. JR

Davrian (GB)

Most Davrian GT two-seaters were sold as road cars, and some 50 had been produced by early 1970 (manufacture began in 1965). The London Works, however, pursued a successful racing policy in the 1,150cc class with a version fitted with the 998cc Imp Sport motor. Construction was based on a built-up lightweight glass-fibre monocoque, designed to accept Hillman Imp mechanical components to whatever degree of tune required by the customer. DF

DB (F)

The first product of the Charles Deutsch-René Bonnet partnership was seen in 1939, when some Citroën-based fwd machines supported lesser French events, among them the Bol d'Or. The partners had two cars running again in time for the Bois de Boulogne race in Septembe 1945, and for three seasons they pursued their pre-war theme, turning out 1·5-litre and 2-litre sports streamliner and single-seaters. Seventy-five bhp were extracted from the 11CV Citroën unit with the aid of twin carburettors and Bossu won the 2-litre category at Chimay in 1947. The 1·5-litre of Lachaize and Debille also secured a clas victory in the 1948 12-Hour sports-car race at Montlhéry By 1949 Deutsch and Bonnet had discovered a smaller fwd design, the ohv flat-twin Dyna-Panhard, and Arnau won the 1950 Bol d'Or in one of their Panhard-derivatives at 64·58mph (103·93kph). Next, the 500cc Formul 3 engaged their attention, and they produced some neat single-seaters in 1950, though these were never a seriou challenge to the Coopers. Trouis and Gatsonides won their class in the 1951 TT and Bonnet came in 7th at Sebring in 1952.

Meanwhile there had been some odd experiments: 1951 brought a twin-engined 4 × 4 racer using a pair of 750cc Panhard units, which was considered as a possibl basis for a Formula 2 challenge; and towards the end of 1952 they had a rear-engined Renault-based *berlinette* o the stocks. Neither of these, however, was raced, thoug during 1953 Bonnet won at Roubaix and collected the Index of Performance at Sebring. The star performance of 1954 was the outright victory of Laureau and Armagnac in the TT (a handicap event), but Bonnet and Bayo won the Index of Performance at Le Mans, and there wa a class victory in the Mille Miglia, not to mention some further successful record work. Chancel took the Class H 50-mile record at 124·98mph (201·13kph), the 610cc Panhard unit being boosted to 85bhp on this occasion.

A use was also sought for the unsuccessful Formula 3 cars, which reappeared in 850cc, 55bhp form as the Monomills — a new idea for one-class racing reminiscen of the earlier Cisitalia circus. The first Monomill race wa staged at Montlhéry in April but though the cars performed at Albi, Aix-les-Bains and Comminges, and wei

Above, 1951 DB 750cc sports car, class winner in the TT. Drivers Trouis (right) and ...tsonides beside the car. *Photo: Autosport*

...ght, 1955 DB 750cc supercharged Formula ...ar. Paul Armagnac at the wheel. *Photo: ...ociated Press*

...7 De Coucy straight-8 racing car. *Photo: ...S. O. Mathieson Collection*

still racing on their own at Pau as late as 1958, they achieved little, even as trainers. In 1955 a pair of them were run in blown 750cc form in the Pau GP (the only cars to take advantage of the 'alternative' size permitted under the prevailing 2·5-litre Formula 1), but they were outclassed. The regular DBs, however, marched on, with Laureau and Armagnac winning their class in the 1955 TT, and in 1956 they took 10th place at Le Mans to secure the Index of Performance once more.

Although the presence of a 750cc Lotus at Le Mans in 1957 put the DBs out of the running, the class victories continued: in the Mille Miglia, and in America at Sebring and less important events. The leading DB protagonist in America was Howard Hanna, who was three times class H national champion: in 1958, 1961 and 1962. Ray Heppenstall captured 1959 H production honours in a Hanna-owned DB, and they were solid contenders up to 1966. By 1959 the 850cc DB coupés were also making their mark in rallies, and along with the usual creditable performances at Sebring and the Nürburgring, and yet another Index of Performance at Le Mans (Cornet and Cotton, who finished 9th), there was a class victory in the alpine, a 3rd in the Monte Carlo for Surles and Piniers, and the Index of Performance award in the Tour de France for Guilhardin and Rey. The next season was the same story, Laureau and Armagnac taking their 2nd Index (and DBs 4th) at Le Mans, Vinatier winning his class at Rouen (with three other DBs in the first five), and another class victory in the Nürburgring 1,000 kilometres.

The company also took up the new Formula Junior, using 70bhp engines, and Bouharde finished 2nd in the Coupe de Montlhéry: some of the superannuated Monomills found a new lease of life as FJs. In 1961 the make again won an Index of Performance at Le Mans. Another DB (Moynet and Vidilles) had its Panhard engine mounted at the rear, but these were the last cars to bear the name. Deutsch and Bonnet parted company, the former continuing to work on Panhard-based specials, while the latter turned to sports and FJ machines using rear-mounted Renault units — a venture which ultimately evolved into the Matra. MCS

Decauville (F)

The first Decauville Voiturelles had 479cc twin-cylinder rear-mounted air-cooled engines and the curious combination of transverse ifs and no springs at all at the back. One of these won the voiturette class of the Paris–Amsterdam–Paris in 1898, but their chief fame was that among their drivers were such later celebrities as Gabriel and Théry, both of whom drove in the 1899 Tour de France. Gabriel's was the best of the voiturettes, and the team finished intact. By the end of the year front-mounted engines and water cooling had arrived. In 1900 Ravenez took the voiturette class in the Bordeaux–Biarritz, and Théry was also successful in this category of the Paris–Rouen–Paris, averaging 28mph (45·06kph). By 1901 the firm had progressed to 1·5-litre 8hp twins with conventional suspension, first seen at the Pau meeting, but for the Paris–Bordeaux and Paris–Berlin they fielded 3-litre fours, with little success.

Decauville light racers in 1902 ran to 4·2 litres, and they tried hard, with seven entries in the Paris–Vienna and six in the Circuit des Ardennes. In the latter event, 6th and 7th places in their class represented their best performance. In 1903 moiv were adopted, and Théry was 6th in the *voiture legère* category in the Paris–Madrid. Apart from a few appearances at early Brooklands meetings, Decauvilles were never again seen in serious competition. MCS

De Coucy (F)

Le comte Enguerrand de Coucy, who was a descendant of Raoul de Coucy, one of the architects of Reims cathedral, designed a number of interesting racing cars over a period of 20 years. These can be divided into four groups:
(1) 1926–1932. A number of 1,100cc straight-8s, with twin overhead camshafts and Roots blowers, made in various engine sizes such as 48 × 70mm, 50 × 76mm, 51 × 67mm, and 51 × 76mm, the last being slightly over the 1,100 limit at 1,243cc. The first engines were bi-bloc, the later ones monobloc. Maximum engine speed was in the range of 8,500rpm, and the crankshaft rotated anticlockwise. A De Coucy was entered for the 1927 Coupe de la Commission Sportive, and the 1,243cc car ran in the 1931 French Grand Prix under the name Demo.
(2) 1934–1937. A 4-cylinder car with tiny 500cc twin-ohc engine developing 60bhp at the very high speed of 10,500rpm was built for record-breaking rather than racing. Clément beat the 10-mile world record for Class 1

cars at 87·9mph (141·5kph) in 1937. A streamlined closed version was built in 1939, but it never ran, and was destroyed during World War 2.
(3) 1945–1948. The Guerin-De Coucy 1·5-litre Formula 1 racing car, built for de Coucy by the Sté d'Etudes Automobiles Guerin. It had a supercharged twin-ohc straight-8 engine of 58 × 70mm, giving 255bhp at 8,200rpm. The gearbox was integral with the rear axle, and the car had 4-wheel independent suspension. Financial difficulties prevented development work on the engine, and when the car appeared at Reims in 1948 it had an old 1,100cc engine, and so was completely outclassed. A 4·5-litre unsupercharged engine was projected, but never built.
(4) 1952. The Longchamp-De Coucy record-breaking car, which had a very small 4-cylinder supercharged engine of 350cc. GNG

De Dietrich, Lorraine-Dietrich (D/F)

Though Amédée Bollée's curious front-engined horizontal-twins had been made under licence by De Dietrich since 1897, and the cars were extensively raced, they did not compete under the De Dietrich name until 1899, when de Turckheim took 5th place in the Nice–Castellane–Nice. In 1903, the De Dietrichs, though still using flitch-plate frames and Loyal-type tubular radiators, were beginning to win sprints and hill-climbs, though sometimes (as in the 1904 Gordon Bennett Trials) they also ran as Turcat-Mérys. Cars with 5,797cc 30hp, and 9,896cc 45hp engines were entered for the Paris–Madrid, Jarrott on one of the bigger machines finishing 3rd. De Brou followed this up with a 2nd in the Circuit des Ardennes. Capacity went up to 12·8 litres for 1904, but the best performance by a De Dietrich in the French Gordon Bennett Trials was Gabriel's 4th place, although Rougier's sister Turcat-Méry went on to represent the ACF at Homburg.

Moiv, steel frames, and Mercedes-type radiators came in 1905, when the works drivers were Gabriel, Duray and Rougier, a combination that was to last unbroken for two further seasons. One of these 17-litre cars driven by Duray was 6th in the Gordon Bennett, and the De Dietrichs were the only team to finish intact in the Coppa Florio, in 2nd, 5th, and 10th places. In 1906 the cars ran as Lorraine-Dietrichs, and a poor showing in the Grand Prix was balanced by Duray's 3rd place in the Vanderbilt Cup in America, and a 'benefit' in the Circuit des Ardennes, where the *team* average was 63mph (101·39kph). Duray won at 65·8mph (105·89kph), and his team-mates were 3rd, 5th and 7th.

Although Lorraine-Dietrich were expanding and had gained control of Isotta Fraschini, 1907 was a difficult year. They were actually racing three different types of car: a more or less stock 130 × 160mm 4-cylinder for the Targa Florio; an oversquare 8-litre for the Kaiserpreis; and a 15·3-litre machine for the Grand Prix. Results were patchy: Gabriel's 4th places in the Grand Prix and the Coppa della Velocita at Brescia, and Duray's 4th in the Targa contrasted with a poor showing in the German race. At the very first Brooklands meeting in that year Jarrott's Lorraine-Dietrich dead-heated with Edge's Napier in the Byfleet Plate. Though Gabriel moved on in 1908, Duray and Rougier remained to drive the new 13-litre ohv GP cars, still with chain drive. These were unsuccessful, and the firm abandoned racing for three seasons (although Duray turned out for the 1911 Grand Prix de France with one of the 1906 racers). Some new cars were prepared for 1912 using 15,095cc ohv 4-cylinder engines and chain drive, and closely resembling

Left, 1908 Lorraine-Dietrich at the start [of] the Savannah Grand Prize. *Photo: Veteran Car Club of Great Britain*

Below, 1926 Lorraine-Dietrich 15CV at [Le] Mans in 1931. Trebor at the wheel. *Photo Autocar*

the Blitzen Benz. In that year's Grand Prix at Dieppe they made a poor showing, but one of them later came to England, where as 'Vieux Charles Trois' it had a long and distinguished career at Brooklands.

Lorraine-Dietrich, however, staged a comeback in the 1920s with the 3,446cc ohv 15CV designed by Marius Barbarou of Benz-Parsifal fame. This started life as a rather American-style family tourer, but an 8th place at Le Mans in 1923 was promising, and in 1924 Stoffel finished 2nd and de Courcelles 3rd. In 1925 came their first victory there, which fell to de Courcelles and Rossignol at 57·83mph (93·07kph), followed by the Brisson and Stalter car in 3rd place. They won again in 1926, the Bloch and Rossignol partnership being the first to average over 62mph (100kph) for the 24 hours. Their actual speed was 66·08mph (106·35kph) and another Lorraine was 2nd. This was the end of works participation, but 15CVs appeared spasmodically at Le Mans until 1935 and one finished 4th in 1931. They were seldom seen in other events, though Brisson won the 5-litre class of the Paris–Nice in 1927, and a 22-year-old unknown named Jean-Pierre Wimille was 2nd in the 1931 Monte Carlo Rally in a second-hand sports saloon. MCS

De Dion-Bouton (F)

This firm can truly be said to have entered motor racing on the ground floor, as Albert de Dion was one of the founders of the ACF in 1895, and Bouton's light steamers won the first two motor races on record, both sponsored by *Le Vélocipède*. That of 1887 was a walkover, but the 1888 tricycle actually had a Serpollet to beat. De Dion

nself was also the moral victor of the Paris–Rouen in
94, though his articulated steam brake was disquali-
d on the grounds that it required a permanent crew of
o. De Dion steamers won both the Marseilles–Nice–
Turbie and the four-seater class of the Paris–Dieppe
1897, but for the next four years the firm's racing
orts were concentrated on tricycles.

The single-cylinder De Dion car, introduced in 1899,
s a commercial success from its introduction and the
mpany virtually gave up racing, though the cars did
ll in all manner of touring-car events, winning (for
tance) a silver medal in the British small-car trials of
04, and their class in the following year's Melbourne-
dney Trial. The prototype of the front-engined series
nched in 1902 was tested in the touring-car category of
Paris–Berlin (1901), but 'works' entries were other-
se rare. De Dion ran four 3,054cc 4-cylinder *voitures
ères* (their first fours) and four 1,059cc single-cylinder
turettes in the Paris–Madrid Race of 1903, Pélisson
ishing 4th in the former class and Holley 5th in the
ter. There was support for *L'Auto's* first abortive
turette event in 1905, and in the early Sicilian Cup
turette races and the Targa Florio there was always a
inkling of stripped, locally-entered touring De Dions.
cenzo Florio himself was 2nd in the 1907 Sicilian Cup,
d Berra on one of the later V-8s managed 4th place in
1913 Targa Florio.

De Dion's main significance in racing, however, stems
m their successful proprietary engines, used in a
ersity of voiturettes up to 1910. Among early users
re Renault, de Boisse, and Prunel, not to mention
uis Delage's first competition machines. Their last
ort was a fantastic 100 × 300mm (2,350cc) single
de for Corre-La Licorne in 1910; it was 39in (about
) high. MCS

ep Sanderson (GB)

is Formula Junior design was produced in 1960 by
ris Lawrence, previously a noted Morgan exponent
sports-car racing. The frame was constructed on the
rahedron principle, the cockpit narrowing towards
rear, a principle reversed for the 1961 version in
erence to human anatomy. The car was never promi-
t in the results. More successful was the 301 coupé
ich was available for several years, with Mini
chanical parts, and this model ran in long-distance
orts-car events as well as British short-circuit races.
e 501 version featured a Downton-Cooper engine at
h end, but this car was never fully sorted for the
cuits. In 1970 a new Deep Sanderson became available,
T saloon with Martin V-8 engine, but this was
igned explicitly as a road car. DF

lage (F)

uis Delage plunged into racing almost before he had
ablished himself as a manufacturer, one of his voitu-
tes with a single-cylinder De Dion engine finishing 2nd
he 1906 Coupe de l'Auto race. Delage were unsucess-
in 1907, but for 1908 they fielded two twins with a De
n engine and a new single with a Causan-designed
t developing 28bhp. Guyot drove this to victory at
8mph (80·15kph), but De Dion had to be given the
dit, since Delage badly needed their bonus to pay his
enses. The twins finished 5th and 12th, giving Delage
team prize, but by 1911, when the firm once again
tested the Coupe de l'Auto, they were making their
n engines, 3-litre 4-cylinder horizontal-valve units,
ed to (a favourite Delage feature, this) 5-speed boxes

Above, 1897 De Dion-Bouton steam brake,
winner of the Marseilles–Nice–La Turbie
Race. *Photo: Veteran Car Club of Great
Britain*

Right, 1903 De Dion-Bouton 9hp Paris–
Madrid voiturette. *Photo: T. A. S. O.
Mathieson Collection*

Above, 1907 De Dion-Bouton voiturette in
the Sicilian Cup. Vincenzo Florio at the
wheel. *Photo: T. A. S. O. Mathieson Collection*

Right, 1961 Deep Sanderson Formula Junior
car. *Photo: Autosport*

with an overdrive top. Drivers were Bablot, Thomas, Guyot and Rigal, and the first three came in 1st, 3rd and 4th, Bablot's average being 55·3mph (89·00kph). Similar in concept and appearance were the firm's 1913 GP machines, only this time capacity was 6,234cc and these engines developed about 130bhp. In the French GP at Amiens a burst tyre robbed Guyot of victory, but he finished 5th and Bablot was 4th. In the Sarthe race at Le Mans, Bablot and Guyot finished 1st and 2nd. W. F. Bradley took two of these cars to Indianapolis in 1914, and René Thomas won the 500 at 82·47mph. Less successful were Delage's 1914 4·5-litre GP cars, for all their 4-wheel brakes, twin ohc, desmodromic valves, twin carburettors (described as 'the latest modern horror' in a contemporary report) and 5-speed boxes.

In the early post-World War 1 years Delage concentrated on sprints and hill-climbs, producing a 6-cylinder 5,136cc ohv machine with which Thomas broke the record at Mont Ventoux in 1922 and 1923, and at La Turbie in 1923 and 1924, as well as making ftd in 1924 at Zbreslav-Jíloviště in Czechoslovakia. This was the car brought to England by Alastair Miller in 1928 as Delage I: its stablemate, Delage II, had a 6-litre dohc engine based on the GL luxury model and was built for a similar purpose in 1925. Its record included fastest times of the day at Mont Ventoux and La Turbie and it survives in Britain to this day in the hands of Nigel Arnold-Forster. An even more effective sprint machine was the 10,688cc push-rod V-12, built in 1923, which broke the record at Gaillon in 1925; like the earlier 350hp Sunbeam, it also took the World's Land Speed Record — in July

Top left, 1908 Delage GP des Voiturettes car. Albert Guyot at the wheel. *Photo: Ferdinand Hediger Collection*

Top right, 1913 Delage GP car. Albert Guyot at the wheel. *Photo: Montagu Motor Museum*

Above left, 1922 Delage I 5·1-litre racing car, at Brooklands in 1928. Alastair Miller at the wheel. *Photo: Montagu Motor Museum*

Above right, 1923 Delage 10·6-litre V-12 record car. René Thomas at the wheel. *Photo: Montagu Motor Museum*

1924, when René Thomas recorded 143·29mph (230·54kph) at Arpajon. This one also crossed the Channel in 1929, and had a long career at Brooklands driven by John Cobb and Oliver Bertram. It did a standing lap at 115·29mph (185·54kph) in 1931, and Bertram took it round at 135·34mph (217·86kph). Mo remarkably, Mrs Kay Petre lapped at 134·75mph (216·78kph), though it was retired after 1935 and did reappear until 1949 in Vintage events.

The first of a new generation of GP Delages appear in 1923, the complex 2-litre, 4-ohc, Planchon-designe roller-bearing V-12s, giving 105bhp in their original guise. Thomas retired in the French GP, and though there were experiments with twin blowers in 1924, the cars ran normally aspirated in the 1924 French GP, D finishing 2nd and Benoist 3rd, while Morel and Divo w 3rd and 4th respectively in the Spanish GP. In 1925 th blowers were back again and with 190bhp on tap the Delages provided worthy competition for Alfa Rome though the Italian cars stayed away from the Spanish race (which was a 1-2-3 Delage procession) and the Delages from Monza. They met in the French GP at Montlhéry, but the Alfas withdrew after Antonio Ascari's fatal crash, so the Divo/Benoist win at 69·7m (112·17kph) was a foregone conclusion. Wagner was 2nd. Some magnificent 1·5-litre dohc straight-8s came from the drawing-board of Albert Lory in 1926, with dry-sump lubrication, twin Roots-type superchargers 5-speed overdrive gearboxes and 165/170bhp, giving top speed of 130mph (209kph). In their first season th proved to be foot-friers, hence a 2nd place by Bourlie and Sénéchal at San Sebastian and an uncomfortable passage for the drivers in the British GP at Brooklands, in spite of which the Wagner/Sénéchal car won at 71·61mph (115·25kph), the Bourlier/Dubonnet machine being 3rd. These snags were ironed out by 1927, when the cars reappeared with raked radiators and dominated the Grand Prix season. Benoist won the Grand Prix de l'Ouverture at Montlhéry; there was a 1-2-3 victory (Benoist–Bourlier–Morel) in the French GP against Talbot opposition; and a similar triumph (headed again by Benoist) in the British GP, the opponents this time being the Bugattis. Benoist also won the Spanish and Italian GPs, in spite of being the sole Delage entry in the latter race.

Louis Delage retired from racing in 1928, but the cars soldiered on continuously for another eight years. There were victories for Malcolm Campbell in 1928 in the Junior GP and the 200 at Brooklands, and also at Boulogne; Chiron took one to Indianapolis in 1929 and finished 7th; and Earl Howe had a good run in voiturette racing winning at Dieppe (1931), Avus (1932) and the Nürburgring (1933), and even in 1935 he managed 3rd at Albi and Berne. Incredibly, Richard Seaman raced a reworked example with hydraulic brakes during 1936, and it was his success with this car that attracted the attention of Mercedes-Benz. Starting off with a victory in the Isle of Man 1,500cc race at 69·76mph (112·27kph), he progressed, via crashes on the Eifelrennen and at Péronne, to wins at Pescara, Berne, and the 200, now revived at Donington.

Delage merged with Delahaye in 1935 and benefited by that firm's unexpected renaissance, though a rival V-12 4·5-litre laid down by Lory (parallel with Jean François's Type-145 Delahaye) achieved nothing beyond Joseph Paul's crash at Brooklands in May 1938, which killed the designer Murray Jamieson. The 2·7-litre D-6-70, how-ever, was made into an excellent sports-racer, its short-stroke engine proving happier at high revs than the better-known Type-135 Delahaye. An elegant sports coupé finished 4th at Le Mans in the hands of Louis Gérard and de Valence, but it was not until it was re-bodied in Delahaye style that Gérard was able to score a major win—in the 1938 TT at Donington. Gérard and Monneret finished 2nd at Le Mans in 1939 with a more streamlined version.

In 1945 a batch of six similar cars with 142bhp engines was laid down for the *Union Sportive Automobile*. These were more successful than the contemporary 2-litre Salmsons. Early in 1948 Louveau won a minor sports-car event at Montlhéry, and he and Brunet collected their class later in the year at the same venue, in the 12-Hour Race. Le Mans reappeared on the agenda in 1949, and there was another Delage 2nd place, only this time Lou-veau and Jover were the drivers, and they were beaten by a Ferrari instead of a Bugatti. Gérard was 2nd in the 1950 GP de Paris, but by this time Delage were only in token production, and the cars faded from the competition scene. MCS

Delahaye (F)

The Delahaye's effective sporting life began at 40. In the 1896–9 period the firm had supported town-to-town events with ponderous belt-driven tourers (in the Paris–Ostend they entered a wagonnette), but for the next 38 years their only other contribution was a team of unsuc-cessful 4-cylinder light cars which ran in the Paris–Vienna and the Circuit des Ardennes in 1902.

However, 1934 brought the 18CV Superlux, an ordin-

Top, c 1923 Delage 14/40 at San Remo speed trials. *Photo: Montagu Motor Museum*

Above, 1927 Delage 1½-litre GP car. Edmond Bourlier at the wheel. *Photo: Montagu Motor Museum*

ary if better-than-average fast tourer using a 3·2-litre 4-bearing ohv 6-cylinder truck engine in a modern chassis with transverse ifs and Bendix brakes. This was soon developed into the 18 Sport, and ultimately into the 3,557cc Type 135, which in competition form would give 125mph (201·2kph) on 160bhp, and managed a Brook-lands lap at 126·09mph (204·2kph) in 1937. It was also reliable and an excellent all-rounder. As early as 1934 Perrot had made fastest touring-car time in the Château-Thierry hill-climb; a streamlined saloon version had circulated at Montlhéry for 48 hours at 107·685mph (175·3kph); the works team had taken the over 3-litre class in the Alpine Trial (at the same time that great Delahaye exponent Mme Lucy Schell collected an indi-vidual Coupe des Glaciers); and Perrot had won the Grand Prix de Tourisme in Algeria—clear evidence of versatility. There was a victory in the 1935 Monte Carlo Rally's Coupe des Dames for Mme Schell, and the cars won the Circuit d'Orléans and the Marne GP; Mongin and Paris finished 5th at Le Mans and 3rd in the Italian Targa Abruzzo.

With the new Talbots still in the teething stage, only Bugatti's Type 57 could beat the Delahayes in 1936.

Type 135s filled the first five places at Miramas, and in the French sports-car GP at Montlhéry they came in 2nd, 3rd, 4th and 5th behind the 'tank' Bugatti. A record lap in the Ulster TT and Schell's 2nd place in the Monte Carlo Rally rounded off an excellent season, though in 1937 the Talbots were finding their feet, and the Delahayes, now raced by the Schells' *Ecurie Bleue*, were also-rans in the French GP and had to be content with 2nd and 3rd at Le Mans. On the credit side the Bira and Dobbs car dominated the 12-Hour Sports-Car Race at Donington Park, winning at 57·63mph (92·75kph). Schell and Carrière did brilliantly to finish 3rd in the Mille Miglia, and a similar two-seater (Le Bègue and Quinlin) won the Monte Carlo Rally.

By 1938 the 135 was definitely outclassed, the Chaboud and Tremoulet victory at Le Mans being a triumph of reliability after the Alfa Romeos and the V-12 Delahayes had faded out. Willing and Jarvis won the 3-hour sports-car race at Brooklands on the ex-'Bira' DUV 870, which Arthur Dobson also drove to victory in 1939 in the controversial Fastest Road Car event at Brooklands. This was another victory on reliability, for Hunter's 2·9-litre Alfa Romeo retired. In rallies the 135s did excellently in the last year of peace: a tie (with Hotchkiss) in the Monte Carlo; 2nd in the Paris–St Raphael; and 1st and 2nd in the Paris–Nice.

Meanwhile the ACF 'Race for the Million', aimed at breeding new French Grand Prix contenders, had produced Jean François's Type 145, a 4,482cc unblown push-rod V-12 with De Dion axle and 4-speed Cotal gearbox. It won the race, though Delahaye did not get

Left top, 1937 Delahaye 135 sports cars in practice at Pau. *Photo: Cyril Posthumus Collection*

Left above, 1938 Delahaye V-12 single-seater in practice for the German GP. Comotti at the wheel. *Photo: Cyril Posthumus Collection*

Right top, 1938 Delahaye V-12 two-seater in German GP. Comotti at the wheel. *Photo: Motor*

Above, 1953 Dellow on Fingle Hill, Devon. *Photo: Charles Dunn*

1954 Denzel in the Alpine Rally. *Photo: A. Zardini*

the money. This ugly car, originally a two-seater capable of road use, managed over 160mph (257·5kph) on 238bhp, but 4·5 unblown litres were not really the answer when Mercedes-Benz could extract 468bhp from a 3-litre supercharged engine. Hence the 145's reign was brief: frugality won Dreyfus the Pau GP from Mercedes-Benz, and he scored another impressive (though emptier) victory at Cork, where his average was 92·95mph (149·59kph). In the German, Tripoli, Swiss and Donington races the cars were outclassed, and 1939 was even worse, although the Schells were now fielding a single-seater version. Dreyfus and Varet brought a road-equipped V-12 into 4th place in the 1938 Mille Miglia.

The Type 135 could still win races in the early post-war years: at Brussels in 1946; in the 1947 and 1948 Grands Prix des Frontières; and at Comminges in 1949, when a pre-war car also won the Australian GP in which it had finished 2nd ten years before. The company's only novelty was the 4·5-litre Type 175, a new 7-bearing six which was too heavy and unreliable for the circuits, though the engine was put into the 135 chassis for sports-car events, and a Delahaye was 5th at Le Mans in 1949. In 1951 Trevoux and Crovetto won the Monte Carlo Rally on a Type 175 saloon, Chiron and Mahé finishing 5th. Delahaye's last victory was in that year's Algiers-Cape event, but the laurels went to a 4 × 4 jeep-type vehicle entered by the French Army. MCS

Dellow (GB)
Both K. C. Delingpole and Ron Lowe had been successful trials drivers before embarking on production of their Ford Ten engined trials cars. During the early 1950s they were very popular, but as the 'specials' became more specialized, even the supercharged versions became no longer competitive with them. The weight distribution was unsuitable for other forms of motor sport, though the manoeuvrability and acceleration were used to good effect in some types of events. Four-seater versions (Mark III) became available, and a sports-racing type (Mark VI) was offered by a re-formed company operating from Oldbury, near Birmingham, but sales fell off. DF

Deltal see Mercer

De Luca see Daimler (GB)

Demo see De Coucy

Denzel (A)
Wolfgang Denzel of Vienna built sports cars based on the Volkswagen from 1948 to 1960. He altered the 75mm bore of the VW engine to either 73·5mm or 80mm, giving capacities of 1,085cc or 1,284cc, bringing the cars into the 1,100cc or 1,300cc classes. Outputs were 38bhp and 45bhp respectively. Porsche engines were also available. The chassis was shorter and wider than that of the normal VW. Denzels were raced in the United States by Richard Toland, and a number of class wins were achieved in European rallies. Notable among these was the 1,300cc class in the 1954 International Alpine Rally (Denzel and Stroinigg). They were 2nd in the same class in 1955. HON

Derby (F)
One of a multitude of assembled French 1,100cc sports cars, the Derby made little impact in the early 1920s, though a special model with twin-carburettor 12-valve ohv Chapuis-Dornier engine was driven by Heaton in

the 1923 200 Miles Race at Brooklands. The make's
racing reputation, however, was won with the Derby-
Miller, originally a 1,500cc fwd Miller 91 racer brought
to France by Douglas Hawkes, which grew more Derby
and less Miller with the years. In 1930 Mrs Gwenda
Stewart took the 1·5-litre class one-mile, one-hour and
200km records at Montlhéry, her speed over the former
distance being 118·13mph (190·15kph). Numerous
records followed, the Derby-Miller graduating to the
2-litre class when the engine was bored out to 1,670cc, in
which form the centrifugally-blown unit developed
200bhp at 6,500rpm. The world 100km record was
broken in 1930, and twice in 1931, when Mrs Stewart
also raised the Montlhéry lap record to 141·37mph
(227·51kph). The 2-litre mile record was taken twice in
1933, Mrs Stewart recording 143·29mph (130·54kph) on
the second occasion, and in this year she beat her own
lap record at Montlhéry with a speed of 145·94mph
(234·86kph). The car was less successful at Brooklands,
though she set up an all-time ladies' lap record at
135·95mph (218·78kph), and in 1934 she once again made
a record lap of Montlhéry (irrespective of sex) at
147·79mph (237·84kph): it took nothing less than Raymond Sommer's 3-litre GP Alfa Romeo to beat it in
1939. She also ran Derby's 2-litre fwd sports eoi V-8s at
Le Mans in 1934 and 1935, but retired on both these
occasions.

The last racing Derby was a fwd single-seater with all-
round independent suspension and 1,500cc blown 4-
cylinder dohc 8-valve Maserati engine built in 1935, with
which Mrs Stewart tried her luck in road racing. It re-

Top, 1928 Derby 1,100cc sports car in a 1930
JCC Trial. *Photo: Montagu Motor Museum*

Left, 1930 Derby-Miller at Montlhéry,
c 1934. Gwenda Stewart at the wheel.
Photo: William Boddy Collection

1959 De Sanctis Formula Junior at
Vallelunga. *Photo: Cerreti & Pellegrini*

tired at Dieppe that year, and subsequent appearances at
Brooklands were equally unsuccessful. MCS

De Sanctis (I)
The de Sanctis family, father and son, ran a large FIAT
dealership in Rome, and Luciano came to prominence
when he finished 2nd in a 30-lap FJ race at Monza in
June 1958. He was driving a rear-engined car of his own
design, powered by a FIAT 750 engine; its lack of power
was compensated for by its light weight—the car scaled
706lb (320kg) compared to the 882lb (400kg) 1100s.
He ran this car for the rest of the season, gaining
third fastest time overall at the Coppa Gallenga hill-
climb behind two Maserati 2000s. An 1100cc engine was
installed for the end of the season and de Sanctis became
the pacemaker in FJ, going into production in 1959 with
improved replicas of his car using a tubular spaceframe,
coil-and-wishbone front suspension and swing-axle rear.
Drivers such as Maglione, Boffa and Roberto Lippi
raced these early de Sanctis cars, but their FIAT engines
were to prove no match for the British Ford 105Es and
BMC 'A'-series units as they were developed.

In later seasons de Sanctis produced Brabham-like
spaceframe FJ and F3 cars using Ford-based engines, and
these were driven with considerable national success by
Jonathan Williams. They have seldom ventured outside
Italy, however, and the Roman constructor has never
quite regained the aura of advance and promise offered
by his early FJs. DCN

De Tomaso (I)
Alessandro de Tomaso is an expatriate Argentinian racing
driver who settled in Modena while racing Osca sports
cars in Europe. When he retired from driving he stayed
on in Modena and set up the company which has since
produced a great number of interesting and exotic cars,
although few of them have been properly developed.

He decided to sell cars to amateur drivers, and in 1961
produced a neat little 1·5-litre F1 chassis, available with
either Osca or Alfa Romeo engines. There were few
takers, and as the 1960s progressed so de Tomaso's
fertile mind evolved a series of competition car projects,
including a cast monocoque sports car and an Indianapolis machine based on a similar cast alloy unit. A flat
8-cylinder 1·5-litre F1 car appeared in practice for the
1963 Italian GP but was seen no more, and this became a
familiar de Tomaso pattern.

But in the latter part of the 1960s de Tomaso negotiated
a very good deal with Ford of America over his Man-
gusta mid-engined road car design, which sealed an order
for a quite large production run of the cars to be ex-

425

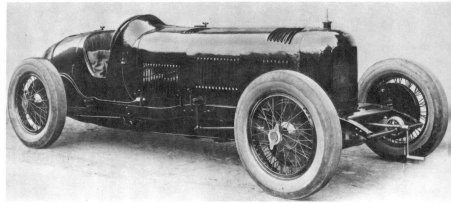

ported to the United States, using Ford V-8 engines. Gian-Paolo Dallara, the engineer responsible for the Lamborghini Miura, joined de Tomaso, and during the 1969 season they produced a compact little monocoque F2 car, unique in using the Cosworth FVA engine as a partially-stressed chassis member. Jonathan Williams drove the car in its first outing, and at the Italian GP meeting de Tomaso approached Frank Williams (no relation), the independent British entrant, with a scheme for running an F1 car in 1970. Williams agreed to provide Cosworth engines, Hewland gearboxes, mechanics and organization for a team that season, with his driver Piers Courage in the cockpit. Dallara produced a solid-looking monocoque using Brabham-like suspension, and a total of five of these cars were built for Courage's use. Their best performance was 3rd in the non-championship *Daily Express* Silverstone meeting, and Courage's death at the Zandvoort circuit was a very grave setback for the team. DCN

DFP (F)

This make stemmed from the Doriot-Flandrin, produced by a firm of which the senior partner had been one of Peugeot's first competition drivers. Doriot-Flandrin was one of the unsuccessful competitors in the 1907 Coupe des Voiturettes. That would probably have been the end of their racing history but for the acquisition of DFP's English agency by the brothers W. O. and H. M. Bentley, who entered 2-litre 12/15hp cars in hill-climbs and sprints. 'W.O.' himself was first in his class on time and formula at Aston Clinton in 1912, and first on time again in 1913. He also drove the cars at Brooklands, and went after class records later in the year with a special streamlined single-seater, snatching all the relevant ones from Tuck's Humber. The DFP managed a flying half-mile at 89·7mph (144·36kph). In 1914 there was more competition work, including a class win at Caerphilly. More important, Bentley fitted aluminium pistons to the 2-litre engine, and ran a car so equipped in the TT. Though that year's formula allowed a 3·3-litre capacity, he managed an astonishing 6th place at 48·38mph (77·86kph).

World War 1 put a stop to any further development, and the post-Armistice decline at Courbevoie where the cars were made coincided with the Bentley brothers' own distinguished essay into manufacture. Sir Henry Birkin drove a 1920-model 12/40 at Brooklands without much success, but 1922 brought a sporting voiturette in the Salmson-Amilcar idiom, the DF Petite with 1,100cc push-rod CIME engine, and one of these started in the 1923 Brooklands 200. One of these little DFPs took 2nd

Left, 1970 De Tomaso-Ford 505 Formula 1 car. Brian Redman at the wheel. *Photo: Autosport*

1925 Diatto straight-8 GP car. *Photo: Cyril Posthumus Collection*

1914 DFP 12/15hp. W. O. Bentley at the wheel. *Photo: Montagu Motor Museum*

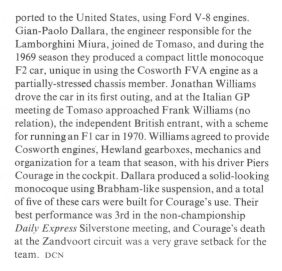

place in its class in the 1926 Bol d'Or, and in 1927 won the race outright at 43·7mph (70·33kph). By this time, however, Doriot, Flandrin and Parant were moribund. MCS

Diatto (I)

Diatto was a railway engineering and iron-casting company who took to car manufacture in 1905 by building the excellent French Clément-Bayard under licence as the Diatto-Clément. These cars were raced spasmodically and with little success before they disappeared again in the financial crash of 1908. Diatto re-emerged as an all-Italian concern, and after World War 1 built a few Brescia Bugattis under licence; one was driven in 1921 by Conelli to win the 215-mile (346km) Circuit of Brescia race for nationals, and also the 2-litre flying kilometre sprints at Brescia at 74·32mph (119·60kph).

At the same time Diatto developed 2- and 3-litre 4-cylinder sporting models with shaft-driven ohc. These were raced by the works and by independents, and driver/development engineer Alfieri Maserati got very good performance from them. With a 2-litre car Guido Meregalli won the Circuit of Garda race three years running, in 1922, 1923 and 1924, besides doing well in hill-climbs and Maserati won the 3-litre class of the Autumn GP at Monza in 1922.

Other notable Diatto victories in the face of considerable opposition from FIAT, Ceirano, Alfa Romeo etc. include the 1923 Montenero Cup race, 3-litre class (Brilli-Peri); the 2-litre class of the 1924 Monza 24 Hours

'Night' GP for sports cars (Schieppati and Ferretti); the 1925 Circuit of Mugello, 2-litres (Stefanelli); the 1926 Circuit of Alessandria (Aimini); and the 1926 Cascine circuit, 2-litres (Barsanti).

In 1924 Diatto gave Alfieri Maserati *carte blanche* to build a 2-litre Diatto GP car. The resultant super-charged straight-8 was not complete until the 1925 Italian GP, when it was driven by Materassi. Far from race-worthy, it retired early with supercharger trouble, but from it sprang the first Maserati racing car, the design being taken over by the famous *fratelli* when they launched their own make in 1926. SA Autocostruzione Diatto itself finally closed down in 1930. CP

Diaz y Grillo (E)

The Diaz y Grillo, or D y G, was one of the Spanish cyclecars which flourished in the period 1917 to 1922, and like its contemporaries the David, the America and the Ideal, took part in many local races and trials. The firm originally used 2-stroke MAG engines, but later built their own 4-cylinder 4-stroke 1,100cc units. The most interesting aspect of the make was the torsion bar suspension with inter-connected front and rear springs which helped the cars to win rallies on bad roads. They did well in the gruelling Barcelona-Madrid-Barcelona Rally, and won their class in the 1920 Vuelta Cataluña. JRV

Diva (GB)

A. J. D. Sim had offered the Yimkin racer from his workshops in London W1 from 1959 onwards, in 2-seater or Formula Junior guise. As an 1172 Formula car, he had a most successful season, and the first Diva of 1962, offered by Tunex Conversions, was based on this model. These cars were leaders in their class, noted Diva drivers who graduated to Formula 1 including John Miles and Jacky Oliver. The most consistent driver was Doug Mockford, who gained 22 first places in British events in 1965 alone, and continued to race after production had ceased. Before this happened the original GT had received homologation as a Group 4 car, and rear-engined models had also been built and raced with some success, including an Imp-engined car and the larger Valkyr for Coventry-Climax or 1600 Ford engine. DF

Dixi (D)

This was the brand name under which cars, built by the Fahrzeugfabrik Eisenach, were sold from 1904 onwards. Previously they had been known as Wartburgs or Eisenachs. In 1902 two Eisenachs ran in the Paris-Vienna race: a 15hp light car with five-speed gearbox and an 8hp voiturette. Two cars developed from the normal touring Dixi cars were entered for the Kaiserpreis of 1907, one of them reaching the final run and finishing 11th. The 7.3-litre engine developed about 60bhp. This model also appeared among the winners at the Ostend meetings. Dixi was represented at various smaller national events as well as at the Herkomer, the Prince Henry, and the Austrian Alpine Trials.

The 6/24PS of 1920 with a 1,570cc unit was the basis for a sports version developing 35bhp. This car took part in a number of national events in the 1920s, including the Avusrennen in 1921 and 1922; in the latter Dixis finished 1-2-3, the average speed of Gebser's winning car being 70mph (112.65kph). Several more victories were gained in hill-climbs and races and the long-distance ADAC Reichsfahrt. An Austin Seven-based Dixi in a specially prepared version driven by Gerhard Macher took part in the 1928 German Grand Prix. He failed to finish but

Above, 1916 Diaz y Grillo at Los Bruchs races, Barcelona. *Photo: Courtesy Mario Grillo*

Right, 1960 Yimkin (Diva) 1,172cc sports car. A. J. D. Sim at the wheel. *Photo: Michael Ware*

Right, c 1966 Diva Valkyr 2.7-litre coupé. *Photo: Autosport*

Right below, 1902 Wartburg (Dixi) 15hp Paris-Vienna car. *Photo: Neubauer Collection*

Below, 1962 Diva GT 997cc coupé at Wiscombe Park Hill-Climb. A. J. D. Sim at the wheel. *Photo: Michael Ware*

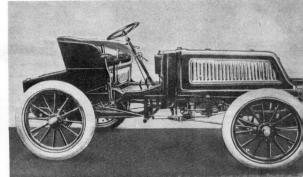

gained a 4th place with the same car in the 750cc class in the Eifelrennen of that year, also held at the Nürburgring. He achieved some more class victories in hill-climbs during the year. At the end of 1928 Dixi was taken over by BMW. HON

Djelmo (F)

In 1923 an Egyptian nobleman, Prince Djellaledin, financed the building of a Land Speed Record car, designed by the engineer Edmond Moglia. It had a straight-8 twin-ohc engine of 10,071cc capacity, with a claimed output of 400bhp. Jules Foresti made several attempts on the record at Pendine Sands in 1927, but at that time it stood at 203·79mph (Segrave's Sunbeam) and Djelmo never approached that figure. In December 1927 the car crashed, and although Foresti was not seriously hurt, he did not drive the Djelmo again. Incidentally, this was the last attempt on the Land Speed Record to be made in the British Isles. Moglia planned another LSR car with two 10-litre engines, and also a 1·5-litre 8-cylinder Grand Prix car, but neither of these was built. GNG

DKW (D)

The first car of this name appeared in 1928, built by the firm which had the world's biggest motorcycle production at that time. It had a 2-cylinder 2-stroke engine of 584cc an output of 16bhp and featured the typical wood-framed chassis-less construction which DKW pioneered. In 1929 Gerhard Macher drove one of these cars in the Monte Carlo Rally. Macher, an engineer with DKW, also developed the handsome sports version of this model with a slightly increased output of 18bhp; it was popular as a cheap means of taking part in competitions. In 1930 and 1931 DKW captured 15 international records on the Montlhéry circuit, the driver being Baron von Koenig-Fachsenfeld. For this purpose the normal sports car was equipped with a 2-cylinder 500cc motorcycle engine with charging pump. Gerhard Macher, Toni Bauhöfer and Hans Simons gained many victories for DKW with specially prepared cars, using either the 500cc motorcycle engine or a combination of two of them.

Another version was derived from the normal 4-cylinder 800cc engine. These had either 1,040cc (70 × 68mm) or 746cc (59 × 68mm), both developing about

60bhp. They took part in national and international events, as did the sports version of the front-driven 490cc and 584cc DKWs with their 2-cylinder transverse engines. After the formation of Auto Union, of which DKW became a part, no more sports versions were built, although one type appeared in 1935 with a smart-looking sports body, the Front Luxus with 684cc engine.

The various German cross-country competitions of the 1930s had DKW entries, mostly with special-purpose bodies but no engine modifications. Gerhard Macher privately produced a unique and interesting twin-engined 'DKW-Macher Special', using two 684cc engines mounted in the front and the rear and driving the front and rear wheels respectively. It also featured an aerodynamic body.

After World War 2 3-cylinder 2-stroke DKW engines were used in Formula Junior racing by Mitter and the Swiss MBM. Mention should also be made of the DKW-Monza, a special version built by Fritz Wenk of Heidelberg and consisting of a DKW chassis and a specially-built glassfibre coupé body. The DKW 1000 engine was tuned to 55bhp and in this form captured five international records on the Monza circuit in 1958. HON

Dodge (US)

Dodge sedans have been regular NASCAR entries since 1953, winning a total of 104 championship stock-car events from their début until the close of the 1970 season. Dodge won the NASCAR 1970 Manufacturers' championship and Boddy Isaac drove a Dodge to capture the 1970 Grand National title. Ron Grable's Dodge Dart won the SCCA A sedan championship in 1966 and a factory-supported Dodge Challenger, driven by Sam Posey, finished 3rd in the 1970 Trans-Am series. In drag racing, Dodge drivers Gene Snow and Dick Landy are frequent winners in their class. ARB

DRW (GB)

Probably no make with such a small total production can have achieved such consistent success as David Warwick's tiny firm in Highgate, London. The early Clubman's cars in 1959 were inspired by the Lotus Seven, the Mark 1 using a Ford 1172 engine and the 1960 model, with independent rear suspension, the Ford 105E unit. The

1970 Dodge Challenger sedan at Daytona. Bobby Allison at the wheel. *Photo: Daytona International Speedway*

Left, 1930 DKW racing car with two 500cc engines. Gerhard Macher at the wheel. *Photo: Neubauer Collection*

Below, 1960 DKW-Hartmann Formula Junior car, at Freiburg hill-climb. *Photo: O. T. Wall*

Above, 1970 DRW Mark 8C Formula Ford. *Photo: Autosport*

Right, 1914 Duesenberg with 'walking beam' engine. Eddie Rickenbacker at the wheel. *Photo: Indianapolis Motor Speedway*

Mark 3 cars, made in 1961 (one originally built as a Formula Junior machine but subsequently converted), were winning their classes in races up to nearly a decade later, in the hands of G. E. Oliver, D. Soley, J. D. A. Bromilow, D. Cook and Warwick's partner Jack Murrell.

The Mark 4 was developed from a Len Terry design, with crossed-linkage rear suspension and Renault gearbox, and one of these was rebuilt with modified suspension and a Hewland 5-speed gearbox as the Mark 5. The Mark 6 was the Hillman Imp rear-engined car used very successfully in hill-climbs by Peter Voigt, and the Mark 7C a 1968 1,500cc Clubman's car. For 1970 new cars were constructed for three different racing classes, bringing total production of new cars actually made in the works up to 10. These were the Mark 7CB Clubman's car, the Mark 8F Formula Ford, and Garo Nigogosian's F100 Mark 9S. The glassfibre bodies, spaceframe chassis and most chassis parts were designed and fabricated entirely by the virtually two-man firm. DF

Duesenberg (US)

The cars built by the brothers Fred and August Duesenberg excelled in several spheres; with Miller they were the most famous make of American racing car, and the

only one to win the French Grand Prix, while the Models J and SJ were outstanding luxury cars. In addition, a Duesenberg-built special held the unofficial Land Speed Record.

The brothers built their first car in about 1907; a 24hp flat-twin with planetary transmission and single chain drive, it was known as the Mason because it was financed by a lawyer of that name. The plant was at Des Moines, Iowa. In 1910 Fred Duesenberg built a 4-cylinder car for racing; the engine had two horizontal valves per cylinder, operated by large rocker arms which gave the engine the name 'walking beam'. Capacity was 351ci (5,752cc), and by 1912 output was 100bhp. Cars so equipped were raced under the name Mason until 1914, then as Duesenbergs. The Mason company changed its name to Maytag in 1910, and moved to Waterloo, Iowa. When the new owners began to lose interest in racing, the Duesenberg brothers set up their own small works in rented property in St Paul, Minn. Masons took 1st and 2nd places in the Wisconsin Trophy at Milwaukee, and at Brighton Beach, N.Y., in 1912, and the following year they ran at Indianapolis for the first time. Willy Haupt finished 9th, and Robert Evans 13th, with cars whose engines were 100ci (1,639cc) smaller than most of their rivals. With engines bored out to 360ci (5,899cc), the same models ran at

1920 Duesenberg Land Speed Record car. Tommy Milton at the wheel. *Photo: Indianapolis Motor Speedway*

Indianapolis in 1914, this time under the name Duesenberg. Eddie Rickenbacker finished 10th, and Haupt 12th. Later in the year, Rickenbacker won a 300-mile race at Sioux City. During 1915 and 1916 the design was gradually improved, a 16-valve engine being introduced in the latter year. Victories included road races at Glendale, Calif., and the Corona Grand Prize, Ascot dirt track, and the Des Moines Board Speedway, with 2nd places at Indianapolis and on the board speedways at Tacoma and Cincinnati. Drivers during these two seasons included Ralph Mulford, Wilbur d'Alene, Eddie Rickenbacker, and Tommy Milton.

The war prevented racing in 1917 and 1918, but during this period the Duesenbergs moved into a new factory at Elizabeth, N.J., where they built aircraft engines, and began to turn out 'walking beam' engines for sale to other car manufacturers. Among their customers were Biddle, Revere, and Roamer. This engine was built by the Rochester Motors Corp from 1919, being known as the Rochester-Duesenberg.

In the 1919 Indianapolis 500 Miles Race, five cars with 4-cylinder Duesenberg engines of 299·5ci (4,980cc) ran, but the race was a disaster for the firm, for two drivers and a mechanic were killed, and all five cars retired. In addition, Tommy Milton drove a new single-ohc straight-8, but he, too, retired on the 49th lap. Later in the year, Milton won the Elgin Road Race with a 4-cylinder car, and Jimmy Murphy, Eddie O'Donnell, Dan Lewis, and Milton set 52 new records at Sheepshead Bay. For the 1920 season of the 183ci (2,999cc) formula, Duesenberg built a new straight-8 with single-ohc and three valves per cylinder. With these cars Milton, Murphy, and Eddie Hearne came 3rd, 4th, and 6th at Indianapolis, and won on the Uniontown and Fresno Board Speedways. Two of the 300ci (4,916cc) straight-8 engines were mounted side-by-side in the special car which Milton covered a mile at 156·046mph (251·17kph) at Daytona in April 1920. This was not recognized as an International Land Speed Record, but was nevertheless nearly 25mph (40kph) faster than the existing record set up by Barney Oldfield's Benz in 1910, and was not exceeded until Parry Thomas's 169·23mph (272·35kph) in 1926.

Up to this time Duesenberg had not built a passenger car for sale to the public, but in December 1920 they announced the Model A, with a 4·2-litre single-ohc straight-8 engine similar to the racing unit, but with only two valves per cylinder. It developed 100bhp. Four-wheel hydraulic brakes were used, a feature also seen on the 1921 racing cars. These finished 2nd, 4th, 6th, and 8th at Indianapolis, and Jimmy Murphy's car won the French Grand Prix at Le Mans. This was the first victory by an American car or driver in a major European event. Murphy's team-mates Dubonnet and Guyot were 4th and 6th. The team manager was George Robertson who had won the 1908 Vanderbilt Cup on a Locomobile. Murphy's car was later purchased by its driver who replaced the engine with a Miller, christened the car the Murphy Special, and won at Indy in 1922. That year, seven of the next nine finishers were also Duesenbergs. For 1922 Duesenberg introduced a twin-ohc head which was also used on 1923's smaller engines of 122ci (1,983cc). This was the year that Miller swept all before them, and thereafter Duesenberg were constantly trying to fight off the Miller challenge, not always successfully. The 1924 season was not particularly good, despite Slim Corum and Joe Boyer's victory at Indy with a supercharged car, for the make won only one other major race, but in 1925 Peter DePaolo turned the tables on Miller, winning at Indy at a

record speed of 101·13mph (162·75kph), and in five major board speedway races to give Duesenberg the AAA Championship. For 1926 the capacity limit was reduced to 91·5ci (1,499·4cc), and Duesenberg produced a supercharged straight-8 with five main bearings in place of three. They also entered a 2-stroke engined car at Indianapolis which ran up to 7,000rpm, but it gave less power than the conventional machines, and heavy consumption of plugs was a further disadvantage. Ben Jones drove the car but it crashed on the 55th lap. Duesenberg's best performance was DePaolo's 5th place. They won again in 1927 — George Souders at 97·54mph (156·97kph) — but this was their last Indianapolis victory. In 1928, 1929, and 1930, they were constantly defeated by Millers, their only important victory being on the Atlantic City Board Speedway in 1928: Fred Winnai at 101mph (162·5kph). Duesenbergs continued to run at Indianapolis into the early 1930s, but with competition from Miller, and semi-stock cars with capacities of up to 366ci (5,998cc), they did not shine. In 1933 August Duesenberg built a special 4,376cc twin-ohc straight-8 engined car for Count Trossi to drive in European events, entered by the Scuderia Ferrari. It did not have a successful career in Grands Prix, but was raced at Brooklands by Whitney Straight and George Duller, lapping at 138·4mph (222·7kph) on one occasion.

In 1926 the Duesenberg company had been acquired by E. L. Cord who gave Fred Duesenberg *carte blanche* to produce a brand-new passenger car that would exceed all standards of luxury and speed. The result was the Model J, introduced at the end of 1928 and made, with its companion the SJ, until all Duesenberg production ceased in 1937. It had a 420ci (6,882cc) twin-ohc straight-8 engine made by Lycoming to Duesenberg's design, which developed 265bhp at 4,250rpm. This was an extraordinary figure at a time when 120bhp was regarded as really powerful, and no less outstanding was the Model J's top speed of 116mph (187kph) with a four-seater body. The even more powerful SJ introduced in 1932 had a centrifugal supercharger and developed 320bhp. Several very handsome roadster bodies were built on the SJ chassis, but despite its sporting potential it was hardly ever seen in competitions. Prince Nicholas of Rumania

1925 Duesenberg, winner at Indianapolis. Peter DePaolo at the wheel. *Photo: Indianapolis Motor Speedway*

entered a Model J at Le Mans in 1933, 1934, and 1935, but never completed the course. The SJ was used by Ab Jenkins as the basis for his Mormon Meteor, but this is dealt with under its own entry.

Fred Duesenberg died after a road accident in 1932. August worked with Auburn-Cord on the supercharged Auburn, and was associated with an abortive plan to launch a new Duesenberg in 1947. He died in 1955 at the age of 76. GNG

Dufaux (CH)

The brothers Frédéric and Charles Dufaux of Geneva built a number of giant racing cars, mostly with straight-8 engines, between 1904 and 1907. Their first car, built in the Piccard-Pictet works, was a 12·75-litre straight-8 intended for the 1904 Gordon Bennett race. It did not start, but later in the year, Frédéric Dufaux won the Coupe Monod with a flying kilometre in 31sec, and came 2nd in a speed trial at Dourdan. The straight-8 was again entered for the Gordon Bennett in 1905, and again did not start. Another 1905 Dufaux was an astonishing 4-cylinder car with a claimed output of 150bhp. Cylinder dimensions were 225 × 166mm, giving a capacity of 26·4 litres, or over 6·5 litres per cylinder. There was no conventional radiator or bonnet, but cooling surfaces were incorporated in the cylinder heads. With this car Frédéric Dufaux covered a flying kilometre at Arles in 23sec, equal to a speed of 97·257mph (156·521kph). In 1907 another straight-8 was built for the Grand Prix, with similar engine to that of the 1904 car, although output was now given as 100/110bhp, compared with 70/90bhp for the earlier machine. Driven by Dufaux again, it lasted for seven out of the ten laps before retiring. GNG

Dulon (GB)

'Dulon' was compounded from the names of the precision engineer Andy Duncan and the electronics engineer and designer Bill Longley, being first applied to 750 and 1172 Formula specials. The LD3 and LD4 were prototype Formula Ford cars, and during 1968 twelve of the LD4B production models were sold. The car purchased by Ian Taylor was particularly successful, and for 1969, when a dozen of the LD4C models were made, he acted as works driver. The LD5 and LD6 were one-off road and racing GTs respectively, and the LD7 a road-going GT vehicle offered for 1970. A Formula 5000 machine carried the designation LD8, and the 1970 cars for FF, F3 or FB were the LD9 and the LD9B, constructed to high standards with no less than 47 rose joints being used.

1970 Dulon LD9 Formula Ford. *Photo: Autosport*

By 1970 this small firm in Didcot, Berkshire, had expanded to offer production cars for F100 (LD10) and Group 6 sports-car racing (LD10B and LD11), based on a substantial steel monocoque chassis. Several of the Formula Ford cars were exported, and others continued to gain success on British circuits, in the hands of Baillie, Rouse and McLeod.

Typical Dulon features were a very wide track, the extensive use of square-section chassis tubing, and an effort to reduce costs without compromising quality by manufacturing a very high proportion of parts within the works. Fibreglass bodies for all models were made on the premises. DF

Dupont (US)

Dupont cars were first made in 1919, but the only sporting model appeared in 1928. This was the Model G, powered by a 5·2-litre 125bhp straight-8 engine built by Continental to Dupont specification. Most Model Gs were two-seater speedsters, but two four-seater sports tourers were built for Le Mans in 1929. Only one ran in the race, driven by Louis Miranda and Charles Moran. It retired on the 20th lap after ballast had fallen through the floor and broken the propeller shaft. In 1930 Moran drove a lightened speedster at Indianapolis but crashed on the 23rd lap. The car was repaired and subsequently raced at the Roosevelt Speedway. GNG

Durant Special *see Miller*

Dürkopp (D)

The first competition cars built by Dürkopp of Bielefeld were three 7·5-litre machines built for the 1907 Kaiserpreis, one finishing 19th. Dürkopp's first real sports car

Left, 1904 Dufaux 70/90hp racing car, now in the Fritz Schlumpf Collection. *Photo: Ferdinand Hediger Collection*

Right, 1905 Dufaux 26·4-litre record car. Frédéric Dufaux at the wheel. *Photo: Ferdinand Hediger Collection*

was the P8A of 1924. It had a 2-litre sv engine but was equipped with a Zoller supercharger, attached to the crankshaft and constantly running. The output of this version was about 60bhp, maximum speed about 95mph (152kph). It gained a number of class victories in hill-climbs and a 2nd place in the German 2,500 kilometres Trial of 1924.

In 1925 the P8B followed with a new 2-litre shaft-driven ohc engine with overhead valves. The output was again 60bhp, and maximum speed about 100mph (160kph). This type was very successful in 1925/6 in national events, mainly hill-climbs. Hans Stuck gained his first victories in a P8B at events like the Salzberg, Regensburg and Oberjoch hill-climbs and on the Solitude circuit. Dürkopp ceased car production in 1927. HON

D'Yrsan (F)

Built by Raymond Siran in Asnières, the d'Yrsan was one of the best-known French sporting 3-wheelers, and un-like its rivals Darmont and Sandford it was a wholly-French design and not a crypto-Morgan. A 972cc Ruby engine powered the touring models, and there was a sports car with pointed tail. The early models had the anachronism of acetylene lighting. A 1,100cc Ruby engine was used in the more powerful sports model which ran in the Bols d'Or, and a streamlined version of the 1100 called the Scarabée was driven by Siran at over 85mph (136kph). A very small number of Scarabées were sold to the public. A 750cc version of the unstreamlined 3-wheeler was built for record-breaking.

In 1927 a 4-wheeled sports car was introduced, and the 3-wheelers were discontinued the following year. The 4-wheelers had Ruby engines of 972cc, 1,097cc (35bhp), or 1,088cc (55/65bhp with supercharger). Again a special 750cc version was built, and with this Siran came 2nd in the 1928 Voiturette Grand Prix at Comminges. Four-wheeler d'Yrsans also competed in the Bol d'Or, the Coppa Florio at St Brieuc, and at Le Mans. A 6-cylinder model with 1,455cc or 1,645cc engines built by Michel Aviation of Strasbourg was planned, but never went into production. GNG

Eagle (US)

All-American Racers of Santa-Ana, Calif., was founded in 1964 by Dan Gurney and Carroll Shelby, with Gurney acquiring sole ownership in 1967. Except for Formula Vee builders, AAR, with a 50-man shop, was one of the lagest U.S. racing car constructors. From 1966 until mid-1970 AAR produced a total of five Formula 1, 18 Formula A (Formula 5000) and 54 Indianapolis Eagle racing cars. Anglo-American Racers, originally located in Rye, Sussex, England (adjacent to shops of Harry Weslake) later moved to Ashford, Kent, before their closure in 1968 when Gurney dropped Formula 1 participation, Len Terry and Tony Southgate were largely responsible for AAR Indianapolis and Formula 1 Eagle chassis and body design. Cylinder head expert Harry Weslake and engine specialist Aubrey Woods built the 3-litre V-12 Formula 1 engine first raced by Gurney at Monza in 1966. Five AAR Eagle-Fords qualified for the 1966 Indianapolis 500 with Lloyd Ruby's Eagle leading for most laps although failing to finish. In addition to Formula 1 and Indianapolis engines, Gurney-Weslake cylinder heads were successfully used by Ford-powered sports cars and drag racers. Denny Hulme drove an Eagle to earn 1967 Indy 'Rookie of the Year' honors for his fourth place finish. Of the four Eagles entered in the 1968 Indianapolis, Bobby Unser was first, Gurney

Above, 1929 d'Yrsan 750cc at Le Mans. *Photo: Montagu Motor Museum*

Right above, 1967 Eagle Formula 1 car at Silverstone. Dan Gurney at the wheel. *Photo: Al Bochroch*

Right, 1969 Eagle Indianapolis car. *Photo: Ozzie Lyons*

second and Hulme fourth. Gurney's stock-block Eagle-Ford was second in 1969 and 1970 and ten Eagles, more than double the next make, were part of the 33 car 1970 Indy grid. Gurney brought the AAR Formula 1 Eagle its first victory at Spa in 1967, the first American car and driver Grand Prix victory since Jimmy Murphy's Duesenberg won the French GP at Le Mans in 1921. Following his retirement as a driver in October 1970, Gurney announced plans to remain in racing as a car builder and team manager. ARB

Effyh (S)

Adding some much needed international interest to the 500cc Formula 3 racing scene in the early 1950s, the Swedish Effyh was a fast, robust little machine with tubular chassis and, transverse-leaf independent sus-pension, powered generally by a Speedway JAP single-cylinder motorcycle unit, although ohc Norton units were also used later. The makers were the Håkansson brothers, headed by Frans Yngve Håkansson from whose initials the name Effyh derived.

Effyh 500s gained many successes in Scandinavian events, particularly at Hedemora, Karlskoga and Skarpnäck, near Stockholm, and on frozen lakes and dirt track courses. Prominent drivers included Åke Jonsson, Eiler Svensson, Sven Andersson, Olle Nygren and Nils Gagnér. An Effyh driven by O. Hansen of Denmark placed 2nd to a Cooper in the 1951 AVUS Formula 3 GP in Germany, and two or three Effyhs were sold to private owners in the United States, where they scored several successes. The Swedish cars also visited Britain on occasions without affecting British domination of the 500cc racing class. Production continued until 1954. CP

EHP (F)

Built by the Etablissements Henri Précloux, the first EHP of 1921 was a typical French sporting cyclecar with 903cc side-valve Ruby engine and no differential. It was entered in competitions soon after its introduction; Chabreiron finished 3rd in the 1921 Cyclecar Grand Prix at Le Mans, and won the cyclecar race at Provins, both successes being with the special 1,095cc ohv engine used in the competition cars. Chabreiron came 6th in the 1922 Coupe des Voiturettes and Ivanowski was 2nd in the 1924 Bol d'Or. M. Benoist won the 1924 La Baule voiturette Grand Prix. In 1925 a larger EHP with 1,496cc CIME engine was introduced; two cars ran at Le Mans and in the Touring Car Grand Prix that year, but did not distinguish themselves. In 1926 three cars ran at Le Mans, one with a streamlined body; their best position was 9th overall, but in 1927 Bouriat and Bussienne drove a 1,094cc car into 4th place overall, and came 2nd in the Rudge-Whitworth Biennial Cup for 1926-7. They repeated this achievement in 1927-8.

The original EHP cyclecar was the basis for the Spanish Loryc. GNG

Elden (GB)

In 1966 Brian and Peter Hampshire had built the interesting Briham Formula 4 car, with a composite fibreglass/Mallite sandwich monocoque, the tubular bulkheads being bonded into the fibreglass. For Formula Ford their London workshops produced the compact Elden in 1969, and this spaceframe design was developed through 1970, though few were made. Spaceframe designs for F100 and Group 6 racing were also available. DF

Eldridge Specials (GB)

Ernest Eldridge built three cars known as Eldridge Specials, in addition to an enormous aero-engined Brooklands special, the Isotta-Maybach, and the even larger Fiat 'Mephistopheles' (see page 451). The first of the smaller Eldridge Specials appeared in 1925, and consisted of a 1·5-litre Anzani engine in an Amilcar chassis. It finished 4th behind the Talbot-Darracq team in the Grand Prix de l'Ouverture at Montlhéry, and was succeeded by a second Special with twin-ohc head on the Anzani block, vertical supercharger, underslung chassis and streamlined body. This car ran in the Italian and San Sebastian Grands Prix of 1925, but was not so successful as the earlier sv-engined car. Both it and a single-seater ran at Indianapolis in 1926, driven by Eldridge and Douglas Hawkes, but both retired. They were the last British cars to run at Indy until Jack Brabham's Cooper in 1959. GNG

Elfe (F)

The Elfe was a spidery cyclecar built in single- and two-seater form, which its designer Eugène Mauve drove in a number of cyclecar events between 1920 and 1922. As raced in the 1920 Coupe des Voiturettes at Le Mans, the Elfe was a tandem two-seater whose occupants sat on sketchy seats with one leg on each side of the frame. Behind the passenger was an air-cooled V-twin Anzani engine with a lozenge-shaped fuel tank above it. It did not distinguish itself, nor did it do any better at the same event in 1921, when it was the slowest car on the course.

Mauve was a lively character, however, and a reporter remarked that his repartee was quicker than his car.

In 1923 he began to make under his own name a conventional light car with front-mounted 7·5hp engine, and shaft drive. He drove one in the 1923 Cyclecars Grand Prix, but as opposition came from three Salmsons, he did not stand much chance of success. GNG

Elfin (AUS)

Now one of the leading Australian constructors, Elfin was started in a small shed in Adelaide, South Australia, in 1959 by Garrie Cooper and his father. Cooper, himself a skilled driver, started with a Formula Junior chassis that represented an improvement on the Lotus 18. A number were bought by Australian drivers, and Formula 3 versions followed. Elfin added a Clubman-type sports car which was very successful, and then a Mallala version to compete with the Lotus 23, but few were sold. The turning point was undoubtedly the monocoque chassis which appeared in 1965, ready to be fitted with Ford 1,100 and 1,500cc engines for the current Australian Formulas 2 and 3. That car is still in production in improved form, and the Type 600 development of it was raced by Cooper in 1969-70 with a 2·5-litre Repco V-8 engine. The factory, still small but highly efficient, also turns out Formula Vee and Formula Ford chassis, although construction of the former category has tended to pass to more specialized constructors. Elfin built their first big Group 7 sports car in conjunction with Frank Matich, but whereas Matich went on to manufacture his SR3 and SR4 versions Elfin continued with its Type 400 and later a smaller Type 300, both of which raced successfully in 1970. TBF

Elizalde (E)

The first Elizalde model was a 2·3-litre 4-cylinder car made in 1915, which won its class in the Vuelta Cataluña of that year. It was followed in 1916 by a 2·7-litre car which achieved a similar success in the 1916 Vuelta

Left above, 1921 Elfe cyclecar. Eugene Mauve at the wheel. *Photo: Montagu Motor Museum*

Above, 1926 EHP 1,239cc at Arnage Corner, Le Mans. Bussienne at the wheel. *Photo: Autocar*

Below, 1925 Eldridge Special. Ernest Eldridge at the wheel. *Photo: T. A. S. O. Mathieson Collection*

Left, 1922 Elizalde Type 5181 at Rabassada hill-climb. Pierre de Vizcaya at the wheel. *Photo: J. Rodriguez-Vina Collection*

Below, 1970 Elfin 600B with 2·5-litre Repco V-8 engine. Garrie Cooper at the wheel. *Photo: Thomas B. Floyd*

Cataluña. In 1918 came a 3·3-litre car with 90bhp and 4-wheel brakes, known as the Reina Victoria Eugenia. This too was entered in competitions, but the most sporting car the firm made was the Type 5181 of 1922. This had a 3·4-litre straight-8 engine and a long-tailed two-seater racing body. It won the 4-litre class in the 1922 Rabassada hill-climb, and made ftd there in 1924. There were also smaller Elizalde racing cars, including the 1·5-litre Type 511 which finished 6th in the 1922 Penya Rhin Grand Prix, and a light car using a 1,100cc engine in the Type 511 chassis which was 5th in the 1922 Armangué Trophy Race, and 4th and 6th in the same event in 1923. Among the best-known Elizalde drivers were the constructor Arturo Elizalde, his brother Salvador, Marc d'Huilier and the two de Vizcaya brothers. Production ended in 1928. JRV

Elva (GB)

Elva cars — the name derived from the French 'elle va' (she goes) — were the brainchild of Frank Nichols. The progenitor of the line was the 1954 CSM Special (Chapman Sports Motors), built in Hastings with multi-tubular frame, divided axle ifs, and modified Ford power unit. In the following year the Elva overhead-valve conversion for Ford engines was introduced, and two Mark 1 Elvas were made by Nichols and Mac Witts at Bexhill, featuring Standard ifs. The Mark 1B used wishbone ifs and the Mark 2 was distinguished by a De Dion rear end. Archie Scott-Brown and Dennis Taylor were among the successful British drivers using these cars, and an export link with the United States was firmly established by 1957. The Mark 3 was designed for the FWA 1,098cc Coventry-Climax engine, and alternatives included the 1·5-litre flap-valve Butterworth unit. The ingenious Mark 4 appeared in 1958, with inboard rear brakes and drive shafts acting as the upper links of the irs. Engines included the Alfa Romeo Giulietta, BMC B-series, and Coventry-Climax twin-ohc 1·5-litre.

In this year also the Courier road car was introduced, made in a new works at Hastings. Based on a simple ladder frame, and using many BMC B-series parts, this model was still being sold ten years later as a race trainer in the United States from Trojans of Croydon, who took over manufacture in 1962. One or two suitably tuned Couriers also made quite an impact on British Club racing, mainly in the Modsports category.

The racing line was continued in 1959 with the sports Mark 5, and its Formula Junior derivative. This car gained some initial success, but was no match for the Lotus and Lola rear-engined machines which appeared

later, although this was due partly to the unreliability of the Elva's BMC or Mitter-DKW engine when highly stressed. The export version, built at Rye, was known as the Scorpion. Rather surprisingly, sales of the Mark 5 reached 182 before production ceased in 1961, despite the introduction of a new rear-engined model in 1960.

A financial crisis intervened in 1961, and a new company was formed to make the Formula Junior car with rear-mounted Cosworth engine, and the rear-engined 1,100cc Mark 6 sports car, some 60 of which were sold. In 1962 the firm moved to Rye, and Keith Marsden's Mark 7 design was introduced, with angled driving position, simpler and lighter frame, revised front suspension and Coventry-Climax or Ford-Cosworth engines of various types.

The following year brought the début of the very successful version with BMW 2-litre engine, developed by Frank Webb, and available also in 1964 as a road car with coachwork by Fissore. This development proved too expensive for sales on a successful scale, despite a take-over by the Lambretta-Trojan group. In sports and GT racing, Bill Moss did well with a Ford-engined Mark 7, and Tony Lanfranchi earned the make's earliest successes with the Elva-BMW. Racing Mark 7s were also used with Porsche engines; Herbert Muller's came 2nd in the European Hill-Climb Championship in 1964 and 1965.

The Mark 8 Elva-BMW was produced at Rye until 1966. After this date no true Elva racing cars were made, although the Trojan-built McLaren models were designated 'McLaren-Elva' for some time. Production of the Courier sports car was transferred to Shenley, Herts, where it continued until 1967. DF

Left, 1959 Elva-Austin Formula Junior car. *Photo: Autosport*

Above, 1961 Elva-Ford Formula Junior car on test at Brands Hatch. John Bolster at the wheel. *Photo: Autosport*

1961 Elva-Ford Mark VI sports car. *Photo: Alan Fulwood*

Above, 1949 Emeryson-Duesenberg 4·5-litre Formula I car in the Isle of Man. *Photo: Motor*

Right above, 1963 Scirocco-BRM (Emeryson) 1·5-litre Formula I car at Solitude. Tony Settember at the wheel. *Photo: Gunther Molter*

Below, 1950 Emeryson 500 at Brands Hatch. Paul Emery at the wheel. *Photo: Guy Griffiths*

Above, 1951 EMW 2-litre racing car. Edgar Barth at the wheel. *Photo: Vladimir Havranek Collection*

Below, 1954 AWE (EMW) 1·5-litre sports car. Edgar Barth at the wheel. *Photo: Vladimir Havranek Collection*

Right, 1921 Enfield-Allday 200-Mile Race car. J. Chance at the wheel. *Photo: Montagu Motor Museum*

Emeryson: Emery (GB)

Paul Emery and E. S. Limpus put a 4·5-litre Duesenberg engine into a Rapier chassis for the post-war Formula 1, but this imaginative project could not compete with the more monied teams in either speed or reliability. In 1949 a tubular-framed 500 was constructed, with independent suspension to all wheels, by rubber up to the 1952 model, and fwd. This unorthodox car was fairly successful in minor British races, other drivers besides Paul Emery himself including A. J. Barrett, J. S. Burnett, J. Caddy, Frank Kennington and ex-motorcyclist Harold Daniell.

After 1952 Emery turned his attention to larger cars, with Aston Martin, Alta and fuel-injected Jaguar engines, and a Connaught-engined Cooper-based Formula 1 car in 1958. The situation was confused when Paul Emery's son Peter produced a Velocette-engined 250cc racing car in 1959, which he also (but more logically) called an Emeryson. Peter's next design was a front-drive Formula Junior of 1960, christened the Elfin, while Paul was at the same time developing a spaceframed rear-engined Formula Junior Emeryson which was to be made by Lister and sold by Connaught. Mike Spence took one of these cars to victory in the 1961 Silverstone 100-mile FJ race.

The Ecurie Nationale Belge bought three Formula 1 cars based on the Formula Junior design for 1961. Both Maserati and Coventry-Climax engines were tried without doing very much good, and they often failed to make the grid. The American-financed Scirocco project later took over the cars, rebuilding and renaming them without improving their fortunes.

The spaceframe Emery GT, with rear-mounted Ford or Hillman Imp engine, was raced successfully by R. Markey and others in the mid-1960s, but Paul Emery then dropped this model also in order to concentrate on the much-modified and highly tuned Emery Imp GT saloon. DF

EMW (D)

EMW was one of the post-World War 2 derivations of the BMW and in fact the cars were built in the former BMW works at Eisenach which were nationalized after the war. Pre-war 2-litre BMW models were resumed and a sports car, the S1, appeared with a 2-litre engine following the BMW 328 layout. From 1953 EMW built a 1·5-litre sports car which had been developed and manufactured by DAMW. It had already been quite successful and continued to be so until 1956, running under the name of AWE (Automobilwerk Eisenach) during the last year before EMW gave up racing. At the time of their with-

drawal from racing the 6-cylinder engine with bore and stroke of 66 × 73mm had an output of about 155bhp at 7,000rpm and a maximum speed of about 155mph (248kph) was recorded. The most successful drivers were Rosenhammer and Barth. HON

Enfield-Allday (GB)

The 10hp Enfield-Allday of 1920 was a brilliant stop-gap effort by A. C. Bertelli after the firm had failed to get their odd radial-engined 5-cylinder Bullet into production. No more than 100 of these pleasant sporting cars were made, but a development of the original sv design, with two overhead inlet valves per cylinder, side exhaust valves, twin carburettors, and an output of 40bhp, was entered for the 1921 200 Miles Race at Brooklands. The model had no success on this occasion, but Bertelli drove a similar car with fwb in the 1922 Isle of Man International 1500 event run in conjunction with the TT, and finished, albeit well down the list. For the 200 Miles Race there were two ioe cars (Barnato and Bertelli) and a single sv machine with touring engine (Chance), but only the latter finished, taking 4th place in the 1·5-litre class.

Enfield-Allday had given up competitions by 1923, and the three Bertellis which started in the 1923 race were in fact Enfield-Allday chassis with 4-cylinder Burt-McCollum single sleeve-valve engines made by Bertelli. They failed, but in 1926 Bertelli and W. S. Renwick produced a prototype ohc sports car with Enfield-Allday chassis and cylinder block. This R and B Special evolved into the Feltham-built Aston Martin. MCS

ERA (GB)

The ERA is unique in several ways. To begin with, it

1936 ERA B-type at Silverstone in c 1949
John Bolster at the wheel. *Photo: Autosport*

Below, 1939 ERA E-type at Albi. Arthur
Dobson at the wheel. *Photo: Klementaski
Studio*

Right, 1952 ERA G-type at Rufforth. Stirling
Moss at the wheel. *Photo: W. K. Henderson*

upheld national prestige in the voiturette category at a time when a decade had passed without a British GP victory. Secondly, the firm never built a road-going car: the 4-litre sports project of 1937 was stillborn, and the 2·7-litre V-8 Raymond Mays of 1939 an independent venture which appeared only in a few rallies. Thirdly, it could be bought off the peg for £1,500 — rather more than the price of Geoffrey Taylor's rival Altas, and almost twice the £795 asked for a K3-type MG. Fourthly, though only 17 of the basic models were built, they were seen all over Europe in the 1935-9 period, as well as in Australia and South Africa, and ERA was in fact the top-scoring racing make in 1937, with 14 victories to Mercedes-Benz's seven. A single car, Prince Chula of Siam's 'Romulus' (R2B) scored 10 1st places, eight 2nds, five 3rd, one 4th and one 5th, with only five retirements, in five pre-war racing seasons.

Conceived in 1933-4 by Raymond Mays, Humphrey Cook, and Peter Berthon, with the assistance of Reid Railton, the ERA made use of a tuned and modified version of the 1·5-litre 6-cylinder high-camshaft ohv Riley engine in a conventional chassis, with 4-speed Wilson preselector gearbox. A Roots-type blower of Murray Jamieson design was fitted, and the cars could be supplied in 1,100cc and 2-litre forms as well as in standard guise. Output of the original 1·5-litre version was 150bhp at 6,500rpm, though in later years the Zoller-blown 2-litre was worked up to 340bhp, and even in 1959 a similar unit with Shorrock supercharger was said to give 300bhp. On a weight of 1,624lb (736·6kg) 125mph (200kph) was possible. The car's first appearances were inauspicious; it was withdrawn from the 1934 Mannin Beg in the Isle of Man after some unsuccessful practice and retired in the British Empire Trophy at Brooklands, though at the track's August Bank Holiday meeting Humphrey Cook's 1,100cc machine won a handicap race at 76·37mph (122·90kph). Mays fielded 1·5-litre and 2-litre machines at Shelsley Walsh that September, winning both his classes and making ftd in 44sec. The ERA's first victory was in the Nuffield Trophy at Donington Park, which Mays won at 61·51mph (98·99kph).

Real advances began to be made in 1935, when a failure in the International Trophy at Brooklands was followed by the two first-ever ascents of Shelsley Walsh in under

40sec by Mays's 1·5-litre and 2-litre cars: the latter set a new record of 39·6sec. In the Mannin Beg the 1,100cc engine had to be used because of a ban on supercharged 1,500cc cars, but Fairfield won, all the same, though Mays's 2-litre retired in the Mannin Moar. The South African driver also won the Nuffield Trophy. Four ERAs were fielded for the Eifelrennen, Mays winning at 68·99mph (111·02kph). Rose-Richards was 3rd, Richard Seaman (who had just bought his car) 4th, and Cook 5th. Fairfield and another rising star, 'B. Bira', were 1st and 2nd at Dieppe. Seaman had an excellent European season, winning the Coppa Acerbo, the Prix de Berne, and the Masaryk race in Czechoslovakia. He also recorded 2nd ftd in both the Gross Glockner and Freiburg hill-climbs. During the season the B-type with stiffer frame had made its appearance, and this formed the bulk of ERA production, 13 cars, of which the last one was delivered in 1938. The later C- and D-types were merely conversions of these.

Zoller blowers which increased output came in 1936, and more victories. At home Fairfield had to be content with 2nd in the British Empire Trophy behind the 'Bira' 3-litre Maserati, but the Thai driver's ERA just pipped Mays at the finish of the International Trophy. Tongue was victorious at Cork, and the Nuffield Trophy was a 1-2-3 victory (Charles Martin, Arthur Dobson and Peter Whitehead). Mays collected fastest times of day at both Shelsley meetings, and in the RAC 1,500cc race in the Isle of Man no fewer than ten ERAs (three works cars and seven private entries), faced 16 opponents, including the redoubtable Delage, which won. However, 'Bira' was only 77sec behind, and ERAs filled the next four places. Abroad, Fairfield collected a 2nd and a 3rd in South Africa, but the British 1·5-litres gave a good account of themselves against Maseratis and Delage alike, collecting four of the first five places at Monaco. 'Bira' won, followed by Lehoux and Embiricos. The Maseratis triumphed in the Eifelrennen, though 'Bira' was 3rd. Péronne saw revenge, 'Bira', Fairfield and Howe leading the field home, but the Coppa Acerbo was a disaster, and 2nd and 3rd ERA's best performances at Berne. At the Roosevelt Raceway in the United States Fairfield was 5th, behind GP Alfa Romeos and a Bugatti, but ahead of all the American cars.

ERA's peak year was 1937, and the works fielded the C-types with Porsche trailing-arm ifs and hydraulic brakes. Success in Britain began with the Coronation Trophy at the new Crystal Palace circuit, where Fairfield led Dobson home at 53·77mph (86·53kph). 'Bira' on 'Romulus' beat the Maseratis in the Isle of Man, averaging 70·69mph (113·76kph) in the rain, and followed by an ERA procession — Mays, Fairfield, Tongue, and Whitehead. Another 1-2-3 in the Nuffield Trophy (Fairfield, Dobson, Mays); 1st and 2nd for 'Bira' and Connell in the London GP; 1st and 4th for Mays and Dobson in the International Trophy; 1st and 3rd (Dobson and Whitehead) in the Brooklands 200; another 1st and 3rd (Mays and Cotton) at Phoenix Park; and a final victory over the Maseratis at the Crystal Palace (where one of the celebrated 'Bira'-Dobson duels ended with a victory for the former by half a length) enlivened a crowded season, even if Mays's absence in Ireland meant the loss of laurels at Shelsley Walsh to Fane's Frazer Nash.

Abroad the situation was just as good. Fairfield opened the season by winning the South African GP with his 1,100cc machine, and Howe's 3rd place in the Grosvenor race sounds better when it is realized that his was beaten only by a pair of Auto Unions. The ERAs defeated the Maseratis at Turin, where Bjørnstadt on the original R1A was 1st and Tongue 3rd; in the Avus-rennen (Martin); at Péronne (Mays); at Albi (Mays, Martin and Tongue); and at Berne (Dobson, Mays and 'Bira').

Lack of finances began to tell in 1938, though the ERAs could still win at home, and did: 3rd in the Coronation Trophy at the Crystal Palace; 1st, 2nd and 3rd in the similarly-named event at Donington; another 'Bira'-Dobson photo-finish in the London GP; a victory for 'Bira' in the Nuffield Trophy; 1st and 3rd for Wakefield and Howe in the Brooklands 200; and a 1-2-3 triumph in the BRDC Brooklands Road Race (successor to the 500), the drivers being 'Bira', Mays, Aitken and Howe. Though Howe won the South African Grosvenor GP against Maserati opposition, and Whitehead the Australian GP against lesser opponents, the ERAs' showing on the Continent was less strong. Albi, Berne and Milan were all Maserati victories, and only at Péronne did Mays win. However, he set up a new record (37·86sec) at Shelsley Walsh, and Ansell made ftd (48·91sec) at a new hill-climb venue, Prescott.

The next season, 1939, was more disappointing, for Humphrey Cook found that he could no longer stand the financial strain, and a subscription fund was opened by the newly-formed ERA Club to keep the wheels turning at Bourne. The works supported the first few races of the season without much success, for the Maseratis dominated the usually-fruitful South African season, and a 5th place in the International Trophy was discouraging. Thereafter the factory shut down; Mays ran as an independent, and won the Campbell Trophy as well as taking the unlimited Brooklands Road Course record at 77·79mph (125·19kph). 'Bira' won the Sydenham Trophy at the Crystal Palace and the Nuffield Trophy at Donington, ERAs (Mays, Whitehead and Ansell) coming in 2nd, 3rd and 4th on the latter occasion.

There was also a new aerodynamic ERA, the E-type, of which great things were promised. It had a shorter stroke (63 × 80mm as against 57·5 × 95·2mm) 1·5-litre engine on the usual lines, said to give 260bhp with the aid of a Zoller blower. Its Porsche ifs and hydraulic brakes were inherited from the C-type, but new were the synchromesh gearbox and De Dion back axle. It was lighter than the old cars, at 1,456lb (660·4kg), but it ran only once during 1939, at Albi, where Dobson crashed it after quite a good showing. Its subsequent record was a tragi-comedy of non-starts and retirements, though it struggled on until 1950, racing in later days under Leslie Johnson's sponsorship after he acquired ERA Ltd in 1948. Whitehead drove it at Turin in 1946, when it retired with supercharger trouble, but it was entered for six races in 1947, and finished only once (in the British Empire Trophy at Douglas, Isle of Man) and then well down the list. Another six retirements followed in 1948, but it actually managed two 2nds, two 3rds and a 5th in 1949, coming in less than 1¼min behind Ascari's winning Ferrari in the International Trophy. One of the cars was written off at Douglas in 1950, and its engine went into a 1926 GP Delage. The other reappeared in 1955 as a sports car with a Jaguar XK engine.

While the E-type farce was being played out, the older cars reappeared in private hands after World War 2. Though Mays retired at Geneva in 1946, he collected his two traditional fastest times of day at Shelsley Walsh, and 'Bira' won the Ulster Trophy, F. R. Gerard being 3rd. Gerard, indeed, campaigned with his ERA to good purpose: 1947 brought wins in the Ulster and British Empire Trophy Races, 3rd at Reims, 4th at Spa, and two fastest times of day at Prescott; and in 1948 he was 3rd in the British GP at Silverstone, and won the British Empire Trophy twice more, in 1949 and 1950. Ansell had won it in 1948, from the sister cars of Hampshire and Brooke, and Gerard and Harrison took 2nd and 3rd places in the 1950 Ulster Trophy. As late as 1951 Shawe-Taylor could still manage a 3rd in this event, and the cars were still good enough for hill-climb work: Mays won the British Championship in 1947 and 1948.

By 1950 the new ERA management had abandoned the E-type in favour of work on what became the Jowett Jupiter sports car, but there was a final fling in 1952 with a Hodkin-designed Formula 2 racer, the G-type, using a 1,971cc Bristol engine converted to dry-sump lubrication. Other features included a 4-speed box in unit with the De Dion back end, coil-and-wishbone ifs, and a twin-tube frame, but though Stirling Moss was placed in minor F2 events at Boreham and Goodwood, the project was abandoned and the car sold to Bristol, who used it as a basis for their Type 450 sports-racer.

The old ERAs have been raced continuously since then, and 16 of the original 17 still survive, almost all of them being active. The Seaman Trophy Race for historic racing cars was long a happy hunting-ground for the make, and they won every event in the series from 1954 to 1963; it was only when post-World War 2 'historic' machines became eligible that their domination was brought to an end by a Cooper-Bristol in 1964. MCS

Eric Campbell (GB)

The Eric Campbell was a typical assembled light car with 1,505cc Coventry-Simplex engine, made in the former Handley-Page aircraft works at Cricklewood, Middlesex. It was introduced in September 1919, and made its sporting debut in the Targa Florio only two months later. This was remarkable at a time when international competition had hardly restarted after the war, and participation in Italian events was generally confined to Italian cars. Two Eric Campbells were entered, but only one started, driven by Jack Scales; he retired with a broken steering gear. The next appearance of an Eric Campbell in a major race was in the 1922 200 Miles Race when H. J. C. Smith drove a specially-built car with single-ohc

1,352cc engine and streamlined body. It retired, and although entered again in 1923 it never reached the starting line. Away from the track Eric Campbells did well in trials and hill-climbs, winning Gold Medals in the London–Manchester, London–Edinburgh and London–Lands End trials. Production ceased in 1926. GNG

Ermini (I)

Prominent in 1950–55 among the numerous *ameliorazioni Fiat* available on the Italian sports car market was the Ermini, produced by a former driver and pre-war racing mechanic of great experience. Low, light, and with excellent roadholding, the attractive Erminis came into direct conflict with rivals such as Stanguellini, Giaur and Abarth, to the betterment of the racing. Pasquale Ermini specialized largely in the 1,100cc national class, notable owners including Piero Scotti, who won his class in the 1950 Giro di Sicilia, Targa Florio, Tuscany Cup and other important races, becoming Italian 1,100cc Champion before moving on to Ferraris. Other successful *Erministi* were Aldo Terigi, who placed 4th overall in the 1952 Targa Florio behind three works Lancias; Attilio Brandi; Lo Manaco; E. Manzini; L. Pagliani; and L. Binda. CP

Estonia (SU)

The most significant Russian racing cars come from the Estonia works at Tallinn in the former independent republic of Estonia. The first was a rear-engined Formula Junior car built in 1961, but from 1964 the Estonia, designed by Ants Seiler, has been a Formula 3 car powered by a rear-mounted Wartburg 3-cylinder 2-stroke engine. Design is generally similar to that of the Polish Promot, but the engine is mounted on its side, giving the Estonia a lower profile than the Polish car. A Formule Libre Estonia used the 5-litre 200bhp V-8 Chaika engine. On the whole Estonias have not been as successful as their competitors from Poland, Czechoslovakia or the German Democratic Republic. In 1970 an Estonia was fitted with a 1,600cc Moskvitch engine, in anticipation of the 1971 Formula 3. GNG

Excelsior (B)

This make was first seen in serious competition at Ostend in 1910, but the following year a team of 3-litre cars was prepared for the Coupe des Voitures Legères. They were credited with 3,000rpm, and 88mph (141·62kph), but none of them was placed. However there was a win in the Liedekerke Cup and further successes at Ostend. Some

Left, 1919 Eric Campbells for the Targa Florio. Cyril Snipe and Jack Scales at the wheels. *Photo: T. A. S. O. Mathieson Collection*

Above, 1920 Eric Campbell at Brooklands. *Photo: Autocar*

Left, c 1951 Ermini 1100 sports car. Mike Hawthorn at the wheel. *Photo: Gino Portieri*

Below, 1970 Estonia-Wartburg Formula 3. *Photo: Federation of Automobile Sports of the USSR*

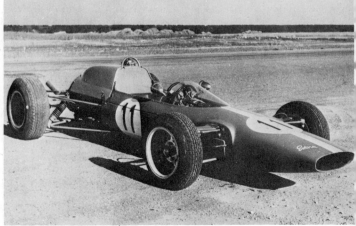

big 9·1-litre machines appeared in 1912 for the French GP, these being the first racing sixes of their period: side valves were still used; Christiaens finished 6th in the race. Some smaller 6·1-litre developments were fielded under the fuel-consumption rules in force in 1913, but the Excelsiors did less well, their best showing being Christiaens' 8th place at 63·6mph (102·35kph), as against the 72·2mph (116·19kph) of the victorious Peugeot. Once again the cars failed to distinguish themselves in the GP de France, though Christiaens won the Brussels–St Petersburg Race at over 50mph on a touring 6-cylinder, and managed 6th place at Indianapolis in 1914 on a 1913-type racer.

The arrival of the ohc 5·3-litre 6-cylinder Albert I model after World War 1 was responsible for a return to sports-car racing, Excelsiors being placed 6th and 9th at Le Mans in 1923, as well as taking 5th and 7th places in the Georges Boillot Cup at Boulogne. The Excelsiors did not turn out in 1924, and they failed to finish in the 1925 Belgian 24-Hour event. Charlier, however, broke the lap record in the Circuit des Routes Pavées, and came 3rd, Caerels winning the 1926 event as well as coming in 2nd (partnered by Dils) in the Belgian race. The make's final appearance was in the 1927 Belgian 24-Hour race, when the Caerels/Sénéchal car won at 57·12mph (91·92kph), with Ledure and Dils in 2nd place. MCS

Facetti (I)

Carlo Facetti made up for what little his car lacked in design sophistication by driving with tremendous verve. In 1960 his Formula Junior Facetti-Lancia was rear-engined, the narrow-angle V-4 unit being mounted in a Cooper-like frame of quite large-diameter tubing, with transverse-leaf rear suspension and coil-and-wishbone arrangement at the front. The car had considerable initial success, and with Baghetti's Dagrada was one of the few Lancia-powered cars to split the Stanguellini-Fiats. DCN

Fageol Twin Coach Special see
Indianapolis Cars

Fairthorpe (GB)

Early Fairthorpes were economy cars with motorcycle engines, but following the introduction of the Electron in 1958 the cars were seen extensively in competition. These very light two-seaters, with 1100cc Coventry-Climax engines, enjoyed quite a vogue in Club racing, and teams were entered regularly in relay races. The

1961 Ferguson at Teretonga Park in 1963. Innes Ireland at the wheel. *Photo: Autosport*

Left, 1913 Excelsior GP car. Christiaens at the wheel. *Photo: T. A. S. O. Mathieson Collection*

Right, 1963 Fairthorpe 948cc sports car at Silverstone. T. Scharff at the wheel. *Photo: Michael Ware*

cheaper Triumph-engined models were also raced for a time, but the later cars were heavier, and the more complex TX models (developed by proprietor Air Vice-Marshal Bennett's son Torix) were not suitable for circuit use. DF

Felday (GB)

Four Felday cars were built near Dorking, Surrey by Felday Engineering Ltd. The proprietor of the firm, Peter Westbury, won the 1963 British hill-climb championship with Felday 1, a 4wd machine of his own design, fitted with a Daimler 2·5-litre V-8 engine. Feldays 2 and 3 were stillborn hill-climb cars; Felday 4 was a 4wd sports car with a BRM 2-litre V-8 engine, completed in 1965 and raced with some success by Westbury, Mac Daghorn and Jim Clark.

In 1966 the Felday 5 was introduced, being a design by Mike Hillman allying a 7-litre Ford V-8 engine, tuned by Holman and Moody to give 510bhp, to the Ferguson 4wd transmission. Development ceased when Group 7 racing was dropped in Britain. Felday 6 was a 4·7-litre Ford V-8 engined hill-climb car with orthodox transmission, used by Tony Griffiths and John T. Williamson. Feldays 7 and 8 were abortive projects for a road car and an F2/F3 monocoque respectively. In 1967 Westbury concentrated on running a Formula 3 Brabham team, and thereafter no more Feldays were made. DF

Ferguson (GB)

The Ferguson Project 99 stemmed from experimental work on 4wd machines carried out before World War 2 by Freddy Dixon and Tony Rolt. The Irish tractor magnate Harry Ferguson ran the project after 1950, Claude Hill also joining the design team at that time. The Formula 1 racing car was built in 1961 at the Ferguson Research works near Coventry, primarily to test under racing conditions the 3-differential transmission and the Dunlop Maxaret anti-lock brake system. The handling, especially in the wet, was up to expectations, and Stirling Moss won the Oulton Park Gold Cup race in September. The engine used at this time was a front-mounted 1·5-litre Coventry-Climax 4-cylinder F1 unit, but this was later replaced with a 2·5-litre unit, similarly canted and angled. In this form the car was loaned to Peter Westbury for the 1964 season, winning the RAC Hill-climb Championship. It was then felt that the car had achieved all that had been hoped for it, and it was retired from competition. DF

Ferrari (I)

Enzo Ferrari, the man, counts for much more than the companies he has founded and run: Scuderia Ferrari; Societa Auto Avio Costruzioni Ferrari; SEFAC Ferrari (Ferrari SpA Esercio Fabbriche Automobili e Corsi). Ferrari's life has been high-performance and competition cars since the end of World War 1, and only when FIAT acquired a majority holding in his company at the end of the 1960s did his spasmodically-expressed wish to give it all up ring true (then he found he was bound by the terms of the agreement to serve on, outwardly as before).

In 1939 Ferrari left the Alfa Corse team which he had managed in succession to Scuderia Ferrari, and founded Auto Avio Costruzioni where the 815 was built. Vettura 815 was built around Fiat running gear and engine (two 508C cylinder heads on a specially cast straight-8 block, 63×60mm, 1,496cc, approximately 75bhp at 5,500rpm), with a Touring body. Two were run in the 1940 Brescia GP 'pseudo Mille Miglia', driven by Ascari and Rangoni; both led the 1·5-litre class, but neither lasted the race.

The first Ferrari—in name as well as in all other respects—was built around a Colombo-designed V-12, which first ran late in 1946. This 60° engine was to serve in various forms, but for the 1947 sports 125 was a single-ohc 1,498cc ($55 \times 52·5$mm) unit; in the 1948 GP 125 a Roots-type single-stage supercharger was added (maximum power 225bhp at 7,500rpm compared with the basic unit's 118bhp at 6,800rpm). The two sports 125s (Sport with full-width body, Competizione with cycle wings) were essentially straightforward, with welded oval-tube cross-braced frames, transverse leaf ifs, rigid back axle and 5-speed gearbox. The first cars were extensively raced in Italy, for the first time by Cortese at Piacenza in May 1947 (Nuvolari later that year won at Forli and Parma with a 125. Sommer at Turin with a 159 derivative).

In effect, the 125s became 159s late in 1947 (engines altered to 59×58mm) and 166s early in 1948 (engines $60 \times 58·8$mm, 1,992cc). With cycle wings and distinctively ponderous nose, the spyder 166 was the first Ferrari to become familiar, and the first to win major races (notably Biondetti the 1948 Targa Florio/Tour of Sicily, and the Mille Miglia, the latter with the car in coupé form). Later the more elegant Touring Barchetta appeared; with one of these Chinetti and Selsdon gained Ferrari's first Le Mans victory, in 1949. Biondetti again

won the Targa Florio/Tour of Sicily and the Mille Miglia, with 166MMs, and Chinetti and Lucas won the Spa 24 Hours. The 195 (2,341cc engine) was raced alongside the 166 in 1950, by which time Ferraris had appeared in competition in Britain (1st and 2nd in the Silverstone International Trophy sports car race) and America (where Cunningham raced the first Ferrari, a 166, to cross the Atlantic). The Colombo V-12 was also used in the 212 and 225 (2,562cc and 2,715cc engines), and subvariants began to proliferate. In 1951, when Ferraris had become almost common in racing (over 30 were run in the Mille Miglia), the 212 and 225 accounted for most successes: most notably Marzotto's 1951 Tour of Sicily win with a 212. These 'Colombo-engined' cars continued as larger-engined Ferraris became increasingly prominent, until effectively supplanted by 4- and 6-cylinder competition units in 1954.

Meanwhile, Grand Prix racing had always been uppermost in Ferrari's mind, and initially he attempted to challenge Alfa Romeo on their terms, with 1·5-litre supercharged engines. The first 125 Gran Premio ran in 1948, when Farina gained the first Ferrari F1 victory at Garda at 72·7mph (117kph). Two-stage superchargers were first used in 1949 (in the Italian GP, power being increased to 300bhp at 7,500rpm). In the same year the wheelbase was extended in an attempt to overcome road-holding deficiencies, while in 1950 De Dion rear suspension was essayed, and power went up to 315bhp at 7,800rpm. The 125 was competitive in races not contested by Alfa Romeo, Ascari winning the Swiss and Italian GPs in 1949, and Villoresi the Zandvoort GP. By 1950 Ferrari attention had turned to an unsupercharged engine as an answer to Alfa supremacy; private 125s continued in racing, notably in the hands of Whitehead, Sommer and Landi.

A 2-litre unsupercharged version of the engine was also used in F2, 1948–50, first in stripped 166 chassis and in 1950 in 125GP chassis. These were very successful, the works team winning all ten races entered in 1950.

In 1949 Lampredi started work on the 'long-block' unsupercharged 60° V-12, which at the outset was intended primarily for GP use, but was to see considerable sports car service. It first appeared in 3,322cc (72×68mm) form in a 275F1 in the 1950 Belgian GP (Ascari, 5th), and in two sports 225s in the Mille Miglia; both retired with

1950 Ferrari 166 at Le Mans. *Photo: Montagu Motor Museum*

Left, 1940 Ferrari 815 at the start of the shortened Mille Miglia. *Photo: David Hodges Collection*

Centre, 1948 Ferrari 125 Sport/48 in the GP des Nations, Geneva. Raymond Sommer at the wheel. *Photo: Cyril Posthumus Collection*

Below, 1951 Ferrari 340 in the British Empire Trophy, Isle of Man. Hans Ruesch at the wheel. *Photo: Francis N. Penn*

rear axle failure, a weakness which was to linger on. For the Geneva Grand Prix des Nations a 4,101cc (80 × 68mm) version was ready, and Ascari held one securely 2nd until he retired just before the end of the race. In the Italian GP he finished 2nd with a 375F1 (80 × 75·5mm, 4,498cc engine), and in the absence of Alfa won the Penya Rhin GP. In 1951 the engine was giving 380bhp at 7,000rpm, and Ferrari at last ended the long unbroken reign of the Alfa Romeo 158/159, a car which he considered he fathered, when Gonzalez fairly and squarely won the British GP at Silverstone. Ascari took the German and Italian GPs with the 375, then suddenly the main purpose of the car disappeared when Alfa Romeo withdrew from racing and the 1·5s/4·5us Formula was to all intents and purposes abandoned. The 4·5 Ferraris were raced in some Formule Libre events; in Britain the increasingly modified Thinwall Special was raced on until 1954; the 430bhp Indianapolis version was a failure, only Ascari ever qualifying one at the Brickyard.

In the F2 Grands Prix of 1952-3 Ferraris were supreme. The 500F2 was a straightforward tubular-framed car with a 1,985cc (90 × 78mm) twin-ohc 4-cylinder engine designed in 1951 by Lampredi. This car was extensively raced in 1951, and thus was fully developed for the Championship in 1952. These Ferraris were beaten only occasionally (by a Gordini in 1952 and a Maserati in 1953). Ascari won the Championship in 1952 and 1953, and Farina, Hawthorn and Taruffi also won *grandes épreuves* with the 500. The marginally different 553 was raced only once.

The 340 sports car with 4·1-litre Lampredi engine was officially introduced at the 1950 Paris Show; its first race, and first victory, came in the 1951 Mille Miglia (Villoresi, driving a Vignale coupé). Thereafter this car was not extensively, or very successfully, raced, but its 375MM successor was; this had a 84 × 68mm, 4,522cc, engine, in 1953 giving 340bhp at 7,000rpm. After unsuccessful first outings at Le Mans and Reims, the 375MMs went on to win the Spa 24 Hours and the Nürburgring 1,000 kilometres (Farina/Hawthorn, and Farina/Ascari) in 1953, when Ferrari took the first Sports Car Championship, and the Buenos Aires 1,000 kilometres in 1954 (Farina/Maglioli). A 4,954cc (84 × 74·5mm) engine was reputedly fitted in the car driven in the 1953 Carrera Panamericana by Maglioli, and officially appeared in the 1954 375Plus, which again had a De Dion rear axle and generally improved handling. This was first raced in the Circuit of Agadir (Farina winning), in June Gonzalez and Trintignant narrowly and dramatically won the Le Mans 24-Hour Race with one, and at the end of the year Maglioli took the last Carrera Panamericana. Successes with other models secured for Ferrari the Championship, and at the end of the year the long-stroke V-12s were set aside in favour of developments of these.

In most respects the Ferraris contesting the first two seasons of the 2·5-litre GP formula sprang from the 500 and 553, the 625 and 555 Squalo respectively (similar in chassis but with 2,490cc, 94 × 90mm, and 2,498cc, 100 × 79·5mm, 4-cylinder engines, both giving some 250bhp in 1954). Gonzalez won three early-season events, and at the end of the year Hawthorn won the Spanish GP in a 555 as his faster opposition disappeared; but generally the cars were outclassed. The 1955 Super Squalo had a considerably revised chassis, better handling and 270bhp — and an undistinguished career, best placings being 3rds at Spa (Farina) and Monza (Castellotti). Ferrari's only *grande épreuve* victory of the season was gained by Trintignant at Monaco, with a 625. Both models were

1951 Ferrari 375 in the British GP at Silverstone. Froilan Gonzalez at the wheel. *Photo: Motor*

1951 Ferrari 'Thinwall Special' at Goodwood in 1952. Giuseppe Farina at the wheel. *Photo: Central Press*

precipitately withdrawn when Ferrari took over the D50 Lancias.

In 1952 the forerunner of the famous 250GT series, the 250 Sport, had appeared, with a square (68 × 68mm) 2,963cc version of the Lampredi V-12. Bracco gained a brilliant victory in the Mille Miglia, then in the 250MM definitive version a 2,950cc variant of the original V-12 was substituted. This was little raced by Scuderia Ferrari, which turned to 4- and 6-cylinder sports cars in 1953-4.

This sometimes unhappy episode was inspired by the success of the F2 Grand Prix cars, and coincided with one of the spasmodic experimental periods (this one even embraced a twin-cylinder engine). The first 2·5- and 3-litre derivatives of the 625 engine were raced in 1953, and versions of the 555 engine appeared in 1954. The first (2,999cc) powered the Monza, a car which failed to live up to its first-time-out promise (2nd in the Supercortemaggiore GP); the 860 version (3,431cc) was raced in 1955-6, in the latter year finishing 1st in the Sebring 12 Hours (Fangio/Castellotti) and Tour of Sicily (Collins) and 2nd in the Mille Miglia and the Nürburgring 1,000 kilometres. The 2-litre (1,985cc) 4-cylinder Mondials and (first) Testa Rossa did not have outstanding careers, best performances being Marzotto's virtuoso 2nd in the 1954 Mille Miglia and the Collins/Hawthorn Supercortemaggiore victory. A 2·5-litre prototype, 625LM, was built primarily for Le Mans, where Trintignant and Gendebien placed one 3rd in 1956.

Above, 1953 Ferrari 500 Formula 2. *Photo: Motor*

Left, 1954 Ferrari 375, driven at Le Mans by Maglioli and Marzotto. *Photo: Motor*

Above, 1956 Ferrari 290MM in the Sebring 12-Hours Race. Phil Hill at the wheel. *Photo: James M. Sitz*

Left, 1958 Ferrari 250 Testa Rossa, the Le Mans-winning car driven by Phil Hill and Olivier Gendebien. *Photo: Motor*

The sixes also derived from the 625 engine, and were used in the 118LM (3,747cc) and 121LM (4,412cc, 360bhp at 6,000rpm); the only real success for either wa Taruffi's 1st in the 1955 Tour of Sicily with a 118LM. When Lampredi left under a cloud in the summer of 1955, Ferrari dropped his engines and reverted to V-12s for sports cars.

Ferrari's Grand Prix standing was restored through Lancia misfortune and FIAT finance. When the former company were forced to withdraw from racing, Ferrari inherited their Jano-designed D50 F1 cars, and thus was reinstated as an equal front-rank contender with Maserat (Mercedes withdrew at the end of 1955). These D50s became known as Lancia-Ferraris (801), but gradually many of the Lancia features were modified out of them. The 1956 season was brilliantly successful, Fangio driving for Ferrari and winning four Championship races, and Collins won the Belgian and French GPs (and gave Fangio the Championship by handing over his own car to the Argentinian at Monza). Modifications for 1957 were substantial, the engine being revised to 80 × 62mm (2,490cc), and to give 245bhp; chassis and suspension were changed, and the characteristic 'tween-wheels panniers discarded. Fortunes were reversed in 1957, Fangio—like others before and since—turning his back on Ferrari and driving for Maserati, while Vanwall became a real force. Scuderia Ferrari failed to win a single Championship race.

During the season, however, Ferrari was turning to another engine format, V-6. The original Dino 156 (named after Ferrari's son) was a Jano design for Formula 2, conventional with a tubular frame, ifs, De Dion transverse-leaf rear suspension, and 1,490cc (70 × 64·5mm) engine, initially producing some 180bhp. This handsome little front-engined car first ran in the Naples GP (Musso 3rd behind two F1 cars), and won at Reims (Trintignant). Through the year the engine was enlarged towards 2·5 litres; 2,417cc versions were run in the last (Moroccan) race of 1957 and in 1958, when the chassis and suspension were also revised. Fortunes were mixed, Hawthorn and Collins winning only one Championship race each; the former, however, accumulated sufficient points to take the title). For Ferrari the price was high: the only ranking Italian GP driver, Musso, was killed in French GP accident, and Collins at the Nürburgring.

Late in 1958, capacity was increased to 2,474cc (295bhp at 8,500rpm); details were revised and disc brakes fitted for 1959. The Dino served on in the face of the gathering rear-engined strength, and Ferrari alone upheld the honour of Italy, a position which bore heavil on the Scuderia. The GP cars won twice, on fast circuits (Brooks, at Reims and the AVUS). Wishbone irs replaced De Dion in 1960, but in a rearguard action Ferrar won only once (Phil Hill the Italian GP, in the absence of most British teams). A rear-engined car designed by Chiti appeared spasmodically, but was not persisted wit to full raceworthiness.

Meanwhile, the 1955 Le Mans accident had accelerate a movement—which proved only transitory—back towards 'true' sports cars, and towards the establishment o GT categories. Out of this was to come one of the classi Ferraris, the 250, which in various forms was to run through to the mid-1960s. Odd V-12 sports-racing cars had been built during the four/six period, and almost as an aside the 4,962cc 410S was raced, unsuccessfully, in South America in 1956, then discarded. The V-12 theme was fully revived in the 130S engine, a new design owing something to both its illustrious forebears. This 3,490cc

3 × 69·5mm) 320bhp single-ohc unit was first used in
he 290MM, which failed in its first race, the Tour of
icily, when two retired, but won its second, the Mille
Miglia, driven by Castellotti, then the Swedish GP in the
ands of Trintignant and Hill, and the 1957 Buenos
ires 1,000 kilometres (four drivers). Early that year the
ngine was equipped with twin-ohc (330bhp); then en-
rged to 3,780cc (76 × 69·5mm) to develop 360bhp in
15; then to 4,022cc (77 × 72mm), to develop 420bhp in
he 335. With one of these Taruffi won the Mille Miglia;
another de Portago crashed, and that great race was
ever run again. The only other victory for this model
me in the Venezualan GP (Collins and Hill), then
hanged regulations made it redundant.

The 2,953cc (73 × 58·8mm) 250GT V-12 had mean-
hile shown considerable promise, and in 1957 a full
ompetition version was developed (300bhp at 7,200rpm),
nd in 1958 raced in the 250 Testa Rossa (chassis de-
eloped from the 4-cylinder Testa Rossa, from mid-1958
ith De Dion rear suspension). These cars won the
uenos Aires 1,000 kilometres, Sebring 12 Hours, Targa
lorio and Le Mans 24 Hours, and thus the 1958 Manu-
cturers' Championship. At the end of the year disc
rakes were fitted, frames were lightened and bodies
odified, right-hand drive became standard, and 5-
peed gearboxes were used. Ferrari lost the 1959 Cham-
ionship to Aston Martin, but took it in 1960 when the
50 TRs were further modified (these won only the
uenos Aires 1,000 kilometres and Le Mans, but Testa
ossas and the V-6 Dino 246 gained sufficient sub-
diary placings to clinch the matter). Bodies were again
odified for 1961, and power was marginally up, to
05bhp at 7,500rpm. Although rear-engined sports-racing
erraris were coming on the scene, the TR61s were
rimarily responsible for gaining the Championship
gain, with victories at Sebring, Le Mans and Pescara.
revised TR61 won the 1962 Sebring 12 Hours, and a
milar car with a 4-litre engine the Le Mans 24-Hour
ace: the last major sports car victory for a front-
ngined Ferrari.

In that 1962 Le Mans race a 250GTO was 2nd, thus
ontinuing the excellent GT record of the 250 'family'
e Portago had scored the first victory, at Nassau in
956). In effect, these cars ended the competitive life of
e Mercedes 300SL, and were little challenged until the
obra appeared, they dominated events like the Tour de
rance as well as race classes. After considerable bicker-
g, the model was finally homologated in 1962 (hence
e designation 250GTO), with the 300bhp Testa Rossa
-12, first essayed in the basic model in 1961. The GTO
rst raced at Sebring (2nd), and then just went successfully
n until rear-engined cars displaced it.

Offshoots of the 250s included the handsome 330LMB,
ith 3,976cc engine; the first (front-engined) 250LM;
nd the 275GTB/GTS, with 3,286cc engine. None of these
ad outstanding, or long, competition careers, as Ferrari
as turning to rear-engined sports-racing cars.

In parallel with the 250s, however, work had started on
e Dino family of V-6 engines in 1956; these, together
ith a V-8, were used in monoposto cars, and in front-
nd rear-engined sports cars. The first Dino-engined
ports car to be raced, early in 1958, was a 2-litre 206;
ter a 3-litre 296 was raced once. The definitive 2-litre
ngine (77 × 71mm, 1983cc, 200bhp at 7,200rpm) then
ppeared in the Dino 196. This was notably unsuccessful
racing in 1959, and gained only one good placing in
960, 2nd in the Targa Florio, and that with a 246 engine.
Ferrari reaped full benefit from preparedness for the

Above, 1958 Ferrari 250 Testa Rossa,
driven to 2nd place in the Nürburgring
1,000 Kilometres by Mike Hawthorn and
Peter Collins. *Photo: Bernard Cahier*

Right, 1958 Ferrari Dino 246 in the French
GP. Peter Collins at the wheel. *Photo: Motor*

Above, 1960 Ferrari 250GT coupé. *Photo:
Motor*

Right, 1961 Ferrari Testa Rossa leads a
Dino 246SP through the esses at Le Mans.
The Testa Rossa, driven by Phil Hill and
Olivier Gendebien, was the winning car.
Photo: Motor

first year of 1·5-litre GP racing. Cars which were in effect prototypes, the 156 with a 65° V-6 (73 × 58·8mm, 1,476cc) were raced at the end of 1960. The 156 was conventionally spaceframed, with wishbone/coil spring/damper independent suspension front and rear, transmission at the rear, and initially characterized by 'nostril' noses. The 65° engine produced 180bhp, its 120° successor in 1961, 190bhp. Ferrari were defeated only twice in 1961, by Moss rather than other cars. Hill, von Trips and Baghetti took five of the *grandes épreuves* and two lesser events (and Hill the Championship).

As they had before, Ferrari fortunes slumped from a pinnacle in one season to the depths in the next—no Championship races fell to the make in 1962. The cars were revised in detail, but outrun by British V-8s; the drivers were not really top-flight; many of Ferrari's senior staff, including Chiti and Tavoni, left during the off-season. Matters improved in 1963: cars were lighter, had revised suspension and fuel-injected engines giving 200bhp, at 9,800rpm; Surtees joined the team, and won the German GP. A V-8 engine was raced alongside the V-6 in 1964, in a new monocoque chassis (the 158). Surtees won the German and Italian GPs, and the Championship, Bandini the Austrian GP. The V-8 was raced again in 1965, together with a flat-12 (220bhp and 235bhp respectively), but the Ferrari effort tailed off in this last 1·5-litre year, 2nd placings being the best the cars achieved.

The first rear-engined sports Ferrari, which came in 1961, owed much to its F1 contemporaries. This 246P had the Chiti divided nose, and a transverse spoiler on the tail—a device to become familiar. Its only 1961 success was in the Targa Florio with Gendebien and von Trips. In 1962 the 248SP and 286SP appeared, similar in most respects but with 2,458cc V-8 and 2,862cc V-6, then the

268 and the 196SP (1,985cc): the numbers and variants proliferated. And they won races, notably in 1962 the Targa Florio and the Nürburgring 1,000 kilometres; Scarfiotti won the European Mountain Championship for Ferrari for the first time, with a Dino 196SP.

In 1963 SEFAC came close to a deal with Ford, which would presumably have resulted in a Ford-Ferrari (and the subsequent history of racing would have been very different). As this fell through, Ford in effect set out to beat Ferrari in the prototype field. Coincidentally, Ferrari was returning once again to the V-12 engine. A 246SP was tested with a Testa Rossa V-12 in 1962, and out of this came the 1963 250P (3-litre engine rated at 310bhp), and a series of cars which were to dominate their category until the Fords became raceworthy.

The 250P won its first race at Sebring in 1963, Surtees making his team début, with Scarfiotti; and won the Nürburgring 1,000 kilometres, Le Mans 24 Hours and lesser events such as the Canadian GP. The 250LM and 3·3-litre 275LM customers' cars appeared in 1964, when the 3·3-litre 275P and 4-litre 330P were introduced for works/works-supported teams. These won at Sebring, the Nürburgring and Le Mans, and a string of secondary events fell to rear-engined Ferraris: Reims and Paris 12 Hours, the TT, Road America 500 and Canadian GP among them. For 1965 front-line use a twin-ohc V-12, based on the 290S engine rather than the Testa Rossa unit, was installed in a new chassis, the 330P2. As well as this 4-litre unit, a 4·4-litre version was used, in the 365. These cars helped keep Ferrari on top for another year, although the mixed 330P2/330P/275P team failed in the Sebring 12 Hours, and all the works 330P2s retired at Le Mans, where a private 250LM won. 275P2s (twin-ohc variant of the engine) won the Monza 1,000 kilometres and Targa Florio; a 265P2 won the Reims 12 Hours;

Left top, 1961 Ferrari 156 in the German GP, Phil Hill at the wheel. *Photo: Motor*

Top, 1962 Ferrari 156 in the German GP. Lorenzo Bandini at the wheel. *Photo: David Phipps*

Left, 1963 Ferrari 330GTO coupé in Le Mans practice. Mike Parkes at the wheel. *Photo: Autosport*

Above, 1965 Ferrari Dino 206SP driven by Ludovico Scarfiotti in hill-climbs. *Photo: Autosport*

1962 Ferrari Testa Rossa, the Le Mans-winning car driven by Phil Hill and Olivier Gendebien. *Photo: Autosport*

Ferrari gained the Prototype Championship; and various private cars won events as diverse as the Enna Cup, Austrian GP and Kyalami 9 Hours.

The functionally beautiful 330P3, in berlinetta and spyder forms, smaller and lighter, with new chassis and 4-litre twin-ohc V-12 developing some 420bhp at 8,000rpm, appeared in 1966. With it came a decline in fortunes, although there was early encouragement when Surtees returned to racing after his Mosport accident and, with Parkes, won the Monza 1,000 kilometres. The Spa 1,000 kilometres also fell to a P3 (Parkes and Scarfiotti).

Le Mans was a Ferrari fiasco: car preparation hampered by the recurrent Maranello strikes; the team riven by the clash between Surtees and Ferrari (in the person of team manager Dragoni); the best-placed Ferrari at the end a 275GTO in 8th place. The P4 succeeded the P3, with a new twin-ohc 4 litre V-12 designed by Rocchi, a new chassis and sleek body. Under team manager Lini initial 1967 prospects appeared bright, with a spectacular 1-2-3 P4 debut at Daytona, and a 1-2 in the Monza 1,000 kilometres. Then came a series of defeats, including Le Mans, but a 2nd place in the last Championship event, the

low, 1965 Ferrari 275LM, the Le Mans-
inning car driven by Jochen Rindt (at the
heel) and Masten Gregory. Photo: Al
chroch

ght, 1966 Ferrari 330P2/3, Le Mans test
y. Photo: Motor

ight, 1968 Ferrari 312 in the French GP.
ackie Ickx (the winner) at the wheel.
hoto: David Hodges Collection

elow, 1970 Ferrari 312B. Clay Regazzoni
t the wheel. Photo: David Phipps

BOAC 500 at Brands Hatch, was enough to secure this for Ferrari. Then the regulations were changed and Ferrari renounced this class of racing—at least for two seasons.

In 1968 Ferrari made a hesitant entry into Can-Am racing, with a 6·2-litre V-12-engined 612 (NART also essayed a P4). The 612 started in the last race of the series, retiring very early as a consequence of another car's accident. A 6·9-litre engine was used in the 1969 712, which showed lack of development but promise, Amon challenging the reigning McLarens on occasion.

At the other end of the scale, the little Dino (166) with 1,592/1,985cc V-6s had sometimes challenged the Porsches in these classes: notably on their own ground, 4th overall in the 1965 Nürburgring 1,000, 2nd and 3rd overall in 1966. Scarfiotti had a successful run in the 1965 Mountain Championship with a 2-litre car. The Dino was put into production in road-going form by FIAT, and thus its engine qualified for use in Formula 2 from 1967.

In that year the monocoque F2 Dino appeared only once, and in 1968 was generally outclassed by Cosworth FVA-engined cars (Ickx won a heat at Zolder, in Belgium, Bell a heat at Zandvoort, Brambilla two end-of-season races at Hockenheim and Vallelunga). But the Argentine Temporada was dominated by de Adamich, who scored three out of four possible outright victories. The car failed to reproduce this form in Europe in 1969, and the effort faded. Perhaps surprisingly, this basic model, with a 2,410cc version of the engine, turned out to be the most successful monoposto Ferrari of the late 1960s. In 1968 Amon won two Tasman races with it, and finished runner-up in the Championship; in 1969 he won the Championship decisively with four victories in seven races. In 1970 Lawrence took the Tasman title with it, albeit against weaker opposition and on the basis of good placings rather than his one victory. Curiously few single-seater Ferraris have got into private hands; most of those which have since the 125 have gone to Austra-lasians.

The first year of the 3-litre GP Formula, 1966, should have been Ferrari's, as the team mechanically best-pre-pared for it. There was nothing novel about the car, or its 60° V-12 unit, initially producing some 375bhp, and of course backed by vast Ferrari V-12 experience (a 2·4-litre V-6 was also used in early races). Bandini was 2nd with the smaller car at Monaco, and Surtees won the first 'fast' race, at Spa, with the V-12. Then he left the team, and the season went Brabham's way until the Italian GP, where revised 36-valve Ferrari engines appeared. These finished 1st and 2nd, Scarfiotti becoming the first Italian to win an Italian GP since 1952.

Accidents and Ferrari dissension effectively reduced the effort to below the level where it could be expected to succeed in 1968: three cars were run in one GP, but Amon was often the only driver. He did not enjoy the best of fortune, but nevertheless gained four 3rds for Ferrari. Early in 1969 a 48-valve 410bhp engine was used and from mid-season the chassis was lighter; the car was com-petitive, the team stronger. But Ferrari gained only one victory—Ickx, in the French GP, although Amon led four *grandes épreuves*. Ferrari started 1969 promisingly, then faded: the reputedly 435bhp engine was discarded, and the effort often seemed half-hearted. The reward was proportionate—no victories. This was the year when FIAT fully and openly acquired control of Ferrari, and an injection of greater tangible support was expected for 1970. In the first Grand Prix of that year, the 312B with

flat-12 engine, troublesome in late-1969 tests, appeared and failed to finish. Gradually through the first half of the season problems with the engine, primarily in its lubrication system, were ironed out and in the second half the 312B became the car to beat (Ickx winning the Austrian, Canadian and Mexican GPs, while to the great joy of the Monza crowd Regazzoni won the Italian GP).

Ferrari re-entered the sports-racing arena in 1969 with the Group 6 3-litre 312P, which came close to winning its first race, the Sebring 12 Hours. That 2nd place was re-peated in the Spa 1,000 kilometres, but these were the best results of the season. For 1970 Ferrari followed the Porsche example and built sufficient cars to homologate a 5-litre Group 5 car, the 512S. This did win at Sebring (Giunti-Vaccarella-Andretti), but failed to score maximum points in another championship event—not only did the team fail to 'click' for manager Mauro Foghieri as the F1 team had, but at times luck seemed to conspire against it (for example at Le Mans, where four works and private Ferraris were involved in a single accident!). At the end of the year Ickx and Giunti drove the single 512s entered in the Kyalami 9-hour Race to victory.

Despite this paper failure in 1970 sports car racing—the single Championship victory did not fairly represent the potential of the car—the Grand Prix comeback meant that the constructor with the longest unbroken competition record entered the seventies more strongly placed than for several years. The 1971 Grand Prix Season began encouragingly with Andretti and Regazzoni finishing 1st and 3rd in the South African GP. DWH

Ferrari in America

It is appropriate for Ferrari to have done well in America. According to *Ferrari* by Fitzgerald & Merritt, it was Ferrari's admiration of the Packard twin-six that led to his devotion to the 12-cylinder engine. Luigi Chinetti, one of the better Ferrari endurance drivers, has been the eastern United States concessionaire for Ferrari cars and sponsor of NART, the North American Racing Team, that brought Ferrari the 1965 Le Mans and other notable victories.

The first Ferrari to be raced in the United States was a Type 166, No 0161-1, owned by Briggs Cunningham and now on display in his Costa Mesa, Calif., museum.

1970 Ferrari 512s, driven by John Surtees and Chris Amon in Monza 1,000 kilometre *Photo: Geoffrey Goddard*

1970 Ferrari 512 Can-Am car. *Photo: Al Bochroch Collection*

Sam Collier was killed in the Cunningham Ferrari at Watkins Glen in October 1949, but it was later raced by George Rand in the Argentine and the U.S. In July 1950, Jim Kimberley won the race at Elkhart Lake, then held over public roads, and, on the West Coast, Jack McAfee, Phil Hill and later Carroll Shelby and Dan Gurney entered big-time racing in the Italian cars.

Twice Ferrari finished 1-2 in the car-breaking Carrera Panamericana. Piero Taruffi and Chinetti won in 1951, followed by Ascari and Villoresi, and in 1954 Maglioli was 1st and Phil Hill 2nd. Beginning with Fangio and Castelotti, Ferrari captured the Sebring 12 Hours in 1956, 1958, 1959, 1961, 1962, 1963, 1964 and 1970. At Daytona, Pedro Rodriguez brought Ferrari overall victories in 1963 and 1964. And in 1967 Bandini and Amon, Scarfiotti and Parkes and Guichet and Rodriguez piloted P4s to a thunderous three abreast, 1-2-3 finish.

But success in international competition is only a part of Ferrari's US story. In the beginning of the American road racing renaissance coming drivers found Ferrari patrons with surprising regularity. Well-to-do Americans such as John Edgar, Temple Buell, Tony Parravano and Allen Guiberson supplied Phil Hill, Shelby, Masten Gregory and others with the red machines. The high point of many early SCCA races were the Ferrari duels between red-uniformed Jim Kimberly of Chicago and Bill Spear, who represented the eastern establishment. Spear won the no longer contested SCCA National Racing Championship in 1953; Ferrari earned national 'modified' (later to be known as 'sports racing') honours for Kimberly in 1954 and for Sherwood Johnson in 1955. E. Lunken and a young Swiss emigrée, Gaston Andrey, were E modified national champions from 1956 through 1959. Bill Lloyd and Phil Hill captured D modified championships in 1954 and 1955; and the Ferraris of James Johnston, Alan Connell and Tom O'Brien won D Modified titles in 1958, 1959 and 1964. George Reed and Bob Grossman took SCCA national production championships in 1958 and 1959 and the Berlinettas of Grossman, Charley Hayes and Bob Hathaway tied for 1961 class A production honours. In 1963 Carroll Shelby's Ferrari won the now obsolete SCCA Formule Libre title.

Stirling Moss, the Rodriguez brothers and the Marquis de Portago were among the Ferrari drivers bringing home trophies from Nassau during Bahama Speed Weeks. But at Indianapolis in 1956 Nino Farina tried to fit a 4·4-litre sports car engine into a Kurtis chassis and failed to qualify.

However, by 1960 Ferrari's fortunes in US road racing had begun to decline. Between 1956 and 1959 the late Walt Hansgen drove Cunningham Jaguars to four consecutive SCCA national championships; V-8 powered Scarabs, Chaparrals, Corvettes and Ford-Cobras began to dominate SCCA modified and production categories. In professional road racing Anglo-American hybrids—British chassis and American V-8 power, usually Chevrolet—became the winning combination. Unlimited displacement Group 7 sports cars left Ferrari without a large enough engine to be competitive in the Can-Am, which, beginning in 1966, became America's premier road racing series. Amon drove a P-4 in the three final 1967 Can-Ams; a 5th at Monterey was his best finish. In 1969 Pedro Rodriguez was 5th at Bridgehampton in a 312 and Chris Amon mounted the first serious, albeit belated, Ferrari Can-Am attack, his 612 gathering a 3rd at Watkins Glen, a 2nd at Edmonton, and a 3rd at Mid-Ohio. ARB

Below, 1907 Fiat GP car. Felice Nazzaro at the wheel. *Photo: Montagu Motor Museum*

Bottom, 1912 Fiat GP car. Louis Wagner at the wheel. *Photo: Veteran Car Club of Great Britain*

Ferry *see Renault*

F.I.A.T.; Fiat (I)

FIAT (the periods were dropped from the name after 1906) was the first Italian make to make any impression in racing outside its homeland. As early as 1900 Lancia and Nazzaro had taken 1st and 2nd places in the Padua-Padua Race, and by 1901 the firm had progressed to a 3·8-litre 4-cylinder car on Mercedes lines, with which Felice Nazzaro won the Giro d'Italia at 26·7mph (49·97kph). Lancia won the 1902 Moncenisio hill-climb, beating a Mercedes, but the cars did not venture abroad before 1903, if a victory in Portugal's first motor race (1902) is excepted. In 1903, however, a 16hp touring model was entered in the ACGBI 1,000 Miles Trial, and two rather large *voitures légères* with moiv and over-square engines were driven unsuccessfully in the Paris-Madrid by Lancia and Storero. Cagno, however, managed 3rd place in his class in the Circuit des Ardennes, and FIAT sent three Mercedes-like 14,112cc sv 4-cylinder cars (painted black) to Homburg for the 1904 Gordon Bennett Cup. Lancia's 8th place was not very encouraging, but he won the Coppa Florio and in America Paul Sartori was timed at over 105mph (168kph) on the Empire City track — some compensation for his early retirement in that year's Vanderbilt Cup. The 1905 Fiats had 16·3 litres, 100bhp, and full overhead valves. In the Gordon Bennett Lancia made the running before his retirement, but Nazzaro's 2nd place and Cagno's 3rd were followed by a 3rd for Lancia in the Coppa Florio, and a 4th in the Vanderbilt Cup, in which the company tried hard, entering four cars, two of them of 1904 type. Nazzaro won the Susa-Moncenisio hill-

climb. Much the same cars were raced in 1906, though some smaller 7·4-litre machines were used in the Targa Florio. Results were less good: 2nd and 5th in the Grand Prix, 2nd in the Vanderbilt Cup, and a clean sweep only in the Italian Coppa d'Oro, which Lancia won.

The next season, 1907, was FIAT's golden year—and Nazzaro's. He won the Targa Florio; the Grand Prix; and the Kaiserpreis with a special 8-litre car, after he and Lancia had won their respective heats. Folkin's 3rd place in the St Petersburg-Moscow rounded off an excellent season, but FIAT's new 155 × 160mm GP cars failed in the 1908 French Grand Prix, though Nazzaro won the Coppa Florio, and Wagner averaged 90mph (144·8kph) to take the American Grand Prize, with his team-mates Nazzaro and DePalma 3rd and 9th respectively. Lancia was 2nd in the Targa Florio, and during the season Nazzaro brought the vast 18,155cc racer 'Mephistopheles' to Brooklands for his famous match race against Frank Newton's Napier, which he beat. It is a matter of debate whether he really did lap the track at 121·64mph (195·78kph), but Mephistopheles continued to race at Brooklands until 1922, when John Duff blew the engine up. Ralph DePalma campaigned with his Cyclone racer in America during this period.

In 1909 and 1910 there was no GP racing in Europe, though Mathis scored a number of successes for FIAT in minor German events, and Ed Parker was 2nd in the 1909

Vanderbilt Cup in the United States. A new record car appeared in 1910, the immense S76 with pear-shaped radiator and a 28,362cc, 300bhp ohc 4-cylinder engine which resulted in a bonnet line about 5ft (1·5m) off the ground. Pietro Bordino did an unofficial 125mph (201·2kph) in this at Saltburn, Yorkshire, in 1911, but two years later Arthur Duray was timed at 132·37mph (213·01kph) over the kilometre at Ostend. The 1911 Grand Prix de France was won by Victor Hémery on a 10·5-litre ohc FIAT S61, in effect a stripped sports car which later had a distinguished record at Brooklands, winning thirteen 1st places between 1920 and 1927. More serious were the last of the chain-driven giants, the 14·1-litre ohc S74s. David Bruce-Brown won that year's American Grand Prize on one of these, and nearly won the 1912 Grand Prix at Dieppe, being timed at 101mph (162·5kph) before he retired. Louis Wagner was 2nd in the race; Caleb Bragg and Barney Oldfield were 1st and 2nd in the Grand Prize after Bruce-Brown had been killed in a practice crash. In 1913 Frank Verbeck won the Los-Angeles–Sacramento Race in a stripped touring model. Ralph DePalma campaigned his Cyclone racer in America with considerable success during this period.

More important, there was a complete break with tradition in 1914, when FIAT GP cars were modern dohc 4·5-litre fours with fwb. These failed at Lyons, but during World War 1 the engines were enlarged to 4·9 litres (with

Left, 1914 Fiat GP car. Biagio Nazzaro at the wheel, with Attilio Marinoni. *Photo: Montagu Motor Museum*

Above, 1922 Fiat GP car. Felice Nazzaro (the winner) at the wheel. *Photo: Montagu Motor Museum*

Opposite, John Surtees. *Photo: Geoff Goddard*

1922 Fiat GP car. Pietro Bordino at the wheel. *Photo: Hugh Conway Collection*

Above, 1922 Fiat 502SS in the Targa Florio. Giaccone at the wheel. *Photo: T. A. S. O. Mathieson Collection*

Right, 1924 Fiat 805 1·5-litre twin-ohc in the Targa Florio. Pietro Bordino at the wheel. *Photo: T. A. S. O. Mathieson Collection*

Opposite, Alfa Romeo 33-3 (Rolf Stommelen) in the Monza 1000km Race, 1970. *Photo: Motor Sport*

Indianapolis in mind) and output went up from 130 to 150bhp. In this guise they did quite well, Nando Minoia making ftd at Fanø in 1919; Masetti's 3rd place in that year's Targa Florio was followed by an outright victory in 1921. More important, Fornaca produced a new 3-litre dohc straight-8 (Tipo-802) with roller-bearing big ends and a taper tail body for that season's Grand Prix. It gave 115bhp, but was not ready for the French race, and was beaten by the Ballots at Brescia. Nazzaro retired in its last race, the 1922 Targa Florio. Greater success was earned by its 2-litre 6-cylinder development raced in the latter year, which inspired the later Sunbeams. This one had servo-assisted fwb, and was used by Nazzaro to win that year's French GP; rear-axle failure eliminated the other two cars, with fatal results for Nazzaro's nephew Biagio. Bordino won the Italian GP, Nazzaro coming 2nd, and there were also some 1·5-litre voiturette versions, designated Tipo-501SS and initially using the chassis of the touring sv 501. In this form, with 8-valve engines giving over 60bhp as against the 92 of the sixes, they ran in the Targa Florio, where Giaccone was 5th, but for the Italian Voiturette GP they were given new frames and bodies like those of the 2-litre, and occupied the first four place in the race. Bordino won at 83·25mph (133·98kph).

There was a new departure in 1923: Wittig-type superchargers on the 2-litre engines, which were now straight-8s and gave 130bhp. These Tipo-805s were the first successful blown GP machines, but on their first outing at Strasbourg they all retired, and it was not until Roots-type blowers were substituted that Carlo Salamano was able to win the Italian GP. There were also some 1·5-litre 4-cylinder cars with engines of similar type developing 80–85bhp. Cagno won a race at Brescia with one of these in June 1923, but though they dominated the early stages of the Brooklands 200 both Malcolm Campbell and Salamano retired. Meanwhile Ernest Eldridge had acquired Mephistopheles and installed a 21,714cc ohc 6-cylinder FIAT airship engine developing 320bhp. In this device he raised the World Land Speed Record to 146·01mph (235·02kph) at Arpajon in 1924, and subsequently took further records, as well as appearing in match races at Montlhéry. Thereafter Mephistopheles was retired until 1961. FIAT continued to race their 1923 cars in 1924, Bordino driving a 1·5-litre into 4th place in the Targa Florio, though all three 2-litres retired in the French GP, and the factory scratched from the Italian race. This was to all intents and purposes the end of *grandes épreuves* for FIAT, though Bordino had a brief season in America in 1925. There was, however, a minor

revival in 1926/7 with a Zerbi-designed triple-ohc twin-six (the crankshafts were geared together) built for the 1·5-litre Formula. Its output of 187bhp (125bhp per litre) was remarkable, but it ran only once, in the 1927 Milan GP, which it won at 94·57mph (152·19kph). A supercharged opposed-piston 2-stroke engine was tried in the same period and gave 170bhp, but it never went into a car.

Not that FIAT were out of competitions. From 1919 onward they were Italy's general providers, and the cheapest way to go racing was to buy a FIAT tourer and tune it. In succession the 1,460cc sv 501, the 990cc ohc 509, and the 1,438cc sv 514 received the attentions of amateur and professional tuners. As early as 1921 Bergese's 501 sports 2-seater had won the 2-litre class of the Targa Florio at 33mph (53·11kph), and the 509, which disposed of 22bhp in standard form, was made to give as much as 35bhp in its hottest (509SM) manifestations. Cars of this type, driven by Jacques Bignan and Malaret, took 1st and 2nd places in the 1928 Monte Carlo Rally, and a year earlier the advent of the Mille Miglia had given the make an opportunity to show its paces. Two classes (1,100cc and 5-litre) were taken in 1928: the former category remained FIAT's preserve for the next two events, after which they moved up to the 1,500cc 'utility' class with the 514. There was also a works entry of 3·7-litre 6-cylinder sports cars for the 1929 Alpine Trial, but not even the presence of Nazzaro, Cagno and Salamano could win the team award, although on this occasion FIAT were testing the hydraulic brakes they were soon to adopt. Costa's sports 514 was the overall winner of the 1930 Italian Coppa delle Tre Venezie, an alpine event, and in 1931 the firm tried really hard in the Mille Miglia with both the 514 and the big 6-cylinder 525; the latter was sold to amateurs for the equivalent of £240 plus the promise of technical help. The works entries did not, however, materialize on this occasion. The 995cc short-stroke Balilla (Tipo-508) appeared in 1933 and won them an 8th place in the 'Monte', while though the cars could not take on the MG Magnettes in the Mille Miglia, the SIATA conversions with ohv and 4-speed boxes motored to good purpose, the fastest 508 (Ambrosini and Menchetti) averaging 54·67mph (87·98kph), and even the so-called standard saloons were not much slower.

By 1934 FIAT had their own ohv 4-speeder in production, and this later version of the 508S enjoyed a virtual domination of the 1,100cc sports category for several years. It could do 75mph (120kph) on 36bhp, blown units (not encouraged by the factory) gave 48bhp, and in stripped form 105mph (168kph) was possible at Brook-

Left, 1935 Fiat Balilla in an English trial.
Photo: Montagu Motor Museum

Above, 1953 Fiat 8V coupé at Le Mans.
Photo: Klementaski Studio

Below, 1970 Fireball racing car. *Photo: E. Setchell*

lands. The model's principal exponent was Amédée Gordini, who won the 1,100cc class of the Bol d'Or, as well as collecting class honours in the Circuit d'Orleans and the Lorraine and Marne Grands Prix. Other 1935 successes included class wins in the Eifelrennen, the Czechoslovak 1,000 Miles Stock-Car Race, the Circuit des Vosges, and numerous hill-climbs. Cars were made under licence in Germany by NSU and in Czechoslovakia by Walter; by this time Gordini's French-assembled specials called themselves Simcas. The first eighteen places in the 1,100cc section of the Mille Miglia were inevitable, but a 7th in general classification was not; the rest of the score amounted to countless minor events, plus a 1-2-3 in class in the Eifelrennen and a class victory for W. Sullivan in the TT. The Kozma and Martinek Balilla saloon won the light-car category of the Monte Carlo Rally, a feat repeated in 1937 by Villoresi in a 6-cylinder 1500. This new model enabled FIAT to win the 1·5-litre touring class of the Mille Miglia as well as both 1,100cc subsections (touring and sports): one of that year's 1500 drivers was Vittorio Mussolini, the dictator's son. By 1938 the 570cc Topolino was joining in, Cecchini taking some international 500cc records with a linered-down example, and Simca victories were matched by the impressive showing of the 1,089cc Millecento sports coupés. There was no Mille Miglia in 1939, but in the 980-mile (1,577km) Tobruk–Tripoli Race, Rossi won the 1,100cc class at 74·49mph (119·88kph)—quicker than the fastest 1·5-litre, a Lancia. The best of the Topolini averaged 63·85mph (102·76kph), and in the shortened 1940 Mille Miglia the class-winning FIAT 1100 did 82·4mph (132·61kph).

Since World War 2 FIAT have taken a back seat. They have provided finance for Ferrari and purchased Lancia: the Topolino's suspension arrangements formed the basis on which the 500cc Formula 3 was founded: and countless competition makes—Stanguellini, Abarth, Cisitalia, SIATA, etc—have made use of FIAT ingredients. Nonetheless, the 1100S carried on into the later 1940s, winning its class in the 1948 and 1949 Belgian 24-Hour Races, as well as making a considerable impression in the Mille Miglia (2nd and 3rd in 1948, and 4th in 1949) and in the Targa Florio (3rd in 1948). The cars also distinguished themselves in early Tulip and Lisbon Rallies, but the company's first serious attempt at a GT coupé—the 1,996cc push-rod 8-cylinder 8V of 1952— was not overly successful, and the model's outright victories came in minor events such as the Pescara 12 Hours

and the Giro d'Umbria. O. Capelli did, however, finish 5th both at Bari and in the Targa Florio in 1952, and as late as 1956/7 the 8V could still win its class in the Mille Miglia. Nor were the company particularly interested in rallies, and before late 1970 there was no works team to compare with the efforts of Ford, BMC or Lancia. MCS

Fireball (GB)

Designed by Frank Boyle and produced with the assistance of Ian Bayley at JB Developments of Aldershot, Hampshire, the Fireball laid claim to being the cheapest serious racing car in production in 1970. Made for the track races sponsored by Spedeworth Ltd, it incorporated a BLMC Mini engine fitted transversely at the rear. An all-up weight of less than 600lb (272kg) ensured an exceptional power to weight ratio, and the cars proved faster on some circuits than Formula Ford machines. DF

FN (B)

FN were always primarily interested in ordnance and motorcycles, and never built a serious racing car. Before World War 1 their appearances were infrequent, though two 12hp *voitures légères* ran in the Paris–Berlin in 1901. Both retired.

After the war, FN tended to concentrate on the Belgian 24-Hour Race at Spa, where by choosing the right class they could score wins on reliability. The little ohv 1300 Sport models took the first three places in the 1,500cc class in 1925 and 1926, respective winners being de Kervyn and Lecomte and Georges and de Grady. A single 10CV of similar type ran in the 1928 TT, but retired. In 1932 FN chose the big-car class at Spa and their modest 3·3-litre sv straight-8s had to be content with tailing the 2·3-litre straight-8 Alfa Romeos home at a respectful distance. Meanwhile Lamarche had done well in the Monte Carlo Rally, taking 3rd place in 1925 and 4th in 1927, and a team of standard ohv 4-cylinder 1625 saloons were only just beaten by the German Wanderers in the 1931 Alpine Trial.

The straight-8 of Georges and Collon won the Liège–Rome–Liège in 1933, and the firm's last competition effort was at Spa once again that year, where some nearly-stock 2-litre sv 4-cylinder Baudouins, with streamlined sports two-seater bodies were 1st, 2nd and 3rd in their class. MCS

Foglietti (I)

Foglietti was one of the earliest manufacturers to support

1958 Foglietti Formula Junior. *Photo: A. Ceci*

Formula Junior, running cars from 1958 until British domination began to make itself felt in 1960. The Fiat engine was in the front of a tubular chassis frame, built up from a lattice of small-diameter tubes based on two large-diameter main longerons. The engine was mounted with a pronounced offset, the drive-line passing to the right of the cockpit, which was itself offset to the left. Foglietti had little real success although their cars, with wire wheels and a pronounced tail-fin behind the cockpit, were among the better-looking of the Formula. DCN

Ford (US)

Henry Ford chose to publicize his first cars through racing and spasmodically through six decades the companies bearing his name have participated in motor sport, becoming a major force in American and international racing during the 1960s. Henry drove in one race, at Grosse Point in October 1901, won it, and left his first company to build a pair of 'specials', the 999 and Arrow. Usually these crude devices were raced by Barney Oldfield and Tom Cooper, save for Ford's famous outing on the ice of Lake St Clair in 1904, when he set an AAA-recognized record of 91·37mph (147·04kph) over a mile.

Throughout the years preceding World War 1, Ford continued to promote through competition in American events, fairground, dirt and board, and duration races. The cars were based, sometimes very loosely, on the Models A, K and T; the most prominent driver—in effect a works driver—was Frank Kulick. By 1913 this effort had been discontinued, as the relatively simple Fords were outclassed and outmoded in a new era, and the Model T was in any case selling itself. Perhaps the most notable single achievement of the period had been in 1909, when two stripped Model Ts were run in the New York—Seattle race and finished 1st (in 22 days 55 minutes) and 3rd: it certainly made for great publicity.

After World War 1, privately-tuned Model Ts proliferated, in widely-varying degrees of sophistication. Single-ohc 16-valve versions of the engine appeared, the best-known being the Chevrolet brothers' Frontenac—the Fronty-Ford. These raced and won on local tracks throughout the States, although they were outclassed at the highest level (5th in 1923 was the best placing for a Fronty-Ford at Indianapolis).

The company briefly flirted with racing again in the mid-1930s, collaborating with Miller in his fwd Ford V-8-engined Indianapolis cars. The four which started in the 1935 Indianapolis 500 failed, abysmally, and were hidden by Ford until quietly sold years later. However, the flathead V-8 (introduced in 1932) was successful in American road races of the period, in events for roadsters and racing cars (these had chassis in great variety, from Bugatti to simple home-made). In the post-war resurgence of American road racing, Ford V-8s played a substantial part, until outclassed by refined engines from Europe. Ford power was not so prominent in the growing hot-rod movement (although in 1951 a machine with an engine built up around Ford parts broke Auto Union's flying-start mile record).

Through the V-8s, American Fords also began to make an impact on motor sport outside the United States in the 1930s. The Monte Carlo Rally—in those days a true mid-winter adventure—fell to Fords in 1936 and 1938. In the wild throw-back of South American open road city-to-city events, Fords were generally dominant, and in open local works competition with General Motors which lasted unabated into the 1950s.

The Galvez brothers were the outstanding Ford *turismo carretera* drivers. The Chevrolet challenge was really successful only when Fangio turned to that make (ironically, he had started his racing career in Ford-powered specials).

The Carrera Panamericana was an event in the same vein, and perhaps a curious one for Ford to choose for their official return to racing. This was through their Lincoln-Mercury Division, in the names of dealers, in 1952. The three works entries finished 1-2-3 in the touring car category, the winner (Chuck Stevenson) averaging 91·2mph (146·77kph) over the 1,913 miles (3,079km). In 1953 Lincoln Capris took the first four in class (Stevenson 7th overall), and the event fell to

1903 Ford Arrow on Lake St Clair in January 1904. Henry Ford at the wheel.
Photo: Ford Archives, Henry Ford Museum

1923 Fronty-Ford (Barber-Warnock Special) at Indianapolis. Slim Corum at the wheel.
Photo: Indianapolis Motor Speedway

Above, 1964 Ford GT40 at the Nürburgring, the model's first competition appearance. Drivers were Phil Hill and Bruce McLaren. *Photo: David Hodges Collection*

Right, 1966 Ford Falcon, followed by a Mustang and a V-8 engined British Ford Cortina at Crystal Palace. *Photo: E. Gerry Stream*

Below, 1965 Ford GT40 in the Targa Florio. Driven by Bob Bondurant, it crashed on the 9th lap. *Photo: Peter Miller*

Right, 1966 Ford Mark II open car, driven to victory in the Sebring 12-Hours Race by Ken Miles and Lloyd Ruby. *Photo: Ford News Department*

Lincoln again in 1954, Ray Crawford averaging 92·25mph (148·46kph).

Ford attention turned to NASCAR stock car races, their hand virtually forced by the sales response to rivals' successes. Initial Ford efforts did little to reverse this, but by mid-1956 their teams were sorted out and cars raceworthy (in the Grand National division Fords and Mercury gained nineteen victories in 56 events, Fords gained 27 of a possible 48 in the Convertible division). In 1957 stronger teams and supercharged 312ci (5,113cc) engines brought 27 victories in 53 races in the former category, and 26 in 40 races in the latter. But halfway through the year came the AMA agreement to abstain from racing, with which Ford complied.

The racing continued of course, Holman and Moody coming together to take over much Ford equipment and become the front-running team racing Fords, in USAC as well as NASCAR stock events. In general, the ban harmed Ford more than their rivals, and as it increasingly appeared not to be honoured in the letter, let alone the spirit, Ford moved back towards direct involvement, and repudiated the agreement in 1962. From this point the greatest motor sport programme ever embarked on by a manufacturer built up, and in time was allowed to run down. This was on four major fronts: stock, drag, track and international sports/prototype racing, with side ventures into Can-Am racing and international rallies. Broadly, Ford delegated racing responsibility, and some development work, to affiliated teams.

For production models the emphasis was on the

stock-racing programme. On the NASCAR and USAC circuits in 1962 Fords were at a disadvantage in engine size and power (their biggest V-8 was a 6·65-litre unit producing some 430bhp; the rival Pontiacs, for example had 6·9-litre, 465bhp engines), and in reliability. In 1963 Ford and Mercury teams had 427ci (6,997cc) engines, and the year started well when Gurney won the 500-mile event at Riverside. Then Fords took the first four places in the Daytona 500, and when GM withdrew their support from teams using their cars, appeared set for domination. But the Chrysler effort was stepped up, and their Plymouths and Dodges cut into the Ford run of successes.

Through a period of changing rules (and internecine strife about them) Ford successes continued (Gurney took the Riverside event in four successive years). In 1966 Plymouth became a real force, while Ford tried to get a single-ohc engine accepted as a production unit, actually withdrawing for a period to force this issue. In 1967 the company returned to the bitterly-fought NASCAR and Trans-Am races—without their single-ohc unit, which could have damaged their 'safety' image, and concentrating on the Fairlane and Shelby Mustang respectively (the Shelby Mustangs in effect took over where the Cobras left off in the American racing scene, and won the first two Trans-Am series).

In 1969 the Fords (Talladegas and Torinos) were hard-pressed in the NASCAR Grand National division, as much by competition from Mercury Cyclones as from Dodges. So the Mercury programme was tapered

John Wyer's Gulf-sponsored JWA team was competitive at international championship level in 1968 and 1969. This team campaigned with their Mirage derivative until it was ruled out by the 3-litre limit imposed on Group 6 prototypes in 1968. For two years their GT40s, with 4·7- and 5-litre engines, were unexpectedly successful in competition with later designs. The Le Mans 24-Hour Race fell to one Gulf-JWA GT40 in 1968 and 1969, and in 1969 the team took the International Championship of Makes as well.

The Ford Division of the Ford Motor Company made a tremendous impact on international motor sport in the 1960s; as the parent company withdrew into North America at the end of the decade, its principal overseas subsidiary, Ford of Britain, had coincidentally become a significant force in motor sport throughout the world.

The sporting activities of other Ford companies outside Europe have been loosely controlled by Dearborn, in Commonwealth countries such as Australia traditionally through the Canadian company. Generally, these subsidiaries have undertaken sporting programmes most applicable to local markets, and this has meant that they have used locally-made cars, European and American, and sometimes hybrids (for example, Ford sponsored the construction of a batch of British Capris with 289ci (4,736cc) V-8 engines in South Africa in 1970, to homologate this variant for racing under local rules, while in Australia the 5·7-litre Falcon GT HO was built in sufficient quantity to qualify it for production saloon car racing, and these cars took the 1970 Tasman Touring Series). DWH

Ford (GB)

The Ford Motor Company Limited has been involved in motor sport since the late 1950s, but on a substantial scale only since the end of the following decade. Pre-war sporting interest in British Ford products was slight, although they did appear in some of the gentle events of the period, and in 1937 an 1100 Ford was even run in the Le Mans 24-Hour Race (it finished 14th). During the immediate post-war years the 1,172cc engines were easily available and cheap, so with all their limitations sporting uses were found for them: around the 100E was built the 1172 Formula, a steadily healthy cheap racing class, and the 98E was popular almost to the exclusion of other engines among trials specialists.

In 1949 the company took its first tentative steps into motor sport, running two 1,172cc Anglias in rallies. During that year Ken Wharton won the Tulip and Joy Cooke took the Coupe des Dames in the Lisbon Rally. Ford ran 3·6-litre V-8-engined Pilots in 1950, Wharton repeating his Tulip success and winning the Lisbon Rally outright. In 1952 he gained his third Tulip victory with a 1·5-litre Consul.

At the end of 1952 the 2·3-litre Zephyr became available to the rally team, and with it came the professional approach to rallies which within a short time was to become prerequisite. Thorough car preparation and detailed reconnaisances paid off in a victory for Gatsonides in the one rally which invariably catches the public eye, the Monte Carlo. On the other side of the coin, tuning departed too far from standard for some scrutineers, and the three team Zephyrs in the Tulip Rally were disqualified at the finish.

The 1,172cc Anglia/Prefect models were rallied alongside the Zephyrs from 1954, but gained no significant European victories: Harrison's 3rd in the RAC Rally was the best Ford placing in an international rally in 1954;

Burgess's 4th in the Monte Carlo the best in 1955. Outside Europe, Marwaha won the East African Safari with a Zephyr in 1955, and the Canadian Winter Rally fell to a Prefect in 1956. Through the 1950s Fords found increasing favour with private entrants, while the team carried on rallying with Anglias and, from its introduction in 1956, with the Mk 2 Zephyr. They gained no more outright victories, but numerous secondary awards: class

Below, 1955 Ford Anglia in the 1956 Monte Carlo Rally. *Photo: Autosport*

Below centre, 1956 Ford Zephyr in Monte Carlo Rally. *Photo: Autosport*

Bottom, 1961 Ford Anglia in 1963 Acropolis Rally. *Photo: Autosport* prizes, team prizes and ladies' cups. The Zephyr was used on into the 1960s, best performances being in the Safari, where Zephyrs took the team prize in 1960 and 1961, but the emphasis swung to new models in rallying, to racing, and to power units which carried the name of Ford into single-seater racing.

Ford had made a tentative entry into racing in 1958, running three Zephyrs (with automatic transmission) at Silverstone, and in 1959 had supported Jeff Uren's effective programme: he won the British Saloon Car Championship. Late that year a new Anglia was introduced, with a new 997cc, 80·96 × 48·41mm engine. Its over-square bore-stroke ratio and 8-port cylinder head promised much, and it proved an ideal unit for tuning specialists. Coincidentally, Formula Junior gained International status in 1960; within a year it was dominated by 105E engines, modified by such firms as Cosworth and Holbay, and usually in Lotus, Lola or Brabham chassis.

While private Anglias were increasingly seen in competition, Ford introduced the Cortina, and concentrated their sporting programmes, including those of affiliated teams on it. In Mk I form it had a 1,498cc 4-cylinder engine, which had considerable development potential. In 1964 it was followed by the Lotus Cortina, evolved by Lotus with a twin ohc 1,557cc version of the engine and revised suspension (which was far from perfect in its early days), and this became the principal Ford competition car. Although this was the period of Mini superiority in rallies, the Cortinas piled up a worthwhile score of victories in major events from 1963 to 1967. In racing they were run by Ford-affiliated teams, as well as purely private owners. In 1963 Sears took the British Saloon Car Championship in Willment Cortina GTs; in 1964 this fell to Clark, driving Team Lotus-entered Lotus Cortinas, and nine other national championships fell to this model. In 1965 Sir John Whitmore won the European Touring Car Championship, and 10 national racing championships and three rally championships fell to Cortina drivers.

Anglias remained competitive in their class throughout the 1960s, and with the British championship basis revised in 1966, Fitzpatrick was able to win this with his successes in the 1-litre class. The following season was the last full one for the Cortina as a works car, although a

1·6-litre version appeared. In private hands it was by no means displaced; in 1967 the RAC World Manufacturers' Championship (for rally performances) went to the Lotus Cortina for the second successive year. Thereafter the Escort largely took its place, a notable exception being in the London–Sydney Marathon, where Lotus Cortinas set the pace to Australia.

The increasing successes of Ford products in racing car classes drew the company in that direction—a reversal of the usual process. The company played some part in the GT40 programme from 1964, but although by the late 1960s this was more a British than an American car, it is normally considered a child of Dearborn rather than Dagenham. The track use which others were making of their engines could hardly escape the notice of the Ford board, and largely through members Harley Copp and Walter Hayes the company began to promote and encourage this. The first positive step was to contribute towards the development costs of the Cosworth SCA single-ohc adaptation of the Cortina unit for the 1-litre Formula 2, which in this class was second only to the much more sophisticated Honda engines used in works Brabhams. Other tuning establishments, such as Holbay, whose F3 engines scored 54 1st places in 1964, for example, also began to receive encouragement.

A major step was taken in October 1965, when Ford decided to back an engine to be built by Cosworth for the 3-litre Grand Prix formula. Ford granted £100,000, plus considerable assistance in kind, to the programme, which was to progress by way of a 1·6-litre unit (the FVA F2 engine built around the Cortina block) towards the DFV F1 V-8, which initially was supplied only to Team Lotus for use in their 49.

Both engines were successful beyond reasonable expectation—indeed, Ford executives were concerned that in the Grands Prix the DFV was too successful once it had been made available to other teams in 1968 and 1969, when it powered every Grand Prix winner. Ford certainly reaped abundant publicity from their very modest investment in Cosworth engines, but their interest did not end there—unobtrusively, the company did much more than buy the right to have 'Ford' cast in the valve-gear covers of engines. Its leading personnel were active in the sport beyond the call of publicity, and the resources of its

1965 Ford Lotus-Cortina at Zandvoort. Sir John Whitmore at the wheel. *Photo: Autosport*

Left, 1962 Ford Zodiac Mark 3 in 1963 Monte Carlo Rally. Peter Riley at the wheel. *Photo: Autosport*

Below, 1964 Ford Lotus-Cortina on Lake Freden, Sweden. Erik Berger, 1964 Swedish Ice Race Champion, at the wheel. *Photo: Ford of Britain*

technical departments were quietly useful to F1 manufacturers.

The DFV was used, less successfully, in prototypes. The P68/P69 cars built by Alan Mann Racing in the name of Ford promised much, but were never properly developed, never finished a race, and were quietly discarded. Only when the DFV was substituted for the original BRM V-12 in the JWA Gulf-Mirage did that car become a potential race-winner; the DFV even found its way into the Argentinian Berta.

Formula 2 cars with the FVA were occasionally beaten by Ferraris or BMW-engined cars, but generally it dominated this class in British, French and Italian chassis, as did Ford-based engines in Formula 3, and in the equivalent American single-seater Formulas B and C.

In racing history there have been numerous attempts to establish economical single-seater classes on cars built around production model components; none have succeeded as has Formula Ford. The first FF cars appeared in 1967, simply as initial training machines at racing drivers' schools, but almost immediately these became the basis of a low-cost racing class.

In saloon car competition a new period opened with the introduction of the Escort, in 1968, and the Capri, in 1969. The basic versions of both were common to Ford's principal plants in Britain and Germany, and their racing and rally roles, particularly in the case of the Escort, became complementary under the Ford of Europe umbrella.

Competition roles were envisaged for the Escort almost from its inception, and very soon after its introduction it appeared on the race and rally circuits, usually in GT (1,298cc) and, as soon as it was homologated, Twin Cam (1,558cc) forms. In the course of time a very comprehensive list of performance equipment was homologated, and made available, and as European collaboration became closer a wide range of variants appeared in the developing sporting programme: for example, German rear axles and gearboxes were used to overcome weaknesses in the original British equipment when an 1,800cc engine was fitted; a V-6-engined version was used in two 1969 rallies; a 'fan-charged' Escort was used by Alan Mann Racing in 1968 and a turbo-charged one in 1969. National company divisions increasingly tended to disappear, and apart from the dovetailed work of English and German competition departments, entries for notable drivers were often identified with their own countries: thus Piot usually ran in rallies under the Ford France banner, and Staepelaere as a Ford of Belgium entry.

In its first year the Escort TC won six international rallies, and Ford gained the Rally Constructors' Championship, and on the circuits Gardner won the British Saloon Car Championship in Alan Mann Escorts. One of the two cars used by this team had a nominally-supercharged FVA engine, which put it into the same capacity class as the Falcons, where it held its own.

In 1969, Escort TCs won four Championship rallies, enough to secure the Championship again. In Group 5 racing, the British Saloon Car Championship did not fall to Ford (British or American) for the first time since 1962: while Ford teams were pre-occupied in other classes, a Mini Cooper built up an unassailable score of 1-litre class victories. The Alan Mann effort in the over 2-litre class, with TC Escorts in place of the FVA-engined car, faded; in their rightful 1,600cc class, TCs were worried only occasionally by Porsche 911Ss; in the 1,300cc class, Broadspeed Escorts were outstanding (and in another category came close to winning outright the British round of the European championship). At the end of the

1970 Ford Escort with 2·1-litre TC engine at Brands Hatch. Dave Brodie at the wheel. *Photo: Paul Cohen*

1970 Ford Escort TC driven by Ken Coffery and John Myerscough in the Spa 24-Hour Race. *Photo: Autosport*

year, Escorts held eight of nine British circuit records in the 1,300cc and 1,600cc classes.

By and large, German Ford was responsible for competition versions of the Capri, although some work was done at the Boreham performance centre in England: for example, in producing 4wd versions, which ran in rally-cross events.

A Ford of Europe tendency to diversify competition activities further became evident in 1970. under overall competitions manager Stuart Turner. This did not mean withdrawal from major activities, although the scale of support for F1 teams using the DFV engine, for example in the form of bonuses, was reduced, and entries into championship rallies were selective. Thus the World Cup Rally became a major objective, at the expense of some traditional regular events on the calendar, and one successfully achieved in that Mikkola and Palm won in an 1834cc Escort 'special' (the same pair also won the 1000 Lakes in an Escort TC conforming to recognizable regulations). The spread of private use of Ford cars in competitions at all levels was further encouraged; towards this end two specialist and primarily sporting variants of the Escort (RS1600 and Mexico) were put

into production in 1970 by Ford's Advanced Vehicle Operations, which had been set up to cater for a definable and worthwhile enthusiast sector of the market. Early in 1971, AVO announced the GT70, a mid-engined coupé to take either the 1600TC, 2·6-litre or 3-litre V-6 engines. Initially the GT70 was intended to provide the works team with an up-to-date rally car, and production for sale to the public was not envisaged immediately.

At the beginning of the 1970s, Ford was thoroughly involved in motor sport at all levels, to the extent that a precipitate withdrawal would be impossible, if indeed it were contemplated. The benefits to the company of this sport-oriented policy could probably have been amply demonstrated to the most dubious board, had this been necessary: an extraordinarily high number of Ford executives in any case fostered it. The competition budget was modest by the standards of the parent company, and a worthwhile market for specialized components had built up to offset it partly. From modest, almost accidental, beginning early in the decade, Ford had come to be one of the largest, most influential, and respected, factors in British motor sport. DWH

Ford (D)

Although German Fords were run privately in rallies from the early 1950s, and the company tentatively—and unsuccessfully—entered the international field with the 20TS saloon in the mid-1960s, this branch of the Ford empire began to become a substantial force only in the late 1960s, as an instrument of Ford of Europe policy.

A team of three 2·3-litre V-6 20M RS saloons was run in the London–Sydney Marathon in 1968; one briefly led, and two finished 7th and 16th. Two 20M RS, together with a Lotus Cortina, were entrusted to Hughes of Nairobi as a works team for the 1969 East African Safari; each led in turn, and the sole survivor (a 20M RS) won clearly. This was the first victory for the competition department which had been set up under one-time Porsche works driver Jochen Neerspach, and which later came under the overall direction of Stuart Turner.

This outing apart, the Cologne emphasis in 1969 was on the Capri and Escort. The basic German versions of the Capri have 1·7-litre (V-4) and 2·3-litre (V-6) engines. Rally work was concentrated on the larger engine, and through the year these units were run in increasingly high states of tune (and with capacity increased late in the year to 2·6 litres). These gained worthwhile placings, although no outright victories (Piot's 3rd in the Tour of Corsica and 6th in the Tour de France being the best performances). In 1970 a fuel-injected 2·6-litre 230bhp version of the V-6 was developed for circuit racing. Escort TCs were raced in Group 2 form in 1968 and 1969 with engines prepared in England, and with these Dieter Glemser won the 1969 German Saloon Car Championship.

The 1970 effort was concentrated on the Capri, on circuits and in rallies, but without achieving victories in major championships, the best result being a win in the Tour of Europe for Kleint and Klapporth in one of the works 2·6-litre rally cars. DWH

Frayer-Miller (US)

The Frayer-Miller was one of the few air-cooled American cars to be entered in major races. For the 1906 Vanderbilt Cup the Columbus, Ohio firm built three special cars with 110hp 4-cylinder engines of $7\frac{1}{4} \times 6$in cylinder dimensions, and huge air-scoops above the engines. Only one car ran in the race itself, driven by Lawwell, and it retired on the 5th lap. GNG

Frazer Nash (GB)

Archibald Frazer-Nash founded the firm of Frazer Nash Ltd in 1922 at Kingston-upon-Thames, Surrey. He had previously been a partner in the GN company, and one of the terms of his departure from them was that he could take with him the works racing cars. These comprised the three 200 Miles Race cars with at least two spare engines, as well as the specials Kim II and Mowgli, and 'sundry racing spares' as Archie put it. As the chassis of the GN and the first Frazer Nashes had a lot in common, these spares were invaluable in the first few years of the new company. All the racing GNs under the new regime were entered as Frazer Nashes in events. The first Frazer Nash proper with 4-cylinder engine was a single-seater special, Rikki-Tikki, which was used largely for hill-climbs, and especially Frazer-Nash's regular attempts on the Brooklands Test Hill Record. By 1932 he had reduced his time for this hill to 7·691sec. Another famous hill-climb car was 'the Terror' with supercharged Anzani engine, with which R. G. J. Nash made two fastest times of day at Shelsley Walsh in the early 1930s. Clive Gallop won the Boulogne GP in 1925 in a privately-entered car, and the name Boulogne was

1968 Ford-Cosworth P68 Group 6 coupé in the Brands Hatch 500. Bruce McLaren at the wheel. *Photo: Geoffrey Goddard*

Below, 1925 Frazer Nash before the start of the Boulogne GP. Clive Gallop at the wheel *Photo: Thirlby Collection*

Below, c 1925 Frazer Nash 'Rikki Tikki' breaking the Brooklands Test Hill record. Archie Frazer Nash at the wheel. *Photo: Thirlby Collection*

current right through to the end of chain-drive production cars in 1939.

H. J. Aldington took over the firm in late 1928, and transferred the factory to Isleworth in 1929. The years 1930 to 1935 were the most successful for the chain-drive Frazer Nash cars, but it must be said that, on analysis of their racing successes, the make could not be regarded as at all significant in the history of motor sport; however, the fact that practically every car built has been used in competition meant that the make had achieved much greater recognition than might be supposed from its humble production rate. Their greatest achievements were in the Alpine Trials of 1932 to 1934, where they won four Glacier Cups for losing no marks. They also took part in the TT, Le Mans (in 1935 only) and the BRDC 500 Miles Race at Brooklands. Private owners entered their Frazer Nashes in a wide variety of club events at Brooklands, hill-climbs and long-distance trials. In a special single-seater car A. F. P. Fane took the record for Shelsley Walsh hill-climb in 1937. Fane also raced this car at Brooklands, and in July 1939 made ftd at Wetherby Speed Trials. From 1936 onwards the works were racing the German BMWs, sold in England as Frazer Nash-BMWs, and with the Type 328 they had a number of successes. S. C. H. Davis put over 102 miles (164km) into the hour in an observed run at Brooklands, and in the 1936 TT, Fane led for a considerable time, eventually finishing 3rd. 'Bira' was 3rd in the 1937 TT in a similar car.

After World War 2 Aldington persuaded the Bristol Aeroplane Company to manufacture under licence the 2-litre BMW engines, which in the first instance were exclusively supplied to Frazer Nash, before Bristol put their own cars into production. The post-war Frazer Nash was made in very small numbers, only 105 in all, but their competition record was more inspiring than that of the pre-war chain-drive cars. In 1949 Norman Culpan and H. J. Aldington finished 3rd overall at Le Mans in the High Speed model, henceforth known as the Le Mans Replica. AFN Ltd (as the company had been called since 1927) did not have a works car until Ken Wharton's lightweight Mark II Le Mans Replica of 1952, but they helped private owners with special parts, and were rewarded with some remarkable victories. These included Franco Cortese's outright victory in the 1951 Targa Florio, the first time a British car had won this gruelling Sicilian event, Stirling Moss's victory in the 1951 British Empire Trophy in the Isle of Man, with Bob Gerard's Frazer Nash 2nd, and the victory by Harry Grey and Larry Kulok in the 1952 Sebring 12 Hours. The lightweight Mark II Le Mans Replica

appeared in 1952, and was driven in a number of events by Ken Wharton, his best placing being 2nd in the 1952 Jersey Road Race. By now the Frazer Nash was being heavily outpointed by specialized competition cars, and AFN Ltd withdrew from active support of sports car racing in 1955. Five years later manufacture ceased altogether. DAT

Freikaiserwagen (GB)

Specials based on the GN cyclecar chassis were very popular in the 1930s for sprints and hill-climbs in Britain. What distinguished the Freikaiserwagen was that the engine was situated behind the driver, driving direct to the bevel box. Devised by Dick Caesar with David and Joe Fry, the car first appeared in 1936, with Morgan ifs and 1,097cc Blackburne V-twin, tuned by Robin R. Jackson. ('Freikaiserwagen' was a punning germanization of the designers' names.) For the next three years numerous class victories were achieved, the Fry cousins sharing the driving.

During World War 2 the chassis was scrapped, and the car was rebuilt afterwards with the GN frame from the Watkins special. In this form the car was developed steadily until 1948, when an Iota 500 tubular chassis, fitted with swing-axle rear suspension by rubber in tension, was substituted. Jackson developed the engine, with two-stage Marshall supercharging, to give 110bhp; weight on the line was only 784lb (356kg). With Joe Fry driving, many fastest times of day were recorded at both sprint and hill-climb venues, including the coveted Shelsley Walsh record in 1949. Fry was killed at Blandford in 1950, and plans to add another cylinder never came to fruition. DF

Frontenac (US)

The name Frontenac has been applied to no fewer than five different makes of American or Canadian car, but only one has any sporting history. These were the racing cars built by Louis Chevrolet between 1916 and 1922. The Frontenac Motor Corporation was founded in 1914, but owing to board room difficulties no cars appeared until two years later. Of the cars which ran at Indianapolis in 1916, one had a 4·9-litre twin-ohc 4-cylinder engine not unlike that of the 1914 Peugeot but with cast-iron head and block, and aluminium crankcase. The other two cars had single-ohc engines in which the majority of components were of aluminium, including cylinder block, crankcase, pistons, intake manifold and camshaft cover. Only two of the three qualified at Indy, and both retired in the race. Several failures followed during the first season, but in December 1916 Louis Chevrolet won

Left, c 1935 Frazer Nash TT Replica in a Brooklands Relay Race. *Photo: Thirlby Collection*

Above, 1952 Frazer Nashes at Silverstone; Peacock in a Le Mans Replica leads Stoop in a Mille Miglia. *Photo: Motor*

Below, 1935 Frazer Nash single-seater at Shelsley Walsh. A. F. P. Fane at the wheel. *Photo: Thirlby Collection*

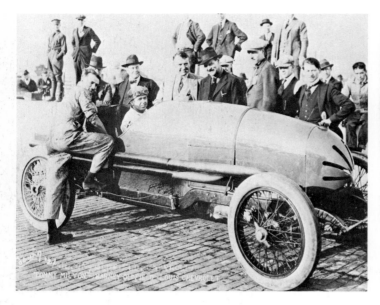

the inaugural race at the Uniontown Board Speedway at 102mph (164·2kph). In 1917 Frontenacs won at Cincinnati (1st and 3rd) Providence, R.I. (1st, 2nd, 4th), Sheepshead Bay, and Chicago. The drivers were Louis Chevrolet, Ralph Mulford, Joe Boyer, and Dario Resta. In 1919 the same cars won four major races on the board tracks and finished 9th at Indianapolis.

In 1920 Louis Chevrolet moved his activities to Indianapolis where he was given space in the premises of the William Small Company, makers of the Monroe car. Here, aided by Cornelius van Ranst, he built seven cars of identical design, four of which were raced under the Monroe name, the other three as Frontenacs. They had modernized versions of the original 1916 cast-iron twin-ohc engine, but with a smaller capacity of 182ci (2,982cc). In the 1920 Indianapolis race no fewer than five cars retired or crashed because of broken steering arms (thus outdoing Singer's performance in the 1935 TT, although the Frontenacs did not pile up one on top of the other) but Gaston Chevrolet in a Monroe won at a speed of 88·17mph (141·73kph). This was the first Indianapolis win by an American car since 1912. For the 1921 season Chevrolet and van Ranst designed a completely new 183ci (2,999cc) twin-ohc straight-8 engine. With one of these cars Tommy Milton won at Indianapolis, a 4-cylinder driven by P. Ford and J. Ellingboe was 3rd, and another straight-8 was 9th. In 1922 Frontenac were

Left, 1921 Frontenac 3-litre at Indianapolis. Tommy Milton at the wheel, to his left, Barney Oldfield and Louis Chevrolet. *Photo: Indianapolis Motor Speedway*

Right, 1916 Frontenac 4·5-litre at Indianapolis in 1919. Ralph Mulford at the wheel. *Photo: Indianapolis Motor Speedway*

Left, 1922 Frontenac 3-litre straight-8. E. G. 'Cannon Ball' Baker at the wheel. *Photo: Indianapolis Motor Speedway*

Below, 1959 Gemini Formula Junior. *Photo: Geoffrey Goddard*

much less successful, and although they entered eleven cars at Indy, their best performance was Tom Alley's 9th place with a 4-cylinder car.

Meanwhile Louis Chevrolet had been fitting ohv heads to Ford Model T engines, and the resulting Fronty-Fords soon became invincible on the dirt tracks and midwest ovals. Among famous drivers who began their careers on Fronty-Fords were Wilbur Shaw and Frank Lockhart. In 1923 a Fronty-Ford known as the Barber-Warnock Special finished 5th at Indy, driven by L. L. Corum, and in 1924 three Barber-Warnocks ran, one driven by A. E. Moss, Stirling's father. They ran consistently and all finished, but their speed was no match for the Millers. In 1926 Chevrolet built a Fronty-Ford using front-wheel drive; called the Hamlin Special, its Ford engine was reduced in bore and stroke to bring it within the prevailing 91ci (1·5-litre) limit. It retired in the race, but did well on the dirt tracks until 1932. The last Fronty-Ford to run at Indianapolis was Gene Hanstein's in 1931. GNG

Fuzzi (GB)
One of the most remarkable British specials of the 1930s, Robert Waddy's Fuzzi had two 500cc single-cylinder dirt-track JAP engines, one driving the front wheels, and another behind the driver for the rear wheels. Each engine drove through its own Rudge gearbox. The engines could be controlled separately. They were mounted in a spaceframe of chrome molybdenum tubing. Suspension was independent all round, by trailing arms and torsion bars at the front, and a transverse leaf spring and a system of wishbone-like links at the rear. Fuzzi did well in sprints from 1936 to 1939, covering the standing half mile in 25·8sec, and climbing Shelsley Walsh in 44·08sec.
After World War 2 Waddy lengthened the chassis and installed a Mercury V-8 engine in place of the JAPs, but still driving by chains to all four wheels. This version of Fuzzi never ran successfully. GNG

Gemini (GB)
Derived from the Moorland Formula Junior designed by Les Redmond, the Gemini Mark 1 of 1959 featured a conventional spaceframe chassis and BMC mechanical parts. The Mark 2 employed a Cosworth engine, but

was still no match for the Cooper and Lotus works cars. The rear-engined Mark 3 of 1960, however, was campaigned with considerable success by Peter Ashdown, Mike Beuttler, Geoff Duke, Tony Maggs, Bill Moss, Mike Parkes and Graham Warner, the firm's sponsor. Later models failed to develop this promise, and the 'Chequered Flag' team turned their allegiance to Lotus products. DF

Genie see Huffaker

Georges Irat (F)

The Georges Irat was a good example of the medium-sized French fast tourer of the 1920s, but it did more racing than most of its contemporaries. The first Georges Irat of 1921 had a 1,991cc ohv 4-cylinder engine and 4-wheel brakes assisted by Dewandre vacuum servo. It was made without major change until 1927, and most of the firm's racing successes were achieved by this model. They were never particularly successful at Le Mans, although they ran there in 1923, 1924 and 1926, but they did much better in the Circuit des Routes Pavées. Here they won outright in 1923 and 1925, came 3rd in 1926, and covered the greatest distance in 1927, though yielding victory on handicap to a smaller car. They also won the Spanish and Moroccan Touring Car Grands Prix in 1927. In all these successes the driver was Maurice Rost, aided in the Spanish event by Marcel Lehoux. With Burie as co-driver, Rost also won the 2-litre class for Georges Irat in the Belgian 24-Hour Race in 1926, 1927 and 1928.

Georges Irat made a 3-litre 6-cylinder car from 1928 to 1929, and small Ruby-engined sports cars with fwd from 1935 to 1938, but neither of these models was seen in serious competitions. GNG

Georges Richard; Richard-Brasier; Brasier (F)

Georges Richard's first success was in the voiturette category of the Paris-Marseilles-Paris on one of his belt-driven rear-engined twins at a mere 12·7mph (20·44kph). Not much more was heard of the firm in competition until 1902, when three 16hp *voitures légères* and two 10hp voiturettes ran unsuccessfully in the Paris-Vienna race. In 1903, Richard fielded some more powerful 2,262cc 4-cylinder types with moiv and shaft drive, designed by Brasier, formerly of Mors. They ran in the voiturettes class of the Paris-Madrid race, in which Barillier was 2nd and Combier 4th.

The name Richard-Brasier was first seen on a more powerful 6,817cc light racer with which Danjean did over 72mph (115kph) to win his class at Dourdan Speed Trials later in the year, and for the French Gordon Bennett

1908 Germain GP car. Roch-Brault at the wheel. *Photo: T. A. S. O. Mathieson Collection*

Trials, Brasier produced some 9·9-litre 80bhp cars with T-head engines. Théry won both the eliminating trials and the race proper, his speed in the latter being 54·5mph (87·71kph). Capacity and output went up to 11,259cc and 96bhp in 1905, by which time Richard had started the manufacture of Unic cars and Brasier was on his own. The result, was, however, even better: two cars (Théry and Caillois) selected for the Gordon Bennett, and two cars among the leaders. Théry won again at 48·4mph (77·89kph), and Caillois was 4th.

Brasier design changed little thereafter, though bigger engines were used for the Grand Prix in 1906, and Barillier was 4th both in this event and in the Circuit des Ardennes. Baras finished 3rd in the 1907 Grand Prix. Smaller engines with 155mm bores were used in 1908, when Théry was back in the Grand Prix team, but these cars were unsuccessful, though Bablot later took the 60bhp class record at Brooklands at nearly 102mph (164kph), and also made fastest times of day at Gaillon and Mont Ventoux. He repeated these successes in 1909, but by this time the Brasier was a little elderly, and the firm, like many another great French name, never fully recovered from World War 1.

Surprisingly, some quite advanced 2·1-litre push-rod 4-cylinder cars with 5-bearing crankshaft and fwb turned out for Le Mans in 1923. They were not highly placed that year, but a pair of these TC4s finished 7th and 8th in the 1924 race. MCS

Left, 1927 Georges Irat 2-litre at San Sebastian. Maurice Rost at the wheel, with Marcel Lehoux. *Photo: T. A. S. O. Mathieson Collection*

Right, 1905 Richard-Brasier before the Gordon Bennett Eliminating Trials. Léon Théry at the wheel. *Photo: T. A. S. O. Mathieson Collection*

Germain (B)

Early Germains had a lot of Panhard in their specification, and the cars that competed in the 1902 Circuit des Ardennes had 4,894cc aiv engines and tube as well as electric ignition. Neither these nor Chisoque's 20hp *voiture légère* achieved anything, but for the 1903 event the make's offerings had grown up to 9·9-litres and boasted moiv. Coppée took 6th place, but for the next few years Germain stayed out of major events. The excellent 3-litre 4-cylinder 'chainless' touring model appeared in 1906 and did well in the Low Countries, winning classes at Scheveningen, Ostend and Orignie, as well as putting up a creditable performance in the Herkomer Trophy, and taking a 3rd in class in the Scottish Trials. Degrais and Roch-Brault drove Germains in the 1907 Grand Prix, but these, though conventional enough in specification with shaft drive and side valves in a T-head, were very small for their period, capacity being a mere 4·3 litres. Their 13th and 14th places were therefore good. Much bigger machines with chain drive were entered for the 1908 race, when Perpère finished 10th. The 1912 Germain range included a 15hp with chain-driven ohc, but apart from an appearance in that year's Belgian GP the make's racing days were over. MCS

Giaur (I)

Domenico Giannini, a FIAT tuning specialist since 1925, and Berardo Taraschi, builder of the BMW twin-cylinder-engined Urania 750cc sports-racing car since 1947, combined their efforts in 1950 to produce a new Italian car called the Giaur (*Gia*-nnini-*Ur*-ania), based at Teramo. With Giannini-prepared ohv engines of remote FIAT origin, high, reliable output and low weight the cars won innumerable Italian national 750cc sports car events between 1950 and 1955. Taraschi himself and Sesto Leonardi both garnered many class victories, the latter winning the 750cc class of the Mille Miglia four years running. When 500cc racing became established internationally as Formula 3, Giaur built a pretty 'miniature GP' single-seater with front-mounted 4-cylinder engine of FIAT Topolino origin. In Taraschi's hands it won the 500cc race at Caracalla, Rome, in 1950, but was too heavy and underpowered to match the British Norton motorcycle-engined Coopers and other cars. Giaur were Italian national 750cc sports car champions in 1951 and 1953, and 750cc racing champions in 1954. CP

Gilbern (GB)

The Gilbern GT, product of Giles Smith and Bernard Friese from Pontypridd in Wales, was raced quite frequently by private owners in Britain during the early 1960s. This model was most commonly seen with MGB engine and running parts, but when it was superseded by the larger Ford V-6-engined type in 1966, the cars were too heavy for further track development. DF

Gilby (GB)

Syd Greene's Gilby Engineering Company had entered Maserati sports and Grand Prix cars during the 1950s, and when Syd's son Keith reached 17 in 1956 he began racing Coopers. After a troubled 1959 season with Lotus 16 and 17 cars, the Greenes' enthusiasm evolved cars of their own.

Len Terry designed an 1100 Climax-engined space-frame sports-racer for 1960 which was competitive with the Lolas, but was rolled by Keith at Silverstone's Abbey Curve. He was running a 2·5 Cooper-Maserati in Formula 1, and for the 1961 1·5-litre Formula, Terry designed a

conventional, rear-engined spaceframe F1 car around the Climax 4-cylinder engine. This was built by Racing Frames at Edmonton, London, and assembled in a garage at Ongar by Keith Greene, Peter Ashcroft and Terry Hoyle. Keith's restrained yet quick driving gave the car some good results, including 3rd behind two works Ferraris in the 1962 Naples GP.

Later that year the Gilby-Climax's frame was modified, lowered by 2in and narrowed overall by 4in, and fitted with a 1·5-litre BRM V-8 engine and Colotti 34 6-speed gearbox. Keith found the V-8 down on torque compared to the 147bhp Climax and after an unequal season's racing sold the car to Ian Raby. He raced it in Formula 1 in 1963 and placings included 3rd in the Rome GP. DCN

Ginetta (GB)

Designed and built by the four Walklett brothers at Woodbridge, Suffolk, the first Ginettas were kit cars for Ford components, based on multi-tubular spaceframes, which were used with some good results in British Club racing around 1960. Current from 1961 to 1964 was the G4, with open or closed fibreglass body and Ford mechanical parts. This model was even more conspicuous

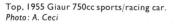

on the circuits, in the hands of John Burton, Chris Meek and numerous others. Operating now from Witham, Essex, the firm had produced an F2/3 monocoque in 1965, but the next really successful competition car was the G12 of 1966, raced with a variety of rear engines from 105E Ford through BRM 2-litre to Ford, Oldsmobile and Chevrolet V-8s. This type was succeeded in 1968 by the G16, still based on a tubular frame, and normally offered with either BRM V-8 or Cosworth FVC engine for Group 6 racing. This type was continued in 1969 and 1970 as the G16A, often with Coventry-Climax power unit.

The single-seaters were generally less successful, though Peter Voigt in a G17 Imp-powered Formula 4 car achieved an enviable hill-climbing record in 1970, and Clark Sturdgess, later to become a F100 constructor, managed some good runs in 1969 with the G18 Formula Ford machine. For 1971 the Formula Ford side was taken over by Ennerdale Racing of Canterbury. The successful road going G15 coupé was supplemented in 1970 by the larger G21. DF

GN (GB)

In late 1910 the firm of GN was founded by H. R. Godfrey and Archibald Frazer-Nash to make cyclecars. Their first entry at Brooklands was for a reliability trial in March 1913, and this was also the first public showing of the new Grand Prix GN. This car had been designed for the 1913 Cyclecar GP at Amiens, and although both cars retired in the race the Grand Prix model became the standard sporting GN of the pre-1914 period. Also in 1913 GN built a special car known as the Streamer with a very narrow single-seater body. Although for various reasons it never tried for the 1-hour Cyclecar Record for which it was built, it did win the first British Cyclecar race at Brooklands on Whit Monday 1913. Archie Frazer-Nash was at the wheel, and another GN driven by Whitehead was 2nd. Another special car, known as Kim (Frazer-Nash was a great enthusiast for Rudyard Kipling) was built for the 1914 Dangerfield Trophy race for cyclecars in the Isle of Man. Because of the outbreak of World War 1 the race never took place, but Kim had a highly successful career after the war. The engine was constantly improved during the 1920s and during its lifetime up to 1927 Kim had over 50 victories in races, sprints and hill-climbs. In 1920 Frazer-Nash had a bad accident at Brooklands in Kim which was then rebuilt with a steering box in place of the pre-war wire and

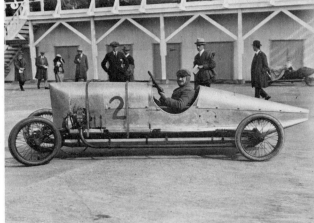

Above, 1913 GN in the make's first appearance at Brooklands. *Photo: Thirlby Collection*

Right above, 1920 GN 'Mowgli' at Brooklands. Archie Frazer-Nash at the wheel. *Photo: Temple Press*

Below, 1926 GN special 'Spider' at Shelsley Walsh, with its builder Basil Davenport. *Photo: Thirlby Collection*

Right, 1912 GN-JAP. Archie Frazer-Nash at the wheel, with H. R. Godfrey. *Photo: Thirlby Collection*

Left, 1913 GN 'The Streamer'. Archie Frazer-Nash at the wheel. *Photo: Thirlby Collection*

bobbin system. In its new form it was known as Kim II.

Needing a car more suitable for Brooklands outer-circuit racing than Kim, Frazer-Nash built Mowgli in 1920. This had a longer wheelbase, achieved by the simple expedient of adding another axle behind the normal rear axle, driven by a single chain from the latter. This was intended to counteract the odd wind effects that were often obtained at Brooklands. The original capacity of Mowgli's engine was 1,087cc, but both bore and stroke were increased so that by 1921 its capacity was nearly 1,500cc, and in this form it took many records. In 1926 Basil Davenport installed Mowgli's engine in his GN-based special Spider which had many successes in the late 1920s, and was constantly modified and brought up to date by Davenport over a period of 20 years.

In 1921 Frazer-Nash won the 1,100cc class of the JCC 200 Miles Race at Brooklands with a new design of engine with ohc drive, and a team of three of these was built for the 1922 race. A piston collapsed in Frazer-Nash's car during the race, but Frazer-Nash and L. A. Cushman fitted a new one during a pit stop, and the GNs won the team prize. In the autumn of 1922 both Frazer-Nash and Godfrey left the GN company, the former to found his own company which announced its first car in 1924. Godfrey became one of the partners in the HRG concern which began car building in 1936.

The French Salmson company had been licenced to build the GN in 1919, and French-built cars had a number of successes in races and rallies. In the 1921

Cyclecar GP at Boulogne, Honel and Lombard finished 1st and 2nd, and Honel won Gold Medals in the Paris-Nice and Paris-Pyrenees-Paris trials. DAT

Gobron-Brillié; Gobron (F)

Technically the Gobron-Brillié was renowned for its opposed-piston engine, but in the world of competition it shone as a sprint machine, as well as running happily on alcohol. The cars were also made in France under licence as Nancéennes and in Belgium as Nagants and raced on occasions under both names. The make's first serious appearance in competition was in 1900 when Brillié himself drove a 16hp rear-engined machine in the Paris-Toulouse-Paris, while 3·6-litre Gobron-Brilliés and Nancéennes supported the light-car category of the Paris-Berlin (1901), one of the former being driven by Louis Rigolly. A Nancéenne also won the Paris-Roubaix alcohol trials, and in the famous Circuit du Nord alcohol race Rigolly finished 3rd in the light-car class, using a new 2-cylinder with front-mounted vertical engine. In the Paris-Vienna it was noted that the old type of rear-engined Gobron-Nagant did better than the new models from the French factory, but Rigolly's Gobron-Brillié was the fastest light car in the Château-Thierry hill-climb, and also in the Circuit des Ardennes. On the latter occasion his average was 43mph (69·20kph) and the car ran on alcohol.

In 1903 came the greatest of the Gobrons with vast 110bhp 13·5-litre L-head 4-cylinder engines, still of opposed-piston type, in light tubular frames with side-chain drive. Three cars ran in the Paris-Madrid and two in the Circuit des Ardennes without success, but sprints and hill-climbs were an entirely different matter, Duray recording 83·74mph (134·76kph) at Ostend in July, and 84·73mph (136·36kph) at Dourdan four months later. At Gaillon Rigolly set up a new record of 33·6sec, which he

Opposite, Alpine-Renault (Cheinesse Henriod) winner of the Index of Thermal Efficiency at Le Mans, 1966. *Photo: Geoff Goddard*

Below, 1903 Gobron-Brillié 110hp before the 1904 Gordon Bennett Eliminating Trials. *Photo: Montagu Motor Museum*

Bottom, 1929 Golden Arrow at Beaulieu in 1961. *Photo: Michael Sedgwick*

slashed to 29sec in 1904. Further, the car carried all before it at the Nice Speed Trials that March, recording 94·78mph (152·53kph) and in July Rigolly became the first man officially to be timed at over 100mph, achieving 103·55mph (166·68kph) at Ostend. There was also a 4th place in the Circuit des Ardennes. Incredibly, Rigolly's museum piece ran in the Grands Prix of 1906 and 1907, and only failed to start in 1908 because it no longer conformed with the formula in force. Neither of the firm's two entries for the 1907 Kaiserpreis achieved anything, and the racing voiturettes announced for 1908 were stillborn.

After 1922 even the opposed-piston engines had gone, but at the very end, in 1928, there was an impressive 1·5-litre Cozette-blown sports car said to give 88bhp in spite of side valves. Chabreiron used one of these to win the 1,500cc class of the Six Hours of Burgundy, and there was a class victory in the 1930 Circuit des Rontes Pavées but the firm closed its doors before further development was possible. MCS

Golden Arrow (GB)

Sir Henry Segrave first became associated with the Land Speed Record when he drove the 4-litre Sunbeam at 152·33mph in 1926, at Southport, in Lancashire, following this with 203·792mph (327·943kph) in the 1,000hp Sunbeam the next year, at Daytona Beach, Fla. In 1928 the record was raised by Ray Keech in the enormous and crude Triplex Special to 207·552mph (333·983kph). Segrave's reply was the Irving-Napier, familiarly known as the Golden Arrow because of the golden finish of its aluminium bodywork. It was designed by Captain J. S. Irving, formerly with Sunbeam, and was powered by a W-12 Napier Lion engine as used in the Schneider Trophy racing sea-plane. Capacity was 23,970cc and power over 900bhp. Final drive was by twin propeller shafts. The very low body, built by Thrupp & Maberly, had large fairings between the front and rear wheels which contained the cooling surfaces. In case the water in these boiled Irving arranged that ice chests should come into contact with the boiling water, by the operation of a thermostat. In fact this device was not needed. In March 1929 Segrave took the car to Daytona Beach, Fla., and with very little difficulty raised the Record to 231·44mph (372·46kph). Golden Arrow made no subsequent attempt on the record, and never ran again. (It is now in the Montagu Motor Museum, Beaulieu). Its total mileage was not more than 50. For his achievement Segrave was knighted later in 1929, the first man to be so honoured for achievement in the motoring world. GNG

Gordini (F)

Amédée Gordini set up on his own in 1952 as a constructor of competition cars, and struggled along for five-and-a-half seasons, always short of money, and beset by mechanical troubles of which the most prevalent were rear-end failures. His staple in the first year was a square (75 × 75mm) 2-litre dohc six derived from the last racing Simca-Gordinis, which gave 155bhp with the aid of three Weber dual-choke carburettors. There was a 5-speed synchromesh gearbox, and the parallel-tube frame, coil ifs, and rigid axles with torsion bars at the rear derived directly from previous Gordini designs.

The all-too-familiar axle troubles eliminated the cars from the Swiss and Paris Grands Prix, and Manzon also retired in the British Empire Trophy Race, although Behra took 2nd place on one of the old Simca-Gordini 1·5-litres. He also won at Reims, averaging 105·33mph

169·65kph) to beat Ascari's Ferrari. The 2-litre engine
was used as well in a centrally-steered sports car: for the
Monaco event a 2,000cc limit was imposed, and Manzon
was able to win, though he retired while leading the field
at Le Mans. Loyer won his class in the sports-car race at
Reims, and Manzon set new sports and racing-car records
at the Mont Ventoux hill-climb. In 1953 a Gordini beat
the Ferraris in the Formula 2 race at Chimay, but though
Trintignant, Schell and Behra took the first three places
at Cadours, they had no serious opposition. A new 9-
bearing, 3-litre straight-8 with dry-sump lubrication
evolved for sports-car racing was not a success, despite an
output of 235bhp. Gordinis had a way of going very fast
and then fading away, as they had in the 1952 Carrera
Panamericana, but at Le Mans the straight-8 did not
even start. A 2·5-litre 6-cylinder car, however, saved the
day: driven by Trintignant and Schell it came in 5th with
a class win, and the same drivers took 6th place and their
class at Reims.

A new GP Formula was introduced in 1954, so the
existing Formula 2 Gordinis were extended to 2,475cc,
and Bayol, Pilette and Behra engaged as drivers. The
season was indifferent: there was only one victory (at
Cadours) for Behra, but he and Simon managed 2nd and
3rd in the British Empire Trophy at Silverstone. At
AVUS, Behra briefly challenged the Mercedes-Benz
before retiring, and Pilette was 4th. The bigger sports
cars, however, did better, with a 2nd in the Coppa
Toscana, 2nd and 3rd at Agadir, and 4th in the Portuguese GP. The Pollet/Gauthier 2·5-litre six won the Tour
de France outright, and a similar car driven by Pollet and
Guelfi managed 6th at Le Mans: the eight, now with disc
brakes, was entrusted to Behra and Simon, but retired,
and after a promising start at Reims it ran into the back of
Moss's Jaguar and was too badly damaged to continue.

A 5th place at Bordeaux was the make's best Formula 1
performance in 1955, though Pilette won the Coupe de
Paris with a six, an accomplishment which is less impressive when it is considered that this was strictly a
sports-car event. By the end of the year Gordini had put a
2·5-litre version of his 8-cylinder sports engine into a new
chassis with all-round independent suspension by torsion
bars and straight bevel final drive. Messier disc brakes
(the rear ones were inboard) were provided, and the 5-
speed box incorporated an emergency low gear, but
output was only 230bhp; 1956 was another disappointing
season. The old sixes were still raced, and at Caen, Simon
was 2nd and Burgraff 4th. In major events, however, the
Gordinis were never to the fore, although Manzon's 6-
cylinder car won at Naples. The firm tried hard with their
sports cars, running a 1·5-litre dohc 4-cylinder as well as

the sixes and eights. All three types turned up for the
1,000 kilometre Race at Montlhéry, but only Loyer on
the 1,500 finished—in 8th place, without even a class
win. Although Manzon won the 2·5-litre category at
Pescara, both the Gordini entries retired at Le Mans.

There were plenty of promising plans for 1957:
Amédée Gordini was said to be experimenting with
desmodromic valves; a 3-litre 8-cylinder sports car was
prepared for the Cuban GP (in which it did not run); and
a new 1·5-litre, 175bhp six with drum brakes was announced for Formula 2. But reality was less impressive.
The old familiar sixes and eights turned up at Pau, where
da Silva Ramos was 6th and Guelfi 7th. Da Silva Ramos
ran again at Naples, but retired. Meanwhile Gordini had
accepted an invitation to work for Renault on the development of 'hot' versions of their 845cc Dauphine
engine, and his little works closed down for good.
(For his later activities see Renault.) MCS

GRAC (F)
Serge Aziosmanoff's Groupe de Recherche de l'Automobile Compétition is based at Valence, and his spaceframe cars achieved considerable Formule France
success from the inception of the class. He also built F3
machines which were notably unattractive, and in 1969
the wedge-shaped MT8 appeared with rear-mounted
radiators, and a very short wheelbase. Drivers objected
to having their feet entangled with the front suspension
and the older, more conventional type was returned to.
GRAC have had few major successes to their credit, but
seem an enterprising concern. DCN

Grégoire (F)
In 1905, when voiturette racing was in decline, this firm
entered a pair of 3·6-litre 4-cylinder shaft-driven cars
rated at 40hp against the Darracqs in the Circuit des
Ardennes, Tavenaux finishing 2nd in his class at 39mph
(62·76kph). There were also three 2-cylinder Grégoires in
that year's first abortive Coupe de l'Auto, but 1906 saw
some much bigger machines with 7·4-litre ohv engines
entered in the Grand Prix. Only one Grégoire started, and
that retired on the first lap. For the 1907 Coupe des
Voiturettes 1,100cc twins were fielded; the firm also
supported the 1908 Grand Prix des Voiturettes, success
still eluding them. A team of 3-litre T-head 4-cylinder
cars with the classic dimensions of 80 × 149mm and
4-speed overdrive gearboxes was entered for the Coupe
des Voitures Légères: Porporato was 5th and de Marne
9th.

Some interesting designs followed—by the end of 1911
Grégoire had a 4-cylinder ohc 90 × 300mm unit ready for

1955 Gordini Formula 1 8-cylinder car.
Photo: Autosport

1955 Gordini 6- and 8-cylinder cars at
Monaco, in 1956, driven by Manzon and
Pilette respectively. *Photo: Autosport*

Opposite, Aston Martin DBR1 (Stirling
Moss) in the 1958 Tourist Trophy at
Goodwood, 1958. *Photo: Geoff Goddard*

Right, 1952 Gordini Formula 2. *Photo: F.
Taylor*

Left, 1952 Gordini 3-litre sports car, driven
in the Carrera Panamericana by Harry
Schell and Elie Bayol. *Photo: Dr Vicente
Alvarez*

motorboat racing, and were playing with some 4-carburettor hemi-head engines on the eve of the following year's Coupe de l'Auto. Nevertheless, the cars that started at Dieppe were straightforward T-head types noted only for their 2-speed back axles giving a choice of 6 forward ratios. Engines were placed well back in the frames, and the last of the cars was withdrawn (because it was considered unsafe) at the end of the first day's racing. Porporato won the 1913 Coupe de la Sarthe on one of these at 64·2mph (103·32kph), but he was the only finisher. Though the name is found in post-1918 competitions, the bigger 'Grégoire-Campbells' were in fact early Bignans made in the Grégoire factory, and the 'Little Gregs' were Hinstin products. Some horizontal valve 4-cylinder cars were prepared for Indianapolis in 1920, but proved even worse failures than their compatriots, the Peugeots. MCS

GSM (ZA)

The Glassport Motor Company was a South African concern whose Ford-powered, fibreglass bodied small GT cars had a certain amount of European and national club racing success in the early 1960s. Their GSM Delta in particular was a successful and very competitive car, Keith Holland's private model scoring a number of club-level successes in England during this period. It was no match for the rapidly-developing range of club racing specials such as the Diva GTs, however, and GSM's successes and fortunes waned sharply from 1963 on. DCN

Guyot Spéciale (F)

Albert Guyot had been a member of the 1923 Rolland-Pilain Grand Prix team, and in 1925 he built a racing car of his own, using the Rolland-Pilain chassis and a 1,984cc sleeve-valve engine of Burt McCollum type, which developed 125bhp at 5,800rpm. This car ran in the Spanish and Italian Grands Prix of 1925, but did not finish in either event. Three cars were built for Indianapolis in 1926; they were similar to the 1925 car, but had their capacity reduced to 1,481cc to bring them within the 91ci (1,491·2cc) limit then prevailing at Indianapolis. Two were sold to Albert Schmidt who prepared and raced them under the name of Schmidt Specials, and the third was driven by Guyot himself. They did not distinguish themselves, the best performance being that of Corum who lasted for 44 laps. The last appearance of a Guyot under its own name was in a Formule Libre race at Montlhéry in July 1927, when de Courcelles crashed fatally. However, the car which de Maleplane drove in 1928 under the name Bucciali was, in fact, a Guyot.

Guyot afterwards made a small number of touring cars with Continental engines, which he also called Guyot Spéciales. GNG

Halford Special (GB)

In 1925 Major Frank Halford built a racing car powered by a 1·5-litre twin-ohc engine of his own design. The 6-cylinder unit had forged aluminium con rods and pistons. An exhaust-driven turbo-supercharger of aircraft type was fitted at first, but was replaced by a Roots-type blower which was more suitable for the varying conditions of road racing. The engine developed 96bhp at 5,300rpm, and maximum speed was in the region of 120mph (170kph). The chassis and gearbox came from an sv Aston Martin; the gearbox was hard put to it, to cope with the greater power of the Halford engine, and was gradually redesigned over the two years, as were the suspension and brakes. In 1926 the Halford won several short races at Brooklands, and held 4th place in the British Grand Prix until the 82nd lap when it retired with a broken universal joint. It was later raced by G. E. T. Eyston, and was eventually converted to a road car. Apart from being an interesting and individual design, the Halford was one of the last specials to compete on anything like equal terms with the best contemporary Grand Prix cars.

For 1927 Halford planned a 1·5-litre V-12 engine with maximum speed of 9,000rpm, but this was not built. GNG

Hanomag (D)

Hanomag started to participate in motor sports in 1926 with the first private car they produced. This Hanomag 2/10PS with its single-cylinder 499cc engine sounded very unsuitable for competitions. But it became a quite successful little car in a number of very specialized conversions. The normal all-enveloping body was extensively lightened and in some cases the car even appeared with a wickerwork body. This reduction of weight and an increased output as a result of mild tuning made up a successful and reliable racer. These cars were driven by Höpfner and Butenuth in Freiburg and Klausen hillclimbs, the opening meeting at the Nürburgring, the Taunus 24-Hour Race and others, gaining class victories or places in the 1,000cc class.

The successor to the 2/10PS was the front-engined 3/16PS that appeared in sports form for a period. Its normal engine capacity was 776cc, but it was also available with 745cc to compete in the 750cc class. Hanomag entered it in competitions, including the Nürburgring race of 1929, when it appeared with blown engine, but it

Above, 1951 Healey Silverstone. *Photo: Wilson McComb Collection*

Right, 1968 Healey-Climax SR coupé. *Photo: Wilson McComb Collection*

1951 Nash-Healey coupé at Le Mans. *Photo: Montagu Motor Museum*

did not finish. The later 4-cylinder 1,494cc Rekord and the 6-cylinder 2,241cc Sturm were supplied with handsome two-seater sports bodies. They did not race, but concentrated on long-distance events, such as the Alpine Trials, the Liège-Rome-Liège, the Montlhéry 12 Hours, and the Morocco Trial, gaining class or overall victories. Hanomags were also successful in the cross-country trials popular in Germany during the 1930s. An aerodynamic version of the Hanomag Rekord Diesel set up a number of world records for diesel-engined cars in 1939 on the Dessau autobahn. HON

Hawk see Brawner

Hawke (GB)
Designed by David Lazenby and driven and promoted by Tony Roberts, the Hawke Formula Ford cars emanated originally from Waltham Cross, Hertfordshire. They had a very promising season in 1969, spearheaded by Tom Walkinshaw, who took the Scottish Championship. The basic spaceframe design remained unchanged, though the suspension was revised for the DL2A of 1970 and again for the DL2B of 1971. In 1970 the firm started to diversify, moving to larger premises at Hoddesdon, and in 1971 they offered new models for Formula Super Vee (DL5) and FA/5000, the DL7 steel and alloy monocoque. DF

HCS see Miller

Healey (GB)
After an apprenticeship at Sopwith's and World War 1 service with the Royal Flying Corps, Donald Healey started trials driving in 1924, then competed in many rallies and won the Monte Carlo Rally outright, in an Invicta, in 1931. From 1934 to 1939 he was with Triumph, designing and driving their cars. During World War 2 Healey, Sampietro and Bowden designed a new car with a light chassis frame, ifs, 2,443cc Riley engine giving 104bhp in modified form, and a wind-tunnel tested body. This appeared in October 1946 as the Healey Elliott saloon and Healey Westland roadster. The saloon was tested by *Motor* at 104·65mph (168·48kph), making it the fastest British production car. The roadster ran in the 1947 Alpine Trial, winning its class and gaining a concours award. Soon after, a saloon achieved 110·8mph (178·3kph) at Jabbeke in Belgium.

In 1948 the Healey family commenced a courageous series of entries in Continental events. There were class victories in the Targa Florio, the Mille Miglia and the

Alpine, in saloons and roadsters driven by Lurani, Haines and others, including Donald Healey himself and his son Geoffrey. One of the saloons finished 2nd in a sports car class in the Spa 24 Hours Race. In October, Wisdom covered 101·7 miles (163·6km) in 1 hour from a standing start at Montlhéry; it was the first time this had been done by a production saloon. In the 1949 Mille Miglia a roadster won its class and a saloon finished 4th in class.

In July 1949 the new Silverstone appeared with the same engine set 18in (45·72cm) farther back in the same chassis, modified suspension, and a light, stressed body. A single car was immediately entered for the Alpine and finished 2nd overall. In the Production Car event at Silverstone, three Healey Silverstones took the team prize, though outshone by the XK 120 Jaguars.

For the 1950 Palm Beach races, Cunningham fitted a 5·5-litre Cadillac engine to his Silverstone and finished 2nd overall, with another 2nd at Watkins Glen later in the year. Two standard Silverstones took a class 1st and 2nd at Palm Beach. One car was 4th in class in the Targa Florio, but two crashed in the Mille Miglia; two others finished, one of them a new prototype fitted with a 3·8-litre American Nash engine. This car was then entered for Le Mans and finished a remarkable 4th overall driven by Rolt and Hamilton. In a Silverstone, Hamilton beat Sommer's Aston Martin for a class victory in the Production Car race. The Astons were too fast for the Healeys at the TT, but five out of six cars finished, Wilkinson's Silverstone in 9th place overall and 4th in class.

In private hands, further successes were achieved later by Riley-engined cars, but Healey production now concentrated on the Nash-Healey, which was eventually given a Farina body and dubbed the 'three-nation sports car'. In 1951 a Nash-Healey finished 4th in class in the Mille Miglia and 6th overall at Silverstone. A coupé version finished 6th at Le Mans and ran well in the following year's Mille Miglia until a burst tyre caused it to crash. The remains were brought back to Warwick and rebuilt with a new cylinder head giving 200bhp. Driven by Johnson and Wisdom at Le Mans in 1952, this car earned Healey's greatest success by finishing 3rd overall behind two Mercedes. It was a fitting climax to this small company's achievements in international racing and rallying, for the new Austin-Healey appeared later in the year.

Some Nash-Healeys were raced in 1953 without notable success, but Warwick continued their development work for another 16 years with a number of successful Austin-Healeys for racing, and the make earned a great reputation in the hands of the BMC rally team.

They also built one more car under the name of Healey:
the exciting SR prototype with 2-litre V-8 Coventry
Climax engine at the rear. It was entered for Le Mans
1968, but retired after 1½ hours with clutch trouble. It ran
again in 1969 but again retired. For 1970 Healey entered
a 3-litre Repco-engined car which returned just before
the finish. FWMCC

HH (D)

Hermann Holbein built BMW specials after World War
2, these being two-seater sports cars based on the pre-war
BMW 328 and designated HH47. In 1948 his new monoposto HH48 appeared with a tuned BMW 2-litre engine
developing about 125bhp. HH cars appeared in a number
of national competitions, most successfully driven by
Fritz Riess, in F2 as well as in the 2-litre sports car class:
in 1949, for example, he finished 3rd in both classes on
the Hockenheim circuit. Sales were limited by the
economic conditions then prevailing in Germany. HON

Hillman (GB)

The make's first public appearance was in the 1907 TT,
when a Hillman driven by its designer Louis Coatalen
made the running in the early stages before being eliminated in a crash. In 1908 the firm built a vast 6-cylinder
60hp racer but this never saw action, and neither their
entries in the RAC's 2,000 Miles Trial nor the solitary
modified 25hp which ran in the Four-Inch TT were
successful. When Coatalen moved to Sunbeam, interest
in competitions evaporated, although Nelson-Smith's
9hp car performed well at Brooklands in 1914, and an
abortive if interesting 2·7-litre parallel-8 with twin gearboxes and propeller shafts was seen there once. In 1919
one of the best small sports cars of its day appeared, the
10hp Brooklands. This had a 3-speed box and a 3·5:1
back axle, but could do 60mph (96kph) in standard form
and over 80 after tuning.

In the 1919–23 period this model was campaigned by
works driver George Bedford, and also by such amateurs
as Raymond Mays, being seen in action at South Harting
within a year of the Armistice. A class win at Southport
followed in 1920, and there were further wins at Aston
Clinton, Westcliff and Holme Moss — among other
venues — in 1921, when an ohv version was tried at
Brooklands. The works racer, however, continued to use

side valves on the circuits, though it dispensed with a
differential, and Bedford did well to take 6th place in the
Coupe Internationale des Voiturettes and 7th in the
JCC 200 against strong opposition. The cars were frequently encountered in the sprints and hill-climbs of
1922. Thereafter Hillmans disappeared from the competition scene apart from some appearances in long-
distance rallies during the 1930s.

Rootes took up rallies seriously in 1948, but rather
naturally they favoured the Sunbeam-Talbot family,
Hillmans seldom being seen. Minxes did, however, win
the appropriate class of the South African Tour of Natal
in 1961 and 1962, as well as in the 1962 Trans-Canada
Rally. In 1963 the ohc 875cc rear-engined Imp was first
seen as a private entry in rallies, tuners of the calibre of
Nathan and Hartwell soon transforming it into a 100mph
vehicle with saloon-car racing potential. The works Imps
achieved little in 1964 beyond I. D. L. Lewis's class
victory in the Welsh Rally, but the following year brought
progress. Rosemary Smith took 8th place (and the ladies'
award) in the Circuit of Ireland as well as winning the
Tulip outright; another Imp (Lewis and Pollard) was 2nd.
Lewis also finished 2nd in the Scottish event, and Thistle-

1965 Hillman Imp driven by Rosemary
Smith and Margaret Mackenzie in the
Monte Carlo Rally. *Photo: Rootes Motors
Ltd*

Left, 1921 Hillman 200-Mile Race car.
George Bedford at the wheel. *Photo:
Montagu Motor Museum*

Below, 1933 Hillman Aero Minx tourer on
Fingle Hill, Devon. *Photo: Montagu Motor
Museum*

thwaite's privately entered car won its class in the Polish Rally.

In 1966 the Imp became a force in saloon-car racing through the endeavours of Alan Fraser's team (Calcutt, Unett, and Brittan), and an impressive season closed with thirty 1sts, nineteen 2nds, and thirteen 3rds, not to mention a 2nd place in their class in the British Saloon-Car Championships. The improved and more powerful 998cc Rallye Imps were also homologated, though from 1967 onward works machines were Sunbeams rather than Hillmans. By 1968, the saloons were also used on the circuits, but not before Fraser had another excellent season, with 20 victories in 29 events, thanks to the use of fuel injection or twin Webers which gave the 1-litre version an output of 115bhp. Once again, however, they came 2nd, defeated by the Broadspeed Ford Anglias in the Saloon-Car Championship.

The end of 1968 saw a brilliant success for the medium-sized 1,725cc Hunter saloon when the factory-entered car of Malkin, Coyle and Cowan won the London–Sydney Marathon against strong opposition from French, German, Russian and Australian teams. MCS

Hispano-Suiza (E)

It is convenient to regard all pre-1914 competition Hispano-Suizas as Spanish as there was no actual manufacture in France until 1919. In fact, however, post-1911 competition cars were prepared by Marc Birkigt at the Levallois-Perret works. Though the 'Alfonso' was already known as such in 1909 when the King of Spain received his first example of the model as a birthday gift from his wife, there was no serious racing before this season, when a team of 65 × 140mm (1,852cc) T-head monobloc-engined 4-cylinder cars was prepared for the Catalan Cup light-car race. They failed to distinguish themselves, but in the ensuing Coupe des Voiturettes the entire team finished in 5th, 6th and 7th places, and there were class victories for the make in the Mont Ventoux and Monte Iguedo hill-climbs.

For the 1910 Catalan Cup piston stroke was lengthened to 170mm, and Zucarelli finished 3rd behind two Lion-Peugeots. In the Coupe des Voiturettes the cars, now with 200mm strokes and 60bhp, were victorious, Zucarelli winning at 55·6mph (89·48kph), while Chassagne was 2nd and Pilliverdier 6th. In 1911 Birkigt designed a new ohc

1911 Hispano-Suiza (E) Alfonso. Photo: Hispano-Suiza S. A.

engine (which Zucarelli and Henry later sold to Peugeot) and a team of 85 × 130mm supercharged cars was planned for the 1912 race. These engines developed 100bhp at 3,000rpm, but troubles with their blowers caused them to be scratched, though a small batch of unblown cars with tall narrow radiators and tandem seating on similar lines, nicknamed 'Sardines', was built and ran in minor events. One of them, driven by Rossiter, won a race at Brooklands in 1914 at 86mph (138·40kph), at a time when 3·6-litre T-head Alfonsos were lapping at around the 81mph mark. In 1912 the ohc cars did quite well in Continental hill-climbs, and Valentin's Hispano-Suiza won the 1st prize of the Imperial Russian Automobile Club in the Czar's Cup event. Some bigger ohc Hispanos were also made and at least one of these was still being raced in Spain as late as 1922. MCS

Left, 1909 Hispano-Suiza (E) Alfonso in the GP des Voiturettes. Photo: T. A. S. O. Mathieson Collection

Right, 1909 Hispano-Suiza (E) Alfonso in the Catalan Cup. Pilliverdier at the wheel. Photo: Hispano-Suiza S. A.

Hispano-Suiza (F)

The outstanding luxury car of the immediate post-1918 period was Marc Birkigt's magnificent 6·6-litre 6-cylinder ohc H6 Hispano-Suiza with its servo-operated 4-wheel brakes. It was capable of 85mph in standard form, and was first seen in competition in 1921, when

Left, 1924 Hispano-Suiza (F) Boulogne in the Targa Florio. André Dubonnet at the wheel. *Photo: T. A. S. O. Mathieson Collection*

Above, 1926 Hisparco 6/8CV sports car. *Photo: J. Rodriguez-Viña Collection*

André Dubonnet won the Boillot Cup at Boulogne. Bablot also won at Boulogne, in 1922, averaging 64mph (103·00kph). The Autumn Cup race at Monza saw Dubonnet at the wheel of a new bored-out 6·9-litre version of the H6, said to do 107mph (172·2kph) on 150bhp; it beat a Ballot into 1st place.

In 1923 an 8-litre engine had been introduced, and works teams ran in the Boillot Cup and at Lasarte. In the French race Garnier was fastest of all at 70·5mph (113·46kph); though he lost on formula to a Chenard-Walcker, production short-chassis 8-litres were subsequently sold as 'Boulogne' models. In Spain, Dubonnet finished 2nd and made the fastest lap. Amazingly he entered a similar car with exotic tulipwood coachwork for the 1924 Targa Florio, and even more amazingly he lay 2nd at the end of the first lap. Thereafter he had tyre troubles and finished 6th.

In 1928 the famous match race took place at Indianapolis between Weymann's 8-litre and Moskovics's smaller Stutz; the Hispano-Suiza had a well-publicized walkover at 70·14mph (128·88kph), though the American car turned the tables in a less well-publicized return match. MCS

Hisparco (E)

The Hisparco was a light sports car whose makers bought many components from Marguerite of Courbevoie and used Chapuis-Dornier engines of 961 or 1,095cc, the latter from 1926 onwards. Two- and two/three-seater sports bodies were fitted, and the cars did well in a number of races including the 1925 Subida Monserrat, (4th in class); the 1925 San Sebastian Cyclecar GP (2nd in class); and best of all, the 12-Hour Mountain Circuit of Guadarrama, which Ramon Uribesalgo won at an average speed of 38mph (61·16kph). Hisparco cars were made between 1923 and 1928. JRV

Holden (AUS)

The Holden holds a unique place in Australian history; as the first car wholly manufactured in that country, starting in 1948, it was always promoted as 'Australia's Own Car' The engine's first moments of glory came when drivers started running highly-modified Holden sedans from about 1953 onwards. In 1963, the end of effective life for the original cars, the best were doing 125mph (200kph); the original iron-headed cars of Jack Myers and Leo Geoghegan were good for only about 110mph (176kph). Holdens have regained dominance in touring car racing

since, but mainly through the arrival of big V-8-engined two-door coupé models.

The two most famous Holden specials in Australian history were the short-lived Centaur-Waggott and the Repco Special. Queensland driver John French had the Centaur-Waggott built for him by brilliant Queensland engineer Tim Harlock. It was a functional but attractive front-engined close-coupled GT coupé, using a very special dohc Waggott-engineered head on a Holden block, the engine developing 220bhp. French used it to win the 1961 Australian GT Championship; the car was later written off in a track accident. Earlier, fellow Queenslander Glyn Scott had developed a single-seater using a Holden engine modified by Repco, who through Charlie Dean — later responsible for much work on the Repco F1 engines — had extracted a lot of power from the humble Holden. Scott's Repco Special dominated Queensland racing for three years and ran in several Australian Grands Prix.

There have been a number of Holden-engined sports cars, but unusual monopostos included Murray Tremberth's Alta fitted with a Holden and fellow South Australian Dud Dansie's BBM Special with a locally-designed Holden engine fitted with a rotary valve system. Western Australian Syd Negus campaigned in a rear-engined Cooper fitted with a Holden in 1959. Holden 5-litre V-8 engines, developed for F5000 racing by Repco, are expected to replace the imported Chevrolet stock-block engines after the 1970 racing season. TBF

Honda (J)

Soichiro Honda's motorcycle company grew from Japan's post-war ruination into a massive industrial giant in the early 1960s. Entries were made in international motorcycle racing from the early 1960s. Despite early reversals Honda's specialized lightweight and extremely powerful multi-cylinder machines soon established a complete domination.

Car production had begun and in 1964 Honda entered Formula 1 with an experimental monocoque car at the German GP. This carried a transversely-mounted 1·5-litre V-12 engine in a tubular rear subframe and was driven by American sports car driver Ron Bucknum, who had an interest in a Honda dealership. The car was poorly finished but Bucknum impressed at Nürburgring, Monza and Watkins Glen.

For 1965 Richie Ginther joined Bucknum in the team and the cars were modified with 58·1 × 47mm, 1,495·3cc,

1965 Honda 1·5-litre Formula 1, before testing at Suzuka. *Photo: Peter Bellamy*

60° quad-cam V-12 engines using Honda fuel injection and producing around 230bhp at a prodigious 12,000rpm. Transmission was via a 6-speed gearbox, and suspension included inboard front spring/damper units. The cars were plagued with overheating and injection troubles, but Ginther won the final 1·5-litre GP at Mexico City and was 6th in the Belgian and Dutch GPs. Bucknum came 5th in Mexico.

Slow development produced the 3-litre V-12-engined RA273 model in time for the 1966 Italian GP. The new engine was a massive 60° V-12 quad-cam with four valves per cylinder, main roller bearings and drive taken from the centre of the crankshaft to prevent whip. This feature dictated a large and heavy unit, and on its début the Honda was 243kg over the 500kg minimum weight limit. Nonetheless, the 78 × 52·2mm, 2,992cc unit produced around 400bhp at 10,000rpm. The car crashed at high speed on its début, Ginther escaping unhurt, and the team later ran a car for Bucknum as well. Ginther was 4th in Mexico and set fastest lap, while Bucknum finished 8th.

For 1967 John Surtees was attracted to the team from Cooper, and he ran the team under the 'Honda Racing' name until the end of 1968. The RA273 was developed but never shed the burden of its overweight engine. Lightweight crankcases were cast but the chassis itself was too heavy. Surtees came 3rd in the South African GP, 4th in the German and 6th in the British before appearing in a new car at Monza. This RA300 was built in Surtees' workshops using many Indy Lola parts and won the Italian GP, then finished 4th in Mexico.

Engineer Nakamura's team developed the V-12 engine to produce some 430bhp in this period, working well between 8,000–11,000rpm but still suffering from excessive weight.

Surtees, Nakamura, Broadley of Lola, and Derrick White developed the RA301 monocoque for 1968 but late delivery delayed its development. Meanwhile Honda politics dictated the introduction of an air-cooled car (all their production models were then air-cooled) and work on a lightweight water-cooled V-12 lapsed. The RA302 air-cooled V-8 had the banks arranged at 120°, with dimensions of 88 × 61·4mm giving 2,987cc. There were four valves per cylinder, four overhead camshafts and Honda injection; output of this very light unit was around 430bhp at 10,000rpm. The car was hurriedly prepared and driven by Jo Schlesser in the French GP at Rouen, a move dictated by Honda against Surtees' wishes. Schlesser crashed in pouring rain, the magnesium monocoque caught fire and he was killed. Surtees was 2nd in this race with the RA301, 3rd in the United

1969 Honda 1300R. *Photo: J. K. Yamaguchi*

States GP, 5th in the British, and set fastest lap at Spa (a new record) in the Belgian. A second RA302 appeared late in the season, but Honda withdrew to ponder their mistakes at the end of the year.

While the RA273 was being developed Honda also produced a very small number of 1-litre fuel-injected F2 engines for the sole use of the Brabham works team. Jack Brabham and Denny Hulme dominated F2 entirely in 1966, winning every race except three with the powerful and reliable units. A Honda subsidiary also built the interesting 1300R two-seater powered by an air-cooled 1300 saloon engine. The production S600 and S800 sports cars and small saloons have been raced widely in club and international events the world over. DCN

Horch (D)

Horch cars of the inter-war period were too ponderous to be effective even in rallies, but the firm's pre-1914 record, mainly in central and northern Europe, was impressive. August Horch himself drove one of the three team cars in the first Herkomer Trophy Trial of 1905, but success came the following year, when Rudolf Stöss's modest 2·7-litre ioe 18/22 PS was overall victor, Horch taking 10th place on a big 5·8-litre car, also shaft-driven. An attempt to run some modified versions of their six with capacity reduced to the regulation 8 litres in the 1907 Kaiserpreis was a failure (as well as leading to Horch's resignation in 1909), and the 1908 Prince Henry cars also failed to distinguish themselves. These, however, are historically important since their low-profile dual-cowl four-seater bodies by Käthe anticipated Neumann-Neander's 1910 Austro-Daimlers, and on 2·7 litres they could do 55mph (88kph): good aerodynamics were said to

Left, 1967 Honda RA273 3-litre V-12 Formula I at Silverstone. John Surtees at the wheel. *Photo: Al Bochroch*

Right, 1968 Honda RA302 3-litre V-8 Formula I in practice at Monza. John Surtees at the wheel. *Photo: David Phipps*

add the equivalent of 6bhp.

Most of Horch's latter-day successes were in Scandinavia: wins in the 1910 Danish Reliability Trials, the 1911 and 1912 Swedish Ice Races, and the 1911 Jutland Trials, for which the Horch company gave the victorious driver Svenning 1,000 marks. Paulmann, Horch's successor as Chief Engineer, drove his own cars, scoring a clean sheet in the 1913 Austrian Alpine Trials, a gold plaque in the 1913 Swedish Winter Trials, and a 3rd place in the 1914 event. These successes were won on sv models such as the 4·2-litre 17/45 PS which had succeeded the ioe types of the August Horch era. MCS

Horstman (GB)
Built in Bath, Somerset, by Sydney Horstmann from 1914 to 1929, Horstman light cars took part in a number of competitions during the 1920s. Coventry-Simplex or Anzani engines were used, the Super Sports model having a 1,440cc Anzani unit. Horstmans ran in the JCC 200 Miles Race at Brooklands from 1921 to 1923, finishing 5th in the 1923 event with a twin-carburettor version. The firm also experimented with supercharged Anzani engines. DAT

Hotchkiss (F)
Hotchkiss were racing almost before their famous round-radiatored cars had reached the public, a team of vast 17,813cc aiv fours with chain drive being entered for the 1904 Gordon Bennett Eliminating Trials. They failed to distinguish themselves there, though Le Blon took 5th place in the Circuit des Ardennes. Moiv and shaft drive came in 1905, when the cars were even bigger at 18·8 litres, but major success eluded both these and the 1906 GP machines; the latter wore wire wheels. Shepard was lying 4th at the end of the first day, but subsequently retired, and he crashed in the Vanderbilt Cup. The car, however, had a long career in America, where it was still racing in 1911: in 1907 George Robertson broke the track record at Morris Park, and in the 24-hour race staged on this course a 35hp touring car finished 3rd. Thereafter Hotchkiss abandoned racing in disgust, though Ainsworth took a standard 3·8-litre car through the 1914 Austrian Alpine Trials, and the smaller AM-type did have some minor European hill-climb successes in the middle 1920s.

Hotchkiss made their great impact in the Monte Carlo Rallies of the 1930s, with their excellent 3·5-litre 6-cylinder ohv models. Vasselle won in 1932 on a prototype of this car, repeating his success in 1933. Winners in 1934 were Gas and Trevoux; the Rumanian Zamfirescu was 4th in 1937; Trevoux was 2nd in 1938; and he and Lesurque tied for 1st place with a Delahaye in 1939. There

was a 3-litre team prize in the 1933 Alpine Trial, and two individual Glacier Cups in 1934, not to mention a victory in the Paris–St Raphael and a 3rd place in the Paris–Nice (which event gave its name to one of Hotchkiss's fast tourers) in 1936. There was another 3rd in the Paris–Nice in 1937. The sixes raced occasionally, Falck gaining a class victory in the 1931 Circuit des Routes Pavées, and Vasselle did well in the Belgian 24-Hour event. The 3·5-litre cars finished 2nd in both the Belgian 10 Hours and the Algiers Grand Prix de Tourisme of 1934. Some long-distance record work was undertaken, first with a stock 3-litre in 1929 and then with a special streamliner based on the bread-and-butter 2-litre four in 1934, on which Eyston and Denly did 6 hours at 101·5mph (163·3kph).

In the early post-World War 2 years the 6-cylinder Hotchkisses were back in rallying, two class wins being scored in the 1946 French Alpine event. Trevoux and Lesurque won the first post-war Monte Carlo in 1949, Becquart and Secret achieving Hotchkiss's final win the following year. MCS

Howmet Turbine (US)
Two turbine-powered sports cars were built by Bob McKee of Palatine, Ill., in 1967 for Howmet Corporation, an American conglomerate with an interest in space-age metals. Designed by Ray Heppenstall of Philadelphia, the cars had chassis of tube construction, unequal A-arms, coil suspension and bodies of aluminium panels. The Continental turbine unit turned at 57,000rpm, reduced to 670rpm at the output shaft where it rated 330bhp. The power train-turbine and differential weighed 250lb (113·4kg); the car's dry weight was 1,430lb (648·64kg); the length was 171in (4·343m), width 69in (1·753m), and height 37in (0·939m). In 1968 the Sports Car Club of America and the Fédération Internationale de l'Automobile granted the Howmet turbine the status of Group 6 prototype, unlike the Rover turbine that had been placed in a special 'exhibition class'. The type was raced widely in 1968, including the Daytona 24 Hours, Sebring and Le Mans, but failed to finish a race until Ray Heppenstall won two SCCA nationals at Huntsville, Ala. He then finished 2nd at the Cumberland nationals and with Dr Richard Thompson won the Marlboro 300 Miles.

In 1969 turbines were banned from SCCA sanctioned professional road races. On 21 August 1970, Ray Heppenstall drove the Howmet Mark 2 to six standing start turbine acceleration records on a certified course near Talladega, Ala. Two records, formerly held by Russia's Pioneer II and England's Rover, were earned with runs of 105·599 and 93·505mph. ARB

Left, 1908 Horch 40hp in the Prince Henry Trial. *Photo: Neubauer Collection*

Above, 1921 Horstman 200-Mile Race Car. Douglas Hawkes at the wheel. *Photo: Thirlby Collection*

Below, 1938 Hotchkiss 3·5-litre saloon in the final tests of the Monte Carlo Rally. Trevoux at the wheel. *Photo: Autocar*

1967 Howmet TX turbine-powered coupé. *Photo: Al Bochroch Collection*

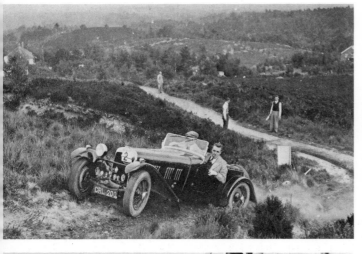

Top, 1937 HRG 1·5-litre sports car in the Lawrence Cup Trial. *Photo: Montagu Motor Museum*

Top right, 1947 HRG 1·5-litre aerodynamic sports car. *Photo: Montagu Motor Museum*

Above, 1948 HRG 1·5-litre aerodynamic coupé. *Photo: Montagu Motor Museum*

Above right, 1949 HRG 1·5-litre lightweight sports cars at Spa. *Photo: Montagu Motor Museum*

HRG (GB)

This tough, traditional sports car was designed with competitions in mind and the original 1·5-litre two-seater with 4ED Meadows engine was stated to do 92mph (148·06kph) in road trim and 100mph stripped—though in practice not all of them were quite as fast as that. HRGs competed in every type of minor event, and one 1948 car still active has in fact won more awards than it has competed in events. There was never a works team; the manufacturers, however, sent a tender van to accompany Alpine Rally competitors as early as 1949. In 1937 Halford and Scott took 2nd place in the 1·5-litre category at Le Mans, this performance being repeated by Clark and Chambers in 1938; the latter partnership won their class again in 1939. The 1·5-litres, by now Singer-engined, did well at Spa in 1948, and some revised cars with lightweight bodies swept the board in the 1·5-litre class in 1949 as well as winning the team prize. The same machines ran at Le Mans, scoring another class victory for Thompson and Fairman. There were class and team wins in the 1948 Alpine Rally, and another class victory, and a Coupe des Alpes for John Gott in 1951, in which year HRGs also finished 1st and 2nd in their class in the RAC Rally. The cars scored class wins in the 1949 and 1950 Production Touring Car Races at Silverstone. In 1955 the HRG company unveiled an exciting twin-ohc sports two-seater on modern lines with all-independent suspension, but it never progressed beyond minor club events. MCS

Hudson (US)

Hudson did not start racing in earnest until the advent of the 4·5-litre sv Super Six, a new model for 1916; towards the end of 1915, one of these, driven by Ralph Mulford, went after stock-car records at Sheepshead Bay, covering 100 miles at 74·9mph (120·54kph). With the aid of a 2·6:1 back axle a similar car achieved 102·5mph (165·0kph) over the mile in 1916. Mulford raised the American 24-hour stock-car record to 75·8mph (121·99kph), as well as using a standard tourer to break the transcontinental record in both directions. He made ftd at Pikes Peak, Colo., though he did not win the coveted Penrose Trophy. Other 1916 Hudson placings included two 3rds at Sheepshead Bay for Ira Vail; a 3rd in the Grand Prix for Patterson; and 4th, 5th and 6th places in the Vanderbilt Cup.

In 1917 there was a factory-entered team of racers with Rudge-Whitworth wire wheels; output was worked up from 76bhp to 115bhp. Despite World War 1 they managed firsts at Omaha and Minneapolis, a 2nd at Cincinnati, and 4th, 5th and 6th at Sheepshead Bay. There were hardly any races in 1918, but the Hudsons were out again in 1919, Pullen coming in 4th in the Santa Monica 250, and Vail a creditable 9th at Indianapolis. A 4th at Los Angeles Speedway in 1920 heralded a decline, but in 1921 Rhiley won the Penrose Trophy at Pikes Peak, and there was another class victory for his short-chassis Hudson Special in 1922.

The 'Junk Formula' in force at Indianapolis in the

477

early 1930s bred a new generation of machines based on stock-car components. A Hudson Eight-engined Marr Special was placed 10th in 1931, though similar cars failed in 1932 (when they were works-sponsored) and in 1933.

In 1951 Hudson began serious racing in the NASCAR Grand Nationals with their 5,048cc 6-cylinder Hornets. They were 3rd in 1951, but from 1952 to 1954 they dominated stock car racing, winning 47 out of 60 events in 1952 alone. Leading drivers were Marshall Teague, Frank Mundy, and Tim Flock who had previously driven for Oldsmobile. The 1954 merger of Hudson and Nash, to form American Motors, meant the end of Hudson's stock-car racing, but it had been a remarkable era, with more decisive dominance by one make than has been seen since on the stock-car scene. MCS

Huffaker (US)

Joseph Huffaker, a native of Indiana, moved to California in 1945 where he began building midgets and sprint cars. In 1959 he became manager of Kjell Qvale's (one of California's largest foreign car dealers) competition department in San Francisco and in ten years built about 80 Formula Juniors, Genie sport cars and Indianapolis entries. Walt Hansgen and Bob Veith drove rear-engined, Offenhauser-powered, MG Liquid Suspension Specials at the Speedway in 1964 and 1965, and in 1966 Eddie

Johnson and Bobby Unser finished 7th and 8th in Huffaker-built machines. Ed Lowther won the 1964 Sports Car Club of America 'C' modified national title in a Genie-Ford and 1966 United States Road Racing champion, Chuck Parsons, drove a Genie-Chevrolet during the first half of his award-winning season. ARB

Humber (GB)

Although generally thought of as one of the staidest makes, Humber had a distinguished competition career in the pre-1914 period. As early as 1903 Cross's 20hp 4-cylinder beat the already rapid Coventry-Daimlers at Phoenix Park, Castlewellan and Killorglin in the Irish Fortnight that followed the Gordon Bennett Cup race, and by 1905 their standard T-head tourers, in 2-litre, 2·4-litre and 3·5-litre sizes, had gained class victories at Brighton, Blackpool, Skegness and South Harting.

In 1906 the firm fielded a 3·3-litre Beeston-Humber for the TT driven by T. C. Pullinger and a 3·3-litre Coventry-Humber for Louis Coatalen. The cars finished 5th and 6th respectively. Humber supported both TTs in 1907, all their four entries having engines of different sizes. In the regular race Tuck (later to be the mainstay of Humber's competition activities) drove a Coventry-built 5·8-litre machine with 4-speed overdrive gearbox, and Reid a smaller 4·5-litre Beeston car; in the Heavy-Car category (where entries had to carry huge rear screens to simulate

Left, 1916 Hudson Super Six at Sheepshead Bay after 24-Hour stock-car record. Ralph Mulford at the wheel. *Photo: American Motors Corp.*

Above, 1953 Hudson Hornet sedan, with Marshall Teague. *Photo: American Motors Corp.*

Left, c 1963 Huffaker Genie Mark I. *Photo: Al Bochroch*

Below, 1914 Humber TT car. *Photo: Veteran Car Club of Great Britain*

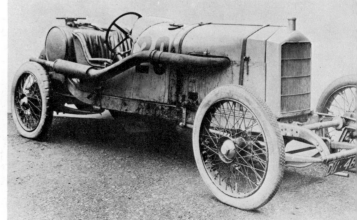

the drag of landaulette coachwork) Cooper had a 6·3-litre 3-speed car and Mills a large 7·2-litre with 4-speed box. Humbers did well, Reid being the 2nd of only two finishers in his class, and Mills winning the Heavy event at 28·1mph (45·22kph).

Tuck continued to support sprints and hill-climbs until 1914, and by 1912 his 1·9-litre sv monobloc 4-cylinder car (and its bigger 14hp sister) could offer serious opposition to W. O. Bentley's rapid DFP. Tuck even went after class records at Brooklands with a single-seater, managing 70·82mph (113·97kph) over the flying mile, and raising this to 74·32mph (119·60kph) with a 2·3-litre engine installed. In 1914 F. T. Burgess produced what amounted to a copy of the Peugeot for the TT, fitted with 8-valve twin-ohc 4-cylinder engines of 3·3 litres' capacity, developing 100bhp, or sufficient for an 85mph (136kph) top speed. Drivers were Burgess, Wright and Tuck, but though the cars achieved little, Tuck later won a race at Brooklands at over 92mph, and as late as 1929 Wallbank was timed there at 104mph (167·4kph), as well as lapping at 91·72mph (147·61kph). The only surviving example of the model appears regularly in VSCC events in the hands of Kenneth Neve.

Although a 14hp similar to Tuck's 1913 sprint car was still to be seen in Welsh hill-climbs as late as 1923, this was the effective end of Humber's competition work, with the possible exception of the appearance of a 1,669cc 12hp in the 1933 Alpine Trial, and Maurice Gatsonides' remarkable 2nd place in the 1950 Monte Carlo Rally on a stock 4·1-litre sv Super Snipe saloon. MCS

Huron (GB)

Formed at the end of 1970 by Canadian Jack Smith, Englishman Ray Ireland and Swiss ex-Lotus and McLaren designer, Jo Marquart, Huron Auto Race Developments planned to build racing and sports cars. The single-seater was a monocoque for Formula 2/Atlantic with inboard front suspension, while the Group 6 sports car was planned to take Cosworth FVC and other engines. Three sports cars were entered for the 1971 Le Mans race. Formula 3 and Formula Ford cars were also planned for the ambitious first season. GNG

Hutton (GB)

The 1904 6-cylinder Gordon Bennett Hutton with Barber infinitely variable gear almost certainly never existed, though two engines were probably made and used for motorboat racing. By contrast, the 1908 TT Hutton built for the 'Four Inch' Rally not only existed,

1953 HWM-Jaguar sports car at Snetterton. George Abecassis at the wheel. *Photo: I. C. B. Pearce*

Left, 1908 Hutton 'Four Inch' TT car, possibly at Westerham Hill-Climb, 1909. W. Watson at the wheel. *Photo: Sedgwick and Marshall Collection*

Right, 1951 HWM 2-litre Formula 2. Peter Collins at the wheel. *Photo: Geoffrey Goddard*

but won its race in the Isle of Man at 50·3mph (80·95kph), and still survives. The Huttons were in fact Acton-built Napiers, the *nom de guerre* being the consequence of their 4-cylinder sv power units at a time when S. F. Edge was identifying himself (and Napier) with 6-cylinder cars. An even larger engine with 8-in stroke was used in J. E. Hutton's own car, but neither this nor P. D. Stirling's standard model finished.

The Hutton later had a long and distinguished career in North of England sprints and hill-climbs in the hands of Hoyle and Bradwell, making ftd at Pateley Bridge in 1910 and 1911. It was rediscovered in 1939 and perhaps its best-known Vintage appearance was in the Anglo-American Vintage Car Rally in the U.S. in 1957. MCS

HWM (GB)

The original HW-Alta of 1948 was adapted by George Abecassis and John Heath of Hersham and Walton Motors as a dual-purpose Formula 2 and sports-racing car. The twin-tube chassis that was used for all HWM cars was evolved in 1949, and for 1950 a full team of three cars was made. New cars were built for 1951, being similar in general appearance, but with single-seater bodies. Coil front suspension replaced the earlier transverse leaf, and a De Dion layout was adopted at the rear instead of a fully independent arrangement. Power was increased for 1952 from 125 to approximately 150bhp, but the cars could still hope only to score on reliability against their lighter, more powerful and better-financed Continental rivals. In 1953 183bhp was achieved with twin Webers and a Weslake head but the composite Alta engine, constructed from metals with differing expansion rates, required very careful assembly to remain reliable when exerted to this extent.

Several leading drivers, including Stirling Moss and Peter Collins, cut their teeth in Heath's team. Principal successes with the Formula 2 cars included the 1949 Manx Cup (Heath), the 1950 Grand Prix des Frontières (Johnny Claes), the 1952 *Daily Express* Trophy at Silverstone (Lance Macklin) and the 1952 GP des Frontières (Paul Frère).

Two cars were made with the 2·5-litre engine, but thereafter Heath turned to long-distance sports car racing. A few cars were sold with special engines, including the 5·4-litre Cadillac, but the works models were raced with Jaguar engines and transmissions. The first of these was made in 1953, and used the early type chassis with transverse leaf suspension. By 1956 D-type engines and a new aerodynamic body were in use, but in the Mille

Miglia of that year Heath was killed and manufacture ceased. Several of the sports cars were used successfully for some years in British sprints and hill-climbs. DF

Ideal (E)

The Ideal, built at Barcelona, 1915–22, was a light car powered by a 6/8hp 4-cylinder engine. It was built by Laureano Hereter, and the most successful tuner and driver was Sebastian Nadal, an agent who was appointed chief engineer of the company. Ideal cars took 1st and 2nd places in the 1917 Vuelta Cataluña, and also did well in the Penya Rhin races of 1917 and 1918, and in the Barcelona–Madrid–Barcelona Rally of 1916. In 1918 the car's name was changed to TH (Talleres Hereter), and a new 15hp model introduced. This did not take part in races. JRV

Imperia (B)

The first Imperias to race were a team of oversquare 4-cylinder 8-litres entered for the 1907 Kaiserpreis: they achieved nothing, though one of the drivers was their designer, the German Paul Henze. By 1908 Imperias had been seen at Brooklands (where they made occasional appearances before 1914) as well as scoring class victories at Mont Ventoux and Château-Thierry. Sauvenière's 3-litre car also won a light-car race at Ostend in that year. Imperia's great victory was, however, that of de Tornaco on the 3-litre 16-valve 4-cylinder sohc sports model in the 1922 Belgian GP: almost the only appearance anywhere of a promising machine.

A slide-valve 1,100cc failed to start in the 1923 200 Miles Race at Brooklands, but a team of these machines took the first three places in their class in the 1925 Belgian 24-Hour Race. The model also dominated the light-car category of that year's Monte Carlo Rally; in this case the winner was M. A. van Roggen, then head of Imperia. A further entry in the 1930 Belgian 24 Hours with 6-cylinder slide-valve cars in 1930 failed, and the so-called sports Imperias raced in 1938 were in fact only Adler *Rennlimousinen* in Belgian colours. MCS

Indianapolis Cars, 1946–1970

Limitations of the 2½-mile (4km) Indianapolis oblong speedway with its four banked left-hand corners retarded American racing car design in the 1930s, and the success

of Wilbur Shaw's Grand Prix-type 3-litre 8CTF supercharged straight-8 Maserati in the 1939 and 1940 500 Miles races had a marked influence on post-World War 2 Indianapolis machinery. Cars became lower, better suspended and sleeker, but beneath the new shapes 'the establishment' continued to rely on the famous Offenhauser 4-cylinder twin-cam engine, born in 1931 and still going strong, whereas nonconformists such as the famous series of Novi Specials provided much technical interest.

Outstanding right into the 1960s, the front-drive torsion bar ifs Novi first appeared in the 1941 race, powered by a centrifugally supercharged, 90° V-8 4-cam 2,762cc engine designed by Ed and Bud Winfield and Leo Goosen, and giving over 450bhp. It came 4th that year, one of its best placings in a dramatic career marked by spectacular speeds, awesome crashes and numerous mechanical mishaps. Power rose through the years to a fantastic claimed 700bhp, but unreliability dogged the Novis. In 1965 one car, sponsored by STP, was rebuilt with Ferguson 4wd, but oiling troubles forced it out and the career of these fabulous machines ended without the outright victory they merited.

A remarkable design of 1946 was the Fageol Twin Coach Special, which had two 1·5-litre Roots-blown Offenhauser engines, one driving the front wheels, the other the rear, with the driver in between. It crashed in the race but reappeared in 1948, only to retire with less than 50 miles of the race to go. Still more bizarre was the Pat Clancy Special which ran in the 1948 500 and came 12th. This car had six cast magnesium wheels, the rear four on twin 'midget racer' quick-change axles, driven by a front-mounted Meyer-Drake Offenhauser engine; objectives were better traction and a steadier ride, but though it raced again in 1949 the weight and friction penalties denied this unique 4wd 6-wheeler any real success.

The most successful Indianapolis cars during the first post-war decade were the Blue Crown Specials and the Kurtis-Krafts. The Blue Crowns, exquisitely built, were designed by Lou Moore around the inevitable Offenhauser engine, driving the front wheels; wishbone and torsion bar independent front suspension and inboard brakes were features, and these cars won the 500 in 1947, 1948 and 1949. After finishing 2nd in 1949 the

Left, Indianapolis cars: 1946 Fageol Twin Coach Special. Paul Russo at the wheel. *Photo: Indianapolis Motor Speedway*

Below, Indianapolis cars: 1946 Novi Special. Ralph Hepburn at the wheel. *Photo: Indianapolis Motor Speedway*

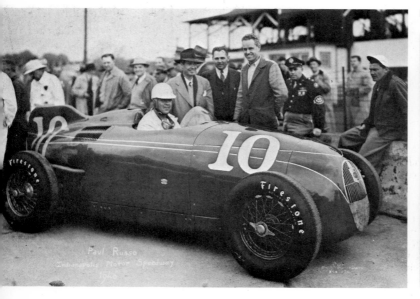

RALPH HEPBURN IN NOVI GOVERN
FASTEST LAP EVER MADE - I
Indianapolis Motor Speedwa

Top, Indianapolis cars: 1948 Pat Clancy Special. *Photo: Indianapolis Motor Speedway*

Top right, Indianapolis cars: 1948 Blue Crown Special. Mauri Rose at the wheel. *Photo: Indianapolis Motor Speedway*

Above, Indianapolis cars: 1958 George Salih lay-down roadster with horizontal engine. Jimmy Bryan at the wheel. *Photo: Indianapolis Motor Speedway*

Above right, Indianapolis cars: 1959 Watson roadster. Roger Ward at the wheel. *Photo: Indianapolis Motor Speedway*

Right, Indianapolis cars: 1967 STP turbine car. Parnelli Jones at the wheel. *Photo: Indianapolis Motor Speenway*

Kurtis-Kraft, designed by former midget race car builder Frank Kurtis of Los Angeles, appeared as a production racing car for sale to private owners in 1950, when one won the race outright. It had a lattice-type multi-tube frame, torsion bar suspension all round, inboard rear braking, Halibrand magnesium wheels, and Offenhauser engine driving the rear wheels.

As the Kurtis design evolved, its chassis and suspension were improved, and the engine inclined and transmission offset to reduce frontal area; the resultant Kurtis '500 roadster' dominated the Indianapolis scene for several years under diverse sponsors' names. An interesting variant was the Cummins Diesel Special of 1950, with big 6-cylinder supercharged compression ignition engine in a Kurtis chassis with Goodyear disc brakes. In 1952, rebuilt with the engine laid flat on its side, the Cummins made fastest practice lap at over 138mph (222kph) but retired in the race. Following the Cummins example, Offenhauser engines were also laid almost flat on their sides in many subsequent roadsters built, not only by Kurtis but by A. J. Watson, Quinn Epperly and George Salih, Eddie Kusma and others.

In 1961 the Australian Jack Brabham ran a 2·7-litre rear-engined Cooper-Climax in the 500, his performance with this small, underpowered machine against the big roadsters launching a design revolution which the highly successful rear-engined Lotus-Fords of 1963–5 accelerated. First American constructor to move the engine behind the driver was Mickey Thompson in 1962, using a stock Buick V-8 engine. His 1963 cars, sensationally low and wide, had Chevrolet V-8 engines and notably small wheels with broad-tread tyres; they proved too

new to do well, and in 1964 an improved Ford-powered, Thompson-built car was eliminated in a fatal Lap 1 crash.

By 1966 the front-engined 'dinosaurs' had gone, and since then American racing cars have closely followed European principles in chassis and suspension, though using Ford or Offenhauser engines giving phenomenal outputs with turbo supercharging. Well-known modern US makes include the Coyote, 500 winner in 1967; the

Eagle, founded by Dan Gurney and 1968 race winner; the Brawner Hawk, 1969 winner; the Colt, 1970 winner; and Vollstedt, Gerhardt, Shrike, Watson and Mongoose.

The most startling Indianapolis development in recent years, however, is the turbine-powered car. STP-sponsored Lotuses fitted with Pratt & Whitney light aircraft-type turbine units driving all four wheels narrowly lost the 500 in 1967 and 1968 through last-minute mechanical trouble. New restrictions imposed by USAC, the controlling authority, on annulus intake area subsequently reduced the turbine menace, although more may yet be heard of so effective a source of performance. CP

Invicta (GB)

The Invicta was conceived as a top-gear car *par excellence,* and its creators' attitude to competitions reflected itself in a refusal to fit rev-counters for several years. As early as 1925 Parry Thomas was racing one at Brooklands, but this was fitted with a 4-cylinder Italian FAST engine in place of the regular Meadows six, and was soon forgotten. The first of Violet Cordery's exploits was in 1926, when she led a team of six drivers who went after long-distance records at Monza with one of the first 3-litres: 15,000 miles were covered at 55·76mph (89·74kph). There followed a 10,000-mile world tour, and in 1929 the Cordery sisters won the RAC's Dewar Trophy by covering 30,000 miles in 30,000 minutes at Brooklands Track on a standard 4·5-litre four-seater. This actual car won Donald Healey his class in the 1930 Alpine Trial, in spite of having been driven (by the Corderys) from London to Edinburgh in bottom gear.

Better suited to competition work was the low-chassis S-type introduced at the 1930 London Show. On one of these Healey won the 1931 Monte Carlo Rally, and finished 2nd in the 1932 event. The model did just as well in the Alpine. Though Healey's was the only Coupe des Glaciers in 1931, there were four such awards in 1932. In 1933 Healey took 2nd place in the appropriate class of the RAC Rally. Invicta had neither the money nor the inclination to race seriously and the special 4·5-litre single-seater prepared for the 1931 BRDC 500 Miles Race never came under starter's orders, being demolished in a practice crash. S-types started in the TTs of 1931, 1933 and 1934, in the 1931 Double-Twelve, and in the 1933 Mannin Moar, but never figured in the result. More

successful was Raymond Mays's white four-seater, which he ran in connection with a tyre-testing programme for the India company. Meadows managed to extract 158bhp from an engine which normally gave 115/120bhp, and the car took 2nd place in the 1932 Brooklands Mountain Championship, as well as setting up a new sports-car record (45·6sec) at Shelsley Walsh. Some exciting 5-litre twin-cam cars with Wilson gearboxes announced late in 1932 were, unfortunately, stillborn, and by the following summer the little factory at Cobham was assembling Railtons. MCS

Iota (GB)

Pioneer of the 500 class, which later received international recognition as Formula 3, Dick Caesar's 1947 Iota design was basically a pair of 2·5in diameter tubes, linked by two cross-members, with suspension to choice. The 'works' layout was Morgan ifs and transverse-leaf rear, with speedway JAP engine, but the specification varied with each of the dozen or so that were built. Early specials based on the Iota included the Stromboli, Milli-Union, Buzzie Mark 2, and one of E. J. Moor's Wasps, but most of these were frequently rebuilt and renamed. Of the cars actually raced as Iotas, the Triumph-engined version of Wing-Cdr Frank Aikens was most successful, defeating Stirling Moss' Cooper in the Silverstone race of 1950. DF

Iso (I)

The remarkable little 236cc bubble-car produced by this firm in 1952 and later made in large numbers by BMW in Germany was actually raced, the fastest one entered for the 1954 Mille Miglia averaging close on 45mph (72·5kph), a speed which had been worked up to 50mph (80·47kph) by 1955.

A more serious proposition was the Chevrolet-engined V-8 Grifo GT coupé of 1965, which was tried at Le Mans and in the Nürburgring 1,000 kilometres. Despite the use of fibreglass bodies and irs in place of a De Dion axle, the cars did not distinguish themselves. De Montemart and Fraissenet came in 9th on the Sarthe Circuit, but both cars retired in Germany. MCS

Isotta Fraschini (I)

As early as 1901 there were entries in a minor race at Brescia and in the Giro d'Italia, but at this stage the cars

1931 Invicta 4·5-litre in Brooklands Double 12-Hour Race. *Photo: Montagu Motor Museum*

1948 Iota-JAP 500 at Bo'ness Hill-Climb. *Photo: Motor*

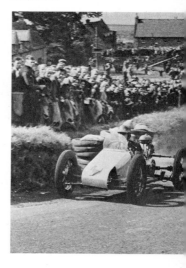

1907 Isotta Fraschini team for the Targa Florio. *Photo: Montagu Motor Museum*

were at least 70 per cent Renault. The car in which Oreste Fraschini took 2nd place in the 1902 Sassi-Superga hill-climb is also of suspect ancestry. The first true Isotta racers, designed by Giustino Cattaneo in 1905, were vast affairs with 17,195cc oversquare ohc 4-cylinder engines and chain drive, which were completed only four days before the Coppa Florio. Understandably Le Blon failed to survive the first lap, though Trucco took 4th place for Isotta Fraschini in the Milan-Florence-Rome-Milan. In 1907, however, came some 8-litre sv cars which were rather more successful, even if undersquare dimensions were used for the Targa Florio, and oversquare units for the Kaiserpreis formula. Though the latter could manage no better than 7th in the German race, Minoia went on to win the Coppa Florio at 64·7mph (104·12kph), while Trucco was 4th. The more conventional Targa Florio machines all finished the race, in 7th, 9th and 10th places. An allegedly standard 50hp car won at Briarcliff in the United States, even if its 'stock' specification was later disputed.

The Isottas did even better in America in 1908, where Strang won at Lowell and Briarcliff as well as in the Savannah Challenge Trophy, and Lyttle won the Long Island Motor Parkway Sweepstake. In Europe, Trucco was victorious in the Targa Florio, and some exciting little 1,327cc ohc monobloc 4-cylinder cars were prepared for the Coupe des Voiturettes. Output was 18bhp, but the engines were said to run up to 3,500rpm. Drivers were Trucco, Buzio and Carlo Maserati, whose brothers Bindo, Ettore and Alfieri were later to work for Isotta Fraschini. Buzio's 8th place was the best by a 4-cylinder car that year, and Lorraine-Dietrich, then in financial control at Milan, were quick to claim credit for these successes, though in fact they were never responsible for any Isotta design.

In 1910 Alfieri and Ettore Maserati were sent to Argentina to supervise the construction of a racer being put together there, but though the firm were pioneers of 4-wheel brakes and made some magnificent chain-driven sports cars in the immediate pre-1914 period, their racing relatives were not very distinguished. The cars sent to Indianapolis in 1913 for Grant, Tetzlaff and Trucco to drive were 7·2-litre, 130bhp machines with ohc and fwb, but all retired.

The big ohv straight-8s of the post-1918 period were hardly driver's cars, but they raced on occasions, Arati di San Pietro winning the Targa Abruzzo twice (1925 and 1926); Maggi, partnered by Bindo Maserati, finished 6th in the first Mille Miglia of 1927. MCS

Isuzu (J)

One of the smaller Japanese manufacturers, Isuzu have dabbled in competition with their specially-tuned and developed GTX coupé and the even more specialized Isuzu R6 Spyder G7 car of the late 1960s. This had considerable success in national 2-litre class races in 1969-70.

Basis of the car was a light alloy monocoque tub with conventional coil and wishbone suspension and a mid-mounted Isuzu Bellet GT-R G161W 4-cylinder dohc engine resembling the Lotus-Ford unit. Bore and stroke were 82 × 75mm, 1,584cc, and with twin 40PHH Solex carburettors output was 180bhp at 8,500rpm. A Hewland FT200 transmission was fitted.

Naturally ordinary Isuzu saloons have been tuned for competition use, and one of these appeared in England in 1964, driven by John Sprinzel. Its performances were not outstanding. DCN

Top, 1969 Isuzu R6 1·6-litre Group 6 coupé.
Photo: J. K. Yamaguchi

Above, 1969 Isuzu R7 5-litre Group 7 car.
Photo: J. K. Yamaguchi

Itala (I)

Fabbrica Automobili Itala SA was formed in 1904 by Matteo Ceirano whose brothers Giovanni and Giovanni Batista later built Rapid, SCAT and Ceirano cars. The first Itala was a 24hp 4-cylinder car of 8 litres' capacity which followed, as did its rival FIAT, the Mercedes pattern of honeycomb radiator, paircast cylinders, and side valves in a T-head. However, Itala used shaft drive from the start, an interesting feature considering that other large Italian cars such as Bianchi and Isotta Fraschini were still using chains ten years later. One of the first Italas won the light car class of the Susa-Moncenisio hill-climb in 1904, following this with a similar class victory in that year's Coppa Florio. Three 15·5-litre cars with overhead inlet valves ran in the 1905 Coppa Florio, Raggio's car winning the event at a record average speed of 65·39mph. The period 1906 to 1908 was Itala's most active in racing. With Cagno as their leading driver they put up some sound performances, but Felice Nazzaro and FIAT were a difficult combination to beat, and Itala's outright victories were few. They entered the Grands Prix of 1906 and 1908, the Kaiserpreis, Coppa Florio and Targa Florio. Cagno won the 1906 Targa (other Italas finished 2nd, 4th and 5th), and the 1907 Coppa della Velocita, but his best performance in a Grand Prix was 11th place in 1908.

Away from the race courses, Italas put up some remarkable speeds on long-distance runs. H. R. Pope averaged 31mph (49·89kph) between Monte Carlo and London in 1907 with his Targa Florio car, and in 1911 drove from London to Turin at a speed of 41·25mph (66·38kph). The incredibly gruelling Peking to Paris Race of 1907 was won by Prince Scipione Borghese's Itala in a journey which included driving for hundreds of miles along a railway track.

CAGNO sur voiture ITALA

L'Birondelle - Paris

Above, 1908 Itala GP car. Allesandro Cagno at the wheel. *Photo: Montagu Motor Museum*

Right, 1923 Itala Type 41SS 2·8-litre in 1926 Targa Florio. *Photo: Montagu Motor Museum*

Right, 1951 Jaguar C-type at Le Mans. Peter Whitehead at the wheel. *Photo: Klementaski Studio*

Below right, 1954 Jaguar Mark VII saloon at Silverstone. Ian Appleyard at the wheel. *Photo: T. C. March*

With the temporary abeyance of Grand Prix racing after 1908 Italas were not seen until 1913 when they entered a team of three in the Grand Prix. They had 8·5-litre 4-cylinder engines with the rotary valves which Itala were using in their production cars. This time the great Nazzaro was driving for them, but he was eliminated by a broken rear spring, and his team-mates retired also. One of the Grand Prix cars was raced successfully at Brooklands during 1914 by Robertson Shersbie-Harvie. Another finished 2nd in the 1919 Targa Florio.

Italas of the 1920s were smaller than their pre-1914 ancestors; the 2·8-litre Tipo 55 took first three places in its class in the 1921 Targa Florio, and 1st in its class in 1922. An Itala chassis was the basis of the special which Emilio Materassi built in 1923, and drove with great success for four years. In 1924 the new chief engineer Giulio Cesare Cappa designed the 2-litre 6-cylinder Tipo 61 with aluminium block and pistons, and 7-bearing crankshaft. Two Tipo 61s ran at Le Mans in 1928, the Benoist and Dauvergne car finishing 8th. A more sporting version followed in the shape of the Tipo 65, with twin-ohc 2-litre engine and a lowered frame through whose side members the rear axle passed. It was more expensive than its highly successful rival the Alfa Romeo 1750, and never won a race. In 1926 Cappa designed a highly complex Grand Prix car powered by a 1·5-litre V-12 engine driving the front wheels. A supercharger was used to scavenge the exhaust from the engine on one stroke and to compress an over-rich mixture on another, all through ports in the cylinder. In the interests of lightness, the frame was of wood. This Tipo 15 was never built, and although an 1100cc version was completed it never ran under its own power. However it still exists in the Biscaretti Museum in Turin. The final Itala was the Tipo 75 with 2·3-litre version of the Tipo 61 engine. Very few were made, and all production ceased in 1934. GNG

Jaguar (GB)

Britain's most successful competition make of the 1950s presents something of an anomaly. Unlike Ferrari or Aston Martin, Jaguar never won the Sports Car Constructors' Championship, they achieved little in the Mille Miglia, and the sports cars were never at home on the Nürburgring, although saloons did well there. Yet by 1960 they had five Le Mans victories to their credit, as against Ferrari's four and only one for Aston Martin.

Before 1949 most of Jaguar's competition successes

had been scored by 2,663cc or 3,485cc push-rod SS 100s of pre-war manufacture, though in September 1948, when Major A. T. G. Gardner attacked international Class E records at Jabbeke, Belgium, with his famous MG streamliner, he used a 2-litre dohc 4-cylinder XJ-type Jaguar engine, forerunner of the famous twin-cam six still in production in 1971. This latter unit was first seen in 3,442cc 160bhp form at the 1948 London Motor Show under the bonnet of the legendary XK 120 sports two-seater. In the summer of 1949 one of these cars recorded 132·6mph (213·4kph) over the flying mile at Jabbeke, and a team of XK 120s took the honours in that year's One-Hour Production Car Race at Silverstone, Leslie Johnson winning at 82·8mph (133·25kph). The XKs won again in 1950 and 1951, but meanwhile in 1950 they had made

Above, 1957 Jaguar D-type, the Le Mans winner, driven by Ron Flockhart and Ivor Bueb. *Photo: David Hodges Collection*

Right, 1957 Jaguar 3·4-litre saloon in 1958 Monte Carlo Rally. Phil Walton at the wheel. *Photo: Teespic*

their first bid for international laurels. Johnson's 5th place in the Mille Miglia was Jaguar's best showing in the Italian classic. Stirling Moss won the TT at 75·15mph (120·94kph), the XKs also taking the team prize.

At Le Mans their best was 12th place, but before its retirement when lying 3rd the Johnson/Hadley car had lapped at 97mph (156·11kph), a promising start which was followed up in 1951 by the introduction of a true competition version, the C-type. This had a new tubular frame and redesigned rear suspension, and with some 200bhp under the bonnet it enabled Moss to repeat his TT victory, as well as recording the make's first Le Mans win, gained by Whitehead and Walker at 93·49mph (150·45kph). There were other successes in Europe and America, and the rally season was a triumphal progress, with outright victories in the Rallye Soleil, the Tulip, the Morecambe, the Scottish, the Liège-Rome-Liège, and Alpine; in the last event Jaguar also won the team award. In addition, the cars won their class in the Edinburgh and RAC Rallies, and the Tour de France, and Vard's Mk V saloon was 3rd in the Monte Carlo.

In 1952 the Appleyards were awarded the first Alpine Gold Cup in history for three successive Coupes des Alpes, though they used one of the new twin-cam Mk VII saloons instead of their familiar white XK 120 for the Tulip, and were rewarded with 2nd place. The racing season was less impressive, being marred by an igno-minious failure at Le Mans: there was, however, some compensation in a 2nd place at Sebring (Schott and Carroll), Moss's victories at Reims (average speed 98·2mph — 158·04kph) and in the Goodwood Nine Hours, and class wins by a youthful Phil Hill at Elkhart Lake and John Fitch at Watkins Glen in America. Also notable was the debut of the Ecurie Ecosse, which had begun as a team of enthusiastic XK 120 owners. The first major success for David Murray's famous Scottish team came that year when Ian Stewart won the last Jersey (Channel Islands) road race in the team's new C-type. This was the first of many new (and ex-works) C- and D-type Jaguars to be raced by Ecurie Ecosse.

In 1953 all the factory cars had disc brakes when Jaguars redeemed themselves at Le Mans. The Rolt/Hamilton car won at 105·85mph (170·38kph), with Moss and Walker 2nd, this latter crew winning its class in the TT. Jaguars also finished 1st at Reims (Moss and White-head). A significant victory (though one little noticed at the time) was that of Moss in the Production Touring

Car event staged during the International Trophy Meeting at Silverstone. He used a Mk VII, and these big and unwieldy saloons were to dominate the new sport of saloon-car racing until 1956-7. In rallies, Jaguar were still doing well, winning the Acropolis and RAC Rallies as well as their class in the Alpine with three Coupes des Alpes; the Appleyards were 2nd in both the Monte Carlo and the Lisbon event, using a Mk VII on the former occasion and an XK 120 on the latter.

Meanwhile William Heynes, who was responsible for all Jaguar engineering until his retirement (as Vice-Chairman) in 1969, was working on a new sports racer. This D-type was based on an experimental two-seater which had recorded 178·383mph (287·135kph) at Jabbeke the previous October — at the same time a nearly standard XK 120 had been timed at over 172mph (276kph) at Montlhéry. The D-type had a monocoque structure, was 7in (177·8mm) shorter than previous racers, and the engine now had dry-sump lubrication and output went up to 250bhp. On the optional 2·53:1 back end nearly 200mph (320kph) was achieved. The Rolt/Hamilton car had to be content with 2nd place at Le Mans only 1½ minutes behind a Ferrari, but in the absence of the Italian cars Whitehead and Wharton headed a 1-2-3 procession at Reims. The TT was a disaster for Jaguars, though on this occasion with a view to countering the handicap system, they tried a 2·5-litre version of their XK engine. This was the effective ancestor of the '2·4' unit fitted into their first unitary-construction saloon un-veiled for the 1956 season. The 1955 Le Mans race was overshadowed by Pierre Levegh's appalling accident and the subsequent withdrawal of the Mercedes-Benz team. Hawthorn and Bueb won for Jaguar at 107mph (172·2kph), Claes and Swaters taking 2nd place. There were also victories for Hawthorn and Walters at Sebring, and for Titterington in the Ulster Trophy. The 1955 and 1956 seasons represented Jaguar's zenith in minor events, with privately-owned C- and D-types racing as well as sundry XKs and the saloons.

Fuel injection pushed the output of 1956 racing engines up to 300bhp, and a 3-litre version was tried at Rouen. Ecurie Ecosse scored Jaguar's fourth Le Mans victory, the drivers being Flockhart and Sanderson, even if the cars were literally boiled out of business at Sebring, where a private entry took 3rd place. Duncan Hamilton won the Coupe de Paris and the Reims race. Sanderson in a D-type won the sports category of the Belgian Pro-

duction-Car Race, and one of the new 2·4-litre saloons, driven by Paul Frère, was the fastest touring car. The Mk VII of Adams and Biggar won the Monte Carlo Rally, but at the end of the season Jaguar retired officially from racing. Their greatest triumph, however, was to come, for at Le Mans in 1957 five cars started, and five finished, in 1st, 2nd, 3rd, 4th and 6th places, Flockhart and Bueb leading the D-type procession home. That summer Ecurie Ecosse supported the curious 'Monza-napolis' race at Monza which attracted a whole squad of American-entered Indianapolis specials; though the D-type's best placing was 4th, Fairman contrived to lap at 152mph (244·6kph) on the banked track. The cars ran in 1958, as did a single-seater Lister-Jaguar special.

After 1957 the clock was running down for the D-type, hastened by the introduction of the 3-litre limit. Ecurie Ecosse persevered with 3-litre versions at Le Mans in 1958, unfortunately to no purpose, and in 1960 Hansgen drove an interesting 3-litre prototype entered by Briggs Cunningham which was really a preview of the E-type, complete with irs and the fuel injection of later D-types. It retired after making fastest practice lap, but subsequently won a race at Bridgehampton and took 3rd place at Elkhart Lake before vanishing from the scene. More impressive was the firm's record in saloon-car racing; by 1958 the big Mk VIIs had given way to the 3·4-litre (and late 3·8-litre) saloons sponsored by T. E. B. Sopwith and others. There were ten major victories that year, six in 1959, and in 1962 the Mk 2 versions had at least 14 victories to their credit. Jaguars could still win rallies. The Morley brothers' 2·4-litre won its class in the 1958 Tulip, and Donald Morley won the event outright in 1959 in a 3·4-litre. Da Silva Ramos and Estager also won the touring-car category in the Tour de France, which led to a virtual monopoly for the 'compact' Jaguars in this event. Consten won the Touring category outright from 1960 to 1963 inclusive, and was 3rd in 1964. Though Mercedes-Benz dominated the 1960 Monte Carlo Rally, Jaguar were on top in that year's Alpine, finishing 1st and 3rd in the touring category. The Sears/Cave 3·8-litre Mk 2 won its class in the RAC British event. The all-independently-sprung E-type arrived in 1961 as a road car design based on sports car experience. It had a 3·8-litre, 265bhp engine, but though this was a best-seller at home and abroad it was giving away nearly 60bhp to contemporary GT

Left, 1960 Jaguar 3-litre prototype entered at Le Mans by Briggs Cunningham. *Photo: Jaguar Cars Ltd*

Right, 1962 Jaguar E-type coupé at Silverstone. The Earl of Denbigh at the wheel. *Photo: Michael Ware*

Ferraris, and Graham Hill's win at 83·22mph (133·93kph) in the Oulton Park GT Trophy Race a few weeks after the model's introduction proved to be 'the first of the few'. Briggs Cunningham tried twice more at Le Mans with the new Jaguar; in 1962 he and Roy Salvadori achieved a creditable 4th at 108·87mph (175·21kph), only 5mph slower than the D-type's fastest winning average, but in 1963 the best he could do was 9th. Between 1962 and 1964 a limited number of special lightweight E-types were turned out by the factory, and in some cases further modified by their owners. There was no standard specification, but cars were produced with aluminium cylinder blocks, aluminium bodies, and fuel injection or Weber carburettors. In West Germany, Lindner and Nöcker continued to campaign the Mk II saloons, winning at Hockenheim in 1962, and following this up with a 1-2-3 victory at the Nürburgring. Nöcker won this 6-hour event again in 1963, and the European Touring Car Challenge Trophy as well. In England that year had seen the rise of the big Ford Galaxies in saloon-car racing, and thereafter Jaguar faded quietly from serious international competition. However the E-type became dominant in club production car races.

Jaguar engines have been used in some specialist competition cars, notably HWM, Lister and Tojeiro. MCS
Jaguar in America: Long before Mike Hawthorn and Phil Walters won the 1955 Sebring in Briggs Cunningham's D-type, the XK 120 was achieving success in SCCA racing. In 1951 Sherwood Johnson's 120M finished 3rd in total car points, and in 1952 Johnson won the SCCA National Championship, his Jaguar Special heading the car point standings then awarded. The XK 120M of Charley Wallace, a hairdresser in Washington D.C., earned national C production honours in 1954 and 1955. Walt Hansgen began his domination of SCCA modified racing in 1956 when he brought Cunningham Jaguars the first of their four consecutive national championships. ARB

Jappic (GB)

Jarvis and Sons of Wimbledon offered the light Jappic, powered by 350 or 500cc JAP engine, for aspiring record-breakers at Brooklands in the mid-1920s. It was sufficiently robust to achieve this object, and took world records in both Class 1 and Class J. DF

Javelin (US)

The Javelin sports sedan, American Motors 'pony car', is raced in NASCAR's Grand American (formerly Grand Touring) championship and in the SCCA club racing and Trans-American series. A Javelin driven by Jim Paschal won 11 oval track races to finish 2nd in the 1970 Grand American series; Roger Penske's Sunoco Special Javelins were 2nd in the 1970 Trans-Am championship; and Roy Woods' victory in the American Road Race of Champions at Road Atlanta gave Javelin the 1970 A sedan national championship in club racing. ARB

Jawa (CS)

The name Jawa is derived from Janaček and Wanderer, formed after the Czech firm Ing. F. Janaček of Prague had acquired the licence to build the German Wanderer motorcycle. Later they built DKW motorcycles, and their first cars, in 1934, were also of DKW design. The sports model was the Jawa 700, with a 750cc 2-cylinder 2-stroke engine developing 22bhp and giving a maximum speed of 80mph (128kph). Several were fitted with stream-lined bodies by Jaray, both open and closed; these came 2nd in the 750cc class of the 1934 Czech Thousand Miles Rally, and won the class in 1935. They also did well in racing. In 1937 a new car, the Jawa Minor with 616cc engine and fwd, was introduced. This was the basis of the post-war Aero Minor, sports versions of which ran at Le Mans, in the Spa 24 Hour Race, and in the Bol d'Or in 1949, as well as in Czech events. The Aero Minor engine was very suitable for tuning, and many amateur-built racing cars used this unit, even after production ceased in 1951. VH

JB (F)

Designed by Jean Bernadet, the JB was the first 500cc racing car to be built in France, and one of the most successful. The first JB, built in 1949, had a Norton engine, and was particularly successful in hill-climbing. It was followed by two more cars, with BMW and JAP engines respectively. During the 1951 season these cars ran in 500 events in Germany and Spain, as well as in France, and performed creditably, although seldom managing to defeat the best of the Coopers. GNG

JBS (GB)

Alf Bottoms acquired the Cowlan Special when he took up 500cc racing and modified this very considerably to form the first JBS car, its first victory being at Blandford at Easter 1950. For 1951 a series of cars were made, buyers including Frank Aikens and Peter Collins. Unfortunately both Bottoms himself and R. M. Dryden crashed fatally later in the year, after Bottoms had shown that he could offer a serious threat to Cooper dominance. A new model was on the stocks and the firm continued to produce this for 1952, but then ceased. DF

Jeantaud (F)

Charles Jeantaud was one of the pioneer builders of electric vehicles in France. In the 1895 Paris–Bordeaux race he entered a large chain-driven carriage with 38 batteries and a 7hp motor. It soon retired with a broken axle which must have been a great disappointment to Jeantaud, who had sent 15 relays of batteries ahead to various points on the route. Jeantaud raced no more, but in 1898 the Comte de Chasseloup-Laubat entered his Jeantaud electric car in a speed competition at Achères. Over a flying kilometre he averaged 39·3mph

Above, 1925 Jappic cyclecar. *Photo: Montagu Motor Museum*

Right, 1934 Jawa 648cc sports car. *Drawing: Jiry Nejedly*

Below, 1950 JB-JAP Formula 3. J. Dabere at the wheel. *Photo: H. Joriaux*

Bottom, 1951 JBS Formula 3 at Silverstone in 1953. Allan Moore at the wheel. *Photo: Harold Barker*

(63·25kph), defeating two Amédée Bollées and a De Dion tricycle, although his was the heaviest vehicle. It was not so called at the time, but this was in effect the Land Speed Record, being the first occasion when a car had been officially timed over a measured length of road. Camille Jenatzy promptly challenged the Comte to a match, and on 17 January 1899 the two electric cars competed against each other. Chasseloup-Laubat did 43·7mph (70·33kph), but Jenatzy raised this to 50mph (80·47kph) a few days later, the Comte replying with 57·6mph (92·70kph). Up to now both cars had been modified touring cars, although the Jeantaud had a wind-cutting body for its later runs, but Jenatzy then built his famous 'La Jamais Contente' with which he raised the record to 65·75mph (105·81kph). Chasseloup-Laubat was unable to improve on this, and neither Jeantaud nor Jenatzy electric cars featured in any kind of competitions after this. GNG

JGS (GB)

Built in 1967 by Geoff Smith and John Giles, the JGS 750 with sv Reliant engine was one of the most successful cars ever made for the 750 Formula, achieving maximum points in the 1969 Goodacre Championship. DF

Jomo (GB)

Keith Vickery's Redditch-based project started with a 750 Formula car in 1967, and then progressed to a Formula Ford design, which was offered at £998 less engine. Several cars were built, but their circuit impact was limited. DF

Jowett (GB)

The little flat-twin Jowett was the classic antithesis of a competition car, and among its few pre-World War 2 appearances was J. J. Hall's and A. H. Grimley's successful attack on the International Class G 12-Hour Record at Brooklands in 1928, at 54·86mph (88·29kph). It is of interest to note that a Jowett Car Club was formed in Bradford as early as May 1922, thus sparking off the one-make movement so popular today. In Britain, the Southern Jowett Car Club is probably the oldest such organization with a continuous history.

Gerald Palmer's ohv flat-4 Javelin of 1947 was the most advanced 1·5-litre saloon of its day, and in 1949 Wise won his class in both the Monte Carlo and Lisbon Rallies. More important, an almost-standard car driven by T. H. Wisdom and A. Hume won the 2-litre touring category of the Belgian 24-Hour Race at Spa, averaging 65·6mph (105·57kph) and lapping at 74mph (119·09kph). Then in 1950 Jowett tried serious racing with their new Jupiter sports convertible, an Eberan von Eberhorst design featuring a form of space-frame. If the Wisdom and Wise victory in the 1,500cc category at Le Mans was rather an empty one (there was only one other finisher in this class) their average of 75·84mph (122·05kph) was a 1·5-litre record for the Sarthe Circuit. In the TT Wisdom could match the speed of the HRGs but retired with bearing failure. However, 1951 was a good year for both Javelin and Jupiter. The former dominated the 1·5-litre class in the Monte Carlo Rally, the Robinson and Ellison car was 6th in general classification, and Jowett won the Manufacturers' Team Prize. On the circuits Jowett fielded two standard Jupiters and a special light-weight car at Le Mans—this retired but Becquart and Wilkins scored a second 1·5-litre win, even if they were slower than Panhard and Porsche entries in the 1,100cc class. Hadley and Wise scored a class victory in the TT, and a Jowett won the 1·5-litre race at Watkins Glen.

Once again the Becquart and Wilkins partnership were the sole 1,500cc survivors at Le Mans in 1952, but good rally performances included 5th in the Monte Carlo; best of the closed cars in the RAC event; a 2nd in class in the Tulip; and a Ladies' Cup for Mrs Mitchell and Mrs Leavens in the Lisbon.

Jowetts did not race in 1953, but Elliott won his class in the RAC Rally, and the Graaf van Zuylen won the Tulip outright on a Javelin. At the 1953 Motor Show the company unveiled the short-chassis R4 Jupiter with a 65bhp engine based on Le Mans experience, but though this one was seen in club racing, Jowett were forced to close down before series manufacture got under way. Another class victory in the 1954 RAC Rally was almost their last achievement. MCS

JP (GB)

Prominent on the northern circuits in Britain in the early fifties were the products of Joseph Potts of Bellshill, Lanarks. Design, especially of the suspension, was at first quite similar to the successful Cooper, and the engines used were 500s or 1,000s by Norton, JAP or Vincent. Leading protagonists included Ron Flockhart, Comish Hunter and Ninian Sanderson. DF

Junior 8 see Miller

JW see Walker

JWA see Mirage

1949 Jowett Javelin in 1951 Bolton-le-Moors Rally. *Photo: Francis Penn*

Below, 1951 JP Formula 3. Billy McMillan at the wheel. *Photo: W. A. C. McCandless*

Left, 1950 Jowett Jupiter in a *Daily Express* Production Car Race at Silverstone. A. H. Grimley at the wheel. *Photo: Geoffrey Goddard*

Below, 1951 Jowett Jupiter Le Mans sports car. *Photo: Francis Penn*

Kieft (GB)

The original Kieft was a 500, with suspension by rubber in torsion, designed by Ray Martin, John A. Cooper and Dean Delamont for Stirling Moss. In the light of experience gained in 1950, including the taking of Class I and J records, a revised design was produced for 1951. With Norton 'double-knocker' engine Moss won the 500 races at the British GP, the Dutch GP and Goodwood International Trophy meetings, repeating the victory at the British event in 1952, when André Loens won the Circuit de Draguignan.

By 1953, when the company moved to Birmingham from Bridgend, Glamorgan, a number of Kiefts were circulating on the tracks, but seldom sufficient to withstand all the Coopers. Models had been built also with V-twin JAP and Vincent engines for hill-climbs, and there was an unsuccessful Formula 2 car with flat-4 Butterworth engine. The new company introduced a sports model, at first with an MG engine and central driving position. In 1954, following a class victory in the Tourist Trophy, a 1,098cc sports car was shown at the London Motor Show, with similar suspension (by coil front and transverse-leaf rear) to the MG-engined car. Other engines used included Chrysler Firedome V-8, Mead 2-litre flat-4, and the ubiquitous Bristol. Don Parker still upheld the make in the 500 class with his very quick maroon car which he assembled himself. A GP car was designed for the Coventry-Climax Godiva V-8, but never saw the light of day.

Left, 1951 Kieft Formula 3 at Brough in 1953. Photo: Norman Burnitt

Right, c 1955 Kieft-Climax sports car G. R. Eden at the wheel. Photo: Bruce Edwards

Below, 1954 Kieft-Climax sports car at Silverstone. Photo: Charles Dunn

Left, 1965 Kincraft 4·7-litre Formule Libre car. Photo: Brian Foley

Right, 1970 Kitchiner K3A Formula 5000 being lapped by Reine Wisell's McLaren Formula 1 at Silverstone. Photo: Autosport

The company was re-formed again in 1956, and the fibreglass-bodied 1,098cc Coventry-Climax-engined sports car was continued, but it was no longer competitive with later designs. Following the firm's final reorganization, a rear-engined Triumph Herald-powered Formula Junior designed by Ron Timmins was offered for 1960 by Lionel Mayman & Co. but this was unsuccessful. DF

Kincraft (GB)

Jack Pearce, an enthusiastic Midlands club racer, had the Kincraft spaceframe Formule Libre car built for him, to a Les Redmond design, in 1965. Power came from a tuned 4·7-litre Ford V-8 engine and Pearce had many Formule Libre successes in it before being involved in Adam Wyllie's fatal accident at Dunboyne, Eire. He sold the car to Robin Darlington, a young Cheshire farmer, and Darlington drove it to an unprecedented series of Formule Libre victories during 1967. Jim Moore had further success in this remarkable car despite crashing it quite regularly, until it was superseded by the advent of Formula 5000. Kincraft, of Tipton, Staffordshire, also built a 5·9 Chevrolet-engined sports racing car, but this was put up for sale before completion. DCN

Kitchiner (GB)

Tony Kitchiner's small racing car company began by producing a light and simple single-seater chassis designed for Formula 3 use in 1968-9. He continued to build the K2AF3 and the K3A Formula A/5000 mono-

coque to be driven by Gordon Spice in Guards European Championship events but finances were too restricted to make the most of an interesting project. DCN

Knox (US)

This American make made its name with air-cooled cars and as early as 1902 H. A. Knox himself handled one of his machines in an ACA Reliabilty Trial. By 1908, however, the firm had progressed to big luxury tourers using water-cooled 4-cylinder engines, and a pair of 'semi-stock' 40hp Knoxes were driven by Bourque and Dennison in the Vanderbilt Cup. Both were flagged off at the end, but better things were in store, for Bourque finished 2nd in the Cobe Trophy at Indianapolis in 1909. Tragically, he and his mechanic were killed in a subsequent 250-mile event at the same meeting, and Knox withdrew his cars. Meanwhile the firm had produced a 60hp six with separately-cast cylinders, 3-speed gearbox, and chain drive, and the first of these Model-Ss was acquired by Barney Oldfield, who campaigned it energetically in stock-car events at Syracuse, New Orleans, Ormond Beach, Daytona, Salt Lake City, Kansas City, Columbus, Philadelphia, Hartford and Worcester. At Philadephia he won the Point Breeze 6-Hour Race in 1910, and also covered five miles in 5min 27·4sec on this circuit. The six also made a good showing in the year's Vanderbilt Cup: Belcher was lying 2nd behind Chevrolet's Buick when an exhaust valve gave up the unequal struggle on the 4th lap. He was 9th in the first Indianapolis 500 of 1911, and Ralph Mulford finished 10th in the 1912 event. The same driver also ran a Knox in the Vanderbilt Cup at Milwaukee, but retired. Thereafter Knox became increasingly committed to commercial vehicles and lost interest in competitions. MCS

Kurtis (US)

Frank Kurtis, born in Colorado in 1908, began building race cars in the early1930s and then established the Kurtis Kraft shops in 1938. Kurtis midgets were the first race cars to use full torsion-bar suspension and as early as 1936 Frank Kurtis built racers with an offset engine, an innovation not seen at Indianapolis until 1952. In addition to making over 800 midgets and selling several hundred midget kits, Kurtis built 58 Indianapolis cars, including the 1950, 1951, 1953, 1954 and 1955, '500' winners. Kurtis also constructed the Cummins Diesel in which Freddy Agabashian earned the pole at India-

napolis 1952, establishing one- and four-lap qualifying records. Also built by Kurtis were the famed Novis, which, while failing to win, were great crowd-pleasers at the Speedway.

In 1949 Kurtis started building sports cars. On the West Coast, Bill Stroppe, later to become associated with Holman Moody as well as other Ford Motor Co. high-performance efforts, successfully drove Ford-powered Kurtis sports cars. And in 1954 Jack Ensley won the Sports Car Club of America 'B' modified national championship driving a Kurtis Special. Frank Kurtis built over 2,000 race cars between 1938 and 1962 when he made his last Indianapolis roadster. The Kurtis plant, now devoted to experimental automotive work, is in Glendale, California. ARB

La Buire (F)

Despite rumours of some big cars in 1905, the La Buire concern never supported racing seriously, and their only major appearance was in the 1907 Coupe de la Commission Sportive race, a fuel-consumption event for which they entered three 3,402cc 4-cylinder machines. Mottard was 2nd, and the following year this design figured in their catalogue. More significant were the endeavours of Joseph Higginson in Britain. He first made his name in 1906 with a 7·5-litre machine at Snake Hill, but a year later had progressed to the immense 13·6-litre 80, a machine which dominated North of England events for nearly six years. Among its best performances were fastest time of day at Werneth Low (1907), Rivington Pike (1908 and 1912), Cornist Hall (1911), Pateley Bridge (1911), and Shelsley Walsh (1912), but thereafter Higginson felt the need for something smaller, and commissioned the first of the 30/98hp Vauxhalls.

Characteristically, La Buire chose another fuel-consumption race, the 1924 GP de Tourisme, for their return to the circuits in 1924, but despite well-streamlined saloon bodywork on their new 4-cylinder ohv machines, none of the cars finished. MCS

Lagonda (GB)

Lagonda cars first took part in serious competition in 1910, when Wilbur Gunn won a gold medal in the Russian Reliability Trials on his 16/20hp tourer. After World War 1 the works entered their 11·1hp ioe light cars in long-distance trials, and in the 1921 JCC 200 Miles Race at Brooklands, Oates and Hammond drove

Above, 1924 La Buire streamlined saloon designed for the Touring Car GP. *Photo: Autocar*

Left, 1912 Knox Six at Elgin. Ralph Mulford at the wheel. *Photo: Peter Helck Collection*

Right, 1953 Kurtis-Offenhauser, winner at Indianapolis. Bill Vukovitch at the wheel. *Photo: Indianapolis Motor Speedway*

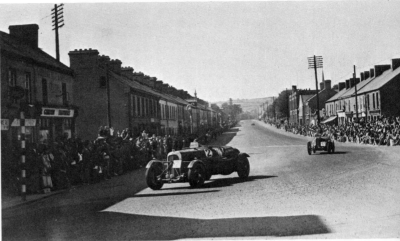

a pair of 1,496cc racing versions, both of which finished. Oates retired in the 1922 event, and it was not until 1928 that the high-camshaft 2-litres ran in the Le Mans 24-Hour Race, the Hawkes and D'Erlanger machine finishing 11th. Lord de Clifford's supercharged 2-litre took 4th place in the 1931 Monte Carlo Rally, and a similar car driven by W. M. Couper won a Glacier Cup in the 1932 Alpine.

Lagonda's real impact on sports-car racing came with the appearance in 1934 of the Fox and Nicholl-prepared 4·5-litres with push-rod Meadows engines. In the TT, Lewis's Lagonda fought a savage duel with Hall's Derby Bentley, but finished 4th, the other cars taking 5th and 8th places. The 7th and 8th places for Hindmarsh and Dodson in 1935 were less impressive, but meanwhile the Hindmarsh and Fontes car had scored Britain's first Le Mans victory since 1930 at 77·85mph (125·29kph), breaking Alfa Romeo's four-year run of success. In 1936 the cars won the big-car classes of both the French GP and the Belgian 24-Hour Race; in the TT, Fairfield and Howe were 4th and 5th respectively; and Brian Lewis drove a stripped example into 3rd place in the BRDC 500 at Brooklands. A solitary car (Brackenbury) ran without success at Le Mans in 1937, but 1938 brought the new Bentley-designed chassis with ifs and the short-stroke 4,480cc ohc V-12, capable of 175/180bhp in stock form. Late in 1938 Earl Howe achieved 101·5mph (163·3km) in one hour at Brooklands in a standard

Left, 1930 Lagonda 2-litre low-chassis tourer in the MCC Buxton Trial. *Photo: Montagu Motor Museum*

Right, 1935 Lagonda 4·5-litre at Newtonards in the TT. C. L. Dodson at the wheel. *Photo: Autocar*

Above, 1949 Lambert 1100 in the Bol d'Or. Germain Lambert at the wheel. *Photo: Lucien Loreille Collection*

Left, 1954 Lagonda V-12 (left) with an Aston Martin DB3S coupé at Silverstone. *Photo: Alan R. Smith*

12-cylinder saloon. For the 1939 Le Mans race Bentley prepared a couple of lightweight two-seaters with 220bhp engines which ran with great regularity, Dobson and Brackenbury finishing 3rd and Lords Waleran and Selsdon 4th. The cars made one more appearance at Brooklands before World War 2. One of them was sent to Indianapolis in 1946 but failed to qualify.

The last competition car to bear the name of Lagonda was an Aston Martin-based 4·5-litre 4-ohc V-12, with triple 4-choke Weber carburettors, 5-speed gearbox, and DB 3S-type Aston chassis tried in 1954. This car was eliminated by a crash at Le Mans, though in the British GP Sports Car Race at Silverstone, Parnell managed to bring it in 4th behind the factory Astons. The design reappeared in 1955 with a new space-frame and disc brakes, but it retired again at Le Mans, and David Brown abandoned his 12-cylinder experiments. MCS

Lago-Talbot see Darracq

La Licorne see Corre; La Licorne

Lambert (F)
Germain Lambert built his first experimental car with independent suspension all round in 1926, and from 1934 to 1936 made a few small fwd sports cars powered by the 1,075cc Ruby engine. After the war, in new premises at Giromagny, Belfort, he built a more conventional sports car, still with Ruby-type engine, but with rwd and conventional suspension by semi-elliptic leaf springs. It had a tubular frame, and could be had with sports or racing bodies, with supercharger optional on all models. Speeds ranged from 75 to 100mph (120·70 to 160·9kph). Lambert competed regularly in his own cars in the Bol d'Or from 1947 to 1951, coming 3rd in 1949 and 1st in 1951, in the 1,100cc class. Lamberts also took part in local races such as the Circuit des Villes d'Eaux des Vosges in which they were 2nd in 1949, and in rallies and hill-climbs. GNG

Lanchester (GB)
The advanced and individual twin-cylinder Lanchester won a Gold medal at the ACGBI's 1899 Richmond Trials, though the make performed less well in the British Thousand Miles Trial of 1900, and the cars appeared infrequently in hill-climbs. George Lanchester, however, won his class at Gorcot in 1902, and in 1914 two 38hp 6-cylinder tourers competed with distinction in the

Swedish Winter Trials. In the 1921–3 period Tommy Hann built up an ingenious Brooklands car from a 1911 25hp landaulette; this ran originally as an aerodynamic tandem two-seater saloon but ended up as the open single-seater 'Softly-Catch-Monkey'.

Other Brooklands Lanchesters were a pair of 6·2-litre ohc Forties, the first of which, a two-seater, took seven International Class G records in the hands of S. F. Edge. The single-seater was built for Lionel Rapson, and in addition to tyre-testing work it went after records, Parry Thomas taking the World's Hour title at 109·09mph (175·54kph) in 1924, as well as putting in the fastest lap at Brooklands to date at 124·12mph (199·83kph). This one was retired after three seasons' racing in 1926. One of the later Daimler-built 15/18hp saloons won the premier award in the 1932 RAC Torquay Rally. MCS

Lancia (I)

Despite Vincenzo Lancia's long and successful career as a works driver for FIAT, his own cars took little part in competition during the twenty years he was in charge at Turin. The early sv 4-cylinder machines were modern in concept and quite fast (a 3·1-litre lapped Brooklands at 66mph (106·22kph) as early as 1909), but its impact was limited to such victories as Hillard's in the 1908 International Light Car Race at Savannah. On the same course Knipper won the 1910 Tiedeman Trophy at

1923 Lanchester 40hp at Shelsley Walsh.
Photo: Francis Hutton-Stott Collection

Left, 1909 Lancia 20hp at Brooklands. W. L. Stewart, the London Lancia concessionaire, at the wheel. *Photo: Montagu Motor Museum*

Right, 1929 Lancia Lambda team for the San Sebastian Sports Car GP. *Photo: Fotocar*

58·48mph (94·12kph). Lancias did well in the Targa Florio races of the period: Airoldi was 3rd in 1909, Cortese 2nd in 1911, Garetto 2nd again in 1912, and Bordino 8th in 1913.

The brilliant 2,121cc V-4 Lambda with its ifs and unitary construction was in production by 1922, but this was always strictly a fast tourer in Italy. Private entrants, however, raced them, and Scarfiotti took 2nd place in the 1925 Targa Abruzzo; in that year, too, Lambdas were 2nd and 3rd in the Rome GP. Gouvion drove one into 3rd place in the 1927 Circuit des Routes Pavées in France, and in the first three Mille Miglia (1927, 1928 and 1929) the Strazza and Varallo partnership took 4th place.

The Lambdas were out of everything save British club racing in 1934, when Lancia's best place in the Mille Miglia was 9th at 59mph (94·95kph) for a stock 3-litre V-8 Astura saloon driven by Pintacuda and Nardilli. Lancias filled the first four places in the shortened and rather tame Targa Florio of 1936, the winner being Magistri's 1·2-litre Augusta. In the immediate pre-World War 2 period this model's successor, the 1,352cc Aprilia, had the 1,500cc sports class to itself in Italy, even if competition Aprilias were slower than the fiercer brands of 1,100cc FIAT. Some aerodynamic two-seaters tried in the 1938 TT retired, and the fastest of the 1940 Mille Miglia cars failed to better 78mph (125·53kph).

The last two pre-war Monte Carlo Rallies, however, showed the Aprilia to advantage: in 1938 Descollas was 8th, Lord Waleran 9th, and the cars filled five of the top six places in the small-car class, and they were 2nd and 3rd in this section in 1939. Aprilias were made until the end of 1949, and had quite a good post-war record, dominating the 1,500cc category of the 1947 and 1948 Alpine Rallies, and winning their classes in the 1948 Lisbon and 1950 Sestrières events.

First of the post-war generation was the 1,754cc V-6 Aurelia saloon which had evolved by 1951 into a very fine 75bhp 2-litre GT coupé. A victory in the Sestrières Rally and a 2nd in class in the Alpine were backed by some racing successes. Bracco and Maglioli drove an Aurelia into 2nd place in the Mille Miglia at 73·7mph (118·61kph), Ippocampo and Mori being 7th. There was a class victory and a 12th at Le Mans, and the Pescara 6

Above, 1935 Lancia D20 2·9-litre coupé in the
Mille Miglia. Photo: Montagu Motor Museum

Right, 1954 Lancia D25 3·7-litre sports car
in the TT. Alberto Ascari at the wheel.
Photo: Doug Nye Collection

Below, 1955 Lancia D50 2·5-litre Formula I
car. Photo: Museo dell'Automobile, Turin

Right, 1967 Lancia Fulvia NF in the Targa
Florio. Photo: Geoffrey Goddard

Hours was a Lancia benefit, with Bracco, Anselmi and
Valenzano taking the first three places. The score in 1952
was a 3rd in the Mille Miglia for Fagioli; 6th and 8th
(Valenzano/Ippocampo, and Bonetto/Anselmi) at Le
Mans; 2nd, 3rd and 4th places in the 2-litre category of
the Tour of Sicily; and a victory for Bonetto in the Targa
Florio, in which he averaged 49·7mph (79·98kph).
Lancias were 2nd and 3rd, and Maglioli closed an
excellent season by finishing 4th in the Carrera Panamericana on a supercharged Aurelia. Valenzano won
the Sestrières Rally, and a 6th in the Liège-Rome-Liège
was a prelude to the outright victory of Claes and
Trasenster in 1953.

The GT Aurelia grew up to 2·5 litres and 118bhp, but
it was now largely reserved for rallies, 1953 representing
its peak. In addition to the Belgian win, there were the
first three places in class and three Coupes des Alpes in
the Alpine (in which the Lancias ran as 2-litres), and a
2nd in the Paris–St Raphael. Meanwhile, Lancia had set
up a competition department and were racing dohc V-6
sports cars with multi-tube frames, inboard brakes,
transverse ifs and rear-axle gearboxes. Blown 2·6-litre
engines were used unsuccessfully at Le Mans, but otherwise capacity was 2·9 litres (later increased to 3·3 litres).
A good season included outright victories in the Coppa
Toscana; the Targa Florio (Maglioli); the GP of

Portugal (Bonetto); and the Carrera Panamericana,
which was a Lancia procession led by Fangio followed by
his team-mates Taruffi and Castellotti at 2nd and 3rd.
Bonetto was 2nd in the Monza Autodrome GP (which
saw the adoption of De Dion axles on competition
Lancias): other 2nd places were Taruffi's in the Dolomite
Cup and Valenzano's in the Circuit of Sicily.

For the 1954 season 3·3-litre units were fitted to the
D24 sports cars. Ascari, Villoresi, Fangio and Taruffi
all retired at Sebring, but the Valenzano and Rubirosa
car came in 2nd. Taruffi's win in the Giro di Sicilia was
backed by the Aurelia's domination of the GT class. The
same pattern is detectable in the Mille Miglia, where
Ascari won and Serafini's Aurelia was 7th; and in the
Targa Florio, where the winner was Taruffi, Piodi's being
the best Aurelia in 3rd place. In the Coppa Toscano the
D24s retired, leaving Piodi's Aurelia to take 3rd place
again. The make did not compete in the 1954 Le Mans.
The TT, as a handicap race, offered little hope to Lancia,
and for all their impressive race average of 85·64mph
(137·82kph), Taruffi and Fangio could not improve
upon 4th place. Rally wins were scored by Chiron in the
Monte Carlo, and by Gatta and Mazzaris at Sestrières.

With good performances to their credit in rallies and
sports-car racing, Lancia were now ready to tackle
Formula 1. The D50 GP car was first seen unsuccessfully

Above, 1969 Lancia Fulvia HF spyder at Mugello, driven by Claudio Maglioli and Pinto Raffaele. *Photo: Autosport*

Right, 1970 Lancia Fulvia 1600 in the Monte Carlo Rally. Drivers Ballestrieri and Andretto finished 6th overall. *Photo: Hugh W. Bishop*

in the 1954 Spanish and Argentinian Grands Prix. This was a 2,487cc 4-ohc V-8 with a tubular frame and De Dion axle inherited from the D24. Other features included the distinctive pannier fuel tanks, the double wishbone ifs, and the 5-speed box. Output was 260bhp at 8,200rpm, and 1955 got away to a promising start when Ascari won the Turin GP at 87·88mph (141·43kph), with Villoresi 3rd and Castellotti 4th. At Pau their best was 2nd after brake trouble had robbed Ascari of almost certain victory. However, Ascari won at Naples, and Castellotti took 2nd place at Monaco after Ascari had driven into the harbour. The latter's tragic death a week later at Monza took all the spirit out of Lancia's racing, and soon after this financial reasons dictated the sale of the GP cars and spares to Ferrari, who campaigned with them as Lancia-Ferraris in 1956 and 1957.

Lancia had managed a 5th place in the 1955 Monte Carlo Rally, and in 1956 the Aurelia was capable of finishing 2nd in the appropriate class of the Mille Miglia. The old type's last major success was Villoresi's win in the 1958 Acropolis Rally. It was not until 1961 that the make made a reappearance in serious competitions, a 1,100cc Appia winning its class in the Pescara 4 Hours.

1970 Lancia Fulvia 1600 driven by Sandro Munari and Lofty Drews in the East African Safari. *Photo: Lancia & Cia*

Two works 6-cylinder Flaminia coupés were at Brand's Hatch for the 6-Hour Saloon Car Race in 1962, the Frescobaldi and Fiorio car taking 5th place. There was also a class victory in the Targa Florio, repeated in 1963.

There was a revival of interest in rallies in 1963, in which Lancia campaigned with the 4-cylinder fwd Flavias. The cars took 3rd, 5th, 6th and 7th places in the Italian Flowers event; and 8th in the Polish. Trautmann and Bouchet won the 1965 Alpine, and there were a 2nd and a 3rd in the Vltava. By 1966 the firm had switched to the Fulvia in 1,298cc 101bhp coupé form and 2nds followed in the Monte Carlo (Andersson and Davenport) and the Three Cities (Cella and Lombardini). They won the team prize in the Flowers, and Ove Andersson was 4th in the Acropolis. The cars scored class wins in the Targa Florio and the Nürburgring 1,000 kilometres.

Competition Lancias in 1967 ran to 1,440cc and 120bhp. There were 1st and 2nd places in the Spanish Rally and the Tour de Corse, with a 2nd in the Acropolis and a 6th in the Swedish event. In 1968 the rally team was spearheaded by Andersson and Davenport and Pat Moss-Carlsson and Liz Nyström, the latter crew winning the Coupes des Dames in the Monte Carlo Rally, and taking 2nd place in the San Remo. Lancias also finished in the first ten in the Acropolis and the Alpine. In 1969, 1·6-litre engines were used. The Kallström/Häggbom car won the San Remo and RAC Rallies; Fall and Liddon were 3rd in the latter event. Other high placings for the make were 2nd in the Monte Carlo, 6th in the Swedish, and 4th and 5th in the Alpine.

GT racing continued, with Lancia entries in the 1,000km races at Monza and the Nürburgring, a 9th in the Targa Florio, and a 6th at Mugello. In 1970 Munari won the GT class in the Targa; Kallström and Häggbom won the RAC Rally for the 2nd time, and Lampinen and Davenport the Portuguese TAP Rally. MCS

Landar (GB)
Peter and Clive Radnall's first production vehicle was the R2 Group 6 sports-racing car of 1965, of which four were made. The R3 and R4 were Formula Vee machines sold as the 'Smithfield'; the R5 was a Formula Ford car which was not developed. The R6, of which 15 were made, was a very successful Group 6 car, gaining victories in the 1150cc class in the 1968 Sports Car Championship of Canada and in the 1969 *Yorkshire Evening Post* Championship, and coming 2nd in the 1969 *Motoring News* Championship, in the hands of R. Peart, D. Boler and C. Radnall respectively.

Most vehicles were exported with BMC 1300 or 850

bove, 1970 Landar Formula F100. *Photo:*
utosport

ight, 1921 La Perle 1,400cc at Le Mans.
evaux at the wheel. *Photo: T. A. S. O.*
Mathieson Collection

ight, 1909 Laurin-Klement Type FCR.
hoto: Motokov

engines for SCCA Class C or D racing. In 1970 the R7
Group 6 car was available, and an F100 version of this
was also marketed. DF

La Perle (F)

The La Perle was built at Boulogne-sur-Seine by the
brothers Louis and Frantz Lefèvre, and achieved considerable success between 1921 and 1930. The very first
La Perle was a cyclecar of 1913, but in 1921 the brothers
built a series of five racing cars powered by the Bignan
1,400cc T-head 4-cylinder engine. They ran in the
Voiturette Grand Prix at Le Mans (finished 5th), at
Boulogne where Louis Lefèvre won his class; and at
Penya Rhin, where Revaux came 3rd behind two
Bugattis. In 1922 the first production La Perle appeared,
of which over 300 were made up to the end of 1925. This
had a 1·5-litre engine designed by Causan which retained the Bignan's twin camshafts mounted in the
crankcase, but sported overhead valves driven by push-
rods. Output was 33bhp. Most of the cars made carried
three/four-seater sports bodies with pointed tails, but
some were racing cars with twin-carburettor engines.
These won the Boulogne Grand Prix des Voiturettes in
1922, and achieved class victories at Boulogne in 1923,
and in hill-climbs at Poitiers and Montaigne. In 1924 a
new racing car with cowled radiator and more streamlined body appeared. This achieved many hill-climb
successes all over France, and also at the Klausen Pass
in Switzerland, and had class victories in racing at St Lo,
Tours, and Boulogne. Louis Lefèvre was the most
successful driver, although his brother Frantz and others
also had their share of success.

From 1924 to 1928 a series of 75 1·5-litre single-ohc
6-cylinder cars were made. With a racing model, Frantz
Lefèvre did a standing-start kilometre in 35·6sec, equalling a blown 6-cylinder Amilcar, and beating Chiron in
an unblown Type 37 Bugatti. Although general production of La Perles ceased in 1928, one low-chassis 6-
cylinder racing car was specially built in 1930. The
engine developed 85bhp, giving a speed of 115mph
(185kph). With this car Casoli finished 2nd in the
1·5-litre class of the 1930 Pau Grand Prix, behind
Sénéchal's Delage; it was also 2nd in the Grand Prix de
la Marne. It was later fitted with a roadster body, and
one more roadster was built up from parts. GNG

Larubia *see* Bertelli

Laurin-Klement (A)

Before World War 1 this make did well in Central and

East European events, the principal drivers being Otto
Hieronymus and Count Sascha Kolowrat. As early as
1906 Laurin-Klements took 1st and 2nd places in the
1,500cc class of the Semmering hill-climb. In 1908 there
were three class victories at the same venue, not to
mention good performances in the Austrian Riesrennen
and the St Petersburg-Moscow, in which event Hieronymus in a 2·5-litre 14/16 won his class. In 1909 the firm
produced a 4-cylinder racer, the FCR-type, with cylinder
dimensions of 85 × 250mm, and in it Hieronymus
scored one of the four class victories achieved at Semmering that year. The FCR also won its class at Gaillon
in 1911. Laurin-Klement had a distinguished record in the
Austrian Alpine Trials, collecting three gold medals and
the team prize in 1910, when Kolowrat clinched matters
by making ftd in the associated Vienna Speed Trials. In
1911 there was a clean run for Hieronymus in a 4,250cc
Model K, as well as another Russian success when he
won his class in the St Petersburg-Sevastopol event.
Three Model Ks and a smaller 1·8-litre car turned out
for the 1912 Austrian Alpine, the big ones going through
without loss of marks, and there were two more clean

sheets (and the War Office Prize for Hieronymus) in
1913. Cars with 4·7-litre Knight engines were used to
good purpose in the 1914 Trials, and Laurin-Klement
also won the principal honours in the two Hungarian
Alpine events, the Tatra-Adria Trial of 1913, and the
1914 Circuit of the Carpathians. The post-World War 1
cars, made under the Czechoslovak flag, were far less
sporting and were seldom seen in competitions. MCS

Lea-Francis (GB)

Like many British light cars, the Lea-Francis made its
first impact in trials. The 1,247cc Meadows-engined
D-types scored 16 major awards in 1924, including a

Special Gold Medal in the RAC Small-Car Trials. Another 80 followed in 1925, but after this works participation in trials was banned, and Lea-Francis turned to racing proper, preparing some blown single-seaters for Brooklands in 1926. These 'Lobsters' had 3-bearing 4ED Meadows engines with Berk superchargers, in which form they had 88bhp under their bonnets, but had only minor successes.

Lea-Francis did not make their name in competition until 1928, when the supercharged S-type, or Hyper Sports, was introduced. In standard form 61bhp were developed, but the special roller-bearing units in works cars disposed of 79bhp, and five were entered for that year's TT, Kaye Don taking 1st place from Cushman's Alvis by only 13 seconds. Don and Sutton finished 3rd in the Brooklands 200 behind two out-and-out racers, a Delage and a Bugatti. Four of the five cars entered for the 1929 Double-Twelve finished in good order, though their best showing was 7th. The Peacock/Newsome Hyper came in 8th at Le Mans, improving on this with a 6th place in 1930. In the 1929 Saorstat Cup at Phoenix Park, Dublin, S. C. H. Davis took 2nd place, Green's sister car being 3rd. Financial troubles eliminated the works cars after 1930, but C. T. Delaney continued to do well at Brooklands with his S-type, averaging a remarkable 95·41mph (153·55kph) in the 1933 Canada Trophy.

The redesigned 1·5-litre model with Rose-designed engine in Riley style made a few successful appearances at Brooklands in 1938, but Lea-Francis never returned

to serious competition, though the post-war 2·5-litre cars were occasionally seen in rallies in the early 1950s, and early Connaughts used Lea-Francis units. An interesting departure in 1947 was a special 1·5-litre engine which the company hoped to sell for use in American midget speedway cars, but this project petered out. MCS

Leda (GB)

Sponsored by the Malaya Garage Group, the Leda LT 20 Formula 5000 monocoque was designed in 1969 by the prolific Len Terry. Ten cars were laid down for 1970, with the unusual feature of identical suspension wishbones for all wheels. The bodywork was by Fibreglass Mouldings Ltd. DF

LeGrand (US)

Alden 'Red' LeGrand began building race cars, primarily single-seaters, in Southern California in the early 1960s. Bruce Eglington won a professional Formula car race at Willow Springs, Calif., in 1964 and in 1965 Karl Knapp won the SCCA Formula C (up to 1,100cc) Pacific division championship driving a Le Grand. LeGrand cars, Sylmar, Calif., are contenders in Formula Ford and SCCA Formula B and C racing. ARB

Lenham (GB)

The Lenham GT was first seen in 1968, and in 1969 replicas of the P70GT model, as raced successfully by Ray Calcutt, were offered in open or closed form. A

Left, 1928 Lea-Francis Hyper 1·5-litre sports car in the TT. *Photo: Montagu Motor Museum*

Above, 1930 Lea-Francis Hyper 1·5-litre sports car at the pits in the Irish GP. *Photo: Montagu Motor Museum*

Left, 1970 Leda LT20 Formula 5000. *Photo: Autosport*

Below, 1970 Lenham GT at Lydden Hill. *Photo: Autosport*

tubular spaceframe with stressed-panel centre section was employed, the fibreglass bodies being built by the firm to the designs of Julian Booty. The Group 6 cars were available with a variety of engines, though few were sold, and an F100 variation was also made in 1970. Part of the Lenham-Hurst Racing Organization workshops at Harrietsham, Kent, was let for the production of the Hamlen Formula Ford cars, designed by Peter Coleman, and when this project ceased the T80 Lenham FF single-seater was offered instead. The sports-racing cars continued to be available for 1971 as the P70 in open or closed form, and the P80 spyder. DF

Léon Bollée (F)

Like the contemporary De Dion tricycle, Léon Bollée's belt-driven tricar contrived to travel a lot faster than its heavier and more orthodox rivals, although it was highly temperamental. Its 640cc horizontal single-cylinder engine was laterally mounted, developed 3bhp, and drove the single rear wheel by belt. The ACF always found difficulty in classifying it, since it was neither motorcycle nor car, but on the make's first appearance, in the Paris–Marseilles–Paris (1896) Lejane's average speed of 19·9mph (32·03kph) put him comfortably ahead of the official winner, Mayade on a Panhard. Both Léon Bollée and his brother Camille came to England for the Motor Car Club's Emancipation Run that winter, and in 1897 Léon won the French Coupe des Motorcycles.

Better things were, however, to follow, for in Paris–Dieppe, Jamin's Bollée made the best performance of all, tricycles included, averaging 25·2mph (40·56kph). He was even faster in the Paris–Trouville, and in 1898 was timed at 37mph over 60km, but by this time the ACF were well aware of the Bollée's eccentricities, and amended their voiturette-class regulations to include a minimum weight limit of 200kg and compulsory side-by-side seating. A twin-engined tricar, capable of 47mph (75·69kph), made its appearance that year, and was the fastest petrol car in the Chanteloup hill-climb. Some 4-wheeled Léon Bollée voiturettes (probably of the unfortunate type later built under licence by Darracq) ran in the Paris–Amsterdam–Paris race, but thereafter the company lost interest in the sport. MCS

Lester (GB)

In the late 1940s one of the most successful British Club racing cars was Harry Lester's MG special, with independent coil front suspension and twin-tube ladder frame of his own design. Replicas were built on a very small scale at Knebworth, Hertfordshire, until Lester moved to larger premises at Thatcham, Berkshire, in 1951. Lester built his own lightweight two-seater bodies, and modified the engines considerably, altering the capacity from the original 1,250cc to 1,087cc or 1,467cc to suit the 1,100cc and 1·5-litre classes then popular. Among the make's major successes was the 1952 British Empire Trophy race in the Isle of Man, when Pat Griffith and Gerry Ruddock finished 1st and 2nd. This model also formed the basis of the early Tojeiro and the very successful Leonard-MG.

A further expansion was put in hand for 1955, with new cars including a fibreglass-bodied two-seater coupé and an 1100 Coventry-Climax-engined model. This project was abandoned following the death of two of the main sponsors, Mike Keen at Goodwood and Jim Mayers in the Tourist Trophy; the latter had achieved a long run of successes with the early model Lester. DF

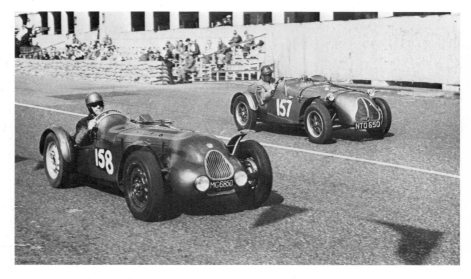

Leyland-Thomas see Thomas Specials

Lightweight Special (GB)

Alec Issigonis began the design of his Lightweight Special in 1933, although the car did not appear in competitions until some six years later. It had an Austin Seven 'Ulster' engine, monocoque stressed-skin construction of plywood faced on both sides with aluminium sheets, ifs by double wishbones and rubber in compression, and irs by swing axles and rubber in tension. The engine was worked on by Murray Jamieson, and in 1939 the Lightweight beat a works Austin Seven with the same engine at Prescott. Its overall weight was only 587lb (266·26kg). After World War 2 a new engine with single ohc and capacity of 748cc, Zoller-blown, was fitted. Weight went up to 720lb (326·59kg), but power was now 95bhp. The new car competed with great success in speed trials and hill-climbs from 1946 to 1950, but appeared much less frequently when Issigonis became increasingly absorbed on design work for Morris Motors, and subsequently BMC. It has competed from time to time in VSCC events. GNG

Ligier (F)

Guy Ligier, head of one of France's largest construction companies, and a rugby international before taking up race driving, began to lay down a series of small lightweight competition coupés in 1969. They appeared in 1970 as the Ligier JS1. These were in fact prototype road cars which Ligier intended to put into limited production, and were based on a Y-shaped backbone chassis, clad in a glassfibre body and powered by a 1·8-litre Cosworth FVC engine. Ligier himself scored a number of minor victories with the car during the 1970 season. DCN

Lincoln see Ford (US)

Lion-Peugeot (F)

From 1906 to 1910 the Lion-Peugeot made at Valentigney was an independent make under the direction of Robert Peugeot, and the chain-driven voiturettes designed by Michaux bore no relation to the more orthodox Peugeots from Audincourt. Some 3-speed single-cylinder cars with side-chain drive ran in the 1906 Coupe de l'Auto, taking a 3rd place, and Goux was 3rd again in the 1907 event. By 1908 the fashion for extreme stroke/bore ratios had crept into small car racing, and though the Lion-

1951 Lester-MG (nearest camera) with a Cooper-MG at Brighton Speed Trials. *Photo: Montagu Motor Museum*

1939 Lightweight Special at Oulton Park in 1961. Alec Issigonis at the wheel. *Photo: Montagu Motor Museum*

Guippone, who averaged 47·5mph (76·44kph). There was also a class victory in the voiturette category at Gaillon; and interestingly enough Boillot on one of the now-obsolete singles won at Mont Ventoux in 1910. By contrast Goux's formula win at Gaillon was accomplished on a new VX5 twin, a formidable machine with an 80 × 280mm engine, which meant that the price of a 95mph (152kph) top speed on a 4-speed overdrive box was that driver and mechanic had to look *round* the engine. As always, these cars were chain-driven, and there was also an ultra-long-stroke (65 × 260mm) V-4 of 3,440cc. Once again the Lion-Peugeots had a good season, winning both the Sicilian and Catalan Cups. However, cooling and tyre troubles took their toll in the Coupe de l'Auto, and the orthodox Hispano-Suizas triumphed, leaving Goux's twin in 2nd place, while Boillot's 4-cylinder came in 4th. There were victories at Val Suzon and in the Coupe de la Meuse, although in the Ostend Trials, Hispano-Suiza once again beat Lion-Peugeot.

By 1911 the two strains of Peugeot were reunited, but the Lions still raced, the last 4-cylinder voiturettes having the more moderate cylinder dimensions of 78 × 156mm. In spite of this they remained hard on tyres, and Boillot did well to finish 2nd in the Coupe de l'Auto. From 1912 onwards competition Peugeots had in-line engines and were based on Zuccarelli-Henry designs. MCS

Lister (GB)

Brian Lister of Cambridge had a good look at Tojeiro practice before building his first car in 1953, with large-diameter tubular chassis, De Dion rear end, and MG engine and gearbox. After the RAC had been persuaded

that Archie Scott-Brown could drive a racing car, it was found that he was invincible in the 2-litre sports class with a Bristol-engined version, and in 1955 a 'production' model was offered. The 1956 type, based on the slightly lighter 1954 car, was raced by Scott-Brown with A6GCS Maserati engine, and was equally successful. The F2 single-seater of the same year used too many standard proprietary parts to be competitive, and its successor of 1958, although a very good-looking car, also carried too much of a weight penalty to merit development.

However, 1957 brought the first Lister-Jaguar, which in its first season took four major sports-car races. Production expanded in 1958, and despite engine troubles with the 2,986cc Jaguar engine, Masten Gregory and Scott-Brown scored consistently until the latter's

Peugeots were still low-built, their 1·3-litre engines had dimensions of 100 × 170mm. Generally speaking, they could not yet match the Sizaire-Naudins, though they beat them in two Italian races, the Chari-La Ressa and the Sicilian Cup. More typical were their 3rd places in the Grand Prix des Voiturettes and the Coupe de l'Auto.

The legendary and towering racers with pointed radiators and complete lack of forward vision came in 1909, when the firm fielded two 2-litre designs, a 100 × 250mm single and an 80 × 192mm narrow-angle V-twin, the latter of orthodox proportions. The singles were more successful, Goux beating the Hispano-Suizas into 1st place in the Catalan Cup. He also won the Sicilian Cup, though on his 2-cylinder model he was beaten into first place in the Coupe de l'Auto by his team-mate

Top, 1908 Lion-Peugeot for the GP des Voiturettes. Georges Boillot at the wheel. *Photo: Montagu Motor Museum*

Centre, 1909 Lion-Peugeot at the start of the Sicilian Cup. Guippone at the wheel. *Photo: Montagu Motor Museum*

Bottom, 1912 Lion-Peugeot Coupe de l'Auto car. *Photo: Montagu Motor Museum*

Right, 1954 Lister-Bristol sports car. *Photo: Autosport*

above, 1956 Lister-Maserati sports car at
Silverstone. Archie Scott-Brown at the
wheel. Photo: J. H. Horsman

right, 1958 Lister-Jaguar sports car at
Virginia International Raceway. Ed
Crawford at the wheel. Photo: Warren
Allard

1906 Locomobile 90hp in the Vanderbilt
Cup. Joe Tracy at the wheel. Photo: Peter
Helck Collection

untimely death on the Spa-Francorchamps circuit in
Belgium. Cars supplied to the Ecurie Ecosse included a
single-seater 3·8 Jaguar-engined version built for the
Race of Two Worlds at Monza, which Phil Scragg later
made good use of at hill-climbs. Stirling Moss, Ivor Bueb
and Bruce Halford were among the sports-car race
results lists for Lister in 1958.

The only major success of the redesigned 1959 cars,
with bodies by Frank Costin, was by Walt Hansgen at
Watkins Glen, and this unfortunate season virtually
finished the make. Halford won a race at Brands Hatch
with a new spaceframe design in 1960, and for several
years the Janguar-engined models, such as that of Gordon
Lee, were prominent in minor events. Lister also built
the chassis for the later Emerysons, but these never did
well. DF

LMB (GB)

Leslie Ballamy's name was well-known in the trials
world before World War 2, his work on Ford suspension
systems, including conversions to ifs, giving these cars a
truly sporting image on occasion. He was responsible for
the suspension of the original Allard, and his designs were
used on several kit-built cars, such as the Falcon, which
were seen in competition in the late 1950s. In 1960 he
marketed his own chassis from premises in Guildford,
Surrey, and this too was used by several Club racers
as a basis for their specials. DF

Locomobile (US)

The Locomobile Company of America were originally
famous for steam cars, but a 4-cylinder petrol-engined
car of 1902 designed by A. L. Riker was the foundation
of a line of high-quality machines which included the
first American racing car to triumph over European
competition. For the 1905 Gordon Bennett Race Locomobile entered a conventional car with 17,657cc
(1,077·5ci) 90bhp 4-cylinder T-head engine and chain
drive. Driven by Joe Tracy it fell out during the 3rd lap,
fatally handicapped on such a mountainous course as
the Auvergne by lack of 2nd gear, which had been broken
before the race started. However, in the Vanderbilt Cup
later in the year Tracy finished 3rd. For 1906 Locomobile built a special racing car with 90bhp ioe engine of
16 litres (976ci) capacity, still with chain drive. With this
car Tracy won the American Eliminating Trials and made
fastest lap in the race itself, but tyre troubles plagued
him and he finished no higher than 10th. The same car,
together with a similar one, ran in the 1908 Vanderbilt
Cup. George Robertson averaged 64·3mph (103·48kph)

to win the race; his team-mate Jim Florida came in 3rd.
The winning car, known as 'Old 16' from the number it
bore in the 1908 Vanderbilt, survives today in the hands
of historian and artist Peter Helck. Robertson also won
the 24-Hour Races at Brighton Beach and Fairmount
Park for Locomobile in 1908, but thereafter the company
took no part in major racing events, although they made
cars until 1929. The 1925 Junior 8 racing car, though named
after a Locomobile model, was in fact a Miller. GNG

Lola (GB)

Eric Broadley took the name for his 1172 Formula
special of 1956 from the song title 'Whatever Lola wants,
Lola gets', and it certainly seemed to work. Next a well-
tuned 1,098cc Coventry-Climax engine was fitted in a
multi-tubular spaceframe weighing only 60lb (27kg), in
which the upper suspension wishbones were formed by
the rear drive shafts. Peter Ashdown with this car was the
leading driver in the class during 1959, winning at
Clermont Ferrand and (with M. Ross) in the TT;
replicas were built at Bromley, Kent.

In 1960 a front-engined Formula Junior (Mark 2) was
available, superseded by a rear-engined car (Mark 3),
with fully triangulated frame, the following year.
Ashdown, Dick Prior, the Fitzwilliam team and the
Speedwell car of Dennis Taylor achieved some good
results, but were sometimes hampered through not having
the fastest engines. In 1963 Dick Attwood of the Midland
Racing Partnership team also did well, with the then
current Mark 5A.

Meanwhile, in 1962, Bowmaker-Yeoman had sponsored a Formula 1 team, the design (Mark 4) being based
on the Formula Junior, but with Coventry-Climax V-8
driving through a Colotti Type 32 5-speed gearbox/final
drive unit. Despite a victory by John Surtees in the
Mallory Park 2,000 Guineas and several other promising
placings, the team was disbanded at the end of the year.
The cars were campaigned privately in 1963 by the
Parnell team and Bob Anderson, who won the non-
championship Rome GP.

The Lola Mark 6 was the sensational GT with central
monocoque and mid-mounted 4·2 Ford V-8 engine,
which led to an 18-month interregnum in Lola designs
while Broadley fulfilled a contract with Fords to assist
in the development of this model towards the Ford
GT40. Late in 1964 Broadley set up again, in Slough, at
first rebuilding earlier single-seaters for the current F2
and F3 regulations, and then producing the T60 series of
monocoque single-seaters and the T70 Group 9 (later
Group 7) sports cars. Chris Amon, Attwood and Surtees

Above, 1956 Lola 1172 at Kirkistown in 1958. A. R. Wershat at the wheel. *Photo: B. E. Swain*

Left, 1961 Lola-Climax sports car at Prescott. *Photo: Michael Ware*

Opposite, BMW 328 (Tony Hutchings) in a Vintage Sports Car Club race at Oulton Park, 1966. *Photo: Geoff Goddard*

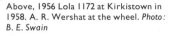

Above, 1961 Lola Formula Junior. *Photo: David Phipps*

Left, 1964 Lola-Chevrolet GT at Brands Hatch. Augie Pabst at the wheel. *Photo: Doug Nye Collection*

Below, 1969 Lola-Chevrolet T70 Mark 3B at Magny Cours in 1970. David Prophet at the wheel. *Photo: DPPI*

with T60s each won a major F2 race in 1965. Surtees was at this time playing a leading part in development as well as racing, and his successes with the T70 included the Guards Trophy at Brands Hatch, the Players 200 at Mosport, and the Players Quebec.

For 1966 the T70 Mark 2 was announced, with aluminium central monocoque section in place of steel, and Surtees won the Can-Am Championship with three 1st places. By 1967 this model had been eclipsed in the Can-Am series by the McLaren team, but was homologated in Groups 4 and 6, winning countless races throughout the world, such as the Capetown Three Hours (Paul Hawkins). The usual engine was the Chevrolet V-8, although others were tried, such as the 5-litre Aston Martin V-8 used at Le Mans. By 1968 the car was a regular race winner, with Hulme winning the TT, the Players and Martini Trophies at Silverstone, Jo Bonnier the Circuit of Anderstorp in Sweden, de Udy the Circuit de Vila Real and the Oulton Park Speedworld Trophy, Frank Gardner the Brands Hatch and Mallory Park Guards Trophies and the Croft Birthday Cup, and Chris Craft the Circuit of Innsbruck.

An even better year followed in 1969, with T70 sales doing well, and a road-going version, the GTR, also being listed. Further major victories were achieved by Bonnier, Craft, Gardner, Hawkins, Hans Herrmann, Hulme, David Piper, Brian Redman, Trevor Taylor and Mike de Udy. Most of these successes were recorded with the T76 Group 4 car, usually known as the T70 Mark 3B.

In 1970, although international race successes continued, production of the T70 ceased; it had been the most successful car ever in its class.

Despite the pressure of development on the early T70, Broadley found time in 1965 to prepare the T80 Indianapolis cars, with 4·2-litre Ford V-8 engine in a bath-tub type monocoque, and Al Unser finished 9th in the race. The following year Graham Hill scored his unexpected and significant victory with the similar rear-engined T90. In 1967 a team of three cars was run, Jackie Stewart retiring but Al Unser finishing 2nd. For 1968 there was a new model, the T150, distinguished by the option of 2-wheel or 4-wheel drive. Al Unser, with turbocharged Ford engine, crashed his 4-wheel drive car when lying 6th, but his brother Bobbie made amends in 1969 by placing 3rd with Offenhauser engine. In 1970 a similar car was used (T154), but with 2-wheel drive, and Mark Donohue achieved a very creditable 2nd.

In 1967 the T100 with light-alloy monocoque, had appeared in Formula 2. Surtees won the Mallory Park Guards Trophy and Circuit of Zolder (Belgium) races, and this model was adopted by BMW as the basis of their F2 car. The T102 was used similarly in 1969 when Hubert Hahne did well and was backed in the team by Gerhard Mitter and Jo Siffert. However, no further models were offered in the class until the appearance of the T240 at the end of 1970. The T110 was a proposed F1 machine, T120 a prototype Group 7 hill-climb car with BMW engine, and T130 the 1968 Honda GP chassis, in the design of which Broadley was involved.

In 1968 production began of the T140, and a new Can-Am (Group 7) car, the T160, was also announced. The T142 of 1969 was one of the more successful cars in Formula 5000, ex-motorcyclist Mike Hailwood and Mike Walker both featuring frequently in the results. Group 7 continued to be dominated by McLaren, however, and the improved T162 for 1969 did not achieve the desired object. By 1970 the T140 series cars

1970 Lola-Cosworth T120 at Mugello. Carlo Zuccoli at the wheel. *Photo: Autosport*

Opposite top, Chevron-BMW (B. Classick/ D. Martland) in the BOAC 500 at Brands Hatch, 1968. *Photo: Motor Sport*

Opposite bottom, Cobra (Phil Hill) passing through Cerda in the 1964 Targa Florio. *Photo: Geoff Goddard*

1927 Lombard AL-3 racing car. Alistair Miller at the wheel. *Photo: T. A. S. O. Mathieson Collection*

were somewhat outclassed in Formulas A and 5000, and the new T190 at first displayed disappointing handling characteristics. Frank Gardner, however, lengthened the wheelbase on his car and found an enormous improvement, so other owners followed suit, and Frank was enrolled in the Lola development staff. In the United States, Ron Grable had some success with his T190 in Formula A. Quite a number of T160 series cars had run in Group 7 races with few top placings despite good drivers, and there was interest when Peter Revson had some very promising runs in the new T220 car in 1970.

Lola entered a new field when the T200 Formula Ford car was introduced for 1970, and this model showed well in its first season with some good runs in Europe in the hands of Peter Hull, Tony Trimmer and others, and in the States by Ron Dykes and Mike Hiss. The T210 was designed for 2-litre sports-car racing, and Jo Bonnier just failed to take the European Championship in this class with the works car. The T230 was another F1 project which was not completed.

At the end of 1970 Lola moved from Slough to Huntingdon, near their main suppliers of chassis and body components, Arch Motors and Specialized Mouldings. The wide range of 1971 cars included two new models, the T240 Formula 2/B/Atlantic and the T250 Super Vee, as well as improved versions of existing Formula A/5000, Formula Ford, 2-litre sports and Can-Am cars. DF

Lombard (F)

Designed by former Salmson racing driver André Lombard, the Lombard was a high-quality small sports car built from 1927 to 1929. It had a 1,095cc twin-ohc 4-cylinder engine developing 45bhp, and Perrot-Piganeau 4-wheel brakes. The first Lombard made, the AL-1, won its class in the 1927 Circuit des Routes Pavées, and this was followed by the AL-2 with 'tank' body rather like

those of the contemporary Chenard-Walckers. Only one AL-1 and two AL-2s were made, but the AL-3 which could be had with a Cozette supercharger boosting power to 70bhp went into production, and a total of 94 were made. Among other successes Dhôme won the 1929 Bol d'Or and Girod, the 1932 Circuit de Picardie. Lombards ran in the Mille Miglia and took 6-hour records at Montlhéry. In 1929 André Lombard ceased to sell the cars under his own name: the BNC factory took over the stock of parts, and assembled a few cars which they sold under their own name, and with their own radiator. At least one of the 'BNCs' which ran at Le Mans was in fact a Lombard. GNG

Lorraine-Dietrich *see* De Dietrich

Lotus (GB)

The Lotus story started in 1948, when the youthful Colin Chapman modified an Austin Seven for trials use, with a distinctive copper radiator cowl of Rolls-Royce shape. The Mark 2 was a more ambitious machine, incorporating a Ford 10 engine in an Austin chassis, boxed and with added tubular bracing for rigidity. Ingenious features included lights behind the grille that moved with the steering. This car won a 16-lap scratch race at Silverstone in 1950, being later sold to Mike Lawson for use in trials. The Mark 3 was the famous 750 formula car, which caused the rules to be changed because of the performance margin gained over its rivals by the expedient of 'de-siamesing' the inlet ports.

In 1952 the Mark 4 trials car was produced for Mike Lawson, and continued the run of successes achieved by the Mark 2. The Mark 5 designation was allotted to a projected 100mph (160kph) 750 car. The Mark 6 was a multi-tubular spaceframed sports car, with coil swing-axle suspension, and the engines used included Ford Consul and 1172, BMW, and MGs of 746, 1,087, 1,250 and 1,467cc. With the latter Peter Gammon won 14 races out of 17 entered in 1954, and among the many other successful drivers was Chapman himself, who won the 1500 class at the BRDC Silverstone meeting. Mark 7 was allocated to an abandoned project (being used again later for the successor to the Mark 6) and the Mark 8 was a sports-racing model with aerodynamic body, designed by Frank Costin, clothing an elaborate spaceframe. This achieved some promising results in the 1500 class, with wins at the *Daily Express* and British GP Silverstone meetings, Castle Combe and Snetterton. From it was developed the 1955 Mark 9, with attention given to maintenance problems, and a variety of options in the engine, transmission and rear-axle specifications. This model was successful with both the Coventry-Climax 1100 and 1·5-litre MG engines, handled by Chapman, Jopp, Davis, Nurse and others, but the 'Le Mans' version did not live up to its name in that race. The slightly larger Mark 10 usually accommodated the 2-litre Bristol motor, although cars were built with Offenhauser, Connaught and Turner engines.

In 1956 the Mark 11 sports car appeared, and victories in major events were scored by Peter Ashdown, Reg Bicknell, Chapman, J. Hall, Mike Hawthorn, Mackay Fraser, B. Naylor and David Piper. When the Coventry-Climax engine was used, this was canted at 10° to the horizontal. The Bicknell and Jopp car came 4th in the Index of Performance at Le Mans and won the 1100 class at 87·97mph (141·57kph).

The following year the Fraser and Chamberlain car scored again in the 1100 class, and the 750 model of

Far left, 1954 Lotus-MG Mark 6 at Silverstone. Peter Gammon at the wheel. *Photo: Charles Dunn*

Left, 1954 Lotus-MG Mark 8 at Gosport Speed Trials. John Coombs at the wheel. *Photo: Alex Tulloch*

Far left, 1958 Lotus-Climax Mark 16 Formula 1 at Monaco. Graham Hill at the wheel. *Photo: Autosport*

Left, 1958 Lotus-Climax Mark 11 at Kirkistown. M. Templeton at the wheel. *Photo: T. L. Irwin*

Allison and Hall won the Index of Performance. Chapman and Chamberlain also took the 1100 class at Sebring. Numerous detail improvements were made to the specification of the 1957 Series II cars, but more improtant was the Mark 12 F2 model, at first with a De Dion rear end similar to that of some Mark 11s, but later with the 'Chapman strut' combined coil spring/damper unit, with lateral location of the wheel by the drive-shaft, the body again being a Costin design.

In 1957 the Elite (Mark 14) was introduced, although production did not start for another two years. Major racing successes of this frameless fibreglass coupé, with 1,216cc Coventry-Climax engine, included class victories in the 1959 Nürburgring 1,000 kilometres and the Le Mans races of 1959, 1960, 1962, 1963 and 1964. This model was also extremely successful in national GT and club racing, such cars as Graham Warner's LOV 1 being favourites on the tracks for several years.

In 1958 the Mark 15 was developed from the Mark 11, featuring strut rear suspension and 5-speed gearbox in unit with the final drive, and this car in turn was succeeded

by the Mark 17 for 1959, with further chassis development and body designed by Len Terry. Victories that year were achieved in major races at Goodwood (Chichester Cup), Circuit d'Auvergne, Aintree, Silverstone, the Roskilde Ring, Brands Hatch (Farningham Trophy) and Oulton Park (International). Development of the relatively unsuccessful Mark 12 continued to the Mark 16, with which Cliff Allison won the 1959 Silverstone International Trophy.

The Mark 18 was the first rear-engined single-seater, being used for everything from Formula 1 to Formula Junior. The chassis was a multi-tubular spaceframe in three sections. In 1960, with Coventry-Climax FPF engine, Innes Ireland won the Silverstone *Daily Express* Trophy and the Richmond Trophy at Goodwood; Stirling Moss succeeded in the Oulton Park Gold Cup and the Monaco and US Grand Prix. The Formula Junior version, with Renault gearbox and fibreglass panelling, won 18 major races, led by the works team of Jim Clark, Peter Arundell and Trevor Taylor.

In 1961 Innes Ireland with the Mark 21 took the

Far left, 1959 Lotus-Climax Mark 14 Elite at Silverstone. Sir John Whitmore at the wheel. *Photo: Autosport*

Left, 1963 Lotus-Climax Mark 25 Formula 1 in the British GP at Silverstone. Jim Clark (the winner) at the wheel. *Photo: Central Press*

1967 Lotus-Ford Mark 49 Formula 1. *Photo: Lotus Cars Ltd*

1970 Lotus-Ford Mark 72 Formula I in practice at Silverstone. Jochen Rindt at the wheel. *Photo: Trevor B. Morgan*

American GP, and Moss scored in the Monaco, German and non-championship Modena GPs. The Mark 19 or 'Monte Carlo' rear-engined sports cars, with aerodynamic fibreglass bodies, were run by the UDT-Laystall team with considerable success.

Tony Marsh showed the adaptability of the make with some fastest times of day in international hill-climbs. The current model in Formula Junior was the Mark 20, and altogether Balsiger, Boyer, Peter Arundell, Andy Hyslop, John Love, Gerhard Mitter, Peter Proctor, Alan Rees, Jim Russell, Jo Siffert and Trevor Taylor took 26 of the 45 major races.

A similar pattern emerged in 1962, when the Mark 22 scored 24 victories in Formula Junior, and Masten Gregory, Dan Gurney, Graham Hill, Innes Ireland and Vogele with the Mark 19 in sports-car racing carried off 12 out of 16 major events. Meanwhile the Mark 23 sports car had impressed on its first showing at the Nürburgring, where the Essex Racing Team car of Jim Clark led for 11 laps with a Ford Classic-based twin-ohc 1,499cc engine. The 23B was made from 1963 to 1966, with the 1,598cc

140bhp Cosworth-Ford motor as standard. The multi-tubular spaceframed Mark 24 appeared at the Brussels GP, cars being purchased subsequently by Brabham, Jo Siffert, Rob Walker and UDT-Laystall. Clark won the Lombank Trophy at Snetterton and the Aintree 200, Jack Brabham took the Roskilde Races in Denmark, and Ireland won at Crystal Palace. The Mark 25 pioneered the riveted box monocoque type of frame construction in GP cars, and created an immediate stir. This was enhanced when Jim Clark took the laurels in the Belgian, British and American GPs, helping Lotus to their third successive 2nd place in the Manufacturers' Championship. During this year the Mark 26 Elan was also introduced, and Mark 28 was allotted to the Lotus-Cortina saloon which Lotus assembled up to 1966. The Seven continued to sell well in kit form.

For 1963 the Coventry-Climax V-8 of the Mark 25 was converted to fuel injection, the resultant 200bhp contributing towards Clark's unprecedented record of 7 wins from 10 Grand Epreuves, plus another 5 non-ranking F1 races. Against this, it was of little importance

505

Left, 1968 Lotus-Pratt & Whitney Mark 56 gas turbine car. *Photo: David Phipps*

Above, 1969 Lotus-Ford Mark 61 Formula Ford making ftd at St Ursannes-les Rangiers Hill-Climb in 1970. *Photo: Autosport*

that the make's fortunes declined in Formula Junior and sports-car racing, despite the introduction of the monocoque Mark 27 in the former category. Of more consequence was the Mark 29 Indianapolis car, with 4·2-litre Ford V-8 fitted with twin-choke Webers, which Clark used to gain 2nd place.

In the interests of easier and cheaper repairs, the company reverted to a spaceframe for the Mark 31, produced for the new Formula 3 of 1964, but this was a Cooper year in the class. The Mark 32 monocoque used by the Harris team in F2, and driven by Clark and Mike Spence, won several races. Different versions of the Mark 25 F1 car were made, with new ZF gearbox, suspension and steering. Clark won the Goodwood *News of the World* Trophy, at Zandvoort and at Spa, but more frequently retired with minor maladies. Private teams continued their habit of running older cars with BRM engines and mixed fortunes. The Mark 30 4·7-litre Ford V-8 engined sports car was never very successful, and the Mark 34 Indianapolis car suffered minor misfortunes, Clark and Gurney both retiring. The Mark 33 also had some bad luck and teething troubles, and did not regain the Championship until 1965, when Clark scored 6 more victories in Grandes Epreuves. Thanks to Clark again, the firm also shone in Formula 2 with the Mark 35 monocoque, with Cosworth SCA or BRM twin-cam engine, but did not do so well in Formula 3.

Marks 36 and 37 were given to the Elan coupé and a Clubman's Seven with irs. At Indianapolis in 1965 Clark drove to victory again in the monocoque Mark 38, designed by Len Terry with 3in offset engine, backed in 2nd place to Parnelli Jones. The Mark 39 was designed for the 16-cylinder 1·5-litre Coventry-Climax engine which never became available; the Mark 40, developed from the Mark 30 for Can-Am racing, was no more successful than its predecessor.

For 1966 another spaceframe design, the Mark 41, was brought out for F3 and F2, and this model with variations was continued through 1967. In its first year it proved equal to the Brabham in Formula 3, Piers Courage, Roy Pike and Peter Revson sharing in seven major victories, and Clark and Jackie Oliver between them won five major 1967 Formula 2 races. The Mark 42 was an Indianapolis design that was shelved because of engine problems, and the Mark 43 was the GP car with the controversial H16 power unit, which surprised everyone with its victory in the United States. Mark 44 was an improved 41 used by the semi-works Ron Harris team in Formula 2, and Mark 45 an improved Elan. Although designed as a road car, the Elan was seen very frequently on the tracks, being at one time the most popular model for 'make' and GT racing, effectively

taking over the mantle of the Elite. The Mark 46 Europa, also with backbone chassis but with rear engine, appeared at the end of the year, the Group 4 competition version, with Cosworth-Ford engine, being the Mark 47. John Miles took the 1968 1600cc Special GT Championship with this model. The Mark 42F ran unsuccessfully at Indianapolis in 1967, but the Mark 48 Cosworth-FVA-engined car picked up a few victories in Formula 2. The Mark 49 F1 car designed by Maurice Phillipe won on its début at Zandvoort and on five subsequent occasions. The Elan Plus Two was the Mark 50. Lotus took an early initiative in Formula Ford with the spaceframed Mark 51.

In 1968 the Players Gold Leaf Team Lotus cars included the Mark 48 F2 model, in one of which Clark lost his life at Hockenheim. In Formula 1 Graham Hill and Jo Siffert assisted Lotus to another Championship season with the 49B, which had improved suspension. The 49T was the Tasman version with 2·5-litre engine. Marks 52 and 53 were experimental sports models, Mark 54 a refined Europa, and Mark 55 the new wedge-bodied monocoque design for F3, usually known on the tracks as the 41X. Morris Nunn's victories with a 1966 Mark 41 earned him a place in the 1969 Players Gold Leaf Team Lotus F3 team. A particularly interesting design was the Mark 56, the Indianapolis car with Pratt and Whitney turbine motor and Ferguson 4wd, which so nearly succeeded despite a practice accident in which the experienced Spence was killed. Marks 57 and 58 were a F1 design with De Dion rear end and a F2 prototype, and Mark 59 the 1969 F2/3/B car which during the next two years fully regained the Lotus's earlier reputation in these classes. Leading drivers in the subordinate formulas included Ian Ashley, Bev Bond, Emerson and Wilson Fittipaldi, James Hunt, Freddy Kottulinsky, Tetsu Ikusawa, Carlos Pace, Roy Pike, Tony Trimmer, Dave Walker and Reine Wisell.

Throughout the years the stark Seven kit-built sports car had been almost the mainstay of Clubman's racing, and the numbers of successes and unsuccessful imitators in the cheaper forms of motor sport can probably never be calculated accurately. Tim Goss won the 1970 Clubmans Championship in a 7X. Mark 60 was allotted to the Series 4 version of this model, with fibreglass bodywork. Mark 61 was the 1969 wedge FF car. With the Mark 62 Lotus turned to Vauxhall to supply a strong basic unit for the racing version of the Europa. The Mark 63 was the 4wd monocoque F1 car, with inboard suspension and brakes, with which John Miles persevered for several races. The STP-sponsored Indianapolis cars were Mark 64, still with 4wd but with 2·65-litre turbocharged Ford V-8 engines and Hewland DG300 4-speed transmission. Trouble with hubs caused withdrawal from the race.

In 1970 the Mark 69 succeeded the 59 for F2/3/B/F, and the Mark 70 was produced for F5000.

The Lotus 72 F1 car appeared in the 1970 Spanish GP, and Jochen Rindt won four consecutive races before his tragic fatal accident in practice for the Italian GP.

It has always been a feature of Lotus that they would come springing back whenever they seemed down, and Emerson Fittipaldi spearheaded their recovery on this occasion by winning the United States GP, with what was undoubtedly the quickest car racing with the Ford-sponsored Cosworth DFV engine. With the 72, Lotus won the 1970 F1 Manufacturers' Cup. This resilience has enabled the organization to maintain its position as the most successful motor-racing make of all time.

In 1971 the 72s were driven by Emerson Fittipaldi and Reine Wissell, and Fittipaldi occasionally also drove the 56B gas-turbine car. DF

Lozier (US)

The Lozier was one of the highest quality cars built in America before World War 1, and also achieved considerable renown in major racing events. To a greater extent than most of their contemporaries, the firm relied on stock chassis for these successes, and the catalogued roadster model could be had with special long-distance fuel tanks and easily demountable wings and lamps to make it ready for the race track after it had been driven there from the owner's home. The Loziers of the best period, up to the end of 1911, all had conventional T-head engines; quality and stamina rather than inspired design were the cornerstones of their success.

Lozier's first season of racing was 1907, when their drivers were Ralph Mulford, Harry Michener, L. M. Smelzer, and W. H. Linkroum. Michener won the 24-Hour Race at Point Breeze, Pa., and Loziers were 2nd in two other events. These successes were achieved with 40hp chain-driven cars, but in 1908 the company went over to shaft-drive for their new 45hp Type H, and 50hp Type 1, the latter with 6 cylinders. Mulford (with co-driver Harry Cole) won the Brighton Beach 24-Hour Race in a Type 1, with Michener and Tom Lynch in a Type H in 2nd place. The next three years saw Lozier established as the most successful American make on the circuits; apart from major victories with works drivers, there were many private owners who competed successfully in local events, encouraged by the works who would send professional drivers to give advice. Mulford won again at Brighton Beach in 1909 and led for a while in the Savannah Grand Prize in 1908. In the latter event his car was powered by a special oversize 4-cylinder engine of 735ci (12,045cc): the stock Type H was 000ci. This was the only non-standard engine used by Lozier, and the car was never raced again.

1962 Lynx Mark 3 Formula Junior. *Photo: Michael Gilmore*

1911 Lozier at Elgin. Ralph Mulford at the wheel. *Photo: Peter Helck Collection*

Lozier's best year was 1910, with victories at Elgin, Atlanta Speedway, and Santa Monica. Mulford was their star driver, and all victories from then on were achieved by the 4-cylinder car, now called the Type 46. In 1911 Mulford won the Vanderbilt Cup at Savannah ahead of two 90hp Mercedes (another Lozier was 4th), and was classified 2nd in the inaugural 500 Miles Race at Indianapolis, although there is evidence that he deserved to have been awarded 1st place. At the peak of their fame, Lozier withdrew from racing at the end of the 1911 season, saying that they had proved how durable the cars were, and that the necessity for participation in racing events no longer existed. Shortage of capital was undoubtedly the real reason. The team cars were raced for a few years afterwards by private owners. GNG

Lynx (AUS)

The first six Lynx cars, built in 1960, were basically Ralts, a type designed by Ron Tauranac before he moved to England. A relatively straightforward car incorporating independent coil front suspension and transverse leaf at the back, it was intended primarily as a sprint machine to be fitted with a Vincent motorcycle engine. Several used blown engines and some normally aspirated versions were used for road racing, one of which took the under 1,100cc lap record at Warwick Farm.

In 1961, the original chassis was redesigned to use a twin-wishbone independent coil/damper rear suspension to enable it to accept Ford, BMC and Borgward 1,100cc engines for Formula Junior racing. At the same time the fibreglass body was redesigned to take a radiator and to reduce frontal area. Nine of these cars were made.

The Mark III, which came on to the market early in 1962, was a completely new spaceframe car with front steering box and a new body which was both lower and smaller than its nearest competitor, the Lotus 20. It was the first car to be seen in Australia with low pivot, top-strut rear suspension. Eight of these FJ-type Lynx cars were sold, although some were bought as hill-climb cars with blown engines. With the exception of the body-work, the cars were all built entirely by Lynx, even down to the rack-and-pinion steering and cast wheels. The engines were also prepared by Lynx and the company always supported at least one works car of each mark. Price of a Mark III without engine was £A1,300. Production ceased in 1962 because of lack of trade sponsorship, but at least eight Lynxs were still in active competition in 1970. TBF

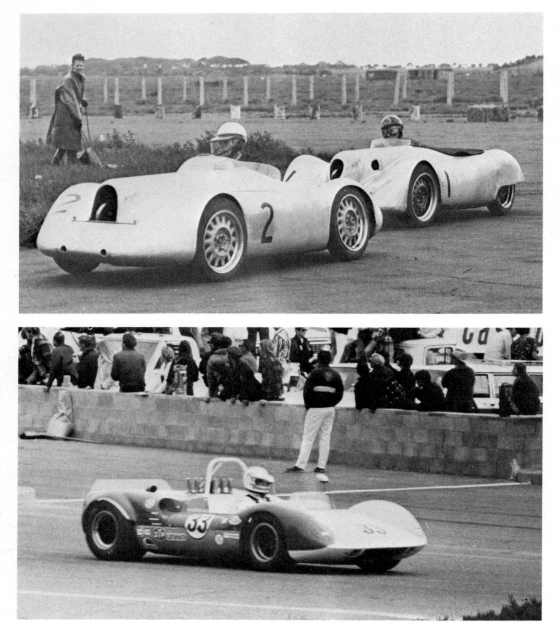

Right, 1964 McLaren-Oldsmobile M1A on its first outing at Goodwood, still using Cooper wheels. Bruce McLaren at the wheel. Photo: Geoffrey Goddard

Far right, 1967 McLaren-BRM M4B 2-litre at Oulton Park. Bruce McLaren at the wheel. Photo: Doug Nye Collection

Centre right, 1968 McLaren-Chevrolet M6B GT at Crystal Palace. David Prophet at the wheel. Photo: Autosport

Centre far right, 1968 McLaren-Ford M7A Formula 1 at Silverstone. Bruce McLaren at the wheel. Photo: Michael Cooper Ltd

Bottom right, 1970 McLaren-Chevrolet M8D in the Mid-Ohio Can-Am race. Denny Hulme, the winner, at the wheel. Photo: Autosport

Bottom far right, 1970 McLaren-Offenhauser M15 Indianapolis car. Bruce McLaren at the wheel. Photo: Autosport

McCandless (GB)
One of the most interesting designs produced under the old 500cc Formula 3 formula was the 4wd McCandless, with front-mounted engine, designed, built and raced by Rex and Cromie McCandless with Laurie McGladery in Belfast. These cars were quite successful in Ireland, but had few confrontations with the top-ranking runners in the international field. Later a sports car was also marketed, using Ford mechanical parts, but did not achieve much impact. DF

McKee (US)
After working in Chicago on drag racers and stock cars, Bob McKee served as crew chief for Dick Rathmann at Indianapolis. He made the first McKee transaxle and installed a Buick engine in Rodger Ward's Cooper chassis for his initial experience in sports cars. Usually powered by American V-8 engines, McKee cars have been raced by Ralph Salyer, 1966 winner of the Sports Car Club of America national 'C' sports racing cham-

pionship in a McKee-Oldsmobile; by Mak Kron, Augie Pabst and by Charlie Hayes, who finished 4th in the 1967 Las Vegas Can-Am driving a McKee-Olds. McKee's works are at Palatine, Ill. ARB

Mackson (GB)
This Formula 3 design was similar in layout to the Kieft, with swing-axle rear suspension, and a team of cars was constructed in 1952 for G. Shillito, B. Gill and designer Gordon Bedson. Other drivers during the following two years included Ian Burgess, G. Baird, J. Lockett, B. A. Manning, M. G. Thomas and Ken Wharton, but no noteworthy success was recorded by the Guildford-built cars. DF

McLaren; McLaren-Elva (GB)
The ancestor of the McLaren cars was the Cooper-Zerex special raced in the United States by Roger Penske with a Coventry-Climax engine. Bruce McLaren purchased this in 1964, installed an Oldsmobile motor, and used it

Top, 1951 McCandless 500s at Kirkistown in 1955. Drivers are Laurie McGladery (No 2) and Rex McCandless (No 1) Photo: W. A. C. McCandless

Above, c 1966 McFee Mark 6B at the 1970 Laguna Seca Can-Am. Chuck Frederick at the wheel. Photo: Al Bochroch

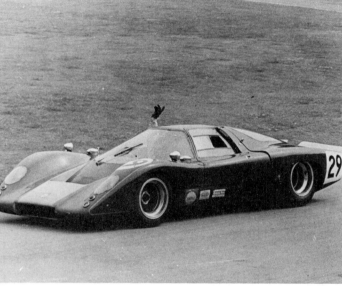

to win races at Mosport and at Brands Hatch. Using the experience thus gained, the first McLaren sports-racing car was also fitted with a Traco-modified Oldsmobile engine. An agreement was concluded with the Lambretta-Trojan group, who had earlier taken over manufacturing rights of the Elva Courier, whereby they would make and sell about two dozen annually of the successful Group 7 models, while manufacture of the team cars, and design and experimental work, were carried out in McLaren's own workshops at Slough. In addition, some F2 and F3 models were made, featuring a Mallite aluminium/wood sandwich construction, but these were soon dropped.

In 1965 McLaren had an encouraging season with the new cars, winning at Silverstone and Nassau and obtaining other good placings. Private owners, including John Coundley and L. Heimrath, also achieved some good results.

After the 1965 season McLaren left the Cooper Formula 1 team, and built cars for this category also. Three different engines were tried — the Serenissima (or ATS) V-8, and two versions of the Ford V-8 4·2-litre, lowered to 3 litres by reductions in bore and stroke. The highest placing was a 2nd at Rouen. However, the McLaren Mark 2, with Chevrolet engine and McLaren at the wheel, won three of the season's Group 7 races, and further points in the Can-Am series were gained by Mk 1B cars driven by Chris Amon, Chuck Parsons, John Cannon, Peter Revson, Lothar Motschenbacher and Masten Gregory.

For 1967 a new Formula 1 model was introduced, with 2-litre V-8 (M4B) or 3-litre V-12 (M5A) BRM engine, being based on a 1966 F2 model. These models were plagued with petty troubles, and McLaren could only muster one 4th place to show for the season. The picture was very different in Group 7, where a number of Mark 3s were sold, and McLaren became Can-Am Champion with victories in the Monterey and Times GPs, and two 2nds, with the M6A car. Runner-up Denny Hulme had three victories to his credit — at Elkhart Lake, Bridge-hampton and Mosport. The specification of this car embraced a monocoque chassis designed by Robin Herd, fibreglass body by Specialised Mouldings, and a fuel-injected 5·8-litre Chevrolet engine transmitting over 500bhp through a Hewland LG600 gearbox.

In 1968 the neater M7A 'bath-tub' monocoque was raced in Formula 1, with Cosworth-Ford DFV V-8 engine developing 400bhp at 9,000rpm. This enabled McLaren to win on the car's début at the Race of the Champions at Brands Hatch, and in the Belgian GP; Hulme scored in the Italian and Canadian GPs. The 'customer car' built by Trojans that year for Group 7 was the M6B which, with the works M8A models of McLaren and Hulme, enabled the make to clear all seven races in the season's Can-Am series, other wins being by Mark Donohue, Cannon and Revson. Piers Courage had a good run in the Tasman Series with an M4A Formula 2 car.

In common with several other British Formula 1 constructors, McLaren experimented with a 4wd car in 1969. This, the M9A, was a stubby monocoque design with drive-shaft running to the driver's left, and large side monocoque sections carrying the fuel tanks. The design was dropped when the conventional M7C proved to be consistently quicker, and Hulme won the Mexican GP late in the year with this model.

Both the M7C and the M10A Formula 5000 car were developed by Jo Marquandt from Herd's original monocoque design. Peter Gethin, with the latter model,

won the British 'Guards' Championship for the year, and Sam Posey in the United States finished well up in the Formula A Championship. The 'for sale' Group 7 vehicle was the M12, based on the M6B and M8A body-work and suspension. The works M8Bs continued their fantastic run of successes, McLaren taking six Can-Am wins and Hulme the remaining five.

The staple 1970 Formula 1 car was the M14A, but there were several variations, including models with Alfa Romeo engines as an alternative to the Cosworth V-8. The M10B, at £4,850 without engine, was raced by many of the leading F5000 contenders, including Gethin (who took the Championship again), David Prophet, Reine Wisell, Howden Ganley and Graham McRae in Britain. The model was found to be suitable also for hill-climbing, and was favoured by several of the leading British contenders in this field, including David Good, Sir Nicholas Williamson and Martin Brain. Development of the Group 7 cars progressed from M8C through M8D to the lightweight M8E, but it was the M8D that was usually raced, and in one of which Bruce McLaren lost his life in a tragic testing accident at Goodwood. Hulme,

Below, 1969 McNally Formula 4. *Photo: Gordon McNally*

Bottom, 1968 McNamara Sebring Formula Vee. *Photo: G. N. Georgano*

Gethin and Dan Gurney between them won the first six races in the Can-Am series, but the make's unprecedented run came to an end at the Road Atlanta race, having gained 26 consecutive victories since the first event in the 1968 series. For the Indianapolis 500 the M15A was produced to a design by Roy Coppuck, and raced by Revson and C. Williams. This design was based on the Can-Am cars, with the monocoque ending behind the cockpit, and the 2·8-litre turbocharged Offenhauser engine forming a stressed member.

Despite the loss of McLaren, plans went ahead for the orange-coloured cars to continue on the circuits in 1971. The M8E Group 7 car was largely unchanged, as was the M18 Formula A/5000. For USAC Championship races the M16 with side radiators succeeded the M15A, while McLaren's F1 car was the Ralph Bellamy-designed M19 with frontal radiator and inboard suspension. DF

McNally (GB)
Gordon McNally had designed a V-12 BRM-engined Formula 1 car for Bob Anderson in 1966, so it was armed with good experience that he embarked in 1969 at Gateshead-on-Tyne on production of his neat Formula 4 car, with honeycomb monocoque and cast alloy bulkheads. However, the hoped-for success did not attend the venture. DF

McNamara (D)
Francis McNamara began racing Formula Vees as a US serviceman in Germany, and later established his own company at Lengreiss on the Rhine. A number of his Formula Vee models proved extremely successful, and in 1969 a Dan Hawkes original spaceframe design was tidied up by Austrian Jo Karasek to produce an F3 car. Two were run for ex-F Vee stars Werner Reidl and Helmut Marko, with Peter Arundell as team manager, but success at first eluded them. Karasek was an ex-Lola designer and his F3 McNamara Sebring Mk 3 was an attractive and well-built machine. But at the start of 1970 Andy Granatelli's STP Corporation chose McNamara to build Andretti's Indianapolis contender for that year and they set to work on their first monocoque design: a clean and workmanlike machine with the compact, chunky look so typical of this American-German make.

1970 McNamara-STP Indianapolis car. Mario Andretti at the wheel. *Photo: Al Bochroch*

The cars were not very successful. Later in the year McNamara modified STP's March F1 car for Andretti, but it was written-off in Austria. DCN

Macon (GB)

Macon Race Cars' production Formula Ford models started with the MR6 in 1967. The first MR7 was a Formula B car, but later versions, and the subsequent MR8, were improved Formula Ford machines. The larger part of production was exported, but successes were achieved in Britain in the hands of Sid Fox and others. Price of the MR8, complete with full-race engine, was £1,375. The 1971 programme included the Formula Ford MR8B, the Super Vee MR9 and Formula Atlantic MR10. DF

Major (F)

The Major was a descendant of Marcel Violet's 1913 Violet-Bogey and retained the pre-war chassis with friction and chain drive. The engine was now a 1,058cc 2-stroke with crankcase compression, and its designer drove it to victory in the 1920 Grand Prix des Cyclecars at Le Mans, averaging 44·1mph (70·97kph), though he was less lucky in the 1,500cc event on the following day, retiring through loss of water. The cars were rallied and raced in 1921, 1922 and 1923, but changed their name once more, appearing as Mourres and Welers. The former seems to have been identical to the Major, but the Weler, although using the same engine, had a conventional gearbox and shaft drive. In the 1921 GP des Cyclecars, Violet was 2nd on a Mourre, and Sabipa 4th on a Weler. MCS

Mallock U2 (GB)

Constant features of the U2 cars since manufacture began in 1958 have been their easy adaptability to the various formulae in vogue, and their straightforward, cost-saving, front-engined design. Most early cars were built for Formula 1172, and up to the end of 1963 some 18 kits had been sold. The Mark 2 utilized a leaf-sprung BMC rear axle, and a modified Ford swing-axle front assembly, but from the Mark 3 onwards rear coil springs were used, and a cross-over front suspension linkage. From the Mark 8 of 1968 a wishbone type front suspension was adopted.

Very few road cars were sold (the Mark 6R of 1967 and the 1970 Mark 10 being examples), and most models were quasi-two-seaters which qualified for the sports classes (Formula 1172, 1200 and Clubman's) while still being competitive in the single-seater Formula Junior,

2, 3 and Ford. Only since the introduction of the Mark 7 Formula Ford car in 1968 have true single-seaters also been made. Engines have included most versions of the BMC 'A' range and all Fords up to the 1,600cc twin-cam.

Designer-constructor Arthur Mallock, with his colleague John Harwood, achieved a remarkable list of successes, including several championships, and from 1968 onwards the standard was ably maintained by Arthur's sons Richard and Raymond. Other drivers of particular note include Andy Diamond (1969 1,000cc Clubman's Champion), David Darby (19 victories in 1966), Geoff Bremner (1969 F1200 Champion), Peter Gaydon, Jeremy Lord (1968 Clubman's Champion and 1969, 1,600 class Clubman's Champion), Ken Miller, Max Mosley, Malcolm Smith and David Wragg (1965 Clubman's Champion).

The 1970 range included the Mark 8B Clubman's or dual-purpose racer, the Mark 10 full-width 2-seater, and the Mark 9, the only production front-engined Formula Ford, ready to race and competitive in every sense at £970. DF

March (GB)

Late in 1969 March burst on the motor racing scene, when Max Mosley, Alan Rees, Graham Coaker and

Left, 1970 Mallock U2 Mark 8B Clubman's racing car. Photo: Autosport

Above, 1970 Mallock U2 Mark 9 Formula Ford. Photo: Arthur Mallock

Left, 1970 March 701 Formula 1. Jackie Stewart at the wheel. Photo: Autosport

Below left, 1970 March 707 Group 7 at Croft. Helmut Kelleners at the wheel. Photo: Motor

Below, 1970 Macon R8 Formula Ford. Photo: Macon Racing Cars Ltd

designer Robin Herd, assisted by outside sponsorship, opened their factory at Bicester, Oxfordshire. The 1969 prototype car was a Formula 3 machine (Model 693), but the ambitious 1970 programme was spearheaded by the 701 design for Formula 1. Following proven principles in the interests of quick manufacture and development, this car had a monocoque body/chassis unit, with Cosworth-Ford DFV 90 V-8 engine and Hewland DJ 300 5-speed gearbox hung on the rear bulkhead. The first March victory came with Jackie Stewart's win in the Tyrrell car in the Race of Champions at Brands Hatch, and he also won the Spanish GP on 19 April 1970. Fortunes drooped in the later half of the season mainly because of weight and handling problems, despite the cars being driven also by Chris Amon, Mario Andretti, François Cevert, Ronnie Peterson, Johnny Servoz-Gavin and Jo Siffert.

Xavier Perrot achieved a surprise Formula 2 victory at the Nürburgring in August 1970, and the first 'Can-Am' car, the 707 driven by Kelleners, won a minor race on its debut. Larger than most Can-Am cars, the 707 had a 96in wheelbase, 68in front track and 62in rear track. It was powered by a 7·6-litre Chevrolet engine. Tom Walkinshaw and others achieved a few good placings in Formula 3, and in Formula Ford Ian Taylor had a successful run with the 708. March had a disappointing first season in 1970, failing to develop a consistent winner in any class, despite great publicity and early promise. Nevertheless, the range of success achieved in such a short space of time was almost without precedent in motor racing history.

Their Formula 1 car for 1971 was the 711 with Frank Costin-designed low-drag body, and side radiators. Engines were either Cosworth-Ford DFV or Alfa Romeo, and the STP-sponsored works cars were run under the name STP Oil Treatment. March also made cars for Formula 2, 3, B, Atlantic and Ford. DF

Marcos (GB)

This make derives its name from Jem Marsh and Frank Costin. The early Marcos was renowned chiefly for its plywood chassis unit, built on principles proven with the de Havilland Mosquito aircraft during World War 2.

Above, 1925 Marguerite Model BO in the Bol d'Or. *Photo: T. A. S. O. Mathieson Collection*

Right, 1913 Marlborough in the Cyclecar GP at Amiens. Sir Francis Samuelson at the wheel, with his wife as mechanic. *Photo: T. A. S. O. Mathieson Collection*

1960 Marcos 1172cc coupé at Silverstone. Jem Marsh at the wheel. *Photo: Michael Ware*

Marsh and Bill Moss proved the prototypes in races during 1959 and 1960, and examples of the 'gull-wing' model driven by John Sutton and Steve Minoprio won a number of British GT races in 1961 and 1962.

In 1963 the firm moved from Luton to Bradford-on-Avon, Wiltshire, enrolling Dennis Adams to design more attractive fibreglass bodies, the line reaching its apogee with the impressive Mantis GT saloon. From this time the make's importance in competition declined, although a Mini-Marcos, with fibreglass monocoque body and BMC Mini mechanical parts, was the only British car to finish at Le Mans in 1966, and a special discount was offered in 1970 to those purchasing the larger GT coupé for competition use. These elegant cars, available with a variety of Ford or Volvo engines, had by this time abandoned the marine-ply chassis construction in the interests of cost-saving. DF

Marguerite (F)

A. Marguerite of Courbevoie made a number of interesting sports cars, and was unusual in that he sold many cars to other firms who marketed them under their own name. These included Induco, Madou, and MS in France, and Hisparco in Spain. The Type A Marguerite appeared in 1922; it was a cyclecar powered by a 995cc Train V-twin engine, and two ran in the first Bol d'Or. The first proper sports Marguerite was the Type BO of 1925; this had a 1,095cc Chapuis-Dornier ohv engine as fitted to the BO 5 tourer, but a lowered chassis which could be supplied with road-going sports or racing body. One of these finished 3rd in the 1926 Bol d'Or. Some BOs had the 12-valve Chapuis-Dornier engine, giving a speed of 85mph (136kph). The 1927 Type BO 2 was similar to the BO but had a twin-carburettor engine giving 88mph (141kph), or the SCAP T-11, with which over 90mph (144kph) was possible. Thirty BO 2s were made, of which five were called Morano-Marguerites, because at this time the bulk of the company's finance came from one Zamorano de Biedema. In 1928 he lost all his fortune at the Deauville Casino, and the company had to close.

The cars continued to be raced in the Bol d'Or and similar events for several years. Raymond Sommer began his career with a Morano-Marguerite in the Bol d'Or; author Roger Labric also drove one. GNG

Marlborough; Marlborough-Thomas (F; GB)

Sir Francis Samuelson drove one of the pre-war 1,100cc 4-cylinder versions in the 1913 Cyclecar GP at Amiens, his wife acting as his mechanic. Unfortunately he retired,

and the make was next seen in a major race in 1921, when the company nominated three cars for the Brooklands 200 Mile Race: a 1,400cc machine for Harris; a 1·5-litre for Martin; and an interesting 1,100cc rotary-valve machine for T. B. André, which did not start in the race. The other two finished without distinction, but the 1923 race saw something far more interesting, the 1·5-litre Marlborough-Thomas, which mechanically was really a scaled-down version of Parry Thomas's Leyland 8, down to the 8-valve ohc engine and torsion-bar suspension. It had already been tried at Brooklands with a 1·9-litre unit of similar design, but the smaller units were not ready, and neither Thomas nor Duller achieved anything. The car appeared as a catalogued sports model at that year's Olympia Show. The last Marlborough to appear at Brooklands was André's 'Submarine', entered in 1924, which used a 1·5-litre sv Anzani engine in a narrow chassis with single-seater bodywork. MCS

Marmon (US)

As early as 1906 one of Howard Marmon's ingenious air-cooled V-4s came through the Glidden Tour without loss of marks, and in 1908 this performance was repeated by the firm's first water-cooled model, the 40/50hp T-head 4-cylinder Model H. These cars also did well in several sealed-bonnet trials, but serious racing started in 1909 with Model 32, a 318ci (5·2-litre) development of the Model H. Officially the make's first race was a 10-mile free-for-all at Indianapolis Speedway, which Ray Harroun won, but the cars went on to score ten 1st places in the 20 events they supported. Even better was 1910: 93 races, twenty-five 1sts, twenty-four 2nds, and thirteen 3rds. The victories included the Cobe, Wheeler-Schebler and Remy Trophies at Indianapolis, four at Los Angeles, and single ones at Atlanta, Elgin and Savannah, though the Harroun and Dawson combination could manage no better than 6th in the Grand Prize. For that year's Vanderbilt Cup Harroun entered a new 6-cylinder car based on the 32, but a broken crankshaft put him out. Dawson in the 4-cylinder was unlucky to finish 2nd at 65·08mph (104·74kph); he would have won had he not stopped to report hitting a spectator on the course. The six was out again for the first Indianapolis 500 Miles Race in 1911: exceptionally for its time it ran with single-seater bodywork and no riding mechanic, Harroun fitting a rear-view mirror, the first of its kind. Appropriately the Marmon won on its home ground at 74·61mph (120·08kph), Dawson taking 5th place. A few sports developments of this Wasp were made, but Marmon never followed up their success, though Ball's 6-cylinder car managed a good 2nd place behind Pullen's

1923 Marlborough-Thomas at Brooklands. Parry Thomas at the wheel. *Photo: Autocar*

1908 Martini Coupe des Voiturettes car. Beck at the wheel. *Photo: Ferdinand Hediger Collection*

Mercer in the 1914 Grand Prize at Santa Monica, Calif.

As late as 1916 Jackson was running a Marmon in the bigger American races, though that year Howard Marmon launched the big 74bhp aluminium-alloy 6-cylinder 34 with a successful attack on the transcontinental record. In 1920 a similar car in full road trim did a standing lap of Indianapolis at 63·2mph (101·71kph) to prove that stock tourers were good for mile-a-minute speeds. The fwd Marmons that ran at Indianapolis in 1928 were merely Millers wearing their sponsors' colours. Production of all Marmons ceased in 1933. MCS

Martin (GB)

Ray Martin, who had been associated with the Kieft Formula 3 design, made several similar cars on his own account between 1954 and 1956. These employed swing-axle rear suspension with rubber in torsion, and were generally fitted with Norton engines. C. D. Headland scored several wins, but the weight of the Cooper opposition and the declining interest in the formula militated against further development.

The Martin Formula 3 cars were not connected with the projects of Ted Martin of Haddenham, Buckinghamshire, whose Formula 1 aspirations went up in smoke at Silverstone in 1967 with the loss of the Pearce Racing Organization's team of three cars equipped with his light alloy V-8 engines.

Meanwhile the unrelated Brian Martin from Dagenham, Essex, had started building some one-off sports cars, leading to the 1969 BM6 GT coupé, with 2 litre BMW engine, with which he won 9 races in the season, and the 1970 BM7 open version which earned no less than 14 victories. DF

Martini (CH)

The first sporting achievement of this well-known Swiss make was an unusual endurance test, the ascent of the rack railway from Montreux to Rochers de Naye in 1903. Captain H. H. P. Deasy drove a 16hp car (which was in fact a licence-built Rochet-Schneider) up the track, which included gradients of up to 1 in 4. By 1907 Martinis were of indigenous design, though still thoroughly conventional. Two racing cars with large 7·5-litre 4-cylinder engines and chain drive ran in the 1907 Kaiserpreis. Beutler finished 12th, and Beck 15th. As they were the only Swiss cars entered, Switzerland could claim that 100% of their cars finished, beating the record of any other country. In the 1908 voiturette races

Martini entered three cars with 4-cylinder 1,086cc single-ohc engines; in the Coupes des Voiturettes they finished 7th, 8th and 10th, and won the team prize. Up to 1914 Martini had a number of successes in sprints and hill-climbs, including the Coupe Monod, when a 12/16hp five-seater tourer was 3rd in general classification; the Coupe de la Gruyère; and Gaillon. Post-World War 1 Martinis were not especially sporting, but as late as 1927 one ran in the Klausen hill-climb. GNG

Martini (F)

Tico Martini, of Channel Islands origin, surprised hill-climbing circles in 1963 when he ran his Martini kart at several of the RAC Championship climbs and set a number of ftd records. A minimum wheelbase regulation was introduced to maintain big car appeal and, in more recent years he moved to France and settled at Magny-Cours with the Winfield Racing Drivers' School, and there has produced a number of Formula France and Formula 3 cars. These have been Brabham-like space-frame cars using differing suspension geometry, and have shown quite well in the hands of Lafitte, Mieusset and Salomon in 1969 and 1970. DCN

Marwyn (GB)

The Bournemouth-built Marwyn 500 of 1947 was intended to compete with the contemporary Cooper, but a high centre of gravity and inadequate engine cooling limited the cars' major successes to the shorter sprint type of events. Many of the cars sold were subsequently extensively modified and renamed, these including the Marott, MHW and SMS. The longer, lower 1949 car with improved suspension, with body by Gray of Emsworth, and produced by a reorganized company in Wareham, Dorset, was no more successful. DF

Maserati (I)

The make Maserati—Officine Alfieri Maserati—had a long and honourable sporting history, which apart from World War 2 was unbroken over three decades. In effect it grew out of the company—to all intents and purposes a tuning shop—which three of the Maserati brothers (see page 254), Alfieri, Bindo and Ernesto, built up in Bologna. During the early 1920s Alfieri had demonstrated the competition potential in Diattos, and that company entrusted the brothers with tuning and then the construction of a 2-litre straight-8 Diatto GP engine. When Diatto withdrew from racing in 1926, the brothers took over this design.

A 1·5-litre (1,491cc) version of the eight was the basis of the first Maserati, Tipo 26. Alfieri drove this to 9th place overall, 1st in class, in the 1927 Targa Florio, and two were run in the Italian GP that year, both retiring. As Maseratis surprisingly quickly became popular with private owners, the 2-litre 26B followed, and then the 8C-1500 replacement for the 26. But failure was the most common lot of Maserati drivers in 1927-8.

New cars at different ends of the scale in 1929 were the 8C-1100 (supercharged twin-ohc 1,078cc eight), and, as it was not feasible to enlarge the original eight, the *Sedici Cilindri*. The 16-cylinder engine of this V-4 was made up of two straight-8s mated on a common crankcase. It had 3,958cc and approximately 300bhp at 5,200rpm. This engine performed well, but the V-4 suffered the roadholding weaknesses common to all early Maseratis. Apart from an international class record, its 1929 performance was poor, but in 1930 Borzacchini won the Tripoli GP at 91·05mph (146·53kph).

Above, 1947 Marwyn 500 at Shelsley Walsh in 1949. Lord Strathcarron at the wheel. *Photo: Temple Press*

Above right, 1926 Maserati Tipo 26 in the 1927 Targa Florio. Alfieri Maserati at the wheel. *Photo: Cyril Posthumus Collection*

1929 Maserati Tipo V4 16-cylinder car. Borzacchini at the wheel. *Photo: Cyril Posthumus Collection*

In that year Maserati achieved a full works team equipped with the 8C-2500 successor to the 26B. The 2,495cc supercharged eight was in many respects a new design, and gave 175bhp at 6,000rpm; the car was utterly conventional, outwardly with the now firmly-established Maserati characteristics: notably a sloping radiator and rather slabby sides. In 1930 GP racing it was very successful, victories including the Coppa Ciano (Fagioli), Rome GP (Arcangeli), Monza and Spanish GPs (Varzi). It continued to be raced into 1931—and later in private hands—when at Monza its 8C-2800 (2,795cc, 198bhp at 6,000rpm) successor made its début, Fagioli winning his GP heat and the final.

Meanwhile, the first Maserati four, the 4C-1100, had appeared. Only modestly successful it was replaced by the 4C TR-1100 in 1932. This model was also popular with private owners, and like most Maseratis of the period was raced open-wheeled or in sports trim. A new version of the 16-cylinder car, the V-5 (4,905cc, 330bhp at 5,200rpm), came in 1932, Fagioli winning the Rome and Monza GPs with it, and Ernesto Maserati finishing 2nd in the Italian GP. At the end of the year Ruggeri was killed in it when he crashed during a record attempt at Montlhéry. The V-5 last raced at Tripoli in 1934, when Taruffi crashed while leading the GP.

In an attempt to recover their 1931 position, Maserati introduced the 8C-3000 and 8CM-3000 in 1933, using a 2,992cc straight-8 engine in their near-standard chassis with usual running gear, although with hydraulic brakes. In 1933 Campari won the French GP for the brothers, and when Nuvolari turned from Alfa Romeo to Maserati

Above, 1930 Maserati Tipo 8C after winning San Sebastian GP. Varzi at the wheel. *Photo: Fotocar*

Above top right, 1934 Maserati Tipo 8CM in Dieppe GP. Etancelin at the wheel. *Photo: David Hodges Collection*

Above right, 1938 Maserati Tipo 8CTF at Donington Park. Luigi Villoresi at the wheel. *Photo: Motor*

Below, 1934 Maserati Tipo 8CM on the Campbell Road Circuit at Brooklands, c 1936. Bira at the wheel has just passed Lord Howe's ERA. *Photo: Montagu Motor Museum*

Right, 1938 Maserati Tipo 6CM after winning the 1945 Coupe des Prisonniers in the Bois de Boulogne, the first post-war motor race in Europe. Henri Louveau at the wheel. *Photo: Planet News*

he won the Belgian GP, Coppa Ciano and Nice GP. German cars and rejuvenated Alfas relegated effective Maserati contention to second-rank events in 1934 and the following years (the 8Cs raced on successfully in such backwaters as British racing until the war). A half-hearted attempt to make the basic car competitive in 1935, with ifs and 3·2-litre engine, predictably achieved little.

During this year Maserati followed the Alfa lead in entrusting their 'works' team to an independent organization, Scuderia Subalpina, with the eight and a developed version of the Type 34 six. In 1934 this had a 3,325cc 260bhp engine, in what was basically the 8C chassis. Nuvolari won two lesser events with it in this form. For 1935 the engine was enlarged to 3,729cc; odd flashes of promise, notably in the Mille Miglia and Monaco GP, were the sum of this car's achievements. Another 1935 essay, the 4,785cc 320bhp V-8 engined V8RI, was no more successful, although it was interesting as the first Maserati to have all-round independent suspension. In 1936 Etancelin gained this model's only victory, in the poorly-supported Pau GP.

The last pre-war GP Maserati, the 8CTF, had a similar European career, on occasion having the speed to lead the German cars, although not the stamina to do so for long. But at Indianapolis it was a very different proposition, and outstandingly successful as the Boyle

Special driven by Shaw. Very much in the direct Maserati line, it had a straightforward welded box-section chassis, ifs and live rear axle, and a 2,990cc twin-ohc straight-8, in effect a 'doubled' 4CL engine, initially giving about 355bhp. Shaw won the 500 Miles in 1939 and 1940, and Horn placed the car 3rd in 1946 and 1947. The first 8CL (2,980cc, 420bhp) derivative was built in 1940; after the war three were raced in Europe and at Indianapolis, without the success of the 8CTF.

Meanwhile in lesser European events, where although the competition was stiff no one manufacturer had the advantage of large resources, Maseratis were more successful. In place of the 4- and 8-cylinder voiturettes, the 6CM was introduced in 1936. In appearance, chassis and basic make-up of engine (a twin-ohc 1,493cc unit initially giving 155bhp at 6,200rpm), this followed in train from the contemporary eights. In 1936–8 it was more or less competitive with the ERAs, and numerically swamped Italian events. In 1938 the Alfa Romeo 158 set new standards, and Maserati returned to four cylinders in an attempt to match these.

The 1938 4CM used the 6CM chassis, with 1,088cc and 1,496cc twin-ohc engines. In performance the larger of these marginally improved on the 6CM, but was still not a match for the Alfetta. This was hoped of the 1939 4CL, but the 220bhp produced by its 1,489cc square (78 × 78mm) engine, which save in the use of four valves per cylinder was a 4-cylinder version of the 8CTF unit, was still not adequate, so that it won only when the Alfettas were not present.

In 1941 Maserati moved from the city of their trident emblem, Bologna, to Modena; in 1947 the surviving brothers, Bindo, Ernesto and Ettore, sold the company to Orsi and returned to Bologna to set up Osca. The 4CLs reappeared on the circuits in 1946, when the semi-works Scuderia Milano cars gained several victories. A 2-stage supercharged version of the engine kept the car competitive in 1947, when it won eight leading secondary races (drivers Villoresi, 'Bira', Kautz, Pagani and Parnell).

The 4CLT/48, popularly the 'San Remo' after its first-time-out victory in the hands of Ascari, came in 1948. Chassis and suspension were revised from the outset, but the engine was only gradually modified during the rest of its life. In 1948 it was producing 260bhp at 7,000rpm. However, in the works-representative Scuderia Ambrosiana or in private hands, it was still no match for the Alfa Romeo. The next year began better — and Fangio started his F1 career in a 4CLT/48 at Albi — but the challenge from Ferrari gained strength. Worthwhile Maserati victories during the season came in the San Remo, Pau and Albi GPs (Fangio) and in the British GP (de Graffenried). In 1950-1 the cars were increasingly outclassed. An attempt by the independent Scuderia Milano to face-lift the basic car as the Maserati-Milan, or simply Milan, primarily with revamped 305bhp engine, larger brakes and eventually De Dion rear suspension, achieved little. Other 'spin-offs' were cars with 1,720cc engines prepared for the 1949-50 South American series, the Maserati-Plate, devised to meet the 2-litre F2 regulations with ifs, lightened, shortened chassis and 1,980cc engine, and the use of an A6G engine in the chassis. None justified the effort put into them.

Under Orsi, true Maserati sports cars, as distinct from adapted single-seaters, appeared. The first of these, the A6G, had been initiated by the brothers, and appeared in 1947. A 2-litre car, it was seldom raced, and outclassed by equivalent Ferraris. Out of it however came the A6GCM F2 car, a Grand Prix car in 1952-3, with 1,988cc engine substantially reworked by Colombo (to give 165bhp in the 1952 A6GCM, up to 190bhp in the 1953 A6SSG). This formula was Ferrari-dominated, but the Maseratis consistently improved and won their last *grande épreuve*, the 1953 Italian GP (Fangio). A version of this engine was the basis of the A6GCS sports car, and was further detuned in a genuine touring model. The competition A6GCS was very successful in the 2-litre classes of international events in 1953-5 (in 1954 Musso drove one to 3rd place overall in the Mille Miglia).

For the 2·5-litre Formula, Colombo designed the outstanding Grand Prix Maserati, the 250F. This was an unsophisticated and workmanlike machine: tubular spaceframe, coil-spring/wishbone ifs, De Dion rear suspension, 5-speed gearbox in unit with final drive, 2,493cc (84 × 72mm) straight-6 engine, and perhaps the most satisfying body lines of all latter-day front-engined cars. Altogether, 32 were built for the works team and private owners, who were well served by the car. In 1954 Fangio won the Argentine and Belgian GPs with 250Fs, then joined Mercedes, to be challenged on occasion by Moss in a 250F. In the front line in 1955 the cars were out run, but very successful in secondary F1 racing. That the 250F was not supreme in 1956 was probably due to Fangio in the Ferrari team, but Moss won the Monaco GP for Maserati and finished runner-up to Fangio in the Championship, while private owners had another good season (no less than 12 250Fs appeared on the same grid for one race). Fangio joined Maserati in 1957, and took the Championship with the 250F, winning the Argentine, Monaco, French and German GPs.

A V-12 Maserati GP engine, 68·5 × 56mm and 2,449cc, appeared spasmodically and noisily in 1957, in 250F chassis. This showed promise, but the varied follies of sports car racing had cost Maserati dear, and the company was forced to withdraw almost completely from racing. A lightweight 250F (250F3) was built for 1958, and driven by Fangio in his last race, the French GP. The Scuderia Centro-Sud raced 250Fs in the Grands Prix, as did several private owners, but effectively the car faded. Plans for a lighter, smaller successor had been prepared, and these were translated into metal in the Tec Mec, which ran in one 2·5-litre Formula race: a decade later its performance in Historic Car Races showed that if developed when planned it might have been effective in the twilight season of front-engined cars.

In 1958 a 250F 'special' with a 4·2-litre engine was sponsored by Eldorado Ice Cream for the Monza Indianapolis regulations race (Race of Two Worlds). Driven by Moss, it crashed. The name Maserati did not altogether disappear from single-seater racing with the 250F: Centro-Sud in particular persevered with the engine in Cooper chassis until the end of the Formula; a V-12 engine was built for the 1·5-litre Formula, but not a chassis for it; the abortive Emeryson used the 150S 4-cylinder unit; in 1966 the older V-12 was revived in 3 litre form, in cumbersome combination with a Cooper chassis for the opening years of the 3-litre Formula.

Sports cars were the downfall of Maserati in racing, and almost as a company. Yet in the mid-1950s all seemed promising, as the company entered this field

Below, 1950 Maserati Tipo 4CLT/48 at Zandvoort. Varzi at the wheel. *Photo: Motor*

Centre, 1953 Maserati Tipo A6SSG at Zandvoort. Gonzalez at the wheel. *Photo: Autosport*

Right, 1953 Maserati Tipo A6GCS 2000. Roy Salvadori at the wheel. *Photo: Marcus W. Taylor*

seriously with the 150S, 200S and 300S. Fairly closely based on the 250F, the 300S was a handsome machine in the contemporary vogue, with a 2,991cc (approximately 250bhp) version of the 'pure' racing engine. This generally trailed Mercedes in 1955 Championship races. Behra gained a first victory in the Portugese GP, and after the Mercedes withdrawal Fangio drove one to win the Venezuelan GP, otherwise good placings were the lot of the 300S in 1955. In 1956, however, it won the Buenos Aires, Nürburgring and Paris 1,000 kilometre races, as well as minor events. Variants appeared, notably and unsuccessfully a 3·5-litre version in 1956, while the basic 300S served on into 1957, reliably backing up the later cars in the team.

The parallel smaller cars were fours, with engines based on the 250F unit. The 1,484cc 150S appeared late in 1955, and was similar in constructional respects to the 300S; in general it was no match for Porsches, except in its first race, the Nürburgring 500 kilometres, won by Behra. The 200S, with bored-out 1,994cc engine and modified body, had to face the competition of smaller Ferraris, and was therefore even less successful.

The 450S was potent, promising—and financially ruinous. It was built around a 4,478cc twin-ohc 90° V-8, which developed some 420bhp at 6,800rpm. A tubular chassis was used, with coil-spring/wishbone ifs and a De Dion rear end. The car was fast, but few other components seemed to equal the engine in reliability; although it won the Sebring 12 Hours (Fangio and Behra) and the Swedish GP (Moss and Behra), between these races there were numerous and varied failures, most notoriously perhaps that of the ill-executed Costin coupé at Le Mans. The works team started three cars in the Venezuelan GP, where all were damaged or destroyed. This was a heavy financial blow to the relatively small company, which

then in effect had to write off the whole investment in these large cars, at least from the sporting point of view, as new regulations imposed a 3-litre limit. Almost inevitably, and certainly realistically, Maserati withdrew from racing.

However, production of sports-racing cars for private owners was for a while continued, primarily with the 'bird cage' cars: their nickname derived from the chassis of multitudinous small-diameter tubes. First came the Type 60, a 2-litre car using a developed 150S engine canted in front of the driver, which made its racing début at Rouen in 1959, Moss gaining a first-time-out victory. The Type 61 with a 2,888cc engine followed; three of these were run in Championship events by Casner's Camoradi Racing Team, proving fast but fragile. Moss won the 1960 Cuban GP and with Gurney the Nürburgring 1,000 kilometres, but once again there was a disproportionate number of failures to offset these two victories. The 1961 Nürburgring 1,000 kilometres also fell to a Type 61 (Gregory-Casner).

In the 1961 Type 63 the engine was rear-mounted; initially the 2,888cc 4-cylinder unit was used, later, in the T64, a 3-litre V-12. The principal cars were raced by Briggs Cunningham (a Maserati distributor) and the Serenissima team. These had dubious handling qualities, and were unreliable in the extreme, although they sometimes came close to success. The 1965 Type 65 belongs to this family, although it was a one-off built by Maserati-France, more or less expressly for Le Mans. It had a substantially modified V-8, of 5,044cc. The Le Mans record of this 'special', the last sports-racing Maserati was even more dismal than those of its purer Modena predecessors.

Three years earlier in the Type 151, Maserati had reverted to a front-mounted engine, a 360bhp 3,996cc

Top left, 1954 Maserati Tipo 250F. Photo: Corrado Millanta

Top, 1954 Maserati Tipo 250F in practice for the British GP at Silverstone. Bira at the wheel. Photo: Central Press

Above, 1957 Maserati Tipo 450S at Le Mans; Behra in the open car, Moss in the coupé. Photo: Motor

Above left, 1960 Maserati Tipo 61 at the Nürburgring. Masten Gregory at the wheel. Photo: Autosport

Bottom, 1962 Maserati Tipo 151 at Reims in 1963. André Simon at the wheel. Photo: Autosport

Opposite top, Cooper-Bristol (Bob Gerrard), one of the first rear-engined GP cars, in the British GP, 1957. Photo: Geoff Goddard

Opposite bottom, Cooper-Maserati V-12 (Jochen Rindt) in the French GP at Reims, 1966. Photo: Geoff Goddard

V-8 based on the 450S unit. These cars were fast, and unlucky in racing rather than unreliable: all three retired at Le Mans in 1962. One was modified, and a 4·9-litre engine installed, for 1963 and 1964. In the first year it at least led the 24-hour Race in the opening phase; in 1964 it at least returned the fastest recorded speed on the Mulsanne straight.

Apart from the 1966-7 association with Cooper, Col. Simone's Le Mans car ended Maserati's long involvement in motor racing, and the company turned exclusively to the production of high-class road cars. DWH

Mason see Duesenberg

Mathis (D; F)

Emile Mathis's speciality was entering cars of the wrong size for races, but in his early days as a German manufacturer his competition cars were in fact Stoewers which he 'manufactured under licence' by adding his own radiators and hubcaps. The car Mathis himself drove into last place in the 1911 Coupe de l'Auto was a Stoewer, though at least it conformed to the capacity rules, unlike his 1912 entry with a 1,847cc 3-bearing sv 4-cylinder engine, which was set to run with the big cars in the concurrent Grand Prix. It showed reliability rather than speed, but another attempt with an undersized voiturette in 1913 led to a retirement. His entries of 1,057cc 4-cylinder Babylette light cars for that year's cyclecar events at Amiens and Le Mans were also unable to match the performance of the true cyclecars, and the make's best effort was 6th in the former race, though a similar small Mathis was raced with some success at Brooklands in 1920 by B. S. Marshall.

The 1921 French Grand Prix was run under a 3-litre formula, which did not stop Mathis entering a 1·5-litre sohc 4-cylinder with 4-wheel brakes. This time, however, the effort was not in vain, for the engine was used as a basis for the firm's entries in the Touring-Car GPs run under fuel consumption rules in 1923, 1924 and 1925. Twin-carburettor 1,100cc versions were used in 1923, when strict discipline (limiting drivers to 2,800rpm) ensured a 1-2-3 victory in the appropriate class. In 1924 form capacity was back to 1·5 litres with 45bhp, and Lahms once again led his team home, the only finishers in a class with nine starters. The 1925 cars had aerodynamic bodies with long tails and vertical spare wheels, as well as coil ignition, but water leaks led to the retirement of the whole team.

Apart from some long-distance record work with a narrow-track single-seater at Montlhéry in 1929, Mathis never officially raced again, though the Huascar with which Violet won the 1931 Bol d'Or was a disguised 1·2-litre PY-type sv four. Mathis, who had refused to have his name on the car, was only too glad to exhibit it in his Paris showroom after its triumph. MCS

Matich (AUS)

The most successful cars ever designed in Australia — the Matich SR series — are the brainchild of five times Australian sports car champion Frank Matich. Thirty-four-year-old Matich took his original design from a basic Lotus 19 sports car — but since then has developed it immensely to take powerful 5-litre V-8 units. Matich built his first car in 1965, calling it a Traco, after the American engine tuners: Travis and Coons. The car used a 390bhp Traco Oldsmobile V-8 of 4,990cc fed by four twin-throat Weber 48mm carburettors on a Traco manifold. The drive ran through a 5-speed ZF gearbox

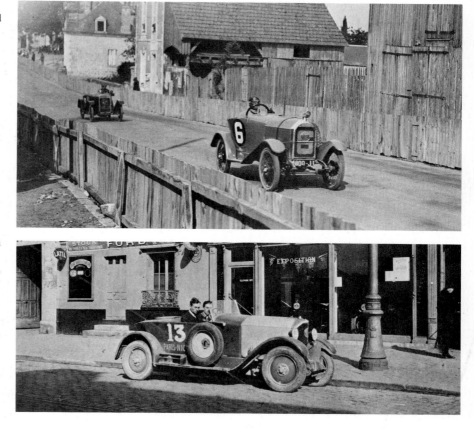

Top, 1923 Mathis 1,100cc in Touring Car GP at Tours. *Photo: Autocar*

Above, 1926 Mathis 11CV driven in Paris–Nice Rally by J. A. Gregoire. *Photo: courtesy J. A. Gregoire*

Opposite top, Ferrari 512 driven by John Surtees and Peter Schetty in the Monza 1000km Race, 1970. *Photo: Motor Sport*

Opposite bottom, Porsche 917 driven by Pedro Rodriguez and Leo Kinnunen in the Monza 1000km Race, 1970. *Photo: Motor Sport*

1969 Matich-Repco SR4. Frank Matich at the wheel. *Photo: Thomas B. Floyd*

similar to that used in most F1 cars.

In July 1967 Matich switched to a Melbourne designed Repco engine, and since then has used four of them in his cars. The original Repco produced 421bhp, the latest is attaining 460bhp. Matich's first car was of tubular 20 gauge steel with 18 gauge reinforcing pipes. It had a 91·75in (2·33cm) wheelbase, a 55in (1·397m) track front and rear, 10in (254mm) front wheels and 12in (304·8mm) rear—all of 15in (381·0mm) diameter. The original car weighed 1,450lb (657·709kg) but his later ones are much lighter. Matich no longer makes cars for sale, although at one stage he did build four in a seven-month period for sale to the United States and New Zealand.

His latest car, the Matich SR8, was still on the design board in mid-1970 but Matich sees it as being the most revolutionary he has built to date. Each new series in the Matich range cost approximately (Aus) $40,000 to design and build. TBF

Above, 1966 Matra-BRM team at Le Mans.
Photo: Matra

Left, 1966 Matra-Ford MS5 Formula 2 at
Goodwood. Jackie Stewart at the wheel,
signalling his return to the pits. *Photo:
David Hodges Collection*

Above, 1966 Matra-Ford MS5 winning the
Nürburgring F2 race. Jean-Pierre Beltoise
at the wheel. *Photo: Matra*

Left, 1970 Matra-Simca 650 in the Monza
1,000 Kilometres Race. Jack Brabham at the
wheel. *Photo: Doug Nye*

Matra (F)

SA Engins Matra, an aeronautical and missile engineering firm since 1941, entered the automotive field in 1964,
through the acquisition of René Bonnet's small specialist
car firm. Production of a refined version of Bonnet's
Djet continued until 1968. Early in 1965 Matra-Sports
(hence designations MS) and a competition department
were set up under Claude le Guezec at Villacoublay.
MS1 appeared that spring, a monocoque Ford-Cosworth-
engined F3 car which by the summer was fully competitive: a fact dramatically demonstrated by Beltoise's
victory over an international field at the Reims 12-hours
meeting (Beltoise went on to win the French championship). During 1965 five single-seaters were built (of
considerable moment, Stewart tested one for Tyrrell),
and the 610 derivative of the Djet as a development car.

Out of this for 1966 came the 2-litre BRM-engined 620
Group 6 coupé, a heavy space-framed car which was
not fully competitive. The opposite, however, was true
of the MS5 single-seater, similar to the 1965 car save that
the hull was of aluminium instead of steel. In F2 and F3
forms, both with Ford-based engines, this characteristically square-cut car was the equal of the British pace-
setters, particularly in the Tyrrell F2 team with Stewart
and Ickx driving.

The 1967 monocoques were lighter, but stronger and
very rigid. In F2, FVA-engined MS5s, and later in the
year MS7s, were run by Tyrrell and the works team;
Tyrrell's drivers gained five victories and Ickx won the
European Championship; for the works Beltoise and
Servoz-Gavin won no races, but the former gained
several 2nd and 3rd placings. Superior Matra handling
paid perhaps greater dividends in F3; Beltoise started
the year by winning all four rounds of the Argentine
Temporada, and Pescarolo and Jaussaud followed this
up in Europe. The MS7 remained competitive in F2 for
the next two years, Beltoise winning the Championship
in works MS7s in 1968, Servoz-Gavin in Coombs' Matra
International MS7s in 1969; then changes in tank
regulations ruled it ineligible. MS5s remained in use
until 1969, although by then not competitive.

The sports/prototype programme continued with the
630, lighter than the 620, with more powerful BRM V-8s
and in one case a 4·7-litre Ford V-8; late in the season
both versions won minor French races, driven by
Pescarolo and Servoz-Gavin.

Meanwhile, Matra had moved quickly towards
Formula 1 and, except in the detail of some components,
towards all-Matra cars. Of primary importance, a
Matra V-12 (79·7 × 50mm, 2,992cc) ran for the first
time at the very end of 1967. Backed by a government
loan of 6 million francs, this 4ohc 48-valve unit was
conventional in all respects, and at the outset intended
for F1 and Group 6 cars. In 1968 it appeared in the MS11
F1 car and in the 630. Georges Martin was primarily
responsible for the engine, Bernard Boyer for chassis.

The MS11 first raced at Monaco, and Beltoise achieved
its best placing, 2nd, at Zandvoort. At the end of 1968,
this F1 effort was set aside in favour of the Group 6
programme. In 1968, the V-12-engined 630 made an
inauspicious debut at Spa and did not run again until Le
Mans, where despite high fuel consumption and minor
delays Pescarolo and Servoz-Gavin at one stage got it
into 2nd place (before retiring).

The sole 640 crashed during 1969 Le Mans trials. An
open 630/650 ran in the Monza 1,000 kilometres, and for
Le Mans a new 650, with revised spaceframe and suspension closely similar to the F1 car, was ready. In the 24-

our race Matras finished 4th, 5th and 7th. Encouraging performances during the rest of 1969 culminated with a 1st and 2nd (650 and 630/650) in the Paris 1,000 kilometres. A 630/650 was sent to the Argentine Temporada, winning the Buenos Aires 1,000 kilometres and finishing 3rd in the Buenos Aires 200 Miles.

Apart from Beltoise's 2nd place in the Dutch GP, the Matra GP team had a mediocre first season, and Tyrrell's Matra International team really established the make as a force in racing's premier class. Their Matra chassis were on loan, and powered by the Cosworth DFV engine. In the South African GP a substantially modified F2 chassis (MS9) was used, and for the European season the MS10 was ready. A straightforward monocoque, this did not use the engine as a load-bearing chassis member; through the year the fashionable aerodynamic aids were added to it. Tyrrell's principal driver, Jackie Stewart, was out of action early in the season; he returned to racing to win the Dutch, German and American GPs, and finished runner-up in the World Championship. His team-mate of the second half of the year, Servoz-Gavin, gained a 2nd at Monza.

Stewart and the Tyrrell Matras dominated the 1969 GP season, the Scot winning the South African, Spanish, Dutch, British, German and Italian GPs, and quite decisively the Championship. Save in the opening race, the Tyrrell car was the bulbous MS80, in which the engine played a stressed role. Matra also produced a second GP car, the spaceframed 4wd MS84. This was driven by Beltoise and Servoz-Gavin, and at least performed more creditably than its contemporaries, albeit at the end in 2-wheel-drive form.

Thus an English team and engine, and a Scottish driver, combined with a French chassis to set the seal on the renaissance of French motor racing. However, this collaboration was then abandoned, because out of their urgent need to market their road-going 530, Matra merged with Simca. This led to substantial changes (le Guezec left), and meant that entries (first in the Daytona 24 Hour Race in 1970) were as Matra-Simcas, and that Matra picked up their solo F1 effort again, building the MS 120 around a developed version of the V-12. Like its predecessors, this car had a first-class chassis—if inelegant appearance—and road-holding, but the engine was the least powerful of any in use by front-line teams, and minor problems (e.g. with the fuel system) dogged the team. So although Beltoise led the French GP, until a pit-stop delayed him, best placing for the MS120 was third (at Monaco, Spa and Monza), and Matra-Simca were equal sixth (with BRM) in the 1970 Constructors'

Left, 1970 Matra-Simca MS120 Formula 1 on test at Montlhéry. *Photo: Matra*

Right, 1916 Maxwell Indianapolis car. Pete Henderson at the wheel. *Photo: Indianapolis Motor Speedway*

1948 Maybach Special in the Bathurst 100, c 1954. Stan Jones at the wheel. *Photo: Australian Motor Sports*

Championship.

The sports car effort was no better rewarded in Championship races, where 3-litre cars were in any case out-run by 4·5/5-litre Porsches and 5-litre Ferraris, and Matra-Simca scored points in only two events. But Brabham and Cevert won the end-of-season Paris 1000km in an MS660, and Matra F1 team drivers Beltoise and Pescarolo finished first and second in the Tour de France with MS650s, these sports-racing cars showing remarkable reliability in this event. DWH

Mauve see Elfe

Maxwell (US)
Early in its life the Maxwell-Briscoe company of Tarrytown, N.Y. built two enormous and unusual cars for the 1906 Vanderbilt Cup. One had two 40hp 4-cylinder engines in tandem, while the other had a horizontal 12-cylinder engine; neither reached the starting line. In 1908 the company built another monster racing car, with 180hp 12-cylinder engine consisting of two 6-cylinder units mounted side by side. This was apparently never raced. For the next six years Maxwell's participation in sport was restricted to reliability trials, where they did very well, twice winning the Glidden Tour outright, in 1911 and 1912.

In 1914 Carl Fisher of the Indianapolis Speedway encouraged Maxwell to build a team of racing cars. These had 4-cylinder single-ohc engines of 298ci (4,885cc) and were designed by Ray Harroun. Their best result at Indy was Rickenbacker's 6th place in 1916, but in 1915 they had major wins at Venice, Calif. (Oldfield), Sioux City, Omaha, Nebraska, and Providence, R.I., (Rickenbacker), and in 1916 at Sheepshead Bay, N.Y. and Tacoma, Washington. GNG

Maybach Special (AUS)
The most successful Australian special, and one of the most remarkable in the world, was Charles Dean's and Jack Joyce's Maybach, so called because of its 4·2-litre 6-cylinder ohc Maybach engine taken from a German scout car. It was built in Melbourne in 1948 as a hill-climb car, and subsequently raced by Stan Jones. So successful was it that in 1954 it was taken to New Zealand where Jones won the New Zealand GP from a field which included two Cooper-Bristols and Ken Wharton in a V-16 BRM. Re-built as a single seater, the Maybach crashed badly in the Australian GP later in 1954, and was re-built again by Repco's experimental department (Dean was now chief engineer to Repco). This Mark III

version had its engine, now with fuel injection, inclined at 60°, but a connecting rod broke, destroying the engine at Orange in 1955, and the project was abandoned. TBF

Mazda (J)

The Toyo Kogyo company's Mazda factory has licences for the production of Wankel engines and its sleek 110S coupé and dumpy R100 saloons have both been developed for fast and reliable competition work. The Wankel rotary engines are shatteringly noisy in this trim but show considerable output figures allied to good reliability.

The 110S has been raced nationally, and the R100s have appeared in international endurance events such as the *Marathon de la Route* at the Nürburgring and in the Spa 24-Hour saloon car race. Mazda's first appearance there in 1969 was marred by a fatal accident to Léon Dernier ('Eldé') at Masta, but the cars were going very well. They returned there in 1970 and lasted the distance, although outpaced by the Porsches and faster BMWs. They also contested the RAC TT at Silverstone but without notable success. DCN

MBM (CH)

Peter Monteverdi of Basle built his first special in 1951, at the age of 17, and in 1959 began construction of

Formula Junior racing cars. The first models had rear-mounted DKW 1-litre engines developing 85bhp and with a maximum speed of 133·6mph (215kph). Twelve were made, mostly being sold in the U.S.A. Later Formula Junior cars of 1960 to 1962 had 95bhp DKW or 90bhp Ford 1,100cc engines. In 1961 Monteverdi built a single Formula 1 car powered by a 1·5-litre Porsche engine. It ran in only one Grand Prix, the 1961 Solitude where it crashed on the first lap, and was written off in a later crash in a Swiss event. Three sports MBMs were also made during this period, one with an Osca engine, and two Ford-powered cars. No further cars were made until the Chrysler-powered Monteverdi GT in 1967. Neither this nor the mid-engined Hai 450 SS has appeared in competition at the time of writing. GNG

Melkus (D)

The most successful builder of racing cars in the German Democratic Republic, Heinz Melkus began in 1956 with small cars powered by BMW motorcycle engines. In 1959 he turned to Formula Junior, and in 1963 to Formula 3. The cars were rear-engined, mostly powered by the readily available Wartburg 3-cylinder 2-stroke unit. Tuned by Melkus, output was as high as 90bhp, giving speeds of over 125mph (200kph). Melkus Formula 3 cars are among the most successful currently being built in Eastern Europe. They are of spaceframe con-

1965 Melkus-Wartburg Formula 3. Photo: Vladimír Havránek Collection

struction, with inboard front and rear suspension. Drum brakes were used until the 1970 models on which discs were introduced. Melkus has also built a few sports cars, though not in series. In 1969 he built the RS 1000, a mid-engined coupé with Wartburg engine and fibreglass two-seater body. Maximum speed was 103mph (165kph). VH

Mercedes (D)

Although Mercedes cars were seen regularly in competition from their introduction in 1901 to 1908, six years separated Lautenschlager's victory at Dieppe from his next triumph at Lyons, and during that period Mercedes did little of any real significance in Europe. The vital importance, however, of Wilhelm Maybach's creation was that its pressed-steel chassis, selective gate change, honeycomb radiator and mechanically-operated inlet valves set the fashion for a generation of racing models just as it had proved the exemplar for luxury touring models of the epoch. Among those who copied the idiom directly were FIAT in Italy, Locomobile in America, Peugeot (briefly) in France, and Star in Great Britain.

The make's first appearance was at Pau on 17 February 1901. These first 35hp cars had T-head pair-cast 4-cylinder engines of 5·9 litres. Barrow's machine expired almost within sight of the start with clutch and gearbox troubles—Thorn's car, listed as a Mercedes, was in fact an 1899 24hp Cannstatt-Daimler. The Mercedes redeemed itself, however, in Nice where Wilhelm Werner did the flying-start kilometre at 53·5mph (86·1kph), beating all the other petrol cars, if not Léon Serpollet's steamer. He also won the Nice–Salon–Nice race and Mercedes took the first three places at La Turbie hill-climb. At Semmering that September von Stern and Werner made the two fastest times, though the new car's racing record continued less impressively. Thorn and Foxhall-Keene entered their 35s in Paris–Bordeaux, but both retired, and the works machines (Werner, Degrais and Lemaître) which contested the Paris–Berlin achieved little. More sprint and hill-climb successes came in 1902, with a bigger 6·8-litre model rated at 40hp. Stead, the winner at La Turbie, was a good one-and-a-half minutes quicker up the hill than Werner had been in 1901, and Werner managed a standing-start mile in 69·6sec at Nice, although he was still 6sec slower than Serpollet's latest machine. It was also noteworthy that the American W. K. Vanderbilt could only equal Jenatzy's 1899 electric-car record over the kilometre—65·79mph (105·87kph) at Achères that April, and even his 69·04mph (111·1kph) at Ablis later in the year still lagged behind steam's best. The best racing performance in the year was Eliot Zborowski's controversial 2nd place in Paris–Vienna: his Mercedes was the only one to get through.

Mercedes began to advance in 1903. The new 9·2-litre 60 featured an ioe engine and was capable of 75mph (120kph), and it showed its mettle early in the season when it knocked 3·5min off the record at La Turbie, and 5·9sec off the standing-start mile at Nice, this latter being achieved in a car destined for Alfred Harmsworth and still in existence with a tonneau body. Some even bigger 11,974cc 90hp cars on similar lines turned out for the Paris–Madrid, but Mercedes' best performance was Warden's 5th in a 60. Gasteaux on a similar car was 9th, and Jenatzy on the best 90 only 11th. Despite their excessive weight, however, they seem to have been quite fast, for Werner was lying 3rd when his back axle broke and the car overturned. These 90s were later destroyed in a fire at Cannstatt; thus the 60s had again to be used in the Gordon Bennett Cup in Ireland, where Jenatzy

on the circuits. Jenatzy finished 2nd in the Gordon Bennett Cup losing the race to Théry's Richard-Brasier after trouble on his 4th lap. Mercedes left the Circuit des Ardennes alone, though privately-owned examples of the 90 and 60 took part. None of the five cars entered for the first Vanderbilt Cup got anywhere, although Campbell's 60 was still running at the end. In the Coppa Florio the donor himself drove a 60hp Mercedes into 3rd place at 70mph (112·65kph). In sprints, Mercedes carried all before them at the Ormond and Daytona Beach Trials that January, when Vanderbilt covered a mile at 92·3mph (148·54kph) with his 90hp. De Caters, not to be outdone, managed a kilometre at 97·54mph (156·97kph) at Ostend in April, and Braun clipped 36sec off the record at Semmering.

Mercedes enlarged their 1905 racing engines to 14 litres and 115bhp, though they did not follow FIATs example in adopting full overhead valves. These cars were, however, hard on tyres and a combination of this and poor pit work upset their chances in the Gordon Bennett, where Jenatzy retired, and his team-mates Werner and de Caters came in 5th and 7th. A 6th in the Ardennes race, 9th in the Coppa Florio, and a complete blank in the Vanderbilt Cup after an early challenge by Jenatzy, left only the world of sprints to cheer Mercedes' flagging

Above, 1901 Mercedes 35hp at the GP de Pau. Lorraine Barrow at the wheel. This was the first appearance of a Mercedes car in racing. *Photo: Montagu Motor Museum*

Right, 1903 Mercedes 60hp with cowled radiator for record-breaking. Baron de Caters at the wheel. *Photo: Courtesy Baron Guy de Caters*

1906 Mercedes 90hp tourer in the Herkomer Trial. Hieronymus at the wheel. *Photo: Autocar*

scored a resounding victory at 49·2mph (79·18kph) after Jellinek had involved himself in a dispute with the German club over the employment of the professional drivers he wanted (but on this occasion did not get). De Caters was 5th, but Foxhall-Keene on the third Mercedes retired. The season was rounded out by further good performances at Semmering and Ostend, and also in British sprints, where 60s recorded two fastest times of day in the Irish Fortnight that followed the Gordon Bennett Cup.

The 90s reappeared in 1904, but victories eluded them

fortunes. Here they did well, with fastest times of day at Kesselberg, Semmering, and Gaillon. Among the drivers who turned out for the Ormond–Daytona Speed Week were automobile manufacturer E. R. Thomas in a 90hp Mercedes, and H. L. Bowden, who had fabricated an extraordinary straight-8 out of two racing 4-cylinder Mercedes engines (one German and the other Austrian), and was timed at 109·75mph (177·08kph). The 1906 season was less than impressive, though de Jochems and Guinness dominated the Ostend meeting and Braun once again made ftd at Semmering, this time on an experimental 12·9-litre ohc six, ancestor of the 10·2-litre production 6-cylinder T-headers which reached the market in 1907. Three privately-entered 1905-type racers (Jenatzy, Florio and Mariaux) contested the French GP without any great success, and Jenatzy finished 5th in the Vanderbilt Cup.

The same basic design of racer ran in 1907, but Mercedes were now claiming 130bhp, and there were the usual successes at Semmering, Gaillon and Daytona. The 8-litre Kaiserpreis cars were not a success, Salzer's 9th being the make's best performance, and of the Grand Prix entries only Hémery was placed, a rather dismal

10th. Both types of racer turned out in the Ardennes: Théodore Pilette achieved nothing in the Kaiserpreis category, and though the Grand Prix section was dominated by Belgium's two best-known Mercedes exponents, Jenatzy and de Caters, the opposition was insignificant.

For the 1908 GP, Mercedes entered some new 12·8-litre cars, still ioe but now with ht magneto ignition in the manner of the rival Benz. The race developed into a duel between the two future partners, Lautenschlager's Mercedes leading the Benz of Hémery and Hanriot home at 69mph (111·04kph), while Poege was 5th; Salzer led for his first and only effective lap. The cars were less successful in the Vanderbilt Cup, but Salzer set up a new record at Semmering, and Poege took 2nd place in the Prince Henry Trials with a new 9·1-litre ioe four which could exceed 80mph on something more than 95bhp.

From 1909 to 1912 the Grandes Epreuves lapsed, and Mercedes were totally uninterested in voiturettes, though the hill-climbs continued. Poege also finished 2nd in the Prince Henry Trials, this time behind an Opel, and in 1910 Jenatzy made 2nd ftd at Gaillon on a bored-out 1908 GP car. In Russia, the Tsar Nicholas II event was notable for a 1-2-3 victory, the Mercedes of Poege, Fritsch and Lude being the new 4·1-litre 16/45PS shaft-driven fours with Knight engines.

In 1911 the amateur Soldatenkoff finished 3rd in the Targa Florio. That year and 1912 were to mark the

zenith of Gordon Watney's rebodied Mercedes at Brooklands — these were elderly 60s with racing coachwork by Ewarts of geyser fame. More important, the 1908 GP Mercedes were beginning to make their mark in the United States, where their great exponent was Ralph DePalma, hitherto noted for his performances in Fiats. In his first Vanderbilt Cup (1911) he finished 2nd behind Mulford's Lozier, Wishart taking 3rd place in another Mercedes. He also took 3rd place in the Grand Prize and Wishart's record was equally impressive. After an unsuccessful attempt at the Vanderbilt Cup in 1910, he was 4th in the Indianapolis 500 Miles and 2nd at Fairmount Park. The 1912 season was another triumphant one for DePalma: he won the Elgin Trophy and the Vanderbilt Cup (in which latter Wishart was 3rd and Clark 5th), and took 3rd place at Indianapolis, though he overturned his car in the Grand Prize while chasing Caleb Bragg in the faster FIAT S74.

There was a resurgence of Mercedes' interest in racing in 1913. Pilette took one of the small 16/45PS Knight-Mercedes to Indianapolis, where it was easily the smallest car in the race, in spite of which the machine (wearing one of the new V-radiators) took 5th place at 68·14mph (109·66kph). Mulford in an older Mercedes was 6th, and Elskamp's 16/45 was placed 3rd in the Belgian GP. For the Grand Prix de France at Le Mans the factory entered two modified 1908 GP machines with wire wheels, and an entirely new racer. Its side-chain drive was archaic,

Left, 1907 Mercedes 80hp Kaiserpreis car. Salzer at the wheel. *Photo: Montagu Motor Museum*

Above, 1908 Mercedes GP car, at Brooklands in 1910. Lord Vernon at the wheel. *Photo: Montagu Motor Museum*

Below, 1908 Mercedes GP car, Lautenschlager at the wheel. *Photo: T. A. S. O. Mathieson Collection*

Left, c 1909 Mercedes, re-bodied by Gordon Watney, at Brooklands in 1911. *Photo: Montagu Motor Museum*

Below, 1914 Mercedes GP team. *Photo: Daimler-Benz AG*

but the engine was an advanced six with separately-cast cylinders, 24 valves, and an overhead camshaft, prototype both of the firm's World War 1 aero-engine and of their 28/95PS fast tourer announced in 1914 and produced in series after the Armistice. The combination was none too successful, and Mercedes' best showing in the race was put up by Pilette on one of the old fours. Salzer's six finished 4th. The model never ran again in Europe, but Ralph DePalma bought one of them and entered it for Indianapolis in 1914. It did not start, but he later scored four victories at Brighton Beach that year, and took two major 4th places in the 1914 Grand Prize and the 1915 Vanderbilt Cup. He was also driving his 12·8-litre in 1914, winning the Vanderbilt Cup after a disagreement with the Mercer company (whose team captain he had been) over the inclusion of Barney Oldfield in the team; 2nd place in the race went, ironically, to Oldfield in a Mercer. DePalma also finished 4th in the Grand Prize.

In 1914 Mercedes brought out some new 4·5-litre 4-cylinder GP cars which were the first such machines from Untertürkheim to feature shaft-drive. The engines derived from the 1913 six with overhead valves and camshaft, hemispherical heads, dual magneto ignition and 4 sparking plugs per cylinder. Output was 110bhp, and top speed around 100mph (160km). These figured in the dramatic French GP, when Sailer set the pace against Georges Boillot's Peugeot before blowing his engine up. Lautenschlager and Wagner then moved up the field, harrying Boillot until his car expired. The three German cars finished in line ahead, Lautenschlager's average being 65·83mph (105·94kph) to the 65·3mph (105·09kph) and 64·8mph (104·29kph) of his team-mates Wagner and Salzer. One of these 4·5-litres came to England where it was studied by Henry Royce; another was sold by the factory to Ralph DePalma for $6,000, and ended up in Packard's experimental department in Detroit, though not before it had enjoyed a chequered career in America. As early as August, 1914 DePalma had won the Chicago Cup at 73·9mph (118·93kph), following this with a victory in the Elgin Trophy at 73·53mph (118·34kph). In 1915 he won the Indianapolis 500 at 89·84mph (144·58kph) and in 1916 there was a continuing battle with Dario Resta in the Mercedes' former rival, the 4·5-litre Peugeot. DePalma won at Kansas City and Omaha, lost to Resta at Chicago, and retired at Tacoma.

Recovery was slow after World War 1, though a new use was found in the immediate post-Armistice years for old chain-driven Mercedes chassis, which were fitted with wartime aero-engines. The factory's first post-war competition machine was the 7,250cc ohc 6-cylinder 28/95PS: Max Sailer bravely entered one for the 1921 Targa Florio in Sicily, Continental providing him with sufficient tyres to reach the start. This car had fwb but not, as has often been stated, a supercharger. Sailer was rewarded for his enterprise with 2nd place. In the same year Minoia won the Italian Alpine Cup and Masetti drove one of the pre-war 4·5-litres into 1st place in the Italian GP at Brescia as well as winning the kilometre sprint which preceded the race.

The Mercedes supercharger arrived on the scene in 1922, though the factory's racing programme was still restricted, since Italy was the only Allied country which permitted German participation. Hence all Mercedes' efforts were concentrated on the Targa Florio in which they entered seven cars (two pre-war 4·5-litres for Lautenschlager and Salzer, plus Masetti's privately-

Above, 1914 Mercedes before the start at Elgin. *Photo: Peter Helck Collection*

Right, 1914 Mercedes, winner at Indianapolis in 1915. Ralph DePalma at the wheel. *Photo: Indianapolis Motor Speedway*

Above, 1914 Mercedes GP car driven in the 1922 Targa Florio by Count Masetti. *Photo: Montagu Motor Museum*

Right, 1921 Mercedes 28/95, winner of the Targa Florio. Max Sailer at the wheel. *Photo: Daimler-Benz AG*

Below, 1923 Mercedes 2-litre in which Werner won the 1924 Coppa and Targa Florios. *Photo: Daimler-Benz AG*

owned example, Sailer and Christian Werner in blown 28/95s, and a pair of new 1·5-litre supercharged 4-cylinder machines for Scheef and Minoia). The 1·5-litres had dohc engines said to develop 80bhp if pushed to the limit, but their chassis design was indifferent, and Scheef's showing amounted only to 20th and 3rd in class. Of the others, Masetti won outright at 39·2mph (63·09kph), Sailer was 6th, Werner 8th, and Lautenschlager 10th. In 1923 came some new 16-valve blown 2-litre fours from which 120bhp were extracted, and in Germany Salzer made ftd at the Solitude hill-climb. This time the factory tried their luck at Indianapolis with Lautenschlager, Sailer and Werner as drivers: Sailer crashed in practice and Lautenschlager in the race. The other two cars carried on, with some changing of drivers, to take 8th and 11th places, a good showing for a team whose crews were relatively elderly.

By contrast, 1924 was a better season with an excellent performance at Solitude (1-2-3 in the 2-litre category and 1st and 2nd in the 1,500cc class), and at Klausen, Merz and Caracciola led the 1·5-litre class. At Semmering Werner made ftd and won the 2-litre section, followed home by Alfred Neubauer, Stuttgart's future team manager; he was beaten on time, however, by Salzer in one of the old 1914 4·5-litres. The 28/95s scored two 3rd places in Italy in the Coppa Acerbo and the Circuit of Mugello, and Caracciola won the Eifelrennen in a blown 1·5-litre. The 2-litre fours achieved nothing at San Sebastian, but there was compensation in another Targa Florio victory, this time for Werner in a similar car at 41·02mph (66·03kph): an extra lap gave him the Coppa Florio into the bargain, and in the Targa, Lautenschlager was 10th and Neubauer 15th. At the close of the season Ferdinand Porsche's 1,980cc blown dohc straight-8 with four valves per cylinder, sodium-cooled exhaust valves, 9-bearing crankshaft and dry-sump lubrication made its appearance in the Italian GP at Monza. Though the engine disposed of 160bhp at over 7,000rpm, it was never a good handler, and its début was marred by a fatal accident to Count Louis Zborowski, after which the remaining cars were withdrawn. (The factory's claim of 269 victories during the season includes Benz's score, though the amalgamation was still two years away.) In 1925 there was a Mercedes triumph in the German

Batschari Prize Contest with the top four places filled; Merz won at Solitude with a 2-litre four; and Werner made ftd at Freiburg on the straight-8. New to the circuits that year was the first of Porsche's supercharged sohc big sixes, the 24/100/140PS K (33/140 in Britain), with a capacity of 6,240cc and road-holding that verged on the perilous. The Italian Cesaroni finished 3rd in the Coppa della Perugia.

The last year of Mercedes without Benz was 1926, and surprisingly pre-war designs were still winning. At Semmering Caracciola not only put up best touring-car performance in one of the new blown sixes, but made ftd in a supercharged 1914 4·5-litre. Orti-Manara's 28/95 was fastest at Merluzzo in Italy, a similar car being 2nd in its class. There were further class victories for this ancient in France, Williams of Bugatti fame scoring one at La Turbie; the modern 2-litre straight-8s triumphed at Freiburg, Solitude and Klausen. At the last-named venue Caracciola showed his mettle by taking one of the lethal Mercedes Ks up in only 13·2sec slower than Rosenberger in the GP car. This latter type turned out for the German GP at the AVUS, and Caracciola won his reputation as *the Regenmeister* by storming through to win from Riecken's NAG. For the Spanish GP the factory entered three K-types (Merz and Gärtner, Caracciola and Kühnke, and Werner and Walb), but twelve hours' racing proved too much for the cars' brakes and road-holding alike, and they were soundly beaten by Minoia in a 2-litre sv OM.

In 1927 the cars became Mercedes-Benz, and henceforward the accent was on the K's more successful descendants, the S and SS. Raymond Mays, however, drove one of the 2-litre blown 4-cylinder cars to some purpose both at South port and Sheesley Walsh (where he made 2nd ftd), and Werner won at the opening Nürburgring meeting in a straight-8. (Raymond Mays tried such a car at Brooklands, but the road-holding defeated even him.) Incredibly, the 1914 GP car was still soldiering on, for Rosenberger made ftd and set up a new record in the Herkules hill-climb, and an extraordinary hill-climb special was evolved by installing one of these blown engines in a 2-litre chassis. With this combination Rosenberger rounded off the old company's career with fastest times of day at Freiburg and Klausen. MCS

Left, 1924 Mercedes 1·5-litre at Klausen Hill-Climb. Otto Merz at the wheel. *Photo: Daimler-Benz AG*

Above, 1924 Mercedes 2-litre 8-cylinder. Raymond Mays at the wheel. *Photo: Montagu Motor Museum*

Mercedes-Benz (D)

The amalgamation of the Daimler and Benz firms at the end of 1926 coincided with a concentration on the big-lhc supercharged 6-cylinder sports cars. By this time the lower and better-handling 6·8-litre S model had supplanted the K, and a good season was crowned with victories for Caracciola and Merz respectively in the opening race at the Nürburgring and the German GP. The S also distinguished itself in hill-climbs and in the Batschari Prize, which was won by Caracciola. Though both the K and S were still racing in 1928 — Calfisch was 2nd at Caserta on one of the old 1925 models — the season brought both the 7·1-litre 225bhp SS and its short-chassis two-seater variant, the SSK, as well as a 1-2-3 victory against Bugatti in the German GP. The TT handicap rules eliminated Thistlethwayte's S from the running, though he made fastest lap at 74·39mph (119·71kph), but there was a 2nd at La Baule for von Wentzel-Mosau, and the usual run of hill-climb victories. Also in 1928 Carlos Zatuszek had his first success in Argentina, in a 12-hour production car race which he won on a K-type.

In the 1929 GP of the Nations at the Nürburgring Bugatti had their revenge, and Mercedes' best placing was 3rd for the Momberger/Arco car, though Caracciola led until he had engine trouble. He scored an amazing 3rd at Monaco, only the SSK's consumption of tyres letting the Bugattis into the lead. A wet Ulster TT saw Caracciola well and truly on form to defeat his handicap and win at 78·82mph (126·85kph), though Merz was only 13th, after he had torn a damaged wing off with his bare hands. The Wiesbaden-Rennen were another triumph, the cars filling the first five places in the road

section, and the first three in the ensuing race. Momberger was 3rd at Monza after beating a Maserati in his heat, and the SSKs dominated the Central European hill-climb season. Zatuszek had exchanged his old car for an SSK and won at Cordoba, and in the Alpine Trials Mercedes-Benz did well, Glacier Cups going to Kimpel's SSK and (surprisingly) to Christian Werner's 2·6-litre sv Stuttgart model, a most unsporting car.

Mercedes contested the major sports-car events of 1930. Caracciola won the Irish GP at Phoenix Park and set up a new lap record. But his oversize supercharger caused him to be barred from the TT; 6th was the best he could manage in the Mille Miglia; and his duel with Birkin's 4½-litre supercharged Bentley at Le Mans ended with an electrical failure. On the credit side Caracciola established a new sports-car record at Shelsley Walsh, and nine major victories on the Continent gave him the European Hill-Climb Championship, which he repeated in 1931. The fiercest of the Porsche-era Mercedes came in 1931, the 300bhp SSKL with drilled chassis, which could reach 140mph (225kph) and won the Mille Miglia outright on its first outing. Caracciola followed this up with victories in the Eifel-rennen and the German GP; in the latter his car ran stripped. Von Brauchitsch was 2nd, and the two drivers scored a 1st and a 3rd respectively at the AVUS. Stuck won the Polish GP and was 2nd in the Masaryk in Czechoslovakia, but the cars retired in the Monaco and French GPs. Ivanowski and Stoffel would have beaten the new 2·3-litre Alfa-Romeo at Le Mans but for persistent tyre trouble: as it was they finished 2nd after a switch from Engleberts to Dunlops during the race.

By 1932 the cars were becoming a little too heavy, but

Below left, 1928 Mercedes-Benz SSK at Semmering Hill-Climb. Carraciola at the wheel. *Photo: Neubauer Collection*

Below, 1930 Mercedes-Benz SS, driven at Le Mans by Carraciola and Werner. *Photo: Motor*

Bottom left, 1931 Mercedes-Benz SSKL in the Czechoslovak GP. Hans Stuck at the wheel. *Photo: T. A. S. O. Mathieson Collection*

Bottom, 1932 Mercedes-Benz SSKL streamlined car. Manfred von Brauchitsch at the wheel. *Photo: Erwin Tragatsch Collection*

Above, 1935 Mercedes-Benz W25 in the French GP at Montlhéry. Manfred von Brauchitsch at the wheel. *Photo: T. A. S. O. Mathieson Collection*

Below, 1937 Mercedes-Benz W125. *Photo: Daimler-Benz AG*

Above, 1937 Mercedes-Benz W125/DAB streamliner at AVUS. Hermann Lang at the wheel. *Photo: Daimler-Benz AG*

Below, 1939 Mercedes-Benz W163 in the Pau GP. Winner Hermann Lang at the wheel. *Photo: Daimler-Benz AG*

with the aid of new aerodynamic coachwork von Brauchitsch won at the AVUS, averaging over 120mph (192kph), and he was 3rd in the Eifelrennen. Broscheck was 3rd at Lwow, and Widengren and Ebb were 1st and 2nd in the Finnish GP. While Zatuszek's South American successes continued, Stuck also ventured across the South Atlantic to take the Brazilian hill-climb championship, and he went on to win the European title as well. By contrast 1933, was a dull year enlivened only by a 1st in Finland for Ebb and a 2nd in the Eifelrennen for von Brauchitsch.

In 1934 came the 750kg formula and the first of the legendary Silver Arrows, subsidized by the Nazi government and managed with consummate skill by Alfred Neubauer: he was probably the main reason why Mercedes-Benz always fared better than Auto Union, who lacked a dictatorial *Rennleiter*. The first of the cars, the W25, was a dohc straight-8 with four valves per cylinder developing 354bhp. This unit was housed in a box-section frame with the all-independent suspension used on the otherwise dull Mercedes touring cars since 1931, hydraulic brakes and aerodynamic single-seater bodywork. Output rose during the season to 398bhp thanks to an increase in capacity, and the cars started off well with a victory in the Eifelrennen for the usually unlucky Brauchitsch at 76·12mph (122·50kph). Auto Union won the German GP though Fagioli was 2nd and Geier 5th (for Mercedes). However, Fagioli won again in the Coppa Acerbo. Mercedes-Benz won the Spanish GP (Fagioli) and the Italian GP (Fagioli and Caracciola), but were unsuccessful in the French and Swiss GPs. Hill-climb honours were divided: at Klausen Caracciola set up a new record, and he was defeated by Auto Union at Freiburg. In December he took a *Renn-limousin* version with 430bhp 4-litre engine and no front brakes to Gyon in Hungary and recorded 196·78mph (316·63kph) over the flying-start mile.

The 4-litre unit was standardized on the 1935 cars, which also incorporated limited-slip differentials. The season was a good one for Mercedes-Benz, with wins at Monaco, Tripoli, Eifelrennen, AVUS, and in the French, Swiss, Spanish, and Belgian GPs. Mercedes had, in fact, won nine of the ten races they entered: the humiliating exception was the German GP, in which Brauchitsch burst a tyre after leading the field and breaking the lap record, and Caracciola's 3rd place was the make's best showing.

The next season, 1936, was a catastrophe, and Auto Union's year. Mercedes had a new, lower chassis, and a 4·7-litre engine developing 474bhp, but despite a promising start at Monaco, where Caracciola won at 51·69mph (83·18kph), there was defeat at Tripoli (Fagioli came in 3rd behind a pair of Auto Unions), and Caracciola's revenge at Tunis was probably due to the elimination of two Auto Unions (one crashed spectacularly and the other caught fire). The Barcelona race went to Alfa Romeo, though Caracciola was 2nd. The cars failed in the Eifelrennen, and their best in the German and Swiss Grands Prix were 5th and 4th respectively. There was compensation in Ebb's 2nd place in an SSK (behind an equally old Alfa Romeo) in the Swedish Winter race, and eight major victories for the irrepressible Zatuszek and his SSK in Argentina. In November Caracciola took a new streamliner with a 5·5-litre 12-cylinder engine over the mile at 228·05mph (366·95kph).

Mercedes had, however, learnt their lesson, and 1937 brought the amazing W125, styled after the 1936 cars, but with a new twin-tube frame, redesigned front suspen-

sion, De Dion back axle, and a 5·7-litre engine from which 646bhp were extracted at 5,800rpm — the apotheosis of the 750kg formula. The 4-speed gearbox was in the back axle. Lang led off to an excellent season by winning in Tripoli at 134·25mph (215·98kph). For the AVUS, two of the cars (Caracciola's and Lang's) were streamliners closely resembling the 1936 V-12. Lang won at 162·6mph (261·7kph), putting in a lap at 171·63mph (276·25kph). That Mercedes were only 2nd and 3rd in the Eifelrennen was due to the one man who really mastered the rear-engined Auto Union — Bernd Rosemeyer. The American Vanderbilt Cup saw a duel between the two aces, Caracciola and Rosemeyer, which ended when the Mercedes' supercharger failed. There was some compensation, however, in the 2nd place scored by a new recruit to the team, Richard Seaman. Lang and Kautz tailed the Auto Unions in 3rd and 4th places in the Belgian GP, but Caracciola won the German GP at the Nürburgring, and Brauchitsch beat Rosemeyer to take 2nd place. Monaco was a Mercedes triumph, with Brauchitsch 1st, Caracciola 2nd, Kautz 3rd and Zehender 5th, and at Pescara, Brauchitsch was 2nd. Three Mercedes processions followed: the first four places on the very fast round-the-houses circuit at Livorno used for that year's Italian GP; another first four in the Masaryk and a 1-2-3 at Berne, Caracciola winning. The 1937 season closed with the descent of the Germans on Donington Park, a spectacle still remembered with awe in Britain. Rosemeyer's Auto Union won, but Brauchitsch and Caracciola were very close behind.

For the new 3-litre formula of 1938 Mercedes had much the same chassis, though power now came from a blown 4-ohc V-12 developing 420bhp, set at an angle in the frame with the rear end tilted downwards. The gearbox had five forward speeds. This year Mercedes beat Auto Union (who had lost Delius and Rosemeyer in fatal accidents, and their designer Porsche to Hitler's KdF project) off the mark, but their opening race at Pau was a humiliating defeat at the hands of the French unblown 4·5-litre Delahaye. Their 1-2-3 victory at Tripoli was achieved in the face of opposition from Alfa Romeo only. Nor was the French GP at Reims a real test, for the serious challengers (Auto Union) faded, and the show of Talbot, Bugatti and SEFAC was poor — hence a demonstration run for Brauchitsch, Caracciola and Lang, in that order. At the Nürburgring Brauchitsch's car first caught fire and then crashed, leaving Seaman to win from a second W154 shared by Caracciola and Lang. Lang was the sole Mercedes survivor in the Coppa Ciano, which he won, and Berne just a repeat of the car 1938 performance, only Seaman won instead of Caracciola. In the Coppa Acerbo Caracciola's was the sole German entry to stay the course, but he came 1st all the same. By this time the Auto Unions were at their peak, and they collected the honours both in the Italian and Donington Park Grands Prix, though Mercedes were 2nd and 3rd on the latter occasions. Zatuszek had been killed in an accident, but Broscutti upheld the honour of the aged SSK by winning the 500-miles (800km) Rafaele race in Argentina.

The 1939 Mercedes-Benz (Type W163) featured a two-stage blower, which boosted output to 480bhp, and this time they made no mistake at Pau, where Lang won. Nuvolari all but snatched the Eifelrennen for Auto Union by going through without a change of tyres, but once again Lang was victorious, Caracciola taking 3rd place. The Belgian GP was marred by a fatal accident to Seaman, Lang scoring his third victory of the year. At

Above, 1939 Mercedes-Benz 3-litre record car. *Photo: Daimler-Benz AG*

Left, 1939 Mercedes-Benz W163s at the start of the 1948 Argentine GP. *Photo: Associated Press*

Above, 1952 Mercedes-Benz 300SL at the start of the Mille Miglia. Caracciola at the wheel. *Photo: Associated Press*

Left, 1952 Mercedes-Benz 300SL driven at Le Mans by Helfrich and Niedermayer. *Photo: Autosport*

the cars retired in the French GP, but Caracciola added the German GP to his score, and in the Swiss race the Mercedes once again finished 1-2-3. A 2nd place for Brauchitsch at Belgrade in September closed the W163's career in formula events, but during the season Daimler-Benz had been exploring other avenues. The W125 was still in service for hill-climbs, Lang making ftd at Grossglöckner. The 1939 Tripoli race had been transformed into a voiturette event in an attempt to stem the tide of German victories. It was all to no avail: Uhlenhaut came up with an oversquare 1·5-litre 260bhp V-8 based on the W163, and Lang won from Caracciola at 122·91mph (197·72kph), on this, the model's only appearance, after Farina had blown his Alfa Romeo up. Two 3-litre streamliners were given an airing on the autobahn at Dessau, doing a standing-start kilometre at 107·9mph (173·6kph) and the flying-start distance at 247·44mph (298·16kph). Finally Porsche designed a huge 6-wheeler with removable bodywork, 29ft (8·84m) long, with an eye on the World Land Speed Record. Power was to come from a 3,030hp V-12 Daimler-Benz aero-engine, but the car never ran under its own power, though it survives in the factory museum at Untertürkheim.

Daimler-Benz were devastated by World War 2. The 'bread-and-butter' Type 170 saloon was back in production by 1948, but there was as yet no prospect of racing. A W163 was taken to America and ran at Indianapolis in 1947 and 1948; on neither occasion did it distinguish itself, although Nalon was lying 4th at the 100-mile mark on its first outing. The model did a little better in Argentina with 2nd places in the Peron Cup and the Grand Prix Eva Peron. However, 1952 started off well with a works entry of the new 6-cylinder ohc 220 saloons in the Monte Carlo Rally: none of the cars finished in the first 15, but they won the team prize. More important, the factory had produced a super-sports car, the legendary 300SL gull-wing coupé. The 7-bearing engine was a development of the existing 220 and 300 series, and gave 175bhp in its original form with three Solex carburettors. Caracciola, Lang and Kling turned out for the Mille Miglia, where the cars were more than a match for the biggest Ferraris and the Jaguar C-type, but could not beat Bracco on the 3-litre Ferrari. Kling was 2nd, and the veteran Caracciola finished 4th. Switzerland was once again lucky for Mercedes, Kling winning from his team-mates Lang and Riess, but a bad crash put Caracciola out of racing for good. At Le Mans, Pierre Levegh's Talbot led until driver-fatigue caused the obstinate Frenchman to make a mistake, and Lang won at the record speed of 96·67mph (155·57kph). The cars had no trouble at all at the Nürburgring (1-2-3-4), and for the Carrera Panamericana they produced an open two-seater version to accommodate the tall American driver John Fitch. Kling won from Lang at over 102mph (164kph) when the Ferraris expired.

The 1953 season was a poor one, and by 1954 the 300SL was a production tourer with fuel injection. It was also the year in which Daimler-Benz returned with some new Silver Arrows, the 2·5-litre W196 straight-8s with dohc and desmodromic valve gear, not to mention fuel injection (tried on the 1·5-litre W165 just before the war), 5-speed gearboxes, spaceframes and inboard brakes. These engines developed 270bhp, and the cars were first seen in the French GP as true streamliners. Fangio's victory from Kling was not unduly significant, since the Ferraris were off form, and at Silverstone the W196 did not shine, partly because the drivers did not

know the course, and partly because the streamliners were ill-suited to the circuit. Fourth and 7th places were a disappointment, but a more orthodox body with exposed wheels was ready in time for the German GP (only Herrmann retained the earlier type on this occasion) and Fangio won. The remainder of the 1954 season was 1937-9 all over again, apart from the Spanish GP, in which garbage was sucked into the air intakes, and the cars ended up 3rd and 5th. Fangio won the Swiss and Italian GPs, and Kling the German.

The cars were back with a vengeance in 1955, brought to meetings on a 300SL-powered transporter, itself capable of 100mph (160kph), and with Moss in the team. If Monaco was a failure for Mercedes-Benz, nothing else was: the season started off with two victories in the Argentine Temporada series, both appropriately for Fangio, and the Argentinian driver proceeded to win the Eifelrennen, the Belgian GP (in which Moss was 2nd), the Dutch GP, and the Italian GP. Moss won at Aintree. Fangio was 2nd and Kling 3rd. Further, Fangio's World Championship and the company's position as top constructor were capped by the sports-car championship, for alongside the W196 the factory raced the 300SLR, a streamlined open-cockpit machine with a 3-litre version of the existing straight-8 engine. Stirling Moss led off with a magnificent victory in the Mille Miglia, with Fangio 2nd and stock 300SLs in 5th, 7th and 10th places. There were other victories in the TT (1st, 2nd and 3rd);

the Targa Florio (1st, 2nd and 4th); the Swedish race (1st and 2nd); and the 300SLs dominated the touring-car category. The only reverse was Le Mans, where the air-brake had its debut and Levegh was introduced into the team: the surviving cars were withdrawn after his fatal crash, and people still argue as to whether the D-type Jaguar would have beaten the 300SLR in a straight fight to the finish.

Thereafter rallies were the firm's principal interest: 300SLs won the Sestrières, Acropolis, Liège-Rome-Liège and Iberian events, and Schock and Moll became European Rally Champions, while Moss and Houel were 2nd and Cotton and Leclerc 4th in the Tour de France. The touring 300SLs could still give a good account of themselves in sports-car events, with a class victory (and 6th, 7th, 8th and 10th in general classification) in the Mille Miglia. The Italian Zampiero came 4th in the Targa Florio and 7th in the Giro di Sicilia, and won the Coppa Inter-Europa outright. By 1957, however, the gull-wings and the roadsters which succeeded them in production were no longer competitive in racing. The rally picture was rather better: if the Moss/Garnier 300SL could manage no better than 5th in the Tour de France there were two class victories (for a 220A and a 300SL) in the Tulip and a 2nd in Liège-Rome-Liège rally. The sole triumphs in 1958 were those of Manussis and Savage on a 219 in the Kenya Coronation Safari, and of Cotton and Simon (300SL) in the Snow and Ice

Top left, 1954 Mercedes-Benz W196 streamliner in French GP. Fangio at the wheel. *Photo: Autosport*

Top, 1955 Mercedes-Benz 300SLR in the T *Photo: Geoffrey Goddard*

Above left, 1955 Mercedes-Benz W196 open-wheel car winning the British GP at Aintree. Stirling Moss at the wheel. *Photo Geoffrey Goddard*

Above, 1960 Mercedes-Benz 220SE driver to victory in the Monte Carlo Rally by Schock and Moll. *Photo: Planet News*

lly. The 1959 score, once again, was limited to tough
ents suited to the company's rather heavy saloons: a
0 collected the Safari, Karl Kling won the Cape-
giers event on a diesel-powered 190, a petrol-engined
0 was victorious in the South African Winter Rally,
d one of the new fuel-injected 220SEs was driven to
tory in the 2,900-mile (4,660km) Argentine road race
Schock and Schiek.

From 1960 to 1964 there was a works-supported rally
m which, among other successes had a 1-2-3 victory
the 1960 Monte Carlo Rally. Mercedes-Benz won the
st African Safari in 1960 and 1961, while other
hievements for works or private entries were victories
the Polish and 1,000 Lakes Rallies (1961), Acropolis,
lish, and Liège–Sofia–Liège (1962), and Polish and
ège–Sofia–Liège in 1963. Mercedes-Benz cars also won
e Argentine Road Race in 1962, 1963, and 1964.

By 1965, Daimler-Benz were out of it, and their only
ajor showing was in the Safari, where a 300SE was 6th
d a 190 7th. The advanced Wankel-engined C-111
upé appeared in 1969, but the factory do not seem
clined to race this, though they turned out for the Spa
-Hour Race with a team of 600SEL saloons powered
their biggest touring engine, the 300bhp 6·3-litre V-8
olved for the vast 'Grand Mercedes' in 1963. The cars
actised, but tyre trouble persuaded the firm to withdraw
em before the event. MCS

ercer (US)

he Mercer Automobile Company of Trenton, N.J.,
as founded in 1910, but its racing career followed the
troduction of the famous Type 35 Raceabout in 1911.
rly successes were achieved by stripped stock chassis,
t from 1913 onwards the company used the special
ype 45 for their top-line drivers. Successes during 1911
cluded 3rd place at Elgin, Ill., behind cars of double the
ercer's capacity such as Alco and National, and class
ins at Fairmount Park, Phila., Savannah Challenge
rophy (Ga.), and the Panama Pacific Light Car Race.
ercers came 12th and 14th in the Indianapolis 500,
oth cars being driven home afterwards. In 1912 Hughes
nished 3rd at Indy with the smallest engine in the race,

1913 Mercer Indianapolis car. Spencer
Wishart at the wheel. *Photo: Indianapolis
Motor Speedway*

at an average of 76·3mph (122·79kph). Ralph de Palma
won the 300ci (4,916cc) class of the Santa Monica Road
Race, and established Class C records from 1 to 20 miles.
Spencer Wishart on a stock Type 35C won a 200-mile
dirt-track race at Columbus, Ohio, and established world
dirt-track records from 75 to 200 miles. Mercers were
also 1st and 2nd in their class at Elgin. More specialized
racing cars were introduced in 1913, the Model F which
used the 300ci Type 35 engine with lighter reciprocating
parts and balanced crankshaft, and the Type 45 which
had a special racing engine with no production counterpart, of 445ci (7,292cc) capacity and 150bhp. This
engine was used almost exclusively in 1914, except for
events in the 300ci class. 1913 successes included Wishart's
2nd place at Indy in a Type F, de Palma's win at Elgin
also in a Type F, and his three wins out of five races at
San Antonio on a Type 45. Mercers had many other
successes in 1913, including six wins, five 2nds, and five
3rds. The highlight of 1914 was Eddie Pullen's victory
in the Grand Prize at Santa Monica on a Type 45, the
first time that an American car had won this event. In
celebration, the whole Mercer works was given a half-
day holiday. Barney Oldfield was 2nd in the Vanderbilt
Cup, and Pullen won the Corona, Calif., Road Race at
an average of 87·89mph (141·44kph), the fastest speed
in a road race at that time. Unfortunately Wishart
crashed fatally when leading in the Elgin National
Trophy. In 1915 Pullen was 3rd in the Vanderbilt Cup,
and he and G. E. Ruckstell won two races on the new
Tacoma Board Speedway.

In 1913 Mercer engineer Erik H. Delling built an
L-head racing car, the Deltal, which finished 2nd to a
Model F at Elgin, and so impressed Mercer directors
that they bought the design and introduced it as the
22/70 production car for 1915. This model was raced
much less than the F-head cars, as the company felt that
racing success was going increasingly to specialized cars.
However, in 1916 a special car based on the Deltal but
with gear-driven single ohc and a V-radiator was raced
by Joe Thomas. It was not very successful, and although
Mercers were made until 1925, no further racing cars
were built. GNG

Mercury *see* Ford (US)

Merlyn (GB)

Colchester Racing Developments progressed steadily as
car manufacturers after a hesitant start in 1960, despite
somewhat uneven fortunes on the track. Design and
construction were managed by Clive Maskery and
Selwyn Hayward, and generally followed orthodox
principles, with an increasing proportion of components
made by the firm as production expanded.

The early mark numbers were Formula Junior
machines, which made comparatively little impact. The
Marks 4 and 6 were sports cars, of conventional spaceframe chassis design, taking various Coventry Climax or
Ford-based engines. More than 50 were made and some
of these, such as Clive Lacey's machine, figured in the
results list over several years. The Mark 5 was the
Formula Junior car for 1963, when the works drivers
were Roy Pike and Jonathan Williams.

In 1964 the Mark 7 was introduced for F2 or F3, and
Chris Irwin managed some good placings in major
events. The Mark 8 was a V-8-engined sports car of which
only two were made, and Marks 9 and 9A the 1965 and
1966 Formula 3 cars. These were lean years, but the tide
turned again in 1967, mainly due to some good drives in

Left, 1963 Merlyn Mark 3 Formula Junior at Brunton Hill-Climb. H. M. Bennett at the wheel. *Photo: Michael Ware*

Above, 1970 Merlyn Mark 17 Formula Ford at Brands Hatch. John Elliott at the wheel. *Photo: Autosport*

Below, 1960 Merlyn Formula Junior. *Photo: Colchester Racing Developments*

the Mark 10 F3 by Tony Lanfranchi. The following year Tim Schenken was Formula Ford Champion with the Mark 11, and Tony Lanfranchi was runner-up in the F3 class using Marks 10, 10A and 14 cars. The Mark 12 Formula 2 car was also produced in 1968, being run by Bob Gerard's team without conspicuous success.

Schenken repeated his FF triumph in 1969 with the Mark 11A, earning Merlyn the STP Constructors' Trophy, and many other drivers took Merlyns to victories in this class. However, the firm's F3 promise was not fulfilled by the Mark 14A model, and the Mark 15 Formula B version was little more successful. For 1970 the Mark 16 was offered in the F100 class, Mark 17 for FF, Mark 18 for F3, Mark 19 for Group 6 sports-car racing and Mark 20 for FB. Once again the results proved disappointing in all but the FF class, where Merlyns virtually swept the board, with wins by some 25 different drivers, of whom Colin Vandervell became almost invincible and won the Les Leston FF Championship. DF

Métallurgique (B)

The Métallurgique was a very fine fast tourer in its day and from 1904 won many prizes in touring car trials. A 3·8-litre 4-cylinder machine (Métallurgique never made a six) was entered for the TT but scratched, and though Cüpper's similar car led the 1907 race for a lap he ran out of petrol and had to give up. In fact, 1907 was not a good year for the breed: in both the Circuit des Ardennes and the Liedekerke Cup they retired while well up in the field, and one of the two 8-litre Kaiserpreis cars (Lucke's) made the final, only to retire on the first lap.

For the Four-Inch TT of 1908 the firm prepared some very fast ioe cars with 172mm piston strokes said to be capable of 105bhp, but though Brabazon and Cüpper motored to some purpose, a broken valve (in Brabazon's case) and ignition troubles eliminated them. In 1910 some magnificent 5·7-litre machines (also ioe) were entered in the Russian and Prince Henry Trials: one of these later did 105mph (169·0kph) at Brooklands. There were victories in the Tour de France and the Circuit du Maroc in 1912, and in the former event the make again figured in the awards list in 1914. That year Duray finished 3rd in the Russian GP. A 3-litre car was entered in the 1921 Belgian GP, but retired after making the fastest lap; the last of the Métallurgiques, Paul Bastien's ohc 2-litre, was never raced. MCS

MG (GB)

Though the make is always associated with racing, MG were never in a position to maintain a full works team of cars, and their active involvement as a factory is limited to two fairly short periods: 1930–5 and 1963–8. The pre-World War 2 racing cars were catalogued and sold to private owners, who enjoyed works support until the competitions department was closed by Morris edict in 1935. It reopened 20 years later under the watchful eye of BMC with a largely non-racing policy until 1963, when a limited programme of participation was permitted until the Leyland takeover of 1968. Between the two, MG necessarily concentrated on record-breaking.

The first Morris Garages sports cars were 'chummy'-bodied 11·9mph Morris Cowleys, with one of which Kimber gained a gold medal in the 1923 Land's End Trial. Further awards were won by Billy Cooper, Russell Chiesmann and others in 1924/5 with the MG versions of the 13·9hp Oxford. Then Kimber built a stark two-seater with ohv Hotchkiss engine in much-modified Morris chassis, and with this won another gold medal in the 1925 Land's End.

MGs first racing victory came in 1927 when a sv 1802cc tourer won an event near Buenos Aires. In 1928 two new ohc models appeared, the 847cc Midget and 2,468cc 18/80 Six. The latter was developed through a second production model (the 18/80 Mk II or A-type) into the first MG designed specifically for racing. It was the Mk III or Tigress, with twin-plug ignition, dry sump, and body built to AIACR regulations, selling at £895. However, its first appearance in the 1930 Double-Twelve was unsuccessful and development was discontinued.

Meanwhile the standard 18/80 models were being eclipsed in trials by the M-type Midget. Two enthusiasts named Edmondson and Randall asked the factory to prepare a team for the Double-Twelve, and these Midgets won the team prize. Two M-types also ran at Le Mans in 1930 without success, but Samuelson took his car on to the Spa 24 Hours and completed the distance. Then J. A. Palmes and George Eyston sought MGs assistance in preparing a Class H record car, for which they had an M-type engine with capacity reduced to 743cc. This was fitted into a factory prototype chassis known as EX120. With its Eyston covered 100km at 87·3mph (140·50kph) in December 1930. A supercharger was then fitted, and on 16 February 1931 this MG became the smallest car in the world to achieve 100mph (160kph).

Two weeks later the production racing Midget was announced. It was the C-type or 'Montlhéry' Midget, costing £295 unsupercharged. The first 14 were delivered Brooklands in time to practise for the 1931 Double-twelve, and took the first five places in that race. They then finished 1-2-3 in the Saorstat Cup, gaining 1st and 3rd overall in the Irish GP, and went on to secure 1st and 3rd in the Ulster TT; supercharged for that event, they established a new class record on the Ards circuit. September the 750cc handicap speed for the 500 Miles was fixed at 93·97mph (151·23kph), but Hall's Midget managed a 92·17mph (148·33kph) average to finish 3rd, and MG again took the team prize.

Though cars entered for Le Mans and the German GP 1100cc class gained no awards, it was a triumphant first full season backed up by many successes in lesser events, and made handicappers very wary of MG in 1932. Norman Black, winner of the Irish GP and the TT, came 3rd in the 1932 1000 Miles at 75·5mph (121·51kph), running unsupercharged. Mille Miglia and Le Mans entries were again unsuccessful, but Hugh Hamilton's C-type gained MGs first major Continental victory in the 800cc class of the German GP, beating many 1·5-litre cars. In the TT, Hall came 3rd behind the Rileys, Horton, with a single-seater body on his C-type, won the 500 Miles at a 96·29mph (154·96kph) average; in an earlier Brooklands event he had taken the Outer Circuit 750cc class record at 115·29mph (185·54kph). He was awarded the BRDC Gold Star for 1932, as

Eyston had been the previous year. With his new record car, the 'Magic Midget', Eyston achieved 120·56mph (194kph) in December, just two years after his first MG record at 87·3mph (140·50kph), and went on to take all international Class H records up to 24hr at 70·61mph (113·64kph).

In late 1931 a new small Six had appeared, the F series Magna (one of which Dick Seaman bought to use in trials and rallies), together with the four-seater D-type Midget. Mid-1932 brought the J series Midget, which in two-seater form set a fashion that lasted more than 20 years. The Magna gave birth to the K series Magnette, first seen as an 1,100cc saloon at the 1932 Motor Show in London; racing versions of this were also catalogued. Earl Howe offered to finance a daring attack against the Maseratis on their home ground in the Mille Miglia. Two prototypes were built, one for the 1933 Monte Carlo (where it made ftd in the Mont des Mules hill-climb), the other for extensive tests in Italy. The new K3, a supercharged 1,100cc Six with preselector gearbox, was driven in the Mille Miglia by Howe, Hamilton, Eyston, Lurani, Birkin and Rubin. It won its class and gained the team prize. Even the Prince of Wales attended the triumphal dinner held afterwards in London.

The MG range now included the unsupercharged J2 at £200 (popular in trials), the supercharged J3 (successful in Continental rallies) and the 'full-race' J4 Midget at £445 (later increased to £495). For 6-cylinder enthusiasts there were the L-type Magna at £285, its engine similar

Left, 1930 MG 18/100 Tigress sold to Viscount Rothschild. *Photo: Wilson McComb Collection*

Above, 1930 MG M-type Midgets in the Brooklands Double Twelve, driven by Randall and Stisted. *Photo: Wilson McComb Collection*

Below, 1933 MG J2 Midget on Nailsworth Ladder. *Photo: Wilson McComb Collection*

Below, 1933 MG J4 Midget. *Photo: BMC*

Left, 1934 MG Q-type Midget at Donington Park. R. G. Everitt at the wheel. *Photo: Wilson McComb Collection*

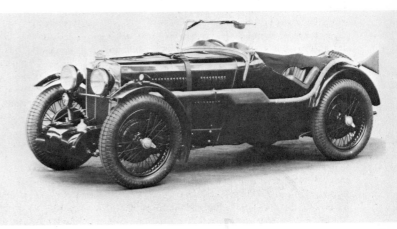

to the K3 but unsupercharged, various types of K-series Magnette, and the impressive K3 at £650 (later £795), ready to race. Entry lists became peppered with the initials MG.

Only a few of the next two years successes can be mentioned. Whitney Straight's K3 beat the dohc single-seater Maseratis to win the 1933 Coppa Acerbo Junior. Horton's old C-type beat the works Austins to win the 800cc class of the German GP at 90·9mph (146·29kph). Hamilton's J4 won the Eifelrennen 800cc event by 25 minutes, made 4th ftd at Freiburg with a faster climb than the best 1·5-litre, and 3rd ftd at Riesengebirge. MG's many other hill-climb successes in 1933 included a record ftd by Hall's K3 at Craigantlet. Hall also won the 1,100cc class of the International Trophy, finishing 2nd overall ahead of three other K3s, and won the 500 Miles outright at an average of 106·53mph (171·46kph), with Martin's Magna 2nd. Hall was awarded the BRDC Gold Star for 1933. MGs were also 3rd and 4th in the British Empire Trophy, 2nd and 3rd in the Isle of Man Mannin Beg (with a new lap record), and 1st in the 1,100cc class at Le Mans with Ford's C-type a surprising 6th overall. There were countless other successes, but the race of the year was the 1933 Ulster TT, which Nuvolari, in a well-used K3 demonstrator, won by less than 1 minute from Hamilton's J4. Nuvolari's race-winning average of 78·65mph (126·57kph) remained unbeaten until 1951, when Moss won at 83·55mph (134·46kph) in a C-type Jaguar.

In 1934 the K3 was fitted with a slim, long-tailed body, modified brakes and new supercharger. A similar body was fitted to the new Q-type racing Midget, sold at £550. Like the production P-type this had a 3-bearing crankshaft, and chassis enlarged to cope with increased power output. The racing 750cc MG was now almost as fast as its 1,100cc stablemate. Pomeroy has pointed out that the Q engine gave a far higher specific output (145bhp/litre) than the contemporary V-16 Auto Union

(85bhp/litre). However, Hall's sprint K3 engine was developed to give 200bhp, or 182bhp/litre.

Home successes in 1934 included the first five places in the Mannin Beg; 1st overall and team prize in the British Empire Trophy; 3rd in the 500 Miles; 2nd and 3rd in the Nuffield Trophy and the County Down Trophy; and class victories in the International Trophy, Shelsley and Craigantlet. Abroad, MGs gained class wins in the Eifelrennen, the Avusrennen, and more than a dozen hill-climbs including Freiburg (Kohlrausch), Mont Ventoux (Seaman) and Stelvio (Cecchini). Seaman, who had Straight's old K3, also won the Prix de Berne and, in the Coppa Acerbo Junior, came 3rd behind the K3s of Hamilton and Cecchini. Cecchini also won the Circuit of Modena, beating Farina's Maserati, and gained the 1,100cc championship of Italy. Maillard-Brune's J4 tied for 1st place in the Bol d'Or 24 hours. At Le Mans, Ford returned with a K3 to hold 2nd place until hit by another car, when the Martin and Eccles K3 finished 4th overall and won the 2-litre class. For the Ulster TT, superchargers were banned. MG built a modified version of the production N Magnette known as the NE, and a team of three came 3rd in the Relay Race. In the TT, Dodson's NE scored MGs third victory in that event at 74·65mph (120·14kph), only 17 seconds ahead of Hall's Bentley.

For Eyston, MG had built a special offset-transmission K3, the Magic Magnette, with one body for racing and another for records. With this, Eyston put the Class G flying start mile up to 128·70mph (207·1kph), while Denly came close in the Magic Midget with 128·63mph (207·05kph) in the Magic Midget. MG still held all Class H and most Class G records. The Q-type's standing start mile 85·59mph (137·74kph) was faster than that of the K3 83.2mph (133·90kph).

With the arrival of the ERA, MG scored fewer out-right victories in 1935, though the class awards continued. In May they announced the remarkable R-type at £750.

Far left, 1935 MG R-type Midget chassis. *Photo: Wilson McComb Collection*

Left, 1934 MG EX135 in original (Magic Magnette) form. *Photo: Wilson McComb Collection*

Far left, 1947 MG TC Midget at a 1950s Snetterton meeting. *Photo: C. Duke*

Left, 1950 MG TD Midget competing in the Highland Three Days Rally. *Photo: W. K. Henderson*

It had a basically Q-type engine in a backbone chassis with independent suspension all round. A similar Magnette version, the S-type, was also planned, and Kimber was campaigning for a 1,500cc GP Formula. But Kimber had pushed Morris's reluctant acquiescence too far. The MG racing department was closed down overnight.

Ten R-types were built and sold, but they lacked the factory backing to overcome teething troubles, though they took class victories in the 1935 International Trophy and various sprints, won at Albi and Montlhéry, and came 3rd in the Nuffield Trophy. The older cars continued to do well in private hands, Kohlrausch in

Below, 1950 MG TD Midget racing in California. Photo: Wilson McComb Collection

Bottom, 1962 MGA 1600 at Brands Hatch. F. Wilson McComb at the wheel. Photo: Wilson McComb Collection

particular gaining many awards with a K3 and the old Magic Midget: the latter made 2nd ftd at Felsberg behind Stuck's Auto Union. He also raised the flying start kilometre to 130·51mph (210·02kph) in Class H. Maillard-Brune won the Bol d'Or at record speed and the 2-litre class at Le Mans, came 4th in the Albi GP and 2nd in the Orléans GP, ahead of Hertzberger's K3. At home, MGs were second only to Bugatti in the number of awards gained at Brooklands.

In 1936, MGs won a quarter of all the races at Brooklands, but they were minor events compared to those of previous years, and not a single MG finished the British Empire Trophy or the International Trophy. Several road races were won in Ireland, Australia and South Africa, a K3 won the Grand Prix des Frontières in Belgium, and Kohlrausch and Maillard-Brune gained many hill-climb awards. Kohlrausch also raised the

flying start kilometre to 140·51mph (226·12kph), a figure unbeaten until 1946. The Abingdon factory turned to more active participation in trials, their 'Cream Crackers' and 'Three Musketeers' rapidly becoming unbeatable, though they had to make do with push-rod ohv cars when Morris discontinued the ohc MG range. The old racing MGs continued to win events in various parts of the world, and MG built for Goldie Gardner a new record car which was, in fact, Eyston's 1934 car rebodied. The outstanding achievement of this was 203·54mph (327·56kph) over the fs kilometre in 1939 with the 1,100cc K3 engine. War came in 1939 with three Brooklands records permanently held by MGs: Campbell Circuit Class G (70·60mph; 113·62kph), Outer Circuit Class G (124·40mph; 200·2kph) and Class H (122·40mph; 196·90kph).

After World War 2 Gardner returned to record-breaking with a succession of figures in various capacity classes. Several old MGs were revived to win various events with new drivers, including Salvadori and Duncan Hamilton, and Monkhouse's 14-year-old K3 made fastest lap in the 1947 Reims GP. Abingdon now built one sports car only, the basically pre-war TC Midget with 1,250cc push rod ohv engine. It sold well abroad and, for those who raced this model, MG produced 'stage tuning' instructions. More than any other make the MG TC and its successor the TD furnished the base of the American sports car boom. George Valentine's TC earned SCCA G production honours as late as 1955. Phil Hill, Ron Flockhart, Bob Holbert and Carroll Shelby were among many who started their racing careers with the MG TC. Overseas successes brought useful publicity, and sales began to soar. Late in 1949 the TD, with ifs and more comfortable (but heavier) body, was produced to meet American demand. Three cars were built unobtrusively for Jacobs, Phillips and Lund, who raced them in British events. They took a class 1-2-3 in the 1950 TT, but were beaten by an HRG 1500 at Silverstone.

George Phillips had raced a home-made TC special at Le Mans in 1949 and 1950. For the 1951 events, MG built him a TD-based car which was, in fact, the first prototype of the MGA. It did not last the race, but the Gardner record car was now fitted with a supercharged engine. It took some records at 137·4mph (221·1kph) in 1951, and some at 189·5mph (305kph) in 1952. That year the first Sebring 12 Hours was held and MGs won the team prize; the best TD finished 6th overall. British 1,500cc racing was gradually dominated by Lester, Lister, Lotus and Kieft, all using the very tunable MG engine. The TDs won their class again in the 1953 TT, but were beaten easily by an Osca at Sebring.

Meanwhile, MG had completed their designs for a new car similar to the Phillips Le Mans entry of 1951, but with a different and much lower chassis frame. This was submitted to BMC late in 1952, but turned down in favour of the new Austin-Healey 100. As a stopgap, the TD was modified to become the TF.

The spare MGA prototype frame was fitted with Gardner-type body and unsupercharged TF engine. This car, EX179, achieved 120·74mph (194·26kph) for 12hr and 153·69mph (247·34kph) for 10 miles at Utah in 1954. The new production TF, its engine stretched to 1,500cc by mid-1954, proved a popular rally car but no match for the new 2-litre Triumph in top speed or acceleration. Also successful in rallies was the ZA Magnette, with BMC 1·5-litre engine and Wolseley-based body.

By late 1954 the new Competition Department of

1965 MGB Le Mans sports car. *Photo: BMC*

BMC was ready to open at Abingdon, and permission had been given for production of the MGA, with engine similar to that of the ZA Magnette. Great plans were made to re-enter racing, and teams entered for Le Mans and the TT, but disastrous accidents at both events caused an understandable change of attitude by BMC. Attention returned to rallies, and Nancy Mitchell drove an MGA and Magnette to win the ladies' championship in 1956 and 1957. In both those years, local drivers with MGAs won the team award at Sebring. At home, the MGA won the *Autosport* production sports car championship in 1956. Jacobs, his own career ended by his crash at Le Mans in 1955, prepared two Magnettes which gained their class in the BRSCC saloon racing championship in 1958. Abingdon built a new record car, EX181, to attempt four miles a minute in Class F. It had a tear-drop body and sc prototype of the 2ohc MGA engine at the rear. This gave 290bhp from 1,500cc, providing an interesting comparison with the Formula 1 Ferraris and Maseratis of a few years before. Moss attained 245·64mph (395·36kph) at Utah in 1957. Two years later the same car, enlarged to 1,506cc for Class E, reached 254·91mph (410·22kph) driven by Phil Hill in what proved to be MGs last record attempt.

In 1957 two MGAs ran in the Mille Miglia to take 2nd and 3rd in the limited-price class behind the Austin-Healey. In 1958 the production 1,600cc dohc MGA was announced. Though too easily damaged in unsympathetic hands (and therefore discontinued after two years), the engine gave good results when rpm limits were observed, and two cars run by Dick Jacobs had three successful seasons without mechanical mishap. They took a class 3rd in the TT races of 1958 and 1960, and won their class of the *Autosport* championship in both 1959 and 1960. For the American MG importers, MG prepared dohc coupés which came 2nd and 3rd in class at Sebring in 1959 and again in 1960. A private syndicate of MG Car Club members entered a car (built 'under the counter' at Abingdon) for Le Mans; it retired after hitting a dog in 1959, but won the 2-litre class in 1960.

The new Sprite-based Midget won its class in the 1961 RAC Rally, and in the Monte Carlo of 1962, where the new MGA 1600 (with push rod engine) also gained a class victory, as in the Tulip Rally of that year. The 1600 coupés came 1st and 2nd in class at Sebring in 1961, but gained no awards in 1962. At the 1962 Motor Show in London the MGB was announced, with new

bodywork and 1,800cc engine. Two cars were prepared for Sebring, but the severe 1962-3 winter in England prevented proper testing, and both ran their bearings because of oil surge.

However, in 1963 MG were at last allowed to prepare some cars for selected long-distance races apart from Sebring, and of course rallying. A lone MGB completed the 1963 Le Mans race at a 92mph (148·06kph) average to score MG's fifth class victory in that event. In 1964 the works MGB won the GT category of the Monte Carlo outright, came 3rd in class at Sebring, and averaged 99·95mph (160·85kph) at Le Mans to win the *Motor* Trophy. The single MGB made its last appearance at Le Mans in 1965 to take a class 2nd at 98·26mph (158·14kph); thereafter, the Le Mans qualifying speed was obviously too high for a standard-bodied car of such an engine capacity. At Sebring, too, it was 2nd in class, but it won the 1965 Brands Hatch 1,000 Miles outright, MGBs also coming 1-2-3 in class.

In their usual unobtrusive way, the Abingdon works built two lightweight Midgets for Dick Jacobs, and these cars won many awards including class victories at the Nürburgring 1,000 Kilometres, the Silverstone and Brands Hatch GT races, the Sebring 12 Hours, and a class 2nd in the 1965 Targa Florio.

In 1966 the MGBs gained category victories in the Targa Florio and Spa 1000 Kilometres, and class wins in the Sebring 12 Hours, the Circuit of Ireland, the Rothman's 12 Hours in Australia, and the Montlhéry 1,000 Kilometres. In the 84-hour Marathon at the Nürburgring, successor to the Liège road event, the works MGB won outright and was the only GT car to finish. The following year brought class victories at Sebring, the Monza 1,000 Kilometres and the Spa Sports Car GP. These cars were enlarged to 2004cc, but still had standard bodywork. Six lightweight GT bodies were now made, and the first car completed ran well in the 1967 Targa Florio. With 3-litre MGC engine installed it came 3rd in the prototype category at Sebring in 1968, while a Midget won the sports car category outright. Carson Baird and W. Koch won SCCA Class G championships in Midgets in 1966 and 1970. Development of the 3-litre engine looked promising, with 200bhp available and more to come. Then came the Leyland takeover in May 1968. MG racing activities came to an end, and the remaining lightweight bodies were left unused in store. FWMcC

1970 Mildren-Waggott 2-litre. *Photo: R. L. Mackenzie*

Mildren-Waggott (AUS)

The two Mildren-Waggott racing cars burst on to the Australian motor racing scene late in 1969 with a spectacular one-two victory in the Hordern Trophy Race at Warwick Farm. In their first racing year the two cars took out the Australian F1 and F2 championships— the F1 with a larger 2·5-litre V-8 Alfa Romeo engine. Both cars designed by Alex Mildren, a former winner of the Australian Grand Prix in a Cooper-Climax who now runs a successful Alfa Romeo dealership in Australia's eastern states.

The first rolling chassis was built in England in late 1968, designed in conjunction with Alex Mildren by Len Bailey and built in Alan Mann's workshops. It was fitted with the Alfa Romeo engine and raced first by British saloon car champion Frank Gardner in the 1969 Tasman Series and later by Australian Gold Star Champion Kevin Bartlett. In late 1969, the monocoque tub was fitted with a 2-litre Waggott FVA engine designed and built by Sydney constructor Mervyn Waggott. The second Mildren car was built in Sydney by Bob Britten. Of spaceframe construction it was first fitted with a drogue 1,600cc Waggott engine for testing purposes, and later with a replica 2-litre engine. Using the 1,600cc Waggott, the car won the Formula 2 Championship of Australia with Max Stewart at the wheel.

In 1970 both cars placed equal third in the Tasman Championship—Kevin Bartlett's monocoque-bodied vehicle being slightly faster than the less sophisticated spaceframe car. TBF

Miller (US)

The cars of Harry Armenius Miller were the most famous American racing cars of their day. The first Miller engines, built in 1916, were 4-cylinder 16-valve single-ohc units of 289ci (4,740cc) capacity. They had desmodromic, or positively closed, valves. One was used in Barney Oldfield's Miller-built Golden Submarine, a remarkable car with streamlined, fully-enclosed cockpit and almost perfect teardrop form in plan view. During 1917 Oldfield won at least seven match races against Ralph DePalma's Packard Twin Six, and also broke international dirt track records from one to fifty miles. In 1918 he ran the car with open cockpit, probably because the noise in its closed form was insupportable. At least one other open car was built with the 289ci Miller engine.

During 1920 design went ahead with Miller's new engine, a 183ci (2,999cc) straight-8. The team of Miller, Leo Goossen and Fred Offenhauser incorporated ideas from Duesenberg, (3-bearing crankshaft straight-8 layout), Peugeot (inclined ohvs, four per cylinder, operated by twin overhead camshafts) and Ballot (piston type cam followers). With this engine installed in a Duesenberg chassis, Jimmy Murphy won the 1922 Indy 500 and four other important races to become AAA National Champion for the year. Under the name Durant Special six more 183ci cars were commissioned by Cliff Durant, son of William Crapo Durant, and these won seven races in the last few months of 1922. The following year saw the new 122ci (1,999cc) formula and almost universal adoption of single-seater bodies for racing cars. Durant ordered from Miller a team of 121ci (1,983cc) straight-8s, now with five-bearing crankshafts and hemispherical combustion chambers. They developed 120bhp at 5,000rpm. Harry C. Stutz also bought two cars, raced as HCS Specials, while Miller himself raced one car as a Miller Special. At the 1923 Indianapolis race, no fewer than nine Miller-built cars started. Tommy Milton's HCS won from Harry Hartz' Durant, with Durants in 3rd and 4th places. Six out of the first seven places went to Miller-built cars. For the rest of 1923 Miller continued to triumph, winning all the major races on the board tracks. A team of three Millers ran at Monza in the European Grand Prix, and Jimmy Murphy finished 3rd, behind the Fiats of Salamano and Nazzaro. Count Zborowski finished 2nd at Sitges, the best performance of a Miller in long-distance European racing. (Gwenda Stewart's Derby-Miller won a number of short races at Brooklands.) For 1924 the design was not greatly changed. Although Duesenberg won at Indy with a supercharged car, the majority of the year's honours went to Miller, including AAA records at 141·2mph (227·2kph) with a 121ci (1983cc) car, and 151·3mph (243·5kph) with a 183ci (2,999cc) car. At the Culver City board speedway Benny Hill averaged 126·9mph (204·2kph) for the 250-mile race, while Hartz covered several laps at 133mph (214·0kph). The first of the fwd Millers appeared in 1925, with 121ci (1,983cc) engines and De Dion axles. The second fwd car built was bought by Cliff Durant and named Junior 8 after one of the models of the Locomobile company which had recently been acquired by his father. Dave Lewis and Benny Hill drove it into 2nd place at Indy, while rear-wheel-drive Millers were 4th, 5th, 6th, 7th and 9th. Over the whole 1925 season Duesenberg won more races than Miller, but from 1926 onwards Miller's position improved dramatically. The 91ci (1,491·2cc) formula came in for 1926, and Miller produced what was one of the most beautiful racing cars ever made, a narrow single-seater machine with twin-ohc supercharged engine developing 154bhp at 7,000rpm in its original form, and up to 285bhp at 8,000rpm when tuned by Frank Lockhart. The first appearance of the Miller 91 was at Indy when Lockhart won a race curtailed by rain to 400 miles. Apart from de Paolo's 5th place in a Duesenberg, all the first nine places were taken by Miller 91s. Lockhart's car had rwd, but an fwd model was available at $15,000, compared with the price of $10,000 for the rwd cars. Fifty 91s were built, of which not more than a dozen had front-wheel-drive. Although the fwd car was faster over a straight line, the rwd had a better racing record, the winning Indy cars in 1926 (Lockhart), 1928 (Meyer) and 1929 (Keech) all driving on the rear wheels. In 1927 Lockhart covered a flying mile at Muroc Dry Lake at a

1923 Miller HCS Special, winner at Indianapolis. Tommy Milton at the wheel.
Photo: Indianapolis Motor Speedway

Centre, 1929 Miller 91, winner at Indianapolis. Ray Keech at the wheel.
Photo: Indianapolis Motor Speedway

Left, 1932 Miller-Hartz fwd, winner at Indianapolis. Fred Frame at the wheel.
Photo: Indianapolis Motor Speedway

two way average of 164mph (263·9kph). Whichever wheels drove, the Miller 91 dominated American racing from 1926 to 1929, winning nearly all the important races on dirt tracks and board speedways. They also took many world records, and here the fwd cars really did shine. In 1929 Leon Duray bought two Millers, known as Packard Cable Specials, to Europe. At Montlhéry he raised the 5-mile class record to 139·22mph (224·03kph), and the 10-mile record to 135·33mph (217·85kph). In the Monza Grand Prix he made fastest lap at 118·147mph (190·17kph), and led for three laps of the first heat before retiring. For the second heat he used the reserve car, but again retired. These fwd cars were subsequently acquired by Ettore Bugatti in exchange for three Type 43s (with which Duray set up a short-lived Bugatti agency in Hollywood). It was no coincidence that the Type 50 Bugatti which appeared in 1930 was the first of the make to use a twin-ohc layout. Another famous record car was the Derby-Miller, developed by Douglas Hawkes and driven by his wife Gwenda. The bore was increased to give a capacity of 103ci (1,673cc), and in this form it took many Class E records at Montlhéry including the lap record at 147·8mph (237·9kph). Gwenda also took the Brooklands ladies lap record at 135·95mph (218·78kph) in 1935.

In 1930 the 91ci formula was replaced in American racing by the so-called Junk Formula which permitted production engines of up to 366ci (6 litres) but banned superchargers and forbade more than two valves per cylinder. Miller sold his business in disgust, but Goossen and Offenhauser remained with the firm, modifying Miller engines to suit the new formula. They did this so well that Miller-engined cars won every Indianapolis race from 1930 to 1938. The 151ci (2·5-litre) straight-8 Miller-Hartz with which Lou Arnold won in 1930 had front-wheel drive, giving the first Indy victory to this system. A similar 183ci (2,999cc) car driven by Fred Frame won in 1932. A 4-cylinder engine developed by Offenhauser from a marine unit powered the 2nd place car in 1930, and this was the basis of the Offenhauser engines used in so many Indy cars over the next 35 years.

Miller, Goossen, and Offenhauser came together again in 1931 in the Rellimah Company (H. A. Miller spelt backwards) when, as well as Frame's Miller-Hartz, they built several unorthodox cars including a V-16 and two 4-wheel-drive V-8s for Indianapolis. They were not successful. Miller's next venture was unconnected with Goossen and Offenhauser who continued to build engines but not complete cars. With Ford backing, Miller designed a new all-independently sprung car powered by a 221ci (3,622cc) Ford V-8 engine driving the front wheels. Four of these ran at Indy in 1935 but were insufficiently prepared, and all retired. Henry Ford withdrew his support and Miller was on his own once more. For 1938 he built two Offenhauser-powered all-independent cars but failed to qualify them for Indy. However, in 1938 he was commissioned by the Gulf Oil Company to design a completely new car which would run under their name. It had a rear-mounted 180·4ci (2,957cc) 6-cylinder engine (the first and only six Miller ever designed) developing 246bhp at 6,500rpm. The 45° inclined engine drove all four wheels via a 4-speed gearbox. Fuel tanks were built into the channel frame. Four Gulf-Millers were built but none had any success. They ran at Indy in 1939, 1940, and 1941, but never completed a race. Miller also built two road-going sports cars, a 325bhp V-8 in 1928, and a four-wheel-drive V-16 in 1932. He died in May 1943. GNG

Above, 1938 Gulf-Miller at Indianapolis in 1941. Al Miller at the wheel. *Photo: Indianapolis Motor Speedway*

Below, 1963 Milmor Mark 5 1172cc at Brunton Hill-Climb. B. A. M. Small at the wheel. *Photo: Michael Ware*

1907 Minerva team for the Kaiserpreis. *Photo: Montagu Motor Museum*

Milmor (GB)

This was the name given to a small-production series of club-racing 1172 and Clubman's Formula cars built during the 1960s by Howard Milborrow. Each succeeding model was better-finished and equipped but apart from club appearances they have made little impact on the motor racing scene. DCN

Minerva (B)

Minerva's participation in sporting events was spasmodic. In 1905, when the Hon. C. S. Rolls was still responsible for British sales, he entered a pair of 2·9-litre 4-cylinder cars with 4-speed overdrive gearboxes for the TT, but both retired, while the same fate attended the 22hp cars entered by Warwick Wright in 1906. Minerva prepared a team of chain-driven cars with 8-litre ioe 5-bearing engines for the Kaiserpreis in 1907, but none of them reached the final, which makes it surprising that that year's Circuit des Ardennes turned out to be a Minerva benefit, in which Moore-Brabazon

Above, 1914 Minerva in the TT. Léon Molon at the wheel. *Photo: Montagu Motor Museum*

Right, 1928 Minerva AKS at Brooklands in the 1930s. G. L. Baker at the wheel. *Photo: Montagu Motor Museum*

Below, 1967 Mirage GT at the Nürburgring in 1969. *Photo: Autosport*

Right, 1969 Mirage-Cosworth 3-litre at Watkins Glen. *Photo: David Hodges Collection*

averaged 59·6mph (95·92kph) to win. The other cars finished in 2nd, 3rd and 6th places, while the same machines, driven by Porlier and Moore-Brabazon, came in 1st and 2nd in the Liedekerke Cup. Minerva supported the Herkomer and Prince Henry Trials with equal lack of success, but their sleeve-valve cars, introduced in 1909, were less sluggish than contemporary Daimlers, and had quite a good record in the tougher trials.

Janek won the 1911 Swedish Winter Cup (in which Minerva gained five other trophies), this success being followed up by Hans Osterman, who took 1st place in 1913, and again in 1914. Minerva also won the 1913 Swedish Summer Cup; took 3rd place in that year's Spanish Touring-Car GP; and did progressively better in successive Austrian Alpine Trials — one clean sheet in 1912, two in 1913, and the Alpine Wanderpreis in 1914. If the good performance of a team of virtually standard 2·5-litre 4-cylinder cars in the Belgian GP of 1912 meant little, the 3·3-litre machines which ran in the 1914 TT were excellent performers. Riecken finished 2nd, Molon 3rd, and Porporato 5th, though unkind people credited this to their smoke-screens which made the Minervas difficult to pass.

After World War 1 Minerva lost interest in competi-

tions until 1928, when a team of 12CV saloons ran in the Alpine Trial, and they also fielded a team of vast 5,954cc 6-cylinder AKS tourers for the Belgian 24-Hour Race. These found difficulty in staying on the course, and none of them qualified, though Baker campaigned in a similar car at Brooklands between 1930 and 1933, and lapped at over 96mph (154·50kph). MCS

Minijem (GB)

Although designed primarily as a miniature road-going GT, this BMC Mini-based kit-built car achieved a remarkable 2nd in class in 1967 at the Nürburgring in the hands of its progenitor, Jeremy Delmar-Morgan. Production was later taken over by Daniel Pearce and Robin Statham of Fellpoint Ltd, and minor improvements were introduced, with a new glassfibre body mould for the Mark II version announced in 1968. Total production had exceeded 300 by 1970. DF

Mirage (GB)

JW Automotive Engineering was established by John Wyer and John Willment late in 1966, in effect to take over Ford Advanced Vehicles, and responsibility for GT40 production and maintenance. GT40s were also raced in a team sponsored by the Gulf Oil Corporation,

and new cars produced under the name Mirage.

Designed by Len Bailey, the first Mirage was a lightweight version of the GT40, with a smoother body and powered by 4·7-, 5- or 5·7-litre Ford V-8s. It was first raced in the 1967 Monza 1,000 Kilometres and gained its first victory in the Spa 1,000 Kilometres; others, less important, followed in the Paris 1,000 Kilometres, in Scandinavia and in South Africa. Changed regulations made it ineligible for Championship races in 1968; one of three built survived, and was sold to Guthrie, who raced it successfully for two years.

A Group 6 Gulf-Mirage M2/300 was designed by Len Terry for 1968, but did not appear until 1969. It was a straightforward monocoque built around the 385bhp BRM V-12 engine, but with this was obviously not competitive. Another version powered by the Cosworth DFV was built by mid-season. This showed more promise, especially in open form (it led the Austrian GP until the steering failed, and won the Imola 500). Then it was sidelined when Gulf-JWA agreed to run the front-line Porsche team in 1970.

Early in 1970 the first single-seater Mirage appeared, the conventional Mk 5 Formula Ford Car designed by Pat Rochefort, which used engines tuned by JWA. DWH

Mitsubishi (J)
This Japanese concern is well known for its Colt series of small capacity vans and saloons, but during the 1960s a limited number of F2 cars were built mainly for national use, but also appearing in such international events as the Macau GP. These were rather crudely-built machines at first but later were remodelled on Brabham spaceframe lines. In the 1970 JAF GP, Ikusawa drove a 'Mitsubishi Colt F2' which was nothing less than an original Brabham-Cosworth BT30 painted in black and white tiger stripes. DCN

Mitter (D)
Gerhard Mitter specialized in tuning DKW 2-stroke engines, and introduced a Formula Junior racing car in 1959. He enlarged the capacity of the normal 998cc DKW engine to 1,100cc and obtained 85bhp at 5,500rpm. Mitter very often drove his own cars and gained a number of wins including the Gaisberg Hill-Climb in 1959, when he defeated the works Porsche RSK, and the 1960 FJ Championship. Later, until his death in racing, he became well-known as a driver for Porsche. HON

Mongoose see Indianapolis Cars

Monopol; Monopoletta (D)
Helmut Polensky, the successful BMW driver of pre-World War 2 years, designed and built a Formula 2 racing car in 1948. His basic components were tuned 2-litre BMW 328 engines—placed in the rear and giving about 130bhp—and drilled ladder-type tubular frames. Polensky drove his own cars and won the Schotten Race in 1949. When Formula 3 came into being, Polensky built the Monopoletta using a 500cc opposed-twin BMW engine. HON

Monopole see Panhard

Monroe see Frontenac

Montier (F)
The Garage Montier of rue Pierre Charron, Paris specialized in sporting conversions of Fords, beginning with

Above, 1951 Monopoletta 500. *Photo: Autosport*

Right, 1927 Montier-Ford. Guy Montier at the wheel. *Photo: T. A. S. O. Mathieson Collection*

the Model T in 1923. They fitted an ohv head, light aluminium pistons, more powerful brakes, and a lowered chassis, and sold their Montier Spéciales to the public as well as racing them. From 1923 to 1925 they entered a car at Le Mans, and their best performance was that of Montier *père* and Ourion who finished 14th in 1923. They were more successful with single-seater racing cars, coming 2nd in the 1927 La Baule Grand Prix and in the 1929 Torvilliers Circuit, while they also entered the Coupe de la Commission Sportive at Montlhéry in 1927, and the 1930 San Sebastian GP. In the 1933 Circuit de Dieppe, Montier *fils* drove a 'straight-8' consisting of two Model A engines in line, and in 1934 the Ford V-8 engine was used in a car which finished 5th in the Belgian GP. GNG

Moorland see Gemini

Morano-Marguerite see Marguerite

Moretti (I)
Aquilino Branca built the range of Moretti production cars at a factory at Buscate, a suburb of Milan, and entered small-capacity sports car racing and later Formula Junior during the 1950s. The true Moretti racing car, the FJ, was based on sports components, and a rear-engined model appeared in 1959 with which Branca put up some fine performances. More recently the name Branca has appeared on a line of small production F3 and National Formula cars, which have been run with little success outside Italy. As with many of the later model FJ and early model F3 cars from Italian manufacturers, these were virtually copies of the Brabham spaceframe designs. DCN

Morgan (GB)
The Morgan 3-wheeler always suffered from an anomalous status, since it lay in the no-man's land between the ACU and the car clubs. As early as 1911 H. F. S. Morgan himself drove one of his cars in the ACU Six Days' Trial, and a gold medal was won in the make's first London–Exeter. In 1912 one example put 59 miles (94·95km) into the hour at Brooklands to set up a new cyclecar record. Lambert finished 3rd in the first race for cyclecars and sidecars at the track in 1913, when McMinnies won the Cyclecar GP at Amiens in an ohv JAP-engined Morgan at 41·9mph (67·43kph), only to be disqualified as being a 'sidecar'. Ware's 773cc machine lapped Brooklands at 63·76mph (102·62kph) in 1914, and the cars were back in competitions in 1919, when 'HFS' won gold medals in the London–Edinburgh and the ACU Six Days, and Honel won the cyclecar class of the Circuit de l'Eure in France.

Top, 1920 Morgan 3-wheeler, winner of Whitsun Long Handicap at Brooklands. E. B. Ware at the wheel. Photo: Montagu Motor Museum

Top right, 1924 Morgan 3-wheeler in 200-Mile Race at Brooklands. E. B. Ware's car at the pits. Photo: Montagu Motor Museum

Above, c 1925 Morgan 3-wheeler on Beggars' Roost Hill in the MCC Lands End Trial. Photo: Montagu Motor Museum

Above right, 1929 Morgan 3-wheeler. Robin Jackson at the wheel. Photo: Montagu Motor Museum

By 1920 the French Darmont company was manufacturing its own version of the Morgan, and the Malvern-built cars were henceforth campaigned across the Channel only by British drivers. Ware's 1914 980cc car, built for the cancelled 1914 Cyclecar GP, won the BMCRC 3-wheeler race at Brooklands in 1920, though his challenge in the cyclecar race at Amiens came to an end when a cylinder blew. There were the usual successes in trials: three gold medals in the 1921 ACU Six Days; the premier award for H.F.S. Morgan in the 1922 ACU Stock Trial; three golds in the Six Days and no fewer than eight in the London–Edinburgh, victories for Ware in the 1923 and 1924 JCC General Efficiency events; a silver cup for HFS in the 1924 Scottish Six Days; and three golds and the team prize (Goodall, Horton and Carr) in the 1926 International Six Days. A star performance was put up in the 1927 London–Edinburgh Trial, when fourteen Morgans were entered, collecting eleven golds and three silvers. In 1929 the make added another nine golds to the score.

Racing successes were, of course, handicapped by the usual problems with 3-wheelers. Morgans were never successful in the JCC 200 Mile Race, and from 1924 to 1928, 3-wheelers were forbidden to compete in car races at Brooklands. Morgans, however, took many records in the appropriate categories. As early as 1921, Ware's 1,096cc machine had covered a kilometre at 86·04mph (138·46kph), and by 1922 Hawkes's Anzani-engined car

had done 86·94mph (139·91kph) over the same distance, this figure being improved to 92·38mph (148·67kph) in 1923, when a 1,100cc Morgan-Blackburne won the Brooklands 3-Wheeler Championship at an average speed of 86·77mph (139·64kph). There were also some successful bids in the 750cc category, and in 1925 Beart's 1,100cc car covered the flying start kilometre at 103·37mph, (166·4kph), the first time a 3-wheeler had been officially timed at over 100mph. Special single cylinder cars were built with engines of 494cc and 350cc, and with these Class I and J records were captured, by Eric Fernihough and H. C. Lones respectively.

Trials were the 3-wheeled Morgan's happiest hunting-ground after 1930, though the Australian T. N. Sulman evolved some interesting 4-wheeler conversions for dirt-track racing. Some very fierce road-going cars were also produced, notably Henry Laird's blown 1931 1,100cc water-cooled 2-speeder, which did the standing-start mile at 81·56mph (131·26kph) in 1935, and Clive Lones's 1932 750cc ohv twin from which 51bhp were extracted. The adoption of the 'softer' Matchless twins in 1934, however, marked a slow decline in the 3-wheeler's competition career, and even these gave way altogether to sv 4-cylinder Fords after 1946.

However, 1936 had brought a new departure in the shape of a 4-wheeled sports car, the 4-4 with 1,122cc ioe Coventry-Climax engine and the traditional Morgan ifs, and this carried on the tradition in rallies and trials, being handled (as had the 3-wheelers before) by the men who built it — the Morgans and the Goodalls, father and son. George Goodall collected the small open-car class in the 1937, 1938 and 1939 RAC Rallies, and the introduction of a drophead coupé in the last pre-war season extended Morgan domination to the closed-car category as well, 'H.F.S' himself winning in England, and Goodall in the Scottish event. The cars were also raced, receiving their baptism of fire in the 1937 Ulster Trophy, won by R. Campbell. He was only 5th in the Leinster race, but the honour of the Malvern Link company was upheld by McCracken, who came in 1st. Campbell was also 2nd at Limerick in 1938, in which year 4-4s ran at Le Mans and in the TT. Laird was flagged off unplaced at Donington, but on the Sarthe Circuit Miss Fawcett and White took 13th place in one of Britain's leaner years. White and Anthony were 15th in 1939, these competition Morgans retaining the Coventry-Climax unit, although by the outbreak of World War 2 the touring machine used a 1,267cc push-rod Standard engine.

Morgans did not figure prominently in competition again until 1951, when the 4-4 gave way to the Plus Four, a more powerful car with the 2,088cc Standard Vanguard engine. This turned the sports Morgan into a club-racer *par excellence,* and one which has figured prominently in minor events in the United States and Australia as well as at home. In 1951 Morgan took the team award in the RAC Rally, as well as class victories in the Lisbon and the Evian–Mont Blanc; the cars repeated their successes in the British and Portuguese events in 1952. Ray won the 1952 and 1953 London Rallies. The 1953 MCC Rally was almost a Morgan benefit, for Clarkson was 2nd overall, the Misses Neil won the ladies' prize, and the Plus Four also collected two classes and the team award. In 1954 a more powerful engine, the 1,991cc Triumph TR, was adopted. Ray won the Scottish Rally, and Yarranton was 2nd in the MCC National. There was a class victory in the 1955 Scottish; in the 1956 RAC event Dr Spare was 3rd and Peter Morgan (son of H.F.S) won his class with one of the smaller 1,172cc Ford-engined 4-4 Series IIs. Yarranton scored another class victory in the 1958 RAC Rally, and 1959 brought the rise of Chris Lawrence and his fast Lawrencetune Plus Fours, which put up an impressive performance in club racing (notably at Goodwood) and also scored a class victory in the Grand Touring Race

that formed part of the International Trophy Meeting at Silverstone. The Morgan team won the National 6-Hour Relay Race, and Peter Morgan took 6th place in the RAC Rally. Though Lawrence retired his Morgan in the 1960 TT, Shepherd-Barron's car took 2nd place in its class in the 1961 Spa GP for GT cars, and there was also a class victory in the Guards Trophy at Brands Hatch, along with a whole string of minor successes. In 1962 a Super Sports 2,138cc version was catalogued capable of 115mph (185kph) on 116bhp; the Lawrence/Shepherd-Barron car averaged 94mph (151·28kph) to finish 13th at Le Mans, there was an 8th place in the TT, and a 27th in the Nürburgring 1,000 Kilometres. Though Morgans continued to support major events, their subsequent successes have been at the club level only. MCS

Mormon Meteor (US)

In 1935 Ab Jenkins took a specially-prepared Duesenberg SJ known as the Duesenberg Special to the Bonneville Salt Flats where he captured international Class B records for one hour at 152·145mph (244·868kph), and for 24-hours at 135·47mph (218·01kph). The former was 17·2mph (27·68kph) faster than Stuck's record with a GP Auto Union in 1934. In 1936 the Duesenberg Special was fitted with a Curtiss Conqueror aero engine, and renamed 'Mormon Meteor', Salt Lake City near Bonneville being the headquarters of the Mormon faith. This car took unlimited class records from 50 miles to 48 hours inclusive. The average for the latter was 148·64mph (239·26kph).

In 1937, with a larger tail-fin, the car was named Mormon Meteor II, and raised the 24-hour unlimited record to 157·27mph (253·01kph). The following year the SJ engine was re-installed and the car used on the road by Jenkins and his son for five years. The final Mormon Meteor was the Mark III of 1938, which used a 750bhp Curtiss-Wright V-12 aero engine, and was assembled by Jenkins in his own workshop opposite the former Duesenberg plant. This car covered 3,868 miles (6,225km) in 24 hours in 1940. GNG

Morris (GB)

Although the name of Morris is seldom associated with motor sport, a single-seater Morris Oxford Sports was catalogued as long ago as 1914. W. R. Morris himself is

Above, 1934 Morris Minor Skinner Special at Shelsley Walsh. At the wheel, Barbara Skinner who set a new Ladies' Record. *Photo: Wilson McComb Collection*

Below left, 1939 Morgan 4-4 dh coupé fording a watersplash in Cornwall. *Photo: Montagu Motor Museum*

Below, 1955 Morgan Plus Four at Prescott Hill-Climb in 1964. *Photo: Montagu Motor Museum*

said to have won an Oxford hill-climb with a de Dietrich in 1908, and he certainly took a gold medal with one of his own cars in the 1913 London-Edinburgh Trial. Other Morrises competed successfully in several hill-climbs and trials, including the Dutch six-day event, before World War 1. In the 1920s the Cowley Sports, though priced at nearly £400 when first announced, was popular in trials and successful in the hands of Billy Cooper, among others. Summers had a modified Cowley racing at Brooklands in 1922. Alf Keen, apprenticed to Morris in bicycle days, built a much-modified single-seater Cowley which was timed at 92mph (148·06kph) unsupercharged, and won several awards.

Cecil Kimber was one of several who offered sporting versions of the contemporary Morris. The Morris Garages 'Chummy' which he drove in the 1923 Land's End certainly came in this category, but his 1925 mount, with ohv Hotchkiss engine and specially-built chassis, was a different proposition. At the 1923 Show, Morris Motors offered an Occasional Four at £215—to the annoyance of Morris Garages, whose equivalent MG Chummy cost £350.

In 1927, Crickmay raced at Brooklands with a modified Cowley which did 6 hours at 64·58mph (103·93kph) and was timed at 93mph (149·67kph). In 1928, Wellsteed was getting a similar performance from his Oxford-based 'Red Flash'. That year came the announcement of the ohc Morris Minor and the first MG Midget, which was little more than a rebodied Minor in original form. When the £100 sv Minor came in 1931, von der Becke did a publicity stunt to achieve 100mph (160kph) supercharged and 100mpg unsupercharged. This car was later adopted by the Skinner family (of SU) together with a sister Minor; supercharged, they achieved remarkable performances at Shelsley Walsh. Another successful supercharged Minor was the Sullivan Special, raced in Ireland.

The Skinners also evolved the 'Smoky', which had a basically Isis engine with an MG Tigress head, Cowley chassis, and four-seater body. It was capable of over 90mph (145kph), and won awards in hill-climbs and rallies, driven by Barbara Skinner.

The second Morris Motors attempt to jump on the MG bandwagon came at the 1933 Motor Show in London with two 'sports' tourers based on the sv Morris 10-4 and 10-6, and priced below the four-seater MGs; they were unsuccessful. The more honest Morris 8 was later rebodied by Cunard and Jensen. Standard versions ran in the 1936 and 1939 Monte Carlo Rallies.

Good roadholding made the post-World War 2 Issigonis Minor popular in tuned form for sporting activities, and one of the first ohv versions did a non-stop 10,000 miles at Goodwood in 1952. Later they were entered in international rallies by the BMC Competitions Department. A classic example was 'Granny', a 1957 Minor saloon usually driven by Pat Moss and Ann Wisdom. It completed the marathon Liège-Rome-Liège, did a Tulip, a Monte Carlo, a Viking, two RAC Rallies and a Circuit of Ireland, actually finishing 4th overall in the 1957 RAC Rally and winning several other awards.

The sporting career of the Morris Mini-Minor is dealt with under BMC. FWMcC

Mors (F)

This make was first seen in the hands of Emile Mors himself in the Paris-Dieppe race of 1897. These earliest Mors racers were 850cc rear-engined twins with lt magneto ignition and belt drive, which by 1898 had given way to 1·5-litre water-cooled V-4s. In the Paris-Amsterdam-Paris, Alfred Levegh finished 9th, behind even the 2-cylinder Peugeots. However, in 1899 there was a bigger 4·2-litre 4-cylinder racer in the Panhard idiom, its make-and-break ignition apart, and this had quite a promising season, with victories in some of the minor events, such as the Paris-St Malo (Antony), the Bordeaux-Biarritz and the Paris-Ostend Races (Levegh). This driver tied with Girardot's Panhard at an average speed of 32·5mph (52·30kph) in the latter event, but 5th and 6th places in the Paris-Bordeaux and a promising turn of speed but no awards in the Tour de France were more truly indicative of Mors's position relative to Panhard. The 1899 season closed with a ftd at Gaillon, and the next opened with another ftd at La Turbie. Levegh's new 7·3-litre racing Mors won the two big events of 1900: the Bordeaux-Périgueux-Bordeaux fell at 48·4mph (77·89kph) with another Mors 4th, in spite of which the make was not chosen to represent France in the Gordon Bennett Cup; and Panhard were defeated again in the Paris-Toulouse-Paris.

1902 Mors 60hp Paris-Vienna car at Phoeni Park, Dublin in 1903. On the right, J. E. Hutton's 60hp Mercedes. *Photo: Autoca*

A Mercedes victory in the 1901 Nice–Salon–Nice was a warning to both Panhard and Mors; the latter's cars, at 60hp and 10·1-litres, were now bigger and more powerful than their rivals, which allowed Henri Fournier to pull off a double—1st in the Paris–Bordeaux at 53·1mph (85·46kph) and in the Paris–Berlin at 44·1mph (70·97kph). Smaller, 9,236cc engines and primitive shock absorbers came in 1902, but Mors left the Circuit du Nord alcohol race alone, and their showing in the Paris–Vienna was poor, even if Fournier's car was extremely fast in the early stages. Gabriel was 2nd and Vanderbilt 3rd in the Circuit des Ardennes. Although the company lost two of their designers (Brasier and Terrasse) in 1903, their Paris–Madrid cars were quite advanced. Still chain-driven, they had mechanically-

Top, 1903 Mors 70hp Paris–Madrid car. Gabriel at the wheel. *Photo: Autocar*

Above left, 1904 Mors Gordon Bennett Trials car, in 1905. J. T. C. Moore-Brabazon at the wheel. *Photo: Montagu Motor Museum*

Above right, 1908 Mors GP car. Camille Jenatzy at the wheel. *Photo: Montagu Motor Museum*

operated inlet valves, and Gabriel won this event. His showing in the Gordon Bennett was, by contrast, disappointing: 4th behind a Mercedes and two Panhards, though de Forest's speed of 84·09mph (136·63kph) in the subsequent Phoenix Park Speed Trials was impressive, and a tonneau-equipped 11,559cc racer won the tourist class at Château-Thierry. Mors were using T-head 13·6-litre engines in 1904, but though their Gordon Bennett Trials cars were among the fastest in terms of straight-line speed and Salleron qualified for a place in the team, he could manage no better than 7th at Homburg. Mors refused to support the 1905 Gordon Bennett, there were no racers in 1906, and only a single abortive entry for the Kaiserpreis in 1907.

For all practical purposes Mors's last effort in motor

sport was the 1908 GP car, a 12·8-litre ohv 4-cylinder, still with lt magneto and side-chain drive, said to develop 100bhp. Despite the presence of Jenatzy in the team, the cars achieved nothing. A planned comeback in the 1914 Coupe de l'Auto was frustrated by World War 1, though at least one 2·5-litre sleeve-valve racer was built. In 1921 Malcolm Campbell was the English concessionaire, and he tried his luck at Brooklands with a 3·5-litre 4-cylinder Knight-engined car. Nothing, however, could sell the Mors by now, and he soon gave up. MCS

Motobloc (F)

This Bordelais make was first seen in the Bordeaux–Périgueux–Bordeaux race of 1900, under its original name of Schaudel, Versein taking 7th place. Some conventional chain-driven twins of 2,614cc took part in the *voiture légère* section of the Paris–Madrid (1903), one of them driven by the Motobloc designer, Dombret. There were some 165 × 140mm 4-cylinder chain-driven Motoblocs in the Grand Prix in 1907, but only Courtade's finished, in 12th position. The 1908 cars were more advanced, with undersquare 12·8-litre engines and hemispherical heads, but it availed the firm nothing, though that year two Motoblocs finished in 13th and 14th places. The cars continued to appear in hill-climbs, Pierron winning two classes at Mont Ventoux in 1909. There was also a class victory at Gaillon in 1911, and Motoblocs were seen in the 1912 Boulogne Speed Trials. MCS

Mourre *see* Major

Multi-Union (I/GB)

One of the handsomest specials ever made, the Multi-Union began life as a 2·9-litre Alfa Romeo Tipo B, and was re-built in 1937 by Fairey Aviation test pilot Chris Staniland. The engine was modified, power being increased from 255bhp to 340bhp, and speed from 5,300rpm to 6,500rpm. Two superchargers were used, and other modifications included a new 4-speed gearbox with remote control right-hand gear lever replacing the central one, Lockheed hydraulic brakes, and a new body very like that of the contemporary Grand Prix Mercedes-Benz. Later modifications included Tecnauto ifs, and coil springs in place of leaves at the rear. The Multi-Union won the Brooklands Outer Circuit Handicaps at 127 and 133mph (204·4 and 214kph) in 1938, and gained the Class D Outer Circuit Record at 141·45mph (227·38kph) as well as several International Class D records. The improved 1939 car should have been able to

beat the Napier-Railton's Outer Circuit Record at 143·44mph (230·76kph), but a hole in a piston prevented this, and less than a month later war broke out. The Multi-Union was less successful on road circuits, but did win the Phoenix Park Race in 1938 at 97·45mph (156·83kph). It was always driven by Staniland.

Recently the Multi-Union has been completely rebuilt, and is now owned by the Hon Patrick Lindsay. GNG

Nacional Pescara (E)

The Fabrica Nacional de Automoviles was founded in 1929 by the Marquis Raul de Poteras Pescara, with finance obtained from the Garriga bank and the moral support of King Alfonso XIII. The chief engineer was the Marquis' brother Enrique Pescara, and plans for the car were laid at a series of banquets at the Ritz hotel in Barcelona. It was said that champagne was used in place of ink for the plans. Nevertheless, it was a sound and modern design, with a twin-ohc 3-litre straight-8 engine developing 100bhp at 4,800rpm, a very low chassis and hydraulic brakes. Electron alloy was widely used in engine and chassis components.

Nacional Pescaras had a number of successes in Spanish events, including the 1930 Cuesta Rabassada and Cuesta del Cristo (Bilbao), but their greatest success was the winning of the European Mountain Championship in 1931, with Juan Zanelli and Esteban Tort driving the victorious cars. In 1934 Sameiro finished 4th in the Penya Rhin Grand Prix, and Zanelli won the 3-litre class at La Turbie hill-climb in 1934, and at Val de Cuech and Kesselberg hill-climbs in 1935, but by this time the cars were no longer being made. Alfonso had gone into exile, and the new Republican government did not encourage credit for motor-racing activities. JRV

NAG (D)

This company did little serious racing, though one Gossi took a first and a second place in Berlin's 1903 Westendrennen, as well as a 3rd place at Hamburg in 1904. An NAG was 16th in the Kaiserpreis of 1907, and the make gained some awards in the Austrian Alpine and Swedish Winter Trials between 1910 and 1914.

More interesting were the successes of the 2·5-litre C4b in the 1922–6 period. This was an old-fashioned sv four with a Delaunay-Belleville-like radiator and a specification redolent of 1914, said to give 70mph (112kph) on 45bhp. Chief Engineer Riecken's victory at the AVUS in 1922 at a startling 84·3mph (135·67kph) was one thing, but when he and Berthold averaged 69mph (111·04kph) for 24 hours in July 1926 to win the

1930 Nacional Pescara at Shelsley Walsh in 1931. Juan Zanelli at the wheel. *Photo: Montagu Motor Museum*

Left, 1908 Motobloc GP car. Garcet at the wheel. *Photo: Geoffroy de Beauffort Collection*

Below, 1937 Multi-Union at Brooklands in 1938. Chris Staniland at the wheel. *Photo: Klementaski Studio*

Grand Premio della Notte at Monza in July 1926, the result was a tribute to good preparation. Even more remarkable was Riecken's 2nd place in the 1926 German GP, in which he was beaten only by Caracciola's 2-litre straight-8 Mercedes, with 160bhp (admittedly allied to terrible handling). Altogether at peak the C4bs won 78 1st places in three seasons, but though they were still seen in German events in 1928 they were by then hopelessly outclassed. MCS

Nagant (B)

The first Nagants had opposed-piston engines mounted at the rear and were made under Gobron-Brillié licence. Cars of this type ran in both the Paris–Vienna and the Circuit des Ardennes in 1902, finishing 11th in the *voiture legère* class of the former event. Busson's win in the 1907 Belgian Critérium de Regularité was the only major success for some years thereafter, but in 1914 the firm entered a pair of 4·5-litre dohc 4-cylinder cars (Esser and Elskamp) for the French GP, and Esser took 6th place at 60·69mph (97·67kph). In 1925 ohv 4-cylinder sports cars with Dewandre servo brakes (de Tozée/ Cheville and Wery/Scholeur) took the first two places in the 3-litre category of the Belgian 24-Hour race, but though Nagant later experimented with supercharged touring engines they did not support a major event again. MCS

Napier (GB)

Napier's last cars, delivered in 1925, were strictly luxury tourers for all their ohc power units, but a quarter of a century before their great salesman and propagandist, Selwyn Francis Edge, had won a Bronze Medal in the Thousand Miles Trial at the wheel of a still-unpainted 8hp 2-cylinder car with chain drive. Edge went on to enter a 4·9-litre 16hp Napier with 4-cylinder engine for the Paris–Toulouse–Paris, in which he retired, but a more serious effort followed in 1901. For that year's Gordon Bennett Cup, Montague Napier prepared a vast 17,157cc 4-cylinder car, still with aiv, chain drive, and flitchplate frame, though it was debarred from the race for wearing foreign-made tyres, and for all its output of 103bhp it was far too heavy at just over 2 tons. It retired in both the Paris–Bordeaux and the Paris–Berlin, but was timed at 66·93mph (107·72kph) and won two classes at Gaillon. The '50hp' Napier probably did more than any other machine to inspire the 1,000kg rule of 1902, in which year Edge and Napier went to the other extreme with a shaft-driven lightweight of only 6·5-litres capacity, rated at 30hp but actually giving around 45bhp. This car won Edge his victory in the third Gordon Bennett Cup, run concurrently with the Paris–Vienna, while in the same year the American Charles J. Glidden started his marathon tour of 50 countries and 50,000 miles.

The year 1903 was less successful. Only one car (Mayhew's) turned out for the Paris–Madrid without success, and though three 45s and a new 13·7-litre 80hp with pressed-steel frame were prepared for the Irish Gordon Bennett, none of the three Napiers to run at Athy distinguished themselves. Crashes eliminated Jarrott and Stocks, and Edge on the 80hp finished last, only to be disqualified for receiving a push-start. At the 1904 Nice Speed Trials Mayhew fielded the first racing Napier with moiv (inlet valves were overhead), and Edge had six racers running during the season, although Earp's spectacular crash during the 1904 British Eliminating Trials lost him his place in the Gordon Bennett team, and only Edge (on his 1903 car) actually competed at

Top, 1901 Napier 50hp Paris–Berlin car. S. F. Edge at the wheel. *Photo: Veteran Car Club of Great Britian*

Above, 1903 Napier 35hp Paris–Madrid car at the *pesage*. This was Mark Mayhew's car. *Photo: T. A. S. O. Mathieson Collection*

1924 NAG C4b at Monza in 1926. Christian Riecken at the wheel. *Photo: Neubauer Collection*

Homburg. Neither his 12th place nor Mayhew's 9th in the Circuit des Ardennes were inspiring, though Edge had practised at Homburg on a new and exciting 15·1-litre six, the celebrated L48 (later known as 'Samson') with 2-speed gearbox. Early in the car's career the ortho-dox Napier radiator was replaced by a wrap-round tubular affair, and during the year Macdonald made ftd at Portmarnock Speed Trials, the car also making 3rd fastest time at Gaillon.

Only one new racer (an improved 4-cylinder for

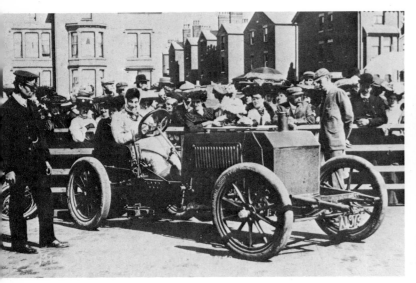

Hargreaves) appeared in the Isle of Man for the 1905 Gordon Bennett Trials, and the solitary Napier chosen for the last Gordon Bennett was L48, driven by Earp. With only two forward speeds it was not at its best on the mountainous circuit, though some people considered it the fastest car in the race. Nevertheless, it shone in sprints. Macdonald covering the mile at 104·65mph (168·48kph) during the AAA's Speed Trials at Daytona Beach, while Earp later made ftd at Brighton, as well as taking a new British kilometre record at 97·25mph (156·51kph).

Napier's entry in the 1907 Kaiserpreis was a failure, but on the credit side there were numerous hill-climb successes. Further, Edge found a new interest in the freshly-opened Brooklands Motor Course, and as a curtain-raiser he covered 24 hours at 65·91mph (106·08kph) on a stripped 60hp 6-cylinder model. The season's sport at the track alone brought him nine 1st places and £1,760 in prize money, and Tryon won the first race ever staged there, the Marcel Renault Memorial Plate. By this time L48 had had its piston stroke lengthened to 7in, bringing output up to 212bhp and capacity to over 20 litres. Frank Newton averaged 84·7mph (136·31kph) for two hours, even if the famous match race against Nazzaro's Fiat in 1908 ended in the Napier's retirement. Newton also took the 90hp Short

Record at an impressive 119·34mph (192·06kph).

1908 was the make's last official racing season. The TT cars, having 4-cylinder engines, ran under the *nom de guerre* of Hutton; some 6-cylinder machines prepared for the Grand Prix were withdrawn by Edge after the ACF had disallowed their Rudge-Whitworth quick-detachable wire wheels. Though C. A. Bird continued to drive his 65hp 6-cylinder car in sprints and hill-climbs to good purpose, and Napier were awarded the RAC's Dewar Trophy in 1910 for a top-gear run from London to Edinburgh, the last noteworthy competition appearance was an entry in the 1912 Russian Army Trials. Napier's aero-engines, however, were destined to figure in such record-breakers as Malcolm Campbell's Bluebird, Sir Henry Segrave's Golden Arrow, and John Cobb's Railton Mobil Special, as well as in the last-mentioned driver's Napier-Railton of 1933. Between the two World Wars the World Land Speed Record stood on seven occasions to the credit of Napier-powered cars. MCS

Napier-Railton (GB)

The Napier-Railton was built for John Cobb by Thomson and Taylor, to the design of Reid Railton, and was originally intended for an attack on the World 24-Hour Record. It used a 23,970cc broad-arrow 12-cylinder Napier Lion aero engine developing 505bhp in a massive chassis with cantilever rear springs. There were 3 forward speeds but no fwb. Gurney Nutting were responsible for the single-seater body. Tyre consumption was always its limiting factor, in spite of which it started its career well in 1933 by setting up a new standing-start lap record at Brooklands at 120·59mph (194·04kph), later recording a flying kilometre at 143·67mph (231·2kph). A number of world records of up to 1,000km were also taken, but a first attack on the 24-hour title failed in 1934 when F. W. Dixon crashed the car at Montlhéry. Bad weather conditions caused the car's withdrawal from that year's BRDC 500 Miles Race, but on two occasions the Napier-Railton broke the Brooklands lap record—its second performance, in August, was at 140·93mph (226·75kph) —as well as putting up the highest race average to date in the history of the track, at 131·53mph (211·65kph).

The World 24-Hour Record finally fell to Cobb, Rose-Richards and Dixon in 1935, at 137·40mph (221·124kph); and at Bonneville the team also took the World Hour Record at 152·7mph (245·7kph). Back in

Left, 1904 Napier 100hp at Blackpool in 1905. Dorothy Levitt at the wheel. *Photo: D. Napier & Son Ltd*

Above, 1904 Napier L48 90hp 'Samson', at Brooklands in 1907. S. F. Edge at the wheel. *Photo: Veteran Car Club of Great Britain*

Left, 1933 Napier-Railton at a VSCC Silverstone meeting in 1963. The Hon Patrick Lindsay at the wheel. *Photo: Studio 3*

England Cobb won the BRDC 500 at 121·28mph (195·13kph), and in October 1935 he raised the Brooklands lap record to 143·44mph (230·76kph), a figure which still stands, as it was never successfully attacked during the remainder of the track's history. Cobb also recorded a flying kilometre at 151·97mph (244·51kph), and in 1936 raised the 24-Hour Record to 150·6mph (245·4kph). The car's last appearance in his hands was in 1937, when it won the BRDC 500 once more.

After World War 2 the Napier-Railton took the role of a contender for the World Land Speed Record in the film *Pandora and the Flying Dutchman*, and subsequently served GQ Parachutes Ltd as a test-bed for aircraft tail chutes; for this work Dunlop disc brakes were used at the rear. In 1962 it reappeared in Vintage events in the hands of the Hon. Patrick Lindsay, who has driven it to some purpose at both Oulton Park and Silverstone. MCS

Nardi (I)

A name still famous in Italy for its 'go faster' equipment such as special manifolds, camshafts, crankshafts, and steering wheels, Nardi of Turin was founded before World War 2 by Ing Enrico Nardi, a former racing mechanic and engineer. In 1932 he had built the intriguing Nardi-Monaco miniature racing car designed by Augusto Monaco and known as the 'Chichibio'. This car had a front-mounted 998cc JAP V-twin engine driving the front wheels through a 5-speed gearbox, and with 65bhp and a weight of only 672lb (304·81kg) it scored several class wins in Italian hill-climbs. 'Chichibio' can be seen today in the Biscaretti Museum in Turin.

After a spell with Lancia, then with Enzo Ferrari as tester of the first-ever Ferrari, the 815 of 1940, Enrico Nardi went into partnership with Renato Danese after the war. Jointly they produced Nardi-Danese (or N-D) sports cars with optional FIAT 500 and 1,100cc 4-cylinder or BMW air-cooled flat-twin engines of 500 and 750cc driving the rear wheels. With tubular chassis, light weight and nimble handling, the BMW-engined cars in particular enjoyed considerable success in Italian national races and hill-climbs, notably in the hands of Gino Valenzano, who later graduated to GP racing.

Cylinder blocks and other components built for the Ferrari 815 were built into two rare N-D models, 1·5-litre and 2-litre straight-8s, but little came of these projects. In 1951 Nardi on his own built an unsuccessful 500cc single-seater racing car with Carru vertical-twin engine. He also projected a rear-engined Formula 2 car with Lancia Aurelia V-6 engine which unfortunately was never built, and in 1955 produced a remarkable twin-fuselaged sports car for Le Mans, powered by a 4-cylinder

1969 Astra RNR (Nathan) at Crystal Palace. Roger Nathan at the wheel. *Photo: Motor*

750cc Giannini twin-ohc engine, located together with the transmission in one boom, in the fashion set by Piero Taruffi's Tarf *bisiluro*. The car retired early in the race, and thereafter the Officine Enrico Nardi concentrated on manufacturing speed equipment. CP

Nash-Healey see Healey

Nathan (GB)

Roger Nathan's early successes as a racing driver were gained with Lotus Elite and Brabham BT8 cars. At the end of 1965 production started of the Costin-Nathan sports racing cars, with open or closed fibreglass body-work, and Hillman Imp engines race-prepared in Nathan's London workshops. The monocoque chassis unit, like Frank Costin's earlier Marcos design, was constructed of Gaboon plywood.

Particularly in Nathan's own hands, these cars were quite successful, and in 1968 took the *Motoring News* and *Tootal* Championships in Britain. At the Nürburgring that year Nathan won his class and finished 8th overall in the ADAC 500 kilometres race.

For 1969 the Astra RNRI Group 6 car was introduced, with similar chassis construction, tubular subframes, 5-speed Hewland gearbox and 2-litre FPF 4-cylinder Coventry-Climax or 1,600cc FVA Ford-Cosworth engines. This model also was successful in its class, earning Nathan six victories out of eight 1969 outings, and in 1970 important wins included the AMOC Martini

Left, 1932 Nardi-Monaco 'Chichibio'. *Photo: Museo dell' Automobile, Turin*

Right, 1948 Nardi-Danese sports car with 750cc BMW engine. *Photo: Cyril Posthumus Collection*

100 at Silverstone, with the RNR2 version; Jeremy Lord took the *Motoring News* GT Championship with the older RNR1 FVA model. Sales, however, were somewhat disappointing, and towards the end of the year the decision was taken to cease production, which had reached a total of about 45. DF

National (US)

It was only natural that National cars should compete at Indianapolis as the firm was one of the city's better-known automobile manufacturers, and moreover one of its directors, Arthur C. Newby, was a founder of the Speedway. During 1909 and 1910 the firm had a number of successes in short races with drivers Tom Kincaid and John Aitken, and in the first 500 of 1911 three Nationals were entered, although the best result was Charles Merz's 7th place. In 1912 however, Joe Dawson won the race, with Howard Wilcox in 9th place in a larger car than Dawson's. Successes away from their home ground included Livingstone and Greiner's 2nd and 3rd places at Elgin in 1910, and Zengle's 1st place at Elgin in 1911. National's racing career was short-lived, and they played little part in the sport after 1912. GNG

Nazzaro (I)

Following his former racing colleague Vincenzo Lancia's example, Felice Nazzaro founded his own make of car in 1912. The Nazzaro was a solid, well-built, 4·4-litre 4-cylinder sv machine of established rather than enterprising design, but this ruggedness stood it in good stead in the gruelling races of the time. One car ran in the 1912 Giro di Sicilia (Targa Florio) driven by Losa and Catalano who finished 12th. In the 1913 event Nazzaro

Top, 1911 National at Fairmount Park, Philadelphia. *Photo: Peter Helck Collection*

Above, 1913 4·4-litre 60hp Nazzaro which won that year's Targa Florio. Felice Nazzaro at the wheel. *Photo: Montagu Motor Museum*

Opposite top, Gordini straight-8 (André Pilette) in the 1956 British GP at Silverstone. *Photo: Geoff Goddard*

Opposite bottom, Vanwall (Tony Brooks) in the 1958 British GP at Silverstone. *Photo: Geoff Goddard*

1970 Nemo Formula 3 at Brands Hatch. B. McInerney at the wheel. *Photo: Autosport*

himself entered the two-day, 652-mile (1049·3km) drive around Sicily and came through to a convincing victory for the new make. The following year he won the 279-mile (449km) Coppa Florio over the 93-mile (149·67km 'long' Madonie mountain circuit as well, heading a SCAT and two Alfa cars, while another Nazzaro was 9th, driven by Mario Cortese.

For the French GP at Lyons in 1914 three special GP Nazzaros were built; these had single shaft-driven ohc engines with four valves per cylinder and ball-bearing crankshafts, and 4-speed gearboxes in unit with the engine. Drivers were Nazzaro, Porporato and de Morac but none finished. After World War 1, Guido Meregall raced a much modified pre-war Nazzaro, winning the 5-litre class of the Consuma hill-climb, with Baldoni in another 2nd. Meregalli scored again in the 6-litre class of the 1920 Parma-Poggio di Berceto climb, where the famous Alfa Romeo driver Campari drove a Nazzaro for a change, and won the over 6-litre class. Meregalli's greatest success, however, was to win the 1920 Targa Florio in terrible conditions of rain and mud, leading Enzo Ferrari's Alfa Romeo home by over 8 minutes in race lasting over 8 hours. Nazzaro himself won the 5-lit class of the Aosta Grand St Bernard mountain climb in 1920, while Brilli-Peri scored two seconds at Mugello and Consuma with another Nazzaro. By 1922 Nazzaro had rejoined the FIAT team and had no more connection with the Nazzaro make, which died in 1923. CP

Neander (D)

Ernst Neumann-Neander was known for his remarkab designs of motorcycles and cyclecar-type 4-wheelers during the 1920s and the 1930s. His Pionier, a tandem-two-seater with 1,000cc JAP engine, appeared in a number of sports car races in Germany during 1938 and 1939, its results including a 3rd place in the 1,100cc clas on the Nürburgring in 1938, driven by Vollmer. After World War 2, Vollmer again appeared with his Neande car in various competitions. At Hockenheim in 1947 he gained a 2nd place in the 1,100cc sports car class. His average speed was 71·2mph (114·59kph); the maximum speed of this car was about 90mph (144kph). HON

Nemo (GB)

During 1970 the prototype Nemo car for Formula 2 or Formula 3 was raced by Brendan McInerney. Produce by Race Cars International, the car was a notably neat and compact design, the work of Canadian Max Boxstrom. DF

Nerus (GB)

During 1970 the Silhouette model of Nick Cole was runner-up in the 'Tarmac' Formula 100 championship. Design was by Cedric Seltzer, with a tubular frame incorporating semi-stressed panels, and fibreglass body by Marchant and Rose of Hastings. For 1971 the car wa available also in Group 6 form. Nerus Engineering wer associated with the Checkpoint organization, who had been connected with the ephemeral Camber GT of 1966. DF

Newton (I)

Despite their name the advanced little Newton racing cars were built in Italy by a small firm near Milan, and designed by the Italian engineer Olivo Pellegatti. They were commissioned by Noel Newton of Newton & Bennett, importers of the Newton-Ceirano. They had 1,095cc twin-ohc 4-cylinder engines, 4-speed gearboxes

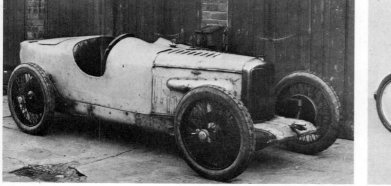

Above, 1923 Newton 200-Mile Race car.
Photo: G. M. Hare

Right, 1935 Nibbio I. *Photo: Museo dell'Automobile, Turin*

Opposite top, Ford GT40 (Paul Hawkins/David Hobbs) in the BOAC 500 at Brands Hatch, 1968. *Photo: Motor Sport*

Opposite bottom, Lola-Chevrolet T70 (Jo Bonnier/S. Axelsson) in the BOAC 500 at Brands Hatch, 1968. *Photo: Motor Sport*

and 4-wheel brakes. Two were entered for the 1923 200 Miles Race, but did not start. A chassis and a complete car were shown at Olympia in 1923 and 1924, and it was intended that the Newtons should be built in England, but they never were. In 1926 the name was changed to Newton-Ceirano, although they were very different from the sv 1·5-litre touring cars of that name. One was owned by Sydney Cummings and driven by his daughter Ivy, but was never very successful. GNG

Nibbio (I)

Count Giovanni Lurani first broke International Class I records with this neat little machine in 1935. It was built at the Quadrio engineering works in Milan, had a frame of welded steel tubes, a Fiat Balilla front axle, coil-sprung rear axle, a rear-mounted 500cc Guzzi 120°. V-twin racing motorcycle engine, motorcycle type wheels, and a streamlined single-seater body. The engine gave 45bhp and the car weighed 644lb (292·11kg). In November 1935, on an autostrada near Lucca, Lurani topped 100mph (160kph) in a 500cc car for the first time, setting the flying kilometre at 100·76mph (162·10kph) and the flying mile at 100·52mph (161·73kph), also breaking standing mile and kilometre records.

The car was then fitted with Tecnauto ifs suspension and the streamlining improved, and Lurani set a flying 10-mile record at 100·8mph (162·2kph) at Dessau, Germany, in 1939. In 1947 a supercharged 250cc Guzzi engine was fitted, and Nibbio went to the Jabbeke-Aeltre highway in Belgium, where Lurani broke six Class J (350cc) records, the quickest the flying kilometre at 105·2mph (169·3kph). In 1956 a more modern Nibbio II appeared, with chassis by Volpini, enclosed bodywork by Ghia, and a 350cc unsupercharged single-cylinder

Guzzi engine. Driving it in relay, Count Lurani, Pietro Campanella and Angelo Poggio jointly succeeded in establishing a new 3-hour record at 81·6mph (132·32kph) on the Monza speedway in June of that year. CP

Nike (GB)

The original Nike, emanating from Bideford in Devon, was a front-engined Formula Junior dating from 1961. The Mark 2 was a 105E Ford-engined sports car, and Mark 3 (the first production model) a Formula Vee design In late 1968 the Mark 4 Formula Ford car appeared, and during 1969 some dozen were made, achieving success particularly in the United States. Mark 5 was a Formula 5000 car, and Mark 6 the 1970 Formula Ford model, redesigned for the Hewland Mk 8 gearbox. In Britain Lou Demarco had some success, but more impact was made in the United States, where they were sometimes known as Bakers, being handled by Jim Baker of Atlanta, Ga. (Tom Fraser Racing). The Mark 7 was another one-off sports car, and Mark 8 a hill-climb car with NSU Wankel engine. Mark 9 was a F100 design, and Marks 10 and 11 respectively the FF and FB designs for 1971. DF

Nissan-Datsun (J)

Nissan were among the first Japanese manufacturers to enter international competition when their Cedric saloons appeared at Macau and in Australia in the early 1960s. Since a true competition department was formed they have produced specialist Group 6 and 7 machines in the form of the Nissan R380, 381 and 382 models. The early 380 was an experimental exercise leading to the development of the spaceframe R381, powered by a 5,461cc 90° V-8 Chevrolet engine developing 450bhp

Below, 1970 Nike Mark 6 Formula Ford. In the background, the Mark 5 Formula 5000. *Photo: Ken Nicholls Engineering Ltd*

Right, 1968 Nissan R381 Group 7. Note the twin aerofoils. *Photo: Doug Nye Collection*

and driving through a Hewland 5-speed LG500 transaxle. The R381 featured twin aerofoils mounted on the rear suspension and operating independently of each other to load the inside wheel during cornering, pre-dating Porsche's adoption of a similar system before both were banned.

Later a Nissan-built V-12 6-litre engine was adopted of which few details have been released. With the national club's ban on wings the cars did not handle well and were markedly over-powered during 1969, although Kitano was notably quick with his car. Later in 1969 the R382 appeared, using a central monocoque section with tubular subframes at front and rear carrying 5·5- or 6·5-litre 60° V-12 engines with four valves per cylinder, still mated to a Hewland gearbox. These engines used Lucas fuel injection and the 382s proved consistently quicker than the 5-litre Toyota opposition.

Competition developments transformed the Skyline 2000GT road car into the GTB track version, using a highly-tuned 1,988cc 6-cylinder sohc engine. The GT-R

was another saloon car variant for circuit work. The Datsun 510 proved itself a very useful rally car, showing particularly well in the East African Safari and similar events. Edgar Herrmann won the 1970 Safari in a 1600SSS saloon. These cars proved very tough and reliable if not very fast, and won the RAC Rally team prize in the UK in 1969. For 1970 Datsun returned to the RAC Rally, running four 240-Z sports coupés with 2·4-litre 6-cylinder front-mounted engines driving the rear wheels. These proved extremely fast and stable, but suffered recurrent differential failures in the event due to an oversight in preparation. DCN

Datsun in America: Backed by substantial factory support, Datsun sports cars have become an important factor in Sports Car Club of America Club racing as well as in the SCCA national rally programme. Bob Sharp's 1600 won F production honours in 1967; Datsun 2000's earned D production national championships in 1969 and 1970, and John Morton's 240Z sports coupé captured the SCCA C production title in 1970. ARB

Top, 1969 Nissan R382 Group 7, winning the Japanese GP. Motoharu Kurosawa at the wheel. *Photo: J. K. Yamaguchi*

Above, 1970 Datsun 1600SSS in the East African Safari. *Photo: DPPI*

Above, 1967 Nomad-Ford GT coupé.
Photo: Autosport

Right, 1970 Nomad-BRM at Mugello. Mark
Konig at the wheel. *Photo: Autosport*

1923 NSU team of 5/30PS cars at the AVUS.
Photo: Neubauer Collection

Nomad (GB)

Bob Curl's Group 6 sports-racing design dated from
1966 and consisted of a multi-tubular space frame
cloaked in a Williams and Pritchard fibreglass body,
with BRM Tasman 2-litre V-8 or 1·6-litre twin-cam Ford
engine, predictably linked to a Hewland gearbox. The
driving force, literally and figuratively, was Mark Konig,
and on the strength of a successful 1967 racing season on
the Continent, replicas were offered for sale. The Nomad
2 of 1969 was an equally strong contender in the 2-litre
sports class, and this model was offered from the
Hastings works at £5,960 for 1970. DF

Novi Special see Indianapolis Cars

NSU (D)

The 1·3-litre 5/20PS model was the basis for the first
NSU competition car. In sports form it was designated
the 5/30PS. A 4-cylinder 1,230cc sv engine gave 30bhp
at 3,100rpm, and a maximum speed of about 65mph
(104kph) was attained. At the 1923 small car race at the
AVUS circuit 5/30PS machines appeared with Roots
blowers and secured a 1-2-3 finish. Several more victories
followed during 1923–5. With blown engine the car was
capable of about 75mph (120kph) and the output was
between 40 and 50bhp. The 1924 Taunus small car race
was won by August Momberger, who started his career
on the small supercharged NSU, and later became one
of Germany's great drivers.

In 1925 NSU launched a successor to the 5/30PS, a
6-cylinder 1·5-litre. It also featured a Roots blower;
output was about 60bhp and the maximum speed
exceeded 100mph (160kph). In both models the blower
ran constantly, driven from the gearbox. The first
success was obtained in the first German Grand Prix at
the AVUS circuit in 1926. NSU had entered four cars
which finished 1-2-3-4 in their class and 5-7-8-10 overall.
In the 1926 Solitude race Seiffert placed his NSU 3rd
behind Merz (Mercedes) and Kimpel (Bugatti).

Financial difficulties did not allow further participation in racing and led to the sale of the automobile
department to FIAT in 1929.

In 1951 NSU took six world records with specially
built cars with blown NSU motorcycle engines of 350cc
and 500cc. Drivers were G. von Opel (350cc) and F.
Lehder (500cc); the latter attained a speed of 162·5mph
(261·5kph) over the flying kilometre.

NSU resumed car production in 1957 and in the
following years a series of models appeared which
gained some success in touring car events. The Spider of
1964 was the first car on the world market with the
Wankel rotary piston engine. The output of the 3-
chambered 500cc engine was normally 50bhp, but in
works cars it was developed to 90bhp and more. The
Spider appeared in the GT class in various competitions;
in 1966 it won the German Rally Championship in the
hands of Panowitz and in 1967 and 1968 Siegfried Spiess
was German Hill-Climb Champion in this car. Also very
successful were the NSU saloons in touring car races
and rallies. NSU engines are used in some sports specials
such as the NSU-Spiess and the NSU-Gepard. HON

Oldsmobile (US)

Until after World War 2 Oldsmobile played little part in
motor sport, although a spidery sprint version of the
Curved Dash 2-seater covered a mile in 42 seconds at
Daytona in 1903. However, the introduction of the
short-stroke ohv V-8 Rocket engine in 1949 gave Oldsmobile a new performance image, and by a happy
coincidence the first NASCAR Grand National season
took place in the same year. Oldsmobile 88s won five of
the year's eight events, while in 1950 McGriff/Elliott
won the first Carrera Panamericana. With drivers such
as Tim, Fonty and Bob Flock, and Curtis Turner,
Oldsmobiles dominated stock car racing in 1951,
earning nearly twice as many points as their nearest
rival, Plymouth. In 1952 the Hudson Hornets appeared
on the scene, and although Oldsmobile still did well, they
were never again NASCAR champions. Their last great

victory was at the 1959 Daytona 500, when Lee Petty won on a photo-finish from Johnny Beauchamp's Thunderbird.

During the 1960s Oldsmobile V-8 engines were used in a number of competition cars including McKee and McLaren. MCS/GNG

OM (I)

The OM (Officine Meccaniche) contrived to do exceedingly well in touring and sports-car events on sv engines, the ohv species being peculiar to England. During their ten years of competition the firm used the same basic design for everything except their brief excursion into Grand Prix racing. As early as 1920 one of the little 1,327cc Tipo 465s had won the Coppa del Garda. In the 1922 Coppa del Garda, Tarchini was 2nd in general classification as well as winning his class. Minoia won the 1923 Coppa delle Alpi, and 1·5-litre 4-cylinder machines developed from the original 465 finished 1st, 2nd, and 3rd in their class.

The 2-litre 6-cylinder 665 joined in in 1924 when Balestrero was 2nd in the Circuito del Montenero, and OMs started to appear in competition outside Italy in 1925. The Tripoli GP, which Balestrero won at 58mph (93·34kph), was technically on Italian territory, but there was also a class victory in a 12-hour touring-car event at San Sebastian. Two OMs tied for 4th place at Le Mans, where Minoia and Foresti won the Rudge-Whitworth Cup in 1926. They were 4th, and the Danieli brothers 5th. In that year R. F. Oats started to race OMs seriously in Britain, fielding a 2-litre ohv conversion using the smaller 4-cylinder frame. Less successful was the firm's supercharged dohc straight-8 for the 1,500cc GP Formula, which handled deplorably. Though cars of this type took 2nd and 4th places in the 1927 GP del'Europe, it did not find its form until Oats brought one of the cars to England and ran it at Brooklands. It eventually lapped at over 117mph (188·3kph), and was still competing as late as 1933.

The first Mille Miglia in 1927 saw an OM procession, Minoia's and Morandi's winning car being followed home by two others of the make. In 1928 Rosa and Mazzotti had to be content with 2nd place, but OMs filled the first eight places in the 2-litre class. The make also took the team prize in the Coppa delle Alpi, and Oats finished 7th in the TT. In 1929 Oats entered ohv cars for both the Double-Twelve at Brooklands and the TT: the latter was a disaster, Clark succumbing to a

fatal accident, but at Brooklands the cars won the team prize. Meanwhile Oats's successful tuning methods had spurred the works to produce some new competition cars, and a team of 2,350cc sv supercharged four-seaters came to the British Isles in 1930, running in both the Irish GP and the TT. Brake troubles dogged them on the first occasion, and fuel feeds on the second, but in Italy the OM went out with a bang. Rosa and Morandi won the Giro di Sicilia, and an unsupercharged production-type 2·2-litre car finished 6th in the Targa Florio. As for the Mille Miglia, the adoption of a 67mm bore in 1930 had moved the cars up to the 3-litre class, out of range of Alfa Romeo's all-conquering 1750s, and once again this category was led by eight OMs. Thereafter private-car production virtually ceased, and with it all competition activity. MCS

Opel (D)

The Opel brothers built Lutzmann cars after they had acquired the production rights in 1898. A Lutzmann had been the winner in the first motorcar competition in Germany in 1897, a trial run from Berlin to Potsdam and back against Benz and Daimler entries. The first international competition was held in 1899, a run from Aachen to Koblenz. A Lutzmann-based Opel was entered but had to withdraw. As the Lutzmann design proved not too successful Opel acquired a licence to build Darracq cars in Germany. An 8PS Opel-Darracq was entered in the second Frankfurt Meeting in 1902 and Brauda won in the voiturette class. Several more victories, mainly in national events, were gained in the following years and two of the Opel brothers—Heinrich and Fritz—were actively taking part as drivers. Fritz Opel was one of three German drivers in the 1904 Gordon Bennett Race. The 100hp Darracq-based car did not distinguish itself.

From 1902 the Opel-Darracq range was supplemented by Opel's own designs, and in 1906 Opel gave up production of Darracq cars altogether. In the Herkomer Trials Fritz Opel finished 4th behind three Mercedes in 1905; in 1906 Heinrich reached the same place and in 1907 he was 2nd. The Kaiserpreis Race of 1907 saw Opels driven by Jörns and Michel in 3rd and 4th places. For this race a 4-cylinder sv engine with a capacity of 8 litres and an output of about 80bhp was used. A new design with 4-cylinder 12-litre engine entered in the 1908 French GP. Jörns and Fritz Opel came in 6th and 21st.

The second Prince Henry Trial of 1909 brought an overall victory for another Opel brother, Wilhelm, and

Below, 1926 OM 2-litre racing car at Brooklands. R. F. Oats at the wheel. *Photo: Montagu Motor Museum*

Right, 1930 OM 2-litre TT car. *Photo: Montagu Motor Museum*

Above, 1914 Opel 4·5-litre GP car, c 1920. Sir Henry Segrave at the wheel. Photo: Montagu Motor Museum

Below, 1939 Opel 2-litre sports car in a cross-country trial. Photo: Neubauer Collection

Below, 1970 Opel Rallye Kadett driven by Ragnotti and Thimonnier in the Monte Carlo Rally. Photo: Hugh W. Bishop

Right, 1970 Opel Commodore GS driven by Pilette and Gosselin in the Spa 24-Hour Race. Photo: Autocar

models. The 14/38PS with 3·5-litre engine was a special sports version—the 14/38 unit installed in the 8/25 chassis—and a quite successful car. Another sports version was developed from the small 4PS 1·1-litre model. The tuned engines developed 28bhp and with blower 36bhp. These were the last sports cars made by Opel. After these few but very successful competition years, Opel retired from motor sport to concentrate on mass production of their standard models. During the 1930s there was one sports car, especially designed as a two-seater roadster for cross-country trials and based mechanically on the ordinary 6-cylinder 2-litre model. Opel's abstinence from motor sport continued after World War 2. Only since 1967, when Opel introduced the Rallye Kadett, have they again taken part in competitions. The Kadett has been rallied quite extensively, and these cars finished in 2nd, 3rd and 4th places in the 1970 RAC Rally. The larger GS Commodore has been seen in saloon car races such as the Spa 24-Hours. HON

Osca (I)

Ernesto and Bindo Maserati sold their own company to Omer Orsi in 1947, returned to Bologna, where they had started, and established a new concern, known as the Officine Specializate Costruzione Automobili Fratelli Maserati, this being abbreviated to OSCA Maserati, and later to just Osca.

They built a series of small 1,100cc sports cars, but were engine men at heart and soon developed a 4·5-litre V-12 unblown engine which was designed to update their 4CLT/48 Maserati frames for the current Formula 1. The V-12 had dimensions of 78 × 78mm and produced close on 300bhp but customers were few. 'B. Bira' fitted one in his Maserati in 1951 with little success, and the accent was quickly changing to 2-litre cars. Late that season a complete Osca 4·5-litre F1 car appeared at Monza for the Italian GP, but this was not seen again. In 1952 the brothers produced a 6-cylinder 2-litre engine, with measurements of 76 × 73mm and a true capacity of 1,987cc. This was fitted in a single-seater chassis looking like a scaled-down 4·5, and these were raced on into 1953 by Chiron and Bayol.

Osca withdrew from Formula 1 from 1954, but their sports cars, using twin-ohc engines of 750, 1,100 and 1,500cc, appeared in many races of every status. Their greatest success was in 1954 when Moss and Lloyd won the Sebring 12-Hour race. In 1959 they produced one of the neatest and best-made of the early front-engined

also 3rd, 5th, 6th and 10th places for Opel cars. In 1910 Opel came in 4th with Herbert Ephraim behind the three winning Austro-Daimler cars. The successful cars in the 1909 event were 2-litre types reaching 55mph (88kph) in the speed tests, in 1910 it was a 4-cylinder 7·3-litre type, with 100bhp and a speed of 85mph (136kph) in the speed test. With this model Opel—particularly with Carl Jörns as a driver—also competed successfully in various events during the next few years and as the 28/70PS type it was also available to other sports-minded customers.

In 1909 Opel introduced a 1·5-litre sports car, based on their standard 6/16PS type. This model developed into the 1,950cc sports car of 1913, which started its real career a few years later. There was also a high-performance car, the 40/100PS, an ohv 4-cylinder of 10·2 litres and 100bhp, capable of 65mph (104kph). A 4-cylinder 12-litre with 260bhp was developed for works entries only, but this car also achieved most of its successes after World War 1. Opel sent works teams to the French GPs of 1913, when neither of their cars finished and 1914, when Jörns finished only in 10th place.

After the war Opel was again active in motor sports with improved designs of the pre-war 1,950cc and 12-litre

Formula Junior cars. This used a Fiat 1100 engine tuned by the brothers, and was conventional in having an offset cockpit with the drive line passing to the left of the driver. Front suspension was by coil-springs and wishbones, with the live rear axle also on coils. Power output was some 78bhp at 7,500rpm. Colin Davis drove an Osca and a Taraschi to win the Italian-inspired FJ International Championship in 1960. At that time Osca were developing a 1,500cc F2 single-seater, although it never appeared. They sold 1,500cc dohc engines to De Tomaso for his 1961 F1 customer car, and developed some delightfully smooth and free-revving power units, including one with desmodromic valve gear.

But the brothers were ageing, and with resources at a low ebb they sold out to Count Agusta's MV concern in the early 1960s. Today, the Osca name is kept alive by the occasional glimpse one has of their cars in historic races and in various collections. In the late 1960s it also appeared on a 1,699cc production car, using a German Taunus V-4 engine, with disc brakes all round and boasting a 110mph (177kph) maximum speed. DCN

Pacey-Hassan see Bentley

Packard (US)
In 1903 Krarup and Fetch succeeded in crossing the American continent in a Packard in 61 days. The make's subsequent racing appearances were infrequent, though the works-built 4-cylinder racer, 'Gray Wolf', was mentioned as a possible contender for the Gordon

Top left, 1951 Osca-Maserati 4·5-litre GP car. Bira at the wheel. *Photo: Geoffrey Goddard*

Above left, 1953 Osca 1·5-litre sports car. A. A. Garthwaite Jr at the wheel. *Photo: Ruth Sands Bentley*

Top right, 1954 Osca 1·5-litre coupé at Amiens. *Photo: Autosport*

Above right, 1923 Packard Indianapolis car. Joe Boyer at the wheel. *Photo: Indianapolis Motor Speedway*

1970 Palliser Formula 3 at Castle Combe. Roger Keele at the wheel. *Photo: Edward G. Hodgkins*

Bennett race, and managed 4th place in the 1904 Vanderbilt Cup. Thereafter Packard dropped out of racing until 1917 when an experimental 12-cylinder car was built to test a new aero-engine design. This averaged 102·8mph (165·5kph) for 6 hours in the hands of Ralph DePalma and finished 6th at Indianapolis in 1919. Even fiercer was a car with a 905ci (14,830·34cc) engine built for record work in 1919. Also a V-12: this one was timed over the mile at Daytona at a speed of 149·87mph (241·21kph), at the time when the official World Land Speed Record stood at only 124mph (200kph). This performance was never internationally recognized, and there was no more official racing by Packard after 1923, when a team of three special cars were produced for Indianapolis. These were not strictly Packards, and were built in Los Angeles under DePalma's supervision. All retired in the race, and apart from Wade's and Wells's successful attack on the Transcontinental Record in 1925, using a stock straight-8, Packard took no further part in competition, until the 1951 Carrera Panamericana, in which a works-entered car driven by Trevoux and Lesurque finished 5th. MCS

Packard Cable Special see Miller

Palliser (GB)
Designed by Len Wimhurst, the London-built Palliser was so-called as this was the middle name of sponsor Hugh Dibley, racing driver and BOAC pilot. The first production model was the 1968 F2/B car, campaigned

successfully by Bob Winkelmann in the United States, who later marketed the cars under his own name. This model was followed by the WDF1 Formula Ford and WDB2 cars for 1969. The following year Jim Jenkins won the IMSA Formula Ford series with a WDF2, while in Britain the leading Palliser drivers were Bob Evans and Peter Lamplough. For 1971 there were also available the WD31 Formula 3, the WD3 for Formula Atlantic and Formula B, the WDV1 Formula Super Vee, and the Palliser-Franklen WDA1 for Formula A/5000.

All cars were based on simple spaceframe designs built by Arch Motors, with an unusually high proportion of the pieces affixed thereto being of Palliser's own design and make. DF

Panhard (F)

Panhard entered several cars for the Paris–Rouen Trials of 1894: these had front-mounted V-twin engines of 1,100cc and 1·5-litres, tube ignition, and chain drive, though Emile Levassor's machine had an experimental Maybach-type spray carburettor. Though they could not improve on 4th and 5th places, they shared the laurels with Peugeot. In 1895 4bhp vertical twins appeared with the new carburettors; also in the Paris–Bordeaux–Paris was a 4-cylinder car with wheel steering, driven by Boulanger. Levassor averaged 15mph (24·14kph) to score a moral victory, though he was placed 2nd. These 2·4-litre fours ran again in the Paris–Marseilles–Paris, 1896, Mayade winning the race. Levassor and d'Hostingue (who took over at Avignon after Levassor had been injured in an accident) came in 4th. Levassor died in 1897 from the effects of this crash. That year the firm was using 2·5-litre wheel-steered twins, and a rear-mounted tubular radiator tried by Girardot in the Paris–Dieppe was standardized. Hourgières won the Paris–Dieppe and Paris–Trouville, both at over 25mph (40kph): in the former race Fernand Charron took 2nd place.

Racing Panhards in 1898 were 2·4-litre fours with pneumatic tyres, and they dominated the season. Charron took the Marseilles–Nice and the Paris–Amsterdam–Paris; Leys was the victor in the Course de Périgueux, and de Knyff was 1st in the Paris–Bordeaux. Girardot ('the eternal second') followed Charron home in the Paris–Amsterdam–Paris. His unwonted victory in the 1899 Nice–Castellane–Nice event was gained in an 1898 car, but during the season Panhard fielded some successful 3·3-litre machines with frontal radiators, which gained them the Paris–Bordeaux: Charron won at 29·9mph (48·12kph), followed by de Knyff, Girardot, Archambault, and Hourgières. For the Tour de France

Top, 1901 Panhard 40hp Paris–Berlin car. Charles Jarrott at the wheel. *Photo: Veteran Car Club of Great Britain*

Above, 1903 Panhard 60hp at Gaillon Hill-Climb. George Heath at the wheel. *Photo: Veteran Car Club of Great Britain*

Left, 1899 Panhard 12hp Paris–Bordeaux car. René de Knyff at the wheel. *Photo: Veteran Car Club of Great Britain*

capacity was increased to 4·4-litres and output to a nominal 16hp, and the firm were rewarded with another victory for Charron, plus 2nd, 3rd and 4th places. The make also won the Paris–Boulogne and Paris–Ostend.

Even more powerful 5,322cc cars with electric as well as tube ignition came in 1900, but Mors were now challenging strongly, and Panhard won only three of the five major races: the Circuit du Sud-Ouest, which went to de Knyff at 43·8mph (70·49kph); the Nice–Marseilles; and the indifferently-supported Gordon Bennett Cup, in which Charron and Girardot were the sole finishers. In addition, the Hon. C. S. Rolls won the ACGBI Gold Medal for the best performance irrespective of class in the British 1,000 Miles Trial. Tube ignition had gone for good from the 7·4-litre racers of 1901, but the season was patchy. Though Maurice Farman won at Pau and Coltelletti was 2nd in the Giro d'Italia, 2nd places in both the Paris–Bordeaux and Paris–Berlin (for Maurice Farman and Girardot respectively) were a warning of the Mors ascendancy, and in the Nice–Salon–Nice the new Mercedes dealt firmly with the Panhards. Admittedly Girardot won the Gordon Bennett Cup, but

that year all the entries were French, and he was the only driver to last out to Bordeaux. More promising were some 3·3-litre 4-cylinder *voitures légères* on classic Panhard lines, with which Giraud won the appropriate category in both the Paris–Bordeaux and Paris–Berlin. Panhards were 2nd and 3rd as well in the latter event.

Things started to go downhill in 1902, though the magnificent 13,672cc 70hp, still with aiv — 3 of them per cylinder — and flitchplate frame, was very fast, winning Henry Farman the big-car class of the Paris–Vienna, and Jarrott the Circuit des Ardennes at 54mph (86·90kph). A 1901-type 40hp driven by Maurice Farman won the Circuit du Nord alcohol race, with Jarrott 2nd on a similar car. Nevertheless though Panhard's light cars now ran to 4·1 litres, the Darracqs were on top, and even the Paris–Vienna victory was less impressive than it seemed since all the heavy cars were beaten by Renault's *voiture légère*, and between Farman and the other Panhards in 3rd, 4th, 5th, 6th and 7th places lay Zborowski's Mercedes. Moiv in a T-head, pressed-steel frames, and shells enclosing the untidy tubular coolers

came in 1903, but the light racers were dropped, and Pierre de Crawhez's home win in the Ardennes was achieved in the absence of Mercedes. Fourth was Panhard's best in the Paris–Madrid, and de Knyff and Henry Farman had to be content with 2nd and 3rd places behind a 60hp Mercedes in the Irish Gordon Bennett.

In 1904, for the first time in the history of the race, Panhards were not automatically allocated a place in the French Gordon Bennett team, and for that year's Trials they entered some enormous 15,435cc affairs with ht magnetos and shaft drive, all to no avail. The American driver, Heath, however, won both the Circuit des Ardennes (at 56·4mph — 90·77kph) and the Vanderbilt Cup (at 52·2mph — 84·01kph), and Teste was 2nd both in the former race and in the Coppa Florio. Output was up from 100 to 120bhp on the 1905 cars, but once again they failed in the Gordon Bennett Trials, and 2nd places in both the Ardennes and the Vanderbilt Cup were indicative of decline. For three more seasons Panhard turned out for the Grand Prix: immense 18·3-litre engines were used in 1906, and 15·5-litre units and dash-

Top, 1908 Panhard French GP team. *Photo: Montagu Motor Museum*

Above, 1927 Panhard 5-litre sports car in the 1928 Georges Boillot Cup at Boulogne. *Photo: Montagu Motor Museum*

board radiators in 1907. There was a reversion to chain drive on the more modest 1908 12,831cc racers. The results were dismal: Heath was 6th in 1906, all the cars retired in 1907, and the American was down to 9th in 1908.

Between the World Wars Panhard confined themselves to record work, which started in 1925 on a big 4·8-litre sleeve-valve 4-cylinder sports car driven by Ortmans. It took the World Hour Record at 115·3mph (185·6kph), and was followed a year later by a 6·4-litre straight-8 which pushed this up to 120·24mph (193·46kph), as well as covering 100km at 125·38mph (201·83kph). An ingenious 'razor-blade' single-seater of 1926, with 3-carburettor 1,500cc engine, steered by a hoop encircling the cockpit, was abandoned after a fatal accident. But in 1932 the 8-cylinder car, now bored out to 8 litres, was out again in the hands of G. E. T. Eyston, managing a new Hour Record of 130·73mph (210·35kph), and winning that year's British Empire Trophy Race at Brooklands at over 126mph (200kph), only to be disqualified. In 1934 the big Panhard was retired after raising the hour to 133·01mph (214·02kph).

There was a renaissance after World War 2 with the brilliant Dyna series of air-cooled fwd flat-twins inspired by J. A. Grégoire. These formed the basis of such makes as the DB and the German Dyna-Veritas, but also raced in their own right. The first Dynas had 610cc engines, but capacity went up to 750cc and finally to 850cc. In 1950 a Monopole-Panhard driven by Hémard and de Montrémy won the Index of Performance at Le Mans, a feat they repeated in 1951 and 1952, and a 750cc class victory was scored in the 1952 Mille Miglia. The new Panhards also made their mark in rallies, with class victories in the Lisbon and Monte Carlo, not to mention 2nd, 3rd, 4th and 5th places, with Coupes des Alpes, in the Alpine. In 1953 Panhard ran some works cars at Le Mans, with pancake-like bodies of Riffard design, rhd, and 610cc and 850cc engines, the latter giving 44bhp. They won the Index of Performance there and at Nîmes; at Caen, a handicap event. Chancel was 1st overall.

By this time the closely related DBs were taking most of the honours on the circuits, but the 1954 score included a 750cc class win at Reims, and victory in both expert and novice categories of the Paris-St Raphael. Gillard and Dugart were 2nd in the 1955 Monte Carlo Rally, and the Panhards took two classes in the Nürburgring 500 Kilometres Race. Monopoles won their class at Reims in 1956 and 1957. The next major Panhard success

1962 CD-Panhard 701cc Le Mans coupé.
Photo: Citroën Cars Ltd

came in the controversial 1961 Monte Carlo Rally, where the 60bhp 850cc Tigre saloons took the first three places. This, unfortunately, did not lead to a run of rally victories. The works 702cc cars fared badly at Le Mans in 1962, even though Gilhaudin and Bertaut won Panhard their final Index of Performance, and the ban on cars of less than 1,000cc in the race was the final blow. Charles Deutsch (by now separated from René Bonnet) tried to circumvent this by running three supercharged CD coupés (under the Le Mans rules, forced induction doubles the cylinder capacity) in 1964. These 848cc machines had 5-speed boxes and Girling disc brakes and outputs of 70bhp were quoted, but they retired. Ogier's 24CT Panhard coupé finished 3rd in the 1965 Geneva Rally, but this was the make's last major success, and in 1967 Citroën (the firm's owners) discontinued the Dyna after a 20-year run. MCS

Parsenn (GB)
Keith Steadman's Parsenn was an interesting 500 special of the same family as the post-war Freikaiserwagen, suspension being by rubber in torsion and the usual driver being Jeremy Fry. The engine was based on a Freikaiserwagen-type Blackburne cylinder, developed by Robin Jackson. A form of spaceframe chassis construction was employed, and the car was exceptionally light, but after some initial success development was curtailed and plans for production abandoned. DF

Pat Clancy Special see Indianapolis Cars

Peerless (US)
The well-known Cleveland, Ohio firm of Peerless built a number of racing cars which were made famous by their colourful driver Barney Oldfield. In 1903 Peerless

Left, 1953 Panhard 850cc coupé at Le Mans.
Photo: Associated Press

Right, 1961 Panhard Tigre 850cc saloon, the Monte Carlo Rally-winning car driven by Maurice Martin and Roger Bateau. Photo: Planet News

Above, 1903 Peerless 80hp Gordon Bennett car. Louis Mooers at the wheel. *Photo: Veteran Car Club of Great Britain*

Right, 1958 Peerless coupé at Le Mans. *Photo: Geoffrey Goddard*

Below, 1904 Peerless Green Dragon. Barney Oldfield at wheel. *Photo: Automobile Manufacturers' Association*

c 1953 Pegaso Z-102 at Rabassada Hill-Climb. *Photo: Autosport*

engineer Louis P. Mooers designed an 80hp 4-cylinder T-head engine with full pressure lubrication for the firm's Gordon Bennett Cup entry. Driven by Mooers, the car retired on the 2nd lap after averaging only 19·8mph (31·87kph). This car was rebuilt for the 1904 Gordon Bennett Cup with a tubular radiator down the sides of the bonnet. It failed the qualifying trials, but passed into the hands of Barney Oldfield who christened it 'The Green Dragon'. With it he commenced a series of demonstrations at dirt tracks and country fairs in every corner of the United States and Canada that lasted until the end of 1907. In August 1904 he set new records for 3 miles at Toronto, and followed this up with other successes before being involved in a serious crash at St Louis in which two spectators were killed, Oldfield put in hospital and the Green Dragon wrecked.

He was soon back with another Green Dragon which used the same engine as the previous car but had an underslung chassis and radiator mounted well behind the front axle. With this car he set new records from one to 50 miles, and in a famous match at Yonkers, N.Y., he beat Théry's Gordon Bennett-winning Richard-Brasier, Benin's 60hp Renault, and Sartori's 90hp Fiat. In 1905 he had another crash, and there is some doubt as to whether the next Green Dragon was a new car, or the old one rebuilt. Oldfield continued to campaign with his car through 1906 and 1907, on one occasion 'driving' on a treadmill on the stage of a Broadway theatre in a play entitled *The Vanderbilt Cup*.

After Oldfield sold the Green Dragon it was raced for a season or two longer, but without distinction. The last appearance of a Peerless in racing was in 1917, when Irving Fetterman won a 112-mile race on the Uniontown Board Speedway. GNG

Peerless (GB)

The Peerless GT was designed by Bernie Rodger, who had earlier been responsible for the Raybern, Warrior-Bristol and Beart-Rodger-Climax sports cars, the latter two proving quite successful in their classes. An early Peerless finished the 1958 Le Mans race, covering over 2,000 miles (3,220km) in the hands of Jopp and Crabb, and thereafter the cars were raced quite successfully in make and GT races. The introduction of a slightly heavier de luxe model a year later failed to stimulate sales, and the company was re-formed to produce the very similar Warwick, also with Triumph TR3 engine and other mechanical parts, in 1960. Even after a Buick

V-8 engine had been adopted, the new name seldom featured in the results. DF

Pegaso (E)

Built in the training works of the former Hispano-Suiza factory at Barcelona, the Pegaso was a complex and very expensive sports car of which only 125 were made between 1951 and 1957. Various models were made, mostly with 4-ohc V-8 engines, dry-sump lubrication and a 5-speed gearbox located in the rear axle. The first model had a capacity of 2·5 litres, and this was increased on subsequent models to 2·8, 3·2, 4·0, 4·5, and 4·7 litres. Very few of the cars of 4 litres and over were made; these had push-rod engines.

The Pegaso was more of a GT car than a competition machine, although it did take part in a number of sporting events. In Spain, Pegasos did well at hill-climbs such as Rabassada (where the record is still held by a Pegaso) and Cuesta de las Perdices. A Pegaso owned by the son of President Trujillo of Cuba and driven by Joaquin Palacio ran in the 1954 Carrera Panamericana, and had reached 2nd place when it was eliminated by an accident In 1953 a Pegaso covered the flying mile at Jabbeke, Belgium, at 152·001mph (244·602kph). The same year a curious asymmetrical car with the driver's seat in a perspex (plexiglass) compartment on the offside was entered for Le Mans, but it did not start. JRV

Perigee (GB)

Home-built by electronics engineer Peter Rhodes at Didcot, Berks., the Perigee C was a typical British F1200 sports-racing car, except for the use of a beam axle layout, in the interests of reducing wheel angles. The car was runner-up in the class championships of 1968 and 1969, and attracted such interest that in 1970 Rhodes offered replica chassis for sale. DF

Peugeot (F)

This pioneer firm was in at the birth of the sport, for a 2-cylinder car driven by Doriot and Rigoulot followed the Paris–Brest Cycle Race in 1891, and succeeded in finishing the course. Peugeot turned out for the Paris–Rouen Trials of 1894, entering five 954cc rear-engined machines powered by Daimler-type V-twins of Panhard manufacture, and blessed with hollow tubular frames through which the cooling water circulated. Lemaître finished 2nd at 11·5mph (18·51kph) and Doriot was 3rd There was also energetic support for the Paris–Bordeaux

Above, 1912 Peugeot Grand Prix car. Jules
Goux at the wheel. Photo: T. A. S. O.
Mathieson Collection

Right, 1914 Peugeot Grand Prix car.
Georges Boillot at the wheel. Photo:
T. A. S. O. Mathieson Collection

Below, 1922 Peugeot 3·8-litre in the Touring
Car GP. André Boillot at the wheel. Photo:
Montagu Motor Museum

Below, 1914 Peugeot Bébé at Brooklands,
c 1921. Photo: Montagu Motor Museum

Right, 1929 Peugeot 3·8-litre French GP car.
Henri Stoffel at the wheel. Photo: T. A. S. O.
Mathieson Collection

Paris in 1895. The mode of awarding prizes in this 732-mile (1,178km) event was peculiar: the fastest car was Levassor's Panhard, but the winner was Koechlin's Peugeot which had, in fact, finished 3rd behind Rigoulot's sister car. A significant if unsuccessful entry was André Michelin's Peugeot, the first racer to fit pneumatic tyres. In 1896 the Daimler engine was replaced by a new Peugeot-designed horizontal-twin, and in 1897 form this had a capacity of 2·2 litres. That year Lemaître was 2nd both in the Marseilles–Nice–La Turbie and in the Paris–Trouville, and Prévost averaged 22·8mph (36·69kph) to take 3rd place in the Paris–Dieppe. Though engines were enlarged twice more — to 3·3 litres in 1898 and to 5·9 litres in 1899, when dimensions were a formidable 140 × 190mm — the traditionally-designed Peugeots were becoming an anachronism now that the Panhard system was pre-eminent, and their successes were confined to relatively minor events such as the Bordeaux–Biarritz (1898) when Koechlin finished 2nd out of only seven starters in the heavy-car category. The next year was a little better: Lemaître won the Nice–Castellane–Nice and was 3rd in the Paris–Ostend. Peugeot also took 1st and 2nd place in the Italian Limone–Cuneo–Turin event. Doriot added a ftd at Chanteloup to the score, but a mysterious '100hp 8-cylinder' car commissioned by Lemaître for the 1900 Gordon Bennett Cup was, perhaps fortunately, stillborn. For the Paris–Berlin Peugeot prepared some 3·3-litre 2-cylinder light cars with front-mounted vertical engines, one of which, driven by

Kroeutler, took 6th place in its class. In 1902 Peugeot adopted the Mercedes arrangement with honeycomb radiators and pressed-steel frames. Both the 16hp light cars and their big 50hp stablemates had oversquare cylinder dimensions, but only the latter had moiv. Rouquette's 19th place on a 50hp marked the end of Peugeot's competition career for ten years.

From 1906 to 1910 the rival Lion-Peugeots had built up an enviable reputation in voiturette racing, and when the two Peugeot companies were reunited in 1910, Michaux's V-engined, chain-driven eccentricities survived for another season. However, 1912 brought designs which were the true progenitors of the modern racing car, and were the brainchildren of Ernest Henry and Paul Zucarelli, though inspired by Marc Birkigt's 1911 ohc Hispano-Suiza. The Henry Peugeots were shaft-driven and had 16-valve 4-cylinder engines with twin bevel-driven overhead camshafts. Long strokes were still the order of the day — the 3-litre Coupe de l'Auto type had dimensions of 78 × 156mm — but this unit developed 80bhp. In Grand Prix guise the engine was extended to 7·6 litres, giving 130bhp at 2,200rpm. Thomas's solitary Coupe de l'Auto car (called a Lion-Peugeot in contemporary reports) retired, but in the concurrently-run Grand Prix Georges Boillot beat the enormous chain-driven Fiats, winning at 68·45mph (110·16kph). Zucarelli later vindicated the 3-litre's honour by a victory in the less important GP de France at Le Mans, and Goux won the Coupe de la

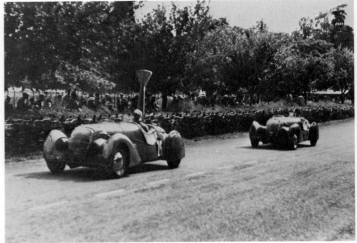

Left, 1932 Peugeot 301C 1,467cc sports car which took the Class F 24-Hour record at Miramas. *Photo: Peugeot SA*

Above, 1937 Peugeot Darl'mat 2-litre sports cars at Le Mans. *Photo: Autocar*

Sarthe on one of the big cars. In 1913 he showed America what the new order could do by winning the Indianapolis Race at 75·93mph (122·20kph) on a similar machine.

In 1913 the cars had ball-bearing crankshafts, dry-sump lubrication, and camshafts driven by a train of gears. Dimensions of the Coupe de l'Auto racers were unchanged, but the big Peugeots now used 5·6-litre engines, and in both the GP and the voiturette race Boillot and Goux led the rest of the field home. In the same year Goux brought one of the 1913 GP machines to Brooklands, and took the World Hour Record at 106·22mph (170·93kph), while at the other end of the scale the factory supported the Le Mans Cyclecar GP with a team of three 856cc T-headed Bébés, which finished 3rd, 5th and 6th. For the 4·5-litre GP formula of 1914 Henry produced some new 92 × 169mm, 112bhp cars with streamlined tails and, most important, fwb. Boillot's lengthy and ultimately unsuccessful duel with Lautenschlager's Mercedes is now part of legend, but despite his retirement and the German triumph Goux finished 4th and Rigal 7th. Meanwhile in America the 1913 racers had had a good season, Duray finishing 2nd at Indianapolis with a 3-litre, while Goux was 4th on a 5·6-litre version. During 1915 Resta carried on the good work. Starting the season with a 1913 GP Peugeot, he won the Grand Prize and the Vanderbilt Cup before progressing to a 1914 4·5-litre and even greater laurels — 1st at Chicago and Cincinnati and 2nd in Indianapolis, followed by an outright victory in the 1916 500 at 84mph (135·18kph). That year he also won at Chicago, and Aitken was victorious at Sheepshead Bay and Wilcox in the Grand Prize at Santa Monica.

The twin-ohc engines inspired a whole generation of American designers, some of whom started by making direct copies — one of Harry Miller's first assignments was to build a replacement unit for Bob Burman, who had blown his up. Wilcox and Goux fielded 4·5-litre cars once more in the first post-World War 1 race at Indianapolis in 1919, the former winning at 88·05mph (141·70kph), and the latter following in 3rd place. Though the 80bhp 2·5-litre cars built for the 1914 Coupe de l'Auto had spent the war in storage (this race was, of course, cancelled) these also emerged in 1919, in time for André Boillot to win the Targa Florio at 34·2mph (55·04kph). As late as 1921 Réville won the voiturette race at Boulogne on a similar machine. After Henry's departure to Ballot, Peugeot's last GP cars represented a sad diminuendo. Their Gremillon-designed engines had

triple ohc and five valves per cylinder and they made unsuccessful appearances at Indianapolis in 1920 and 1921 before being conveniently forgotten. Peugeot never returned to *grandes épreuves*.

Instead, they turned to sports-car events, and for the next decade André Boillot campaigned energetically with some very successful Knight-engined 4-cylinder machines. The basic unit was a 3·8-litre 5-bearing affair which was giving 140bhp by 1925. It made its debut in the Touring Car GP, a fuel consumption event staged in 1922, in which Boillot was 4th behind the Voisins. The engine was then put into the unsuccessful 1921 GP chassis, in which guise the cars finished 1st and 3rd in the Coppa Florio. In 1923 there were two teams in the Touring Car GP: in the five-seater class the 3·8-litres were again used, but in the four-seater category Peugeot prepared some 2·5-litre 15CV machines. There were 1-2-3 victories in each case, the class winners being Boillot and Cabaillot. In 1924 Boillot was 4th in the Targa Florio, and Dauvergne won the Touring Car GP. The next year was even better: Wagner and Boillot came 2nd and 3rd in the Targa Florio; the make won the Coppa Florio outright; and some special streamlined saloons were prepared for the Touring Car race at Montlhéry. Careful discipline limited lap speed, but Boillot won.

In 1926 Peugeot won the 3-litre class of the Paris-Nice. The big sleeve-valvers had an excellent season, Boillot and Louis Rigal winning the Belgian 24-Hour Race, and taking 1st and 2nd places in the 24-Hour touring-car event at Monza. Wagner was 6th in the Targa Florio, Peugeot won their class at San Sebastian, and in addition to the sleeve-valve cars at Monza there was also a 719cc sv 4CV driven by Camouzet which came in 6th — an amazing effort by a completely unsporting car. Rigal managed a 2nd place on a similar machine in the 1927 8-Day Small Car Trial at Montlhéry, and the big Peugeots continued successfully — 4th in the Targa Florio and 2nd at San Sebastian. For the Coupe de la Commission Sportive, another fuel-consumption event, the company produced some special 2·6-litre 4-cylinder cars, still with Knight engines. These dispensed with fwb and circulated in top gear alone, and once again ingenuity was rewarded with victory for Boillot.

By 1928 the 3·8-litre was nearing the end of its career, though Boillot could still finish 2nd at Monaco in 1929, and 6th in 1931, when the model ran in the French GP as well. Morillon took 4th place in the 1929 Monte Carlo Rally, and de Lavalette was 2nd in the light-car section in 1931, but though there was a 996cc ohc racing Peugeot, the 201X, in that year's programme, and its engine was half a Type 35 Bugatti, its only claim to fame is that André Boillot was killed while testing one. Coupes des Dames in the 1933 and 1934 Monte Carlo Rallies represented Sochaux's limit in the mid-1930s but in the 1937 Le Mans 24-Hour Race there were three 2-litre ohv Darl'Mat-Peugeot aerodynamic two-seaters based on the contemporary 402 saloon, and all of them finished, in 7th, 8th and 10th places. De Cortanze and Contet did even better in 1938, taking 5th place, and Miss Patten was 4th in the 1939 Paris–St Raphael Rally. Emile Darl'Mat had a further development of this theme ready for long-distance record work in 1939, but war once again intervened.

Since World War 2 Peugeot's main interest has been in rallies, though various Peugeot-based specials have been seen in sports-car events. A 202-based Darl'Mat 1,100cc special coupé took international class records at Montlhéry in 1947, and Sigrand and Celerier won the 1954 Bol d'Or on an M. D.-Peugeot. Peugeots finished 3rd and 4th in the 1955 Bol d'Or, and another Coupe des Dames in the Monte Carlo Rally fell to the 1·3-litre 203 in 1951. There was a class victory in 1953, a 2nd place overall in 1954, and another class win in 1960, but Peugeot's latter-day speciality has been a tougher type of event. The victory of Tubman and Marshall in the 1953 Australian Redex Trial (over 6,500 miles — 10,460km) was followed by an outright win in the 1956 Ampol event, and the East African Safari has become almost the preserve of the fuel-injection 404 saloons. Nowicki and Cliff won in 1963, there was a class victory in 1964, and a 2nd in 1965, after which the Shankland and Rothwell team won it twice in succession (1966 and 1967). Nowicki and Cliff scored a second victory in 1968, and the Armstrong and Pavely car was 4th in 1969. In 1965 a special 404 coupé with 1,948cc diesel engine took 22 International Class E records, including 200km at 100·75mph (162·08kph). MCS

Right, 1914 Pic-Pic Grand Prix cars. Tournier on the left, Clarke on the right. *Photo: T. A. S. O. Mathieson Collection*

Below, 1965 Peugeot 404 driven by Bert Shankland and Chris Rothwell in the Tanganyika 1000 Rally. *Photo: Camerapix, Dar es Salaam*

Pic-Pic (CH)

The first cars to come from the Piccard-Pictet works in Geneva were the Dufaux racing cars of 1904, but in 1906 the firm began to make their own cars, under the name SAG until 1910, and Piccard-Pictet or Pic-Pic thereafter. A 12CV single-seater did well at hill-climbs and sprints in the pre-1914 period, including Limonest, Mayenne, and Gurnigel, driven by works driver Tournier. The make also won races at San Sebastian and as far away as Buenos Aires. In 1912 a sleeve-valve model was introduced, and the two cars entered for the 1914 Grand Prix used a slightly smaller version of a production sleeve-valve engine. They had a capacity of 4,434cc, front-wheel brakes (in common with Fiat, Delage and Peugeot GP cars) and hydraulic shock absorbers. Driven by Tournier and a young Englishman, Thomas Clarke, both cars retired. The company made a few cars after the war, but their sporting activities were confined to private entries in hill-climbs. GNG

Pipe (B)

As early as 1901 a 4·1-litre 4-cylinder car of Panhard-like aspect put up an undistinguished performance in the Paris–Berlin. More interesting was the *grande voiture* driven by Hautvast in the 1902 Circuit des Ardennes, which claimed 24bhp from 2·5 litres at a time when comparable Panhards ran to 13,672cc. Pipe's 1903 racers retained flitchplate frames, but had 7·2-litre engines with mechanically-operated overhead valves and magnetic clutches. These were unsuccessful in the Paris–Madrid, and took 7th and 8th places in the Ardennes race.

For the 1904 Gordon Bennett Cup the company entered some bigger, 13·5-litre ohv cars with hemi-spherical heads and twin low-mounted camshafts, but Hautvast could do no better than 6th, though victories followed for smaller cars in the 1905 Liedekerke Cup and the 1906 Belgian Criterium. In the latter year there were also class victories at Ostend and Orignie.

Even more successful were the 8-litre cars with similar valve gear built for the Kaiserpreis, in one of which Hautvast finished 2nd behind Nazzaro's Fiat at 51·8mph (83·36kph). The team retired in the Circuit des Ardennes, leaving the race to Minerva. Thereafter the make was seen infrequently in serious competition, though a cup was won in the 1909 Russian Reliability Trials, a touring model did well at Gaillon in 1911, and another Pipe ran at Boulogne in 1912. MCS

Piper (GB)

The name 'Piper' derives from the trademark of Campbell's Garages of Hayes, Kent, managed by the former driver George Henrotte, who had built his own car for the original 500cc formula and was also concerned with the Gemini project. The original Piper GTA of 1965 was designed by Tony Hilder for BMC 'A' series mechanical components, but the production version standardized Ford 1600 engine and transmission. In 1968 the rear-engined GTR was introduced for Group 6 racing, with multi-tubular chassis and Mallite undertray, and Piper-tuned twin-cam Ford engine. BMW and BRM power units were to have been available also.

A new company was organized under Brian Sherwood, and operations transferred to Wokingham, Berkshire, the Piper tuning business remaining at the ex-Gurney Eagle works at Ashford. A car was entered for Le Mans, but failed to start after practice troubles. A Formula 3 car was also built, but neither this nor the Formula Ford car developed from it was put into production.

In 1969 development on the racing side was cut short when Sherwood died in a road accident. Only a handful of GTRs had been built. The firm continued under his widow, with Bill Atkinson as Works Manager. By mid-1970 some 40 GTT coupés had been sold, one with an Alfa Romeo engine for a German customer, and the remainder Ford-equipped. DF

Pluto (D)

Pluto was a German version of the French Amilcar. The first Pluto, the 4/22PS, appeared in 1924 and was based on the Amilcar C4 with 1,004cc ohv engine. It was supplemented a year later by the 5/30PS, which was the original Amilcar CGS with 1,074cc engine. The

5/30PS was also available with Roots or Cozette supercharger. The output for the Roots-equipped version was about 65bhp. The Pluto was very successful in national sports car events in its class. Plutos took part twice in the German Grand Prix, in 1926 on the AVUS circuit and in 1927 on the Nürburgring, but they failed to finish in either of these. Driven by Gockenbach a Pluto gained a 1,100cc class victory in the 1927 Nürburgring inaugural meeting. Late in 1927 production of Pluto cars ceased. HON

Plymouth (US)

Plymouth sedans have been a part of stock car racing since the beginning of NASCAR, winning 162 Grand Nationals between 1949 and the end of the 1970 season; a total second only to the 269 GN victories achieved by Ford. Except for 1969, when he drove for Ford, Richard Petty has been the mainstay of Plymouth's NASCAR effort, his Petty Blue No. 43 winning 18 Grand Nationals in 1970 alone. Roger McCluskey won the 1970 USAC stock car division title, which has been taken by Plymouth in five of the past seven years. In 1969 Art Pollard drove the Plymouth-powered STP Special to victory in the 200-mile USAC Championship Trail over the steeply banked one-mile oval at Dover Downs. Plymouth earned the 1965 and 1966 SCCA Manufacturers Rally Championship and Dan Gurney and Swede Savage raced works-supported Plymouth Barracudas in the 1970 Trans-Am series, but failed to win a single race. In drag racing Plymouth won the 1970 NHRA Manufacturers Cup. ARB

Poggi (I)

Designer Eugenio Poggi produced his Formula Junior car with backing from a new organization set up by Massimino, following his break with Vittorio Stanguellini. The Poggi was very similar to the other Fiat-powered, front-engined spaceframe designs of the time, and used modified Fiat 1100 front suspension with a live rear axle. In appearance it was reminiscent of the successful Stanguellinis, with a long tapering nose cone, but the cockpit sides were higher and it had a steeply sloping tail section. It was not a success. DCN

Pontiac (US)

Between 1957 and 1963 Pontiac sedans captured a total of 69 NASCAR Grand Nationals, winning 30 stock car races in 1961 and 22 in 1962. Pontiac Firebirds raced in the NASCAR Grand American division in 1969 and 1970, the veteran Buck Baker winning once in 1969 and twice in 1970. In the SCCA Trans-American Sedan championship, Pontiac Firebirds finished 3rd in the 1969 series, failing to win but finishing 2nd in three

Left, 1968 Piper GTR coupé at Lydden Hill. Bobby Bell at the wheel. *Photo: Autosport*

Above, 1970 Plymouth Road Runner driven in NASCAR events by Richard Petty. *Photo: Chrysler-Plymouth*

Left, 1924 Pluto 4/22PS at Solitude. *Photo: Neubauer Collection*

Below, 1959 Poggi Formula Junior. *Photo: Autosport*

races. In the 1969 Daytona 24 Hours the Firebird of Jon Ward and Jerry Titus finished 3rd overall and first GT. ARB

Pope-Toledo (US)

The Pope-Toledo was the most expensive of the five makes of car in Colonel Pope's empire, and also the most important from a sporting point of view. For the 1904 Vanderbilt Cup the company entered two cars, a 24hp and a 40hp. Both were virtually stock tourers and the makers had no expectation of winning, merely wishing to gain experience. Webb's 40hp car hit a telegraph pole on the 6th lap, but Lytle's 24hp was running in 3rd place when the race was stopped. For the 1905 Gordon Bennett Race two 60hp cars were built; Lytle finished 12th. In that year's Vanderbilt, Lytle drove a 90hp and Dingley a 60hp; the latter was still running when the race ended, but Lytle retired. For the 1906 Vanderbilt a still larger car of 120hp was built for Lytle to drive, but he was disqualified because the car was started by being towed. Both the 90hp and 120hp cars had enormous radiators whose frontal area was said to have counteracted the power developed. GNG

Porsche (D)

Porsche has existed as a car-producing company since 1948, and has been active in motor sport since 1951, although among the many and varied designs of Dr Ferdinand Porsche were oustanding competition cars and a team under his son Ferry designed the Cisitalia Type 360. The first cars carrying the name Porsche were produced by Porsche Konstruktions-GmbH at Gmünd in Austria; in 1950 the company moved to Zuffenhausen, Stuttgart, as Dr Ing. h.c. F. Porsche KG. During that year privately-owned Porsches appeared in rallies, and in 1951 the first Porsche works entries ran at Le Mans. Since then, under Dr Ferry Porsche, the company has been continuously committed to motor sport, almost as an article of faith.

One of the Porsches at Le Mans in 1951 finished, 20th overall—covering 1,766·3 miles (2,842·5km)—and winning the 1,100cc class. Later, at Montlhéry, 1,100cc and 1·5-litre cars took 17 international class records, from 500km to 10,000km, from six to 72 hours. The competition department behind these efforts was correspondingly modest; significantly it has grown as part of the company's experimental department, not as a section apart from the mainstream. Development of the 356 model continued into the next decade, and this basic Porsche shape became familiar on circuits on both sides of the Atlantic, and in rallies. Engines were of course air-cooled, normally 1,498cc and 1,588cc, and from 1955 sometimes in 4-ohc form. Notable in the 356-165C

Left, 1970 Pontiac Firebird driven by Jerry Titus leading Sam Posey's Dodge in Laguna Seca Trans-Am race. *Photo: SCCA*

Right, 1953 Porsche 356 coupé. *Photo: Marcus W. Taylor*

1954 Porsche 550 Spyder at Le Mans. *Photo: Motor*

series were the Carrera versions (named for 550 successes in the Mexican race), the Super 75 and Super 90 (both numbers denoting bhp outputs), 1,600C and SC 356, and Abarth-bodied Carreras. By the 1960s, the weight of the integral chassis/body increasingly told against the basic models. During the 1950s international rally successes had begun to accrue to Porsche: 1st and 2nd in the Liège–Rome–Liège in 1952, and 2nd in 1955; 1st in the 1957 Alpine, and 2nd in 1955; 1st in the Lisbon, 1952; 1st in the Midnight Sun, 1954; 2nd in the 1954 Tour de France.

In top-class racing the emphasis shifted to the 550, with 4-ohc 1,498cc engine and lighter multi-tubular frame. Prototypes with humbler tuned 1500 engines won the 1·5-litre class at Le Mans and minor German races in 1953; the definitive 550 first ran in the 1953 Carrera Panamericana in spyder form (both cars retiring).

In 1954 the 550s gained class successes in the Mille Miglia (plus 6th overall); at Le Mans (1,100cc and 1·5-litre); in the Reims 12-Hour Race; and the Carrera Panamericana. They were seen more frequently in 1955, when they became available to private owners. The best performance was again at Le Mans, where apart from 1,100cc and 1·5-litre class victories, Porsche spyders were placed 4-5-6 overall, took the Biennial Cup and Index of Performance. Class victories were also gained in the Mille Miglia and Tourist Trophy, and outright victories in lesser races.

The RS, developed from the 550 with lighter space-frame and 5-speed gearbox, first ran in the 1956 Nürburgring 1,000 kilometres (von Trips-Maglioli, 4th overall). In June, Maglioli gained for Porsche their first 'classic' victory, winning the Targa Florio at 56·53mph

(90·66kph). At Sebring, 550s were 6th and 7th; an RS (von Frankenberg-Storez) won the 1·5-litre Reims 12 Hours; at Le Mans a coupé RS was 5th overall. Porsche's Sarthe record was not maintained in 1957, when the works RS and RSK retired (the RSK had revised rear suspension, normally a 1,587cc engine, and in 1957–8 was outwardly distinguished by twin rear fins). The works also ran 1·5-litre spyder versions in the German GP F2 class, Barth winning it and completing 21 laps of the 22-lap race distance.

The 1958 programme was heavier, and after the 1957 débâcle Porsches were highly-placed at Le Mans again (Barth-Herrmann 1·6-litre RSK 3rd overall, 1·5-litre RSKs 4th and 5th); von Hanstein and Pucci were 2nd in the Targa Florio in a Carrera/RSK hybrid. This Le Mans result seemed to inspire Porsche to set their sights (and camshaft lift) too high in 1959, and all their cars retired with engine failures. The Targa Florio, however, went to the Barth-Seidel RSK, at 56·74mph (91·31kph), and for the first time Porsche took the European Mountain Championship.

Meanwhile a single-seater Porsche had appeared, in three 1958 F2 races. This was an RSK with central driving position and a 1,498cc engine giving 164bhp. Behra won the Reims F2 race with it, Gurney won at the AVUS, and Barth placed it 2nd in the German GP F2 class. Less makeshift F2 cars appeared in 1959, when in fact the 'Behra-Porsche' conversion of an RSK was more successful (2nd at Reims) than the bulky works cars (3rd at Reims being the best placing for this version). A full F2 programme was undertaken in 1960; Bonnier and Graham Hill were the regular works drivers, reinforced on occasion, and a car was lent to Walker for Moss to drive. The season ended with Porsche sharing the

Left, 1962 Porsche Formula I at Nürburgring. Dan Gurney at the wheel. *Photo: David Hodges Collection*

Right, 1960 Porsche Formula 2. Stirling Moss at the wheel. *Photo: Autosport*

Opposite top, Invicta 4½-litre S-type owned by R. C. J. Wood. *Photo: Motor Sporting Photographers*

Opposite bottom, Lotus 47 (Jack Oliver/ John Miles) in the BOAC 500 at Brands Hatch, 1968. *Photo: Motor Sport*

Left, 1963 Porsche 904 (Carrera GTS) 2-litre coupé. *Photo: Porsche*

Right, 1966 Porsche 906 at Le Mans Test Day. R. Buchet at the wheel. *Photo: Motor*

Championship with Cooper, the German cars winning at Aintree and Zeltweg (Moss) and the Nürburgring and Modena (Bonnier). Porsche were thus encouraged to contest the Grands Prix under the 1·5-litre formula.

Formula 1 Porsches, in fact the F2 cars, first raced in the 1961 Brussels GP; both cars retired, but then finished 2nd and 3rd in the Syracuse GP. A new car, somewhat slimmer, shorter in the wheelbase and with coil-spring front suspension, but still with the 4-cylinder engine, appeared at Monaco (Herrmann 9th, Bonnier 12th, Gurney 5th in one of the old cars). Thereafter Porsche obtained good placings only in the French, Italian and United States GPs (Gurney was 2nd in each, and only a minor tactical error cost him the French race). Second places were also gained in lesser events at Solitude, Karlskoga and Modena. Two of the cars were raced in 1962 by SSS Venezia, and one with great determination by de Beaufort until his fatal accident in practice for the 1964 German GP.

The long-awaited car with the air-cooled horizontally-opposed flat-8 first appeared for the 1962 Dutch GP. The gestation period of this 1,494cc (66 × 54·6mm) engine had been long drawn out, and it was known to be less powerful than contemporary British V-8s (giving approximately 180bhp at 9,200rpm, some power being wasted in driving the horizontal cooling fan). Four twin-choke carburettors were fitted, as fuel injection experiments (Bosch and Kügelfischer) on the company's fours had been inconclusive. The tubular chassis was reasonably slim, but because of the engine format the car was bulky beside its rivals. Suspension was orthodox, with inboard coil springs; Porsche disc brakes and an all-synchromesh 6-speed gearbox in unit with the final drive were fitted. Handling problems encountered in

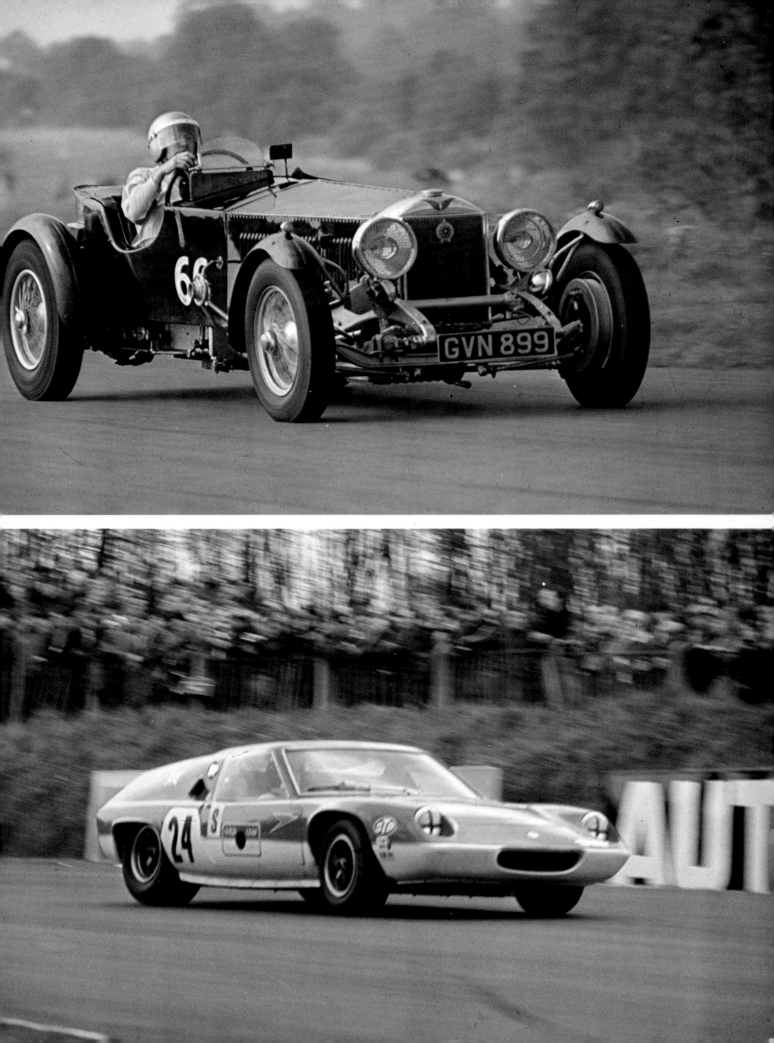

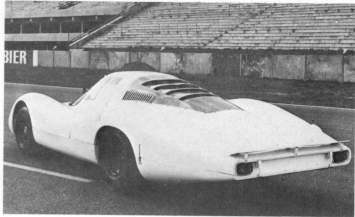

Above, 1969 Porsche 911S at Clermont-Ferrand during the Tour de France. Claude Ballot-Lena at the wheel. *Photo: John Davenport*

Right, 1968 Porsche 908 *langheck* (long-tailed) coupé. *Photo: Porsche*

Opposite, Lotus-Ford 72 (John Miles) in the 1970 French GP at Clemont Ferrand. *Photo: Motor Sport*

Hockenheim tests had not been resolved before the first race, but at least practice performance was sufficient to encourage Porsche to continue the programme. This achieved modest results: Gurney profited as British cars fell out of the French GP and won for Porsche their only *grande épreuve*; their next-best Championship placing was in the German GP (Gurney 3rd), although the American did win the Solitude GP. After the American GP, Porsche withdrew from GP racing, where they were obviously out of their depth, but officially because of lack of support.

This single-seater had distracted them from their normal sports car activities, and in this field results were more satisfactory. At the end of 1960 Porsche were runners-up in the truncated Sports Car Championship —as well as another Targa Florio victory (Bonnier-Herrmann, RS60), Porsche gained a first in the Sebring 12 Hours (Gendebien-Herrmann, RSK). The principal 1961 competition model was the RS61, a refined RS60 which was raced in varying forms, open and coupé and with engines up to 1,987cc. The season brought no outright victories in important races (best placings being a 2-3 in the Targa Florio, and 5ths at Le Mans and Sebring) to complement the by that time inevitable class wins.

New international regulations for GT cars and Prototypes applied in 1962, and new Porsche machines appeared to race under them, in that year most notably an 8-cylinder 1,982cc engine (similar to the F1 unit, even to power output). This first raced in Sicily, in a spaceframed Prototype (6-speed gearbox and trailing-link ifs, discarded in 1963 in favour of a double wishbone coil-spring arrangement). Vaccarella and Bonnier placed a coupé version 3rd in the Targa Florio, Hill and Herrmann an open car 3rd in the Nürburgring 1,000 kilometres. Bonnier and Abate gained for Porsche a 4th Targa Florio victory at 64·57mph (103·91kph) in 1964, a year when the front-line 8-cylinder cars seldom appeared, and achieved only one other finish (8th at Le Mans).

The 904 (otherwise Carrera GTS) appeared late in 1963 as a successor to the Abarth-bodied cars, was homologated as a GT car (minimum production 100) and as such became familiar on circuits, where private owners found it somewhat unforgiving of their errors. Its 1,966cc 4-cylinder engine (180bhp at 7,000rpm in competition tune) was mounted ahead of the rear axle line; a glassfibre body went some way to offset the weight of its box-section chassis. It was first raced, to class victories, at Daytona and Sebring, and first won in Sicily—Pucci and Davis, at 62·28mph (100·23kph). Class

victories in other European events secured the championship for Porsche. In racing the 8-cylinder Prototypes consistently failed, but compensation came in Barth's Mountain Championship (he usually drove an Elva powered by a Porsche flat-8) and in the success of the first Porsche team to run in the Tour de France. This led to a rally programme in 1965; apart from the Monte Carlo (when a 904—of all cars—was 2nd overall, and a 911 won its class), all that was demonstrated in this field was potential.

Apart from numerous private cars, Porsche racing in 1965 was confined to a handful of events contested with 8-cylinder Prototypes and 6/8-cylinder 904s (a racing version of the 1,991cc six of the forthcoming 911 had first appeared in a 904 at Montlhéry in 1964). Once again the best showing was in the Targa Florio, where Davis and Mitter placed a lightweight and most unattractive 8-cylinder open car 2nd (after top-line drivers had rejected it because of poor road-holding), while 904s were 3-4-5; in the Nürburgring 1,000 kilometres 904s were 3-5-6-9, at Le Mans 4-5. But 'Porsche's property', the Mountain Championship, went to Scarfiotti, driving a Ferrari.

The Carrera 6 (or 906) succeeded the 904 in racing in 1966. It was considerably more handsome, lighter, had better road-holding qualities, and the 6-cylinder engine produced some 235bhp at 8,000rpm. It was homologated as a Group 4 car, and thus frequently seen in private hands; some non-standard cars ran as Group 6 Prototypes (with fuel injection or 2·2-litre flat-8s, one at Le Mans with a long-tailed body). One of these Prototypes won the 50th Targa Florio—Mairesse and Muller, at 61·47mph (98·92kph); 906s were 4th at Sebring, Monza, the Nürburgring and Le Mans (and also gained lesser placings). Mitter, using 8-cylinder specials, took the Mountain Championship.

The 2·2-litre 270bhp 910 development of the 906 came in 1967, and with it a stepped-up racing programme; with the 911 (and 912) Porsche also became a very real force in rallies. Two Championship events were won outright (Targa Florio, Hawkins and Stommelen, and the Nürburgring 1,000 kilometres, Schutz and Buzetta); lightweight 910 Bergs won all seven rounds of the Mountain Championship; Elford and Stone won the Group 2 category of the European Rally Championship, winning outright the Tulip, Geneva and Lyons-Charbonnières, and coming 3rd in the Monte Carlo, in a 911; Zasada and Dobrzansky won the Austrian Alpine in a Group 1 912. The 911 also appeared in saloon racing on both sides of the Atlantic, dominating the 2-litre class in America

until ruled out at the end of 1969, but without the same success in British Group 5 racing.

In 1968 Porsche became level-terms contenders under the 3-litre Group 6/5-litre Group 4 regulations, notably with the 3-litre 908 (84 × 66mm, 2,924cc; later 85 × 66 mm, 2,996cc). Early races were contested with 2·2-litre 907s, taking first three places at Daytona — the winning car being driven by five drivers, the first two at Sebring, and first in the Targa Florio. The 908 appeared in the Monza 1,000 kilometres, hamstrung by minor troubles, then won at the Nürburgring and Zeltweg. Then Porsche Systems Engineering took to Le Mans four *langheck* (long-tailed) 908s, supported by three private/semi-private 907s, four 911Ts, a 910 and a 906, with an excellent chance of victory and of ensuring the Group 4/6 Championship. They failed, with the minor mechanical ailments too common in 1968: the only 908 to survive was 3rd, and a 907 was 2nd. Mitter won seven of eight Mountain rounds, but the sometimes dubious handling of the Berg sprint cars caught out Scarfiotti, who crashed fatally at Rossfeld. The rally season started with Swedish and Monte Carlo victories, but tailed off (although Porsche driver Toivonen won the driver's championship).

Rico Steinemann took over from von Hanstein as competitions manager in 1969, when the 908 problems seemed to be left behind (and spyder versions appeared). Further to this, Porsche took advantage of weaknesses

Top left, 1970 Porsche 908 at Sebring, driven by Steve McQueen and Pete Revson. *Photo: David Hodges Collection*

Top right, 1969 Porsche 907 (left) and 910 (right) at Mugello in 1970. *Photo: Autosport*

Above left, 1970 Porsche 908/3 in Campo-felice during the Targa Florio. Brian Redman at the wheel. *Photo: Geoffrey Goddard*

Above right, 1970 Porsche 917 flat-12 air-cooled engine. *Photo: Doug Nye*

in the regulations, and built 25 of the 917s, to qualify this startling model as a Group 4 car — a vastly expensive exercise aimed at the Championship and that elusive Le Mans victory. It had a 4,495cc flat-12 engine, producing some 520bhp at 8,000rpm, was very fast — it was timed at 206mph (331·5kph) at Le Mans, and was theoretically capable of 240mph (384kph) — and had tremendous acceleration. But its handling qualities were not equal to this performance. In Group 6, 908s started in 10 events, and won at Brands Hatch, Monza, Spa, the Nürburgring and Watkins Glen (all driven by Siffert/Redman) and in Sicily (Mitter/Schutz), thus conclusively gaining the Championship. The 917 ran unsuccessfully at Spa, the Nürburgring and Le Mans and was 1st at Zeltweg. Camshaft failures put all five cars out at Daytona, and the Le Mans effort failed for a variety of reasons (just one 908 coupé of the six works cars ran through, to an incredibly close 2nd place). An ugly lightened spyder 917 was run in Can-Am races by Porsche-Audi, Siffert placing it five times in seven starts (the highest being 3rd) although it was considerably underpowered in this field. Porsches (911S, 911T and 911R) were first in the Monte Carlo, Swedish, Acropolis and Polish rallies, but once again lost the constructors' championship (to Ford).

At the end of this very ambitious season, Porsche severely cut back their own direct racing commitments, entrusting the principal teams of 917s for 1970 to JW

Automotive and Porsche Konstruktionen KG of Salzburg, an arrangement which was to lead to some undesirable rivalry. After the 1970 Monte Carlo and Swedish events (both won by 911S), Porsche partly rested on their rally laurels, but despite this and the near-humiliation of the works team in the RAC Rally, the constructors' championship fell to the make.

During the winter, JWA sorted out the 917 to good effect, with high tails which transformed handling; their cars gained 1st and 2nd places in the opening Championship event, at Daytona; the only Championship defeat for Porsche came in the next race, at Sebring. A 5-litre engine (85 × 66mm; 4907cc) first appeared in a 917 at the Monza 1,000km race, and 908/3 lightweight 'specials' derived from the space-framed 909 hill-climb car were raced in the Targa Florio and Nürburgring 1000km. The Gulf/JWA team won seven of the ten championship races, the Salzburg team two, at last gaining for Porsche an outright Le Mans victory (Attwood and Herrmann). During the season the 914/6 was also competitive, at its level in races and rallies. The 1969 Can-Am effort was not followed up directly, although 917s which were at Watkins Glen primarily for the 6-hour race finished 2-3-4-6-7 in a Can-Am race there, and in an admittedly freak race at Atlanta, Tony Dean broke the long run of McLaren Can-Am victories, with his 3-litre 908!

The first two Championship events of 1971, Buenos Aires 1,000km and Daytona 24-Hours, both went to JW 917s driven by Bell and Siffert, and Rodriguez and Oliver respectively. DWH

Porsche in America: It has been said that half of Porsche's entire production is shipped to the United States, and that half of the US total is sold in California. Porsche have ranged from under 2-litre winners to contenders for overall honours and have an outstanding American record in SCCA club racing, international events and SCCA professional racing. At Daytona Roberto Mieres and Antonio Von Dory won the 1959 inaugural sports

car 6 Hours in their RSK; in 1968, 907s finished 1-2-3 in the 24 Hours and in 1970 the 917 of Rodriguez and Kinnunen established a Daytona 24 Hours record of 2,758·44 miles (4,439·66km), with a 114·866mph (184·91kph) race average. At Sebring, in addition to winning the Index of Performance and being first in class 10 times between 1956 and 1970, Porsche enjoyed outright victories in 1960 with Gendebien and Herrmann, and in 1968 with Herrmann and Siffert.

At the Watkins Glen 6 Hours for the manufacturers' championship a 908 was first in 1969, a 917 in 1970. In 1963 Bob Holbert won the first US Road Racing championship driving a Porsche RS61 and a Shelby Cobra. George Follmer won the USRRC in a Porsche-powered Lotus in 1965, and Scooter Patrick's 906 captured the under 2-litre USRRC title in 1966, tying with Joe Buzzetta for the same honours in 1967. From 1955 until 1963 Porsche drivers Pete Lovely, Jack McAfee, Charley Wallace, Bob Holbert, Don Sessler, Roger Penske and Bob Bucher won the SCCA 'F' modified title. Holbert, Buzzetta and Don Wester were five times E Modified champions. Patrick, who with Holbert, Buzzetta and Peter Gregg, were honoured with works rides in European and US events, won the 1968 B Modified championship. Alan Johnson of California and Peter Gregg of Florida won SCCA national sedan titles in 1968 and 1969. In production racing Porsche won 24 national championships between 1954 and 1970, with Bengt Söderström, Lake Underwood, Bruce Jennings and Alan Johnson earning multiple titles. Porsche 911s won the 1967, 1968 and 1969 under 2-litre Trans-Am championship. An increase in engine size, coupled with a new Trans-Am regulation, eliminated the 911 as a sedan and Porsche left the series. In the American Road Race of Champions, the SCCA club racing run-offs, Milt Minter in a Porsche 906 won the 'B' sports racing national championship at Road Atlanta in November 1970. ARB

Below, 1970 Porsche 917 in the Monza 1,000km, driven by Pedro Rodriguez and Leo Kinnunen. *Photo: David Hodges Collection*

Right, 1970 Porsche 916 (Chasseul and Ballot-Lena) leading a 911TH (Hanroud and Verrier) at Le Mans. *Photo: Autocar*

Praga (CS)

The Praga company began by manufacturing cars of
Charron and Isotta Fraschini design under licence.
Early in 1910 Františka Kec began to produce original
designs. The first sports car was the Praga Grand of 1912,
with a 3,824cc 4-cylinder engine devloping nearly 45bhp.
These cars competed in the 1912, 1913, and 1914
Austrian Alpine Trials, and won the 1913 Kielmannsegg
Cup. Later versions of the Grand competed in rallies and
hill-climbs during the 1920s. The 1,790cc 6-cylinder Alfa
of 1932 and onwards competed in the Monte Carlo
Rally, and in hill-climbs at Gaisberg, Schreber, and
other places. In 1935 a team of three Praga Super
Piccolos with 1,660cc 4-cylinder engines and special
streamlined saloon bodies was built for the Czech
Thousand Miles Rally. They achieved the best performance of any Czech cars in the Rally. VH

Premier (US)

Several Indianapolis-built Premier cars took part in the
Glidden Tours, finishing 1st and 4th in the 1910 event,
but it was not until 1916 that they appeared in racing. In

Top, 1935 Praga Super Piccolo coupé built
for Czech 1,000 Miles Trial. *Drawing: Jiry
Nejedly*

Centre, 1916 Premier Indianapolis car.
Tom Rooney at the wheel. *Photo:
Indianapolis Motor Speedway*

Bottom, 1967 Protos-Cosworth Formula 2
at Crystal Palace. Brian Hart at the wheel.
Photo: Autosport

that year three cars were built for the Indianapolis 500;
they were almost exact replicas of the 1914 4·5-litre
twin-ohc Peugeots, except for the use of lighter pistons.
Like the Harroun-designed single-ohc Maxwells,
these Premiers were commissioned by the Speedway
organization in order to provide more interesting racing,
as World War 1 had eliminated foreign competitors.
Wilcox, Rooney, and Anderson drove them in 1916;
Wilcox finished 7th, but the others retired. In 1919, when
Goux cracked a cylinder block of his 1914 Peugeot in
practice, a Premier block was used as a replacement, and
enabled Goux to finish 3rd in the race. GNG

Pringett (GB)

Designed by Pat Rochfort and produced by Gerry
Corbett at Eastbourne, Sussex, the Pringett Mistrale
Formula Ford single-seater was introduced for 1969,
with conventional spaceframe and four-piece glassfibre
body. By mid-1970, some dozen cars had been sold,
including those used by the drivers' school Motor
Racing Stables, and victories had been achieved by M.
Blackie, S. Fox and P. Wardle. DF

Promot see Rak

Protos-Cosworth (GB)

The Protos-Cosworth was an unusual Formula 2 car
built in 1967 by Ron Harris. He ordered from Frank
Costin a number of monocoque chassis formed from
bonded plywood sheet with metal bulkheads and a
mild-steel rear subframe to carry the engine and gearbox.
This was clad in streamlined glassfibre body panels with
a high domed windscreen almost covering the driver; a
slot was cut in it to give adequate forward vision. Power
came from the usual Cosworth-Ford FVA engine,
driving through a Hewland FT200 transaxle unit.
Harris followed a full F2 season, with Brian Hart and
Pedro Rodriguez as his regular drivers. The cars were
well overweight, unfortunately, but their good shape
showed well on the faster circuits, Hart coming 2nd to
Gardner's works Brabham at Hockenheim. Generally,
however, the cars were an expensive failure, and Harris
abandoned the project at the end of 1967. DCN

Puch (A)

Puch took part in the Prince Henry Trials of 1909 and
1910, which they finished unpenalized. A special sports
version of 1909 had a 4-cylinder 4-litre engine and with it
Karl Slevogt, at that time Puch's chief engineer, achieved
a number of class victories, e.g. in the Semmering hill-
climb. Puch also entered the Austrian Alpine Trials, and
were particularly successful in the 1914 event. After
World War 1 they introduced a 1·5-litre sports version of
their Type XII. This had a detachable cylinder head, twin
ohc driven by chain and an output of about 45bhp. It
was seen especially in Austrian hill-climbs, gaining innumerable victories and places. Competition entries
ended with the 1922 season. HON

Pygmée (F)

Marius dal Bo originally built a spidery-looking F3
single-seater for his son Patrick in the mid-1960s, and
from this original F3 Pygmée stemmed a line of improved
machines, culminating in Formula 2 models in 1969 and
1970. The early F3 car had a reputation for being very
light and fragile, and the F2s later encountered similar
problems. They had a very short wheelbase and handled
badly, but team drivers dal Bo and Eric Offenstadt

occasionally showed that their cars had promise. An ambitious F2 programme was planned for 1970, with Beltoise as one of the drivers, and the cars were more competitive than ever before. Beltoise was enthusiastic, insisting that they had great potential, but the dal Bo products could never quite match the opposition. Lack of finance for such an ambitious project was a major hindrance. DCN

Railton (GB)

The Anglo-American Railton based on the 4,168cc straight-8 Hudson was at its best in sprints, recording class victories at Shelsley, Syston and Bo'ness, as well as a class record at Wetherby in 1936. Though on two occasions S. C. H. Davis drove a Railton through the Monte Carlo Rally, the make's best performance in this event was 3rd, by the Portuguese Ribeiro-Ferreira in 1934. The Railton Light Sports made the fastest sports-car ascent of Brooklands Test Hill, and Charles Follett ran this car in the 1938 3-Hour Sports-Car Race at the track, but could manage no better than 7th place. MCS

Left, 1970 Pygmée Formula 2 at Barcelona. J-P Jabrouille at the wheel. *Photo: Autosport*

Right, 1938 Railton-Mobil Special chassis. *Photo: William Boddy Collection*

1935 Railton Light Sports at Shelsley Walsh. *Photo: Montagu Motor Museum*

Railton-Mobil Special (GB)

This was the second of Reid Railton's designs for John Cobb: the first was the 1933 Napier-Railton. Its 1938 successor was intended for attacks on the World's Land Speed Record, and broke completely with tradition in that it used an angled backbone frame in which the two engines (24-litre supercharged 12-cylinder Napier Lions, each developing 1,250bhp) each drove a pair of wheels. Other features included ifs, a solid rear axle, ice-tank cooling, and low weight: about 3 tons as against the 6 tons of Eyston's Thunderbolt. The driver sat in the nose and the body was detachable in one piece for servicing. The late summer of 1938 saw a duel between Eyston and Cobb at Bonneville, the latter collecting his first record at 350·2mph (563·6kph) in September. This record stood for only a day, and it was not until the following year that he was able to regain the record from his rival with a speed of 369·7mph (594·9kph). In September 1947, Cobb improved upon this figure with a mean 394·2mph (594·9kph); the car was clocked at well over 400mph (644kph), but he thereafter turned his

attention to the World's Water Speed Record, and was killed on Loch Ness with his Crusader in 1952. MCS

Raineri (I)

The prototype Raineri FJ appeared on the grid at Monza on 25 April 1958, and there was little unusual about its layout, with a spaceframe chassis and front-mounted Fiat 1100 engine, with all-independent suspension from a Fiat 600. Like the Volpini and Conrero cars it had a central drive-line passing beneath the cockpit, and was a neat and workmanlike-looking little car. Luigi Nobile put up some notable performances in his car, and later Raineri fitted the V-4 Lancia Appia engine. However, with the fall in Italian fortunes in Formula Junior, Raineri cars disappeared from the scene. DCN

Rak (PL)

Rak is Polish for crab, and the cars took this name as the four men behind the project were all born under this sign of the zodiac. The head of the team was Jerzy Jankowski, and his assistants were Zbigniew Kulczynski, Jerzy Przybysz and Krzysztof Brun. The first Raks, made from 1957 to 1960, were sports cars, but in 1961 there appeared a rear-engined Formula Junior car with tubular frame and Triumph T-110 engine. In 1963 the Rak was built to the new Formula 3 regulations, and since then the Polski Swiazek Motorowy (Polish Motoring Association) workshops have turned out a number of Formula 3 cars powered by Ford, Renault and Wartburg engines. Maximum output was 80bhp and speed 118mph (190kph). For the first time, Polish drivers had a car which could hold its own with Czech and East German machines. After a serious accident in 1966 Jankowski retired from driving and concentrated on design. His latest Formula 3 car is called the Promot. It is of spaceframe construction with suspension by two unequal length wishbones and hub carrier at the front, and single top link with twin radius arms with outboard springs at the rear. The most commonly used engine in the Promot is the 3-cylinder Wartbug, coupled to a Wartburg gearbox, but one or two use Holbay engines and Hewland gear boxes. VH

Rapier (GB)

Made and sold by Lagonda in 1934 and 1935, and thereafter produced in Hammersmith, London, as an independent make, Ashcroft's dohc 4-cylinder Rapier

Left, 1958 Raineri Formula Junior. Photo: A. Ceci

Right, 1963 Rak Formula Junior. Jerzy Jankowski at the wheel. Photo: Vladimír Havránek Collection

Below, 1960 Rejo Mark 2 in an 1172 Formula race at Brands Hatch in 1961. Photo: Michael Ware

Right, 1903 Renault 30hp Paris–Madrid car. Louis Renault at the wheel. Photo: Montagu Motor Museum

sports car suffered by virtue of its cylinder capacity— 1,104cc. A 1,080cc version was driven into 16th place at Le Mans in 1934 by de Clifford and Brackenbury, and R. H. Eccles did quite well at Brooklands from 1935 onwards in a special Zoller-blown single-seater. A Rapier engine was also used in 1947 to power the first of the Emerysons. MCS

Rejo (GB)

Some half dozen Rejo Clubman's sports-racing cars were built by Rod Easterling in London, generally powered by the 1,172cc side-valve Ford engine. The last of these (Mark 6) was a rear-engined design. Although built in the early 1960s, one or two, such as Geoff Ward's, were still competitive in 1969 in F1200. DF

Renault (F)

In 1899 Louis Renault's tiny shaft-driven voiturette, with 239cc air-cooled De Dion engine under a meat-safe bonnet, and 3-speed gearbox, made its début in the Paris–Rambouillet, winning its class. By 1900 he had progressed to water cooling with lateral radiators, and capacity was up to 499cc; Aster engines were also being tried. The Renaults were the sole survivors in the voiturette category of the Paris–Toulouse–Paris, and there was a class victory at Brescia for Fraschini, then the make's Italian concessionaire. In 1901, racers retained the lateral coolers but had assumed the classic coal-shovel bonnet; their 1-litre units were rated at 8hp. With

Darracq contesting the *voiture legère* category, a clean sweep of the voiturette section of Paris–Bordeaux was predictable, and Renault himself was followed home by his brother Marcel, Oury and Grus. Louis repeated his success in the Paris–Berlin, where his average was 36.3mph (58·42kph).

In 1902 there were still Renault voiturettes, powered by 9hp Aster engines, but for the *voiture legère* class Renault was now building his own 3,758cc 4-cylinder units, the work of Viet, formerly of De Dion-Bouton. These failed in the Circuit du Nord, though Grus's Renault was the best voiturette. Thus Marcel Renault's showing in the Paris–Vienna was somewhat unexpected, as he was not only fastest of the light cars, but also led the whole race. After this it did not matter unduly if Darracq beat Renault in the voiturette category. 'Light' Renaults of 1903 had 6·3 litres and 30hp, thanks to new L-head moiv engines. The 1903 voiturettes were twins, but after Marcel Renault's fatal crash at Couhé-Verac, Louis withdrew all his surviving cars from the Paris–Madrid. He himself was leading the *voitures legères* when the race was stopped at Bordeaux.

Marcel Renault's death called a temporary halt to works-supported racing, but in 1904 the company built a special car to the 1,000kg formula for the American Gould Brokaw. It had a circular dashboard radiator. It retired in that year's Vanderbilt Cup, and Renault had little better luck with the interesting machines he sent to Clermont-Ferrand for the 1905 French Gordon Bennett

Left, 1904 Renault 60hp Vanderbilt Cup car. *Photo: Montagu Motor Museum*

Right, 1906 Renault 90hp Grand Prix car, before the start. Ferenc Szisz at the wheel. *Photo: Vladimir Havránek Collection*

Left, 1925 Renault 40CV long-distance record car. *Photo: Sedgwick and Marshall Collection*

Right, 1926 Renault 40CV long-distance record car. *Photo: Montagu Motor Museum*

Trials. These had 13-litre engines in underslung frames, but unfortunately Renault chose pump cooling, and the cars overheated. Ferenc Szisz took one to America and finished 5th in the Vanderbilt Cup.

For the 1906 Grand Prix, cylinder capacity was unchanged, but there was a reversion to thermo-syphon circulation and a conventional chassis. More important were the quick-detachable rims, which helped Szisz to hold his lead on the first day's racing, and to win at 62·97mph (101·34kph). These cars could approach 100mph (160·9kph), and were little changed for 1907, when the fuel consumption rules caused Szisz to restrain his style, allowing Nazzaro's Fiat to take the lead. The Hungarian took 2nd place, but in 1908 the Renaults, for all their new and higher-revving engines, did not figure among the leaders. Two cars ran in the American Grand Prize race: Szisz retired, though Strang finished 6th. Touring Renaults of 35hp with GP Replica raceabout coachwork also did well in the 24-hour 'grinds' then fashionable in the United States, Bernin and Lacroix winning at Morris Park in 1907, and Basle at Brighton Beach in 1909.

By this time Renault was the best-selling French make, and there were no notable competition activities until 1925, when Repusseau won the Monte Carlo Rally on one of the large 9,123cc 6-cylinder 4OCVs. In the same year a torpedo version was used by Garfield and Plessier to attack International Class A records at Montlhéry, covering 24 hours at 87·63mph (141·03kph). In 1926 the

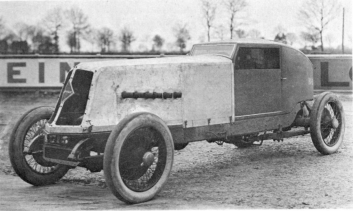

same team returned to the attack with a lightweight fabric single-seater saloon version minus fwb, and took the World 24-Hour Record at 107·9mph (173·6kph) — the first time this had been achieved at over 100mph. A small 6CV also won some long-distance records in Class G.

A team of the new 4·2-litre straight-8 Nervas was entered for the 1930 TT, but were withdrawn after Garfield's death. They had to make their début in a less-well-publicized rally in Morocco, which they won. The Nerva series, in fact, were responsible for all Renault's remaining pre-World War 2 successes: a new World 48-Hour Record at 101·979mph (164·024kph) in 1934; and victories in the 1935 Monte Carlo and Liège-Rome-Liège rallies. The car's 5,448cc engine made it the biggest Monte winner since 1925.

The advent of the 760cc ohv rear-engined 4CV saloon in 1946 brought Renault back into the sport, and quite early in its career capacity was reduced to 747cc to bring it within the smallest competition category. It inspired numerous derivatives, among them the VP and Ferry seen in the 1,000 kilometre Race at Montlhéry in 1956. Other competition cars based on later rear-engined Renaults include the Alpine, and the René Bonnets and Matras that succeeded the Panhard-based DBs. There were class victories in the 1949, 1950, 1951 and 1953 Monte Carlo Rallies, with a Coupe des Dames as well in the last-mentioned year.

Though the little Renaults performed well at Le Mans, they were unfortunate enough to arrive on the scene at a time when the air-cooled Dyna-Panhards dominated both their category and the Index of Performance, and thus rallies became their forte. However, Michel won the 1951 and 1952 Bols d'Or, and the cars had an excellent run of successes in the Mille Miglia of the 1952–7 era.

The 4CV's rally record became even better after the tuners had worked on it, and 4-speed gearboxes became available. In 1952 there was a class win and a Coupe des Alpes for de Regibus in the Alpine; a class win and a Coupe des Dames in the Tour de France; and an outright victory for Mme Simon in the all-feminine Paris–St Raphael event. There were further class victories in the 1954 Alpine and 1955 Paris–St Raphael, and the 4CVs reign came to a close in 1956 with another class win in the Monte Carlo and an 8th place in the Acropolis. This year also saw a successful attack on the world's gas-turbine

Left, 1953 Renault 4CV sports car at Le Mans. *Photo: Autosport*

Right, 1970 Renault-Gordini R8 driven by Swanepoel and Crous in the Monte Carlo Rally. *Photo: Hugh W. Bishop*

Below, 1951 Renault 4CV saloon at Le Mans. *Photo: Autosport*

car speed record with the experimental *Etoile Filante* at 191·2mph (307·7kph).

In 1957 Amédée Gordini gave up the unequal struggle as a specialist manufacturer, and went to work for Renault, boosting the Dauphine's output from 26·5 to 38bhp, and turning a 65mph saloon into something that could approach 80mph (128·75kph) in catalogued form. Renault won the Tour de Corse in 1958: they also scored another victory in the Monte Carlo Rally, the drivers being Monraisse and Feret. The next season was nearly as good: 2nd, 3rd, and a class victory at Monte Carlo, and best performance (by Condrillier and Robin) in the Alpine. Dauphines collected the class honours again in 1960, with a 4th place for Greder and Charron in 1961: that year's score also included another class victory, in the Lyons–Charbonnières. The customary honours in the 1963 Alpine went to the Dauphine.

Then in 1964 came the new R8. This made a good start with Vinatier's victory in the Tour de Corse, in which Renaults were also placed 3rd, 4th and 5th. A 1,300cc Gordini-tuned variant (Orsini and Canonicci) won this event again in 1965. Although the works were relying increasingly on the Dieppe-built Alpines (now running under Renault sponsorship), the Gordini R8s had two big wins in 1967. Piot came 1st in the Italian Flowers event, partnered by Roure, and with Brenard he won the Three Cities. The Alpines were even more strongly in evidence in 1968, and 1969 was another Alpine year, with Renaults finishing no higher than 7th in both the Monte Carlo and in the Alpine. MCS

RGS-Atalanta (GB)

R. G. Shattock of Winkfield, Berkshire, purchased the Atalanta designs after World War 2 and used their coil suspension system for his own multi-tubular frame sports cars. Only a handful were made, the most successful being Shattock's own Lea-Francis engined car in the early years and the C-type Jaguar-engined model of the mid-1950s. DF

Ricart y Perez; Ricart-España (E)

Designed by Wilfredo Ricart, later responsible for the Alfa Romeo Tipo 158 and Pegaso cars, the Ricart y Perez was a 1·5-litre racing car with 16-valve twin-ohc 4-cylinder engine developing 58bhp. Built in 1922, it ran in a number of Spanish events in 1923, including the

Grand Prix des Voiturettes at Sitges, and made ftd in its class in the Rabassada hill-climb. Another Ricart-designed racing car was the Ricart-España, a 1·5-litre twin-ohc 6-cylinder engine. Built in 1927, this also ran at Sitges, but was not a great success. GNG

Richard-Brasier see Georges Richard

Ridley Special (GB)

Lord Ridley's little car was remarkable in that it was a private venture which intervened successfully in the great Austin/MG battle for Class H records in 1931. It had a specially designed and built 4-cylinder twin-ohc engine of 66 × 54·5mm (746cc), originally mounted horizontally, but installed in a vertical position for the successful record-breaking attempts. With a Powerplus supercharger, maximum output was 54bhp at 6,500rpm, and top speed 105mph (168kph). The car had a 5-speed gearbox. The transmission was offset, the driver's legs extending next to the engine, and appearance was very low, rather like that of Parry Thomas's Flat-Iron Specials. In August 1931 Lord Ridley took Class H records for the mile at 104·56mph (168·30kph), and the kilometre at 105·42mph (169·63kph), beating the records of both MG and Austin. Three months later the car crashed during further record attempts at Brooklands, badly injuring its driver. GNG

Riley (GB)

The first Riley to win a race was probably a bicycle, about the turn of the century. Then came quadricycles and tricycles before Riley reverted to two wheels with the 'Moto-Bi'. By 1905 the V-twin Tri-car had appeared. With various engine capacities, this model was notably successful in sporting events, with a long list of successes to its credit; Singer Tri-cars, too, were powered by Riley engines. A similar engine was used for the 4-wheeler of late 1906, which made ftd in nine hill-climbs the following year, often driven by Victor Riley. The 12/18hp version of 1908 was even more successful. It was followed by a 10hp of which a 'Semi-Racing Model' was listed.

Most of these cars were fitted with Rileys' own detachable wire wheel, also supplied to notable English and European makes. Two vertical 4-cylinder engines made brief appearances before World War 1, together with the famous 'silent third' gearbox.

Left, 1952 RGS-Atalanta 3·4-litre sports car. R. G. Shattock at the wheel. Photo: Richmond Pike

Right, 1923 Ricart y Perez at Sitges Speedway. Photo: T. A. S. O. Mathieson Collection

Below, 1927 Ricart-España on the banking at Sitges Speedway. Photo: courtesy W. P. Ricart

Below, 1929 Riley Nine Monaco saloon in the London–Edinburgh Trial, early 1930s. Photo: Arnold Farrar Collection

Right, 1930 Riley Brooklands Nine sports car. Photo: Arnold Farrar Collection

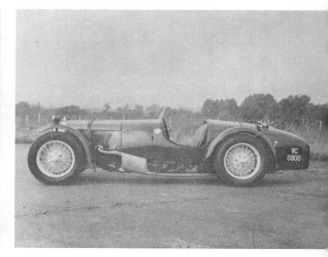

Late in 1919 came the sv 10·8hp four which quickly earned a reputation for good roadholding and reliability, with gold medals in most of the long-distance trials. It featured light-alloy pistons, gave 35bhp at 3200rpm, and first appeared with a straight-cut final drive. A sports two-seater was seen at the 1921 Show; a year later it was accompanied by a sports tourer, and the two-seater carried a 70mph (112kph) guarantee. These were the well-loved 'Redwings' or 'Redwingers', which won countless awards in the Exeter, Edinburgh, Lands End and Scottish Six Days. Late in 1924 an alternative 11·9hp engine was introduced, and a new competition version offered. At the 1926 Motor Show there was even a 10·8 with ohv head, Riley-designed supercharger and a promise of 80mph (128kph), but patent troubles caused its abandonment.

For many years, Victor Gillow and Frank Ashby were prominent at Brooklands with their rebodied sv cars. They won many races, and Ashby's car was capable of lapping at 103mph (165·8kph).

But the 1926 London Motor Show also introduced the brilliant Riley Nine, a well-designed four with ohv operated by short push-rods from two high camshafts, and crossflow head designed by Percy Riley. Despite a 2-bearing crankshaft and plunger oil-pump, it was a tuner's dream. Parry Thomas quickly started work on it,

Above, 1933 Riley 1·5-litre 6-cylinder in the TT. C. R. Whitcroft at the wheel. *Photo: T. A. S. O. Mathieson Collection*

Right, 1933 Riley 1·5-litre 6-cylinder rebodied for record work at Montlhéry. G. E. T. Eyston at the wheel. *Photo: Arnold Farrar Collection*

Below, 1935 Riley Nine Lynx tourer in the 1939 Welsh Rally. *Photo: Arnold Farrar Collection*

Below, 1935 Riley-engined Appleton Special, at a VSCC Silverstone meeting in the 1960s. R. P. Barker at the wheel. *Photo: Montagu Motor Museum*

Right, 1936 Riley 2-litre racing car with ifs. *Photo: T. A. S. O. Mathieson Collection*

and Reid Railton took over when Thomas was killed in March 1927. The first half-dozen of these 'Brooklands Speed Models' were built by Thomson and Taylor. With a double-cranked chassis frame underslung at the rear, they were exceptionally low. A small radiator called for the use of a water-pump, and with two carburettors the 1,100cc engine gave 50bhp at 5000rpm. The fabric-bodied prototype was said to weigh about 1,120lb (508kg), but production versions (built at Coventry and sold for £395 with road equipment) were over 1,680lb (762kg).

In its production life of some 12 years the Nine engine was subjected to many detail improvements, and sired all subsequent Riley engines of four or six cylinders and capacities up to 2,443cc, not to mention the V-8 Autovia. The clean design of the 'PR' head gave amazing results with multiple carburettors, so that the cars could outpace supercharged rivals of equal and sometimes greater capacity.

Until the Nuffield takeover of 1938 the company produced far too many different models, but were never afraid to enter them in races and rallies; and private owners could count on enthusiastic support. The Speed Model won its very first race at Brooklands at 91·37mph (147·04kph) late in 1927, driven by Railton himself. The original Riley Brooklands established several international Class G records in 1928, including 500 miles at 87·09mph (140·15kph). Trouble intervened when a team of three ran in the Six Hours, but Peacock finished 4th and won the 1,100cc class. There were five in the 1928 TT: three crashed, one retired, but Peacock again

won his class. In 1929 the Brooklands Speed Model wa only 6th in the Double-Twelve and 8th in the 500 Miles but won the 1,100cc class of the Irish GP, took many Shelsley awards, and again won the 1,100cc class in the TT. It finished 12th overall, the highest-placed unblow car, but its team-mates did not finish.

Riley Nines took 2nd to 5th places in class at the 193 Monte Carlo. Whitcroft was 3rd overall at 69·96mph (112·59kph) in the Double-Twelve, Gillow won the Saorstat Cup and came 2nd overall in the Irish GP, an Horton finished 8th in the TT to win the 1,100cc class the third time. Using a supercharged car, Davis lapped Brooklands at 111·17mph (178/91kph). Ashby startled the handicappers with his 4-carburettor Nine.

There were now two versions of the Brooklands Spee model: the 'ordinary' one with little more than twin carburettors and a raised compression ratio, and the plus Series or Ulster Brooklands with counterbalanced crankshaft, special rods, bigger rear main bearing, stiffened bell housing (seven webs), and, if required, fo carburettors. Ashby's special Nine was even more advanced. By modifying the camshafts he fitted two carburettors on each side of the head, allowing more room than with four on one side. He developed the engine intensively over the next few years, using a special aluminium-bronze head with 14mm plugs and 15 : 1 compression ratio or higher on alcohol fuel, with nitrided crankshaft. It gave 71bhp at 5,500rpm. With i orange-painted 'flat-iron' body it was said to be capabl of 130mph (209kph), lapping at 112mph (180·2kph).

The Monte Carlo Rally of 1931 justified the Monaco

name with Leverett winning the Light Car Class and Hobbs 4th. Ashby took the 1,100cc class of the Double-Twelve, and the works cars gained a class 1-2-3 in the Irish GP. Froy drove a well-prepared Brooklands all the way from Coventry to the Nürburgring, won the 1,100cc race, then drove it back again. A Nine won the 1,100cc class of the Brooklands 500 Miles at 92·83mph (149·40kph). Staniland broke the Ards 1,100cc lap record and gained the fourth 1,100cc class victory in the TT, where Rileys also won the team prize. Eyston took a host of records with a Nine at Montlhéry, including 108·11 miles (174·02km) in the hour and 1,000km at 99·24mph (159·71kph).

Nine Rileys were entered for the 1932 Monte Carlo, three of them driven to the start overland from Australia. All finished, with 3rd, 4th and 5th overall. In the RAC Rally the Rileys took more than 40 awards. Leverett, highest placed in both, also won his class in the Alpine. A Nine tourer broke the Durban–Johannesburg record in 1932 and again in 1933.

A new racing model appeared, with a basically 14/6 engine reduced from 1,633cc to 1,486cc and a water-cooled centre main bearing. The chassis of this Brooklands Six, unlike that of the Brooklands Nine, was not cranked but sloped from front to tail. It ran first in the 1932 1,000 Miles, which Elsie Wisdom and Joan Richmond won outright at 84·41mph (135·85kph) with a Brooklands Nine.

Then a completely new driver, Freddie Dixon, came on the scene with a Nine which he had laboriously rebuilt himself to make it lighter but stronger. His début in the TT was meteoric: he broke the class lap record in practice, worked all night at his car, and after leading the race for some time, disappeared over a hedge at high speed. However, the works Nines of Whitcroft and Eyston finished 1st and 2nd overall, Whitcroft at a record 74·23mph (119·46kph). Edgar Maclure, giving the new Six its first road outing, came 8th and won the 1,500cc class.

Dixon's next surprise was the 'Red Mongrel', with home-made chassis, Nine engine, streamlined body and one-spoke steering wheel. As modified by Dixon, the engine gave 68bhp at 6,000rpm, later improved to 77bhp. It appeared at the 1932 500 Miles, but the body wilted on the Brooklands bumps. Cyril Paul finished 2nd overall at 99·61mph (160·31kph), the highest speed by an unblown car, with two more Rileys 4th and 5th, giving them a class 1-2-3. Dixon later covered 200km at 110·67mph (178·11kph) with the Mongrel. Eyston did 200 miles at 111·65mph (179·68kph) with the new Six at Brooklands. At Montlhéry, with Denly and Maclure, he covered 112 miles (180·2km) in the hour, ran for 12hr at 92·82mph (149·38kph) and 24hr at 82·41mph (132·63kph).

At Le Mans in 1933, Peacock and von der Becke finished a splendid 4th overall with a Nine to win the 1,500cc class and set a new 1,100cc record. The Mannin Beg on the Isle of Man brought Dixon's first victory, though not in the 'Mongrel', which seldom finished a race. He also finished the TT in 4th place, but was disqualified because of a faulty exhaust. Whitcroft saved the day again by winning the 1,500cc class with yet another new Six, the prototype of the production MPH model. In August, Mays brought out his modified Six with Berthon-designed supercharger, giving over 150bhp. At Shelsley Walsh it made 2nd ftd to Straight's Maserati in 1933 and 1934. This was the famous 'White Riley', from which sprang the ERA. With it Mays established a new Mountain Circuit class record in 1933.

The 'Mongrel' led the Brooklands 500 Miles for a time but eventually had to retire. In Dixon's Mannin Beg car, Paul and Turner finished 3rd at 88·87mph (143·02kph). In 1934 Rileys announced their two-seater Imp on a shortened Monaco frame. All models now had centre-lock wheels.

In 1934 a Riley won the Australian GP for the second year running. Eyston and Edgar Maclure, with a stream-lined Six, covered 1,000 miles at 102·35mph (164·78kph), 12hr at 101·10mph (162·70kph) and 2,000km at 1,242 miles 101·04mph (162·56kph). Dobbs appeared at Brooklands with the first of several fast, offset single-seaters. O'Clery came 3rd in the Leinster Trophy.

Dixon's Mannin Moar entry consisted of two bored-out (1,808cc) Sixes, with one of which Paul finished 3rd. His two Mannin Beg cars were Nines, and Paul brought one home 6th. At Le Mans, however, six works cars started and six finished. Sebilleau and de la Roche were 2nd overall at 70·0mph (112·65kph) with a Six, Dixon and Paul 3rd with another.

The Imp had made its first competition appearance earlier, in the Scottish Rally, winning the 1,100cc class for the third year running, and Rileys took the ladies' award and the team prize. In September a new 1·5-litre engine appeared with only four cylinders. Based on the Nine, it was designed by Hugh Rose, who later designed an engine for Lea-Francis.

In the Brooklands 500 Miles of 1934, Dixon had used a Six bored out to 1,986cc to win, with von der Becke 2nd in the works Six. Rileys won the Team prize. The four Imps entered for the TT had fared badly in Dixon's absence, finishing well down the field.

The Mannin Beg of 1935 had only two finishers: Fairfield's ERA and Dixon's Riley 1·5. For the International Trophy, Dixon had his 1,986cc Six and loaned his 1,808cc car to Tom and Elsie Wisdom. Dixon finished 2nd and the Wisdom family 4th. The British Empire Trophy brought a sweeping 1-2-3 win, with Dixon and Maclure in 2-litre cars followed by Cyril Paul's 1,808cc Riley to win the team prize. At Le Mans, von der Becke finished 4th overall with a 1·5-litre.

The new Sprite now appeared with a basically MPH chassis and 1·5-litre 4- or 2-litre 6-cylinder engine. With a car based on the 1·5, Dixon scored a resounding victory in the 1935 TT at 76·9mph (123·76kph), breaking the class lap record four times. No 1,100cc cars finished. Dixon reverted to his 2-litre for the Brooklands 500 Miles and ran well at first, lapping at about 130mph (209kph). But his co-driver wrecked the engine, leaving von der Becke to finish 2nd at 112·49mph (180·94kph) with the very handsome works 2-litre Six. Again Rileys won the team prize. At Shelsley Walsh, von der Becke took two classes and another went to the Riley-powered Appleton Special. Three Rileys were entered for the British GP at Donington, but all retired.

Yet another new Riley racing model, with 2-litre engine and coil-spring ifs, was seen in the 1936 British Empire Trophy. It lacked the usual sleek Riley lines, having a rounded and rather bulbous nose. Dobbs now had a new car with 2-litre engine and Sprite chassis, which gained many successes and finished 3rd behind two ERAs in the International Trophy, with the new works 2-litre in 6th place. That year the French GP was run as a sports car race at Montlhéry. Riley entered their 1·5-litre TT Sprites to score a 1-2-3-4 in the 2-litre class. In the final Ards TT, Dixon won again at 78·01mph (125·55kph). This was the fastest pre-World War 2 TT victory by an unsupercharged car, and very close to the

1951 Riley 2·5-litre saloon in 1953 Production Car Race at Silverstone. Harold Grace at the wheel. *Photo: Arnold Farrar Collection*

fastest of all — Nuvolari's 78·65mph (126·57kph) with the supercharged Magnette in 1933.

With Charlie Martin, Dixon achieved his last big victory in the 1936 500 Miles, his car averaging 116·86mph (188·01kph). Yet again, Rileys took the team prize.

Possibly because of financial pressure, there was less works participation in the sport during 1937. Two Rileys were 2nd and 3rd behind an ERA in the South African GP. In the British Empire Trophy, now transferred to Donington, Percy Maclure came 2nd, sandwiched between two ERAs. Riley teams were 2nd and 3rd in the Donington 12 Hours, but the TT at Donington only saw A. C. Dobson finish 7th to win the 1,500cc class. Charlie Dobson drove Dixon's 2-litre to finish 2nd in the 500 Kilometres, successor to the 500 Miles. In 1·5-litre Rileys, Percy Maclure was 3rd and A. C. Dobson 5th — and of course they won the team prize. At Montlhéry, in a 186-mile (300km) race, Dobson headed Contet and Forestier for a Riley 1-2-3. During the year, Coventry announced the 2,443cc 'Big Four' engine which was to power the successful Healey many years later.

With an ex-Dobbs car, Meyer won the 1938 South African GP at 86·53mph (139·26kph) and a Brooklands Nine was 3rd. Young Percy Maclure scored a popular victory in the International Trophy, his 1738cc Riley ahead of two ERAs. Rileys were 1st and 2nd in the 1,500cc class of the Paris 12 Hours at Montlhéry, and of the Donington TT, where they also took the team award. It came as a shock to racing enthusiasts when, in September, they heard that Lord Nuffield was taking over. Like MG a few years before, and many others too, Riley found that accountants seemed to lack real enthusiasm for racing.

But private successes continued. At Prescott in 1939, Percy Maclure made ftd with the ex-works ifs car, now with a supercharged 1·5-litre engine. In one of the first races held after the war, Brunet came 2nd in a 1,100cc event in the Bois de Boulogne. The Manx Cup Race saw Rileys 2nd in 1947, 1st in 1948, 2nd in 1949 and again in 1950.

A youthful Mike Hawthorn won the *Motor Sport* Trophy with one of the TT Sprites used in the 1935 and the 1936 French GP. He also won the 1951 Leinster Trophy. Jack Fairman and Don Beauman were also prominent with their Rileys; Harold Grace raced post-war saloons with distinction. Bob Porter made a successful records foray. Even the BMC-designed Riley 1·5 won many races, especially in the hands of Leston, Grace

and Hutcheson, and was used successfully in international rallies by Pat Moss and others.

A great many of the old works cars still survive and win races in the hands of enthusiastic VSCC members. Riley's record of racing successes is unlikely to be forgotten. FWMCC

Rochdale (GB)

One of the earliest production monocoque fibreglass designs was the Rochdale Olympic GT coupé, made in the town of Rochdale, Lancashire, in 1961. At first Riley 1·5-litre mechanical parts were used, but with the Phase 2 version of 1964 a Ford 116E engine and Triumph front suspension were adopted. Although no major competition programme was embarked upon, the car's light weight and good roadholding induced several private owners to use it for racing. DF

Rochet-Schneider (F)

Lyonnais makes tended to be more stolid and less likely to be entered for competitions than their Parisian counterparts, and the Rochet-Schneider was no exception, appearing generally in minor events. As early as 1896 some Benz-like cars were seen in the Paris–Mantes–Paris and the Paris–Marseilles–Paris. Ferradje's retirement in the latter event was caused by an aggressive bull, but their subsequent performances — 13th in the Marseilles–Nice, 1898, and 14th in the Nice–Castellane–Nice, 1899 — were indicative of a lack of interest. Roche won his class at Laffrey in 1901, and for the Nice–Salon–Nice the firm prepared some large and Panhard-like chain-driven machines which have the distinction of being the first cars to be defeated by the Mercedes. In spite of this, Degrais finished 2nd and Schneider and Marge took 4th and 7th places respectively. There was a class victory at Susa-Moncenisio, some crypto-Mercedes were seen at Laffrey and Nice, and Capt. H. H. P. Deasy entered a 4·7-litre tourer in the same idiom (with flitch-plate frame) for the ACGBI 1,000 Miles Trial, winning gold medal. Ironically, however, the Coupe Rochet-Schneider Reliability event in France was won (in 1903 and 1904 alike) by a Martini built under Rochet-Schneider licence in Switzerland.

The 1904 Mont Ventoux hill-climb was almost a Rochet-Schneider benefit, Ollin's being the fastest touring car. However, talk of a Gordon Bennett entry in 1905 came to nothing, and even in 1906 the firm did not venture outside the narrow world of sprints in which they did well. Though the 5-day Coupe de l'Auvergne race over the old Gordon Bennett circuit was dominated by Gobron-Brillié, Rochet-Schneiders took a 2nd and a 3rd in their class.

The firm at long last went back to serious racing in 1907, with an 8-litre car for Viton to drive in the Kaiserpreis, but he was last but one of the qualifiers in his heat, and retired in the final. The Coppa Florio was better, with a 5th place at 59mph (94·95kph); his team-mate Thieulin finished 6th. Both their cars, however, retired in the 1908 event, and other makes were moving into the field of sprints. A Rochet-Schneider won the 6-cylinder category at Nice in 1909, but thereafter the firm's products were conservative and unsporting. MCS

Rolland-Pilain (F)

The famous Tours firm supported racing spasmodically between 1908 and 1926. Their first effort was a team of 1,526cc 4-cylinder cars with 4-speed overdrive gearboxes entered for the 1908 GP des Voiturettes: all finished well

Above, 1908 Rolland-Pilain GP des
Voiturettes car. Louison at the wheel.
Photo: Montagu Motor Museum

Right, 1922 Rolland-Pilain GP car. Louis
Wagner at the wheel. *Photo: T. A. S. O.
Mathieson Collection*

down the list. Surprisingly, Rolland-Pilain chose to build
some new cars for that perambulating motor museum,
the 1911 Grand Prix de France. These had chain drive
and 16-valve 4-cylinder ohc engines of 6·1 litres capacity.
They were handled by Rigal and Gabriel, but proved a
failure, doing nearly as badly in the Grand Prix proper
of 1912, for which engine size was increased to 6,274cc.
There was a victory in the biggest touring-car class at
Gaillon in 1920, and class victories at Fanø and elsewhere
in 1921, but more serious were the Grillot-designed 2-
litre straight-8 GP cars of 1922. The specification embraced twin ohc, desmodromic valves and fwb with
hydraulic actuation on the front only, but all three
machines (driven by Guyot, Hémery and Wagner)
failed at Strasbourg. By 1923 the Rolland-Pilains (now
without the desmodromy) were joined by a new cuff-
valve six, the work of Henry and Schmid, but this failed
to start in the French GP at Tours, and the eights
retired both in this event and at Monza. Guyot and
Delalande took 1st and 2nd places in the Spanish GP at
San Sebastian; the opposition, however, was confined to
Ballots and Bignans. Also in 1923 four 2-litre 4-cylinder
sports cars ran at Le Mans, but though all qualified,
there were no high placings.

The cuff-valve racers ran in blown form in 1924, now
under the name Schmid. Drivers were Goux and Foresti,
and retirements in the French and Spanish GP were
balanced by rather poor 5th and 6th places in the Italian

1906 Rolls-Royce Light Twenty in the TT.
C. S. Rolls at the wheel. *Photo: Rolls-Royce
Ltd*

race. There was also a 6th for the Rolland-Pilains at Le
Mans, but though the cars turned out again in 1925 and
1926, they never improved on this. In 1927 a touring 1·5-
litre finished 11th in the Monte Carlo Rally. MCS

Rolls-Royce (GB)

The Hon. C. S. Rolls's enthusiasm for racing survived
his partnership with F. H. Royce, and in 1905 he entered
two ioe 4-cylinder Light Twenties for the first TT,
Northey's having the standard engine and his own (which
retired on the first lap) an overbored 4-litre unit. Northey
finished 2nd at 33·7mph (54·23kph), and Rolls followed
this up in 1906 with a win at 39·3mph (63·25kph). Four-
and 6-cylinder cars also competed in the 1906 Scottish
Trials, and Claude Johnson staged a long-distance match
against Deasy's big 4-cylinder Martini. This was intended
to settle the 'battle of the cylinders', but in fact proved
nothing, any more than did Rolls' successful attack on
the Monte Carlo–London record in the same year. His
time of 28hr 4min as far as Boulogne was exactly two
hours longer than Radley's time for the whole distance
when he regained the record for Rolls-Royce in 1913.
Though Rolls raced his 20hp car in a few American
events and a machine of this type took part in the Morris
Park, N.Y., 24-Hour Race in 1907, the advent of the sv
6-cylinder Silver Ghost and the adoption of a one-model
policy marked the firm's withdrawal from the sport. But
not immediately—for the original Silver Ghost's
celebrated 15,000 miles RAC-observed trial in 1907
took in the Scottish Trials, in which Johnson gained a
gold medal. Then for the 2,000 Miles Trial in 1908 the firm
prepared a pair of 70hp ioe cars with lengthened strokes.
Platford won his class, but this version was considered
too noisy for series production.

There was another impressive performance in 1911,
when a car was driven from London to Edinburgh in top
gear (as a counterblast to S. F. Edge and Napier), and
then lapped Brooklands at 78·26mph (125·95kph).
E. W. Hives later drove a similar car with light single-
seater body round at over 101mph, but Rolls-Royce were
not goaded into competition again until 1913, after a
privately-entered Silver Ghost had failed in the Katschberg during the 1912 Austrian Alpine Trial. Though an
accident robbed the make of the team award in the 1913
event, Platford and Friese made the best individual
performance, and seven cups were taken back to their
headquarters at Derby. Carlos de Salamanca also won
that year's Spanish Touring Car GP at 54mph (86·9kph),

though even this could not make a customer of Alfonso XIII. The factory left the 1914 Alpine alone, but Radley entered his own car and was the only British competitor to finish without loss of marks.

This was the end of Rolls-Royce's competition career, though their aero engines have powered three subsequent holders of the World Land Speed Record: Campbell's 1933 and 1935 Bluebirds and Eyston's Thunderbolt. There have been two unusual appearances in post-World War 2 rallies: in the 1957 Ampol Round Australia Rally a 30-year-old Phantom I driven by Mrs Brown finished 5th, and two Rolls-Royces ran in the 1970 World Cup event without success. MCS

Rover (GB)

The original 8hp single-cylinder Rover of 1904 was launched straight into competitions, winning its class at Bexhill Speed Trials, and a year later Dr R. L. Jefferson successfully drove one of these small cars from London to Constantinople. For the 1905 Tourist Trophy the factory prepared some 3·1-litre 4-cylinder sv tourers with shaft drive, which finished 5th and 12th in the race, and the firm entered for subsequent TTs. In 1906 the cars were excluded for late arrival, but in the 1907 event Courtis drove his 3·5-litre L-head 20 to victory at an average speed of 28·8mph, being one of only two finishers. The 1908 Four-Inch version was driven by H. B. Browning, later to be famous for long-distance

drives across Africa. He retired, and Rover lost interest in competition, apart from a few promotional exploits.

The Poppe-designed ohc 4-cylinder 14/45 and 16/50 were both raced in 1925-6, a modified version of the latter lapping Brooklands at 102·9mph (165·6kph); its smaller sister was awarded the RAC's Dewar Trophy for 30 consecutive ascents of Bwlch-y-Groes. In 1930 Dudley Noble used a 2-litre Light Six to beat the Blue Train from St Raphael to Calais, and 1931 brought the 2,565cc ohv Speed 20, a potent sporting six which did quite well in club events at Brooklands, and won its class in the 1933 and 1934 RAC Rallies.

In 1949 Maurice Wilks of the Rover Co. campaigned with a fast single-seater based on the contemporary 2·1-litre ioe 6-cylinder 75, but far more important was the 1950 turbocar, JET 1, also using Rover 75 parts. This won the firm their second Dewar Trophy, and also (in 1952) set the first world records for reaction-propelled cars, covering a flying kilometre at 151·965mph (224·58kph). Later developments of this theme were saloons and coupés, but 1963 saw the Rover-BRM propelled by a 150bhp gas turbine motor. This car, driven by Hill and Ginther, was allowed to run unofficially at Le Mans in 1963, averaging 108mph.

Meanwhile, in 1962, Rover had returned to works-supported rallying with the ioe 3-litre saloons, supporting the East African Safari and managing a 6th place (James and Hughes) in the Liège-Sofia-Liège. The same

Left, 1935 Rover Fourteen tourer in the 1937 Welsh Rally. *Photo: Montagu Motor Museum*

Above, 1963 Rover-BRM gas-turbine car. *Photo: Rover Co Ltd*

Left, 1963 Rover 3-litre saloon driven by Logan Morrison and Johnston Syer in the 1964 Acropolis Rally. *Photo: John Davenport*

Below, 1970 Rover 4500 V-8 saloon at Castle Combe, on the way to its first win. R. F. Pierpoint at the wheel. *Photo: Edward G. Hodgkins*

Above, 1928 Rovin 750cc racing car at the pits during the National Trophy at Boulogne. *Photo: Motor*

Right, 1969 Royale RP2 Formula Ford at Brands Hatch. *Photo: London Art Tech*

crew came in 8th in 1963, and in 1964 the factory switched its allegiance to the new and advanced ohc 4-cylinder 2000, obtaining 6th place in the Acropolis and 12th in the Alpine. Rover's best performance in 1965 was Clark and Porter's 5th in the Monte Carlo Rally, and Mabbs and Porter were 10th in 1966 on a similar car. A month later Rover withdrew officially from the sport.

In 1970 a Group 2 saloon car was introduced, using a 345bhp 4·5-litre version of the regular 3·5-litre V-8 unit in a 2000 hull, and a 4-speed manual gearbox. MCS

Rovin (F)

Robert de Rovin was a motorcycle maufacturer who built a few cyclecars for his own amusement in the 1920s. The first of these was a bodyless affair with all-chain transmission, powered by one of his 175cc 2-carburettor, 2-stroke units: it was persuaded to lap Montlhéry at 46mph (74·03kph). A more powerful version with a 500cc JAP engine went after international class records in 1927 and 1928, eventually covering the flying kilometre at over 85mph (136kph), and a neat and substantially-bodied single-seater took part in road events. In 1928 de Rovin won the 750cc category both at Comminges and at Boulogne in the National Trophy, his average in the latter race being 55mph (88·51kph). By contrast, the post-1945 Rovin cyclecar was a 425cc tourer built in the Delaunay-Belleville plant; even this was raced, Bernardet winning the 500cc class of the 1952 Bol d'Or. MCS

1970 Royale RP4 Formula F100 driven by Ray Allen, leading Martin Ray's Daren at Brands Hatch. *Photo: Paul Cohen*

Royale (GB)

Produced by Robert King of Racing Preparations Ltd, Park Royal, London, some 40 Formula Ford cars were sold during 1969, at £1,350 complete. Successes were achieved particularly by Ray Allen in Britain, and in the United States by Kevin Glynn and Bill Scott, the latter with the 1970 RP3 version. The RP4 was the Formula F 100 car, an example of which (in the hands of Ray Allen) won 7 of its first 8 races, and the RP5 was a one-off Formula B single-seater which Tony Lanfranchi campaigned in successfully. Specifications of all cars followed conventional lines, with multi-tubular space-frames and glassfibre bodies, but these were distinguished by a very high standard of appearance and finish. For 1971 Royale offered the RP6A for Formula Ford, RP8 for Formula B/Atlantic, RP9 for Formula Super Vee, and RP4 and RP10 all-enveloping cars for F100 and Group 6 respectively. DF

Saab (S)

The little DKW-inspired fwd twin 2-strokes with their aerodynamic saloon bodywork did not become a major force in rallying until the later 1950s, but they figured in the awards list of their native Midnight Sun Rally as early as 1953, and the veteran driver Greta Molander took 9th place and the Coupé des Dames in the 1955 Tulip. A 748cc 3-cylinder engine was adapted in 1956, and that year's Midnight Sun event included some names that were soon to become famous: Carl-Magnus Skogh was 3rd and Erik Carlsson 4th. However, the Wehrman and Brown victory in the Great American Mountain Rally attracted more publicity, as an excellent send-off for a new make in the United States. Saabs ran in the last Mille Miglia of 1957, and there were more rally successes: a Coupe des Dames in the Sestrières; 5th in the Midnight Sun; and a class win in the Rallye Trifels. The following year was still relatively unremarkable, though a Saab came in 4th (behind three Volvos) in the Lime Rock saloon-car race in America. It also collected the Index of Performance award.

By 1959 Erik Carlsson had taken 2nd place in the European Rally Championship, on the strength of a victory in the Midnight Sun (Skogh was 2nd), a 2nd in the Adriatic and a 5th in the Tulip. A new GT version with 50bhp engine and 4-speed gearbox had finished 12th at Le Mans. In 1960 Carlsson scored his first victory in the RAC Rally and won the RAC and Acropolis events in 1961, Skogh was 3rd in the Tulip, and the make took four of the first eight places. Among Carlsson's 1962

victories were the RAC and the Monte Carlo. Although he had to be content with a 3rd in the 1963 RAC Rally, he and Palm won the Monte Carlo again, and there was a 2nd place in the Liège–Rome–Liège for the make as well.

Carlsson's marriage to Pat Moss produced an almost invincible team for 1964, and his score for the season ran to 1st in the Italian Targa Florio, 2nd in the Polish and the Spa–Sofia–Liège, and 3rd in the Monte Carlo and the Geneva. His wife recorded one 2nd (the Targa Florio), two 3rds (the Acropolis and the Polish), and several other good places. In addition Lampinen won the 1,000 Lakes. In 1965 the Carlssons were back again, even if Saab did not win a single rally outright thanks to the rise of the BMC Minis. There were, however, three 2nds (Andersson's in the Swedish, Carlsson's in the Acropolis, and Larsson's in the Gulf London); three 3rds (one each to the Carlssons in the Polish and the Monte Carlo and one to Larsson in the RAC); and three 4ths (in the 1,000 Lakes, the Acropolis and the RAC).

The 2-strokes were getting a little tired by 1966, but in spite of this the Swedish Rally was a 1-2 victory for Andersson and Lampinen. Andersson won again in the Gulf London, and Pat Moss-Carlsson was 2nd in this event. The Carlsson and Johanssen 850cc Saab won its class in the 6-Hour Saloon-Car Race at Nürburgring.

At long last a 4-stroke engine, the 1,498cc German Ford V-4, made its appearance in 1967, but Saab were beset with gearbox troubles, and their best achievements were a victory in the Czechoslovak Rally, and 2nds in the Swedish and the Austrian Alpine. They were, however, back in winning form in 1968, when 1st and 2nd places in the RAC event went to Lampinen and Davenport and Orrenius and Schröderheim. In the two big Scandinavian events, the Swedish and the 1,000 Lakes, Saabs came in 2nd, the cars also filled 3rd, 6th, 7th and 8th places in the former.

The make had a good season in 1969, with a victory in the Scottish for Lampinen and Hertz (Saab also took the team prize), and 2nd in both the Swedish Rally and in the 1,000 Lakes. In 1970 Blomqvist and Reinicke were 2nd in the Swedish Rally, and Lindberg and Andreasson 2nd in the Austrian Alpine. MCS

Sacha Gordine (F)

One of a number of post-World War 2 Grand Prix cars which never reached a circuit, the Sacha Gordine was financed by the film producer of that name, and designed by Vigna, a student of Ferdinand Porsche. It had a rear-mounted four-ohc V-8 engine with 5-speed gearbox and De Dion axle. Two engine sizes were planned, a 1·5-litre supercharged unit developing 380bhp, and a 2-litre unsupercharged unit. Nearly all castings were in expensive magnesium alloy. A car was entered for the Pau Grand Prix in April 1952, but did not reach the starting line. A coupé version of the 2-litre car was planned for Le Mans, but never built. GNG

Salih see Indianapolis Cars

Salmson (F)

This was probably the most successful of the small sporting 1100s produced in France during the 1920s, and it is astonishing to recall that the factory team relied between 1922 and 1928 on only four 4-cylinder cars laid down by Emile Petit in the competition department at Billancourt. Further, there were only about another 18 cars sold to the public which were to full Grand Prix specification, though the standard 2-bearing Salmson GS could be bought in England for £265 and was extensively used in trials, sprints, and minor events throughout Europe. In 1925 Salmson recorded 76 first places, 14 records and 8 fastest times of day on the Continent alone, and even in 1935, five years after the last of the GS family had been delivered, the make had 14 class wins to its credit just in French hill-climbs, and this on the eve of FIAT's domination of the 1,100cc sports-car class.

Left, 1963 Saab 850cc in the final tests of the Monte Carlo Rally. Erik Carlsson at the wheel. *Photo: Autosport*

Above, 1969 Saab V4 1·7-litre driven by Erik Carlsson and Torsten Aman in the Mexican Baja 1000. *Photo: SAAB*

1922 Salmson 200-Mile Race car. André Lombard at the wheel. *Photo: Montagu Motor Museum*

bove, 1926 Salmson San Sebastian in the
P des Voiturettes at Boulogne, 1927.
eorges Casse at the wheel. *Photo: T. A. S. O.
athieson Collection*

ght, 1954 Salmson 2·3-litre coupé in the
56 Monte Carlo Rally. *Photo: Autosport*

The first Salmson cars were licence-produced GNs, and these did well in events such as the Boulogne Speed Week, the Paris–Nice, and the Swiss Six-Day Motorcycle Trial, in which latter event (1921) Petit's famous 62 × 90mm twin-ohc 1,100cc 4-cylinder engine made its first appearance in a shaft-driven chassis without differential. This 3-bearing 8-valve unit was giving 33bhp by 1922, but it had a magnificent season in 1921: André Lombard (whose Christian name inspired the St Andrew's Cross on Vintage Salmson radiators) won the French Cyclecar GP, and took 2nd place in the 1,100cc class of the 200 Miles Race at Brooklands. Benoist won this category in 1922, being beaten overall only by three 1,500cc cars, two Talbot-Darracqs and an Aston Martin. Salmsons also won the French GP des Voiturettes; the Tour de France; took 2nd and 3rd places in the Bol d'Or; and won the 1,100cc class of the Paris–Nice Rally.

A 750cc version appeared in 1923 which Lombard drove on two occasions, winning his class in the Cyclecar GP; Salmsons were of course 1st and 2nd in the 1,100cc category. The Bol d'Or saw a tie between Benoist and Desvaux for 1st place, and other class wins were in the first Le Mans 24-Hour Race, and in the appropriate classes of the Swiss Motorcycle GP, at Sitges, San Sebastian, and Monza. Although 1924 was a quiet season (Petit did not always find it easy to obtain funds from his directors), Wilson-Jones won the 1,100cc category of the 200 on a works racer, and class victories in the Grand Prix de l'Ouverture at Montlhéry, at Fanø, Parma, and San Sebastian were encouraging. The Brooklands and San Sebastian victories were repeated in 1925 (the latter giving its name to one of the fiercer versions of the twin-cam engine), drivers being Goutte and Casse respectively. Blowers were used for the first time at Miramas in 1926, allowing Casse to finish ahead of the new 6-cylinder Amilcars. A GS won the JCC Production Car Race at Brooklands, beating all the 1·5-litre cars in the process.

By 1927 the 4-cylinder engines were giving 52bhp unblown and 106bhp blown, but Amilcar opposition was taking its toll, despite Salmson's 2nd and 3rd places and the Biennial Cup at Le Mans, and 2nd place in the Coupe de la Commission Sportive, a fuel-consumption event at Montlhéry. The basic design's last big success was yet another Biennial Cup win for Casse and Rousseau at Le Mans in 1928, but meanwhile Petit had come up with an advanced twin-ohc 1,100cc straight-8 complete with desmodromic valve gear. This was a bi-block unit rather in the Alfa Romeo idiom, and in original blown

form it gave 140bhp, later worked up to 170 with twin Cozette superchargers—150bhp per litre. Only two chassis were built, and Salmson's racing department closed down before it could be properly developed, though it was timed over a mile at 125·5mph (202kph) and made ftd at Gaillon in 1929. Armand Girod bought both the eights in 1930, and had about six years' racing out of them, winning the 1,100cc category of the Grand Prix de France and taking 2nd place in Picardy in 1934.

After World War 2 Salmson made 20 single-seater 'racing trainers' for the Union Sportive Automobile. Their 1,997cc twin-cam 4-cylinder engines, ifs and 4-speed Cotal boxes had close affinities to the contemporary S-4-61 touring model, but they never achieved anything. Despite a few abortive appearances by privately-entered cars at Le Mans in the 1950s, the last Salmson to distinguish itself in competition was the 2·3-litre G85 GT coupé which won its class in the 1954 Tulip, Lyons–Charbonnières and Alpine Rallies (beating Stirling Moss's Sunbeam in the latter). It also finished 5th (best French car) in the Liège–Rome–Liège event. MCS

Sam (PL)

The Sam was the first sporting car built in post-war Poland. Between 1954 and 1956 twelve Sams were made, under the direction of Antonin Weiner. They were powered either by motorcycle engines such as Triumph 650, DKW 750 or BMW 750, or by IFA F9, Syrena 750, Fiat 1300 or Lancia 1500 car engines. Other components came from Syrena, Volkswagen, or Fiat cars. Most Sams were two-seaters, but at least one single-seater was made. Driven by Weiner, Jerzy Szulczewski and Ludwig Bielak, they won the Polish Championships in the 750cc, 1,300cc and 1,600cc classes. They were also raced in Czechoslovakia, East Germany and the Soviet Union, but were not particulary successful there. VH

Sandford (F)

Built by Stuart Sandford, an Englishman resident in France, the Sandford 3-wheeler resembled the Morgan in its ifs, but had a 4-cylinder Ruby engine and 3-speed gearbox from the first model of 1922, and front-wheel brakes from 1924. Although more civilized than their rivals the Darmonts, Sandfords did well in their capacity class in events such as the Bol d'Or; in 1932 they won the 3-wheeler class outright in a race during which rain fell for 21 out of the 24 hours. From 1934 some 4-wheeler Sandfords were made, but there is no record of their performance in competitions. GNG

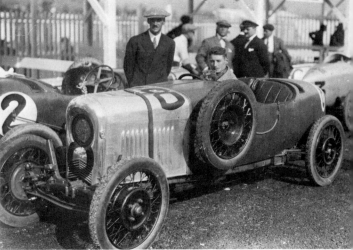

SARA (F)

One of the most successful air-cooled cars of the 1920s, the SARA (Société des Automobiles à Refroidissement par Air) ran at Le Mans every year from 1923 to 1929. The company never entered less than two cars, and sometimes three. Up to 1927 the Le Mans SARAs were 1,100cc 4-cylinder machines, and thereafter 1,800cc sixes, although the latter were less successful than the smaller cars. The make's best performance was Marandet and Lecureul's 5th place overall in 1927. Two 1,100s also ran in the 1925 Cyclecar Grand Prix at San Sebastian. Production ceased in 1930, but in 1933 Gaston Mottet, who had been a works driver, entered for Le Mans a modified 6-cylinder car with improved engine and new body. This was the last air-cooled car to run at Le Mans until the DBs of the early 1950s. GNG

Scampolo (D)

The Scampolo was developed by Kraftfahrzeugtechnischer Versuchsbau in Recklinghausen and was one of the first serious attempts to build racing cars in Germany after World War 2. The man behind the project were Walter Arnold and Walter Komossa; the latter was also a successful driver who won the German Championship in 1949 and 1952. They used a double-piston 2-stroke DKW engine of 600cc with charging pump. This was mounted in the rear and utilized a DKW front-drive component fitted back to front. Later versions abandoned the charging pump. After the introduction of Formula 3 a 500cc Scampolo appeared, and again a DKW engine was used. After the introduction of Formula 3 a 500cc Scampolo also appeared, at first DKW-powered, later with a BMW engine. HON

SCAP (F)

The Société de Construction Automobiles Parisiennes was more famous for their proprietary engines than for their complete cars, although a number of the latter were made. Two SCAPs were entered for the 1914 Coupe de l'Auto which never took place, but thereafter car production was suspended until 1925, when two models, an 1100 and a 1200, were introduced. The former was available with a supercharger, and was a small sports car in the BNC class, although not so popular. Louis Rosier began his career on a blown 1100 in 1928. A 2-litre straight-8 whose engine was basically two blocks of the 1200 with reduced bore was made in very small quantities in 1927. Two straight-8s ran at Le Mans in 1927 (one finished 3rd), and one eight and one 1100 in 1928 when both retired. GNG

Scarab (US)

After racing in Europe in 1957, Lance Reventlow, son of Woolworth heiress Barbara Hutton, decided to build an American race car and formed Reventlow Automobiles Inc. Warren Olson, owner of a Los Angeles sports car shop, headed a group that included driver-engine specialist Chuck Daigh, builders Dick Troutman and Tom Barnes and, on occasion, Ken Miles, who prepared some of the original sports car plans. Using Chevrolet engines and Corvette gearboxes the Scarab first raced in March 1958 at Luke Field, Ariz. Following a string of West Coast victories Chuck Daigh won over Phil Hill's Ferrari at Riverside in 1958. In 1960 and 1961 Augie Pabst and Harry Heuer drove Scarabs to Sports Car Club of America 'B' modified national championships. In December 1963, Indianapolis star A. J. Foyt won

Above, 1925 SARA in the San Sebastian Cyclecar GP. Marandet at the wheel. *Photo Fotocar*

Left, 1948 Scampolo 600cc racing car at Hockenheim. Walter Komossa at the wheel. *Photo: Leica-Studio Worner*

Far left, 1953 Scampolo 750cc sports car with experimental perspex top. *Photo: M. Gatsonides*

Centre, 1960 Scarab Formula 1, with Chuck Daigh. *Photo: Lester Nehamkin*

Below, c 1960 Scarab sports car. Lance Reventlow at the wheel. *Photo: Griffith Borgeson*

two Nassau Speed Week features in the rear-engined Scarab-Chevy, owned by John Mecom, Jr. And in September 1964 Walt Hansgen drove the same machine, a 365ci (5,981cc) Chevy engine replacing the original lightweight Buick, to victory over Pedro Rodriguez at Bridgehampton.

The Formula 1 Scarab arrived on the Grand Prix scene in 1960, the final year of the 2·5-litre capacity limit. A relatively heavy, front-engined machine, close to being obsolete when introduced, the Scarab was withdrawn from Formula 1 racing after poor performances in the season's first three Grands Prix. In four years Reventlow Automobiles built seven race cars, three front-engined sports cars, three front-engined Formula 1 cars and one rear-engined sports car. ARB

SCAT (I)

Another offspring of the remarkable Ceirano family, the make SCAT (Societa Ceirano Automobili Torino) was founded in 1906 and first appeared in racing in 1908 in the Isle of Man 'Four-Inch' TT. Three cars, based on the firm's sturdy 4-cylinder sv standard models, took part but had no success. A big 120hp car appeared in 1909, which Ernesto Ceirano took to France for the Mont Ventoux hill-climb, making ftd. He and Borsari also scored class victories in the Modena flying mile sprints, but SCAT's most significant performances came in the Targa Florio, which they won three times. In 1911 the Sicilian classic fell to Ernesto Ceirano; in 1912 SCAT's English tester/driver Cyril Snipe won; and in 1914 Ernesto Ceirano scored his second victory. A 1913 racing SCAT was acquired by a 22-year-old Mantuan named Tazio Nuvolari, but the outbreak of war in 1914 prevented him from racing it, and his illustrious career began with other makes. CP

Schaudel see Motobloc

Schmid see Roland-Pilain

Scirocco see Emeryson

Scorpion (GB)

The Scorpion 1200 was designed and built by Wally Hayward, of Christian Malford, Wiltshire, on similar lines to the earlier Terrier 1172 Formula cars. A spaceframe with large-diameter tubing was clothed with a sleek needle-nose all-enveloping body, and front suspension was by swing axles with horizontal coil springs. Replicas were offered for sale for 1970. DF

SEFAC (F)

Conceived by Petit and Vareille of Salmson fame as a new French challenger for the 750kg Formula of 1934, the SEFAC (Société d'Etude et de Fabrication d'Automobile de Course) was an interesting machine: a 2·8-litre parallel-8 (as tried before World War 1 by Itala and Hillman) with twin-ohc per block, desmodromic valve gear, and crankshafts rotating in opposite directions, though the gearbox and transmission were conventional. All four wheels were independently sprung. It was entered for the French GP that year, but did not start. It also failed to start in 1935, but was unable to enter in 1936 and 1937 because the French turned their Grand Prix into a sports-car race. As it conformed equally well to the new Formula of 1938, it put in an appearance at Reims that year, and Chaboud actually persuaded it to cover one lap, though this was too much for the car, and

Top, 1934 SEFAC at the *pesage* for the 1935 French GP at Montlhéry. Marcel Lehoux at the wheel. *Photo: Cyril Posthumus Collection*

Above, 1924 Selve SL40 in the 1925 Hainberg Hill-Climb. Karl Slevogt at the wheel. *Photo: Neubauer Collection*

it was a non-starter again in 1939. Nor was this quite the end of the story, for in 1948 details were released of a new 3·6-litre unsupercharged racer, the Dommartin. This turned out to be the SEFAC under a new name, with the addition of a Cotal gearbox. Giraud-Cabantous was named as the driver, but it did not race. MCS

Selve (D)

The first Selve cars to be prepared for competitions were derived from the standard models and appeared in 1922. These were developed by Ernst Lehmann, who drove them himself, mainly in hill-climbs. His last design was the SL40 with a 4-cylinder 2,090cc engine of 50bhp. Lehmann was killed during practice for the Teutoburgerwald Race in 1924. He was succeeded as chief engineer by Karl Slevogt, who was already renowned as an engineer and driver with Apollo. He developed the SL40 to 60bhp and fitted aerodynamic bodies to the competition versions. The maximum speed of these cars was about 85mph. They were successful at hill-climbs, such as Klausen, Semmering, Hainberg and Herkules. In 1926 Selve ceased to take part in racing. HON

Sénéchal (F)

Robert Sénéchal's cyclecar-voiturette was first seen at the Gaillon hill-climb in 1921: standard versions had 903cc 4-cylinder Ruby engines, 2-speed gearboxes (though 3-speeds were regular practice by 1922), and differential-less back axles, but the make made its first impact in the 750cc class. Sénéchal retired in the 1922 Bol d'Or, but won his category in both the year's major Cyclecar Grands Prix, averaging 53·22mph (85·65kph) at Montargis, and 53·73mph (86·47kph) at Le Mans. He

repeated his success at the former venue in 1923, as well as taking 4th place and 750cc honours in the Bol d'Or, but was beaten in the Le Mans cyclecar race by André Lombard on a 750cc dohc Salmson. An unsuccessful ohv Sénéchal was entered for the Grand Prix de Tourisme, but in the Spanish touring-car event at San Sebastian, Palazon recorded yet another 750cc win.

Sénéchal had graduated to 1,100cc cars by 1924, and was thus able to win the Bol d'Or outright, Doré scoring a class win in the Circuit des Routes Pavées. Two mysterious 2-litre Sénéchals (Sénéchal and Léonard) contested the Grand Prix de Tourisme, but although the firm had now been taken over by Chenard-Walcker these were in fact re-worked ohc 4-cylinder Bignans. Apart from a defeat at the hands of the slide-valve Imperias in the Belgian 24-Hour Race, 1925 was quite a good year, and Doré won both the Montlhéry Cyclecar GP and the Bol d'Or, as well as taking 5th place in the Circuit des Routes Pavées. Sénéchal scored yet another victory in the 1926 Bol d'Or. MCS

Serenissima see ATS

Serpollet (F)

A Serpollet steamer was the unsuccessful challenger in the second race staged by the magazine *Le Vélocipede* in 1888 — though it lost, it at least prevented Georges Bouton from claiming a walkover. Although a Serpollet made one of the first serious motor journeys (from Paris to Lyons) in 1890, the make did not as yet race to any purpose. Serpollet himself drove one of the two steamers entered for the Paris–Bordeaux–Paris in 1895, but a narrow front track upset balance, and neither finished.

It was not until 1900 that Serpollet was adequately financed (by the American Frank Gardner), and the cars, now with petroleum burners, were seen in hill-climbs though they could not yet challenge the fastest petrol-engined machinery. In 1901 Nice Speed Trials, however, Léon Serpollet beat the newly-introduced Mercédès with a time of 35·8sec for the flying kilometre, even if this could not match the speed of Jenatzy's *La Jamais Contente*, which had been nearly two seconds quicker in 1899. The cars entered in the Paris–Berlin were, by contrast, hopelessly unsuccessful, and the Serpollets which ran in the 1902 Circuit du Nord alcohol race were said to dislike that fuel, in spite of which four of them finished in line behind the two leading Panhards. Chanliaud's 15th place in the Paris–Vienna was uninspiring, but meanwhile Serpollet's streamlined short-chassis 'Easter Egg' had carried all before it at Nice, where he had clocked 75·06mph (120·80kph), defeating all the internal-combustion brigade. At Gaillon, Le Blon lowered the record to 35sec and in the light-car class Rutishauser's Serpollet was fastest, with 40·8sec. In 1903 all the seven cars entered for the Paris–Madrid reached Bordeaux safely — albeit not among the leaders, although Le Blon was 4th in the Circuit des Ardennes. Serpollets were still supporting hill-climbs and sprints to good purpose in 1904, with two classes to their credit at Dourdan, and another two at Château-Thierry, where racers were barred that year. They also fielded three odd-looking cars with streamlined, boot-shaped noses, 6-cylinder single-acting engines, and the usual central chain drive for the French Gordon Bennett Trials, but Le Blon's 5th place was not sufficient to gain him a place in the team. MCS

Far left, 1922 Sénéchal in the GP des Voiturettes at Boulogne. Robert Sénéchal at the wheel. *Photo: T. A. S. O. Mathieson Collection*

Top, 1902 Serpollet. *Photo: Veteran Car Club of Great Britain*

Left, 1902 Serpollet 'Easter Egg'. Léon Serpollet at the wheel. *Photo: Montagu Motor Museum*

Shadow (US)

The Shadow was one of the most unconventional Can-Am cars to appear during the 1970 season. Built by Advanced Vehicle Systems (AVS), it was designed by Trevor Harris. Among its unusual features were smaller than average wheels (10in (254mm) at front, 12in (304·8mm) at rear) giving a very low profile, air fans to cool the small diameter disc brakes, and semi-automatic transmission. The engine was a Bartz-modified 7-litre Chevrolet. Its first appearance was at Mosport Park in June 1970, when George Follmer drove it and retired with overheating. A month later it was wrecked on its trailer in a road accident. GNG

Shelby see Cobra and Shelby-GT

Siata (I)

From 1926 SIATA specialized in tuning Fiats for

competition, boosting the output of the 995cc Balilla S unit of 1934 to 55bhp with the aid of a blower. From the mid-1950s they made a number of sports cars using a variety of power units. These included Fiat 4- and 8-cylinder units, 725cc Crosleys and even Chrysler V-8s and these were raced nationally although with no great success. However, they were very popular in the United States in the smaller SCCA classes. The firm turned their hands to single-seaters with a 1,100cc model, but this too had little competition success. DCN

Silver Hawk (GB)

This was originally a 1,498cc competition version of the 10hp Eric-Campbell, retaining that car's sv Coventry-Simplex unit, but using a special crankshaft and alloy pistons. The radiator was suggestive of the later Invicta, also to be made at Cobham, Surrey, and to involve the same personalities, including Noel Macklin. These cars did well in sprints and by the beginning of 1921 the Silver Hawk Motor Co. were claiming 'more than 20 awards since June'. In June 1920, C. M. Harvey took the 1·5-litre standing-mile record at 61·53mph (99·02kph), and more class records were taken (also at Brooklands) that October, including 250 miles at 61·09mph (98·31kph). The car was shared by Gedge and Violet Cordery: the first occasion on which a woman driver had taken part in a record attempt.

A team of Silver Hawks ran in the Coupe Internationale des Voiturettes at Le Mans in 1920, but though René Thomas drove one of them, they failed to distinguish themselves. Gedge was 6th and Thomas 7th. By 1921 the company was out of business after making about ten cars. MCS

Sima-Violet (F)

The basic Sima-Violet was a 4-wheeled cyclecar with 2-speed gearbox in unit with a differential-less back end, powered by a 500cc air-cooled flat-twin 2-stroke engine on the usual Violet lines. It cost £57 10s in its country of origin and sold quite well. Violet raced it tirelessly, finishing 4th (and 1st in his class) in the 1925 Bol d'Or. He also won the 750cc category of the small-car races at Montlhéry with the 723cc flat-4 version (not marketed commercially), Doré and Stanton tying for 1st place in the 500cc section and crossing the line hand-in-hand. In 1926 Sima-Violet collected the two smallest racing-car classes at Boulogne. Already, however, Violet was

Left, 1953 Siata sports car at Bridgehampton. Isabel Haskell at the wheel. *Photo: Ruth Sands Bentley*

Above, 1970 AVS Shadow at the Mid-Ohio Can-Am. Vic Elford at the wheel. *Photo: Autosport*

Left, 1920 Silver Hawk in the GP des Voiturettes at Le Mans. *Photo: T. A. S. O. Mathieson Collection*

changing allegiance, and that year he ran one of his fours in the Coupe de la Commission Sportive as a Leroy, as well as driving one of the new water-cooled Deguingands at Boulogne. Less successful was a 1,484cc flat-4 intended for Grands Prix. This had a 4-speed all-indirect box, an underslung frame, transverse front suspension, and no differential, and was said to develop 100bhp unblown. Violet finished 3rd at Boulogne in 1926, and was up-rated to 2nd place after he had protested against a Bugatti. A rear-engined 500cc car, curiously anticipatory of post-war Formula 3 machines, ran in the 1928 National Trophy race at Boulogne. MCS

Simca-Gordini (F)

Amédée Gordini was an Italian who made his home in France, and during his first serious competition season, 1935, he raced 995cc ohv Balilla Fiats tuned by himself. By 1936, Pigozzi's Simca company was firmly established as FIAT's licensee in France, and Gordini's cars ran as Simcas, with new bodies and engine output boosted from 36 to 55bhp. Gordini, Zanardi and Martin took the first three places in the sports-car category of the Bol d'Or, and there were also class wins in the Reims voiturette race, the Coupe de Provence at Miramas, and the Belgian 24-Hour Race. In 1937 Gordini turned his attention to Simca's version of the 570cc Fiat Topolino, from which he extracted 18bhp. One of these (Viale/Alin) averaged 51mph (82·08kph) at Le Mans, where Vernet and Largeot won the 1,100cc category.

In 1938 le sorcier (the wizard), as Gordini was called, had some new raw material: the Millecento with 1,089cc push-rod engine, which emerged as an aerodynamic two-seater with 60bhp, and there were also experiments with an ohv version of the 500. Gordini's 1100 won the Bol d'Or and there were class victories at Reims (where a 1,221cc unit was used); at Spa; the TT at Donington; and the Montlhéry 12 Hours, on which occasion the 750cc category was also won by Lapchin/Plantivaux. Another 500 (Aimé and Plantivaux) won the Index of Performance at Le Mans, and one of these miniatures went after long-distance records at Montlhéry, covering 48 hours at 64mph (103·00kph). Simca also won the Paris–Nice Rally. In 1939 he was back with some even better streamlined 65bhp 1100s, which could reach nearly 110mph (176kph) on 65bhp. A win in the 2·5-litre class at Comminges was backed by victories in the Index of Performance, the Rudge-Whitworth Cup, and the appropriate class at Le Mans, while le sorcier himself broke the 1,100cc record at the La Turbie hill-

climb. The cars were out again in time for the first post-war race meeting in Paris late in 1945, Simca collecting the Benoist Cup for 1,500cc machines.

Some new single-seater 1100s appeared in 1946: the 65bhp push-rod engine was retained, but new was the tubular frame with coil and wishbone ifs, and the combination of a rigid axle and torsion bars at the rear. The sports cars took 2nd and 3rd places in their class of the Belgian GP, and there were victories for the new racers in minor events like the Coupe de l'Entr 'Aide Français and the St Cloud Municipal Cup. The cars were matched for the first time against their great rivals, the Italian Cisitalias, in that year's Coppa Brezzi at Turin: they were defeated on this occasion.

Gordini had hopes of a V-8 in 1947, but Simca (who were sponsoring him) would not consent to this—any more than they did later to a proposed 4·5-litre unblown car to be evolved in association with OSCA—so he had to be content with increasing output to 74bhp. The cars had quite a good season: Cayla and Vernet were 1st and 2nd in the Bol d'Or; Wimille beat the Cisitalias at Nîmes and Lausanne; while in the Coupe des Petites Cylindrées at Reims, 'Bira', Simon and Trintignant took the first three places. 'Bira' also won the Manx Cup Race run in conjunction with the British Empire Trophy Race in the Isle of Man, his average speed qualifying him for 3rd overall. Both at Albi and Nice the cars found themselves up against real Formula 1 machines and acquitted themselves well, Sommer finishing 2nd and Trintignant 6th on the former occasion, and Wimille taking 2nd place on the latter. The season closed with a victory for Wimille in the Formule Libre race staged at Rosario, Argentina.

There was a new 1,433cc engine with cross-push-rod valve gear and a 5-bearing crankshaft in 1948; this was worked up to 105bhp, and the cars did fairly well in minor events. Trintignant won at Perpignan, Troubet-zkoy at Angoulême, and 'Bira' at Stockholm. The first of the sports-racers with central steering, a 1,500cc machine, turned up for the Belgian 24-Hour Race at Spa, where Scaron and Veyron finished 2nd in their class. Simcas scored a 1-2-3 victory in the Bol d'Or, Scaron being the winner at 53·67mph (86·37kph); Aldo Gordini, Amédée's son, won the 1·5-litre category of the Coupe du Salon; and the Molinari and Prat 500 won the 750cc class of the Montlhéry 12 Hours. Successes in 1949 included a 1-2-3 at Lausanne, and victories at Marseilles for Fangio (then a new star) and at Angoulême for Trintignant. There was a new 1,500cc class record at

Left, 1947 Simca-Gordini 1,220cc racing car. J-P Wimille at the wheel. *Photo: G. N. Georgano Collection*

Below, c 1950 Simca-Gordini sports car. Roger Barlow at the wheel. *Photo: Autosport*

Mont Ventoux and Manzon's 1,221cc Simca came 1st in the Bol d'Or, followed by Fièbre on a 1939 sports-racer.

In 1950 Gordini sought to compete on equal terms with the GP cars by trying a Wade-blown 1·5-litre, but this failed, apart from a new record for supercharged machines at Mont Ventoux, and it was left to the normally-aspirated cars to fly the flag. The victories were minor: the Circuit du Médoc, Geneva, and Périgueux; 2nd places at Aix-les-Bains, Angoulême, Roubaix, and the Formula 2 event run at the Swiss GP meeting. Victories in the 1,100cc and 1,500cc classes at the first post-war Nürburgring event were balanced by a failure at Le Mans, despite the presence of Fangio in the team. Only in 1951 did the Simca-Gordinis come out with new square (78 × 78mm) dohc engines developing 105bhp. These cars were quite fast, as witness Trintignant's victory in the Albi GP, and they took the first three places at Mettet, Sables d'Olonne, and Cadours, and also won at Chimay. Scaron won another Bol d'Or, while Lesurque and Trintignant were placed 2nd in the Liège-Rome-Liège Rally. By 1952, Gordini had severed his connection with Simca, but the late 1,500cc machines still raced occasionally, and as late as 1960 Flynn drove one into 4th place in the Leinster Trophy in Ireland.

Apart from Gordini's activities, Simcas have appeared infrequently in competitions. They did, however, have a brief moment of glory in the 1950 Monte Carlo Rally, when three of the five unpenalized competitors drove their cars. MCS

Simplex (US)

This Mercedes-like chain-driven machine was first marketed in 1904 as the Smith and Mabley Simplex, and in that year Frank Croker campaigned with a 14·7-litre 4-cylinder racer rated at 75hp. It proved very fast in the early stages of that year's Vanderbilt Cup, but the over-drilled frame sagged, and it was soon out of the running. Croker met with a fatal accident at the 1905 Ormond Beach-Daytona Speed Trials, and it was not until 1907 that the cars were again seen in action, Al Poole and George Robertson driving 597ci (10-litre) 50s in the Morris Park 24-hour 'grind'. Though Seymour's car was unplaced in the 1908 Vanderbilt Cup, Robertson was victorious in one of the Brighton Beach 24-hour races in spite of striking a track policeman. The make's best year was 1909, with three major victories for Robertson: in July's '24' at Brighton Beach, in the National Stock Car Championship at Lowell, and in the

Fairmount Park Race at Philadelphia, in which he averaged 55·4mph (89·16kph). Mitchell's 50hp, which had been eliminated with a broken crankshaft in the 1908 Vanderbilt Cup, managed a 7th place in 1910, in which the Poole and Basle car scored another 24-hour win at Brighton Beach, and Robertson managed to defeat Ralph DePalma in his Fiat in a 5-mile match race at the same venue. This victory was scored on one of the more powerful 90hp models, the only Simplex ever to be built with left-hand drive. This car later passed into the hands of Louis Disbrow, a well known barn-storming driver of the period. Though Simplex concentrated on touring cars thereafter, Disbrow continued to support major events, taking 8th place in the 1914 Vanderbilt Cup, and 6th in the 1915 Grand Prize at San Francisco. MCS

Simson-Supra (D)

This armaments factory started car production on a small scale just before World War 1. In 1924 Simson introduced their first sports car, one of the finest produced in Germany in that period. This was the Type S, designed by Paul Henze, who had formerly been with Steiger. The engine was a 4-cylinder of 1,950cc with two overhead camshafts, driven by vertical shaft and four overhead valves per cylinder. A normal version with tourer body and a short-wheelbase two-seater sports version were available. Adex 4-wheel brakes were fitted. Engine output was 60bhp. There was also a competition version with modified wheelbase and front track, twin carburettors and an increased output of about 80bhp. It was capable of about 90mph (144kph). This competition version appeared in a number of national events. Karl Kappler was the most successful driver, mainly in hill-climbs, like the Freiburg, Feldberg, Gabelbach and Herkules, and also in long-distance trials such as the Taunus 24 Hours and the Robert Batschari Prize. Another model of Henze's design was the 6-cylinder Type R with 3·1 litres capacity. It was a fast tourer rather than a sports car, and several competed in Monte Carlo Rallies between 1928 and 1930. HON

Singer (GB)

The first phase of Singer's competition career centred round the White- and Poppe-engined T-headed fours. As early as 1907 the 1·8-litre 12/14 was scoring class wins in hill-climbs, and in 1908 it won its class in the RAC 2,000 Miles Trial. Later versions, notably the 2·8-litre 16/20hp, distinguished themselves at Brooklands, where

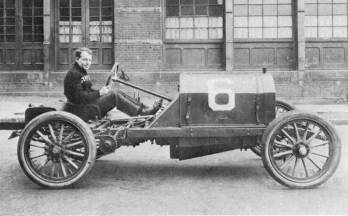

Below, 1950 Simca-Gordini 1·5-litre Le Mans coupé. *Photo: Montagu Motor Museum*

Right, 1910 Simplex 90 single-seater track car. George Robertson at the wheel. *Photo: Peter Helck Collection*

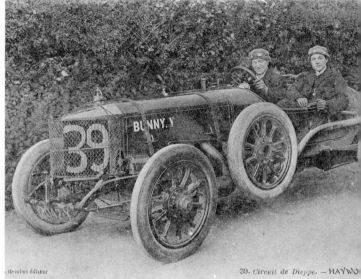

39. Circuit de Dieppe. — HAYWO

Far left, 1911 Singer 15·9hp 'Bunny III' at Brooklands. *Photo: Montagu Motor Museum*

Left, 1912 Singer 15·9hp 'Bunny V' for the Coupe de l'Auto. Haywood at the wheel. *Photo: Veteran Car Club of Great Britain*

Below left, 1935 Singer Nines driven by Norman Black (No 38) and S. C. H. Davis (No 37) passing ffrench-Davies' Fiat Balilla in the TT. *Photo: Autocar*

Top right, 1921 Singer Ten 200-Mile Race car. W. Bicknell at the wheel. *Photo: Montagu Motor Museum*

Right, 1935 Singer 1·5-litre 6-cylinder at Le Mans. J. S. Hindmarsh in car. *Photo: Montagu Motor Museum*

G. O. Herbert's 'Bunny Junior' proved capable of running up to 3,000rpm, and snatched more than one record from Coatalen's Sunbeam. Although the 3-litre ioe cars entered for the 1912 Coupe de l'Auto both retired, the T-head Singers continued to race until the outbreak of World War 1, one of those who favoured the breed being Cecil Kimber, the founder of MG.

In 1912 there appeared the new 1,100cc Ten with 3-speed rear-axle gearbox, which in stripped form scraped in 20lb (9kg) below the maximum permitted weight for a cyclecar, and managed 72 miles (115·87km) in the hour at Brooklands in September 1913. It achieved nothing in the Cyclecar GP at Le Mans, but its sprint record was impressive. Lionel Martin, who offered a tuned sports version, actually beat a 25hp Vauxhall at Kop in 1914, and also won his class at Caerphilly. Singers themselves catalogued a sports Ten in 1919; this could only do about 50mph (80kph), but in 1921 they prepared a special offset single-seater with two speeds and rear tank for Brooklands, unfortunately without success. A more orthodox model (its engine was said to give 33bhp) was driven by Bicknell in that year's Brooklands 200 Miles Race, but retired, and Singer steered clear of competitions for a long time, except for the marathon exploits of the Deeleys at Montlhéry in the winter of 1927, when they drove a stock 848cc ohc Junior for 6 days and nights to average 39·39mph (63·39kph).

For the 1933 season Singer marketed a new 972cc Nine Sports based on the two-bearing ohc Junior. As sold to the public it offered 65–70mph (104–112kph) on about 33bhp; but it was an immediate success in reliability trials, 1933 alone bringing 8 premier awards in the London–Exeter, 11 in the London–Lands End and 12 in the London–Edinburgh, as well as 4 silver cups in the Scottish Six Days. During the sports Singers' two first seasons (1933 and 1934) 578 cars took 495 awards in trials alone. There were a 2nd and 3rd in class in the RAC Rally, a 9th (and 1,100cc class honours) in Liège–Rome–Liège for Miss Labouchere; and a 2nd in the 1,100cc team event of the Alpine Trial for the works cars of Barnes, Black and Langley. A four-seater with its rear seats replaced by extra tankage finished 13th at Le Mans, and cars also scored successes in Australia, New Zealand and Switzerland. 'Le Mans' slab-tank two-seaters were available both on the 9hp model and the new 1,493cc Six in 1934, when Spikins' 4-cylinder won its class in the RAC Rally, Barnes won a class in the Scottish, and the Nines put up an excellent performance in the Alpine, where the team's 2nd in class was backed by three individual Glacier Cups and a silver-gilt plaque. At Le Mans the 972cc machines were backed by a pair of 6-cylinders, the Fox and Nicholl-prepared machine of Lewis and Hindmarsh—which could do 103mph (165kph)—finishing 7th and 2nd in the Rudge-Whitworth Cup, one place ahead of the works-entered 1·5-litre of Barnes and Langley. Two Nines also finished, encouraging Singer to produce some special lightweights for the 1935 season.

These weighed only 1,288lb (584·23kg) as against the 1,764lb (800·14kg) of the standard article, sumps and gearboxes were of elektron and body panels of duralumin, and crash boxes and straight bevel back axles were fitted when regulations permitted such deviations from catalogue specification. Top speed was 90mph (144kph), and they won the Light Car Club's Relay Race at Brooklands as well as finishing in good order, if low down the list, at Le Mans. The TT, however, was a

disaster, steering failures eliminating all three entries (Barnes, Langley and Davis), and wrecking the sports Singer's reputation overnight. Singer closed down their competition department at the end of 1935, both the sports-racing Nines and the trials 1·5-litres being taken over by Autosports, a team run by the Barnes brothers. The successes continued, Godfrey Imhof's 'Le Mans' Nine winning its category in both the Scottish and Welsh events. In the latter Singer also collected the manufacturers' and club team prizes, and there were the usual class victories in the RAC and MCC rallies. In racing, the Fiat entries proved faster both in the TT and the French Sports-Car GP at Montlhéry.

There was a further decline in 1937, despite a new 59bhp 1·5-litre 4-cylinder sports car said to be capable of 85–90mph (136–144kph). This was campaigned through the season by Autosports, but never went into series production. High spots of the year were the club team prize in the RAC Rally, and a surprising win in the smallest closed-car category of the MCC's Torquay Rally for a 'Super Nine' saloon driven by Tett (from the rival Fiat team). Jacques Savoye, the company's Paris agent, drove a Nine into 5th place in the Paris–Nice, but all the Singers retired at Le Mans. Much better was the TT at Donington, where the two best British cars were the old 1935 TT two-seaters of Barnes and Black, in 4th and 6th places. There were no sports cars in the 1938 catalogue, but in a lean year for Britain at Le Mans the nation's best placing was 8th (for the Savoye brothers) and even in 1939 the Jones and Wilkins TT car came in 18th.

The Savoyes had their Nine running in the first postwar French races of 1945, and Leeper's similar machine managed to beat the MGs to win the 1948 Leinster Trophy. However, the make's only other racing appearance was in the 1953 TT, when the Reece and Tyrer 1·5-litre roadster finished 13th. In the later 1960s, Hillman Imp-based Chamois models were sometimes seen alongside their cheaper sisters in saloon-car races. MCS

Sizaire-Naudin (F)

The brothers Georges and Maurice Sizaire and Louis Naudin built the most successful racing voiturettes in France. Their car first appeared in 1905, with a 918cc single-cylinder engine, armoured wood frame, and ifs by transverse leaf springs and sliding pillars. Its first major success was the 1906 Coupe des Voiturettes which Georges Sizaire won at 36·2mph (58·26kph). Another Sizaire-Naudin finished 6th. Later victories included the 1907 Sicilian Cup, and 1st and 2nd in that year's Coupe des Voiturettes; 1st and 2nd in the 1908 Coupe des Voiturettes and 2nd in the Grand Prix des Voiturettes; and 2nd in the 1909 Catalan Cup. The 1908 Coupes des Voiturettes cars were the largest of the singles, with a capacity of 1,963cc (100 × 250mm) and 42bhp. From 1910 onwards the voiturette class of racing began to be dominated by 4-cylinder cars, and the Sizaires no longer won major races. The 1912 Coupe de l'Auto cars had 4-cylinder horizontal-ohv engines of nearly 3 litres, but were underpowered and failed to finish the two-day event. The single and 4-cylinder cars achieved many class successes at hill-climbs such as Gaillon and Mont Ventoux, and were among the first cheap sporting cars to become popular with the public.

In 1920 the name appeared again, with three cars entered for the Coupe des Voiturettes. None of the original founders was now with the firm, and the engines were 4-cylinder sv Ballots. Although the drivers included Hémery and Guyot none of the cars finished. GNG

Skirrow (GB)

Harry Skirrow's dirt-track racing cars were the only such machines built commercially in any numbers for the British dirt-track boom of the mid-1930s. Introduced in 1936, the Skirrow used a 1,000cc JAP V-twin engine developing 80bhp, driving all four wheels by chains. They had narrow single-seater bodies and a wheelbase of 6ft. About 100 Skirrows were made between 1936 and 1939, selling for £175 each. A number were exported to Australia, and among many drivers who cut their teeth on the Skirrow in the early post-war period was Jack Brabham. GNG

Skoda (CS)

Skoda's activities in motor sport started in the second half of the 1930s. For the 1936 Monte Carlo rally a Popular was equipped with the Rapid 1·4-litre engine and driven by Pohl and Hausmann finished 2nd in their class and 8th overall. In 1937 they again took part, this time with a streamlined coupé version of the Popular-Rapid combination and again they finished 8th overall. A number of further victories were achieved by Skoda cars, especially in rallies and long-distance trials.

After World War 2 the standard models 1101 and 1102 were the basis for a line of sports and racing cars. A new 1,089cc twin-ohc engine was used for sports cars from 1958. These cars mainly appeared in national competitions, not in the big international events. An interesting development was the Formula 3 racing car which appeared in 1965 with a modified engine of the standard 1000 MB type capable of about 100bhp. The works ran a team of these cars in Eastern European events from 1966 to 1969. During 1970 the new Formula Skoda was announced, for single-seater racing cars using the 100/110 and 1000 and 1100 MB engines. HON

Snoeck see Bolide

SPA (I)

Founded by Matteo Ceirano in 1906, SPA (Societa Piemontese Automobile) built well-engineered, lively, conventional 4- and 6-cylinder cars before World War 1. They also manufactured lorries and aero engines, and apart from Francesco Ciuppa's 1909 Targa Florio victory, the make did not figure greatly in racing. However, de Zara made ftd in the 1909 Modena flying mile meeting at a rousing 87·15mph (140·25kph) with a 60hp SPA, and Cyril Snipe recorded a class victory in the same event the following year. In 1922 SPA produced the 30/40, a fine twin-ohc, 24-valve, 6-cylinder sports model of considerable competition potential. This was never realized, however, and Beria d'Argentina's outright victory in the 1924 Aosta-Great St Bernard hill-climb, and a 1-2 victory in the 3-litre class of the 3,000km Alpine Cup contest were its main successes. SPA were merged with FIAT in 1925, and still operate as a commercial vehicle and engineering division today. CP

Left, 1909 Sizaire-Naudin 6·2hp at Brooklands. *Photo: Montagu Motor Museum*

Below, 1969 Skoda 1000 MB in the Austrian Alpine Rally. *Photo: Vladimir Havránek Collection*

1935 Squire single-seater raced by Luis Fontes. *Photo: Montagu Motor Museum*

Spyker (Spijker) (NL)

Though as early as 1901 Jacobus Spijker drove one of his own designs in the Dutch Trials, the most famous Spyker racing car of all never raced, and it is doubtful if there was ever any serious intention of running it in the 1904 Gordon Bennett Cup. It was an 8·7-litre T-head six rated at 60hp with 4-wheel drive by cardan shafts running fore-and-aft from the gearbox. A front transmission brake endowed it with a primitive form of fwb. The car still exists. Godard drove a standard, if overburdened 15hp in the 1907 Pekin–Paris Race, but though the car gave little trouble, its driver's unscrupulous scrounging caused him to be removed from the crew before the finish. Spyker's proposed Kaiserpreis entry, at 9·9-litres, was too big to conform with the rules. A touring version was later marketed. In 1922 S. F. Edge used a stripped two-seater 30/40hp car with an sv 5·7-litre 6-cylinder Maybach engine to beat his Double-Twelve Record at Brooklands, which he did handsomely at 74·27mph (119·52kph). MCS

Squire (GB)

Adrian Squire was a perfectionist who built seven sports cars between 1934 and 1936. They had 1·5-litre twin-ohc 4-cylinder Anzani engines, with Roots blower giving 110bhp, and a maximum speed of over 110mph (177kph). Several were raced and rallied by their owners, and Luis Fontes drove a special single-seater at Brooklands. He ran in the 1935 BRDC 500 Miles Race, but retired with a cracked dumb iron. The nearest to victory that Fontes ever came with this car was 3rd in a Mountain Handicap in October 1935. GNG

SS (GB)

As originally conceived in 1932, the SS I, even in its more powerful form with 2·5-litre sv 20hp 6-cylinder Standard engine was purely a promenade sports car; the works team of four-seaters bravely entered for the 1933 Alpine Trial met with no success, though two private entries managed 6th and 8th places in their class, and a team of 2,664cc cars which ran in 1934 were 3rd in the team event behind the Talbots and Adlers. The next year produced nothing better than eight 1st-class awards in the RAC Rally, but in 1936 there were two class victories in the Welsh Rally for the new Jaguar models. More promising still was McEvoy's victory in the 3-litre class of the Marne sports car GP. He beat two of the new 2·5-litre Amilcars. In that year's Alpine Trial best overall performance was put up by the Wisdoms on a 2½-litre SS 100 2-seater, and this new short-chassis model distinguished itself in sprints, rallies and club events, though its rather tricky handling placed it at a disadvantage on road circuits.

The 3,485cc version introduced for 1938 was even better, being capable of 100mph (160kph) in standard form. Rally victories were numerous: 1st and 2nd overall, the Manufacturers' Team Prize, and a class victory in the 1937 RAC event; best individual performance in the 1937 Welsh Rally; and class victories in both again in 1938, when Wisdom's 2½-litre also took its class in the Paris–Nice and in the associated La Turbie hill-climb. Norton's 100 won its class in the 1939 RAC Rally, and in the immediate post-war years, while new sports models were still scarce, the 100s continued to distinguish themselves in sprints and hill-climbs. In the

1948 Alpine Rally Ian Appleyard won his first Coupe des Alpes on the only post-war example of the model. In 1949 the same combination of car and driver took 2nd place in the Tulip Rally, but by this time the twin-cam XK Jaguars were beginning to be seen. MCS

Stanguellini (I)

Vittorio Stanguellini, a FIAT dealer in Modena, used to modify and race 1,100cc Balillas in pre-war days and established his own make in 1946 around FIAT components. He developed special twin-ohc heads and strengthened bottom ends, and Stanguellini 750cc and 1,100cc sports cars gained countless successes in Italian national class events, notably in the hands of Sesto Leonardi.

With the introduction in Italy of Formula Junior as a substitute for the Cooper-dominated Formula 3 in 1958, Stanguellini built a large batch of single-seater Junior cars which met with immediate success in national races, Cammarota winning the 1958 Italian Junior Championship. In 1959, when Formula Junior became international, Stanguellini proved the dominant make: the Swiss driver Michel May headed a 1-2-3 victory in the Monaco Junior GP, won at Solitude and the Nürburgring, and became the first International Junior Champion; Juan-Manuel Bordeu, Fangio's protégé, won at Monza; Wolfgang von Trips won the Eifelrennen; and Lorenzo Bandini won at Innsbruck. The new formula thus justified itself as a training ground for future Grand Prix drivers.

Top left, 1938 SS 100 photographed at Silverstone in July 1970. *Photo: G. N. Georgano*

Top right, 1953 Stanguellini at the start of the Circuito del Castello; the winning car, driven by Casella. *Photo: Autosport*

Above left, 1958 Stanguellini Formula Junior. *Photo: A. Ceci*

Above right, 1959 Stanguellini at Le Mans. *Photo: Theo Page*

The beautifully made Stanguellini with which these victories were secured followed GP conventions of the late 1950s in being front-engined; it used a Fiat-based 1,100cc engine and Fiat gearbox in a tubular frame with Fiat front suspension and a coil-sprung live rear axle located by radius arms. By 1960 it was eclipsed by the British rear-engined Coopers and Lotuses, and although Stanguellini in turn built a rear-engined car, the make never regained its former winning ways. CP

Stanley (US)

The Stanley steamer was the world's most celebrated and long-lived steam car, and with the White the only one to enter competitions on an important scale. Like Alexander Winton and Henry Ford, the Stanley twins believed in the advertising value of racing successes, and regularly entered their cars in demonstration events from 1902 onwards. Originally they used the little 5½hp folding front-seat models, sometimes with the seat removed and the driver crouching on the floor; they frequently beat larger petrol-engined cars such as Stevens-Duryea, Winton, and Daimler. In 1903 F. E. Stanley built a special car with highly-streamlined cigar-shaped body. With it he covered a mile in 1min 2sec in May 1903. It was nicknamed the 'Wogglebug', and this name was applied to other streamlined Stanleys built over the next three years. They were also called 'Teakettle', 'Beetle', or 'Rocket'. The most famous of these was the 20hp car driven by Fred Marriott at Daytona, Fla., in January 1906. He covered the mile in 28·2sec, equal to a speed of

127·66mph (205·5kph). This was nearly 20mph faster than the existing Land Speed Record, though like all American records up to 1927 it was not recognized by the AIACR in Paris. The following year Marriott attempted to break his own record, and reached a speed of over 150mph (240kph) when 'Wogglebug' crashed and was totally destroyed.

In 1906 Stanley built two cars for the Vanderbilt Cup. They had a much more conventional appearance than the streamlined cars, with typical Stanley coal-scuttle bonnet, and driver's seat over the rear axle. They never reached the Eliminating Trials, but were frequently raced at Daytona and elsewhere by F. E. Stanley, Marriott, and others. From 1906 to 1908 the firm offered three models of roadster to the public, in 10, 20, and 30hp form. The 20hp Gentleman's Speedy Roadster claimed the title of Fastest Stock Car in the World after averaging 68·18mph (109·57kph) over a 15-mile handicap at Ormond Beach. Its maximum speed was 75mph (120kph). These Stanleys were unbeaten in hill-climbs at this time, and it is said the Stanley challenge led to Chadwick's experiments with supercharging. The roadsters were discontinued after 1909, and although Stanley production lasted a further 18 years, they played no more part in sport. GNG

Star (GB)

During its first quarter century of existence this Wolverhampton make supported a surprising number of sprints and minor events, the cars often being handled by Edward and Joseph Lisle, the sons of the founder. Star contested both the 1903 and 1905 British Gordon Bennett Eliminating Trials with equal lack of success, a solitary T-head 11-litre of Panhard aspect appearing in 1903, and two 10-litre crypto-Mercedes, handled by the brothers Goodwin, in 1905. Star were equally unfortunate in the TT, which they supported in 1906, 1907, and 1914 with modified touring types. Both their 1907 18hp entries ran well before retiring, but the 1914 sv 5-bearing 3-litres with bolster-tank two-seater bodies made no impression at all. Better performances were achieved in hill-climbs and at Brooklands, using heavily-modified 12 and 15hp cars: the degree of tuning is indicated by the car fielded by Richard Lisle at the Wolverhampton AC event in 1909, which was said to run up to 4,000rpm, and beat strong opposition from Sunbeam, Vauxhall and Napier.

A 2·4-litre 15·9hp driven by Cathie won the RAC's Standard Car Race at Brooklands in 1911, but Star's

1912 'production' entries were disqualified as non-standard. A 3,817cc Twenty with single-seater aerodynamic body took more records (from the Coupe de l'Auto Sunbeam) in 1913 — as these fiercer Wolverhampton cars were capable of 90–95mph (144–152kph) it must have been fast, and covered 500 miles at 78·8mph (126·82kph). There were still 'works' hill-climb Stars as late as 1922, but the last serious appearance of the make was in 1925 when Sir Malcolm Campbell on a stripped ohv 12/40hp sports model won a Short Handicap at Brooklands. MCS

Staride (GB)

Between 1952 and 1955 a dozen Erskine Staride Formula 3 cars were built at Mike Erskine's Southampton workshops. They were generally similar in layout to the Kieft 500, with swinging-arm rear suspension. Dean Delamont collaborated in the design of both cars.

A few minor race victories were achieved, such as Ninian Sanderson's win at Oulton Park in 1953, and good placings were obtained by a variety of drivers, including Rob Anderson, Reg Bicknell, Dickson, A. Eccles, Fenning, P. Green, B. Manning, J. D. Habin, André Loens and Dennis Taylor. In its time the make offered a challenge to the Coopers, but the lack of major international victories did not encourage support, and after 1955 the cars faded from the scene. DF

Steiger (D)

A Steiger sports car first appeared in 1921 in the Grünewald race in Berlin and took part in the 1922 Avusrennen. The 4-cylinder ohv 2·6-litre engine developed 60bhp; it had an extremely long stroke for that period — 160mm, while the bore was 72mm. The overhead camshaft was driven by vertical shaft. Suspension was by half-elliptic springs, underslung at the rear axle. In 1925 a 2·9-litre version appeared with an increased bore of 76mm. A team of these cars was sent to the 1924 Targa Florio. The engine output was raised from 70bhp to about 100bhp and they were capable of about 90mph (144kph). Although the Targa Florio was not a success for Steiger they took part successfully in a number of events in Germany, Austria and Czechoslovakia such as the German Long-Distance Trial, Klausen and Semmering hill-climbs and the Solitude races. A Steiger driven by Kaufmann finished 2nd in the 1923 Italian Grand Prix; in 1925 Fuld was the overall winner of the Robert Batschari Trial. One car driven by Hofer took part in the first German Grand Prix on the AVUS

1953 Staride 500 at Brands Hatch. Reg Bicknell at the wheel. *Photo: Autosport*

Left, 1906 Stanley 'Wogglebug' at Daytona. *Photo: Montagu Motor Museum*

Below, 1905 Star 70hp in the Gordon Bennett Eliminating Trials. F. R. Goodwin at the wheel. *Photo: Sedgwick and Marshall Collection*

Above left, 1924 Steiger Targa Florio car.
Ernst Kaufmann at the wheel. *Photo:
Neubauer Collection*

Above, 1924 Steyr Type VI saloon for the
Touring Car GP. *Photo: Neubauer Collection*

Left, 1926 Steyr Klausen in the Schwaben-
berg race. Count Kinsky at the wheel.
Photo: Neubauer Collection

circuit in 1926 but it had to retire in the second lap.
Production of Steiger cars ceased in 1926 as a result of
financial difficulties. Alfred Noll of Düsseldorf, a Steiger
competition driver, bought the remaining parts and
built a few cars in singles for two or three years. HON

Steyr (A)

Steyr cars were first built in 1920, the early models being
designed by Hans Ledwinka. The 6-cylinder Type II of
3,325cc capacity was used in competitions as well as the
4-cylinder Type IV with 2-litre engine. They were seen in
various competitions in Austria, Hungary and Czechoslovakia, but did not become internationally known
until they were entered for the 1922 Targa Florio, when
Otto Hieronymus drove a Type II into 7th place, while
Hermann Rutzler was 3rd in his class on a Type IV. In
1923 Ferdinand Minoia finished 3rd overall in the Targa
Florio, on a special car with 4,890cc engine. Based on
the Type II, the Type 60 was introduced in 1924, with
two carburettors, overhead camshaft, and an increased
output of 60bhp. This model was further developed into
the Type VI, with increased bore giving a capacity of
4,014 and power of 100bhp. A team of three Type VIs
with streamlined saloon bodies ran in the 1924 and 1925
French Touring Grands Prix; Gauderman finished 2nd
in 1925. From the Type VI came the more famous Type
VI Klausen Sport, with 4,890cc 145bhp engine and
shorter chassis. A further developed model known as the
SS-Klausen Sport, with 153bhp, appeared in 1927.
These cars were built in small numbers (51 Klausens and
9 SS-Klausens), but they competed very successfully,
especially in hill-climbs. There were also some specially-

prepared works entries with power output of up to
200bhp. The most successful drivers were Hermann..
Ritzler, responsible for sports and racing car development
at Steyr, and the Swiss driver Huldrich Heusser. In 1928
August Momberger launched a racing car based on the
Klausen, available with blown engine. From the coming
of the Depression until World War 2, Steyr took no
further part in competition.

After the war Steyr again appeared in motor sport with
the Steyr-Puch 500, using a Fiat 500 body shell and
their own flat-twin 493cc engine. Since its introduction
in 1957 the Steyr-Puch has done very well in hill-climbs,
touring car races and rallies, especially in Austria,
Germany, Hungary and Poland. Among the most successful drivers has been Sobieslaw Zasada who won the
Polish Rally in 1964, was 2nd in 1965, and won the
European Championship in 1966. Like most of the
competition Steyr-Puchs, Zasada's car had an engine
increased to 650cc. The Steyr-Puch engine was also used
in the IMP GT coupé made in 1960 and 1961. HON

Stoddard-Dayton (US)

In 1907 Stoddard-Daytona abandoned Rutenber engines
in favour of their own design of T-head four, launching
this with an entry in the Glidden Tour, in which it took
the Hewer Trophy for runabouts. The firm also distributed box lunches to all the competitors. To the make
belongs the honour of winning the first race ever staged
at the Indianapolis Speedway, a 5-mile affair in 1909.
More important, however, was Clement's 2nd place
behind a Buick in a 250-mile race at the same meeting.
After this brief essay into competition, the company
officially retired from sport, but in the 1910 Vanderbilt
Cup Harding finished 9th at 60·99mph (98·15kph). MCS

Stoewer (D)

Like many a German make, this Stettin car entered
competition via the Herkomer and Prince Henry Trials,
the 1907 factory team being headed by Bernhard Stoewer
himself on an 8·8-litre shaft-driven P6 6-cylinder tour-

c 1921 Stoewers at Fanø: 11·2-litre D7
(left) and 2·5-litre special racing car (right).
Photo: Neubauer Collection

ing model. Both Bernhard and his brother Emil drove sixes in 1908, but though some new 4-cylinder machines with 'marine-form' bodies were prepared for the 1910 Prince Henry they were as unsuccessful as the identical Mathis entries from Strasbourg. In fact some of Emile Mathis's first serious competition successes were obtained on thinly-disguised Stoewers. The Stettin make did not appear in serious competition again until the 1921–4 period when Kordewan was a regular competitor at Denmark's Fanø Speed Trials on one of the aero-engined 6-cylinder 42/120PS ohv cars. Due to formidable opposition, the best it could do was ftd in the touring-car class in 1922, though a smaller 4-cylinder car won the 2·5-litre category in 1924.

Touring sv Stoewers of the period did well in the tougher types of rally, winning the 1922 Estonian Trials and the 1923 All-Russian Reliability Trial. Latterly Stoewer supported the Alpine Trial, running a team of sv straight-eight tourers in 1929, and Kordewan drove one of the new fwd 1·2-litre V-5s in 1931. MCS

STP Oil Treatment see March

Straker-Squire (GB)

This firm's first petrol cars were based on the French Cornilleau-Sainte Beuve, and one of these big 4·9-litre T-headed fours was entered for the 1907 Heavy-Car TT without success. For the RACs 2,000 Miles Trial of 1908 they tried a square-engined 1·9-litre machine, the Shamrock, which gave them a 3rd place in class, but the standard Straker-Squire of the period was the 3-litre 15, a Fedden design which distinguished itself in hill-climbs and at Brooklands alike. Witchell's streamlined single-seater, 'PDQ', ran in 2·8-litre form at the track, and managed a flying mile at over 95mph (153kph) in 1912, while in that year there were class wins at Aston Clinton, Saltburn, Caerphilly, and Pateley Bridge. In the short 1914 season Straker-Squire added 2nd fastest times of day at Caerphilly and Beacon Hill to the score, and for that year's TT they prepared a brace of 3·3-litre 4-cylinder machines for Witchell and Clement to drive. An ohc engine was tried in one of them, but was not used in the race, in spite of which Witchell finished 4th. The firm's last competition machine was the prototype of the 24/80hp ohc six, a dazzle-painted machine raced to some purpose at Brooklands in 1920–1 by Kensington Moir. With 115bhp available from 3,921cc, it attained a lap speed of 104mph (167·4kph). MCS

Strang (GB)

The success of Formula 500 racing in Britain after World War 2 possibly owed more to Colin Strang than any other, for it was he who first showed that this class could provide reasonably cheap, yet competitively fast motor sport.

His special appeared in May 1946, pioneering the classic layout of Fiat suspension and single-cylinder motorcycle engine at the rear, in this case a Vincent-HRD. For the first year he was unbeaten in the class, but thereafter the Coopers gained the ascendancy and Strang, with no interest in development or production of his design, sold his special in 1949. DF

Studebaker (US)

Up to 1930 this firm's main interest was in long-distance endurance runs. As early as 1916 a car was used to drive from Perth to Sydney in Australia, and Ab Jenkins broke the American transcontinental record twice — in

Top, 1918 Straker-Squire 24/80hp at Brooklands, c 1920. *Photo: Montagu Motor Museum*

Right, 1946 Strang 500 at Prescott. Colin Strang at the wheel. *Photo: Murray Hardy*

1926 and 1927 using a Commander Six. On the latter occasion he made the journey in 77hr 40min. In 1926, too, Harry Hartz had covered 5,000 miles in less than 5,000mins on a stock Studebaker at Culver City Speedway. A more ambitious demonstration was staged to launch the company's new straight-8s at Atlantic City track in 1928, when four cars did 30,000 miles in well under 30,000min. The fastest of them, a Commander roadster, averaged 65·31mph (105·11kph) for the first 25,000 miles and put 81·08 miles (130·49km) into the hour. A pair of 8-cylinder Presidents with sports four-seater bodywork ran steadily, if without distinction, in the 1929 Double-Twelve at Brooklands.

Studebaker took the Indianapolis 'Junk Formula' of 1930 more seriously than other makers, even sponsoring an entry in 1932 (when their finances were most uncertain) and marketing their successful racing straight-8 units, complete with four downdraught carburettors, at $750 a time in 1934. Two Studebaker Specials ran in 1930, but success came a year later, when Snowberger finished 4th. Cliff Bergere's 3rd place, at 102·6mph (165·2kph), in 1932 represented the best performance by a racer based on touring-car components, and in 1933 Studebakers filled all places from 6th to 12th inclusive. Snowberger was 8th in 1934, and Studebaker-powered independent entries ran at Indianapolis until 1939.

In 1939 one of the first 164ci (2·7-litre) Champions won the Gilmore-Yosemite event, and class victories in the 1951 and 1952 Mobilgas contests were followed by outright victories in 1954 and 1955. In 1962 there was

Stutz

a brave attempt at a GT, the 289ci (4·7-litre) V-8 Avanti, and though this failed to save Studebaker, Andy Granatelli took 29 stock-car records with the model, fitted with the optional supercharger which boosted output to 315bhp. A flying half-mile was covered at 168·15mph (270·68kph). MCS

Stutz (US)

Harry C. Stutz was the designer of the American Under-slung car and in 1911 he formed the Ideal Motor Company of Indianapolis. The first car to bear his name was completed in five weeks, and entered in the inaugural Indianapolis 500 Miles Race in 1911. Driven by Gil Anderson it finished 11th, and earned the title 'The Car that Made Good in a Day'. This remained the company's slogan for many years. It was a conventional machine with 4-cylinder T-head Wisconsin engine of 6·3 litres, and shaft drive. Production Stutzes used the same engine; a roadster was included in the range, and from 1914 onwards was named the Bearcat, one of America's most famous sporting cars. Successes in 1912 included 4th and 6th at Indianapolis (behind much larger cars), 1st and 2nd in the Illinois Trophy at Elgin, and 3rd in the Grand Prize at Milwaukee. Anderson led the 1913 Indianapolis race for a while before retiring, and Charlie Merz finished 3rd. Later in the year Anderson won the Elgin National Trophy, and on the West Coast Earl Cooper and Reeves Dutton won four important races including one at Corona, Calif., in which Cooper defeated such famous names as Oldfield, DePalma, Tetzlaff and Wishart, all in larger cars. Cooper earned the title of National Champion that year, but 1914 was a disappointing year, the most notable performance being Oldfield's 5th place at Indy, where he and his Stutz were the first American driver and car to finish. He also won the 671-mile (1,079·9km) Cactus Derby from Los Angeles to Phoenix, Arizona.

Up to 1915 all Stutz successes had been achieved with near-stock cars similar to the Bearcats that anyone could buy, but in that year Harry Stutz ordered from Wisconsin a special engine with single-ohc and 16 valves. Capacity was 296ci (4,851cc) and output 130bhp. Three of these cars were built, and were known as the 'White Squadron' Stutzes. They ran in all the major races of 1915, finishing 3rd, 4th, and 7th at Indy; 1st and 2nd at Sheepshead Bay; and 1st at Point Loma, Calif., Minneapolis, and the Elgin Road Race. The leading drivers were Cooper and Anderson, 1st and 3rd

respectively in the Drivers' National Championship, while Stutz took the AAA National Championship for makes. They achieved no important victories in 1916, although Cooper came 2nd in the Vanderbilt Cup, and only one in 1917 when Cooper again won the 250 miles race at the Chicago Board Speedway. The White Squadron cars ran again at Indy in 1919, when Eddie Hearne finished 2nd. Thereafter they were outclassed, and the company did not build any more special racing cars.

The early 1920s were a lean period for Stutz, but in 1922 the company was acquired by steel magnate Charles M. Schwab who brought in a new president, Fred E. Moskovics, and two new designers, C. R. Greuter and Paul Bastien. This team produced the Model AA Vertical Eight, a 289ci (4,736cc) single-ohc straight-8 with underslung worm final drive which allowed very low sedan bodies, as well as a speedster. Moscovics entered the speedster (known as the Black Hawk from 1927) in most of the AAA Stock Car Races on the board speedways, and had many victories in 1927 and 1928. In the latter year, the speedster had a larger engine than the touring cars, with a capacity of 298ci (4,883cc) giving 115bhp. With this car Gil Anderson set a new U.S. Stock Car record of 106·52mph (171·43kph) at Daytona, and also in 1928 there took place the famous match between Stutz and Hispano-Suiza at India-napolis. Moscovics bet C. T. Weymann that a Stutz could beat an 8-litre Hispano-Suiza on a 24-hour run; the Stutz fell out with valve trouble after 19 hours and the Hispano went on to win $25,000 for its backer. However, another Stutz later defeated the Hispano in a 3½-hour race. Stutz did not support racing after 1928, but Weymann entered a four-seater tourer at Le Mans that year. Driven by Bloch and Brisson it finished 2nd behind the Barnato/Rubin 4½-litre Bentley. Three speedsters with Weymann fabric bodies and Roots-type super-chargers ran at Le Mans in 1929 but their best place was 5th (Bouriat and Philippe). Stutzes also ran at Le Mans in 1930 and 1932 but none of these entries finished the course. In 1930 a near-standard Stutz speedster finished in 10th place at Indy at an average of 85·34mph (137·34kph) driven by L. L. Corum.

The name Black Hawk was also used for a Land Speed Record car built in the Stutz works in 1928, and designed by Frank Lockhart. It was the smallest-engined Land Speed Record car ever built, with a 16-cylinder power unit of only 3 litres' capacity, being in fact two modified

Opposite, March-Ford 701 (Chris Amon) in the 1970 Italian GP at Monza. *Photo: Geoff Goddard*

Left, 1915 Stutz 'White Squadron' car at Indianapolis. Gil Anderson at the wheel. *Photo: Indianapolis Motor Speedway*

Below, 1929 Stutz at Arnage Corner, Le Mans. G. E. T. Eyston at the wheel. *Photo: Autocar*

1912 Sunbeam team for the Coupe de l'Auto. *Photo: Montagu Motor Museum*

Opposite top, Maserati 8CM (Colin Crabbe) in a Vintage Sports Car Club meeting at Oulton Park. This car is part of the Tom Wheatcroft Grand Prix Collection at Donington Park. *Photo: Geoff Goddard*

Opposite bottom, Maserati 250F (Hans Herrmann) in the 1959 French GP at Reims. *Photo: Al Bochroch*

1914 Sunbeam in the TT. K. Lee Guinness at the wheel. *Photo: Montagu Motor Museum*

91ci (1,491·2cc) Miller engines mounted side-by-side. With twin superchargers turning at 40,000rpm, power was 400bhp, or almost as much as a 1971 Formula 1 engine delivers, from the same capacity. The Black Hawk had a highly streamlined body and spatted wheels, and ice-filled surface radiators. In February 1928 Lockhart took the car to Daytona, and reached a speed of approximately 225mph (360kph) when Black Hawk overturned and crashed into the sea. Lockhart survived but two months later, on a second attempt, a tyre blew, and he was killed instantly. GNG

Sunbeam (GB)

This famous make was first seen in competition in 1907, when Eastmead's 16/20hp came through the Irish Trials without loss of marks. By 1909 the first of Louis Coatalen's designs, the 14/18hp, was doing well in sprints and hill-climbs and before the year was out it had been joined by the original 12/16hp model with pair-cast cylinders and side valves in a T-head, a car which was to help win seven 1st places in 1910 and thirteen more (on time and formula) in 1911. Coatalen's odd-looking 'Nautilus', a racing machine with 4,256cc ohv engine, a conical nose (which caused overheating) and side-chain drive, had appeared in 1910. Much more promising was its successor, 'Toodles II', which incorporated chain-driven ohc and won three races at Brooklands in the hands of its designer, as well as doing a flying-start mile at 86·16mph (138·66kph). Coatalen's third Brooklands machine, a 6·1-litre six, reverted to side valves, but the most important development in 1911 was the entry in the Coupe de l'Auto race of a 3-litre car with monobloc engine derived from the 12/16hp. It retired, but Coatalen was back in 1912 with four improved cars, still with side valves, but with 74bhp under their bonnets which gave them a top speed of at least 90mph. This year the voiturette event was run concurrently with the Grand Prix at Dieppe, and Rigal, Resta and Caillois not only took the first three places in the Coupe de l'Auto, but also finished 3rd, 4th and 5th in the main race. The winner's average was 65·35mph (105·17kph), and the model later collected over 30 class and world records in original and modified single-seater forms, being timed

over the mile at 99·45mph (160·21kph). More creditable still was Coatalen's equal ftd at Pateley Bridge on a car with unsuitable ratios.

More power and differential-less back axles characterized the 1913 racing voiturettes, but side valves were now a trifle old-fashioned and Kenelm Lee Guinness had to be content with 3rd place. Also without differentials were Sunbeam's first GP machines, 4·5-litre sixes, which finished 3rd and 6th that year. One of these was later used for record work, averaging 90mph (144·84kph) for 1,000 miles. Another record car of 1913 used a 9-litre V-12 aero-engine, and this one put 107·95 miles (173·68km) into the hour at Brooklands, beating recent performances by Goux' Peugeot. 1914 was also a busy year for the company. The V-12 took more records; the 1913 GP cars went to America and ran without distinction at Santa Monica and Indianapolis (Grant finished 7th in the 500); and some new and Peugeot-inspired dohc 4-cylinder 16-valve machines with hemispherical combustion chambers were prepared for the TT and the Grand Prix. The TT car had 3·3 litres and 94bhp, and the Grand Prix 4·5-litre and 108bhp. In the TT, Kenelm Lee Guinness won at 56·4mph (90·77kph), putting in a record lap for the Isle of Man circuit at 59·3mph (95·43kph), but at Lyons, Resta's 5th place in the GP was Sunbeam's best. By 1915 the 1913 and 1914 GP cars and the sprint V-12 were all in America, competing at Indianapolis, Chicago (where Porporato scored a 2nd place in the 1914 car), and Sheepshead Bay; Coatalen (like Antoine Lago in World War 2) even sent a pair of cars to Indianapolis in the third year of war; the 1916 Sunbeams were entirely new 4·9-litre 6-cylinder machines credited with 157bhp. Christiaens took 4th place, Louis Chevrolet drove one later in the season, and though the cars did not start in the 1919 race, they were back in England by 1920, being handled at Brooklands by Hawker and Geach. In 1922 their engines were installed in 1921 GP chassis for the Coppa Florio, in which Segrave was 2nd and Chassagne 4th.

The first post-war racer from Wolverhampton was the fearsome 350hp, powered by an 18,322cc V-12 aero-engine. Réné Thomas made ftd with this at Gaillon in 1920. In 1921 came some new GP cars: these were 3-

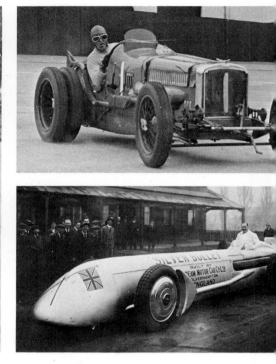

litre dohc straight-8s with dry-sump lubrication and fwb. Their output equalled that of the 1914 4·5-litres, and they ran both as Sunbeams and Talbot-Darracqs, a confusing outcome of the STD merger of 1920. Their 5th, 7th and 8th places in the Grand Prix were unimpressive, even if Haibe managed 5th at Indianapolis, and half Coatalen's new engine was used to good purpose in the invincible Talbot-Darracq voiturettes.

The 2-litre formula introduced in 1922 saw Sunbeam get away to a poor start with a 4-cylinder car. However, in the TT, Chassagne's 3-litre straight-8 defeated the Bentley opposition, and the 350hp made its first successful attack on the World Land Speed Record, Lee Guinness attaining 133·75mph (215·18kph) at Brooklands. The 1923 GP cars were much better: these were the famous 'Fiats in green paint' designed by Bertarione, with roller-bearing dohc 6-cylinder engines capable, once again, of 108bhp. They defeated the supercharged Fiats in the French GP at Strasbourg, Segrave's 1st place at 75·3mph (121·18kph) being the first British victory in this series, and also the last one in a Formula GP for 32 years. Divo came in 2nd and Guinness 4th; the former also won the Spanish GP.

A new lowered chassis and a 146bhp supercharged engine featured in 1924, but the cars did not repeat their 1923 success in France, although Segrave won at San

Top left, 1914 Sunbeam GP car. K. Lee Guinness at the wheel. *Photo: Montagu Motor Museum*

Above left, 1924 Sunbeam 2-litre 6-cylinder at Brooklands in 1928. Kaye Don at the wheel. *Photo: Montagu Motor Museum*

Above, 1926 Sunbeam 3-litre twin-cam sports car at Shelsley Walsh in 1933. *Photo: Montagu Motor Museum*

Top right, 1926 Sunbeam 4-litre V-12 at Brooklands in 1934, after re-build by Thompson & Taylor. Sir Malcolm Campbell at the wheel. *Photo: Montagu Motor Museum*

Above right, 1930 Sunbeam Silver Bullet Land Speed Record car. Kaye Don at the wheel. *Photo: Montagu Motor Museum*

1926 Sunbeam 4-litre V-12 as built for Segrave's Land Speed Record at Southport. *Photo: Montagu Motor Museum*

Sebastian. (The fatal accident to Guinness' mechanic in that race was probably more significant, since it led to the abolition of riding mechanics in *grandes épreuves*). Masetti finished 3rd in the 1925 French GP, and the 2-litre 6-cylinder had a long innings at Brooklands, taking over 30 international class records by 1930. In 1931 the engine was bored out, and it went on to collect another 16 records in the 3-litre class. Another 1925 success was 2nd place at Le Mans by the Chassagne and Davis 3-litre twin-ohc sports car.

There were no GP Sunbeams in 1926, but record cars still engaged the Company's attention. Campbell's early efforts with the 350hp V-12 had been unlucky, for successful attacks on the World Land Speed Record at Saltburn and Fanø in 1923 had been disallowed by the CSI because of the absence of approved timing apparatus. It was not until 1924 that he achieved his objective with a speed of 146·16mph (235·30kph) at Pendine, raised a year later to 150·87mph (242·81kph). In 1926 Sunbeam produced a very different type of car—a supercharged, 296bhp 4-litre V-12 made up of two 2-litre GP blocks, with which Segrave raised the record to 152·308mph (296·113kph). This Sunbeam Tiger was the last World Land Speed Record machine to be raced, at San Sebastian and Boulogne as well as at Brooklands, where it won a race at over 128mph (206kph) in 1928, and gave Malcolm Campbell the Mountain Championship in 1932.

In 1927 came Sunbeam's last successful record-breaker, the chain-driven twin-engined 1,000hp monster, a cut-price item which disposed of nearly 45 litres. On this car Segrave became the first man to exceed 200mph (320kph), his speed being 203·79mph (327·94kph). The 'Silver Bullet', built for Kaye Don in 1930, was an unsuccessful contender, and by this time STD's finances could no longer run to any kind of racing, though Duller's 3-litre sports car had won the Essex MC's Six-Hour Race at Brooklands in 1927, and Campbell tried a supercharged version of this model without success at Phoenix Park in 1929.

The Sunbeam name did not reappear in competitions until 1953, when the successful 2·3-litre Sunbeam-Talbot 90 MkII was evolved into the Alpine roadster. Sheila van Damm introduced the new model by recording 120mph (193·1kph) over the kilometre at Jabbeke, Belgium, and before the year was out Sunbeams had won the Team Prize in the Monte Carlo and Great American Mountain Rallies, four Coupes des Alpes and a Coupe des Dames in the Alpine, and an outright victory in the Victorian Alpine event in Australia. The 1954 Monte Carlo brought another team award, and in a great season Sheila van Damm captured the ladies' prizes in the Alpine, Tulip, Geneva, Viking and Austrian Alpine events. Stirling Moss also became the second driver to win an Alpine Gold Cup for three clean sheets in succession (the first had been Ian Appleyard in a Jaguar). The 1955 and 1956 Monte Carlo Rallies were also rewarding for the company. The Norwegians Malling and Fadum were outright winners in 1955, and Peter Harper was 3rd in 1956, in which year Sunbeams once again collected the team honours.

A new Sunbeam appeared in 1956, the 1,390cc 62bhp Rapier based on the Hillman Minx, and this was destined to be the most successful rally car produced by a Rootes group company. The Rapier and its sports two-seater derivative, the Alpine which joined the range for 1960, had countless successes: class victories in the 1956 and 1957 Tulip Rallies, the 1958 Scottish, the 1958 and 1960 Circuits of Ireland, the 1959 Liège-Rome-Liège, the 1960 and 1962 Acropolis, the 1961 East African Safari, the 1962 RAC British Rally (the Harper and Deane Rapier had won this event outright in 1958), and the 1962 Tour de France. There were also outright victories in both Scottish and Irish events in 1961 and 1962, and in the Monte Carlo and Alpine rallies the cars had an impressive record. These machines were also raced to some purpose: in 1956, when the Hillman ancestry was only too visible, Peter Harper and Sheila van Damm finished 2nd and 3rd in their class in the Mille Miglia, and another 2nd place was recorded in 1957. The Harper and Proctor Alpine won the Index of Thermal Efficiency at Le Mans in 1961 despite its low placing (16th) and in 1961 Rapiers took the first three places in the Improved Touring Car event at Spa. That year Peter Harper won the BRSCC Saloon Car Racing Championship.

Lean years came in 1963 and 1964, though Rootes tried hard with a new version of the Alpine, the 4·3-litre Tiger powered by an American Ford V-8 engine.

Both their 1964 Le Mans entries retired, but Harper came in 4th in the Monte Carlo, and was unlucky enough to be disqualified on a technicality in the Alpine when he was an almost certain winner.

The Chrysler-Rootes merger was fatal for a sports car powered by a rival American maker's unit, and the name of Sunbeam vanished from major rallies until 1967, when the 1-litre Rallye Imps changed emblems and ceased to be Hillmans. That year Peter Harper took 10th place in the Tulip and Rosemary Smith won the ladies' award in the Canadian Shell event. Thereafter Rootes virtually withdrew from rallying, and the Imps also appeared less frequently in saloon-car events.

It is interesting to note that quite a few of the early racers from Wolverhampton still survive in running order. Operational in Britain alone are a 1912 Coupe de l'Auto 3-litre, two 1914 TT cars, the 1920 350hp, a 1921 3-litre, a 1924 supercharged 2-litre, and the 1926 4-litre Tiger. MCS

Sunbeam-Talbot (GB)

The first cars to bear this illustrious name were Hillman- and Humber-based machines of 'promenade' type, but the advent of the 2-litre ohv 90 saloon in 1948 brought Rootes into active rallying. Murray Frame won a Coupe des Alpes that season, and the following year the Monkhouse and Hartwell car was placed 5th. By 1952 the 90 had ifs and a more powerful 2·3-litre engine. Stirling Moss took 2nd place in the Monte Carlo Rally, and the Alpine was a foretaste of later Rootes achievements: the team included Stirling Moss and Mike Hawthorn, and took three Coupes des Alpes, the first four places in their class, and the manufacturers' team prize. For their year's endeavours the firm were awarded the RAC's Dewar Trophy.

Though the saloons rallied in 1953 and 1954 were still strictly Sunbeam-Talbots, the Alpine two-seaters introduced in the former year were always Sunbeams, and the make's later exploits are described under this name. MCS

Surtees (GB)

Team Surtees introduced the TS5 from their Slough workshops for the 1969 season. Although virtually the least-experienced car-producing firm in the Formula 5000 field, they were the most successful, with victories by David Hobbs at Mondello Park and by Trevor Taylor at Koksijde, Zandvoort, Snetterton and Hockenheim. Hobbs went to America and finished as runner-up in the 1969 SCCA Formula A Championship.

Left, 1955 Sunbeam Mark III team for the Monte Carlo Rally. *Photo: Rootes Motors Ltd*

Right, 1959 Sunbeam Rapier in the Alpine Rally. *Photo: Rootes Motors Ltd*

Left, 1970 Surtees TS7 Formula 1 at Hockenheim. John Surtees at the wheel. *Photo: J. Mayrhofer*

Above, 1930 Talbot 90s before the start of the Irish GP. *Photo: Montagu Motor Museum*

In mid-1970, by which time a dozen or so TS5 and TS5A cars had been completed, the TS7 Formula 1 machine was announced, using the Cosworth-Ford DFV V-8 engine. Surtees' first victory with this model was the Oulton Park Gold Cup on 22 August, his highest placing in a Championship race being 5th in the Canadian GP.

Both models were based on a full monocoque unit, and featured Surtees' special 'Adjusta' three-piece magnesium wheels. The cars were designed by Len Terry, developed by Surtees himself, and built by his subsidiary firm TS Research and Development Ltd, who moved (with the rest of the organization) in 1969 to Edenbridge, Kent. The 1971 cars were the TS5B and TS8 Formula A/5000 and TS9 Formula 1. The latter finished 3rd in the Race of Champions at Brands Hatch. DF

Talbot (i) (GB)

It was not until 1906 that the London Talbot started to shake off its Clément-Bayard ancestry and in that year a factory-entered 12/16hp 4-cylinder machine driven by H. G. Day won its class at Blackpool Speed Trials. The 25hp Talbots with pair-cast T-head 4,155cc engines were first seen in 1908, and by 1912 these had been developed into the L-head 4·5-litres designed by G. W. A. Brown. The special sprint cars driven by Leslie Hands and Percy Lambert were the fastest machines in their class: output was around 130bhp and late in 1912 Lambert did 113·28mph (182·33kph) over the mile at Brooklands. The following February his streamlined single-seater became the first car to put over 100 miles

(160km) into the hour, and an excellent sprint and hill-climb season followed, with many class wins and fastest times of day. Although Lambert was killed at Brooklands that November, Hands continued to campaign with the 25hp Talbot during 1914, with further hill-climb successes. The ex-Lambert engine was used to good purpose in a 25/50hp driven by C. A. Vandervell in the immediate post-World War 1 period, but during Sunbeam-Talbot-Darracq's golden-years on the circuits (1921–6) their competition cars hailed from Wolverhampton or Suresnes rather than the Talbot works in London, and renaissance did not come until 1930, with the 90, descended from Georges Roesch's brilliant 1,666cc 6-cylinder 14/45 tourer unveiled at the Olympia Motor Show in 1926.

The ohv push-rod Talbot was amazingly efficient, and the racing models, sponsored by Fox and Nicholl of Tolworth, extracted 93bhp from 2·3 litres, as well as going about their business in a silence that aroused as much comment in its day as did the first XK 120 Jaguars to appear on the circuits in 1949. Their début in the Double-Twelve at Brooklands was inauspicious, as a fatal crash eliminated both Rabagliati's and Hebeler's cars, But at Le Mans they showed their form, the Lewis/Eaton 90 finished 3rd and winning the Index of Performance, while the second Talbot (Hindmarsh/Rose-Richards) was 4th. They took the first three places in their class in the TT and in the BRDC 500-Mile Race at Brooklands. In 1931 came the bigger 3-litre 105 engine, giving 140bhp in competition guise, and the Fox and Nicholl team had an excellent season. Lewis achieved a

Left, 1913 Talbot 25hp at Porthcawl Sands speed trials. *Photo: Montagu Motor Museum*

Below, 1913 Talbot 25hp single-seater. Percy Lambert at the wheel. *Photo: Montagu Motor Museum*

3rd in the Irish GP, a 4th in the TT, and 2nd in the BRDC
500 on the single-seater version. Talbots made a clean
sweep of the 3-litre category in the Double-Twelve, and
the Rose-Richards/Saunders-Davies 105 took 3rd
place at Le Mans, averaging 73·5mph (118·29kph).
Finally, Symons's 90 won a Coupe des Glaciers in the
Alpine Trial, encouraging Fox and Nicholl to enter a
full team of three cars (with standard rather than racing
four-seater bodies) for the 1932 event. All emerged with
clean sheets, sharing class honours with the German
Wanderers. Other 1932 successes included 3rd yet again
at Le Mans; 2nd, 4th and 7th places in the 1,000 Miles
Race at Brooklands; and a 3rd place for Lewis and Cobb
in the BRDC 500. Lewis and Rubin were unlucky to
skid when lying 2nd in the Mille Miglia: they finished
well down the list in 25th place. At the end of the season
the Fox and Nicholl team was disbanded, but three
105s with Wilson gearboxes (W. M. Couper, T. H.
Wisdom and H. S. Eaton) turned out for the 1934
Alpine and repeated their 1932 performance: three
Coupes des Alpes, and a tie with a German team (Adler,
this time) in the 3-litre category.

One of these Talbots, the famous BGH 23, was
subsequently acquired by Couper and fitted with the
3,378cc 110 engine, in which guise it could do 140mph
(226kph), and won an Outer Circuit Race at Brooklands
in 1938 at 119·85mph (192·88kph). MCS

Talbot (ii) see Darracq

Taraschi (I)

After building the Urania sports car and subsequently
the Giaur in partnership with Giannini, designer/driver
Berardo Taraschi of Teramo began constructing racing
cars under his own name to the newly introduced Formula
Junior of 1958–9. The FJ Taraschi had the usual Fiat-
based engine mounted at the front, the driver's cockpit
was set left of the transmission line, and suspension was
by coil springs and wishbones at the front, with—
unusually on an FJ—a De Dion type rear axle.

Early successes fell to this car in Italian National
races at Syracuse and Vallelunga in 1958, with Zannini
driving, and in 1959 Colin Davis, son of S. C. H. Davis
of Le Mans and Bentley fame, won FJ races at Naples,
Pau and Albi with a Taraschi. Berardo Taraschi himself
won at Castello and Salerno that season, and in 1960
was 1st at Caserta, but by then the British rear-engined

Juniors were proving much faster, and Taraschi went
back to tuning and purveying 'souped up' Fiats. CP

Tarf (I)

Two Italcorsa 'Tarf' record cars were built in Rome in
1948–50 by racing driver and engineer Piero Taruffi, in
collaboration with Ing. Giannini and Luigi Forzi. Both
cars were of *bisiluro* or twin-fuselage construction, with
the driver and two wheels encased in one nacelle, the
engine, chain transmission and two wheels in the other,
and low-drag housings connecting the two, the top layer
hingeing to act as an air brake. The objectives were
reduced frontal area, less weight, and aerodynamic
stability, aided by an anti-lift aerofoil between the
fuselages. Levers replaced the steering wheel, and Tarf I,
fitted with a Guzzi 120° V-twin racing motorcycle
engine, weighed only 560lb (254·01kg).

With this car Taruffi broke the Class I (500cc) International flying kilometre record at 128·86mph
(207·40kph) on the Bergamo-Brescia autostrada in
1948. Between then and 1957 he set over 20 further
records, replacing the Guzzi unit with a 4-cylinder
Gilera, and using first a stretch of the Appian Way,
then Montlhéry, then Monza, for his forays. His highest
speed in Tarf I was 133mph (214·8kph) with the engine
bored out to 550cc to take Class H records; he also
fitted a 350cc Gilera engine for Class J figures, taking the
1-hour record at 118·1mph (190·1kph).

In 1949–50 Taruffi built Tarf II to take a bigger 1,720cc
two-stage supercharged Maserati engine. This time the
nacelles were frameless—i.e. self-supporting monocoques as later used on F1 cars—and the radiator was
housed in one of the aerofoils. With this clever machine
Taruffi broke the Class E flying kilometre record at
185·41mph (294·32kph) in 1951, and set 10 further,
longer-distance records between then and 1956, including
the 100 miles at 140·30mph (225·8kph). The Maserati-
engined Tarf II was subsequently taken to England in
1957 for demonstration at Silverstone by Taruffi. CP

Tatra (CS)

The make of Tatra is one of the European pioneers. It
first appeared in 1897 as the Nesselsdorf, taking its
name from the town of its production (now called
Kopřivnice) in the old Austro-Hungarian monarchy.
The first competition entry was for a meeting in Vienna,
held on a racecourse and won by Theodor von Liebieg

Below, 1934 Talbot 105. W. M. Couper at
the wheel. *Photo: Monty Bowers*

Right, 1924 Tatra Type II, class winner in
Solitude races. Josef Vermirovsky at the
wheel. *Photo: Vladimír Havránek Collection*

in his Nesselsdorf car. In 1900 he competed in many events in Austria, Germany and France and was very successful, using a special, stripped version of the standard model. But these first promising attempts came to an end very soon when Nesselsdorf concentrated on touring cars and gave up competitions, with the exception of the Austrian Alpine Trial of 1911. After World War 1, with their home town now part of the new Czechoslovakia, the firm adopted the name Tatra and returned to motor sport.

The 3·5-litre type T and 6·5-litre Type U which had originated in 1914 as Nesselsdorfs, were used for long-distance trials as well as for hill-climbs. But Hans Ledwinka, technical director of Tatra, introduced his revolutionary Type 11 with central tubular frame and air-cooled 2-cylinder opposed engine in 1923. This became the basis for a number of very successful competition cars. The Type 11 with two-seater body, increased engine output of about 35bhp and a maximum speed of 90mph (144kph) gained a 1-2-3 class victory in the Solitude Race of 1924 and in 1925 two of them won their class in the Targa Florio. The Type 17 of 1926, a water-cooled 6-cylinder of 1,930cc followed and in its sports version participated in many events, mainly hill-climbs. Tatra won the 1,500cc team award in the 1932 Alpine Trial. The rear-engined streamlined Types 77, 87 and 97 were only seen in long-distance trials, such as the Czechoslovak 1000 Miles.

After World War 2 several versions appeared with a V-8 cylinder engine, mounted ahead of the rear axle. There were 2-litre sports cars and Formula 2 cars and a 2·5-litre Formula 1 monoposto. They were seen mainly in Czechoslovakia and did not compete in international events. The same happened to a Formula Junior Tatra of 1963 with 4-cylinder 1·1-litre engine. The Tatra 603, a streamlined 2·5-litre V-8 saloon, did appear in various international events, and gained 4th and 5th places in the 1967 Marathon de la Route at the Nürburgring. HON

Taydec (GB)

Originally known as the Tadec, this was a Group 6 sports car built in 1970 by Tom Clapham of Keighley, Yorkshire, powered by a Cosworth FVC 2-litre engine. Design was based on a central monocoque, and suspension followed orthodox principles. The 1971 Mark 3 sold for £5,250 with engine and gearbox. DF

Tecno (I)

The largest and currently the most successful of the specialist Italian competition car constructors is Tecno. After building karts for two years, they introduced their first Formula 4 cars, powered by 250cc Ducati engines, in 1964, and the following year a Fiat 850-engined car was produced for the national 850 Formula. Their first F3 car appeared in July 1966; Cosworth-powered, it was an unusual-looking machine with a centre fuel tank and

Left, 1949 Tatra Formula 1 in practice for the 1950 Czech GP. Adolf Vermirovsky at the wheel. *Photo: Vladimír Havránek Collection*

Right, 1949 Tatraplan Type 602 sports car before the start of the Czech GP. *Photo: Vladimír Havránek Collection*

its seat very far forward. Carlo Facetti drove the car in its début at Mugello, finished 4th. Facetti, Baghetti and Regazzoni drove a team of similar cars in the 1967 Temporada with little success, but back in Europe that season a stumpy but conventional F3 car was built which scored immediate success. That season Tecnos became the F3 cars to beat in Italy and Europe, and in 1968 many orders were taken and a Cosworth-powered F2 car made its first appearance at Barcelona in Regazzoni's hands. No fewer than 10 F2 and 43 F3 cars were sold that year, and many F3 successes were scored by Wissel, Jaussaud and Cevert. The cars were small, well-balanced and extremely manageable, but as more were produced the spares situation became almost impossible for a serious racing programme. But they were inexpensive and the company stuck to early delivery dates; above all they were extremely competitive. Tecno produced their own Ford 105E-based engine, together with the normal Novamotor, Holbay and other options.

Their Formula 2 programme had rather stretched the Pederzani brothers' resources, and in 1969 they stuck to a two-car Shell-backed works team with Cevert and Galli driving, Cevert scoring their first major success at Reims that season. In Formula 3, two successive Monaco victories headed their list of successes, but during the 1969 season many owners were upset by the spares situation and by the short life of some components, particularly wheels. At the start of 1969 the younger

Left, 1964 Tatra Type 603 in the Vltava Rally. *Photo: Vladimir Havránek Collection*

Right, 1960 Terrier Mark 2 at Brands Hatch. Brian Hart at the wheel. *Photo: R. C. Loveday*

Left, 1966 Tecno Formula 3 at Mugello. Carlo Facetti at the wheel. *Photo: Attualfoto*

Right, 1969 Tecno Formula 2 at Tulln-Langenlebarn. Francois Cevert at the wheel. *Photo: Autosport*

brother, Gianfranco, took over sole control of the company, which continued as Italy's fastest-growing and most successful single-seater constructor.

In 1970 Regazzoni's F2 Team won the European Championship with four outright victories, and team-mates Cevert and Salvati scored one major F2 win each. In F3, Tecno notched seven major wins and the company continued in these classes for 1971. DCN

Terrier (GB)
The original Terrier of 1959 was an 1172 Formula car designed by Len Terry and raced by Brian Hart, with spaceframe chassis and aluminium bodywork. Further examples were made at Thornwood, Essex, and other designs were developed, including a Formula Junior single-seater. Although produced for only a relatively short period. Terriers proved competitive in the 1172 Formula and its successor F1200 throughout the next decade. DF

Thomas (US)
The E. R. Thomas Company of Buffalo, N.Y., is chiefly celebrated in motoring history for their victory in the New York to Paris Race of 1908, but they had made several sorties into racing before that. For the 1905 Vanderbilt Cup the company built a 60hp 6-cylinder car with very long bonnet and drivers' seat behind the rear axle, in the manner of some modern dragsters. Driven

Seine-Inférieure
Grand Prix de l'A. C. F. - 6 et 7 Juillet 1908
STRANG sur voiture THOMAS
L'Hirondelle - Paris

Top, 1908 Thomas GP car. Lewis Strang at the wheel. *Photo: Montagu Motor Museum*

Top right, 1923 Leyland Eight (Thomas Special) at Brooklands. J. G. Parry Thomas at the wheel. *Photo: Montagu Motor Museum*

Above, 1926 Thomas 'flat-iron' Special at the pits at Brooklands, c 1928. *Photo: David Hodges Collection*

Above right, 1923 Higham Special 'Babs' as raced at Brooklands in 1926 by Parry Thomas. *Photo: Montagu Motor Museum*

by Montague Roberts this car finished 5th in the eliminating trials, but was not chosen for the race itself. For the 1906 Vanderbilt Thomas secured the services of the French drivers Le Blon and Caillois, in addition to Roberts. Three 115hp cars ran in the Eliminating Trials, Le Blon qualifying for the race itself. He finished 8th (still running when the race was stopped), making the fastest lap at 67·6mph (108·79kph), and being the highest placed American entrant. In 1908 Thomas made their first and only entry into European racing, sending one 115hp car to the French Grand Prix. It had a 11,321cc 4-cylinder engine and chain drive. Driven by Lewis Strang, it retired on the 5th lap. Three cars ran again in the 1908 Vanderbilt Cup, the best result being George Salzman's 4th place.

Three months before the Vanderbilt Cup, in July 1908, Thomas achieved their greatest fame with victory in the New York to Paris Race. Driven by George Schuster and Montague Roberts, a stock 72hp 6-cylinder tourer covered the 12,116 miles (19,500km) of motoring in 170 days. GNG

Thomas Specials (GB)

The Thomas Specials were built at Brooklands by the great Welsh designer–driver, J. G. Parry Thomas. The first two were developed from Leyland Eight luxury cars and, with increasingly streamlined bodywork, became the most famous cars at Brooklands from 1924 to 1926,

running quietly on soft suspension to take the lap record to over 125mph (200kph), win races innumerable and break a great many World and International class records, including the coveted one-hour honour. Thomas built a second of these 7·2-litre straight-8 ohc racing cars with torsion-bar suspension for Capt J. E. P. Howey and another for himself after he had written the first off in a crash at Boulogne.

He also built a Thomas Special at the opposite extreme, in the form of the 1·8-litre single-seater which was successful at Brooklands in 1925, winning a *News of the World* long-distance handicap. Thomas then turned to making two ultra-low straight-8 Thomas Specials intended for long duration races with road-circuit type corners. These were delayed but ran in a number of 1926 events and Thomas used one of them to capture the class hour record at an impressive 115mph (185·1kph).

Anxious to go even faster than the speeds of which his big Leyland-Thomas was capable, Thomas bought the Liberty aero-engined Higham Special, a chain-drive monster with the biggest engine ever used in a Brooklands two-seater, after the death of its creator, Count Zborowski. He modified it to his own ideas, with improved streamlining. Renamed 'Babs', this enormous car broke the Land Speed Record several times at Pendine, in Wales, took short distance Class A records at Brooklands and was raced there by Thomas and Cobb. In the attempt to take the fastest-ever title from Campbell in March 1927, 'Babs' crashed on Pendine sands, killing its driver. It lay buried under the beach until dug up for restoration by Owen Wyn Owen in 1969. WB

Thorne Engineering Special (US)

Joel Thorne, a 23-year-old millionaire who had driven an Alfa Romeo into 6th place in the 1937 Vanderbilt Cup, came to prominence in 1938 when he entered a pair of cars designed by Leo Goossen for the Indianapolis 500 Miles, run that year under European formula rules. Thorne favoured a centrifugally-blown dohc 3-litre 6-cylinder unit mounted in a chassis with all-round transverse suspension. Jimmy Snyder retired early after leading the race, but Thorne himself (who carried two-way radio on his car) came in 9th. The same machines and drivers contested the 1939 race, Snyder taking 2nd place at 114·245mph (183·868kph) while Thorne was 7th, following this up with 5th in 1940. For the 1941 event he entered a 3-litre with six Winfield carburettors and an unblown 4·5-litre, but the new version failed to qualify and Thorne crashed the blown car. More successful was a comeback staged in 1946, when George Robson drove a supercharged 3-litre to victory at 114·82mph (184·83kph), one of only two 6-cylinder cars to win at Indianapolis. Output of this engine may have been as high as 400bhp: a 4·5-litre entrusted to Rudolf Caracciola was crashed with near-fatal results in practice. Though Thorne entered again in 1947 and 1948, on neither occasion did his car qualify. MCS

Th. Schneider (F)

Théophile Schneider had been one of the founders of the Rochet-Schneider company before he started building cars on his own at Besançon in 1910. For the 1912 Coupe de l'Auto, Schneider entered two cars powered by 2·8-litre 4-cylinder engines as used in the firm's touring cars, and sharing with the latter the dashboard-radiator layout which characterized all pre-1914 Th. Schneiders. Croquet finished 4th. In the 1912 Grand Prix de France Th. Schneiders finished 2nd, 4th and 6th (Champoiseau, Croquet, and Nicodemi respectively), and encouraged by these successes with largely standard cars the firm entered four 5·5-litre cars in the next year's Grand Prix de l'Automobile Club de France. It was remarked that they lacked speed but that their cornering powers were good, and their best position was Champoiseau's 7th. Three cars ran in the 1914 Grand Prix, this time with 4·4-litre engines; again Champoiseau was their best performer but he could manage no higher than 9th.

During the 1920s the firm made a good 2-litre sports tourer, but did not figure very prominently in the sport. Two cars ran at Le Mans in 1926 and 1927, the best performance being that of Tabourin and Lefranc who finished 6th in the 1926 event. The firm continued until 1929. GNG

Thunderbolt (GB)

This was the car built in 1937 by Capt G. E. T. Eyston to raise the Land Speed Record above the 301mph (484kph) achieved by Campbell's Bluebird in 1935. It was powered by two Rolls-Royce 'R' type engines totalling over 73 litres capacity and developing 6,000bhp. The engines were mounted side-by-side at the front of the car, and were geared together driving the rear wheels. There were six wheels, a 4-wheel bogie at the front steering, as on a heavy lorry. A 3-speed gearbox was fitted giving 100mph (160kph) in bottom gear, and 220mph (354kph) in second. Thunderbolt was built at

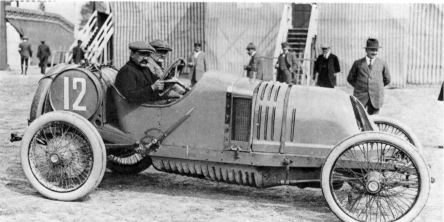

Top, 1938 Thorne Engineering Special, winner at Indianapolis in 1946. George Robson at the wheel. *Photo: Indianapolis Motor Speedway*

Centre, 1913 Th Schneider GP car. Fernand Gabriel at the wheel. *Photo: Montagu Motor Museum*

Above, 1937 Thunderbolt at Bonneville, refuelling between runs. *Photo: Keystone*

the Bean works at Tipton, Staffordshire. In October 1937 Eyston set a new record of 312mph (502·1kph) at Bonneville. The following year the car was modified, with coil springs instead of leaves, and without the tail-fin. In this form it achieved 345·49mph (555·94kph) in August 1938, only to see John Cobb's Railton Mobil Special cap this with 350·20mph (563·60kph). The next day Eyston did 357·50mph (575·30kph), the highest speed that Thunderbolt reached. The car is still in existence in New Zealand. GNG

Above, 1967 Titan Formula 3. *Photo: Doug Nye Collection*

Left, 1952 Tojeiro-Bristol. *Photo: Autosport*

Titan (GB)

The first Titan was a 1965 sports-racing one-off, used by Picko Troberg in Sweden for some time with a 2·5-litre Maserati engine. The Mark 2 car was a Formula 2 design, raced by Roy Pike, who in 1967 scored several major wins with the Formula 3 Mark 3 model. The proprietor of the firm, Charles Lucas, was also very successful in 1968 and 1969 with the Mark 3A. Other successful drivers of this period included Tony Trimmer, Tony Dron and Nick Brittan. The firm started in the ex-BRP Highgate workshops, moving after a spell in

Above left, 1960 Tojeiro Formula Junior at Little Rissington sprint meeting in 1962. E. Pound at the wheel. *Photo: Michael Ware*

Left, 1959 Tornado Typhoon at Silverstone in 1961. David Wansborough at the wheel. *Photo: Michael Ware*

King's Lynn to more extensive premises at Huntingdon when the engine preparation and general engineering side of the business expanded. A Formula Ford variant had been available in 1968 (the Mark 4), with space-frame chassis and Specialized Mouldings body similar to the F3 machines, and the Mark 5 constituted the majority of 1969 car sales. During 1970 production of the Mark 6 FF car exceeded 80, most being sold to the United States, although Chris Meek won the FF Tate Championship in the North of England. DF

Tojeiro (GB)

The twin-tube Tojeiro chassis of 1950 was based on the Lester, being used successfully with JAP, Lea-Francis and MG engines. The car that put John Tojeiro's little Hertfordshire works on the map was Cliff Davis' LOY 500 of 1952, a Bristol-engined sports car with Cooper-type transverse-leaf independent suspension and 'Barchetta' body styling copied from the Ferrari Mille Miglia Type 166. This car achieved an incredible run of successes in British Club racing, and subsequently became the prototype of the production AC Ace.

In 1955 Tojeiro adopted a multi-tubular space-frame, with De Dion rear end, available in various sizes up to the 250bhp D-type Jaguar-engined model which Jack Brabham raced in 1957. This type was raced also for the Ecurie Ecosse by various drivers, but never proved as successful as the smaller cars of such drivers as Jim Fiander and Chric Threlfall. Another space-frame model, with single disc transmission brake, ran in the 1958 Le Mans with 1,098cc Coventry-Climax engine.

In 1960 some rear-engined Formula Juniors were made, both under the Tojeiro name and as the Britannia, a firm for which Tojeiro had done some design work, and which he took a further interest in after it had failed. The cars were not successful under either name.

Rear-engined prototypes were designed for GT racing up to 1962, for Buick, Jaguar, Ford and Coventry-Climax engines. The last-named type was adopted by the Ecurie Ecosse to race at Le Mans, but handling problems supervened after teething troubles had been overcome. Ecurie Ecosse developed the design and built some more Coventry-Climax-engined cars, but these were attended by no better fortune. DF

Tornado (GB)

The Tornado, built at Rickmansworth, Hertfordshire, from 1958 to 1964, started as just another kit-built sports car, using a straightforward ladder frame. The company built their own bodies in a variety of styles. The two directors, however, pursued a very active competitions policy, and regularly entered teams in club relay races with considerable success. With the Ford Classic-engined Talisman saloon model, both Colin Hextall and Bill Woodhouse achieved many class successes, and private owners also raced several examples. Eventually, however, the firm became insolvent, and their successors were less interested in the sport. DF

Toyota (J)

One of the mighty Japanese combines actively concerned with motor sport, Toyota see Nissan-Datsun as their deadly rival. Their aggressive-looking 2000GT of 1966 first commanded European attention, with its mid-mounted 6-cylinder 1,998cc dohc engine producing some 200bhp at 7,200rpm. Disc brakes were featured all round and top speed was quoted as 155mph (250kph).

Above, 1969 Toyota 7, winner of the Fuji 200-Mile Race. Minoru Kawai at the wheel. *Photo: J. K. Yamaguchi*

Right, 1928 Tracta at Le Mans. J. A. Grégoire at the wheel. *Photo: courtesy J. A. Grégoire*

Below, 1935 Triumph Southern Cross on a trials hill in Devonshire. *Photo: Montagu Motor Museum*

Right, 1928 Triplex Special at Daytona. *Photo: Montagu Motor Museum*

Right below, 1954 Triumph TR2 in driving tests of Thames Estuary Anniversary Rally, 1956. *Photo: Charles Dunn*

The type was used quite widely in national racing, and Toyota then developed specialized Group 7 machines which raced successfully from 1968.

The 1968 car was a 3-litre lightweight model, using a 2,988cc 90° V-8 quad-cam engine producing some 330bhp at 8,000rpm. Transmission was via a 5-speed ZF gearbox and with an all-alloy monocoque chassis the Toyota G7 won most of the major home events and finished 4th, 5th and 6th behind much more powerful Can-Am G7 machines in the Fuji 200 of 1968.

A new spaceframe chassis was later devised to accept a 5-litre V-8 engine developed from the 3-litre unit. This eventually appeared with twin exhaust-driven turbochargers in 1969–70, producing 800bhp at 8,000rpm. The all-alloy engine had four valves per cylinder, Nippondenso fuel injection (Bosch licenses) and dimensions of 102mm × 76mm. The 5-litre units performed admirably against the larger 6-litre Nissan R-series cars and attracted interest from Trojan in England, who acquired an engine for evaluation in a McLaren M8C chassis owned by Ecurie Evergreen. The Toyota G7 itself featured a large chassis-mounted wing and was driven through an indigenous ASCO 5-speed transaxle system.

The company also showed interest in rallying with specially-developed Monte Corona GSS models, and the 1600GT coupé also made competition appearances. This used a front-mounted, rear-drive, 4-cylinder 1,587cc engine with dohc, producing 110bhp at 6,200rpm. DCN

Tracta (F)

Designed and built by Jean Grégoire, the Tracta was a typical light French sports car of the 1920s, unusual only in employing front-wheel drive. It was powered by a 1,100cc SCAP engine, and often ran with a supercharger. Its first event was the 1926 Coupe de l'Armistice rally, after which Grégoire took it straight to the Lévy-Saint-Nom hill-climb where he made fastest time of the day. Tractas ran regularly at Le Mans between 1927 and 1930, finishing 2nd in their class in 1928 and winning it in 1929 (Balard and Debeugny). In 1929 Grégoire's partner and backer Pierre Fenaille designed an unconventional car with 2-cylinder opposed piston 2-stroke Cozette engine and aerodynamic body not unlike that of the 'tank' Chenard-Walckers. It ran under the Tracta name at Le Mans but retired after four hours. Tractas also competed in the 1927 Florio Cup, where one was 2nd in class; the Georges Boillot Cup, Bol d'Or, and other races as well as numerous hill-climbs. After 1930 Grégoire did not race his cars any longer, although private entrants continued to do so. One Tracta ran at

Le Mans in 1933, finishing 9th, and two in 1934, of which one finished 19th and the other retired. GNG

Triplex Specials (US)

The Philadelphia-built Triplex Special of 1928 was probably the crudest Land Speed Record car ever built. It certainly had the largest capacity, with three Liberty V-12 aero engines totalling 81 litres, and developing about 1,200bhp. Two of the engines were mounted side-by-side behind the driver, with the third ahead of him. The rear engines were connected by bevel gears to the axle, while the front engine drove by shaft between the other two to its own bevel gear in the centre of the rear axle. The car was sponsored by J. H. White (hence its alternative name of White-Triplex), and driven by Ray Keech, who reached a speed of 207·55mph (333·98kph) in 1928, beating Campbell's record by less than 1mph. During an untimed run Keech estimated that he was doing 220mph (354kph). Later, Segrave took the record to 231·44mph (372·46kph) with the Golden Arrow, and in attempting to beat this, the Triplex crashed at Daytona, killing its driver Lee Bible. GNG

Triumph (GB)

The 832cc hydraulic-braked Super 7 of 1928, like the MG Midget, was produced in 750cc blown form in 1929 and 1930, though it lacked the success of either the

Austin or the MG, and was strictly an also-ran in the TT as well as at Brooklands. The little Triumphs did much better in the Antipodes, where they won three of the first four places in the Royal Australian Automobile Club's 1930 trials, and went on to break the Brisbane–Sydney light-car record in 1931. Donald Healey, however, finished 7th in the 1930 Monte Carlo Rally, and in 1932 Mrs Vaughan's Triumph took the Coupe des Dames. Altogether faster were the ioe Southern Cross 4-cylinder cars first seen in action in the 1933 Alpine Trial; the following year the works machines (Leverett, Ridley and Holbrook) collected the 1,100cc team award, and there were also a couple of individual Glacier Cups for the make.

A 2-litre dohc straight-8 on Alfa Romeo lines, the first car to bear the name of Dolomite, was, by contrast, an ill-starred venture: Healey charged a train in the road section of the 1935 Monte Carlo, and only managed 8th in 1936. Apart from a record lap by a youthful A. P. R. Rolt in the 1937 Leinster Trophy the 8-cylinder Triumph faded quickly out of the picture.

The 1936 Welsh Rally saw Boughton's 2-litre ioe 6-cylinder Southern Cross the outright winner, and there was another Glacier Cup for Healey in the Alpine, this time on a prototype ohv 14hp saloon. These 4-cylinder models were destined to do well in British rallies, figuring in the road sections as well as the *concours d'élégance*.

Under Standard ownership, Triumph produced nothing sporting until the arrival of the tough, simple and economical TR2 in 1953; this used a 1,991cc 90bhp version of the 4-cylinder push-rod Standard Vanguard unit. It was a natural for club-racing and rallies, and had a long career, its major 1954 successes being 1st and 2nd

places in the RAC Rally (Wallwork and Cooper), and the team prize and a Coupe des Alpes in the Alpine (Gatsonides was their star performer). There were also demonstrations of reliability both at Le Mans and in the TT, though their best placings were 15th and 19th respectively. In 1955 the Triumphs turned out for the Mille Miglia and Le Mans, the three TRs finishing 14th, 15th and 19th on the latter occasion. During 1958 the factory tried 2·2-litre engines in their competition cars, and continued to achieve good placings in rallies.

From 1959 onwards the company tried different models in different events. In the 1959, 1960 and 1961 Le Mans races they entered 2-litre TRS-type dohc prototypes, these being seen at first with the traditional TR shape. All retired in 1959, but they took 15th, 18th and 19th places in 1960, and had worked up as high as 9th by the time they disappeared from racing. The new all independently sprung 948cc Herald appeared in rallies in 1959, and Lewis won a Coupe des Alpes in the Alpine. The small cars were used again in 1960, but the make's principal honours (team prize in the RAC and a class win for Seigle-Morris and Elford in the Tulip) were scored on the old TRs. Mabbs' Herald won the 1961 Tulip Rally, and in 1962 Triumph fielded their improved 2,138cc TR4s, these gaining a class victory and a Coupe des Alpes in the Alpine.

In 1963 there was a brief try with the small 6-cylinder Vitesse saloon, and at Le Mans in 1964 the firm ran a couple of 1,147cc Spitfire hardtops with all-synchromesh boxes, Hobbs and Slotemaker finishing 21st. Spitfires were used again in 1965 for the Monte Carlo Rally, Le Mans (where they took 13th and 14th places) and the Alpine (where they won their class). A 3-carburettor 2000 saloon had also been prepared for the Monte Carlo, and

Left, 1959 Triumph TR3 driven by Eric Hodson in 1960 Monte Carlo Rally. *Photo: Autosport*

Above, 1960 Triumph TRS at Le Mans Test Day. Peter Bolton at the wheel. *Photo: Standard-Triumph Ltd*

Left, 1964 Triumph Spitfire Le Mans coupé. *Photo: Standard-Triumph Ltd*

Below, 1970 Triumph GT6 leads a Datsun in SCCA club racing. *Photo: Al Bochroch Collection*

later in the season this model took 2nd and 3rd places in the Welsh Rally, and 5th in the RAC.

Both the 2000 and the Spitfire were campaigned in 1966, when the make's best showings were 4th in the Circuit of Ireland and 7th in the Geneva Rally. TR4s finished (though well down on the list) in both the Sebring 12 Hours and the Daytona Continental 24 in America. In 1968 the Mandeville and Allison 2000 was 3rd in the East African Safari, but Triumph were transferring their allegiance to derivatives of the 2000 with 2·5-litre fuel-injection engines, these cars turning out both for the Safari and the RAC Rally. An 11th place in the latter indicated a degree of promise, and in the 1970 World Cup Rally the 2·5 PIs were 2nd and 4th (Culcheth/Syer and Hopkirk/Nash/Johnston respectively). MCS

Triumph in America: The Triumph TR series has been a winner in US club racing since 1954 when Robert Salzgaber won the national SCCA E production title. The most consistent TR driver has been Bob Tullius, four times national champion, of Falls Church, Va. As SCCA production sports car classes are based on performance potential, rather than engine displacement, 1971 regulations moved the Triumph GT6, class E winner in 1970, up to class D, where it faces such competition as the class-winning Datsun-SRL. In the small-bore category, a Triumph Spitfire, driven by John Kelly of Group 44, captured the 1970 F production title. ARB

Tui (GB)

This Formula 3 design, the work of Alan McCall, was unusual in featuring a full monocoque up to the seat bulkhead, the engine then forming a fully stressed member. Production of this and a Formula 2/B/Atlantic model was planned for 1971. DF

Turcat-Méry (F)

From 1902 to 1911 the Turcat-Méry was the lesser-known *alter ego* of the De Dietrich, though in fact Turcat and Méry were responsible for the design of both cars. Competition machines, however, tended to carry the De Dietrich name. Rougier finished 9th in the Paris–Madrid in 1903 on a Turcat-Méry, later breaking the record at Mont Ventoux hill-climb in the snow. Yet another ftd in this event followed in 1904, when the French Gordon Bennett Eliminating Trials saw two 12·8-litre 4-cylinder Turcat-Mérys as well as an identical team of De Dietrichs; Rougier on one of the former was selected for the ACF's team at Homburg. He finished 3rd in the big race at 46·8mph (75·32kph), but though De Dietrichs continued to race, nothing more was heard of Turcat-Méry until 1911, when Rougier won the first

Above, 1970 Triumph 2·5 PI in Swedish Rally. *Photo: John Davenport*

Right, 1961 Turner-Climax at a Yorkshire sprint meeting. Mike Brown at the wheel. *Photo: Peter Craven*

1956 Turner 950 at Gerard's Bend, Mallory Park in 1959. Bob Gerard at the wheel. *Photo: Dr K. E. Jolles*

Left, 1970 Tui Formula 3. *Photo: Autosport*

Right, 1921 Turcat-Méry team for the Circuit de Corse. *Photo: T. A. S. O. Mathieson Collection*

Monte Carlo Rally in a 4-cylinder saloon.

The make's post-1918 appearances were less frequent, but in the 1921 Circuit de Corse, Rougier's sports model came in 2nd behind a Bignan, other Turcat-Mérys finishing 3rd, 4th, 5th and 6th. Some advanced 4-cylinder ohc sports cars were made in 1923–4, but by this time the company was on its last legs, and they distinguished themselves only in hill-climbs such as Alpilles and Mont Ventoux. MCS

Turner (GB)

John H. Turner of Wolverhampton indulged in a variety of interesting projects during the 1950s, including a 4-cylinder 500 engine and a 2-litre engine (used in the 1955 Phoenix sports car), both with ohc. Success throughout the world was earned by the neat Turner Sports, available as standard with 803 or 948cc BMC engine, and for sports racing with Coventry-Climax units. From 1960 to 1962 the car to beat in the small production sports class was the incredible 'Tatty Turner' of Pat Fergusson. Such up-and-coming drivers as Warwick Banks and John Miles were earning their laurels in British Club races in 1963, and ex-ERA driver Bob Gerard was at one time a leading Turner exponent. In 1962 a new design was introduced, retaining the original chubby shape but with a fibreglass semi-monocoque body reinforced with steel tubing. Although production ceased in 1966, Geoff Daryn was still winning regularly in 1970 with his 1600 Ford-engined car. DF

TVR (GB)

Designed initially in 1954 as a kit-built sports car, the first well-known model of this Blackpool, Lancashire, firm was the Grantura of 1957. There was a choice of

car in the Canadian, United States and Mexican GPs at the close of the season and proved its worth beyond all doubt. He led at St Jovite until a front stub axle broke, and repeated the performance at Watkins Glen, lapping all but Rodriguez in 2nd place then suffering engine failure at three-quarters distance. In Mexico his was the only car to challenge the Ferraris until steering problems slowed him and a collision with a dog put him out. Two cars were run in 1971, for Stewart and Cevert. Stewart was 2nd in the South African, and won the Spanish GP. DCN

U2 see Mallock

Unipower (GB)
The Unipower GT was built in Perivale, Middlesex, by Universal Power Drives Ltd, from 1966 to 1970 and featured a fibreglass body cloaking a tubular space-frame accepting Mini components. Under the guidance of Andrew Hedges, a long-distance race exponent, several special competition cars were prepared and ran with some success, the most ambitious being Stanley Robinson's FVA Cosworth-powered version. DF

Urania see Giaur

Vanwall (GB)
C. A. (Tony) Vandervell had achieved some success with his 4·5-litre Ferrari, modified and known as the Thinwall Special in recognition of the bearings of his own manufacture that were used, before embarking as a manufacturer of racing cars in his own right. The first chassis, built by Cooper, clearly borrowed from Ferrari

Above left, 1961 TVR at Silverstone in 1963. J. Woollen at the wheel. *Photo: Michael Ware*

Left, 1970 Tyrrell-Ford Formula 1 at Oulton Park. Jackie Stewart at the wheel. *Photo: Autocar*

Right, 1969 Unipower GT driven at Mugello by Piers Weld-Forester and Dominique Martin. *Photo: Autosport*

Centre right, 1956 Vanwall Formula 1 at Silverstone. Stirling Moss at the wheel. *Photo: Autosport*

Bottom right, 1961 Vanwall Formula 1 at Silverstone. John Surtees at the wheel. *Photo: Keystone*

Ford or other engines, but with the notably short wheelbase and Volkswagen-type suspension, the handling at high speed was not such as to encourage competitive use. This was changed in 1962 with a new multi-tubular chassis and double wishbone suspension, and thereafter the cars achieved success in various branches of the sport. In 1963 Tom Entwistle, with an MGB-engined Grantura, won the Freddie Dixon Trophy in British make races. In 1966 Gerry Marshall scored a number of victories with his Griffith model, with Ford V8 engine, and John Akers proved the make's suitability for autocross. A similar situation prevailed in 1969 and 1970, when Mike Day was the British National Autocross Champion and Rod Longton took the STP sports-car racing championship, both with examples of the Ford V-6-engined Tuscan. DF

Tyrrell (GB)
When British entrant Ken Tyrrell bought March chassis for the 1970 Formula 1 season, he hedged his bet by commissioning a car of his own. Design of this car was the responsibility of Derek Gardner, an engineer whom Tyrrell had met when Harry Ferguson Research co-operated on development of the Matra MS84 4-wheel-drive vehicle.

Work began early in 1970 and half-way through the season outside contractors began construction of a simple, sturdy and lightweight monocoque chassis designed to accept the Cosworth-Ford DFV engine in which Tyrrell and driver Jackie Stewart had so much faith. The car was very conventional in appearance, with a Matra MS80-like concentration of weight within the wheelbase, and its existence was a well-kept secret until its press unveiling the day after the Austrian GP.

Stewart gave it its début in the Oulton Park Gold Cup, and although put out of the contest by a sticking throttle he rejoined and put up a great display of sheer driving skill, established a new lap record in the process. The team were not happy with the car's development as yet and the March ran in the Italian GP, but Tyrrell's declared policy was to run whichever chassis proved quickest in practice for any given event. Stewart ran the

practice. The 2-litre 4-cylinder twin-ohc engine was designed by Leo Kuswicki who, like Vandervell himself, had been concerned with Norton motorcycles, and the bottom end was by courtesy of Rolls-Royce. This model was developed through 1954 and 1955, the engine enlarged in stages to the full 2·5 litres of the current Formula 1, and the external radiator on the nose abandoned. For 1956 Colin Chapman developed a new multi-tubular frame, and Frank Costin designed the body. A 5-speed gearbox was fitted in unit with the ZF limited slip final drive unit, and Goodyear disc brakes were employed. With Bosch fuel injection and alcohol fuel, over 280bhp was developed. The cars were driven by Peter Collins, Mike Hawthorn and Ken Wharton before Stirling Moss started them on the winning path with the 1956 Silverstone *Daily Express* Trophy.

In 1957 Moss succeeded in the Pescara, Italian and (with Tony Brooks) British GPs. In 1958 came the reward for Vandervell's perseverance—a really firm foothold for Britain in GP racing for the first time—the World Manufacturers' Championship with wins in six Grands Prix, three each for Moss and Brooks, with backing from Stuart Lewis-Evans. At the end of the year the team was disbanded following advice from Vandervell's doctor, but Brooks raced a lightened car occasionally in 1959 and 1960 without success. An unwieldy rear-engined car, nicknamed the 'Beast', was built for the Intercontinental Formula, and raced a little by John Surtees in 1961. DF

Vauxhall (GB)

Even in pre-Laurence Pomeroy days Vauxhall had made a prentice effort at racing, running one of their 12/14hp chain-drive 3-cylinder cars (with an overdrive top) in the 1905 TT, albeit without success. Then in 1908 came Pomeroy's famous sv 4-cylinder 20hp of 3 litres' capacity, which developed 38bhp at an unheard-of 2,400rpm and formed the basis of all sporting Vauxhalls produced up to the General Motors takeover. This one was built for the RAC 2,000 Miles Trial, in which it not only won its class, but also made best individual performance, and during the year Vauxhalls performed with distinction in speed events, winning on time at Aston Clinton and on formula at Shelsley Walsh. Percy Kidner also took a car to Gaillon where he won his class with a time of 51·4sec and was 2nd overall on Index of Performance. A Gold Medal followed in the 1909 Scottish Trials, and Vauxhall turned their attention to Brooklands, where that year's O'Gorman Trophy Race resolved itself into a battle between Hancock and Kidner on stripped 20hp chassis. More important, one of these 3,053cc cars was fitted with a narrow streamlined single-seater body (this was the famous 'KN'), and did a flying-start half-mile at 88·62mph (142·62kph). The next year was even better, for not only did Hancock win the O'Gorman Trophy (against two other Vauxhalls) but also recorded 100·08mph (161·03kph) over the kilometre in the KN— the first vehicle of this type to reach 100mph.

The hill-climb successes continued, and a pair of 3-litre sports cars (Hancock and Kidner) were entered for the Prince Henry Trials. On a mere 60bhp they were no match for Porsche's 5·7-litre ohc Austro-Daimlers, but they had a trouble-free run and proved capable of 72mph (116kph). A new model had been born. A special sprint car appeared in 1911 with cylinder dimensions of 80 × 200mm, which ran at Shelsley, and recorded 94·91mph (152·75kph) over the mile at Brooklands.

Above, 1913 Vauxhall Prince Henry at Shelsley Walsh. N. A. Barber Lomax at the wheel. *Photo: Radio Times Hulton Picture Library*

Below, 1913 Vauxhall Coupe de l'Auto car. *Photo: Montagu Motor Museum*

Bottom, 1914 Vauxhall GP car, at Brooklands in 1921. Swain at the wheel. *Photo: Montagu Motor Museum*

Hancock drove a 3-litre sv Vauxhall in the Coupe des Voiturettes, but retired, though Kidner won his class in the Russian Reliability Trials. In the 1912 Swedish Winter Trials he could do no better than 11th with his Prince Henry Vauxhall; Kjellgren's touring model, however, finished a creditable 2nd, even if none of the Coupe de l'Auto team (now with 80bhp) finished the course at Dieppe.

A new Brooklands car (KN2 with the 3,969cc edition of the Prince Henry engine) went after records in 1913, when Vauxhalls came in 1st and 4th on formula in the St Petersburg Winter Race, and Hancock at last managed a 4th place in the Coupe de l'Auto. More important, however, was the appearance of the first of the 30/98hp sports cars. This had a 4·5-litre, 90bhp engine, still with sv, and was produced for Joseph Higginson, who badly needed a successor for his all-conquering La Buire in hill-climbs. It was first seen that year at Waddington Fells, where it made ftd with 47·2sec: other Vauxhall successes that season included fastest times of day at Aston Clinton, Shelsley Walsh (55·2sec) and Caerphilly, and a best performance over the flying kilometre at Saltburn, Yorkshire. A 30/98 also finished 2nd in the 1914 Russian GP at 70·8mph (113·94kph); but meanwhile Pomeroy had progressed to some exciting machines with twin bevel-driven ohc, cantilever rear suspension, and hydraulic dampers. These were made in 4·5-litre, 130bhp form for the Grand Prix at Lyons, and with 3·3-litre engines for the TT. The former version could do nearly 120mph (192kph), but both teams failed in their appointed races, even though Swain and Park did well at Brooklands after the war with the TT cars.

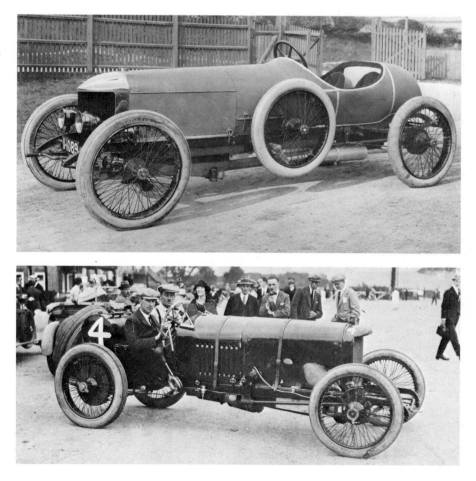

During the World War 1 years the energetic Boyd Edkins, Vauxhall's Australian agent, had successfully attacked both the Sydney–Melbourne and Brisbane–Sydney records, but after the Armistice the 30/98 emerged as the fast tourer *par excellence* of its generation. In the 1919 Westcliff Speed Trials Lees made ftd at 60·1mph (96·72kph), but the cars were never officially raced. Pearce-Jones won his class at Gaillon in 1920, 30/98s performed at Brooklands, Boulogne and elsewhere, and Humphrey Cook's *Rouge et Noir* was an outstanding hill-climber of its day which commenced its career with class victories at Kop and Irondown in 1921. The firm's last competition car was the complex and expensive 3-litre produced for the 1922 Tourist Trophy—this had twin gear-driven ohc, a 5-bearing crankshaft, power-assisted brakes, and no differential—it also gave 112bhp per ton, but it did not distinguish itself in the Isle of Man. In private hands, however, the TT Vauxhall's story is quite a different one: one of the three won 17 1sts between 1922 and 1928, and another took international class records. The most famous was Raymond Mays's sprint car (variously known during its career as the Vauxhall Villiers and the Villiers Supercharge). In unblown form it ascended Shelsley Walsh in 48sec in 1928: after the addition of the Amherst Villiers blower this was reduced to 45·4sec in 1930, 43·6sec in 1931, and 42·4sec in 1933, when Mays turned his allegiance to the new ERA. The Vauxhall still exists, and has been restored to nearly original condition.

In the post-World War 2 period, Vauxhalls have ignored competitions though the 30/98 remains a favourite in Vintage events. In 1953 T. H. Plowman took a 29-year-old OE-type to Montlhéry and put 106·9

miles (172km) into the hour. In a typical International Veteran and Vintage event—the 1965 FIVA Rally in New Zealand—the make won two classes, in the timed sections two OE-types tied for 1st place with a 1914 Prince Henry as a runner-up, and the Prince Henry won the hill-climb. Specially prepared Vivas (the work of W. B. Blydenstein of Borgward fame) appeared in saloon-car racing in 1969. MCS

Veritas (D)

Veritas was the best known of the various BMW derivations after World War 2 in Germany. Designed by Ernst Loof—formerly with BMW—the first versions appeared in 1947. The 1,971cc BMW 328 engine was used in a tuned version, giving 115/125bhp at 5,500rpm. The tubular frame enabled either two-seater or single-seater light-metal bodies to be fitted for use in the sports car or Formula 2 class. A 1·5-litre version was also available; the engine was again a BMW 328 with stroke reduced to 73mm by use of a different crankshaft. The output of this engine is stated to have been 100bhp. Competition was not too strong and the entries were limited to German events during the first few years. At Hockenheim in 1948 Veritas won the racing car class with Georg Meier driving, and the over 1,500cc sports car class with Karl Kling. In 1951 the 2-litre sports car version averaged 131·6mph (211·8kph) on the Grenzlandring driven by Toni Ulmen.

In 1950 Veritas introduced a new engine of their own design, built for them by Heinkel. It was also a 6-cylinder with single chain-driven overhead camshaft; capacity was 1,988cc (75 × 75mm) and output 140bhp at 6,000rpm. It was known as the Meteor and was built

Left, 1921 Vauxhall 30/98 'Rouge et Noir'. *Photo: Montagu Motor Museum*

Above, 1914 Vauxhall TT car. W. Watson at the wheel. *Photo: Montagu Motor Museum*

Opposite, Matra-Simca (Jack Brabham) in the 1970 BOAC 1000km at Brands Hatch. *Photo: Geoff Goddard*

Left, 1948 Veritas Comet sports car at Nürburgring. *Photo: Cyril Posthumus Collection*

Below, 1912 Vinot Coupe de l'Auto car. Lucien Molon at the wheel. *Photo: T. A. S. O. Mathieson Collection*

mainly as a single-seater for Formula 2 racing. On the Grenzlandring it achieved 126·8mph (204·1kph) in 1950. Financial problems did not allow a thorough development of this promising design. However, this engine with a reduced output of 100bhp was used in sports and touring car versions.

Production of all models was very limited and the firm of Veritas disappeared in 1953. HON

Vinot (F)

The firm of Vinot et Deguingand, founded in 1901, entered serious competition in 1908 with a team of three cars in the Four-Inch Race; Ross Browne finished 6th. In 1912 they ran a team of three cars in the Coupe de l'Auto, with 4-cylinder ioe engines of 3 litres, and streamlined pointed tails. The brothers Léon and Lucien Molon, and Vonlatum drove them, the best placing being Vonlatum's 7th. The same cars were driven by the Molon brothers in the Grand Prix de France, Léon finishing 3rd and Lucien 5th. Vinots failed to finish in the 1913 Coupe de la Sarthe, and the firm took no further part in competitions until 1923, when a normal four-seater tourer was entered in the first Le Mans 24-Hour Race. Driven again by the Molons, it finished 25th out of 29 cars to complete the course. Production ended in 1926. GNG

Violet-Bogey (F)

This was Marcel Violet's first successful racing cyclecar, but unlike his later efforts it had overhead inlet valves; output from the 1,088cc water-cooled vertical-twin engine was 22bhp at 2,400rpm. It also had friction drive, and Violet was unlucky to be disqualified for shedding a wing in the 1913 Cyclecar GP at Amiens, though his team-mate Pouliez finished 5th. In the later race at Le Mans, Violet was 2nd. The cars reappeared in 1920 under the name of Major. MCS

Vixen (GB)

In 1966 Alex Bottoms offered a straightforward space-frame Formula 4 design, which rapidly became the leader in the class. With Hillman Imp engines they were competitive in higher classes also, but plans for expansion into Formula 3, with Honda engines, were not developed. In Formula 4, however, the Cheshunt-built cars maintained complete domination. DF

Voisin (F)

Gabriel Voisin's contribution to motor sport lies mainly in the field of aerodynamics and the sleeve-valve engine, of which he was an uncompromising devotee, but his first competition success came in 1921, when a stock 4-litre 4-cylinder car won its class in the Fuel Consumption Trials at Le Mans, averaging 43·9mpg (15·54kpl). A 2nd place on formula followed in 1922, but more interesting were the cars prepared for that year's Grand Prix de Tourisme, also a fuel-consumption event. Once again he used the standard 4-litre chassis, but managed to circumvent regulations which stipulated a 52in (132cm) body width by adding cigar-shaped bulges at the sides — shades of the Prince Henry Trials. Rougier won the race,

Right, 1969 Vixen-Honda Formula 3 at Lydden Hill. David Palmer at the wheel. *Photo: Doug Nye Collection*

Opposite top, Mercedes-Benz W196 (Juan Fangio) in the 1954 Spanish GP. *Photo: Geoff Goddard*

Opposite bottom, 1966 Honda V-12. *Photo: Geoff Goddard*

1913 Violet-Bogey before the Le Mans Cyclecar GP. Marcel Violet at the wheel. *Photo: T. A. S. O. Mathieson Collection*

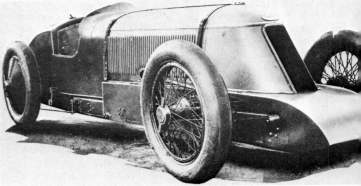

Left, 1923 Voisin team for the French GP.
Photo: T. A. S. O. Mathieson Collection

Above, 1927 Voisin 8-cylinder record car.
Photo: Montagu Motor Museum

Duray being 2nd and Gaudermans 3rd. Gaudermans also won the 1,500cc four-seater class of the Circuit des Routes Pavées on one of the little 1,244cc C4s.

Even more exciting were Voisin's entries for the 1923 French GP, for, like Adler at a later date, he sought to make aerodynamics do the work of horsepower. The cars had unitary tubular-steel structures of aerofoil section, and streamlining was carried to the limit, with an entirely flat under-surface. Even the steering wheels had angular sides, and there were no differentials. Unfortunately the 2-litre 6-cylinder engines (in effect prototypes of his 1927 touring model) developed 75bhp at the most, and the Voisins turned out to be merely slow and reliable. Fifth place was the best they could manage. In 1924 he was back with some slab-sided unitary-construction machines for the Grand Prix de Tourisme, using 2- and 4-litre 4-cylinder engines. They managed 2nd, 3rd and 4th places, and similar 'laboratory' models were actually catalogued in 1925: the bigger cars were said to be capable of 105mph (169·0kph).

Thereafter Voisin abandoned racing for long-distance record work, and made several attempts to capture the World 24-Hour title. His first efforts, with the old 4-litre, were unsuccessful, though he managed to extract 150bhp from the engine and in 1926 Lefèbvre covered 50 miles at over 118mph (189·9kph). By 1927 he had installed an experimental 7,938cc straight-8 engine in an underslung frame with no front-wheel brakes, and Marchand's team wrested the 24-hour record from Renault at 113·4mph (182·5kph). Marchand was seriously hurt in a further attempt in 1928, and a crash put a stop to an

elaborately-organized campaign at Montlhéry, when an aerodynamic single-seater V-12 was prepared to run for 25,000 miles. In 1930, however, a stock 12-cylinder saloon achieved 30,000 miles at 74mph (119·09kph). MCS

Vollstedt see Indianapolis Cars

Volvo (S)

This well-known Swedish company has never made an out-and-out sports car, and their P.1800 sports coupé has been seen relatively little in competitions, but their saloons have been remarkably successful in rallying and saloon car racing.

The ugly but effective PV444 with 1,420cc 4-cylinder ohv engine first appeared unobtrusively in rallies in 1952, when one of them won the ladies' award in the Swedish Midnight Sun Rally. In 1957 the PV444 received a 1,580cc 85bhp engine, and the successes began in earnest. Over the next eight years the round-backed, 2-door saloons (called PV544 from 1959) had innumerable rally victories, including the Tulip in 1958 (Kolwes and Lautmann), the Acropolis and Midnight Sun in 1964 (Trana), and the East African Safari (Singh brothers), Swedish (Trana and Thermaenius) and Acropolis (Skogh) in 1965. This was the last season for the PV544s, for during the year the 120/130 series was adopted for rally work. These did not have such a distinguished career as the smaller cars, but among their good results were 2nd in the 1,000 Lakes and 3rd in the RAC (Trana and Andreasson), 3rd in the East African Safari (Singh and Bhardwaj) in 1966 and 3rd in the

Left, c 1962 Volvo PV544, winner of the 1963 RAC Rally driven by Tom Trana and Sune Lindström. Photo: Autosport

Below, 1963 Volvo 121 in the Acropolis Rally. Carl-Magnus Skogh at the wheel. Photo: Autosport

Thousand Lakes in 1967 (Mikkola). In recent years Volvos have appeared less frequently in rallies, but Singh and Bhardwaj managed 2nd place in the 1969 Safari.

In saloon-car racing Volvos competed widely in the United States as well as in Europe. At Lime Rock the PV444s finished 1-2-3-4 in 1957 and 1-2-3 in 1958. Andersson won his class in the BRDC saloon-car race at Silverstone in 1959. This was the first of several important racing successes in England, including Trana and Skogh's class victory in the 1963 6-Hour Saloon Car Race at Brands Hatch. Volvos were 2nd and 3rd in the 1963 Argentine Saloon Car GP, and both the PV544 and the P1800 coupé ran in the 1963 Nürburgring 1,000 kilometres. The 120 series was not raced so much, although two figured in the first 20 in the 1967 Daytona Continental 24-Hour Race. MCS

VP see Renault

Wainer (I)

During 1958 Gianfranco Mantovani from Milan developed and produced his first Wainer FJ car. It used a large number of standard Fiat 1100 and 600 parts, and this feature allowed it to be offered very cheaply with a full-race 1,100cc engine, quoted price being 1,900,000 lire compared to 2,250,000 lire for a new Stanguellini. In appearance the car was very similar to an Arnott 500, and it was one of the earliest rear-engined Italian FJ machines. Fiat 600 transverse leaf front suspension was allied to the coil-and-wishbone rear suspension system from the same source, and the frame itself was based on two large-diameter main longerons with a tubular superstructure built up from them. Fiat 600 transmission was used, modified with a set of quick-change gears being sandwiched between the clutch and the differential.

The car first appeared in the Cortina GP ice race, driven by Corrado Manfredini, and won. Fortunes sagged after that, apart from a few minor victories, notably in the wet where the Wainer's layout made it an easier car to drive. However, Mantovani continued producing later FJ and F3 cars for Manfredini and for sale. But production ceased in the mid-sixties. DCN

Walker (GB)

Johnny Walker, the bearded industrialist from south Gloucestershire, was virtually the 'father' of Formula 4

1930 Walter 6B racing car. *Drawing: Jiří Nejedlý*

Left, 1958 Wainer Formula Junior winning the Cortina ice-race. Corrado Manfredini at the wheel. *Photo: A. Ceci*

Right, 1965 Walker JW4 Formula 4. Johnny Walker at the wheel. *Photo: Rea Publicity (Western) Ltd*

in Britain. A number of his JW4 models were sold in 1966, usually with Villiers Starmaker 250 engine, but this unit proved less reliable behind a bulkhead than in the frame of a scrambles motorcycle. The emphasis in the class moved towards the Imp-engined 875cc division, and Frank Costin designed the Costin-Walker to this configuration for 1969, but this model was not successful. Walker also offered the Costin-designed Amigo GT coupé, which was later sold by Costin from his own works in North Wales. DF

Walter (CS)

Although they had built motorcycles and 3-wheeled cars for several years, the Prague firm of Josef Walter did not make a 4-wheeler until 1913. This was a 1,250cc light car with 2-cylinder air-cooled engine which was entered for a number of sporting events in the Austro-Hungarian empire. Successes included class victories at hill-climbs such as Semmering, Riedsburg and Zbraslav-Jíloviště. A water-cooled version appeared in 1914, and after World War 1 came the Walter W12 with 4-cylinder water-cooled engine of 1,540cc. This also did well in hill-climbs. The first high-performance Walter was the 2000 of 1924, with 2-litre single-ohc engine developing 78bhp, and giving a speed of 103mph (165kph) in racing form. In 1928 came the 6B with 2,980cc 6-cylinder ohv engine, followed in 1931 by the 3,250cc 6B Super. These were mostly made as touring cars but sports and racing models were developed. A team of three touring 6Bs won the foreign car class of the Germany ADAC 10,000km trial in 1931, and in 1934 a 6B Super won the

Czech 1,000km trial outright. A short-chassis racing car was built by Jindrich Knapp, and in blown form its 3,250cc engine developed 115bhp. This car was successful in hill-climbs, but in racing was no match for the contemporary Bugattis and Alfa Romeos. From 1933 Walter built the Fiat Balilla under licence, in sports as well as saloon form, and in 1934 Knapp disguised his 3·2-litre car with a body exactly like that of the Balilla sports. Production of all Walters ceased in 1936. VH

Wanderer (D)

The Wanderer 1·3-litre—originating from before World War 1—appeared in an improved form after the war. After 1921 it was supplemented by the 1·5-litre, which was similar to the smaller model in basic technical details, such as overhead valves and detachable cylinder heads. These models were also the basis for some specially-built competition cars; the most characteristic change was the fitting of an overhead camshaft. They had some successes in national events during 1923–5, mostly driven by Huldreich Heusser before he changed to Steyr cars. During 1929–32 Wanderer concentrated on long-distance trials and their principal successes were gained in the Alpine Trials, where the 6-cylinder W11 and 12/65Ps with capacities of 2·5 and 3·-litres respectively were used.

In 1936 there appeared an attractive 2-litre sports car, the W25K. However, performance was disappointing, and its competition appearances were few. HON

Wartburg see Dixi

Watson see Indianapolis Cars

Weigel (GB)

The production cars built by D. M. Weigel between 1906 and 1909 were close copies of Italas, but in 1907 and 1908 he built teams of more original cars for the Grand Prix. The 1907 cars had straight-8 engines con-

Top, 1924 Wanderer 1·5-litre at Zbraslav-Jíloviště Hill-Climb. Huldrich Heusser at the wheel. *Photo: Neubauer Collection*

Left, 1908 Weigel GP car. Shannon at the wheel. *Photo: T. A. S. O. Mathieson Collection*

1905 White Vanderbilt Cup car. Walter White at the wheel. *Photo: Peter Helck Collection*

sisting of two 40hp 4-cylinder units coupled together. Capacity was 14,866cc, the cars had 2-speed gearboxes and shaft drive. Driven by Harrison and Laxen, the former did best, but retired on the 6th lap. Laxen and Harrison, in that order, were 5th and 6th in the section of the Circuit des Ardennes devoted to Grand Prix cars. For 1908 Weigel entered three 4-cylinder cars, with a capacity of 12,781cc. They were driven in the Grand Prix by Harrison, Laxen, and Shannon, but had no better luck than in 1907; Harrison was again the best, and again he fell out on the 6th lap. GNG

Weler see Major

Whico (GB)

A line of 750 Formula specials under this name were built by Jim White, who included in his successes the Goodacre Championship, and three times runner-up. The 1969 model was notable for its very low build, with offset transmission line, and featured independent front suspension by rubber bands. DF

White (US)

After Stanley, White was the most famous American make of steam car, its history beginning in 1900. The two most celebrated racing Whites were the 1905 Vanderbilt Cup car, and the special raced by Webb Jay and known as Whistling Billy. The Vanderbilt car was the only steam automobile to compete in these races, as the 1906 Stanleys failed to start. Driven by Walter White, the car was long and low, with a 40hp engine and condenser wrapped around the bonnet in the manner of the early Wolseleys' radiators. It retired on the 5th lap, but restarted and was still running when the race was ended because the crowd was out of control. This car later competed at Morris Park and other American tracks. Whistling Billy was another long, low car with underslung frame. It owed its name to the noise made by the burners on humid days.

Webb Jay drove it in many demonstration races and gasoline versus steam challenges, defeating such powerful cars as a 90hp Fiat. In 1905 he set a World Mile Track Record at 74·07mph (119·20kph) As late as 1912 Whistling Billy was still being raced, now with a maximum speed of over 90mph (145kpg). White touring cars did well in the Glidden Tours from 1905 to 1910. Production ceased in 1918. GNG

Wikov (CS)

The sporting era of Wikov cars was between 1929 and 1934 and the most successful model was the 1·5-litre. Its 4-cylinder engine was based on an Ansaldo design featuring ohc and rocker-operated overhead valves. The output was about 45bhp and a maximum speed of about 85mph (136kph) could be achieved. The most successful Wikov driver was Szcyzycky who gained a 1st place in the 1929 Ecce Homo hill-climb. Further successes were gained in the Tatra Rally of 1930 and 1931, the Czech 1,000 Miles Trial and in hill-climb events. Szcyzycky also competed in the racing car class, coming 4th in the Polish GP of 1931 behind an SSKL Mercedes and two Type 35 Bugattis, and 2nd in the 1932 Polish Mountain Race. HON

Willment (GB)

John Willment worked as a spare-time Bugatti mechanic before embarking on construction of his own cars. Offshoots of the family engineering firm prepared, projected, built and modified a variety of racing cars during the 1950s and 1960s, from the unfulfilled blown 750cc sports car of 1953 to the Godiva V-8-engined Formula 1 Willment-Climax of 1966. More successful were the spaceframe Willment-Climax sports cars, available with 1·5-litre or 2-litre engine from 1957 to 1959. Although often non-starters, Ian Walker won the Easter Trophy race at Brands Hatch in 1959 with one of these. Also promising, but never fully developed, was the Group 7 Willment-BRM of 1965, designed by Brian Waite, featuring box section fuel carriers on each side of the car, which was sometimes raced by Innes Ireland. DF

Left, 1957 Willment-Climax at Brands Hatch.'Ian Walker at the wheel. *Photo: Kentish Mercury*

Right, 1903 Winton 40hp Gordon Bennett car. Percy Owen at the wheel. *Photo: Autocar*

1903 Winton 80hp Gordon Bennett car. Alexander Winton at the wheel. *Photo: Veteran Car Club of Great Britain*

Winklemann see Palliser

Winton (US)

One of the earliest builders of production cars in the United States, Alexander Winton also supported racing in his own country and in Europe for a few years. He entered a 16hp single-cylinder car in the first Gordon Bennett race of 1900, driven by himself, but retired at Orleans. For the 1903 Gordon Bennett Winton prepared two cars, both with in-line horizontal engines with cylinder heads to the right. One had a 4-cylinder engine of 8·5-litres, rated at 40hp, and the other an 8-cylinder engine of 17 litres, rated at 80hp. The latter car had only one forward speed. The 'small' Winton was driven by Percy Owen, the larger by Winton himself, but both retired. The larger car was subsequently acquired by Barney Oldfield who drove it to a number of victories on American tracks. Among records he established were a mile in 55sec, and 10 miles in 9min 45sec. GNG

Wolseley; Wolseley-Siddeley (GB)

The Wolseley was one of the first British competition cars. Herbert Austin campaigned with his horizontal-engined singles, twins and fours in sprints and hill-climbs, and the first 4-wheeler of all won its class in the British 1,000 Miles Trial of 1900. By 1901 Austin had built a large chain-driven racing car with flat-four engine and a 5-speed gearbox. But it was not until 1902 that Wolseley actually raced, a 4-speed 6·4-litre 30hp based on the 1901 design being joined by a low-slung affair with 8·2-litre horizontal 3-cylinder engine said to give 45bhp. This was a complete failure, but Austin's 30 did quite well in the Bexhill Speed Trials, even if neither of his Paris–Vienna entries achieved anything. Some even larger 11,082cc machines (variously described as 50 and 70hp) supported both the Paris–Madrid and the Circuit des Ardennes in 1903, but once again there were no successes. This design, enlarged to 11·9 litres and endowed with a curiously-shaped nose which earned it the soubriquet of 'Beetle', reappeared in 1904 along with a transverse horizontal-four of similar capacity rated at 96hp, but though crankshafts remained a Wolseley weakness, and the Circuit des Ardennes was once again unfruitful, both the cars (Girling's and Jarrott's) selected for the British Gordon Bennett team finished at Homburg; what is more, they did better than the much-vaunted Napier. In that year's Blackpool Speed Trials a Wolseley also won the 1,000kg category.

Austin had nothing new to offer in 1905, when Rolls and Bianchi drove two 96hp cars in the Isle of Man Trials, but Wolseley also entered a J. D. Siddeley design. This still had chain drive, but was powered by a vertical

ioe engine of over 15 litres' capacity. Though Girling crashed this one, both the older cars ran in the Gordon Bennett Cup. Rolls put up the best British performance (8th), once again beating the faster Napiers.

This was the end of the Austin régime, and Siddeley was quick to discard the expensive racing programme. In 1907 some so-called Wolsits ran in the Coppa Florio and other Italian events: these were Wolseley-Siddeleys made under licence in Italy by the Legnano firm.

In 1921 there was a return to competition with 1,261cc 10hp and 2·7-litre 15bhp ohc 4-cylinder cars sponsored by A. G. Miller. Both types took numerous class records at Brooklands; the smaller Moth lapped at 88mph (141·62kph), and the Tens ran in the 200-Mile Races of 1922 and 1923. The 1,271cc 6-cylinder Hornet Special of the early 1930s was seen in minor races and trials, a team of them winning the 1932 LCC Relay Race at Brooklands. Even more surprisingly, a standard 1935 model with the 1,645cc 14hp engine won its class in the Donington 12-Hour Race as late as 1937. Wolseley's last exploit was Symons's and Browning's attack on the London–Cape record in 1939 with a specially-prepared 18/85hp saloon. Though the car fell through a bridge in the Congo, the journey was successfully completed in 31 days 22hr. MCS

Left, 1903 Wolseley 50hp Paris–Madrid car. *Photo: T. A. S. O. Mathieson Collection*

Right, 1922 Wolseley 10hp 200-Mile Race car at Brooklands. George Newman at the wheel. *Photo: Autocar*

Above, 1969 Wren Formula Ford. *Photo: Thomas B. Floyd*

Below, 1922 Wolseley 15hp record car. Alistair Miller at the wheel. *Photo: T. A. S. O. Mathieson Collection*

Wren (AUS)

Bill Reynolds of Melbourne had built a few sports/racing cars to order before he began to manufacture the Wren Formula Ford car in 1969. It had a multi-tube space frame and colour-impregnated fibreglass body made by Lumalite Industries. Four Wrens had been made by early 1970. TBF

Yenko Stinger (US)

This was a modified Corvair Corsa 2-door coupé, used primarily for club racing. The Chevrolet dealer and race driver Don Yenko of Cannonsbury, Pa., produced 185 Stingers between 1966 and 1969. The normal 164ci (2,687·48cc) engine was overbored to 168ci (2,753·03cc) for the production and to 176ci (2,884·12cc) for the modified model. Jerry Thompson was victorious in the 1967 SCCA 'D' production national championship driving a Stinger. ARB

Z (CS)

A. S. Československa Zbrojovka of Brno was founded just after World War 1, and began car production in 1926. Their first sports car was the Z18 with a 987cc 33bhp 2-cylinder 2-stroke engine. It won the under-1,000cc class at the Ecce Homo and Brno-Soběšice hill-climbs in 1927. The following year the first racing model appeared, the Z2 with a 6-cylinder 1,100cc opposed-piston 2-stroke engine and a Roots blower, developing 60bhp. This car won its class at Zbraslav-Jíloviště and the Ecce Homo, and also finished 2nd at the Nürburgring in 1929. It was followed by another remarkable racing car, the Z13 of 1932, with a 1·5-litre 8-cylinder engine consisting of four parallel pairs of cylinders, each pair with a common combustion chamber. With Roots or Cozette blower, output of this engine was 65bhp, and maximum speed over 100mph (160kph). Z13s finished 3rd to 6th in their class in the 1934 Masaryk Grand Prix. The production model Z4 with a 990cc 2-cylinder 2-stroke unit was successful in the 1934 Monte Carlo Rally, and won its class in the 1935 Czech Thousand Miles Rally. VH

Zoller (D)

Arnold Zoller was a 2-stroke specialist and his first racing cars, which appeared in 1935, were on this principle. The 6-cylinder opposed-piston engine of 1·5 litres developed about 160bhp with supercharger. They did not appear very often in competitions and proved

none too reliable. After Zoller's death development ended, although Gerhard Macher tried to carry on the project. He completed a sports car with a Zoller engine in 1938, but it did not take part in competitions and the outbreak of war prevented further experiments. HON

Zvezda (SU)

From 1946 to 1957 a series of remarkable little record-breaking cars were built in Russia under the name Zvezda (Star). Designed by Alexander Pelzer they had tear-drop shaped all-enveloping bodies, with wider track

Left, 1928 Z2 sports car. *Photo: Vladimir Havránek Collection*

Right, 1928 Z2 racing car at Brno-Soběšice Hill-Climb. *Photo: Vladimir Havránek Collection*

Left, 1934 Z4 coupé. *Drawing: Jiří Nejedlý*

Right, 1935 Zoller 1·5-litre racing car. *Photo: Neubauer Collection*

at the front than at the rear. Engines were motorcycle units of 250cc, 350cc or 500cc. In 1949 Andrei Ponisovkin broke the International Class J (350cc) record for the flying kilometre at 107·37mph (172·8kph), and in 1953 Alexei Ambrosenkov in a 500cc Zvezda covered 50km at 105·576mph (169·907kph). By 1958 Edouard Lorent had raised the Class J record to 137·63mph (221·5kph), and in 1961 in a 250cc Zvezda he set Class K records at 138·69mph (223·2kph). These later records were achieved on a dried-out salt lake at Baskuntshak, similar to the Bonneville Salt Flats in Utah. GNG

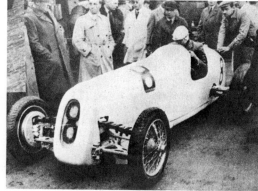

Glossary

A guide to the more frequently used technical terms and those general terms which have a different meaning, or spelling, in the U.S. and UK. No attempt has been made to give a complete glossary of motor sport.

A-Arm American term for **Wishbone** (UK) Suspension component, formed in a rough A-shape and providing location between the road wheels' uprights and the actual chassis of the car.

Aerodynamics In general use defined as the study of air-flow effects on and around a moving body. As applied to competition car design, first experiments began with 'wind-cheating' body shapes as early as 1898 with Amédée Bollée cars, and received remarkable attention in Jenatzy's Land Speed Record vehicle— 'La Jamais Contente'—in 1899. These early efforts all concentrated on providing a boat or torpedo-like shape, with a sharp 'bow' to cut into the air. More recently aerodynamic downthrust has proved of vital importance in maintaining contact between a lightweight, fast-moving racing car and the ground, and the prevention of aerodynamic lift at high speed has become something of a subscience in its own right.

These 'down-thrust' or 'negative-lift' characteristics were first achieved in sports cars with down-swept nose panels and similar devices, but during the 'sixties the addition of 'spoilers' and 'aerofoils' have brought negative lift effects of hitherto undreamed-of proportions. Clever design of the basic body shape can produce many pounds down-thrust at high-speed but extra drag is a natural companion and disadvantage of such effects. The great advantage of aerodynamic downthrust is that the extra loading on the front or rear wheels of the car at speed does not affect the actual mass of the car, and therefore, does not represent extra weight to be accelerated and braked.

Left, Aerofoils: Front and rear stayed aerofoils on Brabham-Repco BT26. *Photo: Al Bochroch*

Right, Aerofoils: The rear-mounted aerofoil on the Chaparral 2G. *Photo: Autosport*

In the pre-war years ultra-streamlined bodywork was fitted to works Mercedes-Benz and Auto Union cars for record runs and for races on such high-speed circuits as AVUS or Tripoli. Long tapering tails were much in evidence and aesthetically at least looked right. But during the 'thirties Professor Kamm proved conclusively that a short cut-off tail promoted less drag than a long streamlined cowling, and during the 'fifties his theories were practised in such cars as the 'Manx-tailed' Cooper sports cars. In the 'sixties most Formula 1 and sports car designers did not even bother to cover the tails of their cars, as good penetration and down-thrust effects were apparently deemed more important than the production of a turbulent slip-stream, and drag still did not reach disadvantageous proportions.

Aerofoils Technically, a device of aerodynamic section which produces a lift component when placed in a moving air-stream. In the competition car sense, aerofoils have been used on and off for several years. Opel's rocket car used side-mounted stub wings to keep it 'ground-borne' in the 'twenties, and in 1956 Michel May's private Porsche Spyder appeared in practice for the Nürburgring 1,000km with an aerofoil section mounted high above the tail. The scrutineers refused to accept the car and the idea of loading the rear wheels aerodynamically to ensure better adhesion lapsed for nearly ten years.

Texan Jim Hall's Chaparral concern resurrected the idea with their type 2E Can–Am sports car in 1966, and brought the system to Europe in 1967 with their Type 2F coupé. In 1968 Ron Tauranac of Brabham and Caliri

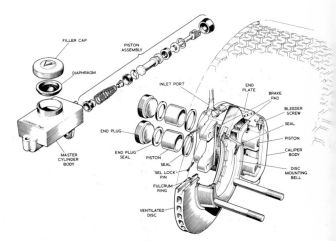

of Ferrari introduced stayed aerofoils into Formula 1, arriving simultaneously at Spa with small 'wings' mounted above their cars' tails. The vogue was immediately established and aerofoils grew bigger and better with almost every meeting. Bad accidents due to aerofoil collapse occurred in the 1969 Spanish GP, and regulations drastically limiting their size and character were introduced at Monaco and Zandvoort later that year.

Limited aerofoils are now permitted on single-seater cars, usually being standardized with canard wings mounted either side of the nose cone and a larger wing of maximum permitted height and width mounted above the rear wheels. These tractive aids are also seen in most other single-seater racing classes, and in Can–Am racing. See *Aerodynamics; Spoiler.*

A-Frame A term usually applied to a chassis component, like an A-Arm suspension linkage, being formed in a rough figure 'A' shape. These components, usually of tubular steel, are often used to provide engine mountings on the back of monocoque sports car or single-seater tubs. The front of the engine mounts on the monocoque itself, A-frames extend rearwards along either side of the block, and provide rearward engine mounts at their tips. Recent cars using this method of construction include the Can–Am and Indianapolis McLarens, and the F1 BRMs of 1970 and 1971.

ALAM see **Horsepower**

Alcohol Alcohol fuels were extensively used in all forms of motor racing for many years until the sponsoring oil companies decided they wanted to advertize successes on gasoline (petrol) 'just like you can buy', and persuaded the FIA to limit F1 and other European style racing to pump or Aviation grade fuels. Alcohol fuels are still used for USAC and Drag-racing competition. Its great advantage is its internal cooling property, which is six times that of 100 octane petrol (the latent heat of methanol is three times that of the petrol, and its maximum power air/fuel ratio is 6 to 1 against 12 to 1 for the petrol. Alcohol is slower burning, with lower flame temperatures than petrol and permits high-boost super- and turbocharging with a higher compression ratio and therefore greater power outputs.

Anti-Roll bar Suspension component, a torsion bar mounted transversely at front or rear and connected to the suspension links locating the wheel on either end of the common axle. The effect is to limit the amount the body rolls in a corner, and adjustment of these limitations can alter a car's cornering characteristics. Stiffening a front anti-roll bar induces more understeer, and a rear anti-roll bar can produce an oversteering characteristic. See *Oversteer; Understeer.*

Aquaplaning Loss of traction due to riding on top of rain on the track.

Armco Proprietary name of a brand of corrugated steel crash barrier much used in modern racing circuit design. The name is now virtually accepted as indicative of all barriers of this kind.

Automatic inlet valve (air) A type of inlet valve much in evidence in early petrol/gasoline engines, operated by the suction created by the descending piston on its induction stroke. Gave rise to the wheezing and gurgling noise made by many early engines in starting.

Belt drive A simple transmission system, consisting of a driven pulley connected by leather, textile or rubber belt to a drive pulley. In recent applications synthetic polymer belts have been devised with internal tooth formations, driving toothed wheels connected to such timed components as camshafts. Advantages are lightweight and ease of maintenance. System widely used in racing engines since *c* 1966 and in driving dragster superchargers since well before that.

Top, Brakes: An exploded view of the Formula I Lockheed disc brake and its associated master cylinder used on the McLaren-Ford M7A. *Photo: Automotive Products Group*

Above, Brakes: Close-up of the offside front wheel of the McLaren-Ford M7A showing the Lockheed disc brake. *Photo: Automotive Products Group*

bhp see **Horsepower**

Bialbero (Italian: twin-camshaft). Applied to Abarth, Siata models etc.

Blower Colloquial term for supercharger. See *Supercharger.*

Bonnet UK term for **Hood** (U.S.) Usually applied to the engine cover in production cars.

Boot UK term for **Trunk** (U.S.) Luggage compartment of a production car.

Brake Colloquial term for 'Dynamometer'; engine power-testing equipment. Two power outputs may be quoted for any given engine, the SAE figure being that obtained with all auxiliaries being run by outside agencies or removed entirely, and the DIN figure being that obtained with such auxiliaries as fan, dynamo etc being run off the engine itself and therefore absorbing some of its power as will be the case with the engine installed in a car.

Brakes Retarding agents in motor car design. In the early days brakes operated on the rear wheels only and sometimes on the transmission line, but front-wheel brakes were considered dangerous for many years. In 1914 Peugeot appeared with front-wheel brakes for the French GP and they were accompanied by Delage, Fiat and Piccard-Pictet in this advance. These were shaft-operated drum brakes, and not until 1921 were hydraulically-operated brakes introduced, on the French GP-winning Duesenberg which used a mixture of glycerine and water as the operating fluid.

Hydraulically-operated drum brakes were to dominate the field for many years, but in 1906 Lanchester had devised a disc brake in which pads of friction material clamped onto a disc revolving with the wheel in order to retard it. In 1953 Jaguar C-Type sports cars used Dunlop disc brakes with great success at Le Mans, and Vandervell's Thinwall Special Ferraris in England were using experimental Goodyear-type discs. When the Thinwalls developed into the Vanwalls and won the Manufacturers' Championship in 1958 the drum brake was well and truly dying, and the disc brake is now universally used in competition cars. Its main advantages are its stable braking effort, better resistance to fade, excellent recovery from water immersion and better directional stability under operation.

Bulkhead Effectively a partition in the structure of the car, often bearing considerable loads. Since the introduction of monocoque racing car construction, the bulkheads have taken on new importance as they locate and give shape to the stressed skinning which forms the monocoque shell. Normally these bulkheads are fabricated from mild steel sheet or tube, but in some cases cast magnesium bulkheads have been used, as in the 1970 March 701 design. In production cars modified for racing or rallying, the front and fear bulkheads separating the engine bay and tail section from the cabin are sheathed and proofed to act as fire- and fluid-proof walls.

Bumper UK term for **Fender** (U.S.)

Camshaft A shaft with a number of cams, or eccentric lobes, projecting from it used to operate engine valve gear. Camshaft positioning and drive has been the subject of much diversification in automotive design, and pure racing engines have featured overhead camshaft valve operation for around 50 years.

In these designs the camshaft is mounted on top of the cylinder head (or heads in a Vee- or Flat-engine design), driving the valves through bucket tappets driven direct from the cams and contacting the valve stems. Camshaft drives vary from gear-trains to chains and internal toothed belts in more recent designs. Push-rod valve operation, with the cams operating linking rods which in turn contact rockers operating the actual valves has been the norm in production or stock engines for many years, but in the competition application its great disadvantage is springiness in the system leading to largely uncontrolled oscillations. Control is much more direct with overhead camshafts and tappet operation; valve performance is more rigidly controlled and much more precise. The reciprocating parts of the valve gear are kept to a minimum in these designs and this in itself allows higher engine speeds to be contemplated, which give greater potential power output. Peugeot's Swiss engineer, Ernest Henry, introduced the twin-ohc system to racing with the 1912 GP car, and the latest dohc F1 power plant is the Ferrari 312B, introduced in 1969–70 and retaining the almost 60-year-old system.

Capacity UK term for **Displacement** (U.S.) Swept volume of a conventional piston engine; in other words the capacity of the cylinders through which the pistons move during their cycle. Measured in cubic centimetres (cc) or cubic inches (ci), sometimes rounded-up in litres.

Carburation Internal combustion engines run on a fuel/air mixture, and this term describes the mixing process which produces the necessary fuel/air charge for each firing cycle of the engine. The mixing apparatus is a carburettor, but a modern alternative is found in fuel injection. See *Fuel injection*.

Catch-tank A residue or overflow tank designed to prevent fluids being dropped onto racing circuits. Water catch-tanks are quite widely-used in connection with cooling systems, while FIA regulations demand the fitting of oil catch-tanks in modern Formula and sports/racing cars to prevent track fouling. For the same reason it is prohibited to add oil during a single-seater race.

Chain drive Literally just that; a transmission system in which the wheels are attached to a sprocket, driven by chain from an engine-powered sprocket usually on the output side of a gearbox. Term also applied to chain-and-sprocket-driven camshafts and auxiliary gear.

Chassis Nowadays accepted as the major structural component of a motor car, although the vast majority of modern competition cars are technically of chassis-less construction. The traditional chassis frame is a strong channel or box-section frame, suitably cross-braced to provide a fair degree of rigidity in bending, torsion and tension. Today's unitary construction or monocoque 'chassis' and advanced spaceframes have almost completely replaced the original so-called ladder-frames and twin-tube structures.

In traditional form the chassis frame's main shortcoming was its lack of torsional rigidity, and to overcome this its side-sections had to be made very deep and heavy. Later in its development the chassis became a frame of parallel, large diameter, thin-wall tubing, with strong cross-bracing, and later still this frame was reinforced with a superstructure of thinner tubes providing body and component mounts. Natural development reduced the size of the base tubes and increased that of the superstructure tubes until they were approximately equal, giving rise to the so-called spaceframe still used by many manufacturers today in preference to the expensive and difficult-to-repair monocoque. See *Spaceframe*.

Chicane A diversion in the route, a tight Ess-bend. Chicanes have been used in circuit design for a number of varying reasons. At Brooklands a series of artificial bends or chicanes were introduced into the main Finishing Straight as a form of handicapping. Each chicane was tighter than the next and cars of larger capacity and performance potential had to pass through the tighter chicanes while the smallest cars had a virtually free run. This simple handicapping system allowed spectators to follow the race much more easily but was very difficult to contrive with any accuracy. Chicanes were introduced in a number of races—mainly in Europe—to deprive the faster (usually foreign!) cars of any advantage they might have over the local (possibly better-handling) machines. Races at Montlhèry and Monza contested by the German teams of Mercedes-Benz and Auto Union were notable for their Bugatti- and Alfa Romeo-favouring chicanes respectively. More recently the introduction of chicanes has become a crowd-pleasing factor, as at Goodwood and Thruxton, while at Hockenheim and Enna chicanes were introduced during 1970 to break up slip-streaming groups. Chicanes were another safety feature in 1,000km sports car races at Monza and Montlhèry, where they slowed the entry of cars to the difficult and dangerous banking sections, and slowed them down past the exposed pits.

Combustion chambers The area at the top of the cylinders in an internal combustion engine in which the petrol/air charge is actually ignited and burned to produce the power stroke. Combustion chamber design is a rather mysterious art, but efficient combustion is a pre-requisite of good engine performance. Combustion chambers have been introduced into the recessed crowns of pistons, rather than being recessed into the cylinder heads, in some modern engines.

Compression ratio The ratio of cylinder volume with the piston at bottom dead centre to that with the piston at top dead centre. Higher compression ratios usually demand more potent fuels unless combustion chamber design and efficiency are outstandingly good.

Cuff valve Literally a short sleeve-valve. See *Sleeve Valve*.

CV see **Horsepower**

Cyclecar A term used to describe the very lightweight production (stock) cars built from 1910 to about 1924 from mainly motor-cycle components, usually powered by single- or twin-cylinder engines. The provision of a 4-cylinder engine made them 'respectable', whereupon they were termed 'light cars'.

De Dion axle Count de Dion's axle principle of the nineteenth century was revived in 1924 by the American engineer Harry Miller. The De Dion axle has the wheels tied by a transverse tube, usually curved to clear a final drive unit rigidly mounted to the car's chassis frame. Drive is taken to the wheels by universally-jointed half-shafts, and the tube itself is allowed to move vertically on a slide in its centre to allow the wheels to rise and fall against their separate springing medium independently, but maintaining a vertical movement. Miller used the system on his front-wheel drive cars, as did Alvis in 1927. Mercedes-Benz adapted the system to the rear of their W125 cars in 1937, and Alfa Romeo in their type 159A of 1951. The system subsequently became generally used during the 2½-litre Formula 1 from 1954–1958, when the wishbone-suspended rear-engined cars began to establish their dominance, and has since appeared in production road cars. Lotus attempted to revive the system in experimental F2 designs in the late 'sixties but the cars never raced.

Displacement (U.S.) American term for **Capacity** (UK)

Drift Term describing a balanced 4-wheel slide, sustained through wide radius corners by only the most skilful of drivers. The classic demonstration of the so-called '4-wheel drift' was in the 1957 French Grand Prix at Rouen, where Fangio demonstrated his virtuosity by hurling his Maserati 250F through the down-hill sweeps after the start in tremendous drifts, balancing steering effect against the throttle and maintaining the car in a slide, travelling in a sideways attitude with the nose pointing into the inside of the corner but the car sliding parallel with the kerb.

Drive Imprecise term applied to power applications as in camshaft-drive, tachometer-drive, fwd, 4wd, and rwd. In the automotive transmission sense, fwd systems transmit engine power to the road through the front wheels, rwd through the rear wheels and 4wd through all four wheels simultaneously.

Rear-wheel drive is the classic and traditional system, because the use of the front wheels for steering made it difficult to power them. The American Christie concern produced a fwd racing car as early as 1905, while 1924 saw Miller producing a front-drive track car at the instigation of Jimmy Murphy, the idea being to achieve higher cornering speeds at Indianapolis and on the short board tracks which then abounded in the United States. Four-wheel drive appeared in 1932 on the Bugatti Type 53, which was confined to hill-climbing, and Miller built two 5·1-litre quad-cam V-8 cars with this transmission system for Indianapolis but was also unsuccessful. Maserati toyed with front-wheel drive in this period, and after the war Dr Porsche's Cisitalia design (presumably the '1941 Auto-Union') also had 4wd. But not until 1961 was the system proved worthwhile when Stirling Moss won the Oulton Park Gold Cup in the Ferguson P99. After this successful showing in the wet, the system disappeared from F1 use, although appearing in Felday sports cars and an experimental BRM (unraced) in 1964–66. In 1969 a resurgence of interest saw 4wd cars built by Matra, McLaren, Lotus and Cosworth but they all failed because of their inability to match the easy-to-control rwd cars under all condi-tions. Four-wheel drive cars had been run successfully at Indianapolis, but the challenge of road racing with corners of varying radii and changing gradient and surface was a different matter . . . for the moment the theoretical advantages of 4wd lie untapped.

Epicyclic gearbox UK term for **Planetary gearbox** (U.S.) An epicycle is literally a small circle whose centre moves around the circumference of a larger circle. In the epicyclic gearbox as seen in Wilson 'Pre-selector' form there is no normal clutch, the left-hand foot pedal being connected to a series of contracting external bands which lock onto the periphery of planetary gears. A number of gear systems and contracting bands are laid out in the gearbox, and gears could be pre-selected by moving a quadrant lever within the cockpit. Dipping the clutch pedal and returning it allowed the contracting bands to pick up the ratio thus selected and so the system allowed the driver to make his changes along the straight and actually select the gears in the corner without moving his hands from the steering wheel.

The Wilson transmission was produced by Armstrong-Siddeley and used in such competition cars as the HWMs and Connaughts, while Lago-Talbot also fitted the system. Its great disadvantage was its greater power absorption as compared to the conventional 'cog-box'.

Exhaust Appertaining to the exit system of burned gas from an engine system. Exhaust technology has recognised the advantages to be gained from having a precisely tuned pipe length, and this is the reason for the convoluted pipe systems seen on modern multi-cylinder engines, the idea being to give each cylinder the same exhaust-pipe length. Connaught and Vanwall were among the first in cleaning up their body designs and recessing the exhaust system into the body panels out of the air-stream, while in recent years exhaust-driven turbochargers and very complex pipe systems have become a relatively common — and untidy — sight. One of the big problems with the H16 BRM engine was that it only began to run properly after Tony Rudd had altered the plane of the crankshafts, which then required a cross-over exhaust system with the pipes from one bank interlinking with the other. It was impossible to devise a cross-over system for the lower bank of eight cylinders unless the designer was prepared to run the engine an extra 6in off the ground. This no chassis designer was prepared to do, and Lotus, for example, ran their engines in late 1966 with a cross-over system to the upper bank and a split-system down below, which was hardly satisfactory.

Fender American term for **Bumper** (UK)

F-head engine see **Inlet over exhaust** (ioe) valves

Flags An internationally-recognized code of motor racing signal flags is used at every meeting. Their colours and meaning are as follows: *National flag*: start of race. *Blue flag*: held steady warns of another competitor following closely, if waved means another competitor is attempting to pass. *Yellow flag*: held steady warns of obstruction ahead, if waved warns of great danger ahead, be prepared to stop; *Yellow and red striped flag*: held steady warns of slippery track ahead, probably due to oil, if waved warns of extremely slippery surface ahead, great danger. *Green flag*: the course is now clear. *Black flag*: displayed beside board with an offending car's number on it, means that car must stop at pits on next lap. Usually used if car is seen to be trailing pieces, or dropping oil. *Red flag*: all cars stop immediately, racing terminated. *White flag*: held steady, caution: service or ambulance vehicles on circuit, if waved, great caution: vehicles directly ahead. *Chequered flag*: end of race, technically should only be waved at the winning car and held steady for the rest.

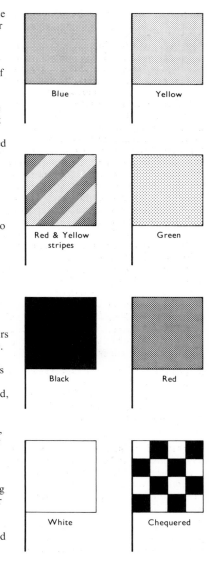

Blue

Yellow

Red & Yellow stripes

Green

Black

Red

White

Chequered

Flat engines Otherwise known as horizontally-opposed engines; ie, those with opposing banks of cylinders lying at 180° to each other, as in the un-raced Alfa Romeo 512 and Cisitalia and the more recent Coventry Climax 16-cylinder 1½-litre engine and Porsche units. Offers very low centre of gravity and compact silhouette.

Forest rally A rally, usually held in the British Isles or Scandinavia, where the competitive part of the rally comprises special stages of which the majority are forest roads.

Four-wheel drive (4wd) see **Drive**

Friction transmission A drive system which was much in evidence in certain French cyclecars and also produced by GWK (Grice, Wood & Keiller Ltd) in England. Cones drove onto drums, literally transferring their power by friction.

Fuel injection A system which injects metered charges of fuel into an engine system, offering marginal increase in power and more precisely metered fuel/air charges than carburettors. Because of these advantages fuel injection is now almost universal on competition cars where allowed by the regulations. Injection pressure is provided by an electronic or mechanical pump, and a specially-designed metering unit then gauges the charge requirement of the engine and delivers accordingly.

Fuels Term normally applied to fuel mixtures other than standard pump gasoline (petrol). American 'Fuel' classes in drag-racing for example are run purely on specialized mixes such as methanol, while petrol-classes are termed 'Gas' or 'Gasser' classes, after 'Gasoline'. Gas turbine engines run on aviation 'jet' fuels such as paraffin/kerosene, as used by Rover-BRM at Le Mans, and STP-Paxton at Indianapolis.

Gasoline American term for **Petrol** (UK)

Gas turbines Form of engine much used in aviation and industrial application, commercial vehicles and more recently in competition cars such as the Le Mans Rover-BRMs of 1963 and 1965, the STP-Paxton Turbocar at Indianapolis in 1967 and Lotus since at Indy and in Formula 1. Air enters the engine and is compressed by a radial or axial compressor, being delivered via diffusers to the combustion chambers. There a primary combustion zone finds the fuel sprayed under pressure from a central burner, and burning fuel atomizes into the air as it passes down the chamber, completing the combustion process. Hot exhausting gases are then channeled through a first turbine stage which drives the initial compressor, and the gas is then guided by variable nozzle

Gas Turbines: The Continental TS325-1 turboshaft engine used to power the Howmet TX experimental sports car. *Photo: Al Bochroch Collection*

blades to drive a second turbine stage, this power stage being connected by reduction gear to the output shaft. Early automotive turbine applications were extremely uneconomical, such as the Rover JET 1's 4mpg consumption in 1950. Ceramic regenerators have since been developed to take as much heat as possible from the gases, and this device gave the 1965 Le Mans Rover-BRM a 14·2mpg consumption figure.

The FIA have established an equivalency formula to match turbines to internal combustion engines, which is:

$$A = \frac{C \times 0·09625}{(3·10 \times R) - 7·63}$$

This equation has A as the permitted high-pressure nozzle area, in square centimetres at maximum opening; C is the competing piston engine capacity in cc; R is the total pressure ratio of the compressor, obtained by a further complex calculation, multiplying together a definite value for each stage, calculated as follows:

Subsonic axial compressors — 1·15 per stage
Trans-sonic axial compressors — 1·5 per stage
Radial compressors — 4·25 per stage.

The great advantage of the aviation-developed turbine is its fantastic reliability. Racing disadvantages include slow throttle response demanding tremendous anticipation, and poor braking effect.

Gear ratios The ratios effected by a transmission gearbox effectively allying engine speed to road speed. Choice of gear ratios is vital in circuit racing. High-speed circuits will need a very high overall gear ratio so that the engine reaches its maximum speed near the end of the straights rather than right at the beginning. At Spa, for example, speeds of 190mph may be achieved with the engine running at a limit of say 10,500rpm. If the car had been undergeared the engine would reach 10,500rpm but the maximum speed reached might only be 180mph —this putting the car at a distinct disadvantage. On tight circuits much lower gear ratios would be used, with the accent on acceleration rather than high maximum speed. As engine development brings higher rpm and greater power because of that increase, a further advantage may be gained since lower gear ratios may be fitted, thus increasing acceleration even further. Hewland transmissions have quick-change gears on the end of the gearbox which allow very simple ratio changes, but the ZF (Zahnradfabrik Friedrichshafen) transmissions once used by Lotus for example had to be stripped completely to change ratios. This was one of the main reasons behind Lotus adopting the British-made 'boxes.

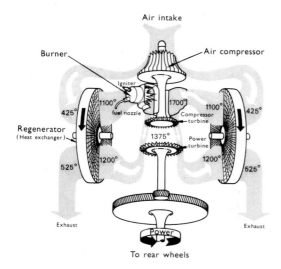

Air intake

Burner

Air compressor

Igniter

1100°
fuel nozzle

1700°

1100°

425°

425°

Compressor turbine

Regenerator
(Heat exchanger)

1375°

Power turbine

1200°

1200°

525°

525°

Exhaust

Exhaust

Power

To rear wheels

Left, Gas Turbines: Schematic diagram to show the flow of air.

Grande èpreuve Strictly a World Championship-qualifying round for Formula 1. A title awarded to the most important races of the international calendar.

Grid positions Starting order at the beginning of a race. Standing starts as generally used in road racing have the starting order normally decided on lap times established in practice. The fastest qualifier will be placed on 'pole position', on the front row of the grid and normally on the side of the road which forms the inside of the first bend. The next fastest qualifier will be beside him, and so on back through a number of rows to the slowest qualifier on the back of the grid. A number of grid arrangements are used, sometimes 3-2-3, with three cars on the front row, two behind, and three behind that and so on, but 2-2-2 and 4-3-4 grids are also seen. Positions are normally staggered so that cars on one row are not precisely behind the cars on the row ahead, and in order to prevent obstruction by cars broken down on the starting grid a dummy grid system is often used. Here the field forms up on a grid some way from the starting line, engines are started and the field rolls forward onto the proper grid, pauses and is flagged away. In American Can-Am and Indianapolis-type racing a rolling-start behind a pace car is common, the cars circulating in grid formation behind a starter's car which flags them off as it approaches the starting line and peels off into the pit lane.

Halda A name deriving from a firm in Sweden which makes very accurate mileometers which have become universally accepted as essential equipment on rally cars.

Homologation The process by which the international governing body of the sport recognises and accepts a new model into one of its racing classes. An homologation board will visit the manufacturer to ensure that minimum production numbers have been reached in order to qualify the car in question for whichever class it is intended to run in.

Hood American term for **Bonnet** (UK)

Horsepower (hp, bhp, CV, PS). The unit used for measuring the power output of the engine, defined mechanically as 33,000 foot-pounds per minute. Up to about 1910 the hp quoted by makers was meant to correspond to the actual output. Sometimes a double figure would be quoted, such as 10/12 or 24/30; the first figure represented the power developed at 1,000rpm, while the second was the power developed at the engine's maximum speed. In 1904 the Automobile Club of Great Britain & Ireland's rating (the RAC rating from 1907 onwards) was introduced, calculated on the bore of the engine only, and as engine efficiency improved, the discrepancy between rated and actual hp grew. Thus by the mid-1920s a car might be described as a 12/50 or a 14/40, where the first figure was the rated hp, and the second the actual hp developed at maximum revs. RAC ratings were widely used until after World War 2 when taxation by horsepower in the UK was abandoned in January 1948.

The American ALAM (later NACC) horsepower rating followed the English system of calculation on the cylinder bore alone, but French (CV) and German (PS) ratings were based on different formulae, with the result that a 15hp English car might be called an 11CV in France and a 9PS in Germany. The French rating was introduced in 1912, and the German at about the same time. Prior to this, the terms CV and PS were used to denote actual brake horsepower. Today hp rating has largely been abandoned; engine capacity is indicated in cc or litres and ci, and power in developed or brake horsepower (bhp).

Ignition Appertaining to the firing of fuel/air charges in an engine system. Early cars from Panhard and Daimler used 'hot-tube' ignition with a high-melting point tube (normally platinum) inserted through the wall of the valve chest, its exterior end being heated by a blow-lamp until the interior end glowed red hot and began to fire the charges.

Benz used electric ignition, by coil and spark-plug, from the beginning. Although early batteries and plugs were very unreliable this system allowed the timing to be altered whereas the hot-tube system was nonadjustable. In 1901 Mercedes used a low-tension magneto, effectively just a generator with current led to each sparking plug by a single wire in series. The magneto proved capable of firing racing engines for many years and only when really high-revving multi-cylinder engines began to be used did problems arise in producing sufficient sparks in a short time. Hence the development of transistorised electronic ignition systems with as few actual mechanical moving parts as possible. Systems from Lucas, Bosch and Marelli are used, triggered by impulses from pole pieces on the flywheel or one of the ancillary drives. These timed impulses are amplified by a transformer, operate a transistorized spark generator and then pass via a conventional rotary distributor to the plugs.

Induction Appertaining to the inlet side of any engine system; where the induction of fuel and air occurs. See *Fuel Injection*; *Carburation*.

Inlet over exhaust (ioe) **valves** Cylinder head design, known as F-head, incorporating overhead inlet and side exhaust valves.

In-line engines Otherwise known as 'straight' engines, having the cylinders in a single line rather than disposed at 'Vee' or 'Flat' angles. CGV in France produced the first straight eight-cylinder engine in 1902, but it really found reliability and power in Bugatti's WW1 aero engine, and entered the racing world on 31 May 1919 when Duesenburg and Ballot brought eights to the line at Indianapolis. The straight-eight power unit subsequently became a classic racing layout, terminating in the Mercedes-Benz W196 F1 and 300SLR sports-racing designs of 1954–55.

Intercom A microphone and earphone attachment for crash helmets usually connected by flexible leads to an amplifier mounted in a rally car to provide communication between driver and co-driver when the noise of engine, exhaust and stones being thrown up underneath the car would prevent normal conversation. Since the introduction of sophisticated pace notes these have become almost essential in international events.

Jump-start To anticipate the fall of the starting flag and so start racing before your competitors. Usually penalized by a 1-minute penalty which is severe enough to deter taking a split-second advantage.

Kerosene American term for **Paraffin** (UK). See **Gas turbine.**

Lap of honour Sometimes known as a 'slowing down lap'. Final lap made by the race winner before pulling into his pit or in the case of major races usually something of a carnival event after the presentation, with the winner, and perhaps his car, circulating on a trailer.

Lap, to Lapping one's competitors is the process of gaining sufficient lead over them to close up behind them — on a closed circuit — and to overtake them, thus putting them one lap behind; in other words to establish a lead in excess of the length of the circuit.

Lay-down engine Sometimes known as a canted engine, the cylinder block (normally of in-line layout) being angled steeply to one side in order to lower the centre of gravity, provide a low silhouette and so allow the car to be built lower overall. The 1954–55 Mercedes-Benz W196 featured such an installation, and the term was particularly used of the Indianapolis roadsters designed by George Salih.

L-head engine see **Side valves**

Line Path a racing car follows through a corner. The classic racing line effectively makes the corner as gentle as possible, entering wide, clipping the inside apex and exiting wide; the line of least resistance. Once committed at racing speeds it is very difficult to alter the line safely.

Litre (l) Unit of capacity (displacement): 1,000cc. See *Capacity*; *Displacement*.

Monocoque Literally 'single shell'; a method of so-called chassisless or stressed skin construction. Introduced to competition by the 1915 Indianapolis Cornelian, monocoque centre sections appeared in the D-type Jaguar sports-racing cars and were popularized in Formula 1 by Colin Chapman's Lotus 25 of 1962. Strictly the monocoque should be an unpierced single-tube structure, but the racing car application needs holes for cockpit and general access, hence 'bath-tub' monocoque with an open top, and 'full monocoque' with complete tubular sections enclosing driver's legs and forming an enclosed bay behind his back. See *Chassis*.

Monoposto Literally 'single-seat', Italian term as applied to the classic 1932 Alfa Romeo Tipo B 'Monoposto', Europe's first Grand Prix single-seater. Monoposto Formula is a British club-racing class.

Motor American term for **Engine** (UK)

Muffler American term for **Silencer** (UK)

Overhead camshafts (ohc) see **Camshafts**

Overhead valves (ohv) see **Valves**

Over-rev To exceed permitted maximum engine revolutions, usually with disastrous results.

Oversquare Expression relating to the ratio between cylinder bore and stroke measurements. If the bore dimension exceeds the stroke the engine is said to be 'oversquare'. Gives good piston area, low piston speed and high revolutions — most modern racing engines are oversquare. See *Under-square*; *Square*.

Pace notes A form of shorthand used in rallying, varying considerably from crew to crew which describes the speed, length and spacing of the various bends that go together to make up a hill-climb or a special stage. Experiments with tape recorders have been tried but pace notes are nearly always written out in notebooks.

Paddock Term borrowed from horse-racing, describing the area at a motor-sporting venue in which the cars are kept and prepared during a meeting.

Paraffin UK term for **Kerosene**. See **Gas turbine**

Pesage (French: weighing-in) In races where a weight limit was applied to the cars, such as in the early town-to-town races, part of the scrutineering involved the weighing of each car. This operation was known as the *pesage*.

Petrol UK term for **Gasoline**. See **Alcohol, Fuels**

Pits Service depots at a race circuit, accessible to cars while the race is in progress. The term stems from the 1908 Grand Prix at Dieppe where service depots were arranged in a deep trench dug before the tribunes, divided by wire netting into pens for each manufacturer.

Planetary gearbox American term for **Epicyclic gearbox** (UK)

Pole position Place taken at start by fastest practise qualifier. See *Grid positions*.

Production car American term for **Stock car** (U.S.) *qv*

PS see **Horsepower**

Push start A start in which the engine of the car is fired by the clutch being engaged while the car is being pushed forward. F1 regulations demand self-starting, and push-starts normally entail disqualification. At Indianapolis and in other forms of U.S. motor sport push-starts are generally accepted; self-starters and associate electrical gear not being fitted.

Radius rod Suspension component normally locating road wheels or axles in the fore-and-aft plane, pivoted on the chassis at the inboard end. Hence the outboard end moves through a radius.

Rear-wheel drive (rwd) see **Drive**

Rolling start see **Grid positions**

Rotary engines Strictly speaking an engine in which the cylinder banks revolve around the crank as in WW1 Gnome aero engine etc. More recently, term applied to Wankel engines with their rotating 'piston' in an epitrochoidal chamber.

Rotary valves Itala produced an 8,344cc model for the 1913 Grand Prix using a rotary valve system. This featured a vertical valve to each pair of cylinders, pierced at intervals and rotating at one-quarter engine speed. Charges were induced and exhausted by the coincidence of the plate holes with the ports on the cylinders. Modern rotary valve engines are confined to small motor-cycle and kart racing units in which the valve layout allows very high crankshaft speeds to be maintained.

Saloon UK term for **Sedan** (U.S.)

Sedan American term for **Saloon** (UK)

Selective Any piece of public road not closed to other traffic over which rally cars have to achieve a target time, which is normally calculated at an average higher than the rest of the rally route.

Set-up American term for suspension modifications (see *Tuning*).

Shock absorbers An accepted term for what should truly be called 'dampers'; fittings designed to absorb the energy the vertical movement of the road wheels imparts to the springing medium. Without dampers, springs would continue to rebound until their minimal internal damping qualities dissipated the imparted energy. Early dampers were of the friction

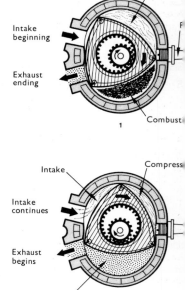

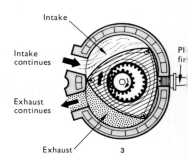

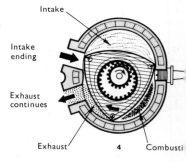

Above, Rotary engines: A series of diagrams showing the cycle of the 3-sided, eccentrically mounted, rotor of the basic Wankel engine.

Left, Monocoque: A 1963 Lotus Type 29 Indianapolis car under construction. *Photo: Geoffrey Goddard*

type in which pads of friction material affectively braked the action of the springs, but as early as 1899 a racing Mors used a form of hydraulic damper, now used almost universally in competition cars, although German Bilstein gas-filled dampers are becoming increasingly popular.

Shunt Colloquial term for crash, accident.

Side valves (sv) Valve mounting position with the ports actually offset to one side of the head, alongside the cylinder. A side-valve engine is known as a flat-head, or L-head engine in the United States.

Silencer UK term for **Muffler** (U.S.)

Slant engine Unit similar to lay-down engine, with the in-line cylinder bank canted over to one side, reducing overall height, size of silhouette and lowering centre of gravity. Really used where engine has been developed from half of vee unit, or is intended to form the basis of a vee unit.

Sleeve valve An alternative to the now almost universal poppet valves used in internal combustion engines. The sleeve fitted around the cylinder liner, and its ports were arranged to coincide with those of the cylinder liner when the sleeve was moved in a vertical or twisting action. Short sleeve valves were known as 'cuff valves', as used in the Schmid-engined Rolland-Pilain of 1922. Theoretical advantages include very large port area, freedom to form a perfectly hemispherical combustion chamber unmarred by poppet valves, rapid covering and uncovering of the ports and the removal of valve bounce problems at high speed. In practice the engine was underpowered, beset by heat-flow problems and with a vast oil consumption. See *Valves.*

Space-frame Form of multi-tubular chassis structure, in its strict sense meaning a frame in which every rectangular bay is cross-braced or triangulated. In the competition car this is impossible since access must be preserved to cockpit, engine bay and other parts, but careful design has produced frames which are extremely light and yet strong torsionally, despite the lack of triangulation in some parts. Maserati's 'bird-cage' chassis are perhaps the apotheosis of space-frame design, while more recent developments include the tubular frame/stressed skin 'monocoques' used by Ferrari in the 'sixties and 'seventies.

Special stage Any piece of public or private road closed to other traffic over which rally cars are timed to the second and their penalties calculated either against a target time or on scratch.

Spoiler Normally applied to an aerodynamic fin or tab attached to the nose or tail of a competition car. See *Aerodynamics*; *Aerofoils.*

Springs Suspension medium providing bearable ride for driver or crew and ensuring the wheels maintain contact with the ground. The original leaf or 'cart' springs have been replaced by coil-springs, torsion bars and even rubber blocks and elastic bands in recent years.

Left, Space frame: A 1958 Lotus 15 sports car before the addition of the body panels. *Photo: Geoffrey Goddard*

Right, Sucker devices: The diagram shows how the system functioned in the Can-Am Chaparral 2J. **1** the path of air under the skirts, whose height is kept nearly constant; **2** the path of the air drawn out from under the car by fans powered by an auxiliary 2-cycle, 2-cylinder Rockwell JL0 engine, causing the rear section of the car to become a vacuum reservoir; **3** the down force of more than 1,000lb (over one-half the weight of the car) caused by the pressure differential between the outside and inside of the car; **4** the skirts, extending from the body to within one-quarter of an inch of the ground. *Drawing: General Electric Co*

Spyder Open-topped two-seater sporting car in the strict sense. A term borrowed from the coaching days of old, and applied to a sporting Alfa Romeo of the 'thirties by stylist Zagato. Since accepted into general usage to describe this type of car.

Square engine Unit whose bore and stroke measurements are equal. See *Oversquare*; *Undersquare.*

Starting grid see **Grid positions**

Stock car American term for **Production car** (UK) For an explanation of European stock cars see page 29.

Straight engines see **In-line engines.**

Sucker devices In 1970 Can-Am events, Chaparral ran their Type 2J car which had a handling and cornering aid in the form of a 'hovercraft in reverse'. An auxiliary engine drove fans which sucked air from a chamber below the car roughly sealed from the outside by 'Lexan' skirts. The low pressure area thus created sucked the car closer to the ground and enabled it to corner at extremely high speeds. Since the device employed moving parts as recently limited in use by the FIA (see *Aerofoils*), the sucker device was banned, but designer Don Gates patented another similar system under the Antares Engineering banner and early in 1971 was looking forward to the regulations being liberalized.

Supercharging The use of a compressor to raise induction pressure above that normally provided by atmospheric conditions. This allows more fuel to be burned in each cycle and thereby produces more power. Superchargers were used briefly by Chadwick in the U.S. in 1908–09, and Hispano-Suiza experimented with the system in 1911, but Fiat introduced it to GP racing in 1923. Three types of blower are used generally, vane-type, Roots and centrifugal. The vane-type has sliding vanes mounted on an eccentric rotor. The vanes contact the sides of the casing, and slide into the rotor shaft as they reach the 'close' part of their sweep where the distance between eccentric and wall is smallest. The air trapped between vanes and wall is compressed and exits here through a port. The Roots type has the advantage that no contact is required between the casing wall and the rotors are geared to revolve in opposite directions, compressing air between them. The centrifugal blower, as used by BRM and now seen in exhaust driven turbochargers, compresses air by centrifugal force. See *Turbocharger.*

Suspension The springing and locating medium arranged between chassis frame and road wheels. In most recent form has to maintain wide modern tyres (tires) in virtually vertical positions at all times, as up-edged tyres lose adhesion very rapidly.

Tire American spelling of **Tyre** (UK)

T-race Rally-style special stage speed event peculiar to Sweden.

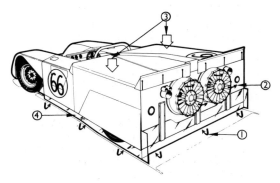

Track UK term for **Tread** (U.S.) The measurement from one wheel centre to another on the same axle line.

Tread Term for part of the tyre which actually contacts the road surface. Also U.S. term for *Track*.

Trunk American term for **Boot** (UK)

Tubular frame see **Chassis Spaceframe**

Tuning The science—some would say art—of extracting the optimum amount of power and reliability from a basic engine design. May also be applied to adjusting suspension settings, such as spring rates, camber and castor angles and damper settings, for optimum cornering performance (*set-up* in U.S.).

Turbocharger An exhaust-driven supercharger, which has come into motor racing in recent years. The flow of exhaust gases from the engine is fed into a turbine stage, which is coupled to a centrifugal supercharger in an integral casing. As exhaust gases drive the impeller turbine, so the supercharger pressurizes the induction system, allowing the engine to burn more fuel and hence produce more power. This, in turn, increases the supercharge and so on. American Airesearch and Schwitzer turbochargers have been used very successfully in USAC racing and similar systems have appeared in Can-Am and touring-car racing. BMW have led developments in Europe. See *Supercharging*.

Two-cycle American term for **Two-stroke** (UK) Engine design in which every second stroke is a power stroke as opposed to the conventional four-stroke automotive engine in which every fourth-stroke produces power. Basically difficult to cool adequately and only really efficient—or as efficient as a four-stroke—if very precisely tuned.

Two-stroke UK term for **Two-cycle** (U.S.)

Tyre UK spelling of **Tire** (U.S.)

Undersquare Engine whose bore and stroke dimensions are unequal, the stroke being longer than the bore. See *Over-square*; *Square*.

Valves When appertaining to automotive engines, this term describes the devices used to allow the induction and exhaust of gas charges and which close in order to allow charge compression before the firing stroke. See *Cuff valve*; *Rotary valve*; *Sleeve valve* etc.

Vee-engine Unit with in-line banks of cylinders arranged on a common crankcase at an included angle of less than 180°, usually 60° in a V12, 90° in a V8 and 60° or 120° in a V6. The opposition of firing impulses in these arrangements gives generally smooth operation.

Voiture légère see below

Voiturette Early term for a small-car racing class. Racing in classes was tentatively initiated in 1898, and in 1901 classes were firmly established as Unlimited (over 650kg, or 1,456lb); Voitures Légères (250–400kg) and Voiturettes (less than 250kg). Incredible by today's standards, a 1-litre single-cylinder Renault of 1901 weighed only 560lb. Later the Voiturette class was for . 1,100cc and 1,500cc cars, such as the ERAs at a time when the massive Mercedes and Auto Unions dominated Grand Prix racing. After 1950 the archaic nomenclature was replaced by Formula 1, Formula 2 and Formula 3 classification.

Windshield American term for **Windscreen** (UK)

Windscreen UK term for **Windshield** (U.S.) A fitting non-existent in the earliest racing cars, the windscreen was adopted in miniscule aero-screen form before World War 1 and remained virtually unchanged until the 'fifties when Maserati began using wrap-round perspex screens. Now the wheel has come virtually full circle with several 1971 F1 cars having no transparency around the cockpit at all, merely an aerodynamic glass fibre coaming.

Wishbone UK term for **A-Arm** (U.S.)

Yump Scandinavian term used in rallying to describe a bump big enough to throw a fast-travelling car bodily into the air. Also applied in recent years to the notorious bumps at the Nürburgring sections of Brunnchen and the Flugplatz (although both have been eased) and similar sections elsewhere.

Index